CW00797587

סידור קורן לימות החול • נוסח אשכנז

The Koren Weekday Siddur • Nusaḥ Ashkenaz

קורן ירושלים

THE LOBEL EDITION

סידור קורן לימות החול
THE KOREN WEEKDAY SIDDUR

WITH INTRODUCTION, TRANSLATION
AND COMMENTARY BY

Rabbi Lord Jonathan Sacks שליט״א

•

KOREN PUBLISHERS JERUSALEM

THE KOREN EDITION

סידור קורן לימות החול

THE KOREN WEEKDAY SIDDUR

WITH INTRODUCTION, TRANSLATION
AND COMMENTARY BY

Rabbi Lord Jonathan Sacks

KOREN PUBLISHERS JERUSALEM

The Koren Weekday Siddur
The Lobel Edition
Nusaḥ Ashkenaz
First Hebrew/English Edition, 2014

Koren Publishers Jerusalem Ltd.
POB 4044, Jerusalem 91040, ISRAEL
POB 8531, New Milford, CT 06776, USA

www.korenpub.com

The creation of this Siddur was made possible with the generous support of
Torah Education in Israel.

Compact Size, Hardcover, ISBN 978 965 301 713 9
Compact Size, Softcover, ISBN 978 965 301 714 6
Compact Size, Hardcover, artwork by Emanuel, ISBN 978 965 301 715 3
Compact Size, Hardcover, Leather, ISBN 978 965 301 716 0

SWA1

CONTENTS

PREFACE TO THE FIRST HEBREW EDITION

"My help comes from the LORD…"

"And their fear toward Me is as a commandment of men learned by rote" (Is. 29:13) laments the prophet, referring to those who turn prayer into routine habit. Even when they pray before the LORD, "With their mouth and with their lips do [they] honor Me, but have removed their heart far from Me." This is precisely as our sages cautioned, saying: "When you pray, do not do so as a fixed routine, but as a plea for mercy and grace before God" (*Avot* 2:18). Bartenura elaborates, "[Do not say] as a person who has a duty to fulfill says: I shall relieve myself from this burden." Thus is the nature of ritual duties: when they become routine habit, their original meaning is diminished.

The prayers in this Siddur – the same words, those same sentences we repeat daily and even several times each day – become routine verbiage, "a chirping of a starling" which lacks the deep concentration and the vital sense of "knowing before whom one stands."

This unfortunate situation – which is natural – became our inspiration to present worshipers with the means to connect to prayer, both to the words of the prayers and to the content and meaning our sages infused into the phrases. We resolved to bring the prayers before the worshiper not in a secular form, as a regular book, but in a more sacred manner, so as to enable the worldly structure to become a source of inspiration, reverence, sanctity and awe.

To achieve this, we created an original design of the printed font and the layout of the words in accordance with the meaning of the prayers, line-by-line, page-by-page. From a visual standpoint, the contents of the prayers are presented in a style that does not spur habit and hurry, but rather encourages the worshiper to engross his mind and heart in prayer.

One possible hazard that undermines the beauty and the purity of the prayers is carelessness of diction when pronouncing the words. Disregard for grammar and punctuation, disrespect, or lack of knowledge of the laws of the *dagesh*, the quiescent *sh'va* and the mobile *sh'va*, and so forth, that our sages – the authors of the *Mesora*, the scholars of the linguistic form of the language, the adjudicators of the laws and students of the Torah

◀ and Kabbala

and Kabbala – were so meticulous about perfecting. In parts of prayers (such as the Shema and the Blessing of the Kohanim), they viewed this meticulous pronunciation as obligatory.

In order to relieve the worshiper of these details – for the sake of his praying – we have presented him (excluding Biblical quotations) with a different notation between the two *sh'va*s (the mobile *sh'va* is more predominant, which is a sign for the worshiper to express the vowel as a brief *segol*, while the quiescent *sh'va* is smaller, as it is not pronounced), and a special form of the *kamatz* (the "small *kamatz*" has a longer foot).

"A window thou shalt make to the ark," says God to Noaḥ, and our sages took this also to mean that the correct pronunciation of the words is an embellishment to the prayers. It is fitting that our conversations with God be clear, pure and unblemished, open and lit as this window.

The Nusaḥ Ashkenaz edition of this Siddur is based upon that of the "first Ashkenazic scholars," incorporating the revisions that were accepted in the land of Israel by the pupils of the Vilna Ga'on, and are customary in synagogues in Israel and the Diaspora (with different customs indicated).

I am very grateful to the excellent proofreaders Shmuel Vexler and Abraham Frankel, for their diligent work, and to Esther Be'er, who skillfully prepared the difficult typesetting of this Siddur.

All this would not have been possible without the help and guidance of my friend Meir Medan, who helped us reach this goal. Using his vast knowledge and careful comparison between different versions, we strived together to make this Siddur as perfect as humanly possible.

And let the beauty of the LORD *our God be upon us: and establish the work of our hands upon us; O prosper it, the work of our hands.*

Eliyahu Koren

PREFACE TO THE HEBREW/ENGLISH EDITION

"One generation will praise Your works to the next…"

It is with gratitude and pride that we introduce this first Hebrew/English Edition of the Koren Weekday Siddur. Since its publication in 1981, The Koren Siddur has been recognized for its textual accuracy and innovative graphic design. We have remained committed to these qualities, as we have had the privilege of enriching the Siddur with the eloquent English translation and insightful commentary of one of the most articulate and original Jewish thinkers of our time, Rabbi Lord Jonathan Sacks.

Since the very successful introduction of the full Koren Siddur five years ago, we have had many requests for a compact edition for weekday prayer, that provides these same qualities in a convenient and portable format. By not including prayers for Shabbat, Ḥagim and Ḥol HaMo'ed, but still retaining the textual integrity and aesthetics that Koren is renowned for, we hope this new edition fulfills the need for a dedicated Weekday Siddur.

It is also our hope that through this project we have realized the aim of master typographer Eliyahu Koren, founder of Koren Publishers Jerusalem, "to present to worshipers a means to draw and connect them not only to the words of the prayers, but also to the contents and meaning that were before our sages when engraving the phrases of the prayers, and our rabbis throughout the ages when compiling versions of the prayers."

It is always a privilege to collaborate on a project with those who share our commitment and enthusiasm for bringing out the beauty of *Tefilla*. We are grateful to Judith and David Lobel for their support and proud to have their name grace this edition. On behalf of the scholars, editors and designers of this volume, we thank you; on behalf of the users of this Siddur, we are forever in your debt.

Those new to The Koren Siddur will note several unique features:

- ▸ Two, distinct fonts, designed by Eliyahu Koren and recently digitized, are used throughout the Siddur. Koren Tanakh Font is used for Tanakh texts (except when embedded in prayers,) and Koren Siddur Font is used for prayers, in keeping with Mr. Koren's belief that the presentation of Tanakh text should be distinctive.

◂ Reading

▸ Reading aids, fully explained in the Guide to the Reader, facilitate correct reading.
▸ The graphic layout distinguishes poetry from prose, and provides space to allow pages to "breathe." We have developed a parallel style for the English text that balances the weight of the Hebrew letters to further Mr. Koren's intention of presenting the texts "in a style that does not spur habit and hurry, but rather encourages the worshiper to engross his mind and heart in prayer."

This Hebrew/English Edition also includes new features. We have added Rabbi Sacks' commentary to illuminate and clarify practice and tradition. We have introduced concise instructions and practical *halakha* guides. Finally, we have incorporated prayers for visitors to Israel, for Yom HaZikaron and Yom HaAtzma'ut to reflect the essential and integral connection between the Jewish people in Israel and around the world, and the centrality of Jerusalem to us all.

We wish to thank Rabbi Sacks שליט״א for his exceptional translation and commentary, and his dedicated involvement throughout the preparation of this Siddur; and Rabbi Eli Clark for his extraordinarily helpful section on *Halakha*.

Raphaël Freeman designed the full edition of the Siddur, from which this is derived; an outstanding team at Koren, including Rabbi David Fuchs, Rachel Hanstater Meghnagi and Esther Be'er, brought it to life.

We can only hope that we have extended the vision of Eliyahu Koren to a new generation and a larger audience, furthering *Avodat HaShem* for Jews everywhere.

Matthew Miller, Publisher
Jerusalem 5775 (2014)

סידור קורן
THE KOREN SIDDUR

ימות החול

WEEKDAYS

Shaḥarit

*The following order of prayers and blessings, which departs from that of most prayer books,
is based on the consensus of recent halakhic authorities. See laws 2–9.*

ON WAKING

*On waking, our first thought should be that we are in the presence of God. Since
we are forbidden to speak God's name until we have washed our hands, the
following prayer is said, which, without mentioning God's name, acknowledges
His presence and gives thanks for a new day and for the gift of life.*

מוֹדָה I thank You, living and eternal King,
for giving me back my soul in mercy.
Great is Your faithfulness.

*Wash hands and say the following blessings.
Some have the custom to say "Wisdom begins" on page 10 at this point.*

בָּרוּךְ Blessed are You, LORD our God, King of the Universe,
who has made us holy through His commandments,
and has commanded us about washing hands.

בָּרוּךְ Blessed are You, LORD our God, King of the Universe,
who formed man in wisdom
and created in him many orifices and cavities.
It is revealed and known before the throne of Your glory
that were one of them to be ruptured or blocked,
it would be impossible to survive
and stand before You.
Blessed are You, LORD,
Healer of all flesh who does wondrous deeds.

אֲשֶׁר יָצַר *Who formed man in wisdom:* A blessing of thanks for the intricate
wonders of the human body. *Were one of them to be ruptured or blocked* – even
the smallest variation in the human genome can cause potentially fatal illness.
The more we understand of the complexity of life, the more we appreciate
"How numerous are Your works, LORD; You made them all in wisdom; the
earth is full of Your creations" (Psalm 104:24). This blessing is a rejection of
the idea that the spirit alone is holy, and physical life bereft of God.

שחרית

The following order of prayers and blessings, which departs from that of most prayer books,
is based on the consensus of recent halakhic authorities. See laws 2–9.

השכמת הבוקר

On waking, our first thought should be that we are in the presence of God. Since
we are forbidden to speak God's name until we have washed our hands, the
following prayer is said, which, without mentioning God's name, acknowledges
His presence and gives thanks for a new day and for the gift of life.

מוֹדֶה/ *women* מוֹדָה/ אֲנִי לְפָנֶֽיךָ מֶֽלֶךְ חַי וְקַיָּם

שֶׁהֶחֱזַֽרְתָּ בִּי נִשְׁמָתִי בְּחֶמְלָה

רַבָּה אֱמוּנָתֶֽךָ.

Wash hands and say the following blessings.
Some have the custom to say רֵאשִׁית חָכְמָה *on page 11 at this point.*

בָּרוּךְ אַתָּה יהוה אֱלֹהֵֽינוּ מֶֽלֶךְ הָעוֹלָם

אֲשֶׁר קִדְּשָֽׁנוּ בְּמִצְוֺתָיו וְצִוָּֽנוּ עַל נְטִילַת יָדָֽיִם.

בָּרוּךְ אַתָּה יהוה אֱלֹהֵֽינוּ מֶֽלֶךְ הָעוֹלָם

אֲשֶׁר יָצַר אֶת הָאָדָם בְּחָכְמָה

וּבָרָא בוֹ נְקָבִים נְקָבִים, חֲלוּלִים חֲלוּלִים.

גָּלוּי וְיָדֽוּעַ לִפְנֵי כִסֵּא כְבוֹדֶֽךָ

שֶׁאִם יִפָּתֵֽחַ אֶחָד מֵהֶם אוֹ יִסָּתֵם אֶחָד מֵהֶם

אִי אֶפְשָׁר לְהִתְקַיֵּם וְלַעֲמֹד לְפָנֶֽיךָ.

בָּרוּךְ אַתָּה יהוה, רוֹפֵא כָל בָּשָׂר וּמַפְלִיא לַעֲשׂוֹת.

מוֹדֶה אֲנִי *I thank You:* These words are to be said immediately on waking from
sleep. In them we thank God for life itself, renewed each day. Sleep, said the
sages, is "one-sixtieth of death" (*Berakhot* 57b). Waking, therefore, is a miniature rebirth. Despite its brevity, this sentence articulates a transformative act
of faith: the recognition that life is a gift from God. Expressing gratitude at the
fact of being alive, we prepare ourselves to celebrate and sanctify the new day.

אֱלֹהַי My God,
the soul You placed within me is pure.
You created it, You formed it, You breathed it into me,
and You guard it while it is within me.
One day You will take it from me,
and restore it to me in the time to come.
As long as the soul is within me,
I will thank You,
Lord my God and God of my ancestors,
Master of all works, Lord of all souls.
Blessed are You, Lord,
who restores souls to lifeless bodies.

TZITZIT

*The following blessing is said before putting on tzitzit. Neither it
nor the subsequent prayer is said by those who wear a tallit.
The blessing over the latter exempts the former. See laws 10–16.*

בָּרוּךְ Blessed are You, Lord our God, King of the Universe,
who has made us holy through His commandments,
and has commanded us about the command of tasseled garments.

After putting on tzitzit, say:

יְהִי רָצוֹן May it be Your will, Lord my God and God of my ancestors,
that the commandment of the tasseled garment be considered before You
as if I had fulfilled it in all its specifics,
details and intentions,
as well as the 613 commandments
dependent on it, Amen, Selah.

_____

them. The blessing ends with a reference to the resurrection of the dead,
returning to the theme of the first words said in the morning.

אֱלֹהַי

נְשָׁמָה שֶׁנָּתַתָּ בִּי טְהוֹרָה הִיא.

אַתָּה בְרָאתָהּ, אַתָּה יְצַרְתָּהּ, אַתָּה נְפַחְתָּהּ בִּי

וְאַתָּה מְשַׁמְּרָהּ בְּקִרְבִּי, וְאַתָּה עָתִיד לִטְּלָהּ מִמֶּנִּי

וּלְהַחֲזִירָהּ בִּי לֶעָתִיד לָבוֹא.

כָּל זְמַן שֶׁהַנְּשָׁמָה בְקִרְבִּי, מוֹדֶה/ women מוֹדָה/ אֲנִי לְפָנֶיךָ

יהוה אֱלֹהַי וֵאלֹהֵי אֲבוֹתַי

רִבּוֹן כָּל הַמַּעֲשִׂים, אֲדוֹן כָּל הַנְּשָׁמוֹת.

בָּרוּךְ אַתָּה יהוה, הַמַּחֲזִיר נְשָׁמוֹת לִפְגָרִים מֵתִים.

לבישת ציצית

The following blessing is said before putting on a טלית קטן. *Neither it nor* יְהִי רָצוֹן *is said by those who wear a* טלית. *The blessing over the latter exempts the former. See laws 10–16.*

בָּרוּךְ אַתָּה יהוה אֱלֹהֵינוּ מֶלֶךְ הָעוֹלָם

אֲשֶׁר קִדְּשָׁנוּ בְּמִצְוֹתָיו וְצִוָּנוּ עַל מִצְוַת צִיצִית.

After putting on the טלית קטן, *say:*

יְהִי רָצוֹן מִלְּפָנֶיךָ, יהוה אֱלֹהַי וֵאלֹהֵי אֲבוֹתַי

שֶׁתְּהֵא חֲשׁוּבָה מִצְוַת צִיצִית לְפָנֶיךָ

כְּאִלּוּ קִיַּמְתִּיהָ בְּכָל פְּרָטֶיהָ וְדִקְדּוּקֶיהָ וְכַוָּנוֹתֶיהָ

וְתַרְיַ״ג מִצְוֹת הַתְּלוּיוֹת בָּהּ, אָמֵן סֶלָה.

אֱלֹהַי *My God, the soul You placed within me is pure:* An affirmation of Jewish belief in the freedom and responsibility of each human being. The soul as such is pure. We have good instincts and bad, and we must choose between

BLESSINGS OVER THE TORAH

*In Judaism, study is greater even than prayer. So, before beginning to pray, we engage in a
miniature act of study, preceded by the appropriate blessings. The blessings are followed by
brief selections from Scripture, Mishna and Gemara, the three foundational texts of Judaism.*

בָּרוּךְ Blessed are You, LORD our God, King of the Universe,
who has made us holy through His commandments,
and has commanded us to engage in study
of the words of Torah.
Please, LORD our God, make the words of Your Torah
sweet in our mouths and in the mouths of Your people,
the house of Israel,
so that we, our descendants (and their descendants)
and the descendants of Your people,
the house of Israel,
may all know Your name
and study Your Torah for its own sake.
Blessed are You, LORD,
who teaches Torah to His people Israel.

בָּרוּךְ Blessed are You, LORD our God, King of the Universe,
who has chosen us from all the peoples
and given us His Torah.
Blessed are You, LORD, Giver of the Torah.

---

chosenness means responsibility, and is inseparably linked to the study and
practice of Torah.

So as to follow the blessings immediately with an act that fulfills the commandment, we read three texts whose recitation forms an act of study. The
Talmud (*Kiddushin* 30a) rules that Torah study must be divided into three:
study of (1) Torah, (2) Mishna, and (3) Gemara. Hence we read: (1) a biblical
text – the priestly blessings, (2) a passage from the Mishna about commandments that have no fixed measure, and (3) a passage from the Gemara about
the reward of good deeds in this world and the next.

ברכות התורה

*In Judaism, study is greater even than prayer. So, before beginning to pray, we engage in a
miniature act of study, preceded by the appropriate blessings. The blessings are followed
by brief selections from* משנה ,תנ״ך *and* גמרא, *the three foundational texts of Judaism.*

בָּרוּךְ אַתָּה יהוה אֱלֹהֵינוּ מֶלֶךְ הָעוֹלָם
אֲשֶׁר קִדְּשָׁנוּ בְּמִצְוֹתָיו
וְצִוָּנוּ לַעֲסֹק בְּדִבְרֵי תוֹרָה.
וְהַעֲרֶב נָא יהוה אֱלֹהֵינוּ אֶת דִּבְרֵי תוֹרָתְךָ
בְּפִינוּ וּבְפִי עַמְּךָ בֵּית יִשְׂרָאֵל
וְנִהְיֶה אֲנַחְנוּ וְצֶאֱצָאֵינוּ (וְצֶאֱצָאֵי צֶאֱצָאֵינוּ)
וְצֶאֱצָאֵי עַמְּךָ בֵּית יִשְׂרָאֵל
כֻּלָּנוּ יוֹדְעֵי שְׁמֶךָ וְלוֹמְדֵי תוֹרָתְךָ לִשְׁמָהּ.
בָּרוּךְ אַתָּה יהוה, הַמְלַמֵּד תּוֹרָה לְעַמּוֹ יִשְׂרָאֵל.

בָּרוּךְ אַתָּה יהוה אֱלֹהֵינוּ מֶלֶךְ הָעוֹלָם
אֲשֶׁר בָּחַר בָּנוּ מִכָּל הָעַמִּים
וְנָתַן לָנוּ אֶת תּוֹרָתוֹ.
בָּרוּךְ אַתָּה יהוה, נוֹתֵן הַתּוֹרָה.

BLESSINGS OVER THE TORAH
The history of Judaism is a story of the love of a people for the Book of Books,
the Torah. As a preliminary to study, we pronounce two blessings and a
prayer. The first, "who has made us holy through His commandments," is a
blessing over the commandment to engage in study of the Torah, a declaration that we do not simply study as an intellectual or cultural exercise but as
the fulfillment of a divine commandment. This is followed by a prayer that
God make Torah study sweet, and help us to hand it on to our children. The
final blessing, "who has chosen us," is a blessing of acknowledgment that

יְבָרֶכְךָ May the Lord bless you and protect you.
May the Lord make His face shine on you
and be gracious to you.
May the Lord turn His face toward you
and grant you peace.

Num. 6

אֵלּוּ These are the things
for which there is no fixed measure:
the corner of the field, first-fruits,
appearances before the Lord
[on festivals, with offerings],
acts of kindness and the study of Torah.

Mishna
Pe'ah 1:1

אֵלּוּ These are the things
whose fruits we eat in this world
but whose full reward awaits us
in the World to Come:

> honoring parents; acts of kindness;
> arriving early at the house of study
> morning and evening;
> hospitality to strangers; visiting the sick;
> helping the needy bride; attending to the dead;
> devotion in prayer;
> and bringing peace between people –
> but the study of Torah is equal to them all.

Shabbat
127a

Some say:

רֵאשִׁית חָכְמָה Wisdom begins in awe of the Lord;
all who fulfill [His commandments] gain good understanding;
His praise is ever-lasting.
The Torah Moses commanded us
is the heritage of the congregation of Jacob.
Listen, my son, to your father's instruction,
and do not forsake your mother's teaching.
May the Torah be my faith and Almighty God my help.
Blessed be the name of His glorious kingdom for ever and all time.

Ps. 111

Deut. 33

Prov. 1

במדברו

יְבָרֶכְךָ יהוה וְיִשְׁמְרֶךָ:

יָאֵר יהוה פָּנָיו אֵלֶיךָ וִיחֻנֶּךָּ:

יִשָּׂא יהוה פָּנָיו אֵלֶיךָ וְיָשֵׂם לְךָ שָׁלוֹם:

משנה,
פאה א: א

אֵלּוּ דְבָרִים שֶׁאֵין לָהֶם שִׁעוּר

הַפֵּאָה וְהַבִּכּוּרִים וְהָרֵאָיוֹן

וּגְמִילוּת חֲסָדִים וְתַלְמוּד תּוֹרָה.

שבת קכז.

אֵלּוּ דְבָרִים שֶׁאָדָם אוֹכֵל פֵּרוֹתֵיהֶם בָּעוֹלָם הַזֶּה

וְהַקֶּרֶן קַיֶּמֶת לוֹ לָעוֹלָם הַבָּא

וְאֵלּוּ הֵן

כִּבּוּד אָב וָאֵם, וּגְמִילוּת חֲסָדִים

וְהַשְׁכָּמַת בֵּית הַמִּדְרָשׁ שַׁחֲרִית וְעַרְבִית

וְהַכְנָסַת אוֹרְחִים, וּבִקּוּר חוֹלִים

וְהַכְנָסַת כַּלָּה, וּלְוָיַת הַמֵּת

וְעִיּוּן תְּפִלָּה

וַהֲבָאַת שָׁלוֹם בֵּין אָדָם לַחֲבֵרוֹ

וְתַלְמוּד תּוֹרָה כְּנֶגֶד כֻּלָּם.

Some say:

תהלים קיא

רֵאשִׁית חָכְמָה יִרְאַת יהוה

שֵׂכֶל טוֹב לְכָל־עֹשֵׂיהֶם

תְּהִלָּתוֹ עֹמֶדֶת לָעַד:

דברים ל׳
משלי א

תּוֹרָה צִוָּה־לָנוּ מֹשֶׁה, מוֹרָשָׁה קְהִלַּת יַעֲקֹב:

שְׁמַע בְּנִי מוּסַר אָבִיךָ וְאַל־תִּטֹּשׁ תּוֹרַת אִמֶּךָ:

תּוֹרָה תְּהֵא אֱמוּנָתִי, וְאֵל שַׁדַּי בְּעֶזְרָתִי.

בָּרוּךְ שֵׁם כְּבוֹד מַלְכוּתוֹ לְעוֹלָם וָעֶד.

TALLIT

*Say the following meditation before putting on the tallit. Meditations before
the fulfillment of mitzvot are to ensure that we do so with the requisite intention
(kavana). This particularly applies to mitzvot whose purpose is to induce in
us certain states of mind, as is the case with tallit and tefillin, both of which are
external symbols of inward commitment to the life of observance of the mitzvot.*

בָּרְכִי נַפְשִׁי Bless the LORD, my soul. LORD, my God, You are very   *Ps. 104*
great, clothed in majesty and splendor, wrapped in a robe of light,
spreading out the heavens like a tent.

Some say:

For the sake of the unification of the Holy One, blessed be He, and His Divine Presence,
in reverence and love, to unify the name *Yod-Heh* with *Vav-Heh* in perfect unity in the
name of all Israel.

I am about to wrap myself in this tasseled garment (tallit). So may my soul, my 248
limbs and 365 sinews be wrapped in the light of the tassel (*hatzitzit*) which amounts to
613 [commandments]. And just as I cover myself with a tasseled garment in this world,
so may I be worthy of rabbinical dress and a fine garment in the World to Come in the
Garden of Eden. Through the commandment of tassels may my life's-breath, spirit,
soul and prayer be delivered from external impediments, and may the tallit spread its
wings over them like an eagle stirring up its nest, hovering over its young. May the   *Deut. 32*
commandment of the tasseled garment be considered before the Holy One, blessed
be He, as if I had fulfilled it in all its specifics, details and intentions, as well as the 613
commandments dependent on it, Amen, Selah.

Before wrapping oneself in the tallit, say:

בָּרוּךְ Blessed are You, LORD our God, King of the Universe,
who has made us holy through His commandments,
and has commanded us to wrap ourselves
in the tasseled garment.

*According to the Shela (R. Isaiah Horowitz), one should say
these verses after wrapping oneself in the tallit:*

מַה־יָּקָר How precious is Your loving-kindness, O God, and the   *Ps. 36*
children of men find refuge under the shadow of Your wings. They
are filled with the rich plenty of Your House. You give them drink
from Your river of delights. For with You is the fountain of life; in
Your light, we see light. Continue Your loving-kindness to those
who know You, and Your righteousness to the upright in heart.

_____

an undergarment *beneath* our outer clothes. Though they fulfill a single commandment, they were deemed so different as to warrant two different blessings.

עֲטִיפַת טַלִּית

Say the following meditation before putting on the טלית. *Meditations before the fulfillment of* מצוות *are to ensure that we do so with the requisite intention* (כַוָּנָה). *This particularly applies to* מצוות *whose purpose is to induce in us certain states of mind, as is the case with* טלית *and* תפילין, *both of which are external symbols of inward commitment to the life of observance of the* מצוות.

תהלים קד

בָּרְכִי נַפְשִׁי אֶת־יהוה, יהוה אֱלֹהַי גָּדַלְתָּ מְּאֹד, הוֹד וְהָדָר לָבָשְׁתָּ: עֹטֶה־אוֹר כַּשַּׂלְמָה, נוֹטֶה שָׁמַיִם כַּיְרִיעָה:

Some say:

לְשֵׁם יִחוּד קֻדְשָׁא בְּרִיךְ הוּא וּשְׁכִינְתֵּהּ בִּדְחִילוּ וּרְחִימוּ, לְיַחֵד שֵׁם י"ה בו"ה בְּיִחוּדָא שְׁלִים בְּשֵׁם כָּל יִשְׂרָאֵל.

הֲרֵינִי מִתְעַטֵּף בַּצִּיצִית. כֵּן תִּתְעַטֵּף נִשְׁמָתִי וּרְמַ"ח אֵבָרַי וּשְׁסַ"ה גִידַי בְּאוֹר הַצִּיצִית הָעוֹלֶה תַּרְיַ"ג. וּכְשֵׁם שֶׁאֲנִי מִתְכַּסֶּה בְּטַלִּית בָּעוֹלָם הַזֶּה, כָּךְ אֶזְכֶּה לַחֲלוּקָא דְרַבָּנָן וּלְטַלִּית נָאֶה לָעוֹלָם הַבָּא בְּגַן עֵדֶן. וְעַל יְדֵי מִצְוַת צִיצִית תִּנָּצֵל נַפְשִׁי רוּחִי וְנִשְׁמָתִי וּתְפִלָּתִי מִן הַחִיצוֹנִים. וְהַטַּלִּית תִּפְרֹשׂ כְּנָפֶיהָ עֲלֵיהֶם וְתַצִּילֵם, כְּנֶשֶׁר יָעִיר קִנּוֹ, עַל גּוֹזָלָיו יְרַחֵף: וּתְהֵא חֲשׁוּבָה מִצְוַת צִיצִית לִפְנֵי הַקָּדוֹשׁ בָּרוּךְ הוּא, כְּאִלּוּ קִיַּמְתִּיהָ בְּכָל פְּרָטֶיהָ וְדִקְדּוּקֶיהָ וְכַוָּנוֹתֶיהָ וְתַרְיַ"ג מִצְוֹת הַתְּלוּיוֹת בָּהּ, אָמֵן סֶלָה.

דברים לב

Before wrapping oneself in the טלית, *say:*

בָּרוּךְ אַתָּה יהוה אֱלֹהֵינוּ מֶלֶךְ הָעוֹלָם אֲשֶׁר קִדְּשָׁנוּ בְּמִצְוֹתָיו וְצִוָּנוּ לְהִתְעַטֵּף בַּצִּיצִית.

According to the Shela (R. Isaiah Horowitz), one should say these verses after wrapping oneself in the טלית:

תהלים לו

מַה־יָּקָר חַסְדְּךָ אֱלֹהִים, וּבְנֵי אָדָם בְּצֵל כְּנָפֶיךָ יֶחֱסָיוּן: יִרְוְיֻן מִדֶּשֶׁן בֵּיתֶךָ, וְנַחַל עֲדָנֶיךָ תַשְׁקֵם: כִּי־עִמְּךָ מְקוֹר חַיִּים, בְּאוֹרְךָ נִרְאֶה־אוֹר: מְשֹׁךְ חַסְדְּךָ לְיֹדְעֶיךָ, וְצִדְקָתְךָ לְיִשְׁרֵי־לֵב:

TALLIT AND TEFILLIN

The mitzva of tzitzit, placing tassels on the corner of our garments, is to recall us constantly to our vocation: "Thus you will be reminded to keep all My commandments, and be holy to your God" (Num. 15:40). Over the course of time, the fulfillment of this commandment took two different forms: the tallit, worn as a robe during prayer, *over* our clothes, and the tallit katan, worn as

TEFILLIN

Some say the following meditation before putting on the tefillin.

For the sake of the unification of the Holy One, blessed be He, and His Divine
Presence, in reverence and love, to unify the name *Yod-Heh* with *Vav-Heh* in
perfect unity in the name of all Israel.

> By putting on the tefillin I hereby intend to fulfill the commandment of
> my Creator who commanded us to wear tefillin, as it is written in His
> Torah: "Bind them as a sign on your hand, and they shall be an emblem *Deut. 6*
> on the center of your head." They contain these four sections of the
> Torah: one beginning with *Shema* [Deut. 6:4–9]; another with *Vehaya
> im shamo'a* [ibid. 11:13–21]; the third with *Kadesh Li* [Ex. 13:1–10]; and
> the fourth with *Vehaya ki yevi'akha* [ibid. 13:11–16]. These proclaim the
> uniqueness and unity of God, blessed be His name in the world. They
> also remind us of the miracles and wonders which He did for us when
> He brought us out of Egypt, and that He has the power and the domin-
> ion over the highest and the lowest to deal with them as He pleases. He
> commanded us to place one of the tefillin on the arm in memory of
> His "outstretched arm" (of redemption), setting it opposite the heart,
> to subject the desires and designs of our heart to His service, blessed
> be His name. The other is to be on the head, opposite the brain, so that
> my mind, whose seat is in the brain, together with my other senses and
> faculties, may be subjected to His service, blessed be His name. May the
> spiritual influence of the commandment of the tefillin be with me so that
> I may have a long life, a flow of holiness, and sacred thoughts, free from
> any suggestion of sin or iniquity. May the evil inclination neither incite
> nor entice us, but leave us to serve the LORD, as it is in our hearts to do.

And may it be Your will, LORD our God and God of our ancestors, that the
commandment of tefillin be considered before You as if I had fulfilled it in all its
specifics, details and intentions, as well as the 613 commandments dependent
on it, Amen, Selah.

———————————————————————————————

this is the head-tefillin opposite the seat of consciousness, the soul. *All your
might:* this is the strap of the hand-tefillin, symbolizing action, power, might.
Tefillin thus symbolize the love for God in emotion (heart), thought (head)
and deed (hand).

הנחת תפילין

Some say the following meditation before putting on the תפילין.

לְשֵׁם יִחוּד קֻדְשָׁא בְּרִיךְ הוּא וּשְׁכִינְתֵּהּ בִּדְחִילוּ וּרְחִימוּ, לְיַחֵד שֵׁם י״ה בו״ה בְּיִחוּדָא שְׁלִים בְּשֵׁם כָּל יִשְׂרָאֵל.

הִנְנִי מְכַוֵּן בַּהֲנָחַת תְּפִילִין לְקַיֵּם מִצְוַת בּוֹרְאִי, שֶׁצִּוָּנוּ לְהָנִיחַ תְּפִילִין, כַּכָּתוּב בְּתוֹרָתוֹ: וּקְשַׁרְתָּם לְאוֹת עַל־יָדֶךָ, וְהָיוּ לְטֹטָפֹת בֵּין עֵינֶיךָ: דברים ו וְהֵן אַרְבַּע פָּרָשִׁיּוֹת אֵלּוּ, שְׁמַע, וְהָיָה אִם שָׁמֹעַ, קַדֶּשׁ לִי, וְהָיָה כִּי יְבִאֲךָ, שֶׁיֵּשׁ בָּהֶם יִחוּדוֹ וְאַחְדוּתוֹ יִתְבָּרַךְ שְׁמוֹ בָּעוֹלָם, וְשֶׁנִּזְכֹּר נִסִּים וְנִפְלָאוֹת שֶׁעָשָׂה עִמָּנוּ בְּהוֹצִיאוֹ אוֹתָנוּ מִמִּצְרָיִם, וַאֲשֶׁר לוֹ הַכֹּחַ וְהַמֶּמְשָׁלָה בָּעֶלְיוֹנִים וּבַתַּחְתּוֹנִים לַעֲשׂוֹת בָּהֶם כִּרְצוֹנוֹ. וְצִוָּנוּ לְהָנִיחַ עַל הַיָּד לְזִכָּרוֹן זְרוֹעַ הַנְּטוּיָה, וְשֶׁהִיא נֶגֶד הַלֵּב, לְשַׁעְבֵּד בָּזֶה תַּאֲווֹת וּמַחְשְׁבוֹת לִבֵּנוּ לַעֲבוֹדָתוֹ יִתְבָּרַךְ שְׁמוֹ. וְעַל הָרֹאשׁ נֶגֶד הַמֹּחַ, שֶׁהַנְּשָׁמָה שֶׁבְּמֹחִי עִם שְׁאָר חוּשַׁי וְכֹחוֹתַי כֻּלָּם יִהְיוּ מְשֻׁעְבָּדִים לַעֲבוֹדָתוֹ, יִתְבָּרַךְ שְׁמוֹ. וּמִשֶּׁפַע מִצְוַת תְּפִילִין יִתְמַשֵּׁךְ עָלַי לִהְיוֹת לִי חַיִּים אֲרוּכִים וְשֶׁפַע קֹדֶשׁ וּמַחְשָׁבוֹת קְדוֹשׁוֹת בְּלִי הִרְהוּר חֵטְא וְעָוֹן כְּלָל, וְשֶׁלֹּא יְפַתֵּנוּ וְלֹא יִתְגָּרֶה בָּנוּ יֵצֶר הָרָע, וְיַנִּיחֵנוּ לַעֲבֹד אֶת יהוה כַּאֲשֶׁר עִם לְבָבֵנוּ.

וִיהִי רָצוֹן מִלְּפָנֶיךָ, יהוה אֱלֹהֵינוּ וֵאלֹהֵי אֲבוֹתֵינוּ, שֶׁתְּהֵא חֲשׁוּבָה מִצְוַת הֲנָחַת תְּפִילִין לִפְנֵי הַקָּדוֹשׁ בָּרוּךְ הוּא, כְּאִלּוּ קִיַּמְתִּיהָ בְּכָל פְּרָטֶיהָ וְדִקְדּוּקֶיהָ וְכַוָּנוֹתֶיהָ וְתַרְיַ״ג מִצְוֹת הַתְּלוּיוֹת בָּהּ, אָמֵן סֶלָה.

───────────────────────────────

Tefillin: The word tefillin (called *totafot* in the Torah) means "emblem, sign, insignia," the visible symbol of an abstract idea. Tefillin are our reminder of the commandment of the Shema: "Love the LORD your God your with all your heart, with all your soul and with all your might" (Deut. 6:5). *All your heart:* this is the tefillin on the upper arm opposite the heart. *All your soul:*

Stand and place the hand-tefillin on the biceps of the left arm (or right arm if you are left-handed), angled toward the heart, and before tightening the strap, say:

בָּרוּךְ Blessed are You, LORD our God,
King of the Universe,
who has made us holy through His commandments,
and has commanded us to put on tefillin.

*Wrap the strap of the hand-tefillin seven times around the arm.
Place the head-tefillin above the hairline, centered between the eyes, and say quietly:*

בָּרוּךְ Blessed are You, LORD our God,
King of the Universe,
who has made us holy through His commandments,
and has commanded us about the commandment of tefillin.

Adjust the head-tefillin and say:
בָּרוּךְ Blessed be the name of His glorious kingdom for ever and all time.

Some say:
From Your wisdom, God most high, grant me [wisdom], and from Your
understanding, give me understanding. May Your loving-kindness be
greatly upon me, and in Your might may my enemies and those who rise
against me be subdued. Pour Your goodly oil on the seven branches of
the menora so that Your good flows down upon Your creatures. You open   *Ps. 145*
Your hand, and satisfy every living thing with favor.

Wind the strap of the hand-tefillin three times around the middle finger, saying:

וְאֵרַשְׂתִּיךְ I will betroth you to Me for ever;   *Hos. 2*
I will betroth you to Me in righteousness and justice,
loving-kindness and compassion;
I will betroth you to Me in faithfulness;
and you shall know the LORD.

---

like a wedding ring, we remind ourselves of God's love for Israel, and Israel's
love for God.

Stand and place the תפילין של יד *on the biceps of the left arm (or right arm if you are left-handed), angled toward the heart, and before tightening the strap, say:*

בָּרוּךְ אַתָּה יהוה אֱלֹהֵינוּ מֶלֶךְ הָעוֹלָם
אֲשֶׁר קִדְּשָׁנוּ בְּמִצְוֹתָיו
וְצִוָּנוּ לְהָנִיחַ תְּפִילִין.

Wrap the strap of the תפילין של יד *seven times around the arm.*
Place the תפילין של ראש *above the hairline, centered between the eyes, and say quietly:*

בָּרוּךְ אַתָּה יהוה אֱלֹהֵינוּ מֶלֶךְ הָעוֹלָם
אֲשֶׁר קִדְּשָׁנוּ בְּמִצְוֹתָיו
וְצִוָּנוּ עַל מִצְוַת תְּפִילִין.

Adjust the תפילין של ראש *and say:*

בָּרוּךְ שֵׁם כְּבוֹד מַלְכוּתוֹ לְעוֹלָם וָעֶד

Some say:

וּמֵחָכְמָתְךָ אֵל עֶלְיוֹן תַּאֲצִיל עָלַי, וּמִבִּינָתְךָ תְּבִינֵנִי, וּבְחַסְדְּךָ תַּגְדִּיל
עָלַי, וּבִגְבוּרָתְךָ תַּצְמִית אוֹיְבַי וְקָמַי. וְשֶׁמֶן הַטּוֹב תָּרִיק עַל שִׁבְעָה
קְנֵי הַמְּנוֹרָה, לְהַשְׁפִּיעַ טוּבְךָ לִבְרִיּוֹתֶיךָ. פּוֹתֵחַ אֶת־יָדֶךָ וּמַשְׂבִּיעַ
לְכָל־חַי רָצוֹן:

תהלים
קמה

Wind the strap of the תפילין של יד *three times around the middle finger, saying:*

הושע ב

וְאֵרַשְׂתִּיךְ לִי לְעוֹלָם
וְאֵרַשְׂתִּיךְ לִי בְּצֶדֶק וּבְמִשְׁפָּט וּבְחֶסֶד וּבְרַחֲמִים:
וְאֵרַשְׂתִּיךְ לִי בֶּאֱמוּנָה, וְיָדַעַתְּ אֶת־יהוה:

————————————————————————

וְאֵרַשְׂתִּיךְ *I will betroth you to Me:* These exquisite lines from the book of Hosea
speak of God's covenant with Israel as a marriage – a mutual pledge of faith,
born of love. Wrapping the strap of the hand-tefillin around the middle finger

After putting on the tefillin, say the following:

וַיְדַבֵּר The LORD spoke to Moses, saying, "Consecrate to Me every   Ex. 13
firstborn male. The first offspring of every womb among the Israelites,
whether man or beast, belongs to Me." Then Moses said to the people,
"Remember this day on which you left Egypt, the slave-house, when
the LORD brought you out of it with a mighty hand. No leaven shall be
eaten. You are leaving on this day, in the month of Aviv. When the LORD
brings you into the land of the Canaanites, Hittites, Amorites, Hivites and
Jebusites, the land He swore to your ancestors to give you, a land flowing
with milk and honey, you are to observe this service in this same month.
For seven days you shall eat unleavened bread, and make the seventh day
a festival to the LORD. Unleavened bread shall be eaten throughout the
seven days. No leavened bread may be seen in your possession, and no
leaven shall be seen anywhere within your borders. On that day you shall
tell your son, 'This is because of what the LORD did for me when I left
Egypt.' [These words] shall also be a sign on your hand, and a reminder
above your forehead, so that the LORD's Torah may always be in your
mouth, because with a mighty hand the LORD brought you out of Egypt.
You shall therefore keep this statute at its appointed time from year to year."

וְהָיָה After the LORD has brought you into the land of the Canaanites, as
He swore to you and your ancestors, and He has given it to you, you shall
set apart for the LORD the first offspring of every womb. All the firstborn
males of your cattle belong to the LORD. Every firstling donkey you shall
redeem with a lamb. If you do not redeem it, you must break its neck.
Every firstborn among your sons you must redeem. If, in time to come,
your son asks you, "What does this mean?" you shall say to him, "With a
mighty hand the LORD brought us out of Egypt, out of the slave-house.
When Pharaoh stubbornly refused to let us leave, the LORD killed all the
firstborn in the land of Egypt, both man and beast. That is why I sacrifice
to the LORD the first male offspring of every womb, and redeem all the
firstborn of my sons." [These words] shall be a sign on your hand and
as an emblem above your forehead, that with a mighty hand the LORD
brought us out of Egypt.

After putting on the תפילין, *say the following:*

שמות יג

וַיְדַבֵּר יהוה אֶל־מֹשֶׁה לֵּאמֹר: קַדֶּשׁ־לִי כָל־בְּכוֹר, פֶּטֶר כָּל־רֶחֶם
בִּבְנֵי יִשְׂרָאֵל, בָּאָדָם וּבַבְּהֵמָה, לִי הוּא: וַיֹּאמֶר מֹשֶׁה אֶל־הָעָם, זָכוֹר
אֶת־הַיּוֹם הַזֶּה, אֲשֶׁר יְצָאתֶם מִמִּצְרַיִם מִבֵּית עֲבָדִים, כִּי בְּחֹזֶק יָד
הוֹצִיא יהוה אֶתְכֶם מִזֶּה, וְלֹא יֵאָכֵל חָמֵץ: הַיּוֹם אַתֶּם יֹצְאִים, בְּחֹדֶשׁ
הָאָבִיב: וְהָיָה כִי־יְבִיאֲךָ יהוה אֶל־אֶרֶץ הַכְּנַעֲנִי וְהַחִתִּי וְהָאֱמֹרִי
וְהַחִוִּי וְהַיְבוּסִי, אֲשֶׁר נִשְׁבַּע לַאֲבֹתֶיךָ לָתֶת לָךְ, אֶרֶץ זָבַת חָלָב
וּדְבָשׁ, וְעָבַדְתָּ אֶת־הָעֲבֹדָה הַזֹּאת בַּחֹדֶשׁ הַזֶּה: שִׁבְעַת יָמִים תֹּאכַל
מַצֹּת, וּבַיּוֹם הַשְּׁבִיעִי חַג לַיהוה: מַצּוֹת יֵאָכֵל אֵת שִׁבְעַת הַיָּמִים,
וְלֹא־יֵרָאֶה לְךָ חָמֵץ וְלֹא־יֵרָאֶה לְךָ שְׂאֹר, בְּכָל־גְּבֻלֶךָ: וְהִגַּדְתָּ לְבִנְךָ
בַּיּוֹם הַהוּא לֵאמֹר, בַּעֲבוּר זֶה עָשָׂה יהוה לִי בְּצֵאתִי מִמִּצְרָיִם: וְהָיָה
לְךָ לְאוֹת עַל־יָדְךָ וּלְזִכָּרוֹן בֵּין עֵינֶיךָ, לְמַעַן תִּהְיֶה תּוֹרַת יהוה בְּפִיךָ,
כִּי בְּיָד חֲזָקָה הוֹצִאֲךָ יהוה מִמִּצְרָיִם: וְשָׁמַרְתָּ אֶת־הַחֻקָּה הַזֹּאת
לְמוֹעֲדָהּ, מִיָּמִים יָמִימָה:

וְהָיָה כִּי־יְבִאֲךָ יהוה אֶל־אֶרֶץ הַכְּנַעֲנִי כַּאֲשֶׁר נִשְׁבַּע לְךָ וְלַאֲבֹתֶיךָ,
וּנְתָנָהּ לָךְ: וְהַעֲבַרְתָּ כָל־פֶּטֶר־רֶחֶם לַיהוה, וְכָל־פֶּטֶר שֶׁגֶר בְּהֵמָה
אֲשֶׁר יִהְיֶה לְךָ הַזְּכָרִים, לַיהוה: וְכָל־פֶּטֶר חֲמֹר תִּפְדֶּה בְשֶׂה, וְאִם־
לֹא תִפְדֶּה וַעֲרַפְתּוֹ, וְכֹל בְּכוֹר אָדָם בְּבָנֶיךָ תִּפְדֶּה: וְהָיָה כִּי־יִשְׁאָלְךָ
בִנְךָ מָחָר, לֵאמֹר מַה־זֹּאת, וְאָמַרְתָּ אֵלָיו, בְּחֹזֶק יָד הוֹצִיאָנוּ יהוה
מִמִּצְרַיִם מִבֵּית עֲבָדִים: וַיְהִי כִּי־הִקְשָׁה פַרְעֹה לְשַׁלְּחֵנוּ, וַיַּהֲרֹג יהוה
כָּל־בְּכוֹר בְּאֶרֶץ מִצְרַיִם, מִבְּכֹר אָדָם וְעַד־בְּכוֹר בְּהֵמָה, עַל־כֵּן אֲנִי
זֹבֵחַ לַיהוה כָּל־פֶּטֶר רֶחֶם הַזְּכָרִים, וְכָל־בְּכוֹר בָּנַי אֶפְדֶּה: וְהָיָה
לְאוֹת עַל־יָדְכָה וּלְטוֹטָפֹת בֵּין עֵינֶיךָ, כִּי בְּחֹזֶק יָד הוֹצִיאָנוּ יהוה
מִמִּצְרָיִם:

PREPARATION FOR PRAYER

On entering the synagogue:

HOW GOODLY

Num. 24

are your tents, Jacob, your dwelling places, Israel.
As for me,
in Your great loving-kindness,
I will come into Your House.
I will bow down to Your holy Temple
in awe of You.
Lᴏʀᴅ, I love the habitation of Your House,
the place where Your glory dwells.

Ps. 5

Ps. 26

As for me,
I will bow in worship;

> I will bend the knee
> before the Lᴏʀᴅ my Maker.

As for me,
may my prayer come to You, Lᴏʀᴅ,

Ps. 69

> at a time of favor.
> God, in Your great loving-kindness,
> answer me with Your faithful salvation.

הכנה לתפילה

On entering the בית כנסת:

במדבר כד

מַה־טֹּבוּ

אֹהָלֶיךָ יַעֲקֹב, מִשְׁכְּנֹתֶיךָ יִשְׂרָאֵל:

תהלים ה

וַאֲנִי בְּרֹב חַסְדְּךָ אָבוֹא בֵיתֶךָ
אֶשְׁתַּחֲוֶה אֶל־הֵיכַל־קָדְשְׁךָ
בְּיִרְאָתֶךָ:

תהלים כו

יהוה אָהַבְתִּי מְעוֹן בֵּיתֶךָ
וּמְקוֹם מִשְׁכַּן כְּבוֹדֶךָ:

וַאֲנִי אֶשְׁתַּחֲוֶה

וְאֶכְרָעָה
אֲבָרְכָה לִפְנֵי יהוה עֹשִׂי.

תהלים סט

וַאֲנִי תְפִלָּתִי־לְךָ יהוה

עֵת רָצוֹן
אֱלֹהִים בְּרָב־חַסְדֶּךָ
עֲנֵנִי בֶּאֱמֶת יִשְׁעֶךָ:

*The following poems, on this page and the next, both from the Middle Ages,
are summary statements of Jewish faith, orienting us to the spiritual contours
of the world that we actualize in the mind by the act of prayer.*

LORD OF THE UNIVERSE,
who reigned before the birth of any thing –

When by His will all things were made
then was His name proclaimed King.

And when all things shall cease to be
He alone will reign in awe.

He was, He is, and He shall be
glorious for evermore.

He is One, there is none else,
alone, unique, beyond compare;

Without beginning, without end,
His might, His rule are everywhere.

He is my God; my Redeemer lives.
He is the Rock on whom I rely –

My banner and my safe retreat,
my cup, my portion when I cry.

Into His hand my soul I place,
when I awake and when I sleep.

The LORD is with me, I shall not fear;
body and soul from harm will He keep.

The following poems, on this page and the next, both from the Middle Ages,
are summary statements of Jewish faith, orienting us to the spiritual contours
of the world that we actualize in the mind by the act of prayer.

אֲדוֹן עוֹלָם

אֲשֶׁר מָלַךְ בְּטֶרֶם כָּל־יְצִיר נִבְרָא.

לְעֵת נַעֲשָׂה בְחֶפְצוֹ כֹּל אֲזַי מֶלֶךְ שְׁמוֹ נִקְרָא.

וְאַחֲרֵי כִּכְלוֹת הַכֹּל לְבַדּוֹ יִמְלֹךְ נוֹרָא.

וְהוּא הָיָה וְהוּא הֹוֶה וְהוּא יִהְיֶה בְּתִפְאָרָה.

וְהוּא אֶחָד וְאֵין שֵׁנִי לְהַמְשִׁיל לוֹ לְהַחְבִּירָה.

בְּלִי רֵאשִׁית בְּלִי תַכְלִית וְלוֹ הָעֹז וְהַמִּשְׂרָה.

וְהוּא אֵלִי וְחַי גּוֹאֲלִי וְצוּר חֶבְלִי בְּעֵת צָרָה.

וְהוּא נִסִּי וּמָנוֹס לִי מְנָת כּוֹסִי בְּיוֹם אֶקְרָא.

בְּיָדוֹ אַפְקִיד רוּחִי בְּעֵת אִישַׁן וְאָעִירָה.

וְעִם רוּחִי גְּוִיָּתִי יהוה לִי וְלֹא אִירָא.

GREAT

is the living God and praised.
He exists, and His existence is beyond time.

He is One, and there is no unity like His.
Unfathomable, His oneness is infinite.

He has neither bodily form nor substance;
His holiness is beyond compare.

He preceded all that was created.
He was first: there was no beginning to His beginning.

Behold He is Master of the Universe; and every creature
shows His greatness and majesty.

The rich flow of His prophecy He gave
to His treasured people in whom He gloried.

Never in Israel has there arisen another like Moses,
a prophet who beheld God's image.

God gave His people a Torah of truth
by the hand of His prophet, most faithful of His House.

God will not alter or change His law
for any other, for eternity.

He sees and knows our secret thoughts;
as soon as something is begun, He foresees its end.

He rewards people with loving-kindness according to their deeds;
He punishes the wicked according to his wickedness.

At the end of days He will send our Messiah
to redeem those who await His final salvation.

God will revive the dead in His great loving-kindness.
Blessed for evermore is His glorious name!

יִגְדַּל

אֱלֹהִים חַי וְיִשְׁתַּבַּח, נִמְצָא וְאֵין עֵת אֶל מְצִיאוּתוֹ.

אֶחָד וְאֵין יָחִיד כְּיִחוּדוֹ, נֶעְלָם וְגַם אֵין סוֹף לְאַחְדּוּתוֹ.

אֵין לוֹ דְּמוּת הַגּוּף וְאֵינוֹ גוּף, לֹא נַעֲרֹךְ אֵלָיו קְדֻשָּׁתוֹ.

קַדְמוֹן לְכָל דָּבָר אֲשֶׁר נִבְרָא, רִאשׁוֹן וְאֵין רֵאשִׁית לְרֵאשִׁיתוֹ.

הִנּוֹ אֲדוֹן עוֹלָם, וְכָל נוֹצָר יוֹרֶה גְדֻלָּתוֹ וּמַלְכוּתוֹ.

שֶׁפַע נְבוּאָתוֹ נְתָנוֹ אֶל־אַנְשֵׁי סְגֻלָּתוֹ וְתִפְאַרְתּוֹ.

לֹא קָם בְּיִשְׂרָאֵל כְּמֹשֶׁה עוֹד נָבִיא וּמַבִּיט אֶת תְּמוּנָתוֹ.

תּוֹרַת אֱמֶת נָתַן לְעַמּוֹ אֵל עַל יַד נְבִיאוֹ נֶאֱמַן בֵּיתוֹ.

לֹא יַחֲלִיף הָאֵל וְלֹא יָמִיר דָּתוֹ לְעוֹלָמִים לְזוּלָתוֹ.

צוֹפֶה וְיוֹדֵעַ סְתָרֵינוּ, מַבִּיט לְסוֹף דָּבָר בְּקַדְמָתוֹ.

גּוֹמֵל לְאִישׁ חֶסֶד כְּמִפְעָלוֹ, נוֹתֵן לְרָשָׁע רָע כְּרִשְׁעָתוֹ.

יִשְׁלַח לְקֵץ יָמִין מְשִׁיחֵנוּ לִפְדּוֹת מְחַכֵּי קֵץ יְשׁוּעָתוֹ.

מֵתִים יְחַיֶּה אֵל בְּרֹב חַסְדּוֹ, בָּרוּךְ עֲדֵי עַד שֵׁם תְּהִלָּתוֹ.

MORNING BLESSINGS

The following blessings are said aloud by the Leader, but each individual
should say them quietly as well. It is our custom to say them standing.

בָּרוּךְ Blessed are You, LORD our God,
King of the Universe,
who gives the heart understanding
to distinguish day from night.

Blessed are You, LORD our God,
King of the Universe,
who has not made me a heathen.

Blessed are You, LORD our God,
King of the Universe,
who has not made me a slave.

Blessed are You, LORD our God,
King of the Universe,
men: who has not made me a woman.
women: who has made me according to His will.

שֶׁלֹּא עָשַׂנִי *Who has not made me a heathen, a slave, a woman:* These three
blessings are mentioned in the Talmud (*Menaḥot* 43b). Before we bless God
for the universalities of human life, we bless Him for the particularities of
our identity. We belong to the people of the covenant; we are free; and we
have differentiated responsibilities as women and men. These blessings have
nothing to do with hierarchies of dignity, for we believe that every human
being is equally formed in the image of God. Rather, they are expressions
of acknowledgment of the special duties of Jewish life. Heathens, slaves and
women are exempt from certain commands which apply to Jewish men. By
these blessings, we express our faith that the commandments are not a burden but a cherished vocation.

ברכות השחר

The following blessings are said aloud by the שְׁלִיחַ צִבּוּר*, but each individual should say them quietly as well. It is our custom to say them standing.*

בָּרוּךְ אַתָּה יהוה אֱלֹהֵינוּ מֶלֶךְ הָעוֹלָם
אֲשֶׁר נָתַן לַשֶּׂכְוִי בִינָה
לְהַבְחִין בֵּין יוֹם וּבֵין לָיְלָה.

בָּרוּךְ אַתָּה יהוה אֱלֹהֵינוּ מֶלֶךְ הָעוֹלָם
שֶׁלֹּא עָשַׂנִי גּוֹי.

בָּרוּךְ אַתָּה יהוה אֱלֹהֵינוּ מֶלֶךְ הָעוֹלָם
שֶׁלֹּא עָשַׂנִי עָבֶד.

בָּרוּךְ אַתָּה יהוה אֱלֹהֵינוּ מֶלֶךְ הָעוֹלָם
women שֶׁלֹּא עָשַׂנִי אִשָּׁה. / *men* שֶׁעָשַׂנִי כִּרְצוֹנוֹ.

בָּרוּךְ אַתָּה *Blessed are You:* These blessings, itemized in the Talmud (*Berakhot* 60b), were originally said at home to accompany the various stages of waking and rising. "Who gives sight to the blind" was said on opening one's eyes, "Who clothes the naked" on putting on clothes, and so on. Several medieval authorities, however, held that they should be said in the synagogue.

Their purpose is to make us conscious of what we might otherwise take for granted. Praise is an act of focused attention, foregrounding what is usually in the background of awareness. "The world is full of the light of God, but to see it we must learn to open our eyes" (Rabbi Naḥman of Bratslav).

אֲשֶׁר נָתַן לַשֶּׂכְוִי *Who gives the heart:* This is the translation according to Rabbeinu Asher (Rosh); Rashi and Abudarham read it, "who gives the cockerel." According to Rosh's reading, the first blessing mirrors the first request of the Amida, for human understanding, as well as the first act of creation in which God created light, separating it from darkness.

Blessed are You, LORD our God,
    King of the Universe,
      who gives sight to the blind.

Blessed are You, LORD our God,
    King of the Universe,
      who clothes the naked.

Blessed are You, LORD our God,
    King of the Universe,
      who sets captives free.

Blessed are You, LORD our God,
    King of the Universe,
      who raises those bowed down.

Blessed are You, LORD our God,
    King of the Universe,
      who spreads the earth above the waters.

Blessed are You, LORD our God,
    King of the Universe,
      who has provided me with all I need.

Blessed are You, LORD our God,
    King of the Universe,
      who makes firm the steps of man.

Blessed are You, LORD our God,
    King of the Universe,
      who girds Israel with strength.

Blessed are You, LORD our God,
    King of the Universe,
      who crowns Israel with glory.

Blessed are You, LORD our God,
    King of the Universe,
      who gives strength to the weary.

בָּרוּךְ אַתָּה יהוה אֱלֹהֵֽינוּ מֶֽלֶךְ הָעוֹלָם
פּוֹקֵֽחַ עִוְרִים.

בָּרוּךְ אַתָּה יהוה אֱלֹהֵֽינוּ מֶֽלֶךְ הָעוֹלָם
מַלְבִּישׁ עֲרֻמִּים.

בָּרוּךְ אַתָּה יהוה אֱלֹהֵֽינוּ מֶֽלֶךְ הָעוֹלָם
מַתִּיר אֲסוּרִים.

בָּרוּךְ אַתָּה יהוה אֱלֹהֵֽינוּ מֶֽלֶךְ הָעוֹלָם
זוֹקֵף כְּפוּפִים.

בָּרוּךְ אַתָּה יהוה אֱלֹהֵֽינוּ מֶֽלֶךְ הָעוֹלָם
רוֹקַע הָאָֽרֶץ עַל הַמָּֽיִם.

בָּרוּךְ אַתָּה יהוה אֱלֹהֵֽינוּ מֶֽלֶךְ הָעוֹלָם
שֶׁעָֽשָׂה לִי כָּל צָרְכִּי.

בָּרוּךְ אַתָּה יהוה אֱלֹהֵֽינוּ מֶֽלֶךְ הָעוֹלָם
הַמֵּכִין מִצְעֲדֵי גָֽבֶר.

בָּרוּךְ אַתָּה יהוה אֱלֹהֵֽינוּ מֶֽלֶךְ הָעוֹלָם
אוֹזֵר יִשְׂרָאֵל בִּגְבוּרָה.

בָּרוּךְ אַתָּה יהוה אֱלֹהֵֽינוּ מֶֽלֶךְ הָעוֹלָם
עוֹטֵר יִשְׂרָאֵל בְּתִפְאָרָה.

בָּרוּךְ אַתָּה יהוה אֱלֹהֵֽינוּ מֶֽלֶךְ הָעוֹלָם
הַנּוֹתֵן לַיָּעֵף כֹּֽחַ.

בָּרוּךְ Blessed are You, Lᴏʀᴅ our God, King of the Universe,
who removes sleep from my eyes
and slumber from my eyelids.
And may it be Your will, Lᴏʀᴅ our God
and God of our ancestors,
to accustom us to Your Torah,
and make us attached to Your commandments.
Lead us not into error, transgression,
iniquity, temptation or disgrace.
Do not let the evil instinct dominate us.
Keep us far from a bad man and a bad companion.
Help us attach ourselves to the good instinct and to good deeds
and bend our instincts to be subservient to You.
Grant us, this day and every day,
grace, loving-kindness and compassion in Your eyes
and in the eyes of all who see us,
and bestow loving-kindness upon us.
Blessed are You, Lᴏʀᴅ,
who bestows loving-kindness on His people Israel.

יְהִי רָצוֹן May it be Your will, Lᴏʀᴅ my God and God of my ancestors, to
save me today and every day, from the arrogant and from arrogance itself, *Berakhot*
from a bad man, a bad friend, a bad neighbor, a bad mishap, a destructive *16b*
adversary, a harsh trial and a harsh opponent, whether or not he is a son of
the covenant.

---

us of the verse from Psalms (92:3): "To proclaim Your loving-kindness in the
morning and Your faithfulness at night."

יְהִי רָצוֹן *May it be Your will:* A meditation composed by Rabbi Judah the
Prince (late second–early third century), redactor of the Mishna and leader
of the Jewish community in Israel. We are social beings, influenced by our
environment (Maimonides); therefore, we pray to be protected from harmful
people, events and temptations. The prayer reflects the "social fabric of faith"
(Rabbi Lord Jakobovits).

בָּרוּךְ אַתָּה יהוה אֱלֹהֵינוּ מֶלֶךְ הָעוֹלָם
הַמַּעֲבִיר שֵׁנָה מֵעֵינָי וּתְנוּמָה מֵעַפְעַפָּי.
וִיהִי רָצוֹן מִלְּפָנֶיךָ יהוה אֱלֹהֵינוּ וֵאלֹהֵי אֲבוֹתֵינוּ
שֶׁתַּרְגִּילֵנוּ בְּתוֹרָתֶךָ
וְדַבְּקֵנוּ בְּמִצְוֹתֶיךָ
וְאַל תְּבִיאֵנוּ לֹא לִידֵי חֵטְא
וְלֹא לִידֵי עֲבֵרָה וְעָוֹן
וְלֹא לִידֵי נִסָּיוֹן וְלֹא לִידֵי בִזָּיוֹן
וְאַל תַּשְׁלֶט בָּנוּ יֵצֶר הָרָע
וְהַרְחִיקֵנוּ מֵאָדָם רָע וּמֵחָבֵר רָע
וְדַבְּקֵנוּ בְּיֵצֶר הַטּוֹב וּבְמַעֲשִׂים טוֹבִים
וְכֹף אֶת יִצְרֵנוּ לְהִשְׁתַּעְבֶּד לָךְ
וּתְנֵנוּ הַיּוֹם וּבְכָל יוֹם לְחֵן וּלְחֶסֶד וּלְרַחֲמִים
בְּעֵינֶיךָ, וּבְעֵינֵי כָל רוֹאֵינוּ
וְתִגְמְלֵנוּ חֲסָדִים טוֹבִים.
בָּרוּךְ אַתָּה יהוה, גּוֹמֵל חֲסָדִים טוֹבִים לְעַמּוֹ יִשְׂרָאֵל.

ברכות טז: יְהִי רָצוֹן מִלְּפָנֶיךָ יהוה אֱלֹהַי וֵאלֹהֵי אֲבוֹתַי, שֶׁתַּצִּילֵנִי הַיּוֹם וּבְכָל יוֹם
מֵעַזֵּי פָנִים וּמֵעַזּוּת פָּנִים, מֵאָדָם רָע, וּמֵחָבֵר רָע, וּמִשָּׁכֵן רָע, וּמִפֶּגַע רָע,
וּמִשָּׂטָן הַמַּשְׁחִית, מִדִּין קָשֶׁה, וּמִבַּעַל דִּין קָשֶׁה בֵּין שֶׁהוּא בֶן בְּרִית וּבֵין
שֶׁאֵינוֹ בֶן בְּרִית.

הַמַּעֲבִיר *Who removes sleep from my eyes:* Having thanked God for the blessings with which we are surrounded, we conclude by asking for His help in
dedicating our lives to His service, undeterred by obstacles that may stand
in our way. The prayer ends with thanksgiving for God's kindness, reminding

THE BINDING OF ISAAC

*On the basis of Jewish mystical tradition, some have the custom of saying daily
the biblical passage recounting the Binding of Isaac, the supreme trial of faith
in which Abraham demonstrated his love of God above all other loves.*

Our God and God of our ancestors, remember us with a favorable memory, and recall
us with a remembrance of salvation and compassion from the highest of high heavens.
Remember, LORD our God, on our behalf, the love of the ancients, Abraham, Isaac
and Yisrael Your servants; the covenant, the loving-kindness, and the oath You swore
to Abraham our father on Mount Moriah, and the Binding, when he bound Isaac his
son on the altar, as is written in Your Torah:

It happened after these things that God tested Abraham. He said to him, *Gen. 22*
"Abraham!" "Here I am," he replied. He said, "Take your son, your only
son, Isaac, whom you love, and go to the land of Moriah and offer him
there as a burnt-offering on one of the mountains which I shall say to you."
Early the next morning Abraham rose and saddled his donkey and took
his two lads with him, and Isaac his son, and he cut wood for the burnt-
offering, and he set out for the place of which God had told him. On the
third day Abraham looked up and saw the place from afar. Abraham said
to his lads, "Stay here with the donkey while I and the boy go on ahead.
We will worship and we will return to you." Abraham took the wood
for the burnt-offering and placed it on Isaac his son, and he took in his
hand the fire and the knife, and the two of them went together. Isaac said
to Abraham his father, "Father?" and he said "Here I am, my son." And
he said, "Here are the fire and the wood, but where is the sheep for the
burnt-offering?" Abraham said, "God will see to the sheep for the burnt-
offering, my son." And the two of them went together. They came to the
place God had told him about, and Abraham built there an altar and
arranged the wood and bound Isaac his son and laid him on the altar on
top of the wood. He reached out his hand and took the knife to slay his
son. Then an angel of the LORD called out to him from heaven, "Abraham!
Abraham!" He said, "Here I am." He said, "Do not reach out your hand
against the boy; do not do anything to him, for now I know that you fear
God, because you have not held back your son, your only son, from Me."
Abraham looked up and there he saw a ram caught in a thicket by its horns,
and Abraham went and took the ram and offered it as a burnt-offering
instead of his son. Abraham called that place "The LORD will see," as is
said to this day, "On the mountain of the LORD He will be seen." The

פרשת העקדה

*On the basis of Jewish mystical tradition, some have the cu~~~
the biblical passage recounting the Binding of Isaac, the ~~~saying daily
in which Abraham demonstrated his love of God abo~~~ a other of faith*

אֱלֹהֵינוּ, זָכְרֵנוּ בְּזִכְרוֹן טוֹב לְפָנֶיךָ, וּפָקְדֵנוּ בִּפְקֻדַּת יְשׁוּעָה וְרַחֲמִים
מִקֶּדֶם, זְכָר לָנוּ יהוה אֱלֹהֵינוּ, אַהֲבַת הַקַּדְמוֹנִים אַבְרָהָם יִצְחָק וְיִשְׂרָאֵל
אֶת בְּרִית וְאֶת הַחֶסֶד וְאֶת הַשְּׁבוּעָה שֶׁנִּשְׁבַּעְתָּ לְאַבְרָהָם אָבִינוּ בְּהַר
הַמֹּרִיָּה, וְאֶת הָעֲקֵדָה שֶׁעָקַד אֶת יִצְחָק בְּנוֹ עַל גַּבֵּי הַמִּזְבֵּחַ, כַּכָּתוּב בְּתוֹרָתֶךָ:

בראשית כב

וַיְהִי אַחַר הַדְּבָרִים הָאֵלֶּה, וְהָאֱלֹהִים נִסָּה אֶת־אַבְרָהָם, וַיֹּאמֶר אֵלָיו אַבְרָהָם,
וַיֹּאמֶר הִנֵּנִי: וַיֹּאמֶר קַח־נָא אֶת־בִּנְךָ אֶת־יְחִידְךָ אֲשֶׁר־אָהַבְתָּ אֶת־יִצְחָק,
וְלֶךְ־לְךָ אֶל־אֶרֶץ הַמֹּרִיָּה, וְהַעֲלֵהוּ שָׁם לְעֹלָה עַל אַחַד הֶהָרִים אֲשֶׁר אֹמַר
אֵלֶיךָ: וַיַּשְׁכֵּם אַבְרָהָם בַּבֹּקֶר, וַיַּחֲבֹשׁ אֶת־חֲמֹרוֹ, וַיִּקַּח אֶת־שְׁנֵי נְעָרָיו אִתּוֹ
וְאֵת יִצְחָק בְּנוֹ, וַיְבַקַּע עֲצֵי עֹלָה, וַיָּקָם וַיֵּלֶךְ אֶל־הַמָּקוֹם אֲשֶׁר־אָמַר־לוֹ
הָאֱלֹהִים: בַּיּוֹם הַשְּׁלִישִׁי וַיִּשָּׂא אַבְרָהָם אֶת־עֵינָיו וַיַּרְא אֶת־הַמָּקוֹם מֵרָחֹק:
וַיֹּאמֶר אַבְרָהָם אֶל־נְעָרָיו, שְׁבוּ־לָכֶם פֹּה עִם־הַחֲמוֹר, וַאֲנִי וְהַנַּעַר נֵלְכָה עַד־
כֹּה, וְנִשְׁתַּחֲוֶה וְנָשׁוּבָה אֲלֵיכֶם: וַיִּקַּח אַבְרָהָם אֶת־עֲצֵי הָעֹלָה וַיָּשֶׂם עַל־יִצְחָק
בְּנוֹ, וַיִּקַּח בְּיָדוֹ אֶת־הָאֵשׁ וְאֶת־הַמַּאֲכֶלֶת, וַיֵּלְכוּ שְׁנֵיהֶם יַחְדָּו: וַיֹּאמֶר יִצְחָק
אֶל־אַבְרָהָם אָבִיו, וַיֹּאמֶר אָבִי, וַיֹּאמֶר הִנֶּנִּי בְנִי, וַיֹּאמֶר, הִנֵּה הָאֵשׁ וְהָעֵצִים,
וְאַיֵּה הַשֶּׂה לְעֹלָה: וַיֹּאמֶר אַבְרָהָם, אֱלֹהִים יִרְאֶה־לּוֹ הַשֶּׂה לְעֹלָה, בְּנִי, וַיֵּלְכוּ
שְׁנֵיהֶם יַחְדָּו: וַיָּבֹאוּ אֶל־הַמָּקוֹם אֲשֶׁר אָמַר־לוֹ הָאֱלֹהִים, וַיִּבֶן שָׁם אַבְרָהָם
אֶת־הַמִּזְבֵּחַ וַיַּעֲרֹךְ אֶת־הָעֵצִים, וַיַּעֲקֹד אֶת־יִצְחָק בְּנוֹ, וַיָּשֶׂם אֹתוֹ עַל־הַמִּזְבֵּחַ
מִמַּעַל לָעֵצִים: וַיִּשְׁלַח אַבְרָהָם אֶת־יָדוֹ, וַיִּקַּח אֶת־הַמַּאֲכֶלֶת, לִשְׁחֹט אֶת־
בְּנוֹ: וַיִּקְרָא אֵלָיו מַלְאַךְ יהוה מִן־הַשָּׁמַיִם, וַיֹּאמֶר אַבְרָהָם אַבְרָהָם, וַיֹּאמֶר
הִנֵּנִי: וַיֹּאמֶר אַל־תִּשְׁלַח יָדְךָ אֶל־הַנַּעַר, וְאַל־תַּעַשׂ לוֹ מְאוּמָה, כִּי עַתָּה
יָדַעְתִּי כִּי־יְרֵא אֱלֹהִים אַתָּה, וְלֹא חָשַׂכְתָּ אֶת־בִּנְךָ אֶת־יְחִידְךָ מִמֶּנִּי: וַיִּשָּׂא
אַבְרָהָם אֶת־עֵינָיו, וַיַּרְא וְהִנֵּה־אַיִל, אַחַר נֶאֱחַז בַּסְּבַךְ בְּקַרְנָיו, וַיֵּלֶךְ אַבְרָהָם
וַיִּקַּח אֶת־הָאַיִל, וַיַּעֲלֵהוּ לְעֹלָה תַּחַת בְּנוֹ: וַיִּקְרָא אַבְרָהָם שֵׁם־הַמָּקוֹם
הַהוּא יהוה יִרְאֶה, אֲשֶׁר יֵאָמֵר הַיּוֹם בְּהַר יהוה יֵרָאֶה: וַיִּקְרָא מַלְאַךְ יהוה

angel of the Lord called to Abraham a second time from heaven, and
said, "By Myself I swear, declares the Lord, that because you have done
this and have not held back your son, your only son, I will greatly bless
you of the seashore, and your descendants, as the stars of heaven and the
gates of their enemies. Through your descendants, all the nations of the
earth will be blessed, because you have heeded My voice." Then Abraham
returned to his lads, and they rose and went together to Beersheba, and
Abraham stayed in Beersheba.

verse, just as Abraham our father suppressed his compassion to
wholeheartedly, so may Your compassion suppress Your anger from us
Your compassion prevail over Your other attributes. Deal with us, Lord
God, with the attributes of loving-kindness and compassion, and in Your great
ness may Your anger be turned away from Your people, Your city, Your land and
inheritance. Fulfill in us, Lord our God, the promise You made in Your Torah
the hand of Moses Your servant, as it is said: "I will remember My covenant   *Lev. 26*
with Jacob, and also My covenant with Isaac, and also My covenant with Abraham I
will remember, and the land I will remember."

ACCEPTING THE SOVEREIGNTY OF HEAVEN

לְעוֹלָם A person should always be God-fearing, privately and publicly,   *Tanna*
acknowledging the truth and speaking it in his heart.   *DeVei*
He should rise early and say: *Eliyahu,*
ch. 21

> Master of all worlds,
> not because of our righteousness   *Dan. 9*
>   do we lay our pleas before You,
>   but because of Your great compassion.

"privately" and "speaking it [truth] in his heart" (that is, the secret practice of
Judaism) and the recitation here of the first lines of the Shema, which could
not be said at the normal time. The final blessing, "Who sanctifies His name
among the multitudes," refers to the martyrdom of those who went to their
deaths rather than renounce their faith. Martyrdom is called *Kiddush HaShem*,
"sanctifying [God's] name."

רִבּוֹן *Master of all worlds:* This passage also appears in the *Ne'ila* prayer on Yom

אֶל־אַבְרָהָם שֵׁנִית מִן־הַשָּׁמָיִם: וַיֹּאמֶר, בִּי נִשְׁבַּעְתִּי נְאֻם־יהוה, כִּי יַעַן אֲשֶׁר
עָשִׂיתָ אֶת־הַדָּבָר הַזֶּה, וְלֹא חָשַׂכְתָּ אֶת־בִּנְךָ אֶת־יְחִידֶךָ: כִּי־בָרֵךְ אֲבָרֶכְךָ,
וְהַרְבָּה אַרְבֶּה אֶת־זַרְעֲךָ כְּכוֹכְבֵי הַשָּׁמַיִם, וְכַחוֹל אֲשֶׁר עַל־שְׂפַת הַיָּם, וְיִרַשׁ
זַרְעֲךָ אֵת שַׁעַר אֹיְבָיו: וְהִתְבָּרְכוּ בְזַרְעֲךָ כֹּל גּוֹיֵי הָאָרֶץ, עֵקֶב אֲשֶׁר שָׁמַעְתָּ
בְּקֹלִי: וַיָּשָׁב אַבְרָהָם אֶל־נְעָרָיו, וַיָּקֻמוּ וַיֵּלְכוּ יַחְדָּו אֶל־בְּאֵר שָׁבַע, וַיֵּשֶׁב
אַבְרָהָם בִּבְאֵר שָׁבַע:

רִבּוֹנוֹ שֶׁל עוֹלָם, כְּמוֹ שֶׁכָּבַשׁ אַבְרָהָם אָבִינוּ אֶת רַחֲמָיו לַעֲשׂוֹת רְצוֹנְךָ בְּלֵבָב שָׁלֵם,
כֵּן יִכְבְּשׁוּ רַחֲמֶיךָ אֶת כַּעַסְךָ מֵעָלֵינוּ וְיָגֹלּוּ רַחֲמֶיךָ עַל מִדּוֹתֶיךָ. וְתִתְנַהֵג עִמָּנוּ יהוה
אֱלֹהֵינוּ בְּמִדַּת הַחֶסֶד וּבְמִדַּת הָרַחֲמִים, וּבְטוּבְךָ הַגָּדוֹל יָשׁוּב חֲרוֹן אַפְּךָ מֵעַמְּךָ
וּמֵעִירְךָ וּמֵאַרְצְךָ וּמִנַּחֲלָתֶךָ. וְקַיֶּם לָנוּ יהוה אֱלֹהֵינוּ אֶת הַדָּבָר שֶׁהִבְטַחְתָּנוּ בְּתוֹרָתֶךָ
ויקרא כו עַל יְדֵי מֹשֶׁה עַבְדֶּךָ, כָּאָמוּר: וְזָכַרְתִּי אֶת־בְּרִיתִי יַעֲקוֹב וְאַף אֶת־בְּרִיתִי יִצְחָק, וְאַף
אֶת־בְּרִיתִי אַבְרָהָם אֶזְכֹּר, וְהָאָרֶץ אֶזְכֹּר:

קבלת עול מלכות שמים

תנא דבי
אליהו,
פרק כא לְעוֹלָם יְהֵא אָדָם יְרֵא שָׁמַיִם בְּסֵתֶר וּבְגָלוּי
וּמוֹדֶה עַל הָאֱמֶת, וְדוֹבֵר אֱמֶת בִּלְבָבוֹ
וְיַשְׁכֵּם וְיֹאמַר
רִבּוֹן כָּל הָעוֹלָמִים
דניאל ט לֹא עַל־צִדְקוֹתֵינוּ אֲנַחְנוּ מַפִּילִים תַּחֲנוּנֵינוּ לְפָנֶיךָ
כִּי עַל־רַחֲמֶיךָ הָרַבִּים:

לְעוֹלָם *A person should always:* This whole section until "Who sanctifies His
name among the multitudes" appears in the tenth-century Midrash, *Tanna
DeVei Eliyahu* (chapter 21). Some believe that it dates from a period of persecution under the Persian ruler Yazdegerd II who, in 456 CE, forbade the
observance of Shabbat and the reading of the Torah. Jews continued to practice their faith in secret, saying prayers at times and in ways that would not
be detected by their persecutors. This explains the reference to fearing God

What are we? What are our lives?
What is our loving-kindness? What is our righteousness?
What is our salvation? What is our strength?
What is our might? What shall we say before You,
Lᴏʀᴅ our God and God of our ancestors?
Are not all the mighty like nothing before You,
the men of renown as if they had never been,
the wise as if they know nothing,
and the understanding as if they lack intelligence?
For their many works are in vain,
and the days of their lives like a fleeting breath before You.
The pre-eminence of man over the animals is nothing,   *Eccl. 3*
for all is but a fleeting breath.

אֲבָל Yet we are Your people, the children of Your covenant,
the children of Abraham, Your beloved,
to whom You made a promise on Mount Moriah;
the offspring of Isaac his only one who was bound on the altar;
the congregation of Jacob Your firstborn son
whom – because of the love with which You loved him
and the joy with which You rejoiced in him –
You called Yisrael and Yeshurun.

לְפִיכָךְ Therefore it is our duty
to thank You, and to praise, glorify, bless, sanctify
and give praise and thanks to Your name.
Happy are we, how good is our portion,
how lovely our fate, how beautiful our heritage.

_____

empty, futile." However, it literally means "a short breath." It conveys a sense
of the brevity and insubstantiality of life as a physical phenomenon. All that
lives soon dies, and is as if it had never been. *Yet:* You created us, made us,
chose us. We are infinitesimally small, yet brushed by the wings of Infinity.
We are dust; yet *we are Your people, children of Your covenant*, descendants

מַה אָנוּ, מֶה חַיֵּינוּ, מֶה חַסְדֵּנוּ, מַה צִּדְקוֹתֵינוּ
מַה יְשׁוּעָתֵנוּ, מַה כֹּחֵנוּ, מַה גְּבוּרָתֵנוּ
מַה נֹּאמַר לְפָנֶיךָ, יהוה אֱלֹהֵינוּ וֵאלֹהֵי אֲבוֹתֵינוּ
הֲלֹא כָּל הַגִּבּוֹרִים כְּאַיִן לְפָנֶיךָ
וְאַנְשֵׁי הַשֵּׁם כְּלֹא הָיוּ
וַחֲכָמִים כִּבְלִי מַדָּע, וּנְבוֹנִים כִּבְלִי הַשְׂכֵּל
כִּי רֹב מַעֲשֵׂיהֶם תֹּהוּ, וִימֵי חַיֵּיהֶם הֶבֶל לְפָנֶיךָ
וּמוֹתַר הָאָדָם מִן־הַבְּהֵמָה אָיִן
כִּי הַכֹּל הָבֶל:

קהלת ג

אֲבָל אֲנַחְנוּ עַמְּךָ בְּנֵי בְרִיתֶךָ
בְּנֵי אַבְרָהָם אֹהַבְךָ שֶׁנִּשְׁבַּעְתָּ לּוֹ בְּהַר הַמּוֹרִיָּה
זֶרַע יִצְחָק יְחִידוֹ שֶׁנֶּעֱקַד עַל גַּבֵּי הַמִּזְבֵּחַ
עֲדַת יַעֲקֹב בִּנְךָ בְּכוֹרֶךָ
שֶׁמֵּאַהֲבָתְךָ שֶׁאָהַבְתָּ אוֹתוֹ, וּמִשִּׂמְחָתְךָ שֶׁשָּׂמַחְתָּ בּוֹ
קָרָאתָ אֶת שְׁמוֹ יִשְׂרָאֵל וִישֻׁרוּן.

לְפִיכָךְ אֲנַחְנוּ חַיָּבִים
לְהוֹדוֹת לְךָ וּלְשַׁבֵּחֲךָ וּלְפָאֶרְךָ
וּלְבָרֶךְ וּלְקַדֵּשׁ וְלָתֵת שֶׁבַח וְהוֹדָיָה לִשְׁמֶךָ.
אַשְׁרֵינוּ, מַה טּוֹב חֶלְקֵנוּ
וּמַה נָּעִים גּוֹרָלֵנוּ, וּמַה יָּפָה יְרֻשָּׁתֵנוּ.

Kippur. It expresses the paradox of the human condition in the presence of God. We know how small we are and how brief our lives. *Fleeting breath*: the Hebrew word *hevel* – the key word of the opening chapters of Ecclesiastes, from which this line is taken – has been translated as "vain, meaningless,

▸ Happy are we who, early and late,
  evening and morning,
  say twice each day –

> ## Listen, Israel: the LORD is our God, the LORD is One.
> *Deut. 6*
>
> *Quietly:* Blessed be the name of His glorious kingdom for ever and all time.

Some congregations say the entire first paragraph of the Shema (below) at this point.
If there is a concern that the Shema will not be recited within the prescribed
time, then all three paragraphs should be said. See law 26.

Love the LORD your God with all your heart, with all your soul, and with all your
might. These words which I command you today shall be on your heart. Teach them
repeatedly to your children, speaking of them when you sit at home and when you
travel on the way, when you lie down and when you rise. Bind them as a sign on your
hand, and they shall be an emblem between your eyes. Write them on the doorposts
of your house and gates.

> אַתָּה הוּא It was You who existed
> before the world was created,
> it is You now that the world has been created.
> It is You in this world
> and You in the World to Come.
> ▸ Sanctify Your name
> through those who sanctify Your name,
> and sanctify Your name
> throughout Your world.
> By Your salvation may our pride be exalted;
> raise high our pride.
> Blessed are You, LORD,
> who sanctifies His name among the multitudes.

---

the refusal of Jews to abandon their faith. God does not alter or revoke His
covenant; therefore, we may not renounce our religion or identity: "I, God, do
not change; so you, children of Jacob, are not destroyed" (Mal. 3:6).

◆ אַשְׁרֵינוּ, שֶׁאֲנַחְנוּ מַשְׁכִּימִים וּמַעֲרִיבִים עֶרֶב וָבֹקֶר
וְאוֹמְרִים פַּעֲמַיִם בְּכָל יוֹם

דברים ו

שְׁמַע יִשְׂרָאֵל, יהוה אֱלֹהֵינוּ, יהוה אֶחָד:

Quietly בָּרוּךְ שֵׁם כְּבוֹד מַלְכוּתוֹ לְעוֹלָם וָעֶד.

Some congregations say the entire first paragraph of the שמע (below) at this point.
If there is a concern that the שמע will not be recited within the prescribed
time, then all three paragraphs should be said. See law 26.

וְאָהַבְתָּ אֵת יהוה אֱלֹהֶיךָ, בְּכָל־לְבָבְךָ, וּבְכָל־נַפְשְׁךָ, וּבְכָל־מְאֹדֶךָ: וְהָיוּ הַדְּבָרִים
הָאֵלֶּה, אֲשֶׁר אָנֹכִי מְצַוְּךָ הַיּוֹם, עַל־לְבָבֶךָ: וְשִׁנַּנְתָּם לְבָנֶיךָ, וְדִבַּרְתָּ בָּם, בְּשִׁבְתְּךָ
בְּבֵיתֶךָ, וּבְלֶכְתְּךָ בַדֶּרֶךְ, וּבְשָׁכְבְּךָ וּבְקוּמֶךָ: וּקְשַׁרְתָּם לְאוֹת עַל־יָדֶךָ וְהָיוּ לְטֹטָפֹת
בֵּין עֵינֶיךָ: וּכְתַבְתָּם עַל־מְזֻזוֹת בֵּיתֶךָ וּבִשְׁעָרֶיךָ:

אַתָּה הוּא עַד שֶׁלֹּא נִבְרָא הָעוֹלָם

אַתָּה הוּא מִשֶּׁנִּבְרָא הָעוֹלָם.

אַתָּה הוּא בָּעוֹלָם הַזֶּה

וְאַתָּה הוּא לָעוֹלָם הַבָּא.

◆ קַדֵּשׁ אֶת שִׁמְךָ עַל מַקְדִּישֵׁי שְׁמֶךָ

וְקַדֵּשׁ אֶת שִׁמְךָ בְּעוֹלָמֶךָ

וּבִישׁוּעָתְךָ תָּרוּם וְתַגְבִּיהַּ קַרְנֵנוּ.

בָּרוּךְ אַתָּה יהוה

הַמְקַדֵּשׁ אֶת שְׁמוֹ בָּרַבִּים.

_____

of those You singled out to be witnesses to the world of Your existence
and majesty.

אַתָּה הוּא *It was You who existed:* This prayer, with its emphasis on the changeless-
ness of God, may have been incorporated at a time of persecution, expressing

אַתָּה הוּא You are the LORD our God
in heaven and on earth,
and in the highest heaven of heavens.
Truly, You are the first
and You are the last,
and besides You there is no god.
Gather those who hope in You
from the four quarters of the earth.
May all mankind recognize and know
that You alone are God
over all the kingdoms on earth.

You made the heavens and the earth,
the sea and all they contain.
Who among all the works of Your hands,
above and below,
can tell You what to do?

Heavenly Father,
deal kindly with us
for the sake of Your great name
by which we are called,
and fulfill for us,
LORD our God,
that which is written:

> "At that time I will bring you home, and at that time *Zeph. 3*
> I will gather you, for I will give you renown and praise
> among all the peoples of the earth when I bring back
> your exiles before your eyes, says the LORD."

---

ingathering of Jews and of a time when "I will give you renown and praise
among all the peoples of the earth." This entire sequence of prayers is eloquent testimony to how Jews sustained faith and hope, dignity and pride,
during some of the most prolonged periods of persecution in history.

אַתָּה הוּא יהוה אֱלֹהֵינוּ
בַּשָּׁמַיִם וּבָאָרֶץ.
וּבִשְׁמֵי הַשָּׁמַיִם הָעֶלְיוֹנִים.
אֱמֶת, אַתָּה הוּא רִאשׁוֹן
וְאַתָּה הוּא אַחֲרוֹן
וּמִבַּלְעָדֶיךָ אֵין אֱלֹהִים.
קַבֵּץ קֹוֶיךָ מֵאַרְבַּע כַּנְפוֹת הָאָרֶץ.
יַכִּירוּ וְיֵדְעוּ כָּל בָּאֵי עוֹלָם
כִּי אַתָּה הוּא הָאֱלֹהִים לְבַדְּךָ לְכֹל מַמְלְכוֹת הָאָרֶץ.

אַתָּה עָשִׂיתָ אֶת הַשָּׁמַיִם וְאֶת הָאָרֶץ
אֶת הַיָּם וְאֶת כָּל אֲשֶׁר בָּם
וּמִי בְּכָל מַעֲשֵׂי יָדֶיךָ בָּעֶלְיוֹנִים אוֹ בַתַּחְתּוֹנִים
שֶׁיֹּאמַר לְךָ מַה תַּעֲשֶׂה.

אָבִינוּ שֶׁבַּשָּׁמַיִם
עֲשֵׂה עִמָּנוּ חֶסֶד
בַּעֲבוּר שִׁמְךָ הַגָּדוֹל שֶׁנִּקְרָא עָלֵינוּ
וְקַיֶּם לָנוּ יהוה אֱלֹהֵינוּ
מַה שֶּׁכָּתוּב:

צפניה ג

בָּעֵת הַהִיא אָבִיא אֶתְכֶם, וּבָעֵת קַבְּצִי אֶתְכֶם,
כִּי־אֶתֵּן אֶתְכֶם לְשֵׁם וְלִתְהִלָּה בְּכֹל עַמֵּי הָאָרֶץ,
בְּשׁוּבִי אֶת־שְׁבוּתֵיכֶם לְעֵינֵיכֶם, אָמַר יהוה:

───

אַתָּה הוּא *You are the* LORD *our God:* This second prayer, for the end of
exile, culminates with the verse from Zephania (3:20) which speaks of the

OFFERINGS

The sages held that, in the absence of the Temple, studying the laws of sacrifices is the equivalent of offering them. Hence the following texts. There are different customs as to how many passages are to be said, and one should follow the custom of one's congregation. The minimum requirement is to say the verses relating to The Daily Sacrifice on the next page.

THE BASIN

The Lord spoke to Moses, saying: Make a bronze basin, with its bronze *Ex. 30* stand for washing, and place it between the Tent of Meeting and the altar, and put water in it. From it, Aaron and his sons are to wash their hands and feet. When they enter the Tent of Meeting, they shall wash with water so that they will not die; likewise when they approach the altar to minister, presenting a fire-offering to the Lord. They must wash their hands and feet so that they will not die. This shall be an everlasting ordinance for Aaron and his descendants throughout their generations.

TAKING OF THE ASHES

The Lord spoke to Moses, saying: Instruct Aaron and his sons, saying, *Lev. 6* This is the law of the burnt-offering. The burnt-offering shall remain on the altar hearth throughout the night until morning, and the altar fire shall be kept burning on it. The priest shall then put on his linen garments, and linen breeches next to his body, and shall remove the ashes of the burnt-offering that the fire has consumed on the altar and place them beside the altar. Then he shall take off these clothes and put on others, and carry the ashes outside the camp to a clean place. The fire on the altar must be kept burning; it must not go out. Each morning the priest shall burn wood on it, and prepare on it the burnt-offering and burn the fat of the peace-offerings. A perpetual fire must be kept burning on the altar; it must not go out.

May it be Your will, Lord our God and God of our ancestors, that You have compassion on us and pardon us all our sins, grant atonement for all our iniquities and forgive all our transgressions. May You rebuild the Temple swiftly in our days so that we may offer You the continual-offering that it may atone for us as You have prescribed for us in Your Torah through Moses Your servant, from the mouthpiece of Your glory, as it is said:

---

about sacrifice was a substitute for sacrifice itself (*Ta'anit* 27b). The passage from the Mishna (*Zevaḥim* 5) is also about sacrifices, and was chosen because it does not contain any disagreement between the sages, and thus accords with the rule that one should pray "after a decided *halakha*," that is, an item of Jewish law about which there is no debate.

סדר הקרבנות

חז״ל held that, in the absence of the Temple, studying the laws of sacrifices is the equivalent of offering them. Hence the following texts. There are different customs as to how many passages are to be said, and one should follow the custom of one's congregation. The minimum requirement is to say the verses relating to the קרבן תמיד on the next page.

פרשת הכיור

שמות ל

וַיְדַבֵּר יהוה אֶל־מֹשֶׁה לֵּאמֹר: וְעָשִׂיתָ כִּיּוֹר נְחֹשֶׁת וְכַנּוֹ נְחֹשֶׁת לְרָחְצָה: וְנָתַתָּ אֹתוֹ בֵּין־אֹהֶל מוֹעֵד וּבֵין הַמִּזְבֵּחַ, וְנָתַתָּ שָׁמָּה מָיִם: וְרָחֲצוּ אַהֲרֹן וּבָנָיו מִמֶּנּוּ אֶת־יְדֵיהֶם וְאֶת־רַגְלֵיהֶם: בְּבֹאָם אֶל־אֹהֶל מוֹעֵד יִרְחֲצוּ־מַיִם, וְלֹא יָמֻתוּ, אוֹ בְגִשְׁתָּם אֶל־הַמִּזְבֵּחַ לְשָׁרֵת, לְהַקְטִיר אִשֶּׁה לַיהוה: וְרָחֲצוּ יְדֵיהֶם וְרַגְלֵיהֶם וְלֹא יָמֻתוּ, וְהָיְתָה לָהֶם חָק־עוֹלָם, לוֹ וּלְזַרְעוֹ לְדֹרֹתָם:

פרשת תרומת הדשן

ויקרא ו

וַיְדַבֵּר יהוה אֶל־מֹשֶׁה לֵּאמֹר: צַו אֶת־אַהֲרֹן וְאֶת־בָּנָיו לֵאמֹר, זֹאת תּוֹרַת הָעֹלָה, הִוא הָעֹלָה עַל מוֹקְדָה עַל־הַמִּזְבֵּחַ כָּל־הַלַּיְלָה עַד־הַבֹּקֶר, וְאֵשׁ הַמִּזְבֵּחַ תּוּקַד בּוֹ: וְלָבַשׁ הַכֹּהֵן מִדּוֹ בַד, וּמִכְנְסֵי־בַד יִלְבַּשׁ עַל־בְּשָׂרוֹ, וְהֵרִים אֶת־הַדֶּשֶׁן אֲשֶׁר תֹּאכַל הָאֵשׁ אֶת־הָעֹלָה, עַל־הַמִּזְבֵּחַ, וְשָׂמוֹ אֵצֶל הַמִּזְבֵּחַ: וּפָשַׁט אֶת־בְּגָדָיו, וְלָבַשׁ בְּגָדִים אֲחֵרִים, וְהוֹצִיא אֶת־הַדֶּשֶׁן אֶל־מִחוּץ לַמַּחֲנֶה, אֶל־מָקוֹם טָהוֹר: וְהָאֵשׁ עַל־הַמִּזְבֵּחַ תּוּקַד־בּוֹ, לֹא תִכְבֶּה, וּבִעֵר עָלֶיהָ הַכֹּהֵן עֵצִים בַּבֹּקֶר בַּבֹּקֶר, וְעָרַךְ עָלֶיהָ הָעֹלָה, וְהִקְטִיר עָלֶיהָ חֶלְבֵי הַשְּׁלָמִים: אֵשׁ, תָּמִיד תּוּקַד עַל־הַמִּזְבֵּחַ, לֹא תִכְבֶּה:

יְהִי רָצוֹן מִלְּפָנֶיךָ יהוה אֱלֹהֵינוּ וֵאלֹהֵי אֲבוֹתֵינוּ, שֶׁתְּרַחֵם עָלֵינוּ, וְתִמְחֹל לָנוּ עַל כָּל חַטֹּאתֵינוּ וּתְכַפֵּר לָנוּ עַל כָּל עֲוֹנוֹתֵינוּ וְתִסְלַח לָנוּ עַל כָּל פְּשָׁעֵינוּ, וְתִבְנֶה בֵּית הַמִּקְדָּשׁ בִּמְהֵרָה בְיָמֵינוּ, וְנַקְרִיב לְפָנֶיךָ קָרְבַּן הַתָּמִיד שֶׁיְּכַפֵּר בַּעֲדֵנוּ, כְּמוֹ שֶׁכָּתַבְתָּ עָלֵינוּ בְּתוֹרָתֶךָ עַל יְדֵי מֹשֶׁה עַבְדֶּךָ מִפִּי כְבוֹדֶךָ, כָּאָמוּר

OFFERINGS

There now follows a second cycle of study, with the same structure as the first, with passages from (1) the Torah, (2) the Mishna, and (3) the Gemara. The passages from the Torah relate to the daily, weekly and monthly sacrifices because, in the absence of the Temple, the sages held that study of the laws

THE DAILY SACRIFICE

וַיְדַבֵּר The LORD said to Moses, "Command the Israelites and *Num. 28* tell them: 'Be careful to offer to Me at the appointed time My food-offering consumed by fire, as an aroma pleasing to Me.' Tell them: 'This is the fire-offering you shall offer to the LORD – two lambs a year old without blemish, as a regular burnt-offering each day. Prepare one lamb in the morning and the other toward evening, together with a meal-offering of a tenth of an ephah of fine flour mixed with a quarter of a hin of oil from pressed olives. This is the regular burnt-offering instituted at Mount Sinai as a pleasing aroma, a fire-offering made to the LORD. Its libation is to be a quarter of a hin [of wine] with each lamb, poured in the Sanctuary as a libation of strong drink to the LORD. Prepare the second lamb in the afternoon, along with the same meal-offering and libation as in the morning. This is a fire-offering, an aroma pleasing to the LORD.'"

וְשָׁחַט He shall slaughter it at the north side of the altar before *Lev. 1* the LORD, and Aaron's sons the priests shall sprinkle its blood against the altar on all sides.

May it be Your will, LORD our God and God of our ancestors,
that this recitation be considered accepted and favored before You
as if we had offered the daily sacrifice at its appointed time and place, according to its laws.

It is You, LORD our God, to whom our ancestors offered fragrant incense when the Temple stood, as You commanded them through Moses Your prophet, as is written in Your Torah:

THE INCENSE

The LORD said to Moses: Take fragrant spices – balsam, onycha, galbanum *Ex. 30* and pure frankincense, all in equal amounts – and make a fragrant blend of incense, the work of a perfumer, well mixed, pure and holy. Grind it very finely and place it in front of the [Ark of] Testimony in the Tent of Meeting, where I will meet with you. It shall be most holy to you.

And it is said:

Aaron shall burn fragrant incense on the altar every morning when he cleans the lamps. He shall burn incense again when he lights the lamps toward evening so that there will be incense before the LORD at all times, throughout your generations.

פרשת קרבן התמיד

במדבר כח

וַיְדַבֵּר יהוה אֶל־מֹשֶׁה לֵּאמֹר: צַו אֶת־בְּנֵי יִשְׂרָאֵל וְאָמַרְתָּ
אֲלֵהֶם, אֶת־קָרְבָּנִי לַחְמִי לְאִשַּׁי, רֵיחַ נִיחֹחִי, תִּשְׁמְרוּ לְהַקְרִיב
לִי בְּמוֹעֲדוֹ: וְאָמַרְתָּ לָהֶם, זֶה הָאִשֶּׁה אֲשֶׁר תַּקְרִיבוּ לַיהוה,
כְּבָשִׂים בְּנֵי־שָׁנָה תְמִימִם שְׁנַיִם לַיּוֹם, עֹלָה תָמִיד: אֶת־הַכֶּבֶשׂ
אֶחָד תַּעֲשֶׂה בַבֹּקֶר, וְאֵת הַכֶּבֶשׂ הַשֵּׁנִי תַּעֲשֶׂה בֵּין הָעַרְבָּיִם:
וַעֲשִׂירִית הָאֵיפָה סֹלֶת לְמִנְחָה, בְּלוּלָה בְּשֶׁמֶן כָּתִית רְבִיעִת
הַהִין: עֹלַת תָּמִיד, הָעֲשֻׂיָה בְּהַר סִינַי, לְרֵיחַ נִיחֹחַ אִשֶּׁה לַיהוה:
וְנִסְכּוֹ רְבִיעִת הַהִין לַכֶּבֶשׂ הָאֶחָד, בַּקֹּדֶשׁ הַסֵּךְ נֶסֶךְ שֵׁכָר
לַיהוה: וְאֵת הַכֶּבֶשׂ הַשֵּׁנִי תַּעֲשֶׂה בֵּין הָעַרְבָּיִם, כְּמִנְחַת הַבֹּקֶר
וּכְנִסְכּוֹ תַּעֲשֶׂה, אִשֵּׁה רֵיחַ נִיחֹחַ לַיהוה:

ויקרא א

וְשָׁחַט אֹתוֹ עַל יֶרֶךְ הַמִּזְבֵּחַ צָפֹנָה לִפְנֵי יהוה, וְזָרְקוּ בְּנֵי אַהֲרֹן
הַכֹּהֲנִים אֶת־דָּמוֹ עַל־הַמִּזְבֵּחַ, סָבִיב:

יְהִי רָצוֹן מִלְּפָנֶיךָ, יהוה אֱלֹהֵינוּ וֵאלֹהֵי אֲבוֹתֵינוּ
שֶׁתְּהֵא אֲמִירָה זוֹ חֲשׁוּבָה וּמְקֻבֶּלֶת וּמְרֻצָּה לְפָנֶיךָ
כְּאִלּוּ הִקְרַבְנוּ קָרְבַּן הַתָּמִיד בְּמוֹעֲדוֹ וּבִמְקוֹמוֹ וּכְהִלְכָתוֹ.

אַתָּה הוּא יהוה אֱלֹהֵינוּ שֶׁהִקְטִירוּ אֲבוֹתֵינוּ לְפָנֶיךָ אֶת קְטֹרֶת הַסַּמִּים בִּזְמַן שֶׁבֵּית
הַמִּקְדָּשׁ הָיָה קַיָּם, כַּאֲשֶׁר צִוִּיתָ אוֹתָם עַל יְדֵי מֹשֶׁה נְבִיאֶךָ, כַּכָּתוּב בְּתוֹרָתֶךָ:

פרשת הקטורת

שמות ל

וַיֹּאמֶר יהוה אֶל־מֹשֶׁה, קַח־לְךָ סַמִּים נָטָף וּשְׁחֵלֶת וְחֶלְבְּנָה, סַמִּים וּלְבֹנָה
זַכָּה, בַּד בְּבַד יִהְיֶה: וְעָשִׂיתָ אֹתָהּ קְטֹרֶת, רֹקַח מַעֲשֵׂה רוֹקֵחַ, מְמֻלָּח, טָהוֹר
קֹדֶשׁ: וְשָׁחַקְתָּ מִמֶּנָּה הָדֵק, וְנָתַתָּה מִמֶּנָּה לִפְנֵי הָעֵדֻת בְּאֹהֶל מוֹעֵד אֲשֶׁר
אִוָּעֵד לְךָ שָׁמָּה, קֹדֶשׁ קָדָשִׁים תִּהְיֶה לָכֶם:

וְנֶאֱמַר

וְהִקְטִיר עָלָיו אַהֲרֹן קְטֹרֶת סַמִּים, בַּבֹּקֶר בַּבֹּקֶר בְּהֵיטִיבוֹ אֶת־הַנֵּרֹת
יַקְטִירֶנָּה: וּבְהַעֲלֹת אַהֲרֹן אֶת־הַנֵּרֹת בֵּין הָעַרְבַּיִם יַקְטִירֶנָּה, קְטֹרֶת תָּמִיד
לִפְנֵי יהוה לְדֹרֹתֵיכֶם:

The rabbis taught: How was the incense prepared? It weighed 368 manehs, 365 *Keritot 6a*
corresponding to the number of days in a solar year, a maneh for each day, half
to be offered in the morning and half in the afternoon, and three additional
manehs from which the High Priest took two handfuls on Yom Kippur. These
were put back into the mortar on the day before Yom Kippur and ground again
very thoroughly so as to be extremely fine. The incense contained eleven kinds
of spices: balsam, onycha, galbanum and frankincense, each weighing seventy
manehs; myrrh, cassia, spikenard and saffron, each weighing sixteen manehs;
twelve manehs of costus, three of aromatic bark; nine of cinnamon; nine kabs
of Carsina lye; three seahs and three kabs of Cyprus wine. If Cyprus wine was
not available, old white wine might be used. A quarter of a kab of Sodom salt,
and a minute amount of a smoke-raising herb. Rabbi Nathan the Babylonian
says: also a minute amount of Jordan amber. If one added honey to the mixture,
he rendered it unfit for sacred use. If he omitted any one of its ingredients, he is
guilty of a capital offence.

Rabban Simeon ben Gamliel says: "Balsam" refers to the sap that drips from the
balsam tree. The Carsina lye was used for bleaching the onycha to improve it.
The Cyprus wine was used to soak the onycha in it to make it pungent. Though
urine is suitable for this purpose, it is not brought into the Temple out of
respect.

It was taught, Rabbi Nathan says: While it was being ground, another would say,
"Grind well, well grind," because the [rhythmic] sound is good for spices. If it
was mixed in half-quantities, it is fit for use, but we have not heard whether this
applies to a third or a quarter. Rabbi Judah said: The general rule is that if it was
made in the correct proportions, it is fit for use even if made in half-quantity, but
if he omitted any one of its ingredients, he is guilty of a capital offence.

It was taught, Bar Kappara says: Once every sixty or seventy years, the accumu- *JT Yoma 4:5*
lated surpluses amounted to half the yearly quantity. Bar Kappara also taught:
If a minute quantity of honey had been mixed into the incense, no one could
have resisted the scent. Why did they not put honey into it? Because the Torah
says, "For you are not to burn any leaven or honey in a fire-offering made to *Lev. 2*
the LORD."

The following three verses are each said three times:
The LORD of hosts is with us; the God of Jacob is our stronghold, Selah. *Ps. 46*
LORD of hosts, happy is the one who trusts in You. *Ps. 84*
LORD, save! May the King answer us on the day we call. *Ps. 20*

כריתות ו

תָּנוּ רַבָּנָן: פִּטּוּם הַקְּטֹרֶת כֵּיצַד, שְׁלֹשׁ מֵאוֹת וְשִׁשִּׁים וּשְׁמוֹנָה מָנִים הָיוּ בָהּ. שְׁלֹשׁ מֵאוֹת וְשִׁשִּׁים וַחֲמִשָּׁה כְּמִנְיַן יְמוֹת הַחַמָּה, מָנֶה לְכָל יוֹם, פְּרָס בְּשַׁחֲרִית וּפְרָס בֵּין הָעַרְבָּיִם, וּשְׁלֹשָׁה מָנִים יְתֵרִים שֶׁמֵּהֶם מַכְנִיס כֹּהֵן גָּדוֹל מְלֹא חָפְנָיו בְּיוֹם הַכִּפּוּרִים, וּמַחֲזִירָן לְמַכְתֶּשֶׁת בְּעֶרֶב יוֹם הַכִּפּוּרִים וְשׁוֹחֲקָן יָפֶה יָפֶה, כְּדֵי שֶׁתְּהֵא דַקָּה מִן הַדַּקָּה. וְאֶחָד עָשָׂר סַמָּנִים הָיוּ בָהּ, וְאֵלּוּ הֵן: הַצֳּרִי, וְהַצִּפֹּרֶן, וְהַחֶלְבְּנָה, וְהַלְּבוֹנָה מִשְׁקַל שִׁבְעִים שִׁבְעִים מָנֶה, מוֹר, וּקְצִיעָה, שִׁבֹּלֶת נֵרְדְּ, וְכַרְכֹּם מִשְׁקַל שִׁשָּׁה עָשָׂר שִׁשָּׁה עָשָׂר מָנֶה, הַקֹּשְׁטְ שְׁנֵים עָשָׂר, קִלּוּפָה שְׁלֹשָׁה, קִנָּמוֹן תִּשְׁעָה, בֹּרִית כַּרְשִׁינָה תִּשְׁעָה קַבִּין, יֵין קַפְרִיסִין סְאִין תְּלָת וְקַבִּין תְּלָתָא, וְאִם לֹא מָצָא יֵין קַפְרִיסִין, מֵבִיא חֲמַר חִוַּרְיָן עַתִּיק. מֶלַח סְדוֹמִית רֹבַע, מַעֲלֶה עָשָׁן כָּל שֶׁהוּא. רַבִּי נָתָן הַבַּבְלִי אוֹמֵר: אַף כִּפַּת הַיַּרְדֵּן כָּל שֶׁהוּא, וְאִם נָתַן בָּהּ דְּבַשׁ פְּסָלָהּ, וְאִם חִסַּר אַחַד מִכָּל סַמָּנֶיהָ, חַיָּב מִיתָה.

רַבָּן שִׁמְעוֹן בֶּן גַּמְלִיאֵל אוֹמֵר: הַצֳּרִי אֵינוֹ אֶלָּא שְׂרָף הַנּוֹטֵף מֵעֲצֵי הַקְּטָף. בֹּרִית כַּרְשִׁינָה שֶׁשָּׁפִין בָּהּ אֶת הַצִּפֹּרֶן כְּדֵי שֶׁתְּהֵא נָאָה, יֵין קַפְרִיסִין שֶׁשּׁוֹרִין בּוֹ אֶת הַצִּפֹּרֶן כְּדֵי שֶׁתְּהֵא עַזָּה, וַהֲלֹא מֵי רַגְלַיִם יָפִין לָהּ, אֶלָּא שֶׁאֵין מַכְנִיסִין מֵי רַגְלַיִם בַּמִּקְדָּשׁ מִפְּנֵי הַכָּבוֹד.

תַּנְיָא, רַבִּי נָתָן אוֹמֵר: כְּשֶׁהוּא שׁוֹחֵק אוֹמֵר, הָדֵק הֵיטֵב הֵיטֵב הָדֵק, מִפְּנֵי שֶׁהַקּוֹל יָפֶה לַבְּשָׂמִים. פִּטְּמָהּ לַחֲצָאִין כְּשֵׁרָה, לִשְׁלִישׁ וְלִרְבִיעַ לֹא שָׁמָעְנוּ. אָמַר רַבִּי יְהוּדָה: זֶה הַכְּלָל, אִם כְּמִדָּתָהּ כְּשֵׁרָה לַחֲצָאִין, וְאִם חִסַּר אֶחָד מִכָּל סַמָּנֶיהָ חַיָּב מִיתָה.

ירושלמי יומא ד, הלכה ה

תַּנְיָא, בַּר קַפָּרָא אוֹמֵר: אַחַת לְשִׁשִּׁים אוֹ לְשִׁבְעִים שָׁנָה הָיְתָה בָאָה שֶׁל שִׁירַיִם לַחֲצָאִין. וְעוֹד תָּנֵי בַּר קַפָּרָא: אִלּוּ הָיָה נוֹתֵן בָּהּ קוֹרְטוֹב שֶׁל דְּבַשׁ אֵין אָדָם יָכוֹל לַעֲמֹד מִפְּנֵי רֵיחָהּ, וְלָמָּה אֵין מְעָרְבִין בָּהּ דְּבַשׁ, מִפְּנֵי שֶׁהַתּוֹרָה אָמְרָה: כִּי ויקרא ב כָל־שְׂאֹר וְכָל־דְּבַשׁ לֹא־תַקְטִירוּ מִמֶּנּוּ אִשֶּׁה לַיהוה:

The following three verses are each said three times:

תהלים מו   יהוה צְבָאוֹת עִמָּנוּ, מִשְׂגָּב לָנוּ אֱלֹהֵי יַעֲקֹב סֶלָה:

תהלים פד   יהוה צְבָאוֹת, אַשְׁרֵי אָדָם בֹּטֵחַ בָּךְ:

תהלים כ   יהוה הוֹשִׁיעָה, הַמֶּלֶךְ יַעֲנֵנוּ בְיוֹם־קָרְאֵנוּ:

You are my hiding place; You will protect me from distress and surround *Ps. 32*
me with songs of salvation, Selah.

Then the offering of Judah and Jerusalem will be pleasing to the LORD as *Mal. 3*
in the days of old and as in former years.

THE ORDER OF THE PRIESTLY FUNCTIONS

Abaye related the order of the daily priestly functions in the name of tradi- *Yoma 33a*
tion and in accordance with Abba Shaul: The large pile [of wood] comes
before the second pile for the incense; the second pile for the incense
precedes the laying in order of the two logs of wood; the laying in order of
the two logs of wood comes before the removing of ashes from the inner
altar; the removing of ashes from the inner altar precedes the cleaning of
the five lamps; the cleaning of the five lamps comes before the blood of
the daily offering; the blood of the daily offering precedes the cleaning
of the [other] two lamps; the cleaning of the two lamps comes before the
incense-offering; the incense-offering precedes the burning of the limbs;
the burning of the limbs comes before the meal-offering; the meal-offering
precedes the pancakes; the pancakes come before the wine-libations; the
wine-libations precede the additional offerings; the additional offerings
come before the [frankincense] censers; the censers precede the daily
afternoon offering; as it is said, "On it he shall arrange burnt-offerings, and *Lev. 6*
on it he shall burn the fat of the peace-offerings" – "on it" [the daily offering]
all the offerings were completed.

Please, by the power of Your great right hand, set the captive nation free.
Accept Your people's prayer. Strengthen us, purify us, You who are revered.
Please, mighty One, guard like the pupil of the eye those who seek Your unity.
Bless them, cleanse them, have compassion on them,
grant them Your righteousness always.
Mighty One, Holy One, in Your great goodness guide Your congregation.
Only One, exalted One, turn to Your people, who proclaim Your holiness.
Accept our plea and heed our cry, You who know all secret thoughts.
    Blessed be the name of His glorious kingdom for ever and all time.

Master of the Universe, You have commanded us to offer the daily sacrifice at
its appointed time with the priests at their service, the Levites on their platform,
and the Israelites at their post. Now, because of our sins, the Temple is destroyed
and the daily sacrifice discontinued, and we have no priest at his service, no
Levite on his platform, no Israelite at his post. But You said: "We will offer in *Hos. 14*
place of bullocks [the prayer of] our lips." Therefore may it be Your will, LORD
our God and God of our ancestors, that the prayer of our lips be considered,
accepted and favored before You as if we had offered the daily sacrifice at its
appointed time and place, according to its laws.

אַתָּה סֵתֶר לִי, מִצַּר תִּצְּרֵנִי, רָנֵּי פַלֵּט תְּסוֹבְבֵנִי סֶלָה: תהלים לב

וְעָרְבָה לַיהוה מִנְחַת יְהוּדָה וִירוּשָׁלָֽםִ מלאכי ג
כִּימֵי עוֹלָם וּכְשָׁנִים קַדְמוֹנִיּוֹת:

סדר המערכה

אַבַּיֵּי הֲוָה מְסַדֵּר סֵדֶר הַמַּעֲרָכָה מִשְּׁמָא דִגְמָרָא, וְאַלִּבָּא דְאַבָּא שָׁאוּל: יומא לג
מַעֲרָכָה גְדוֹלָה קוֹדֶֽמֶת לְמַעֲרָכָה שְׁנִיָּה שֶׁל קְטֹֽרֶת, וּמַעֲרָכָה שְׁנִיָּה שֶׁל
קְטֹֽרֶת קוֹדֶֽמֶת לְסִדּוּר שְׁנֵי גִזְרֵי עֵצִים, וְסִדּוּר שְׁנֵי גִזְרֵי עֵצִים קוֹדֵם לְדִשּׁוּן
מִזְבֵּֽחַ הַפְּנִימִי, וְדִשּׁוּן מִזְבֵּֽחַ הַפְּנִימִי קוֹדֵם לַהֲטָבַת חָמֵשׁ נֵרוֹת, וַהֲטָבַת
חָמֵשׁ נֵרוֹת קוֹדֶֽמֶת לְדַם הַתָּמִיד, וְדַם הַתָּמִיד קוֹדֵם לַהֲטָבַת שְׁתֵּי
נֵרוֹת, וַהֲטָבַת שְׁתֵּי נֵרוֹת קוֹדֶֽמֶת לִקְטֹֽרֶת, וּקְטֹֽרֶת קוֹדֶֽמֶת לָאֵבָרִים,
וְאֵבָרִים לְמִנְחָה, וּמִנְחָה לַחֲבִתִּין, וַחֲבִתִּין לִנְסָכִין, וּנְסָכִין לְמוּסָפִין,
וּמוּסָפִין לְבָזִיכִין, וּבָזִיכִין קוֹדְמִין לְתָמִיד שֶׁל בֵּין הָעַרְבָּֽיִם: שֶׁנֶּאֱמַר:
וְעָרַךְ עָלֶֽיהָ הָעֹלָה, וְהִקְטִיר עָלֶֽיהָ חֶלְבֵי הַשְּׁלָמִים: עָלֶֽיהָ הַשְׁלֵם כָּל ויקרא ו
הַקָּרְבָּנוֹת כֻּלָּם.

אָנָּא, בְּכֹֽחַ גְּדֻלַּת יְמִינְךָ, תַּתִּיר צְרוּרָה.
קַבֵּל רִנַּת עַמְּךָ, שַׂגְּבֵֽנוּ, טַהֲרֵֽנוּ, נוֹרָא.
נָא גִבּוֹר, דּוֹרְשֵׁי יִחוּדְךָ כְּבָבַת שָׁמְרֵם.
בָּרְכֵם, טַהֲרֵם, רַחֲמֵם, צִדְקָתְךָ תָּמִיד גָּמְלֵם.
חֲסִין קָדוֹשׁ, בְּרֹב טוּבְךָ נַהֵל עֲדָתֶֽךָ.
יָחִיד גֵּאֶה, לְעַמְּךָ פְּנֵה, זוֹכְרֵי קְדֻשָּׁתֶֽךָ.
שַׁוְעָתֵֽנוּ קַבֵּל וּשְׁמַע צַעֲקָתֵֽנוּ, יוֹדֵֽעַ תַּעֲלוּמוֹת.
בָּרוּךְ שֵׁם כְּבוֹד מַלְכוּתוֹ לְעוֹלָם וָעֶד.

רִבּוֹן הָעוֹלָמִים, אַתָּה צִוִּיתָֽנוּ לְהַקְרִיב קָרְבַּן הַתָּמִיד בְּמוֹעֲדוֹ וְלִהְיוֹת כֹּהֲנִים
בַּעֲבוֹדָתָם וּלְוִיִּם בְּדוּכָנָם וְיִשְׂרָאֵל בְּמַעֲמָדָם, וְעַתָּה בַּעֲוֹנוֹתֵֽינוּ חָרַב בֵּית
הַמִּקְדָּשׁ וּבָטֵל הַתָּמִיד וְאֵין לָֽנוּ לֹא כֹהֵן בַּעֲבוֹדָתוֹ וְלֹא לֵוִי בְּדוּכָנוֹ וְלֹא
יִשְׂרָאֵל בְּמַעֲמָדוֹ, וְאַתָּה אָמַֽרְתָּ: וּנְשַׁלְּמָה פָרִים שְׂפָתֵֽינוּ: לָכֵן יְהִי רָצוֹן מִלְּפָנֶֽיךָ הושע יד
יהוה אֱלֹהֵֽינוּ וֵאלֹהֵי אֲבוֹתֵֽינוּ, שֶׁיְּהֵא שִֽׂיחַ שִׂפְתוֹתֵֽינוּ חָשׁוּב וּמְקֻבָּל וּמְרֻצֶּה
לְפָנֶֽיךָ, כְּאִלּוּ הִקְרַֽבְנוּ קָרְבַּן הַתָּמִיד בְּמוֹעֲדוֹ וּבִמְקוֹמוֹ וּכְהִלְכָתוֹ.

On Rosh Ḥodesh:

וּבְרָאשֵׁי חָדְשֵׁכֶם On your new moons, present as a burnt-offering to the
LORD, two young bulls, one ram, and seven yearling lambs without
blemish. There shall be a meal-offering of three-tenths of an ephah of
fine flour mixed with oil for each bull, two-tenths of an ephah of fine
flour mixed with oil for the ram, and one-tenth of an ephah of fine flour
mixed with oil for each lamb. This is the burnt-offering – a fire-offering
of pleasing aroma to the LORD. Their libations shall be: half a hin of
wine for each bull, a third of a hin for the ram, and a quarter of a hin
for each lamb. This is the monthly burnt-offering to be made at each
new moon throughout the year. One male goat should be offered as a
sin-offering to God, in addition to the regular daily burnt-offering and
its libation.

Num. 28

LAWS OF OFFERINGS, MISHNA ZEVAHIM

אֵיזֶהוּ מְקוֹמָן What is the location for sacrifices? The holiest offerings were slaughtered on the north side. The bull and he-goat of Yom Kippur were slaughtered
on the north side. Their blood was received in a sacred vessel on the north side,
and had to be sprinkled between the poles [of the Ark], toward the veil [screen-
ing the Holy of Holies], and on the golden altar. [The omission of] one of these
sprinklings invalidated [the atonement ceremony]. The leftover blood was to be
poured onto the western base of the outer altar. If this was not done, however,
the omission did not invalidate [the ceremony].

Zevaḥim
Ch. 5

The bulls and he-goats that were completely burnt were slaughtered on the north
side, their blood was received in a sacred vessel on the north side, and had to
be sprinkled toward the veil and on the golden altar. [The omission of] one
of these sprinklings invalidated [the ceremony]. The leftover blood was to be
poured onto the western base of the outer altar. If this was not done, however,
the omission did not invalidate [the ceremony]. All these offerings were burnt
where the altar ashes were deposited.

The communal and individual sin-offerings – these are the communal sin-
offerings: the he-goats offered on Rosh Ḥodesh and Festivals were slaughtered
on the north side, their blood was received in a sacred vessel on the north side,
and required four sprinklings, one on each of the four corners of the altar. How
was this done? The priest ascended the ramp and turned [right] onto the surrounding ledge. He came to the southeast corner, then went to the northeast,
then to the northwest, then to the southwest. The leftover blood he poured onto
the southern base. [The meat of these offerings], prepared in any manner, was

51

בראש חודש:

במדבר כח

וּבְרָאשֵׁי חָדְשֵׁיכֶם תַּקְרִיבוּ עֹלָה לַיהוה, פָּרִים בְּנֵי־בָקָר שְׁנַיִם, וְאַיִל אֶחָד, כְּבָשִׂים בְּנֵי־שָׁנָה שִׁבְעָה, תְּמִימִם: וּשְׁלֹשָׁה עֶשְׂרֹנִים סֹלֶת מִנְחָה בְּלוּלָה בַשֶּׁמֶן לַפָּר הָאֶחָד, וּשְׁנֵי עֶשְׂרֹנִים סֹלֶת מִנְחָה בְּלוּלָה בַשֶּׁמֶן לָאַיִל הָאֶחָד: וְעִשָּׂרֹן עִשָּׂרוֹן סֹלֶת מִנְחָה בְּלוּלָה בַשֶּׁמֶן לַכֶּבֶשׂ הָאֶחָד, עֹלָה רֵיחַ נִיחֹחַ, אִשֶּׁה לַיהוה: וְנִסְכֵּיהֶם, חֲצִי הַהִין יִהְיֶה לַפָּר, וּשְׁלִישִׁת הַהִין לָאַיִל, וּרְבִיעִת הַהִין לַכֶּבֶשׂ יָיִן, זֹאת עֹלַת חֹדֶשׁ בְּחָדְשׁוֹ לְחָדְשֵׁי הַשָּׁנָה: וּשְׂעִיר עִזִּים אֶחָד לְחַטָּאת לַיהוה, עַל־עֹלַת הַתָּמִיד יֵעָשֶׂה, וְנִסְכּוֹ:

דיני זבחים

זבחים פרקה

אֵיזֶהוּ מְקוֹמָן שֶׁל זְבָחִים. קָדְשֵׁי קָדָשִׁים שְׁחִיטָתָן בַּצָּפוֹן. פָּר וְשָׂעִיר שֶׁל יוֹם הַכִּפּוּרִים, שְׁחִיטָתָן בַּצָּפוֹן, וְקִבּוּל דָּמָן בִּכְלִי שָׁרֵת בַּצָּפוֹן, וְדָמָן טָעוּן הַזָּיָה עַל בֵּין הַבַּדִּים, וְעַל הַפָּרֹכֶת, וְעַל מִזְבַּח הַזָּהָב. מַתָּנָה אַחַת מֵהֶן מְעַכָּבֶת. שְׁיָרֵי הַדָּם הָיָה שׁוֹפֵךְ עַל יְסוֹד מַעֲרָבִי שֶׁל מִזְבַּח הַחִיצוֹן, אִם לֹא נָתַן לֹא עִכֵּב.

פָּרִים הַנִּשְׂרָפִים וּשְׂעִירִים הַנִּשְׂרָפִים, שְׁחִיטָתָן בַּצָּפוֹן, וְקִבּוּל דָּמָן בִּכְלִי שָׁרֵת בַּצָּפוֹן, וְדָמָן טָעוּן הַזָּיָה עַל הַפָּרֹכֶת וְעַל מִזְבַּח הַזָּהָב. מַתָּנָה אַחַת מֵהֶן מְעַכָּבֶת. שְׁיָרֵי הַדָּם הָיָה שׁוֹפֵךְ עַל יְסוֹד מַעֲרָבִי שֶׁל מִזְבַּח הַחִיצוֹן, אִם לֹא נָתַן לֹא עִכֵּב. אֵלּוּ וָאֵלּוּ נִשְׂרָפִין בְּבֵית הַדֶּשֶׁן.

חַטֹּאת הַצִּבּוּר וְהַיָּחִיד. אֵלּוּ הֵן חַטֹּאת הַצִּבּוּר: שְׂעִירֵי רָאשֵׁי חֳדָשִׁים וְשֶׁל מוֹעֲדוֹת. שְׁחִיטָתָן בַּצָּפוֹן, וְקִבּוּל דָּמָן בִּכְלִי שָׁרֵת בַּצָּפוֹן, וְדָמָן טָעוּן אַרְבַּע מַתָּנוֹת עַל אַרְבַּע קְרָנוֹת. כֵּיצַד, עָלָה בַכֶּבֶשׁ, וּפָנָה לַסּוֹבֵב, וּבָא לוֹ לְקֶרֶן דְּרוֹמִית מִזְרָחִית, מִזְרָחִית צְפוֹנִית, צְפוֹנִית מַעֲרָבִית, מַעֲרָבִית דְּרוֹמִית. שְׁיָרֵי הַדָּם הָיָה שׁוֹפֵךְ עַל יְסוֹד דְּרוֹמִי.

eaten within the [courtyard] curtains, by males of the priest-hood, on that day and the following night, until midnight.

The burnt-offering was among the holiest of sacrifices. It was slaughtered on the north side, its blood was received in a sacred vessel on the north side, and required two sprinklings [at opposite corners of the altar], making four in all. The offering had to be flayed, dismembered and wholly consumed by fire.

The communal peace-offerings and the guilt-offerings – these are the guilt-offerings: the guilt-offering for robbery; the guilt-offering for profane use of a sacred object; the guilt-offering [for violating] a betrothed maidservant; the guilt-offering of a Nazirite [who had become defiled by a corpse]; the guilt-offering of a leper [at his cleansing]; and the guilt-offering in case of doubt. All these were slaughtered on the north side, their blood was received in a sacred vessel on the north side, and required two sprinklings [at opposite corners of the altar], making four in all. [The meat of these offerings], prepared in any manner, was eaten within the [courtyard] curtains, by males of the priesthood, on that day and the following night, until midnight.

The thanksgiving-offering and the ram of a Nazirite were offerings of lesser holiness. They could be slaughtered anywhere in the Temple court, and their blood required two sprinklings [at opposite corners of the altar], making four in all. The meat of these offerings, prepared in any manner, was eaten anywhere within the city [Jerusalem], by anyone during that day and the following night until midnight. This also applied to the portion of these sacrifices [given to the priests], except that the priests' portion was only to be eaten by the priests, their wives, children and servants.

Peace-offerings were [also] of lesser holiness. They could be slaughtered any-where in the Temple court, and their blood required two sprinklings [at opposite corners of the altar], making four in all. The meat of these offerings, prepared in any manner, was eaten anywhere within the city [Jerusalem], by anyone, for two days and one night. This also applied to the portion of these sacrifices [given to the priests], except that the priests' portion was only to be eaten by the priests, their wives, children and servants.

The firstborn and tithe of cattle and the Pesaḥ lamb were sacrifices of lesser holi-ness. They could be slaughtered anywhere in the Temple court, and their blood required only one sprinkling, which had to be done at the base of the altar. They differed in their consumption: the firstborn was eaten only by priests, while the tithe could be eaten by anyone. Both could be eaten anywhere within the city, prepared in any manner, during two days and one night. The Pesaḥ lamb had to be eaten that night until midnight. It could only be eaten by those who had been numbered for it, and eaten only roasted.

וְנֶאֱכָלִין לִפְנִים מִן הַקְּלָעִים, לְזִכְרֵי כְהֻנָּה, בְּכָל מַאֲכָל, לְיוֹם וָלַיְלָה עַד חֲצוֹת.

הָעוֹלָה קֹדֶשׁ קָדָשִׁים. שְׁחִיטָתָהּ בַּצָּפוֹן, וְקִבּוּל דָּמָהּ בִּכְלִי שָׁרֵת בַּצָּפוֹן, וְדָמָהּ טָעוּן שְׁתֵּי מַתָּנוֹת שֶׁהֵן אַרְבַּע, וּטְעוּנָה הֶפְשֵׁט וְנִתּוּחַ, וְכָלִיל לָאִשִּׁים.

וְזִבְחֵי שַׁלְמֵי צִבּוּר וַאֲשָׁמוֹת. אֵלּוּ הֵן אֲשָׁמוֹת: אֲשַׁם גְּזֵלוֹת, אֲשַׁם מְעִילוֹת, אֲשַׁם שִׁפְחָה חֲרוּפָה, אֲשַׁם נָזִיר, אֲשַׁם מְצֹרָע, אָשָׁם תָּלוּי. שְׁחִיטָתָן בַּצָּפוֹן, וְקִבּוּל דָּמָן בִּכְלִי שָׁרֵת בַּצָּפוֹן, וְדָמָן טָעוּן שְׁתֵּי מַתָּנוֹת שֶׁהֵן אַרְבַּע. וְנֶאֱכָלִין לִפְנִים מִן הַקְּלָעִים, לְזִכְרֵי כְהֻנָּה, בְּכָל מַאֲכָל, לְיוֹם וָלַיְלָה עַד חֲצוֹת.

הַתּוֹדָה וְאֵיל נָזִיר קָדָשִׁים קַלִּים. שְׁחִיטָתָן בְּכָל מָקוֹם בָּעֲזָרָה, וְדָמָן טָעוּן שְׁתֵּי מַתָּנוֹת שֶׁהֵן אַרְבַּע, וְנֶאֱכָלִין בְּכָל הָעִיר, לְכָל אָדָם, בְּכָל מַאֲכָל, לְיוֹם וָלַיְלָה עַד חֲצוֹת. הַמּוּרָם מֵהֶם כַּיּוֹצֵא בָהֶם, אֶלָּא שֶׁהַמּוּרָם נֶאֱכָל לַכֹּהֲנִים, לִנְשֵׁיהֶם, וְלִבְנֵיהֶם וּלְעַבְדֵיהֶם.

שְׁלָמִים קָדָשִׁים קַלִּים. שְׁחִיטָתָן בְּכָל מָקוֹם בָּעֲזָרָה, וְדָמָן טָעוּן שְׁתֵּי מַתָּנוֹת שֶׁהֵן אַרְבַּע, וְנֶאֱכָלִין בְּכָל הָעִיר, לְכָל אָדָם, בְּכָל מַאֲכָל, לִשְׁנֵי יָמִים וְלַיְלָה אֶחָד. הַמּוּרָם מֵהֶם כַּיּוֹצֵא בָהֶם, אֶלָּא שֶׁהַמּוּרָם נֶאֱכָל לַכֹּהֲנִים, לִנְשֵׁיהֶם, וְלִבְנֵיהֶם וּלְעַבְדֵיהֶם.

הַבְּכוֹר וְהַמַּעֲשֵׂר וְהַפֶּסַח קָדָשִׁים קַלִּים. שְׁחִיטָתָן בְּכָל מָקוֹם בָּעֲזָרָה, וְדָמָן טָעוּן מַתָּנָה אֶחָת, וּבִלְבַד שֶׁיִּתֵּן כְּנֶגֶד הַיְסוֹד. שִׁנָּה בַאֲכִילָתָן, הַבְּכוֹר נֶאֱכָל לַכֹּהֲנִים וְהַמַּעֲשֵׂר לְכָל אָדָם, וְנֶאֱכָלִין בְּכָל הָעִיר, בְּכָל מַאֲכָל, לִשְׁנֵי יָמִים וְלַיְלָה אֶחָד. הַפֶּסַח אֵינוֹ נֶאֱכָל אֶלָּא בַלַּיְלָה, וְאֵינוֹ נֶאֱכָל אֶלָּא עַד חֲצוֹת, וְאֵינוֹ נֶאֱכָל אֶלָּא לִמְנוּיָיו, וְאֵינוֹ נֶאֱכָל אֶלָּא צָלִי.

THE INTERPRETIVE PRINCIPLES OF RABBI YISHMAEL

רַבִּי יִשְׁמָעֵאל Rabbi Yishmael says:

The Torah is expounded by thirteen principles:

1. An inference from a lenient law to a strict one, and vice versa.
2. An inference drawn from identical words in two passages.
3. A general principle derived from one text or two related texts.
4. A general law followed by specific examples
   [where the law applies exclusively to those examples].
5. A specific example followed by a general law
   [where the law applies to everything implied in the general statement].
6. A general law followed by specific examples and concluding with a general
   law: here you may infer only cases similar to the examples.
7. When a general statement requires clarification by a specific example,
   or a specific example requires clarification by a general statement
   [then rules 4 and 5 do not apply].
8. When a particular case, already included in the general statement,
   is expressly mentioned to teach something new, that special provision
   applies to all other cases included in the general statement.
9. When a particular case, though included in the general statement,
   is expressly mentioned with a provision similar to the general law,
   such a case is singled out to lessen the severity of the law, not to increase it.
10. When a particular case, though included in the general statement,
    is explicitly mentioned with a provision differing from the general law,
    it is singled out to lessen in some respects, and in others to increase,
    the severity of the law.
11. When a particular case, though included in the general statement, is explic-
    itly mentioned with a new provision, the terms of the general statement no
    longer apply to it, unless Scripture indicates explicitly that they do apply.
12. A matter elucidated from its context, or from the following passage.
▸ 13. Also, when two passages [seem to] contradict each other,
      [they are to be elucidated by] a third passage that reconciles them.

May it be Your will, LORD our God and God of our ancestors, that the Temple be speedily rebuilt in our days, and grant us our share in Your Torah. And may we serve You there in reverence, as in the days of old and as in former years.

Torah is interpreted" (Maimonides, Laws of Torah Study 1:11). It was chosen because it appears at the beginning of the *Sifra*, the halakhic commentary to Leviticus, which is the source of most of the laws of offerings. It also reminds us of the indissoluble connection between the Written Law (the Mosaic books) and the Oral Law (Mishna, Midrash and Talmud). Rabbi Yishmael's principles show how the latter can be derived from the former.

בְּרַיְתָא דְרַבִּי יִשְׁמָעֵאל
רַבִּי יִשְׁמָעֵאל אוֹמֵר: בִּשְׁלֹשׁ עֶשְׂרֵה מִדּוֹת הַתּוֹרָה נִדְרֶשֶׁת

א מִקַּל וָחֹמֶר

ב וּמִגְּזֵרָה שָׁוָה

ג מִבִּנְיַן אָב מִכָּתוּב אֶחָד, וּמִבִּנְיַן אָב מִשְּׁנֵי כְתוּבִים

ד מִכְּלָל וּפְרָט

ה מִפְּרָט וּכְלָל

ו כְּלָל וּפְרָט וּכְלָל, אִי אַתָּה דָן אֶלָּא כְּעֵין הַפְּרָט

ז מִכְּלָל שֶׁהוּא צָרִיךְ לִפְרָט, וּמִפְּרָט שֶׁהוּא צָרִיךְ לִכְלָל

ח כָּל דָּבָר שֶׁהָיָה בִּכְלָל, וְיָצָא מִן הַכְּלָל לְלַמֵּד
לֹא לְלַמֵּד עַל עַצְמוֹ יָצָא, אֶלָּא לְלַמֵּד עַל הַכְּלָל כֻּלּוֹ יָצָא

ט כָּל דָּבָר שֶׁהָיָה בִּכְלָל, וְיָצָא לִטְעֹן טֹעַן אֶחָד שֶׁהוּא כְעִנְיָנוֹ
יָצָא לְהָקֵל וְלֹא לְהַחֲמִיר

י כָּל דָּבָר שֶׁהָיָה בִּכְלָל, וְיָצָא לִטְעֹן טֹעַן אַחֵר שֶׁלֹּא כְעִנְיָנוֹ
יָצָא לְהָקֵל וּלְהַחֲמִיר

יא כָּל דָּבָר שֶׁהָיָה בִּכְלָל, וְיָצָא לִדּוֹן בַּדָּבָר הֶחָדָשׁ
אִי אַתָּה יָכוֹל לְהַחֲזִירוֹ לִכְלָלוֹ
עַד שֶׁיַּחֲזִירֶנּוּ הַכָּתוּב לִכְלָלוֹ בְּפֵרוּשׁ

יב דָּבָר הַלָּמֵד מֵעִנְיָנוֹ, וְדָבָר הַלָּמֵד מִסּוֹפוֹ

יג וְכֵן שְׁנֵי כְתוּבִים הַמַּכְחִישִׁים זֶה אֶת זֶה
עַד שֶׁיָּבוֹא הַכָּתוּב הַשְּׁלִישִׁי וְיַכְרִיעַ בֵּינֵיהֶם.

יְהִי רָצוֹן מִלְּפָנֶיךָ, יהוה אֱלֹהֵינוּ וֵאלֹהֵי אֲבוֹתֵינוּ, שֶׁיִּבָּנֶה בֵּית הַמִּקְדָּשׁ
בִּמְהֵרָה בְיָמֵינוּ, וְתֵן חֶלְקֵנוּ בְּתוֹרָתֶךָ, וְשָׁם נַעֲבָדְךָ בְּיִרְאָה כִּימֵי עוֹלָם
וּכְשָׁנִים קַדְמוֹנִיּוֹת.

THE INTERPRETIVE PRINCIPLES OF RABBI YISHMAEL
This passage is included as an item of Talmud, defined in its broadest sense as
"deducing conclusions from premises, developing implications of statements,
comparing dicta, and studying the hermeneutical principles by which the

THE RABBIS' KADDISH

The following prayer, said by mourners, requires the presence of a minyan.
A transliteration can be found on page 698.

Mourner: יִתְגַּדַּל Magnified and sanctified
may His great name be,
in the world He created by His will.
May He establish His kingdom in your lifetime
and in your days,
and in the lifetime of all the house of Israel,
swiftly and soon –
and say: Amen.

All: May His great name be blessed for ever and all time.

Mourner: Blessed and praised,
glorified and exalted,
raised and honored,
uplifted and lauded
be the name of the Holy One,
blessed be He,
beyond any blessing,
song, praise and consolation uttered in the world –
and say: Amen.

---

mark the end of the Amida and its associated meditations; (3) the Mourner's
Kaddish; (4) The Rabbis' Kaddish, said after a passage from the Oral Law;
(5) the Kaddish of Renewal, said only at the conclusion of a tractate of the
Talmud, or by a child at the funeral of a parent.

The Rabbis' Kaddish is a prayer not only for the establishment of God's
kingdom but also for the teachers of Torah and their disciples. It is charac-
teristic of Judaism's value system that this is the first Kaddish we say each
morning. Judaism is a faith whose passion is education, whose heroes are
teachers, and whose citadels are schools and houses of study. To learn, to
teach, to internalize God's will, to join our minds with the great sages and
scholars of the past – this is a supreme expression of Judaism, and the one
from which all else flows.

קדיש דרבנן

The following prayer, said by mourners, requires the presence of a מנין.
A transliteration can be found on page 698.

אבל יִתְגַּדַּל וְיִתְקַדַּשׁ שְׁמֵהּ רַבָּא (קהל: אָמֵן)

בְּעָלְמָא דִּי בְרָא כִרְעוּתֵהּ

וְיַמְלִיךְ מַלְכוּתֵהּ

בְּחַיֵּיכוֹן וּבְיוֹמֵיכוֹן וּבְחַיֵּי דְּכָל בֵּית יִשְׂרָאֵל

בַּעֲגָלָא וּבִזְמַן קָרִיב

וְאִמְרוּ אָמֵן. (קהל: אָמֵן)

קהל יְהֵא שְׁמֵהּ רַבָּא מְבָרַךְ לְעָלַם וּלְעָלְמֵי עָלְמַיָּא.
ואבל

אבל יִתְבָּרַךְ וְיִשְׁתַּבַּח וְיִתְפָּאַר וְיִתְרוֹמַם וְיִתְנַשֵּׂא

וְיִתְהַדָּר וְיִתְעַלֶּה וְיִתְהַלָּל

שְׁמֵהּ דְּקֻדְשָׁא בְּרִיךְ הוּא (קהל: בְּרִיךְ הוּא)

לְעֵלָּא מִן כָּל בִּרְכָתָא

/ בעשרת ימי תשובה: לְעֵלָּא לְעֵלָּא מִכָּל בִּרְכָתָא/

וְשִׁירָתָא, תֻּשְׁבְּחָתָא וְנֶחֱמָתָא, דַּאֲמִירָן בְּעָלְמָא

וְאִמְרוּ אָמֵן. (קהל: אָמֵן)

THE RABBIS' KADDISH

The Kaddish, one of the most important of all prayers, had its origins not in the synagogue but in the house of study. It grew out of a custom, still widely practiced, of ending every discourse or sermon with the hope that we may speedily see the coming of the messianic age, when the sovereignty of God will be recognized by all the dwellers on earth. It is written mainly in Aramaic, the language most widely spoken by Jews in the first centuries of the Common Era.

It has come to have five forms: (1) Half Kaddish, recited to mark the beginning or end of a section of the prayers; (2) Full Kaddish (*Titkabal*), to

To Israel, to the teachers,
their disciples and their disciples' disciples,
and to all who engage in the study of Torah,
in this (*in Israel add:* holy) place or elsewhere,
may there come to them and you great peace,
grace, kindness and compassion,
long life, ample sustenance and deliverance,
from their Father in Heaven –
and say: Amen.

May there be great peace from heaven,
and (good) life for us and all Israel –
and say: Amen.

*Bow, take three steps back, as if taking leave of the Divine Presence,
then bow, first left, then right, then center, while saying:*
May He who makes peace in His high places,
in His compassion make peace for us and all Israel –
and say: Amen.

On Yom HaAtzma'ut and Yom Yerushalayim, continue Shaḥarit on page 428.

A PSALM BEFORE VERSES OF PRAISE

מִזְמוֹר שִׁיר A psalm of David. A song for the dedication of the House. *Ps. 30*
I will exalt You, LORD, for You have lifted me up, and not let my
enemies rejoice over me. LORD, my God, I cried to You for help
and You healed me. LORD, You lifted my soul from the grave; You
spared me from going down to the pit. Sing to the LORD, you His
devoted ones, and give thanks to His holy name. For His anger is
for a moment, but His favor for a lifetime. At night there may be
weeping, but in the morning there is joy. When I felt secure, I said,
"I shall never be shaken." LORD, when You favored me, You made
me stand firm as a mountain, but when You hid Your face, I was
terrified. To You, LORD, I called; I pleaded with my LORD: "What

עַל יִשְׂרָאֵל וְעַל רַבָּנָן

וְעַל תַּלְמִידֵיהוֹן וְעַל כָּל תַּלְמִידֵי תַלְמִידֵיהוֹן

וְעַל כָּל מָאן דְּעָסְקִין בְּאוֹרַיְתָא

דִּי בְאַתְרָא (בארץ ישראל: קַדִּישָׁא) הָדֵין, וְדִי בְּכָל אֲתַר וַאֲתַר

יְהֵא לְהוֹן וּלְכוֹן שְׁלָמָא רַבָּא

חִנָּא וְחִסְדָּא, וְרַחֲמֵי, וְחַיֵּי אֲרִיכֵי, וּמְזוֹנֵי רְוִיחֵי

וּפֻרְקָנָא מִן קֳדָם אֲבוּהוֹן דִּי בִשְׁמַיָּא

וְאִמְרוּ אָמֵן. (קהל: אָמֵן)

יְהֵא שְׁלָמָא רַבָּא מִן שְׁמַיָּא

וְחַיִּים (טוֹבִים) עָלֵינוּ וְעַל כָּל יִשְׂרָאֵל, וְאִמְרוּ אָמֵן. (קהל: אָמֵן)

Bow, take three steps back, as if taking leave of the Divine Presence,
then bow, first left, then right, then center, while saying:

עֹשֶׂה שָׁלוֹם/ בעשרת ימי תשובה: הַשָּׁלוֹם/ בִּמְרוֹמָיו

הוּא יַעֲשֶׂה בְרַחֲמָיו שָׁלוֹם, עָלֵינוּ וְעַל כָּל יִשְׂרָאֵל

וְאִמְרוּ אָמֵן. (קהל: אָמֵן)

On יום העצמאות *and* יום ירושלים, *continue* שחרית *on page 429.*

מזמור לפני פסוקי דזמרה

מִזְמוֹר שִׁיר־חֲנֻכַּת הַבַּיִת לְדָוִד: אֲרוֹמִמְךָ יהוה כִּי דִלִּיתָנִי, וְלֹא־ ‏תהלים ל

שִׂמַּחְתָּ אֹיְבַי לִי: יהוה אֱלֹהָי, שִׁוַּעְתִּי אֵלֶיךָ וַתִּרְפָּאֵנִי: יהוה,

הֶעֱלִיתָ מִן־שְׁאוֹל נַפְשִׁי, חִיִּיתַנִי מִיָּרְדִי־בוֹר: זַמְּרוּ לַיהוה חֲסִידָיו,

וְהוֹדוּ לְזֵכֶר קָדְשׁוֹ: כִּי רֶגַע בְּאַפּוֹ, חַיִּים בִּרְצוֹנוֹ, בָּעֶרֶב יָלִין בֶּכִי

וְלַבֹּקֶר רִנָּה: וַאֲנִי אָמַרְתִּי בְשַׁלְוִי, בַּל־אֶמּוֹט לְעוֹלָם: יהוה, בִּרְצוֹנְךָ

הֶעֱמַדְתָּה לְהַרְרִי עֹז, הִסְתַּרְתָּ פָנֶיךָ הָיִיתִי נִבְהָל: אֵלֶיךָ יהוה

אֶקְרָא, וְאֶל־אֲדֹנָי אֶתְחַנָּן: מַה־בֶּצַע בְּדָמִי, בְּרִדְתִּי אֶל שָׁחַת,

gain would there be if I died and went down to the grave? Can dust
thank You? Can it declare Your truth? Hear, LORD, and be gracious
to me; LORD, be my help." ▸ You have turned my sorrow into dancing. You have removed my sackcloth and clothed me with joy, so
that my soul may sing to You and not be silent. LORD my God, for
ever will I thank You.

MOURNER'S KADDISH

*The following prayer, said by mourners, requires the presence of a minyan.
A transliteration can be found on page 699.*

Mourner: יִתְגַּדַּל Magnified and sanctified
may His great name be,
in the world He created by His will.
May He establish His kingdom
in your lifetime and in your days,
and in the lifetime of all the house of Israel,
swiftly and soon – and say: Amen.

All: May His great name be blessed for ever and all time.

Mourner: Blessed and praised, glorified and exalted,
raised and honored, uplifted and lauded
be the name of the Holy One,
blessed be He,
beyond any blessing,
song, praise and consolation
uttered in the world – and say: Amen.

May there be great peace from heaven,
and life for us and all Israel – and say: Amen.

*Bow, take three steps back, as if taking leave of the Divine Presence,
then bow, first left, then right, then center, while saying:*

May He who makes peace in His high places,
make peace for us and all Israel –
and say: Amen.

הַיּוֹדְךָ עָפָר, הֲיַגִּיד אֲמִתֶּךָ: שְׁמַע־יהוה וְחָנֵּנִי, יהוה הֱיֵה־עֹזֵר לִי:

◆ הָפַכְתָּ מִסְפְּדִי לְמָחוֹל לִי, פִּתַּחְתָּ שַׂקִּי, וַתְּאַזְּרֵנִי שִׂמְחָה: לְמַעַן

יְזַמֶּרְךָ כָבוֹד וְלֹא יִדֹּם, יהוה אֱלֹהַי, לְעוֹלָם אוֹדֶךָּ:

קדיש יתום

The following prayer, said by mourners, requires the presence of a מִנְיָן.
A transliteration can be found on page 699.

אבל: יִתְגַּדַּל וְיִתְקַדַּשׁ שְׁמֵהּ רַבָּא (קהל: אָמֵן)

בְּעָלְמָא דִּי בְרָא כִרְעוּתֵהּ

וְיַמְלִיךְ מַלְכוּתֵהּ

בְּחַיֵּיכוֹן וּבְיוֹמֵיכוֹן וּבְחַיֵּי דְכָל בֵּית יִשְׂרָאֵל

בַּעֲגָלָא וּבִזְמַן קָרִיב, וְאִמְרוּ אָמֵן. (קהל: אָמֵן)

קהל
ואבל: יְהֵא שְׁמֵהּ רַבָּא מְבָרַךְ לְעָלַם וּלְעָלְמֵי עָלְמַיָּא.

אבל: יִתְבָּרַךְ וְיִשְׁתַּבַּח וְיִתְפָּאַר

וְיִתְרוֹמַם וְיִתְנַשֵּׂא וְיִתְהַדָּר וְיִתְעַלֶּה וְיִתְהַלָּל

שְׁמֵהּ דְּקֻדְשָׁא בְּרִיךְ הוּא (קהל: בְּרִיךְ הוּא)

לְעֵלָּא מִן כָּל בִּרְכָתָא / בעשרת ימי תשובה: לְעֵלָּא לְעֵלָּא מִכָּל בִּרְכָתָא/

וְשִׁירָתָא, תֻּשְׁבְּחָתָא וְנֶחֱמָתָא

דַּאֲמִירָן בְּעָלְמָא, וְאִמְרוּ אָמֵן. (קהל: אָמֵן)

יְהֵא שְׁלָמָא רַבָּא מִן שְׁמַיָּא

וְחַיִּים, עָלֵינוּ וְעַל כָּל יִשְׂרָאֵל, וְאִמְרוּ אָמֵן. (קהל: אָמֵן)

Bow, take three steps back, as if taking leave of the Divine Presence,
then bow, first left, then right, then center, while saying:

עֹשֶׂה שָׁלוֹם/ בעשרת ימי תשובה: הַשָּׁלוֹם/ בִּמְרוֹמָיו

הוּא יַעֲשֶׂה שָׁלוֹם עָלֵינוּ וְעַל כָּל יִשְׂרָאֵל

וְאִמְרוּ אָמֵן. (קהל: אָמֵן)

PESUKEI DEZIMRA

The introductory blessing to the Pesukei DeZimra (Verses of Praise) is said standing, while holding the two front tzitziot of the tallit. They are kissed and released at the end of the blessing at "songs of praise" (on next page). From the beginning of this prayer to the end of the Amida, conversation is forbidden. See table on pages 695–697 for which congregational responses are permitted.

Some say:

I hereby prepare my mouth to thank, praise and laud my Creator, for the sake of the unification of the Holy One, blessed be He, and His Divine Presence, through that which is hidden and concealed, in the name of all Israel.

BLESSED IS HE WHO SPOKE

and the world came into being, blessed is He.

> Blessed is He who creates the universe.
> Blessed is He who speaks and acts.
> Blessed is He who decrees and fulfills.
> Blessed is He who shows compassion to the earth.
> Blessed is He who shows compassion to all creatures.
> Blessed is He who gives a good reward
>   to those who fear Him.
> Blessed is He who lives for ever and exists to eternity.
> Blessed is He who redeems and saves.
> Blessed is His name.

---

structed in three movements, whose themes are: (1) *Creation:* God as He is in nature; (2) *Revelation:* God as He is in Torah and prayer; and (3) *Redemption:* God as He is in history and our lives. The theme of the Verses of Praise is Creation – God as Architect and Maker of a universe of splendor and diversity, whose orderliness testifies to the single creative will that underlies all that exists. The psalms tell this story not in scientific prose but majestic poetry, not *proving* but *proclaiming* the One at the heart of all.

The core elements of *Pesukei DeZimra* are: (1) Psalm 145 (*Ashrei*), a prayer to which the sages attached particular significance, specifying that it should be said three times daily; and (2) Psalms 146–150, which form the culmination and crescendo of the book of Psalms as a whole. These six psalms

פסוקי דזמרה

The introductory blessing to the פסוקי דזמרה *is said standing, while holding the two front* ציצית *of the* טלית *of the* בתשבחות*. They are kissed and released at the end of the blessing at* (on next page)*. From the beginning of this prayer to the end of the* עמידה*, conversation is forbidden. See table on pages 695–697 for which congregational responses are permitted.*

Some say:

הֲרֵינִי מְזַמֵּן אֶת פִּי לְהוֹדוֹת וּלְהַלֵּל וּלְשַׁבֵּחַ אֶת בּוֹרְאִי, לְשֵׁם יִחוּד קֻדְשָׁא בְּרִיךְ הוּא וּשְׁכִינְתֵּהּ עַל יְדֵי הַהוּא טָמִיר וְנֶעְלָם בְּשֵׁם כָּל יִשְׂרָאֵל.

בָּרוּךְ
שֶׁאָמַר
וְהָיָה הָעוֹלָם, בָּרוּךְ הוּא.

בָּרוּךְ עוֹשֶׂה בְרֵאשִׁית
בָּרוּךְ אוֹמֵר וְעוֹשֶׂה
בָּרוּךְ גּוֹזֵר וּמְקַיֵּם
בָּרוּךְ מְרַחֵם עַל הָאָרֶץ
בָּרוּךְ מְרַחֵם עַל הַבְּרִיּוֹת
בָּרוּךְ מְשַׁלֵּם שָׂכָר טוֹב לִירֵאָיו
בָּרוּךְ חַי לָעַד וְקַיָּם לָנֶצַח
בָּרוּךְ פּוֹדֶה וּמַצִּיל
בָּרוּךְ שְׁמוֹ

___

PESUKEI DEZIMRA / VERSES OF PRAISE

"A person should first recount the praise of the Holy One, blessed be He, and then pray" (*Berakhot* 32b), hence the passages that follow, known as the "Verses of Praise." The morning service from this point until the end is con-

Blessed are You, LORD our God,
King of the Universe,
God, compassionate Father,
extolled by the mouth of His people,
praised and glorified by the tongue of His devoted ones and
those who serve Him.
With the songs of Your servant David
we will praise You, O LORD our God.
With praises and psalms
we will magnify and praise You, glorify You,
Speak Your name and proclaim Your kingship,
our King, our God, ‣ the only One, Giver of life to the worlds,
the King whose great name is praised
and glorified to all eternity.
Blessed are You, LORD,
the King extolled with songs of praise.

הוֹדוּ לַיהוה Thank the LORD, call on His name, make His acts known   *1 Chr. 16*
among the peoples. Sing to Him, make music to Him, tell of all
His wonders. Glory in His holy name; let the hearts of those who
seek the LORD rejoice. Search out the LORD and His strength; seek
His presence at all times. Remember the wonders He has done,

Blessed are You: The second half of the blessing is a prelude to the biblical
verses that follow, mainly from the book of Psalms ("With the songs of Your
servant David we will exalt You") but also from the books of Chronicles
and Nehemiah ("extolled by the mouth of His people"). To emphasize the
significance of this declaration, we recite it standing and, at the end, kiss the
two front fringes of the tallit.

הוֹדוּ לַיהוה *Thank the LORD:* A psalm of thanksgiving composed by King
David to celebrate the moment when the Ark of the Covenant was brought
to Jerusalem. In many communities, the Leader says the verse, "For all the
gods," aloud to emphasize the need to make a pause between the word "idols"
and the name of God.

בָּרוּךְ אַתָּה יהוה אֱלֹהֵינוּ מֶלֶךְ הָעוֹלָם
הָאֵל הָאָב הָרַחֲמָן הַמְהֻלָּל בְּפִי עַמּוֹ
מְשֻׁבָּח וּמְפֹאָר בִּלְשׁוֹן חֲסִידָיו וַעֲבָדָיו
וּבְשִׁירֵי דָוִד עַבְדֶּךָ
נְהַלֶּלְךָ יהוה אֱלֹהֵינוּ.
בִּשְׁבָחוֹת וּבִזְמִירוֹת
נְגַדֶּלְךָ וּנְשַׁבֵּחֲךָ וּנְפָאֶרְךָ
וְנַזְכִּיר שִׁמְךָ וְנַמְלִיכְךָ
מַלְכֵּנוּ אֱלֹהֵינוּ, ‧ יָחִיד חֵי הָעוֹלָמִים
מֶלֶךְ, מְשֻׁבָּח וּמְפֹאָר עֲדֵי עַד שְׁמוֹ הַגָּדוֹל
בָּרוּךְ אַתָּה יהוה, מֶלֶךְ מְהֻלָּל בַּתִּשְׁבָּחוֹת.

הוֹדוּ לַיהוה קִרְאוּ בִשְׁמוֹ, הוֹדִיעוּ בָעַמִּים עֲלִילֹתָיו: שִׁירוּ לוֹ,   דברי
הימים
א, טז
זַמְּרוּ־לוֹ, שִׂיחוּ בְּכָל־נִפְלְאוֹתָיו: הִתְהַלְלוּ בְּשֵׁם קָדְשׁוֹ, יִשְׂמַח

---

correspond to the six days of creation; others are added on Shabbat and
festivals. Around this inner core other passages have been woven: some from
other biblical books and others from selected verses in the book of Psalms.
The section begins and ends with a paragraph of blessings: "Blessed is He
who spoke" (*Barukh She'Amar*) at the beginning, and "May Your Name be
praised for ever" (*Yishtabaḥ*) at the end.

בָּרוּךְ שֶׁאָמַר *Blessed is He who spoke* (*previous page*): An introductory blessing
to the Verses of Praise, in two parts. The first is a ten-part litany of praise
to God as Creator, each phrase introduced with the word "Blessed" (the
second phrase, *barukh hu*, "blessed is He," is not a separate verse but was
originally a congregational response). The number ten corresponds to the
ten times the word *Vayomer*, "And He said," appears in the story of creation
in Genesis 1, hence the rabbinic saying that "With ten utterances the world
was created."

His miracles, and the judgments He pronounced. Descendants of Yisrael His servant, sons of Jacob His chosen ones: He is the LORD our God. His judgments are throughout the earth. Remember His covenant for ever, the word He commanded for a thousand generations. He made it with Abraham, vowed it to Isaac, and confirmed it to Jacob as a statute and to Israel as an everlasting covenant, saying, "To you I will give the land of Canaan as your allotted heritage." You were then small in number, few, strangers there, wandering from nation to nation, from one kingdom to another, but He let no man oppress them, and for their sake He rebuked kings: "Do not touch My anointed ones, and do My prophets no harm." Sing to the LORD, all the earth; proclaim His salvation daily. Declare His glory among the nations, His marvels among all the peoples. For great is the LORD and greatly to be praised; He is awesome beyond all heavenly powers. ‣ For all the gods of the peoples are mere idols; it was the LORD who made the heavens.

Before Him are majesty and splendor; there is strength and beauty in His holy place. Render to the LORD, families of the peoples, render to the LORD honor and might. Render to the LORD the glory due to His name; bring an offering and come before Him; bow down to the LORD in the splendor of holiness. Tremble before Him, all the earth; the world stands firm, it will not be shaken. Let the heavens rejoice and the earth be glad; let them declare among the nations, "The LORD is King." Let the sea roar, and all that is in it; let the fields be jubilant, and all they contain. Then the trees of the forest will sing for joy before the LORD, for He is coming to judge the earth. Thank the LORD for He is good; His lovingkindness is for ever. Say: "Save us, God of our salvation; gather us and rescue us from the nations, to acknowledge Your holy name and glory in Your praise. Blessed is the LORD, God of Israel, from this world to eternity." And let all the people say "Amen" and "Praise the LORD."

לֵב מְבַקְשֵׁי יהוה: דִּרְשׁוּ יהוה וְעֻזּוֹ, בַּקְּשׁוּ פָנָיו תָּמִיד: זִכְרוּ
נִפְלְאֹתָיו אֲשֶׁר עָשָׂה, מֹפְתָיו וּמִשְׁפְּטֵי־פִיהוּ: זֶרַע יִשְׂרָאֵל עַבְדּוֹ,
בְּנֵי יַעֲקֹב בְּחִירָיו: הוּא יהוה אֱלֹהֵינוּ בְּכָל־הָאָרֶץ מִשְׁפָּטָיו:
זִכְרוּ לְעוֹלָם בְּרִיתוֹ, דָּבָר צִוָּה לְאֶלֶף דּוֹר: אֲשֶׁר כָּרַת אֶת־
אַבְרָהָם, וּשְׁבוּעָתוֹ לְיִצְחָק: וַיַּעֲמִידֶהָ לְיַעֲקֹב לְחֹק, לְיִשְׂרָאֵל
בְּרִית עוֹלָם: לֵאמֹר, לְךָ אֶתֵּן אֶרֶץ־כְּנָעַן, חֶבֶל נַחֲלַתְכֶם:
בִּהְיוֹתְכֶם מְתֵי מִסְפָּר, כִּמְעַט וְגָרִים בָּהּ: וַיִּתְהַלְּכוּ מִגּוֹי אֶל־
גּוֹי, וּמִמַּמְלָכָה אֶל־עַם אַחֵר: לֹא־הִנִּיחַ לְאִישׁ לְעָשְׁקָם, וַיּוֹכַח
עֲלֵיהֶם מְלָכִים: אַל־תִּגְּעוּ בִמְשִׁיחָי, וּבִנְבִיאַי אַל־תָּרֵעוּ: שִׁירוּ
לַיהוה כָּל־הָאָרֶץ, בַּשְּׂרוּ מִיּוֹם־אֶל־יוֹם יְשׁוּעָתוֹ: סַפְּרוּ בַגּוֹיִם
אֶת־כְּבוֹדוֹ, בְּכָל־הָעַמִּים נִפְלְאֹתָיו: כִּי גָדוֹל יהוה וּמְהֻלָּל מְאֹד,
וְנוֹרָא הוּא עַל־כָּל־אֱלֹהִים: ‹ כִּי כָּל־אֱלֹהֵי הָעַמִּים אֱלִילִים,
וַיהוה שָׁמַיִם עָשָׂה:

הוֹד וְהָדָר לְפָנָיו, עֹז וְחֶדְוָה בִּמְקֹמוֹ: הָבוּ לַיהוה מִשְׁפְּחוֹת
עַמִּים, הָבוּ לַיהוה כָּבוֹד וָעֹז: הָבוּ לַיהוה כְּבוֹד שְׁמוֹ, שְׂאוּ מִנְחָה
וּבֹאוּ לְפָנָיו, הִשְׁתַּחֲווּ לַיהוה בְּהַדְרַת־קֹדֶשׁ: חִילוּ מִלְּפָנָיו כָּל־
הָאָרֶץ, אַף־תִּכּוֹן תֵּבֵל בַּל־תִּמּוֹט: יִשְׂמְחוּ הַשָּׁמַיִם וְתָגֵל הָאָרֶץ,
וְיֹאמְרוּ בַגּוֹיִם יהוה מָלָךְ: יִרְעַם הַיָּם וּמְלֹאוֹ, יַעֲלֹץ הַשָּׂדֶה
וְכָל־אֲשֶׁר־בּוֹ: אָז יְרַנְּנוּ עֲצֵי הַיָּעַר, מִלִּפְנֵי יהוה, כִּי־בָא לִשְׁפּוֹט
אֶת־הָאָרֶץ: הוֹדוּ לַיהוה כִּי טוֹב, כִּי לְעוֹלָם חַסְדּוֹ: וְאִמְרוּ,
הוֹשִׁיעֵנוּ אֱלֹהֵי יִשְׁעֵנוּ, וְקַבְּצֵנוּ וְהַצִּילֵנוּ מִן־הַגּוֹיִם, לְהֹדוֹת
לְשֵׁם קָדְשֶׁךָ, לְהִשְׁתַּבֵּחַ בִּתְהִלָּתֶךָ: בָּרוּךְ יהוה אֱלֹהֵי יִשְׂרָאֵל
מִן־הָעוֹלָם וְעַד־הָעֹלָם, וַיֹּאמְרוּ כָל־הָעָם אָמֵן, וְהַלֵּל לַיהוה:

‣ Exalt the LORD our God and bow before His footstool: He is   *Ps. 99*
holy. Exalt the LORD our God and bow at His holy mountain; for
holy is the LORD our God.

He is compassionate. He forgives iniquity and does not destroy.   *Ps. 78*
Repeatedly He suppresses His anger, not rousing His full wrath.
You, LORD: do not withhold Your compassion from me. May Your   *Ps. 40*
loving-kindness and truth always guard me. Remember, LORD,   *Ps. 25*
Your acts of compassion and love, for they have existed for ever.
Ascribe power to God, whose majesty is over Israel and whose   *Ps. 68*
might is in the skies. God is awesome, God, in Your holy places.
It is the God of Israel who gives might and strength to the people,
may God be blessed. God of retribution, LORD, God of retribu-   *Ps. 94*
tion, appear. Arise, Judge of the earth, to repay the arrogant their
just deserts. Salvation belongs to the LORD; may Your blessing rest   *Ps. 3*
upon Your people, Selah! ‣ The LORD of hosts is with us, the God   *Ps. 46*
of Jacob is our stronghold, Selah! LORD of hosts, happy is the one   *Ps. 84*
who trusts in You. LORD, save! May the King answer us on the day   *Ps. 20*
we call.

Save Your people and bless Your heritage; tend them and carry   *Ps. 28*
them for ever. Our soul longs for the LORD; He is our Help and   *Ps. 33*
Shield. For in Him our hearts rejoice, for in His holy name we have
trusted. May Your loving-kindness, LORD, be upon us, as we have
put our hope in You. Show us, LORD, Your loving-kindness and   *Ps. 85*
grant us Your salvation. Arise, help us and redeem us for the sake   *Ps. 44*
of Your love. I am the LORD your God who brought you up from   *Ps. 81*
the land of Egypt: open your mouth wide and I will fill it. Happy   *Ps. 144*
is the people for whom this is so; happy is the people whose God
is the LORD. ‣ As for me, I trust in Your loving-kindness; my heart   *Ps. 13*
rejoices in Your salvation. I will sing to the LORD for He has been
good to me.

---

of King David to today. We may no longer have the Ark, but we still have
the covenant.

‹ רוֹמְמוּ יהוה אֱלֹהֵינוּ וְהִשְׁתַּחֲווּ לַהֲדֹם רַגְלָיו, קָדוֹשׁ הוּא: תהלים צט
רוֹמְמוּ יהוה אֱלֹהֵינוּ וְהִשְׁתַּחֲווּ לְהַר קָדְשׁוֹ, כִּי־קָדוֹשׁ יהוה
אֱלֹהֵינוּ:

וְהוּא רַחוּם, יְכַפֵּר עָוֹן וְלֹא־יַשְׁחִית, וְהִרְבָּה לְהָשִׁיב אַפּוֹ,   תהלים עח
וְלֹא־יָעִיר כָּל־חֲמָתוֹ: אַתָּה יהוה לֹא־תִכְלָא רַחֲמֶיךָ מִמֶּנִּי, חַסְדְּךָ   תהלים מ
וַאֲמִתְּךָ תָּמִיד יִצְּרוּנִי: זְכֹר־רַחֲמֶיךָ יהוה וַחֲסָדֶיךָ, כִּי מֵעוֹלָם   תהלים כה
הֵמָּה: תְּנוּ עֹז לֵאלֹהִים, עַל־יִשְׂרָאֵל גַּאֲוָתוֹ, וְעֻזּוֹ בַּשְּׁחָקִים: תהלים סח
נוֹרָא אֱלֹהִים מִמִּקְדָּשֶׁיךָ, אֵל יִשְׂרָאֵל הוּא נֹתֵן עֹז וְתַעֲצֻמוֹת
לָעָם, בָּרוּךְ אֱלֹהִים: אֵל־נְקָמוֹת יהוה, אֵל נְקָמוֹת הוֹפִיעַ:   תהלים צד
הִנָּשֵׂא שֹׁפֵט הָאָרֶץ, הָשֵׁב גְּמוּל עַל־גֵּאִים: לַיהוה הַיְשׁוּעָה,   תהלים ג
עַל־עַמְּךָ בִרְכָתֶךָ סֶּלָה: ‹ יהוה צְבָאוֹת עִמָּנוּ, מִשְׂגָּב לָנוּ אֱלֹהֵי   תהלים מו
יַעֲקֹב סֶלָה: יהוה צְבָאוֹת, אַשְׁרֵי אָדָם בֹּטֵחַ בָּךְ: יהוה הוֹשִׁיעָה,   תהלים פד / תהלים כ
הַמֶּלֶךְ יַעֲנֵנוּ בְיוֹם־קָרְאֵנוּ:

הוֹשִׁיעָה אֶת־עַמֶּךָ, וּבָרֵךְ אֶת־נַחֲלָתֶךָ, וּרְעֵם וְנַשְּׂאֵם עַד־   תהלים כח
הָעוֹלָם: נַפְשֵׁנוּ חִכְּתָה לַיהוה, עֶזְרֵנוּ וּמָגִנֵּנוּ הוּא: כִּי־בוֹ יִשְׂמַח   תהלים לג
לִבֵּנוּ, כִּי בְשֵׁם קָדְשׁוֹ בָטָחְנוּ: יְהִי־חַסְדְּךָ יהוה עָלֵינוּ, כַּאֲשֶׁר
יִחַלְנוּ לָךְ: הַרְאֵנוּ יהוה חַסְדֶּךָ, וְיֶשְׁעֲךָ תִּתֶּן־לָנוּ: קוּמָה עֶזְרָתָה   תהלים פה / תהלים מד
לָּנוּ, וּפְדֵנוּ לְמַעַן חַסְדֶּךָ: אָנֹכִי יהוה אֱלֹהֶיךָ הַמַּעַלְךָ מֵאֶרֶץ   תהלים פא
מִצְרָיִם, הַרְחֶב־פִּיךָ וַאֲמַלְאֵהוּ: אַשְׁרֵי הָעָם שֶׁכָּכָה לּוֹ, אַשְׁרֵי   תהלים קמד
הָעָם שֶׁיהוה אֱלֹהָיו: ‹ וַאֲנִי בְּחַסְדְּךָ בָטַחְתִּי, יָגֵל לִבִּי בִּישׁוּעָתֶךָ,   תהלים יג
אָשִׁירָה לַיהוה, כִּי גָמַל עָלָי:

רוֹמְמוּ *Exalt:* These paragraphs (until כִּי גָמַל עָלָי, "for He has been good to me")
are a selection of verses from the book of Psalms on the theme of hope and
trust in God. It forms a moving transition from then to now, from the days

The following psalm recalls the thanksgiving-offering in Temple times.
It is not said on Erev Pesaḥ, or Erev Yom Kippur
since no thanksgiving-offerings were brought on these days.
To emphasize its sacrificial nature, the custom is to say it standing.

מִזְמוֹר A psalm of thanksgiving. Shout joyously to the Lord, *Ps. 100*
all the earth. Serve the Lord with joy. Come before Him with
jubilation. Know that the Lord is God. He made us and we are
His. We are His people and the flock He tends. Enter His gates
with thanksgiving, His courts with praise. Thank Him and
bless His name. ‣ For the Lord is good, His loving-kindness is
everlasting, and His faithfulness is for every generation.

יְהִי כְבוֹד May the Lord's glory be for ever; may the Lord rejoice in His *Ps. 104*
works. May the Lord's name be blessed, now and for ever. From the *Ps. 113*
rising of the sun to its setting, may the Lord's name be praised. The
Lord is high above all nations; His glory is above the heavens. Lord, *Ps. 135*
Your name is for ever. Your renown, Lord, is for all generations. The *Ps. 103*
Lord has established His throne in heaven; His kingdom rules all. Let *1 Chr. 16*
the heavens rejoice and the earth be glad. Let them say among the
nations, "The Lord is King." The Lord is King, the Lord was King,
the Lord will be King for ever and all time. The Lord is King for ever *Ps. 10*
and all time; nations will perish from His land. The Lord foils the plans *Ps. 33*
of nations; He frustrates the intentions of peoples. Many are the inten- *Prov. 19*
tions in a person's mind, but the Lord's plan prevails. The Lord's plan *Ps. 33*
shall stand for ever, His mind's intent for all generations. For He spoke
and it was; He commanded and it stood firm. For the Lord has chosen *Ps. 132*
Zion; He desired it for His dwelling. For the Lord has chosen Jacob as *Ps. 135*
His own, Israel as His special treasure. For the Lord will not abandon *Ps. 94*
His people; nor will He forsake His heritage. ‣ He is compassionate. He *Ps. 78*
forgives iniquity and does not destroy. Repeatedly He suppresses His
anger, not rousing His full wrath. Lord, save! May the King answer us *Ps. 20*
on the day we call.

---

birth or danger) in place of the sacrifice. The psalm first appeared as part of
the daily service in Yemenite and French prayer books of the Middle Ages.
Its presence here is to emphasize the mood of thankfulness that dominates
this section of the prayers.

The following psalm recalls the קרבן תודה *in Temple times. It is not said on* ערב פסח, *or* ערב יום כיפור, *since no* קורבנות תודה *were brought on these days. To emphasize its sacrificial nature, the custom is to say it standing.*

תהלים ק

מִזְמוֹר לְתוֹדָה, הָרִיעוּ לַיהוה כָּל־הָאָרֶץ: עִבְדוּ אֶת־יהוה
בְּשִׂמְחָה, בֹּאוּ לְפָנָיו בִּרְנָנָה: דְּעוּ כִּי־יהוה הוּא אֱלֹהִים,
הוּא עָשָׂנוּ וְלוֹ אֲנַחְנוּ, עַמּוֹ וְצֹאן מַרְעִיתוֹ: בֹּאוּ שְׁעָרָיו
בְּתוֹדָה, חֲצֵרֹתָיו בִּתְהִלָּה, הוֹדוּ לוֹ, בָּרְכוּ שְׁמוֹ: ‹ כִּי־טוֹב
יהוה, לְעוֹלָם חַסְדּוֹ, וְעַד־דֹּר וָדֹר אֱמוּנָתוֹ:

תהלים קד
תהלים קג

יְהִי כְבוֹד יהוה לְעוֹלָם, יִשְׂמַח יהוה בְּמַעֲשָׂיו: יְהִי שֵׁם יהוה מְבֹרָךְ,
מֵעַתָּה וְעַד־עוֹלָם: מִמִּזְרַח־שֶׁמֶשׁ עַד־מְבוֹאוֹ, מְהֻלָּל שֵׁם יהוה:

תהלים קלה

רָם עַל־כָּל־גּוֹיִם יהוה, עַל הַשָּׁמַיִם כְּבוֹדוֹ: יהוה שִׁמְךָ לְעוֹלָם,

תהלים קג

יהוה זִכְרְךָ לְדֹר־וָדֹר: יהוה בַּשָּׁמַיִם הֵכִין כִּסְאוֹ, וּמַלְכוּתוֹ בַּכֹּל

דברי הימים
א׳ טז

מָשָׁלָה: יִשְׂמְחוּ הַשָּׁמַיִם וְתָגֵל הָאָרֶץ, וְיֹאמְרוּ בַגּוֹיִם יהוה מָלָךְ:

תהלים י

יהוה מֶלֶךְ, יהוה מָלָךְ, יהוה יִמְלֹךְ לְעוֹלָם וָעֶד. יהוה מֶלֶךְ עוֹלָם

תהלים לג

וָעֶד, אָבְדוּ גוֹיִם מֵאַרְצוֹ: יהוה הֵפִיר עֲצַת־גּוֹיִם, הֵנִיא מַחְשְׁבוֹת

משלי יט,
תהלים לג

עַמִּים: רַבּוֹת מַחֲשָׁבוֹת בְּלֶב־אִישׁ, וַעֲצַת יהוה הִיא תָקוּם: עֲצַת
יהוה לְעוֹלָם תַּעֲמֹד, מַחְשְׁבוֹת לִבּוֹ לְדֹר וָדֹר: כִּי הוּא אָמַר וַיֶּהִי,

תהלים קלב
תהלים קלה

הוּא־צִוָּה וַיַּעֲמֹד: כִּי־בָחַר יהוה בְּצִיּוֹן, אִוָּה לְמוֹשָׁב לוֹ: כִּי־יַעֲקֹב

תהלים צד

בָּחַר לוֹ יָהּ, יִשְׂרָאֵל לִסְגֻלָּתוֹ: כִּי לֹא־יִטֹּשׁ יהוה עַמּוֹ, וְנַחֲלָתוֹ לֹא

תהלים עח

יַעֲזֹב: ‹ וְהוּא רַחוּם, יְכַפֵּר עָוֹן וְלֹא־יַשְׁחִית, וְהִרְבָּה לְהָשִׁיב אַפּוֹ,

תהלים כ

וְלֹא־יָעִיר כָּל־חֲמָתוֹ: יהוה הוֹשִׁיעָה, הַמֶּלֶךְ יַעֲנֵנוּ בְיוֹם־קָרְאֵנוּ:

מִזְמוֹר לְתוֹדָה *A psalm of thanksgiving:* This psalm accompanied the *korban toda*, a thanksgiving-offering (Lev. 7:12), brought to express gratitude for coming safely through a hazardous situation (recovering from illness, completing a potentially dangerous journey or being released from captivity). Nowadays, we make the *HaGomel* blessing (which is said after surviving illness, child-

The line beginning with "You open Your hand" should be said with special concentration, representing as it does the key idea of this Psalm, and of Pesukei DeZimra as a whole, that God is the creator and sustainer of all. Some have the custom to touch the hand-tefillin at °, and the head-tefillin at °°.

אַשְׁרֵי Happy are those who dwell in Your House;   Ps. 84
they shall continue to praise You, Selah!
Happy are the people for whom this is so;   Ps. 144
happy are the people whose God is the Lord.

A song of praise by David.   Ps. 145
 I will exalt You, my God, the King, and bless Your name for ever
 and all time. Every day I will bless You, and praise Your name for
 ever and all time. Great is the Lord and greatly to be praised;
 His greatness is unfathomable. One generation will praise Your
 works to the next, and tell of Your mighty deeds. On the glorious
 splendor of Your majesty I will meditate, and on the acts of Your
 wonders. They shall talk of the power of Your awesome deeds,
 and I will tell of Your greatness. They shall recite the record of
 Your great goodness, and sing with joy of Your righteousness. The
 Lord is gracious and compassionate, slow to anger and great in
 loving-kindness. The Lord is good to all, and His compassion
 extends to all His works. All Your works shall thank You, Lord,
 and Your devoted ones shall bless You. They shall talk of the glory
 of Your kingship, and speak of Your might. To make known to
 mankind His mighty deeds and the glorious majesty of His kingship. Your kingdom is an everlasting kingdom, and Your reign is
 for all generations. The Lord supports all who fall, and raises all
 who are bowed down. All raise their eyes to You in hope, and You
 give them their food in due season. °You open Your hand, °°and
 satisfy every living thing with favor. The Lord is righteous in all
 His ways, and kind in all He does. The Lord is close to all who
 call on Him, to all who call on Him in truth. He fulfills the will
 of those who revere Him; He hears their cry and saves them. The
 Lord guards all who love Him, but all the wicked He will destroy.
 ‣ My mouth shall speak the praise of the Lord, and all creatures
 shall bless His holy name for ever and all time.

We will bless the Lord now and for ever. Halleluya!   Ps. 115

The line beginning with פּוֹתֵחַ אֶת יָדֶךָ should be said with special concentration, representing as it does the key idea of this psalm, and of פְּסוּקֵי דְזִמְרָה as a whole, that God is the creator and sustainer of all. Some have the custom to touch the תפילין של יד at °, and the תפילין של ראש at °°.

תהלים פד
אַשְׁרֵי יוֹשְׁבֵי בֵיתֶךָ, עוֹד יְהַלְלוּךָ סֶּלָה:

תהלים קמד
אַשְׁרֵי הָעָם שֶׁכָּכָה לּוֹ, אַשְׁרֵי הָעָם שֶׁיהוה אֱלֹהָיו:

תהלים קמה
תְּהִלָּה לְדָוִד

אֲרוֹמִמְךָ אֱלוֹהַי הַמֶּלֶךְ, וַאֲבָרְכָה שִׁמְךָ לְעוֹלָם וָעֶד:

בְּכָל־יוֹם אֲבָרְכֶךָּ, וַאֲהַלְלָה שִׁמְךָ לְעוֹלָם וָעֶד:

גָּדוֹל יהוה וּמְהֻלָּל מְאֹד, וְלִגְדֻלָּתוֹ אֵין חֵקֶר:

דּוֹר לְדוֹר יְשַׁבַּח מַעֲשֶׂיךָ, וּגְבוּרֹתֶיךָ יַגִּידוּ:

הֲדַר כְּבוֹד הוֹדֶךָ, וְדִבְרֵי נִפְלְאֹתֶיךָ אָשִׂיחָה:

וֶעֱזוּז נוֹרְאֹתֶיךָ יֹאמֵרוּ, וּגְדוּלָּתְךָ אֲסַפְּרֶנָּה:

זֵכֶר רַב־טוּבְךָ יַבִּיעוּ, וְצִדְקָתְךָ יְרַנֵּנוּ:

חַנּוּן וְרַחוּם יהוה, אֶרֶךְ אַפַּיִם וּגְדָל־חָסֶד:

טוֹב־יהוה לַכֹּל, וְרַחֲמָיו עַל־כָּל־מַעֲשָׂיו:

יוֹדוּךָ יהוה כָּל־מַעֲשֶׂיךָ, וַחֲסִידֶיךָ יְבָרְכוּכָה:

כְּבוֹד מַלְכוּתְךָ יֹאמֵרוּ, וּגְבוּרָתְךָ יְדַבֵּרוּ:

לְהוֹדִיעַ לִבְנֵי הָאָדָם גְּבוּרֹתָיו, וּכְבוֹד הֲדַר מַלְכוּתוֹ:

מַלְכוּתְךָ מַלְכוּת כָּל־עֹלָמִים, וּמֶמְשַׁלְתְּךָ בְּכָל־דּוֹר וָדֹר:

סוֹמֵךְ יהוה לְכָל־הַנֹּפְלִים, וְזוֹקֵף לְכָל־הַכְּפוּפִים:

עֵינֵי־כֹל אֵלֶיךָ יְשַׂבֵּרוּ, וְאַתָּה נוֹתֵן־לָהֶם אֶת־אָכְלָם בְּעִתּוֹ:

°פּוֹתֵחַ אֶת־יָדֶךָ, °°וּמַשְׂבִּיעַ לְכָל־חַי רָצוֹן:

צַדִּיק יהוה בְּכָל־דְּרָכָיו, וְחָסִיד בְּכָל־מַעֲשָׂיו:

קָרוֹב יהוה לְכָל־קֹרְאָיו, לְכֹל אֲשֶׁר יִקְרָאֻהוּ בֶאֱמֶת:

רְצוֹן־יְרֵאָיו יַעֲשֶׂה, וְאֶת־שַׁוְעָתָם יִשְׁמַע, וְיוֹשִׁיעֵם:

שׁוֹמֵר יהוה אֶת־כָּל־אֹהֲבָיו, וְאֵת כָּל־הָרְשָׁעִים יַשְׁמִיד:

◂ תְּהִלַּת יהוה יְדַבֶּר־פִּי, וִיבָרֵךְ כָּל־בָּשָׂר שֵׁם קָדְשׁוֹ לְעוֹלָם וָעֶד:

תהלים קטו
וַאֲנַחְנוּ נְבָרֵךְ יָהּ מֵעַתָּה וְעַד־עוֹלָם, הַלְלוּיָהּ:

הַלְלוּיָהּ Halleluya! Praise the LORD, my soul. I will praise the LORD *Ps. 146* all my life; I will sing to my God as long as I live. Put not your trust in princes, or in mortal man who cannot save. His breath expires, he returns to the earth; on that day his plans come to an end. Happy is he whose help is the God of Jacob, whose hope is in the LORD his God who made heaven and earth, the sea and all they contain; He who keeps faith for ever. He secures justice for the oppressed. He gives food to the hungry. The LORD sets captives free. The LORD gives sight to the blind. The LORD raises those bowed down. The LORD loves the righteous. The LORD protects the stranger. He gives courage to the orphan and widow. He thwarts the way of the wicked. ‣ The LORD shall reign for ever. He is your God, Zion, for all generations. Halleluya!

הַלְלוּיָהּ Halleluya! How good it is to sing songs to our God; how *Ps. 147* pleasant and fitting to praise Him. The LORD rebuilds Jerusalem. He gathers the scattered exiles of Israel. He heals the brokenhearted and binds up their wounds. He counts the number of the stars, calling each by name. Great is our LORD and mighty in power; His understanding has no limit. The LORD gives courage to the humble, but casts the wicked to the ground. Sing to the LORD in thanks; make music to our God on the harp. He covers the sky with clouds. He provides the earth with rain and makes grass grow on the hills. He gives food to the cattle and to the ravens when they cry. He does not take delight in the strength of horses nor pleasure in the fleetness of man. The LORD takes pleasure in those who fear Him, who put their hope in His loving care. Praise the LORD, Jerusalem; sing to your God, Zion, for He has strengthened the bars of your gates and blessed your children in your midst. He has brought peace to your borders, and satisfied you with the finest wheat. He sends His commandment to earth; swiftly runs His word. He spreads snow like fleece, sprinkles frost like ashes, scatters hail like crumbs. Who can stand His cold? He sends His word and melts them; He makes the wind blow and the waters flow. ‣ He has declared His words to Jacob, His statutes and laws to Israel. He has done this for no other nation; such laws they do not know. Halleluya!

תהלים קמו

הַלְלוּיָהּ, הַלְלִי נַפְשִׁי אֶת־יהוה: אֲהַלְלָה יהוה בְּחַיָּי, אֲזַמְּרָה
לֵאלֹהַי בְּעוֹדִי: אַל־תִּבְטְחוּ בִנְדִיבִים, בְּבֶן־אָדָם שֶׁאֵין לוֹ תְשׁוּעָה:
תֵּצֵא רוּחוֹ, יָשֻׁב לְאַדְמָתוֹ, בַּיּוֹם הַהוּא אָבְדוּ עֶשְׁתֹּנֹתָיו: אַשְׁרֵי
שֶׁאֵל יַעֲקֹב בְּעֶזְרוֹ, שִׂבְרוֹ עַל־יהוה אֱלֹהָיו: עֹשֶׂה שָׁמַיִם וָאָרֶץ,
אֶת־הַיָּם וְאֶת־כָּל־אֲשֶׁר־בָּם, הַשֹּׁמֵר אֱמֶת לְעוֹלָם: עֹשֶׂה מִשְׁפָּט
לַעֲשׁוּקִים, נֹתֵן לֶחֶם לָרְעֵבִים, יהוה מַתִּיר אֲסוּרִים: יהוה פֹּקֵחַ
עִוְרִים, יהוה זֹקֵף כְּפוּפִים, יהוה אֹהֵב צַדִּיקִים: יהוה שֹׁמֵר אֶת־
גֵּרִים, יָתוֹם וְאַלְמָנָה יְעוֹדֵד, וְדֶרֶךְ רְשָׁעִים יְעַוֵּת: ◂ יִמְלֹךְ יהוה
לְעוֹלָם, אֱלֹהַיִךְ צִיּוֹן לְדֹר וָדֹר, הַלְלוּיָהּ:

תהלים קמז

הַלְלוּיָהּ, כִּי־טוֹב זַמְּרָה אֱלֹהֵינוּ, כִּי־נָעִים נָאוָה תְהִלָּה: בּוֹנֵה
יְרוּשָׁלַ͏ִם יהוה, נִדְחֵי יִשְׂרָאֵל יְכַנֵּס: הָרֹפֵא לִשְׁבוּרֵי לֵב, וּמְחַבֵּשׁ
לְעַצְּבוֹתָם: מוֹנֶה מִסְפָּר לַכּוֹכָבִים, לְכֻלָּם שֵׁמוֹת יִקְרָא: גָּדוֹל
אֲדוֹנֵינוּ וְרַב־כֹּחַ, לִתְבוּנָתוֹ אֵין מִסְפָּר: מְעוֹדֵד עֲנָוִים יהוה, מַשְׁפִּיל
רְשָׁעִים עֲדֵי־אָרֶץ: עֱנוּ לַיהוה בְּתוֹדָה, זַמְּרוּ לֵאלֹהֵינוּ בְכִנּוֹר:
הַמְכַסֶּה שָׁמַיִם בְּעָבִים, הַמֵּכִין לָאָרֶץ מָטָר, הַמַּצְמִיחַ הָרִים חָצִיר:
נוֹתֵן לִבְהֵמָה לַחְמָהּ, לִבְנֵי עֹרֵב אֲשֶׁר יִקְרָאוּ: לֹא בִגְבוּרַת הַסּוּס
יֶחְפָּץ, לֹא־בְשׁוֹקֵי הָאִישׁ יִרְצֶה: רוֹצֶה יהוה אֶת־יְרֵאָיו, אֶת־
הַמְיַחֲלִים לְחַסְדּוֹ: שַׁבְּחִי יְרוּשָׁלַ͏ִם אֶת־יהוה, הַלְלִי אֱלֹהַיִךְ צִיּוֹן:
כִּי־חִזַּק בְּרִיחֵי שְׁעָרָיִךְ, בֵּרַךְ בָּנַיִךְ בְּקִרְבֵּךְ: הַשָּׂם־גְּבוּלֵךְ שָׁלוֹם,
חֵלֶב חִטִּים יַשְׂבִּיעֵךְ: הַשֹּׁלֵחַ אִמְרָתוֹ אָרֶץ, עַד־מְהֵרָה יָרוּץ דְּבָרוֹ:
הַנֹּתֵן שֶׁלֶג כַּצָּמֶר, כְּפוֹר כָּאֵפֶר יְפַזֵּר: מַשְׁלִיךְ קַרְחוֹ כְפִתִּים, לִפְנֵי
קָרָתוֹ מִי יַעֲמֹד: יִשְׁלַח דְּבָרוֹ וְיַמְסֵם, יַשֵּׁב רוּחוֹ יִזְּלוּ־מָיִם: ◂ מַגִּיד
דְּבָרָו לְיַעֲקֹב, חֻקָּיו וּמִשְׁפָּטָיו לְיִשְׂרָאֵל: לֹא עָשָׂה כֵן לְכָל־גּוֹי,
וּמִשְׁפָּטִים בַּל־יְדָעוּם, הַלְלוּיָהּ:

הַלְלוּיָהּ Halleluya! Praise the LORD from the heavens, praise Him *Ps. 148*
in the heights. Praise Him, all His angels; praise Him, all His hosts.
Praise Him, sun and moon; praise Him, all shining stars. Praise Him,
highest heavens and the waters above the heavens. Let them praise
the name of the LORD, for He commanded and they were created. He
established them for ever and all time, issuing a decree that will never
change. Praise the LORD from the earth: sea monsters and all the deep
seas; fire and hail, snow and mist, storm winds that obey His word;
mountains and all hills, fruit trees and all cedars; wild animals and
all cattle, creeping things and winged birds; kings of the earth and all
nations, princes and all judges on earth; youths and maidens, old and
young. ‣ Let them praise the name of the LORD, for His name alone
is sublime; His majesty is above earth and heaven. He has raised the
pride of His people, for the glory of all His devoted ones, the children
of Israel, the people close to Him. Halleluya!

הַלְלוּיָהּ Halleluya! Sing to the LORD a new song, His praise in the *Ps. 149*
assembly of the devoted. Let Israel rejoice in its Maker; let the children of Zion exult in their King. Let them praise His name with
dancing; sing praises to Him with timbrel and harp. For the LORD
delights in His people; He adorns the humble with salvation. Let
the devoted revel in glory; let them sing for joy on their beds. Let
high praises of God be in their throats, and a two-edged sword in
their hand: to impose retribution on the nations, punishment on
the peoples, ‣ binding their kings with chains, their nobles with iron
fetters, carrying out the judgment written against them. This is the
glory of all His devoted ones. Halleluya!

הַלְלוּיָהּ Halleluya! Praise God in His holy place; praise Him in the *Ps. 150*
heavens of His power. Praise Him for His mighty deeds; praise Him
for His surpassing greatness. Praise Him with blasts of the shofar;
praise Him with the harp and lyre. Praise Him with timbrel and dance;
praise Him with strings and flute. Praise Him with clashing cymbals;
praise Him with resounding cymbals. ‣ Let all that breathes praise the
LORD. Halleluya! Let all that breathes praise the LORD. Halleluya!

תהלים קמח הַלְלוּיָהּ, הַלְלוּ אֶת־יהוה מִן־הַשָּׁמַיִם, הַלְלוּהוּ בַּמְּרוֹמִים: הַלְלוּהוּ
כָל־מַלְאָכָיו, הַלְלוּהוּ כָּל־צְבָאָו: הַלְלוּהוּ שֶׁמֶשׁ וְיָרֵחַ, הַלְלוּהוּ
כָּל־כּוֹכְבֵי אוֹר: הַלְלוּהוּ שְׁמֵי הַשָּׁמָיִם, וְהַמַּיִם אֲשֶׁר מֵעַל הַשָּׁמָיִם:
יְהַלְלוּ אֶת־שֵׁם יהוה, כִּי הוּא צִוָּה וְנִבְרָאוּ: וַיַּעֲמִידֵם לָעַד לְעוֹלָם,
חָק־נָתַן וְלֹא יַעֲבוֹר: הַלְלוּ אֶת־יהוה מִן־הָאָרֶץ, תַּנִּינִים וְכָל־
תְּהֹמוֹת: אֵשׁ וּבָרָד שֶׁלֶג וְקִיטוֹר, רוּחַ סְעָרָה עֹשָׂה דְבָרוֹ:
הֶהָרִים וְכָל־גְּבָעוֹת, עֵץ פְּרִי וְכָל־אֲרָזִים: הַחַיָּה וְכָל־בְּהֵמָה, רֶמֶשׂ
וְצִפּוֹר כָּנָף: מַלְכֵי־אֶרֶץ וְכָל־לְאֻמִּים, שָׂרִים וְכָל־שֹׁפְטֵי אָרֶץ:
בַּחוּרִים וְגַם־בְּתוּלוֹת, זְקֵנִים עִם־נְעָרִים: ‹ יְהַלְלוּ אֶת־שֵׁם יהוה,
כִּי־נִשְׂגָּב שְׁמוֹ לְבַדּוֹ, הוֹדוֹ עַל־אֶרֶץ וְשָׁמָיִם: וַיָּרֶם קֶרֶן לְעַמּוֹ,
תְּהִלָּה לְכָל־חֲסִידָיו, לִבְנֵי יִשְׂרָאֵל עַם קְרֹבוֹ, הַלְלוּיָהּ:

תהלים קמט הַלְלוּיָהּ, שִׁירוּ לַיהוה שִׁיר חָדָשׁ, תְּהִלָּתוֹ בִּקְהַל חֲסִידִים: יִשְׂמַח
יִשְׂרָאֵל בְּעֹשָׂיו, בְּנֵי־צִיּוֹן יָגִילוּ בְמַלְכָּם: יְהַלְלוּ שְׁמוֹ בְמָחוֹל, בְּתֹף
וְכִנּוֹר יְזַמְּרוּ־לוֹ: כִּי־רוֹצֶה יהוה בְּעַמּוֹ, יְפָאֵר עֲנָוִים בִּישׁוּעָה:
יַעְלְזוּ חֲסִידִים בְּכָבוֹד, יְרַנְּנוּ עַל־מִשְׁכְּבוֹתָם: רוֹמְמוֹת אֵל
בִּגְרוֹנָם, וְחֶרֶב פִּיפִיּוֹת בְּיָדָם: לַעֲשׂוֹת נְקָמָה בַּגּוֹיִם, תּוֹכֵחוֹת
בַּלְאֻמִּים: ‹ לֶאְסֹר מַלְכֵיהֶם בְּזִקִּים, וְנִכְבְּדֵיהֶם בְּכַבְלֵי בַרְזֶל:
לַעֲשׂוֹת בָּהֶם מִשְׁפָּט כָּתוּב, הָדָר הוּא לְכָל־חֲסִידָיו, הַלְלוּיָהּ:

תהלים קנ הַלְלוּיָהּ, הַלְלוּ־אֵל בְּקָדְשׁוֹ, הַלְלוּהוּ בִּרְקִיעַ עֻזּוֹ: הַלְלוּהוּ
בִגְבוּרֹתָיו, הַלְלוּהוּ כְּרֹב גֻּדְלוֹ: הַלְלוּהוּ בְּתֵקַע שׁוֹפָר, הַלְלוּהוּ
בְּנֵבֶל וְכִנּוֹר: הַלְלוּהוּ בְּתֹף וּמָחוֹל, הַלְלוּהוּ בְּמִנִּים וְעֻגָב: הַלְלוּהוּ
בְצִלְצְלֵי־שָׁמַע, הַלְלוּהוּ בְּצִלְצְלֵי תְרוּעָה: ‹ כֹּל הַנְּשָׁמָה תְּהַלֵּל
יָהּ, הַלְלוּיָהּ:   כֹּל הַנְּשָׁמָה תְּהַלֵּל יָהּ, הַלְלוּיָהּ:

בָּרוּךְ Blessed be the LORD for ever. Amen and Amen. *Ps. 89*

Blessed from Zion be the LORD *Ps. 135*

who dwells in Jerusalem. Halleluya!

Blessed be the LORD, God of Israel, *Ps. 72*

who alone does wonders.

▸ Blessed be His glorious name for ever,

and may all the earth be filled with His glory.

Amen and Amen.

Stand (see commentary) until after "Bless the LORD" on page 88.

וַיְבָרֶךְ David blessed the LORD in front of the entire assembly. David *1 Chr. 29*
said, "Blessed are You, LORD, God of our father Yisrael, for ever
and ever. Yours, LORD, are the greatness and the power, the glory,
majesty and splendor, for everything in heaven and earth is Yours.
Yours, LORD, is the kingdom; You are exalted as Head over all. Both
riches and honor are in Your gift and You reign over all things. In
Your hand are strength and might. It is in Your power to make great
and give strength to all. Therefore, our God, we thank You and
praise Your glorious name."   You alone are the LORD. You *Neh. 9*
made the heavens, even the highest heavens, and all their hosts,
the earth and all that is on it, the seas and all they contain. You
give life to them all, and the hosts of heaven worship You. ▸ You are
the LORD God who chose Abram and brought him out of Ur of
the Chaldees, changing his name to Abraham. You found his heart
faithful toward You, ◂ and You made a covenant with him to give
to his descendants the land of the Canaanites, Hittites, Amorites,

---

money to charity at this point in the service. Some give this as the reason
we stand at this point of the service, since we stand to fulfill a mitzva, in this
case, giving to charity.

   Others relate the act of standing to the next passage, "You alone," taken
from the gathering in the days of Ezra and Nehemiah after the Babylonian exile and return, when the people renewed their covenant with God.

תהלים פט
בָּרוּךְ יהוה לְעוֹלָם, אָמֵן וְאָמֵן:

תהלים קלה
בָּרוּךְ יהוה מִצִּיּוֹן, שֹׁכֵן יְרוּשָׁלָםִ, הַלְלוּיָהּ:

תהלים עב
בָּרוּךְ יהוה אֱלֹהִים אֱלֹהֵי יִשְׂרָאֵל, עֹשֵׂה נִפְלָאוֹת לְבַדּוֹ:

‣ וּבָרוּךְ שֵׁם כְּבוֹדוֹ לְעוֹלָם

וְיִמָּלֵא כְבוֹדוֹ אֶת־כָּל־הָאָרֶץ

אָמֵן וְאָמֵן:

Stand (see commentary) until after בָּרְכוּ *on page 89.*

דברי
הימים א,
כט
וַיְבָרֶךְ דָּוִיד אֶת־יהוה לְעֵינֵי כָּל־הַקָּהָל, וַיֹּאמֶר דָּוִיד, בָּרוּךְ
אַתָּה יהוה, אֱלֹהֵי יִשְׂרָאֵל אָבִינוּ, מֵעוֹלָם וְעַד־עוֹלָם: לְךָ יהוה
הַגְּדֻלָּה וְהַגְּבוּרָה וְהַתִּפְאֶרֶת וְהַנֵּצַח וְהַהוֹד, כִּי־כֹל בַּשָּׁמַיִם
וּבָאָרֶץ, לְךָ יהוה הַמַּמְלָכָה וְהַמִּתְנַשֵּׂא לְכֹל לְרֹאשׁ: וְהָעֹשֶׁר
וְהַכָּבוֹד מִלְּפָנֶיךָ, וְאַתָּה מוֹשֵׁל בַּכֹּל, וּבְיָדְךָ כֹּחַ וּגְבוּרָה, וּבְיָדְךָ
לְגַדֵּל וּלְחַזֵּק לַכֹּל: וְעַתָּה אֱלֹהֵינוּ מוֹדִים אֲנַחְנוּ לָךְ, וּמְהַלְלִים
לְשֵׁם תִּפְאַרְתֶּךָ:

נחמיה ט
אַתָּה־הוּא יהוה לְבַדֶּךָ, אַתָּ עָשִׂיתָ
אֶת־הַשָּׁמַיִם, שְׁמֵי הַשָּׁמַיִם וְכָל־צְבָאָם, הָאָרֶץ וְכָל־אֲשֶׁר עָלֶיהָ,
הַיַּמִּים וְכָל־אֲשֶׁר בָּהֶם, וְאַתָּה מְחַיֶּה אֶת־כֻּלָּם, וּצְבָא הַשָּׁמַיִם לְךָ
מִשְׁתַּחֲוִים: ‣ אַתָּה הוּא יהוה הָאֱלֹהִים אֲשֶׁר בָּחַרְתָּ בְּאַבְרָם,
וְהוֹצֵאתוֹ מֵאוּר כַּשְׂדִּים, וְשַׂמְתָּ שְּׁמוֹ אַבְרָהָם: וּמָצָאתָ אֶת־
לְבָבוֹ נֶאֱמָן לְפָנֶיךָ, ‣ וְכָרוֹת עִמּוֹ הַבְּרִית לָתֵת אֶת־אֶרֶץ הַכְּנַעֲנִי

_____

וַיְבָרֶךְ דָּוִיד *David blessed:* This passage is part of the prayer of thanksgiving
said by King David at the end of his life after he had gathered the resources
to build the Temple in Jerusalem, to be undertaken by Solomon his son. As
with the Tabernacle, the Temple was made out of the voluntary contribu-
tions of the people as a whole. For that reason, many have the custom to give

Perizzites, Jebusites and Girgashites. You fulfilled Your promise
for You are righteous. You saw the suffering of our ancestors in
Egypt. You heard their cry at the Sea of Reeds. You sent signs and
wonders against Pharaoh, all his servants and all the people of
his land, because You knew how arrogantly the Egyptians treated
them. You created for Yourself renown that remains to this day.
‣ You divided the sea before them, so that they passed through the
sea on dry land, but You cast their pursuers into the depths, like a
stone into mighty waters.

וַיּוֹשַׁע That day the LORD saved Israel from the hands of the Egyp- *Ex. 14*
tians, and Israel saw the Egyptians lying dead on the seashore.
‣ When Israel saw the great power the LORD had displayed against
the Egyptians, the people feared the LORD, and believed in the
LORD and in His servant, Moses.

אָז יָשִׁיר־מֹשֶׁה Then Moses and the Israelites sang this song to the *Ex. 15*
    LORD, saying:
    I will sing to the LORD, for He has triumphed gloriously;
    horse and rider He has hurled into the sea.
The LORD is my strength and song; He has become my salvation.
    This is my God, and I will beautify Him,
    my father's God, and I will exalt Him.
The LORD is a Master of war; LORD is His name.
Pharaoh's chariots and army He cast into the sea;
    the best of his officers drowned in the Sea of Reeds.
The deep waters covered them;
    they went down to the depths like a stone.
Your right hand, LORD, is majestic in power.
    Your right hand, LORD, shatters the enemy.
In the greatness of Your majesty, You overthrew those who rose
    against You.
    You sent out Your fury; it consumed them like stubble.

הַחִתִּי הָאֱמֹרִי וְהַפְּרִזִּי וְהַיְבוּסִי וְהַגִּרְגָּשִׁי, לָתֵת לְזַרְעוֹ, וַתָּקֶם
אֶת־דְּבָרֶיךָ, כִּי צַדִּיק אָתָּה: וַתֵּרֶא אֶת־עֳנִי אֲבֹתֵינוּ בְּמִצְרָיִם,
וְאֶת־זַעֲקָתָם שָׁמַעְתָּ עַל־יַם־סוּף: וַתִּתֵּן אֹתֹת וּמֹפְתִים בְּפַרְעֹה
וּבְכָל־עֲבָדָיו וּבְכָל־עַם אַרְצוֹ, כִּי יָדַעְתָּ כִּי הֵזִידוּ עֲלֵיהֶם, וַתַּעַשׂ־
לְךָ שֵׁם כְּהַיּוֹם הַזֶּה: ◂ וְהַיָּם בָּקַעְתָּ לִפְנֵיהֶם, וַיַּעַבְרוּ בְתוֹךְ־הַיָּם
בַּיַּבָּשָׁה, וְאֶת־רֹדְפֵיהֶם הִשְׁלַכְתָּ בִמְצוֹלֹת כְּמוֹ־אֶבֶן, בְּמַיִם עַזִּים:

שמות יד
וַיּוֹשַׁע יהוה בַּיּוֹם הַהוּא אֶת־יִשְׂרָאֵל מִיַּד מִצְרָיִם, וַיַּרְא יִשְׂרָאֵל
אֶת־מִצְרַיִם מֵת עַל־שְׂפַת הַיָּם: ◂ וַיַּרְא יִשְׂרָאֵל אֶת־הַיָּד הַגְּדֹלָה
אֲשֶׁר עָשָׂה יהוה בְּמִצְרַיִם, וַיִּירְאוּ הָעָם אֶת־יהוה, וַיַּאֲמִינוּ
בַּיהוה וּבְמֹשֶׁה עַבְדּוֹ:

שמות טו
אָז יָשִׁיר־מֹשֶׁה וּבְנֵי יִשְׂרָאֵל אֶת־הַשִּׁירָה הַזֹּאת לַיהוה, וַיֹּאמְרוּ
לֵאמֹר,   אָשִׁירָה לַיהוה כִּי־גָאֹה גָּאָה,   סוּס
וְרֹכְבוֹ רָמָה בַיָּם: עָזִּי וְזִמְרָת יָהּ וַיְהִי־לִי
לִישׁוּעָה,   זֶה אֵלִי וְאַנְוֵהוּ,   אֱלֹהֵי
אָבִי וַאֲרֹמְמֶנְהוּ:   יהוה אִישׁ מִלְחָמָה, יהוה
שְׁמוֹ:   מַרְכְּבֹת פַּרְעֹה וְחֵילוֹ יָרָה בַיָּם,   וּמִבְחַר
שָׁלִשָׁיו טֻבְּעוּ בְיַם־סוּף: תְּהֹמֹת יְכַסְיֻמוּ, יָרְדוּ בִמְצוֹלֹת כְּמוֹ־
אָבֶן: יְמִינְךָ יהוה נֶאְדָּרִי בַּכֹּחַ,   יְמִינְךָ
יהוה תִּרְעַץ אוֹיֵב: וּבְרֹב גְּאוֹנְךָ תַּהֲרֹס

Immediately prior to this passage, we read that the Levites called on the people to "Rise, bless the LORD your God" (Neh. 9:5). Hence we too stand in remembrance of that gathering (Rabbi Eli Munk).

By the blast of Your nostrils the waters piled up.
> The surging waters stood straight like a wall;
> the deeps congealed in the heart of the sea.

The enemy said, "I will pursue. I will overtake. I will divide the spoil.
> My desire shall have its fill of them.
> I will draw my sword. My hand will destroy them."

You blew with Your wind; the sea covered them.
> They sank in the mighty waters like lead.

Who is like You, LORD, among the mighty?
> Who is like You – majestic in holiness, awesome in glory,
> working wonders?

You stretched out Your right hand,
> the earth swallowed them.

In Your loving-kindness, You led the people You redeemed.
> In Your strength, You guided them to Your holy abode.

Nations heard and trembled;
> terror gripped Philistia's inhabitants.

The chiefs of Edom were dismayed,
> Moab's leaders were seized with trembling,
> the people of Canaan melted away.

Fear and dread fell upon them.
> By the power of Your arm, they were still as stone –
> until Your people crossed, LORD,
> until the people You acquired crossed over.

You will bring them and plant them
> on the mountain of Your heritage –
> the place, LORD, You made for Your dwelling,
> the Sanctuary, LORD, Your hands established.
> The LORD will reign for ever and all time.

The LORD will reign for ever and all time.

The LORD's kingship is established for ever and to all eternity.

When Pharaoh's horses, chariots and riders went into the sea,
> the LORD brought the waters of the sea back over them, but
> the Israelites walked on dry land through the sea.

קָמֶיךָ, תְּשַׁלַּח חֲרֹנְךָ יֹאכְלֵמוֹ כַּקַּשׁ: וּבְרוּחַ

אַפֶּיךָ נֶעֶרְמוּ מַיִם, נִצְּבוּ כְמוֹ־נֵד

נֹזְלִים, קָפְאוּ תְהֹמֹת בְּלֶב־יָם: אָמַר

אוֹיֵב אֶרְדֹּף, אַשִּׂיג, אֲחַלֵּק שָׁלָל, תִּמְלָאֵמוֹ

נַפְשִׁי, אָרִיק חַרְבִּי תּוֹרִישֵׁמוֹ יָדִי: נָשַׁפְתָּ

בְרוּחֲךָ כִּסָּמוֹ יָם, צָלֲלוּ כַּעוֹפֶרֶת בְּמַיִם

אַדִּירִים: מִי־כָמֹכָה בָּאֵלִם יהוה, מִי

כָּמֹכָה נֶאְדָּר בַּקֹּדֶשׁ, נוֹרָא תְהִלֹּת עֹשֵׂה

פֶלֶא: נָטִיתָ יְמִינְךָ תִּבְלָעֵמוֹ אָרֶץ: נָחִיתָ

בְחַסְדְּךָ עַם־זוּ גָּאָלְתָּ, נֵהַלְתָּ בְעָזְּךָ אֶל־נְוֵה

קָדְשֶׁךָ: שָׁמְעוּ עַמִּים יִרְגָּזוּן, חִיל

אָחַז יֹשְׁבֵי פְּלָשֶׁת: אָז נִבְהֲלוּ אַלּוּפֵי

אֱדוֹם, אֵילֵי מוֹאָב יֹאחֲזֵמוֹ רָעַד, נָמֹגוּ

כֹּל יֹשְׁבֵי כְנָעַן: תִּפֹּל עֲלֵיהֶם אֵימָתָה

וָפַחַד, בִּגְדֹל זְרוֹעֲךָ יִדְּמוּ כָּאָבֶן, עַד־

יַעֲבֹר עַמְּךָ יהוה, עַד־יַעֲבֹר עַם־זוּ

קָנִיתָ: תְּבִאֵמוֹ וְתִטָּעֵמוֹ בְּהַר נַחֲלָתְךָ, מָכוֹן

לְשִׁבְתְּךָ פָּעַלְתָּ יהוה, מִקְּדָשׁ אֲדֹנָי כּוֹנְנוּ

יָדֶיךָ: יהוה יִמְלֹךְ לְעֹלָם וָעֶד:

יהוה יִמְלֹךְ לְעֹלָם וָעֶד.

יהוה מַלְכוּתֵהּ קָאֵם לְעָלַם וּלְעָלְמֵי עָלְמַיָּא.

כִּי

בָא סוּס פַּרְעֹה בְּרִכְבּוֹ וּבְפָרָשָׁיו בַּיָּם, וַיָּשֶׁב יהוה עֲלֵהֶם אֶת־מֵי

הַיָּם, וּבְנֵי יִשְׂרָאֵל הָלְכוּ בַיַּבָּשָׁה בְּתוֹךְ הַיָּם:

▸ For kingship is the LORD's   *Ps. 22*
   and He rules over the nations.
   Saviors shall go up to Mount Zion   *Ob. 1*
   to judge Mount Esau,
   and the LORD's shall be the kingdom.

Then the LORD shall be King over all the earth;   *Zech. 14*
on that day the LORD shall be One and His name One,

(as it is written in Your Torah, saying:
Listen, Israel: the LORD is our God, the LORD is One.)   *Deut. 6*

יִשְׁתַּבַּח May Your name be praised for ever, our King,
the great and holy God, King in heaven and on earth.
For to You,
LORD our God and God of our ancestors,
it is right to offer song and praise,
hymn and psalm,
strength and dominion,
eternity, greatness and power,
song of praise and glory,
holiness and kingship,
▸ blessings and thanks,
from now and for ever.
Blessed are You, LORD,
God and King,
exalted in praises,
God of thanksgivings,
Master of wonders,
who delights in hymns of song,
King, God, Giver of life to the worlds.

תהלים כב   ‹ כִּי לַיהוה הַמְּלוּכָה וּמֹשֵׁל בַּגּוֹיִם:

עובדיה א   וְעָלוּ מוֹשִׁעִים בְּהַר צִיּוֹן לִשְׁפֹּט אֶת־הַר עֵשָׂו

וְהָיְתָה לַיהוה הַמְּלוּכָה:

זכריה יד   וְהָיָה יהוה לְמֶלֶךְ עַל־כָּל־הָאָרֶץ

בַּיּוֹם הַהוּא יִהְיֶה יהוה אֶחָד וּשְׁמוֹ אֶחָד:

דברים ו   (וּבְתוֹרָתְךָ כָּתוּב לֵאמֹר, שְׁמַע יִשְׂרָאֵל, יהוה אֱלֹהֵינוּ יהוה אֶחָד:)

יִשְׁתַּבַּח

שִׁמְךָ לָעַד, מַלְכֵּנוּ

הָאֵל הַמֶּלֶךְ הַגָּדוֹל וְהַקָּדוֹשׁ בַּשָּׁמַיִם וּבָאָרֶץ

כִּי לְךָ נָאֶה, יהוה אֱלֹהֵינוּ וֵאלֹהֵי אֲבוֹתֵינוּ

שִׁיר וּשְׁבָחָה, הַלֵּל וְזִמְרָה

עֹז וּמֶמְשָׁלָה, נֶצַח, גְּדֻלָּה וּגְבוּרָה

תְּהִלָּה וְתִפְאֶרֶת, קְדֻשָּׁה וּמַלְכוּת

‹ בְּרָכוֹת וְהוֹדָאוֹת, מֵעַתָּה וְעַד עוֹלָם.

בָּרוּךְ אַתָּה יהוה

אֵל מֶלֶךְ גָּדוֹל בַּתִּשְׁבָּחוֹת

אֵל הַהוֹדָאוֹת

אֲדוֹן הַנִּפְלָאוֹת

הַבּוֹחֵר בְּשִׁירֵי זִמְרָה

מֶלֶךְ, אֵל, חֵי הָעוֹלָמִים.

Between Rosh HaShana and Yom Kippur, many congregations open
the Ark and say this psalm responsively, verse by verse.

שִׁיר הַמַּעֲלוֹת A song of ascents. From the depths I have called to You, LORD. *Ps. 130*
LORD, hear my voice; let Your ears be attentive to my plea. If You, LORD,
should keep account of sins, O LORD, who could stand? But with You there
is forgiveness, that You may be held in awe. I wait for the LORD, my soul
waits, and in His word I put my hope. My soul waits for the LORD more than
watchmen wait for the morning, more than watchmen wait for the morning.
Israel, put your hope in the LORD, for with the LORD there is loving-kindness,
and great is His power to redeem. It is He who will redeem Israel from all
their sins.

HALF KADDISH

Leader: יִתְגַּדֵּל Magnified and sanctified
may His great name be,
in the world He created by His will.
May He establish His kingdom
in your lifetime and in your days,
and in the lifetime of all the house of Israel,
swiftly and soon –
and say: Amen.

All: May His great name be blessed
for ever and all time.

Leader: Blessed and praised,
glorified and exalted,
raised and honored,
uplifted and lauded
be the name of the Holy One,
blessed be He,
beyond any blessing,
song, praise and consolation
uttered in the world –
and say: Amen.

During the עשרת ימי תשובה, *many congregations open the*
ארון קדש *and say this psalm responsively, verse by verse.*

שִׁיר הַמַּעֲלוֹת, מִמַּעֲמַקִּים קְרָאתִיךָ יהוה: אֲדֹנָי שִׁמְעָה בְקוֹלִי, תִּהְיֶינָה תהלים קל
אָזְנֶיךָ קַשֻּׁבוֹת לְקוֹל תַּחֲנוּנָי: אִם־עֲוֹנוֹת תִּשְׁמׇר־יָהּ, אֲדֹנָי מִי יַעֲמֹד: כִּי־
עִמְּךָ הַסְּלִיחָה, לְמַעַן תִּוָּרֵא: קִוִּיתִי יהוה קִוְּתָה נַפְשִׁי, וְלִדְבָרוֹ הוֹחָלְתִּי:
נַפְשִׁי לַאדֹנָי, מִשֹּׁמְרִים לַבֹּקֶר, שֹׁמְרִים לַבֹּקֶר: יַחֵל יִשְׂרָאֵל אֶל יהוה,
כִּי־עִם־יהוה הַחֶסֶד, וְהַרְבֵּה עִמּוֹ פְדוּת: וְהוּא יִפְדֶּה אֶת־יִשְׂרָאֵל, מִכֹּל
עֲוֹנֹתָיו:

חצי קדיש

שיץ: יִתְגַּדַּל וְיִתְקַדַּשׁ שְׁמֵהּ רַבָּא (קהל: אָמֵן)

בְּעָלְמָא דִּי בְרָא כִרְעוּתֵהּ

וְיַמְלִיךְ מַלְכוּתֵהּ

בְּחַיֵּיכוֹן וּבְיוֹמֵיכוֹן וּבְחַיֵּי דְכָל בֵּית יִשְׂרָאֵל

בַּעֲגָלָא וּבִזְמַן קָרִיב

וְאִמְרוּ אָמֵן. (קהל: אָמֵן)

קהל יְהֵא שְׁמֵהּ רַבָּא מְבָרַךְ לְעָלַם וּלְעָלְמֵי עָלְמַיָּא.
ושיץ:

שיץ: יִתְבָּרַךְ וְיִשְׁתַּבַּח וְיִתְפָּאַר וְיִתְרוֹמַם וְיִתְנַשֵּׂא

וְיִתְהַדָּר וְיִתְעַלֶּה וְיִתְהַלָּל

שְׁמֵהּ דְּקֻדְשָׁא בְּרִיךְ הוּא (קהל: בְּרִיךְ הוּא)

לְעֵלָּא מִן כָּל בִּרְכָתָא

/ בעשרת ימי תשובה: לְעֵלָּא לְעֵלָּא מִכָּל בִּרְכָתָא/

וְשִׁירָתָא, תֻּשְׁבְּחָתָא וְנֶחֱמָתָא, דַּאֲמִירָן בְּעָלְמָא

וְאִמְרוּ אָמֵן. (קהל: אָמֵן)

BLESSINGS OF THE SHEMA

The following blessing and response are said only in the presence of a minyan.
They represent a formal summons to the congregation to engage in an act of collective
prayer. The custom of bowing at this point is based on 1 Chronicles 29:20, "David said
to the whole assembly, 'Now bless the LORD your God.' All the assembly blessed the
LORD God of their fathers and bowed their heads low to the LORD and the King."
The Leader says the following, bowing at "Bless," standing straight at "the LORD."
The congregation, followed by the Leader, responds, bowing at "Bless,"
standing straight at "the LORD."

Leader: # BLESS
the LORD, the blessed One.

Congregation: Bless the LORD, the blessed One,
for ever and all time.

Leader: Bless the LORD, the blessed One,
for ever and all time.

The custom is to sit from this point until the Amida, since the predominant
emotion of this section of the prayers is love rather than awe.
Conversation is forbidden until after the Amida. See table on pages 695–697.

בָּרוּךְ Blessed are You, LORD our God,
King of the Universe,
who forms light and creates darkness,
makes peace and creates all.

Is. 45

---

prayer). Saying the Shema twice daily (morning and evening, "when you
lie down and when you rise up") is a biblical institution, and was part of the
order of service in Temple times. The transition to congregational prayer is
marked by a call – "Bless the LORD" – to those present to join in prayer as
a community.

קריאת שמע וברכותיה

The following blessing and response are said only in the presence of a מנין.
They represent a formal summons to the קהל *to engage in an act of collective prayer.*
The custom of bowing at this point is based on דברי הימים א' כט, כ, *"David said
to the whole assembly, 'Now bless the* Lord *your God.' All the assembly blessed the*
Lord *God of their fathers and bowed their heads low to the* Lord *and the King."*
The שליח ציבור *says the following, bowing at* בָּרְכוּ, *standing straight at* ה'. *The* קהל,
followed by the שליח ציבור, *responds, bowing at* בָּרוּך, *standing straight at* ה'.

ש״ץ:

אֶת יהוה הַמְבֹרָךְ.

קהל: בָּרוּךְ יהוה הַמְבֹרָךְ לְעוֹלָם וָעֶד.

ש״ץ: בָּרוּךְ יהוה הַמְבֹרָךְ לְעוֹלָם וָעֶד.

The custom is to sit from this point until the עמידה, *since the predominant
emotion of the prayers is love rather than awe.
Conversation is forbidden until after the* עמידה. *See table on pages 695–697.*

ישעיה מה

בָּרוּךְ אַתָּה יהוה אֱלֹהֵינוּ מֶלֶךְ הָעוֹלָם
יוֹצֵר אוֹר וּבוֹרֵא חֹשֶׁךְ
עֹשֶׂה שָׁלוֹם וּבוֹרֵא אֶת הַכֹּל.

───

THE SHEMA AND ITS BLESSINGS
The *Pesukei DeZimra* are a prelude to prayer. We now move to congregational prayer, the heart of which is the Shema and the Amida (the "standing"

הַמֵּאִיר In compassion He gives light to the earth
and its inhabitants,
and in His goodness continually renews the work of creation,
day after day.
How numerous are Your works, LORD;   *Ps. 104*
You made them all in wisdom;
the earth is full of Your creations.
He is the King exalted alone since the beginning of time –
praised, glorified and elevated since the world began.
Eternal God,
            in Your great compassion, have compassion on us,
            LORD of our strength, Rock of our refuge,
            Shield of our salvation, You are our stronghold.
The blessed God,
great in knowledge,
prepared and made the rays of the sun.
He who is good formed glory for His name,
surrounding His power with radiant stars.
The leaders of His hosts,
the holy ones,
exalt the Almighty,
constantly proclaiming God's glory and holiness.
Be blessed, LORD our God,
for the magnificence of Your handiwork
and for the radiant lights You have made.
May they glorify You, Selah!

───────────────────────────────────────

the sun, moon and stars, made on the fourth day of creation, and the spiritual
light created on the first day ("Let there be light"). The prayer modulates from
the first to the second: from the universe as we see it, to the mystical vision
of God enthroned in glory, surrounded by angels.

הַמֵּאִיר לָאָרֶץ וְלַדָּרִים עָלֶיהָ בְּרַחֲמִים

וּבְטוּבוֹ מְחַדֵּשׁ בְּכָל יוֹם תָּמִיד מַעֲשֵׂה בְרֵאשִׁית.

תהלים קד

מָה־רַבּוּ מַעֲשֶׂיךָ יהוה, כֻּלָּם בְּחָכְמָה עָשִׂיתָ

מָלְאָה הָאָרֶץ קִנְיָנֶךָ:

הַמֶּלֶךְ הַמְרוֹמָם לְבַדּוֹ מֵאָז

הַמְשֻׁבָּח וְהַמְפֹאָר וְהַמִּתְנַשֵּׂא מִימוֹת עוֹלָם.

אֱלֹהֵי עוֹלָם

בְּרַחֲמֶיךָ הָרַבִּים רַחֵם עָלֵינוּ

אֲדוֹן עֻזֵּנוּ, צוּר מִשְׂגַּבֵּנוּ

מָגֵן יִשְׁעֵנוּ, מִשְׂגָּב בַּעֲדֵנוּ.

אֵל בָּרוּךְ גְּדוֹל דֵּעָה

הֵכִין וּפָעַל זָהֳרֵי חַמָּה

טוֹב יָצַר כָּבוֹד לִשְׁמוֹ

מְאוֹרוֹת נָתַן סְבִיבוֹת עֻזּוֹ

פִּנּוֹת צְבָאָיו קְדוֹשִׁים, רוֹמְמֵי שַׁדַּי

תָּמִיד מְסַפְּרִים כְּבוֹד אֵל וּקְדֻשָּׁתוֹ.

תִּתְבָּרַךְ יהוה אֱלֹהֵינוּ

עַל שֶׁבַח מַעֲשֵׂה יָדֶיךָ.

וְעַל מְאוֹרֵי אוֹר שֶׁעָשִׂיתָ

יְפָאֲרוּךָ סֶּלָה.

אֵל בָּרוּךְ *The blessed God:* An alphabetical acrostic of twenty-two words. Although the first blessing is about creation as a whole, the morning prayer
emphasizes the element of which we are most conscious at the start of the
day: the creation of light. Of this, there are two forms: the physical light of

תִּתְבָּרֵךְ May You be blessed,
our Rock, King and Redeemer,
Creator of holy beings.
May Your name be praised for ever,
our King, Creator of the ministering angels,
all of whom stand in the universe's heights,
proclaiming together,
in awe, aloud,
the words of the living God, the eternal King.
They are all beloved, all pure, all mighty,
and all perform in awe and reverence the will of their Maker.
‣ All open their mouths in holiness and purity,
with song and psalm,
       and bless, praise, glorify,
             revere, sanctify and declare the sovereignty of – ◂
The name of the great, mighty
and awesome God and King,
holy is He.
‣ All accept on themselves,
one from another,
the yoke of the kingdom of heaven,
granting permission to one another
to sanctify the One who formed them,
in serene spirit,
pure speech and sweet melody.
All, as one,
proclaim His holiness,
saying in awe:

The theme of this section of the service is *revelation*: God as He has disclosed Himself in the words of the Torah. So at its heart are three passages from the Torah, known collectively by their first word, *Shema*. Around it

תִּתְבָּרַךְ
צוּרֵנוּ מַלְכֵּנוּ וְגוֹאֲלֵנוּ, בּוֹרֵא קְדוֹשִׁים
יִשְׁתַּבַּח שִׁמְךָ לָעַד
מַלְכֵּנוּ, יוֹצֵר מְשָׁרְתִים
וַאֲשֶׁר מְשָׁרְתָיו כֻּלָּם עוֹמְדִים בְּרוּם עוֹלָם
וּמַשְׁמִיעִים בְּיִרְאָה יַחַד בְּקוֹל
דִּבְרֵי אֱלֹהִים חַיִּים וּמֶלֶךְ עוֹלָם.
כֻּלָּם אֲהוּבִים, כֻּלָּם בְּרוּרִים, כֻּלָּם גִּבּוֹרִים
וְכֻלָּם עוֹשִׂים בְּאֵימָה וּבְיִרְאָה רְצוֹן קוֹנָם
‹ וְכֻלָּם פּוֹתְחִים אֶת פִּיהֶם בִּקְדֻשָּׁה וּבְטָהֳרָה
בְּשִׁירָה וּבְזִמְרָה
וּמְבָרְכִים וּמְשַׁבְּחִים וּמְפָאֲרִים
‹ וּמַעֲרִיצִים וּמַקְדִּישִׁים וּמַמְלִיכִים ›
אֶת שֵׁם הָאֵל הַמֶּלֶךְ הַגָּדוֹל, הַגִּבּוֹר וְהַנּוֹרָא
קָדוֹשׁ הוּא.
‹ וְכֻלָּם מְקַבְּלִים עֲלֵיהֶם עֹל מַלְכוּת שָׁמַיִם זֶה מִזֶּה
וְנוֹתְנִים רְשׁוּת זֶה לָזֶה
לְהַקְדִּישׁ לְיוֹצְרָם בְּנַחַת רוּחַ
בְּשָׂפָה בְרוּרָה וּבִנְעִימָה
קְדֻשָּׁה כֻּלָּם כְּאֶחָד
עוֹנִים וְאוֹמְרִים בְּיִרְאָה

The three blessings and the three paragraphs of the Shema form six passages, leading up to the seventh, the Amida. In Judaism, seven is the number of the holy.

All say aloud: Holy, holy, holy is the LORD of hosts;   *Is. 6*
the whole world is filled with His glory.

▸ Then the Ophanim and the Holy Ḥayyot,
with a roar of noise,
raise themselves toward the Seraphim and,
facing them, give praise, saying:

All say aloud: Blessed is the LORD's glory from His place.   *Ezek. 3*

לְאֵל To the blessed God they offer melodies.
To the King, living and eternal God,
they say psalms and proclaim praises.
        For it is He alone
            who does mighty deeds and creates new things,
            who is Master of battles, and sows righteousness,
            who makes salvation grow and creates cures,
            who is revered in praises,
            LORD of wonders,
who in His goodness,
continually renews the work of creation, day after day,
as it is said:
            "[Praise] Him who made the great lights,   *Ps. 136*
                for His love endures for ever."
▸ May You make a new light shine over Zion,
and may we all soon be worthy of its light.
Blessed are You, LORD, who forms the radiant lights.

---

renewed daily. The second אַהֲבָה רַבָּה ("You have loved us") is about revelation: the Torah, given in love. The third אֱמֶת וְיַצִּיב ("True and firm") is about
redemption.

ישעיה ו

All say aloud קָדוֹשׁ, קָדוֹשׁ, קָדוֹשׁ יהוה צְבָאוֹת

מְלֹא כָל־הָאָרֶץ כְּבוֹדוֹ:

‹ וְהָאוֹפַנִּים וְחַיּוֹת הַקֹּדֶשׁ

בְּרַעַשׁ גָּדוֹל מִתְנַשְּׂאִים לְעֻמַּת שְׂרָפִים

לְעֻמָּתָם מְשַׁבְּחִים וְאוֹמְרִים

יחזקאל ג

All say aloud בָּרוּךְ כְּבוֹד־יהוה מִמְּקוֹמוֹ:

לָאֵל בָּרוּךְ נְעִימוֹת יִתֵּנוּ, לְמֶלֶךְ אֵל חַי וְקַיָּם

זְמִירוֹת יֹאמֵרוּ וְתִשְׁבָּחוֹת יַשְׁמִיעוּ

כִּי הוּא לְבַדּוֹ

פּוֹעֵל גְּבוּרוֹת, עוֹשֶׂה חֲדָשׁוֹת

בַּעַל מִלְחָמוֹת, זוֹרֵעַ צְדָקוֹת

מַצְמִיחַ יְשׁוּעוֹת, בּוֹרֵא רְפוּאוֹת

נוֹרָא תְהִלּוֹת, אֲדוֹן הַנִּפְלָאוֹת

הַמְחַדֵּשׁ בְּטוּבוֹ בְּכָל יוֹם תָּמִיד מַעֲשֵׂה בְרֵאשִׁית

כָּאָמוּר

תהלים קלו

לְעֹשֵׂה אוֹרִים גְּדֹלִים, כִּי לְעוֹלָם חַסְדּוֹ:

‹ אוֹר חָדָשׁ עַל צִיּוֹן תָּאִיר וְנִזְכֶּה כֻלָּנוּ מְהֵרָה לְאוֹרוֹ.

בָּרוּךְ אַתָּה יהוה, יוֹצֵר הַמְּאוֹרוֹת.

---

are three blessings, two before and one after the Shema. Like the morning service as a whole, their themes are creation, revelation and redemption. The first (continuing the theme of the *Pesukei DeZimra*) is about creation,

אַהֲבָה You have loved us with great love, Lord our God,
and with surpassing compassion
have You had compassion on us.
Our Father, our King,
for the sake of our ancestors who trusted in You,
and to whom You taught the laws of life,
be gracious also to us and teach us.
Our Father, compassionate Father,
ever compassionate,
have compassion on us.
Instill in our hearts
the desire to understand and discern,
to listen, learn and teach,
to observe, perform and fulfill
all the teachings of Your Torah in love.
Enlighten our eyes in Your Torah
and let our hearts cling to Your commandments.
Unite our hearts to love and revere Your name,
so that we may never be ashamed.
And because we have trusted
in Your holy, great and revered name,
may we be glad and rejoice in Your salvation.

At this point, gather the four tzitziot of the tallit, holding them in the left hand.

Bring us back in peace from the four quarters of the earth
and lead us upright to our land.
‣ For You are a God who performs acts of salvation,
and You chose us from all peoples and tongues,
bringing us close to Your great name for ever in truth,
that we may thank You
and proclaim Your oneness in love.
Blessed are You, Lord,
who chooses His people Israel in love.

אַהֲבָה רַבָּה אֲהַבְתָּנוּ, יהוה אֱלֹהֵינוּ

חֶמְלָה גְדוֹלָה וִיתֵרָה חָמַלְתָּ עָלֵינוּ.

אָבִינוּ מַלְכֵּנוּ

בַּעֲבוּר אֲבוֹתֵינוּ שֶׁבָּטְחוּ בְךָ

וַתְּלַמְּדֵם חֻקֵּי חַיִּים

כֵּן תְּחָנֵּנוּ וּתְלַמְּדֵנוּ.

אָבִינוּ, הָאָב הָרַחֲמָן, הַמְרַחֵם

רַחֵם עָלֵינוּ

וְתֵן בְּלִבֵּנוּ לְהָבִין וּלְהַשְׂכִּיל

לִשְׁמֹעַ, לִלְמֹד וּלְלַמֵּד, לִשְׁמֹר וְלַעֲשׂוֹת, וּלְקַיֵּם

אֶת כָּל דִּבְרֵי תַלְמוּד תּוֹרָתֶךָ בְּאַהֲבָה.

וְהָאֵר עֵינֵינוּ בְּתוֹרָתֶךָ, וְדַבֵּק לִבֵּנוּ בְּמִצְוֹתֶיךָ

וְיַחֵד לְבָבֵנוּ לְאַהֲבָה וּלְיִרְאָה אֶת שְׁמֶךָ

וְלֹא נֵבוֹשׁ לְעוֹלָם וָעֶד.

כִּי בְשֵׁם קָדְשְׁךָ הַגָּדוֹל וְהַנּוֹרָא בָּטָחְנוּ

נָגִילָה וְנִשְׂמְחָה בִּישׁוּעָתֶךָ.

At this point, gather the four ציציות of the טלית, holding them in the left hand.

וַהֲבִיאֵנוּ לְשָׁלוֹם מֵאַרְבַּע כַּנְפוֹת הָאָרֶץ

וְתוֹלִיכֵנוּ קוֹמְמִיּוּת לְאַרְצֵנוּ.

◂ כִּי אֵל פּוֹעֵל יְשׁוּעוֹת אָתָּה

וּבָנוּ בָחַרְתָּ מִכָּל עַם וְלָשׁוֹן

וְקֵרַבְתָּנוּ לְשִׁמְךָ הַגָּדוֹל סֶלָה, בֶּאֱמֶת

לְהוֹדוֹת לְךָ וּלְיַחֶדְךָ בְּאַהֲבָה.

בָּרוּךְ אַתָּה יהוה, הַבּוֹחֵר בְּעַמּוֹ יִשְׂרָאֵל בְּאַהֲבָה.

The Shema must be said with intense concentration. In the first paragraph one should accept, with love, the sovereignty of God; in the second, the mitzvot as the will of God. The end of the third paragraph constitutes fulfillment of the mitzva to remember, morning and evening, the exodus from Egypt. See laws 32–41.

When not praying with a minyan, say:

God, faithful King!

The following verse should be said aloud, while covering the eyes with the right hand:

Listen, Israel: the LORD is our God, the LORD is One.

Deut. 6

Quietly: Blessed be the name of His glorious kingdom for ever and all time.

Touch the hand-tefillin at ° and the head-tefillin at °°.

וְאָהַבְתָּ Love the LORD your God with all your heart, with all your soul, and with all your might. These words which I command you today shall be on your heart. Teach them repeatedly to your children, speaking of them when you sit at home and when you travel on the way, when you lie down and when you rise. °Bind them as a sign on your hand, and °°they shall be an emblem between your eyes. Write them on the doorposts of your house and gates.

Deut. 6

Touch the hand-tefillin at ° and the head-tefillin at °°.

וְהָיָה If you indeed heed My commandments with which I charge you today, to love the LORD your God and worship Him with all your heart and with all your soul, I will give rain in your land in its season, the early and late rain; and you shall gather in your grain, wine and oil. I will give grass in your field for your cattle, and you shall eat and be satisfied. Be careful lest your heart be tempted and

Deut. 11

---

biblical readings. It is less a prayer than a prelude to prayer. In prayer, we speak to God. In the Shema, God, through the Torah, speaks to us. The word Shema itself means "listen," and the recital of the Shema is a supreme act of faith-as-listening: to the voice that brought the universe into being, created us in love and guides us through our lives.

The first paragraph represents *kabbalat ol malkhut shamayim,* "acceptance of the yoke of the kingship of heaven." We pledge allegiance to the One God, Sovereign of the universe, to whose authority all earthly powers are answer-

The שמע must be said with intense concentration. In the first paragraph one should accept, with love, the sovereignty of God; in the second, the מצוות as the will of God. The end of the third paragraph constitutes fulfillment of the מצוה to remember, morning and evening, the exodus from Egypt. See laws 32–41.

When not praying with a מנין, say:

אֵל מֶלֶךְ נֶאֱמָן

The following verse should be said aloud, while covering the eyes with the right hand:

דברים ו

שְׁמַע יִשְׂרָאֵל, יהוה אֱלֹהֵינוּ, יהוה ׀ אֶחָד:

בָּרוּךְ שֵׁם כְּבוֹד מַלְכוּתוֹ לְעוֹלָם וָעֶד. *Quietly*

Touch the תפילין של יד at °° and the תפילין של ראש at °.

דברים ו

וְאָהַבְתָּ אֵת יהוה אֱלֹהֶיךָ, בְּכָל־לְבָבְךָ וּבְכָל־נַפְשְׁךָ וּבְכָל־מְאֹדֶךָ: וְהָיוּ הַדְּבָרִים הָאֵלֶּה, אֲשֶׁר אָנֹכִי מְצַוְּךָ הַיּוֹם, עַל־לְבָבֶךָ: וְשִׁנַּנְתָּם לְבָנֶיךָ וְדִבַּרְתָּ בָּם, בְּשִׁבְתְּךָ בְּבֵיתֶךָ וּבְלֶכְתְּךָ בַדֶּרֶךְ, וּבְשָׁכְבְּךָ וּבְקוּמֶךָ: °יוּקְשַׁרְתָּם לְאוֹת עַל־יָדֶךָ °°וְהָיוּ לְטֹטָפֹת בֵּין עֵינֶיךָ: וּכְתַבְתָּם עַל־מְזֻזוֹת בֵּיתֶךָ וּבִשְׁעָרֶיךָ:

Touch the תפילין של יד at °° and the תפילין של ראש at °.

דברים יא

וְהָיָה אִם־שָׁמֹעַ תִּשְׁמְעוּ אֶל־מִצְוֹתַי אֲשֶׁר אָנֹכִי מְצַוֶּה אֶתְכֶם הַיּוֹם, לְאַהֲבָה אֶת־יהוה אֱלֹהֵיכֶם וּלְעָבְדוֹ, בְּכָל־לְבַבְכֶם וּבְכָל־נַפְשְׁכֶם: וְנָתַתִּי מְטַר־אַרְצְכֶם בְּעִתּוֹ, יוֹרֶה וּמַלְקוֹשׁ, וְאָסַפְתָּ דְגָנֶךָ וְתִירֹשְׁךָ וְיִצְהָרֶךָ: וְנָתַתִּי עֵשֶׂב בְּשָׂדְךָ לִבְהֶמְתֶּךָ, וְאָכַלְתָּ וְשָׂבָעְתָּ: הִשָּׁמְרוּ לָכֶם פֶּן יִפְתֶּה לְבַבְכֶם, וְסַרְתֶּם וַעֲבַדְתֶּם

THE SHEMA

The Shema is the oldest and greatest of our prayers, part of the liturgy since Temple times, recited evening and morning, "when you lie down and when you rise." Its opening line is among the first words taught to a Jewish child, and among the last words spoken by those who went to their deaths because they were Jews. It is the supreme declaration of faith.

The Shema contains no human requests, no praise, no plea. It is a set of

you go astray and worship other gods, bowing down to them. Then
the LORD's anger will flare against you and He will close the heavens so that there will be no rain. The land will not yield its crops,
and you will perish swiftly from the good land that the LORD is
giving you. Therefore, set these, My words, on your heart and soul.
°Bind them as a sign on your hand, °°and they shall be an emblem
between your eyes. Teach them to your children, speaking of them
when you sit at home and when you travel on the way, when you
lie down and when you rise. Write them on the doorposts of your
house and gates, so that you and your children may live long in the
land that the LORD swore to your ancestors to give them, for as long
as the heavens are above the earth.

Transfer the tzitziot to the right hand, kissing them at °.

וַיֹּאמֶר The LORD spoke to Moses, saying: Speak to the Israelites   *Num. 15*
and tell them to make °tassels on the corners of their garments
for all generations. They shall attach to the °tassel at each corner
a thread of blue. This shall be your °tassel, and you shall see it
and remember all of the LORD's commandments and keep them,
not straying after your heart and after your eyes, following your
own sinful desires. Thus you will be reminded to keep all My
commandments, and be holy to your God. I am the LORD your
God, who brought you out of the land of Egypt to be your God.
I am the LORD your God.

°True –

The Leader repeats:
‣ The LORD your God is true –

---

commandments." Whereas the first paragraph speaks to us as individuals, the
second speaks to us as a people, defined by our covenant with God and its
613 commandments. "Our nation is only a nation in virtue of its Torah," said
Rabbi Sa'adia Gaon, and our collective fate depends on our collective faith.
The third paragraph speaks of tzitzit, a perennial reminder of God's commandments. It then leads into the theme of the exodus from Egypt, which
we are commanded to remember "all the days of our lives."

אֱלֹהִים אֲחֵרִים וְהִשְׁתַּחֲוִיתֶם לָהֶם: וְחָרָה אַף־יהוה בָּכֶם, וְעָצַר
אֶת־הַשָּׁמַֽיִם וְלֹא־יִהְיֶה מָטָר, וְהָאֲדָמָה לֹא תִתֵּן אֶת־יְבוּלָהּ,
וַאֲבַדְתֶּם מְהֵרָה מֵעַל הָאָֽרֶץ הַטֹּבָה אֲשֶׁר יהוה נֹתֵן לָכֶם:
וְשַׂמְתֶּם אֶת־דְּבָרַי אֵֽלֶּה עַל־לְבַבְכֶם וְעַל־נַפְשְׁכֶם, וּקְשַׁרְתֶּם
אֹתָם לְאוֹת עַל־יֶדְכֶם, °וְהָיוּ לְטוֹטָפֹת בֵּין עֵינֵיכֶם: וְלִמַּדְתֶּם
אֹתָם אֶת־בְּנֵיכֶם לְדַבֵּר בָּם, בְּשִׁבְתְּךָ בְּבֵיתֶֽךָ וּבְלֶכְתְּךָ בַדֶּֽרֶךְ,
וּבְשָׁכְבְּךָ וּבְקוּמֶֽךָ: וּכְתַבְתָּם עַל־מְזוּזוֹת בֵּיתֶֽךָ וּבִשְׁעָרֶֽיךָ: לְמַֽעַן
יִרְבּוּ יְמֵיכֶם וִימֵי בְנֵיכֶם עַל הָאֲדָמָה אֲשֶׁר נִשְׁבַּע יהוה לַאֲבֹתֵיכֶם
לָתֵת לָהֶם, כִּימֵי הַשָּׁמַֽיִם עַל־הָאָֽרֶץ:

Transfer the צִיצִיּוֹת to the right hand, kissing them at °.

במדבר טו

וַיֹּֽאמֶר יהוה אֶל־מֹשֶׁה לֵּאמֹר: דַּבֵּר אֶל־בְּנֵי יִשְׂרָאֵל וְאָמַרְתָּ
אֲלֵהֶם, וְעָשׂוּ לָהֶם °צִיצִת עַל־כַּנְפֵי בִגְדֵיהֶם לְדֹרֹתָם, וְנָתְנוּ
°עַל־צִיצִת הַכָּנָף פְּתִיל תְּכֵֽלֶת: וְהָיָה לָכֶם °לְצִיצִת, וּרְאִיתֶם
אֹתוֹ וּזְכַרְתֶּם אֶת־כָּל־מִצְוֹת יהוה וַעֲשִׂיתֶם אֹתָם, וְלֹא תָתֽוּרוּ
אַחֲרֵי לְבַבְכֶם וְאַחֲרֵי עֵינֵיכֶם, אֲשֶׁר־אַתֶּם זֹנִים אַחֲרֵיהֶם: לְמַֽעַן
תִּזְכְּרוּ וַעֲשִׂיתֶם אֶת־כָּל־מִצְוֹתָי, וִהְיִיתֶם קְדֹשִׁים לֵאלֹהֵיכֶם: אֲנִי
יהוה אֱלֹהֵיכֶם, אֲשֶׁר הוֹצֵֽאתִי אֶתְכֶם מֵאֶֽרֶץ מִצְרַֽיִם, לִהְיוֹת לָכֶם
לֵאלֹהִים, אֲנִי יהוה אֱלֹהֵיכֶם:

אֱמֶת°

The שְׁלִיחַ צִבּוּר repeats:

◂ יהוה אֱלֹהֵיכֶם אֱמֶת

---

able. We do so not in fear but in love and with the totality of our being: all our
heart, our soul, our might. That love suffuses all we do, from our relationships
with our children to the homes we make.

The second paragraph represents *kabbalat ol mitzvot*, "acceptance of the

וְיַצִּיב And firm, established and enduring,
right, faithful,
beloved, cherished, delightful, pleasant,
awesome, mighty, perfect, accepted,
good and beautiful
is this faith for us for ever.

True is the eternal God, our King,
Rock of Jacob,
Shield of our salvation.
He exists and His name exists
through all generations.
His throne is established,
His kingship and faithfulness endure for ever.

At °, kiss the tzitziot and release them.

His words live and persist,
faithful and desirable
°for ever and all time.

► So they were for our ancestors,
so they are for us,
and so they will be for our children
and all our generations
and for all future generations
of the seed of Israel, Your servants. ◄
For the early and the later generations
this faith has proved good and enduring for ever –

True and faithful, an irrevocable law.

Israel," and the beginning of the Amida (*Berakhot* 14b, 9b). The connection
between the two is *redemption*, the theme of this section. The Shema ends by
speaking about redemption in the past. In the Amida we pray for redemption
in the future. Connecting past and future is "truth" – our faith in God and
in His covenant with us.

וְיַצִּיב, וְנָכוֹן וְקַיָּם, וְיָשָׁר וְנֶאֱמָן
וְאָהוּב וְחָבִיב, וְנֶחְמָד וְנָעִים
וְנוֹרָא וְאַדִּיר, וּמְתֻקָּן וּמְקֻבָּל
וְטוֹב וְיָפֶה
הַדָּבָר הַזֶּה עָלֵינוּ לְעוֹלָם וָעֶד.
אֱמֶת אֱלֹהֵי עוֹלָם מַלְכֵּנוּ
צוּר יַעֲקֹב מָגֵן יִשְׁעֵנוּ
לְדוֹר וָדוֹר הוּא קַיָּם וּשְׁמוֹ קַיָּם
וְכִסְאוֹ נָכוֹן
וּמַלְכוּתוֹ וֶאֱמוּנָתוֹ לָעַד קַיֶּמֶת.

At °, kiss the ציצית *and release them.*

וּדְבָרָיו חָיִים וְקַיָּמִים
נֶאֱמָנִים וְנֶחֱמָדִים
°לָעַד וּלְעוֹלְמֵי עוֹלָמִים
‹ עַל אֲבוֹתֵינוּ וְעָלֵינוּ
עַל בָּנֵינוּ וְעַל דּוֹרוֹתֵינוּ
וְעַל כָּל דּוֹרוֹת זֶרַע יִשְׂרָאֵל עֲבָדֶיךָ. ›
עַל הָרִאשׁוֹנִים וְעַל הָאַחֲרוֹנִים
דָּבָר טוֹב וְקַיָּם לְעוֹלָם וָעֶד
אֱמֶת וֶאֱמוּנָה, חֹק וְלֹא יַעֲבֹר.

וְיַצִּיב *And firm:* This section of prayer, joining the Shema to the Amida, goes back to Temple times. The sages emphasized that there must be no separation between the last words of the Shema, "I am the LORD your God," and the first word of the prayer, "*True* and firm," or between its last words, "who redeemed

True You are the LORD: our God and God of our ancestors,
▸ our King and King of our ancestors,
our Redeemer and Redeemer of our ancestors,
our Maker,
Rock of our salvation,
our Deliverer and Rescuer:
this has ever been Your name.
There is no God but You.

עֶזְרַת You have always been the help of our ancestors,
Shield and Savior of their children after them
in every generation.
Your dwelling is in the heights of the universe,
and Your judgments and righteousness
reach to the ends of the earth.
Happy is the one who obeys Your commandments
and takes to heart Your teaching and Your word.
True You are the Master of Your people
and a mighty King who pleads their cause.
True You are the first and You are the last.
Besides You, we have no king,
redeemer or savior.
From Egypt You redeemed us,
LORD our God,
and from the slave-house You delivered us.
All their firstborn You killed,
but Your firstborn You redeemed.
You split the Sea of Reeds
and drowned the arrogant.
You brought Your beloved ones across.
The water covered their foes;   *Ps. 106*
not one of them was left.

אֱמֶת שָׁאַתָּה הוּא יהוה אֱלֹהֵינוּ וֵאלֹהֵי אֲבוֹתֵינוּ

׳ מַלְכֵּנוּ מֶלֶךְ אֲבוֹתֵינוּ

גּוֹאֲלֵנוּ גּוֹאֵל אֲבוֹתֵינוּ

יוֹצְרֵנוּ צוּר יְשׁוּעָתֵנוּ

פּוֹדֵנוּ וּמַצִּילֵנוּ מֵעוֹלָם שְׁמֶךָ

אֵין אֱלֹהִים זוּלָתֶךָ.

עֶזְרַת אֲבוֹתֵינוּ אַתָּה הוּא מֵעוֹלָם

מָגֵן וּמוֹשִׁיעַ לִבְנֵיהֶם אַחֲרֵיהֶם בְּכָל דּוֹר וָדוֹר.

בְּרוּם עוֹלָם מוֹשָׁבֶךָ

וּמִשְׁפָּטֶיךָ וְצִדְקָתְךָ עַד אַפְסֵי אָרֶץ.

אַשְׁרֵי אִישׁ שֶׁיִּשְׁמַע לְמִצְוֹתֶיךָ

וְתוֹרָתְךָ וּדְבָרְךָ יָשִׂים עַל לִבּוֹ.

אֱמֶת אַתָּה הוּא אָדוֹן לְעַמֶּךָ

וּמֶלֶךְ גִּבּוֹר לָרִיב רִיבָם.

אֱמֶת אַתָּה הוּא רִאשׁוֹן וְאַתָּה הוּא אַחֲרוֹן

וּמִבַּלְעָדֶיךָ אֵין לָנוּ מֶלֶךְ גּוֹאֵל וּמוֹשִׁיעַ.

מִמִּצְרַיִם גְּאַלְתָּנוּ, יהוה אֱלֹהֵינוּ

וּמִבֵּית עֲבָדִים פְּדִיתָנוּ

כָּל בְּכוֹרֵיהֶם הָרָגְתָּ, וּבְכוֹרְךָ גָּאָלְתָּ

וְיַם סוּף בָּקַעְתָּ

וְזֵדִים טִבַּעְתָּ

וִידִידִים הֶעֱבַרְתָּ

וַיְכַסּוּ־מַיִם צָרֵיהֶם, אֶחָד מֵהֶם לֹא נוֹתָר:

תהלים קו

For this, the beloved ones praised and exalted God,
the cherished ones sang psalms, songs and praises,
blessings and thanksgivings to the King,
the living and enduring God.
High and exalted, great and awesome,
He humbles the haughty and raises the lowly,
freeing captives and redeeming those in need,
helping the poor
and answering His people when they cry out to Him.

Stand in preparation for the Amida. Take three steps back before beginning the Amida.

‣ Praises to God Most High,
the Blessed One who is blessed.
Moses and the children of Israel
recited to You a song with great joy,
and they all exclaimed:

> "Who is like You, LORD, among the mighty?   Ex. 15
>   Who is like You, majestic in holiness,
>   awesome in praises, doing wonders?"

‣ With a new song, the redeemed people praised
Your name at the seashore.
Together they all gave thanks,
proclaimed Your kingship,
and declared:

> "The LORD shall reign for ever and ever."   Ex. 15

*Congregants should end the following blessing together with the Leader so as to be able to move
directly from the words "redeemed Israel" to the Amida, without the interruption of saying Amen.*

‣ צוּר יִשְׂרָאֵל Rock of Israel! Arise to the help of Israel.
Deliver, as You promised, Judah and Israel.
      Our Redeemer, the LORD of hosts is His name,   Is. 47
      the Holy One of Israel.
Blessed are You, LORD, who redeemed Israel.

עַל זֹאת שִׁבְּחוּ אֲהוּבִים, וְרוֹמְמוּ אֵל

וְנָתְנוּ יְדִידִים זְמִירוֹת, שִׁירוֹת וְתִשְׁבָּחוֹת

בְּרָכוֹת וְהוֹדָאוֹת לְמֶלֶךְ אֵל חַי וְקַיָּם

רָם וְנִשָּׂא, גָּדוֹל וְנוֹרָא

מַשְׁפִּיל גֵּאִים וּמַגְבִּיהַּ שְׁפָלִים

מוֹצִיא אֲסִירִים, וּפוֹדֶה עֲנָוִים וְעוֹזֵר דַּלִּים

וְעוֹנֶה לְעַמּוֹ בְּעֵת שַׁוְּעָם אֵלָיו.

Stand in preparation for the עמידה. *Take three steps back before beginning the* עמידה.

‹ תְּהִלּוֹת לְאֵל עֶלְיוֹן, בָּרוּךְ הוּא וּמְבֹרָךְ

מֹשֶׁה וּבְנֵי יִשְׂרָאֵל

לְךָ עָנוּ שִׁירָה בְּשִׂמְחָה רַבָּה

וְאָמְרוּ כֻלָּם

שמות טו מִי־כָמֹכָה בָּאֵלִם, יהוה

מִי כָּמֹכָה נֶאְדָּר בַּקֹּדֶשׁ, נוֹרָא תְהִלֹּת, עֹשֵׂה פֶלֶא:

‹ שִׁירָה חֲדָשָׁה שִׁבְּחוּ גְאוּלִים

לְשִׁמְךָ עַל שְׂפַת הַיָּם

יַחַד כֻּלָּם הוֹדוּ וְהִמְלִיכוּ

וְאָמְרוּ

שמות טו יהוה יִמְלֹךְ לְעֹלָם וָעֶד:

The קהל *should end the following blessing together with the* שליח ציבור *so as to be able to move directly from the words* גָּאַל יִשְׂרָאֵל *to the* עמידה, *without the interruption of saying* אמן.

‹ צוּר יִשְׂרָאֵל, קוּמָה בְּעֶזְרַת יִשְׂרָאֵל

וּפְדֵה כִנְאֻמֶךָ יְהוּדָה וְיִשְׂרָאֵל.

ישעיה מו גֹּאֲלֵנוּ יהוה צְבָאוֹת שְׁמוֹ, קְדוֹשׁ יִשְׂרָאֵל:

בָּרוּךְ אַתָּה יהוה, גָּאַל יִשְׂרָאֵל.

THE AMIDA

*The following prayer, until "in former years" on page 134, is said standing with feet
together in imitation of the angels in Ezekiel's vision (Ezek. 1:7). The Amida is said
silently, following the precedent of Hannah when she prayed for a child (1 Sam. 1:13).
If there is a minyan, it is repeated aloud by the Leader. Take three steps forward, as if
formally entering the place of the Divine Presence. At the points indicated by ˎ, bend the
knees at the first word, bow at the second, and stand straight before saying God's name.*

O LORD, open my lips,   *Ps. 51*
so that my mouth may declare Your praise.

PATRIARCHS

ˎבָּרוּךְ Blessed are You, LORD our God and God of our fathers,
God of Abraham, God of Isaac and God of Jacob;
the great, mighty and awesome God, God Most High,
who bestows acts of loving-kindness and creates all,
who remembers the loving-kindness of the fathers and will bring
a Redeemer to their children's children
for the sake of His name, in love.

Between Rosh   Remember us for life, O King who desires life,
HaShana &   and write us in the book of life –
Yom Kippur: for Your sake, O God of life.

King, Helper, Savior, Shield:
ˎBlessed are You, LORD, Shield of Abraham.

Several centuries later, it was canonized in a fuller form by Shimon HaPakuli
in the days of Rabban Gamliel II (*Berakhot* 28b).

It is often called the *Shemoneh Esreh*, "Eighteen," because it originally
consisted of eighteen blessings (now, nineteen). It has a three-part structure:
(1) *praise* (blessings 1–3), (2) *requests* (blessings 4–16), and (3) *thanks* (17–19).
Each of these has a tripartite form. The first and last sections each contain
three blessings. The middle section is composed of twelve blessings (4–15),
six personal requests and six collective ones. The first three personal requests
are for spiritual goods (wisdom, repentance and forgiveness). The second
are for physical goods (deliverance, healing and livelihood). The first three
national requests are for physical events (ingathering of exiles, justice, and an
end to internal conflicts). The second three are for the nation's spiritual needs

עמידה

The following prayer, until קַדְמֹנִיּוֹת *on page 135, is said standing with feet together in imitation of the angels in Ezekiel's vision (*יחזקאל א, ז*). The* עמידה *is said silently, following the precedent of Hannah when she prayed for a child (*שמואל א' א', יג*). If there is a* מנין*, it is repeated aloud by the* שליח ציבור*. Take three steps forward, as if formally entering the place of the Divine Presence. At the points indicated by* ˊ*, bend the knees at the first word, bow at the second, and stand straight before saying God's name.*

תהלים נא

אֲדֹנָי, שְׂפָתַי תִּפְתָּח, וּפִי יַגִּיד תְּהִלָּתֶךָ:

אבות

ˊבָּרוּךְ אַתָּה יהוה, אֱלֹהֵינוּ וֵאלֹהֵי אֲבוֹתֵינוּ

אֱלֹהֵי אַבְרָהָם, אֱלֹהֵי יִצְחָק, וֵאלֹהֵי יַעֲקֹב

הָאֵל הַגָּדוֹל הַגִּבּוֹר וְהַנּוֹרָא, אֵל עֶלְיוֹן

גּוֹמֵל חֲסָדִים טוֹבִים, וְקֹנֵה הַכֹּל

וְזוֹכֵר חַסְדֵי אָבוֹת

וּמֵבִיא גוֹאֵל לִבְנֵי בְנֵיהֶם לְמַעַן שְׁמוֹ בְּאַהֲבָה.

בעשרת ימי תשובה: זָכְרֵנוּ לְחַיִּים, מֶלֶךְ חָפֵץ בַּחַיִּים

וְכָתְבֵנוּ בְּסֵפֶר הַחַיִּים, לְמַעַנְךָ אֱלֹהִים חַיִּים.

מֶלֶךְ עוֹזֵר וּמוֹשִׁיעַ וּמָגֵן.

ˊבָּרוּךְ אַתָּה יהוה, מָגֵן אַבְרָהָם.

THE AMIDA: THE STANDING PRAYER

The Amida is the summit of prayer: in it, we enter the holy of holies of religious experience. We say it standing because we are conscious of being in the unmediated presence of God. The name Amida is also related to its earliest setting: prayers said by the people of the *Ma'amad*, groups of laymen who, in Second Temple times, accompanied their local "watch" (*mishmar*) of priests who officiated in the Temple on a one-in-24-week schedule. The *Ma'amad* was one of the prototypes of congregational prayer.

According to tradition, the Amida in embryonic form dates back to the Great Assembly in the time of Ezra following the Jews' return from Babylon.

DIVINE MIGHT

אַתָּה גִּבּוֹר You are eternally mighty, LORD.
You give life to the dead and have great power to save.

> *The phrase "He makes the wind blow and the rain fall" is said from*
> *Simhat Torah until Pesah. In Israel the phrase "He causes the dew to fall"*
> *is said from Pesah until Shemini Atzeret. See laws 49–51.*

In fall & winter: He makes the wind blow and the rain fall.
In Israel, in spring He causes the dew to fall.
& summer:

He sustains the living with loving-kindness,
and with great compassion revives the dead.
He supports the fallen, heals the sick,
sets captives free,
and keeps His faith with those who sleep in the dust.
Who is like You, Master of might,
and to whom can You be compared,
O King who brings death and gives life,
and makes salvation grow?

Between Rosh HaShana Who is like You, compassionate Father,
& Yom Kippur: who remembers His creatures in compassion, for life?

Faithful are You to revive the dead.
Blessed are You, LORD, who revives the dead.

---

who was the first person to heed God's call. לְמַעַנְךָ אֱלֹהִים חַיִּים *For Your sake, O God of life:* the phrase literally means "Living God." The translation, however, conveys the poetic structure of this short but powerful prayer: four phrases, each ending with the word *hayim*, "life."

גבורות *Blessing 2: Divine might.* The fivefold reference to the resurrection of the dead reflects the controversy between the Sadducees and Pharisees in the late Second Temple era. The Sadducees rejected belief in resurrection; the Pharisees, whose heirs we are, affirmed it. Belief that those who died will one day live again is one of Judaism's great principles of hope, set out in the vision of Ezekiel of the valley of dry bones that came to life once more. Jews kept hope alive; hope kept the Jewish people alive.

גבורות

אַתָּה גִּבּוֹר לְעוֹלָם, אֲדֹנָי מְחַיֵּה מֵתִים אַתָּה, רַב לְהוֹשִׁיעַ

The phrase מַשִּׁיב הָרוּחַ *is said from* שמחת תורה *until* פסח. *In* ארץ ישראל *the phrase* מוֹרִיד הַטָּל *is said from* פסח *until* שמיני עצרת. *See laws 49–51.*

בחורף מַשִּׁיב הָרוּחַ וּמוֹרִיד הַגֶּשֶׁם / בארץ ישראל בקיץ: מוֹרִיד הַטָּל

מְכַלְכֵּל חַיִּים בְּחֶסֶד, מְחַיֵּה מֵתִים בְּרַחֲמִים רַבִּים
סוֹמֵךְ נוֹפְלִים, וְרוֹפֵא חוֹלִים, וּמַתִּיר אֲסוּרִים
וּמְקַיֵּם אֱמוּנָתוֹ לִישֵׁנֵי עָפָר.
מִי כָמְוֹךָ, בַּעַל גְּבוּרוֹת
וּמִי דוֹמֶה לָּךְ
מֶלֶךְ, מֵמִית וּמְחַיֶּה וּמַצְמִיחַ יְשׁוּעָה.

בעשרת ימי תשובה: מִי כָמְוֹךָ אַב הָרַחֲמִים
זוֹכֵר יְצוּרָיו לְחַיִּים בְּרַחֲמִים.

וְנֶאֱמָן אַתָּה לְהַחֲיוֹת מֵתִים.
בָּרוּךְ אַתָּה יהוה, מְחַיֵּה הַמֵּתִים.

(the righteous and pious, the rebuilding of Jerusalem, and the restoration of the Davidic monarchy). One blessing, "Listen to our voice" (the sixteenth, last of the "request" blessings), stands outside this structure because it is a prayer about prayer itself. It is also the point at which individuals can add their personal requests.

אבות *Blessing 1: Patriarchs.* In these opening chords we refer back to the dawn of our people's history – the days of the patriarchs, Abraham, Isaac and Jacob. In so doing, we echo Moses, who constantly referred to the patriarchs when praying for forgiveness for the people. God's love for, and covenant with, those who first heard His call is the supreme ground on which we stand when we turn to Him in prayer. The paragraph ends with a reference to Abraham,

When saying the Amida silently, continue with "You are holy" on the next page.

KEDUSHA

> *During the Leader's Repetition, the following is said standing
> with feet together, rising on the toes at the words indicated by ⁺.*

Cong. then Leader:	נְקַדֵּשׁ We will sanctify Your name on earth, as they sanctify it in the highest heavens, as is written by Your prophet, "And they [the angels] call to one another saying:	*Is. 6*
Cong. then Leader:	⁺Holy, ⁺holy, ⁺holy is the LORD of hosts the whole world is filled with His glory." Those facing them say "Blessed – "	
Cong. then Leader:	⁺"Blessed is the LORD's glory from His place." And in Your holy Writings it is written thus:	*Ezek. 3*
Cong. then Leader:	⁺"The LORD shall reign for ever. He is your God, Zion, from generation to generation, Halleluya!"	*Ps. 146*
Leader:	From generation to generation we will declare Your greatness, and we will proclaim Your holiness for evermore. Your praise, our God, shall not leave our mouth forever, for You, God, are a great and holy King. Blessed are You, LORD, the holy God. / *Between Rosh HaShana & Yom Kippur:* the holy King./	

> *The Leader continues with "You grace humanity" on the next page.*

---

do not require a *minyan* and are said sitting. The second requires a *minyan* and is said standing. The reason is that the first and third are descriptions of the song of the angels; the second is a reenactment. We stand, feet together, rising on our toes, as if we too were angels.

In the *Kedusha* we move beyond the priestly prayer-as-sacrifice and the prophetic prayer-as-dialogue, to prayer as a mystic experience. So holy is it that in Israel in ancient times it was said only on Shabbat and festivals. The *Zohar* interprets Jacob's vision of a ladder stretching from earth to heaven, with angels ascending and descending (Gen. 28:12), as a metaphor for prayer, and this, too, is part of the meaning of *Kedusha*. We have climbed the ladder from earth to heaven. As the Leader repeats the prayer on behalf of the entire community, we reach the summit of religious experience.

When saying the עמידה silently, continue with אַתָּה קָדוֹשׁ on the next page.

קדושה

*During חזרת הש״ץ, the following is said standing
with feet together, rising on the toes at the words indicated by ^.*

קהל
then ש״ץ: נְקַדֵּשׁ אֶת שִׁמְךָ בָּעוֹלָם, כְּשֵׁם שֶׁמַּקְדִּישִׁים אוֹתוֹ בִּשְׁמֵי מָרוֹם
כַּכָּתוּב עַל יַד נְבִיאֶךָ, וְקָרָא זֶה אֶל־זֶה וְאָמַר

ישעיהו

קהל
then ש״ץ: ^קָדוֹשׁ, ^קָדוֹשׁ, ^קָדוֹשׁ, יהוה צְבָאוֹת, מְלֹא כָל־הָאָרֶץ כְּבוֹדוֹ:
לְעֻמָּתָם בָּרוּךְ יֹאמֵרוּ

קהל
then ש״ץ: ^בָּרוּךְ כְּבוֹד־יהוה מִמְּקוֹמוֹ:
וּבְדִבְרֵי קָדְשְׁךָ כָּתוּב לֵאמֹר

יחזקאל ג

קהל
then ש״ץ: ^יִמְלֹךְ יהוה לְעוֹלָם, אֱלֹהַיִךְ צִיּוֹן לְדֹר וָדֹר, הַלְלוּיָהּ:

תהלים קמו

ש״ץ: לְדוֹר וָדוֹר נַגִּיד גָּדְלֶךָ, וּלְנֵצַח נְצָחִים קְדֻשָּׁתְךָ נַקְדִּישׁ
וְשִׁבְחֲךָ אֱלֹהֵינוּ מִפִּינוּ לֹא יָמוּשׁ לְעוֹלָם וָעֶד
כִּי אֵל מֶלֶךְ גָּדוֹל וְקָדוֹשׁ אָתָּה.
בָּרוּךְ אַתָּה יהוה, הָאֵל הַקָּדוֹשׁ./בעשרת ימי תשובה: הַמֶּלֶךְ הַקָּדוֹשׁ./

The שליח ציבור continues with אַתָּה חוֹנֵן on the next page.

קדושה *Kedusha*. The *Kedusha* is the supreme moment of holiness in prayer. It takes several different forms. Common to them all is that they are built around the two supreme mystical visions in the Hebrew Bible, of Isaiah (chapter 6) and Ezekiel (chapters 1–3). The prophet sees God enthroned in glory, surrounded by angels singing His praises. Isaiah hears them singing, "Holy, holy, holy is the Lord of hosts; the whole world is filled with His glory." Ezekiel (3:12) hears them singing, "Blessed is the Lord's glory from His place." Together they constitute the most sublime expression of prayer as praise in the presence of God.

In the morning, *Kedusha* is said three times at different points in the service. There is *Kedushat Yotzer*, which appears in the first of the three Shema blessings (page 95), *Kedusha DeAmida*, said here during the Leader's Repetition; and *Kedusha DeSidra*, toward the end of the service. The first and third

HOLINESS

אַתָּה קָדוֹשׁ You are holy and Your name is holy,
and holy ones praise You daily, Selah!
Blessed are You, LORD,
the holy God. / *Between Rosh HaShana & Yom Kippur:* the holy King./
(*If forgotten, repeat the Amida.*)

KNOWLEDGE

אַתָּה חוֹנֵן You grace humanity with knowledge
and teach mortals understanding.
Grace us with the knowledge, understanding
and discernment that come from You.
Blessed are You, LORD, who graciously grants knowledge.

REPENTANCE

הֲשִׁיבֵנוּ Bring us back, our Father,
to Your Torah.
Draw us near, our King,
to Your service.
Lead us back to You in perfect repentance.
Blessed are You, LORD, who desires repentance.

דעת *Blessing 4: Knowledge.* This is the first of the "request" blessings. King Solomon, when asked by God to name the thing he most desired (1 Kings 3:5–15), asked for wisdom; so do we. Knowledge is prior to emotion, because "the heart is deceitful above all things" (Jer. 17:9). Untutored emotion can be misdirected, even destructive.

This paragraph replicates the structure of the Amida as a whole. It begins with praise ("You grace humanity with knowledge"), proceeds to request ("Grace us with the knowledge"), and ends in acknowledgment ("Who graciously grants knowledge").

תשובה *Blessing 5: Repentance.* Knowledge and understanding allow us to see where we have drifted from the right path of life. So we ask God to help us find the way back to repentance.

קדושת השם

אַתָּה קָדוֹשׁ וְשִׁמְךָ קָדוֹשׁ
וּקְדוֹשִׁים בְּכָל יוֹם יְהַלְלוּךָ סֶּלָה.
בָּרוּךְ אַתָּה יהוה, הָאֵל הַקָּדוֹשׁ./בעשרת ימי תשובה: הַמֶּלֶךְ הַקָּדוֹשׁ./
(If forgotten, repeat the עמידה.)

דעת

אַתָּה חוֹנֵן לְאָדָם דַּעַת
וּמְלַמֵּד לֶאֱנוֹשׁ בִּינָה.
חָנֵּנוּ מֵאִתְּךָ דֵּעָה בִּינָה וְהַשְׂכֵּל.
בָּרוּךְ אַתָּה יהוה, חוֹנֵן הַדָּעַת.

תשובה

הֲשִׁיבֵנוּ אָבִינוּ לְתוֹרָתֶךָ
וְקָרְבֵנוּ מַלְכֵּנוּ לַעֲבוֹדָתֶךָ
וְהַחֲזִירֵנוּ בִּתְשׁוּבָה שְׁלֵמָה לְפָנֶיךָ.
בָּרוּךְ אַתָּה יהוה, הָרוֹצֶה בִּתְשׁוּבָה.

קדושת השם **Blessing 3: Holiness.** The threefold reference to holiness ("You are holy and Your name is holy, and holy ones praise You daily") mirrors the threefold declaration of the angels in Isaiah's vision: "Holy, holy, holy is the LORD of hosts." *Kadosh,* "holy," means "set apart, distinct." When used of God, it refers to His transcendence, the fact that He stands outside nature, creating and sustaining it. When used of Israel, it means that we too are summoned to stand apart from the idols of the age, living instead in close and continuous proximity to God.

The first three paragraphs of the Amida (excluding the *Kedusha*), form a composite unit. The first speaks of the beginning of covenantal time in the days of the patriarchs. The second is about the end of time: resurrection. The third is about holiness, beyond space and time.

FORGIVENESS

Strike the left side of the chest at °.

סְלַח לָנוּ Forgive us, our Father, for we have °sinned.

Pardon us, our King, for we have °transgressed;

for You pardon and forgive.

Blessed are You, LORD, the gracious One who repeatedly forgives.

REDEMPTION

רְאֵה Look on our affliction, plead our cause,

and redeem us soon for Your name's sake,

for You are a powerful Redeemer.

Blessed are You, LORD, the Redeemer of Israel.

On Fast Days the Leader adds:

עֲנֵנוּ Answer us, LORD, answer us on our Fast Day, for we are in great distress. Look not at our wickedness. Do not hide Your face from us and do not ignore our plea. Be near to our cry; please let Your loving-kindness comfort us. Even before we call to You, answer us, as is said, "Before they call, I will   *Is. 65* answer. While they are still speaking, I will hear." For You, LORD, are the One who answers in time of distress, redeems and rescues in all times of trouble and anguish. Blessed are You, LORD, who answers in time of distress.

---

or affliction. Rabbi Samson Raphael Hirsch distinguishes between the first two phrases thus: "Look on our affliction" refers to suffering not caused by others, while "Plead our cause" refers to those who seek our harm. Rational argument is often insufficient to cure hatred; therefore we place our fate in the hands of God, asking Him to heal hostility (Rabbi J.H. Hertz). לְמַעַן שְׁמֶךָ *For Your name's sake:* may we be spared suffering not for our own sake but so that we may be free to worship You without distraction (Rabbi Yaakov Tzvi Mecklenburg). גּוֹאֵל יִשְׂרָאֵל *Redeemer of Israel:* in the present, as opposed to the blessing immediately prior to the Amida, which refers to acts of divine redemption in the past.

עֲנֵנוּ *Answer us:* A special prayer to be said on public fasts (*Ta'anit* 11a). The Leader recites it at this point in the Repetition of the Amida.

סליחה

Strike the left side of the chest at °.

סְלַח לָנוּ אָבִינוּ כִּי °חָטָאנוּ

מְחַל לָנוּ מַלְכֵּנוּ כִּי °פָשָׁעְנוּ

כִּי מוֹחֵל וְסוֹלֵחַ אָתָּה.

בָּרוּךְ אַתָּה יהוה, חַנּוּן הַמַּרְבֶּה לִסְלֹחַ.

גאולה

רְאֵה בְעָנְיֵנוּ, וְרִיבָה רִיבֵנוּ

וּגְאָלֵנוּ מְהֵרָה לְמַעַן שְׁמֶךָ

כִּי גוֹאֵל חָזָק אָתָּה.

בָּרוּךְ אַתָּה יהוה, גּוֹאֵל יִשְׂרָאֵל.

———————————————————————————————————

On Fast Days the שליח ציבור *adds:*

עֲנֵנוּ יהוה עֲנֵנוּ בְּיוֹם צוֹם תַּעֲנִיתֵנוּ, כִּי בְצָרָה גְדוֹלָה אֲנָחְנוּ. אַל תֵּפֶן אֶל
רִשְׁעֵנוּ, וְאַל תַּסְתֵּר פָּנֶיךָ מִמֶּנּוּ, וְאַל תִּתְעַלַּם מִתְּחִנָּתֵנוּ. הֱיֵה נָא קָרוֹב
לְשַׁוְעָתֵנוּ, יְהִי נָא חַסְדְּךָ לְנַחֲמֵנוּ, טֶרֶם נִקְרָא אֵלֶיךָ עֲנֵנוּ, כַּדָּבָר שֶׁנֶּאֱמַר:
ישעיה סה וְהָיָה טֶרֶם יִקְרָאוּ וַאֲנִי אֶעֱנֶה, עוֹד הֵם מְדַבְּרִים וַאֲנִי אֶשְׁמָע: כִּי אַתָּה יהוה
הָעוֹנֶה בְּעֵת צָרָה, פּוֹדֶה וּמַצִּיל בְּכָל עֵת צָרָה וְצוּקָה. בָּרוּךְ אַתָּה יהוה,
הָעוֹנֶה בְּעֵת צָרָה.

———————————————————————————————————

סליחה **Blessing 6: Forgiveness.** Repentance involves asking God to forgive us. This applies to sins between us and God. Sins between us and our fellow human beings are only forgiven when we have apologized to, and tried to obtain the forgiveness of, those we have wronged. Knowledge, repentance and forgiveness are the three primary needs of the mind and soul.

גאולה **Blessing 7: Redemption.** The commentators explain that this request is not for national redemption, the subject of later blessings. Here the reference is to release from personal crises: captivity, persecution, misfortune

HEALING

רְפָאֵנוּ Heal us, LORD, and we shall be healed.
Save us and we shall be saved,
for You are our praise.
Bring complete recovery for all our ailments,

The following prayer for a sick person may be said here:
May it be Your will, O LORD my God and God of my ancestors, that You
speedily send a complete recovery from heaven, a healing of both soul and
body, to the patient (*name*), son/daughter of (*mother's name*) among the
other afflicted of Israel.

---

for You, God, King, are a faithful and compassionate Healer.
Blessed are You, LORD, Healer of the sick of His people Israel.

PROSPERITY

*The phrase "Grant dew and rain as a blessing" is said from December 5th
(in the year before a civil leap year, December 6th) until Pesah. In Israel, it is
said from the 7th of Marheshvan. The phrase "Grant blessing" is said from
Hol HaMo'ed Pesah until December 4th (in the year before a civil leap year,
December 5th). In Israel it is said through the 6th of Marheshvan. See laws 52–54.*

בָּרֵךְ Bless this year for us, LORD our God,
and all its types of produce for good.

In winter: Grant dew and rain as a blessing
In other seasons: Grant blessing

on the face of the earth,
and from its goodness satisfy us,
blessing our year as the best of years.
Blessed are You, LORD, who blesses the years.

---

teaches its inhabitants the need for prayer. וְתֵן טַל וּמָטָר *Grant dew and rain:*
unlike the praise "He makes the wind blow and the rain fall" (page 110), which
we begin saying on Shemini Atzeret, the actual prayer for rain is said later to
coincide with the rainy season itself. Outside Israel, it is said from the sixtieth
day after "*Tekufat Tishrei*," the Jewish equivalent of the fall equinox (in the
Northern Hemisphere).

רְפוּאָה

רְפָאֵנוּ יהוה וְנֵרָפֵא

הוֹשִׁיעֵנוּ וְנִוָּשֵׁעָה, כִּי תְהִלָּתֵנוּ אָתָּה

וְהַעֲלֵה רְפוּאָה שְׁלֵמָה לְכָל מַכּוֹתֵינוּ

The following prayer for a sick person may be said here:

יְהִי רָצוֹן מִלְּפָנֶיךָ יהוה אֱלֹהַי וֵאלֹהֵי אֲבוֹתַי, שֶׁתִּשְׁלַח מְהֵרָה רְפוּאָה שְׁלֵמָה

מִן הַשָּׁמַיִם רְפוּאַת הַנֶּפֶשׁ וּרְפוּאַת הַגּוּף לַחוֹלֶה/לַחוֹלָה *name of patient*

בֶּן/בַּת *mother's name* בְּתוֹךְ שְׁאָר חוֹלֵי יִשְׂרָאֵל.

כִּי אֵל מֶלֶךְ רוֹפֵא נֶאֱמָן וְרַחֲמָן אָתָּה.

בָּרוּךְ אַתָּה יהוה, רוֹפֵא חוֹלֵי עַמּוֹ יִשְׂרָאֵל.

בִּרְכַּת הַשָּׁנִים

The phrase וְתֵן טַל וּמָטָר לִבְרָכָה *is said from December 5th (in the year before a civil leap year,*
December 6th) until פֶּסַח. *In* אֶרֶץ יִשְׂרָאֵל, *it is said from* ז. מַרְחֶשְׁוָן. *The phrase* וְתֵן בְּרָכָה
is said from חוֹל הַמּוֹעֵד פֶּסַח *until December 4th (in the year before a civil leap year,*
December 5th). In אֶרֶץ יִשְׂרָאֵל *it is said through* ז. מַרְחֶשְׁוָן. *See laws 52–54.*

בָּרֵךְ עָלֵינוּ יהוה אֱלֹהֵינוּ אֶת הַשָּׁנָה הַזֹּאת

וְאֶת כָּל מִינֵי תְבוּאָתָהּ, לְטוֹבָה

בחורף: וְתֵן טַל וּמָטָר לִבְרָכָה / בקיץ: וְתֵן בְּרָכָה

עַל פְּנֵי הָאֲדָמָה, וְשַׂבְּעֵנוּ מִטּוּבָהּ

וּבָרֵךְ שְׁנָתֵנוּ כַּשָּׁנִים הַטּוֹבוֹת.

בָּרוּךְ אַתָּה יהוה, מְבָרֵךְ הַשָּׁנִים.

───────────────────────────────

רְפוּאָה *Blessing 8: Healing.* We pray that medical treatment be successful, and
that God Himself be part of the healing process. We are both body and soul:
the health of one affects that of the other.

בִּרְכַּת הַשָּׁנִים *Blessing 9: Prosperity.* We pray for God's blessing on our efforts
to earn a livelihood. Israel's agriculture depends on rain, so this blessing
includes – during the winter months – a prayer for rain. Israel is a land that

INGATHERING OF EXILES

תְּקַע Sound the great shofar for our freedom,
raise high the banner to gather our exiles,
and gather us together from the four quarters of the earth.
Blessed are You, Lord,
who gathers the dispersed of His people Israel.

JUSTICE

הָשִׁיבָה Restore our judges as at first,
and our counselors as at the beginning,
and remove from us sorrow and sighing.
May You alone, Lord,
reign over us with loving-kindness and compassion,
and vindicate us in justice.
Blessed are You, Lord,
the King who loves righteousness and justice.

/ *Between Rosh HaShana & Yom Kippur, end the blessing:* the King of justice. /

AGAINST INFORMERS

וְלַמַּלְשִׁינִים For the slanderers let there be no hope,
and may all wickedness perish in an instant.
May all Your people's enemies swiftly be cut down.
May You swiftly uproot, crush, cast down
and humble the arrogant swiftly in our days.
Blessed are You, Lord,
who destroys enemies and humbles the arrogant.

---

leaders of the people (Rabbi Abraham ben HaRambam). The prayer for the restoration of judges, following the ingathering of exiles, is thus a plea for the return of national sovereignty. וְהָסֵר מִמֶּנּוּ יָגוֹן וַאֲנָחָה *Remove from us sorrow and sighing:* the plaint of a people who have known the full precariousness of being dependent on the goodwill of others.

ברכת המינים *Blessing 12: Against Informers.* The text of this paragraph underwent several changes during the centuries. Its original object was the sectarianism that split the Jewish world during the late Second Temple period.

קבוץ גלויות

תְּקַע בְּשׁוֹפָר גָּדוֹל לְחֵרוּתֵנוּ, וְשָׂא נֵס לְקַבֵּץ גָּלֻיּוֹתֵינוּ
וְקַבְּצֵנוּ יַחַד מֵאַרְבַּע כַּנְפוֹת הָאָרֶץ.
בָּרוּךְ אַתָּה יהוה, מְקַבֵּץ נִדְחֵי עַמּוֹ יִשְׂרָאֵל.

השבת המשפט

הָשִׁיבָה שׁוֹפְטֵינוּ כְּבָרִאשׁוֹנָה וְיוֹעֲצֵינוּ כְּבַתְּחִלָּה
וְהָסֵר מִמֶּנּוּ יָגוֹן וַאֲנָחָה
וּמְלֹךְ עָלֵינוּ אַתָּה יהוה לְבַדְּךָ בְּחֶסֶד וּבְרַחֲמִים
וְצַדְּקֵנוּ בַּמִּשְׁפָּט.
בָּרוּךְ אַתָּה יהוה
מֶלֶךְ אוֹהֵב צְדָקָה וּמִשְׁפָּט. / בעשרת ימי תשובה: הַמֶּלֶךְ הַמִּשְׁפָּט. /

ברכת המינים

וְלַמַּלְשִׁינִים אַל תְּהִי תִקְוָה, וְכָל הָרִשְׁעָה כְּרֶגַע תֹּאבֵד
וְכָל אוֹיְבֵי עַמְּךָ מְהֵרָה יִכָּרֵתוּ
וְהַזֵּדִים מְהֵרָה תְעַקֵּר וּתְשַׁבֵּר וּתְמַגֵּר וְתַכְנִיעַ בִּמְהֵרָה בְיָמֵינוּ.
בָּרוּךְ אַתָּה יהוה, שׁוֹבֵר אוֹיְבִים וּמַכְנִיעַ זֵדִים.

─────────

קבוץ גלויות *Blessing 10: Ingathering of exiles.* With this paragraph, the requests change from individual to collective hopes. They begin with three prayers for political-historical renewal: the return of exiles, the restoration of independence, and an end to the factionalism that caused great damage to the Israelites from the biblical era to the end of the Second Temple period. תְּקַע בְּשׁוֹפָר גָּדוֹל *Sound the great shofar:* A reference to Isaiah 27:13, "On that day a great shofar will sound." וְשָׂא נֵס *Raise high the banner:* Isaiah 11:12, "He will raise a banner for the nations and gather the exiles of Israel; He will assemble the scattered people of Judah from the four quarters of the earth."

משפט *Blessing 11: Justice.* A prayer for self-government. The "Judges" in the biblical book of that name were not merely judges in a legal sense; they were

THE RIGHTEOUS

עַל הַצַּדִּיקִים To the righteous, the pious,
the elders of Your people the house of Israel,
the remnant of their scholars,
the righteous converts, and to us,
may Your compassion be aroused,
LORD our God.
Grant a good reward to all who sincerely trust in Your name.
Set our lot with them,
so that we may never be ashamed, for in You we trust.
Blessed are You, LORD,
who is the support and trust of the righteous.

REBUILDING JERUSALEM

וְלִירוּשָׁלַיִם To Jerusalem, Your city,
may You return in compassion,
and may You dwell in it as You promised.
May You rebuild it rapidly in our days
as an everlasting structure,
and install within it soon the throne of David.
Blessed are You, LORD, who builds Jerusalem.

פְּלֵיטַת סוֹפְרֵיהֶם *The remnant of their scholars* is a reference to those Jews who
endured religious persecution under the Greeks and Romans, and later, those
who survived the Crusades and those who lived through the Holocaust. Judaism lost many of its greatest scholars as martyrs.

בנין ירושלים *Blessing 14: Rebuilding Jerusalem.* Jerusalem is the home of the
Jewish soul, the place to which we turn in prayer and for whose restoration
Jews prayed in every generation. The book of Psalms has left us an indelible
description of how Jews felt when the city fell to the Babylonians in the
sixth century BCE: "By the rivers of Babylon we sat and wept when we remembered Zion … May my tongue cling to the roof of my mouth if I do not
remember you, if I do not consider Jerusalem my highest joy" (Psalm 137).
Jerusalem is mentioned more than 600 times in the Hebrew Bible.

עַל הַצַּדִּיקִים

עַל הַצַּדִּיקִים וְעַל הַחֲסִידִים
וְעַל זִקְנֵי עַמְּךָ בֵּית יִשְׂרָאֵל
וְעַל פְּלֵיטַת סוֹפְרֵיהֶם
וְעַל גֵּרֵי הַצֶּדֶק, וְעָלֵינוּ
יֶהֱמוּ רַחֲמֶיךָ יהוה אֱלֹהֵינוּ
וְתֵן שָׂכָר טוֹב לְכָל הַבּוֹטְחִים בְּשִׁמְךָ בֶּאֱמֶת
וְשִׂים חֶלְקֵנוּ עִמָּהֶם, וּלְעוֹלָם לֹא נֵבוֹשׁ כִּי בְךָ בָּטָחְנוּ.
בָּרוּךְ אַתָּה יהוה, מִשְׁעָן וּמִבְטָח לַצַּדִּיקִים.

בִּנְיַן יְרוּשָׁלַיִם

וְלִירוּשָׁלַיִם עִירְךָ בְּרַחֲמִים תָּשׁוּב
וְתִשְׁכֹּן בְּתוֹכָהּ כַּאֲשֶׁר דִּבַּרְתָּ
וּבְנֵה אוֹתָהּ בְּקָרוֹב בְּיָמֵינוּ בִּנְיַן עוֹלָם
וְכִסֵּא דָוִד מְהֵרָה לְתוֹכָהּ תָּכִין.
בָּרוּךְ אַתָּה יהוה, בּוֹנֵה יְרוּשָׁלָיִם.

There were Jews in the Hellenistic age who turned against their own people.
Faith (*emuna*) in Judaism involves the idea of loyalty – to a people and its
heritage. This prayer is a protest against disloyalty.

The Talmud (*Berakhot* 28b) says that, to formulate this prayer, Rabban
Gamliel turned to Shmuel HaKatan. Rabbi Kook pointed out that Shmuel
HaKatan was known for his attachment to the principle, "Do not rejoice
when your enemy falls" (*Avot* 4:24). Only a person who deeply loved his
fellow human beings could be entrusted with the task of constructing this
prayer, which must be free of animosity and *schadenfreude*.

עַל הַצַּדִּיקִים *Blessing 13:* הַצַּדִּיקִים *The righteous.* After mentioning those
who harm the Jewish people, we go on to describe those who endow it
with greatness: the righteous, the pious, the elders, scholars and converts.

KINGDOM OF DAVID

אֶת צֶמַח May the offshoot of Your servant David soon flower,
and may his pride be raised high by Your salvation,
for we wait for Your salvation all day.
Blessed are You, LORD, who makes the glory of salvation flourish.

RESPONSE TO PRAYER

שְׁמַע קוֹלֵנוּ Listen to our voice, LORD our God.
Spare us and have compassion on us,
and in compassion and favor accept our prayer,
for You, God, listen to prayers and pleas.
Do not turn us away, O our King,
empty-handed from Your presence,*
for You listen with compassion
to the prayer of Your people Israel.
Blessed are You, LORD, who listens to prayer.

---

*In times of drought in Israel, add:

וַעֲנֵנוּ And answer us through the attribute of compassion, Creator of the
universe who chooses His people Israel to make known His greatness and
majestic glory. You who listen to prayer, grant dew and rain on the face of the
earth, satisfying the whole universe from Your goodness. Fill our hands from
Your blessings and Your hand's rich gift. Guard and deliver this year from all
evil, all kinds of destruction and punishment, and give it hope and a peaceful
end. Spare us and have compassion on us and on all our produce and fruit,
blessing us with bounteous rain. May we merit life, plenty and peace as in the
good years. Remove from us plague, sword and famine, wild animals, captivity
and plunder, the evil instinct and serious and dangerous illnesses and events.
Decree for us goodly decrees, and may Your compassion prevail over Your
other attributes, that You may act toward Your children through the attribute
of compassion, and in compassion and favor accept our prayer.

Continue with "for You listen" above.

שומע תפלה Blessing 16: *Response to Prayer*. An all-inclusive prayer, that our
prayers be heard. At this point in the silent Amida, the individual can include
any of his or her personal requests.

מלכות בית דוד

אֶת צֶמַח דָּוִד עַבְדְּךָ מְהֵרָה תַצְמִיחַ, וְקַרְנוֹ תָּרוּם בִּישׁוּעָתֶךָ
כִּי לִישׁוּעָתְךָ קִוִּינוּ כָּל הַיּוֹם.
בָּרוּךְ אַתָּה יהוה, מַצְמִיחַ קֶרֶן יְשׁוּעָה.

שומע תפלה

שְׁמַע קוֹלֵנוּ יהוה אֱלֹהֵינוּ
חוּס וְרַחֵם עָלֵינוּ, וְקַבֵּל בְּרַחֲמִים וּבְרָצוֹן אֶת תְּפִלָּתֵנוּ
כִּי אֵל שׁוֹמֵעַ תְּפִלּוֹת וְתַחֲנוּנִים אָתָּה
וּמִלְּפָנֶיךָ מַלְכֵּנוּ רֵיקָם אַל תְּשִׁיבֵנוּ*
כִּי אַתָּה שׁוֹמֵעַ תְּפִלַּת עַמְּךָ יִשְׂרָאֵל בְּרַחֲמִים.
בָּרוּךְ אַתָּה יהוה, שׁוֹמֵעַ תְּפִלָּה.

In times of drought in אֶרֶץ יִשְׂרָאֵל, *add:*

וַעֲנֵנוּ בּוֹרֵא עוֹלָם בְּמִדַּת הָרַחֲמִים, בּוֹחֵר בְּעַמּוֹ יִשְׂרָאֵל לְהוֹדִיעַ גָּדְלוֹ וְהַדְרַת
כְּבוֹדוֹ. שׁוֹמֵעַ תְּפִלָּה, תֵּן טַל וּמָטָר עַל פְּנֵי הָאֲדָמָה, וְתַשְׂבִּיעַ אֶת הָעוֹלָם
כֻּלּוֹ מִטּוּבֶךָ, וּמַלֵּא יָדֵינוּ מִבִּרְכוֹתֶיךָ וּמֵעֹשֶׁר מַתְּנַת יָדֶךָ. שְׁמֹר וְהַצֵּל שָׁנָה
זוֹ מִכָּל דָּבָר רָע, וּמִכָּל מִינֵי מַשְׁחִית וּמִכָּל מִינֵי פֻּרְעָנִיּוֹת, וַעֲשֵׂה לָהּ תִּקְוָה
וְאַחֲרִית שָׁלוֹם. חוּס וְרַחֵם עָלֵינוּ וְעַל כָּל תְּבוּאָתֵנוּ וּפֵרוֹתֵינוּ, וּבָרְכֵנוּ בְּגִשְׁמֵי
בְרָכָה, וְנִזְכֶּה לְחַיִּים וְשָׂבָע וְשָׁלוֹם כַּשָּׁנִים הַטּוֹבוֹת. וְהָסֵר מִמֶּנּוּ דֶּבֶר וְחֶרֶב
וְרָעָב, וְחַיָּה רָעָה וּשְׁבִי וּבִזָּה, וְיֵצֶר הָרָע וָחֳלָיִים רָעִים וְקָשִׁים וּמְאֹרָעוֹת רָעִים
וְקָשִׁים. וּגְזֹר עָלֵינוּ גְּזֵרוֹת טוֹבוֹת מִלְּפָנֶיךָ, וְיִגֹּלּוּ רַחֲמֶיךָ עַל מִדּוֹתֶיךָ, וְתִתְנַהֵג
עִם בָּנֶיךָ בְּמִדַּת הָרַחֲמִים, וְקַבֵּל בְּרַחֲמִים וּבְרָצוֹן אֶת תְּפִלָּתֵנוּ.

Continue with כִּי אַתָּה שׁוֹמֵעַ *above.*

מלכות בית דוד *Blessing 15: Kingdom of David.* David was promised by God that the monarchy would always be the heritage of his children. The Davidic monarchy came to an end with the Babylonian conquest. It will be restored in the messianic age. The word "Messiah" in Hebrew means "anointed"; that is, a duly appointed king of Davidic descent.

TEMPLE SERVICE

רְצֵה Find favor, LORD our God,
in Your people Israel and their prayer.
Restore the service to Your most holy House,
and accept in love and favor
the fire-offerings of Israel and their prayer.
May the service of Your people Israel
always find favor with You.

On Rosh Ḥodesh, say:

אֱלֹהֵינוּ Our God and God of our ancestors, may there rise, come,
reach, appear, be favored, heard, regarded and remembered before
You, our recollection and remembrance, as well as the remembrance of our ancestors, and of the Messiah son of David Your
servant, and of Jerusalem Your holy city, and of all Your people the
house of Israel – for deliverance and well-being, grace, loving-kindness and compassion, life and peace, on this day of Rosh Ḥodesh.
On it remember us, LORD our God, for good; recollect us for blessing, and deliver us for life. In accord with Your promise of salvation
and compassion, spare us and be gracious to us; have compassion
on us and deliver us, for our eyes are turned to You because You,
God, are a gracious and compassionate King.

וְתֶחֱזֶינָה And may our eyes witness
Your return to Zion in compassion.
Blessed are You, LORD,
who restores His Presence to Zion.

Priestly Blessing, but according to Maimonides it means that they said the
prayer beginning שִׂים שָׁלוֹם, "Grant peace."

עבודה

רְצֵה יהוה אֱלֹהֵינוּ בְּעַמְּךָ יִשְׂרָאֵל, וּבִתְפִלָּתָם
וְהָשֵׁב אֶת הָעֲבוֹדָה לִדְבִיר בֵּיתֶךָ
וְאִשֵּׁי יִשְׂרָאֵל וּתְפִלָּתָם בְּאַהֲבָה תְקַבֵּל בְּרָצוֹן
וּתְהִי לְרָצוֹן תָּמִיד עֲבוֹדַת יִשְׂרָאֵל עַמֶּךָ.

ראש חודש *On*, say:

אֱלֹהֵינוּ וֵאלֹהֵי אֲבוֹתֵינוּ, יַעֲלֶה וְיָבוֹא וְיַגִּיעַ, וְיֵרָאֶה וְיֵרָצֶה
וְיִשָּׁמַע, וְיִפָּקֵד וְיִזָּכֵר זִכְרוֹנֵנוּ וּפִקְדוֹנֵנוּ וְזִכְרוֹן אֲבוֹתֵינוּ, וְזִכְרוֹן
מָשִׁיחַ בֶּן דָּוִד עַבְדֶּךָ, וְזִכְרוֹן יְרוּשָׁלַיִם עִיר קָדְשֶׁךָ, וְזִכְרוֹן כָּל עַמְּךָ
בֵּית יִשְׂרָאֵל, לְפָנֶיךָ, לִפְלֵיטָה לְטוֹבָה, לְחֵן וּלְחֶסֶד וּלְרַחֲמִים,
לְחַיִּים וּלְשָׁלוֹם בְּיוֹם רֹאשׁ הַחֹדֶשׁ הַזֶּה. זָכְרֵנוּ יהוה אֱלֹהֵינוּ בּוֹ
לְטוֹבָה, וּפָקְדֵנוּ בוֹ לִבְרָכָה, וְהוֹשִׁיעֵנוּ בוֹ לְחַיִּים. וּבִדְבַר יְשׁוּעָה
וְרַחֲמִים, חוּס וְחָנֵּנוּ וְרַחֵם עָלֵינוּ וְהוֹשִׁיעֵנוּ, כִּי אֵלֶיךָ עֵינֵינוּ, כִּי
אֵל מֶלֶךְ חַנּוּן וְרַחוּם אָתָּה.

וְתֶחֱזֶינָה עֵינֵינוּ בְּשׁוּבְךָ לְצִיּוֹן בְּרַחֲמִים.
בָּרוּךְ אַתָּה יהוה
הַמַּחֲזִיר שְׁכִינָתוֹ לְצִיּוֹן.

עבודה *Blessing 17: Temple Service.* The last three blessings, called by the sages
"Thanksgiving," are linked because they were said by the priests in the Temple
(*Tamid* 5:1). This paragraph was originally a prayer that the day's sacrifices be
accepted. The priests then said *Modim,* "We give thanks to You" and blessed
the people. According to *Tosafot,* this means that they said the threefold

THANKSGIVING

Bow at the first nine words.

מוֹדִים We give thanks to You,
for You are the LORD our God
and God of our ancestors
for ever and all time.
You are the Rock of our lives,
Shield of our salvation
from generation to generation.
We will thank You and
declare Your praise for our lives,
which are entrusted into Your hand;
for our souls,
which are placed in Your charge;
for Your miracles
which are with us every day;
and for Your wonders and favors
at all times, evening,
morning and midday.
You are good –
for Your compassion never fails.
You are compassionate –
for Your loving-
kindnesses never cease.
We have always
placed our hope in You.

*During the Leader's Repetition,
the congregation says quietly:*

מוֹדִים We give thanks to You,
for You are the LORD
our God
and God of our ancestors,
God of all flesh,
who formed us
and formed the universe.
Blessings and thanks are due
to Your great and holy name
for giving us life
and sustaining us.
May You continue
to give us life and sustain us;
and may You gather
our exiles
to Your holy courts,
to keep Your decrees,
do Your will and serve You
with a perfect heart,
for it is for us
to give You thanks.
Blessed be God
to whom
thanksgiving is due.

---

hidden miracles take place within them. God is present not only in signs
and wonders, but also in the very laws that govern the universe. To see the
miraculous in the everyday is part of the Judaic vision, beautifully expressed
in these lines.

הודאה

Bow at the first five words.

During the קהל *says quietly:* חזרת הש"ץ

מוֹדִים אֲנַחְנוּ לָךְ
שָׁאַתָּה הוּא יהוה אֱלֹהֵינוּ
וֵאלֹהֵי אֲבוֹתֵינוּ
אֱלֹהֵי כָל בָּשָׂר
יוֹצְרֵנוּ, יוֹצֵר בְּרֵאשִׁית.
בְּרָכוֹת וְהוֹדָאוֹת
לְשִׁמְךָ הַגָּדוֹל וְהַקָּדוֹשׁ
עַל שֶׁהֶחֱיִיתָנוּ וְקִיַּמְתָּנוּ.
כֵּן תְּחַיֵּנוּ וּתְקַיְּמֵנוּ
וְתֶאֱסֹף גָּלֻיּוֹתֵינוּ
לְחַצְרוֹת קָדְשֶׁךָ
לִשְׁמֹר חֻקֶּיךָ
וְלַעֲשׂוֹת רְצוֹנֶךָ וּלְעָבְדְּךָ
בְּלֵבָב שָׁלֵם
עַל שֶׁאֲנַחְנוּ מוֹדִים לָךְ.
בָּרוּךְ אֵל הַהוֹדָאוֹת.

מוֹדִים אֲנַחְנוּ לָךְ
שָׁאַתָּה הוּא יהוה אֱלֹהֵינוּ
וֵאלֹהֵי אֲבוֹתֵינוּ לְעוֹלָם וָעֶד.
צוּר חַיֵּינוּ, מָגֵן יִשְׁעֵנוּ
אַתָּה הוּא לְדוֹר וָדוֹר.
נוֹדֶה לְּךָ וּנְסַפֵּר תְּהִלָּתֶךָ
עַל חַיֵּינוּ הַמְּסוּרִים בְּיָדֶךָ
וְעַל נִשְׁמוֹתֵינוּ הַפְּקוּדוֹת לָךְ
וְעַל נִסֶּיךָ שֶׁבְּכָל יוֹם עִמָּנוּ
וְעַל נִפְלְאוֹתֶיךָ וְטוֹבוֹתֶיךָ
שֶׁבְּכָל עֵת
עֶרֶב וָבֹקֶר וְצָהֳרָיִם.
הַטּוֹב, כִּי לֹא כָלוּ רַחֲמֶיךָ
וְהַמְרַחֵם, כִּי לֹא תַמּוּ חֲסָדֶיךָ
מֵעוֹלָם קִוִּינוּ לָךְ.

הודאה *Blessing 18: Thanksgiving.* The root *y-d-h* has three meanings: (1) to bow (see *Targum* to II Samuel 16:4), hence we bow at the beginning and end of this blessing; (2) to confess or profess; and (3) to thank. The blessing begins as a confession of faith, and moves to thanks for God's blessings which surround us continually. וְעַל נִסֶּיךָ שֶׁבְּכָל יוֹם עִמָּנוּ *For Your miracles which are with us every day:* Nahmanides explained the difference between a "revealed" and a "hidden" miracle. Revealed miracles stand outside the laws of nature;

On Ḥanukka:

עַל הַנִּסִּים [We thank You also] for the miracles, the redemption, the mighty deeds, the salvations, and the victories in battle which You performed for our ancestors in those days, at this time.

בִּימֵי מַתִּתְיָהוּ In the days of Mattityahu, son of Yoḥanan, the High Priest, the Hasmonean, and his sons, the wicked Greek kingdom rose up against Your people Israel to make them forget Your Torah and to force them to transgress the statutes of Your will. It was then that You in Your great compassion stood by them in the time of their distress. You championed their cause, judged their claim, and avenged their wrong. You delivered the strong into the hands of the weak, the many into the hands of the few, the impure into the hands of the pure, the wicked into the hands of the righteous, and the arrogant into the hands of those who were engaged in the study of Your Torah. You made for Yourself great and holy renown in Your world, and for Your people Israel You performed a great salvation and redemption as of this very day. Your children then entered the holiest part of Your House, cleansed Your Temple, purified Your Sanctuary, kindled lights in Your holy courts, and designated these eight days of Ḥanukka for giving thanks and praise to Your great name.

Continue with "For all these things."

On Purim:

עַל הַנִּסִּים [We thank You also] for the miracles, the redemption, the mighty deeds, the salvations, and the victories in battle which You performed for our ancestors in those days, at this time.

בִּימֵי מָרְדְּכַי In the days of Mordekhai and Esther, in Shushan the capital, the wicked Haman rose up against them and sought to destroy, slay and exterminate   *Esther 3* all the Jews, young and old, children and women, on one day, the thirteenth day of the twelfth month, which is the month of Adar, and to plunder their possessions. Then You in Your great compassion thwarted his counsel, frustrated his plans, and caused his scheme to recoil on his own head, so that they hanged him and his sons on the gallows.

Continue with "For all these things."

וְעַל כֻּלָּם For all these things may Your name be blessed and exalted, our King, continually, for ever and all time.

Between Rosh HaShana   And write, for a good life,
& Yom Kippur: all the children of Your covenant.

Let all that lives thank You, Selah! and praise Your name in truth, God, our Savior and Help, Selah!
▸Blessed are You, LORD, whose name is "the Good" and to whom thanks are due.

בחנוכה:

עַל הַנִּסִּים וְעַל הַפֻּרְקָן וְעַל הַגְּבוּרוֹת וְעַל הַתְּשׁוּעוֹת וְעַל הַמִּלְחָמוֹת שֶׁעָשִׂיתָ לַאֲבוֹתֵינוּ בַּיָּמִים הָהֵם בַּזְּמַן הַזֶּה.

בִּימֵי מַתִּתְיָהוּ בֶּן יוֹחָנָן כֹּהֵן גָּדוֹל חַשְׁמוֹנַאי וּבָנָיו, כְּשֶׁעָמְדָה מַלְכוּת יָוָן הָרְשָׁעָה עַל עַמְּךָ יִשְׂרָאֵל לְהַשְׁכִּיחָם תּוֹרָתֶךָ וּלְהַעֲבִירָם מֵחֻקֵּי רְצוֹנֶךָ, וְאַתָּה בְּרַחֲמֶיךָ הָרַבִּים עָמַדְתָּ לָהֶם בְּעֵת צָרָתָם, רַבְתָּ אֶת רִיבָם, דַּנְתָּ אֶת דִּינָם, נָקַמְתָּ אֶת נִקְמָתָם, מָסַרְתָּ גִבּוֹרִים בְּיַד חַלָּשִׁים, וְרַבִּים בְּיַד מְעַטִּים, וּטְמֵאִים בְּיַד טְהוֹרִים, וּרְשָׁעִים בְּיַד צַדִּיקִים, וְזֵדִים בְּיַד עוֹסְקֵי תוֹרָתֶךָ, וּלְךָ עָשִׂיתָ שֵׁם גָּדוֹל וְקָדוֹשׁ בְּעוֹלָמֶךָ, וּלְעַמְּךָ יִשְׂרָאֵל עָשִׂיתָ תְּשׁוּעָה גְדוֹלָה וּפֻרְקָן כְּהַיּוֹם הַזֶּה. וְאַחַר כֵּן בָּאוּ בָנֶיךָ לִדְבִיר בֵּיתֶךָ, וּפִנּוּ אֶת הֵיכָלֶךָ, וְטִהֲרוּ אֶת מִקְדָּשֶׁךָ, וְהִדְלִיקוּ נֵרוֹת בְּחַצְרוֹת קָדְשֶׁךָ, וְקָבְעוּ שְׁמוֹנַת יְמֵי חֲנֻכָּה אֵלּוּ, לְהוֹדוֹת וּלְהַלֵּל לְשִׁמְךָ הַגָּדוֹל.

Continue with וְעַל כֻּלָּם

בפורים:

עַל הַנִּסִּים וְעַל הַפֻּרְקָן וְעַל הַגְּבוּרוֹת וְעַל הַתְּשׁוּעוֹת וְעַל הַמִּלְחָמוֹת שֶׁעָשִׂיתָ לַאֲבוֹתֵינוּ בַּיָּמִים הָהֵם בַּזְּמַן הַזֶּה.

בִּימֵי מָרְדְּכַי וְאֶסְתֵּר בְּשׁוּשַׁן הַבִּירָה, כְּשֶׁעָמַד עֲלֵיהֶם הָמָן הָרָשָׁע, בִּקֵּשׁ לְהַשְׁמִיד לַהֲרֹג וּלְאַבֵּד אֶת־כָּל־הַיְּהוּדִים מִנַּעַר וְעַד־זָקֵן טַף וְנָשִׁים בְּיוֹם אֶחָד, בִּשְׁלוֹשָׁה עָשָׂר לְחֹדֶשׁ שְׁנֵים־עָשָׂר, הוּא־חֹדֶשׁ אֲדָר, וּשְׁלָלָם לָבוֹז: וְאַתָּה בְּרַחֲמֶיךָ הָרַבִּים הֵפַרְתָּ אֶת עֲצָתוֹ, וְקִלְקַלְתָּ אֶת מַחֲשַׁבְתּוֹ, וַהֲשֵׁבוֹתָ לּוֹ גְּמוּלוֹ בְּרֹאשׁוֹ, וְתָלוּ אוֹתוֹ וְאֶת בָּנָיו עַל הָעֵץ. אסתר ג

Continue with וְעַל כֻּלָּם

וְעַל כֻּלָּם יִתְבָּרַךְ וְיִתְרוֹמַם שִׁמְךָ מַלְכֵּנוּ תָּמִיד לְעוֹלָם וָעֶד.

בעשרת ימי תשובה: וּכְתֹב לְחַיִּים טוֹבִים כָּל בְּנֵי בְרִיתֶךָ.

וְכֹל הַחַיִּים יוֹדוּךָ סֶּלָה, וִיהַלְלוּ אֶת שִׁמְךָ בֶּאֱמֶת הָאֵל יְשׁוּעָתֵנוּ וְעֶזְרָתֵנוּ סֶלָה. יבָּרוּךְ אַתָּה יהוה, הַטּוֹב שִׁמְךָ וּלְךָ נָאֶה לְהוֹדוֹת.

The following is said by the Leader during the Repetition of the Amida,
except in a house of mourning and on Tisha B'Av. In Israel, if Kohanim
bless the congregation, turn to page 386. See laws 62–69.

Our God and God of our fathers, bless us with the threefold blessing in the
Torah, written by the hand of Moses Your servant and pronounced by Aaron
and his sons the priests, Your holy people, as it is said:

May the LORD bless you and protect you.	*Cong:* May it be Your will.	*Num. 6*
May the LORD make His face shine on you and be gracious to you.	*Cong:* May it be Your will.	
May the LORD turn His face toward you, and grant you peace.	*Cong:* May it be Your will.	

PEACE

שִׂים שָׁלוֹם **Grant peace**, goodness and blessing,
grace, loving-kindness and compassion to us and all Israel Your people.
Bless us, our Father, all as one, with the light of Your face,
for by the light of Your face You have given us, LORD our God,
the Torah of life and love of kindness,
righteousness, blessing, compassion, life and peace.
May it be good in Your eyes to bless Your people Israel
at every time, in every hour, with Your peace.

Between Rosh HaShana   In the book of life, blessing, peace and prosperity,
& Yom Kippur: may we and all Your people the house of Israel
                            be remembered and written before You
                            for a good life, and for peace.*

Blessed are You, LORD, who blesses His people Israel with peace.

                    **Between Rosh HaShana and Yom Kippur*
                    outside Israel, many end the blessing:
                    Blessed are You, LORD, who makes peace.

The following verse concludes the Leader's Repetition of the Amida.
Some also say it here as part of the silent Amida. See law 60.

May the words of my mouth and the meditation of my heart   *Ps. 19*
find favor before You, LORD, my Rock and Redeemer.

---

famously in the words of Isaiah: "Nation shall not lift up sword against nation;
neither shall they learn war anymore" (Is. 2:4). Peace is the ultimate hope of
monotheism, with its belief that the world is the product of a single will, not
the blind clash of conflicting elements.

The following is said by the שליח ציבור *during* חזרת הש״ץ *except*
in a house of mourning and on תשעה באב. *In* ארץ ישראל *if*
ברכת כהנים *say* כהנים *turn to page 387. See laws 62–69.*

אֱלֹהֵינוּ וֵאלֹהֵי אֲבוֹתֵינוּ, בָּרְכֵנוּ בַּבְּרָכָה הַמְשֻׁלֶּשֶׁת בַּתּוֹרָה, הַכְּתוּבָה עַל
יְדֵי מֹשֶׁה עַבְדֶּךָ, הָאֲמוּרָה מִפִּי אַהֲרֹן וּבָנָיו כֹּהֲנִים עַם קְדוֹשֶׁיךָ, כָּאָמוּר

במדבר

יְבָרֶכְךָ יהוה וְיִשְׁמְרֶךָ: קהל: כֵּן יְהִי רָצוֹן
יָאֵר יהוה פָּנָיו אֵלֶיךָ וִיחֻנֶּךָּ: קהל: כֵּן יְהִי רָצוֹן
יִשָּׂא יהוה פָּנָיו אֵלֶיךָ וְיָשֵׂם לְךָ שָׁלוֹם: קהל: כֵּן יְהִי רָצוֹן

שָׁלוֹם

שִׂים שָׁלוֹם טוֹבָה וּבְרָכָה
חֵן וָחֶסֶד וְרַחֲמִים עָלֵינוּ וְעַל כָּל יִשְׂרָאֵל עַמֶּךָ.
בָּרְכֵנוּ אָבִינוּ כֻּלָּנוּ כְּאֶחָד בְּאוֹר פָּנֶיךָ
כִּי בְאוֹר פָּנֶיךָ נָתַתָּ לָּנוּ יהוה אֱלֹהֵינוּ
תּוֹרַת חַיִּים וְאַהֲבַת חֶסֶד
וּצְדָקָה וּבְרָכָה וְרַחֲמִים וְחַיִּים וְשָׁלוֹם.
וְטוֹב בְּעֵינֶיךָ לְבָרֵךְ אֶת עַמְּךָ יִשְׂרָאֵל
בְּכָל עֵת וּבְכָל שָׁעָה בִּשְׁלוֹמֶךָ.

בעשרת ימי תשובה: בְּסֵפֶר חַיִּים, בְּרָכָה וְשָׁלוֹם, וּפַרְנָסָה טוֹבָה
נִזָּכֵר וְנִכָּתֵב לְפָנֶיךָ, אֲנַחְנוּ וְכָל עַמְּךָ בֵּית יִשְׂרָאֵל
לְחַיִּים טוֹבִים וּלְשָׁלוֹם.*

בָּרוּךְ אַתָּה יהוה, הַמְבָרֵךְ אֶת עַמּוֹ יִשְׂרָאֵל בַּשָּׁלוֹם.

During the עשרת ימי תשובה *in* ארץ ישראל, *many end the blessing:*
בָּרוּךְ אַתָּה יהוה, עוֹשֶׂה הַשָּׁלוֹם.

The following verse concludes the חזרת הש״ץ.
Some also say it here as part of the silent עמידה. *See law 60.*

תהלים יט

יִהְיוּ לְרָצוֹן אִמְרֵי־פִי וְהֶגְיוֹן לִבִּי לְפָנֶיךָ, יהוה צוּרִי וְגֹאֲלִי:

שלום *Blessing 19: Peace. Shalom* means more than the English word "peace": it
also means "completeness, perfection, harmonious interaction." The prophets of Israel were the first in history to conceive of peace as an ideal, most

אֱלֹהַי **My God,**
guard my tongue from evil and my lips from deceitful speech.
To those who curse me, let my soul be silent;
may my soul be to all like the dust.
Open my heart to Your Torah and let my soul
pursue Your commandments.
As for all who plan evil against me,
swiftly thwart their counsel and frustrate their plans.
    Act for the sake of Your name; act for the sake of Your right hand;
    act for the sake of Your holiness; act for the sake of Your Torah.
That Your beloved ones may be delivered,
save with Your right hand and answer me.
May the words of my mouth and the meditation of my heart
find favor before You, LORD, my Rock and Redeemer.

Bow, take three steps back, then bow, first left, then right, then center, while saying:

May He who makes peace in His high places,
make peace for us and all Israel – and say: Amen.

יְהִי רָצוֹן **May it be Your will,** LORD our God and God of our ancestors,
that the Temple be rebuilt speedily in our days,
and grant us a share in Your Torah. And there we will serve You
with reverence, as in the days of old and as in former years.
Then the offering of Judah and Jerusalem will be pleasing to the LORD
as in the days of old and as in former years.

Berakhot
17a

Ps. 60

Ps. 19

Mal. 3

> *When praying with a minyan, the Amida is repeated aloud by the Leader.*
>
> *On days when Taḥanun is said (see page 144), start Taḥanun on page 152.*
> *On Mondays and Thursdays start Taḥanun on page 144.*
> *In Israel, on days on which Taḥanun is said, some say Viduy and the*
> *Thirteen Attributes of Divine Compassion on page 136. See law 176a.*
>
> *On fast days (except Tisha B'Av) most congregations say Seliḥot*
> *on page 466 before Avinu Malkenu on page 138.*
>
> *Between Rosh HaShana and Yom Kippur (but not on Erev Yom Kippur,*
> *unless it falls on Friday), say Avinu Malkenu on page 138.*
>
> *On Rosh Ḥodesh, Ḥanukka, Yom HaAtzma'ut and*
> *Yom Yerushalayim, say Hallel on page 360.*
>
> *On other days when Taḥanun is not said (see page 144),*
> *the Leader says Half Kaddish on page 156.*

אֱלֹהַי

נְצֹר לְשׁוֹנִי מֵרָע וּשְׂפָתַי מִדַּבֵּר מִרְמָה

וְלִמְקַלְלַי נַפְשִׁי תִדֹּם, וְנַפְשִׁי כֶּעָפָר לַכֹּל תִּהְיֶה.

פְּתַח לִבִּי בְּתוֹרָתֶךָ, וּבְמִצְוֹתֶיךָ תִּרְדֹּף נַפְשִׁי.

וְכָל הַחוֹשְׁבִים עָלַי רָעָה

מְהֵרָה הָפֵר עֲצָתָם וְקַלְקֵל מַחֲשַׁבְתָּם.

עֲשֵׂה לְמַעַן שְׁמֶךָ, עֲשֵׂה לְמַעַן יְמִינֶךָ

עֲשֵׂה לְמַעַן קְדֻשָּׁתֶךָ, עֲשֵׂה לְמַעַן תּוֹרָתֶךָ.

לְמַעַן יֵחָלְצוּן יְדִידֶיךָ, הוֹשִׁיעָה יְמִינְךָ וַעֲנֵנִי:

יִהְיוּ לְרָצוֹן אִמְרֵי־פִי וְהֶגְיוֹן לִבִּי לְפָנֶיךָ, יהוה צוּרִי וְגֹאֲלִי:

Bow, take three steps back, then bow, first left, then right, then center, while saying:

עֹשֶׂה שָׁלוֹם/בעשרת ימי תשובה: הַשָּׁלוֹם/ בִּמְרוֹמָיו

הוּא יַעֲשֶׂה שָׁלוֹם עָלֵינוּ וְעַל כָּל יִשְׂרָאֵל, וְאִמְרוּ אָמֵן.

יְהִי רָצוֹן מִלְּפָנֶיךָ יהוה אֱלֹהֵינוּ וֵאלֹהֵי אֲבוֹתֵינוּ

שֶׁיִּבָּנֶה בֵּית הַמִּקְדָּשׁ בִּמְהֵרָה בְיָמֵינוּ, וְתֵן חֶלְקֵנוּ בְּתוֹרָתֶךָ

וְשָׁם נַעֲבָדְךָ בְּיִרְאָה כִּימֵי עוֹלָם וּכְשָׁנִים קַדְמֹנִיּוֹת.

וְעָרְבָה לַיהוה מִנְחַת יְהוּדָה וִירוּשָׁלָ͏ִם כִּימֵי עוֹלָם וּכְשָׁנִים קַדְמֹנִיּוֹת:

When praying with a מנין, the עמידה is repeated aloud by the שליח ציבור.

On days when תחנון is said (see page 145), start on page 153.
On Mondays and Thursdays start תחנון on page 145.
In ארץ ישראל, on days on which תחנון is said,
some say וידוי and the יג מדות on page 137. See law 176a.

On fast days (except תשעה באב) most congregations say
סליחות on page 467 before אבינו מלכנו on page 139.

During the עשרת ימי תשובה (but not on ערב יום כיפור,
unless it falls on Friday), say אבינו מלכנו on page 139.

On יום ירושלים, יום העצמאות, חנוכה, ראש חודש and הלל, say הלל on page 361.

On other days when תחנון is not said (see page 145),
the שליח ציבור says חצי קדיש on page 157.

VIDUY

In Israel on days on which Tahanun is said (see page 144), some say Viduy and the Thirteen Attributes of Divine Compassion. See law 176a. The congregation stands and says:

אֱלֹהֵינוּ Our God and God of our fathers, let our prayer come before You, and do not hide Yourself from our plea, for we are not so arrogant or obstinate as to say before You, LORD, our God and God of our fathers, we are righteous and have not sinned, for in truth, we and our fathers have sinned.

At each expression, strike the chest on the left side:

אָשַׁמְנוּ We have been guilty, we have acted treacherously, we have robbed, we have spoken slander. We have acted perversely, we have acted wickedly, we have acted presumptuously, we have been violent, we have framed lies. We have given bad advice, we have deceived, we have scorned, we have rebelled, we have provoked, we have turned away, we have committed iniquity, we have transgressed, we have persecuted, we have been obstinate. We have acted wickedly, we have corrupted, we have acted abominably, we have strayed, we have led others astray.

We have turned away from Your commandments and good laws, to no avail, for You are *Neh. 9* just in all that has befallen us, for You have acted faithfully while we have done wickedly.

When praying without a minyan continue with "He is compassionate" on page 144.

THIRTEEN ATTRIBUTES OF DIVINE COMPASSION

אֵל אֶרֶךְ You are a God slow to anger, You are called Master of Compassion, and You have taught the way of repentance. May You remember today and every day the greatness of Your compassion and loving-kindness for the sake of the descendants of Your beloved ones. Turn toward us in compassion, for You are the Master of Compassion. We come before You in plea and prayer, as You in ancient times showed the humble one [Moses]. Turn from Your fierce anger, as is written in Your Torah. In the shadow of Your wings may we shelter and abide, as on the day when the LORD descended in the cloud. ▸ Disregard transgression and erase guilt as on the day You stood with him [Moses] there. Hear our cry and heed our word, as on the day You proclaimed in the name of the LORD, and there it is written:

All say aloud:

וַיַּעֲבֹר And the LORD passed by before him and proclaimed: *Ex. 34*

The LORD, the LORD, compassionate and gracious God, slow to anger,
abounding in loving-kindness and truth, extending loving-kindness to a
thousand generations, forgiving iniquity, rebellion and sin,
and absolving [the guilty who repent]. Forgive us our iniquity and our sin,
and take us as Your inheritance. Forgive us, our Father, for we have sinned.
Pardon us, our King, for we have transgressed. For You, LORD, are good *Ps. 86*
and forgiving, abounding in loving-kindness to all who call on You.

*On Mondays and Thursdays continue with "He is compassionate"
on page 144; on other days with "David said" on page 152.*

וידוי

In ארץ ישראל *on days on which* תחנון *is said (see page 145),*
some say וידוי *and the* י״ג מדות. *See law 176a. The* קהל *stands and says:*

אֱלֹהֵינוּ וֵאלֹהֵי אֲבוֹתֵינוּ, תָּבוֹא לְפָנֶיךָ תְּפִלָּתֵנוּ, וְאַל תִּתְעַלַּם מִתְּחִנָּתֵנוּ, שֶׁאֵין
אֲנַחְנוּ עַזֵּי פָנִים וּקְשֵׁי עֹרֶף לוֹמַר לְפָנֶיךָ, יהוה אֱלֹהֵינוּ וֵאלֹהֵי אֲבוֹתֵינוּ, צַדִּיקִים
אֲנַחְנוּ וְלֹא חָטָאנוּ, אֲבָל אֲנַחְנוּ וַאֲבוֹתֵינוּ חָטָאנוּ.

At each expression, strike the chest on the left side:

אָשַׁמְנוּ, בָּגַדְנוּ, גָּזַלְנוּ, דִּבַּרְנוּ דֹפִי, הֶעֱוִינוּ, וְהִרְשַׁעְנוּ, זַדְנוּ, חָמַסְנוּ, טָפַלְנוּ שֶׁקֶר,
יָעַצְנוּ רָע, כִּזַּבְנוּ, לַצְנוּ, מָרַדְנוּ, נִאַצְנוּ, סָרַרְנוּ, עָוִינוּ, פָּשַׁעְנוּ, צָרַרְנוּ, קִשִּׁינוּ עֹרֶף,
רָשַׁעְנוּ, שִׁחַתְנוּ, תִּעַבְנוּ, תָּעִינוּ, תִּעְתָּעְנוּ.

נחמיה ט
סַרְנוּ מִמִּצְוֹתֶיךָ וּמִמִּשְׁפָּטֶיךָ הַטּוֹבִים, וְלֹא שָׁוָה לָנוּ. וְאַתָּה צַדִּיק עַל כָּל־הַבָּא עָלֵינוּ,
כִּי־אֱמֶת עָשִׂיתָ, וַאֲנַחְנוּ הִרְשָׁעְנוּ:

When praying without a מנין *continue with* וְהוּא רַחוּם *on page 145.*

י״ג מדות

אֵל אֶרֶךְ אַפַּיִם אַתָּה, וּבַעַל הָרַחֲמִים נִקְרֵאתָ, וְדֶרֶךְ תְּשׁוּבָה הוֹרֵיתָ. גְּדֻלַּת רַחֲמֶיךָ
וַחֲסָדֶיךָ, תִּזְכֹּר הַיּוֹם וּבְכָל יוֹם לְזֶרַע יְדִידֶיךָ. תֵּפֶן אֵלֵינוּ בְּרַחֲמִים, כִּי אַתָּה הוּא בַּעַל
הָרַחֲמִים. בְּתַחֲנוּן וּבִתְפִלָּה פָּנֶיךָ נְקַדֵּם, כְּהוֹדַעְתָּ לֶעָנָו מִקֶּדֶם. מֵחֲרוֹן אַפְּךָ שׁוּב,
כְּמוֹ בְתוֹרָתְךָ כָּתוּב. וּבְצֵל כְּנָפֶיךָ נֶחֱסֶה וְנִתְלוֹנָן, כְּיוֹם וַיֵּרֶד יהוה בֶּעָנָן. ◄ תַּעֲבֹר עַל
פֶּשַׁע וְתִמְחֶה אָשָׁם, כְּיוֹם וַיִּתְיַצֵּב עִמּוֹ שָׁם. תַּאֲזִין שַׁוְעָתֵנוּ וְתַקְשִׁיב מֶנּוּ מַאֲמָר,
כְּיוֹם וַיִּקְרָא בְשֵׁם יהוה, וְשָׁם נֶאֱמַר:

All say aloud:

שמות לד
וַיַּעֲבֹר יהוה עַל־פָּנָיו וַיִּקְרָא:

יהוה, יהוה, אֵל רַחוּם וְחַנּוּן, אֶרֶךְ אַפַּיִם וְרַב־חֶסֶד וֶאֱמֶת:
נֹצֵר חֶסֶד לָאֲלָפִים, נֹשֵׂא עָוֹן וָפֶשַׁע וְחַטָּאָה, וְנַקֵּה:
וְסָלַחְתָּ לַעֲוֹנֵנוּ וּלְחַטָּאתֵנוּ, וּנְחַלְתָּנוּ:
סְלַח לָנוּ אָבִינוּ כִּי חָטָאנוּ, מְחַל לָנוּ מַלְכֵּנוּ כִּי פָשָׁעְנוּ
תהלים פו
כִּי־אַתָּה אֲדֹנָי טוֹב וְסַלָּח וְרַב־חֶסֶד לְכָל־קֹרְאֶיךָ:

On Mondays and Thursdays continue with וְהוּא רַחוּם
on page 145; on other days with וַיֹּאמֶר דָּוִד *on page 153.*

AVINU MALKENU

*On fast days (except Tisha B'Av) most congregations say Seliḥot
on page 466 before Avinu Malkenu.*

*Between Rosh HaShana and Yom Kippur (but not on Erev Yom
Kippur, unless it falls on Friday), say Avinu Malkenu below.*

The Ark is opened.

אָבִינוּ מַלְכֵּנוּ Our Father, our King, we have sinned before You.

Our Father, our King, we have no king but You.

Our Father, our King, deal kindly with us for the sake of Your name.

Our Father our King, /*bless us with / a good year.

                    /*Between Rosh HaShana & Yom Kippur: renew for us/

Our Father, our King, nullify all harsh decrees against us.

Our Father, our King, nullify the plans of those who hate us.

Our Father, our King, thwart the counsel of our enemies.

Our Father, our King, rid us of every oppressor and adversary.

Our Father, our King, close the mouths of our adversaries and accusers.

Our Father, our King, eradicate pestilence, sword, famine,
                captivity and destruction, iniquity and eradication
                from the people of Your covenant.

Our Father, our King, withhold the plague from Your heritage.

Our Father, our King, forgive and pardon all our iniquities.

Our Father, our King, wipe away and remove our transgressions and sins
                from Your sight.

Our Father, our King, erase in Your abundant mercy all records of our sins.

The following nine sentences are said responsively, first by the Leader, then by the congregation:

Our Father, our King, bring us back to You in perfect repentance.

Our Father, our King, send a complete healing to the sick of Your people.

Our Father, our King, tear up the evil decree against us.

Our Father, our King, remember us with a memory of favorable deeds
                before You.

---

the second by love, compassion and forgiveness. By placing the words in the
reverse order, we mirror both history and faith: history because God called
us His children ("My child, My firstborn, Israel") at Mount Sinai before He
became Israel's King; faith because we ask God to let His parental love temper
the severity of justice.

אבינו מלכנו

On fast days (except תשעה באב) most congregations say סליחות
on page 467 before אבינו מלכנו.
During the עשרת ימי תשובה (but not on ערב יום כיפור,
unless it falls on Friday), say אבינו מלכנו below.

The ארון קודש is opened.

אָבִינוּ מַלְכֵּנוּ, חָטָאנוּ לְפָנֶיךָ.

אָבִינוּ מַלְכֵּנוּ, אֵין לָנוּ מֶלֶךְ אֶלָּא אָתָּה.

אָבִינוּ מַלְכֵּנוּ, עֲשֵׂה עִמָּנוּ לְמַעַן שְׁמֶךָ.

אָבִינוּ מַלְכֵּנוּ, בָּרֵךְ/ בעשרת ימי תשובה: חַדֵּשׁ/ עָלֵינוּ שָׁנָה טוֹבָה.

אָבִינוּ מַלְכֵּנוּ, בַּטֵּל מֵעָלֵינוּ כָּל גְּזֵרוֹת קָשׁוֹת.

אָבִינוּ מַלְכֵּנוּ, בַּטֵּל מַחְשְׁבוֹת שׂוֹנְאֵינוּ.

אָבִינוּ מַלְכֵּנוּ, הָפֵר עֲצַת אוֹיְבֵינוּ.

אָבִינוּ מַלְכֵּנוּ, כַּלֵּה כָּל צַר וּמַשְׂטִין מֵעָלֵינוּ.

אָבִינוּ מַלְכֵּנוּ, סְתֹם פִּיוֹת מַשְׂטִינֵינוּ וּמְקַטְרִגֵינוּ.

אָבִינוּ מַלְכֵּנוּ, כַּלֵּה דֶּבֶר וְחֶרֶב וְרָעָב וּשְׁבִי וּמַשְׁחִית וְעָוֹן וּשְׁמַד מִבְּנֵי בְרִיתֶךָ.

אָבִינוּ מַלְכֵּנוּ, מְנַע מַגֵּפָה מִנַּחֲלָתֶךָ.

אָבִינוּ מַלְכֵּנוּ, סְלַח וּמְחַל לְכָל עֲוֹנוֹתֵינוּ.

אָבִינוּ מַלְכֵּנוּ, מְחֵה וְהַעֲבֵר פְּשָׁעֵינוּ וְחַטֹּאתֵינוּ מִנֶּגֶד עֵינֶיךָ.

אָבִינוּ מַלְכֵּנוּ, מְחֹק בְּרַחֲמֶיךָ הָרַבִּים כָּל שִׁטְרֵי חוֹבוֹתֵינוּ.

The following nine sentences are said responsively, first by the שליח ציבור, then by the קהל:

אָבִינוּ מַלְכֵּנוּ, הַחֲזִירֵנוּ בִּתְשׁוּבָה שְׁלֵמָה לְפָנֶיךָ.

אָבִינוּ מַלְכֵּנוּ, שְׁלַח רְפוּאָה שְׁלֵמָה לְחוֹלֵי עַמֶּךָ.

אָבִינוּ מַלְכֵּנוּ, קְרַע רֹעַ גְּזַר דִּינֵנוּ.

אָבִינוּ מַלְכֵּנוּ, זָכְרֵנוּ בְּזִכָּרוֹן טוֹב לְפָנֶיךָ.

אָבִינוּ מַלְכֵּנוּ **Our Father, our King:** A prayer attributed, in its earliest form, to Rabbi Akiva. The opening two words juxtapose the two aspects of our relationship with God. He is our King and we are His subjects; He is our Parent and we are His children. The first relationship is governed by justice,

Between Rosh HaShana and Yom Kippur:

Our Father, our King, write us in the
book of good life.

Our Father, our King, write us in the
book of redemption and
salvation.

Our Father, our King, write us in the
book of livelihood and
sustenance.

Our Father, our King, write us in the
book of merit.

Our Father, our King, write us in
the book of pardon and
forgiveness.

On Fast Days:

Our Father, our King, remember
us for a good life.

Our Father, our King, remember
us for redemption
and salvation.

Our Father, our King, remember
us for livelihood and
sustenance.

Our Father, our King, remember
us for merit.

Our Father, our King, remember
us for pardon and
forgiveness.

End of responsive reading.

Our Father, our King, let salvation soon flourish for us.

Our Father, our King, raise the honor of Your people Israel.

Our Father, our King, raise the honor of Your anointed.

Our Father, our King, fill our hands with Your blessings.

Our Father, our King, fill our storehouses with abundance.

Our Father, our King, hear our voice, pity and be compassionate to us.

Our Father, our King, accept, with compassion and favor, our prayer.

Our Father, our King, open the gates of heaven to our prayer.

Our Father, our King, remember that we are dust.

Our Father, our King, please do not turn us away from You empty-handed.

Our Father, our King, may this moment be a moment of compassion
and a time of favor before You.

Our Father, our King, have pity on us, our children and our infants.

Our Father, our King, act for the sake of those who were killed
for Your holy name.

Our Father, our King, act for the sake of those who were slaughtered
for proclaiming Your Unity.

Our Father, our King, act for the sake of those
who went through fire and water
to sanctify Your name.

On Fast Days:	During the עשרת ימי תשובה:
אָבִינוּ מַלְכֵּנוּ, זָכְרֵנוּ לְחַיִּים טוֹבִים.	אָבִינוּ מַלְכֵּנוּ, כָּתְבֵנוּ בְּסֵפֶר חַיִּים טוֹבִים.
אָבִינוּ מַלְכֵּנוּ, זָכְרֵנוּ לִגְאֻלָּה וִישׁוּעָה.	אָבִינוּ מַלְכֵּנוּ, כָּתְבֵנוּ בְּסֵפֶר גְּאֻלָּה וִישׁוּעָה.
אָבִינוּ מַלְכֵּנוּ, זָכְרֵנוּ לְפַרְנָסָה וְכַלְכָּלָה.	אָבִינוּ מַלְכֵּנוּ, כָּתְבֵנוּ בְּסֵפֶר פַּרְנָסָה וְכַלְכָּלָה.
אָבִינוּ מַלְכֵּנוּ, זָכְרֵנוּ לִזְכִיּוֹת.	אָבִינוּ מַלְכֵּנוּ, כָּתְבֵנוּ בְּסֵפֶר זְכִיּוֹת.
אָבִינוּ מַלְכֵּנוּ, זָכְרֵנוּ לִסְלִיחָה וּמְחִילָה.	אָבִינוּ מַלְכֵּנוּ, כָּתְבֵנוּ בְּסֵפֶר סְלִיחָה וּמְחִילָה.

End of responsive reading.

אָבִינוּ מַלְכֵּנוּ, הַצְמַח לָנוּ יְשׁוּעָה בְּקָרוֹב.

אָבִינוּ מַלְכֵּנוּ, הָרֵם קֶרֶן יִשְׂרָאֵל עַמֶּךָ.

אָבִינוּ מַלְכֵּנוּ, הָרֵם קֶרֶן מְשִׁיחֶךָ.

אָבִינוּ מַלְכֵּנוּ, מַלֵּא יָדֵינוּ מִבִּרְכוֹתֶיךָ.

אָבִינוּ מַלְכֵּנוּ, מַלֵּא אֲסָמֵינוּ שָׂבָע.

אָבִינוּ מַלְכֵּנוּ, שְׁמַע קוֹלֵנוּ, חוּס וְרַחֵם עָלֵינוּ.

אָבִינוּ מַלְכֵּנוּ, קַבֵּל בְּרַחֲמִים וּבְרָצוֹן אֶת תְּפִלָּתֵנוּ.

אָבִינוּ מַלְכֵּנוּ, פְּתַח שַׁעֲרֵי שָׁמַיִם לִתְפִלָּתֵנוּ.

אָבִינוּ מַלְכֵּנוּ, זְכֹר כִּי עָפָר אֲנָחְנוּ.

אָבִינוּ מַלְכֵּנוּ, נָא אַל תְּשִׁיבֵנוּ רֵיקָם מִלְּפָנֶיךָ.

אָבִינוּ מַלְכֵּנוּ, תְּהֵא הַשָּׁעָה הַזֹּאת שְׁעַת רַחֲמִים וְעֵת רָצוֹן מִלְּפָנֶיךָ.

אָבִינוּ מַלְכֵּנוּ, חֲמֹל עָלֵינוּ וְעַל עוֹלָלֵינוּ וְטַפֵּנוּ.

אָבִינוּ מַלְכֵּנוּ, עֲשֵׂה לְמַעַן הֲרוּגִים עַל שֵׁם קָדְשֶׁךָ.

אָבִינוּ מַלְכֵּנוּ, עֲשֵׂה לְמַעַן טְבוּחִים עַל יִחוּדֶךָ.

אָבִינוּ מַלְכֵּנוּ, עֲשֵׂה לְמַעַן בָּאֵי בָאֵשׁ וּבַמַּיִם עַל קִדּוּשׁ שְׁמֶךָ.

Our Father, our King, avenge before our eyes
                the spilt blood of Your servants.

Our Father, our King, act for Your sake, if not for ours.

Our Father, our King, act for Your sake, and save us.

Our Father, our King, act for the sake of Your abundant compassion.

Our Father, our King, act for the sake of Your great, mighty and awesome
                name by which we are called.

▸ Our Father, our King, be gracious to us and answer us, though we have
                no worthy deeds; act with us in charity and
                loving-kindness and save us.

The Ark is closed.

During Minḥa continue with Taḥanun on page 252.

---

faces to the ground, even after the destruction of the Temple. We preserve a trace of that gesture by resting our heads on our arms and covering our faces as we say Psalm 6. The Leader's Repetition of the Amida stands in place of the daily sacrifice, which is why we subsequently "fall on our faces."

The custom of attaching special significance to Mondays and Thursdays is also ancient. Already in the Second Temple period, Mondays and Thursdays were days on which the pious would fast. According to tradition, Moses began his ascent of Mount Sinai to receive the second tablets on a Thursday and descended forty days later on a Monday (the 10th of Tishrei, Yom Kippur). The second tablets were a sign of God's forgiveness. Hence, these days were seen as "days of favor." They were also market days when people would come from villages to towns. Congregations were larger; the Torah was read; law courts were in session. The heightened atmosphere was the setting for more extended penitential prayer; therefore, on Mondays and Thursdays, *Taḥanun* is longer.

One of the classic biblical instances of supplication was Daniel's prayer on behalf of the exiles in Babylon (Daniel, chapter 9). Sections of that prayer, together with other verses from the prophetic books and Psalms, form the core of these paragraphs. There are three sections, each containing eighteen mentions of God's name; thus we say them quietly, standing, as if they were forms of the Amida.

A tradition, found in the Geonic literature, dates these prayers to the period of persecution under the Romans, when three exiles crossed the Mediterranean, found temporary refuge and then suffered renewed oppression.

אָבִינוּ מַלְכֵּנוּ, נְקֹם לְעֵינֵינוּ נִקְמַת דַּם עֲבָדֶיךָ הַשָּׁפוּךְ.

אָבִינוּ מַלְכֵּנוּ, עֲשֵׂה לְמַעַנְךָ אִם לֹא לְמַעֲנֵנוּ.

אָבִינוּ מַלְכֵּנוּ, עֲשֵׂה לְמַעַנְךָ וְהוֹשִׁיעֵנוּ.

אָבִינוּ מַלְכֵּנוּ, עֲשֵׂה לְמַעַן רַחֲמֶיךָ הָרַבִּים.

אָבִינוּ מַלְכֵּנוּ, עֲשֵׂה לְמַעַן שִׁמְךָ הַגָּדוֹל הַגִּבּוֹר וְהַנּוֹרָא, שֶׁנִּקְרָא עָלֵינוּ.

‹ אָבִינוּ מַלְכֵּנוּ, חָנֵּנוּ וַעֲנֵנוּ, כִּי אֵין בָּנוּ מַעֲשִׂים
עֲשֵׂה עִמָּנוּ צְדָקָה וָחֶסֶד וְהוֹשִׁיעֵנוּ.

The ארון קודש *is closed.*

During מנחה *continue with* סדר תחנון *on page 253.*

TAḤANUN: PLEADING WITH GOD

This section of the prayers, known as *Taḥanun*, "plea," is a return to private prayer, which began with the silent Amida. The siddur preserves a careful balance between the two ways in which we address God: as individuals with our personal hopes and fears, and as members of a community whose fate and aspirations we share. First we pray individually (the silent Amida), then communally (the Leader's Repetition), then individually in *Taḥanun* again.

Knowing that our time in the direct presence of the Supreme King of kings is drawing to an end, we approach Him directly, seeking, as it were, a private audience. Our voices drop; we whisper our deepest thoughts; we express our feelings of inadequacy and vulnerability. We know we are unworthy: we say nothing in our defense except that we have absolute faith in God.

The word *Taḥanun* derives from the root *ḥ-n-n* meaning, "to show favor, to be gracious, to forgive." What differentiates *Taḥanun* from other modes of prayer is the extent to which we emphasize our failings and our lack of good deeds. We express our dependence on God's unconditional grace and mercy. *Taḥanun* is the chamber music rather than the symphony of the soul, and it has a unique intensity of tone.

The practice of following public prayer with private intercession goes back to Temple times. After the daily sacrifice, "The Levites sang the Psalm [of the day]. When they reached the end of each section [the psalm was divided into three parts] they blew the shofar and the people prostrated themselves" (*Tamid* 7:3). Some communities continued the custom of prostration, with

TAHANUN

On Mondays and Thursdays, when Tahanun is said, begin with "He is compassionate"
below. On other days when Tahanun is said, begin with "David said" on page 152.

Tahanun is not said on: Rosh Hodesh, Hanukka, Tu BiShvat, the 14th and 15th of Adar I,
Purim and Shushan Purim, in the month of Nisan, Yom HaAtzma'ut, the 14th of Iyar
(Pesah Sheni), Lag BaOmer, Yom Yerushalayim, from Rosh Hodesh Sivan
through the day after Shavuot (in Israel through 12th of Sivan), Tisha B'Av,
Tu B'Av, Erev Rosh HaShana, and from Erev Yom Kippur through the day
after Simhat Torah (in Israel through Rosh Hodesh Marheshvan).

Tahanun is also not said: on the morning of a Brit Mila, either where the brit will take place
or where the father, Sandek or Mohel are present; if a groom is present (and some say a bride)
on the day of his wedding or during the week of Sheva Berakhot; in a house of mourning.

In Israel on days on which Tahanun is said, say Viduy and the Thirteen
Attributes of Divine Compassion on page 136. See law 176a.

The following until "David said" on page 152 is said standing.

וְהוּא רַחוּם He is compassionate. He forgives iniquity and does not destroy.   Ps. 78
Repeatedly He suppresses His anger, not rousing His full wrath. LORD, do
not withhold Your compassion from us. May Your loving-kindness and
truth always protect us. Save us, LORD our God, and gather us from among   Ps. 106
the nations, that we may give thanks to Your holy name and glory in Your
praise. If You, LORD, should keep account of sins, O LORD, who could stand?   Ps. 130
But with You is forgiveness, that You may be revered. Do not deal with us   Jer. 14
according to our sins; do not repay us according to our iniquities. Though
our iniquities testify against us, LORD, act for Your name's sake. Remember,   Ps. 25
LORD, Your compassion and loving-kindness, for they are everlasting. May   Ps. 20
the LORD answer us when we are in distress; may the name of Jacob's God
protect us. LORD, save! May the King answer us when we call. Our Father,
our King, be gracious to us and answer us, though we have no worthy deeds;

---

hope defeats tragedy. In these profound and moving words, Jews found the
strength to survive.

With its intense penitential mood, Tahanun is not said on days of festive
joy; nor is it said on the Ninth of Av or in the house of a mourner.

וְהוּא רַחוּם *He is compassionate:* Penitential prayers woven from a variety of
biblical texts, from Genesis and Exodus, Isaiah, Jeremiah and Joel, Lamenta-
tions, Daniel and Psalms. Lacking a Temple and sacrifices, we offer God our
tears in their place: "The sacrifices of God are a broken spirit; a broken and
humbled heart, God, You will not despise" (Psalm 51:19).

סדר תחנון

On Mondays and Thursdays, when תחנון *is said, begin with* וְהוּא רַחוּם *below.*
On other days when תחנון *is said, begin with* וַיֹּאמֶר דָּוִד *on page 153.*

תחנון *is not said on:* פורים, ראש חודש, חנוכה, ט"ו בשבט, *the 14th and 15th of* אדר א' *and* ל"ג בעומר, (פסח שני) י"ד אייר *in the month of* ניסן, *the 14th of* י"ד העצמאות, שושן פורים *through* ראש חודש סיון, יום ירושלים, יום יום חודש סיון (in) ישראל ארץ *through the day after* שבועות, *and from* ערב יום כיפור, ערב ראש השנה, ט"ו באב, תשעה באב, (י"ב סיון) *through*
the day after שמחת תורה (in) ארץ ישראל (ראש חודש מרחשון) *through*

תחנון *is also not said: on the morning of a* ברית מילה, *either where the* ברית *will take place*
or where the father, סנדק *or* מוהל *are present; if a* חתן *is present (and some say a* כלה)
on the day of his wedding or during the week of שבע ברכות; *in a house of mourning.*
In ארץ ישראל *on days on which* תחנון *is said, say* וידוי
and the י"ג מדות *on page 137. See law 176a.*

The following until וַיֹּאמֶר דָּוִד *on page 153 is said standing.*

תהלים עח — וְהוּא רַחוּם, יְכַפֵּר עָוֹן וְלֹא־יַשְׁחִית, וְהִרְבָּה לְהָשִׁיב אַפּוֹ וְלֹא־יָעִיר כָּל־
חֲמָתוֹ: אַתָּה יהוה לֹא־תִכְלָא רַחֲמֶיךָ מִמֶּנִּי, חַסְדְּךָ וַאֲמִתְּךָ תָּמִיד יִצְּרוּנִי.
תהלים קו — הוֹשִׁיעֵנוּ יהוה אֱלֹהֵינוּ וְקַבְּצֵנוּ מִן־הַגּוֹיִם, לְהוֹדוֹת לְשֵׁם קָדְשֶׁךָ, לְהִשְׁתַּבֵּחַ
תהלים קל — בִּתְהִלָּתֶךָ: אִם־עֲוֹנוֹת תִּשְׁמָר־יָהּ, אֲדֹנָי מִי יַעֲמֹד: כִּי־עִמְּךָ הַסְּלִיחָה לְמַעַן
ירמיה יד — תִּוָּרֵא: לֹא כַחֲטָאֵינוּ תַּעֲשֶׂה לָּנוּ, וְלֹא כַעֲוֹנֹתֵינוּ תִּגְמֹל עָלֵינוּ. אִם־עֲוֹנֵינוּ
תהלים כה — עָנוּ בָנוּ, יהוה עֲשֵׂה לְמַעַן שְׁמֶךָ: זְכֹר־רַחֲמֶיךָ יהוה וַחֲסָדֶיךָ, כִּי מֵעוֹלָם
תהלים כ — הֵמָּה: יַעַנְךָ יהוה בְּיוֹם צָרָה, יְשַׂגֶּבְךָ שֵׁם אֱלֹהֵי יַעֲקֹב. יהוה הוֹשִׁיעָה,

Some passages may have been added in the wake of the Gothic and Frankish
persecutions in the seventh century. Their mood bespeaks the tears of Jews
throughout the centuries of exile who experienced persecution, expulsion,
humiliation, and often bloodshed at the hands of those amongst whom they
lived. Even in times of freedom, we continue to say these prayers, keeping
faith with our ancestors and remembering their tears.

What is remarkable about the prayers is the absence of anger or despair. If
we ever doubt the power of prayer to transform the human situation, here we
find an answer. Despite being treated as a pariah people, Jews never allowed
themselves to be defined by their enemies. They wept and gave voice to pain:
"God, see how low our glory has sunk among the nations. They abhor us as
if we were impure." Yet they remained the people of the covenant, children
of the divine promise, unbroken and unbreakable. Prayer sustains hope, and

act charitably with us for Your name's sake. Lord our God, hear the sound of our pleas. Remember for us the covenant of our ancestors, and save us for Your name's sake.

וְעַתָּה And now, My Lord, our God, who took Your people out of the land   *Dan. 9* of Egypt with a mighty hand, creating for Yourself renown to this day: we have sinned and acted wrongly. Lord, in keeping with all Your righteousness, please turn Your wrath and anger away from Jerusalem, Your holy mountain. Because of our sins and the iniquities of our ancestors, Jerusalem and Your people have become the scorn of all those around us. And now, our God, heed Your servant's prayer and pleas, and let Your face shine on Your desolate Sanctuary, for Your sake, O Lord. Incline Your ear, my God, and hear. Open Your eyes and see our desolation and that of the city called by Your name. Not because of our righteousness do we lay our pleas before You, but because of Your great compassion. Lord, hear! Lord, forgive! Lord, listen and act! Do not delay – for Your sake, my God, because Your city and Your people are called by Your name.

אָבִינוּ Our Father, compassionate Father, show us a sign for good, and gather our scattered ones from the four quarters of the earth. Let all the nations recognize and know that You are the Lord our God. And now, Lord, You   *Is. 64* are our Father. We are the clay and You are our Potter; we are all the work of Your hand. Save us for the sake of Your name, our Rock, our King and our Redeemer. Pity Your people, Lord. Let not Your heritage become an object   *Joel 2* of scorn, a byword among nations. Why should they say among the peoples, "Where is their God?" We know we have sinned and that there is no one to stand up for us. Let Your great name stand up for us in time of trouble. We know we have no merits of our own: therefore deal with us charitably for Your name's sake. As a father has compassion on his children, so, Lord, have compassion on us, and save us for the sake of Your name. Have mercy on Your people; have compassion for Your heritage; take pity in Your great

---

The passage weaves together three appeals to God's compassion: (1) we are Your children and You our Parent: have mercy on us as a parent forgives a child; (2) we are Your creation and You are our Creator: save us as an artist saves his most precious works of art; (3) we are Your witnesses, bearers of Your name: therefore save us for the sake of Your name. Let not the nations say, seeing our suffering, "Where is God?"

הַמֶּלֶךְ יַעֲנֵנוּ בְיוֹם־קָרְאֵנוּ: אָבִינוּ מַלְכֵּנוּ, חָנֵּנוּ וַעֲנֵנוּ, כִּי אֵין בָּנוּ מַעֲשִׂים,
צְדָקָה עֲשֵׂה עִמָּנוּ לְמַעַן שְׁמֶךָ. אֲדוֹנֵינוּ אֱלֹהֵינוּ, שְׁמַע קוֹל תַּחֲנוּנֵינוּ,
וּזְכָר לָנוּ אֶת בְּרִית אֲבוֹתֵינוּ וְהוֹשִׁיעֵנוּ לְמַעַן שְׁמֶךָ.

דניאל ט

וְעַתָּה אֲדֹנָי אֱלֹהֵינוּ, אֲשֶׁר הוֹצֵאתָ אֶת־עַמְּךָ מֵאֶרֶץ מִצְרַיִם בְּיָד חֲזָקָה
וַתַּעַשׂ־לְךָ שֵׁם כַּיּוֹם הַזֶּה, חָטָאנוּ רָשָׁעְנוּ: אֲדֹנָי, כְּכָל־צִדְקֹתֶךָ יָשָׁב־נָא
אַפְּךָ וַחֲמָתְךָ, מֵעִירְךָ יְרוּשָׁלַםִ הַר־קָדְשֶׁךָ, כִּי בַחֲטָאֵינוּ וּבַעֲוֹנוֹת אֲבֹתֵינוּ,
יְרוּשָׁלַםִ וְעַמְּךָ לְחֶרְפָּה לְכָל־סְבִיבֹתֵינוּ: וְעַתָּה שְׁמַע אֱלֹהֵינוּ אֶל־תְּפִלַּת
עַבְדְּךָ וְאֶל־תַּחֲנוּנָיו, וְהָאֵר פָּנֶיךָ עַל־מִקְדָּשְׁךָ הַשָּׁמֵם, לְמַעַן אֲדֹנָי: הַטֵּה
אֱלֹהַי אָזְנְךָ וּשֲׁמָע, פְּקַח עֵינֶיךָ וּרְאֵה שֹׁמְמֹתֵינוּ וְהָעִיר אֲשֶׁר־נִקְרָא שִׁמְךָ
עָלֶיהָ, כִּי לֹא עַל־צִדְקֹתֵינוּ אֲנַחְנוּ מַפִּילִים תַּחֲנוּנֵינוּ לְפָנֶיךָ, כִּי עַל־רַחֲמֶיךָ
הָרַבִּים: אֲדֹנָי שֲׁמָעָה, אֲדֹנָי סְלָחָה, אֲדֹנָי הַקְשִׁיבָה וַעֲשֵׂה אַל־תְּאַחַר,
לְמַעֲנְךָ אֱלֹהַי, כִּי־שִׁמְךָ נִקְרָא עַל־עִירְךָ וְעַל־עַמֶּךָ:

אָבִינוּ הָאָב הָרַחֲמָן, הַרְאֵנוּ אוֹת לְטוֹבָה וְקַבֵּץ נְפוּצוֹתֵינוּ מֵאַרְבַּע כַּנְפוֹת
הָאָרֶץ. יַכִּירוּ וְיֵדְעוּ כָּל־הַגּוֹיִם כִּי אַתָּה יהוה אֱלֹהֵינוּ: וְעַתָּה יהוה אָבִינוּ

ישעיה סד

אָתָּה, אֲנַחְנוּ הַחֹמֶר וְאַתָּה יֹצְרֵנוּ וּמַעֲשֵׂה יָדְךָ כֻּלָּנוּ. הוֹשִׁיעֵנוּ לְמַעַן
שְׁמֶךָ, צוּרֵנוּ מַלְכֵּנוּ וְגוֹאֲלֵנוּ. חוּסָה יהוה עַל־עַמֶּךָ, וְאַל־תִּתֵּן נַחֲלָתְךָ

יואל ב

לְחֶרְפָּה לִמְשָׁל־בָּם גּוֹיִם, לָמָּה יֹאמְרוּ בָעַמִּים אַיֵּה אֱלֹהֵיהֶם: יָדַעְנוּ כִּי
חָטָאנוּ וְאֵין מִי יַעֲמֹד בַּעֲדֵנוּ, שִׁמְךָ הַגָּדוֹל יַעֲמָד־לָנוּ בְעֵת צָרָה. יָדַעְנוּ
כִּי אֵין בָּנוּ מַעֲשִׂים, צְדָקָה עֲשֵׂה עִמָּנוּ לְמַעַן שְׁמֶךָ. כְּרַחֵם אָב עַל בָּנִים
כֵּן תְּרַחֵם יהוה עָלֵינוּ, וְהוֹשִׁיעֵנוּ לְמַעַן שְׁמֶךָ. חֲמֹל עַל עַמֶּךָ, רַחֵם עַל

וְעַתָּה *And now:* A prayer uttered by Daniel (9:15–19) in the first year of the
reign of Xerxes, when he foresaw that the desolation of Jerusalem would last
for seventy years. Fasting, dressed in sackcloth and ashes, he pleaded to God
to forgive the people and bring an end to their suffering. These words play a
key part in the Seliḥot (penitential prayers) on Fast Days.

אֲנַחְנוּ הַחֹמֶר *We are the clay and You are our Potter:* A verse from Isaiah (64:7)
which became the basis of one of the liturgical poems on *Kol Nidrei* night.

compassion. Be gracious to us and answer us, for righteousness is Yours, LORD. Always You do wondrous things.

הַבֶּט נָא Please look, please swiftly have compassion for Your people for Your name's sake. In Your great compassion, LORD our God, have pity and compassion, and rescue the flock You tend. Let us not be ruled by wrath, for our eyes are turned toward You. Save us for Your name's sake. Have compassion on us for the sake of Your covenant. Look and answer us in time of trouble, for Yours, LORD, is the power to save. Our hope is in You, God of forgiveness. Please forgive, good and forgiving God, for You are a gracious, compassionate God and King.

אָנָּא מֶלֶךְ Please, gracious and compassionate King, remember and call to mind the Covenant between the Pieces [with Abraham] and let the binding of his only son [Isaac] appear before You for Israel's sake. Our Father, our King, be gracious to us and answer us, for we are called by Your great name. You who work miracles at all times, deal with us according to Your lovingkindness. Gracious and compassionate One, look and answer us in time of trouble, for salvation is Yours, LORD. Our Father, our King, our Refuge, do not act with us according to our evil deeds. Remember, LORD, Your tender mercies and Your love. Save us in Your great goodness, and have mercy on us, for we have no other god but You, our Rock. Do not abandon us, LORD our God, do not be distant from us, for we are worn out by the sword and captivity, pestilence and plague, and by every trouble and sorrow. Rescue us, for in You lies our hope. Put us not to shame, LORD our God. Let Your face shine upon us. Remember for us the covenant of our ancestors and save us for Your name's sake. See our troubles and heed the voice of our prayer, for You heed the prayer of every mouth.

אֵל רַחוּם וְחַנּוּן O Compassionate and gracious God, have compassion on us and on all Your works, for there is none like You, LORD our God. Please, we beg You, forgive our sins, our Father, our King, our Rock, our Redeemer, living and eternal God, mighty in strength, loving and good to all Your works, for You are the LORD our God. O God, slow to anger and full of compassion, act with us according to Your great compassion and save us for Your name's sake. Hear our prayer, our King, and save us from our enemies' hands. Heed our prayer, our King, and save us from all distress and sorrow. You are our Father, our King. We are called by Your name. Do not desert us. Do not abandon us, our Father. Do not cast us away, our Creator. Do not forget us, our Maker – for You are a gracious and compassionate God and King.

נַחֲלָתֶךָ, חוּסָה נָּא כְּרֹב רַחֲמֶיךָ, חָנֵּנוּ וַעֲנֵנוּ. כִּי לְךָ יהוה הַצְּדָקָה, עֹשֶׂה
נִפְלָאוֹת בְּכָל עֵת.

הַבֶּט נָא, רַחֵם נָא עַל עַמְּךָ מְהֵרָה לְמַעַן שְׁמֶךָ בְּרַחֲמֶיךָ הָרַבִּים יהוה
אֱלֹהֵינוּ. חוּס וְרַחֵם וְהוֹשִׁיעָה צֹאן מַרְעִיתֶךָ, וְאַל יִמְשָׁל בָּנוּ קֶצֶף, כִּי לְךָ
עֵינֵינוּ תְלוּיוֹת. הוֹשִׁיעֵנוּ לְמַעַן שְׁמֶךָ. רַחֵם עָלֵינוּ לְמַעַן בְּרִיתֶךָ. הַבִּיטָה
וַעֲנֵנוּ בְּעֵת צָרָה, כִּי לְךָ יהוה הַיְשׁוּעָה. בְּךָ תוֹחַלְתֵּנוּ אֱלוֹהַּ סְלִיחוֹת, אָנָּא
סְלַח נָא אֵל טוֹב וְסַלָּח, כִּי אֵל מֶלֶךְ חַנּוּן וְרַחוּם אָתָּה.

אָנָּא מֶלֶךְ חַנּוּן וְרַחוּם, זְכֹר וְהַבֵּט לִבְרִית בֵּין הַבְּתָרִים, וְתֵרָאֶה לְפָנֶיךָ
עֲקֵדַת יָחִיד לְמַעַן יִשְׂרָאֵל. אָבִינוּ מַלְכֵּנוּ, חָנֵּנוּ וַעֲנֵנוּ, כִּי שִׁמְךָ הַגָּדוֹל
נִקְרָא עָלֵינוּ. עֹשֶׂה נִפְלָאוֹת בְּכָל עֵת, עֲשֵׂה עִמָּנוּ כְּחַסְדֶּךָ. חַנּוּן וְרַחוּם,
הַבִּיטָה וַעֲנֵנוּ בְּעֵת צָרָה, כִּי לְךָ יהוה הַיְשׁוּעָה. אָבִינוּ מַלְכֵּנוּ מַחֲסֵנוּ,
אַל תַּעַשׂ עִמָּנוּ כְּרֹעַ מַעֲלָלֵינוּ. זְכֹר רַחֲמֶיךָ יהוה וַחֲסָדֶיךָ, וּכְרֹב טוּבְךָ
הוֹשִׁיעֵנוּ, וַחֲמֹל נָא עָלֵינוּ, כִּי אֵין לָנוּ אֱלוֹהַּ אַחֵר מִבַּלְעָדֶיךָ צוּרֵנוּ. אַל
תַּעַזְבֵנוּ יהוה אֱלֹהֵינוּ אַל תִּרְחַק מִמֶּנּוּ. כִּי נַפְשֵׁנוּ קָצְרָה, מֵחֶרֶב וּמִשֶּׁבִי
וּמִדֶּבֶר וּמִמַּגֵּפָה. וּמִכָּל צָרָה וְיָגוֹן הַצִּילֵנוּ, כִּי לְךָ קִוִּינוּ. וְאַל תַּכְלִימֵנוּ
יהוה אֱלֹהֵינוּ, וְהָאֵר פָּנֶיךָ בָּנוּ, וּזְכֹר לָנוּ אֶת בְּרִית אֲבוֹתֵינוּ וְהוֹשִׁיעֵנוּ
לְמַעַן שְׁמֶךָ. רְאֵה בְצָרוֹתֵינוּ, וּשְׁמַע קוֹל תְּפִלָּתֵנוּ, כִּי אַתָּה שׁוֹמֵעַ תְּפִלַּת
כָּל פֶּה.

אֵל רַחוּם וְחַנּוּן, רַחֵם עָלֵינוּ וְעַל כָּל מַעֲשֶׂיךָ, כִּי אֵין כָּמוֹךָ יהוה אֱלֹהֵינוּ.
אָנָּא שָׂא נָא פְשָׁעֵינוּ, אָבִינוּ מַלְכֵּנוּ צוּרֵנוּ וְגֹאֲלֵנוּ, אֵל חַי וְקַיָּם הֶחָסִין
בַּכֹּחַ, חָסִיד וְטוֹב עַל כָּל מַעֲשֶׂיךָ, כִּי אַתָּה הוּא יהוה אֱלֹהֵינוּ. אֵל אֶרֶךְ
אַפַּיִם וּמָלֵא רַחֲמִים, עֲשֵׂה עִמָּנוּ כְּרֹב רַחֲמֶיךָ, וְהוֹשִׁיעֵנוּ לְמַעַן שְׁמֶךָ.
שְׁמַע מַלְכֵּנוּ תְּפִלָּתֵנוּ, וּמִיַּד אוֹיְבֵינוּ הַצִּילֵנוּ. שְׁמַע מַלְכֵּנוּ תְּפִלָּתֵנוּ, וּמִכָּל
צָרָה וְיָגוֹן הַצִּילֵנוּ. אָבִינוּ מַלְכֵּנוּ אַתָּה, וְשִׁמְךָ עָלֵינוּ נִקְרָא. אַל תַּנִּיחֵנוּ,
אַל תַּעַזְבֵנוּ אָבִינוּ וְאַל תִּטְּשֵׁנוּ וְאַל תַּשְׁכָּחֵנוּ וְאַל תִּשְׁכָּחֵנוּ בּוֹרְאֵנוּ יוֹצְרֵנוּ, כִּי אֵל מֶלֶךְ
חַנּוּן וְרַחוּם אָתָּה.

אֵין כָּמוֹךָ There is none like You in grace and compassion, LORD our God. There is none like You, God, slow to anger and abounding in loving-kindness and truth. Save us in Your great compassion; rescue us from storm and turmoil. Remember Your servants Abraham, Isaac and Jacob; do not attend to our stubbornness, wickedness and sinfulness. Turn from Your fierce anger, and relent from the evil meant for Your people. Remove from us the scourge of death, for You are compassionate. This is Your way, to show unearned loving-kindness to every generation. Have pity on Your people, LORD, and save us from Your wrath. Remove from us the scourge of plague and the harsh decree, for You are the Guardian of Israel. You are right, my LORD, and we are shamefaced. How can we complain? What can we say? What can we plead? How can we justify ourselves? Let us search our ways and examine them and return to You, for Your right hand is outstretched to receive those who return. Please, LORD, please save. Please, LORD, please send success. Please, LORD, answer us when we call. For You, LORD, we wait. For You, LORD, we hope. For You, LORD, we long. Do not be silent while we suffer, for the nations are saying, "Their hope is lost." To You alone every knee must bend, and those who hold themselves high bow down.

Ex. 32

Dan. 9

Ps. 118

הַפּוֹתֵחַ יָד You who hold out an open hand of repentance to receive transgressors and sinners – our soul is overwhelmed by our great sorrow. Do not forget us for ever. Arise and save us, for we seek refuge in You. Our Father, our King, though we lack righteousness and good deeds, remember for us the covenant of our fathers, and our testimonies daily that "The LORD is One." Look on our affliction, for many are our sufferings and heartaches. Have pity on us, LORD, in the land of our captivity. Do not pour out Your wrath on us, for we are Your people, the children of Your covenant. God, see how low our glory has sunk among the nations. They abhor us as if we were impure. How long will Your strength be captive, and Your glory in the hand of the foe? Arouse Your strength and zeal against Your enemies. Let them be shamed and deprived of power. Let not our hardships seem small to You. Swiftly may Your compassion reach us in the day of our distress. If not for our sake, act for Yours, so that the memory of our survivors be not destroyed. Be gracious to the nation who, in constant love, proclaim twice daily the unity of Your name, saying, "Listen, Israel, the LORD is our God, the LORD is One."

Deut. 6

אֵין כָּמוֹךָ חַנּוּן וְרַחוּם יהוה אֱלֹהֵינוּ, אֵין כָּמוֹךָ אֵל אֶרֶךְ אַפַּיִם וְרַב חֶסֶד וֶאֱמֶת. הוֹשִׁיעֵנוּ בְּרַחֲמֶיךָ הָרַבִּים, מֵרַעַשׁ וּמֵרְגֶז הַצִּילֵנוּ. זְכֹר לַעֲבָדֶיךָ לְאַבְרָהָם לְיִצְחָק וּלְיַעֲקֹב, אַל תֵּפֶן אֶל קַשְׁיֵנוּ וְאֶל רִשְׁעֵנוּ וְאֶל חַטָּאתֵנוּ. שׁוּב מֵחֲרוֹן אַפֶּךָ, וְהִנָּחֵם עַל־הָרָעָה לְעַמֶּךָ: וְהָסֵר מִמֶּנּוּ מַכַּת הַמָּוֶת כִּי

שמות לב

רַחוּם אָתָּה, כִּי כֵן דַּרְכֶּךָ, עֹשֶׂה חֶסֶד חִנָּם בְּכָל דּוֹר וָדוֹר. חוּסָה יהוה עַל עַמֶּךָ וְהַצִּילֵנוּ מִזַּעְמֶךָ, וְהָסֵר מִמֶּנּוּ מַכַּת הַמַּגֵּפָה וּגְזֵרָה קָשָׁה, כִּי אַתָּה שׁוֹמֵר יִשְׂרָאֵל. לְךָ אֲדֹנָי הַצְּדָקָה וְלָנוּ בֹּשֶׁת הַפָּנִים: מַה נִּתְאוֹנֵן, מַה נֹּאמַר,

דניאל ט

מַה נְּדַבֵּר וּמַה נִּצְטַדָּק. נַחְפְּשָׂה דְרָכֵינוּ וְנַחְקֹרָה וְנָשׁוּבָה אֵלֶיךָ, כִּי יְמִינְךָ פְּשׁוּטָה לְקַבֵּל שָׁבִים. אָנָּא יהוה הוֹשִׁיעָה נָּא, אָנָּא יהוה הַצְלִיחָה נָּא:

תהלים קיח

אָנָּא יהוה עֲנֵנוּ בְיוֹם קָרְאֵנוּ. לְךָ יהוה חִכִּינוּ, לְךָ יהוה קִוִּינוּ, לְךָ יהוה נְיַחֵל. אַל תֶּחֱשֶׁה וּתְעַנֵּנוּ, כִּי נֶאֶמְרוּ גוֹיִם, אָבְדָה תִקְוָתָם. כָּל בֶּרֶךְ וְכָל קוֹמָה, לְךָ לְבַד תִּשְׁתַּחֲוֶה.

הַפּוֹתֵחַ יָד בִּתְשׁוּבָה לְקַבֵּל פּוֹשְׁעִים וְחַטָּאִים, נִבְהֲלָה נַפְשֵׁנוּ מֵרֹב עִצְּבוֹנֵנוּ. אַל תִּשְׁכָּחֵנוּ נֶצַח, קוּמָה וְהוֹשִׁיעֵנוּ כִּי חָסִינוּ בָךְ. אָבִינוּ מַלְכֵּנוּ, אִם אֵין בָּנוּ צְדָקָה וּמַעֲשִׂים טוֹבִים, זְכָר לָנוּ אֶת בְּרִית אֲבוֹתֵינוּ וְעֵדוּתֵנוּ בְּכָל יוֹם יהוה אֶחָד. הַבִּיטָה בְעָנְיֵנוּ, כִּי רַבּוּ מַכְאוֹבֵינוּ וְצָרוֹת לְבָבֵינוּ. חוּסָה יהוה עָלֵינוּ בְּאֶרֶץ שִׁבְיֵנוּ, וְאַל תִּשְׁפֹּךְ חֲרוֹנְךָ עָלֵינוּ, כִּי אֲנַחְנוּ עַמְּךָ בְּנֵי בְרִיתֶךָ. אֵל, הַבִּיטָה, דַּל כְּבוֹדֵנוּ בַגּוֹיִם וְשִׁקְּצוּנוּ כְּטֻמְאַת הַנִּדָּה. עַד מָתַי עֻזְּךָ בַּשֶּׁבִי, וְתִפְאַרְתְּךָ בְּיַד צָר. עוֹרְרָה גְבוּרָתְךָ וְקִנְאָתְךָ עַל אוֹיְבֶיךָ. הֵם יֵבוֹשׁוּ וְיֵחַתּוּ מִגְּבוּרָתָם. וְאַל יִמְעֲטוּ לְפָנֶיךָ תְּלָאוֹתֵינוּ, מַהֵר יְקַדְּמוּנוּ רַחֲמֶיךָ בְּיוֹם צָרָתֵנוּ. וְאִם לֹא לְמַעֲנֵנוּ, לְמַעַנְךָ פְּעַל, וְאַל תַּשְׁחִית זֵכֶר שְׁאֵרִיתֵנוּ, וְחֹן אִם הַמְיַחֲדִים שִׁמְךָ פַּעֲמַיִם בְּכָל יוֹם תָּמִיד בְּאַהֲבָה, וְאוֹמְרִים, שְׁמַע יִשְׂרָאֵל, יהוה אֱלֹהֵינוּ, יהוה אֶחָד:

דברים ו

הַפּוֹתֵחַ יָד *You who hold out an open hand:* God's forgiveness stretches beyond strict retribution: "I do not desire the death of the wicked, but rather that they turn from their ways and live" (Ezek. 33:11).

LOWERING THE HEAD

On Sundays, Tuesdays, Wednesdays and Fridays, begin Taḥanun here.
The following, until "We do not know" on page 156, is said sitting. When praying
in a place where there is a Torah scroll, one should lean forward, resting one's
head on the left arm (unless you are wearing tefillin on the left arm, in which case
rest on the right arm out of respect for the tefillin), until in "sudden shame."

וַיֹּאמֶר דָּוִד David said to Gad, "I am in great distress.   *II Sam. 24*
Let us fall into God's hand, for His mercy is great;
but do not let me fall into the hand of man."

Compassionate and gracious One, I have sinned before You.
LORD, full of compassion, have compassion on me and accept my pleas.

LORD, do not rebuke me in Your anger or chastise me in Your wrath. Be gracious to   *Ps. 6*
me, LORD, for I am weak. Heal me, LORD, for my bones are in agony. My soul is in
anguish, and You, O LORD – how long? Turn, LORD, set my soul free; save me for
the sake of Your love. For no one remembers You when he is dead. Who can praise
You from the grave? I am weary with my sighing. Every night I drench my bed, I
soak my couch with my tears. My eye grows dim from grief, worn out because of
all my foes. Leave me, all you evildoers, for the LORD has heard the sound of my
weeping. The LORD has heard my pleas. The LORD will accept my prayer. All my
enemies will be shamed and utterly dismayed. They will turn back in sudden shame.

Sit upright. On Mondays and Thursdays, say the following.
On other days, continue with "Guardian of Israel" on the next page.

LORD, God of Israel, turn away from Your fierce anger,
and relent from the evil against Your people.

Look down from heaven and see how we have become an object of scorn and
derision among the nations. We are regarded as sheep led to the slaughter, to be
killed, destroyed, beaten and humiliated. Yet, despite all this, we have not forgotten Your name. Please do not forget us.

LORD, God of Israel, turn away from Your fierce anger,
and relent from the evil against Your people.

Strangers say, "You have no hope or expectation." Be gracious to the nation
whose hope is in Your name. O Pure One, bring our deliverance close. We are
exhausted. We are given no rest. May Your compassion suppress Your anger
against us. Please turn away from Your fierce anger, and have compassion on the
people You chose as Your own.

---

when prayer becomes the ladder on which we climb from the pit of despair
to the free air of hope.

הַבֵּט מִשָּׁמַיִם *Look down from heaven:* These heart-rending words were already
known in Europe in the eleventh century, and recall the terrible persecutions
Jews suffered during the early Middle Ages.

נפילת אפיים

On Sundays, Tuesdays, Wednesdays and Fridays, begin תחנון *here.*
The following, until וַאֲנַחְנוּ לֹא נֵדַע *on page 157, is said sitting. When praying*
in a place where there is a סֵפֶר תּוֹרָה, *one should lean forward, resting one's*
head on the arm on which the תְּפִילִין *are not worn, until* יָבְשׁוּ רֶגַע.

שמואל ב, כד

וַיֹּאמֶר דָּוִד אֶל־גָּד, צַר־לִי מְאֹד
נִפְּלָה־נָּא בְיַד־יהוה, כִּי־רַבִּים רַחֲמָו, וּבְיַד־אָדָם אַל־אֶפְּלָה:

רַחוּם וְחַנּוּן, חָטָאתִי לְפָנֶיךָ. יהוה מָלֵא רַחֲמִים, רַחֵם עָלַי וְקַבֵּל תַּחֲנוּנָי.

תהלים ו

יהוה, אַל־בְּאַפְּךָ תוֹכִיחֵנִי, וְאַל־בַּחֲמָתְךָ תְיַסְּרֵנִי: חָנֵּנִי יהוה, כִּי אֻמְלַל אָנִי,
רְפָאֵנִי יהוה, כִּי נִבְהֲלוּ עֲצָמָי: וְנַפְשִׁי נִבְהֲלָה מְאֹד, וְאַתָּ יהוה, עַד־מָתָי: שׁוּבָה
יהוה, חַלְּצָה נַפְשִׁי, הוֹשִׁיעֵנִי לְמַעַן חַסְדֶּךָ: כִּי אֵין בַּמָּוֶת זִכְרֶךָ, בִּשְׁאוֹל מִי
יוֹדֶה־לָּךְ: יָגַעְתִּי בְּאַנְחָתִי, אַשְׂחֶה בְכָל־לַיְלָה מִטָּתִי, בְּדִמְעָתִי עַרְשִׂי אַמְסֶה:
עָשְׁשָׁה מִכַּעַס עֵינִי, עָתְקָה בְּכָל־צוֹרְרָי: סוּרוּ מִמֶּנִּי כָּל־פֹּעֲלֵי אָוֶן, כִּי שָׁמַע
יהוה קוֹל בִּכְיִי: שָׁמַע יהוה תְּחִנָּתִי, יהוה תְּפִלָּתִי יִקָּח: יֵבֹשׁוּ וְיִבָּהֲלוּ מְאֹד
כָּל־אֹיְבָי, יָשֻׁבוּ יֵבֹשׁוּ רָגַע:

Sit upright. On Mondays and Thursdays, say the following.
On other days, continue with שׁוֹמֵר יִשְׂרָאֵל *on the next page.*

יהוה אֱלֹהֵי יִשְׂרָאֵל, שׁוּב מֵחֲרוֹן אַפֶּךָ וְהִנָּחֵם עַל הָרָעָה לְעַמֶּךָ.
הַבֵּט מִשָּׁמַיִם וּרְאֵה כִּי הָיִינוּ לַעַג וָקֶלֶס בַּגּוֹיִם, נֶחְשַׁבְנוּ כַּצֹּאן לַטֶּבַח יוּבָל,
לַהֲרֹג וּלְאַבֵּד וּלְמַכָּה וּלְחֶרְפָּה. וּבְכָל זֹאת שִׁמְךָ לֹא שָׁכָחְנוּ, נָא אַל תִּשְׁכָּחֵנוּ.
יהוה אֱלֹהֵי יִשְׂרָאֵל, שׁוּב מֵחֲרוֹן אַפֶּךָ וְהִנָּחֵם עַל הָרָעָה לְעַמֶּךָ.
זָרִים אוֹמְרִים אֵין תּוֹחֶלֶת וְתִקְוָה, חֹן אֹם לְשִׁמְךָ מְקַוֶּה, טָהוֹר יְשׁוּעָתֵנוּ
קָרְבָה, יָגַעְנוּ וְלֹא הוּנַח לָנוּ, רַחֲמֶיךָ יִכְבְּשׁוּ אֶת כַּעַסְךָ מֵעָלֵינוּ. אָנָּא שׁוּב
מֵחֲרוֹנְךָ וְרַחֵם סְגֻלָּה אֲשֶׁר בָּחָרְתָּ.

וַיֹּאמֶר דָּוִד *David said to Gad:* Words spoken by David during a moment of crisis (II Sam. 24:14). The king had sinned by taking a census of the people. God, through the prophet Gad, offered him a choice: famine, war, or punishment directly from heaven. David replied: it is better to be punished by God than suffer the cruelty of man.

יהוה, אַל־בְּאַפְּךָ תוֹכִיחֵנִי *LORD, do not rebuke me in Your anger:* A psalm of intense emotional power, spoken out of fear's heart of darkness. שָׁמַע יהוה *The LORD has heard my pleas:* from the deepest pain, strength is born,

Lord, God of Israel, turn away from Your fierce anger,
and relent from the evil against Your people.

Have pity on us, Lord, in Your compassion, and do not hand us over to cruel
oppressors. Why should the nations say, "Where is their God now?" For Your
own sake, deal kindly with us, and do not delay. Please turn away from Your
fierce anger, and have compassion on the people You chose as Your own.

Lord, God of Israel, turn away from Your fierce anger,
and relent from the evil against Your people.

Heed our voice and be gracious. Do not abandon us into the hand of our
enemies to blot out our name. Remember what You promised our fathers:
"I will make your descendants as many as the stars of heaven" – yet now we
are only a few left from many. Yet, despite all this, we have not forgotten Your
name. Please do not forget us.

Lord, God of Israel, turn away from Your fierce anger,
and relent from the evil against Your people.

Help us, God of our salvation, for the sake of the glory of Your name. Save   *Ps. 79*
us and pardon our sins for Your name's sake.

Lord, God of Israel, turn away from Your fierce anger,
and relent from the evil against Your people.

On all days continue here:

שׁוֹמֵר יִשְׂרָאֵל Guardian of Israel, guard the remnant of Israel,
    and let not Israel perish, who declare, "Listen, Israel."
Guardian of a unique nation, guard the remnant of a unique people,
    and let not that unique nation perish, who proclaim the unity
    of Your name [saying], "The Lord is our God, the Lord is One."
Guardian of a holy nation, guard the remnant of that holy people,
    and let not the holy nation perish, who three times repeat
    the threefold declaration of holiness to the Holy One.
You who are conciliated by calls for compassion and placated by pleas,
    be conciliated and placated toward an afflicted generation,
    for there is no other help.
Our Father, our King, be gracious to us and answer us, though we have no
    worthy deeds; act with us in charity and loving-kindness and save us.

───────────────────────────────
שׁוֹמֵר יִשְׂרָאֵל *Guardian of Israel:* A three-verse prayer set in motion by a
phrase from Psalm 121: "See: the Guardian of Israel neither slumbers nor
sleeps." An example of early liturgical poetry, it has the same structure as

יהוה אֱלֹהֵי יִשְׂרָאֵל, שׁוּב מֵחֲרוֹן אַפֶּךָ וְהִנָּחֵם עַל הָרָעָה לְעַמֶּךָ.

חוּסָה יהוה עָלֵינוּ בְּרַחֲמֶיךָ, וְאַל תִּתְּנֵנוּ בִּידֵי אַכְזָרִים. לָמָּה יֹאמְרוּ הַגּוֹיִם אַיֵּה נָא אֱלֹהֵיהֶם, לְמַעַנְךָ עֲשֵׂה עִמָּנוּ חֶסֶד וְאַל תְּאַחַר. אָנָּא שׁוּב מֵחֲרוֹנְךָ וְרַחֵם סְגֻלָּה אֲשֶׁר בָּחָרְתָּ.

יהוה אֱלֹהֵי יִשְׂרָאֵל, שׁוּב מֵחֲרוֹן אַפֶּךָ וְהִנָּחֵם עַל הָרָעָה לְעַמֶּךָ.

קוֹלֵנוּ תִשְׁמַע וְתָחֹן, וְאַל תִּטְּשֵׁנוּ בְּיַד אוֹיְבֵינוּ לִמְחוֹת אֶת שְׁמֵנוּ. זְכֹר אֲשֶׁר נִשְׁבַּעְתָּ לַאֲבוֹתֵינוּ כְּכוֹכְבֵי הַשָּׁמַיִם אַרְבֶּה אֶת זַרְעֲכֶם, וְעַתָּה נִשְׁאַרְנוּ מְעַט מֵהַרְבֵּה. וּבְכָל זֹאת שִׁמְךָ לֹא שָׁכָחְנוּ, נָא אַל תִּשְׁכָּחֵנוּ.

יהוה אֱלֹהֵי יִשְׂרָאֵל, שׁוּב מֵחֲרוֹן אַפֶּךָ וְהִנָּחֵם עַל הָרָעָה לְעַמֶּךָ.

עָזְרֵנוּ אֱלֹהֵי יִשְׁעֵנוּ עַל דְּבַר כְּבוֹד שְׁמֶךָ, וְהַצִּילֵנוּ וְכַפֵּר עַל חַטֹּאתֵינוּ לְמַעַן שְׁמֶךָ: תהלים עט

יהוה אֱלֹהֵי יִשְׂרָאֵל, שׁוּב מֵחֲרוֹן אַפֶּךָ וְהִנָּחֵם עַל הָרָעָה לְעַמֶּךָ.

On all days continue here:

שׁוֹמֵר יִשְׂרָאֵל, שְׁמֹר שְׁאֵרִית יִשְׂרָאֵל, וְאַל יֹאבַד יִשְׂרָאֵל הָאוֹמְרִים שְׁמַע יִשְׂרָאֵל.

שׁוֹמֵר גּוֹי אֶחָד, שְׁמֹר שְׁאֵרִית עַם אֶחָד, וְאַל יֹאבַד גּוֹי אֶחָד הַמְיַחֲדִים שִׁמְךָ, יהוה אֱלֹהֵינוּ יהוה אֶחָד.

שׁוֹמֵר גּוֹי קָדוֹשׁ, שְׁמֹר שְׁאֵרִית עַם קָדוֹשׁ, וְאַל יֹאבַד גּוֹי קָדוֹשׁ הַמְשַׁלְּשִׁים בְּשָׁלֹשׁ קְדֻשּׁוֹת לְקָדוֹשׁ.

מִתְרַצֶּה בְּרַחֲמִים וּמִתְפַּיֵּס בְּתַחֲנוּנִים, הִתְרַצֵּה וְהִתְפַּיֵּס לְדוֹר עָנִי כִּי אֵין עוֹזֵר.

אָבִינוּ מַלְכֵּנוּ, חָנֵּנוּ וַעֲנֵנוּ, כִּי אֵין בָּנוּ מַעֲשִׂים עֲשֵׂה עִמָּנוּ צְדָקָה וָחֶסֶד וְהוֹשִׁיעֵנוּ.

───

וּבְכָל זֹאת *Yet, despite all this:* After the Holocaust, the concentration camp at Theresienstadt was excavated. A hidden room was discovered, which had served as a secret place in which the prisoners would pray. On one of its walls were written the words: "Yet, despite all this, we have not forgotten Your name. Please do not forget us."

Stand at ˆ.

וַאֲנַחְנוּ We do not know ˆwhat to do, but our eyes are turned to You. Remember, LORD, Your compassion and loving-kindness, for they are everlasting. May Your loving-kindness, LORD, be with us, for we have put our hope in You. Do not hold against us the sins of those who came before us. May Your mercies meet us swiftly, for we have been brought very low. Be gracious to us, LORD, be gracious to us, for we are sated with contempt. In wrath, remember mercy. He knows our nature; He remembers that we are dust. ˈ Help us, God of our salvation, for the sake of the glory of Your name. Save us and grant atonement for our sins for Your name's sake.

II Chr. 12
Ps. 25

Ps. 33

Ps. 79
Ps. 123
Hab. 3
Ps. 103
Ps. 79

HALF KADDISH

Leader: יִתְגַּדַּל Magnified and sanctified
may His great name be,
in the world He created by His will.
May He establish His kingdom
in your lifetime and in your days,
and in the lifetime of all the house of Israel,
swiftly and soon – and say: Amen.

All: May His great name be blessed for ever and all time.

Leader: Blessed and praised, glorified and exalted,
raised and honored, uplifted and lauded
be the name of the Holy One,
blessed be He,
beyond any blessing, song, praise and consolation
uttered in the world – and say: Amen.

וַאֲנַחְנוּ לֹא נֵדַע We do not know: A line taken from the prayer of King Jehoshaphat when the nation was confronted by a coalition of hostile powers intent on war (II Chr. 20:12). Our custom is to stand after these words. Abudarham explains that this is because – like Moses pleading on behalf of the people – we have prayed in every posture, sitting (before the Amida), standing (during the Amida), and "falling on our faces" (during Taḥanun). We have exhausted the repertoire of prayer and do not know what else to do. We stand at this point to signal that our private supplications have come to an end.

Stand at ˄.

דברי
הימים ב׳ כ
תהלים כה
תהלים לג
תהלים עט

וַאֲנַחְנוּ לֹא נֵדַע ׳מַה־נַּעֲשֶׂה, כִּי עָלֶיךָ עֵינֵינוּ: זְכֹר־רַחֲמֶיךָ יהוה וַחֲסָדֶיךָ,
כִּי מֵעוֹלָם הֵמָּה: יְהִי־חַסְדְּךָ יהוה עָלֵינוּ, כַּאֲשֶׁר יִחַלְנוּ לָךְ: אַל־תִּזְכָּר־לָנוּ
עֲוֺנֹת רִאשֹׁנִים, מַהֵר יְקַדְּמוּנוּ רַחֲמֶיךָ, כִּי דַלּוֹנוּ מְאֹד: חָנֵּנוּ יהוה חָנֵּנוּ,
כִּי־רַב שָׂבַעְנוּ בוּז: בְּרֹגֶז רַחֵם תִּזְכּוֹר: כִּי־הוּא יָדַע יִצְרֵנוּ, זָכוּר כִּי־עָפָר

תהלים קכג
חבקוק ג
תהלים קג
תהלים עט

אֲנָחְנוּ: ˄ עָזְרֵנוּ אֱלֹהֵי יִשְׁעֵנוּ עַל־דְּבַר כְּבוֹד־שְׁמֶךָ, וְהַצִּילֵנוּ וְכַפֵּר עַל־
חַטֹּאתֵינוּ לְמַעַן שְׁמֶךָ:

חצי קדיש

ש״ץ: יִתְגַּדַּל וְיִתְקַדַּשׁ שְׁמֵהּ רַבָּא (קהל: אָמֵן)

בְּעָלְמָא דִּי בְרָא כִרְעוּתֵהּ

וְיַמְלִיךְ מַלְכוּתֵהּ

בְּחַיֵּיכוֹן וּבְיוֹמֵיכוֹן וּבְחַיֵּי דְכָל בֵּית יִשְׂרָאֵל

בַּעֲגָלָא וּבִזְמַן קָרִיב, וְאִמְרוּ אָמֵן. (קהל: אָמֵן)

קהל
וש״ץ:

יְהֵא שְׁמֵהּ רַבָּא מְבָרַךְ לְעָלַם וּלְעָלְמֵי עָלְמַיָּא.

ש״ץ: יִתְבָּרַךְ וְיִשְׁתַּבַּח וְיִתְפָּאַר וְיִתְרוֹמַם וְיִתְנַשֵּׂא

וְיִתְהַדָּר וְיִתְעַלֶּה וְיִתְהַלָּל

שְׁמֵהּ דְּקֻדְשָׁא בְּרִיךְ הוּא (קהל: בְּרִיךְ הוּא)

לְעֵלָּא מִן כָּל בִּרְכָתָא

/ בעשרת ימי תשובה: לְעֵלָּא לְעֵלָּא מִכָּל בִּרְכָתָא/

וְשִׁירָתָא, תֻּשְׁבְּחָתָא וְנֶחֱמָתָא

דַּאֲמִירָן בְּעָלְמָא, וְאִמְרוּ אָמֵן. (קהל: אָמֵן)

───

the poem preceding the morning Amida, "Rock of Israel! Arise to the help
of Israel…" and the prayer said on the Ten Days of Penitence, "Remember
us for life, O King who desires life…" In each case every verse contains
four phrases, all ending with the same word (Rabbi Jeffrey Cohen). The
prayer was transferred from the penitential prayers known as Seliḥot to the
Daily Service.

REMOVING THE TORAH FROM THE ARK

On Mondays and Thursdays, Rosh Ḥodesh, Ḥanukka, Purim and
Fast Days, the Torah is read when a minyan is present. On all other
days, continue with "Happy are those" on page 174.

Before taking the Torah out of the Ark, on Mondays and Thursdays, stand while
reciting "God, slow to anger." It is not said on Rosh Ḥodesh, Erev Pesaḥ, Ḥanukka,
the 14th and 15th of Adar 1, Purim and Shushan Purim, Yom HaAtzma'ut,
Yom Yerushalayim, Tisha B'Av or in a house of mourning, and in Israel on
Isru Ḥag. Most people say both paragraphs; some say only the first.

God, slow to anger, abounding in loving-kindness and truth, do not rebuke us in Your anger. Have pity on Your people, LORD, and save us from all evil. We have sinned against You, LORD. Please forgive in accordance with Your great compassion, God.	God, slow to anger, full of compassion, do not hide Your face from us. Have pity on the remnant of Israel Your people, LORD, and deliver us from all evil. We have sinned against You, LORD. Please forgive in accordance with Your great compassion, God.

The Ark is opened and the congregation stands. All say:

וַיְהִי בִּנְסֹעַ **Whenever the Ark set out,** Moses would say, "Arise, LORD, *Num. 10* and may Your enemies be scattered. May those who hate You flee before You." For the Torah shall come forth from Zion, and the word *Is. 2* of the LORD from Jerusalem. Blessed is He who in His holiness gave the Torah to His People Israel.

---

them the entire Book of the Covenant which had been found in the LORD's Temple" (II Chr. 34:30).

The book of Nehemiah (8:1–12) contains a graphic description of the return of the Babylonian exiles to Israel. Ezra gathered the people at the Temple and read the Torah to them "from dawn until midday," assisted by Levites who "interpreted it and explained its meaning, so that they understood the verses."

These were national occasions. At a more local level, tradition holds that Moses instituted the practice that the Torah be read on Shabbat, Yom Tov, Ḥol HaMo'ed, and Rosh Ḥodesh. Ezra ordained that it also be read on Mondays and Thursdays (market days in ancient times) and on Shabbat afternoons (Yerushalmi, *Megilla* 4:1). The public reading of the Torah is as ancient an institution as prayer itself.

The synagogue thus became not only a house of prayer but also a house of study. The result is a dynamic tension between speaking and listening. In

הוצאת ספר תורה

On Mondays and Thursdays, ראש חודש, חנוכה, פורים *and Fast Days,*
the תורה *is read when a* מנין *is present. On all other days, continue with* אשרי *on page 175.*

Before taking the תורה *out of the* ארון קודש, *on Mondays and Thursdays, stand while*
reciting אל ארך אפים. *It is not said on:* ראש חודש, חנוכה, *ערב פסח,* the 14th and 15th of
אדר א', *תשעה באב, יום ירושלים, יום העצמאות, שושן פורים or in a house of mourning, and*
in ארץ ישראל *on* אסרו חג. *Most people say both paragraphs, some say only the first.*

אֵל אֶרֶךְ אַפַּיִם וּמָלֵא רַחֲמִים	אֵל אֶרֶךְ אַפַּיִם וְרַב חֶסֶד וֶאֱמֶת
אַל תַּסְתֵּר פָּנֶיךָ מִמֶּנּוּ.	אַל בְּאַפְּךָ תוֹכִיחֵנוּ.
חוּסָה יהוה עַל שְׁאֵרִית יִשְׂרָאֵל עַמֶּךָ	חוּסָה יהוה עַל עַמֶּךָ
וְהַצִּילֵנוּ מִכָּל רָע.	וְהוֹשִׁיעֵנוּ מִכָּל רָע.
חָטָאנוּ לְךָ אָדוֹן	חָטָאנוּ לְךָ אָדוֹן
סְלַח נָא כְּרֹב רַחֲמֶיךָ אֵל.	סְלַח נָא כְּרֹב רַחֲמֶיךָ אֵל.

The ארון קודש *is opened and the* קהל *stands. All say:*

וַיְהִי בִּנְסֹעַ הָאָרֹן וַיֹּאמֶר מֹשֶׁה, קוּמָה יהוה וְיָפֻצוּ אֹיְבֶיךָ וְיָנֻסוּ   במדבר י
מְשַׂנְאֶיךָ מִפָּנֶיךָ: כִּי מִצִּיּוֹן תֵּצֵא תוֹרָה וּדְבַר־יהוה מִירוּשָׁלָםִ:   ישעיה ב
בָּרוּךְ שֶׁנָּתַן תּוֹרָה לְעַמּוֹ יִשְׂרָאֵל בִּקְדֻשָּׁתוֹ.

READING OF THE TORAH

From earliest times, the public reading of the Torah has been a constitutive
element of the spiritual life of Israel. At Mount Sinai, to confirm the covenant
between the people and God, Moses "took the Book of the Covenant and
read it aloud to the people" (Ex. 24:7). The penultimate commandment of
the Torah specifies that every seven years (on Sukkot following the sabbatical
year) there should be a national assembly at which "the people, men, women,
children and the strangers in your communities" are to hear the Torah proclaimed "so that they may listen and learn to fear the LORD your God and
observe faithfully all the words of this Torah" (Deut. 31:12).

At critical moments during the biblical era, when the people had drifted
from their faith, national renewal was marked by a public Torah reading. King
Jehoshaphat sent out officers who "taught throughout Judah, having with
them a scroll of the LORD's Torah. They circulated throughout the towns of
Judah and taught the people" (II Chr. 17:9).

King Josiah assembled "all the men of Judah, the inhabitants of Jerusalem,
the priests, the Levites, and all the people, young and old alike, and read to

Blessed is the name of the Master of the Universe. Blessed is Your crown and Your *Zohar,* place. May Your favor always be with Your people Israel. Show Your people the *Vayak-hel* salvation of Your right hand in Your Temple. Grant us the gift of Your good light, and accept our prayers in mercy. May it be Your will to prolong our life in goodness. May I be counted among the righteous, so that You will have compassion on me and protect me and all that is mine and all that is Your people Israel's. You feed all; You sustain all; You rule over all; You rule over kings, for sovereignty is Yours. I am a servant of the Holy One, blessed be He, before whom and before whose glorious Torah I bow at all times. Not in man do I trust, nor on any angel do I rely, but on the God of heaven who is the God of truth, whose Torah is truth, whose prophets speak truth, and who abounds in acts of love and truth. • In Him I trust, and to His holy and glorious name I offer praises. May it be Your will to open my heart to the Torah, and to fulfill the wishes of my heart and of the hearts of all Your people Israel for good, for life, and for peace.

The Leader takes the Torah scroll in his right arm, bows toward the Ark and says:

Magnify the LORD with me, and let us exalt His name together. *Ps. 34*

The Ark is closed. The Leader carries the Torah scroll to the bima and the congregation says:

לְךָ Yours, LORD, are the greatness and the power, the glory and the *1 Chr. 29* majesty and splendor, for everything in heaven and earth is Yours. Yours, LORD, is the kingdom; You are exalted as Head over all.

רוֹמְמוּ Exalt the LORD our God and bow to His footstool; He is holy. *Ps. 99* Exalt the LORD our God, and bow at His holy mountain, for holy is the LORD our God.

אַב הָרַחֲמִים May the Father of compassion have compassion on the people borne by Him. May He remember the covenant with the mighty [patriarchs], and deliver us from evil times. May He reproach the evil instinct in the people carried by Him, and graciously grant that we be an everlasting remnant. May He fulfill in good measure our requests for salvation and compassion.

───────────────────────────────

literacy and lifelong learning. The Torah is not just written on parchment; it is meant to be engraved on the Jewish soul.

Keriat HaTorah, translated as "the reading of the Torah," also means "the proclamation of the Torah." The public reading symbolically affirms the Torah as the written constitution of the Jewish people as a nation under the sovereignty of God. It is a reenactment of the revelation at Mount Sinai when the Israelites first became a nation, bound by the Torah's laws, summoned to translate its ideals into life.

בְּרִיךְ שְׁמֵהּ דְּמָרֵא עָלְמָא, בְּרִיךְ כִּתְרָךְ וְאַתְרָךְ. יְהֵא רְעוּתָךְ עִם עַמָּךְ יִשְׂרָאֵל לְעָלַם, וּפֻרְקַן יְמִינָךְ אַחֲזֵי לְעַמָּךְ בְּבֵית מַקְדְּשָׁךְ, וּלְאַמְטוֹיֵי לָנָא מִטּוּב נְהוֹרָךְ, וּלְקַבֵּל צְלוֹתָנָא בְּרַחֲמִין. יְהֵא רַעֲוָא קֳדָמָךְ דְּתוֹרִיךְ לָן חַיִּין בְּטִיבוּ, וְלֶהֱוֵי אֲנָא פְּקִידָא בְּגוֹ צַדִּיקַיָּא, לְמִרְחַם עֲלַי וּלְמִנְטַר יָתִי וְיַת כָּל דִּי לִי וְדִי לְעַמָּךְ יִשְׂרָאֵל. אַנְתְּ הוּא זָן לְכֹלָּא וּמְפַרְנֵס לְכֹלָּא, אַנְתְּ הוּא שַׁלִּיט עַל כֹּלָּא, אַנְתְּ הוּא דְּשַׁלִּיט עַל מַלְכַיָּא, וּמַלְכוּתָא דִּילָךְ הִיא. אֲנָא עַבְדָּא דְּקֻדְשָׁא בְּרִיךְ הוּא, דְּסָגִדְנָא קַמֵּהּ וּמִקַּמֵּי דִּיקַר אוֹרַיְתֵהּ בְּכָל עִדָּן וְעִדָּן. לָא עַל אֱנָשׁ רְחִיצְנָא וְלָא עַל בַּר אֱלָהִין סָמִיכְנָא, אֶלָּא בֵּאלָהָא דִשְׁמַיָּא, דְּהוּא אֱלָהָא קְשׁוֹט, וְאוֹרַיְתֵהּ קְשׁוֹט, וּנְבִיאוֹהִי קְשׁוֹט, וּמַסְגֵּא לְמֶעְבַּד טָבְוָן וּקְשׁוֹט. ◦ בֵּהּ אֲנָא רְחִיץ, וְלִשְׁמֵהּ קַדִּישָׁא יַקִּירָא אֲנָא אֵמַר תֻּשְׁבְּחָן. יְהֵא רַעֲוָא קֳדָמָךְ דְּתִפְתַּח לִבַּאי בְּאוֹרַיְתָא, וְתַשְׁלִים מִשְׁאֲלִין דְּלִבַּאי וְלִבָּא דְכָל עַמָּךְ יִשְׂרָאֵל לְטַב וּלְחַיִּין וְלִשְׁלָם.

The שליח ציבור *takes the* ספר תורה *in his right arm, bows toward the* ארון קודש *and says:*

גַּדְּלוּ לַיהוה אִתִּי וּנְרוֹמְמָה שְׁמוֹ יַחְדָּו:

The ארון קודש *is closed. The* שליח ציבור *carries the* ספר תורה *to the* בימה *and the* קהל *says:*

לְךָ יהוה הַגְּדֻלָּה וְהַגְּבוּרָה וְהַתִּפְאֶרֶת וְהַנֵּצַח וְהַהוֹד, כִּי־כֹל בַּשָּׁמַיִם וּבָאָרֶץ, לְךָ יהוה הַמַּמְלָכָה וְהַמִּתְנַשֵּׂא לְכֹל לְרֹאשׁ:

רוֹמְמוּ יהוה אֱלֹהֵינוּ וְהִשְׁתַּחֲווּ לַהֲדֹם רַגְלָיו, קָדוֹשׁ הוּא: רוֹמְמוּ יהוה אֱלֹהֵינוּ וְהִשְׁתַּחֲווּ לְהַר קָדְשׁוֹ, כִּי־קָדוֹשׁ יהוה אֱלֹהֵינוּ:

אַב הָרַחֲמִים הוּא יְרַחֵם עַם עֲמוּסִים, וְיִזְכֹּר בְּרִית אֵיתָנִים, וְיַצִּיל נַפְשׁוֹתֵינוּ מִן הַשָּׁעוֹת הָרָעוֹת, וְיִגְעַר בְּיֵצֶר הָרָע מִן הַנְּשׂוּאִים, וְיָחֹן אוֹתָנוּ לִפְלֵיטַת עוֹלָמִים, וִימַלֵּא מִשְׁאֲלוֹתֵינוּ בְּמִדָּה טוֹבָה יְשׁוּעָה וְרַחֲמִים.

---

prayer, we speak to God. In study we listen to God speaking to us, His word unchanged and undiminished across the centuries.

The assembly convened by Ezra, when the Torah was not only read but also explained, became the model for educational activities within the synagogue, of which the *derasha* ("sermon," or more precisely, "exposition") is only one of many forms. To an unparalleled degree, Judaism is predicated on universal

The Torah scroll is placed on the bima and the Gabbai calls a Kohen to the Torah. See laws 75–87.
May His kingship over us be soon revealed and made manifest. May He be gracious to
our surviving remnant, the remnant of His people the house of Israel in grace, loving-
kindness, compassion and favor, and let us say: Amen. Let us all render greatness to
our God and give honor to the Torah. *Let the Kohen come forward. Arise (*name*
son of *father's name*), the Kohen.

*If no Kohen is present, a Levi or Yisrael is called up as follows:

/As there is no Kohen, arise (*name* son of *father's name*) in place of a Kohen./

Blessed is He who, in His holiness, gave the Torah to His people Israel.

Congregation followed by the Gabbai:
You who cling to the Lᴏʀᴅ your God are all alive today.   *Deut. 4*

The appropriate Torah portions are to be found from page 614.
The Reader shows the oleh the section to be read. The oleh touches the scroll at that place
with the tzitzit of his tallit, which he then kisses. Holding the handles of the scroll, he says:

Oleh: Bless the Lᴏʀᴅ, the blessed One.

Cong: Bless the Lᴏʀᴅ, the blessed One, for ever and all time.

Oleh: Bless the Lᴏʀᴅ, the blessed One, for ever and all time.

Blessed are You, Lᴏʀᴅ our God, King of the Universe,
who has chosen us from all peoples and has given us His Torah.
Blessed are You, Lᴏʀᴅ, Giver of the Torah.

After the reading, the oleh says:
Oleh: Blessed are You, Lᴏʀᴅ our God, King of the Universe, who has
given us the Torah of truth, planting everlasting life in our midst.
Blessed are You, Lᴏʀᴅ, Giver of the Torah.

One who has survived a situation of danger (see laws 88–89) says:
Blessed are You, Lᴏʀᴅ our God, King of the Universe,
who bestows good on the unworthy,
who has bestowed on me much good.

The congregation responds:
Amen. May He who bestowed much good on you continue to bestow on
you much good, Selah.

After a Bar Mitzva boy has finished the Torah blessing, his father says aloud:
Blessed is He who has released me from the responsibility for this child.

The ספר תורה *is placed on the* שולחן *and the* גבאי *calls a* כהן *to the* תורה. *See laws 75–87.*

וְתִגָּלֶה וְתֵרָאֶה מַלְכוּתוֹ עָלֵינוּ בִּזְמַן קָרוֹב, וְיָחֹן פְּלֵיטָתֵנוּ וּפְלֵיטַת עַמּוֹ בֵּית יִשְׂרָאֵל
לְחֵן וּלְחֶסֶד וּלְרַחֲמִים וּלְרָצוֹן וְנֹאמַר אָמֵן. הַכֹּל הָבוּ גֹדֶל לֵאלֹהֵינוּ וּתְנוּ כָבוֹד לַתּוֹרָה.
כֹּהֵן קְרָב, יַעֲמֹד (פְּלוֹנִי בֶּן פְּלוֹנִי) הַכֹּהֵן.

If no כהן *is present, a* לוי *or* ישראל *is called up as follows:*
/אִם כָּאן כֹּהֵן, יַעֲמֹד (פְּלוֹנִי בֶּן פְּלוֹנִי) בִּמְקוֹם כֹּהֵן./

בָּרוּךְ שֶׁנָּתַן תּוֹרָה לְעַמּוֹ יִשְׂרָאֵל בִּקְדֻשָּׁתוֹ.

קהל *followed by the* גבאי:

וְאַתֶּם הַדְּבֵקִים בַּיהוה אֱלֹהֵיכֶם חַיִּים כֻּלְּכֶם הַיּוֹם:

דברים ד

The appropriate תורה *portions are to be found from page 614.*

The קורא *shows the* עולה *the section to be read. The* עולה *touches the* ספר תורה *at that place*
with the ציצית *of his* טלית, *which he then kisses. Holding the handles of the* ספר תורה, *he says:*

עולה: בָּרְכוּ אֶת יהוה הַמְבֹרָךְ.

קהל: בָּרוּךְ יהוה הַמְבֹרָךְ לְעוֹלָם וָעֶד.

עולה: בָּרוּךְ יהוה הַמְבֹרָךְ לְעוֹלָם וָעֶד.
בָּרוּךְ אַתָּה יהוה, אֱלֹהֵינוּ מֶלֶךְ הָעוֹלָם
אֲשֶׁר בָּחַר בָּנוּ מִכָּל הָעַמִּים וְנָתַן לָנוּ אֶת תּוֹרָתוֹ.
בָּרוּךְ אַתָּה יהוה, נוֹתֵן הַתּוֹרָה.

After the קריאת התורה, *the* עולה *says:*

עולה: בָּרוּךְ אַתָּה יהוה אֱלֹהֵינוּ מֶלֶךְ הָעוֹלָם
אֲשֶׁר נָתַן לָנוּ תּוֹרַת אֱמֶת וְחַיֵּי עוֹלָם נָטַע בְּתוֹכֵנוּ.
בָּרוּךְ אַתָּה יהוה, נוֹתֵן הַתּוֹרָה.

One who has survived a situation of danger (see laws 88–89) says:

בָּרוּךְ אַתָּה יהוה אֱלֹהֵינוּ מֶלֶךְ הָעוֹלָם הַגּוֹמֵל לְחַיָּבִים טוֹבוֹת
שֶׁגְּמָלַנִי כָּל טוֹב.

The קהל *responds:*

אָמֵן. מִי שֶׁגְּמָלְךָ כָּל טוֹב הוּא יִגְמָלְךָ כָּל טוֹב, סֶלָה.

After a בר מצוה *has finished the* תורה *blessing, his father says aloud:*

בָּרוּךְ שֶׁפְּטָרַנִי מֵעָנְשׁוֹ שֶׁלָּזֶה.

FOR AN OLEH
May He who blessed our fathers, Abraham, Isaac and Jacob, bless (*name*, son of *father's name*) who has been called up in honor of the All-Present, in honor of the Torah. As a reward for this, may the Holy One, blessed be He, protect and deliver him from all trouble and distress, all infection and illness, and send blessing and success to all the work of his hands, together with all Israel, his brethren, and let us say: Amen.

FOR A SICK MAN
May He who blessed our fathers, Abraham, Isaac and Jacob, Moses and Aaron, David and Solomon, bless and heal one who is ill, (*sick person's name*, son of *mother's name*), on whose behalf (*name of the one making the offering*) is making a contribution to charity. As a reward for this, may the Holy One, blessed be He, be filled with compassion for him, to restore his health, cure him, strengthen and revive him, sending him a swift and full recovery from heaven to all his 248 organs and 365 sinews, amongst the other sick ones in Israel, a healing of the spirit and a healing of the body, now, swiftly and soon, and let us say: Amen.

FOR A SICK WOMAN
May He who blessed our fathers, Abraham, Isaac and Jacob, Moses and Aaron, David and Solomon, bless and heal one who is ill, (*sick person's name*, daughter of *mother's name*), on whose behalf (*name of the one making the offering*) is making a contribution to charity. As a reward for this, may the Holy One, blessed be He, be filled with compassion for her, to restore her health, cure her, strengthen and revive her, sending her a swift and full recovery from heaven to all her organs and sinews, amongst the other sick ones in Israel, a healing of the spirit and a healing of the body, now, swiftly and soon, and let us say: Amen.

ON THE BIRTH OF A SON
May He who blessed our fathers, Abraham, Isaac and Jacob, Moses and Aaron, David and Solomon, Sarah, Rebecca, Rachel and Leah, bless the woman (*name*, daughter of *father's name*) who has given birth, and her son who has been born to her as an auspicious sign. Her husband, the child's father, is making a contribution to charity. As a reward for this, may father and mother merit to bring the child into the covenant of Abraham and to a life of Torah, to the marriage canopy and to good deeds, and let us say: Amen.

ON THE BIRTH OF A DAUGHTER
May He who blessed our fathers, Abraham, Isaac and Jacob, Moses and Aaron, David and Solomon, Sarah, Rebecca, Rachel and Leah, bless the woman (*name*, daughter of *father's name*) who has given birth, and her daughter who has been

מי שברך לעולה לתורה

מִי שֶׁבֵּרַךְ אֲבוֹתֵינוּ אַבְרָהָם יִצְחָק וְיַעֲקֹב, הוּא יְבָרֵךְ אֶת (פְּלוֹנִי בֶּן פְּלוֹנִי), בַּעֲבוּר שֶׁעָלָה לִכְבוֹד הַמָּקוֹם וְלִכְבוֹד הַתּוֹרָה. בִּשְׂכַר זֶה הַקָּדוֹשׁ בָּרוּךְ הוּא יִשְׁמְרֵהוּ וְיַצִּילֵהוּ מִכָּל צָרָה וְצוּקָה וּמִכָּל נֶגַע וּמַחֲלָה, וְיִשְׁלַח בְּרָכָה וְהַצְלָחָה בְּכָל מַעֲשֵׂה יָדָיו עִם כָּל יִשְׂרָאֵל אֶחָיו, וְנֹאמַר אָמֵן.

מי שברך לחולה

מִי שֶׁבֵּרַךְ אֲבוֹתֵינוּ אַבְרָהָם יִצְחָק וְיַעֲקֹב, מֹשֶׁה וְאַהֲרֹן דָּוִד וּשְׁלֹמֹה הוּא יְבָרֵךְ וִירַפֵּא אֶת הַחוֹלֶה (פְּלוֹנִי בֶּן פְּלוֹנִי) בַּעֲבוּר שֶׁ(פְּלוֹנִי בֶּן פְּלוֹנִי) נוֹדֵר צְדָקָה בַּעֲבוּרוֹ. בִּשְׂכַר זֶה הַקָּדוֹשׁ בָּרוּךְ הוּא יִמָּלֵא רַחֲמִים עָלָיו לְהַחֲלִימוֹ וּלְרַפֹּאתוֹ וּלְהַחֲזִיקוֹ וּלְהַחֲיוֹתוֹ וְיִשְׁלַח לוֹ מְהֵרָה רְפוּאָה שְׁלֵמָה מִן הַשָּׁמַיִם לִרְמַ"ח אֵבָרָיו וּשְׁסָ"ה גִידָיו בְּתוֹךְ שְׁאָר חוֹלֵי יִשְׂרָאֵל, רְפוּאַת הַנֶּפֶשׁ וּרְפוּאַת הַגּוּף, הַשְׁתָּא בַּעֲגָלָא וּבִזְמַן קָרִיב, וְנֹאמַר אָמֵן.

מי שברך לחולה

מִי שֶׁבֵּרַךְ אֲבוֹתֵינוּ אַבְרָהָם יִצְחָק וְיַעֲקֹב, מֹשֶׁה וְאַהֲרֹן דָּוִד וּשְׁלֹמֹה הוּא יְבָרֵךְ וִירַפֵּא אֶת הַחוֹלָה (פְּלוֹנִית בַּת פְּלוֹנִי) בַּעֲבוּר שֶׁ(פְּלוֹנִי בֶּן פְּלוֹנִי) נוֹדֵר צְדָקָה בַּעֲבוּרָהּ. בִּשְׂכַר זֶה הַקָּדוֹשׁ בָּרוּךְ הוּא יִמָּלֵא רַחֲמִים עָלֶיהָ לְהַחֲלִימָהּ וּלְרַפֹּאתָהּ וּלְהַחֲזִיקָהּ וּלְהַחֲיוֹתָהּ וְיִשְׁלַח לָהּ מְהֵרָה רְפוּאָה שְׁלֵמָה מִן הַשָּׁמַיִם לְכָל אֵבָרֶיהָ וּלְכָל גִּידֶיהָ בְּתוֹךְ שְׁאָר חוֹלֵי יִשְׂרָאֵל, רְפוּאַת הַנֶּפֶשׁ וּרְפוּאַת הַגּוּף, הַשְׁתָּא בַּעֲגָלָא וּבִזְמַן קָרִיב, וְנֹאמַר אָמֵן.

מי שברך ליולדת בן

מִי שֶׁבֵּרַךְ אֲבוֹתֵינוּ אַבְרָהָם יִצְחָק וְיַעֲקֹב, מֹשֶׁה וְאַהֲרֹן דָּוִד וּשְׁלֹמֹה, שָׂרָה רִבְקָה רָחֵל וְלֵאָה הוּא יְבָרֵךְ אֶת הָאִשָּׁה הַיּוֹלֶדֶת (פְּלוֹנִית בַּת פְּלוֹנִי) וְאֶת בְּנָהּ שֶׁנּוֹלַד לָהּ לְמַזָּל טוֹב בַּעֲבוּר שֶׁבַּעְלָהּ וְאָבִיו נוֹדֵר צְדָקָה בַּעֲדָם. בִּשְׂכַר זֶה יִזְכּוּ אָבִיו וְאִמּוֹ לְהַכְנִיסוֹ בִּבְרִיתוֹ שֶׁל אַבְרָהָם אָבִינוּ וּלְגַדְּלוֹ לְתוֹרָה וּלְחֻפָּה וּלְמַעֲשִׂים טוֹבִים, וְנֹאמַר אָמֵן.

מי שברך ליולדת בת

מִי שֶׁבֵּרַךְ אֲבוֹתֵינוּ אַבְרָהָם יִצְחָק וְיַעֲקֹב, מֹשֶׁה וְאַהֲרֹן דָּוִד וּשְׁלֹמֹה, שָׂרָה רִבְקָה רָחֵל וְלֵאָה הוּא יְבָרֵךְ אֶת הָאִשָּׁה הַיּוֹלֶדֶת (פְּלוֹנִית בַּת פְּלוֹנִי) וְאֶת בִּתָּהּ

born to her as an auspicious sign; and may her name be called in Israel (*baby's name*, daughter of *father's name*). Her husband, the child's father, is making a contribution to charity. As a reward for this, may father and mother merit to raise her to a life of Torah, to the marriage canopy, and to good deeds, and let us say: Amen.

FOR A BAR MITZVA

May He who blessed our fathers, Abraham, Isaac and Jacob, bless (*name*, son of *father's name*) who has completed thirteen years and attained the age of the commandments, who has been called to the Torah to give praise and thanks to God, may His name be blessed, for all the good He has bestowed on him. May the Holy One, blessed be He, protect and sustain him and direct his heart to be perfect with God, to walk in His ways and keep the commandments all the days of his life, and let us say: Amen.

FOR A BAT MITZVA

May He who blessed our fathers, Abraham, Isaac and Jacob, Sarah, Rebecca, Rachel and Leah, bless (*name*, daughter of *father's name*) who has completed twelve years and attained the age of the commandments, and gives praise and thanks to God, may His name be blessed, for all the good He has bestowed on her. May the Holy One, blessed be He, protect and sustain her and direct her heart to be perfect with God, to walk in His ways and keep the commandments all the days of her life, and let us say: Amen.

MEMORIAL (YAHRZEIT) PRAYER

For a male close relative:

אֵל מָלֵא רַחֲמִים God, full of mercy, who dwells on high, grant fitting rest on the wings of the Divine Presence, in the heights of the holy and the pure who shine like the radiance of heaven, to the soul of (*name*, son of *father's name*) who has gone to his eternal home, and to this I pledge (without formal vow) to give charity in his memory, may his resting place be in the Garden of Eden. Therefore, Master of compassion, shelter him in the shadow of Your wings forever and bind his soul in the bond of everlasting life. The LORD is his heritage; may he rest in peace, and let us say: Amen.

For a female close relative:

אֵל מָלֵא רַחֲמִים God, full of mercy, who dwells on high, grant fitting rest on the wings of the Divine Presence, in the heights of the holy and the pure who shine like the radiance of heaven, to the soul of (*name*, daughter of *father's name*) who has gone to her eternal home, and to this I pledge (without formal vow) to give charity in her memory, may her resting place be in the Garden of Eden. Therefore, Master of compassion, shelter her in the shadow of Your wings forever and bind her soul in the bond of everlasting life. The LORD is her heritage; may she rest in peace, and let us say: Amen.

שֶׁנּוֹלְדָה לָהּ לְמַזָּל טוֹב וְיִקָּרֵא שְׁמָהּ בְּיִשְׂרָאֵל (פלונית בת פלוני), בַּעֲבוּר שֶׁבַּעְלָהּ וְאָבִיהָ נוֹדֵר צְדָקָה בַּעֲדָהּ. בִּשְׂכַר זֶה יְזַכּוּ אָבִיהָ וְאִמָּהּ לְגַדְּלָהּ לְתוֹרָה וּלְחֻפָּה וּלְמַעֲשִׂים טוֹבִים, וְנֹאמַר אָמֵן.

מי שברך לבר מצוה

מִי שֶׁבֵּרַךְ אֲבוֹתֵינוּ אַבְרָהָם יִצְחָק וְיַעֲקֹב הוּא יְבָרֵךְ אֶת (פלוני בן פלוני) שֶׁמָּלְאוּ לוֹ שְׁלֹשׁ עֶשְׂרֵה שָׁנָה וְהִגִּיעַ לְמִצְוֹת, וְעָלָה לַתּוֹרָה, לָתֵת שֶׁבַח וְהוֹדָיָה לְהַשֵּׁם יִתְבָּרַךְ עַל כָּל הַטּוֹבָה שֶׁגָּמַל אִתּוֹ. יִשְׁמְרֵהוּ הַקָּדוֹשׁ בָּרוּךְ הוּא וִיחַיֵּיהוּ, וִיכוֹנֵן אֶת לִבּוֹ לִהְיוֹת שָׁלֵם עִם יהוה וְלָלֶכֶת בִּדְרָכָיו וְלִשְׁמֹר מִצְוֹתָיו כָּל הַיָּמִים, וְנֹאמַר אָמֵן.

מי שברך לבת מצוה

מִי שֶׁבֵּרַךְ אֲבוֹתֵינוּ אַבְרָהָם יִצְחָק וְיַעֲקֹב, שָׂרָה רִבְקָה רָחֵל וְלֵאָה, הוּא יְבָרֵךְ אֶת (פלונית בת פלוני) שֶׁמָּלְאוּ לָהּ שְׁתֵּים עֶשְׂרֵה שָׁנָה וְהִגִּיעָה לְמִצְוֹת, וְנוֹתֶנֶת שֶׁבַח וְהוֹדָיָה לְהַשֵּׁם יִתְבָּרַךְ עַל כָּל הַטּוֹבָה שֶׁגָּמַל אִתָּהּ. יִשְׁמְרֶהָ הַקָּדוֹשׁ בָּרוּךְ הוּא וִיחַיֶּהָ, וִיכוֹנֵן אֶת לִבָּהּ לִהְיוֹת שָׁלֵם עִם יהוה וְלָלֶכֶת בִּדְרָכָיו וְלִשְׁמֹר מִצְוֹתָיו כָּל הַיָּמִים, וְנֹאמַר אָמֵן.

הזכרת נשמות

For a male close relative:

אֵל מָלֵא רַחֲמִים, שׁוֹכֵן בַּמְּרוֹמִים, הַמְצֵא מְנוּחָה נְכוֹנָה עַל כַּנְפֵי הַשְּׁכִינָה, בְּמַעֲלוֹת קְדוֹשִׁים וּטְהוֹרִים, כְּזֹהַר הָרָקִיעַ מַזְהִירִים, לְנִשְׁמַת (פלוני בן פלוני) שֶׁהָלַךְ לְעוֹלָמוֹ, בַּעֲבוּר שֶׁבְּלִי נֶדֶר אֶתֵּן צְדָקָה בְּעַד הַזְכָּרַת נִשְׁמָתוֹ, בְּגַן עֵדֶן תְּהֵא מְנוּחָתוֹ. לָכֵן, בַּעַל הָרַחֲמִים יַסְתִּירֵהוּ בְּסֵתֶר כְּנָפָיו לְעוֹלָמִים, וְיִצְרוֹר בִּצְרוֹר הַחַיִּים אֶת נִשְׁמָתוֹ, יהוה הוּא נַחֲלָתוֹ, וְיָנוּחַ בְּשָׁלוֹם עַל מִשְׁכָּבוֹ, וְנֹאמַר אָמֵן.

For a female close relative:

אֵל מָלֵא רַחֲמִים, שׁוֹכֵן בַּמְּרוֹמִים, הַמְצֵא מְנוּחָה נְכוֹנָה עַל כַּנְפֵי הַשְּׁכִינָה, בְּמַעֲלוֹת קְדוֹשִׁים וּטְהוֹרִים, כְּזֹהַר הָרָקִיעַ מַזְהִירִים, לְנִשְׁמַת (פלונית בת פלוני) שֶׁהָלְכָה לְעוֹלָמָהּ, בַּעֲבוּר שֶׁבְּלִי נֶדֶר אֶתֵּן צְדָקָה בְּעַד הַזְכָּרַת נִשְׁמָתָהּ, בְּגַן עֵדֶן תְּהֵא מְנוּחָתָהּ. לָכֵן, בַּעַל הָרַחֲמִים יַסְתִּירֶהָ בְּסֵתֶר כְּנָפָיו לְעוֹלָמִים, וְיִצְרוֹר בִּצְרוֹר הַחַיִּים אֶת נִשְׁמָתָהּ, יהוה הוּא נַחֲלָתָהּ, וְתָנוּחַ בְּשָׁלוֹם עַל מִשְׁכָּבָהּ, וְנֹאמַר אָמֵן.

HALF KADDISH

After the Reading of the Torah, the Reader says Half Kaddish:

Reader: יִתְגַּדַּל Magnified and sanctified may His great name be,
in the world He created by His will.
May He establish His kingdom
in your lifetime and in your days,
and in the lifetime of all the house of Israel,
swiftly and soon –
and say: Amen.

All: May His great name be blessed for ever and all time.

Reader: Blessed and praised, glorified and exalted,
raised and honored, uplifted and lauded
be the name of the Holy One,
blessed be He,
beyond any blessing,
song, praise and consolation
uttered in the world –
and say: Amen.

The Torah scroll is lifted and the congregation says:

וְזֹאת הַתּוֹרָה This is the Torah   *Deut. 4*
that Moses placed before the children of Israel,
at the LORD's commandment, by the hand of Moses.   *Num. 9*

Some add:

It is a tree of life to those who grasp it, and those who uphold it are happy.   *Prov. 3*
Its ways are ways of pleasantness, and all its paths are peace.
Long life is at its right hand; at its left, riches and honor.
It pleased the LORD for the sake of [Israel's] righteousness,   *Is. 42*
to make the Torah great and glorious.

On those Mondays and Thursdays when Taḥanun is said,
the Leader says the following while the Torah scroll is being bound:

יְהִי רָצוֹן May it be the will of our Father in heaven to establish
(the Temple), home of our life,
and to restore His Presence to our midst,
swiftly in our days – and let us say: Amen.

חצי קדיש

After the קריאת התורה, *the* קורא *says* חצי קדיש:

קורא: יִתְגַּדַּל וְיִתְקַדַּשׁ שְׁמֵהּ רַבָּא (קהל: אָמֵן)
בְּעָלְמָא דִּי בְרָא כִרְעוּתֵהּ
וְיַמְלִיךְ מַלְכוּתֵהּ
בְּחַיֵּיכוֹן וּבְיוֹמֵיכוֹן וּבְחַיֵּי דְכָל בֵּית יִשְׂרָאֵל
בַּעֲגָלָא וּבִזְמַן קָרִיב, וְאִמְרוּ אָמֵן. (קהל: אָמֵן)

קורא וקהל: יְהֵא שְׁמֵהּ רַבָּא מְבָרַךְ לְעָלַם וּלְעָלְמֵי עָלְמַיָּא.

קורא: יִתְבָּרַךְ וְיִשְׁתַּבַּח וְיִתְפָּאַר וְיִתְרוֹמַם וְיִתְנַשֵּׂא
וְיִתְהַדָּר וְיִתְעַלֶּה וְיִתְהַלָּל
שְׁמֵהּ דְּקֻדְשָׁא בְּרִיךְ הוּא (קהל: בְּרִיךְ הוּא)
לְעֵלָּא מִן כָּל בִּרְכָתָא / בעשרת ימי תשובה: לְעֵלָּא לְעֵלָּא מִכָּל בִּרְכָתָא/
וְשִׁירָתָא, תֻּשְׁבְּחָתָא וְנֶחֱמָתָא
דַּאֲמִירָן בְּעָלְמָא, וְאִמְרוּ אָמֵן. (קהל: אָמֵן)

The ספר תורה *is lifted and the* קהל *says:*

דברים ד | וְזֹאת הַתּוֹרָה אֲשֶׁר־שָׂם מֹשֶׁה לִפְנֵי בְּנֵי יִשְׂרָאֵל:

במדבר ט | עַל־פִּי יהוה בְּיַד־מֹשֶׁה:

Some add:

משלי ג | עֵץ־חַיִּים הִיא לַמַּחֲזִיקִים בָּהּ וְתֹמְכֶיהָ מְאֻשָּׁר:
דְּרָכֶיהָ דַרְכֵי־נֹעַם וְכָל־נְתִיבוֹתֶיהָ שָׁלוֹם:
אֹרֶךְ יָמִים בִּימִינָהּ, בִּשְׂמֹאולָהּ עֹשֶׁר וְכָבוֹד:

ישעיה מב | יהוה חָפֵץ לְמַעַן צִדְקוֹ יַגְדִּיל תּוֹרָה וְיַאְדִּיר:

On those Mondays and Thursdays when תחנון *is said,*
the שליח ציבור *says the following while the* ספר תורה *is being bound:*

יְהִי רָצוֹן מִלְּפְנֵי אָבִינוּ שֶׁבַּשָּׁמַיִם, לְכוֹנֵן אֶת בֵּית חַיֵּינוּ
וּלְהָשִׁיב אֶת שְׁכִינָתוֹ בְּתוֹכֵנוּ
בִּמְהֵרָה בְיָמֵינוּ, וְנֹאמַר אָמֵן.

יְהִי רָצוֹן May it be the will of our Father in heaven
        to have compassion on us and our remnant,
        and to keep destruction and plague away from us
        and from all His people the house of Israel –
        and let us say: Amen.

יְהִי רָצוֹן May it be the will of our Father in heaven
        to preserve among us the sages of Israel:
        them, their wives, their sons and daughters,
        their disciples and their disciples' disciples,
        in all their dwelling places – and let us say: Amen.

יְהִי רָצוֹן May it be the will of our Father in heaven
        that we may hear and be given good tidings
        of salvation and consolation,
        and that our dispersed be gathered
        from the four quarters of the earth – and let us say: Amen.

All:

אַחֵינוּ As for our brothers of the whole house of Israel who are in distress
or captivity, on sea or land, may the All-Present have compassion on them
and lead them from distress to relief, from darkness to light, and from
oppression to freedom, now, swiftly and soon – and let us say: Amen.

RETURNING THE TORAH TO THE ARK

The Ark is opened. The Leader takes the Torah scroll and says:

יְהַלְלוּ Let them praise the name of the LORD,
        for His name alone is sublime.
                    Ps. 148

The congregation responds:

הוֹדוֹ His majesty is above earth and heaven.
        He has raised the horn of His people,
        for the glory of all His devoted ones,
        the children of Israel, the people close to Him.
        Halleluya!

יְהִי רָצוֹן מִלִּפְנֵי אָבִינוּ שֶׁבַּשָּׁמַיִם, לְרַחֵם עָלֵינוּ וְעַל פְּלֵיטָתֵנוּ
וְלִמְנֹעַ מַשְׁחִית וּמַגֵּפָה מֵעָלֵינוּ
וּמֵעַל כָּל עַמּוֹ בֵּית יִשְׂרָאֵל, וְנֹאמַר אָמֵן.

יְהִי רָצוֹן מִלִּפְנֵי אָבִינוּ שֶׁבַּשָּׁמַיִם, לְקַיֵּם בָּנוּ חַכְמֵי יִשְׂרָאֵל
הֵם וּנְשֵׁיהֶם וּבְנֵיהֶם וּבְנוֹתֵיהֶם
וְתַלְמִידֵיהֶם וְתַלְמִידֵי תַלְמִידֵיהֶם
בְּכָל מְקוֹמוֹת מוֹשְׁבוֹתֵיהֶם, וְנֹאמַר אָמֵן.

יְהִי רָצוֹן מִלִּפְנֵי אָבִינוּ שֶׁבַּשָּׁמַיִם
שֶׁנִּשְׁמַע וְנִתְבַּשֵּׂר בְּשׂוֹרוֹת טוֹבוֹת, יְשׁוּעוֹת וְנֶחָמוֹת
וִיקַבֵּץ נִדָּחֵינוּ מֵאַרְבַּע כַּנְפוֹת הָאָרֶץ, וְנֹאמַר אָמֵן.

All:

אַחֵינוּ כָּל בֵּית יִשְׂרָאֵל, הַנְּתוּנִים בְּצָרָה וּבְשִׁבְיָה, הָעוֹמְדִים בֵּין בַּיָּם
וּבֵין בַּיַּבָּשָׁה, הַמָּקוֹם יְרַחֵם עֲלֵיהֶם וְיוֹצִיאֵם מִצָּרָה לִרְוָחָה, וּמֵאֲפֵלָה
לְאוֹרָה, וּמִשִּׁעְבּוּד לִגְאֻלָּה, הַשְׁתָּא בַּעֲגָלָא וּבִזְמַן קָרִיב, וְנֹאמַר אָמֵן.

הכנסת ספר תורה

ארון קודש *The* ספר תורה *is opened. The* שליח ציבור *takes the* ארון קודש *and says:*

תהלים קמח

יְהַלְלוּ אֶת־שֵׁם יהוה, כִּי נִשְׂגָּב שְׁמוֹ, לְבַדּוֹ

The קהל *responds:*

הוֹדוֹ עַל־אֶרֶץ וְשָׁמָיִם:
וַיָּרֶם קֶרֶן לְעַמּוֹ
תְּהִלָּה לְכָל־חֲסִידָיו
לִבְנֵי יִשְׂרָאֵל עַם קְרֹבוֹ, הַלְלוּיָהּ:

As the Torah scroll is returned to the Ark, say:

לְדָוִד מִזְמוֹר A psalm of David. The earth is the LORD's and all it con- Ps. 24
tains, the world and all who live in it. For He founded it on the seas
and established it on the streams. Who may climb the mountain
of the LORD? Who may stand in His holy place? He who has clean
hands and a pure heart, who has not taken My name in vain, or sworn
deceitfully. He shall receive blessing from the LORD, and just reward
from God, his salvation. This is a generation of those who seek Him,
the descendants of Jacob who seek Your presence, Selah! Lift up your
heads, O gates; be uplifted, eternal doors, so that the King of glory
may enter. Who is the King of glory? It is the LORD, strong and mighty,
the LORD mighty in battle. Lift up your heads, O gates; lift them up,
eternal doors, so that the King of glory may enter. Who is He, the
King of glory? The LORD of hosts, He is the King of glory, Selah!

As the Torah scroll is placed into the Ark, say:

וּבְנֻחֹה יֹאמַר When the Ark came to rest, Moses would say: "Return, Num. 10
O LORD, to the myriad thousands of Israel." Advance, LORD, to Your Ps. 132
resting place, You and Your mighty Ark. Your priests are clothed in
righteousness, and Your devoted ones sing in joy. For the sake of
Your servant David, do not reject Your anointed one. For I give you Prov. 4
good instruction; do not forsake My Torah. It is a tree of life to those Prov. 3
who grasp it, and those who uphold it are happy. Its ways are ways of
pleasantness, and all its paths are peace. ‣ Turn us back, O LORD, to Lam. 5
You, and we will return. Renew our days as of old.

The Ark is closed.

וּבְנֻחֹה יֹאמַר *When the Ark came to rest:* These words, taken from Numbers 10:36,
recall the journeys of the Israelites through the wilderness in the days of Moses.
They parallel the words we say when the scroll is taken out, "Whenever the
Ark set out" (page 158), said by the Israelites when they began a new journey.
Throughout the centuries, wherever Jews went, they took the Torah with them:
it became their "portable homeland." עֵץ־חַיִּים הִיא לַמַּחֲזִיקִים בָּהּ *It is a tree of life
to those who grasp it:* though Adam and Eve were forbidden to eat the fruit of
the tree of life (Gen. 3:22), the Torah is our intimation of eternity in the midst
of time. Immortality is a matter, not of *how long* we live, but of *how* we live.

As the ספר תורה *is returned to the* ארון קודש, *say:*

תהלים כד

לְדָוִד מִזְמוֹר, לַיהוה הָאָרֶץ וּמְלוֹאָהּ, תֵּבֵל וְיִשְׁבֵי בָהּ: כִּי־הוּא
עַל־יַמִּים יְסָדָהּ, וְעַל־נְהָרוֹת יְכוֹנְנֶהָ: מִי־יַעֲלֶה בְהַר־יהוה,
וּמִי־יָקוּם בִּמְקוֹם קָדְשׁוֹ: נְקִי כַפַּיִם וּבַר־לֵבָב, אֲשֶׁר לֹא־נָשָׂא
לַשָּׁוְא נַפְשִׁי וְלֹא נִשְׁבַּע לְמִרְמָה: יִשָּׂא בְרָכָה מֵאֵת יהוה, וּצְדָקָה
מֵאֱלֹהֵי יִשְׁעוֹ: זֶה דּוֹר דֹּרְשָׁו, מְבַקְשֵׁי פָנֶיךָ, יַעֲקֹב, סֶלָה: שְׂאוּ
שְׁעָרִים רָאשֵׁיכֶם, וְהִנָּשְׂאוּ פִּתְחֵי עוֹלָם, וְיָבוֹא מֶלֶךְ הַכָּבוֹד:
מִי זֶה מֶלֶךְ הַכָּבוֹד, יהוה עִזּוּז וְגִבּוֹר, יהוה גִּבּוֹר מִלְחָמָה: שְׂאוּ
שְׁעָרִים רָאשֵׁיכֶם, וּשְׂאוּ פִּתְחֵי עוֹלָם, וְיָבֹא מֶלֶךְ הַכָּבוֹד: מִי הוּא
זֶה מֶלֶךְ הַכָּבוֹד, יהוה צְבָאוֹת הוּא מֶלֶךְ הַכָּבוֹד, סֶלָה:

As the ספר תורה *is placed into the* ארון קודש, *say:*

במדברי
תהלים קלב

וּבְנֻחֹה יֹאמַר, שׁוּבָה יהוה רִבְבוֹת אַלְפֵי יִשְׂרָאֵל: ‣ קוּמָה יהוה
לִמְנוּחָתֶךָ, אַתָּה וַאֲרוֹן עֻזֶּךָ: כֹּהֲנֶיךָ יִלְבְּשׁוּ־צֶדֶק, וַחֲסִידֶיךָ יְרַנֵּנוּ:

משלי ד

בַּעֲבוּר דָּוִד עַבְדֶּךָ אַל־תָּשֵׁב פְּנֵי מְשִׁיחֶךָ: כִּי לֶקַח טוֹב נָתַתִּי

משלי ג

לָכֶם, תּוֹרָתִי אַל־תַּעֲזֹבוּ: עֵץ־חַיִּים הִיא לַמַּחֲזִיקִים בָּהּ, וְתֹמְכֶיהָ

איכה ה

מְאֻשָּׁר: דְּרָכֶיהָ דַרְכֵי־נֹעַם וְכָל־נְתִיבֹתֶיהָ שָׁלוֹם: ‣ הֲשִׁיבֵנוּ יהוה
אֵלֶיךָ וְנָשׁוּבָה, חַדֵּשׁ יָמֵינוּ כְּקֶדֶם:

The ארון קודש *is closed.*

───────────────────────────────

לְדָוִד מִזְמוֹר *A psalm of David:* A psalm of joyous procession to the Temple.
It begins with creation, "The earth is the Lord's," and moves directly to the
moral requirements of the religious life: "Who may climb the mountain of
the Lord?" Just as God created an orderly universe, so we are commanded to
create an orderly society. Worshiping God at the Temple may not be divorced
from honesty and integrity in everyday life. The latter part of the psalm, "Lift
up your heads, O gates," was said by King Solomon when the Ark, containing the tablets of the covenant, was first brought into the Temple (*Shabbat*
30a). As the Torah scroll is returned to the Ark, we recall that historic scene.

CONCLUSION OF THE SERVICE

Some have the custom to touch the hand-tefillin at °, and the head-tefillin at °°.

אַשְׁרֵי Happy are those who dwell in Your House;   *Ps. 84*
they shall continue to praise You, Selah!
Happy are the people for whom this is so;   *Ps. 144*
happy are the people whose God is the LORD.
A song of praise by David.   *Ps. 145*

    I will exalt You, my God, the King, and bless Your name for
    ever and all time. Every day I will bless You, and praise Your
    name for ever and all time. Great is the LORD and greatly to be
    praised; His greatness is unfathomable. One generation will
    praise Your works to the next, and tell of Your mighty deeds.
    On the glorious splendor of Your majesty I will meditate, and
    on the acts of Your wonders. They shall talk of the power of
    Your awesome deeds, and I will tell of Your greatness. They shall
    recite the record of Your great goodness, and sing with joy of
    Your righteousness. The LORD is gracious and compassionate,
    slow to anger and great in loving-kindness. The LORD is good
    to all, and His compassion extends to all His works. All Your
    works shall thank You, LORD, and Your devoted ones shall bless
    You. They shall talk of the glory of Your kingship, and speak
    of Your might. To make known to mankind His mighty deeds

---

your mouth will not depart from your mouth, or from the mouth of your
children"). Thus are joined study, the *internalization* of God's word, and redemption, the *externalization* of God's word as we prepare to enter the world
of work, striving to live by the Torah's commandments.

אַשְׁרֵי *Happy are those:* Just as we say *Ashrei before* the Shema and the Amida,
so do we say it *after*, following the custom of "the pious of old" who devoted
time before prayer in preparation, and afterward in meditation. According to
the Talmud, the practice was based on the first line of *Ashrei* itself: "Happy
are those who dwell in Your House."

סיום התפילה

Some have the custom to touch the תפילין של יד *at* °, *and the* תפילין של ראש *at* °°.

תהלים פד

תהלים קמד

תהלים קמה

אַשְׁרֵי יוֹשְׁבֵי בֵיתֶךָ, עוֹד יְהַלְלוּךָ סֶּלָה:

אַשְׁרֵי הָעָם שֶׁכָּכָה לּוֹ, אַשְׁרֵי הָעָם שֶׁיהוה אֱלֹהָיו:

תְּהִלָּה לְדָוִד

אֲרוֹמִמְךָ אֱלוֹהַי הַמֶּלֶךְ, וַאֲבָרְכָה שִׁמְךָ לְעוֹלָם וָעֶד:

בְּכָל־יוֹם אֲבָרְכֶךָּ, וַאֲהַלְלָה שִׁמְךָ לְעוֹלָם וָעֶד:

גָּדוֹל יהוה וּמְהֻלָּל מְאֹד, וְלִגְדֻלָּתוֹ אֵין חֵקֶר:

דּוֹר לְדוֹר יְשַׁבַּח מַעֲשֶׂיךָ, וּגְבוּרֹתֶיךָ יַגִּידוּ:

הֲדַר כְּבוֹד הוֹדֶךָ, וְדִבְרֵי נִפְלְאֹתֶיךָ אָשִׂיחָה:

וֶעֱזוּז נוֹרְאֹתֶיךָ יֹאמֵרוּ, וּגְדוּלָּתְךָ אֲסַפְּרֶנָּה:

זֵכֶר רַב־טוּבְךָ יַבִּיעוּ, וְצִדְקָתְךָ יְרַנֵּנוּ:

חַנּוּן וְרַחוּם יהוה, אֶרֶךְ אַפַּיִם וּגְדָל־חָסֶד:

טוֹב־יהוה לַכֹּל, וְרַחֲמָיו עַל־כָּל־מַעֲשָׂיו:

יוֹדוּךָ יהוה כָּל־מַעֲשֶׂיךָ, וַחֲסִידֶיךָ יְבָרְכוּכָה:

CONCLUSION OF THE SERVICE

The final section of the prayers now begins. It interweaves two distinct elements: one is a formal conclusion to the morning service, including *Aleinu* and the Daily Psalm, with an emphasis on the theme of Redemption; and the other is study. It was the custom in ancient times, and in many places today, to devote time after prayer to Torah learning. This originally included texts from the prophetic books. The close of a study session was marked by a series of prayers beginning "You are the Holy One." The Kaddish had its origin in such sessions.

The link between these two ideas – redemption and Torah study – is created in an inspired fashion, by reading two consecutive verses from Isaiah, the first of which speaks of redemption ("A redeemer will come to Zion"), and the second of which talks of Torah study ("My words I have placed in

and the glorious majesty of His kingship. Your kingdom is an
everlasting kingdom, and Your reign is for all generations. The
Lord supports all who fall, and raises all who are bowed down.
All raise their eyes to You in hope, and You give them their food
in due season. °You open Your hand, °°and satisfy every living
thing with favor. The Lord is righteous in all His ways, and
kind in all He does. The Lord is close to all who call on Him,
to all who call on Him in truth. He fulfills the will of those
who revere Him; He hears their cry and saves them. The Lord
guards all who love Him, but all the wicked He will destroy.
‣ My mouth shall speak the praise of the Lord, and all creatures
shall bless His holy name for ever and all time.
We will bless the Lord now and for ever. Halleluya!   Ps. 115

*Omit on Rosh Hodesh, Erev Pesah, Erev Yom Kippur, Hanukka,
the 14th and 15th of Adar 1, Purim and Shushan Purim, Yom HaAtzma'ut,
Yom Yerushalayim, Tisha B'Av, or in a house of mourning, and in Israel on Isru Hag.*

לַמְנַצֵּחַ For the conductor of music. A psalm of David. May the Lord   Ps. 20
answer you when you are in distress; may the name of Jacob's God
protect you. May He send you help from the Sanctuary and support
from Zion. May He remember all your meal-offerings and accept
your burnt-offerings, Selah! May He give you your heart's desire and
make all your plans succeed. We will shout for joy at Your salvation
and lift a banner in the name of our God. May the Lord grant all
your requests. Now I know that the Lord saves His anointed; He
answers him from His holy heaven with the saving power of His
right hand. Some trust in chariots, others in horses, but we call on
the name of the Lord our God. They were brought to their knees
and fell, but we rose up and stood firm. ‣ Lord, save! May the King
answer us on the day we call.

dangers, we ask God to keep us from harm. Because of the solemnity of its
mood, this psalm is omitted on festivals or in a house of mourning, so as not
to subtract from the joy of the former, or add to the grief of the latter.

כְּבוֹד מַלְכוּתְךָ יֹאמֵרוּ, וּגְבוּרָתְךָ יְדַבֵּרוּ:

לְהוֹדִיעַ לִבְנֵי הָאָדָם גְּבוּרֹתָיו, וּכְבוֹד הֲדַר מַלְכוּתוֹ:

מַלְכוּתְךָ מַלְכוּת כָּל־עֹלָמִים, וּמֶמְשַׁלְתְּךָ בְּכָל־דּוֹר וָדֹר:

סוֹמֵךְ יהוה לְכָל־הַנֹּפְלִים, וְזוֹקֵף לְכָל־הַכְּפוּפִים:

עֵינֵי־כֹל אֵלֶיךָ יְשַׂבֵּרוּ, וְאַתָּה נוֹתֵן־לָהֶם אֶת־אָכְלָם בְּעִתּוֹ:

°פּוֹתֵחַ אֶת־יָדֶךָ, °°וּמַשְׂבִּיעַ לְכָל־חַי רָצוֹן:

צַדִּיק יהוה בְּכָל־דְּרָכָיו, וְחָסִיד בְּכָל־מַעֲשָׂיו:

קָרוֹב יהוה לְכָל־קֹרְאָיו, לְכֹל אֲשֶׁר יִקְרָאֻהוּ בֶאֱמֶת:

רְצוֹן־יְרֵאָיו יַעֲשֶׂה, וְאֶת־שַׁוְעָתָם יִשְׁמַע, וְיוֹשִׁיעֵם:

שׁוֹמֵר יהוה אֶת־כָּל־אֹהֲבָיו, וְאֵת כָּל־הָרְשָׁעִים יַשְׁמִיד:

‹ תְּהִלַּת יהוה יְדַבֶּר־פִּי, וִיבָרֵךְ כָּל־בָּשָׂר שֵׁם קָדְשׁוֹ לְעוֹלָם וָעֶד:

וַאֲנַחְנוּ נְבָרֵךְ יָהּ מֵעַתָּה וְעַד־עוֹלָם, הַלְלוּיָהּ:

תהלים קטו

Omit on חֲנֻכָּה, עֶרֶב יוֹם כִּפּוּר, עֶרֶב פֶּסַח, ראש חֹדֶשׁ,
the 14th and 15th of אֲדָר א', שׁוּשַׁן פּוּרִים and פּוּרִים, יוֹם הָעַצְמָאוּת,
אִסְרוּ חַג on אֶרֶץ יִשְׂרָאֵל or in a house of mourning, and in תִּשְׁעָה בְּאָב, יוֹם יְרוּשָׁלַיִם.

תהלים כ

לַמְנַצֵּחַ מִזְמוֹר לְדָוִד: יַעַנְךָ יהוה בְּיוֹם צָרָה, יְשַׂגֶּבְךָ שֵׁם אֱלֹהֵי

יַעֲקֹב: יִשְׁלַח־עֶזְרְךָ מִקֹּדֶשׁ, וּמִצִּיּוֹן יִסְעָדֶךָּ: יִזְכֹּר כָּל־מִנְחֹתֶיךָ,

וְעוֹלָתְךָ יְדַשְּׁנֶה סֶלָה: יִתֶּן־לְךָ כִלְבָבֶךָ וְכָל־עֲצָתְךָ יְמַלֵּא: נְרַנְּנָה

בִּישׁוּעָתֶךָ, וּבְשֵׁם־אֱלֹהֵינוּ נִדְגֹּל, יְמַלֵּא יהוה כָּל־מִשְׁאֲלוֹתֶיךָ: עַתָּה

יָדַעְתִּי כִּי הוֹשִׁיעַ יהוה מְשִׁיחוֹ, יַעֲנֵהוּ מִשְּׁמֵי קָדְשׁוֹ, בִּגְבוּרוֹת יֵשַׁע

יְמִינוֹ: אֵלֶּה בָרֶכֶב וְאֵלֶּה בַסּוּסִים, וַאֲנַחְנוּ בְּשֵׁם־יהוה אֱלֹהֵינוּ

נַזְכִּיר: הֵמָּה כָּרְעוּ וְנָפָלוּ, וַאֲנַחְנוּ קַמְנוּ וַנִּתְעוֹדָד: ‹ יהוה הוֹשִׁיעָה,

הַמֶּלֶךְ יַעֲנֵנוּ בְיוֹם־קָרְאֵנוּ:

לַמְנַצֵּחַ *Psalm 20*: A prayer for protection from harm. As prayer reaches its
close, and we prepare to reenter the outside world with its hazards and

*In a house of mourning and on Tisha B'Av omit the verse beginning
"As for Me" and continue with "You are the Holy One."*

וּבָא לְצִיּוֹן גּוֹאֵל "A redeemer will come to Zion,   *Is. 59*
to those in Jacob who repent of their sins," declares the LORD.
"As for Me, this is My covenant with them," says the LORD.
"My spirit, that is on you, and My words I have placed in your
mouth will not depart from your mouth, or from the mouth of
your children, or from the mouth of their descendants from this
time on and for ever," says the LORD.

▸ You are the Holy One, enthroned on the praises of Israel.   *Ps. 22*
And (the angels) call to one another, saying, "Holy, holy, holy   *Is. 6*
is the LORD of hosts; the whole world is filled with His glory."
And they receive permission from one another, saying: *Targum*
"Holy in the highest heavens, home of His Presence; holy on earth,   *Yonatan*
the work of His strength; holy for ever and all time is the LORD of hosts;   *Is. 6*
the whole earth is full of His radiant glory."

▸ Then a wind lifted me up and I heard behind me the sound of a   *Ezek. 3*
great noise, saying, "Blessed is the LORD's glory from His place."
Then a wind lifted me up and I heard behind me   *Targum*
the sound of a great tempest of those who uttered praise, saying,   *Yonatan*
"Blessed is the LORD's glory from the place of the home of His Presence."   *Ezek. 3*

The LORD shall reign for ever and all time.   *Ex. 15*
The LORD's kingdom is established for ever and all time.   *Targum*
     Onkelos
     Ex. 15

יהוה LORD, God of Abraham, Isaac and Yisrael, our ancestors, may   *1 Chr. 29*
You keep this for ever so that it forms the thoughts in Your people's
heart, and directs their heart toward You. He is compassionate. He   *Ps. 78*
forgives iniquity and does not destroy. Repeatedly He suppresses
His anger, not rousing His full wrath. For You, my LORD, are good   *Ps. 86*

─────────────────────────────────────

service, known as *Kedusha deSidra*. Here, it is incorporated into an act of
study. Hence the verses of the *Kedusha* are followed by their Aramaic trans-
lations and expansions (Aramaic was for a long time the language of study).

In a house of mourning and on תשעה באב *omit the verse*
beginning וַאֲנִי זֹאת בְּרִיתִי *and continue with* וְאַתָּה קָדוֹשׁ

ישעיה נט

וּבָא לְצִיּוֹן גּוֹאֵל, וּלְשָׁבֵי פֶשַׁע בְּיַעֲקֹב, נְאֻם יהוה:

וַאֲנִי זֹאת בְּרִיתִי אוֹתָם, אָמַר יהוה

רוּחִי אֲשֶׁר עָלֶיךָ וּדְבָרַי אֲשֶׁר־שַׂמְתִּי בְּפִיךָ

לֹא־יָמוּשׁוּ מִפִּיךָ וּמִפִּי זַרְעֲךָ וּמִפִּי זֶרַע זַרְעֲךָ

אָמַר יהוה, מֵעַתָּה וְעַד־עוֹלָם:

תהלים כב
ישעיהו

‹ וְאַתָּה קָדוֹשׁ יוֹשֵׁב תְּהִלּוֹת יִשְׂרָאֵל: וְקָרָא זֶה אֶל־זֶה וְאָמַר
קָדוֹשׁ, קָדוֹשׁ, קָדוֹשׁ, יהוה צְבָאוֹת, מְלֹא כָל־הָאָרֶץ כְּבוֹדוֹ:

תרגום
יונתן
ישעיהו

וּמְקַבְּלִין דֵּין מִן דֵּין וְאָמְרִין, קַדִּישׁ בִּשְׁמֵי מְרוֹמָא עִלָּאָה בֵּית שְׁכִינְתֵּהּ
קַדִּישׁ עַל אַרְעָא עוֹבַד גְּבוּרְתֵּהּ, קַדִּישׁ לְעָלַם וּלְעָלְמֵי עָלְמַיָּא
יהוה צְבָאוֹת, מַלְיָא כָל אַרְעָא זִיו יְקָרֵהּ.

יחזקאל ג

‹ וַתִּשָּׂאֵנִי רוּחַ, וָאֶשְׁמַע אַחֲרַי קוֹל רַעַשׁ גָּדוֹל
בָּרוּךְ כְּבוֹד־יהוה מִמְּקוֹמוֹ:

תרגום
יונתן
יחזקאל ג

וּנְטָלַתְנִי רוּחָא, וּשְׁמָעִית בַּתְרַי קָל זִיעַ סַגִּיא, דִּמְשַׁבְּחִין וְאָמְרִין
בְּרִיךְ יְקָרָא דַיהוה מֵאֲתַר בֵּית שְׁכִינְתֵּהּ.

שמות טו
תרגום
אונקלוס
שמות טו

יהוה יִמְלֹךְ לְעֹלָם וָעֶד:
יהוה מַלְכוּתֵהּ קָאֵם לְעָלַם וּלְעָלְמֵי עָלְמַיָּא.

דברי הימים
א כט
תהלים עח

יהוה אֱלֹהֵי אַבְרָהָם יִצְחָק וְיִשְׂרָאֵל אֲבֹתֵינוּ, שָׁמְרָה־זֹּאת לְעוֹלָם
לְיֵצֶר מַחְשְׁבוֹת לְבַב עַמֶּךָ, וְהָכֵן לְבָבָם אֵלֶיךָ: וְהוּא רַחוּם יְכַפֵּר
עָוֹן וְלֹא־יַשְׁחִית, וְהִרְבָּה לְהָשִׁיב אַפּוֹ, וְלֹא־יָעִיר כָּל־חֲמָתוֹ:

וּבָא לְצִיּוֹן גּוֹאֵל *A redeemer will come to Zion:* These two verses (from Isaiah), are
all that remain of the ancient custom of studying prophetic texts after prayer.
וְאַתָּה קָדוֹשׁ *You are the Holy One:* the third and final *Kedusha* of the morning

and forgiving, abundantly kind to all who call on You. Your righ- *Ps. 119*
teousness is eternally righteous, and Your Torah is truth. Grant *Mic. 7*
truth to Jacob, loving-kindness to Abraham, as You promised our
ancestors in ancient times. Blessed is my LORD for day after day *Ps. 68*
He burdens us [with His blessings]; God is our salvation, Selah!
The LORD of hosts is with us; the God of Jacob is our refuge, Selah! *Ps. 46*
LORD of hosts, happy is the one who trusts in You. LORD, save! May *Ps. 84*
the King answer us on the day we call. *Ps. 20*

בָּרוּךְ Blessed is He, our God, who created us for His glory, separating us from those who go astray; who gave us the Torah of truth,
planting within us eternal life. May He open our heart to His Torah,
imbuing our heart with the love and awe of Him, that we may do
His will and serve Him with a perfect heart, so that we neither toil
in vain nor give birth to confusion.

יְהִי רָצוֹן May it be Your will, O LORD our God and God of our ancestors, that we keep Your laws in this world, and thus be worthy to live,
see and inherit goodness and blessing in the Messianic Age and in
the life of the World to Come. So that my soul may sing to You and *Ps. 30*
not be silent. LORD, my God, for ever I will thank You. Blessed is *Jer. 17*
the man who trusts in the LORD, whose trust is in the LORD alone.
Trust in the LORD for evermore, for God, the LORD, is an everlast- *Is. 26*
ing Rock. ‣ Those who know Your name trust in You, for You, LORD, *Ps. 9*
do not forsake those who seek You. The LORD desired, for the sake *Is. 42*
of Israel's merit, to make the Torah great and glorious.

On Rosh Ḥodesh the Leader says Half Kaddish, page 168.
The service then continues with Musaf for Rosh Ḥodesh on page 372.

On other days, the Leader continues with Full Kaddish on the next page.

The prayer, by contrast, looks forward to the future, personal and collective:
personal – may God help us to keep His commandments, and collective –
may we see the coming of the Messianic Age.

תהלים פו
תהלים קיט   כִּי־אַתָּה אֲדֹנָי טוֹב וְסַלָּח, וְרַב־חֶסֶד לְכָל־קֹרְאֶיךָ: צִדְקָתְךָ

מיכה ז   צֶדֶק לְעוֹלָם וְתוֹרָתְךָ אֱמֶת: תִּתֵּן אֱמֶת לְיַעֲקֹב, חֶסֶד לְאַבְרָהָם,

תהלים סח   אֲשֶׁר־נִשְׁבַּעְתָּ לַאֲבֹתֵינוּ מִימֵי קֶדֶם: בָּרוּךְ אֲדֹנָי יוֹם יוֹם יַעֲמָס־

תהלים מו   לָנוּ, הָאֵל יְשׁוּעָתֵנוּ סֶלָה: יהוה צְבָאוֹת עִמָּנוּ, מִשְׂגָּב לָנוּ אֱלֹהֵי

תהלים פד
תהלים כ   יַעֲקֹב סֶלָה: יהוה צְבָאוֹת, אַשְׁרֵי אָדָם בֹּטֵחַ בָּךְ: יהוה הוֹשִׁיעָה,

הַמֶּלֶךְ יַעֲנֵנוּ בְיוֹם־קָרְאֵנוּ:

בָּרוּךְ הוּא אֱלֹהֵינוּ שֶׁבְּרָאָנוּ לִכְבוֹדוֹ, וְהִבְדִּילָנוּ מִן הַתּוֹעִים,
וְנָתַן לָנוּ תּוֹרַת אֱמֶת, וְחַיֵּי עוֹלָם נָטַע בְּתוֹכֵנוּ. הוּא יִפְתַּח לִבֵּנוּ
בְּתוֹרָתוֹ, וְיָשֵׂם בְּלִבֵּנוּ אַהֲבָתוֹ וְיִרְאָתוֹ וְלַעֲשׂוֹת רְצוֹנוֹ וּלְעָבְדוֹ
בְּלֵבָב שָׁלֵם, לְמַעַן לֹא נִיגַע לָרִיק וְלֹא נֵלֵד לַבֶּהָלָה.

יְהִי רָצוֹן מִלְּפָנֶיךָ יהוה אֱלֹהֵינוּ וֵאלֹהֵי אֲבוֹתֵינוּ, שֶׁנִּשְׁמֹר חֻקֶּיךָ
בָּעוֹלָם הַזֶּה, וְנִזְכֶּה וְנִחְיֶה וְנִרְאֶה וְנִירַשׁ טוֹבָה וּבְרָכָה, לִשְׁנֵי

תהלים ל   יְמוֹת הַמָּשִׁיחַ וּלְחַיֵּי הָעוֹלָם הַבָּא. לְמַעַן יְזַמֶּרְךָ כָבוֹד וְלֹא יִדֹּם,

ירמיה יז   יהוה אֱלֹהַי, לְעוֹלָם אוֹדֶךָּ: בָּרוּךְ הַגֶּבֶר אֲשֶׁר יִבְטַח בַּיהוה,

ישעיה כו   וְהָיָה יהוה מִבְטַחוֹ: בִּטְחוּ בַיהוה עֲדֵי־עַד, כִּי בְּיָהּ יהוה צוּר

תהלים ט   עוֹלָמִים: ◄ וְיִבְטְחוּ בְךָ יוֹדְעֵי שְׁמֶךָ, כִּי לֹא־עָזַבְתָּ דֹרְשֶׁיךָ, יהוה:

ישעיה מב   יהוה חָפֵץ לְמַעַן צִדְקוֹ, יַגְדִּיל תּוֹרָה וְיַאְדִּיר:

On ראש חודש the שליח ציבור says חצי קדיש, page 169.
The service then continues with מוסף for ראש חודש on page 373.

On other days the שליח ציבור continues with קדיש שלם on the next page.

בָּרוּךְ הוּא אֱלֹהֵינוּ *Blessed is He, our God:* There now follow a concluding blessing and a prayer. The blessing marks the end of a Torah study session (the
counterpart of the two opening benedictions in the Blessings over the Torah).

FULL KADDISH

Leader: יִתְגַּדַּל Magnified and sanctified may His great name be,
in the world He created by His will.
May He establish His kingdom in your lifetime
and in your days,
and in the lifetime of all the house of Israel,
swiftly and soon –
and say: Amen.

All: May His great name be blessed for ever and all time.

Leader: Blessed and praised,
glorified and exalted,
raised and honored,
uplifted and lauded be
the name of the Holy One,
blessed be He,
beyond any blessing,
song, praise and consolation
uttered in the world –
and say: Amen.

*On Tisha B'Av, omit the next verse and continue
with "May there be great peace."*

May the prayers and pleas of all Israel
be accepted by their Father in heaven –
and say: Amen.

May there be great peace from heaven,
and life for us and all Israel –
and say: Amen.

*Bow, take three steps back, as if taking leave of the Divine Presence,
then bow, first left, then right, then center, while saying:*

May He who makes peace in His high places,
make peace for us and all Israel –
and say: Amen.

קדיש שלם

ש״ץ: יִתְגַּדַּל וְיִתְקַדַּשׁ שְׁמֵהּ רַבָּא (קהל: אָמֵן)
בְּעָלְמָא דִּי בְרָא כִרְעוּתֵהּ
וְיַמְלִיךְ מַלְכוּתֵהּ
בְּחַיֵּיכוֹן וּבְיוֹמֵיכוֹן וּבְחַיֵּי דְּכָל בֵּית יִשְׂרָאֵל
בַּעֲגָלָא וּבִזְמַן קָרִיב, וְאִמְרוּ אָמֵן. (קהל: אָמֵן)

קהל
ושץ: יְהֵא שְׁמֵהּ רַבָּא מְבָרַךְ לְעָלַם וּלְעָלְמֵי עָלְמַיָּא.

ש״ץ: יִתְבָּרַךְ וְיִשְׁתַּבַּח וְיִתְפָּאַר
וְיִתְרוֹמַם וְיִתְנַשֵּׂא וְיִתְהַדָּר וְיִתְעַלֶּה וְיִתְהַלָּל
שְׁמֵהּ דְּקֻדְשָׁא בְּרִיךְ הוּא (קהל: בְּרִיךְ הוּא)
לְעֵלָּא מִן כָּל בִּרְכָתָא
בעשרת ימי תשובה: לְעֵלָּא לְעֵלָּא מִכָּל בִּרְכָתָא/
וְשִׁירָתָא, תֻּשְׁבְּחָתָא וְנֶחֱמָתָא
דַּאֲמִירָן בְּעָלְמָא, וְאִמְרוּ אָמֵן. (קהל: אָמֵן)

On תשעה באב, omit the next verse and continue with יְהֵא שְׁלָמָא.
תִּתְקַבַּל צְלוֹתְהוֹן וּבָעוּתְהוֹן דְּכָל יִשְׂרָאֵל
קֳדָם אֲבוּהוֹן דִּי בִשְׁמַיָּא, וְאִמְרוּ אָמֵן. (קהל: אָמֵן)

יְהֵא שְׁלָמָא רַבָּא מִן שְׁמַיָּא
וְחַיִּים, עָלֵינוּ וְעַל כָּל יִשְׂרָאֵל, וְאִמְרוּ אָמֵן. (קהל: אָמֵן)

Bow, take three steps back, as if taking leave of the Divine Presence,
then bow, first left, then right, then center, while saying:

עֹשֶׂה שָׁלוֹם/ בעשרת ימי תשובה: הַשָּׁלוֹם/ בִּמְרוֹמָיו
הוּא יַעֲשֶׂה שָׁלוֹם עָלֵינוּ וְעַל כָּל יִשְׂרָאֵל
וְאִמְרוּ אָמֵן. (קהל: אָמֵן)

Stand while saying Aleinu. Bow at '.

עָלֵינוּ It is our duty to praise the Master of all,
and ascribe greatness to the Author of creation,
who has not made us like the nations of the lands
nor placed us like the families of the earth;
who has not made our portion like theirs,
nor our destiny like all their multitudes.
(For they worship vanity and emptiness,
and pray to a god who cannot save.)
' But we bow in worship and thank the Supreme King of kings,
the Holy One, blessed be He,
who extends the heavens and establishes the earth,
whose throne of glory is in the heavens above,
and whose power's Presence is in the highest of heights.
He is our God; there is no other.
Truly He is our King, there is none else,
as it is written in His Torah:
"You shall know and take to heart this day that the LORD is God,   *Deut. 4*
in heaven above and on earth below. There is no other."

Therefore, we place our hope in You, LORD our God,
that we may soon see the glory of Your power,
when You will remove abominations from the earth,
and idols will be utterly destroyed,
when the world will be perfected under the sovereignty of the Almighty,
when all humanity will call on Your name,
to turn all the earth's wicked toward You.
All the world's inhabitants will realize and know
that to You every knee must bow and every tongue swear loyalty.
Before You, LORD our God, they will kneel and bow down
and give honor to Your glorious name.

---

statement of the particularity of Jewish faith and its universal aspiration for
humanity.

The first paragraph, was originally used (and still is) as an introduction to the
Blessing of Kingship in the *Musaf* of Rosh HaShana. Less a prayer than a declaration of faith, it speaks of the singular vocation of the Jewish people as bearers

Stand while saying עָלֵינוּ. *Bow at* ˙.

עָלֵינוּ לְשַׁבֵּחַ לַאֲדוֹן הַכֹּל, לָתֵת גְּדֻלָּה לְיוֹצֵר בְּרֵאשִׁית

שֶׁלֹּא עָשָׂנוּ כְּגוֹיֵי הָאֲרָצוֹת, וְלֹא שָׂמָנוּ כְּמִשְׁפְּחוֹת הָאֲדָמָה

שֶׁלֹּא שָׂם חֶלְקֵנוּ כָּהֶם וְגוֹרָלֵנוּ כְּכָל הֲמוֹנָם.

(שֶׁהֵם מִשְׁתַּחֲוִים לְהֶבֶל וָרִיק וּמִתְפַּלְלִים אֶל אֵל לֹא יוֹשִׁיעַ.)

וַאֲנַחְנוּ כּוֹרְעִים וּמִשְׁתַּחֲוִים וּמוֹדִים

לִפְנֵי מֶלֶךְ מַלְכֵי הַמְּלָכִים, הַקָּדוֹשׁ בָּרוּךְ הוּא

שֶׁהוּא נוֹטֶה שָׁמַיִם וְיוֹסֵד אָרֶץ, וּמוֹשַׁב יְקָרוֹ בַּשָּׁמַיִם מִמַּעַל

וּשְׁכִינַת עֻזּוֹ בְּגָבְהֵי מְרוֹמִים.

הוּא אֱלֹהֵינוּ, אֵין עוֹד.

אֱמֶת מַלְכֵּנוּ, אֶפֶס זוּלָתוֹ

כַּכָּתוּב בְּתוֹרָתוֹ

דברים ד

וְיָדַעְתָּ הַיּוֹם וַהֲשֵׁבֹתָ אֶל־לְבָבֶךָ

כִּי יהוה הוּא הָאֱלֹהִים בַּשָּׁמַיִם מִמַּעַל וְעַל־הָאָרֶץ מִתָּחַת, אֵין עוֹד:

עַל כֵּן נְקַוֶּה לְּךָ יהוה אֱלֹהֵינוּ, לִרְאוֹת מְהֵרָה בְּתִפְאֶרֶת עֻזֶּךָ

לְהַעֲבִיר גִּלּוּלִים מִן הָאָרֶץ, וְהָאֱלִילִים כָּרוֹת יִכָּרֵתוּן

לְתַקֵּן עוֹלָם בְּמַלְכוּת שַׁדַּי.

וְכָל בְּנֵי בָשָׂר יִקְרְאוּ בִשְׁמֶךָ לְהַפְנוֹת אֵלֶיךָ כָּל רִשְׁעֵי אָרֶץ.

יַכִּירוּ וְיֵדְעוּ כָּל יוֹשְׁבֵי תֵבֵל

כִּי לְךָ תִּכְרַע כָּל בֶּרֶךְ, תִּשָּׁבַע כָּל לָשׁוֹן.

לְפָנֶיךָ יהוה אֱלֹהֵינוּ יִכְרְעוּ וְיִפֹּלוּ, וְלִכְבוֹד שִׁמְךָ יְקָר יִתֵּנוּ

וִיקַבְּלוּ כֻלָּם אֶת עֹל מַלְכוּתֶךָ

וְתִמְלֹךְ עֲלֵיהֶם מְהֵרָה לְעוֹלָם וָעֶד.

עָלֵינוּ *It is our duty:* Since the twelfth or thirteenth century, it has become the custom to bring all services to a close with the magnificent prayer known as *Aleinu*, a construct of two paragraphs, which together make a striking

They will all accept the yoke of Your kingdom,
and You will reign over them soon and for ever.
For the kingdom is Yours, and to all eternity You will reign in glory,
as it is written in Your Torah: "The LORD will reign for ever and ever."   *Ex. 15*
▸ And it is said: "Then the LORD shall be King over all the earth;   *Zech. 14*
on that day the LORD shall be One and His name One."

Some add:

Have no fear of sudden terror or of the ruin when it overtakes the wicked.   *Prov. 3*
Devise your strategy, but it will be thwarted;   *Is. 8*
propose your plan, but it will not stand, for God is with us.
When you grow old, I will still be the same.   *Is. 46*
When your hair turns gray, I will still carry you.
I made you, I will bear you, I will carry you, and I will rescue you.

MOURNER'S KADDISH

The following prayer, said by mourners, requires the presence of a minyan.
A transliteration can be found on page 699.

Mourner: **יִתְגַּדַּל** Magnified and sanctified
may His great name be,
in the world He created by His will.
May He establish His kingdom
in your lifetime and in your days,
and in the lifetime of all the house of Israel,
swiftly and soon – and say: Amen.

All: May His great name be blessed for ever and all time.

Mourner: Blessed and praised, glorified and exalted,
raised and honored, uplifted and lauded
be the name of the Holy One,
blessed be He,

No prayer more eloquently expresses the dual nature of the Jewish people:
its singular history as the nation chosen to be God's witnesses on earth, and
its universal aspiration for the time when all the inhabitants of earth will
recognize the God in whose image we are formed.

כִּי הַמַּלְכוּת שֶׁלְּךָ הִיא וּלְעוֹלְמֵי עַד תִּמְלֹךְ בְּכָבוֹד

שמות טו

כַּכָּתוּב בְּתוֹרָתֶךָ, יהוה יִמְלֹךְ לְעֹלָם וָעֶד:

זכריה יד

‹ וְנֶאֱמַר, וְהָיָה יהוה לְמֶלֶךְ עַל־כָּל־הָאָרֶץ

בַּיּוֹם הַהוּא יִהְיֶה יהוה אֶחָד וּשְׁמוֹ אֶחָד:

Some add:

משלי ג

אַל־תִּירָא מִפַּחַד פִּתְאֹם וּמִשֹּׁאַת רְשָׁעִים כִּי תָבֹא:

ישעיה ח

עֻצוּ עֵצָה וְתֻפָר, דַּבְּרוּ דָבָר וְלֹא יָקוּם, כִּי עִמָּנוּ אֵל:

ישעיה מו

וְעַד־זִקְנָה אֲנִי הוּא, וְעַד־שֵׂיבָה אֲנִי אֶסְבֹּל, אֲנִי עָשִׂיתִי וַאֲנִי אֶשָּׂא וַאֲנִי אֶסְבֹּל וַאֲמַלֵּט:

קדיש יתום

The following prayer, said by mourners, requires the presence of a מנין.
A transliteration can be found on page 699.

אבל: יִתְגַּדַּל וְיִתְקַדַּשׁ שְׁמֵהּ רַבָּא (קהל: אָמֵן)

בְּעָלְמָא דִּי בְרָא כִרְעוּתֵהּ

וְיַמְלִיךְ מַלְכוּתֵהּ

בְּחַיֵּיכוֹן וּבְיוֹמֵיכוֹן וּבְחַיֵּי דְכָל בֵּית יִשְׂרָאֵל

בַּעֲגָלָא וּבִזְמַן קָרִיב, וְאִמְרוּ אָמֵן. (קהל: אָמֵן)

קהל
ואבל: יְהֵא שְׁמֵהּ רַבָּא מְבָרַךְ לְעָלַם וּלְעָלְמֵי עָלְמַיָּא.

אבל: יִתְבָּרַךְ וְיִשְׁתַּבַּח וְיִתְפָּאַר

וְיִתְרוֹמַם וְיִתְנַשֵּׂא וְיִתְהַדָּר וְיִתְעַלֶּה וְיִתְהַלָּל

שְׁמֵהּ דְּקֻדְשָׁא בְּרִיךְ הוּא (קהל: בְּרִיךְ הוּא)

---

of the message of monotheism. Twice, the prayer uses the expression, "There is no other," forcefully expressed in Hebrew by two monosyllabic words, *ein od*.

The second paragraph turns to God and to the future, to a time when all humanity will acknowledge the One God, a vision eloquently spoken of by the prophet Zechariah, from whose book the final verse is taken. It contains a phrase – "to perfect the world under the sovereignty of God" – which became a leading theme of Lurianic mysticism in the sixteenth century (*tikkun olam*).

beyond any blessing, song, praise and consolation
uttered in the world – and say: Amen.

May there be great peace from heaven,
and life for us and all Israel – and say: Amen.

*Bow, take three steps back, as if taking leave of the Divine Presence,
then bow, first left, then right, then center, while saying:*

May He who makes peace in His high places,
make peace for us and all Israel – and say: Amen.

THE DAILY PSALM

One of the following psalms is said on the appropriate day of the week as indicated.

*After the Daily Psalm, on Rosh Ḥodesh, add Barekhi Nafshi, page 194 (in Israel, some only say
Barekhi Nafshi). On Ḥanukka, add Psalm 30, page 58 followed by Mourner's Kaddish. From
the second day of Rosh Ḥodesh Elul through Shemini Atzeret (in Israel, through Hoshana
Raba), add Psalm 27 on page 196. In a house of mourning the service concludes on page 602.*

Sunday: Today is the first day of the week,
         on which the Levites used to say this psalm in the Temple:

לְדָוִד מִזְמוֹר A psalm of David. The earth is the LORD's and all it contains, the   Ps. 24
world and all who live in it. For He founded it on the seas and established it
on the streams. Who may climb the mountain of the LORD? Who may stand
in His holy place? He who has clean hands and a pure heart, who has not
taken My name in vain or sworn deceitfully. He shall receive a blessing from
the LORD, and just reward from the God of his salvation. This is a generation
of those who seek Him, the descendants of Jacob who seek Your presence,
Selah! Lift up your heads, O gates; be uplifted, eternal doors, so that the King
of glory may enter. Who is the King of glory? It is the LORD, strong and mighty,
the LORD mighty in battle. Lift up your heads, O gates; lift them up, eternal
doors, that the King of glory may enter. ‣ Who is He, the King of glory? The
LORD of hosts, He is the King of glory, Selah!

Mourner's Kaddish (previous page)

לְדָוִד מִזְמוֹר Sunday: Psalm 24. The opening verses mirror the act of creation,
reminding us that each week mirrors the seven days of creation itself. The
psalm also alludes to the Temple, built on "the mountain of the LORD." The
connection between the two is based on the idea that the Temple was a
microcosm of the universe, and its construction a human counterpart to the
divine creation of the cosmos.

‎לְעֵלָּא מִן כָּל בִּרְכָתָא /בעשרת ימי תשובה: לְעֵלָּא לְעֵלָּא מִכָּל בִּרְכָתָא/
‎וְשִׁירָתָא, תֻּשְׁבְּחָתָא וְנֶחֱמָתָא
‎דַּאֲמִירָן בְּעָלְמָא, וְאִמְרוּ אָמֵן. (קהל: אָמֵן)

‎יְהֵא שְׁלָמָא רַבָּא מִן שְׁמַיָּא
‎וְחַיִּים, עָלֵינוּ וְעַל כָּל יִשְׂרָאֵל, וְאִמְרוּ אָמֵן. (קהל: אָמֵן)

*Bow, take three steps back, as if taking leave of the Divine Presence,
then bow, first left, then right, then center, while saying:*

‎עֹשֶׂה שָׁלוֹם /בעשרת ימי תשובה: הַשָּׁלוֹם: בִּמְרוֹמָיו
‎הוּא יַעֲשֶׂה שָׁלוֹם עָלֵינוּ וְעַל כָּל יִשְׂרָאֵל, וְאִמְרוּ אָמֵן. (קהל: אָמֵן)

‎שִׁיר שֶׁל יוֹם

One of the following psalms is said on the appropriate day of the week as indicated.

After ‎שיר של יום, *on* ‎ראש חודש, *add* ‎בָּרְכִי נַפְשִׁי, *page 195 (in* ‎ארץ ישראל, *some only say* ‎בָּרְכִי נַפְשִׁי). *On* ‎חנוכה, *add* ‎מִזְמוֹר שִׁיר־חֲנֻכַּת הַבַּיִת, *page 59 followed by* ‎קדיש יתום. *From the second day of* ‎(הושענא רבה ‎through ‎שמיני עצרת (in ‎ארץ ישראל, *through* ‎ראש חודש ‎add ‎לְדָוִד, יהוה אוֹרִי *on page 197. In a house of mourning the service concludes on page 603.*

‎Sunday ‎הַיּוֹם יוֹם רִאשׁוֹן בְּשַׁבָּת, שֶׁבּוֹ הָיוּ הַלְוִיִּם אוֹמְרִים בְּבֵית הַמִּקְדָּשׁ: ‎תהלים כד

‎לְדָוִד מִזְמוֹר, לַיהוה הָאָרֶץ וּמְלוֹאָהּ, תֵּבֵל וְיֹשְׁבֵי בָהּ: כִּי־הוּא עַל־יַמִּים
‎יְסָדָהּ, וְעַל־נְהָרוֹת יְכוֹנְנֶהָ: מִי־יַעֲלֶה בְהַר־יהוה, וּמִי־יָקוּם בִּמְקוֹם קָדְשׁוֹ:
‎נְקִי כַפַּיִם וּבַר־לֵבָב, אֲשֶׁר לֹא־נָשָׂא לַשָּׁוְא נַפְשִׁי, וְלֹא נִשְׁבַּע לְמִרְמָה:
‎יִשָּׂא בְרָכָה מֵאֵת יהוה, וּצְדָקָה מֵאֱלֹהֵי יִשְׁעוֹ: זֶה דּוֹר דֹּרְשָׁיו, מְבַקְשֵׁי
‎פָנֶיךָ יַעֲקֹב סֶלָה: שְׂאוּ שְׁעָרִים רָאשֵׁיכֶם, וְהִנָּשְׂאוּ פִּתְחֵי עוֹלָם, וְיָבוֹא
‎מֶלֶךְ הַכָּבוֹד: מִי זֶה מֶלֶךְ הַכָּבוֹד, יהוה עִזּוּז וְגִבּוֹר, יהוה גִּבּוֹר מִלְחָמָה:
‎שְׂאוּ שְׁעָרִים רָאשֵׁיכֶם, וּשְׂאוּ פִּתְחֵי עוֹלָם, וְיָבֹא מֶלֶךְ הַכָּבוֹד: • מִי הוּא
‎זֶה מֶלֶךְ הַכָּבוֹד, יהוה צְבָאוֹת הוּא מֶלֶךְ הַכָּבוֹד סֶלָה:

‎קדיש יתום *(previous page)*

THE DAILY PSALM
A special psalm was said in the Temple on each of the seven days of the week.
We say them still, in memory of those days and in hope of future restoration.

Monday: Today is the second day of the week,
on which the Levites used to say this psalm in the Temple:

שִׁיר מִזְמוֹר A song. A psalm of the sons of Koraḥ. Great is the LORD and   *Ps. 48*
greatly to be praised in the city of God, on His holy mountain – beautiful in
its heights, joy of all the earth, Mount Zion on its northern side, city of the
great King. In its citadels God is known as a stronghold. See how the kings
joined forces, advancing together. They saw, they were astounded, they
panicked, they fled. There fear seized them, like the pains of a woman giving
birth, like ships of Tarshish wrecked by an eastern wind. What we had heard,
now we have seen, in the city of the LORD of hosts, in the city of our God.
May God preserve it for ever, Selah! In the midst of Your Temple, God, we
meditate on Your love. As is Your name, God, so is Your praise: it reaches to
the ends of the earth. Your right hand is filled with righteousness. Let Mount
Zion rejoice, let the towns of Judah be glad, because of Your judgments. Walk
around Zion and encircle it. Count its towers, note its strong walls, view its
citadels, so that you may tell a future generation ‣ that this is God, our God,
for ever and ever. He will guide us for evermore.   *Mourner's Kaddish (page 186)*

Tuesday: Today is the third day of the week,
on which the Levites used to say this psalm in the Temple:

מִזְמוֹר לְאָסָף A psalm of Asaph. God stands in the divine assembly. Among   *Ps. 82*
the judges He delivers judgment. How long will you judge unjustly, showing
favor to the wicked? Selah. Do justice to the weak and the orphaned. Vindicate the poor and destitute. Rescue the weak and needy. Save them from the
hand of the wicked. They do not know nor do they understand. They walk
about in darkness while all the earth's foundations shake. I once said, "You
are like gods, all of you are sons of the Most High." But you shall die like mere
men, you will fall like any prince. ‣ Arise, O LORD, judge the earth, for all the
nations are Your possession.   *Mourner's Kaddish (page 186)*

to relate, it ever rises from its ashes to renewed life and glory. It is the
Eternal City of the Eternal People. (Rabbi J.H. Hertz)

מִזְמוֹר לְאָסָף *Tuesday: Psalm 82.* The psalm for Tuesday is about judges and
justice. Justice, the application of law, brings order to society as scientific law
brings order to the cosmos. Justice ultimately belongs to God. A judge must
therefore act with humility and integrity, bringing divine order to human
chaos. "A judge who delivers a true judgment becomes a partner of the Holy
One, blessed be He, in the work of creation" (*Shabbat* 10a).

היום יום שֵׁנִי בְּשַׁבָּת, שֶׁבּוֹ הָיוּ הַלְוִיִּם אוֹמְרִים בְּבֵית הַמִּקְדָּשׁ: *Monday*

תהלים מח : שִׁיר מִזְמוֹר לִבְנֵי־קֹרַח: גָּדוֹל יהוה וּמְהֻלָּל מְאֹד, בְּעִיר אֱלֹהֵינוּ, הַר־קָדְשׁוֹ: יְפֵה נוֹף מְשׂוֹשׂ כָּל־הָאָרֶץ, הַר־צִיּוֹן יַרְכְּתֵי צָפוֹן, קִרְיַת מֶלֶךְ רָב: אֱלֹהִים בְּאַרְמְנוֹתֶיהָ נוֹדַע לְמִשְׂגָּב: כִּי־הִנֵּה הַמְּלָכִים נוֹעֲדוּ, עָבְרוּ יַחְדָּו: הֵמָּה רָאוּ כֵּן תָּמָהוּ, נִבְהֲלוּ נֶחְפָּזוּ: רְעָדָה אֲחָזָתַם שָׁם, חִיל כַּיּוֹלֵדָה: בְּרוּחַ קָדִים תְּשַׁבֵּר אֳנִיּוֹת תַּרְשִׁישׁ: כַּאֲשֶׁר שָׁמַעְנוּ כֵּן רָאִינוּ, בְּעִיר־יהוה צְבָאוֹת, בְּעִיר אֱלֹהֵינוּ, אֱלֹהִים יְכוֹנְנֶהָ עַד־עוֹלָם סֶלָה: דִּמִּינוּ אֱלֹהִים חַסְדֶּךָ, בְּקֶרֶב הֵיכָלֶךָ: כְּשִׁמְךָ אֱלֹהִים כֵּן תְּהִלָּתְךָ עַל־קַצְוֵי־אֶרֶץ, צֶדֶק מָלְאָה יְמִינֶךָ: יִשְׂמַח הַר־צִיּוֹן, תָּגֵלְנָה בְּנוֹת יְהוּדָה, לְמַעַן מִשְׁפָּטֶיךָ: סֹבּוּ צִיּוֹן וְהַקִּיפוּהָ, סִפְרוּ מִגְדָּלֶיהָ: שִׁיתוּ לִבְּכֶם לְחֵילָה, פַּסְּגוּ אַרְמְנוֹתֶיהָ, לְמַעַן תְּסַפְּרוּ לְדוֹר אַחֲרוֹן: כִּי זֶה אֱלֹהִים אֱלֹהֵינוּ עוֹלָם וָעֶד, הוּא יְנַהֲגֵנוּ עַל־מוּת:

קדיש יתום (*page 187*)

היום יום שְׁלִישִׁי בְּשַׁבָּת, שֶׁבּוֹ הָיוּ הַלְוִיִּם אוֹמְרִים בְּבֵית הַמִּקְדָּשׁ: *Tuesday*

תהלים פב : מִזְמוֹר לְאָסָף, אֱלֹהִים נִצָּב בַּעֲדַת־אֵל, בְּקֶרֶב אֱלֹהִים יִשְׁפֹּט: עַד־מָתַי תִּשְׁפְּטוּ־עָוֶל, וּפְנֵי רְשָׁעִים תִּשְׂאוּ־סֶלָה: שִׁפְטוּ־דַל וְיָתוֹם, עָנִי וָרָשׁ הַצְדִּיקוּ: פַּלְּטוּ־דַל וְאֶבְיוֹן, מִיַּד רְשָׁעִים הַצִּילוּ: לֹא יָדְעוּ וְלֹא יָבִינוּ, בַּחֲשֵׁכָה יִתְהַלָּכוּ, יִמּוֹטוּ כָּל־מוֹסְדֵי אָרֶץ: אֲנִי־אָמַרְתִּי אֱלֹהִים אַתֶּם, וּבְנֵי עֶלְיוֹן כֻּלְּכֶם: אָכֵן כְּאָדָם תְּמוּתוּן, וּכְאַחַד הַשָּׂרִים תִּפֹּלוּ: ◄ קוּמָה אֱלֹהִים שָׁפְטָה הָאָרֶץ, כִּי־אַתָּה תִנְחַל בְּכָל־הַגּוֹיִם:

קדיש יתום (*page 187*)

שִׁיר מִזְמוֹר לִבְנֵי־קֹרַח **Monday: Psalm 48.** A hymn of praise to the beauty and endurance of Jerusalem, the city that outlived all those who sought to conquer it.

A score of conquerors have held it as their choicest prize; and more than a dozen times has it been utterly destroyed. The Babylonians burnt it, and deported its population; the Romans slew a million of its inhabitants, razed it to the ground, passed the ploughshare over it, and strewed its furrows with salt; Hadrian banished its very name from the lips of men, changed it to *Aelia Capitolina*, and prohibited any Jew from entering its precincts on pain of death. Persians and Arabs, Barbarians and Crusaders and Turks took it and retook it, ravaged it and burnt it; and yet, marvelous

Wednesday: Today is the fourth day of the week,
on which the Levites used to say this psalm in the Temple:

אֵל־נְקָמוֹת God of retribution, LORD, God of retribution, appear! Rise up, Judge   *Ps. 94*
of the earth. Repay to the arrogant what they deserve. How long shall the wicked, LORD, how long shall the wicked triumph? They pour out insolent words. All the evildoers are full of boasting. They crush Your people, LORD, and oppress Your inheritance. They kill the widow and the stranger. They murder the orphaned. They say, "The LORD does not see. The God of Jacob pays no heed." Take heed, you most brutish people. You fools, when will you grow wise? Will He who implants the ear not hear? Will He who formed the eye not see? Will He who disciplines nations – He who teaches man knowledge – not punish? The LORD knows that the thoughts of man are a mere fleeting breath. Happy is the man whom You discipline, LORD, the one You instruct in Your Torah, giving him tranquility in days of trouble, until a pit is dug for the wicked. For the LORD will not forsake His people, nor abandon His heritage. Judgment shall again accord with justice, and all the upright in heart will follow it. Who will rise up for me against the wicked? Who will stand up for me against wrongdoers? Had the LORD not been my help, I would soon have dwelt in death's silence. When I thought my foot was slipping, Your loving-kindness, LORD, gave me support. When I was filled with anxiety, Your consolations soothed my soul. Can a corrupt throne be allied with You? Can injustice be framed into law? They join forces against the life of the righteous, and condemn the innocent to death. But the LORD is my stronghold, my God is the Rock of my refuge. He will bring back on them their wickedness, and destroy them for their evil deeds. The LORD our God will destroy them.

‣ Come, let us sing for joy to the LORD; let us shout aloud to the Rock of our   *Ps. 95*
salvation. Let us greet Him with thanksgiving, shout aloud to Him with songs of praise. For the LORD is the great God, the King great above all powers.

Mourner's Kaddish (page 186)

Thursday: Today is the fifth day of the week,
on which the Levites used to say this psalm in the Temple:

לַמְנַצֵּחַ For the conductor of music. On the Gittit. By Asaph. Sing for joy to God,   *Ps. 81*
our strength. Shout aloud to the God of Jacob. Raise a song, beat the drum, play the sweet harp and lyre. Sound the shofar on the new moon, on our feast

---

לַמְנַצֵּחַ *Thursday: Psalm 81.* God pleads with His people: a classic expression of one of the great themes of the prophetic literature, the divine pathos – God's love for, but exasperation with, His children. "If only My people would listen to Me."

Wednesday הַיּוֹם יוֹם רְבִיעִי בְּשַׁבָּת, שֶׁבּוֹ הָיוּ הַלְוִיִּם אוֹמְרִים בְּבֵית הַמִּקְדָּשׁ:

תהלים צד אֵל־נְקָמוֹת יהוה, אֵל נְקָמוֹת הוֹפִיעַ: הִנָּשֵׂא שֹׁפֵט הָאָרֶץ, הָשֵׁב גְּמוּל עַל־גֵּאִים: עַד־מָתַי רְשָׁעִים, יהוה, עַד־מָתַי רְשָׁעִים יַעֲלֹזוּ: יַבִּיעוּ יְדַבְּרוּ עָתָק, יִתְאַמְּרוּ כָּל־פֹּעֲלֵי אָוֶן: עַמְּךָ יהוה יְדַכְּאוּ, וְנַחֲלָתְךָ יְעַנּוּ: אַלְמָנָה וְגֵר יַהֲרֹגוּ, וִיתוֹמִים יְרַצֵּחוּ: וַיֹּאמְרוּ לֹא יִרְאֶה־יָּהּ, וְלֹא־יָבִין אֱלֹהֵי יַעֲקֹב: בִּינוּ בֹּעֲרִים בָּעָם, וּכְסִילִים מָתַי תַּשְׂכִּילוּ: הֲנֹטַע אֹזֶן הֲלֹא יִשְׁמָע, אִם־יֹצֵר עַיִן הֲלֹא יַבִּיט: הֲיֹסֵר גּוֹיִם הֲלֹא יוֹכִיחַ, הַמְלַמֵּד אָדָם דָּעַת: יהוה יֹדֵעַ מַחְשְׁבוֹת אָדָם, כִּי־הֵמָּה הָבֶל: אַשְׁרֵי הַגֶּבֶר אֲשֶׁר־תְּיַסְּרֶנּוּ יָּהּ, וּמִתּוֹרָתְךָ תְלַמְּדֶנּוּ: לְהַשְׁקִיט לוֹ מִימֵי רָע, עַד יִכָּרֶה לָרָשָׁע שָׁחַת: כִּי לֹא־יִטֹּשׁ יהוה עַמּוֹ, וְנַחֲלָתוֹ לֹא יַעֲזֹב: כִּי־עַד־צֶדֶק יָשׁוּב מִשְׁפָּט, וְאַחֲרָיו כָּל־יִשְׁרֵי־לֵב: מִי־יָקוּם לִי עִם־מְרֵעִים, מִי־יִתְיַצֵּב לִי עִם־פֹּעֲלֵי אָוֶן: לוּלֵי יהוה עֶזְרָתָה לִּי, כִּמְעַט שָׁכְנָה דוּמָה נַפְשִׁי: אִם־אָמַרְתִּי מָטָה רַגְלִי, חַסְדְּךָ יהוה יִסְעָדֵנִי: בְּרֹב שַׂרְעַפַּי בְּקִרְבִּי, תַּנְחוּמֶיךָ יְשַׁעַשְׁעוּ נַפְשִׁי: הַיְחָבְרְךָ כִּסֵּא הַוּוֹת, יֹצֵר עָמָל עֲלֵי־חֹק: יָגוֹדּוּ עַל־נֶפֶשׁ צַדִּיק, וְדָם נָקִי יַרְשִׁיעוּ: וַיְהִי יהוה לִי לְמִשְׂגָּב, וֵאלֹהַי לְצוּר מַחְסִי: וַיָּשֶׁב עֲלֵיהֶם אֶת־אוֹנָם, וּבְרָעָתָם יַצְמִיתֵם, יַצְמִיתֵם יהוה אֱלֹהֵינוּ:

תהלים צה ‹ לְכוּ נְרַנְּנָה לַיהוה, נָרִיעָה לְצוּר יִשְׁעֵנוּ: נְקַדְּמָה פָנָיו בְּתוֹדָה, בִּזְמִרוֹת נָרִיעַ לוֹ: כִּי אֵל גָּדוֹל יהוה, וּמֶלֶךְ גָּדוֹל עַל־כָּל־אֱלֹהִים:

קדיש יתום (*page 187*)

Thursday הַיּוֹם יוֹם חֲמִישִׁי בְּשַׁבָּת, שֶׁבּוֹ הָיוּ הַלְוִיִּם אוֹמְרִים בְּבֵית הַמִּקְדָּשׁ:

תהלים פא לַמְנַצֵּחַ עַל־הַגִּתִּית לְאָסָף: הַרְנִינוּ לֵאלֹהִים עוּזֵּנוּ, הָרִיעוּ לֵאלֹהֵי יַעֲקֹב: שְׂאוּ־זִמְרָה וּתְנוּ־תֹף, כִּנּוֹר נָעִים עִם־נָבֶל: תִּקְעוּ בַחֹדֶשׁ שׁוֹפָר, בַּכֵּסֶה לְיוֹם חַגֵּנוּ: כִּי חֹק לְיִשְׂרָאֵל הוּא, מִשְׁפָּט לֵאלֹהֵי יַעֲקֹב: עֵדוּת בִּיהוֹסֵף

⸻

אֵל־נְקָמוֹת יהוה *Wednesday: Psalm 94.* Marking the midweek, this is a psalm of intense power about the connection between religious faith and ethical conduct and their opposite: lack of faith and a failure of humanity. When man begins to worship himself, he dreams of becoming a god but ends by becoming lower than the beasts. Appropriately, some communities recite this psalm on Yom HaSho'a, Holocaust Memorial Day (27 Nisan).

day when the moon is hidden. For it is a statute for Israel, an ordinance of the God of Jacob. He established it as a testimony for Joseph when He went forth against the land of Egypt, where I heard a language that I did not know. I relieved his shoulder of the burden. His hands were freed from the builder's basket. In distress you called and I rescued you. I answered you from the secret place of thunder; I tested you at the waters of Meribah, Selah! Hear, My people, and I will warn you. Israel, if you would only listen to Me! Let there be no strange god among you. Do not bow down to an alien god. I am the LORD your God who brought you out of the land of Egypt. Open your mouth wide and I will fill it. But My people would not listen to Me. Israel would have none of Me. So I left them to their stubborn hearts, letting them follow their own devices. If only My people would listen to Me, if Israel would walk in My ways, I would soon subdue their enemies, and turn My hand against their foes. Those who hate the LORD would cower before Him and their doom would last for ever. ‣ He would feed Israel with the finest wheat – with honey from the rock I would satisfy you.

Mourner's Kaddish (page 186)

Friday: Today is the sixth day of the week,
on which the Levites used to say this psalm in the Temple:

יהוה מָלָךְ The LORD reigns. He is robed in majesty. The LORD is robed, girded *Ps. 93* with strength. The world is firmly established; it cannot be moved. Your throne stands firm as of old; You are eternal. Rivers lift up, LORD, rivers lift up their voice, rivers lift up their crashing waves. Mightier than the noise of many waters, than the mighty waves of the sea is the LORD on high. ‣ Your testimonies are very sure; holiness adorns Your House, LORD, for evermore.

Mourner's Kaddish (page 186)

On Rosh Ḥodesh, the following psalm is said:

בָּרְכִי נַפְשִׁי Bless the LORD, my soul. LORD, my God, You are very great, clothed *Ps. 104* in majesty and splendor, wrapped in a robe of light. You have spread out the heavens like a tent. He has laid the beams of His lofts in the waters. He makes the clouds His chariot, riding on the wings of the wind. He makes the winds His messengers, flames of fire His ministers. He has fixed the earth on its foundations so that it will never be shaken. You covered it with the deep like a cloak; the waters stood above the mountains. At Your rebuke they fled; at the sound of Your thunder they rushed away, flowing over the hills, pouring down into the valleys to the place You appointed for them. You fixed a boundary they were not to pass, so that they would never cover the earth again. He makes springs flow in the valleys; they make their way between the hills, giving drink to all

שְׁמוֹ, בְּצֵאתוֹ עַל־אֶרֶץ מִצְרָיִם, שְׂפַת לֹא־יָדַעְתִּי אֶשְׁמָע: הֲסִירוֹתִי מִסֵּבֶל שִׁכְמוֹ, כַּפָּיו מִדּוּד תַּעֲבֹרְנָה: בַּצָּרָה קָרָאתָ וָאֲחַלְּצֶךָּ, אֶעֶנְךָ בְּסֵתֶר רַעַם, אֶבְחָנְךָ עַל־מֵי מְרִיבָה סֶלָה: שְׁמַע עַמִּי וְאָעִידָה בָּךְ, יִשְׂרָאֵל אִם־תִּשְׁמַע־לִי: לֹא־יִהְיֶה בְךָ אֵל זָר, וְלֹא תִשְׁתַּחֲוֶה לְאֵל נֵכָר: אָנֹכִי יהוה אֱלֹהֶיךָ, הַמַּעַלְךָ מֵאֶרֶץ מִצְרָיִם, הַרְחֶב־פִּיךָ וַאֲמַלְאֵהוּ: וְלֹא־שָׁמַע עַמִּי לְקוֹלִי, וְיִשְׂרָאֵל לֹא־אָבָה לִי: וָאֲשַׁלְּחֵהוּ בִּשְׁרִירוּת לִבָּם, יֵלְכוּ בְּמוֹעֲצוֹתֵיהֶם: לוּ עַמִּי שֹׁמֵעַ לִי, יִשְׂרָאֵל בִּדְרָכַי יְהַלֵּכוּ: כִּמְעַט אוֹיְבֵיהֶם אַכְנִיעַ, וְעַל־צָרֵיהֶם אָשִׁיב יָדִי: מְשַׂנְאֵי יהוה יְכַחֲשׁוּ־לוֹ, וִיהִי עִתָּם לְעוֹלָם: ◄ וַיַּאֲכִילֵהוּ מֵחֵלֶב חִטָּה, וּמִצּוּר, דְּבַשׁ אַשְׂבִּיעֶךָ:

(page 187)   קדיש יתום

Friday   הַיּוֹם יוֹם שִׁשִּׁי בְּשַׁבָּת, שֶׁבּוֹ הָיוּ הַלְוִיִּם אוֹמְרִים בְּבֵית הַמִּקְדָּשׁ

תהלים צג   יהוה מָלָךְ, גֵּאוּת לָבֵשׁ, לָבֵשׁ יהוה עֹז הִתְאַזָּר, אַף־תִּכּוֹן תֵּבֵל בַּל־תִּמּוֹט: נָכוֹן כִּסְאֲךָ מֵאָז, מֵעוֹלָם אָתָּה: נָשְׂאוּ נְהָרוֹת יהוה, נָשְׂאוּ נְהָרוֹת קוֹלָם, יִשְׂאוּ נְהָרוֹת דָּכְיָם: מִקֹּלוֹת מַיִם רַבִּים, אַדִּירִים מִשְׁבְּרֵי־יָם, אַדִּיר בַּמָּרוֹם יהוה: ◄ עֵדֹתֶיךָ נֶאֶמְנוּ מְאֹד, לְבֵיתְךָ נַאֲוָה־קֹּדֶשׁ, יהוה לְאֹרֶךְ יָמִים:

(page 187)   קדיש יתום

On ראש חודש, *the following psalm is said:*

תהלים קד   בָּרְכִי נַפְשִׁי אֶת־יהוה, יהוה אֱלֹהַי גָּדַלְתָּ מְּאֹד, הוֹד וְהָדָר לָבָשְׁתָּ: עֹטֶה־אוֹר כַּשַּׂלְמָה, נוֹטֶה שָׁמַיִם כַּיְרִיעָה: הַמְקָרֶה בַמַּיִם עֲלִיּוֹתָיו, הַשָּׂם־עָבִים רְכוּבוֹ, הַמְהַלֵּךְ עַל־כַּנְפֵי־רוּחַ: עֹשֶׂה מַלְאָכָיו רוּחוֹת, מְשָׁרְתָיו אֵשׁ לֹהֵט: יָסַד־אֶרֶץ עַל־מְכוֹנֶיהָ, בַּל־תִּמּוֹט עוֹלָם וָעֶד: תְּהוֹם כַּלְּבוּשׁ כִּסִּיתוֹ, עַל־הָרִים יַעַמְדוּ־מָיִם: מִן־גַּעֲרָתְךָ יְנוּסוּן, מִן־קוֹל רַעַמְךָ יֵחָפֵזוּן: יַעֲלוּ הָרִים, יֵרְדוּ בְקָעוֹת, אֶל־מְקוֹם זֶה יָסַדְתָּ לָהֶם: גְּבוּל־שַׂמְתָּ בַּל־יַעֲבֹרוּן, בַּל־יְשֻׁבוּן לְכַסּוֹת הָאָרֶץ: הַמְשַׁלֵּחַ מַעְיָנִים בַּנְּחָלִים, בֵּין הָרִים יְהַלֵּכוּן: יַשְׁקוּ כָּל־חַיְתוֹ שָׂדָי, יִשְׁבְּרוּ פְרָאִים צְמָאָם: עֲלֵיהֶם עוֹף־הַשָּׁמַיִם יִשְׁכּוֹן, מִבֵּין עֳפָאיִם יִתְּנוּ־קוֹל: מַשְׁקֶה

יהוה מָלָךְ *Friday: Psalm 93.* Speaking as it does of the completion of creation ("the world is firmly established"), this psalm is appropriate for the sixth day, when "the heavens and the earth were completed, and all their array."

the beasts of the field; the wild donkeys quench their thirst. The birds of the sky dwell beside them, singing among the foliage. He waters the mountains from His lofts: the earth is sated with the fruit of Your work. He makes grass grow for the cattle, and plants for the use of man, that he may produce bread from the earth, wine to cheer the heart of man, oil to make the face shine, and bread to sustain man's heart. The trees of the Lord drink their fill, the cedars of Lebanon which He planted. There, birds build their nests; the stork makes its home in the cypresses. High hills are for the wild goats; crags are shelter for the badgers. He made the moon to mark the seasons, and makes the sun know when to set. You bring darkness and it is night; then all the beasts of the forests stir. The young lions roar for prey, seeking their food from God. When the sun rises, they slink away and seek rest in their lairs. Man goes out to his work and his labor until evening. How numerous are Your works, Lord; You made them all in wisdom; the earth is full of Your creations. There is the vast, immeasurable sea with its countless swarming creatures, living things great and small. There ships sail. There is Leviathan You formed to sport there. All of them look to You in hope, to give them their food when it is due. What You give them, they gather up. When You open Your hand, they are sated with good. When You hide Your face, they are dismayed. When You take away their breath, they die and return to dust. When You send back Your breath, they are created, giving new life to the earth. May the glory of the Lord be for ever; may the Lord rejoice in His works. When He looks at the earth, it trembles. When He touches the mountains, they pour forth smoke. I will sing to the Lord as long as I live; I will sing psalms to my God all my life. ▸ May my meditation be pleasing to Him; I shall rejoice in the Lord. May sinners vanish from the earth, and the wicked be no more. Bless the Lord, my soul. Halleluya!

Mourner's Kaddish (page 186)

During the month of Elul (except Erev Rosh HaShana), the shofar is sounded (some sound the shofar after the psalm below). From the second day of Rosh Ḥodesh Elul through Shemini Atzeret, the following psalm is said:

לְדָוִד By David. The Lord is my light and my salvation – whom then shall I fear?   *Ps. 27* The Lord is the stronghold of my life – of whom shall I be afraid? When evil men close in on me to devour my flesh, it is they, my enemies and foes, who stumble and fall. Should an army besiege me, my heart would not fear. Should war break out against me, still I would be confident. One thing I ask of the Lord, only this do I seek: to live in the House of the Lord all the days of my life, to gaze on the beauty of the Lord and worship in His Temple. For He will keep me safe in His pavilion on the day of trouble. He will hide me under the cover of His tent. He will set me high upon a rock. Now my head is high above my enemies who surround me. I will sacrifice in His tent with shouts of joy. I will sing and chant praises to the Lord. Lord, hear my voice when I call. Be

הָרִים מֵעֲלִיּוֹתָיו, מִפְּרִי מַעֲשֶֽׂיךָ תִּשְׂבַּע הָאָֽרֶץ: מַצְמִֽיחַ חָצִיר לַבְּהֵמָה, וְעֵֽשֶׂב לַעֲבֹדַת הָאָדָם, לְהֽוֹצִיא לֶֽחֶם מִן הָאָֽרֶץ: וְיַֽיִן יְשַׂמַּח לְבַב אֱנוֹשׁ, לְהַצְהִיל פָּנִים מִשָּֽׁמֶן, וְלֶֽחֶם לְבַב אֱנוֹשׁ יִסְעָד: יִשְׂבְּעוּ עֲצֵי יהוה, אַרְזֵי לְבָנוֹן אֲשֶׁר נָטָע: אֲשֶׁר שָׁם צִפֳּרִים יְקַנֵּֽנוּ, חֲסִידָה בְּרוֹשִׁים בֵּיתָהּ: הָרִים הַגְּבֹהִים לַיְּעֵלִים, סְלָעִים מַחְסֶה לַשְׁפַנִּים: עָשָׂה יָרֵֽחַ לְמוֹעֲדִים, שֶֽׁמֶשׁ יָדַע מְבוֹאוֹ: תָּֽשֶׁת חֹֽשֶׁךְ וִיהִי לָֽיְלָה, בּוֹ תִרְמֹשׂ כָּל חַיְתוֹ יָֽעַר: הַכְּפִירִים שֹׁאֲגִים לַטָּֽרֶף, וּלְבַקֵּשׁ מֵאֵל אָכְלָם: תִּזְרַח הַשֶּֽׁמֶשׁ יֵאָסֵפֽוּן, וְאֶל מְעוֹנֹתָם יִרְבָּצוּן: יֵצֵא אָדָם לְפָעֳלוֹ, וְלַעֲבֹדָתוֹ עֲדֵי עָֽרֶב: מָה רַבּוּ מַעֲשֶֽׂיךָ יהוה, כֻּלָּם בְּחָכְמָה עָשִֽׂיתָ, מָלְאָה הָאָֽרֶץ קִנְיָנֶֽךָ: זֶה הַיָּם גָּדוֹל וּרְחַב יָדָֽיִם, שָׁם רֶֽמֶשׂ וְאֵין מִסְפָּר, חַיּוֹת קְטַנּוֹת עִם גְּדֹלוֹת: שָׁם אֳנִיּוֹת יְהַלֵּכוּן, לִוְיָתָן זֶה יָצַֽרְתָּ לְשַֽׂחֶק בּוֹ: כֻּלָּם אֵלֶֽיךָ יְשַׂבֵּרוּן, לָתֵת אָכְלָם בְּעִתּוֹ: תִּתֵּן לָהֶם יִלְקֹטוּן, תִּפְתַּח יָדְךָ יִשְׂבְּעוּן טוֹב: תַּסְתִּיר פָּנֶֽיךָ יִבָּהֵלוּן, תֹּסֵף רוּחָם יִגְוָעוּן, וְאֶל עֲפָרָם יְשׁוּבוּן: תְּשַׁלַּח רוּחֲךָ יִבָּרֵאוּן, וּתְחַדֵּשׁ פְּנֵי אֲדָמָה: יְהִי כְבוֹד יהוה לְעוֹלָם, יִשְׂמַח יהוה בְּמַעֲשָׂיו: הַמַּבִּיט לָאָֽרֶץ וַתִּרְעָד, יִגַּע בֶּהָרִים וְיֶעֱשָֽׁנוּ: אָשִֽׁירָה לַיהוה בְּחַיָּי, אֲזַמְּרָה לֵאלֹהַי בְּעוֹדִי: ‹ יֶעֱרַב עָלָיו שִׂיחִי, אָנֹכִי אֶשְׂמַח בַּיהוה: יִתַּֽמּוּ חַטָּאִים מִן הָאָֽרֶץ, וּרְשָׁעִים עוֹד אֵינָם, בָּרְכִי נַפְשִׁי אֶת יהוה, הַלְלוּיָהּ:

קדיש יתום (page 187)

During the month of אלול (except עֶרֶב רֹאשׁ הַשָּׁנָה), the שׁוֹפָר is sounded (some sound the שׁוֹפָר after the psalm below). From the second day of רֹאשׁ חֹדֶשׁ אלול through שְׁמִינִי עֲצֶרֶת, the following psalm is said:

תהלים כז

לְדָוִד, יהוה אוֹרִי וְיִשְׁעִי, מִמִּי אִירָא, יהוה מָעוֹז חַיַּי, מִמִּי אֶפְחָד: בִּקְרֹב עָלַי מְרֵעִים לֶאֱכֹל אֶת בְּשָׂרִי, צָרַי וְאֹיְבַי לִי, הֵֽמָּה כָשְׁלוּ וְנָפָֽלוּ: אִם תַּחֲנֶה עָלַי מַחֲנֶה, לֹא יִירָא לִבִּי, אִם תָּקוּם עָלַי מִלְחָמָה, בְּזֹאת אֲנִי בוֹטֵֽחַ: אַחַת שָׁאַֽלְתִּי מֵאֵת יהוה, אוֹתָהּ אֲבַקֵּשׁ, שִׁבְתִּי בְּבֵית יהוה כָּל יְמֵי חַיַּי, לַחֲזוֹת בְּנֹֽעַם יהוה, וּלְבַקֵּר בְּהֵיכָלוֹ: כִּי יִצְפְּנֵֽנִי בְּסֻכֹּה בְּיוֹם רָעָה, יַסְתִּרֵֽנִי בְּסֵֽתֶר

___

לְדָוִד Psalm 27: A magnificent expression of trust in God's protection and unfailing love. An early Midrash (Vayikra Raba 21:4) relates it to the festivals of Tishrei: "The Lord is my light – on Rosh HaShana, and my salvation – on Yom Kippur." The phrase, "He will keep me safe in His pavilion [beSukko]" suggested Sukkot. It was accordingly adopted as a prayer for the penitential period up to and including these holy days, beginning on Rosh Ḥodesh Elul.

gracious to me and answer me. On Your behalf my heart says, "Seek My face." Your face, LORD, will I seek. Do not hide Your face from me. Do not turn Your servant away in anger. You have been my help. Do not reject or forsake me, God, my Savior. Were my father and my mother to forsake me, the LORD would take me in. Teach me Your way, LORD, and lead me on a level path, because of my oppressors. Do not abandon me to the will of my foes, for false witnesses have risen against me, breathing violence. ▸ Were it not for my faith that I shall see the LORD's goodness in the land of the living. Hope in the LORD. Be strong and of good courage, and hope in the LORD!

Mourner's Kaddish (page 186)

In Israel the following through "Bless the LORD," on the next page, is said:

אֵין כֵּאלֹהֵינוּ **There is** none like our God, none like our LORD, none like our King, none like our Savior. Who is like our God? Like our LORD? Like our King? Like our Savior? We will thank our God, thank our LORD, thank our King, thank our Savior. Blessed is our God, blessed our LORD, blessed our King, blessed our Savior. You are our God, You are our LORD, You are our King, You are our Savior. You are He to whom our ancestors offered the fragrant incense.

פִּטּוּם הַקְּטֹרֶת **The incense** mixture consisted of balsam, onycha, galbanum and frank-   *Keritot 6a* incense, each weighing seventy manehs; myrrh, cassia, spikenard and saffron, each weighing sixteen manehs; twelve manehs of costus, three of aromatic bark; nine of cinnamon; nine kabs of Carsina lye; three seahs and three kabs of Cyprus wine. If Cyprus wine was not available, old white wine might be used. A quarter of a kab of Sodom salt, and a minute amount of a smoke-raising herb. Rabbi Nathan says: Also a minute amount of Jordan amber. If one added honey to the mixture, he rendered it unfit for sacred use. If he omitted any one of its ingredients, he is guilty of a capital offence.

Rabban Shimon ben Gamliel says: "Balsam" refers to the sap that drips from the balsam tree. The Carsina lye was used for bleaching the onycha to improve it. The Cyprus wine was used to soak the onycha in it to make it pungent. Though urine is suitable for this purpose, it is not brought into the Temple out of respect.

It was taught in the Academy of Elijah: Whoever studies [Torah] laws every day is   *Megilla 28b* assured that he will be destined for the World to Come, as it is said, "The ways of the   *Hab. 3* world are His" – read not, "ways" [halikhot] but "laws" [halakhot].

Rabbi Elazar said in the name of Rabbi Ḥanina: The disciples of the sages increase   *Berakhot* peace in the world, as it is said, "And all your children shall be taught of the LORD, and   *64a* great shall be the peace of your children [banayikh]." Read not banayikh, "your children,"   *Is. 54* but bonayikh, "your builders." Those who love Your Torah have great peace; there is   *Ps. 119* no stumbling block for them. May there be peace within your ramparts, prosperity in your palaces. For the sake of my brothers and friends, I shall say, "Peace be within you."   *Ps. 122* For the sake of the House of the LORD our God, I will seek your good. ▸ May the LORD   *Ps. 29* grant strength to His people; may the LORD bless His people with peace.

אָהֳלוֹ, בְּצוּר יְרוֹמְמֵנִי: וְעַתָּה יָרוּם רֹאשִׁי עַל אֹיְבַי סְבִיבוֹתַי, וְאֶזְבְּחָה בְאָהֳלוֹ זִבְחֵי תְרוּעָה, אָשִׁירָה וַאֲזַמְּרָה לַיהוה: שְׁמַע־יהוה קוֹלִי אֶקְרָא, וְחָנֵּנִי וַעֲנֵנִי: לְךָ אָמַר לִבִּי בַּקְּשׁוּ פָנָי, אֶת־פָּנֶיךָ יהוה אֲבַקֵּשׁ: אַל־תַּסְתֵּר פָּנֶיךָ מִמֶּנִּי, אַל תַּט־בְּאַף עַבְדֶּךָ, עֶזְרָתִי הָיִיתָ, אַל־תִּטְּשֵׁנִי וְאַל־תַּעַזְבֵנִי, אֱלֹהֵי יִשְׁעִי: כִּי־אָבִי וְאִמִּי עֲזָבוּנִי, וַיהוה יַאַסְפֵנִי: הוֹרֵנִי יהוה דַּרְכֶּךָ, וּנְחֵנִי בְּאֹרַח מִישׁוֹר, לְמַעַן שׁוֹרְרָי: אַל־תִּתְּנֵנִי בְּנֶפֶשׁ צָרָי, כִּי קָמוּ־בִי עֵדֵי־שֶׁקֶר, וִיפֵחַ חָמָס: ‹ לוּלֵא הֶאֱמַנְתִּי לִרְאוֹת בְּטוּב־יהוה בְּאֶרֶץ חַיִּים: קַוֵּה אֶל־יהוה, חֲזַק וְיַאֲמֵץ לִבֶּךָ, וְקַוֵּה אֶל־יהוה:

קדיש יתום (page 187)

In ארץ ישראל *the following through* בָּרְכוּ, *on the next page, is said:*

אֵין כֵּאלֹהֵינוּ, אֵין כַּאדוֹנֵינוּ, אֵין כְּמַלְכֵּנוּ, אֵין כְּמוֹשִׁיעֵנוּ. מִי כֵאלֹהֵינוּ, מִי כַאדוֹנֵינוּ, מִי כְמַלְכֵּנוּ, מִי כְמוֹשִׁיעֵנוּ. נוֹדֶה לֵאלֹהֵינוּ, נוֹדֶה לַאדוֹנֵינוּ, נוֹדֶה לְמַלְכֵּנוּ, נוֹדֶה לְמוֹשִׁיעֵנוּ. בָּרוּךְ אֱלֹהֵינוּ, בָּרוּךְ אֲדוֹנֵינוּ, בָּרוּךְ מַלְכֵּנוּ, בָּרוּךְ מוֹשִׁיעֵנוּ. אַתָּה הוּא אֱלֹהֵינוּ, אַתָּה הוּא אֲדוֹנֵינוּ, אַתָּה הוּא מַלְכֵּנוּ, אַתָּה הוּא מוֹשִׁיעֵנוּ. אַתָּה הוּא שֶׁהִקְטִירוּ אֲבוֹתֵינוּ לְפָנֶיךָ אֶת קְטֹרֶת הַסַּמִּים.

פִּטּוּם הַקְּטֹרֶת. הַצֳרִי, וְהַצִּפֹּרֶן, וְהַחֶלְבְּנָה, וְהַלְּבוֹנָה מִשְׁקַל שִׁבְעִים שִׁבְעִים מָנֶה, מֹר, וּקְצִיעָה, שִׁבֹּלֶת נֵרְדְּ, וְכַרְכֹּם מִשְׁקַל שִׁשָּׁה עָשָׂר שִׁשָּׁה עָשָׂר מָנֶה, הַקֹּשְׁטְ שְׁנֵים עָשָׂר, קִלּוּפָה שְׁלֹשָׁה, וְקִנָּמוֹן תִּשְׁעָה, בּוֹרִית כַּרְשִׁינָה תִּשְׁעָה קַבִּין, יֵין קַפְרִיסִין סְאִין תְּלָת וְקַבִּין תְּלָתָא, וְאִם אֵין לוֹ יֵין קַפְרִיסִין, מֵבִיא חֲמַר חִוַּרְיָן עַתִּיק. מֶלַח סְדוֹמִית רֹבַע, מַעֲלֶה עָשָׁן כָּל שֶׁהוּא. רַבִּי נָתָן הַבַּבְלִי אוֹמֵר: אַף כִּפַּת הַיַּרְדֵּן כָּל שֶׁהוּא, וְאִם נָתַן בָּהּ דְּבַשׁ פְּסָלָהּ, וְאִם חִסַּר אַחַד מִכָּל סַמְמָנֶיהָ, חַיָּב מִיתָה. כריתות ו

רַבָּן שִׁמְעוֹן בֶּן גַּמְלִיאֵל אוֹמֵר: הַצֳרִי אֵינוֹ אֶלָּא שְׂרָף הַנּוֹטֵף מֵעֲצֵי הַקְּטָף. בּוֹרִית כַּרְשִׁינָה שֶׁשָּׁפִין בָּהּ אֶת הַצִּפֹּרֶן כְּדֵי שֶׁתְּהֵא נָאָה, יֵין קַפְרִיסִין שֶׁשּׁוֹרִין בּוֹ אֶת הַצִּפֹּרֶן כְּדֵי שֶׁתְּהֵא עַזָּה, וַהֲלֹא מֵי רַגְלַיִם יָפִין לָהּ, אֶלָּא שֶׁאֵין מַכְנִיסִין מֵי רַגְלַיִם בַּמִּקְדָּשׁ מִפְּנֵי הַכָּבוֹד.

תָּנָא דְבֵי אֵלִיָּהוּ: כָּל הַשּׁוֹנֶה הֲלָכוֹת בְּכָל יוֹם, מֻבְטָח לוֹ שֶׁהוּא בֶן עוֹלָם הַבָּא, שֶׁנֶּאֱמַר הֲלִיכוֹת עוֹלָם לוֹ: אַל תִּקְרֵי הֲלִיכוֹת אֶלָּא הֲלָכוֹת. מגילה כח חבקוק ג

אָמַר רַבִּי אֶלְעָזָר, אָמַר רַבִּי חֲנִינָא: תַּלְמִידֵי חֲכָמִים מַרְבִּים שָׁלוֹם בָּעוֹלָם, שֶׁנֶּאֱמַר וְכָל־בָּנַיִךְ לִמּוּדֵי יהוה, וְרַב שְׁלוֹם בָּנָיִךְ: אַל תִּקְרֵי בָּנָיִךְ, אֶלָּא בּוֹנָיִךְ. שָׁלוֹם רָב לְאֹהֲבֵי תוֹרָתֶךָ, וְאֵין־לָמוֹ מִכְשׁוֹל: יְהִי־שָׁלוֹם בְּחֵילֵךְ, שַׁלְוָה בְּאַרְמְנוֹתָיִךְ: לְמַעַן אַחַי וְרֵעָי אֲדַבְּרָה־נָּא שָׁלוֹם בָּךְ: לְמַעַן בֵּית־יהוה אֱלֹהֵינוּ אֲבַקְשָׁה טוֹב לָךְ: ‹ יהוה עֹז לְעַמּוֹ יִתֵּן, יהוה יְבָרֵךְ אֶת־עַמּוֹ בַשָּׁלוֹם: ברכות סד ישעיה נד תהלים קיט תהלים קכב תהלים כט

THE RABBIS' KADDISH

The following prayer, said by mourners, requires the presence of a minyan.
A transliteration can be found on page 698.

Mourner: יִתְגַּדַּל Magnified and sanctified
may His great name be, in the world He created by His will.
May He establish His kingdom in your lifetime
and in your days, and in the lifetime of all the house of Israel,
swiftly and soon – and say: Amen.

All: May His great name be blessed for ever and all time.

Mourner: Blessed and praised, glorified and exalted,
raised and honored, uplifted and lauded be
the name of the Holy One, blessed be He,
beyond any blessing,
song, praise and consolation
uttered in the world – and say: Amen.

To Israel, to the teachers,
their disciples and their disciples' disciples,
and to all who engage in the study of Torah,
in this (*in Israel add:* holy) place or elsewhere,
may there come to them and you great peace,
grace, kindness and compassion, long life, ample sustenance
and deliverance, from their Father in Heaven – and say: Amen.

May there be great peace from heaven,
and (good) life for us and all Israel – and say: Amen.

Bow, take three steps back, as if taking leave of the Divine Presence,
then bow, first left, then right, then center, while saying:
May He who makes peace in His high places,
in His compassion make peace for us
and all Israel – and say: Amen.

In Israel, on days when the Torah is not read, the person saying Kaddish adds:
Bless the LORD, the blessed One.

and the congregation responds:
Bless the LORD, the blessed One, for ever and all time.

In Israel during Elul, some congregations blow shofar and say Psalm 27
(*page 196*) *at this point. In a house of mourning the service continues on page 602.*

קדיש דרבנן

The following prayer, said by mourners, requires the presence of a מנין.
A transliteration can be found on page 698.

אבל: יִתְגַּדַּל וְיִתְקַדַּשׁ שְׁמֵהּ רַבָּא (קהל: אָמֵן)
בְּעָלְמָא דִּי בְרָא כִרְעוּתֵהּ
וְיַמְלִיךְ מַלְכוּתֵהּ
בְּחַיֵּיכוֹן וּבְיוֹמֵיכוֹן וּבְחַיֵּי דְּכָל בֵּית יִשְׂרָאֵל
בַּעֲגָלָא וּבִזְמַן קָרִיב, וְאִמְרוּ אָמֵן. (קהל: אָמֵן)

קהל ואבל: יְהֵא שְׁמֵהּ רַבָּא מְבָרַךְ לְעָלַם וּלְעָלְמֵי עָלְמַיָּא.

אבל: יִתְבָּרַךְ וְיִשְׁתַּבַּח וְיִתְפָּאַר וְיִתְרוֹמַם וְיִתְנַשֵּׂא
וְיִתְהַדָּר וְיִתְעַלֶּה וְיִתְהַלָּל, שְׁמֵהּ דְּקֻדְשָׁא בְּרִיךְ הוּא (קהל: בְּרִיךְ הוּא)
לְעֵלָּא מִן כָּל בִּרְכָתָא / בעשרת ימי תשובה: לְעֵלָּא לְעֵלָּא מִכָּל בִּרְכָתָא /
וְשִׁירָתָא, תֻּשְׁבְּחָתָא וְנֶחֱמָתָא, דַּאֲמִירָן בְּעָלְמָא, וְאִמְרוּ אָמֵן. (קהל: אָמֵן)

עַל יִשְׂרָאֵל וְעַל רַבָּנָן, וְעַל תַּלְמִידֵיהוֹן וְעַל כָּל תַּלְמִידֵי תַלְמִידֵיהוֹן
וְעַל כָּל מָאן דְּעָסְקִין בְּאוֹרַיְתָא
דִּי בְאַתְרָא (בארץ ישראל: קַדִּישָׁא) הָדֵין וְדִי בְכָל אֲתַר וַאֲתַר
יְהֵא לְהוֹן וּלְכוֹן שְׁלָמָא רַבָּא, חִנָּא וְחִסְדָּא, וְרַחֲמֵי, וְחַיֵּי אֲרִיכֵי, וּמְזוֹנֵי רְוִיחֵי
וּפֻרְקָנָא מִן קֳדָם אֲבוּהוֹן דִּי בִשְׁמַיָּא, וְאִמְרוּ אָמֵן. (קהל: אָמֵן)

יְהֵא שְׁלָמָא רַבָּא מִן שְׁמַיָּא
וְחַיִּים (טוֹבִים) עָלֵינוּ וְעַל כָּל יִשְׂרָאֵל, וְאִמְרוּ אָמֵן. (קהל: אָמֵן)

Bow, take three steps back, as if taking leave of the Divine Presence,
then bow, first left, then right, then center, while saying:

עֹשֶׂה שָׁלוֹם / בעשרת ימי תשובה: הַשָּׁלוֹם / בִּמְרוֹמָיו
הוּא יַעֲשֶׂה בְרַחֲמָיו שָׁלוֹם, עָלֵינוּ וְעַל כָּל יִשְׂרָאֵל, וְאִמְרוּ אָמֵן. (קהל: אָמֵן)

In ארץ ישראל, on days when the תורה is not read, the person saying קדיש adds:

בָּרְכוּ אֶת יהוה הַמְבֹרָךְ.

and the קהל responds:

בָּרוּךְ יהוה הַמְבֹרָךְ לְעוֹלָם וָעֶד.

In ארץ ישראל during אלול, some congregations blow שופר and say לְדָוִד, יהוה אוֹרִי
(page 197) at this point. In a house of mourning the service continues on page 603.

READINGS AFTER THE SERVICE

Over the centuries, some communities have added various readings
and personal supplications to the end of the service.
The following is based on the text as compiled in Siddur Otzar HaTefillot (Vilna, 1911).

THE SIX REMEMBRANCES

The Exodus from Egypt

That you may remember the day you left the land of Egypt all the days of your life.   *Deut. 16*

The Revelation at Mount Sinai

Only be careful and watch yourself very closely lest you forget the things your eyes   *Deut. 4*
have seen or let them slip from your heart all the days of your life. You shall make them
known to your children and your children's children – the day you stood before the
Lord your God at Horeb when the Lord said to me, "Assemble the people before
Me and I will let them hear My words, so that they may learn to be in awe of Me as
long as they live on earth, and they will teach them to their children."

Amalek

Remember what Amalek did to you on your way out of Egypt, how he met you on the   *Deut. 25*
way, cutting off those who were lagging behind, when you were tired and exhausted,
and he did not fear God. So, when the Lord your God grants you rest from all your
enemies around you in the land the Lord your God is about to give you to possess
as an inheritance, you shall wipe out the memory of Amalek from under the heavens:
you shall not forget.

The Golden Calf

Remember, and do not forget, how you provoked the Lord your God in the wilder-   *Deut. 9*
ness.

Miriam

Remember what the Lord your God did to Miriam on the way when you came out   *Deut. 24*
of Egypt.

The Shabbat

Remember the Sabbath day to hallow it.   *Ex. 20*

---

golden calf reminds us of sins against God; Miriam's fate reminds us of sins
against our fellows, especially through evil speech. Amalek's attack on the
Israelites showed how a failure to fear God leads to cruelty against human
beings.

אמירות לאחר התפילה

Over the centuries, some communities have added various readings
and personal supplications to the end of the service.
The following is based on the text as compiled in סידור אוצר התפילות *(Vilna, 1911).*

שש זכירות

יציאת מצרים

דברים טז   לְמַעַן תִּזְכֹּר אֶת־יוֹם צֵאתְךָ מֵאֶרֶץ מִצְרַיִם כֹּל יְמֵי חַיֶּיךָ:

מעמד הר סיני

דברים ד   רַק הִשָּׁמֶר לְךָ וּשְׁמֹר נַפְשְׁךָ מְאֹד פֶּן־תִּשְׁכַּח אֶת־הַדְּבָרִים אֲשֶׁר־רָאוּ עֵינֶיךָ וּפֶן־יָסוּרוּ מִלְּבָבְךָ כֹּל יְמֵי חַיֶּיךָ וְהוֹדַעְתָּם לְבָנֶיךָ וְלִבְנֵי בָנֶיךָ: יוֹם אֲשֶׁר עָמַדְתָּ לִפְנֵי יהוה אֱלֹהֶיךָ בְּחֹרֵב בֶּאֱמֹר יהוה אֵלַי הַקְהֶל־לִי אֶת־הָעָם וְאַשְׁמִעֵם אֶת־דְּבָרָי אֲשֶׁר יִלְמְדוּן לְיִרְאָה אֹתִי כָּל־הַיָּמִים אֲשֶׁר הֵם חַיִּים עַל־הָאֲדָמָה וְאֶת־בְּנֵיהֶם יְלַמֵּדוּן:

מעשה עמלק ומחייתו

דברים כה   זָכוֹר אֵת אֲשֶׁר־עָשָׂה לְךָ עֲמָלֵק בַּדֶּרֶךְ בְּצֵאתְכֶם מִמִּצְרָיִם: אֲשֶׁר קָרְךָ בַּדֶּרֶךְ וַיְזַנֵּב בְּךָ כָּל־הַנֶּחֱשָׁלִים אַחֲרֶיךָ וְאַתָּה עָיֵף וְיָגֵעַ וְלֹא יָרֵא אֱלֹהִים: וְהָיָה בְּהָנִיחַ יהוה אֱלֹהֶיךָ ׀ לְךָ מִכָּל־אֹיְבֶיךָ מִסָּבִיב בָּאָרֶץ אֲשֶׁר־יהוה אֱלֹהֶיךָ נֹתֵן לְךָ נַחֲלָה לְרִשְׁתָּהּ תִּמְחֶה אֶת־זֵכֶר עֲמָלֵק מִתַּחַת הַשָּׁמָיִם לֹא תִּשְׁכָּח:

מעשי אבותינו במדבר

דברים ט   זְכֹר אַל־תִּשְׁכַּח אֵת אֲשֶׁר־הִקְצַפְתָּ אֶת־יהוה אֱלֹהֶיךָ בַּמִּדְבָּר

מעשה מרים

דברים כד   זָכוֹר אֵת אֲשֶׁר־עָשָׂה יהוה אֱלֹהֶיךָ לְמִרְיָם בַּדֶּרֶךְ בְּצֵאתְכֶם מִמִּצְרָיִם:

שבת

שמות כ   זָכוֹר אֶת־יוֹם הַשַּׁבָּת לְקַדְּשׁוֹ:

THE SIX REMEMBRANCES
These acts of remembrance define three positive and three negative param-
eters of Jewish faith and life. Positively, the exodus reminds us of divine
redemption, Sinai of revelation, and the Sabbath of creation. Negatively, the

THE TEN COMMANDMENTS

God spoke all these words, saying: *Ex. 20*

1. אָנֹכִי I am the Lord your God who brought you out of the land of Egypt, from the slave-house.

2. לֹא־יִהְיֶה Have no other gods besides Me. Do not make a sculptured image for yourself, or any likeness of what is in the heavens above, or on the earth below, or in the waters under the earth. Do not bow down to them or worship them, for I am the Lord your God, a zealous God, visiting the guilt of the parents on the children to the third and fourth generation, if they also reject Me; but showing kindness to thousands of generations of those who love Me and keep My commandments.

3. לֹא תִשָּׂא Do not take the name of the Lord your God in vain. The Lord will not leave unpunished one who utters His name in vain.

4. זָכוֹר Remember the Sabbath and keep it holy. Six days you shall labor and do all your work, but the seventh day is a Sabbath of the Lord your God; on it you shall not do any work – you, your son or daughter, your male or female slaves, your cattle, or the stranger within your gates. For in six days the Lord made heaven and earth and sea, and all that is in them, and rested on the seventh day; therefore the Lord blessed the Sabbath day and made it holy.

5. כַּבֵּד Honor your father and your mother, so that you may live long in the land that the Lord your God is giving you.

6. לֹא תִרְצַח Do not murder.

7. לֹא תִנְאָף Do not commit adultery.

8. לֹא תִגְנֹב Do not steal.

9. לֹא־תַעֲנֶה Do not testify as a false witness against your neighbor.

10. לֹא תַחְמֹד Do not be envious of your neighbor's house. Do not be envious of your neighbor's wife, his male or female slave, his ox, his ass, or anything else that is your neighbor's.

---

when sectarians maintained that only these, and not the other commandments, were from God (*Berakhot* 12a). So deep was the attachment of Jews to this "sublime summary of human duties" (Rabbi J.H. Hertz), however, that the custom developed to say it privately after the end of the morning service.

עשרת הדברות

וַיְדַבֵּר אֱלֹהִים אֵת כָּל־הַדְּבָרִים הָאֵלֶּה לֵאמֹר:

א אָנֹכִי יהוה אֱלֹהֶיךָ אֲשֶׁר הוֹצֵאתִיךָ מֵאֶרֶץ מִצְרַיִם מִבֵּית עֲבָדִים:

ב לֹא־יִהְיֶה לְךָ אֱלֹהִים אֲחֵרִים עַל־פָּנָי: לֹא־תַעֲשֶׂה לְךָ פֶסֶל וְכָל־תְּמוּנָה אֲשֶׁר בַּשָּׁמַיִם מִמַּעַל וַאֲשֶׁר בָּאָרֶץ מִתַּחַת וַאֲשֶׁר בַּמַּיִם מִתַּחַת לָאָרֶץ: לֹא־תִשְׁתַּחֲוֶה לָהֶם וְלֹא תָעָבְדֵם כִּי אָנֹכִי יהוה אֱלֹהֶיךָ אֵל קַנָּא פֹּקֵד עֲוֹן אָבֹת עַל־בָּנִים עַל־שִׁלֵּשִׁים וְעַל־רִבֵּעִים לְשֹׂנְאָי: וְעֹשֶׂה חֶסֶד לַאֲלָפִים לְאֹהֲבַי וּלְשֹׁמְרֵי מִצְוֹתָי:

ג לֹא תִשָּׂא אֶת־שֵׁם־יהוה אֱלֹהֶיךָ לַשָּׁוְא כִּי לֹא יְנַקֶּה יהוה אֵת אֲשֶׁר־יִשָּׂא אֶת־שְׁמוֹ לַשָּׁוְא:

ד זָכוֹר אֶת־יוֹם הַשַּׁבָּת לְקַדְּשׁוֹ: שֵׁשֶׁת יָמִים תַּעֲבֹד וְעָשִׂיתָ כָּל־מְלַאכְתֶּךָ: וְיוֹם הַשְּׁבִיעִי שַׁבָּת לַיהוה אֱלֹהֶיךָ לֹא־תַעֲשֶׂה כָל־מְלָאכָה אַתָּה וּבִנְךָ וּבִתֶּךָ עַבְדְּךָ וַאֲמָתְךָ וּבְהֶמְתֶּךָ וְגֵרְךָ אֲשֶׁר בִּשְׁעָרֶיךָ: כִּי שֵׁשֶׁת־יָמִים עָשָׂה יהוה אֶת־הַשָּׁמַיִם וְאֶת־הָאָרֶץ אֶת־הַיָּם וְאֶת־כָּל־אֲשֶׁר־בָּם וַיָּנַח בַּיּוֹם הַשְּׁבִיעִי עַל־כֵּן בֵּרַךְ יהוה אֶת־יוֹם הַשַּׁבָּת וַיְקַדְּשֵׁהוּ:

ה כַּבֵּד אֶת־אָבִיךָ וְאֶת־אִמֶּךָ לְמַעַן יַאֲרִכוּן יָמֶיךָ עַל הָאֲדָמָה אֲשֶׁר־יהוה אֱלֹהֶיךָ נֹתֵן לָךְ:

ו לֹא תִרְצָח

ז לֹא תִנְאָף

ח לֹא תִגְנֹב

ט לֹא־תַעֲנֶה בְרֵעֲךָ עֵד שָׁקֶר:

י לֹא תַחְמֹד בֵּית רֵעֶךָ לֹא־תַחְמֹד אֵשֶׁת רֵעֶךָ וְעַבְדּוֹ וַאֲמָתוֹ וְשׁוֹרוֹ וַחֲמֹרוֹ וְכֹל אֲשֶׁר לְרֵעֶךָ:

THE TEN COMMANDMENTS

In Temple times, the Ten Commandments were recited as part of the daily prayers, immediately prior to the Shema. The practice was discontinued

THE THIRTEEN PRINCIPLES OF JEWISH FAITH

1. I believe with perfect faith
    that the Creator,
    blessed be His name,
    creates and rules all creatures,
    and that He alone made, makes, and will make, all things.

2. I believe with perfect faith
    that the Creator,
    blessed be His name, is One;
    that there is no oneness like His in any way;
    and that He alone is our God who was, is, and ever will be.

3. I believe with perfect faith
    that the Creator,
    blessed be His name, is not physical,
    that no physical attributes can apply to Him,
    and that there is nothing whatsoever to compare to Him.

4. I believe with perfect faith
    that the Creator,
    blessed be His name, is first and last.

5. I believe with perfect faith
    that the Creator,
    blessed be His name,
    is the only one to whom it is proper to pray,
    and that it is improper to pray to anyone else.

6. I believe with perfect faith
    that all the words of the prophets are true.

7. I believe with perfect faith
    that the prophecy of Moses our teacher,
    peace be to him, was true,
    and that he was the father of the prophets –
    those who preceded him and those who followed him.

---

and (5) the belief that He alone is to be worshiped. The next four are about revelation: (6) belief in prophecy; (7) the unique status of Moses as the

שלושה עשר עיקרים

א אֲנִי מַאֲמִין בֶּאֱמוּנָה שְׁלֵמָה
שֶׁהַבּוֹרֵא יִתְבָּרַךְ שְׁמוֹ הוּא בּוֹרֵא וּמַנְהִיג לְכָל הַבְּרוּאִים
וְהוּא לְבַדּוֹ עָשָׂה וְעוֹשֶׂה וְיַעֲשֶׂה לְכָל הַמַּעֲשִׂים.

ב אֲנִי מַאֲמִין בֶּאֱמוּנָה שְׁלֵמָה
שֶׁהַבּוֹרֵא יִתְבָּרַךְ שְׁמוֹ הוּא יָחִיד
וְאֵין יְחִידוּת כָּמוֹהוּ בְּשׁוּם פָּנִים
וְהוּא לְבַדּוֹ אֱלֹהֵינוּ, הָיָה הֹוֶה וְיִהְיֶה.

ג אֲנִי מַאֲמִין בֶּאֱמוּנָה שְׁלֵמָה
שֶׁהַבּוֹרֵא יִתְבָּרַךְ שְׁמוֹ אֵינוֹ גוּף
וְלֹא יַשִּׂיגוּהוּ מַשִּׂיגֵי הַגּוּף
וְאֵין לוֹ שׁוּם דִּמְיוֹן כְּלָל.

ד אֲנִי מַאֲמִין בֶּאֱמוּנָה שְׁלֵמָה
שֶׁהַבּוֹרֵא יִתְבָּרַךְ שְׁמוֹ הוּא רִאשׁוֹן וְהוּא אַחֲרוֹן.

ה אֲנִי מַאֲמִין בֶּאֱמוּנָה שְׁלֵמָה
שֶׁהַבּוֹרֵא יִתְבָּרַךְ שְׁמוֹ לוֹ לְבַדּוֹ רָאוּי לְהִתְפַּלֵּל
וְאֵין רָאוּי לְהִתְפַּלֵּל לְזוּלָתוֹ.

ו אֲנִי מַאֲמִין בֶּאֱמוּנָה שְׁלֵמָה
שֶׁכָּל דִּבְרֵי נְבִיאִים אֱמֶת.

ז אֲנִי מַאֲמִין בֶּאֱמוּנָה שְׁלֵמָה
שֶׁנְּבוּאַת מֹשֶׁה רַבֵּנוּ עָלָיו הַשָּׁלוֹם הָיְתָה אֲמִתִּית
וְשֶׁהוּא הָיָה אָב לַנְּבִיאִים, לַקּוֹדְמִים לְפָנָיו וְלַבָּאִים אַחֲרָיו.

THE THIRTEEN PRINCIPLES OF JEWISH FAITH
A prose counterpart to the poetic Yigdal, both of which summarize the principles set out by Moses Maimonides (1135–1204). The first five are about God:
(1) His existence; (2) His unity; (3) His incorporeality; (4) His eternity;

8. I believe with perfect faith
>> that the entire Torah now in our hands
>> is the same one that was given to Moses our teacher,
>> peace be upon him.

9. I believe with perfect faith
>> that this Torah will not be changed,
>> nor will there be any other Torah from the Creator,
>> blessed be His name.

10. I believe with perfect faith
>> that the Creator, blessed be His name,
>> knows all the deeds and thoughts of humanity,
>> as it is said, "He fashions the hearts of them all,   *Ps. 33*
>> comprehending all their deeds."

11. I believe with perfect faith
>> that the Creator, blessed be His name,
>> rewards those who keep His commandments,
>> and punishes those who transgress them.

12. I believe with perfect faith
>> in the coming of the Messiah,
>> and though he may delay,
>> I wait daily for his coming.

13. I believe with perfect faith
>> that the dead will live again
>> at a time of the Creator's choosing:
>> blessed be His name and exalted be His mention
>> for ever and all time.

---

ishes; (12) He will send the Messiah; and (13) in time to come, He will bring the dead back to life again. The presence of this passage is a reminder that the siddur is not just a book of prayer but also of faith.

ח אֲנִי מַאֲמִין בֶּאֱמוּנָה שְׁלֵמָה
שֶׁכָּל הַתּוֹרָה הַמְּצוּיָה עַתָּה בְּיָדֵינוּ
הִיא הַנְּתוּנָה לְמֹשֶׁה רַבֵּנוּ עָלָיו הַשָּׁלוֹם.

ט אֲנִי מַאֲמִין בֶּאֱמוּנָה שְׁלֵמָה
שֶׁזֹּאת הַתּוֹרָה לֹא תְהֵא מֻחְלֶפֶת
וְלֹא תְהֵא תוֹרָה אַחֶרֶת מֵאֵת הַבּוֹרֵא יִתְבָּרַךְ שְׁמוֹ.

י אֲנִי מַאֲמִין בֶּאֱמוּנָה שְׁלֵמָה
שֶׁהַבּוֹרֵא יִתְבָּרַךְ שְׁמוֹ
יוֹדֵעַ כָּל מַעֲשֵׂה בְּנֵי אָדָם וְכָל מַחְשְׁבוֹתָם.
שֶׁנֶּאֱמַר: הַיֹּצֵר יַחַד לִבָּם, הַמֵּבִין אֶל־כָּל־מַעֲשֵׂיהֶם:

תהלים לג

יא אֲנִי מַאֲמִין בֶּאֱמוּנָה שְׁלֵמָה
שֶׁהַבּוֹרֵא יִתְבָּרַךְ שְׁמוֹ גּוֹמֵל טוֹב לְשׁוֹמְרֵי מִצְוֹתָיו
וּמַעֲנִישׁ לְעוֹבְרֵי מִצְוֹתָיו.

יב אֲנִי מַאֲמִין בֶּאֱמוּנָה שְׁלֵמָה
בְּבִיאַת הַמָּשִׁיחַ
וְאַף עַל פִּי שֶׁיִּתְמַהְמֵהַּ עִם כָּל זֶה אֲחַכֶּה לּוֹ
בְּכָל יוֹם שֶׁיָּבוֹא.

יג אֲנִי מַאֲמִין בֶּאֱמוּנָה שְׁלֵמָה
שֶׁתִּהְיֶה תְּחִיַּת הַמֵּתִים
בְּעֵת שֶׁיַּעֲלֶה רָצוֹן מֵאֵת הַבּוֹרֵא
יִתְבָּרַךְ שְׁמוֹ וְיִתְעַלֶּה זִכְרוֹ לָעַד וּלְנֵצַח נְצָחִים.

greatest of the prophets; (8) the divine authorship of the Torah; and (9) the immutability of the Torah. The last four are about reward, punishment and justice: (10) God knows our thoughts and deeds; (11) He rewards and pun-

The following is said after morning and evening prayers:

יְהִי יהוה **May the LORD** our God be with us, as He was with our ancestors. *I Kings 8*
May He never abandon us or forsake us, ever; as He turns our hearts toward
Him, to follow all His paths and to keep His commands and His statutes and
laws, as He charged our ancestors. And may these words with which I have
pleaded before the LORD be close to the LORD our God, day and night, that
He do justice for Your servant, and for Your people Israel, day by day. That all
the peoples of the earth shall know that the LORD is God; there is no other.

יהוה נְחֵנִי **Lead me, LORD,** in Your righteousness, because of my foes; make *Ps. 5*
Your way straight before me. As for me, I lead a blameless life; redeem me and *Ps. 26*
show me favor. Turn to me and show me favor, for I am lonely and afflicted. *Ps. 25*
My foot stands on level ground: in the assemblies I will bless the LORD. The *Ps. 26*
LORD is my Guardian; the LORD is my Shade at my right hand. My help comes *Ps. 121*
from the LORD, Maker of heaven and earth. The LORD will guard my coming
and going, for life and for peace, now and for evermore. Gaze down from Your *Deut. 26*
holy dwelling place, from the heavens, and bless Your people Israel, and the
land that You have given us, as You promised our ancestors: a land flowing
with milk and honey.

אֶל הַכָּבוֹד **Glorious God,** I bring before You song and praise; I shall worship
You day and night. Blessed be the One and Only One – who was, who is and
who will always be. LORD God, God of Israel, King, King of kings, Holy One,
blessed be He. He is the living God, the living and ever, forever enduring King.
Blessed be the name of His glorious kingdom for ever and ever. I long for Your *Gen. 49*
salvation, LORD. All the nations will walk, each in the name of its god; and
I will walk in the name of the LORD, the living God and eternal King. My help *Ps. 121*
comes from the LORD, Maker of heaven and earth. The LORD will reign for *Ex. 15*
ever and all time.

לַמְנַצֵּחַ **For the Chief Musician;** with stringed instruments. A psalm. A song. *Ps. 67*
May God be gracious to us and bless us; may He cause His face to shine upon
us, Selah, that Your way may be known on earth, Your salvation, among all nations. May the peoples praise You, God; may all the peoples praise You! The
nations will rejoice and break into song; for You judge the peoples with equity
and guide the nations of the earth, Selah. May the peoples praise You, God;
may all the peoples praise You! The earth has yielded its produce; may God,
our God, bless us. May God bless us, and may all the ends of the earth fear Him!

Some say Adon Olam (page 22) at this point.

The following is said after morning and evening prayers:

מלכים א׳ ח : יְהִי יהוה אֱלֹהֵינוּ עִמָּנוּ כַּאֲשֶׁר הָיָה עִם־אֲבֹתֵינוּ, אַל־יַעַזְבֵנוּ וְאַל־יִטְּשֵׁנוּ: לְהַטּוֹת לְבָבֵנוּ אֵלָיו, לָלֶכֶת בְּכָל־דְּרָכָיו וְלִשְׁמֹר מִצְוֹתָיו וְחֻקָּיו וּמִשְׁפָּטָיו אֲשֶׁר צִוָּה אֶת־אֲבֹתֵינוּ: וְיִהְיוּ דְבָרַי אֵלֶּה אֲשֶׁר הִתְחַנַּנְתִּי לִפְנֵי יהוה, קְרֹבִים אֶל־יהוה אֱלֹהֵינוּ יוֹמָם וָלָיְלָה, לַעֲשׂוֹת מִשְׁפַּט עַבְדּוֹ וּמִשְׁפַּט עַמּוֹ יִשְׂרָאֵל דְּבַר־יוֹם בְּיוֹמוֹ: לְמַעַן דַּעַת כָּל־עַמֵּי הָאָרֶץ כִּי יהוה הוּא הָאֱלֹהִים, אֵין עוֹד:

תהלים ה / תהלים כז : יהוה נְחֵנִי בְצִדְקָתֶךָ לְמַעַן שׁוֹרְרָי, הַיְשַׁר לְפָנַי דַּרְכֶּךָ: וַאֲנִי בְּתֻמִּי אֵלֵךְ, פְּדֵנִי תהלים כה / תהלים כו : וְחָנֵּנִי: פְּנֵה־אֵלַי וְחָנֵּנִי כִּי־יָחִיד וְעָנִי אָנִי: רַגְלִי עָמְדָה בְמִישׁוֹר, בְּמַקְהֵלִים תהלים קכא : אֲבָרֵךְ יהוה: יהוה שֹׁמְרִי, יהוה צִלְּךָ עַל יַד יְמִינֶךָ. עֻזְרִי מֵעִם יהוה, עֹשֵׂה שָׁמַיִם וָאָרֶץ: יהוה יִשְׁמָר צֵאתְךָ וּבוֹאֶךָ לְחַיִּים וּלְשָׁלוֹם, מֵעַתָּה וְעַד עוֹלָם. דברים כו : הַשְׁקִיפָה מִמְּעוֹן קָדְשְׁךָ מִן־הַשָּׁמַיִם, וּבָרֵךְ אֶת־עַמְּךָ, אֶת־יִשְׂרָאֵל, וְאֵת הָאֲדָמָה אֲשֶׁר נָתַתָּה לָנוּ כַּאֲשֶׁר נִשְׁבַּעְתָּ לַאֲבֹתֵינוּ, אֶרֶץ זָבַת חָלָב וּדְבָשׁ:

אֵל הַכָּבוֹד, אֶתֵּן לְךָ שִׁיר וָהַלֵּל וְאֶעֱבֹד לְךָ יוֹם וָלֵיל. בָּרוּךְ יָחִיד וּמְיֻחָד, הָיָה הֹוֶה וְיִהְיֶה, יהוה אֱלֹהֵי יִשְׂרָאֵל, מֶלֶךְ מַלְכֵי הַמְּלָכִים, הַקָּדוֹשׁ בָּרוּךְ הוּא. הוּא אֱלֹהִים חַיִּים, מֶלֶךְ חַי וְקַיָּם לָעַד וּלְעוֹלְמֵי עַד. בָּרוּךְ שֵׁם בראשית מט : כְּבוֹד מַלְכוּתוֹ לְעוֹלָם וָעֶד. לִישׁוּעָתְךָ קִוִּיתִי יהוה: כִּי כָל הָעַמִּים יֵלְכוּ תהלים קכא : אִישׁ בְּשֵׁם אֱלֹהָיו, וַאֲנַחְנוּ נֵלֵךְ בְּשֵׁם יהוה אֱלֹהֵינוּ חַיִּים וּמֶלֶךְ עוֹלָם. עֻזְרִי שמות טו : מֵעִם יהוה, עֹשֵׂה שָׁמַיִם וָאָרֶץ: יהוה יִמְלֹךְ לְעֹלָם וָעֶד:

תהלים סז : לַמְנַצֵּחַ בִּנְגִינֹת, מִזְמוֹר שִׁיר: אֱלֹהִים יְחָנֵּנוּ וִיבָרְכֵנוּ, יָאֵר פָּנָיו אִתָּנוּ סֶלָה: לָדַעַת בָּאָרֶץ דַּרְכֶּךָ, בְּכָל־גּוֹיִם יְשׁוּעָתֶךָ: יוֹדוּךָ עַמִּים אֱלֹהִים, יוֹדוּךָ עַמִּים כֻּלָּם: יִשְׂמְחוּ וִירַנְּנוּ לְאֻמִּים, כִּי־תִשְׁפֹּט עַמִּים מִישֹׁר, וּלְאֻמִּים בָּאָרֶץ תַּנְחֵם סֶלָה: יוֹדוּךָ עַמִּים אֱלֹהִים, יוֹדוּךָ עַמִּים כֻּלָּם: אֶרֶץ נָתְנָה יְבוּלָהּ, יְבָרְכֵנוּ אֱלֹהִים אֱלֹהֵינוּ: יְבָרְכֵנוּ אֱלֹהִים, וְיִירְאוּ אֹתוֹ כָּל־אַפְסֵי־אָרֶץ:

Some say אדון עולם *(page 23) at this point.*

PRAYER UPON LEAVING THE SYNAGOGUE

Say while seated:

אַךְ Surely the righteous will praise Your name;
the upright shall live in Your presence.

Ps. 104

Stand and say:

כִּי All the nations will walk, each in the name of its god;
and I will walk in the name of the Lord, the living God and eternal King.
My help comes from the Lord, Maker of heaven and earth.
The Lord will reign for ever and all time.

Ps. 121

Ex. 15

*Walk toward the door of the synagogue, respectfully, without turning
one's back, as one taking leave of the Divine Presence.*
At the door, bow toward the Ark and say:

יהוה נְחֵנִי Lead me, Lord, in Your righteousness,
because of my foes; make Your way straight before me.

Ps. 5

While leaving, say the following three verses:

גָּד Invaders may invade Gad, but he will invade at their heels.
David was wise in all that he did, and the Lord was with him.
And Noah found favor in the eyes of the Lord.

Gen. 49

1 Sam. 18

Gen. 6

One who will conduct business says:

עֶזְרִי My help comes from the Lord, Maker of heaven and earth. Cast your
cares upon the Lord and He will sustain you. Watch the blameless, observe
the upright, for there is a future for the peace-loving man. Trust in the Lord
and do good, settle the land and cherish faithfulness. Behold, God is my salvation. I will trust and not be afraid. The Lord, the Lord, is my strength and
my song. He has become my salvation. Master of the Universe, it is written
in Your holy scriptures: "Love surrounds him who trusts in the Lord"; and
it is written: "You give life to them all." Lord, God of truth, grant blessing
and success to all the works of my hands. For I place my trust in You, that
through my trade, through my profession, You will send me blessing, allowing me to sustain myself and the people of my household with ease, without
suffering, by legal and not by forbidden means, for life and for peace. And
may what is written be fulfilled in me: "Cast your cares upon the Lord and
He will sustain you." Amen.

Ps. 121
Ps. 55
Ps. 37
Ibid.
Is. 12

Ps. 32

Neh. 9

Ps. 55

תפילה כשיוצא מבית הכנסת

Say while seated:

תהלים קמו

אַךְ צַדִּיקִים יוֹדוּ לִשְׁמֶךָ, יֵשְׁבוּ יְשָׁרִים אֶת־פָּנֶיךָ:

Stand and say:

כִּי כָּל הָעַמִּים יֵלְכוּ אִישׁ בְּשֵׁם אֱלֹהָיו,
וַאֲנַחְנוּ נֵלֵךְ בְּשֵׁם יהוה אֱלֹהֵינוּ חַיִּים וּמֶלֶךְ עוֹלָם.

תהלים קכא

עֶזְרִי מֵעִם יהוה, עֹשֵׂה שָׁמַיִם וָאָרֶץ:

שמות טו

יהוה יִמְלֹךְ לְעֹלָם וָעֶד:

Walk toward the door of the בית כנסת, respectfully, without turning one's back, as one taking leave of the Divine Presence.
At the door, bow toward the ארון קדש and say:

תהלים ה

יהוה נְחֵנִי בְצִדְקָתֶךָ לְמַעַן שׁוֹרְרָי, הַיְשַׁר לְפָנַי דַּרְכֶּךָ:

While leaving, say the following three verses:

בראשית מט

גָּד גְּדוּד יְגוּדֶנּוּ, וְהוּא יָגֻד עָקֵב:

שמואל א׳ יח

וַיְהִי דָוִד לְכָל־דְּרָכָו מַשְׂכִּיל, וַיהוה עִמּוֹ:

בראשית ו

וְנֹחַ מָצָא חֵן בְּעֵינֵי יהוה:

One who will conduct business says:

תהלים קכא
תהלים נה
תהלים לז
שם

עֶזְרִי מֵעִם יהוה, עֹשֵׂה שָׁמַיִם וָאָרֶץ: הַשְׁלֵךְ עַל־יהוה יְהָבְךָ וְהוּא יְכַלְכְּלֶךָ: שְׁמָר־תָּם וּרְאֵה יָשָׁר, כִּי־אַחֲרִית לְאִישׁ שָׁלוֹם: בְּטַח בַּיהוה וַעֲשֵׂה־

ישעיה יב

טוֹב, שְׁכָן־אֶרֶץ וּרְעֵה אֱמוּנָה: הִנֵּה אֵל יְשׁוּעָתִי אֶבְטַח וְלֹא אֶפְחָד, כִּי־עָזִּי וְזִמְרָת יָהּ יהוה וַיְהִי־לִי לִישׁוּעָה: רִבּוֹנוֹ שֶׁל עוֹלָם, בְּדִבְרֵי קָדְשְׁךָ כָּתוּב

תהלים לב
נחמיה ט

לֵאמֹר, הַבּוֹטֵחַ בַּיהוה חֶסֶד יְסוֹבְבֶנּוּ: וּכְתִיב, וְאַתָּה מְחַיֶּה אֶת־כֻּלָּם:

יהוה אֱלֹהִים אֱמֶת, תֵּן בְּרָכָה וְהַצְלָחָה בְּכָל מַעֲשֵׂה יָדַי, כִּי בְּךָ בָטַחְתִּי בָּךְ שֶׁעַל יְדֵי מַשָּׂא וּמַתָּן וַעֲסָקִים שֶׁלִּי תִּשְׁלַח לִי בְּרָכָה, כְּדֵי שֶׁאוּכַל לְפַרְנֵס אֶת עַצְמִי וּבְנֵי בֵיתִי בְּנַחַת וְלֹא בְּצַעַר, בְּהֶתֵּר וְלֹא בְּאִסּוּר,

תהלים נה

לְחַיִּים וּלְשָׁלוֹם. וִיקֻיַּם בִּי מִקְרָא שֶׁכָּתוּב: הַשְׁלֵךְ עַל־יהוה יְהָבְךָ וְהוּא יְכַלְכְּלֶךָ, אָמֵן.

PERSONAL SUPPLICATIONS

Some have the custom to read on a daily basis certain passages from the Torah, either in supplication to God that He may grant us our daily needs (both material and spiritual), or as a reminder that all our blessings come ultimately from Him.

THE CHAPTER OF THE MANNA

After the exodus from Egypt, the Israelites depended each day on the manna for their survival. Nowadays, we risk living under the illusion of self-reliance, and forgetting the true source of our sustenance. As early as the thirteenth century, the pupils of the Maharam of Rothenburg recommended reciting the verses which describe the miracle of the manna, as a declaration of faith and an expression of trust and gratitude.

יְהִי רָצוֹן **May it be Your will**, Lord our God, God of our ancestors, that you call forth sustenance for all Your people Israel, and among them, for me and for the people of my household. May it come with ease, without suffering, honorably, without shame, by legal and not by forbidden means, that we may perform Your service and learn Your Torah; just as You nourished our ancestors in the wilderness, in an arid, desert land.

וַיֹּאמֶר **The** Lord **said to Moses:** I shall rain bread down upon you from the   *Ex. 16* sky. And the people shall go out and gather, each day their daily needs, so that I may test whether they will follow My Law or not. And on the sixth day, as they prepare what they bring home, it shall be twice what they gather every day. And so Moses and Aaron told all the people of Israel, "By evening you shall know that it was the Lord who brought you out of the land of Egypt, and in the morning you shall see the glory of God, who has heard all your protest against Him – as for us, who are we that you should stir up protest against us?" Moses said, "The Lord shall give you meat to eat in the evening, and bread in the morning to satisfy your hunger, when the Lord heeds the protest you have stirred up against Him – as for us, who are we? Your protest is not for us but for the Lord." Then Moses said to Aaron, "Tell all the congregation of Israel: Draw near to the Lord, for He has heard your protest." And when Aaron spoke to all the congregation of Israel, they turned toward the desert and there was the glory of God, revealed in a cloud.

The Lord said to Moses, "I have heard the protest of the people of Israel. Speak to them, tell them, by evening you shall eat meat, and in the morning, bread will satisfy you, and you shall know that I am the Lord your God." When evening came, quail rose up and covered the camp, and in the morning, a layer of dew surrounded the camp. And as the layer of dew lifted – there on the surface of the desert was a fine, round substance, fine as frost upon the land. And the

בקשות אישיות

Some have the custom to read on a daily basis certain passages from the תורה, either in supplication to God that He may grant us our daily needs (both material and spiritual), or as a reminder that all our blessings come ultimately from Him.

פרשת המן

After the exodus from Egypt, the Israelites depended each day on the manna for their survival. Nowadays, we risk living under the illusion of self-reliance, and forgetting the true source of our sustenance. As early as the thirteenth century, the pupils of the Maharam of Rothenburg recommended reciting the verses which describe the miracle of the manna, as a declaration of faith and an expression of trust and gratitude.

יְהִי רָצוֹן מִלְּפָנֶיךָ, יהוה אֱלֹהֵינוּ וֵאלֹהֵי אֲבוֹתֵינוּ, שֶׁתַּזְמִין פַּרְנָסָה לְכָל עַמְּךָ בֵּית יִשְׂרָאֵל, וּפַרְנָסָתִי וּפַרְנָסַת אַנְשֵׁי בֵיתִי בִּכְלָלָם, בְּנַחַת וְלֹא בְצַעַר, בְּכָבוֹד וְלֹא בְבִזּוּי, בְּהֶתֵּר וְלֹא בְאִסּוּר, כְּדֵי שֶׁנּוּכַל לַעֲבֹד עֲבוֹדָתֶךָ וְלִלְמֹד תּוֹרָתֶךָ, כְּמוֹ שֶׁזַּנְתָּ לַאֲבוֹתֵינוּ מָן בַּמִּדְבָּר, בְּאֶרֶץ צִיָּה וַעֲרָבָה.

שמות טז
וַיֹּאמֶר יהוה אֶל־מֹשֶׁה, הִנְנִי מַמְטִיר לָכֶם לֶחֶם מִן־הַשָּׁמָיִם, וְיָצָא הָעָם וְלָקְטוּ דְּבַר־יוֹם בְּיוֹמוֹ, לְמַעַן אֲנַסֶּנּוּ הֲיֵלֵךְ בְּתוֹרָתִי אִם־לֹא: וְהָיָה בַּיּוֹם הַשִּׁשִּׁי, וְהֵכִינוּ אֵת אֲשֶׁר־יָבִיאוּ, וְהָיָה מִשְׁנֶה עַל אֲשֶׁר־יִלְקְטוּ יוֹם יוֹם: וַיֹּאמֶר מֹשֶׁה וְאַהֲרֹן אֶל־כָּל־בְּנֵי יִשְׂרָאֵל, עֶרֶב וִידַעְתֶּם כִּי יהוה הוֹצִיא אֶתְכֶם מֵאֶרֶץ מִצְרָיִם: וּבֹקֶר וּרְאִיתֶם אֶת־כְּבוֹד יהוה, בְּשָׁמְעוֹ אֶת־תְּלֻנֹּתֵיכֶם עַל־יהוה, וְנַחְנוּ מָה כִּי תַלִּינוּ עָלֵינוּ: וַיֹּאמֶר מֹשֶׁה, בְּתֵת יהוה לָכֶם בָּעֶרֶב בָּשָׂר לֶאֱכֹל וְלֶחֶם בַּבֹּקֶר לִשְׂבֹּעַ, בִּשְׁמֹעַ יהוה אֶת־תְּלֻנֹּתֵיכֶם אֲשֶׁר־אַתֶּם מַלִּינִם עָלָיו, וְנַחְנוּ מָה, לֹא־עָלֵינוּ תְלֻנֹּתֵיכֶם כִּי עַל־יהוה: וַיֹּאמֶר מֹשֶׁה אֶל־אַהֲרֹן, אֱמֹר אֶל־כָּל־עֲדַת בְּנֵי יִשְׂרָאֵל, קִרְבוּ לִפְנֵי יהוה כִּי שָׁמַע אֵת תְּלֻנֹּתֵיכֶם: וַיְהִי כְּדַבֵּר אַהֲרֹן אֶל־כָּל־עֲדַת בְּנֵי־יִשְׂרָאֵל, וַיִּפְנוּ אֶל־הַמִּדְבָּר, וְהִנֵּה כְּבוֹד יהוה נִרְאָה בֶּעָנָן:

וַיְדַבֵּר יהוה אֶל־מֹשֶׁה לֵּאמֹר: שָׁמַעְתִּי אֶת־תְּלוּנֹּת בְּנֵי יִשְׂרָאֵל, דַּבֵּר אֲלֵהֶם לֵאמֹר בֵּין הָעַרְבַּיִם תֹּאכְלוּ בָשָׂר וּבַבֹּקֶר תִּשְׂבְּעוּ־לָחֶם, וִידַעְתֶּם כִּי אֲנִי יהוה אֱלֹהֵיכֶם: וַיְהִי בָעֶרֶב, וַתַּעַל הַשְּׂלָו וַתְּכַס אֶת־הַמַּחֲנֶה, וּבַבֹּקֶר הָיְתָה שִׁכְבַת הַטַּל סָבִיב לַמַּחֲנֶה: וַתַּעַל שִׁכְבַת הַטָּל, וְהִנֵּה עַל־פְּנֵי הַמִּדְבָּר דַּק מְחֻסְפָּס, דַּק כַּכְּפֹר עַל־הָאָרֶץ: וַיִּרְאוּ בְנֵי־יִשְׂרָאֵל וַיֹּאמְרוּ

children of Israel saw it and said one to another, "What is this?" not knowing what it could be. And Moses said, "This is the bread that the LORD has given you to eat. This is what the LORD has commanded: gather it, each person as much as he eats, an omer a head, as many as you are; let each man bring enough for the people in his tent." And so the people of Israel did; they each gathered; some much and some but little. And they measured what they had taken by the omer, and the ones who took much had no more, and the ones who took little had no less; each man had gathered as much as he would eat. Moses told them, "Let no man leave any of this behind until the morning." But they did not heed Moses, and some left some until the morning, and it became infested with worms and rotted, and Moses was furious with them. They gathered it early in the morning, each man as much as he would eat; and as the sun grew hot, it melted away. On the sixth day they gathered double bread, two omarim for each person, and all the princes of the congregation came and told Moses of it. And he said, "This is what the LORD has said: Tomorrow is a holy Sabbath of utter rest to the LORD – whatever you will bake, bake now, and whatever you will cook, cook; and all that is left over, save until the morning." So they left it for the morning as Moses had charged them; and it did not rot, and no worm was found in it. And Moses said, "Eat it today, for today is the Sabbath of the LORD; today you shall not find it outside. Six days shall you gather it, and on the seventh, the Sabbath, it will not be there." There were those of the people who went out on the seventh day to gather; but no manna did they find.

And the LORD said to Moses, "How long will you refuse to keep My commands and My Law? Look – the LORD has given you the Sabbath; and so He gave you two days' bread on the sixth day; each of you, sit in your places, and let no man leave his home on the seventh day." And so the people rested on the seventh day. The people of Israel named that substance, "Manna." And it looked like coriander seeds, but white, and its taste was that of flatbread made with honey. And Moses said, "This is what the LORD has commanded: An omer measure of this shall be kept down your generations, that you may see the bread that I fed you with in the desert when I brought you out of the land of Egypt." And Moses said to Aaron, "Take a jar and fill it with an omer of manna, and place it in the LORD's presence to be kept through the generations." So, as the LORD commanded Moses, Aaron placed it before the Testimony to be kept there. And the children of Israel ate the manna for forty years, until they arrived in settled land; they ate manna until they came to the borders of the Land of Canaan. An omer is the tenth of an ephah measure.

אִישׁ אֶל־אָחִיו מָן הוּא, כִּי לֹא יָדְעוּ מַה־הוּא, וַיֹּאמֶר מֹשֶׁה אֲלֵהֶם, הוּא
הַלֶּחֶם אֲשֶׁר נָתַן יְהוָה לָכֶם לְאָכְלָה: זֶה הַדָּבָר אֲשֶׁר צִוָּה יְהוָה, לִקְטוּ
מִמֶּנּוּ אִישׁ לְפִי אָכְלוֹ, עֹמֶר לַגֻּלְגֹּלֶת מִסְפַּר נַפְשֹׁתֵיכֶם, אִישׁ לַאֲשֶׁר בְּאָהֳלוֹ
תִּקָּחוּ: וַיַּעֲשׂוּ־כֵן בְּנֵי יִשְׂרָאֵל, וַיִּלְקְטוּ הַמַּרְבֶּה וְהַמַּמְעִיט: וַיָּמֹדּוּ בָעֹמֶר,
וְלֹא הֶעְדִּיף הַמַּרְבֶּה וְהַמַּמְעִיט לֹא הֶחְסִיר, אִישׁ לְפִי־אָכְלוֹ לָקָטוּ: וַיֹּאמֶר
מֹשֶׁה אֲלֵהֶם, אִישׁ אַל־יוֹתֵר מִמֶּנּוּ עַד־בֹּקֶר: וְלֹא־שָׁמְעוּ אֶל־מֹשֶׁה, וַיּוֹתִרוּ
אֲנָשִׁים מִמֶּנּוּ עַד־בֹּקֶר, וַיָּרֻם תּוֹלָעִים וַיִּבְאַשׁ, וַיִּקְצֹף עֲלֵהֶם מֹשֶׁה: וַיִּלְקְטוּ
אֹתוֹ בַּבֹּקֶר בַּבֹּקֶר אִישׁ כְּפִי אָכְלוֹ, וְחַם הַשֶּׁמֶשׁ וְנָמָס: וַיְהִי בַּיּוֹם הַשִּׁשִּׁי
לָקְטוּ לֶחֶם מִשְׁנֶה, שְׁנֵי הָעֹמֶר לָאֶחָד, וַיָּבֹאוּ כָּל־נְשִׂיאֵי הָעֵדָה וַיַּגִּידוּ
לְמֹשֶׁה: וַיֹּאמֶר אֲלֵהֶם, הוּא אֲשֶׁר דִּבֶּר יְהוָה, שַׁבָּתוֹן שַׁבַּת־קֹדֶשׁ לַיהוָה
מָחָר, אֵת אֲשֶׁר־תֹּאפוּ אֵפוּ וְאֵת אֲשֶׁר־תְּבַשְּׁלוּ בַּשֵּׁלוּ, וְאֵת כָּל־הָעֹדֵף
הַנִּיחוּ לָכֶם לְמִשְׁמֶרֶת עַד־הַבֹּקֶר: וַיַּנִּיחוּ אֹתוֹ עַד־הַבֹּקֶר כַּאֲשֶׁר צִוָּה מֹשֶׁה,
וְלֹא הִבְאִישׁ וְרִמָּה לֹא־הָיְתָה־בּוֹ: וַיֹּאמֶר מֹשֶׁה אִכְלֻהוּ הַיּוֹם כִּי־שַׁבָּת
הַיּוֹם לַיהוָה, הַיּוֹם לֹא תִמְצָאֻהוּ בַּשָּׂדֶה: שֵׁשֶׁת יָמִים תִּלְקְטֻהוּ, וּבַיּוֹם
הַשְּׁבִיעִי שַׁבָּת לֹא יִהְיֶה־בּוֹ: וַיְהִי בַּיּוֹם הַשְּׁבִיעִי יָצְאוּ מִן־הָעָם לִלְקֹט, וְלֹא
מָצָאוּ:   וַיֹּאמֶר יְהוָה אֶל־מֹשֶׁה, עַד־אָנָה מֵאַנְתֶּם לִשְׁמֹר מִצְוֹתַי
וְתוֹרֹתָי: רְאוּ כִּי־יְהוָה נָתַן לָכֶם הַשַּׁבָּת, עַל־כֵּן הוּא נֹתֵן לָכֶם בַּיּוֹם הַשִּׁשִּׁי
לֶחֶם יוֹמָיִם, שְׁבוּ אִישׁ תַּחְתָּיו, אַל־יֵצֵא אִישׁ מִמְּקֹמוֹ בַּיּוֹם הַשְּׁבִיעִי:
וַיִּשְׁבְּתוּ הָעָם בַּיּוֹם הַשְּׁבִעִי: וַיִּקְרְאוּ בֵית־יִשְׂרָאֵל אֶת־שְׁמוֹ מָן, וְהוּא כְּזֶרַע
גַּד לָבָן, וְטַעְמוֹ כְּצַפִּיחִת בִּדְבָשׁ: וַיֹּאמֶר מֹשֶׁה זֶה הַדָּבָר אֲשֶׁר צִוָּה יְהוָה,
מְלֹא הָעֹמֶר מִמֶּנּוּ לְמִשְׁמֶרֶת לְדֹרֹתֵיכֶם, לְמַעַן יִרְאוּ אֶת־הַלֶּחֶם אֲשֶׁר
הֶאֱכַלְתִּי אֶתְכֶם בַּמִּדְבָּר, בְּהוֹצִיאִי אֶתְכֶם מֵאֶרֶץ מִצְרָיִם: וַיֹּאמֶר מֹשֶׁה
אֶל־אַהֲרֹן, קַח צִנְצֶנֶת אַחַת וְתֶן־שָׁמָּה מְלֹא־הָעֹמֶר מָן, וְהַנַּח אֹתוֹ לִפְנֵי
יְהוָה לְמִשְׁמֶרֶת לְדֹרֹתֵיכֶם: כַּאֲשֶׁר צִוָּה יְהוָה אֶל־מֹשֶׁה, וַיַּנִּיחֵהוּ אַהֲרֹן
לִפְנֵי הָעֵדֻת לְמִשְׁמָרֶת: וּבְנֵי יִשְׂרָאֵל אָכְלוּ אֶת־הַמָּן אַרְבָּעִים שָׁנָה, עַד־
בֹּאָם אֶל־אֶרֶץ נוֹשָׁבֶת, אֶת־הַמָּן אָכְלוּ עַד־בֹּאָם אֶל־קְצֵה אֶרֶץ כְּנָעַן:
וְהָעֹמֶר עֲשִׂרִית הָאֵיפָה הוּא:

PRAYER FOR SUSTENANCE

אָנָּא Please, LORD who prepares sustenance for every creation, and calls forth clothing for all who have been made, and sends them their nourishment – grant me nourishment in plenty, provide for me and sustain me, and grant me and all the members of my household, and all of Israel, sustenance in plenty, honorable and obtained in serenity, without suffering, in legal ways and not forbidden ones, with honor and without disgrace, a sustenance with no shame or humiliation. A sustenance by which You will never make me needy of the gifts of other people, but only of Your full, broad hand; a sustenance that will allow me to engage in study of Your holy, pure and perfect Torah, pure meat, easily prepared; my bread and the bread of the people of my household – all our needs before we come to need them – so that my mind may be free of all worry to engage in study of the words of the Torah and to fulfill the commands, and to dwell in peace at my table, honorable, with all my household, without waiting to be invited to the tables of others. So that I will not be subject to any man, and that I will have the yoke of no man upon my shoulders, but only the yoke of Your kingship, making me serve You wholeheartedly, wearing clothes of honor; let our clothing be costly and not shameful. And save us from poverty, from vulnerability and shame, and allow me the merit of welcoming guests and dealing generously with every person. Send opportunities for me to give charity to those who deserve it, and let me not fall at the hands of dishonest people. Amen.

THE CHAPTER OF REVERENCE

In his final address before his death, Moses charges the people of Israel with loving God and holding Him in reverence, reminding them of God's combined majesty and humility (see "May God give you," page 324), and recounting the miracles He has done for them.

וְעַתָּה And now, Israel, what does the LORD your God ask of you, but that you *Deut. 10* hold the LORD your God in awe, walk in His ways and love Him, serving the LORD your God with all your heart and all your soul; keeping the commands of the LORD and His laws, as I charge you on this day, as a blessing. The sky, the highest heavens, the earth and all that fills it, belong to the LORD. Yet the LORD delighted in your ancestors, and loved them, and He chose their children after them – chose you – from all the other nations, as you see this day. Now, open your hearts, and stiffen your necks no longer. For the LORD your God is the God of gods, the LORD of lords, the great, mighty and awesome God, who does not favor the powerful, or accept any bribe. He does justice for the orphan and the widow, and loves the stranger, giving him bread and clothing. And you shall love the stranger, for you were strangers in the land of Egypt. Hold the LORD your God in awe and serve Him, cling to Him and swear by His name. For He

תפילה על הפרנסה

אָנָּא הָאֵל הַמֵּכִין פַּרְנָסָה לְכָל בְּרִיָּה, וּמְזַמֵּן מַלְבּוּשׁ לְכָל נִבְרָא, וְשׁוֹלֵחַ לָהֶם מִחְיָה, שֶׁתִּתֶּן לִי מִחְיָתִי בְּשׁוֹפִי, שֶׁתְּכַלְכְּלֵנִי וּתְפַרְנְסֵנִי לִי וּלְכָל אַנְשֵׁי בֵיתִי וּלְכָל יִשְׂרָאֵל פַּרְנָסָה טוֹבָה שֶׁל כָּבוֹד, בְּנַחַת וְלֹא בְצַעַר, בְּהֶתֵּר וְלֹא בְאִסּוּר, בְּכָבוֹד וְלֹא בְּבִזּוּי. פַּרְנָסָה שֶׁלֹּא תִהְיֶה בָּהּ שׁוּם בּוּשָׁה וּכְלִמָּה, פַּרְנָסָה שֶׁלֹּא תַצְרִיכֵנִי בָּהּ לִידֵי מַתְּנַת בָּשָׂר וָדָם, כִּי אִם לְיָדְךָ הַמְּלֵאָה וְהָרְחָבָה, פַּרְנָסָה שֶׁאוּכַל לַעֲסֹק בְּתוֹרָתְךָ הַקְּדוֹשָׁה וְהַטְּהוֹרָה וְהַתְּמִימָה, וְטֶרֶף נָקִי וּמְזֻמָּן וּמְזוֹנוֹתַי וּמְזוֹנוֹת אַנְשֵׁי בֵיתִי וְכָל צָרְכֵנוּ קֹדֶם שֶׁנִּצְטָרֵךְ לָהֶם, כְּדֵי שֶׁיִּהְיֶה לִבִּי פָנוּי בְּלִי טִרְדָּה לַעֲסֹק בְּדִבְרֵי תוֹרָה וּלְקַיֵּם הַמִּצְוֹת, וְלֵישֵׁב בְּשָׁלוֹם עַל שֻׁלְחָנִי בְּכָבוֹד עִם כָּל בְּנֵי בֵיתִי. וְשֶׁלֹּא אֶצְטָרֵךְ לְשֻׁלְחָן שֶׁל אֲחֵרִים, וְשֶׁלֹּא אֶצְטָרֵךְ לְהִשְׁתַּעֲבֵּד לְשׁוּם אָדָם, וְשֶׁלֹּא יְהֵא עָלַי שׁוּם עֹל בָּשָׂר וָדָם, כִּי אִם עֹל מַלְכוּתְךָ לְעָבְדְּךָ בְּלֵבָב שָׁלֵם. וּבִגְדֵי כָבוֹד יִהְיוּ לְבוּשֵׁנוּ, בִּיקָר וְלֹא בְּבֹשֶׁת פָּנִים. וְהַצִּילֵנוּ מִן עֲנִיּוּת וּמִדַּלּוּת וְשִׁפְלוּת, וְאֶזְכֶּה לְהַכְנִיס אוֹרְחִים וְלִגְמָל חֶסֶד לְכָל אָדָם. וְהָזְמֵן לִי לַעֲשׂוֹת צְדָקָה לְהָרְאוּיִים לָהּ, וְלֹא אֶכָּשֵׁל בִּבְנֵי אָדָם שֶׁאֵינָם הֲגוּנִים, אָמֵן.

פרשת היראה

In his final address before his death, Moses charges the people of Israel with loving God and holding Him in reverence, reminding them of God's combined majesty and humility (see וַיִּתֶּן־לְךָ, *page 325), and recounting the miracles He has done for them.*

דברים

וְעַתָּה יִשְׂרָאֵל, מָה יהוה אֱלֹהֶיךָ שֹׁאֵל מֵעִמָּךְ, כִּי אִם־לְיִרְאָה אֶת־יהוה אֱלֹהֶיךָ לָלֶכֶת בְּכָל־דְּרָכָיו וּלְאַהֲבָה אֹתוֹ, וְלַעֲבֹד אֶת־יהוה אֱלֹהֶיךָ בְּכָל־לְבָבְךָ וּבְכָל־נַפְשֶׁךָ: לִשְׁמֹר אֶת־מִצְוֹת יהוה וְאֶת־חֻקֹּתָיו, אֲשֶׁר אָנֹכִי מְצַוְּךָ הַיּוֹם, לְטוֹב לָךְ: הֵן לַיהוה אֱלֹהֶיךָ הַשָּׁמַיִם וּשְׁמֵי הַשָּׁמָיִם, הָאָרֶץ וְכָל־אֲשֶׁר־בָּהּ: רַק בַּאֲבֹתֶיךָ חָשַׁק יהוה לְאַהֲבָה אוֹתָם, וַיִּבְחַר בְּזַרְעָם אַחֲרֵיהֶם, בָּכֶם מִכָּל־הָעַמִּים, כַּיּוֹם הַזֶּה: וּמַלְתֶּם אֵת עָרְלַת לְבַבְכֶם, וְעָרְפְּכֶם לֹא תַקְשׁוּ עוֹד: כִּי יהוה אֱלֹהֵיכֶם הוּא אֱלֹהֵי הָאֱלֹהִים וַאֲדֹנֵי הָאֲדֹנִים, הָאֵל הַגָּדֹל הַגִּבֹּר וְהַנּוֹרָא, אֲשֶׁר לֹא־יִשָּׂא פָנִים וְלֹא יִקַּח שֹׁחַד: עֹשֶׂה מִשְׁפַּט יָתוֹם וְאַלְמָנָה, וְאֹהֵב גֵּר לָתֶת לוֹ לֶחֶם וְשִׂמְלָה: וַאֲהַבְתֶּם אֶת־הַגֵּר, כִּי־גֵרִים הֱיִיתֶם בְּאֶרֶץ מִצְרָיִם: אֶת־יהוה אֱלֹהֶיךָ תִּירָא, אֹתוֹ תַעֲבֹד, וּבוֹ תִדְבָּק

is your glory and He is the God who performed with you these great and awesome things that your eyes have witnessed. Your ancestors were but seventy souls when they went down to Egypt, and now the LORD your God has made you as many as the stars of the sky.

You shall love the LORD your God, and keep what He gives you to guard, His statutes, His laws and His commands, every day of your lives. And know this day – for your children do not know and did not see what the LORD your God has taught you – His greatness, His mighty hand and His outstretched arm; His signs and the acts He has performed in Egypt, against Pharaoh, king of Egypt and all his land; and what He did to all the army of Egypt, its horses and its chariots, which He drowned in the waters of the Sea of Reeds before their eyes, as they chased after you – and the LORD destroyed them, gone to this very day; and what He did for you in the desert, until you came to this place; and what He did to Datan and to Aviram, the sons of Eliav, son of Reuben, when the earth opened her mouth and swallowed them, their families and their tents and everything that was theirs, in the very midst of all Israel – it is your eyes that have seen all the great work of the LORD that He has done. And you shall keep all the command that I charge you with on this day, that you may be strong and come and inherit the land that you are soon to cross over to and inherit; and so that you may live long upon the land that the LORD promised to give your ancestors and their descendants; a land flowing with milk and honey.

יְהִי רָצוֹן May it be Your will, LORD my God and God of my ancestors, that You plant the love and the awe of You in my heart, and in the hearts of all Israel, Your people, that we may revere Your great, mighty and awesome name, with all our heart and soul – in awe of the sublimity of the Infinite One; may Your name be blessed and raised high, for You are great and Your name is awesome, Amen, Selah.

THE CHAPTER OF REPENTANCE

This passage comes from the end of Moses' final address. After describing the blessings which might be conferred by keeping the covenant and the repercussions of breaking it, Moses promises the people that the punishment incurred will not be irrevocable; the gates of repentance are always open, and by returning to God the people might yet be redeemed. These verses were later interwoven into the prayer for the State of Israel (page 462) to express the hope that this first stage of redemption will lead to its full flowering, with the ingathering of all exiles and the opening of our hearts to truly loving and revering God.

וְהָיָה And when all these things come upon you, the blessing and the curse that   *Deut. 30* I have laid before you now – you shall take this to heart, as you dwell with all the nations among whom the LORD your God has scattered you. And you will

וּבְשָׁמְךָ תִשָּׁבֵעַ: הוּא תְהִלָּתְךָ וְהוּא אֱלֹהֶיךָ, אֲשֶׁר־עָשָׂה אִתְּךָ אֶת־הַגְּדֹלֹת
וְאֶת־הַנּוֹרָאֹת הָאֵלֶּה אֲשֶׁר רָאוּ עֵינֶיךָ: בְּשִׁבְעִים נֶפֶשׁ יָרְדוּ אֲבֹתֶיךָ מִצְרָיְמָה,
וְעַתָּה שָׂמְךָ יהוה אֱלֹהֶיךָ כְּכוֹכְבֵי הַשָּׁמַיִם לָרֹב: וְאָהַבְתָּ אֵת יהוה אֱלֹהֶיךָ,
וְשָׁמַרְתָּ מִשְׁמַרְתּוֹ וְחֻקֹּתָיו וּמִשְׁפָּטָיו וּמִצְוֺתָיו כָּל־הַיָּמִים: וִידַעְתֶּם הַיּוֹם,
כִּי לֹא אֶת־בְּנֵיכֶם אֲשֶׁר לֹא־יָדְעוּ וַאֲשֶׁר לֹא־רָאוּ אֶת־מוּסַר יהוה אֱלֹהֵיכֶם,
אֶת־גָּדְלוֹ אֶת־יָדוֹ הַחֲזָקָה וּזְרֹעוֹ הַנְּטוּיָה: וְאֶת־אֹתֹתָיו וְאֶת־מַעֲשָׂיו אֲשֶׁר
עָשָׂה בְּתוֹךְ מִצְרָיִם, לְפַרְעֹה מֶלֶךְ־מִצְרַיִם וּלְכָל־אַרְצוֹ: וַאֲשֶׁר עָשָׂה לְחֵיל
מִצְרַיִם לְסוּסָיו וּלְרִכְבּוֹ, אֲשֶׁר הֵצִיף אֶת־מֵי יַם־סוּף עַל־פְּנֵיהֶם בְּרָדְפָם
אַחֲרֵיכֶם, וַיְאַבְּדֵם יהוה עַד הַיּוֹם הַזֶּה: וַאֲשֶׁר עָשָׂה לָכֶם בַּמִּדְבָּר, עַד־
בֹּאֲכֶם עַד־הַמָּקוֹם הַזֶּה: וַאֲשֶׁר עָשָׂה לְדָתָן וְלַאֲבִירָם בְּנֵי אֱלִיאָב בֶּן־רְאוּבֵן,
אֲשֶׁר פָּצְתָה הָאָרֶץ אֶת־פִּיהָ וַתִּבְלָעֵם וְאֶת־בָּתֵּיהֶם וְאֶת־אָהֳלֵיהֶם, וְאֵת
כָּל־הַיְקוּם אֲשֶׁר בְּרַגְלֵיהֶם בְּקֶרֶב כָּל־יִשְׂרָאֵל: כִּי עֵינֵיכֶם הָרֹאֹת אֵת כָּל־
מַעֲשֵׂה יהוה הַגָּדֹל, אֲשֶׁר עָשָׂה: וּשְׁמַרְתֶּם אֶת־כָּל־הַמִּצְוָה אֲשֶׁר אָנֹכִי מְצַוְּךָ
הַיּוֹם, לְמַעַן תֶּחֶזְקוּ וּבָאתֶם וִירִשְׁתֶּם אֶת־הָאָרֶץ אֲשֶׁר אַתֶּם עֹבְרִים שָׁמָּה
לְרִשְׁתָּהּ: וּלְמַעַן תַּאֲרִיכוּ יָמִים עַל־הָאֲדָמָה אֲשֶׁר נִשְׁבַּע יהוה לַאֲבֹתֵיכֶם
לָתֵת לָהֶם וּלְזַרְעָם, אֶרֶץ זָבַת חָלָב וּדְבָשׁ:

יְהִי רָצוֹן מִלְּפָנֶיךָ, יהוה אֱלֹהַי וֵאלֹהֵי אֲבוֹתַי, שֶׁתִּטַּע אַהֲבָתְךָ וְיִרְאָתְךָ בְּלִבִּי וּבְלֵב
כָּל יִשְׂרָאֵל עַמֶּךָ, לְיִרְאָה אֶת שִׁמְךָ הַגָּדוֹל הַגִּבּוֹר וְהַנּוֹרָא בְּכָל לְבָבֵנוּ וּבְכָל נַפְשֵׁנוּ,
יִרְאַת הָרוֹמְמוּת שֶׁל אֵין סוֹף בָּרוּךְ הוּא, וְיִתְעַלֶּה שִׁמְךָ. כִּי גָדוֹל אַתָּה וְנוֹרָא שְׁמֶךָ,
אָמֵן סֶלָה.

פרשת התשובה

This passage comes from the end of Moses' final address. After describing the blessings which might be conferred by keeping the covenant and the repercussions of breaking it, Moses promises the people that the punishment incurred will not be irrevocable; the gates of repentance are always open, and by returning to God the people might yet be redeemed. These verses were later interwoven into the תפילה לשלום מדינת ישראל *(page 463) to express the hope that this first stage of redemption will lead to its full flowering, with the ingathering of all exiles and the opening of our hearts to truly loving and revering God.*

דברים ל

וְהָיָה כִי־יָבֹאוּ עָלֶיךָ כָּל־הַדְּבָרִים הָאֵלֶּה, הַבְּרָכָה וְהַקְּלָלָה אֲשֶׁר נָתַתִּי
לְפָנֶיךָ, וַהֲשֵׁבֹתָ אֶל־לְבָבֶךָ בְּכָל־הַגּוֹיִם אֲשֶׁר הִדִּיחֲךָ יהוה אֱלֹהֶיךָ שָׁמָּה:

return to the LORD your God, and you will listen to His voice, just as I charge you on this day, you and your children, with all your heart and all your soul. And the LORD shall restore your fortunes, and have compassion for you, and will return and gather you in from all the nations among whom the LORD has dispersed you. Even if you are scattered to the furthermost lands under the heavens, from there the LORD your God will gather you and take you back. The LORD your God will bring you to the land your ancestors possessed and you will possess it; and He will make you more prosperous and numerous than your ancestors. Then the LORD your God will open up your heart and the heart of your descendants, to love the LORD your God with all your heart and with all your soul, that you may live. And as for all these curses the LORD your God will place them upon your enemies, upon those who hate you and who persecute you. And you will return and listen again to the voice of the LORD, and will fulfill all the commands that I charge you with this day. And the LORD your God will give you plenty in all the works of your hand, your young, the young of your cattle, the fruits of the land, for the good, for the LORD will come back to rejoice in you for the good, just as He rejoiced in your ancestors. For you shall listen to the voice of the LORD your God, keeping His commands and His statutes, as they are written in this scroll of the Torah, for you shall return to the LORD your God with all your heart and with all your soul.

יְהִי רָצוֹן May it be Your will, LORD my God and God of my ancestors, that You dig a passage for us beneath the walls to tunnel through to the throne of Your glory, returning all the sinners of Your people in full repentance – for Your right hand is outstretched to receive those who return, and You desire our repentance, Amen, Selah.

וְשַׁבְתָּ עַד־יהוה אֱלֹהֶיךָ וְשָׁמַעְתָּ בְקֹלוֹ, כְּכֹל אֲשֶׁר־אָנֹכִי מְצַוְּךָ הַיּוֹם, אַתָּה וּבָנֶיךָ בְּכָל־לְבָבְךָ וּבְכָל־נַפְשֶׁךָ: וְשָׁב יהוה אֱלֹהֶיךָ אֶת־שְׁבוּתְךָ וְרִחֲמֶךָ, וְשָׁב וְקִבֶּצְךָ מִכָּל־הָעַמִּים אֲשֶׁר הֱפִיצְךָ יהוה אֱלֹהֶיךָ שָׁמָּה: אִם־יִהְיֶה נִדַּחֲךָ בִּקְצֵה הַשָּׁמָיִם, מִשָּׁם יְקַבֶּצְךָ יהוה אֱלֹהֶיךָ וּמִשָּׁם יִקָּחֶךָ: וֶהֱבִיאֲךָ יהוה אֱלֹהֶיךָ אֶל־הָאָרֶץ אֲשֶׁר־יָרְשׁוּ אֲבֹתֶיךָ וִירִשְׁתָּהּ, וְהֵיטִבְךָ וְהִרְבְּךָ מֵאֲבֹתֶיךָ: וּמָל יהוה אֱלֹהֶיךָ אֶת־לְבָבְךָ וְאֶת־לְבַב זַרְעֶךָ, לְאַהֲבָה אֶת־יהוה אֱלֹהֶיךָ בְּכָל־לְבָבְךָ וּבְכָל־נַפְשְׁךָ, לְמַעַן חַיֶּיךָ: וְנָתַן יהוה אֱלֹהֶיךָ אֵת כָּל־הָאָלוֹת הָאֵלֶּה עַל־אֹיְבֶיךָ וְעַל־שֹׂנְאֶיךָ אֲשֶׁר רְדָפוּךָ: וְאַתָּה תָשׁוּב וְשָׁמַעְתָּ בְּקוֹל יהוה, וְעָשִׂיתָ אֶת־כָּל־מִצְוֹתָיו אֲשֶׁר אָנֹכִי מְצַוְּךָ הַיּוֹם: וְהוֹתִירְךָ יהוה אֱלֹהֶיךָ בְּכֹל מַעֲשֵׂה יָדֶךָ, בִּפְרִי בִטְנְךָ וּבִפְרִי בְהֶמְתְּךָ וּבִפְרִי אַדְמָתְךָ, לְטֹבָה, כִּי יָשׁוּב יהוה לָשׂוּשׂ עָלֶיךָ לְטוֹב כַּאֲשֶׁר־שָׂשׂ עַל־אֲבֹתֶיךָ: כִּי תִשְׁמַע בְּקוֹל יהוה אֱלֹהֶיךָ, לִשְׁמֹר מִצְוֹתָיו וְחֻקֹּתָיו הַכְּתוּבָה בְּסֵפֶר הַתּוֹרָה הַזֶּה, כִּי תָשׁוּב אֶל־יהוה אֱלֹהֶיךָ בְּכָל־לְבָבְךָ וּבְכָל־נַפְשֶׁךָ:

יְהִי רָצוֹן מִלְּפָנֶיךָ, יהוה אֱלֹהַי וֵאלֹהֵי אֲבוֹתַי, שֶׁתַּחְתֹּר חֲתִירָה מִתַּחַת כִּסֵּא כְבוֹדְךָ לְהַחֲזִיר בִּתְשׁוּבָה שְׁלֵמָה לְכָל פּוֹשְׁעֵי עַמְּךָ בֵּית יִשְׂרָאֵל, וּבִכְלָלָם תַּחֲזִירֵנִי בִּתְשׁוּבָה שְׁלֵמָה לְפָנֶיךָ, כִּי יְמִינְךָ פְּשׁוּטָה לְקַבֵּל שָׁבִים וְרוֹצֶה אַתָּה בִּתְשׁוּבָה, אָמֵן סֶלָה.

FOR PROTECTION FROM THE EVIL EYE

The following prayer, based on Rabbi Tzvi Hirsch Kaidanover's Kav HaYashar
(Frankfurt, 1705), incorporates biblical verses as a segula (charm) for God's protection.

When the plague of tzara'at is found in a man, he shall be brought before the priest.	*Lev. 13*
We will pass over armed before the LORD into the land of Canaan, and possess our inheritance here on this side of the Jordan.	*Num. 32*
The LORD your God will raise up a prophet from your midst for you, one of your brethren, like me; and it is him that you shall heed.	*Deut. 18*
There is a river whose streams bring joy to the city of God, the holy dwelling-place of the Most High.	*Ps. 46*
You led Your people like a flock by the hand of Moses and Aaron.	*Ps. 77*
He performed wonders in the sight of their fathers, in the land of Egypt, in the fields of Tzo'an.	*Ps. 78*
I have perfumed my bed with myrrh, aloes, and cinnamon.	*Prov. 7*
The spirit of man is the candle of the LORD, searching out all his inner chambers.	*Prov. 20*
Your lips drip nectar, my bride; honey and milk lie under your tongue, and on your dress lingers Lebanon's scent.	*Song. 4*
Flee out of the midst of Babylonia; depart from the land of the Kasdim; and be as the he-goats running before the flocks.	*Jer. 50*

They were armed with bows, and could use both the right hand
      and the left, slinging stones and shooting arrows from their bows;
        they were Saul's brethren, from Benjamin.
	1 Chr. 12

רִבּוֹנוֹ Master of the Universe, shelter Your people Israel from every kind of sorcery, from every evil eye. And just as You spread Your wings over our ancestors in the desert, and did not allow the evil eye of Balaam son of Beor to have hold over them, so may You spread Your wings over us, in Your great compassion, that we may be protected (protected and guided,) by Your holy names, from every evil eye.

> You are my shelter, You will shield me from distress;   *Ps. 32*
> You will surround me with songs of deliverance. Selah.

שמירה נגד עין הרע

The following prayer, based on Rabbi Tzvi Hirsch Kaidanover's קב הישר *(Frankfurt, 1705), incorporates biblical verses as a* סגולה *(charm) for God's protection.*

ויקרא יג   נֶגַע צָרַעַת כִּי תִהְיֶה בְּאָדָם וְהוּבָא אֶל־הַכֹּהֵן:

במדבר לב   נַחְנוּ נַעֲבֹר חֲלוּצִים לִפְנֵי יהוה אֶרֶץ כְּנָעַן
וְאִתָּנוּ אֲחֻזַּת נַחֲלָתֵנוּ מֵעֵבֶר לַיַּרְדֵּן:

דברים יח   נָבִיא מִקִּרְבְּךָ מֵאַחֶיךָ כָּמֹנִי יָקִים לְךָ יהוה אֱלֹהֶיךָ, אֵלָיו תִּשְׁמָעוּן:

תהלים מו   נָהָר פְּלָגָיו יְשַׂמְּחוּ עִיר־אֱלֹהִים, קְדֹשׁ מִשְׁכְּנֵי עֶלְיוֹן:

תהלים עז   נָחִיתָ כַצֹּאן עַמֶּךָ בְּיַד־מֹשֶׁה וְאַהֲרֹן:

תהלים עח   נֶגֶד אֲבוֹתָם עָשָׂה פֶלֶא בְּאֶרֶץ מִצְרַיִם שְׂדֵה־צֹעַן:

משלי ז   נַפְתִּי מִשְׁכָּבִי מֹר אֲהָלִים וְקִנָּמוֹן:

משלי כ   נֵר יהוה נִשְׁמַת אָדָם חֹפֵשׂ כָּל־חַדְרֵי־בָטֶן:

שיר
השירים ד   נֹפֶת תִּטֹּפְנָה שִׂפְתוֹתַיִךְ כַּלָּה
דְּבַשׁ וְחָלָב תַּחַת לְשׁוֹנֵךְ וְרֵיחַ שַׂלְמֹתַיִךְ כְּרֵיחַ לְבָנוֹן:

ירמיה נ   נֻדוּ מִתּוֹךְ בָּבֶל וּמֵאֶרֶץ כַּשְׂדִּים צֵאוּ, וִהְיוּ כְּעַתּוּדִים לִפְנֵי־צֹאן:

דברי הימים
א יב   נֹשְׁקֵי קֶשֶׁת מַיְמִינִים וּמַשְׂמִאלִים בָּאֲבָנִים וּבַחִצִּים בַּקָּשֶׁת
מֵאֲחֵי שָׁאוּל מִבִּנְיָמִן:

רִבּוֹנוֹ שֶׁל עוֹלָם, הַצֵּל עַמְּךָ בֵּית יִשְׂרָאֵל מִכָּל מִינֵי כְּשׁוּפִים וּמִכָּל מִינֵי עַיִן הָרָע,
וּכְשֵׁם שֶׁפָּרַשְׁתָּ כְּנָפֶיךָ עַל אֲבוֹתֵינוּ שֶׁבַּמִּדְבָּר, שֶׁלֹּא שָׁלַט עֲלֵיהֶם עֵינָא בִּישָׁא
דְּבִלְעָם בֶּן בְּעוֹר, כֵּן תִּפְרֹס כְּנָפֶיךָ עָלֵינוּ בְּרַחֲמֶיךָ הָרַבִּים לְהַצִּילֵנוּ מַכְסֵה (בְּמִכְסֶה
וּבְהַנְהָגָה) בְּשִׁמּוֹתֶיךָ הַקְּדוֹשִׁים מִכָּל עֵינָא בִּישָׁא.

תהלים כב   אַתָּה סֵתֶר לִי מִצַּר תִּצְּרֵנִי רָנֵּי פַלֵּט תְּסוֹבְבֵנִי סֶלָה:

Minḥa for Weekdays

אַשְׁרֵי Happy are those who dwell in Your House;   *Ps. 84*
they shall continue to praise You, Selah!
Happy are the people for whom this is so;   *Ps. 144*
happy are the people whose God is the LORD.
A song of praise by David.   *Ps. 145*

I will exalt You, my God, the King, and bless Your name for ever
and all time. Every day I will bless You, and praise Your name for
ever and all time. Great is the LORD and greatly to be praised;
His greatness is unfathomable. One generation will praise Your
works to the next, and tell of Your mighty deeds. On the glorious splendor of Your majesty I will meditate, and on the acts
of Your wonders. They shall talk of the power of Your awesome deeds, and I will tell of Your greatness. They shall recite
the record of Your great goodness, and sing with joy of Your
righteousness. The LORD is gracious and compassionate, slow
to anger and great in loving-kindness. The LORD is good to all,
and His compassion extends to all His works. All Your works
shall thank You, LORD, and Your devoted ones shall bless You.
They shall talk of the glory of Your kingship, and speak of Your
might. To make known to mankind His mighty deeds and the

Its form is simple. It begins with *Ashrei* as a prelude to prayer, the third of
three daily recitals. The Amida is the same as in the morning with two changes. In the Leader's Repetition, the passage referring to the priestly blessing
is not said, since in the Temple the priests did not bless the congregation in
the afternoon. Likewise, a shorter form of the final blessing (associated with
the priestly blessing in the Temple) is said. *Taḥanun* is also said at Minḥa, on
days when it is said in the morning, except on the afternoon before Shabbat
and Yom Tov and certain other occasions (see page 253). The service ends
with *Aleinu*.

מנחה לחול

אַשְׁרֵי יוֹשְׁבֵי בֵיתֶךָ, עוֹד יְהַלְלוּךָ סֶּלָה:
אַשְׁרֵי הָעָם שֶׁכָּכָה לּוֹ, אַשְׁרֵי הָעָם שֶׁיהוה אֱלֹהָיו:
תְּהִלָּה לְדָוִד
אֲרוֹמִמְךָ אֱלוֹהַי הַמֶּלֶךְ, וַאֲבָרְכָה שִׁמְךָ לְעוֹלָם וָעֶד:
בְּכָל־יוֹם אֲבָרְכֶךָּ, וַאֲהַלְלָה שִׁמְךָ לְעוֹלָם וָעֶד:
גָּדוֹל יהוה וּמְהֻלָּל מְאֹד, וְלִגְדֻלָּתוֹ אֵין חֵקֶר:
דּוֹר לְדוֹר יְשַׁבַּח מַעֲשֶׂיךָ, וּגְבוּרֹתֶיךָ יַגִּידוּ:
הֲדַר כְּבוֹד הוֹדֶךָ, וְדִבְרֵי נִפְלְאֹתֶיךָ אָשִׂיחָה:
וֶעֱזוּז נוֹרְאֹתֶיךָ יֹאמֵרוּ, וּגְדוּלָּתְךָ אֲסַפְּרֶנָּה:
זֵכֶר רַב־טוּבְךָ יַבִּיעוּ, וְצִדְקָתְךָ יְרַנֵּנוּ:
חַנּוּן וְרַחוּם יהוה, אֶרֶךְ אַפַּיִם וּגְדָל־חָסֶד:
טוֹב־יהוה לַכֹּל, וְרַחֲמָיו עַל־כָּל־מַעֲשָׂיו:
יוֹדוּךָ יהוה כָּל־מַעֲשֶׂיךָ, וַחֲסִידֶיךָ יְבָרְכוּכָה:
כְּבוֹד מַלְכוּתְךָ יֹאמֵרוּ, וּגְבוּרָתְךָ יְדַבֵּרוּ:
לְהוֹדִיעַ לִבְנֵי הָאָדָם גְּבוּרֹתָיו, וּכְבוֹד הֲדַר מַלְכוּתוֹ:
מַלְכוּתְךָ מַלְכוּת כָּל־עֹלָמִים, וּמֶמְשַׁלְתְּךָ בְּכָל־דּוֹר וָדֹר:

AFTERNOON SERVICE

The afternoon service corresponds to the daily afternoon sacrifice (Num. 28:4). *Minḥa*, the "meal-offering," was not unique to the afternoon. The prayer may have acquired this name because of the verse in Psalms (141:2): "May my prayer be like incense before You, the lifting up of my hands like the afternoon offering (*minḥat arev*)." The sages attached special significance to this prayer, noting that Elijah's prayer was answered at this time (1 Kings 18:36).

glorious majesty of His kingship. Your kingdom is an everlasting kingdom, and Your reign is for all generations. The LORD
supports all who fall, and raises all who are bowed down. All
raise their eyes to You in hope, and You give them their food in
due season. You open Your hand, and satisfy every living thing
with favor. The LORD is righteous in all His ways, and kind in all
He does. The LORD is close to all who call on Him, to all who
call on Him in truth. He fulfills the will of those who revere
Him; He hears their cry and saves them. The LORD guards all
who love Him, but all the wicked He will destroy. ‣ My mouth
shall speak the praise of the LORD, and all creatures shall bless
His holy name for ever and all time.

We will bless the LORD now and for ever. Halleluya!   *Ps. 115*

HALF KADDISH

Leader: יִתְגַּדַּל Magnified and sanctified may His great name be,
in the world He created by His will.
May He establish His kingdom
in your lifetime and in your days,
and in the lifetime of all the house of Israel,
swiftly and soon –
and say: Amen.

All: May His great name be blessed for ever and all time.

Leader: Blessed and praised, glorified and exalted,
raised and honored, uplifted and lauded
be the name of the Holy One, blessed be He,
beyond any blessing,
song, praise and consolation
uttered in the world –
and say: Amen.

On fast days, go to Removing the Torah from the Ark *on page 158. The Torah reading and Haftara
for fast days are on page 654. After the Torah is returned to the Ark, the Leader says Half Kaddish.*

סוֹמֵךְ יהוה לְכָל־הַנֹּפְלִים, וְזוֹקֵף לְכָל־הַכְּפוּפִים:

עֵינֵי־כֹל אֵלֶיךָ יְשַׂבֵּרוּ, וְאַתָּה נוֹתֵן־לָהֶם אֶת־אָכְלָם בְּעִתּוֹ:

פּוֹתֵחַ אֶת־יָדֶךָ, וּמַשְׂבִּיעַ לְכָל־חַי רָצוֹן:

צַדִּיק יהוה בְּכָל־דְּרָכָיו, וְחָסִיד בְּכָל־מַעֲשָׂיו:

קָרוֹב יהוה לְכָל־קֹרְאָיו, לְכֹל אֲשֶׁר יִקְרָאֻהוּ בֶאֱמֶת:

רְצוֹן־יְרֵאָיו יַעֲשֶׂה, וְאֶת־שַׁוְעָתָם יִשְׁמַע, וְיוֹשִׁיעֵם:

שׁוֹמֵר יהוה אֶת־כָּל־אֹהֲבָיו, וְאֵת כָּל־הָרְשָׁעִים יַשְׁמִיד:

‹ תְּהִלַּת יהוה יְדַבֶּר פִּי, וִיבָרֵךְ כָּל־בָּשָׂר שֵׁם קָדְשׁוֹ לְעוֹלָם וָעֶד:

וַאֲנַחְנוּ נְבָרֵךְ יָהּ מֵעַתָּה וְעַד־עוֹלָם, הַלְלוּיָהּ:

תהלים קמה

חצי קדיש

ש״ץ: יִתְגַּדַּל וְיִתְקַדַּשׁ שְׁמֵהּ רַבָּא (קהל: אָמֵן)

בְּעָלְמָא דִּי בְרָא כִרְעוּתֵהּ

וְיַמְלִיךְ מַלְכוּתֵהּ

בְּחַיֵּיכוֹן וּבְיוֹמֵיכוֹן וּבְחַיֵּי דְכָל בֵּית יִשְׂרָאֵל

בַּעֲגָלָא וּבִזְמַן קָרִיב, וְאִמְרוּ אָמֵן. (קהל: אָמֵן)

קהל
ושׁ״ץ: יְהֵא שְׁמֵהּ רַבָּא מְבָרַךְ לְעָלַם וּלְעָלְמֵי עָלְמַיָּא.

שׁ״ץ: יִתְבָּרַךְ וְיִשְׁתַּבַּח וְיִתְפָּאַר וְיִתְרוֹמַם וְיִתְנַשֵּׂא

וְיִתְהַדָּר וְיִתְעַלֶּה וְיִתְהַלָּל

שְׁמֵהּ דְּקֻדְשָׁא בְּרִיךְ הוּא (קהל: בְּרִיךְ הוּא)

לְעֵלָּא מִן כָּל בִּרְכָתָא / בעשרת ימי תשובה: לְעֵלָּא לְעֵלָּא מִכָּל בִּרְכָתָא/

וְשִׁירָתָא, תֻּשְׁבְּחָתָא וְנֶחֱמָתָא

דַּאֲמִירָן בְּעָלְמָא, וְאִמְרוּ אָמֵן. (קהל: אָמֵן)

On fast days, go to הוצאת ספר תורה *on page 159. The* תורה *reading and* הפטרה *for fast days are on page 654. After the* תורה *is returned to the* ארון קודש, *the* שליח ציבור *says* חצי קדיש.

THE AMIDA

*The following prayer, until "in former years" on page 250, is said silently, standing
with feet together. If there is a minyan, the Amida is repeated aloud by the Leader.
Take three steps forward and at the points indicated by ˈ, bend the knees at the
first word, bow at the second, and stand straight before saying God's name.*

When I proclaim the LORD's name, give glory to our God.   *Deut. 32*
O LORD, open my lips, so that my mouth may declare Your praise.   *Ps. 51*

PATRIARCHS

ˈבָּרוּךְ Blessed are You, LORD our God and God of our fathers,
God of Abraham, God of Isaac and God of Jacob;
the great, mighty and awesome God, God Most High,
who bestows acts of loving-kindness and creates all,
who remembers the loving-kindness of the fathers
and will bring a Redeemer to their children's children
for the sake of His name, in love.

Between Rosh Remember us for life, O King who desires life,
HaShana & and write us in the book of life –
Yom Kippur: for Your sake, O God of life.

King, Helper, Savior, Shield:
ˈBlessed are You, LORD, Shield of Abraham.

DIVINE MIGHT

אַתָּה גִבּוֹר You are eternally mighty, LORD.
You give life to the dead and have great power to save.

*The phrase "He makes the wind blow and the rain fall" is added from
Simḥat Torah until Pesaḥ. In Israel the phrase "He causes the dew to
fall" is added from Pesaḥ until Shemini Atzeret. See laws 49–51.*

In fall & winter: He makes the wind blow and the rain fall.

In Israel, in spring He causes the dew to fall.
& summer:

"I am not a man of words...I am heavy of speech and tongue." Isaiah said, "I
am a man of unclean lips." Jeremiah said, "I cannot speak for I am a child." So
our first prayer is for divine help in the act of prayer itself.

עֲמִידָה

The following prayer, until קַדְמֹנִיּוֹת *on page 251, is said silently, standing with feet together. If there is a* מִנְיָן, *the* עֲמִידָה *is repeated aloud by the* שְׁלִיחַ צִבּוּר. *Take three steps forward and at the points indicated by* ˚, *bend the knees at the first word, bow at the second, and stand straight before saying God's name.*

דברים לב

תהלים נא

כִּי שֵׁם יהוה אֶקְרָא, הָבוּ גֹדֶל לֵאלֹהֵינוּ:
אֲדֹנָי, שְׂפָתַי תִּפְתָּח, וּפִי יַגִּיד תְּהִלָּתֶךָ:

אבות

˚בָּרוּךְ אַתָּה יהוה, אֱלֹהֵינוּ וֵאלֹהֵי אֲבוֹתֵינוּ,
אֱלֹהֵי אַבְרָהָם, אֱלֹהֵי יִצְחָק, וֵאלֹהֵי יַעֲקֹב,
הָאֵל הַגָּדוֹל הַגִּבּוֹר וְהַנּוֹרָא, אֵל עֶלְיוֹן,
גּוֹמֵל חֲסָדִים טוֹבִים, וְקֹנֵה הַכֹּל,
וְזוֹכֵר חַסְדֵי אָבוֹת,
וּמֵבִיא גוֹאֵל לִבְנֵי בְנֵיהֶם לְמַעַן שְׁמוֹ בְּאַהֲבָה.

בעשרת ימי תשובה: זָכְרֵנוּ לְחַיִּים, מֶלֶךְ חָפֵץ בַּחַיִּים,
וְכָתְבֵנוּ בְּסֵפֶר הַחַיִּים, לְמַעַנְךָ אֱלֹהִים חַיִּים.

מֶלֶךְ עוֹזֵר וּמוֹשִׁיעַ וּמָגֵן.
˚בָּרוּךְ אַתָּה יהוה, מָגֵן אַבְרָהָם.

גבורות

אַתָּה גִּבּוֹר לְעוֹלָם, אֲדֹנָי,
מְחַיֵּה מֵתִים אַתָּה, רַב לְהוֹשִׁיעַ

The phrase מַשִּׁיב הָרוּחַ *is added from* שמחת תורה *until* פסח.
In ארץ ישראל *the phrase* מוֹרִיד הַטָּל *is added from* פסח *until* שמיני עצרת. *See laws 49–51.*

בחורף: מַשִּׁיב הָרוּחַ וּמוֹרִיד הַגֶּשֶׁם / בארץ ישראל בקיץ: מוֹרִיד הַטָּל

אֲדֹנָי, שְׂפָתַי תִּפְתָּח / *O Lord, open my lips:* Standing in the presence of God, we feel our inadequacy. The greatest of the prophets felt tongue-tied. Moses said,

He sustains the living with loving-kindness,
and with great compassion revives the dead.
He supports the fallen, heals the sick,
sets captives free,
and keeps His faith with those who sleep in the dust.
Who is like You, Master of might,
and to whom can You be compared,
O King who brings death and gives life,
and makes salvation grow?

Between Rosh HaShana   Who is like You, compassionate Father,
     & Yom Kippur: who remembers His creatures in compassion, for life?

Faithful are You to revive the dead.
Blessed are You, Lᴏʀᴅ, who revives the dead.

      When saying the Amida silently, continue with "You are holy" on the next page.

KEDUSHA

     *During the Leader's Repetition, the following is said standing
     with feet together, rising on the toes at the words indicated by ˄.*

Cong. then   נְקַדֵּשׁ We will sanctify Your name on earth,
    Leader: as they sanctify it in the highest heavens,
       as is written by Your prophet,
       "And they [the angels] call to one another saying: *Is. 6*

Cong. then   ˄"Holy, ˄holy, ˄holy is the Lᴏʀᴅ of hosts
    Leader: the whole world is filled with His glory."
       Those facing them say "Blessed – "

Cong. then   ˄"Blessed is the Lᴏʀᴅ's glory from His place."   *Ezek. 3*
    Leader: And in Your holy Writings it is written thus:

Cong. then   ˄"The Lᴏʀᴅ shall reign for ever. He is your God, Zion,   *Ps. 146*
    Leader: from generation to generation, Halleluya!"

    Leader: From generation to generation we will declare Your greatness,
       and we will proclaim Your holiness for evermore.
       Your praise, our God, shall not leave our mouth forever,
       for You, God, are a great and holy King. Blessed are You, Lᴏʀᴅ,
       the holy God. / *Between Rosh HaShana & Yom Kippur:* the holy King./

     The Leader continues with "You grace humanity" on the next page.

מְכַלְכֵּל חַיִּים בְּחֶסֶד, מְחַיֵּה מֵתִים בְּרַחֲמִים רַבִּים

סוֹמֵךְ נוֹפְלִים, וְרוֹפֵא חוֹלִים, וּמַתִּיר אֲסוּרִים

וּמְקַיֵּם אֱמוּנָתוֹ לִישֵׁנֵי עָפָר.

מִי כָמוֹךָ, בַּעַל גְּבוּרוֹת

וּמִי דוֹמֶה לָּךְ

מֶלֶךְ, מֵמִית וּמְחַיֶּה וּמַצְמִיחַ יְשׁוּעָה.

בעשרת ימי תשובה: מִי כָמוֹךָ אַב הָרַחֲמִים

זוֹכֵר יְצוּרָיו לְחַיִּים בְּרַחֲמִים.

וְנֶאֱמָן אַתָּה לְהַחֲיוֹת מֵתִים.

בָּרוּךְ אַתָּה יהוה, מְחַיֵּה הַמֵּתִים.

When saying the עמידה silently, continue with אַתָּה קָדוֹשׁ on the next page.

---

*During the חזרת הש״ץ, the following is said standing
with feet together, rising on the toes at the words indicated by ˄.*

קהל
then
ש״ץ: נְקַדֵּשׁ אֶת שִׁמְךָ בָּעוֹלָם, כְּשֵׁם שֶׁמַּקְדִּישִׁים אוֹתוֹ בִּשְׁמֵי מָרוֹם

כַּכָּתוּב עַל יַד נְבִיאֶךָ: וְקָרָא זֶה אֶל־זֶה וְאָמַר   ישעיה ו

קהל
then
ש״ץ: ˄קָדוֹשׁ, קָדוֹשׁ, קָדוֹשׁ, יהוה צְבָאוֹת, מְלֹא כָל־הָאָרֶץ כְּבוֹדוֹ:

לְעֻמָּתָם בָּרוּךְ יֹאמֵרוּ

קהל
then
ש״ץ: ˄בָּרוּךְ כְּבוֹד־יהוה מִמְּקוֹמוֹ:   יחזקאל ג

וּבְדִבְרֵי קָדְשְׁךָ כָּתוּב לֵאמֹר

קהל
then
ש״ץ: ˄יִמְלֹךְ יהוה לְעוֹלָם, אֱלֹהַיִךְ צִיּוֹן לְדֹר וָדֹר, הַלְלוּיָהּ:   תהלים קמו

ש״ץ: לְדוֹר וָדוֹר נַגִּיד גָּדְלֶךָ, וּלְנֵצַח נְצָחִים קְדֻשָּׁתְךָ נַקְדִּישׁ

וְשִׁבְחֲךָ אֱלֹהֵינוּ מִפִּינוּ לֹא יָמוּשׁ לְעוֹלָם וָעֶד

כִּי אֵל מֶלֶךְ גָּדוֹל וְקָדוֹשׁ אָתָּה.

בָּרוּךְ אַתָּה יהוה, הָאֵל הַקָּדוֹשׁ./ בעשרת ימי תשובה: הַמֶּלֶךְ הַקָּדוֹשׁ./

The שליח ציבור continues with אַתָּה חוֹנֵן on the next page.

HOLINESS

אַתָּה קָדוֹשׁ You are holy and Your name is holy,
and holy ones praise You daily, Selah!
Blessed are You, LORD,
the holy God. / *Between Rosh HaShana & Yom Kippur:* the holy King./
(*If forgotten, repeat the Amida.*)

KNOWLEDGE

אַתָּה חוֹנֵן You grace humanity with knowledge
and teach mortals understanding.
Grace us with the knowledge, understanding
and discernment that come from You.
Blessed are You, LORD,
who graciously grants knowledge.

REPENTANCE

הֲשִׁיבֵנוּ Bring us back, our Father, to Your Torah.
Draw us near, our King, to Your service.
Lead us back to You in perfect repentance.
Blessed are You, LORD,
who desires repentance.

FORGIVENESS

Strike the left side of the chest at °.

סְלַח לָנוּ Forgive us, our Father, for we have °sinned.
Pardon us, our King, for we have °transgressed;
for You pardon and forgive.
Blessed are You, LORD,
the gracious One who repeatedly forgives.

REDEMPTION

רְאֵה Look on our affliction, plead our cause,
and redeem us soon for Your name's sake,
for You are a powerful Redeemer.
Blessed are You, LORD,
the Redeemer of Israel.

קדושת השם

אַתָּה קָדוֹשׁ וְשִׁמְךָ קָדוֹשׁ
וּקְדוֹשִׁים בְּכָל יוֹם יְהַלְלוּךָ סֶּלָה.
בָּרוּךְ אַתָּה יהוה, הָאֵל הַקָּדוֹשׁ./ בעשרת ימי תשובה: הַמֶּלֶךְ הַקָּדוֹשׁ.
(If forgotten, repeat the עמידה.)

דעת

אַתָּה חוֹנֵן לְאָדָם דַּעַת, וּמְלַמֵּד לֶאֱנוֹשׁ בִּינָה.
חָנֵּנוּ מֵאִתְּךָ דֵּעָה בִּינָה וְהַשְׂכֵּל.
בָּרוּךְ אַתָּה יהוה, חוֹנֵן הַדָּעַת.

תשובה

הֲשִׁיבֵנוּ אָבִינוּ לְתוֹרָתֶךָ, וְקָרְבֵנוּ מַלְכֵּנוּ לַעֲבוֹדָתֶךָ,
וְהַחֲזִירֵנוּ בִּתְשׁוּבָה שְׁלֵמָה לְפָנֶיךָ.
בָּרוּךְ אַתָּה יהוה, הָרוֹצֶה בִּתְשׁוּבָה.

סליחה

Strike the left side of the chest at °.

סְלַח לָנוּ אָבִינוּ כִּי °חָטָאנוּ
מְחַל לָנוּ מַלְכֵּנוּ כִּי °פָשָׁעְנוּ
כִּי מוֹחֵל וְסוֹלֵחַ אָתָּה.
בָּרוּךְ אַתָּה יהוה, חַנּוּן הַמַּרְבֶּה לִסְלֹחַ.

גאולה

רְאֵה בְעָנְיֵנוּ, וְרִיבָה רִיבֵנוּ
וּגְאָלֵנוּ מְהֵרָה לְמַעַן שְׁמֶךָ
כִּי גּוֹאֵל חָזָק אָתָּה.
בָּרוּךְ אַתָּה יהוה, גּוֹאֵל יִשְׂרָאֵל.

On fast days the Leader adds:

עֲנֵנוּ Answer us, Lᴏʀᴅ, answer us on our Fast Day, for we are in great distress.
Look not at our wickedness. Do not hide Your face from us and do not ignore
our plea. Be near to our cry; please let Your loving-kindness comfort us. Even
before we call to You, answer us, as it is said, "Before they call, I will answer. *Is. 65*
While they are still speaking, I will hear." For You, Lᴏʀᴅ, are the One who
answers in time of distress, redeems and rescues in all times of trouble and
anguish. Blessed are You, Lᴏʀᴅ, who answers in time of distress.

HEALING

רְפָאֵנוּ Heal us, Lᴏʀᴅ, and we shall be healed.
Save us and we shall be saved,
for You are our praise.
Bring complete recovery for all our ailments,

The following prayer for a sick person may be said here:

May it be Your will, O Lᴏʀᴅ my God and God of my ancestors, that You
speedily send a complete recovery from heaven, a healing of both soul and
body, to the patient (*name*), son/daughter of (*mother's name*) among the
other afflicted of Israel.

for You, God, King, are a faithful and compassionate Healer.
Blessed are You, Lᴏʀᴅ, Healer of the sick of His people Israel.

PROSPERITY

*The phrase "Grant dew and rain as a blessing" is said from December 5th
(in the year before a civil leap year, December 6th) until Pesaḥ. In Israel, it is
said from the 7th of Marḥeshvan. The phrase "Grant blessing" is said from
Ḥol HaMoʾed Pesaḥ until December 4th (in the year before a civil leap year,
December 5th). In Israel it is said through the 6th of Marḥeshvan. See laws 52–54.*

בָּרֵךְ Bless this year for us, Lᴏʀᴅ our God,
and all its types of produce for good.

In winter: Grant dew and rain as a blessing
In other seasons: Grant blessing

on the face of the earth,
and from its goodness satisfy us,
blessing our year as the best of years.
Blessed are You, Lᴏʀᴅ, who blesses the years.

On fast days the שליח ציבור adds:

עֲנֵנוּ יהוה עֲנֵנוּ בְּיוֹם צוֹם תַּעֲנִיתֵנוּ, כִּי בְצָרָה גְדוֹלָה אֲנַחְנוּ. אַל תֵּפֶן אֶל
רִשְׁעֵנוּ, וְאַל תַּסְתֵּר פָּנֶיךָ מִמֶּנּוּ, וְאַל תִּתְעַלַּם מִתְּחִנָּתֵנוּ. הֱיֵה נָא קָרוֹב
לְשַׁוְעָתֵנוּ, יְהִי נָא חַסְדְּךָ לְנַחֲמֵנוּ, טֶרֶם נִקְרָא אֵלֶיךָ עֲנֵנוּ, כַּדָּבָר שֶׁנֶּאֱמַר:
ישעיה סה וְהָיָה טֶרֶם יִקְרָאוּ וַאֲנִי אֶעֱנֶה, עוֹד הֵם מְדַבְּרִים וַאֲנִי אֶשְׁמָע: כִּי אַתָּה יהוה
הָעוֹנֶה בְּעֵת צָרָה, פּוֹדֶה וּמַצִּיל בְּכָל עֵת צָרָה וְצוּקָה. בָּרוּךְ אַתָּה יהוה,
הָעוֹנֶה בְּעֵת צָרָה.

רפואה

רְפָאֵנוּ יהוה וְנֵרָפֵא, הוֹשִׁיעֵנוּ וְנִוָּשֵׁעָה, כִּי תְהִלָּתֵנוּ אָתָּה,
וְהַעֲלֵה רְפוּאָה שְׁלֵמָה לְכָל מַכּוֹתֵינוּ

The following prayer for a sick person may be said here:

יְהִי רָצוֹן מִלְּפָנֶיךָ יהוה אֱלֹהַי וֵאלֹהֵי אֲבוֹתַי, שֶׁתִּשְׁלַח מְהֵרָה רְפוּאָה שְׁלֵמָה
מִן הַשָּׁמַיִם רְפוּאַת הַנֶּפֶשׁ וּרְפוּאַת הַגּוּף לַחוֹלֶה/לַחוֹלָה name of patient
בֶּן/בַּת mother's name בְּתוֹךְ שְׁאָר חוֹלֵי יִשְׂרָאֵל.

כִּי אֵל מֶלֶךְ רוֹפֵא נֶאֱמָן וְרַחֲמָן אָתָּה.
בָּרוּךְ אַתָּה יהוה, רוֹפֵא חוֹלֵי עַמּוֹ יִשְׂרָאֵל.

ברכת השנים

The phrase וְתֵן טַל וּמָטָר לִבְרָכָה is said from December 5th (in the year before a
civil leap year, December 6th) until פסח. In אֶרֶץ יִשְׂרָאֵל, it is said from מרחשון ז.
The phrase וְתֵן בְּרָכָה is said from חול המועד פסח until December 4th (in the year before a
civil leap year, December 5th). In אֶרֶץ יִשְׂרָאֵל it is said through מרחשון ז. See laws 52–54.

בָּרֵךְ עָלֵינוּ יהוה אֱלֹהֵינוּ אֶת הַשָּׁנָה הַזֹּאת
וְאֶת כָּל מִינֵי תְבוּאָתָהּ, לְטוֹבָה

בחורף וְתֵן טַל וּמָטָר לִבְרָכָה / בקיץ וְתֵן בְּרָכָה

עַל פְּנֵי הָאֲדָמָה, וְשַׂבְּעֵנוּ מִטּוּבָהּ
וּבָרֵךְ שְׁנָתֵנוּ כַּשָּׁנִים הַטּוֹבוֹת.
בָּרוּךְ אַתָּה יהוה, מְבָרֵךְ הַשָּׁנִים.

INGATHERING OF EXILES

תְּקַע Sound the great shofar for our freedom,
raise high the banner to gather our exiles,
and gather us together from the four quarters of the earth.
Blessed are You, LORD,
who gathers the dispersed of His people Israel.

JUSTICE

הָשִׁיבָה Restore our judges as at first,
and our counselors as at the beginning,
and remove from us sorrow and sighing.
May You alone, LORD,
reign over us with loving-kindness and compassion,
and vindicate us in justice.
Blessed are You, LORD,
the King who loves righteousness and justice.

/ *Between Rosh HaShana & Yom Kippur, end the blessing:* the King of justice./

AGAINST INFORMERS

וְלַמַּלְשִׁינִים For the slanderers let there be no hope,
and may all wickedness perish in an instant.
May all Your people's enemies swiftly be cut down.
May You swiftly uproot, crush, cast down
and humble the arrogant swiftly in our days.
Blessed are You, LORD,
who destroys enemies and humbles the arrogant.

THE RIGHTEOUS

עַל הַצַּדִּיקִים To the righteous, the pious,
the elders of Your people the house of Israel,
the remnant of their scholars,
the righteous converts, and to us,
may Your compassion be aroused, LORD our God.

קבוץ גלויות

תְּקַע בְּשׁוֹפָר גָּדוֹל לְחֵרוּתֵנוּ

וְשָׂא נֵס לְקַבֵּץ גָּלֻיּוֹתֵינוּ

וְקַבְּצֵנוּ יַחַד מֵאַרְבַּע כַּנְפוֹת הָאָרֶץ.

בָּרוּךְ אַתָּה יהוה, מְקַבֵּץ נִדְחֵי עַמּוֹ יִשְׂרָאֵל.

השבת המשפט

הָשִׁיבָה שׁוֹפְטֵינוּ כְּבָרִאשׁוֹנָה וְיוֹעֲצֵינוּ כְּבַתְּחִלָּה

וְהָסֵר מִמֶּנּוּ יָגוֹן וַאֲנָחָה

וּמְלֹךְ עָלֵינוּ אַתָּה יהוה לְבַדְּךָ בְּחֶסֶד וּבְרַחֲמִים

וְצַדְּקֵנוּ בַּמִּשְׁפָּט.

בָּרוּךְ אַתָּה יהוה

מֶלֶךְ אוֹהֵב צְדָקָה וּמִשְׁפָּט. / בעשרת ימי תשובה: הַמֶּלֶךְ הַמִּשְׁפָּט./

ברכת המינים

וְלַמַּלְשִׁינִים אַל תְּהִי תִקְוָה, וְכָל הָרִשְׁעָה כְּרֶגַע תֹּאבֵד

וְכָל אוֹיְבֵי עַמְּךָ מְהֵרָה יִכָּרֵתוּ

וְהַזֵּדִים מְהֵרָה תְעַקֵּר וּתְשַׁבֵּר וּתְמַגֵּר וְתַכְנִיעַ בִּמְהֵרָה בְיָמֵינוּ.

בָּרוּךְ אַתָּה יהוה, שׁוֹבֵר אוֹיְבִים וּמַכְנִיעַ זֵדִים.

על הצדיקים

עַל הַצַּדִּיקִים וְעַל הַחֲסִידִים

וְעַל זִקְנֵי עַמְּךָ בֵּית יִשְׂרָאֵל

וְעַל פְּלֵיטַת סוֹפְרֵיהֶם

וְעַל גֵּרֵי הַצֶּדֶק, וְעָלֵינוּ

יֶהֱמוּ רַחֲמֶיךָ יהוה אֱלֹהֵינוּ

Grant a good reward to all who sincerely trust in Your name.
Set our lot with them,
so that we may never be ashamed, for in You we trust.
Blessed are You, LORD,
who is the support and trust of the righteous.

REBUILDING JERUSALEM

וְלִירוּשָׁלַיִם To Jerusalem, Your city, may You return in compassion,
and may You dwell in it as You promised.
May You rebuild it rapidly in our days as an everlasting structure,
and install within it soon the throne of David.
*Blessed are You, LORD,
who builds Jerusalem.

On Tisha B'Av all conclude as follows:

נַחֵם Console, O LORD our God, the mourners of Zion and the mourners of
Jerusalem, and the city that is in sorrow, laid waste, scorned and desolate; that
grieves for the loss of its children, that is laid waste of its dwellings, robbed
of its glory, desolate without inhabitants. She sits with her head covered
like a barren childless woman. Legions have devoured her; idolaters have
taken possession of her; they have put Your people Israel to the sword and
deliberately killed the devoted followers of the Most High. Therefore Zion
weeps bitterly, and Jerusalem raises her voice. My heart, my heart grieves for
those they killed; I am in anguish, I am in anguish for those they killed. For
You, O LORD, consumed it with fire, and with fire You will rebuild it in the
future, as is said, "And I Myself will be a wall of fire around it, says the LORD,   *Zech. 2*
and I will be its glory within." Blessed are You, LORD, who consoles Zion and
rebuilds Jerusalem.   *Continue with "May the offshoot" below.*

KINGDOM OF DAVID

אֶת צֶמַח May the offshoot of Your servant David soon flower,
and may his pride be raised high by Your salvation,
for we wait for Your salvation all day.
Blessed are You, LORD,
who makes the glory of salvation flourish.

וְתֵן שָׂכָר טוֹב לְכָל הַבּוֹטְחִים בְּשִׁמְךָ בֶּאֱמֶת
וְשִׂים חֶלְקֵנוּ עִמָּהֶם
וּלְעוֹלָם לֹא נֵבוֹשׁ כִּי בְךָ בָּטָחְנוּ.
בָּרוּךְ אַתָּה יהוה, מִשְׁעָן וּמִבְטָח לַצַּדִּיקִים.

בניין ירושלים

וְלִירוּשָׁלַיִם עִירְךָ בְּרַחֲמִים תָּשׁוּב
וְתִשְׁכֹּן בְּתוֹכָהּ כַּאֲשֶׁר דִּבַּרְתָּ
וּבְנֵה אוֹתָהּ בְּקָרוֹב בְּיָמֵינוּ בִּנְיַן עוֹלָם
וְכִסֵּא דָוִד מְהֵרָה לְתוֹכָהּ תָּכִין.
*בָּרוּךְ אַתָּה יהוה, בּוֹנֵה יְרוּשָׁלָיִם.

---

*On תשעה באב, all conclude as follows:

נַחֵם יהוה אֱלֹהֵינוּ אֶת אֲבֵלֵי צִיּוֹן וְאֶת אֲבֵלֵי יְרוּשָׁלַיִם, וְאֶת הָעִיר הָאֲבֵלָה
וְהַחֲרֵבָה וְהַבְּזוּיָה וְהַשּׁוֹמֵמָה. הָאֲבֵלָה מִבְּלִי בָנֶיהָ, וְהַחֲרֵבָה מִמְּעוֹנוֹתֶיהָ,
וְהַבְּזוּיָה מִכְּבוֹדָהּ, וְהַשּׁוֹמֵמָה מֵאֵין יוֹשֵׁב. וְהִיא יוֹשֶׁבֶת וְרֹאשָׁהּ חָפוּי, כְּאִשָּׁה
עֲקָרָה שֶׁלֹּא יָלֶדָה. וַיְבַלְּעוּהָ לִגְיוֹנוֹת, וַיִּירָשׁוּהָ עוֹבְדֵי פְסִילִים, וַיָּטִילוּ אֶת
עַמְּךָ יִשְׂרָאֵל לֶחָרֶב, וַיַּהַרְגוּ בְזָדוֹן חֲסִידֵי עֶלְיוֹן. עַל כֵּן צִיּוֹן בְּמַר תִּבְכֶּה,
וִירוּשָׁלַיִם תִּתֵּן קוֹלָהּ. לִבִּי לִבִּי עַל חַלְלֵיהֶם, מֵעַי מֵעַי עַל חַלְלֵיהֶם, כִּי אַתָּה
יהוה בָּאֵשׁ הִצַּתָּהּ, וּבָאֵשׁ אַתָּה עָתִיד לִבְנוֹתָהּ. כָּאָמוּר: וַאֲנִי אֶהְיֶה-לָּהּ, זכריה ב
נְאֻם-יהוה, חוֹמַת אֵשׁ סָבִיב, וּלְכָבוֹד אֶהְיֶה בְתוֹכָהּ: בָּרוּךְ אַתָּה יהוה,
מְנַחֵם צִיּוֹן וּבוֹנֵה יְרוּשָׁלָיִם.
Continue with אֶת צֶמַח below.

משיח בן דוד

אֶת צֶמַח דָּוִד עַבְדְּךָ מְהֵרָה תַצְמִיחַ
וְקַרְנוֹ תָּרוּם בִּישׁוּעָתֶךָ, כִּי לִישׁוּעָתְךָ קִוִּינוּ כָּל הַיּוֹם.
בָּרוּךְ אַתָּה יהוה, מַצְמִיחַ קֶרֶן יְשׁוּעָה.

RESPONSE TO PRAYER

שְׁמַע קוֹלֵנוּ Listen to our voice, LORD our God.
Spare us and have compassion on us,
and in compassion and favor accept our prayer,
for You, God, listen to prayers and pleas.
Do not turn us away, O our King,
empty-handed from Your presence,*
for You listen with compassion
to the prayer of Your people Israel.
Blessed are You, LORD, who listens to prayer.

---

*At this point on fast days, the congregation adds "Answer us" below.
In times of drought in Israel, say "And answer us" on page 124.

עֲנֵנוּ Answer us, LORD, answer us on our Fast Day, for we are in great distress.
Look not at our wickedness. Do not hide Your face from us and do not
ignore our plea. Be near to our cry; please let Your loving-kindness comfort
us. Even before we call to You, answer us, as is said, "Before they call, I will
answer. While they are still speaking, I will hear." For You, LORD, are the
One who answers in time of distress, redeems and rescues in all times of
trouble and anguish.   *Continue with "for You listen" above.*

TEMPLE SERVICE

רְצֵה Find favor, LORD our God,
in Your people Israel and their prayer.
Restore the service to Your most holy House,
and accept in love and favor
the fire-offerings of Israel and their prayer.
May the service of Your people Israel always find favor with You.

On Rosh Ḥodesh, say:

אֱלֹהֵינוּ Our God and God of our ancestors, may there rise, come, reach,
appear, be favored, heard, regarded and remembered before You, our recollection and remembrance, as well as the remembrance of our ancestors,
and of the Messiah son of David Your servant, and of Jerusalem Your
holy city, and of all Your people the house of Israel – for deliverance and

שומע תפלה
שְׁמַע קוֹלֵנוּ יהוה אֱלֹהֵינוּ
חוּס וְרַחֵם עָלֵינוּ
וְקַבֵּל בְּרַחֲמִים וּבְרָצוֹן אֶת תְּפִלָּתֵנוּ
כִּי אֵל שׁוֹמֵעַ תְּפִלּוֹת וְתַחֲנוּנִים אָתָּה
וּמִלְּפָנֶיךָ מַלְכֵּנוּ רֵיקָם אַל תְּשִׁיבֵנוּ*
כִּי אַתָּה שׁוֹמֵעַ תְּפִלַּת עַמְּךָ יִשְׂרָאֵל בְּרַחֲמִים.
בָּרוּךְ אַתָּה יהוה, שׁוֹמֵעַ תְּפִלָּה.

*At this point on fast days, the קהל adds עֲנֵנוּ below.
In times of drought in ארץ ישראל, say וְעֵנֵנוּ on page 125.

עֲנֵנוּ יהוה עֲנֵנוּ בְּיוֹם צוֹם תַּעֲנִיתֵנוּ, כִּי בְצָרָה גְדוֹלָה אֲנָחְנוּ. אַל תֵּפֶן אֶל
רִשְׁעֵנוּ, וְאַל תַּסְתֵּר פָּנֶיךָ מִמֶּנּוּ, וְאַל תִּתְעַלַּם מִתְּחִנָּתֵנוּ. הֱיֵה נָא קָרוֹב
לְשַׁוְעָתֵנוּ, יְהִי נָא חַסְדְּךָ לְנַחֲמֵנוּ, טֶרֶם נִקְרָא אֵלֶיךָ עֲנֵנוּ, כַּדָּבָר שֶׁנֶּאֱמַר:
וְהָיָה טֶרֶם יִקְרָאוּ וַאֲנִי אֶעֱנֶה, עוֹד הֵם מְדַבְּרִים וַאֲנִי אֶשְׁמָע: כִּי אַתָּה
יהוה הָעוֹנֶה בְּעֵת צָרָה, פּוֹדֶה וּמַצִּיל בְּכָל עֵת צָרָה וְצוּקָה.
Continue with כִּי אַתָּה שׁוֹמֵעַ above.

עבודה
רְצֵה יהוה אֱלֹהֵינוּ בְּעַמְּךָ יִשְׂרָאֵל, וּבִתְפִלָּתָם
וְהָשֵׁב אֶת הָעֲבוֹדָה לִדְבִיר בֵּיתֶךָ
וְאִשֵּׁי יִשְׂרָאֵל וּתְפִלָּתָם בְּאַהֲבָה תְקַבֵּל בְּרָצוֹן
וּתְהִי לְרָצוֹן תָּמִיד עֲבוֹדַת יִשְׂרָאֵל עַמֶּךָ.

On ראש חודש, say:

אֱלֹהֵינוּ וֵאלֹהֵי אֲבוֹתֵינוּ, יַעֲלֶה וְיָבֹא וְיַגִּיעַ, וְיֵרָאֶה וְיֵרָצֶה
וְיִשָּׁמַע, וְיִפָּקֵד וְיִזָּכֵר זִכְרוֹנֵנוּ וּפִקְדוֹנֵנוּ וְזִכְרוֹן אֲבוֹתֵינוּ, וְזִכְרוֹן
מָשִׁיחַ בֶּן דָּוִד עַבְדֶּךָ, וְזִכְרוֹן יְרוּשָׁלַיִם עִיר קָדְשֶׁךָ, וְזִכְרוֹן כָּל עַמְּךָ

well-being, grace, loving-kindness and compassion, life and peace, on
this day of Rosh Ḥodesh. On it remember us, LORD our God, for good;
recollect us for blessing, and deliver us for life. In accord with Your
promise of salvation and compassion, spare us and be gracious to us;
have compassion on us and deliver us, for our eyes are turned to You
because You, God, are a gracious and compassionate King.

וְתֶחֱזֶינָה And may our eyes witness Your return
to Zion in compassion.
Blessed are You, LORD, who restores His Presence to Zion.

THANKSGIVING

Bow at the first nine words.

מוֹדִים We give thanks to You,
for You are the LORD our God
and God of our ancestors
for ever and all time.
You are the Rock of our lives,
Shield of our salvation
from generation to generation.
We will thank You and
declare Your praise for our lives,
which are entrusted into Your hand;
for our souls,
which are placed in Your charge;
for Your miracles
which are with us every day;
and for Your wonders and favors
at all times, evening,
morning and midday.
You are good –
for Your compassion never fails.
You are compassionate –
for Your loving-kindnesses never cease.
We have always placed our hope in You.

*During the Leader's Repetition,
the congregation says quietly:*
מוֹדִים We give thanks to You,
for You are the LORD our God
and God of our ancestors,
God of all flesh,
who formed us
and formed the universe.
Blessings and thanks
are due to Your great
and holy name for giving us
life and sustaining us.
May You continue
to give us life
and sustain us;
and may You gather our
exiles to Your holy courts,
to keep Your decrees,
do Your will and serve You
with a perfect heart,
for it is for us
to give You thanks.
Blessed be God to whom
thanksgiving is due.

בֵּית יִשְׂרָאֵל, לְפָנֶיךָ, לִפְלֵיטָה לְטוֹבָה, לְחֵן וּלְחֶסֶד וּלְרַחֲמִים, לְחַיִּים וּלְשָׁלוֹם בְּיוֹם רֹאשׁ הַחֹדֶשׁ הַזֶּה. זָכְרֵנוּ יהוה אֱלֹהֵינוּ בּוֹ לְטוֹבָה, וּפָקְדֵנוּ בוֹ לִבְרָכָה, וְהוֹשִׁיעֵנוּ בוֹ לְחַיִּים. וּבִדְבַר יְשׁוּעָה וְרַחֲמִים, חוּס וְחָנֵּנוּ וְרַחֵם עָלֵינוּ וְהוֹשִׁיעֵנוּ, כִּי אֵלֶיךָ עֵינֵינוּ, כִּי אֵל מֶלֶךְ חַנּוּן וְרַחוּם אָתָּה.

וְתֶחֱזֶינָה עֵינֵינוּ בְּשׁוּבְךָ לְצִיּוֹן בְּרַחֲמִים.
בָּרוּךְ אַתָּה יהוה, הַמַּחֲזִיר שְׁכִינָתוֹ לְצִיּוֹן.

הוֹדָאָה

Bow at the first five words.

יְמוֹדִים אֲנַחְנוּ לָךְ
שָׁאַתָּה הוּא יהוה אֱלֹהֵינוּ
וֵאלֹהֵי אֲבוֹתֵינוּ לְעוֹלָם וָעֶד.
צוּר חַיֵּינוּ, מָגֵן יִשְׁעֵנוּ
אַתָּה הוּא לְדוֹר וָדוֹר.
נוֹדֶה לְּךָ וּנְסַפֵּר תְּהִלָּתֶךָ
עַל חַיֵּינוּ הַמְּסוּרִים בְּיָדֶךָ
וְעַל נִשְׁמוֹתֵינוּ הַפְּקוּדוֹת לָךְ
וְעַל נִסֶּיךָ שֶׁבְּכָל יוֹם עִמָּנוּ
וְעַל נִפְלְאוֹתֶיךָ וְטוֹבוֹתֶיךָ
שֶׁבְּכָל עֵת
עֶרֶב וָבֹקֶר וְצָהֳרָיִם.
הַטּוֹב, כִּי לֹא כָלוּ רַחֲמֶיךָ
וְהַמְרַחֵם, כִּי לֹא תַמּוּ חֲסָדֶיךָ
מֵעוֹלָם קִוִּינוּ לָךְ.

During the ‏חזרת הש״ץ‏
the ‏קהל‏ says quietly:

מוֹדִים אֲנַחְנוּ לָךְ
שָׁאַתָּה הוּא יהוה אֱלֹהֵינוּ
וֵאלֹהֵי אֲבוֹתֵינוּ
אֱלֹהֵי כָל בָּשָׂר
יוֹצְרֵנוּ, יוֹצֵר בְּרֵאשִׁית.
בְּרָכוֹת וְהוֹדָאוֹת
לְשִׁמְךָ הַגָּדוֹל וְהַקָּדוֹשׁ
עַל שֶׁהֶחֱיִיתָנוּ וְקִיַּמְתָּנוּ.
כֵּן תְּחַיֵּנוּ וּתְקַיְּמֵנוּ
וְתֶאֱסֹף גָּלֻיּוֹתֵינוּ
לְחַצְרוֹת קָדְשֶׁךָ
לִשְׁמוֹר חֻקֶּיךָ
וְלַעֲשׂוֹת רְצוֹנֶךָ וּלְעָבְדְּךָ
בְּלֵבָב שָׁלֵם
עַל שֶׁאֲנַחְנוּ מוֹדִים לָךְ.
בָּרוּךְ אֵל הַהוֹדָאוֹת.

On Ḥanukka:

עַל הַנִּסִּים [We thank You also] for the miracles, the redemption, the mighty deeds, the salvations, and the victories in battle which You performed for our ancestors in those days, at this time.

בִּימֵי מַתִּתְיָהוּ In the days of Mattityahu, son of Yoḥanan, the High Priest, the Hasmonean, and his sons, the wicked Greek kingdom rose up against Your people Israel to make them forget Your Torah and to force them to transgress the statutes of Your will. It was then that You in Your great compassion stood by them in the time of their distress. You championed their cause, judged their claim, and avenged their wrong. You delivered the strong into the hands of the weak, the many into the hands of the few, the impure into the hands of the pure, the wicked into the hands of the righteous, and the arrogant into the hands of those who were engaged in the study of Your Torah. You made for Yourself great and holy renown in Your world, and for Your people Israel You performed a great salvation and redemption as of this very day. Your children then entered the holiest part of Your House, cleansed Your Temple, purified Your Sanctuary, kindled lights in Your holy courts, and designated these eight days of Ḥanukka for giving thanks and praise to Your great name.

Continue with "For all these things."

On Purim:

עַל הַנִּסִּים [We thank You also] for the miracles, the redemption, the mighty deeds, the salvations, and the victories in battle which You performed for our ancestors in those days, at this time.

בִּימֵי מָרְדְּכַי In the days of Mordekhai and Esther, in Shushan the capital, the wicked Haman rose up against them and sought to destroy, slay and exterminate *Esther 3* all the Jews, young and old, children and women, on one day, the thirteenth day of the twelfth month, which is the month of Adar, and to plunder their possessions. Then You in Your great compassion thwarted his counsel, frustrated his plans, and caused his scheme to recoil on his own head, so that they hanged him and his sons on the gallows.

Continue with "For all these things."

וְעַל כֻּלָּם For all these things may Your name be blessed and exalted, our King, continually, for ever and all time.

Between Rosh HaShana And write, for a good life,
& Yom Kippur: all the children of Your covenant.

Let all that lives thank You, Selah! and praise Your name in truth, God, our Savior and Help, Selah!
Blessed are You, LORD, whose name is "the Good" and to whom thanks are due.

בחנוכה:

עַל הַנִּסִּים וְעַל הַפֻּרְקָן וְעַל הַגְּבוּרוֹת וְעַל הַתְּשׁוּעוֹת וְעַל הַמִּלְחָמוֹת שֶׁעָשִׂיתָ לַאֲבוֹתֵינוּ בַּיָּמִים הָהֵם בַּזְּמַן הַזֶּה.

בִּימֵי מַתִּתְיָהוּ בֶּן יוֹחָנָן כֹּהֵן גָּדוֹל חַשְׁמוֹנַאי וּבָנָיו, כְּשֶׁעָמְדָה מַלְכוּת יָוָן הָרְשָׁעָה עַל עַמְּךָ יִשְׂרָאֵל לְהַשְׁכִּיחָם תּוֹרָתֶךָ וּלְהַעֲבִירָם מֵחֻקֵּי רְצוֹנֶךָ, וְאַתָּה בְּרַחֲמֶיךָ הָרַבִּים עָמַדְתָּ לָהֶם בְּעֵת צָרָתָם, רַבְתָּ אֶת רִיבָם, דַּנְתָּ אֶת דִּינָם, נָקַמְתָּ אֶת נִקְמָתָם, מָסַרְתָּ גִבּוֹרִים בְּיַד חַלָּשִׁים, וְרַבִּים בְּיַד מְעַטִּים, וּטְמֵאִים בְּיַד טְהוֹרִים, וּרְשָׁעִים בְּיַד צַדִּיקִים, וְזֵדִים בְּיַד עוֹסְקֵי תוֹרָתֶךָ, וּלְךָ עָשִׂיתָ שֵׁם גָּדוֹל וְקָדוֹשׁ בְּעוֹלָמֶךָ, וּלְעַמְּךָ יִשְׂרָאֵל עָשִׂיתָ תְּשׁוּעָה גְדוֹלָה וּפֻרְקָן כְּהַיּוֹם הַזֶּה. וְאַחַר כֵּן בָּאוּ בָנֶיךָ לִדְבִיר בֵּיתֶךָ, וּפִנּוּ אֶת הֵיכָלֶךָ, וְטִהֲרוּ אֶת מִקְדָּשֶׁךָ, וְהִדְלִיקוּ נֵרוֹת בְּחַצְרוֹת קָדְשֶׁךָ, וְקָבְעוּ שְׁמוֹנַת יְמֵי חֲנֻכָּה אֵלּוּ, לְהוֹדוֹת וּלְהַלֵּל לְשִׁמְךָ הַגָּדוֹל.

Continue with וְעַל כֻּלָּם.

בפורים:

עַל הַנִּסִּים וְעַל הַפֻּרְקָן וְעַל הַגְּבוּרוֹת וְעַל הַתְּשׁוּעוֹת וְעַל הַמִּלְחָמוֹת שֶׁעָשִׂיתָ לַאֲבוֹתֵינוּ בַּיָּמִים הָהֵם בַּזְּמַן הַזֶּה.

אסתר ג בִּימֵי מָרְדְּכַי וְאֶסְתֵּר בְּשׁוּשַׁן הַבִּירָה, כְּשֶׁעָמַד עֲלֵיהֶם הָמָן הָרָשָׁע, בִּקֵּשׁ לְהַשְׁמִיד לַהֲרֹג וּלְאַבֵּד אֶת־כָּל־הַיְּהוּדִים מִנַּעַר וְעַד־זָקֵן טַף וְנָשִׁים בְּיוֹם אֶחָד, בִּשְׁלוֹשָׁה עָשָׂר לְחֹדֶשׁ שְׁנֵים־עָשָׂר, הוּא־חֹדֶשׁ אֲדָר, וּשְׁלָלָם לָבוֹז: וְאַתָּה בְּרַחֲמֶיךָ הָרַבִּים הֵפַרְתָּ אֶת עֲצָתוֹ, וְקִלְקַלְתָּ אֶת מַחֲשַׁבְתּוֹ, וַהֲשֵׁבוֹתָ לּוֹ גְּמוּלוֹ בְּרֹאשׁוֹ, וְתָלוּ אוֹתוֹ וְאֶת בָּנָיו עַל הָעֵץ.

Continue with וְעַל כֻּלָּם.

───────────────────────────────

וְעַל כֻּלָּם יִתְבָּרַךְ וְיִתְרוֹמַם שִׁמְךָ מַלְכֵּנוּ תָּמִיד לְעוֹלָם וָעֶד.

בעשרת ימי תשובה: וּכְתֹב לְחַיִּים טוֹבִים כָּל בְּנֵי בְרִיתֶךָ.

וְכֹל הַחַיִּים יוֹדוּךָ סֶּלָה, וִיהַלְלוּ אֶת שִׁמְךָ בֶּאֱמֶת הָאֵל יְשׁוּעָתֵנוּ וְעֶזְרָתֵנוּ סֶלָה.
בָּרוּךְ אַתָּה יהוה, הַטּוֹב שִׁמְךָ וּלְךָ נָאֶה לְהוֹדוֹת.

*On public fast days only, the following is said by the Leader during
the Repetition of the Amida, except in a house of mourning. In Israel, on Fast Days,
if Kohanim bless the congregation, turn to page 386. See laws 62–69.*

Our God and God of our fathers, bless us with the threefold blessing in the
Torah, written by the hand of Moses Your servant and pronounced by Aaron
and his sons the priests, Your holy people, as it is said:

May the LORD bless you and protect you.   *Cong:* May it be Your will.   *Num. 6*

May the LORD make His face shine on you
       and be gracious to you.   *Cong:* May it be Your will.

May the LORD turn His face toward you,
       and grant you peace.   *Cong:* May it be Your will.

PEACE

שָׁלוֹם רָב Grant
great peace
to Your people Israel
for ever,
for You are
the sovereign LORD
of all peace;
and may it be good
in Your eyes
to bless Your people Israel
at every time,
at every hour,
with Your peace.

On fast days:

שִׂים שָׁלוֹם Grant peace,
goodness and blessing,
grace, loving-kindness and compassion
to us and all Israel Your people.
Bless us, our Father, all as one,
with the light of Your face,
for by the light of Your face
You have given us, LORD our God,
the Torah of life and love of kindness,
righteousness, blessing, compassion,
life and peace.
May it be good in Your eyes
to bless Your people Israel
at every time, in every hour,
with Your peace.

*Between
Rosh HaShana
& Yom Kippur:*

In the book of life, blessing, peace and prosperity,
may we and all Your people the house of Israel be remembered
and written before You for a good life, and for peace.*

Blessed are You, LORD, who blesses His people Israel with peace.

**Between Rosh HaShana and Yom Kippur
outside Israel, many end the blessing:*

Blessed are You, LORD, who makes peace.

*The following verse concludes the Leader's Repetition of the Amida.
Some also say it here as part of the silent Amida. See law 60.*

May the words of my mouth and the meditation of my heart   *Ps. 19*
find favor before You, LORD, my Rock and Redeemer.

On public fast days only, the following is said by the שליח ציבור *during the* חזרת הש"ץ *except in a house of mourning. In* ארץ ישראל, *on Fast Days,* *if* כהנים *say* ברכת כהנים *turn to page 387. See laws 62–69.*

אֱלֹהֵינוּ וֵאלֹהֵי אֲבוֹתֵינוּ, בָּרְכֵנוּ בַּבְּרָכָה הַמְשֻׁלֶּשֶׁת בַּתּוֹרָה, הַכְּתוּבָה עַל
יְדֵי מֹשֶׁה עַבְדֶּךָ, הָאֲמוּרָה מִפִּי אַהֲרֹן וּבָנָיו כֹּהֲנִים עַם קְדוֹשֶׁיךָ, כָּאָמוּר:

במדבר ו

יְבָרֶכְךָ יהוה וְיִשְׁמְרֶךָ: קהל: כֵּן יְהִי רָצוֹן

יָאֵר יהוה פָּנָיו אֵלֶיךָ וִיחֻנֶּךָּ: קהל: כֵּן יְהִי רָצוֹן

יִשָּׂא יהוה פָּנָיו אֵלֶיךָ וְיָשֵׂם לְךָ שָׁלוֹם: קהל: כֵּן יְהִי רָצוֹן

ברכת שלום

שָׁלוֹם רָב עַל יִשְׂרָאֵל

עַמְּךָ תָּשִׂים לְעוֹלָם

כִּי אַתָּה הוּא

מֶלֶךְ אָדוֹן לְכָל הַשָּׁלוֹם.

וְטוֹב בְּעֵינֶיךָ

לְבָרֵךְ אֶת עַמְּךָ יִשְׂרָאֵל

בְּכָל עֵת וּבְכָל שָׁעָה

בִּשְׁלוֹמֶךָ.

On fast days:

שִׂים שָׁלוֹם טוֹבָה וּבְרָכָה
חֵן וָחֶסֶד וְרַחֲמִים
עָלֵינוּ וְעַל כָּל יִשְׂרָאֵל עַמֶּךָ.
בָּרְכֵנוּ אָבִינוּ כֻּלָּנוּ כְּאֶחָד בְּאוֹר פָּנֶיךָ
כִּי בְאוֹר פָּנֶיךָ נָתַתָּ לָּנוּ יהוה אֱלֹהֵינוּ
תּוֹרַת חַיִּים וְאַהֲבַת חֶסֶד
וּצְדָקָה וּבְרָכָה וְרַחֲמִים וְחַיִּים וְשָׁלוֹם.
וְטוֹב בְּעֵינֶיךָ לְבָרֵךְ אֶת עַמְּךָ יִשְׂרָאֵל
בְּכָל עֵת וּבְכָל שָׁעָה בִּשְׁלוֹמֶךָ.

בעשרת ימי תשובה:

בְּסֵפֶר חַיִּים, בְּרָכָה וְשָׁלוֹם, וּפַרְנָסָה טוֹבָה
נִזָּכֵר וְנִכָּתֵב לְפָנֶיךָ, אֲנַחְנוּ וְכָל עַמְּךָ בֵּית יִשְׂרָאֵל
לְחַיִּים טוֹבִים וּלְשָׁלוֹם.*

בָּרוּךְ אַתָּה יהוה, הַמְבָרֵךְ אֶת עַמּוֹ יִשְׂרָאֵל בַּשָּׁלוֹם.

During the עשרת ימי תשובה *in* ארץ *חוץ לארץ, many end the blessing:*

בָּרוּךְ אַתָּה יהוה, עוֹשֶׂה הַשָּׁלוֹם.

The following verse concludes the חזרת הש"ץ.
Some also say it here as part of the silent עמידה. *See law 60.*

תהלים יט

יִהְיוּ לְרָצוֹן אִמְרֵי־פִי וְהֶגְיוֹן לִבִּי לְפָנֶיךָ, יהוה צוּרִי וְגֹאֲלִי:

אֱלֹהַי My God,
guard my tongue from evil and my lips from deceitful speech.
To those who curse me, let my soul be silent;
may my soul be to all like the dust.
Open my heart to Your Torah and let my soul
pursue Your commandments. As for all who plan evil against me,
swiftly thwart their counsel and frustrate their plans.

    Act for the sake of Your name; act for the sake of Your right hand;
    act for the sake of Your holiness; act for the sake of Your Torah.
That Your beloved ones may be delivered,
save with Your right hand and answer me.

*May the words of my mouth and the meditation of my heart
find favor before You, Lord, my Rock and Redeemer.

Bow, take three steps back, then bow, first left, then right, then center, while saying:

May He who makes peace in His high places,
make peace for us and all Israel – and say: Amen.

יְהִי רָצוֹן May it be Your will, Lord our God and God of our ancestors,
that the Temple be rebuilt speedily in our days,
and grant us a share in Your Torah.
And there we will serve You with reverence,
as in the days of old and as in former years.
Then the offering of Judah and Jerusalem will be pleasing to the Lord
as in the days of old and as in former years.

On days when Taḥanun is not said, the Leader says Full Kaddish on page 254.

*Berakhot
17a*

Ps. 60

Ps. 19

Mal. 3

---

*A person undertaking a personal fast says the following at Minḥa before the fast:
Master of all worlds, I hereby take upon myself before You a voluntary fast tomorrow.
May it be Your will, Lord my God and God of my ancestors, that You accept me in love
and favor, that my prayer may come before You, and that You may answer my entreaty
in Your great compassion, for You hear the prayer of every mouth.

On the afternoon of the fast, the following is said:
Master of all worlds, it is revealed and known to You that when the Temple stood, a
person who sinned would offer a sacrifice, of which were offered only the fat and blood,
yet You in Your great compassion granted atonement. Now I have fasted, and my fat and
blood have been diminished. May it be Your will that this diminution today of my fat and
blood be as if I had offered them before You on the altar, and may You show me favor.

אֱלֹהַי

נְצֹר לְשׁוֹנִי מֵרָע וּשְׂפָתַי מִדַּבֵּר מִרְמָה

וְלִמְקַלְלַי נַפְשִׁי תִדֹּם, וְנַפְשִׁי כֶּעָפָר לַכֹּל תִּהְיֶה.

פְּתַח לִבִּי בְּתוֹרָתֶךָ, וּבְמִצְוֹתֶיךָ תִּרְדּוֹף נַפְשִׁי.

וְכָל הַחוֹשְׁבִים עָלַי רָעָה

מְהֵרָה הָפֵר עֲצָתָם וְקַלְקֵל מַחֲשַׁבְתָּם.

עֲשֵׂה לְמַעַן שְׁמֶךָ, עֲשֵׂה לְמַעַן יְמִינֶךָ

עֲשֵׂה לְמַעַן קְדֻשָּׁתֶךָ, עֲשֵׂה לְמַעַן תּוֹרָתֶךָ.

לְמַעַן יֵחָלְצוּן יְדִידֶיךָ, הוֹשִׁיעָה יְמִינְךָ וַעֲנֵנִי:

*יִהְיוּ לְרָצוֹן אִמְרֵי־פִי וְהֶגְיוֹן לִבִּי לְפָנֶיךָ, יהוה צוּרִי וְגֹאֲלִי:

Bow, take three steps back, then bow, first left, then right, then center, while saying:

עֹשֶׂה שָׁלוֹם/ בעשרת ימי תשובה: הַשָּׁלוֹם/ בִּמְרוֹמָיו

הוּא יַעֲשֶׂה שָׁלוֹם עָלֵינוּ וְעַל כָּל יִשְׂרָאֵל, וְאִמְרוּ אָמֵן.

יְהִי רָצוֹן מִלְּפָנֶיךָ יהוה אֱלֹהֵינוּ וֵאלֹהֵי אֲבוֹתֵינוּ

שֶׁיִּבָּנֶה בֵּית הַמִּקְדָּשׁ בִּמְהֵרָה בְיָמֵינוּ, וְתֵן חֶלְקֵנוּ בְּתוֹרָתֶךָ

וְשָׁם נַעֲבָדְךָ בְּיִרְאָה כִּימֵי עוֹלָם וּכְשָׁנִים קַדְמוֹנִיּוֹת.

וְעָרְבָה לַיהוה מִנְחַת יְהוּדָה וִירוּשָׁלָ͏ִם כִּימֵי עוֹלָם וּכְשָׁנִים קַדְמוֹנִיּוֹת:

On days when תחנון *is not said, the* שליח ציבור *says* קדיש שלם *on page 255.*

**A person undertaking a personal fast says the following at* מנחה *before the fast:*

רִבּוֹן כָּל הָעוֹלָמִים, הֲרֵי אֲנִי לְפָנֶיךָ בְּתַעֲנִית נְדָבָה לְמָחָר. יְהִי רָצוֹן מִלְּפָנֶיךָ יהוה
אֱלֹהַי וֵאלֹהֵי אֲבוֹתַי, שֶׁתְּקַבְּלֵנִי בְּאַהֲבָה וּבְרָצוֹן, וְתָבֹא לְפָנֶיךָ תְּפִלָּתִי, וְתַעֲנֶה
עֲתִירָתִי בְּרַחֲמֶיךָ הָרַבִּים, כִּי אַתָּה שׁוֹמֵעַ תְּפִלַּת כָּל־פֶּה.

On the afternoon of the fast, the following is said:

רִבּוֹן כָּל הָעוֹלָמִים, גָּלוּי וְיָדוּעַ לְפָנֶיךָ, בִּזְמַן שֶׁבֵּית הַמִּקְדָּשׁ קַיָּם, אָדָם חוֹטֵא וּמַקְרִיב
קָרְבָּן, וְאֵין מַקְרִיבִין מִמֶּנּוּ אֶלָּא חֶלְבּוֹ וְדָמוֹ, וְאַתָּה בְּרַחֲמֶיךָ הָרַבִּים מְכַפֵּר. וְעַכְשָׁו
יָשַׁבְתִּי בְּתַעֲנִית, וְנִתְמַעֵט חֶלְבִּי וְדָמִי. יְהִי רָצוֹן מִלְּפָנֶיךָ, שֶׁיְּהֵא מְעוּט חֶלְבִּי וְדָמִי
שֶׁנִּתְמַעֵט הַיּוֹם, כְּאִלּוּ הִקְרַבְתִּיו עַל־גַּבֵּי הַמִּזְבֵּחַ, וּתְרַצֵנִי.

Between Rosh HaShana and Yom Kippur and on fast days, except days when
Taḥanun is not said (see list below), Avinu Malkenu (on page 138) is said here.

TAḤANUN

Taḥanun is not said on Erev Shabbat and Erev Yom Tov. It is also not said on the following days:
Rosh Ḥodesh, Ḥanukka, Tu BiShvat, the 14th and 15th of Adar I, Purim and Shushan Purim,
Yom HaAtzma'ut, Lag BaOmer, Yom Yerushalayim, Tisha B'Av, Tu B'Av, and the preceding
afternoons, the month of Nisan, the 14th of Iyar (Pesaḥ Sheni), from Rosh Ḥodesh Sivan
through the day after Shavuot (in Israel through 12th of Sivan), and from Erev Yom Kippur
through the day after Simḥat Torah (in Israel through Rosh Ḥodesh Marḥeshvan). Taḥanun
is also not said: on the occasion of a Brit Mila, either where the brit will take place or where
the father, Sandek or Mohel are present; if a groom is present (and some say, a bride) on
the day of his wedding or during the week of Sheva Berakhot; in a house of mourning.

LOWERING THE HEAD

Say while sitting; in the presence of a Torah scroll say until "in sudden shame,"
leaning forward and resting one's head on the left arm.

וַיֹּאמֶר דָּוִד David said to Gad, "I am in great distress.   *II Sam. 24*
Let us fall into God's hand, for His mercy is great;
but do not let me fall into the hand of man."

Compassionate and gracious One, I have sinned before You.
Lord, full of compassion, have compassion on me and accept my pleas.

Lord, do not rebuke me in Your anger or chastise me in Your wrath.   *Ps. 6*
Be gracious to me, Lord, for I am weak.
Heal me, Lord, for my bones are in agony.
My soul is in anguish, and You, O Lord – how long?
Turn, Lord, set my soul free; save me for the sake of Your love.
For no one remembers You when he is dead.
Who can praise You from the grave? I am weary with my sighing.
Every night I drench my bed, I soak my couch with my tears.
My eye grows dim from grief, worn out because of all my foes.
Leave me, all you evildoers,
for the Lord has heard the sound of my weeping.
The Lord has heard my pleas. The Lord will accept my prayer.
All my enemies will be shamed and utterly dismayed.
They will turn back in sudden shame.

Sit upright.

During the עשרת ימי תשובה *and on fast days, except days when*
תחנון *is not said (see list below),* אבינו מלכנו *(on page 139) is said here.*

סדר תחנון

תחנון *is not said on* ערב יום טוב *and* ערב שבת. *It is also not said on the following*
days: שושן פורים *and* פורים, אדר א׳ *, the 14th and 15th of* ט״ו בשבט, חנוכה, ראש חודש,
, and the preceding afternoons, ל״ג בעומר, יום ירושלים, ט״ו באב, תשעה באב, יום העצמאות
the month of ניסן, *the 14th of* אייר (פסח שני)*, from* ראש חודש סיון *through the day*
after שבועות *(in* ארץ ישראל *through* י״ב סיון*), and from* ערב יום כיפור *through the*
day after שמחת תורה *through* ארץ ישראל *(in* ראש חודש מרחשון*).* תחנון *is also not*
said: on the occasion of a ברית מילה, *either where the* ברית *will take place or where*
the father, מוהל *or* סנדק *are present; if a* חתן *is present (and some say, a* כלה*) on the*
day of his wedding or during the week of שבע ברכות*; in a house of mourning.*

נפילת אפים

Say while sitting; in the presence of a ספר תורה *say until* יֵבשׁוּ רָגַע*,*
leaning forward and resting one's head on the left arm.

שמואל ב׳ כד

וַיֹּאמֶר דָּוִד אֶל־גָּד, צַר־לִי מְאֹד
נִפְּלָה־נָּא בְיַד־יהוה, כִּי־רַבִּים רַחֲמָו, וּבְיַד־אָדָם אַל־אֶפֹּלָה:

רַחוּם וְחַנּוּן, חָטָאתִי לְפָנֶיךָ.
יהוה מָלֵא רַחֲמִים, רַחֵם עָלַי וְקַבֵּל תַּחֲנוּנָי.

תהלים ו

יהוה, אַל־בְּאַפְּךָ תוֹכִיחֵנִי, וְאַל־בַּחֲמָתְךָ תְיַסְּרֵנִי:
חָנֵּנִי יהוה, כִּי אֻמְלַל אָנִי, רְפָאֵנִי יהוה, כִּי נִבְהֲלוּ עֲצָמָי:
וְנַפְשִׁי נִבְהֲלָה מְאֹד, וְאַתְּ יהוה, עַד־מָתָי:
שׁוּבָה יהוה, חַלְּצָה נַפְשִׁי, הוֹשִׁיעֵנִי לְמַעַן חַסְדֶּךָ:
כִּי אֵין בַּמָּוֶת זִכְרֶךָ, בִּשְׁאוֹל מִי יוֹדֶה־לָּךְ:
יָגַעְתִּי בְּאַנְחָתִי, אַשְׂחֶה בְכָל־לַיְלָה מִטָּתִי, בְּדִמְעָתִי עַרְשִׂי אַמְסֶה:
עָשְׁשָׁה מִכַּעַס עֵינִי, עָתְקָה בְּכָל־צוֹרְרָי:
סוּרוּ מִמֶּנִּי כָּל־פֹּעֲלֵי אָוֶן, כִּי־שָׁמַע יהוה קוֹל בִּכְיִי:
שָׁמַע יהוה תְּחִנָּתִי, יהוה תְּפִלָּתִי יִקָּח:
יֵבֹשׁוּ וְיִבָּהֲלוּ מְאֹד כָּל־אֹיְבָי, יָשֻׁבוּ יֵבֹשׁוּ רָגַע:

Sit upright.

שׁוֹמֵר יִשְׂרָאֵל Guardian of Israel,
    guard the remnant of Israel,
    and let not Israel perish, who declare, "Listen, Israel."
Guardian of a unique nation, guard the remnant of a unique people,
    and let not that unique nation perish, who proclaim the unity of
    Your name [saying], "The LORD is our God, the LORD is One."
Guardian of a holy nation, guard the remnant of that holy people,
    and let not the holy nation perish, who three times repeat
    the threefold declaration of holiness to the Holy One.
You who are conciliated by calls for compassion and placated by pleas,
    be conciliated and placated toward an afflicted generation,
    for there is no other help.
Our Father, our King, be gracious to us and answer us,
    though we have no worthy deeds;
    act with us in charity and loving-kindness and save us.

Stand at ⌃.

וַאֲנַחְנוּ We do not know ⌃what to do, but our eyes are turned to You. *II Chr. 12*
Remember, LORD, Your compassion and loving-kindness, for they are *Ps. 25*
everlasting. May Your loving-kindness, LORD, be with us, for we have put *Ps. 33*
our hope in You. Do not hold against us the sins of those who came before *Ps. 79*
us. May Your mercies meet us swiftly, for we have been brought very low.
Be gracious to us, LORD, be gracious to us, for we are sated with contempt. *Ps. 123*
In wrath, remember mercy. He knows our nature; He remembers that *Hab. 3*
we are dust. ▸ Help us, God of our salvation, for the sake of the glory of *Ps. 103* *Ps. 79*
Your name. Save us and grant atonement for our sins for Your name's sake.

FULL KADDISH

Leader: יִתְגַּדַּל Magnified and sanctified may His great name be,
    in the world He created by His will.
    May He establish His kingdom
    in your lifetime and in your days,
    and in the lifetime of all the house of Israel,
    swiftly and soon – and say: Amen.

All: May His great name be blessed for ever and all time.

שׁוֹמֵר יִשְׂרָאֵל, שְׁמֹר שְׁאֵרִית יִשְׂרָאֵל, וְאַל יֹאבַד יִשְׂרָאֵל
הָאוֹמְרִים שְׁמַע יִשְׂרָאֵל.

שׁוֹמֵר גּוֹי אֶחָד, שְׁמֹר שְׁאֵרִית עַם אֶחָד, וְאַל יֹאבַד גּוֹי אֶחָד
הַמְיַחֲדִים שִׁמְךָ, יְהוָה אֱלֹהֵינוּ יְהוָה אֶחָד.

שׁוֹמֵר גּוֹי קָדוֹשׁ, שְׁמֹר שְׁאֵרִית עַם קָדוֹשׁ, וְאַל יֹאבַד גּוֹי קָדוֹשׁ
הַמְשַׁלְּשִׁים בְּשָׁלֹשׁ קְדֻשּׁוֹת לְקָדוֹשׁ.

מִתְרַצֶּה בְּרַחֲמִים וּמִתְפַּיֵּס בְּתַחֲנוּנִים, הִתְרַצֵּה וְהִתְפַּיֵּס לְדוֹר עָנִי
כִּי אֵין עוֹזֵר.

אָבִינוּ מַלְכֵּנוּ, חָנֵּנוּ וַעֲנֵנוּ, כִּי אֵין בָּנוּ מַעֲשִׂים
עֲשֵׂה עִמָּנוּ צְדָקָה וָחֶסֶד וְהוֹשִׁיעֵנוּ.

Stand at ▲.

וַאֲנַחְנוּ לֹא נֵדַע מַה־נַּעֲשֶׂה, כִּי עָלֶיךָ עֵינֵינוּ: זְכֹר־רַחֲמֶיךָ יְהוָה
וַחֲסָדֶיךָ, כִּי מֵעוֹלָם הֵמָּה: יְהִי־חַסְדְּךָ יְהוָה עָלֵינוּ, כַּאֲשֶׁר יִחַלְנוּ לָךְ:
אַל־תִּזְכָּר־לָנוּ עֲוֹנֹת רִאשֹׁנִים, מַהֵר יְקַדְּמוּנוּ רַחֲמֶיךָ, כִּי דַלּוֹנוּ מְאֹד:
חָנֵּנוּ יְהוָה חָנֵּנוּ, כִּי־רַב שָׂבַעְנוּ בוּז: בְּרֹגֶז רַחֵם תִּזְכּוֹר: כִּי־הוּא יָדַע
יִצְרֵנוּ, זָכוּר כִּי־עָפָר אֲנָחְנוּ: ▲ עָזְרֵנוּ אֱלֹהֵי יִשְׁעֵנוּ עַל־דְּבַר כְּבוֹד־
שְׁמֶךָ, וְהַצִּילֵנוּ וְכַפֵּר עַל־חַטֹּאתֵינוּ לְמַעַן שְׁמֶךָ:

דברי
הימים ב׳ כ׳
תהלים כה
תהלים לג
תהלים עט
תהלים קכב
חבקוק ג
תהלים קג
תהלים עט

קדיש שלם

שׁ״ץ: יִתְגַּדַּל וְיִתְקַדַּשׁ שְׁמֵהּ רַבָּא (קהל: אָמֵן)
בְּעָלְמָא דִּי בְרָא כִרְעוּתֵהּ
וְיַמְלִיךְ מַלְכוּתֵהּ
בְּחַיֵּיכוֹן וּבְיוֹמֵיכוֹן וּבְחַיֵּי דְכָל בֵּית יִשְׂרָאֵל
בַּעֲגָלָא וּבִזְמַן קָרִיב, וְאִמְרוּ אָמֵן. (קהל: אָמֵן)

קהל
ושׁ״ץ: יְהֵא שְׁמֵהּ רַבָּא מְבָרַךְ לְעָלַם וּלְעָלְמֵי עָלְמַיָּא.

Leader: Blessed and praised,
      glorified and exalted, raised and honored,
      uplifted and lauded be
      the name of the Holy One, blessed be He,
      beyond any blessing,
      song, praise and consolation
      uttered in the world –
      and say: Amen.

May the prayers and pleas of all Israel
be accepted by their Father in heaven –
and say: Amen.

May there be great peace from heaven,
and life for us and all Israel –
and say: Amen.

Bow, take three steps back, as if taking leave of the Divine Presence,
then bow, first left, then right, then center, while saying:

May He who makes peace in His high places,
make peace for us and all Israel –
and say: Amen.

Stand while saying Aleinu. Bow at ˙.

עָלֵינוּ It is our duty to praise the Master of all,
and ascribe greatness to the Author of creation,
who has not made us like the nations of the lands
nor placed us like the families of the earth;
who has not made our portion like theirs,
nor our destiny like all their multitudes.
(For they worship vanity and emptiness,
and pray to a god who cannot save.)
˙But we bow in worship
and thank the Supreme King of kings,
the Holy One, blessed be He,
who extends the heavens and establishes the earth,

ש״ץ: יִתְגַּדַּל וְיִשְׁתַּבַּח וְיִתְפָּאַר

וְיִתְרוֹמַם וְיִתְנַשֵּׂא וְיִתְהַדָּר וְיִתְעַלֶּה וְיִתְהַלָּל

שְׁמֵהּ דְּקֻדְשָׁא בְּרִיךְ הוּא (קהל: בְּרִיךְ הוּא)

לְעֵלָּא מִן כָּל בִּרְכָתָא / בעשרת ימי תשובה: לְעֵלָּא לְעֵלָּא מִכָּל בִּרְכָתָא/

וְשִׁירָתָא, תֻּשְׁבְּחָתָא וְנֶחֱמָתָא, דַּאֲמִירָן בְּעָלְמָא

וְאִמְרוּ אָמֵן. (קהל: אָמֵן)

תִּתְקַבַּל צְלוֹתְהוֹן וּבָעוּתְהוֹן דְּכָל יִשְׂרָאֵל

קֳדָם אֲבוּהוֹן דִּי בִשְׁמַיָּא

וְאִמְרוּ אָמֵן. (קהל: אָמֵן)

יְהֵא שְׁלָמָא רַבָּא מִן שְׁמַיָּא

וְחַיִּים, עָלֵינוּ וְעַל כָּל יִשְׂרָאֵל

וְאִמְרוּ אָמֵן. (קהל: אָמֵן)

*Bow, take three steps back, as if taking leave of the Divine Presence,
then bow, first left, then right, then center, while saying:*

עֹשֶׂה שָׁלוֹם/בעשרת ימי תשובה: הַשָּׁלוֹם/ בִּמְרוֹמָיו

הוּא יַעֲשֶׂה שָׁלוֹם עָלֵינוּ וְעַל כָּל יִשְׂרָאֵל

וְאִמְרוּ אָמֵן. (קהל: אָמֵן)

Stand while saying עָלֵינוּ. *Bow at* ׳.

עָלֵינוּ לְשַׁבֵּחַ לַאֲדוֹן הַכֹּל, לָתֵת גְּדֻלָּה לְיוֹצֵר בְּרֵאשִׁית

שֶׁלֹּא עָשָׂנוּ כְּגוֹיֵי הָאֲרָצוֹת, וְלֹא שָׂמָנוּ כְּמִשְׁפְּחוֹת הָאֲדָמָה

שֶׁלֹּא שָׂם חֶלְקֵנוּ כָּהֶם וְגוֹרָלֵנוּ כְּכָל הֲמוֹנָם.

(שֶׁהֵם מִשְׁתַּחֲוִים לְהֶבֶל וָרִיק וּמִתְפַּלְלִים אֶל אֵל לֹא יוֹשִׁיעַ.)

וַאֲנַחְנוּ כּוֹרְעִים וּמִשְׁתַּחֲוִים וּמוֹדִים

לִפְנֵי מֶלֶךְ מַלְכֵי הַמְּלָכִים, הַקָּדוֹשׁ בָּרוּךְ הוּא

שֶׁהוּא נוֹטֶה שָׁמַיִם וְיוֹסֵד אָרֶץ

whose throne of glory is in the heavens above,
and whose power's Presence is in the highest of heights.
He is our God; there is no other.
Truly He is our King, there is none else,
as it is written in His Torah:
"You shall know and take to heart this day   *Deut. 4*
that the Lord is God,
in heaven above and on earth below. There is no other."

Therefore, we place our hope in You, Lord our God,
that we may soon see the glory of Your power,
when You will remove abominations from the earth,
and idols will be utterly destroyed,
when the world will be perfected
under the sovereignty of the Almighty,
when all humanity will call on Your name,
to turn all the earth's wicked toward You.
All the world's inhabitants will realize and know
that to You every knee must bow and every tongue swear loyalty.
Before You, Lord our God, they will kneel and bow down
and give honor to Your glorious name.
They will all accept the yoke of Your kingdom,
and You will reign over them soon and for ever.
For the kingdom is Yours,
and to all eternity You will reign in glory,
as it is written in Your Torah:
"The Lord will reign for ever and ever."   *Ex. 15*
‣ And it is said: "Then the Lord shall be King over all the earth;   *Zech. 14*
on that day the Lord shall be One and His name One."

Some add:
Have no fear of sudden terror or of the ruin when it overtakes the wicked.   *Prov. 3*
Devise your strategy, but it will be thwarted;   *Is. 8*
propose your plan, but it will not stand, for God is with us.
When you grow old, I will still be the same.   *Is. 46*
When your hair turns gray, I will still carry you.
I made you, I will bear you, I will carry you, and I will rescue you.

וּמוֹשַׁב יְקָרוֹ בַּשָּׁמַיִם מִמַּעַל

וּשְׁכִינַת עֻזּוֹ בְּגָבְהֵי מְרוֹמִים.

הוּא אֱלֹהֵינוּ, אֵין עוֹד.

אֱמֶת מַלְכֵּנוּ, אֶפֶס זוּלָתוֹ

כַּכָּתוּב בְּתוֹרָתוֹ

דברים ד   וְיָדַעְתָּ הַיּוֹם וַהֲשֵׁבֹתָ אֶל־לְבָבֶךָ

כִּי יהוה הוּא הָאֱלֹהִים בַּשָּׁמַיִם מִמַּעַל וְעַל־הָאָרֶץ מִתָּחַת, אֵין עוֹד:

עַל כֵּן נְקַוֶּה לְךָ יהוה אֱלֹהֵינוּ, לִרְאוֹת מְהֵרָה בְּתִפְאֶרֶת עֻזֶּךָ

לְהַעֲבִיר גִּלּוּלִים מִן הָאָרֶץ, וְהָאֱלִילִים כָּרוֹת יִכָּרֵתוּן

לְתַקֵּן עוֹלָם בְּמַלְכוּת שַׁדַּי.

וְכָל בְּנֵי בָשָׂר יִקְרְאוּ בִשְׁמֶךָ לְהַפְנוֹת אֵלֶיךָ כָּל רִשְׁעֵי אָרֶץ.

יַכִּירוּ וְיֵדְעוּ כָּל יוֹשְׁבֵי תֵבֵל

כִּי לְךָ תִּכְרַע כָּל בֶּרֶךְ, תִּשָּׁבַע כָּל לָשׁוֹן.

לְפָנֶיךָ יהוה אֱלֹהֵינוּ יִכְרְעוּ וְיִפֹּלוּ, וְלִכְבוֹד שִׁמְךָ יְקָר יִתֵּנוּ

וִיקַבְּלוּ כֻלָּם אֶת עֹל מַלְכוּתֶךָ

וְתִמְלֹךְ עֲלֵיהֶם מְהֵרָה לְעוֹלָם וָעֶד.

כִּי הַמַּלְכוּת שֶׁלְּךָ הִיא וּלְעוֹלְמֵי עַד תִּמְלֹךְ בְּכָבוֹד

שמות טו   כַּכָּתוּב בְּתוֹרָתֶךָ, יהוה יִמְלֹךְ לְעֹלָם וָעֶד:

זכריה יד   ◄ וְנֶאֱמַר, וְהָיָה יהוה לְמֶלֶךְ עַל־כָּל־הָאָרֶץ

בַּיּוֹם הַהוּא יִהְיֶה יהוה אֶחָד וּשְׁמוֹ אֶחָד:

Some add:

משלי ג   אַל־תִּירָא מִפַּחַד פִּתְאֹם וּמִשֹּׁאַת רְשָׁעִים כִּי תָבֹא:

ישעיה ח   עֻצוּ עֵצָה וְתֻפָר, דַּבְּרוּ דָבָר וְלֹא יָקוּם, כִּי עִמָּנוּ אֵל:

ישעיה מו   וְעַד־זִקְנָה אֲנִי הוּא, וְעַד־שֵׂיבָה אֲנִי אֶסְבֹּל

אֲנִי עָשִׂיתִי וַאֲנִי אֶשָּׂא וַאֲנִי אֶסְבֹּל וַאֲמַלֵּט:

MOURNER'S KADDISH

The following prayer, said by mourners, requires the presence of a minyan.
A transliteration can be found on page 699.

Mourner: **יִתְגַּדַּל** Magnified and sanctified
may His great name be,
in the world He created by His will.
May He establish His kingdom
in your lifetime
and in your days,
and in the lifetime
of all the house of Israel,
swiftly and soon –
and say: Amen.

All: May His great name be blessed for ever and all time.

Mourner: Blessed and praised,
glorified and exalted,
raised and honored,
uplifted and lauded
be the name of the Holy One,
blessed be He,
beyond any blessing,
song, praise and consolation
uttered in the world –
and say: Amen.

May there be great peace from heaven,
and life for us and all Israel –
and say: Amen.

Bow, take three steps back, as if taking leave of the Divine Presence,
then bow, first left, then right, then center, while saying:

May He who makes peace in His high places,
make peace for us and all Israel –
and say: Amen.

קדיש יתום

The following prayer, said by mourners, requires the presence of a מנין.
A transliteration can be found on page 699.

אבל: יִתְגַּדַּל וְיִתְקַדַּשׁ שְׁמֵהּ רַבָּא (קהל: אָמֵן)
בְּעָלְמָא דִּי בְרָא כִרְעוּתֵהּ
וְיַמְלִיךְ מַלְכוּתֵהּ
בְּחַיֵּיכוֹן וּבְיוֹמֵיכוֹן
וּבְחַיֵּי דְכָל בֵּית יִשְׂרָאֵל
בַּעֲגָלָא וּבִזְמַן קָרִיב
וְאִמְרוּ אָמֵן. (קהל: אָמֵן)

קהל: יְהֵא שְׁמֵהּ רַבָּא מְבָרַךְ לְעָלַם וּלְעָלְמֵי עָלְמַיָּא.
ואבל:

אבל: יִתְבָּרַךְ וְיִשְׁתַּבַּח וְיִתְפָּאַר
וְיִתְרוֹמַם וְיִתְנַשֵּׂא וְיִתְהַדָּר וְיִתְעַלֶּה וְיִתְהַלָּל
שְׁמֵהּ דְּקֻדְשָׁא בְּרִיךְ הוּא (קהל: בְּרִיךְ הוּא)
לְעֵלָּא מִן כָּל בִּרְכָתָא
/בעשרת ימי תשובה: לְעֵלָּא לְעֵלָּא מִכָּל בִּרְכָתָא/
וְשִׁירָתָא, תֻּשְׁבְּחָתָא וְנֶחָמָתָא
דַּאֲמִירָן בְּעָלְמָא
וְאִמְרוּ אָמֵן. (קהל: אָמֵן)

יְהֵא שְׁלָמָא רַבָּא מִן שְׁמַיָּא
וְחַיִּים, עָלֵינוּ וְעַל כָּל יִשְׂרָאֵל, וְאִמְרוּ אָמֵן. (קהל: אָמֵן)

Bow, take three steps back, as if taking leave of the Divine Presence,
then bow, first left, then right, then center, while saying:

עֹשֶׂה שָׁלוֹם/ בעשרת ימי תשובה: הַשָּׁלוֹם/ בִּמְרוֹמָיו
הוּא יַעֲשֶׂה שָׁלוֹם עָלֵינוּ וְעַל כָּל יִשְׂרָאֵל
וְאִמְרוּ אָמֵן. (קהל: אָמֵן)

Ma'ariv for Weekdays

*On Motza'ei Shabbat some have the custom to sing Psalm 144 and
Psalm 67 before the Ma'ariv Service (page 314).*

וְהוּא רַחוּם He is compassionate.   *Ps. 78*

He forgives iniquity and does not destroy.

Repeatedly He suppresses His anger, not rousing His full wrath.

LORD, save! May the King, answer us on the day we call.   *Ps. 20*

BLESSINGS OF THE SHEMA

*The Leader says the following, bowing at "Bless," standing straight
at "the LORD"; the congregation, followed by the Leader, responds,
bowing at "Bless," standing straight at "the LORD":*

Leader: # BLESS
the LORD, the blessed One.

Congregation: Bless the LORD, the blessed One,
for ever and all time.

Leader: Bless the LORD, the blessed One,
for ever and all time.

---

prayer: the ladder stretching from earth to heaven on which angels ascended
and descended. During that vision, God promised Jacob that "I will protect
you wherever you go" (Gen. 28:15). The evening service represents our trust
in God during the dark and dangers of night.

וְהוּא רַחוּם *He is compassionate:* A prelude to prayer, from the book of Psalms,
that serves as a brief equivalent to the Verses of Praise in the morning service.
The verse (Psalm 78:38) contains thirteen words that are reminiscent of the
thirteen attributes of divine mercy.

בָּרְכוּ אֶת יהוה *Bless the LORD:* As in the morning service, a call to the congregation to join in communal prayer, derived from the verse: "Magnify the
LORD with me; let us exalt His name together" (Psalm 34:4).

מעריב לחול

On מוצאי שבת *some have the custom to sing* לְדָוִד, בָּרוּךְ יהוה צוּרִי *and* תְּפִלַּת ערבית *before* מִזְמוֹר שִׁיר לַמְנַצֵּחַ בִּנְגִינֹת *(page 315).*

וְהוּא רַחוּם, יְכַפֵּר עָוֹן וְלֹא-יַשְׁחִית
וְהִרְבָּה לְהָשִׁיב אַפּוֹ, וְלֹא-יָעִיר כָּל-חֲמָתוֹ:

יהוה הוֹשִׁיעָה, הַמֶּלֶךְ יַעֲנֵנוּ בְיוֹם-קָרְאֵנוּ:

קריאת שמע וברכותיה

The שליח ציבור *says the following, bowing at* בָּרְכוּ, *standing straight at* ה'; *the* קהל, *followed by the* שליח ציבור, *responds, bowing at* בָּרוּךְ, *standing straight at* ה':

שׁ״ץ: בָּרְכוּ

אֶת יהוה הַמְבֹרָךְ.

קהל: בָּרוּךְ יהוה הַמְבֹרָךְ לְעוֹלָם וָעֶד.

שׁ״ץ: בָּרוּךְ יהוה הַמְבֹרָךְ לְעוֹלָם וָעֶד.

EVENING SERVICE

The saying of Shema at night ("when you lie down") is a biblical imperative. In early post-Temple times there were some who held that the evening Amida was non-obligatory since – unlike the morning and afternoon services – there was no daily sacrifice to which it corresponded (*Berakhot* 27b–28a). So widespread was its observance, however, that it was eventually deemed obligatory. Notwithstanding, since the Amida at night does not correspond to a sacrifice, it is not repeated by the Leader.

Tradition identifies the evening prayer with Jacob, who had his most intense religious experiences at night, especially the vision most associated with

בָּרוּךְ Blessed are You, LORD our God, King of the Universe,
who by His word brings on evenings,
by His wisdom opens the gates of heaven,
with understanding makes time change and the seasons rotate,
and by His will
orders the stars in their constellations in the sky.
He creates day and night,
rolling away the light before the darkness,
and darkness before the light.
▸ He makes the day pass and brings on night,
distinguishing day from night:
the LORD of hosts is His name.
May the living and forever enduring God rule over us for all time.
Blessed are You, LORD, who brings on evenings.

אַהֲבַת עוֹלָם With everlasting love
have You loved Your people, the house of Israel.
You have taught us Torah and commandments,
decrees and laws of justice.
Therefore, LORD our God, when we lie down and when we rise up
we will speak of Your decrees, rejoicing in the words of Your Torah
and Your commandments for ever.
▸ For they are our life and the length of our days;
on them will we meditate day and night.
May You never take away Your love from us.
Blessed are You, LORD, who loves His people Israel.

---

revelation: God's gift to Israel of the Torah and its commandments. In the
same way that God binds Himself to His people through word and deed, so
do we bind ourselves to Him by the words of Torah and the deeds of the
commandments. No simpler or more profound statement exists of the love
of Jews for the life of the commandments than the phrase, "For they are our
life and the length of our days."

בָּרוּךְ אַתָּה יהוה אֱלֹהֵינוּ מֶלֶךְ הָעוֹלָם

אֲשֶׁר בִּדְבָרוֹ מַעֲרִיב עֲרָבִים

בְּחָכְמָה פּוֹתֵחַ שְׁעָרִים

וּבִתְבוּנָה מְשַׁנֶּה עִתִּים וּמַחֲלִיף אֶת הַזְּמַנִּים

וּמְסַדֵּר אֶת הַכּוֹכָבִים בְּמִשְׁמְרוֹתֵיהֶם בָּרָקִיעַ כִּרְצוֹנוֹ.

בּוֹרֵא יוֹם וָלָיְלָה, גּוֹלֵל אוֹר מִפְּנֵי חֹשֶׁךְ וְחֹשֶׁךְ מִפְּנֵי אוֹר

‹ וּמַעֲבִיר יוֹם וּמֵבִיא לָיְלָה

וּמַבְדִּיל בֵּין יוֹם וּבֵין לָיְלָה

יהוה צְבָאוֹת שְׁמוֹ.

אֵל חַי וְקַיָּם תָּמִיד, יִמְלֹךְ עָלֵינוּ לְעוֹלָם וָעֶד.

בָּרוּךְ אַתָּה יהוה, הַמַּעֲרִיב עֲרָבִים.

אַהֲבַת עוֹלָם בֵּית יִשְׂרָאֵל עַמְּךָ אָהָבְתָּ

תּוֹרָה וּמִצְוֹת, חֻקִּים וּמִשְׁפָּטִים, אוֹתָנוּ לִמַּדְתָּ

עַל כֵּן יהוה אֱלֹהֵינוּ בְּשָׁכְבֵּנוּ וּבְקוּמֵנוּ נָשִׂיחַ בְּחֻקֶּיךָ

וְנִשְׂמַח בְּדִבְרֵי תוֹרָתֶךָ וּבְמִצְוֹתֶיךָ לְעוֹלָם וָעֶד

‹ כִּי הֵם חַיֵּינוּ וְאֹרֶךְ יָמֵינוּ, וּבָהֶם נֶהְגֶּה יוֹמָם וָלָיְלָה.

וְאַהֲבָתְךָ אַל תָּסִיר מִמֶּנּוּ לְעוֹלָמִים.

בָּרוּךְ אַתָּה יהוה, אוֹהֵב עַמּוֹ יִשְׂרָאֵל.

הַמַּעֲרִיב עֲרָבִים *Who brings on evenings:* Praise of God as Creator of the universe, and hence of time itself. As with the morning service, the two blessings before the Shema, and the one immediately following, speak in turn of the three key elements of Jewish faith: creation, revelation and redemption.

אַהֲבַת עוֹלָם *With everlasting love:* A counterpart to the morning blessing, "You have loved us with great love." Both speak of divine love in terms of

The Shema must be said with intense concentration. See laws 35–39.
When not with a minyan, say:

God, faithful King!

The following verse should be said aloud, while covering the eyes with the right hand:

Listen, Israel: the LORD is our God, the LORD is One.

Deut. 6

Quietly: Blessed be the name of His glorious kingdom for ever and all time.

וְאָהַבְתָּ Love the LORD your God with all your heart, with all your *Deut. 6* soul, and with all your might. These words which I command you today shall be on your heart. Teach them repeatedly to your children, speaking of them when you sit at home and when you travel on the way, when you lie down and when you rise. Bind them as a sign on your hand, and they shall be an emblem between your eyes. Write them on the doorposts of your house and gates.

וְהָיָה If you indeed heed My commandments with which I charge *Deut. 11* you today, to love the LORD your God and worship Him with all your heart and with all your soul, I will give rain in your land in its season, the early and late rain; and you shall gather in your grain, wine and oil. I will give grass in your field for your cattle, and you shall eat and be satisfied. Be careful lest your heart be tempted and you go astray and worship other gods, bowing down to them. Then the LORD's anger will flare against you and He will close the heavens so that there will be no rain. The land will not yield its crops, and you will perish swiftly from the good land that the LORD is giving you. Therefore, set these, My words, on your heart and soul. Bind them as a sign on your hand, and they shall be an emblem between your eyes. Teach them to your children, speaking of them when you sit at home and when you travel on the way, when you lie down and when you rise. Write them on the doorposts of your house and gates, so that you and your children may live long in the land that the LORD swore to your ancestors to give them, for as long as the heavens are above the earth.

The שמע *must be said with intense concentration. See laws 35–39.*

When not with a מנין, *say:*

אֵל מֶלֶךְ נֶאֱמָן

The following verse should be said aloud, while covering the eyes with the right hand:

שְׁמַ֥ע יִשְׂרָאֵ֑ל יְהֹוָ֥ה אֱלֹהֵ֖ינוּ יְהֹוָ֥ה ׀ אֶחָֽד׃   דברים ו

Quietly

בָּרוּךְ שֵׁם כְּבוֹד מַלְכוּתוֹ לְעוֹלָם וָעֶד.

וְאָהַבְתָּ֕ אֵ֖ת יְהֹוָ֣ה אֱלֹהֶ֑יךָ בְּכָל־לְבָֽבְךָ֛ וּבְכָל־נַפְשְׁךָ֖ וּבְכָל־מְאֹדֶֽךָ׃   דברים ו
וְהָי֞וּ הַדְּבָרִ֣ים הָאֵ֗לֶּה אֲשֶׁ֨ר אָֽנֹכִ֧י מְצַוְּךָ֛ הַיּ֖וֹם עַל־לְבָבֶֽךָ׃ וְשִׁנַּנְתָּ֣ם
לְבָנֶ֔יךָ וְדִבַּרְתָּ֖ בָּ֑ם בְּשִׁבְתְּךָ֤ בְּבֵיתֶ֨ךָ֙ וּבְלֶכְתְּךָ֣ בַדֶּ֔רֶךְ וּֽבְשָׁכְבְּךָ֖
וּבְקוּמֶֽךָ׃ וּקְשַׁרְתָּ֥ם לְא֖וֹת עַל־יָדֶ֑ךָ וְהָי֥וּ לְטֹטָפֹ֖ת בֵּ֥ין עֵינֶֽיךָ׃
וּכְתַבְתָּ֛ם עַל־מְזֻז֥וֹת בֵּיתֶ֖ךָ וּבִשְׁעָרֶֽיךָ׃

וְהָיָ֗ה אִם־שָׁמֹ֤עַ תִּשְׁמְעוּ֙ אֶל־מִצְוֺתַ֔י אֲשֶׁ֧ר אָֽנֹכִ֛י מְצַוֶּ֥ה אֶתְכֶ֖ם   דברים יא
הַיּ֑וֹם לְאַֽהֲבָ֞ה אֶת־יְהֹוָ֤ה אֱלֹֽהֵיכֶם֙ וּלְעָבְד֔וֹ בְּכָל־לְבַבְכֶ֖ם וּבְכָל־
נַפְשְׁכֶֽם׃ וְנָֽתַתִּ֧י מְטַֽר־אַרְצְכֶ֛ם בְּעִתּ֖וֹ יוֹרֶ֣ה וּמַלְק֑וֹשׁ וְאָֽסַפְתָּ֣ דְגָנֶ֔ךָ
וְתִֽירֹֽשְׁךָ֖ וְיִצְהָרֶֽךָ׃ וְנָֽתַתִּ֛י עֵ֥שֶׂב בְּשָׂדְךָ֖ לִבְהֶמְתֶּ֑ךָ וְאָֽכַלְתָּ֖ וְשָׂבָֽעְתָּ׃
הִשָּֽׁמְר֣וּ לָכֶ֔ם פֶּן־יִפְתֶּ֖ה לְבַבְכֶ֑ם וְסַרְתֶּ֗ם וַֽעֲבַדְתֶּם֙ אֱלֹהִ֣ים אֲחֵרִ֔ים
וְהִשְׁתַּֽחֲוִיתֶ֖ם לָהֶֽם׃ וְחָרָ֨ה אַף־יְהֹוָ֜ה בָּכֶ֗ם וְעָצַ֤ר אֶת־הַשָּׁמַ֨יִם֙
וְלֹא־יִֽהְיֶ֣ה מָטָ֔ר וְהָ֣אֲדָמָ֔ה לֹ֥א תִתֵּ֖ן אֶת־יְבוּלָ֑הּ וַֽאֲבַדְתֶּ֣ם מְהֵרָ֗ה
מֵעַל֙ הָאָ֣רֶץ הַטֹּבָ֔ה אֲשֶׁ֥ר יְהֹוָ֖ה נֹתֵ֥ן לָכֶֽם׃ וְשַׂמְתֶּם֙ אֶת־דְּבָרַ֣י
אֵ֔לֶּה עַל־לְבַבְכֶ֖ם וְעַֽל־נַפְשְׁכֶ֑ם וּקְשַׁרְתֶּ֨ם אֹתָ֤ם לְאוֹת֙ עַל־יֶדְכֶ֔ם
וְהָי֥וּ לְטֽוֹטָפֹ֖ת בֵּ֣ין עֵֽינֵיכֶֽם׃ וְלִמַּדְתֶּ֥ם אֹתָ֛ם אֶת־בְּנֵיכֶ֖ם לְדַבֵּ֣ר בָּ֑ם
בְּשִׁבְתְּךָ֤ בְּבֵיתֶ֨ךָ֙ וּבְלֶכְתְּךָ֣ בַדֶּ֔רֶךְ וּֽבְשָׁכְבְּךָ֖ וּבְקוּמֶֽךָ׃ וּכְתַבְתָּ֛ם
עַל־מְזוּז֥וֹת בֵּיתֶ֖ךָ וּבִשְׁעָרֶֽיךָ׃ לְמַ֨עַן יִרְבּ֤וּ יְמֵיכֶם֙ וִימֵ֣י בְנֵיכֶ֔ם עַ֚ל
הָֽאֲדָמָ֔ה אֲשֶׁ֨ר נִשְׁבַּ֧ע יְהֹוָ֛ה לַֽאֲבֹֽתֵיכֶ֖ם לָתֵ֣ת לָהֶ֑ם כִּימֵ֥י הַשָּׁמַ֖יִם
עַל־הָאָֽרֶץ׃

וַיֹּאמֶר The LORD spoke to Moses, saying: Speak to the Israelites *Num. 15* and tell them to make tassels on the corners of their garments for all generations. They shall attach to the tassel at each corner a thread of blue. This shall be your tassel, and you shall see it and remember all of the LORD's commandments and keep them, not straying after your heart and after your eyes, following your own sinful desires. Thus you will be reminded to keep all My commandments, and be holy to your God. I am the LORD your God, who brought you out of the land of Egypt to be your God. I am the LORD your God.

True –

The Leader repeats:
‣ The LORD your God is true –

וֶאֱמוּנָה – and faithful is all this,
and firmly established for us
that He is the LORD our God,
and there is none besides Him,
and that we, Israel, are His people.
He is our King, who redeems us from the hand of kings
and delivers us from the grasp of all tyrants.
He is our God,
who on our behalf repays our foes
and brings just retribution on our mortal enemies;
who performs great deeds beyond understanding
and wonders beyond number;
who kept us alive, not letting our foot slip;   *Ps. 66*
who led us on the high places of our enemies,
raising our pride above all our foes;

---

faithfulness at night echoes the phrase from Psalm 92: "to tell of Your love in the morning, and Your faithfulness at night."

במדבר טו

וַיֹּאמֶר יהוה אֶל־מֹשֶׁה לֵּאמֹר: דַּבֵּר אֶל־בְּנֵי יִשְׂרָאֵל וְאָמַרְתָּ
אֲלֵהֶם, וְעָשׂוּ לָהֶם צִיצִת עַל־כַּנְפֵי בִגְדֵיהֶם לְדֹרֹתָם, וְנָתְנוּ עַל־
צִיצִת הַכָּנָף פְּתִיל תְּכֵלֶת: וְהָיָה לָכֶם לְצִיצִת, וּרְאִיתֶם אֹתוֹ
וּזְכַרְתֶּם אֶת־כָּל־מִצְוֹת יהוה וַעֲשִׂיתֶם אֹתָם, וְלֹא תָתוּרוּ אַחֲרֵי
לְבַבְכֶם וְאַחֲרֵי עֵינֵיכֶם, אֲשֶׁר־אַתֶּם זֹנִים אַחֲרֵיהֶם: לְמַעַן תִּזְכְּרוּ
וַעֲשִׂיתֶם אֶת־כָּל־מִצְוֹתָי, וִהְיִיתֶם קְדֹשִׁים לֵאלֹהֵיכֶם: אֲנִי יהוה
אֱלֹהֵיכֶם, אֲשֶׁר הוֹצֵאתִי אֶתְכֶם מֵאֶרֶץ מִצְרַיִם, לִהְיוֹת לָכֶם
לֵאלֹהִים, אֲנִי יהוה אֱלֹהֵיכֶם:

אֱמֶת

The שליח ציבור *repeats:*

‹ יהוה אֱלֹהֵיכֶם אֱמֶת

וֶאֱמוּנָה כָּל זֹאת וְקַיָּם עָלֵינוּ

כִּי הוּא יהוה אֱלֹהֵינוּ וְאֵין זוּלָתוֹ

וַאֲנַחְנוּ יִשְׂרָאֵל עַמּוֹ.

הַפּוֹדֵנוּ מִיַּד מְלָכִים

מַלְכֵּנוּ הַגּוֹאֲלֵנוּ מִכַּף כָּל הֶעָרִיצִים.

הָאֵל הַנִּפְרָע לָנוּ מִצָּרֵינוּ

וְהַמְשַׁלֵּם גְּמוּל לְכָל אוֹיְבֵי נַפְשֵׁנוּ.

הָעוֹשֶׂה גְדוֹלוֹת עַד אֵין חֵקֶר, וְנִפְלָאוֹת עַד אֵין מִסְפָּר

תהלים סו   הַשָּׂם נַפְשֵׁנוּ בַּחַיִּים, וְלֹא־נָתַן לַמּוֹט רַגְלֵנוּ:

הַמַּדְרִיכֵנוּ עַל בָּמוֹת אוֹיְבֵינוּ

וַיָּרֶם קַרְנֵנוּ עַל כָּל שׂוֹנְאֵינוּ.

אֱמֶת וֶאֱמוּנָה *True and faithful:* A blessing about redemption, parallel to the
blessing אֱמֶת וְיַצִּיב, "True and firm," in the morning. The special emphasis on

who did miracles for us
and brought vengeance against Pharaoh;
who performed signs and wonders
in the land of Ham's children;
who smote in His wrath all the firstborn of Egypt,
and brought out His people Israel from their midst
into everlasting freedom;
who led His children through the divided Reed Sea,
plunging their pursuers and enemies into the depths.
When His children saw His might,
they gave praise and thanks to His name,
‣ and willingly accepted His Sovereignty.
Moses and the children of Israel
then sang a song to You with great joy,
and they all exclaimed:

> מִי־כָמְכָה "Who is like You, Lord, among the mighty?   *Ex. 15*
> Who is like You, majestic in holiness,
> awesome in praises, doing wonders?"

‣ Your children beheld Your majesty
as You parted the sea before Moses.
"This is my God!" they responded,
and then said:

> "The Lord shall reign for ever and ever."   *Ex. 15*

‣ And it is said, "For the Lord has redeemed Jacob   *Jer. 31*
and rescued him from a power stronger than his own."
Blessed are You, Lord, who redeemed Israel.

הַשְׁכִּיבֵנוּ Help us lie down, O Lord our God, in peace,
and rise up, O our King, to life.
Spread over us Your canopy of peace.
Direct us with Your good counsel,
and save us for the sake of Your name.

הָעוֹשֶׂה לָנוּ נִסִּים וּנְקָמָה בְּפַרְעֹה
אוֹתוֹת וּמוֹפְתִים בְּאַדְמַת בְּנֵי חָם.
הַמַּכֶּה בְעֶבְרָתוֹ כָּל בְּכוֹרֵי מִצְרָיִם
וַיּוֹצֵא אֶת עַמּוֹ יִשְׂרָאֵל מִתּוֹכָם לְחֵרוּת עוֹלָם.
הַמַּעֲבִיר בָּנָיו בֵּין גִּזְרֵי יַם סוּף
אֶת רוֹדְפֵיהֶם וְאֶת שׂוֹנְאֵיהֶם בִּתְהוֹמוֹת טִבַּע
וְרָאוּ בָנָיו גְּבוּרָתוֹ, שִׁבְּחוּ וְהוֹדוּ לִשְׁמוֹ

◄ וּמַלְכוּתוֹ בְּרָצוֹן קִבְּלוּ עֲלֵיהֶם.
מֹשֶׁה וּבְנֵי יִשְׂרָאֵל, לְךָ עָנוּ שִׁירָה בְּשִׂמְחָה רַבָּה
וְאָמְרוּ כֻלָּם

שמות טו

מִי־כָמֹכָה בָּאֵלִם יהוה
מִי כָּמֹכָה נֶאְדָּר בַּקֹּדֶשׁ
נוֹרָא תְהִלֹּת עֹשֵׂה פֶלֶא:

◄ מַלְכוּתְךָ רָאוּ בָנֶיךָ, בּוֹקֵעַ יָם לִפְנֵי מֹשֶׁה
זֶה אֵלִי עָנוּ, וְאָמְרוּ

שמות טו

יהוה יִמְלֹךְ לְעֹלָם וָעֶד:

◄ וְנֶאֱמַר

ירמיהו לא

כִּי־פָדָה יהוה אֶת־יַעֲקֹב, וּגְאָלוֹ מִיַּד חָזָק מִמֶּנּוּ:
בָּרוּךְ אַתָּה יהוה, גָּאַל יִשְׂרָאֵל.

הַשְׁכִּיבֵנוּ יהוה אֱלֹהֵינוּ לְשָׁלוֹם, וְהַעֲמִידֵנוּ מַלְכֵּנוּ לְחַיִּים
וּפְרֹשׂ עָלֵינוּ סֻכַּת שְׁלוֹמֶךָ, וְתַקְּנֵנוּ בְּעֵצָה טוֹבָה מִלְּפָנֶיךָ
וְהוֹשִׁיעֵנוּ לְמַעַן שְׁמֶךָ.

הַשְׁכִּיבֵנוּ *Help us lie down:* This blessing, which has no parallel in the morning
service, is a prayer for protection against the hazards of the night.

Shield us and remove from us every enemy,
plague, sword, famine and sorrow.
Remove the adversary from before and behind us.
Shelter us in the shadow of Your wings,
for You, God, are our Guardian and Deliverer;
You, God, are a gracious and compassionate King.
▸ Guard our going out and our coming in,
for life and peace, from now and for ever.
Blessed are You, LORD, who guards His people Israel for ever.

In Israel the service continues with Half Kaddish on page 276.

בָּרוּךְ Blessed be the LORD for ever. Amen and Amen.   *Ps. 89*
Blessed from Zion be the LORD   *Ps. 135*
who dwells in Jerusalem. Halleluya!
Blessed be the LORD, God of Israel,   *Ps. 72*
who alone does wondrous things.
Blessed be His glorious name for ever,
and may the whole earth be filled with His glory. Amen and Amen.
May the glory of the LORD endure for ever;   *Ps. 104*
may the LORD rejoice in His works.
May the name of the LORD be blessed now and for all time.   *Ps. 113*
For the sake of His great name   *1 Sam. 12*
the LORD will not abandon His people,
for the LORD vowed to make you a people of His own.
When all the people saw [God's wonders] they fell on their faces   *1 Kings 18*
and said: "The LORD, He is God; the LORD, He is God."
Then the LORD shall be King over all the earth;   *Zech. 14*
on that day the LORD shall be One and His name One.
May Your love, LORD, be upon us, as we have put our hope in You.   *Ps. 33*

God, was originally recited as a substitute for the evening Amida – possibly
to shorten the evening service in synagogue so that participants could return
home before dark. When conditions changed, the prayer was retained. Since
it was a substitute for the weekday Amida, it is not said on Shabbat or Yom Tov.

וְהָגֵן בַּעֲדֵנוּ, וְהָסֵר מֵעָלֵינוּ אוֹיֵב, דֶּבֶר וְחֶרֶב וְרָעָב וְיָגוֹן
וְהָסֵר שָׂטָן מִלְּפָנֵינוּ וּמֵאַחֲרֵינוּ, וּבְצֵל כְּנָפֶיךָ תַּסְתִּירֵנוּ
כִּי אֵל שׁוֹמְרֵנוּ וּמַצִּילֵנוּ אָתָּה
כִּי אֵל מֶלֶךְ חַנּוּן וְרַחוּם אָתָּה.
‹ וּשְׁמֹר צֵאתֵנוּ וּבוֹאֵנוּ לְחַיִּים וּלְשָׁלוֹם מֵעַתָּה וְעַד עוֹלָם.
בָּרוּךְ אַתָּה יהוה, שׁוֹמֵר עַמּוֹ יִשְׂרָאֵל לָעַד.

In ארץ ישראל the service continues with חצי קדיש on page 277.

תהלים פט	בָּרוּךְ יהוה לְעוֹלָם, אָמֵן וְאָמֵן:
תהלים קלה	בָּרוּךְ יהוה מִצִּיּוֹן, שֹׁכֵן יְרוּשָׁלָםִ, הַלְלוּיָהּ:
תהלים עב	בָּרוּךְ יהוה אֱלֹהִים אֱלֹהֵי יִשְׂרָאֵל, עֹשֵׂה נִפְלָאוֹת לְבַדּוֹ:
	וּבָרוּךְ שֵׁם כְּבוֹדוֹ לְעוֹלָם
	וְיִמָּלֵא כְבוֹדוֹ אֶת־כָּל־הָאָרֶץ, אָמֵן וְאָמֵן:
תהלים קד	יְהִי כְבוֹד יהוה לְעוֹלָם, יִשְׂמַח יהוה בְּמַעֲשָׂיו:
תהלים קיג	יְהִי שֵׁם יהוה מְבֹרָךְ מֵעַתָּה וְעַד־עוֹלָם:
שמואל א, יב	כִּי לֹא־יִטֹּשׁ יהוה אֶת־עַמּוֹ בַּעֲבוּר שְׁמוֹ הַגָּדוֹל
	כִּי הוֹאִיל יהוה לַעֲשׂוֹת אֶתְכֶם לוֹ לְעָם:
מלכים א, יח	וַיַּרְא כָּל־הָעָם וַיִּפְּלוּ עַל־פְּנֵיהֶם
	וַיֹּאמְרוּ, יהוה הוּא הָאֱלֹהִים, יהוה הוּא הָאֱלֹהִים:
זכריה יד	וְהָיָה יהוה לְמֶלֶךְ עַל־כָּל־הָאָרֶץ
	בַּיּוֹם הַהוּא יִהְיֶה יהוה אֶחָד וּשְׁמוֹ אֶחָד:
תהלים לג	יְהִי־חַסְדְּךָ יהוה עָלֵינוּ, כַּאֲשֶׁר יִחַלְנוּ לָךְ:

בָּרוּךְ יהוה לְעוֹלָם **Blessed be the LORD for ever:** This passage originated among
Babylonian Jewry at a time when synagogues were not permitted within the
town and were built in the fields outside. This made attendance at synagogue
potentially hazardous at night. This prayer, with its eighteen references to

הוֹשִׁיעֵנוּ Save us, Lord our God, gather us   *Ps. 106*
and deliver us from the nations,
to thank Your holy name, and glory in Your praise.
All the nations You made shall come and bow before You, Lord,   *Ps. 86*
and pay honor to Your name,
for You are great and You perform wonders:
You alone are God.
We, Your people, the flock of Your pasture, will praise You for ever. *Ps. 79*
For all generations we will relate Your praise.

בָּרוּךְ Blessed is the Lord by day, blessed is the Lord by night.
Blessed is the Lord when we lie down;
blessed is the Lord when we rise.
For in Your hand are the souls of the living and the dead,
[as it is written:] "In His hand is every living soul,   *Job 12*
and the breath of all mankind."
Into Your hand I entrust my spirit: *Ps. 31*
You redeemed me, Lord, God of truth.
Our God in heaven, bring unity to Your name,
establish Your kingdom constantly
and reign over us for ever and all time.

יִרְאוּ May our eyes see, our hearts rejoice,
and our souls be glad in Your true salvation,
when Zion is told, "Your God reigns."
The Lord is King, the Lord was King,
the Lord will be King for ever and all time.
‣ For sovereignty is Yours,
and to all eternity You will reign in glory,
for we have no king but You.
Blessed are You, Lord,
the King who in His constant glory will reign over us
and all His creation for ever and all time.

תהלים קו

הוֹשִׁיעֵנוּ יהוה אֱלֹהֵינוּ, וְקַבְּצֵנוּ מִן־הַגּוֹיִם
לְהֹדוֹת לְשֵׁם קָדְשֶׁךָ, לְהִשְׁתַּבֵּחַ בִּתְהִלָּתֶךָ:

תהלים פו

כָּל־גּוֹיִם אֲשֶׁר עָשִׂיתָ, יָבוֹאוּ וְיִשְׁתַּחֲווּ לְפָנֶיךָ, אֲדֹנָי
וִיכַבְּדוּ לִשְׁמֶךָ:
כִּי־גָדוֹל אַתָּה וְעֹשֵׂה נִפְלָאוֹת, אַתָּה אֱלֹהִים לְבַדֶּךָ:

תהלים עט

וַאֲנַחְנוּ עַמְּךָ וְצֹאן מַרְעִיתֶךָ, נוֹדֶה לְּךָ לְעוֹלָם
לְדוֹר וָדֹר נְסַפֵּר תְּהִלָּתֶךָ:

בָּרוּךְ יהוה בַּיּוֹם, בָּרוּךְ יהוה בַּלָּיְלָה
בָּרוּךְ יהוה בְּשָׁכְבֵנוּ, בָּרוּךְ יהוה בְּקוּמֵנוּ.
כִּי בְיָדְךָ נַפְשׁוֹת הַחַיִּים וְהַמֵּתִים.

איוב יב

אֲשֶׁר בְּיָדוֹ נֶפֶשׁ כָּל־חָי, וְרוּחַ כָּל־בְּשַׂר־אִישׁ:

תהלים לא

בְּיָדְךָ אַפְקִיד רוּחִי, פָּדִיתָה אוֹתִי יהוה אֵל אֱמֶת:
אֱלֹהֵינוּ שֶׁבַּשָּׁמַיִם, יַחֵד שִׁמְךָ וְקַיֵּם מַלְכוּתְךָ תָּמִיד
וּמְלֹךְ עָלֵינוּ לְעוֹלָם וָעֶד.

יִרְאוּ עֵינֵינוּ וְיִשְׂמַח לִבֵּנוּ
וְתָגֵל נַפְשֵׁנוּ בִּישׁוּעָתְךָ בֶּאֱמֶת
בֶּאֱמֹר לְצִיּוֹן מָלַךְ אֱלֹהָיִךְ.
יהוה מֶלֶךְ, יהוה מָלָךְ, יהוה יִמְלֹךְ לְעֹלָם וָעֶד.
‹ כִּי הַמַּלְכוּת שֶׁלְּךָ הִיא, וּלְעוֹלְמֵי עַד תִּמְלֹךְ בְּכָבוֹד
כִּי אֵין לָנוּ מֶלֶךְ אֶלָּא אָתָּה.
בָּרוּךְ אַתָּה יהוה
הַמֶּלֶךְ בִּכְבוֹדוֹ תָּמִיד, יִמְלֹךְ עָלֵינוּ לְעוֹלָם וָעֶד
וְעַל כָּל מַעֲשָׂיו.

HALF KADDISH

Leader: יִתְגַּדַּל Magnified and sanctified
may His great name be,
in the world He created by His will.
May He establish His kingdom
in your lifetime and in your days,
and in the lifetime of all the house of Israel,
swiftly and soon –
and say: Amen.

All: May His great name be blessed for ever and all time.

Leader: Blessed and praised, glorified and exalted,
raised and honored, uplifted and lauded
be the name of the Holy One,
blessed be He,
beyond any blessing,
song, praise and consolation
uttered in the world –
and say: Amen.

THE AMIDA

*The following prayer, until "in former years" on page 296, is said silently, standing with feet
together. Take three steps forward and at the points indicated by ˙, bend the knees at
the first word, bow at the second, and stand straight before saying God's name.*

O Lord, open my lips,
so that my mouth may declare Your praise.

Ps. 51

PATRIARCHS

בָּרוּךְ Blessed are You, Lord our God and God of our fathers,
God of Abraham, God of Isaac and God of Jacob;
the great, mighty and awesome God, God Most High,
who bestows acts of loving-kindness and creates all,

חצי קדיש

ש״ץ: יִתְגַּדַּל וְיִתְקַדַּשׁ שְׁמֵהּ רַבָּא (קהל: אָמֵן)

בְּעָלְמָא דִּי בְרָא כִרְעוּתֵהּ

וְיַמְלִיךְ מַלְכוּתֵהּ

בְּחַיֵּיכוֹן וּבְיוֹמֵיכוֹן וּבְחַיֵּי דְכָל בֵּית יִשְׂרָאֵל

בַּעֲגָלָא וּבִזְמַן קָרִיב, וְאִמְרוּ אָמֵן. (קהל: אָמֵן)

קהל
וש״ץ: יְהֵא שְׁמֵהּ רַבָּא מְבָרַךְ לְעָלַם וּלְעָלְמֵי עָלְמַיָּא.

ש״ץ: יִתְבָּרַךְ וְיִשְׁתַּבַּח וְיִתְפָּאַר וְיִתְרוֹמַם וְיִתְנַשֵּׂא

וְיִתְהַדָּר וְיִתְעַלֶּה וְיִתְהַלָּל

שְׁמֵהּ דְּקֻדְשָׁא בְּרִיךְ הוּא (קהל: בְּרִיךְ הוּא)

לְעֵלָּא מִן כָּל בִּרְכָתָא

/בעשרת ימי תשובה: לְעֵלָּא לְעֵלָּא מִכָּל בִּרְכָתָא/

וְשִׁירָתָא, תֻּשְׁבְּחָתָא וְנֶחֱמָתָא

דַּאֲמִירָן בְּעָלְמָא, וְאִמְרוּ אָמֵן. (קהל: אָמֵן)

עמידה

The following prayer, until קדמוניות *on page 297, is said silently, standing with feet together. Take three steps forward and at the points indicated by *, bend the knees at the first word, bow at the second, and stand straight before saying God's name.*

תהלים נא

אֲדֹנָי, שְׂפָתַי תִּפְתָּח, וּפִי יַגִּיד תְּהִלָּתֶךָ:

אבות
*בָּרוּךְ אַתָּה יהוה, אֱלֹהֵינוּ וֵאלֹהֵי אֲבוֹתֵינוּ
אֱלֹהֵי אַבְרָהָם, אֱלֹהֵי יִצְחָק, וֵאלֹהֵי יַעֲקֹב
הָאֵל הַגָּדוֹל הַגִּבּוֹר וְהַנּוֹרָא, אֵל עֶלְיוֹן
גּוֹמֵל חֲסָדִים טוֹבִים, וְקֹנֵה הַכֹּל

who remembers the loving-kindness of the fathers
and will bring a Redeemer to their children's children
for the sake of His name, in love.

> *Between Rosh* Remember us for life, O King who desires life,
> *HaShana &* and write us in the book of life –
> *Yom Kippur:* for Your sake, O God of life.

King, Helper, Savior, Shield:
▼Blessed are You, LORD, Shield of Abraham.

DIVINE MIGHT

אַתָּה גִבּוֹר You are eternally mighty, LORD.
You give life to the dead
and have great power to save.

> *The phrase "He makes the wind blow and the rain fall" is added from
> Simḥat Torah until Pesaḥ. In Israel the phrase "He causes the dew to
> fall" is added from Pesaḥ until Shemini Atzeret. See laws 49–51.*

> *In fall & winter:* He makes the wind blow and the rain fall.
> *In Israel, in spring* He causes the dew to fall.
> *& summer:*

He sustains the living with loving-kindness,
and with great compassion revives the dead.
He supports the fallen, heals the sick, sets captives free,
and keeps His faith with those who sleep in the dust.
Who is like You, Master of might,
and to whom can You be compared,
O King who brings death and gives life,
and makes salvation grow?

> *Between Rosh HaShana* Who is like You, compassionate Father,
> *& Yom Kippur:* who remembers His creatures in compassion, for life?

Faithful are You to revive the dead.
Blessed are You, LORD, who revives the dead.

וְזוֹכֵר חַסְדֵי אָבוֹת

וּמֵבִיא גוֹאֵל לִבְנֵי בְנֵיהֶם לְמַעַן שְׁמוֹ בְּאַהֲבָה.

בעשרת ימי תשובה: זָכְרֵנוּ לְחַיִּים, מֶלֶךְ חָפֵץ בַּחַיִּים

וְכָתְבֵנוּ בְּסֵפֶר הַחַיִּים, לְמַעַנְךָ אֱלֹהִים חַיִּים.

מֶלֶךְ עוֹזֵר וּמוֹשִׁיעַ וּמָגֵן.

ּבָּרוּךְ אַתָּה יהוה, מָגֵן אַבְרָהָם.

גבורות

אַתָּה גִּבּוֹר לְעוֹלָם, אֲדֹנָי

מְחַיֵּה מֵתִים אַתָּה, רַב לְהוֹשִׁיעַ

The phrase מַשִּׁיב הָרוּחַ *is added from* שמחת תורה *until* פסח. *In* ארץ ישראל *the*
phrase מוֹרִיד הַטָּל *is added from* פסח *until* שמיני עצרת. *See laws* 49–51.

בחורף: מַשִּׁיב הָרוּחַ וּמוֹרִיד הַגֶּשֶׁם / בארץ ישראל בקיץ: מוֹרִיד הַטָּל

מְכַלְכֵּל חַיִּים בְּחֶסֶד

מְחַיֵּה מֵתִים בְּרַחֲמִים רַבִּים

סוֹמֵךְ נוֹפְלִים, וְרוֹפֵא חוֹלִים, וּמַתִּיר אֲסוּרִים

וּמְקַיֵּם אֱמוּנָתוֹ לִישֵׁנֵי עָפָר.

מִי כָמוֹךָ, בַּעַל גְּבוּרוֹת

וּמִי דּוֹמֶה לָּךְ

מֶלֶךְ, מֵמִית וּמְחַיֶּה וּמַצְמִיחַ יְשׁוּעָה.

בעשרת ימי תשובה: מִי כָמוֹךָ אַב הָרַחֲמִים

זוֹכֵר יְצוּרָיו לְחַיִּים בְּרַחֲמִים.

וְנֶאֱמָן אַתָּה לְהַחֲיוֹת מֵתִים.

בָּרוּךְ אַתָּה יהוה, מְחַיֵּה הַמֵּתִים.

HOLINESS

אַתָּה קָדוֹשׁ You are holy and Your name is holy,
and holy ones praise You daily, Selah!
Blessed are You, LORD,
the holy God. / *Between Rosh HaShana & Yom Kippur:* the holy King./

(*If forgotten, repeat the Amida.*)

KNOWLEDGE

אַתָּה חוֹנֵן You grace humanity with knowledge
and teach mortals understanding.

On Motza'ei Shabbat and Motza'ei Yom Tov add:

אַתָּה חוֹנַנְתָּנוּ You have graced us with the knowledge of Your Torah, and
taught us to perform the statutes of Your will. You have distinguished, LORD
our God, between sacred and profane, light and darkness, Israel and the
nations, and between the seventh day and the six days of work. Our Father,
our King, may the days approaching us bring peace; may we be free from
all sin, cleansed from all iniquity, holding fast to our reverence of You. And

---

Grace us with the knowledge, understanding
and discernment that come from You.
Blessed are You, LORD,
who graciously grants knowledge.

REPENTANCE

הֲשִׁיבֵנוּ Bring us back, our Father, to Your Torah.
Draw us near, our King, to Your service.
Lead us back to You in perfect repentance.
Blessed are You, LORD,
who desires repentance.

---

distinction?"). In nature there are no sharp boundaries. Day shades gradually
into night; winter into spring; life into sentience. According to the Torah, what
links man to God is our ability to separate, classify and name, and thus to see
order amidst seeming chaos. As we begin the working week, we acknowledge
the divine order of creation as the necessary prelude to human acts of creation.

קדושת השם

אַתָּה קָדוֹשׁ וְשִׁמְךָ קָדוֹשׁ
וּקְדוֹשִׁים בְּכָל יוֹם יְהַלְלוּךָ סֶּלָה.
בָּרוּךְ אַתָּה יהוה
הָאֵל הַקָּדוֹשׁ. /בעשרת ימי תשובה: הַמֶּלֶךְ הַקָּדוֹשׁ./
(If forgotten, repeat the עמידה.)

דעת

אַתָּה חוֹנֵן לְאָדָם דַּעַת, וּמְלַמֵּד לֶאֱנוֹשׁ בִּינָה.

On מוצאי שבת and מוצאי יום טוב add:

אַתָּה חוֹנַנְתָּנוּ לְמַדַּע תּוֹרָתֶךָ, וַתְּלַמְּדֵנוּ לַעֲשׂוֹת חֻקֵּי רְצוֹנֶךָ, וַתַּבְדֵּל
יהוה אֱלֹהֵינוּ בֵּין קֹדֶשׁ לְחֹל, בֵּין אוֹר לְחְשֶׁךְ, בֵּין יִשְׂרָאֵל לָעַמִּים, בֵּין יוֹם
הַשְּׁבִיעִי לְשֵׁשֶׁת יְמֵי הַמַּעֲשֶׂה. אָבִינוּ מַלְכֵּנוּ, הָחֵל עָלֵינוּ הַיָּמִים הַבָּאִים
לִקְרָאתֵנוּ לְשָׁלוֹם, חֲשׂוּכִים מִכָּל חֵטְא וּמְנֻקִּים מִכָּל עָוֹן וּמְדֻבָּקִים בְּיִרְאָתֶךָ. וְ

חָנֵּנוּ מֵאִתְּךָ דֵּעָה בִּינָה וְהַשְׂכֵּל.
בָּרוּךְ אַתָּה יהוה, חוֹנֵן הַדָּעַת.

תשובה

הֲשִׁיבֵנוּ אָבִינוּ לְתוֹרָתֶךָ, וְקָרְבֵנוּ מַלְכֵּנוּ לַעֲבוֹדָתֶךָ,
וְהַחֲזִירֵנוּ בִּתְשׁוּבָה שְׁלֵמָה לְפָנֶיךָ.
בָּרוּךְ אַתָּה יהוה, הָרוֹצֶה בִּתְשׁוּבָה.

אַתָּה חוֹנַנְתָּנוּ <i>You have graced us:</i> From Talmudic times, this paragraph has
been the way of marking Havdala – the transition between holy and secular time – within the Amida prayer. Havdala is repeated as a separate ceremony in the synagogue after prayer, and then again at home. Its position-
ing here, in the prayer for knowledge, indicates the essential connection
between the human mind and the ability to make distinctions ("If there is no
knowledge," says the Talmud Yerushalmi [<i>Berakhot</i> 5:2], "how can there be

FORGIVENESS

Strike the left side of the chest at °.

סְלַח לָנוּ Forgive us, our Father, for we have °sinned.
Pardon us, our King, for we have °transgressed;
for You pardon and forgive.
Blessed are You, LORD,
the gracious One who repeatedly forgives.

REDEMPTION

רְאֵה Look on our affliction,
plead our cause,
and redeem us soon for Your name's sake,
for You are a powerful Redeemer.
Blessed are You, LORD,
the Redeemer of Israel.

HEALING

רְפָאֵנוּ Heal us, LORD, and we shall be healed.
Save us and we shall be saved,
for You are our praise.
Bring complete recovery for all our ailments,

The following prayer for a sick person may be said here:
May it be Your will, O LORD my God and God of my ancestors, that You
speedily send a complete recovery from heaven, a healing of both soul and
body, to the patient (*name*), son/daughter of (*mother's name*) among the
other afflicted of Israel.

---

for You, God, King, are a faithful and compassionate Healer.
Blessed are You, LORD,
Healer of the sick of His people Israel.

סליחה

Strike the left side of the chest at °.

סְלַח לָנוּ אָבִינוּ כִּי °חָטָאנוּ

מְחַל לָנוּ מַלְכֵּנוּ כִּי °פָשָׁעְנוּ

כִּי מוֹחֵל וְסוֹלֵחַ אָתָּה.

בָּרוּךְ אַתָּה יהוה, חַנּוּן הַמַּרְבֶּה לִסְלֹחַ.

גאולה

רְאֵה בְעָנְיֵנוּ, וְרִיבָה רִיבֵנוּ

וּגְאָלֵנוּ מְהֵרָה לְמַעַן שְׁמֶךָ

כִּי גוֹאֵל חָזָק אָתָּה.

בָּרוּךְ אַתָּה יהוה, גּוֹאֵל יִשְׂרָאֵל.

רפואה

רְפָאֵנוּ יהוה וְנֵרָפֵא

הוֹשִׁיעֵנוּ וְנִוָּשֵׁעָה, כִּי תְהִלָּתֵנוּ אָתָּה

וְהַעֲלֵה רְפוּאָה שְׁלֵמָה לְכָל מַכּוֹתֵינוּ

The following prayer for a sick person may be said here:

יְהִי רָצוֹן מִלְּפָנֶיךָ יהוה אֱלֹהַי וֵאלֹהֵי אֲבוֹתַי, שֶׁתִּשְׁלַח מְהֵרָה רְפוּאָה שְׁלֵמָה
מִן הַשָּׁמַיִם רְפוּאַת הַנֶּפֶשׁ וּרְפוּאַת הַגּוּף לַחוֹלֶה/לַחוֹלָה *name of patient*
בֶּן/בַּת *mother's name* בְּתוֹךְ שְׁאָר חוֹלֵי יִשְׂרָאֵל.

כִּי אֵל מֶלֶךְ רוֹפֵא נֶאֱמָן וְרַחֲמָן אָתָּה.

בָּרוּךְ אַתָּה יהוה, רוֹפֵא חוֹלֵי עַמּוֹ יִשְׂרָאֵל.

PROSPERITY

The phrase "Grant dew and rain as a blessing" is said from December 4th
(in the year before a civil leap year, December 5th) until Pesaḥ. In Israel,
it is said from the 7th of Marḥeshvan. The phrase "Grant blessing" is said from
Ḥol HaMo'ed Pesaḥ until December 3rd (in the year before a civil leap year,
December 4th). In Israel it is said through the 6th of Marḥeshvan. See laws 52–54.

בָּרֵךְ Bless this year for us, LORD our God,
and all its types of produce for good.

In winter: Grant dew and rain as a blessing

In other seasons: Grant blessing

on the face of the earth, and from its goodness satisfy us,
blessing our year as the best of years.
Blessed are You, LORD,
who blesses the years.

INGATHERING OF EXILES

תְּקַע Sound the great shofar for our freedom,
raise high the banner to gather our exiles,
and gather us together from the four quarters of the earth.
Blessed are You, LORD,
who gathers the dispersed of His people Israel.

JUSTICE

הָשִׁיבָה Restore our judges as at first,
and our counselors as at the beginning,
and remove from us sorrow and sighing.
May You alone, LORD,
reign over us
with loving-kindness and compassion,
and vindicate us in justice.
Blessed are You, LORD,
the King who loves righteousness and justice.

/ *Between Rosh HaShana & Yom Kippur, end the blessing:* the King of justice./

ברכת השנים

The phrase וְתֵן טַל וּמָטָר לִבְרָכָה is said from December 4th (in the year before a civil leap year, December 5th) until פסח. In ארץ ישראל, it is said from מרחשון ז׳. The phrase וְתֵן בְּרָכָה is said from חול המועד פסח until December 3rd (in the year before a civil leap year, December 4th). In ארץ ישראל it is said through מרחשון ז׳. See laws 52–54.

בָּרֵךְ עָלֵינוּ יהוה אֱלֹהֵינוּ אֶת הַשָּׁנָה הַזֹּאת
וְאֶת כָּל מִינֵי תְבוּאָתָהּ, לְטוֹבָה
בחורף: וְתֵן טַל וּמָטָר לִבְרָכָה / בקיץ: וְתֵן בְּרָכָה
עַל פְּנֵי הָאֲדָמָה, וְשַׂבְּעֵנוּ מִטּוּבָהּ
וּבָרֵךְ שְׁנָתֵנוּ כַּשָּׁנִים הַטּוֹבוֹת.
בָּרוּךְ אַתָּה יהוה, מְבָרֵךְ הַשָּׁנִים.

קבוץ גלויות

תְּקַע בְּשׁוֹפָר גָּדוֹל לְחֵרוּתֵנוּ
וְשָׂא נֵס לְקַבֵּץ גָּלֻיּוֹתֵינוּ
וְקַבְּצֵנוּ יַחַד מֵאַרְבַּע כַּנְפוֹת הָאָרֶץ.
בָּרוּךְ אַתָּה יהוה, מְקַבֵּץ נִדְחֵי עַמּוֹ יִשְׂרָאֵל.

השבת המשפט

הָשִׁיבָה שׁוֹפְטֵינוּ כְּבָרִאשׁוֹנָה
וְיוֹעֲצֵינוּ כְּבַתְּחִלָּה
וְהָסֵר מִמֶּנּוּ יָגוֹן וַאֲנָחָה
וּמְלֹךְ עָלֵינוּ אַתָּה יהוה לְבַדְּךָ בְּחֶסֶד וּבְרַחֲמִים
וְצַדְּקֵנוּ בַּמִּשְׁפָּט.
בָּרוּךְ אַתָּה יהוה
מֶלֶךְ אוֹהֵב צְדָקָה וּמִשְׁפָּט. / בעשרת ימי תשובה: הַמֶּלֶךְ הַמִּשְׁפָּט./

AGAINST INFORMERS

וְלַמַּלְשִׁינִים For the slanderers let there be no hope,
and may all wickedness perish in an instant.
May all Your people's enemies swiftly be cut down.
May You swiftly uproot, crush, cast down
and humble the arrogant swiftly in our days.
Blessed are You, LORD,
who destroys enemies and humbles the arrogant.

THE RIGHTEOUS

עַל הַצַּדִּיקִים To the righteous, the pious,
the elders of Your people the house of Israel,
the remnant of their scholars,
the righteous converts, and to us,
may Your compassion be aroused,
LORD our God.
Grant a good reward to all
who sincerely trust in Your name.
Set our lot with them,
so that we may never be ashamed,
for in You we trust.
Blessed are You, LORD,
who is the support and trust of the righteous.

REBUILDING JERUSALEM

וְלִירוּשָׁלַיִם To Jerusalem, Your city, may You return in compassion,
and may You dwell in it as You promised.
May You rebuild it rapidly in our days
as an everlasting structure,
and install within it soon the throne of David.
Blessed are You, LORD,
who builds Jerusalem.

ברכת המינים

וְלַמַּלְשִׁינִים אַל תְּהִי תִקְוָה

וְכָל הָרִשְׁעָה כְּרֶגַע תֹּאבֵד

וְכָל אוֹיְבֵי עַמְּךָ מְהֵרָה יִכָּרֵתוּ

וְהַזֵּדִים מְהֵרָה תְעַקֵּר וּתְשַׁבֵּר וּתְמַגֵּר וְתַכְנִיעַ בִּמְהֵרָה בְיָמֵינוּ.

בָּרוּךְ אַתָּה יהוה, שׁוֹבֵר אוֹיְבִים וּמַכְנִיעַ זֵדִים.

על הצדיקים

עַל הַצַּדִּיקִים וְעַל הַחֲסִידִים

וְעַל זִקְנֵי עַמְּךָ בֵּית יִשְׂרָאֵל

וְעַל פְּלֵיטַת סוֹפְרֵיהֶם

וְעַל גֵּרֵי הַצֶּדֶק, וְעָלֵינוּ

יֶהֱמוּ רַחֲמֶיךָ יהוה אֱלֹהֵינוּ

וְתֵן שָׂכָר טוֹב לְכָל הַבּוֹטְחִים בְּשִׁמְךָ בֶּאֱמֶת

וְשִׂים חֶלְקֵנוּ עִמָּהֶם

וּלְעוֹלָם לֹא נֵבוֹשׁ כִּי בְךָ בָּטָחְנוּ.

בָּרוּךְ אַתָּה יהוה, מִשְׁעָן וּמִבְטָח לַצַּדִּיקִים.

בניין ירושלים

וְלִירוּשָׁלַיִם עִירְךָ בְּרַחֲמִים תָּשׁוּב

וְתִשְׁכֹּן בְּתוֹכָהּ כַּאֲשֶׁר דִּבַּרְתָּ

וּבְנֵה אוֹתָהּ בְּקָרוֹב בְּיָמֵינוּ בִּנְיָן עוֹלָם

וְכִסֵּא דָוִד מְהֵרָה לְתוֹכָהּ תָּכִין.

בָּרוּךְ אַתָּה יהוה, בּוֹנֵה יְרוּשָׁלָיִם.

KINGDOM OF DAVID

אֶת צֶמַח May the offshoot of Your servant David soon flower,
and may his pride be raised high by Your salvation,
for we wait for Your salvation all day.
Blessed are You, LORD,
who makes the glory of salvation flourish.

RESPONSE TO PRAYER

שְׁמַע קוֹלֵנוּ Listen to our voice, LORD our God.
Spare us and have compassion on us,
and in compassion and favor accept our prayer,
for You, God, listen to prayers and pleas.
Do not turn us away, O our King,
empty-handed from Your presence,*
for You listen with compassion
to the prayer of Your people Israel.
Blessed are You, LORD,
who listens to prayer.

At this point, in times of drought in Israel, say "And answer us" on page 124.

TEMPLE SERVICE

רְצֵה Find favor, LORD our God,
in Your people Israel and their prayer.
Restore the service to Your most holy House,
and accept in love and favor
the fire-offerings of Israel and their prayer.
May the service of Your people Israel always find favor with You.

On Rosh Ḥodesh, say:
אֱלֹהֵינוּ Our God and God of our ancestors, may there rise,
come, reach, appear, be favored, heard, regarded and remembered before You, our recollection and remembrance, as well
as the remembrance of our ancestors, and of the Messiah son
of David Your servant, and of Jerusalem Your holy city, and

משיח בן דוד

אֶת צֶמַח דָּוִד עַבְדְּךָ מְהֵרָה תַצְמִיחַ
וְקַרְנוֹ תָּרוּם בִּישׁוּעָתֶךָ
כִּי לִישׁוּעָתְךָ קִוִּינוּ כָּל הַיּוֹם.
בָּרוּךְ אַתָּה יהוה, מַצְמִיחַ קֶרֶן יְשׁוּעָה.

שומע תפלה

שְׁמַע קוֹלֵנוּ יהוה אֱלֹהֵינוּ
חוּס וְרַחֵם עָלֵינוּ
וְקַבֵּל בְּרַחֲמִים וּבְרָצוֹן אֶת תְּפִלָּתֵנוּ
כִּי אֵל שׁוֹמֵעַ תְּפִלּוֹת וְתַחֲנוּנִים אָתָּה
וּמִלְּפָנֶיךָ מַלְכֵּנוּ רֵיקָם אַל תְּשִׁיבֵנוּ*
כִּי אַתָּה שׁוֹמֵעַ תְּפִלַּת עַמְּךָ יִשְׂרָאֵל בְּרַחֲמִים.
בָּרוּךְ אַתָּה יהוה, שׁוֹמֵעַ תְּפִלָּה.

*At this point, in times of drought in אֶרֶץ יִשְׂרָאֵל, say וְעֲנֵנוּ on page 125.

עבודה

רְצֵה יהוה אֱלֹהֵינוּ בְּעַמְּךָ יִשְׂרָאֵל, וּבִתְפִלָּתָם
וְהָשֵׁב אֶת הָעֲבוֹדָה לִדְבִיר בֵּיתֶךָ
וְאִשֵּׁי יִשְׂרָאֵל וּתְפִלָּתָם בְּאַהֲבָה תְקַבֵּל בְּרָצוֹן
וּתְהִי לְרָצוֹן תָּמִיד עֲבוֹדַת יִשְׂרָאֵל עַמֶּךָ.

On רֹאשׁ חֹדֶשׁ, say:

אֱלֹהֵינוּ וֵאלֹהֵי אֲבוֹתֵינוּ, יַעֲלֶה וְיָבוֹא וְיַגִּיעַ וְיֵרָאֶה וְיֵרָצֶה וְיִשָּׁמַע,
וְיִפָּקֵד וְיִזָּכֵר זִכְרוֹנֵנוּ וּפִקְדוֹנֵנוּ וְזִכְרוֹן אֲבוֹתֵינוּ, וְזִכְרוֹן מָשִׁיחַ
בֶּן דָּוִד עַבְדֶּךָ, וְזִכְרוֹן יְרוּשָׁלַיִם עִיר קָדְשֶׁךָ, וְזִכְרוֹן כָּל עַמְּךָ

of all Your people the house of Israel – for deliverance and well-
being, grace, loving-kindness and compassion, life and peace, on
this day of Rosh Ḥodesh. On it remember us, LORD our God, for
good; recollect us for blessing, and deliver us for life. In accord
with Your promise of salvation and compassion, spare us and
be gracious to us; have compassion on us and deliver us, for our
eyes are turned to You because You, God, are a gracious and
compassionate King.

וְתֶחֱזֶינָה And may our eyes witness
Your return to Zion in compassion.
Blessed are You, LORD,
who restores His Presence to Zion.

THANKSGIVING
Bow at the first nine words.
מוֹדִים We give thanks to You,
for You are the LORD our God and God of our ancestors
for ever and all time.
You are the Rock of our lives,
Shield of our salvation from generation to generation.
We will thank You and declare Your praise for our lives,
which are entrusted into Your hand;
for our souls, which are placed in Your charge;
for Your miracles which are with us every day;
and for Your wonders and favors at all times,
evening, morning and midday.
You are good –
for Your compassion never fails.
You are compassionate –
for Your loving-kindnesses never cease.
We have always placed our hope in You.

‏בֵּית יִשְׂרָאֵל, לְפָנֶיךָ, לִפְלֵיטָה לְטוֹבָה, לְחֵן וּלְחֶסֶד וּלְרַחֲמִים, לְחַיִּים וּלְשָׁלוֹם בְּיוֹם רֹאשׁ הַחֹדֶשׁ הַזֶּה. זָכְרֵנוּ יהוה אֱלֹהֵינוּ בּוֹ לְטוֹבָה, וּפָקְדֵנוּ בוֹ לִבְרָכָה, וְהוֹשִׁיעֵנוּ בוֹ לְחַיִּים. וּבִדְבַר יְשׁוּעָה וְרַחֲמִים, חוּס וְחָנֵּנוּ וְרַחֵם עָלֵינוּ וְהוֹשִׁיעֵנוּ, כִּי אֵלֶיךָ עֵינֵינוּ, כִּי אֵל מֶלֶךְ חַנּוּן וְרַחוּם אָתָּה.‏

___

‏וְתֶחֱזֶינָה עֵינֵינוּ בְּשׁוּבְךָ לְצִיּוֹן בְּרַחֲמִים.‏
‏בָּרוּךְ אַתָּה יהוה, הַמַּחֲזִיר שְׁכִינָתוֹ לְצִיּוֹן.‏

‏הודאה‏

Bow at the first five words.

‏מוֹדִים אֲנַחְנוּ לָךְ‏
‏שָׁאַתָּה הוּא יהוה אֱלֹהֵינוּ וֵאלֹהֵי אֲבוֹתֵינוּ לְעוֹלָם וָעֶד.‏
‏צוּר חַיֵּינוּ, מָגֵן יִשְׁעֵנוּ‏
‏אַתָּה הוּא לְדוֹר וָדוֹר.‏
‏נוֹדֶה לְּךָ וּנְסַפֵּר תְּהִלָּתֶךָ‏
‏עַל חַיֵּינוּ הַמְּסוּרִים בְּיָדֶךָ‏
‏וְעַל נִשְׁמוֹתֵינוּ הַפְּקוּדוֹת לָךְ‏
‏וְעַל נִסֶּיךָ שֶׁבְּכָל יוֹם עִמָּנוּ‏
‏וְעַל נִפְלְאוֹתֶיךָ וְטוֹבוֹתֶיךָ שֶׁבְּכָל עֵת‏
‏עֶרֶב וָבֹקֶר וְצָהֳרָיִם.‏
‏הַטּוֹב, כִּי לֹא כָלוּ רַחֲמֶיךָ‏
‏וְהַמְרַחֵם, כִּי לֹא תַמּוּ חֲסָדֶיךָ‏
‏מֵעוֹלָם קִוִּינוּ לָךְ.‏

On Ḥanukka:

עַל הַנִּסִּים [We thank You also] for the miracles, the redemption, the mighty deeds, the salvations, and the victories in battle which You performed for our ancestors in those days, at this time.

בִּימֵי מַתִּתְיָהוּ In the days of Mattityahu, son of Yoḥanan, the High Priest, the Hasmonean, and his sons, the wicked Greek kingdom rose up against Your people Israel to make them forget Your Torah and to force them to transgress the statutes of Your will. It was then that You in Your great compassion stood by them in the time of their distress. You championed their cause, judged their claim, and avenged their wrong. You delivered the strong into the hands of the weak, the many into the hands of the few, the impure into the hands of the pure, the wicked into the hands of the righteous, and the arrogant into the hands of those who were engaged in the study of Your Torah. You made for Yourself great and holy renown in Your world, and for Your people Israel You performed a great salvation and redemption as of this very day. Your children then entered the holiest part of Your House, cleansed Your Temple, purified Your Sanctuary, kindled lights in Your holy courts, and designated these eight days of Ḥanukka for giving thanks and praise to Your great name.

Continue with "For all these things."

On Purim:

עַל הַנִּסִּים [We thank You also] for the miracles, the redemption, the mighty deeds, the salvations, and the victories in battle which You performed for our ancestors in those days at this time.

בִּימֵי מָרְדְּכַי In the days of Mordekhai and Esther, in Shushan the capital, the wicked Haman rose up against them and sought to destroy, slay and exterminate *Esther 3* all the Jews, young and old, children and women, on one day, the thirteenth day of the twelfth month, which is the month of Adar, and to plunder their possessions. Then You in Your great compassion thwarted his counsel, frustrated his plans, and caused his scheme to recoil on his own head, so that they hanged him and his sons on the gallows.

Continue with "For all these things."

וְעַל כֻּלָּם For all these things may Your name be blessed and exalted, our King, continually, for ever and all time.

Between Rosh HaShana And write, for a good life,
& Yom Kippur: all the children of Your covenant.

Let all that lives thank You, Selah! and praise Your name in truth, God, our Savior and Help, Selah!

‣Blessed are You, Lord, whose name is "the Good" and to whom thanks are due.

בחנוכה:

עַל הַנִּסִּים וְעַל הַפֻּרְקָן וְעַל הַגְּבוּרוֹת וְעַל הַתְּשׁוּעוֹת וְעַל הַמִּלְחָמוֹת
שֶׁעָשִׂיתָ לַאֲבוֹתֵינוּ בַּיָּמִים הָהֵם בַּזְּמַן הַזֶּה.

בִּימֵי מַתִּתְיָהוּ בֶּן יוֹחָנָן כֹּהֵן גָּדוֹל חַשְׁמוֹנַאי וּבָנָיו, כְּשֶׁעָמְדָה מַלְכוּת יָוָן
הָרְשָׁעָה עַל עַמְּךָ יִשְׂרָאֵל לְהַשְׁכִּיחָם תּוֹרָתֶךָ וּלְהַעֲבִירָם מֵחֻקֵּי רְצוֹנֶךָ,
וְאַתָּה בְּרַחֲמֶיךָ הָרַבִּים עָמַדְתָּ לָהֶם בְּעֵת צָרָתָם, רַבְתָּ אֶת רִיבָם, דַּנְתָּ
אֶת דִּינָם, נָקַמְתָּ אֶת נִקְמָתָם, מָסַרְתָּ גִבּוֹרִים בְּיַד חַלָּשִׁים, וְרַבִּים בְּיַד
מְעַטִּים, וּטְמֵאִים בְּיַד טְהוֹרִים, וּרְשָׁעִים בְּיַד צַדִּיקִים, וְזֵדִים בְּיַד עוֹסְקֵי
תוֹרָתֶךָ, וּלְךָ עָשִׂיתָ שֵׁם גָּדוֹל וְקָדוֹשׁ בְּעוֹלָמֶךָ, וּלְעַמְּךָ יִשְׂרָאֵל עָשִׂיתָ
תְּשׁוּעָה גְדוֹלָה וּפֻרְקָן כְּהַיּוֹם הַזֶּה. וְאַחַר כֵּן בָּאוּ בָנֶיךָ לִדְבִיר בֵּיתֶךָ,
וּפִנּוּ אֶת הֵיכָלֶךָ, וְטִהֲרוּ אֶת מִקְדָּשֶׁךָ, וְהִדְלִיקוּ נֵרוֹת בְּחַצְרוֹת קָדְשֶׁךָ,
וְקָבְעוּ שְׁמוֹנַת יְמֵי חֲנֻכָּה אֵלּוּ, לְהוֹדוֹת וּלְהַלֵּל לְשִׁמְךָ הַגָּדוֹל.

וְעַל כֻּלָּם. *Continue with*

בפורים:

עַל הַנִּסִּים וְעַל הַפֻּרְקָן וְעַל הַגְּבוּרוֹת וְעַל הַתְּשׁוּעוֹת וְעַל הַמִּלְחָמוֹת
שֶׁעָשִׂיתָ לַאֲבוֹתֵינוּ בַּיָּמִים הָהֵם בַּזְּמַן הַזֶּה.

אסתר ג בִּימֵי מָרְדְּכַי וְאֶסְתֵּר בְּשׁוּשַׁן הַבִּירָה, כְּשֶׁעָמַד עֲלֵיהֶם הָמָן הָרָשָׁע, בִּקֵּשׁ
לְהַשְׁמִיד לַהֲרֹג וּלְאַבֵּד אֶת כָּל הַיְּהוּדִים מִנַּעַר וְעַד זָקֵן טַף וְנָשִׁים בְּיוֹם
אֶחָד, בִּשְׁלוֹשָׁה עָשָׂר לְחֹדֶשׁ שְׁנֵים עָשָׂר, הוּא חֹדֶשׁ אֲדָר, וּשְׁלָלָם
לָבוֹז. וְאַתָּה בְּרַחֲמֶיךָ הָרַבִּים הֵפַרְתָּ אֶת עֲצָתוֹ, וְקִלְקַלְתָּ אֶת מַחֲשַׁבְתּוֹ,
וַהֲשֵׁבוֹתָ לּוֹ גְּמוּלוֹ בְּרֹאשׁוֹ, וְתָלוּ אוֹתוֹ וְאֶת בָּנָיו עַל הָעֵץ.

וְעַל כֻּלָּם. *Continue with*

וְעַל כֻּלָּם יִתְבָּרַךְ וְיִתְרוֹמַם שִׁמְךָ מַלְכֵּנוּ תָּמִיד לְעוֹלָם וָעֶד.

בעשרת ימי תשובה: וּכְתֹב לְחַיִּים טוֹבִים כָּל בְּנֵי בְרִיתֶךָ.

וְכֹל הַחַיִּים יוֹדוּךָ סֶּלָה, וִיהַלְלוּ אֶת שִׁמְךָ בֶּאֱמֶת
הָאֵל יְשׁוּעָתֵנוּ וְעֶזְרָתֵנוּ סֶלָה.

בָּרוּךְ אַתָּה יהוה, הַטּוֹב שִׁמְךָ וּלְךָ נָאֶה לְהוֹדוֹת.

PEACE

שָׁלוֹם רָב Grant great peace to Your people Israel for ever,
for You are the sovereign LORD of all peace;
and may it be good in Your eyes
to bless Your people Israel
at every time, at every hour, with Your peace.

Between Rosh HaShana & Yom Kippur: In the book of life, blessing, peace and prosperity,
may we and all Your people the house of Israel be remembered
and written before You for a good life, and for peace.*

Blessed are You, LORD, who blesses His people Israel with peace.

> *Between Rosh HaShana and Yom Kippur
> outside Israel, many end the blessing:
> Blessed are You, LORD, who makes peace.

Some say the following verse (see law 60):
May the words of my mouth and the meditation of my heart
find favor before You, LORD, my Rock and Redeemer.

Ps. 19

אֱלֹהַי My God,
guard my tongue from evil and my lips from deceitful speech.
To those who curse me, let my soul be silent;
may my soul be to all like the dust.
Open my heart to Your Torah
and let my soul pursue Your commandments.
As for all who plan evil against me,
swiftly thwart their counsel and frustrate their plans.
    Act for the sake of Your name; act for the sake of Your right hand;
    act for the sake of Your holiness; act for the sake of Your Torah.
That Your beloved ones may be delivered,
save with Your right hand and answer me.
May the words of my mouth
and the meditation of my heart find favor before You,
LORD, my Rock and Redeemer.

Berakhot 17a

Ps. 60

Ps. 19

Bow, take three steps back, then bow, first left, then right, then center, while saying:
May He who makes peace in His high places,
make peace for us and all Israel – and say: Amen.

ברכת שלום

שָׁלוֹם רָב עַל יִשְׂרָאֵל עַמְּךָ תָּשִׂים לְעוֹלָם
כִּי אַתָּה הוּא מֶלֶךְ אָדוֹן לְכָל הַשָּׁלוֹם.
וְטוֹב בְּעֵינֶיךָ לְבָרֵךְ אֶת עַמְּךָ יִשְׂרָאֵל
בְּכָל עֵת וּבְכָל שָׁעָה בִּשְׁלוֹמֶךָ.

בעשרת ימי תשובה: בְּסֵפֶר חַיִּים, בְּרָכָה וְשָׁלוֹם, וּפַרְנָסָה טוֹבָה
נִזָּכֵר וְנִכָּתֵב לְפָנֶיךָ, אֲנַחְנוּ וְכָל עַמְּךָ בֵּית יִשְׂרָאֵל
לְחַיִּים טוֹבִים וּלְשָׁלוֹם.*

בָּרוּךְ אַתָּה יהוה, הַמְבָרֵךְ אֶת עַמּוֹ יִשְׂרָאֵל בַּשָּׁלוֹם.

*During the עשרת ימי תשובה in חוץ לארץ, many end the blessing:

בָּרוּךְ אַתָּה יהוה, עוֹשֵׂה הַשָּׁלוֹם.

Some say the following verse (see law 60):

תהלים יט   יִהְיוּ לְרָצוֹן אִמְרֵי פִי וְהֶגְיוֹן לִבִּי לְפָנֶיךָ, יהוה צוּרִי וְגֹאֲלִי:

ברכות יז   אֱלֹהַי

נְצֹר לְשׁוֹנִי מֵרָע וּשְׂפָתַי מִדַּבֵּר מִרְמָה
וְלִמְקַלְלַי נַפְשִׁי תִדֹּם, וְנַפְשִׁי כֶּעָפָר לַכֹּל תִּהְיֶה.
פְּתַח לִבִּי בְּתוֹרָתֶךָ, וּבְמִצְוֹתֶיךָ תִּרְדֹּף נַפְשִׁי.
וְכָל הַחוֹשְׁבִים עָלַי רָעָה
מְהֵרָה הָפֵר עֲצָתָם וְקַלְקֵל מַחֲשַׁבְתָּם.
עֲשֵׂה לְמַעַן שְׁמֶךָ, עֲשֵׂה לְמַעַן יְמִינֶךָ
עֲשֵׂה לְמַעַן קְדֻשָּׁתֶךָ, עֲשֵׂה לְמַעַן תּוֹרָתֶךָ.

תהלים ס   לְמַעַן יֵחָלְצוּן יְדִידֶיךָ, הוֹשִׁיעָה יְמִינְךָ וַעֲנֵנִי:

תהלים יט   יִהְיוּ לְרָצוֹן אִמְרֵי פִי וְהֶגְיוֹן לִבִּי לְפָנֶיךָ, יהוה צוּרִי וְגֹאֲלִי:

Bow, take three steps back, then bow, first left, then right, then center, while saying:

עֹשֶׂה שָׁלוֹם/בעשרת ימי תשובה: הַשָּׁלוֹם/ בִּמְרוֹמָיו
הוּא יַעֲשֶׂה שָׁלוֹם עָלֵינוּ וְעַל כָּל יִשְׂרָאֵל, וְאִמְרוּ אָמֵן.

יְהִי רָצוֹן May it be Your will, LORD our God and God of our ancestors,
that the Temple be rebuilt speedily in our days, and grant us a share in Your Torah.
And there we will serve You with reverence,
as in the days of old and as in former years.
Then the offering of Judah and Jerusalem   *Mal. 3*
will be pleasing to the LORD as in the days of old and as in former years.

*On Motza'ei Shabbat (except when Yom Tov or Erev Pesah falls in the following week), the
Leader continues with Half Kaddish (below, until •), then "May the pleasantness" on page 316.
On Motza'ei Shabbat when Yom Tov falls in the following week, the service continues on page 322.
On other evenings the Leader says Full Kaddish:*

FULL KADDISH

Leader: יִתְגַּדַּל Magnified and sanctified may His great name be,
        in the world He created by His will.
        May He establish His kingdom
        in your lifetime and in your days,
        and in the lifetime of all the house of Israel,
        swiftly and soon –
        and say: Amen.

All: May His great name be blessed for ever and all time.

Leader: Blessed and praised,
        glorified and exalted,
        raised and honored,
        uplifted and lauded be
        the name of the Holy One,
        blessed be He, beyond any blessing,
        song, praise and consolation
        uttered in the world –
        and say: Amen. ◂

        May the prayers and pleas of all Israel
        be accepted by their Father in heaven –
        and say: Amen.

יְהִי רָצוֹן מִלְּפָנֶיךָ יהוה אֱלֹהֵינוּ וֵאלֹהֵי אֲבוֹתֵינוּ
שֶׁיִּבָּנֶה בֵּית הַמִּקְדָּשׁ בִּמְהֵרָה בְיָמֵינוּ, וְתֵן חֶלְקֵנוּ בְּתוֹרָתֶךָ.
וְשָׁם נַעֲבָדְךָ בְּיִרְאָה כִּימֵי עוֹלָם וּכְשָׁנִים קַדְמוֹנִיּוֹת.
וְעָרְבָה לַיהוה מִנְחַת יְהוּדָה וִירוּשָׁלָ͏ִם כִּימֵי עוֹלָם וּכְשָׁנִים קַדְמוֹנִיּוֹת: מלאכי ג

On מוצאי שבת (except when עֶרֶב פסח or יום טוב falls in the following week),
the שליח ציבור continues with חצי קדיש (below, until ◄), then וִיהִי נֹעַם on page 317.

On מוצאי שבת when יום טוב falls in the following week, the service continues on page 323.
On other evenings the שליח ציבור says קדיש שלם:

קדיש שלם

שׁ״ץ: יִתְגַּדַּל וְיִתְקַדַּשׁ שְׁמֵהּ רַבָּא (קהל: אָמֵן)
בְּעָלְמָא דִּי בְרָא כִרְעוּתֵהּ
וְיַמְלִיךְ מַלְכוּתֵהּ
בְּחַיֵּיכוֹן וּבְיוֹמֵיכוֹן וּבְחַיֵּי דְכָל בֵּית יִשְׂרָאֵל
בַּעֲגָלָא וּבִזְמַן קָרִיב, וְאִמְרוּ אָמֵן. (קהל: אָמֵן)

קהל ושׁ״ץ: יְהֵא שְׁמֵהּ רַבָּא מְבָרַךְ לְעָלַם וּלְעָלְמֵי עָלְמַיָּא.

שׁ״ץ: יִתְבָּרַךְ וְיִשְׁתַּבַּח וְיִתְפָּאַר וְיִתְרוֹמַם וְיִתְנַשֵּׂא
וְיִתְהַדָּר וְיִתְעַלֶּה וְיִתְהַלָּל
שְׁמֵהּ דְּקֻדְשָׁא בְּרִיךְ הוּא (קהל: בְּרִיךְ הוּא)
לְעֵלָּא מִן כָּל בִּרְכָתָא
/בעשרת ימי תשובה: לְעֵלָּא לְעֵלָּא מִכָּל בִּרְכָתָא/
וְשִׁירָתָא, תֻּשְׁבְּחָתָא וְנֶחֱמָתָא
דַּאֲמִירָן בְּעָלְמָא, וְאִמְרוּ אָמֵן. (קהל: אָמֵן) ◄

תִּתְקַבַּל צְלוֹתְהוֹן וּבָעוּתְהוֹן דְּכָל יִשְׂרָאֵל
קֳדָם אֲבוּהוֹן דִּי בִשְׁמַיָּא, וְאִמְרוּ אָמֵן. (קהל: אָמֵן)

May there be great peace from heaven,
and life for us and all Israel –
and say: Amen.

Bow, take three steps back, as if taking leave of the Divine Presence,
then bow, first left, then right, then center, while saying:

May He who makes peace in His high places,
make peace for us and all Israel –
and say: Amen.

On Yom HaAtzma'ut (in Israel and many communities outside Israel)
the service continues with "Listen, Israel" on page 424.
From the second night of Pesah until the night before Shavuot, the Omer is counted here (page 304).
On Purim, Megillat Esther is read; on Tisha B'Av, Megillat Eikha is read.

Stand while saying Aleinu. Bow at ˙.

עָלֵינוּ It is our duty to praise the Master of all,
and ascribe greatness to the Author of creation,
who has not made us like the nations of the lands
nor placed us like the families of the earth;
who has not made our portion like theirs,
nor our destiny like all their multitudes.
(For they worship vanity and emptiness,
and pray to a god who cannot save.)
˙But we bow in worship
and thank the Supreme King of kings,
the Holy One, blessed be He,
who extends the heavens and establishes the earth,
whose throne of glory is in the heavens above,
and whose power's Presence is in the highest of heights.
He is our God; there is no other.
Truly He is our King, there is none else,
as it is written in His Torah:
"You shall know and take to heart this day
that the LORD is God,
in heaven above and on earth below. There is no other."

Deut. 4

יְהֵא שְׁלָמָא רַבָּא מִן שְׁמַיָּא
וְחַיִּים, עָלֵינוּ וְעַל כָּל יִשְׂרָאֵל, וְאִמְרוּ אָמֵן. (קהל: אָמֵן)

Bow, take three steps back, as if taking leave of the Divine Presence,
then bow, first left, then right, then center, while saying:

עֹשֶׂה שָׁלוֹם/ בעשרת ימי תשובה: הַשָּׁלוֹם/ בִּמְרוֹמָיו
הוּא יַעֲשֶׂה שָׁלוֹם עָלֵינוּ וְעַל כָּל יִשְׂרָאֵל
וְאִמְרוּ אָמֵן. (קהל: אָמֵן)

*(*חוץ לארץ *and many communities in* ארץ ישראל *in)* יום העצמאות
the service continues with שְׁמַע יִשְׂרָאֵל *on page 425.*
From the second night of פסח *until the night before* שבועות, *the* עומר *is counted here (page 305).*
On פורים, מגילת אסתר *is read; on* תשעה באב, מגילת איכה *is read.*

Bow at ﬞ. עָלֵינוּ. *Stand while saying* עָלֵינוּ.

עָלֵינוּ לְשַׁבֵּחַ לַאֲדוֹן הַכֹּל, לָתֵת גְּדֻלָּה לְיוֹצֵר בְּרֵאשִׁית
שֶׁלֹּא עָשָׂנוּ כְּגוֹיֵי הָאֲרָצוֹת, וְלֹא שָׂמָנוּ כְּמִשְׁפְּחוֹת הָאֲדָמָה
שֶׁלֹּא שָׂם חֶלְקֵנוּ כָּהֶם וְגוֹרָלֵנוּ כְּכָל הֲמוֹנָם.
(שֶׁהֵם מִשְׁתַּחֲוִים לְהֶבֶל וָרִיק וּמִתְפַּלְלִים אֶל אֵל לֹא יוֹשִׁיעַ.)
ﬞוַאֲנַחְנוּ כּוֹרְעִים וּמִשְׁתַּחֲוִים וּמוֹדִים
לִפְנֵי מֶלֶךְ מַלְכֵי הַמְּלָכִים, הַקָּדוֹשׁ בָּרוּךְ הוּא
שֶׁהוּא נוֹטֶה שָׁמַיִם וְיוֹסֵד אָרֶץ
וּמוֹשַׁב יְקָרוֹ בַּשָּׁמַיִם מִמַּעַל
וּשְׁכִינַת עֻזּוֹ בְּגָבְהֵי מְרוֹמִים.
הוּא אֱלֹהֵינוּ, אֵין עוֹד.
אֱמֶת מַלְכֵּנוּ, אֶפֶס זוּלָתוֹ
כַּכָּתוּב בְּתוֹרָתוֹ
וְיָדַעְתָּ הַיּוֹם וַהֲשֵׁבֹתָ אֶל־לְבָבֶךָ
כִּי יהוה הוּא הָאֱלֹהִים בַּשָּׁמַיִם מִמַּעַל וְעַל־הָאָרֶץ מִתָּחַת, אֵין עוֹד:

דברים ד

Therefore, we place our hope in You, Lord our God,
that we may soon see the glory of Your power,
when You will remove abominations from the earth,
and idols will be utterly destroyed,
when the world will be perfected under the sovereignty of the Almighty,
when all humanity will call on Your name,
to turn all the earth's wicked toward You.
All the world's inhabitants will realize and know
that to You every knee must bow and every tongue swear loyalty.
Before You, Lord our God, they will kneel and bow down
and give honor to Your glorious name.
They will all accept the yoke of Your kingdom,
and You will reign over them soon and for ever.
For the kingdom is Yours, and to all eternity You will reign in glory,
as it is written in Your Torah: "The Lord will reign for ever and ever."   *Ex. 15*
▸ And it is said: "Then the Lord shall be King over all the earth;   *Zech. 14*
  on that day the Lord shall be One and His name One."

Some add:

Have no fear of sudden terror or of the ruin when it overtakes the wicked.   *Prov. 3*
Devise your strategy, but it will be thwarted;   *Is. 8*
propose your plan, but it will not stand, for God is with us.
When you grow old, I will still be the same.   *Is. 46*
When your hair turns gray, I will still carry you.
I made you, I will bear you, I will carry you, and I will rescue you.

MOURNER'S KADDISH

The following prayer, said by mourners, requires the presence of a minyan.
A transliteration can be found on page 699.

Mourner: יִתְגַּדַּל Magnified and sanctified may His great name be,
in the world He created by His will.
May He establish His kingdom
in your lifetime and in your days,
and in the lifetime of all the house of Israel,
swiftly and soon – and say: Amen.

All: May His great name be blessed for ever and all time.

עַל כֵּן נְקַוֶּה לְּךָ יהוה אֱלֹהֵינוּ, לִרְאוֹת מְהֵרָה בְּתִפְאֶרֶת עֻזֶּךָ

לְהַעֲבִיר גִּלּוּלִים מִן הָאָרֶץ, וְהָאֱלִילִים כָּרוֹת יִכָּרֵתוּן

לְתַקֵּן עוֹלָם בְּמַלְכוּת שַׁדַּי.

וְכָל בְּנֵי בָשָׂר יִקְרְאוּ בִשְׁמֶךָ לְהַפְנוֹת אֵלֶיךָ כָּל רִשְׁעֵי אָרֶץ.

יַכִּירוּ וְיֵדְעוּ כָּל יוֹשְׁבֵי תֵבֵל

כִּי לְךָ תִּכְרַע כָּל בֶּרֶךְ, תִּשָּׁבַע כָּל לָשׁוֹן.

לְפָנֶיךָ יהוה אֱלֹהֵינוּ יִכְרְעוּ וְיִפֹּלוּ, וְלִכְבוֹד שִׁמְךָ יְקָר יִתֵּנוּ

וִיקַבְּלוּ כֻלָּם אֶת עֹל מַלְכוּתֶךָ

וְתִמְלֹךְ עֲלֵיהֶם מְהֵרָה לְעוֹלָם וָעֶד.

כִּי הַמַּלְכוּת שֶׁלְּךָ הִיא וּלְעוֹלְמֵי עַד תִּמְלֹךְ בְּכָבוֹד

שמות טו
כַּכָּתוּב בְּתוֹרָתֶךָ, יהוה יִמְלֹךְ לְעֹלָם וָעֶד:

זכריה יד
‹ וְנֶאֱמַר, וְהָיָה יהוה לְמֶלֶךְ עַל־כָּל־הָאָרֶץ

בַּיּוֹם הַהוּא יִהְיֶה יהוה אֶחָד וּשְׁמוֹ אֶחָד:

Some add:

משלי ג
אַל־תִּירָא מִפַּחַד פִּתְאֹם וּמִשֹּׁאַת רְשָׁעִים כִּי תָבֹא:

ישעיה ח
עֻצוּ עֵצָה וְתֻפָר, דַּבְּרוּ דָבָר וְלֹא יָקוּם, כִּי עִמָּנוּ אֵל:

ישעיה מו
וְעַד־זִקְנָה אֲנִי הוּא, וְעַד־שֵׂיבָה אֲנִי אֶסְבֹּל אֲנִי עָשִׂיתִי וַאֲנִי אֶשָּׂא וַאֲנִי אֶסְבֹּל וַאֲמַלֵּט:

קדיש יתום

The following prayer, said by mourners, requires the presence of a מניָן.
A transliteration can be found on page 699.

אבל: יִתְגַּדַּל וְיִתְקַדַּשׁ שְׁמֵהּ רַבָּא (קהל: אָמֵן)

בְּעָלְמָא דִּי בְרָא כִרְעוּתֵהּ

וְיַמְלִיךְ מַלְכוּתֵהּ

בְּחַיֵּיכוֹן וּבְיוֹמֵיכוֹן וּבְחַיֵּי דְכָל בֵּית יִשְׂרָאֵל

בַּעֲגָלָא וּבִזְמַן קָרִיב, וְאִמְרוּ אָמֵן. (קהל: אָמֵן)

קהל
ואבל: יְהֵא שְׁמֵהּ רַבָּא מְבָרַךְ לְעָלַם וּלְעָלְמֵי עָלְמַיָּא.

Mourner: Blessed and praised, glorified and exalted,
raised and honored, uplifted and lauded
be the name of the Holy One,
blessed be He, beyond any blessing,
song, praise and consolation
uttered in the world – and say: Amen.

May there be great peace from heaven,
and life for us and all Israel – and say: Amen.

*Bow, take three steps back, as if taking leave of the Divine Presence,
then bow, first left, then right, then center, while saying:*

May He who makes peace in His high places,
make peace for us and all Israel – and say: Amen.

*From the second day of Rosh Ḥodesh Elul through
Shemini Atzeret, the following psalm is said:*

לְדָוִד By David. The Lord is my light and my salvation – whom then shall   *Ps. 27*
I fear? The Lord is the stronghold of my life – of whom shall I be afraid?
When evil men close in on me to devour my flesh, it is they, my enemies and
foes, who stumble and fall. Should an army besiege me, my heart would not
fear. Should war break out against me, still I would be confident. One thing
I ask of the Lord, only this do I seek: to live in the House of the Lord all
the days of my life, to gaze on the beauty of the Lord and worship in His
Temple. For He will keep me safe in His pavilion on the day of trouble. He
will hide me under the cover of His tent. He will set me high upon a rock.
Now my head is high above my enemies who surround me. I will sacrifice
in His tent with shouts of joy. I will sing and chant praises to the Lord.
Lord, hear my voice when I call. Be gracious to me and answer me. On
Your behalf my heart says, "Seek My face." Your face, Lord, will I seek. Do
not hide Your face from me. Do not turn Your servant away in anger. You
have been my help. Do not reject or forsake me, God, my Savior. Were my
father and my mother to forsake me, the Lord would take me in. Teach me
Your way, Lord, and lead me on a level path, because of my oppressors. Do
not abandon me to the will of my foes, for false witnesses have risen against
me, breathing violence. ‣ Were it not for my faith that I shall see the Lord's
goodness in the land of the living. Hope in the Lord. Be strong and of good
courage, and hope in the Lord!

Mourner's Kaddish (on previous page)

In a house of mourning the service continues on page 602.

אבל: יִתְבָּרַךְ וְיִשְׁתַּבַּח וְיִתְפָּאַר

וְיִתְרוֹמַם וְיִתְנַשֵּׂא וְיִתְהַדָּר וְיִתְעַלֶּה וְיִתְהַלָּל

שְׁמֵהּ דְּקֻדְשָׁא בְּרִיךְ הוּא (קהל: בְּרִיךְ הוּא)

לְעֵלָּא מִן כָּל בִּרְכָתָא

/בעשרת ימי תשובה: לְעֵלָּא לְעֵלָּא מִכָּל בִּרְכָתָא/

וְשִׁירָתָא, תֻּשְׁבְּחָתָא וְנֶחֱמָתָא

דַּאֲמִירָן בְּעָלְמָא, וְאִמְרוּ אָמֵן. (קהל: אָמֵן)

יְהֵא שְׁלָמָא רַבָּא מִן שְׁמַיָּא

וְחַיִּים, עָלֵינוּ וְעַל כָּל יִשְׂרָאֵל, וְאִמְרוּ אָמֵן. (קהל: אָמֵן)

Bow, take three steps back, as if taking leave of the Divine Presence,
then bow, first left, then right, then center, while saying:

עֹשֶׂה שָׁלוֹם/בעשרת ימי תשובה: הַשָּׁלוֹם/ בִּמְרוֹמָיו

הוּא יַעֲשֶׂה שָׁלוֹם עָלֵינוּ וְעַל כָּל יִשְׂרָאֵל, וְאִמְרוּ אָמֵן. (קהל: אָמֵן)

From the second day of ראש חודש אלול *through* שמיני עצרת,
the following psalm is said:

תהלים כז: לְדָוִד, יהוה אוֹרִי וְיִשְׁעִי, מִמִּי אִירָא, יהוה מָעוֹז־חַיַּי, מִמִּי אֶפְחָד: בִּקְרֹב עָלַי מְרֵעִים לֶאֱכֹל אֶת־בְּשָׂרִי, צָרַי וְאֹיְבַי לִי, הֵמָּה כָשְׁלוּ וְנָפָלוּ: אִם־תַּחֲנֶה עָלַי מַחֲנֶה, לֹא־יִירָא לִבִּי, אִם־תָּקוּם עָלַי מִלְחָמָה, בְּזֹאת אֲנִי בוֹטֵחַ: אַחַת שָׁאַלְתִּי מֵאֵת־יהוה, אוֹתָהּ אֲבַקֵּשׁ, שִׁבְתִּי בְּבֵית־יהוה כָּל־יְמֵי חַיַּי, לַחֲזוֹת בְּנֹעַם־יהוה, וּלְבַקֵּר בְּהֵיכָלוֹ: כִּי יִצְפְּנֵנִי בְּסֻכֹּה בְּיוֹם רָעָה, יַסְתִּרֵנִי בְּסֵתֶר אָהֳלוֹ, בְּצוּר יְרוֹמְמֵנִי: וְעַתָּה יָרוּם רֹאשִׁי עַל אֹיְבַי סְבִיבוֹתַי, וְאֶזְבְּחָה בְאָהֳלוֹ זִבְחֵי תְרוּעָה, אָשִׁירָה וַאֲזַמְּרָה לַיהוה: שְׁמַע־יהוה קוֹלִי אֶקְרָא, וְחָנֵּנִי וַעֲנֵנִי: לְךָ אָמַר לִבִּי בַּקְּשׁוּ פָנָי, אֶת־פָּנֶיךָ יהוה אֲבַקֵּשׁ: אַל־תַּסְתֵּר פָּנֶיךָ מִמֶּנִּי, אַל תַּט־בְּאַף עַבְדֶּךָ, עֶזְרָתִי הָיִיתָ, אַל־תִּטְּשֵׁנִי וְאַל־תַּעַזְבֵנִי, אֱלֹהֵי יִשְׁעִי: כִּי־אָבִי וְאִמִּי עֲזָבוּנִי, וַיהוה יַאַסְפֵנִי: הוֹרֵנִי יהוה דַּרְכֶּךָ, וּנְחֵנִי בְּאֹרַח מִישׁוֹר, לְמַעַן שׁוֹרְרָי: אַל־תִּתְּנֵנִי בְּנֶפֶשׁ צָרָי, כִּי קָמוּ־בִי עֵדֵי־שֶׁקֶר, וִיפֵחַ חָמָס: ◆ לוּלֵא הֶאֱמַנְתִּי לִרְאוֹת בְּטוּב־יהוה בְּאֶרֶץ חַיִּים: קַוֵּה אֶל־יהוה, חֲזַק וְיַאֲמֵץ לִבֶּךָ, וְקַוֵּה אֶל־יהוה:

קדיש יתום (on previous page)

In a house of mourning the service continues on page 603.

COUNTING OF THE OMER

The Omer is counted each night from the second night of Pesaḥ
until the night before Shavuot. See laws 98–100.
Some say the following meditation before the blessing:

For the sake of the unification of the Holy One, blessed be He,
and His Divine Presence, in reverence and love,
to unify the name *Yod-Heh* with *Vav-Heh*
in perfect unity in the name of all Israel.

הִנְנִי I am prepared and ready to fulfill the positive commandment of Counting the Omer, as is written in the Torah, "You shall count seven complete   *Lev. 23*
weeks from the day following the [Pesaḥ] rest day, when you brought the
Omer as a wave-offering. To the day after the seventh week you shall count
fifty days. Then you shall present a meal-offering of new grain to the LORD."
May the pleasantness of the LORD our God be upon us. Establish for us the   *Ps. 90*
work of our hands, O establish the work of our hands.

בָּרוּךְ Blessed are You, LORD our God, King of the Universe,
who has made us holy through His commandments,
and has commanded us about counting the Omer.

16 Nisan	19 Nisan
1. Today is the first day of the Omer.	4. Today is the fourth day of the Omer.
17 Nisan	20 Nisan
2. Today is the second day of the Omer.	5. Today is the fifth day of the Omer.
18 Nisan	21 Nisan
3. Today is the third day of the Omer.	6. Today is the sixth day of the Omer.

Egypt with the giving of the Torah at Mount Sinai, are a time of preparation
and growth – of leaving a world of slavery and getting ready to enter a world
of personal, social and spiritual responsibility. The Jewish mystics attached
special significance to this period of the year as one in which the various
facets of the soul were cleansed, one by one.

סדר ספירת העומר

The עומר *is counted each night from the second night of* פסח
until the night before שבועות. *See laws 98–100.*

Some say the following meditation before the blessing:

לְשֵׁם יִחוּד קֻדְשָׁא בְּרִיךְ הוּא וּשְׁכִינְתֵּהּ בִּדְחִילוּ וּרְחִימוּ
לְיַחֵד שֵׁם י״ה בו״ה בְּיִחוּדָא שְׁלִים בְּשֵׁם כָּל יִשְׂרָאֵל.

הִנְנִי מוּכָן וּמְזֻמָּן לְקַיֵּם מִצְוַת עֲשֵׂה שֶׁל סְפִירַת הָעֹמֶר. כְּמוֹ שֶׁכָּתוּב בַּתּוֹרָה, ויקרא כג
וּסְפַרְתֶּם לָכֶם מִמָּחֳרַת הַשַּׁבָּת, מִיּוֹם הֲבִיאֲכֶם אֶת־עֹמֶר הַתְּנוּפָה, שֶׁבַע
שַׁבָּתוֹת תְּמִימֹת תִּהְיֶינָה: עַד מִמָּחֳרַת הַשַּׁבָּת הַשְּׁבִיעִת תִּסְפְּרוּ חֲמִשִּׁים
יוֹם, וְהִקְרַבְתֶּם מִנְחָה חֲדָשָׁה לַיהוה: וִיהִי נֹעַם אֲדֹנָי אֱלֹהֵינוּ עָלֵינוּ, וּמַעֲשֵׂה תהלים צ
יָדֵינוּ כּוֹנְנָה עָלֵינוּ, וּמַעֲשֵׂה יָדֵינוּ כּוֹנְנֵהוּ:

בָּרוּךְ אַתָּה יהוה אֱלֹהֵינוּ מֶלֶךְ הָעוֹלָם
אֲשֶׁר קִדְּשָׁנוּ בְּמִצְוֹתָיו וְצִוָּנוּ עַל סְפִירַת הָעֹמֶר.

טז בניסן		יד בניסן	
4. הַיּוֹם אַרְבָּעָה יָמִים בָּעֹמֶר.		1. הַיּוֹם יוֹם אֶחָד בָּעֹמֶר.	
נצח שבחסד		חסד שבחסד	
כ בניסן		יז בניסן	
5. הַיּוֹם חֲמִשָּׁה יָמִים בָּעֹמֶר.		2. הַיּוֹם שְׁנֵי יָמִים בָּעֹמֶר.	
הוד שבחסד		גבורה שבחסד	
כא בניסן		יח בניסן	
6. הַיּוֹם שִׁשָּׁה יָמִים בָּעֹמֶר.		3. הַיּוֹם שְׁלֹשָׁה יָמִים בָּעֹמֶר.	
יסוד שבחסד		תפארת שבחסד	

COUNTING THE OMER

When the Temple stood, on the day after the first day of Pesaḥ an offering was
made of an Omer (approximately nine pounds) of new barley grain. There
then began a count of forty-nine days – seven complete weeks – and on the
fiftieth day, the festival of Shavuot was celebrated. When the Temple was
destroyed, the sages ordained that we should continue to count the days as
a memory of this practice. The forty-nine days, connecting the exodus from

22 Nisan

7. Today is the seventh day,
making one week
of the Omer.

23 Nisan

8. Today is the eighth day,
making one week and one day
of the Omer.

24 Nisan

9. Today is the ninth day,
making one week and two days
of the Omer.

25 Nisan

10. Today is the tenth day,
making one week and three
days of the Omer.

26 Nisan

11. Today is the eleventh day,
making one week and four
days of the Omer.

27 Nisan

12. Today is the twelfth day,
making one week and five days
of the Omer.

28 Nisan

13. Today is the thirteenth day,
making one week and six days
of the Omer.

29 Nisan

14. Today is the fourteenth day,
making two weeks
of the Omer.

30 Nisan, 1st day Rosh Ḥodesh

15. Today is the fifteenth day,
making two weeks and one day
of the Omer.

1 Iyar, 2nd day Rosh Ḥodesh

16. Today is the sixteenth day,
making two weeks and two
days of the Omer.

2 Iyar

17. Today is the seventeenth day,
making two weeks and three
days of the Omer.

3 Iyar

18. Today is the eighteenth day,
making two weeks and four
days of the Omer.

4 Iyar

19. Today is the nineteenth day,
making two weeks and five
days of the Omer.

5 Iyar, Yom HaAtzma'ut

20. Today is the twentieth day,
making two weeks and six days
of the Omer.

7. הַיּוֹם שִׁבְעָה יָמִים
שֶׁהֵם שָׁבוּעַ אֶחָד בָּעֹמֶר.
מלכות שבחסד

8. הַיּוֹם שְׁמוֹנָה יָמִים
שֶׁהֵם שָׁבוּעַ אֶחָד וְיוֹם אֶחָד
בָּעֹמֶר.
חסד שבגבורה

9. הַיּוֹם תִּשְׁעָה יָמִים
שֶׁהֵם שָׁבוּעַ אֶחָד וּשְׁנֵי יָמִים
בָּעֹמֶר.
גבורה שבגבורה

10. הַיּוֹם עֲשָׂרָה יָמִים
שֶׁהֵם שָׁבוּעַ אֶחָד וּשְׁלֹשָׁה
יָמִים בָּעֹמֶר.
תפארת שבגבורה

11. הַיּוֹם אַחַד עָשָׂר יוֹם
שֶׁהֵם שָׁבוּעַ אֶחָד וְאַרְבָּעָה
יָמִים בָּעֹמֶר.
נצח שבגבורה

12. הַיּוֹם שְׁנֵים עָשָׂר יוֹם
שֶׁהֵם שָׁבוּעַ אֶחָד וַחֲמִשָּׁה
יָמִים בָּעֹמֶר.
הוד שבגבורה

13. הַיּוֹם שְׁלֹשָׁה עָשָׂר יוֹם
שֶׁהֵם שָׁבוּעַ אֶחָד וְשִׁשָּׁה יָמִים
בָּעֹמֶר.
יסוד שבגבורה

14. הַיּוֹם אַרְבָּעָה עָשָׂר יוֹם
שֶׁהֵם שְׁנֵי שָׁבוּעוֹת
בָּעֹמֶר.
מלכות שבגבורה

15. הַיּוֹם חֲמִשָּׁה עָשָׂר יוֹם
שֶׁהֵם שְׁנֵי שָׁבוּעוֹת וְיוֹם אֶחָד
בָּעֹמֶר.
חסד שבתפארת

16. הַיּוֹם שִׁשָּׁה עָשָׂר יוֹם
שֶׁהֵם שְׁנֵי שָׁבוּעוֹת וּשְׁנֵי יָמִים
בָּעֹמֶר.
גבורה שבתפארת

17. הַיּוֹם שִׁבְעָה עָשָׂר יוֹם
שֶׁהֵם שְׁנֵי שָׁבוּעוֹת וּשְׁלֹשָׁה
יָמִים בָּעֹמֶר.
תפארת שבתפארת

18. הַיּוֹם שְׁמוֹנָה עָשָׂר יוֹם
שֶׁהֵם שְׁנֵי שָׁבוּעוֹת וְאַרְבָּעָה
יָמִים בָּעֹמֶר.
נצח שבתפארת

19. הַיּוֹם תִּשְׁעָה עָשָׂר יוֹם
שֶׁהֵם שְׁנֵי שָׁבוּעוֹת וַחֲמִשָּׁה
יָמִים בָּעֹמֶר.
הוד שבתפארת

20. הַיּוֹם עֶשְׂרִים יוֹם
שֶׁהֵם שְׁנֵי שָׁבוּעוֹת וְשִׁשָּׁה
יָמִים בָּעֹמֶר.
יסוד שבתפארת

6 Iyar

21. Today is the twenty-first day,
    making three weeks
    of the Omer.

7 Iyar

22. Today is the twenty-second
    day, making three weeks and
    one day of the Omer.

8 Iyar

23. Today is the twenty-third day,
    making three weeks and two
    days of the Omer.

9 Iyar

24. Today is the twenty-fourth day,
    making three weeks and three
    days of the Omer.

10 Iyar

25. Today is the twenty-fifth day,
    making three weeks and four
    days of the Omer.

11 Iyar

26. Today is the twenty-sixth day,
    making three weeks and five
    days of the Omer.

12 Iyar

27. Today is the twenty-seventh
    day, making three weeks and
    six days of the Omer.

13 Iyar

28. Today is the twenty-eighth day,
    making four weeks
    of the Omer.

14 Iyar, Pesah Sheni

29. Today is the twenty-ninth day,
    making four weeks and one
    day of the Omer.

15 Iyar

30. Today is the thirtieth day,
    making four weeks and two
    days of the Omer.

16 Iyar

31. Today is the thirty-first day,
    making four weeks and three
    days of the Omer.

17 Iyar

32. Today is the thirty-second day,
    making four weeks and four
    days of the Omer.

18 Iyar, Lag BaOmer

33. Today is the thirty-third day,
    making four weeks and five
    days of the Omer.

19 Iyar

34. Today is the thirty-fourth day,
    making four weeks and six
    days of the Omer.

ו באייר

.21 הַיּוֹם אֶחָד וְעֶשְׂרִים יוֹם
שֶׁהֵם שְׁלֹשָׁה שָׁבוּעוֹת בָּעֹמֶר.
מלכות שבתפארת

ז באייר

.22 הַיּוֹם שְׁנַיִם וְעֶשְׂרִים יוֹם
שֶׁהֵם שְׁלֹשָׁה שָׁבוּעוֹת
וְיוֹם אֶחָד בָּעֹמֶר.   חסד שבנצח

ח באייר

.23 הַיּוֹם שְׁלֹשָׁה וְעֶשְׂרִים יוֹם
שֶׁהֵם שְׁלֹשָׁה שָׁבוּעוֹת
וּשְׁנֵי יָמִים בָּעֹמֶר.   גבורה שבנצח

ט באייר

.24 הַיּוֹם אַרְבָּעָה וְעֶשְׂרִים יוֹם
שֶׁהֵם שְׁלֹשָׁה שָׁבוּעוֹת
וּשְׁלֹשָׁה יָמִים בָּעֹמֶר.

י באייר

.25 הַיּוֹם חֲמִשָּׁה וְעֶשְׂרִים יוֹם
שֶׁהֵם שְׁלֹשָׁה שָׁבוּעוֹת
וְאַרְבָּעָה יָמִים בָּעֹמֶר. נצח שבנצח

יא באייר

.26 הַיּוֹם שִׁשָּׁה וְעֶשְׂרִים יוֹם
שֶׁהֵם שְׁלֹשָׁה שָׁבוּעוֹת
וַחֲמִשָּׁה יָמִים בָּעֹמֶר.   הוד שבנצח

יב באייר

.27 הַיּוֹם שִׁבְעָה וְעֶשְׂרִים יוֹם
שֶׁהֵם שְׁלֹשָׁה שָׁבוּעוֹת
וְשִׁשָּׁה יָמִים בָּעֹמֶר.   יסוד שבנצח

תפארת שבנצח

ג באייר

.28 הַיּוֹם שְׁמוֹנָה וְעֶשְׂרִים יוֹם
שֶׁהֵם אַרְבָּעָה שָׁבוּעוֹת
בָּעֹמֶר.   מלכות שבנצח

יד באייר, פסח שני

.29 הַיּוֹם תִּשְׁעָה וְעֶשְׂרִים יוֹם
שֶׁהֵם אַרְבָּעָה שָׁבוּעוֹת
וְיוֹם אֶחָד בָּעֹמֶר.   חסד שבהוד

טו באייר

.30 הַיּוֹם שְׁלֹשִׁים יוֹם
שֶׁהֵם אַרְבָּעָה שָׁבוּעוֹת
וּשְׁנֵי יָמִים בָּעֹמֶר.   גבורה שבהוד

טז באייר

.31 הַיּוֹם אֶחָד וּשְׁלֹשִׁים יוֹם
שֶׁהֵם אַרְבָּעָה שָׁבוּעוֹת
וּשְׁלֹשָׁה יָמִים בָּעֹמֶר.

תפארת שבהוד

יז באייר

.32 הַיּוֹם שְׁנַיִם וּשְׁלֹשִׁים יוֹם
שֶׁהֵם אַרְבָּעָה שָׁבוּעוֹת
וְאַרְבָּעָה יָמִים בָּעֹמֶר. נצח שבהוד

יח באייר, ל"ג בעומר

.33 הַיּוֹם שְׁלֹשָׁה וּשְׁלֹשִׁים יוֹם
שֶׁהֵם אַרְבָּעָה שָׁבוּעוֹת
וַחֲמִשָּׁה יָמִים בָּעֹמֶר.   הוד שבהוד

יט באייר

.34 הַיּוֹם אַרְבָּעָה וּשְׁלֹשִׁים יוֹם
שֶׁהֵם אַרְבָּעָה שָׁבוּעוֹת
וְשִׁשָּׁה יָמִים בָּעֹמֶר.   יסוד שבהוד

20 Iyar

35. Today is the thirty-fifth day,
    making five weeks
    of the Omer.

21 Iyar

36. Today is the thirty-sixth day,
    making five weeks and one day
    of the Omer.

22 Iyar

37. Today is the thirty-seventh day,
    making five weeks and two
    days of the Omer.

23 Iyar

38. Today is the thirty-eighth day,
    making five weeks and three
    days of the Omer.

24 Iyar

39. Today is the thirty-ninth day,
    making five weeks and four
    days of the Omer.

25 Iyar

40. Today is the fortieth day,
    making five weeks and five
    days of the Omer.

26 Iyar

41. Today is the forty-first day,
    making five weeks and six days
    of the Omer.

27 Iyar

42. Today is the forty-second day,
    making six weeks
    of the Omer.

28 Iyar, Yom Yerushalayim

43. Today is the forty-third day,
    making six weeks and one day
    of the Omer.

29 Iyar

44. Today is the forty-fourth day,
    making six weeks and two days
    of the Omer.

1 Sivan, Rosh Ḥodesh

45. Today is the forty-fifth day,
    making six weeks and three
    days of the Omer.

2 Sivan

46. Today is the forty-sixth day,
    making six weeks and four
    days of the Omer.

3 Sivan

47. Today is the forty-seventh day,
    making six weeks and five days
    of the Omer.

4 Sivan

48. Today is the forty-eighth day,
    making six weeks and six days
    of the Omer.

42. הַיּוֹם שְׁנַיִם וְאַרְבָּעִים יוֹם
שֶׁהֵם שִׁשָּׁה שָׁבוּעוֹת
בָּעֹמֶר.   מלכות שביסוד

43. הַיּוֹם שְׁלֹשָׁה וְאַרְבָּעִים יוֹם
שֶׁהֵם שִׁשָּׁה שָׁבוּעוֹת
וְיוֹם אֶחָד בָּעֹמֶר.   חסד שבמלכות

44. הַיּוֹם אַרְבָּעָה וְאַרְבָּעִים יוֹם
שֶׁהֵם שִׁשָּׁה שָׁבוּעוֹת
וּשְׁנֵי יָמִים בָּעֹמֶר.   גבורה שבמלכות

45. הַיּוֹם חֲמִשָּׁה וְאַרְבָּעִים יוֹם
שֶׁהֵם שִׁשָּׁה שָׁבוּעוֹת וּשְׁלֹשָׁה
יָמִים בָּעֹמֶר.   תפארת שבמלכות

46. הַיּוֹם שִׁשָּׁה וְאַרְבָּעִים יוֹם
שֶׁהֵם שִׁשָּׁה שָׁבוּעוֹת וְאַרְבָּעָה
יָמִים בָּעֹמֶר.   נצח שבמלכות

47. הַיּוֹם שִׁבְעָה וְאַרְבָּעִים יוֹם
שֶׁהֵם שִׁשָּׁה שָׁבוּעוֹת וַחֲמִשָּׁה
יָמִים בָּעֹמֶר.   הוד שבמלכות

48. הַיּוֹם שְׁמוֹנָה וְאַרְבָּעִים יוֹם
שֶׁהֵם שִׁשָּׁה שָׁבוּעוֹת וְשִׁשָּׁה
יָמִים בָּעֹמֶר.   יסוד שבמלכות

35. הַיּוֹם חֲמִשָּׁה וּשְׁלֹשִׁים יוֹם
שֶׁהֵם חֲמִשָּׁה שָׁבוּעוֹת
בָּעֹמֶר.   מלכות שבהוד

36. הַיּוֹם שִׁשָּׁה וּשְׁלֹשִׁים יוֹם
שֶׁהֵם חֲמִשָּׁה שָׁבוּעוֹת
וְיוֹם אֶחָד בָּעֹמֶר.   חסד שביסוד

37. הַיּוֹם שִׁבְעָה וּשְׁלֹשִׁים יוֹם
שֶׁהֵם חֲמִשָּׁה שָׁבוּעוֹת
וּשְׁנֵי יָמִים בָּעֹמֶר.   גבורה שביסוד

38. הַיּוֹם שְׁמוֹנָה וּשְׁלֹשִׁים יוֹם
שֶׁהֵם חֲמִשָּׁה שָׁבוּעוֹת
וּשְׁלֹשָׁה יָמִים בָּעֹמֶר.
תפארת שביסוד

39. הַיּוֹם תִּשְׁעָה וּשְׁלֹשִׁים יוֹם
שֶׁהֵם חֲמִשָּׁה שָׁבוּעוֹת
וְאַרְבָּעָה יָמִים בָּעֹמֶר. נצח שביסוד

40. הַיּוֹם אַרְבָּעִים יוֹם
שֶׁהֵם חֲמִשָּׁה שָׁבוּעוֹת
וַחֲמִשָּׁה יָמִים בָּעֹמֶר. הוד שביסוד

41. הַיּוֹם אֶחָד וְאַרְבָּעִים יוֹם
שֶׁהֵם חֲמִשָּׁה שָׁבוּעוֹת
וְשִׁשָּׁה יָמִים בָּעֹמֶר. יסוד שביסוד

5 Sivan, Erev Shavuot

49. Today is the forty-ninth day,
    making seven weeks of the Omer.

הָרַחֲמָן May the Compassionate One
restore the Temple service to its place
speedily in our days. Amen, Selah.

Some add:

לַמְנַצֵּחַ For the conductor of music. With stringed instruments. A psalm, a song. *Ps. 67*
May God be gracious to us and bless us. May He make His face shine on us, Selah.
Then will Your way be known on earth, Your salvation among all the nations. Let
the peoples praise You, God; let all peoples praise You. Let nations rejoice and
sing for joy, for You judge the peoples with equity, and guide the nations of the
earth, Selah. Let the peoples praise You, God; let all peoples praise You. The earth
has yielded its harvest. May God, our God, bless us. God will bless us, and all the
ends of the earth will fear Him.

אָנָּא Please, by the power of Your great right hand, set the captive nation free.
Accept Your people's prayer. Strengthen us, purify us, You who are revered. Please,
mighty One, guard like the pupil of the eye those who seek Your unity. Bless them,
cleanse them, have compassion on them, grant them Your righteousness always.
Mighty One, Holy One, in Your great goodness guide Your congregation. Only
One, exalted One, turn to Your people, who proclaim Your holiness. Accept our
plea and heed our cry, You who know all secret thoughts. Blessed be the name
of His glorious kingdom for ever and all time.

רִבּוֹנוֹ שֶׁל עוֹלָם Master of the Universe, You commanded us through Your servant
Moses to count the Omer, to cleanse our carapaces and impurities, as You have
written in Your Torah: "You shall count seven complete weeks from the day *Lev. 23*
following the [Pesaḥ] rest day, when you brought the Omer as a wave-offering. To
the day after the seventh week, you shall count fifty days." This is so that the souls
of Your people Israel may be purified from their uncleanliness. May it also be
Your will, Lord our God and God of our ancestors, that in the merit of the Omer
count that I have counted today, there may be rectified any defect on my part in
the counting of (*insert the appropriate sefira for each day*). May I be cleansed and
sanctified with Your holiness on high, and through this may there flow a rich
stream through all worlds, to rectify our lives, spirits and souls from any dross
and defect, purifying and sanctifying us with Your sublime holiness. Amen, Selah.

The service continues with Aleinu on page 298.

ה בסיון, ערב שבועות

49. הַיּוֹם תִּשְׁעָה וְאַרְבָּעִים יוֹם
שֶׁהֵם שִׁבְעָה שָׁבוּעוֹת בָּעֹמֶר.   מַלְכוּת שֶׁבְּמַלְכוּת

הָרַחֲמָן הוּא יַחֲזִיר לָנוּ עֲבוֹדַת בֵּית הַמִּקְדָּשׁ לִמְקוֹמָהּ
בִּמְהֵרָה בְיָמֵינוּ, אָמֵן סֶלָה.

Some add:

לַמְנַצֵּחַ בִּנְגִינֹת, מִזְמוֹר שִׁיר: אֱלֹהִים יְחָנֵּנוּ וִיבָרְכֵנוּ, יָאֵר פָּנָיו אִתָּנוּ סֶלָה: לָדַעַת   תהלים סז
בָּאָרֶץ דַּרְכֶּךָ, בְּכָל־גּוֹיִם יְשׁוּעָתֶךָ: יוֹדוּךָ עַמִּים אֱלֹהִים, יוֹדוּךָ עַמִּים כֻּלָּם: יִשְׂמְחוּ וִירַנְּנוּ
לְאֻמִּים, כִּי־תִשְׁפֹּט עַמִּים מִישֹׁר, וּלְאֻמִּים בָּאָרֶץ תַּנְחֵם סֶלָה: יוֹדוּךָ עַמִּים אֱלֹהִים,
יוֹדוּךָ עַמִּים כֻּלָּם: אֶרֶץ נָתְנָה יְבוּלָהּ, יְבָרְכֵנוּ אֱלֹהִים אֱלֹהֵינוּ: יְבָרְכֵנוּ אֱלֹהִים, וְיִירְאוּ
אוֹתוֹ כָּל־אַפְסֵי־אָרֶץ:

אָנָּא, בְּכֹחַ גְּדֻלַּת יְמִינְךָ, תַּתִּיר צְרוּרָה. קַבֵּל רִנַּת עַמְּךָ, שַׂגְּבֵנוּ, טַהֲרֵנוּ, נוֹרָא. נָא גִבּוֹר,
דּוֹרְשֵׁי יִחוּדְךָ כְּבָבַת שָׁמְרֵם. בָּרְכֵם, טַהֲרֵם, רַחֲמֵם, צִדְקָתְךָ תָּמִיד גָּמְלֵם. חֲסִין קָדוֹשׁ,
בְּרֹב טוּבְךָ נַהֵל עֲדָתֶךָ. יָחִיד גֵּאֶה, לְעַמְּךָ פְּנֵה, זוֹכְרֵי קְדֻשָּׁתֶךָ. שַׁוְעָתֵנוּ קַבֵּל וּשְׁמַע
צַעֲקָתֵנוּ, יוֹדֵעַ תַּעֲלוּמוֹת. בָּרוּךְ שֵׁם כְּבוֹד מַלְכוּתוֹ לְעוֹלָם וָעֶד.

רִבּוֹנוֹ שֶׁל עוֹלָם, אַתָּה צִוִּיתָנוּ עַל יְדֵי מֹשֶׁה עַבְדְּךָ לִסְפֹּר סְפִירַת הָעֹמֶר, כְּדֵי לְטַהֲרֵנוּ   ויקרא כג
מִקְּלִפּוֹתֵינוּ וּמִטֻּמְאוֹתֵינוּ. כְּמוֹ שֶׁכָּתַבְתָּ בְּתוֹרָתֶךָ: וּסְפַרְתֶּם לָכֶם מִמָּחֳרַת הַשַּׁבָּת,
מִיּוֹם הֲבִיאֲכֶם אֶת־עֹמֶר הַתְּנוּפָה, שֶׁבַע שַׁבָּתוֹת תְּמִימֹת תִּהְיֶינָה: עַד מִמָּחֳרַת הַשַּׁבָּת
הַשְּׁבִיעִת תִּסְפְּרוּ חֲמִשִּׁים יוֹם: כְּדֵי שֶׁיִּטָּהֲרוּ נַפְשׁוֹת עַמְּךָ יִשְׂרָאֵל מִזֻּהֲמָתָם. וּבְכֵן יְהִי
רָצוֹן מִלְּפָנֶיךָ יהוה אֱלֹהֵינוּ וֵאלֹהֵי אֲבוֹתֵינוּ, שֶׁבִּזְכוּת סְפִירַת הָעֹמֶר שֶׁסָּפַרְתִּי הַיּוֹם,
יְתֻקַּן מַה שֶּׁפָּגַמְתִּי בִּסְפִירָה (ספירה *for day*) *(insert appropriate)* וְאֶטָּהֵר וְאֶתְקַדֵּשׁ
בִּקְדֻשָּׁה שֶׁל מַעְלָה, וְעַל יְדֵי זֶה יֻשְׁפַּע שֶׁפַע רַב בְּכָל הָעוֹלָמוֹת, לְתַקֵּן אֶת נַפְשׁוֹתֵינוּ
וְרוּחוֹתֵינוּ וְנִשְׁמוֹתֵינוּ מִכָּל סִיג וּפְגָם, וּלְטַהֲרֵנוּ וּלְקַדְּשֵׁנוּ בִּקְדֻשָּׁתְךָ הָעֶלְיוֹנָה, אָמֵן סֶלָה.

The service continues with עָלֵינוּ *on page 299.*

לַמְנַצֵּחַ *Psalm 67:* Selected to be said at this time because the psalm (excluding
the first verse, which is a superscription and not part of the psalm itself) contains forty-nine words, corresponding to the days of the counting of the Omer.

רִבּוֹנוֹ שֶׁל עוֹלָם *Master of the Universe:* a prayer emphasizing the idea that the
counting of the Omer is a time of spiritual purification.

MA'ARIV FOR MOTZA'EI SHABBAT

*In many congregations, the following two psalms are sung
before Ma'ariv at the end of Shabbat.*

לְדָוִד Of David. Blessed is the LORD, my Rock, who trains my hands   *Ps. 144*
for war, my fingers for battle. He is my Benefactor, my Fortress, my
Stronghold and my Refuge, my Shield in whom I trust, He who
subdues nations under me. LORD, what is man that You care for
him, what are mortals that You think of them? Man is no more than
a breath, his days like a fleeting shadow. LORD, part Your heavens
and come down; touch the mountains so that they pour forth
smoke. Flash forth lightning and scatter them; shoot Your arrows
and panic them. Reach out Your hand from on high; deliver me
and rescue me from the mighty waters, from the hands of strangers, whose every word is worthless, whose right hands are raised
in falsehood. To You, God, I will sing a new song; to You I will play
music on a ten-stringed harp. He who gives salvation to kings, who
saved His servant David from the cruel sword: may He deliver me
and rescue me from the hands of strangers, whose every word is
worthless, whose right hands are raised in falsehood. Then our sons
will be like saplings, well nurtured in their youth. Our daughters
will be like pillars carved for a palace. Our barns will be filled with
every kind of provision. Our sheep will increase by thousands, even
tens of thousands in our fields. Our oxen will draw heavy loads.

The story is a parable of Jewish spirituality. Shabbat is our weekly return
to the harmony and serenity of the Garden of Eden. As the day ends we, like
Adam and Eve, prepare to reengage with the world – a world often fraught
with dangers. We pray to God to be with us in the days ahead, to protect us
from harm, and to bless the work of our hands.

לְדָוִד *Psalm 144:* As the arrival of Shabbat is greeted with psalms, so is its de-
parture. Psalm 144 speaks with confidence about facing the battles that may
lie ahead, and the blessings, human and material, that come from hard work.
This is the song of a people who, trusting in God, face the future without fear.

מעריב למוצאי שבת

In many congregations, the following two psalms are sung before מעריב *on* מוצאי שבת.

תהלים קמד

לְדָוִד, בָּרוּךְ יהוה צוּרִי, הַמְלַמֵּד יָדַי לַקְרָב, אֶצְבְּעוֹתַי לַמִּלְחָמָה: חַסְדִּי וּמְצוּדָתִי מִשְׂגַּבִּי וּמְפַלְטִי לִי, מָגִנִּי וּבוֹ חָסִיתִי, הָרוֹדֵד עַמִּי תַחְתָּי: יהוה מָה־אָדָם וַתֵּדָעֵהוּ, בֶּן־אֱנוֹשׁ וַתְּחַשְּׁבֵהוּ: אָדָם לַהֶבֶל דָּמָה, יָמָיו כְּצֵל עוֹבֵר: יהוה הַט־שָׁמֶיךָ וְתֵרֵד, גַּע בֶּהָרִים וְיֶעֱשָׁנוּ: בְּרוֹק בָּרָק וּתְפִיצֵם, שְׁלַח חִצֶּיךָ וּתְהֻמֵּם: שְׁלַח יָדֶיךָ מִמָּרוֹם, פְּצֵנִי וְהַצִּילֵנִי מִמַּיִם רַבִּים, מִיַּד בְּנֵי נֵכָר: אֲשֶׁר פִּיהֶם דִּבֶּר־שָׁוְא, וִימִינָם יְמִין שָׁקֶר: אֱלֹהִים שִׁיר חָדָשׁ אָשִׁירָה לָּךְ, בְּנֵבֶל עָשׂוֹר אֲזַמְּרָה־לָּךְ: הַנּוֹתֵן תְּשׁוּעָה לַמְּלָכִים, הַפּוֹצֶה אֶת־דָּוִד עַבְדּוֹ מֵחֶרֶב רָעָה: פְּצֵנִי וְהַצִּילֵנִי מִיַּד בְּנֵי נֵכָר, אֲשֶׁר פִּיהֶם דִּבֶּר־שָׁוְא, וִימִינָם יְמִין שָׁקֶר: אֲשֶׁר בָּנֵינוּ כִּנְטִעִים, מְגֻדָּלִים בִּנְעוּרֵיהֶם, בְּנוֹתֵינוּ כְזָוִיֹּת, מְחֻטָּבוֹת תַּבְנִית הֵיכָל: מְזָוֵינוּ מְלֵאִים, מְפִיקִים מִזַּן אֶל־זַן, צֹאונֵנוּ מַאֲלִיפוֹת מְרֻבָּבוֹת

CONCLUSION OF SHABBAT

The end of Shabbat is one of the most intense Jewish experiences of time. According to rabbinic tradition (*Pirkei deRabbi Eliezer*, chapter 20), Adam and Eve were created, sinned, and were sentenced to exile from the Garden of Eden, all on the sixth day. God granted them stay of sentence, allowing them to spend one day, Shabbat itself, in the garden. During that day, say the sages, the sun did not set. As Shabbat came to an end, and darkness began to fall, the first human beings prepared to leave paradise and enter the world outside with its conflicts and challenges, hazards and fears. Assuring them that He would be with them, God gave them a gift: the ability to make light. Hence our custom of making a blessing over light in the Havdala service.

There will be no breach in the walls, no going into captivity, no cries of distress in our streets. Happy are the people for whom this is so; happy are the people whose God is the LORD.

לַמְנַצֵּחַ For the conductor of music. With stringed instruments. A *Ps. 67* psalm, a song. May God be gracious to us and bless us. May He make His face shine on us, Selah. Then will Your way be known on earth, Your salvation among all the nations. Let the peoples praise You, God; let all peoples praise You. Let nations rejoice and sing for joy, for You judge the peoples with equity, and guide the nations of the earth, Selah. Let the peoples praise You, God; let all peoples praise You. The earth has yielded its harvest. May God, our God, bless us. God will bless us, and all the ends of the earth will fear Him.

The service continues with Ma'ariv for Weekdays on page 262. After the Amida, the Leader says Half Kaddish and the congregation continues below:

וִיהִי נֹעַם May the pleasantness of the LORD our God be upon us. *Ps. 90* Establish for us the work of our hands, O establish the work of our hands.

יֹשֵׁב He who lives in the shelter of the Most High dwells in the *Ps. 91* shadow of the Almighty. I say of the LORD, my Refuge and Stronghold, my God in whom I trust, that He will save you from the fowler's snare and the deadly pestilence. With His pinions He

⎯⎯⎯⎯⎯⎯⎯⎯⎯⎯⎯⎯⎯⎯⎯⎯⎯⎯⎯⎯⎯⎯⎯⎯⎯⎯⎯⎯⎯⎯⎯⎯

deliverance from harm. It is said at the end of Shabbat as a prayer for God's protection against the dangers that may lie ahead in the coming week. It is prefaced by the last verse of the previous psalm. According to tradition (Rashi, Ex. 39:43), this was the blessing Moses gave to those who had helped build the Sanctuary, adding: "May the Divine Presence rest in the work of your hands." Said here at the beginning of the workday week, it is a prayer that God may send His blessings for our labors.

This and the following section are not said in a week in which a Festival falls, because we do not then face a full working week, and because the merit of the coming Festival itself is an augury of divine protection.

בְּחוּצוֹתֵינוּ: אַלּוּפֵינוּ מְסֻבָּלִים, אֵין פֶּרֶץ וְאֵין יוֹצֵאת, וְאֵין צְוָחָה
בִּרְחֹבֹתֵינוּ: אַשְׁרֵי הָעָם שֶׁכָּכָה לּוֹ, אַשְׁרֵי הָעָם שֶׁיהוה אֱלֹהָיו:

תהלים סז

לַמְנַצֵּחַ בִּנְגִינֹת, מִזְמוֹר שִׁיר: אֱלֹהִים יְחָנֵּנוּ וִיבָרְכֵנוּ, יָאֵר פָּנָיו
אִתָּנוּ סֶלָה: לָדַעַת בָּאָרֶץ דַּרְכֶּךָ, בְּכָל־גּוֹיִם יְשׁוּעָתֶךָ: יוֹדוּךָ עַמִּים
אֱלֹהִים, יוֹדוּךָ עַמִּים כֻּלָּם: יִשְׂמְחוּ וִירַנְּנוּ לְאֻמִּים, כִּי־תִשְׁפֹּט עַמִּים
מִישֹׁר, וּלְאֻמִּים בָּאָרֶץ תַּנְחֵם סֶלָה: יוֹדוּךָ עַמִּים אֱלֹהִים, יוֹדוּךָ
עַמִּים כֻּלָּם: אֶרֶץ נָתְנָה יְבוּלָהּ, יְבָרְכֵנוּ אֱלֹהִים אֱלֹהֵינוּ: יְבָרְכֵנוּ
אֱלֹהִים, וְיִירְאוּ אוֹתוֹ כָּל־אַפְסֵי־אָרֶץ:

The service continues with מעריב לחול *on page 263. After the* עמידה,
the שליח ציבור *says* חצי קדיש *and the* קהל *continues below:*

תהלים צ

וִיהִי נֹעַם אֲדֹנָי אֱלֹהֵינוּ עָלֵינוּ וּמַעֲשֵׂה יָדֵינוּ כּוֹנְנָה עָלֵינוּ וּמַעֲשֵׂה
יָדֵינוּ כּוֹנְנֵהוּ:

תהלים צא

יֹשֵׁב בְּסֵתֶר עֶלְיוֹן, בְּצֵל שַׁדַּי יִתְלוֹנָן: אֹמַר לַיהוה מַחְסִי וּמְצוּדָתִי,
אֱלֹהַי אֶבְטַח־בּוֹ: כִּי הוּא יַצִּילְךָ מִפַּח יָקוּשׁ, מִדֶּבֶר הַוּוֹת:
בְּאֶבְרָתוֹ יָסֶךְ לָךְ, וְתַחַת־כְּנָפָיו תֶּחְסֶה, צִנָּה וְסֹחֵרָה אֲמִתּוֹ:
לֹא־תִירָא מִפַּחַד לָיְלָה, מֵחֵץ יָעוּף יוֹמָם: מִדֶּבֶר בָּאֹפֶל יַהֲלֹךְ,

---

לַמְנַצֵּחַ *Psalm 67: A psalm of thanksgiving whose key phrase is "the earth
has yielded its harvest." The second verse uses language reminiscent of the
Priestly blessings. The word "earth" appears four times in a variety of senses,
suggesting that when we do God's will on earth, the earth yields its blessings
with the result that God is recognized by all nations of the earth. As we prepare to meet the time that recalls Adam's exile from Eden, we do so in a spirit
directly opposite to the mood that prevailed then. Then it was said: "Cursed
be the ground because of you" (Gen. 3:17). Now we pray for it to be blessed.*

וִיהִי נֹעַם *May the pleasantness of the Lord: Psalm 91 which follows immediately is known as the Psalm of Blessing and is the most famous of prayers for*

will cover you, and beneath His wings you will find shelter; His faithfulness is an encircling shield. You need not fear terror by night, nor the arrow that flies by day; not the pestilence that stalks in darkness, nor the plague that ravages at noon. A thousand may fall at your side, ten thousand at your right hand, but it will not come near you. You will only look with your eyes and see the punishment of the wicked. Because you said, "The LORD is my Refuge," taking the Most High as your shelter, no harm will befall you, no plague come near your tent, for He will command His angels about you, to guard you in all your ways. They will lift you in their hands, lest your foot stumble on a stone. You will tread on lions and vipers; you will trample on young lions and snakes. [God says:] "Because he loves Me, I will rescue him; I will protect him, because he acknowledges My name. When he calls on Me, I will answer him; I will be with him in distress, I will deliver him and bring him honor.
▸ With long life I will satisfy him and show him My salvation.
   With long life I will satisfy him and show him My salvation.

▸ You are the Holy One, enthroned on the praises of Israel.   Ps. 22
   And [the angels] call to one another, saying, "Holy, holy, holy   Is. 6
   is the LORD of hosts; the whole world is filled with His glory."

   And they receive permission from one another, saying: Targum
   "Holy in the highest heavens, home of His Presence;   Yonatan
   holy on earth, the work of His strength;   Is. 6
   holy for ever and all time is the LORD of hosts;
   the whole earth is full of His radiant glory."

▸ Then a wind lifted me up and I heard behind me the sound of   Ezek. 3
   a great noise, saying, "Blessed is the LORD's glory from His place."

   Then a wind lifted me up and I heard behind me   Targum
   the sound of a great tempest of those who uttered praise, saying,   Yonatan
   "Blessed is the LORD's glory from the place of the home of His Presence."   Ezek. 3

   The LORD shall reign for ever and all time.   Ex. 15

   The LORD's kingdom is established for ever and all time.   Targum
                                                              Onkelos Ex. 15

מִקְטֶב יָשׁוּד צָהֳרָיִם: יִפֹּל מִצִּדְּךָ אֶלֶף, וּרְבָבָה מִימִינֶךָ, אֵלֶיךָ
לֹא יִגָּשׁ: רַק בְּעֵינֶיךָ תַבִּיט, וְשִׁלֻּמַת רְשָׁעִים תִּרְאֶה: כִּי־אַתָּה
יהוה מַחְסִי, עֶלְיוֹן שַׂמְתָּ מְעוֹנֶךָ: לֹא־תְאֻנֶּה אֵלֶיךָ רָעָה, וְנֶגַע
לֹא־יִקְרַב בְּאָהֳלֶךָ: כִּי מַלְאָכָיו יְצַוֶּה־לָּךְ, לִשְׁמָרְךָ בְּכָל־דְּרָכֶיךָ:
עַל־כַּפַּיִם יִשָּׂאוּנְךָ, פֶּן־תִּגֹּף בָּאֶבֶן רַגְלֶךָ: עַל־שַׁחַל וָפֶתֶן תִּדְרֹךְ,
תִּרְמֹס כְּפִיר וְתַנִּין: כִּי בִי חָשַׁק וַאֲפַלְּטֵהוּ, אֲשַׂגְּבֵהוּ כִּי־יָדַע
שְׁמִי: יִקְרָאֵנִי וְאֶעֱנֵהוּ, עִמּוֹ אָנֹכִי בְצָרָה, אֲחַלְּצֵהוּ וַאֲכַבְּדֵהוּ:

‹ אֹרֶךְ יָמִים אַשְׂבִּיעֵהוּ, וְאַרְאֵהוּ בִּישׁוּעָתִי:
   אֹרֶךְ יָמִים אַשְׂבִּיעֵהוּ, וְאַרְאֵהוּ בִּישׁוּעָתִי:

תהלים כב

‹ וְאַתָּה קָדוֹשׁ יוֹשֵׁב תְּהִלּוֹת יִשְׂרָאֵל: וְקָרָא זֶה אֶל־זֶה וְאָמַר

ישעיה ו

קָדוֹשׁ, קָדוֹשׁ, קָדוֹשׁ, יהוה צְבָאוֹת, מְלֹא כָל־הָאָרֶץ כְּבוֹדוֹ:

תרגום יונתן
ישעיה ו

וּמְקַבְּלִין דֵּין מִן דֵּין וְאָמְרִין, קַדִּישׁ בִּשְׁמֵי מְרוֹמָא עִלָּאָה בֵּית שְׁכִינְתֵּהּ
קַדִּישׁ עַל אַרְעָא עוֹבַד גְּבוּרְתֵּהּ, קַדִּישׁ לְעָלַם וּלְעָלְמֵי עָלְמַיָּא
יהוה צְבָאוֹת, מַלְיָא כָל אַרְעָא זִיו יְקָרֵהּ.

‹ וַתִּשָּׂאֵנִי רוּחַ, וָאֶשְׁמַע אַחֲרַי קוֹל רַעַשׁ גָּדוֹל

יחזקאל ג

בָּרוּךְ כְּבוֹד־יהוה מִמְּקוֹמוֹ:

תרגום יונתן
יחזקאל ג

וּנְטָלַתְנִי רוּחָא, וּשְׁמָעִית בַּתְרַי קָל זִיעַ סַגִּיא, דִּמְשַׁבְּחִין וְאָמְרִין
בְּרִיךְ יְקָרָא דַיהוה מֵאֲתַר בֵּית שְׁכִינְתֵּהּ.

יהוה יִמְלֹךְ לְעֹלָם וָעֶד:

שמות טו
תרגום אונקלוס
שמות טו

יהוה מַלְכוּתֵהּ קָאֵם לְעָלַם וּלְעָלְמֵי עָלְמַיָּא.

וְאַתָּה קָדוֹשׁ *You are the Holy One:* This prayer, with its parallels in the weekday
morning and Shabbat afternoon services, was usually associated with periods
of communal study. Its presence here may hark back to a time when it was
customary to dedicate time to a period of study at the end of Shabbat.

יהוה Lord, God of Abraham, Isaac and Yisrael, our ancestors, may   *1 Chr. 29*
You keep this for ever so that it forms the thoughts in Your people's
heart, and directs their heart toward You. He is compassionate. He   *Ps. 78*
forgives iniquity and does not destroy. Repeatedly He suppresses
His anger, not rousing His full wrath. For You, my Lord, are good   *Ps. 86*
and forgiving, abundantly kind to all who call on You. Your righ-   *Ps. 119*
teousness is eternally righteous, and Your Torah is truth. Grant   *Micah 7*
truth to Jacob, loving-kindness to Abraham, as You promised our
ancestors in ancient times. Blessed is my Lord for day after day He   *Ps. 68*
burdens us [with His blessings]; God is our salvation, Selah! The   *Ps. 46*
Lord of hosts is with us; the God of Jacob is our refuge, Selah!
Lord of hosts, happy is the one who trusts in You. Lord, save!   *Ps. 84*
                                                                     Ps. 20
May the King answer us on the day we call.

בָּרוּךְ Blessed is He, our God, who created us for His glory, separating us from those who go astray; who gave us the Torah of truth,
planting within us eternal life. May He open our heart to His Torah,
imbuing our heart with the love and awe of Him, that we may do
His will and serve Him with a perfect heart, so that we neither toil
in vain nor give birth to confusion.

יְהִי רָצוֹן May it be Your will, O Lord our God and God of our ancestors, that we keep Your laws in this world, and thus be worthy to live,
see and inherit goodness and blessing in the Messianic Age and in
the life of the World to Come. So that my soul may sing to You and   *Ps. 30*
not be silent. Lord, my God, for ever I will thank You. Blessed is   *Jer. 17*
the man who trusts in the Lord, whose trust is in the Lord alone.
Trust in the Lord for evermore, for God, the Lord, is an everlast-   *Is. 26*
ing Rock. ► Those who know Your name trust in You, for You, Lord,   *Ps. 9*
do not forsake those who seek You. The Lord desired, for the sake   *Is. 42*
of Israel's merit, to make the Torah great and glorious.

דברי הימים
א׳ כט
יהוה אֱלֹהֵי אַבְרָהָם יִצְחָק וְיִשְׂרָאֵל אֲבֹתֵינוּ, שָׁמְרָה־זֹּאת לְעוֹלָם

תהלים עח
לְיֵצֶר מַחְשְׁבוֹת לְבַב עַמֶּךָ, וְהָכֵן לְבָבָם אֵלֶיךָ: וְהוּא רַחוּם יְכַפֵּר
עָוֹן וְלֹא־יַשְׁחִית, וְהִרְבָּה לְהָשִׁיב אַפּוֹ, וְלֹא־יָעִיר כָּל־חֲמָתוֹ:

תהלים פו
תהלים קיט
מיכה ז
כִּי־אַתָּה אֲדֹנָי טוֹב וְסַלָּח, וְרַב־חֶסֶד לְכָל־קֹרְאֶיךָ: צִדְקָתְךָ
צֶדֶק לְעוֹלָם וְתוֹרָתְךָ אֱמֶת: תִּתֵּן אֱמֶת לְיַעֲקֹב, חֶסֶד לְאַבְרָהָם,

תהלים סח
אֲשֶׁר־נִשְׁבַּעְתָּ לַאֲבֹתֵינוּ מִימֵי קֶדֶם: בָּרוּךְ אֲדֹנָי יוֹם יוֹם יַעֲמָס־

תהלים מו
לָנוּ, הָאֵל יְשׁוּעָתֵנוּ סֶלָה: יהוה צְבָאוֹת עִמָּנוּ, מִשְׂגָּב לָנוּ אֱלֹהֵי

תהלים פד
תהלים כ
יַעֲקֹב סֶלָה: יהוה צְבָאוֹת, אַשְׁרֵי אָדָם בֹּטֵחַ בָּךְ: יהוה הוֹשִׁיעָה,
הַמֶּלֶךְ יַעֲנֵנוּ בְיוֹם־קָרְאֵנוּ:

בָּרוּךְ הוּא אֱלֹהֵינוּ שֶׁבְּרָאָנוּ לִכְבוֹדוֹ, וְהִבְדִּילָנוּ מִן הַתּוֹעִים,
וְנָתַן לָנוּ תּוֹרַת אֱמֶת, וְחַיֵּי עוֹלָם נָטַע בְּתוֹכֵנוּ. הוּא יִפְתַּח לִבֵּנוּ
בְּתוֹרָתוֹ, וְיָשֵׂם בְּלִבֵּנוּ אַהֲבָתוֹ וְיִרְאָתוֹ וְלַעֲשׂוֹת רְצוֹנוֹ וּלְעָבְדוֹ
בְּלֵבָב שָׁלֵם, לְמַעַן לֹא נִיגַע לָרִיק וְלֹא נֵלֵד לַבֶּהָלָה.

יְהִי רָצוֹן מִלְּפָנֶיךָ יהוה אֱלֹהֵינוּ וֵאלֹהֵי אֲבוֹתֵינוּ, שֶׁנִּשְׁמֹר חֻקֶּיךָ
בָּעוֹלָם הַזֶּה, וְנִזְכֶּה וְנִחְיֶה וְנִרְאֶה וְנִירַשׁ טוֹבָה וּבְרָכָה, לִשְׁנֵי

תהלים ל
יְמוֹת הַמָּשִׁיחַ וּלְחַיֵּי הָעוֹלָם הַבָּא. לְמַעַן יְזַמֶּרְךָ כָבוֹד וְלֹא יִדֹּם,

ירמיה יז
יהוה אֱלֹהַי, לְעוֹלָם אוֹדֶךָּ: בָּרוּךְ הַגֶּבֶר אֲשֶׁר יִבְטַח בַּיהוה,

ישעיה כו
וְהָיָה יהוה מִבְטַחוֹ: בִּטְחוּ בַיהוה עֲדֵי־עַד, כִּי בְּיָהּ יהוה צוּר

תהלים ט
עוֹלָמִים: ◂ וְיִבְטְחוּ בְךָ יוֹדְעֵי שְׁמֶךָ, כִּי לֹא־עָזַבְתָּ דֹרְשֶׁיךָ, יהוה:

ישעיה מב
יהוה חָפֵץ לְמַעַן צִדְקוֹ, יַגְדִּיל תּוֹרָה וְיַאְדִּיר:

FULL KADDISH

Leader: יִתְגַּדַּל Magnified and sanctified may His great name be,
in the world He created by His will.
May He establish His kingdom in your lifetime
and in your days,
and in the lifetime of all the house of Israel,
swiftly and soon –
and say: Amen.

All: May His great name be blessed for ever and all time.

Leader: Blessed and praised,
glorified and exalted,
raised and honored,
uplifted and lauded be
the name of the Holy One,
blessed be He,
beyond any blessing,
song, praise and consolation uttered in the world –
and say: Amen.

*On Purim and Tisha B'Av, omit the next verse and
continue with "May there be great peace."*

May the prayers and pleas of all Israel
be accepted by their Father in heaven –
and say: Amen.

May there be great peace from heaven,
and life for us and all Israel –
and say: Amen.

*Bow, take three steps back, as if taking leave of the Divine Presence,
then bow, first left, then right, then center, while saying:*

May He who makes peace in His high places,
make peace for us and all Israel –
and say: Amen.

קדיש שלם

ש״ץ: יִתְגַּדַּל וְיִתְקַדַּשׁ שְׁמֵהּ רַבָּא (קהל: אָמֵן)

בְּעָלְמָא דִּי בְרָא כִרְעוּתֵהּ

וְיַמְלִיךְ מַלְכוּתֵהּ

בְּחַיֵּיכוֹן וּבְיוֹמֵיכוֹן וּבְחַיֵּי דְכָל בֵּית יִשְׂרָאֵל

בַּעֲגָלָא וּבִזְמַן קָרִיב, וְאִמְרוּ אָמֵן. (קהל: אָמֵן)

קהל ושץ: יְהֵא שְׁמֵהּ רַבָּא מְבָרַךְ לְעָלַם וּלְעָלְמֵי עָלְמַיָּא.

ש״ץ: יִתְבָּרַךְ וְיִשְׁתַּבַּח וְיִתְפָּאַר

וְיִתְרוֹמַם וְיִתְנַשֵּׂא וְיִתְהַדָּר וְיִתְעַלֶּה וְיִתְהַלָּל

שְׁמֵהּ דְּקֻדְשָׁא בְּרִיךְ הוּא (קהל: בְּרִיךְ הוּא)

לְעֵלָּא מִן כָּל בִּרְכָתָא

/בעשרת ימי תשובה: לְעֵלָּא לְעֵלָּא מִכָּל בִּרְכָתָא/

וְשִׁירָתָא, תֻּשְׁבְּחָתָא וְנֶחֱמָתָא

דַּאֲמִירָן בְּעָלְמָא, וְאִמְרוּ אָמֵן. (קהל: אָמֵן)

On פורים and תשעה באב, תשעה, omit the next verse and continue with יְהֵא שְׁלָמָא.

תִּתְקַבֵּל צְלוֹתְהוֹן וּבָעוּתְהוֹן דְּכָל יִשְׂרָאֵל

קֳדָם אֲבוּהוֹן דִּי בִשְׁמַיָּא, וְאִמְרוּ אָמֵן. (קהל: אָמֵן)

יְהֵא שְׁלָמָא רַבָּא מִן שְׁמַיָּא

וְחַיִּים, עָלֵינוּ וְעַל כָּל יִשְׂרָאֵל, וְאִמְרוּ אָמֵן. (קהל: אָמֵן)

Bow, take three steps back, as if taking leave of the Divine Presence,
then bow, first left, then right, then center, while saying:

עֹשֶׂה שָׁלוֹם /בעשרת ימי תשובה: הַשָּׁלוֹם/ בִּמְרוֹמָיו

הוּא יַעֲשֶׂה שָׁלוֹם עָלֵינוּ וְעַל כָּל יִשְׂרָאֵל

וְאִמְרוּ אָמֵן. (קהל: אָמֵן)

Between Pesaḥ and Shavuot the Omer is counted at this point on page 304.

On Ḥanukka, the candles are lit at this point, page 404.

On Tisha B'Av, the following prayers are omitted and the service continues with Aleinu on page 332.

BIBLICAL VERSES OF BLESSING

וְיִתֶּן־לְךָ May God give you dew from heaven and the richness of the earth, and *Gen. 27* corn and wine in plenty. May peoples serve you and nations bow down to you. Be lord over your brothers, and may your mother's sons bow down to you. A curse on those who curse you, but a blessing on those who bless you.

וְאֵל שַׁדַּי May God Almighty bless you; may He make you fruitful and numer- *Gen. 28* ous until you become an assembly of peoples. May He give you and your descendants the blessing of Abraham, that you may possess the land where you are now staying, the land God gave to Abraham. This comes from the *Gen. 49* God of your father – may He help you – and from the Almighty – may He bless you with blessings of the heaven above and the blessings of the deep that lies below, the blessings of breast and womb. The blessings of your father surpass the blessings of my fathers to the bounds of the endless hills. May they rest on the head of Joseph, on the brow of the prince among his brothers. He will love you and bless you and increase your numbers. He will bless the *Deut. 7* fruit of your womb and the fruit of your land: your corn, your wine and oil, the calves of your herds and the lambs of your flocks, in the land He swore to your fathers to give you. You will be blessed more than any other people. None of your men or women will be childless, nor any of your livestock without young. The LORD will keep you free from any disease. He will not inflict on you the terrible diseases you knew in Egypt, but He will inflict them on those who hate you.

הַמַּלְאָךְ May the angel who rescued me from all harm, bless these boys. May *Gen. 48* they be called by my name and the names of my fathers Abraham and Isaac, and may they increase greatly on the earth. The LORD your God has increased *Deut. 1* your numbers so that today you are as many as the stars in the sky. May the LORD, God of your fathers, increase you a thousand times, and bless you as He promised you.

---

to begin the next stage, confident in the knowledge that God is with us. They begin with the blessings of Isaac to Jacob, Jacob to Joseph and his brothers, and Moses' closing addresses to the Israelites in the book of Deuteronomy.

Between פסח *and* שבועות *the* עומר *is counted at this point on page 305.*

On חנוכה, *the candles are lit at this point, page 405.*

On תשעה באב, *the following prayers are omitted
and the service continues with* עלינו *on page 333.*

פסוקי ברכה

וְיִתֶּן־לְךָ הָאֱלֹהִים מִטַּל הַשָּׁמַיִם וּמִשְׁמַנֵּי הָאָרֶץ, וְרֹב דָּגָן וְתִירֹשׁ: יַעַבְדוּךָ בראשית כז
עַמִּים וְיִשְׁתַּחֲווּ לְךָ לְאֻמִּים, הֱוֵה גְבִיר לְאַחֶיךָ וְיִשְׁתַּחֲווּ לְךָ בְּנֵי אִמֶּךָ,
אֹרְרֶיךָ אָרוּר וּמְבָרֲכֶיךָ בָּרוּךְ:

וְאֵל שַׁדַּי יְבָרֵךְ אֹתְךָ וְיַפְרְךָ וְיַרְבֶּךָ, וְהָיִיתָ לִקְהַל עַמִּים: וְיִתֶּן־לְךָ אֶת־ בראשית כח
בִּרְכַּת אַבְרָהָם, לְךָ וּלְזַרְעֲךָ אִתָּךְ, לְרִשְׁתְּךָ אֶת־אֶרֶץ מְגֻרֶיךָ אֲשֶׁר־נָתַן
אֱלֹהִים לְאַבְרָהָם: מֵאֵל אָבִיךָ וְיַעְזְרֶךָּ וְאֵת שַׁדַּי וִיבָרֲכֶךָּ, בִּרְכֹת שָׁמַיִם בראשית מט
מֵעָל בִּרְכֹת תְּהוֹם רֹבֶצֶת תָּחַת, בִּרְכֹת שָׁדַיִם וָרָחַם: בִּרְכֹת אָבִיךָ גָּבְרוּ
עַל־בִּרְכֹת הוֹרַי עַד־תַּאֲוַת גִּבְעֹת עוֹלָם, תִּהְיֶןָ לְרֹאשׁ יוֹסֵף וּלְקָדְקֹד
נְזִיר אֶחָיו: וַאֲהֵבְךָ וּבֵרַכְךָ וְהִרְבֶּךָ, וּבֵרַךְ פְּרִי־בִטְנְךָ וּפְרִי־אַדְמָתֶךָ, דְּגָנְךָ דברים ז
וְתִירֹשְׁךָ וְיִצְהָרֶךָ, שְׁגַר־אֲלָפֶיךָ וְעַשְׁתְּרֹת צֹאנֶךָ, עַל הָאֲדָמָה אֲשֶׁר־נִשְׁבַּע
לַאֲבֹתֶיךָ לָתֶת לָךְ: בָּרוּךְ תִּהְיֶה מִכָּל־הָעַמִּים, לֹא־יִהְיֶה בְךָ עָקָר וַעֲקָרָה
וּבִבְהֶמְתֶּךָ: וְהֵסִיר יהוה מִמְּךָ כָּל־חֹלִי, וְכָל־מַדְוֵי מִצְרַיִם הָרָעִים אֲשֶׁר
יָדַעְתָּ, לֹא יְשִׂימָם בָּךְ, וּנְתָנָם בְּכָל־שֹׂנְאֶיךָ:

הַמַּלְאָךְ הַגֹּאֵל אֹתִי מִכָּל־רָע יְבָרֵךְ אֶת־הַנְּעָרִים, וְיִקָּרֵא בָהֶם שְׁמִי וְשֵׁם בראשית מח
אֲבֹתַי אַבְרָהָם וְיִצְחָק, וְיִדְגּוּ לָרֹב בְּקֶרֶב הָאָרֶץ: יהוה אֱלֹהֵיכֶם הִרְבָּה דברים א
אֶתְכֶם, וְהִנְּכֶם הַיּוֹם כְּכוֹכְבֵי הַשָּׁמַיִם לָרֹב: יהוה אֱלֹהֵי אֲבוֹתֵכֶם יֹסֵף
עֲלֵיכֶם כָּכֶם אֶלֶף פְּעָמִים, וִיבָרֵךְ אֶתְכֶם כַּאֲשֶׁר דִּבֶּר לָכֶם:

פסוקי ברכה *Biblical Verses of Blessing.* Setting out on a journey is a time to
seek blessing and divine protection through the challenges that lie ahead,
hence this long series of verses from Tanakh, including many of the blessings recorded in the Mosaic books. They are clustered around the themes of
blessing, redemption and salvation; rescue and transformation; peace and
consolation. Together they emphasize that time is a journey and we are about

בָּרוּךְ You will be blessed in the city, and blessed in the field. You will be blessed   *Deut. 28*
when you come in, and blessed when you go out. Your basket and your knead-
ing trough will be blessed. The fruit of your womb will be blessed, and the
crops of your land, and the young of your livestock, the calves of your herds
and the lambs of your flocks. The LORD will send a blessing on your barns,
and on everything you put your hand to. The LORD your God will bless you
in the land He is giving you. The LORD will open for you the heavens, the
storehouse of His bounty, to send rain on your land in season, and to bless all
the work of your hands. You will lend to many nations but will borrow from
none. For the LORD your God will bless you as He has promised: you will lend   *Deut. 15*
to many nations but will borrow from none. You will rule over many nations,
but none will rule over you. Happy are you, Israel! Who is like you, a people   *Deut. 33*
saved by the LORD? He is your Shield and Helper and your glorious Sword.
Your enemies will cower before you, and you will tread on their high places.

מָחִיתִי I have wiped away your transgressions like a cloud, your sins like the   *Is. 44*
morning mist. Return to Me for I have redeemed you. Sing for joy, O heavens, for the LORD has done this; shout aloud, you depths of the earth; burst
into song, you mountains, you forests and all your trees, for the LORD has
redeemed Jacob, and will glory in Israel. Our Redeemer, the LORD of hosts is   *Is. 47*
His name, the Holy One of Israel.

יִשְׂרָאֵל Israel is saved by the LORD with everlasting salvation. You will never   *Is. 45*
be ashamed or disgraced to time everlasting. You will eat your fill and praise   *Joel 2*
the name of the LORD your God, who has worked wonders for you. Never
again shall My people be shamed. Then you will know that I am in the midst
of Israel, that I am the LORD your God, and there is no other. Never again
will My people be shamed. You will go out in joy and be led out in peace. The   *Is. 55*
mountains and hills will burst into song before you, and all the trees of the
field will clap their hands. Behold, God is my salvation, I will trust and not   *Is. 12*
be afraid. The LORD, the LORD, is my strength and my song. He has become
my salvation. With joy you will draw water from the springs of salvation. On
that day you will say, "Thank the LORD, proclaim His name, make His deeds
known among the nations." Declare that His name is exalted. Sing to the LORD,
for He has done glorious things; let this be known throughout the world.
Shout aloud and sing for joy, you who dwell in Zion, for great in your midst
is the Holy One of Israel. On that day they will say, "See, this is our God; we   *Is. 25*
set our hope in Him and He saved us. This is the LORD in whom we hoped;
let us rejoice and be glad in His salvation."

דברים כח

בָּרוּךְ אַתָּה בָּעִיר, וּבָרוּךְ אַתָּה בַּשָּׂדֶה: בָּרוּךְ אַתָּה בְּבֹאֶךָ, וּבָרוּךְ אַתָּה בְּצֵאתֶךָ: בָּרוּךְ טַנְאֲךָ וּמִשְׁאַרְתֶּךָ: בָּרוּךְ פְּרִי־בִטְנְךָ וּפְרִי אַדְמָתְךָ וּפְרִי בְהֶמְתֶּךָ, שְׁגַר אֲלָפֶיךָ וְעַשְׁתְּרוֹת צֹאנֶךָ: יְצַו יהוה אִתְּךָ אֶת־הַבְּרָכָה בַּאֲסָמֶיךָ וּבְכֹל מִשְׁלַח יָדֶךָ, וּבֵרַכְךָ בָּאָרֶץ אֲשֶׁר־יהוה אֱלֹהֶיךָ נֹתֵן לָךְ: יִפְתַּח יהוה לְךָ אֶת־אוֹצָרוֹ הַטּוֹב אֶת־הַשָּׁמַיִם, לָתֵת מְטַר־אַרְצְךָ בְּעִתּוֹ,

דברים טו

וּלְבָרֵךְ אֵת כָּל־מַעֲשֵׂה יָדֶךָ, וְהִלְוִיתָ גּוֹיִם רַבִּים וְאַתָּה לֹא תִלְוֶה: כִּי־יהוה אֱלֹהֶיךָ בֵּרַכְךָ כַּאֲשֶׁר דִּבֶּר־לָךְ, וְהַעֲבַטְתָּ גּוֹיִם רַבִּים וְאַתָּה לֹא תַעֲבֹט, וּמָשַׁלְתָּ בְּגוֹיִם רַבִּים וּבְךָ לֹא יִמְשֹׁלוּ:

דברים לג

אַשְׁרֶיךָ יִשְׂרָאֵל, מִי כָמוֹךָ, עַם נוֹשַׁע בַּיהוה, מָגֵן עֶזְרֶךָ וַאֲשֶׁר־חֶרֶב גַּאֲוָתֶךָ, וְיִכָּחֲשׁוּ אֹיְבֶיךָ לָךְ, וְאַתָּה עַל־בָּמוֹתֵימוֹ תִדְרֹךְ:

ישעיה מד

מָחִיתִי כָעָב פְּשָׁעֶיךָ וְכֶעָנָן חַטֹּאותֶיךָ, שׁוּבָה אֵלַי כִּי גְאַלְתִּיךָ: רָנּוּ שָׁמַיִם כִּי־עָשָׂה יהוה, הָרִיעוּ תַּחְתִּיּוֹת אָרֶץ, פִּצְחוּ הָרִים רִנָּה, יַעַר וְכָל־עֵץ בּוֹ,

ישעיה מה

כִּי־גָאַל יהוה יַעֲקֹב וּבְיִשְׂרָאֵל יִתְפָּאָר: גֹּאֲלֵנוּ, יהוה צְבָאוֹת שְׁמוֹ, קְדוֹשׁ יִשְׂרָאֵל:

ישעיה מה

יִשְׂרָאֵל נוֹשַׁע בַּיהוה תְּשׁוּעַת עוֹלָמִים, לֹא־תֵבֹשׁוּ וְלֹא־תִכָּלְמוּ עַד־עוֹלְמֵי עַד:

יואל ב

וַאֲכַלְתֶּם אָכוֹל וְשָׂבוֹעַ, וְהִלַּלְתֶּם אֶת־שֵׁם יהוה אֱלֹהֵיכֶם אֲשֶׁר־עָשָׂה עִמָּכֶם לְהַפְלִיא, וְלֹא־יֵבֹשׁוּ עַמִּי לְעוֹלָם: וִידַעְתֶּם כִּי בְקֶרֶב יִשְׂרָאֵל

ישעיה נה

אָנִי, וַאֲנִי יהוה אֱלֹהֵיכֶם וְאֵין עוֹד, וְלֹא־יֵבֹשׁוּ עַמִּי לְעוֹלָם: כִּי־בְשִׂמְחָה תֵצֵאוּ וּבְשָׁלוֹם תּוּבָלוּן, הֶהָרִים וְהַגְּבָעוֹת יִפְצְחוּ לִפְנֵיכֶם רִנָּה, וְכָל־עֲצֵי

ישעיה יב

הַשָּׂדֶה יִמְחֲאוּ־כָף: הִנֵּה אֵל יְשׁוּעָתִי אֶבְטַח, וְלֹא אֶפְחָד, כִּי־עָזִּי וְזִמְרָת יָהּ יהוה, וַיְהִי־לִי לִישׁוּעָה: וּשְׁאַבְתֶּם־מַיִם בְּשָׂשׂוֹן, מִמַּעַיְנֵי הַיְשׁוּעָה: וַאֲמַרְתֶּם בַּיּוֹם הַהוּא, הוֹדוּ לַיהוה קִרְאוּ בִשְׁמוֹ, הוֹדִיעוּ בָעַמִּים עֲלִילֹתָיו, הַזְכִּירוּ כִּי נִשְׂגָּב שְׁמוֹ: זַמְּרוּ יהוה כִּי גֵאוּת עָשָׂה, מוּדַעַת זֹאת בְּכָל־

ישעיה כה

הָאָרֶץ: צַהֲלִי וָרֹנִּי יוֹשֶׁבֶת צִיּוֹן, כִּי־גָדוֹל בְּקִרְבֵּךְ קְדוֹשׁ יִשְׂרָאֵל: וְאָמַר בַּיּוֹם הַהוּא, הִנֵּה אֱלֹהֵינוּ זֶה קִוִּינוּ לוֹ וְיוֹשִׁיעֵנוּ, זֶה יהוה קִוִּינוּ לוֹ, נָגִילָה וְנִשְׂמְחָה בִּישׁוּעָתוֹ:

בֵּית Come, house of Jacob: let us walk in the light of the Lord. He will be the *Is. 2*
sure foundation of your times; a rich store of salvation, wisdom and knowl- *Is. 32*
edge – the fear of the Lord is a person's treasure. In everything he did, David *1 Sam. 18*
was successful, for the Lord was with him.

פָּדָה He redeemed my soul in peace from the battle waged against me, for the *Ps. 55*
sake of the many who were with me. The people said to Saul, "Shall Jonathan *1 Sam. 14*
die – he who has brought about this great deliverance in Israel? Heaven forbid!
As surely as the Lord lives, not a hair of his head shall fall to the ground, for he
did this today with God's help." So the people rescued Jonathan and he did not
die. Those redeemed by the Lord shall return; they will enter Zion singing; *Is. 35*
everlasting joy will crown their heads. Gladness and joy will overtake them, and
sorrow and sighing will flee away.

הָפַכְתָּ You have turned my sorrow into dancing. You have removed my sackcloth *Ps. 30*
and clothed me with joy. The Lord your God refused to listen to Balaam; in- *Deut. 23*
stead the Lord your God turned the curse into a blessing, for the Lord your
God loves you. Then maidens will dance and be glad; so too will young men and *Jer. 31*
old together; I will turn their mourning into gladness; I will give them comfort
and joy instead of sorrow.

בּוֹרֵא I create the speech of lips: Peace, peace to those far and near, says the Lord, *Is. 57*
and I will heal them. Then the spirit came upon Amasai, chief of the captains, *1 Chr. 12*
and he said: "We are yours, David! We are with you, son of Jesse! Peace, peace to
you, and peace to those who help you; for your God will help you." Then David
received them and made them leaders of his troop. And you shall say: "To life! *1 Sam. 25*
Peace be to you, peace to your household, and peace to all that is yours!" The *Ps. 29*
Lord will give strength to His people; the Lord will bless His people with peace.

אָמַר Rabbi Yoḥanan said: Wherever you find the greatness of the Holy One, *Megilla 31a*
blessed be He, there you find His humility. This is written in the Torah, repeated
in the Prophets, and stated a third time in the Writings. It is written in the
Torah: "For the Lord your God is God of gods and Lord of lords, the great, *Deut. 10*
mighty and awe-inspiring God, who shows no favoritism and accepts no bribe."
Immediately afterwards it is written, "He upholds the cause of the orphan and
widow, and loves the stranger, giving him food and clothing." It is repeated in the
Prophets, as it says: "So says the High and Exalted One, who lives for ever and *Is. 57*
whose name is Holy: I live in a high and holy place, but also with the contrite
and lowly in spirit, to revive the spirit of the lowly, and to revive the heart of the

_____

(*Megilla* 31a) telling us to learn from God that greatness is humility, and humility greatness. The Creator of all cares for all; the Power of powers cares for
the powerless. The deeper our compassion, the higher we stand.

בֵּית יַעֲקֹב לְכוּ וְנֵלְכָה בְּאוֹר יהוה: וְהָיָה אֱמוּנַת עִתֶּיךָ, חֹסֶן יְשׁוּעֹת חָכְמַת
וָדָעַת, יִרְאַת יהוה הִיא אוֹצָרוֹ: וַיְהִי דָוִד לְכָל־דְּרָכָו מַשְׂכִּיל, וַיהוה עִמּוֹ:

(margin: ישעיה ב / ישעיה לג / שמואל א׳ י״ח)

פָּדָה בְשָׁלוֹם נַפְשִׁי מִקְּרָב־לִי, כִּי־בְרַבִּים הָיוּ עִמָּדִי: וַיֹּאמֶר הָעָם אֶל־
שָׁאוּל, הֲיוֹנָתָן יָמוּת אֲשֶׁר עָשָׂה הַיְשׁוּעָה הַגְּדוֹלָה הַזֹּאת בְּיִשְׂרָאֵל,
חָלִילָה, חַי־יהוה אִם־יִפֹּל מִשַּׂעֲרַת רֹאשׁוֹ אַרְצָה, כִּי־עִם־אֱלֹהִים עָשָׂה
הַיּוֹם הַזֶּה, וַיִּפְדּוּ הָעָם אֶת־יוֹנָתָן וְלֹא־מֵת: וּפְדוּיֵי יהוה יְשֻׁבוּן וּבָאוּ צִיּוֹן
בְּרִנָּה, וְשִׂמְחַת עוֹלָם עַל־רֹאשָׁם, שָׂשׂוֹן וְשִׂמְחָה יַשִּׂיגוּ, וְנָסוּ יָגוֹן וַאֲנָחָה:

(margin: תהלים נה / שמואל א׳ י״ד / ישעיה לה)

הָפַכְתָּ מִסְפְּדִי לְמָחוֹל לִי, פִּתַּחְתָּ שַׂקִּי, וַתְּאַזְּרֵנִי שִׂמְחָה: וְלֹא־אָבָה יהוה
אֱלֹהֶיךָ לִשְׁמֹעַ אֶל־בִּלְעָם, וַיַּהֲפֹךְ יהוה אֱלֹהֶיךָ לְּךָ אֶת־הַקְּלָלָה לִבְרָכָה,
כִּי אֲהֵבְךָ יהוה אֱלֹהֶיךָ: אָז תִּשְׂמַח בְּתוּלָה בְּמָחוֹל, וּבַחֻרִים וּזְקֵנִים יַחְדָּו,
וְהָפַכְתִּי אֶבְלָם לְשָׂשׂוֹן, וְנִחַמְתִּים, וְשִׂמַּחְתִּים מִיגוֹנָם:

(margin: תהלים ל / דברים כג / ירמיה לא)

בּוֹרֵא נִיב שְׂפָתָיִם, שָׁלוֹם שָׁלוֹם לָרָחוֹק וְלַקָּרוֹב אָמַר יהוה, וּרְפָאתִיו: וְרוּחַ
לָבְשָׁה אֶת־עֲמָשַׂי רֹאשׁ הַשָּׁלִישִׁים, לְךָ דָוִיד וְעִמְּךָ בֶן־יִשַׁי, שָׁלוֹם שָׁלוֹם
לְךָ וְשָׁלוֹם לְעֹזְרֶךָ, כִּי עֲזָרְךָ אֱלֹהֶיךָ, וַיְקַבְּלֵם דָּוִיד וַיִּתְּנֵם בְּרָאשֵׁי הַגְּדוּד:
וַאֲמַרְתֶּם כֹּה לֶחָי, וְאַתָּה שָׁלוֹם וּבֵיתְךָ שָׁלוֹם וְכֹל אֲשֶׁר־לְךָ שָׁלוֹם: יהוה
עֹז לְעַמּוֹ יִתֵּן, יהוה יְבָרֵךְ אֶת־עַמּוֹ בַשָּׁלוֹם:

(margin: ישעיה נז / דברי הימים א׳ י״ב / שמואל א׳ כ״ה / תהלים כט)

אָמַר רַבִּי יוֹחָנָן: בְּכָל מָקוֹם שֶׁאַתָּה מוֹצֵא גְּדֻלָּתוֹ שֶׁל הַקָּדוֹשׁ בָּרוּךְ
הוּא, שָׁם אַתָּה מוֹצֵא עַנְוְתָנוּתוֹ. דָּבָר זֶה כָּתוּב בַּתּוֹרָה, וְשָׁנוּי בַּנְּבִיאִים,
וּמְשֻׁלָּשׁ בַּכְּתוּבִים. כָּתוּב בַּתּוֹרָה: כִּי יהוה אֱלֹהֵיכֶם הוּא אֱלֹהֵי הָאֱלֹהִים
וַאֲדֹנֵי הָאֲדֹנִים, הָאֵל הַגָּדֹל הַגִּבֹּר וְהַנּוֹרָא, אֲשֶׁר לֹא־יִשָּׂא פָנִים וְלֹא יִקַּח
שֹׁחַד: וּכְתִיב בַּתְרֵהּ: עֹשֶׂה מִשְׁפַּט יָתוֹם וְאַלְמָנָה, וְאֹהֵב גֵּר לָתֶת לוֹ לֶחֶם
וְשִׂמְלָה: שָׁנוּי בַּנְּבִיאִים, דִּכְתִיב: כִּי כֹה אָמַר רָם וְנִשָּׂא שֹׁכֵן עַד וְקָדוֹשׁ

(margin: מגילה לא / דברים י / ישעיה נז)

פָּדָה *He redeemed my soul in peace:* There now follow three verses on the theme of redemption, three on transformation of fortune from bad to good, and three on peace. These three verses, according to the Talmud (*Berakhot* 55b), should be said to banish fear of misfortune.

אָמַר רַבִּי יוֹחָנָן *Rabbi Yoḥanan said:* A magnificent passage from the Talmud

contrite." It is stated a third time in the Writings: "Sing to God, make music for *Ps. 68*
His name, extol Him who rides the clouds – the Lord is His name – and exult
before Him." Immediately afterwards it is written: "Father of the orphans and
Justice of widows, is God in His holy habitation."

יְהִי May the Lord our God be with us, as He was with our ancestors. May He *1 Kings 8*
never abandon us or forsake us. You who cleave to the Lord your God are all *Deut. 4*
alive this day. For the Lord will comfort Zion, He will comfort all her ruins; *Is. 51*
He will make her wilderness like Eden, and her desert like a garden of the Lord.
Joy and gladness will be found there, thanksgiving and the sound of singing. It *Is. 42*
pleased the Lord for the sake of [Israel's] righteousness to make the Torah
great and glorious.

שִׁיר הַמַּעֲלוֹת A song of ascents. Happy are all who fear the Lord, who walk in His *Ps. 128*
ways. When you eat the fruit of your labor, happy and fortunate are you. Your
wife shall be like a fruitful vine within your house; your sons like olive saplings
around your table. So shall the man who fears the Lord be blessed. May the
Lord bless you from Zion; may you see the good of Jerusalem all the days of
your life; and may you live to see your children's children. Peace be on Israel!

HAVDALA IN THE SYNAGOGUE

Some say the full Havdala on page 346.
On Motza'ei Yom Tov that is not a Motza'ei Shabbat, the
blessings for the spices and flame are omitted.

The Leader takes the cup of wine in his right hand, and says:

Please pay attention, my masters.
Blessed are You, Lord our God, King of the Universe, who creates the fruit
of the vine.

Holding the spice box, the Leader says:

Blessed are You, Lord our God, King of the Universe, who creates the various
spices.

The Leader smells the spices and puts the spice box down.
He lifts his hands toward the flame of the Havdala candle, and says:

Blessed are You, Lord our God, King of the Universe, who creates the lights
of fire.

He lifts the cup of wine in his right hand, and says:

Blessed are You, Lord our God, King of the Universe, who distinguishes
between sacred and secular, between light and darkness, between Israel
and the nations, between the seventh day and the six days of work. Blessed
are You, Lord, who distinguishes between sacred and secular.

שְׁמוֹ, מָרוֹם וְקָדוֹשׁ אֶשְׁכּוֹן, וְאֶת־דַּכָּא וּשְׁפַל־רוּחַ, לְהַחֲיוֹת רוּחַ שְׁפָלִים וּלְהַחֲיוֹת לֵב נִדְכָּאִים: מְשֻׁלָּשׁ בַּכְּתוּבִים, דִּכְתִיב: שִׁירוּ לֵאלֹהִים, זַמְּרוּ שְׁמוֹ, סֹלּוּ לָרֹכֵב בָּעֲרָבוֹת בְּיָהּ שְׁמוֹ, וְעִלְזוּ לְפָנָיו: וּכְתִיב בַּתְרֵהּ: אֲבִי יְתוֹמִים וְדַיַּן אַלְמָנוֹת, אֱלֹהִים בִּמְעוֹן קָדְשׁוֹ:

תהלים סח

יְהִי יהוה אֱלֹהֵינוּ עִמָּנוּ כַּאֲשֶׁר הָיָה עִם־אֲבֹתֵינוּ, אַל־יַעַזְבֵנוּ וְאַל־יִטְּשֵׁנוּ: וְאַתֶּם הַדְּבֵקִים בַּיהוה אֱלֹהֵיכֶם, חַיִּים כֻּלְּכֶם הַיּוֹם: כִּי־נִחַם יהוה צִיּוֹן, נִחַם כָּל־חָרְבֹתֶיהָ, וַיָּשֶׂם מִדְבָּרָהּ כְּעֵדֶן וְעַרְבָתָהּ כְּגַן־יהוה, שָׂשׂוֹן וְשִׂמְחָה יִמָּצֵא בָהּ, תּוֹדָה וְקוֹל זִמְרָה: יהוה חָפֵץ לְמַעַן צִדְקוֹ, יַגְדִּיל תּוֹרָה וְיַאְדִּיר:

מלכים א ח
דברים ד
ישעיה נא

ישעיה מב

שִׁיר הַמַּעֲלוֹת, אַשְׁרֵי כָּל־יְרֵא יהוה, הַהֹלֵךְ בִּדְרָכָיו: יְגִיעַ כַּפֶּיךָ כִּי תֹאכֵל, אַשְׁרֶיךָ וְטוֹב לָךְ: אֶשְׁתְּךָ כְּגֶפֶן פֹּרִיָּה בְּיַרְכְּתֵי בֵיתֶךָ, בָּנֶיךָ כִּשְׁתִלֵי זֵיתִים, סָבִיב לְשֻׁלְחָנֶךָ: הִנֵּה כִי־כֵן יְבֹרַךְ גָּבֶר יְרֵא יהוה: יְבָרֶכְךָ יהוה מִצִּיּוֹן, וּרְאֵה בְּטוּב יְרוּשָׁלָיִם, כֹּל יְמֵי חַיֶּיךָ: וּרְאֵה־בָנִים לְבָנֶיךָ, שָׁלוֹם עַל־יִשְׂרָאֵל:

תהלים קכח

הבדלה בבית הכנסת

Some say the full הבדלה *on page 347.*

On מוצאי יום טוב *that is not a* מוצאי שבת, *the blessings for the spices and flame are omitted.*

The שליח ציבור *takes the cup of wine in his right hand, and says:*

סַבְרִי מָרָנָן

בָּרוּךְ אַתָּה יהוה אֱלֹהֵינוּ מֶלֶךְ הָעוֹלָם, בּוֹרֵא פְּרִי הַגָּפֶן.

Holding the spice box, the שליח ציבור *says:*

בָּרוּךְ אַתָּה יהוה אֱלֹהֵינוּ מֶלֶךְ הָעוֹלָם, בּוֹרֵא מִינֵי בְשָׂמִים.

The שליח ציבור *smells the spices and puts the spice box down.*
He lifts his hands toward the flame of the הבדלה *candle, and says:*

בָּרוּךְ אַתָּה יהוה אֱלֹהֵינוּ מֶלֶךְ הָעוֹלָם, בּוֹרֵא מְאוֹרֵי הָאֵשׁ.

He lifts the cup of wine in his right hand, and says:

בָּרוּךְ אַתָּה יהוה אֱלֹהֵינוּ מֶלֶךְ הָעוֹלָם, הַמַּבְדִּיל בֵּין קֹדֶשׁ לְחֹל, בֵּין אוֹר לְחֹשֶׁךְ, בֵּין יִשְׂרָאֵל לָעַמִּים, בֵּין יוֹם הַשְּׁבִיעִי לְשֵׁשֶׁת יְמֵי הַמַּעֲשֶׂה. בָּרוּךְ אַתָּה יהוה, הַמַּבְדִּיל בֵּין קֹדֶשׁ לְחֹל.

Stand while saying Aleinu. Bow at ˙.

עָלֵינוּ It is our duty to praise the Master of all,
and ascribe greatness to the Author of creation,
who has not made us like the nations of the lands
nor placed us like the families of the earth;
who has not made our portion like theirs,
nor our destiny like all their multitudes.
(For they worship vanity and emptiness,
and pray to a god who cannot save.)
˙But we bow in worship and thank the Supreme King of kings,
the Holy One, blessed be He,
who extends the heavens and establishes the earth,
whose throne of glory is in the heavens above,
and whose power's Presence is in the highest of heights.
He is our God; there is no other.
Truly He is our King, there is none else, as it is written in His Torah:
"You shall know and take to heart this day that the Lord is God,   *Deut. 4*
in heaven above and on earth below. There is no other."

Therefore, we place our hope in You, Lord our God,
that we may soon see the glory of Your power,
when You will remove abominations from the earth,
and idols will be utterly destroyed,
when the world will be perfected under the sovereignty of the Almighty,
when all humanity will call on Your name,
to turn all the earth's wicked toward You.
All the world's inhabitants will realize and know
that to You every knee must bow and every tongue swear loyalty.
Before You, Lord our God, they will kneel and bow down
and give honor to Your glorious name.
They will all accept the yoke of Your kingdom,
and You will reign over them soon and for ever.
For the kingdom is Yours, and to all eternity You will reign in glory,
as it is written in Your Torah:
"The Lord will reign for ever and ever."   *Ex. 15*
▸ And it is said: "Then the Lord shall be King over all the earth;   *Zech. 14*
on that day the Lord shall be One and His name One."

Stand while saying עָלֵינוּ. Bow at ˙.

עָלֵינוּ לְשַׁבֵּחַ לַאֲדוֹן הַכֹּל, לָתֵת גְּדֻלָּה לְיוֹצֵר בְּרֵאשִׁית
שֶׁלֹּא עָשָׂנוּ כְּגוֹיֵי הָאֲרָצוֹת, וְלֹא שָׂמָנוּ כְּמִשְׁפְּחוֹת הָאֲדָמָה
שֶׁלֹּא שָׂם חֶלְקֵנוּ כָּהֶם וְגוֹרָלֵנוּ כְּכָל הֲמוֹנָם.
(שֶׁהֵם מִשְׁתַּחֲוִים לְהֶבֶל וָרִיק וּמִתְפַּלְּלִים אֶל אֵל לֹא יוֹשִׁיעַ.)
וַאֲנַחְנוּ כּוֹרְעִים וּמִשְׁתַּחֲוִים וּמוֹדִים
לִפְנֵי מֶלֶךְ מַלְכֵי הַמְּלָכִים, הַקָּדוֹשׁ בָּרוּךְ הוּא
שֶׁהוּא נוֹטֶה שָׁמַיִם וְיוֹסֵד אָרֶץ
וּמוֹשַׁב יְקָרוֹ בַּשָּׁמַיִם מִמַּעַל
וּשְׁכִינַת עֻזּוֹ בְּגָבְהֵי מְרוֹמִים.
הוּא אֱלֹהֵינוּ, אֵין עוֹד.
אֱמֶת מַלְכֵּנוּ, אֶפֶס זוּלָתוֹ, כַּכָּתוּב בְּתוֹרָתוֹ
וְיָדַעְתָּ הַיּוֹם וַהֲשֵׁבֹתָ אֶל־לְבָבֶךָ

דברים ד

כִּי יהוה הוּא הָאֱלֹהִים בַּשָּׁמַיִם מִמַּעַל וְעַל־הָאָרֶץ מִתָּחַת, אֵין עוֹד:

עַל כֵּן נְקַוֶּה לְּךָ יהוה אֱלֹהֵינוּ, לִרְאוֹת מְהֵרָה בְּתִפְאֶרֶת עֻזֶּךָ
לְהַעֲבִיר גִּלּוּלִים מִן הָאָרֶץ, וְהָאֱלִילִים כָּרוֹת יִכָּרֵתוּן
לְתַקֵּן עוֹלָם בְּמַלְכוּת שַׁדַּי.
וְכָל בְּנֵי בָשָׂר יִקְרְאוּ בִשְׁמֶךָ לְהַפְנוֹת אֵלֶיךָ כָּל רִשְׁעֵי אָרֶץ.
יַכִּירוּ וְיֵדְעוּ כָּל יוֹשְׁבֵי תֵבֵל, כִּי לְךָ תִּכְרַע כָּל בֶּרֶךְ, תִּשָּׁבַע כָּל לָשׁוֹן.
לְפָנֶיךָ יהוה אֱלֹהֵינוּ יִכְרְעוּ וְיִפֹּלוּ, וְלִכְבוֹד שִׁמְךָ יְקָר יִתֵּנוּ
וִיקַבְּלוּ כֻלָּם אֶת עֹל מַלְכוּתֶךָ וְתִמְלֹךְ עֲלֵיהֶם מְהֵרָה לְעוֹלָם וָעֶד.
כִּי הַמַּלְכוּת שֶׁלְּךָ הִיא וּלְעוֹלְמֵי עַד תִּמְלֹךְ בְּכָבוֹד
כַּכָּתוּב בְּתוֹרָתֶךָ

שמות טו

יהוה יִמְלֹךְ לְעֹלָם וָעֶד:

זכריה יד

˙ וְנֶאֱמַר, וְהָיָה יהוה לְמֶלֶךְ עַל־כָּל־הָאָרֶץ
בַּיּוֹם הַהוּא יִהְיֶה יהוה אֶחָד וּשְׁמוֹ אֶחָד:

Some add:

Have no fear of sudden terror or of the ruin when it overtakes the wicked.	*Prov. 3*
Devise your strategy, but it will be thwarted;	*Is. 8*
propose your plan, but it will not stand, for God is with us.	
When you grow old, I will still be the same.	*Is. 46*
When your hair turns gray, I will still carry you.	
I made you, I will bear you, I will carry you, and I will rescue you.	

MOURNER'S KADDISH

The following prayer, said by mourners, requires the presence of a minyan.
A transliteration can be found on page 699.

Mourner: יִתְגַּדַּל Magnified and sanctified may His great name be,
in the world He created by His will.
May He establish His kingdom
in your lifetime and in your days,
and in the lifetime of all the house of Israel,
swiftly and soon –
and say: Amen.

All: May His great name be blessed for ever and all time.

Mourner: Blessed and praised, glorified and exalted,
raised and honored, uplifted and lauded
be the name of the Holy One,
blessed be He,
beyond any blessing,
song, praise and consolation
uttered in the world –
and say: Amen.

May there be great peace from heaven,
and life for us and all Israel – and say: Amen.

Bow, take three steps back, as if taking leave of the Divine Presence,
then bow, first left, then right, then center, while saying:

May He who makes peace in His high places,
make peace for us and all Israel –
and say: Amen.

Some add:

אַל־תִּירָא מִפַּחַד פִּתְאֹם וּמִשֹּׁאַת רְשָׁעִים כִּי תָבֹא: — משלי ג

עֻצוּ עֵצָה וְתֻפָר, דַּבְּרוּ דָבָר וְלֹא יָקוּם, כִּי עִמָּנוּ אֵל: — ישעיה ח

וְעַד־זִקְנָה אֲנִי הוּא, וְעַד־שֵׂיבָה אֲנִי אֶסְבֹּל — ישעיה מו

אֲנִי עָשִׂיתִי וַאֲנִי אֶשָּׂא וַאֲנִי אֶסְבֹּל וַאֲמַלֵּט:

קדיש יתום

The following prayer, said by mourners, requires the presence of a מִנְיָן.
A transliteration can be found on page 699.

אבל: יִתְגַּדַּל וְיִתְקַדַּשׁ שְׁמֵהּ רַבָּא (קהל: אָמֵן)

בְּעָלְמָא דִּי בְרָא כִרְעוּתֵהּ

וְיַמְלִיךְ מַלְכוּתֵהּ

בְּחַיֵּיכוֹן וּבְיוֹמֵיכוֹן וּבְחַיֵּי דְּכָל בֵּית יִשְׂרָאֵל

בַּעֲגָלָא וּבִזְמַן קָרִיב, וְאִמְרוּ אָמֵן. (קהל: אָמֵן)

קהל ואבל: יְהֵא שְׁמֵהּ רַבָּא מְבָרַךְ לְעָלַם וּלְעָלְמֵי עָלְמַיָּא.

אבל: יִתְבָּרַךְ וְיִשְׁתַּבַּח וְיִתְפָּאַר

וְיִתְרוֹמַם וְיִתְנַשֵּׂא וְיִתְהַדָּר וְיִתְעַלֶּה וְיִתְהַלָּל

שְׁמֵהּ דְּקֻדְשָׁא בְּרִיךְ הוּא (קהל: בְּרִיךְ הוּא)

לְעֵלָּא מִן כָּל בִּרְכָתָא / בעשרת ימי תשובה: לְעֵלָּא לְעֵלָּא מִכָּל בִּרְכָתָא/

וְשִׁירָתָא, תֻּשְׁבְּחָתָא וְנֶחֱמָתָא

דַּאֲמִירָן בְּעָלְמָא, וְאִמְרוּ אָמֵן. (קהל: אָמֵן)

יְהֵא שְׁלָמָא רַבָּא מִן שְׁמַיָּא

וְחַיִּים, עָלֵינוּ וְעַל כָּל יִשְׂרָאֵל, וְאִמְרוּ אָמֵן. (קהל: אָמֵן)

Bow, take three steps back, as if taking leave of the Divine Presence,
then bow, first left, then right, then center, while saying:

עֹשֶׂה שָׁלוֹם / בעשרת ימי תשובה: הַשָּׁלוֹם / בִּמְרוֹמָיו

הוּא יַעֲשֶׂה שָׁלוֹם עָלֵינוּ וְעַל כָּל יִשְׂרָאֵל

וְאִמְרוּ אָמֵן. (קהל: אָמֵן)

*From the second day of Rosh Ḥodesh Elul through Shemini Atzeret,
the following psalm is said:*

לְדָוִד By David. The Lord is my light and my salvation – whom then shall I fear? *Ps. 27*
The Lord is the stronghold of my life – of whom shall I be afraid? When evil men
close in on me to devour my flesh, it is they, my enemies and foes, who stumble
and fall. Should an army besiege me, my heart would not fear. Should war break
out against me, still I would be confident. One thing I ask of the Lord, only this
do I seek: to live in the House of the Lord all the days of my life, to gaze on the
beauty of the Lord and worship in His Temple. For He will keep me safe in His
pavilion on the day of trouble. He will hide me under the cover of His tent. He will
set me high upon a rock. Now my head is held high above my enemies who surround
me. I will sacrifice in His tent with shouts of joy. I will sing and chant praises to
the Lord. Lord, hear my voice when I call. Be gracious to me and answer me.
On Your behalf my heart says, "Seek My face." Your face, Lord, will I seek. Do
not hide Your face from me. Do not turn Your servant away in anger. You have
been my help. Do not reject or forsake me, God, my Savior. Were my father and
my mother to forsake me, the Lord would take me in. Teach me Your way, Lord,
and lead me on a level path, because of my oppressors. Do not abandon me to
the will of my foes, for false witnesses have risen against me, breathing violence.
‣ Were it not for my faith that I shall see the Lord's goodness in the land of the
living. Hope in the Lord. Be strong and of good courage, and hope in the Lord!

Mourner's Kaddish (previous page)

In a house of mourning the service continues on page 602.

BLESSING OF THE NEW MOON

*Kiddush Levana, the Blessing of the New Moon, is said between the third day
and the middle day of each month. If possible, it should be said at the end
of Shabbat, under the open sky, and in the presence of a minyan. See law 106.*

הַלְלוּיָהּ Halleluya! Praise the Lord from the heavens, praise Him in *Ps. 148*
the heights. Praise Him, all His angels; praise Him, all His hosts. Praise
Him, sun and moon; praise Him, all shining stars. Praise Him, highest
heavens and the waters above the heavens. Let them praise the name of
the Lord, for He commanded and they were created. He established
them for ever and all time, issuing a decree that will never change.

a symbol of Jewish people who have seemed at times to face eclipse, yet they
too have recovered and given light at dark times. Both themes are present in
the Psalms and accompanying blessing. The physical act of stretching out on
tiptoe to the moon is a gesture of faith that as the moon is beyond human
reach and indestructible, so is the people it symbolizes.

From the second day of ראש חודש אלול *through* שמיני עצרת,
the following psalm is said:

תהלים כז

לְדָוִד, יהוה אוֹרִי וְיִשְׁעִי, מִמִּי אִירָא, יהוה מָעוֹז־חַיַּי, מִמִּי אֶפְחָד: בִּקְרֹב עָלַי מְרֵעִים לֶאֱכֹל אֶת־בְּשָׂרִי, צָרַי וְאֹיְבַי לִי, הֵמָּה כָשְׁלוּ וְנָפֶלוּ: אִם־תַּחֲנֶה עָלַי מַחֲנֶה, לֹא־יִירָא לִבִּי, אִם־תָּקוּם עָלַי מִלְחָמָה, בְּזֹאת אֲנִי בוֹטֵחַ: אַחַת שָׁאַלְתִּי מֵאֵת־יהוה, אוֹתָהּ אֲבַקֵּשׁ, שִׁבְתִּי בְּבֵית־יהוה כָּל־יְמֵי חַיַּי, לַחֲזוֹת בְּנֹעַם־יהוה, וּלְבַקֵּר בְּהֵיכָלוֹ: כִּי יִצְפְּנֵנִי בְּסֻכֹּה בְּיוֹם רָעָה, יַסְתִּרֵנִי בְּסֵתֶר אָהֳלוֹ, בְּצוּר יְרוֹמְמֵנִי: וְעַתָּה יָרוּם רֹאשִׁי עַל אֹיְבַי סְבִיבוֹתַי, וְאֶזְבְּחָה בְאָהֳלוֹ זִבְחֵי תְרוּעָה, אָשִׁירָה וַאֲזַמְּרָה לַיהוה: שְׁמַע־יהוה קוֹלִי אֶקְרָא, וְחָנֵּנִי וַעֲנֵנִי: לְךָ אָמַר לִבִּי בַּקְּשׁוּ פָנָי, אֶת־פָּנֶיךָ יהוה אֲבַקֵּשׁ: אַל־תַּסְתֵּר פָּנֶיךָ מִמֶּנִּי, אַל תַּט־בְּאַף עַבְדֶּךָ, עֶזְרָתִי הָיִיתָ, אַל־תִּטְּשֵׁנִי וְאַל־תַּעַזְבֵנִי, אֱלֹהֵי יִשְׁעִי: כִּי־אָבִי וְאִמִּי עֲזָבוּנִי, וַיהוה יַאַסְפֵנִי: הוֹרֵנִי יהוה דַּרְכֶּךָ, וּנְחֵנִי בְּאֹרַח מִישׁוֹר, לְמַעַן שׁוֹרְרָי: אַל־תִּתְּנֵנִי בְּנֶפֶשׁ צָרָי, כִּי קָמוּ־בִי עֵדֵי־שֶׁקֶר, וִיפֵחַ חָמָס: ‹ לוּלֵא הֶאֱמַנְתִּי לִרְאוֹת בְּטוּב־יהוה בְּאֶרֶץ חַיִּים: קַוֵּה אֶל־יהוה, חֲזַק וְיַאֲמֵץ לִבֶּךָ, וְקַוֵּה אֶל־יהוה:

קדיש יתום *(previous page)*

In a house of mourning the service continues on page 603.

קידוש לבנה

קידוש לבנה, the Blessing of the New Moon, is said between the third day
and the middle day of each month. If possible, it should be said at the end
of שבת, under the open sky, and in the presence of a מנין. See law 106.

תהלים קמח

הַלְלוּיָהּ, הַלְלוּ אֶת־יהוה מִן הַשָּׁמַיִם, הַלְלוּהוּ בַּמְּרוֹמִים: הַלְלוּהוּ כָל־מַלְאָכָיו, הַלְלוּהוּ כָּל־צְבָאָו: הַלְלוּהוּ שֶׁמֶשׁ וְיָרֵחַ, הַלְלוּהוּ כָּל־כּוֹכְבֵי אוֹר: הַלְלוּהוּ שְׁמֵי הַשָּׁמָיִם, וְהַמַּיִם אֲשֶׁר מֵעַל הַשָּׁמָיִם: יְהַלְלוּ אֶת־שֵׁם יהוה, כִּי הוּא צִוָּה וְנִבְרָאוּ: וַיַּעֲמִידֵם לָעַד לְעוֹלָם, חָק־נָתַן וְלֹא יַעֲבוֹר:

These prayers, said on seeing the New Moon, have a dual dimension. First, they testify to the presence of God in creation. The regularity of the moon's waxing and waning are a visible reminder of the law-governed nature of the universe and the presence of an underlying order that surrounds us (Rabbenu Yonah). Second, the moon, endlessly reborn after seeming to decline, is

כִּי־אֶרְאֶה When I see Your heavens, the work of Your fingers, the moon   *Ps. 8*
and the stars which You have set in place: What is man that You are
mindful of him, the son of man that You care for him?

Look at the moon, then say:

בָּרוּךְ Blessed are You, Lᴏʀᴅ our God, King of the Universe who by
His word created the heavens, and by His breath all their host. He set
for them laws and times, so that they should not deviate from their
appointed task. They are joyous and glad to perform the will of their
Owner, the Worker of truth whose work is truth. To the moon He said
that it should renew itself as a crown of beauty for those He carried
from the womb [Israel], for they are destined to be renewed like it, and
to praise their Creator for the sake of His glorious majesty. Blessed are
You, Lᴏʀᴅ, who renews the months.

The following five verses are each said three times:

Blessed is He who formed you; blessed is He who made you;
blessed is He who owns you; blessed is He who created you.

The following verse is said rising on the toes.

Just as I leap toward you but cannot touch you,
so may none of my enemies be able to touch me to do me harm.

May fear and dread fall upon them;   *Ex. 15*
by the power of Your arm may they be still as stone.

May they be still as stone through the power of Your arm,
when dread and fear fall upon them.

David, King of Israel, lives and endures.

Turn to three people and say to each:

Peace upon you.

They respond:

Upon you, peace.

Say three times:

May it be a good sign and a good omen for us and all Israel. Amen.

קוֹל Hark! My beloved! Here he comes, leaping over the mountains,   *Song. 2*
bounding over the hills. My beloved is like a gazelle, like a young deer.
There he stands outside our wall, peering in through the windows,
gazing through the lattice.

כִּי־אֶרְאֶה שָׁמֶיךָ מַעֲשֵׂה אֶצְבְּעֹתֶיךָ, יָרֵחַ וְכוֹכָבִים אֲשֶׁר כּוֹנָנְתָּה: תהלים ח
מָה־אֱנוֹשׁ כִּי־תִזְכְּרֶנּוּ, וּבֶן־אָדָם כִּי תִפְקְדֶנּוּ:

Look at the moon, then say:

בָּרוּךְ אַתָּה יהוה אֱלֹהֵינוּ מֶלֶךְ הָעוֹלָם, אֲשֶׁר בְּמַאֲמָרוֹ בָּרָא שְׁחָקִים,
וּבְרוּחַ פִּיו כָּל צְבָאָם, חֹק וּזְמַן נָתַן לָהֶם שֶׁלֹּא יְשַׁנּוּ אֶת תַּפְקִידָם.
שָׂשִׂים וּשְׂמֵחִים לַעֲשׂוֹת רְצוֹן קוֹנָם, פּוֹעֵל אֱמֶת שֶׁפְּעֻלָּתוֹ אֱמֶת.
וְלַלְּבָנָה אָמַר שֶׁתִּתְחַדֵּשׁ, עֲטֶרֶת תִּפְאֶרֶת לַעֲמוּסֵי בָטֶן, שֶׁהֵם
עֲתִידִים לְהִתְחַדֵּשׁ כְּמוֹתָהּ וּלְפָאֵר לְיוֹצְרָם עַל שֵׁם כְּבוֹד מַלְכוּתוֹ.
בָּרוּךְ אַתָּה יהוה, מְחַדֵּשׁ חֳדָשִׁים.

The following five verses are each said three times:

בָּרוּךְ יוֹצְרֵךְ, בָּרוּךְ עוֹשֵׂךְ, בָּרוּךְ קוֹנֵךְ, בָּרוּךְ בּוֹרְאֵךְ.

The following verse is said rising on the toes:

כְּשֵׁם שֶׁאֲנִי רוֹקֵד כְּנֶגְדֵּךְ וְאֵינִי יָכוֹל לִנְגֹּעַ בָּךְ
כָּךְ לֹא יוּכְלוּ כָּל אוֹיְבַי לִנְגֹּעַ בִּי לְרָעָה.

תִּפֹּל עֲלֵיהֶם אֵימָתָה וָפַחַד, בִּגְדֹל זְרוֹעֲךָ יִדְּמוּ כָּאָבֶן: שמות טו
כָּאֶבֶן יִדְּמוּ זְרוֹעֲךָ בִּגְדֹל, וָפַחַד אֵימָתָה עֲלֵיהֶם תִּפֹּל.
דָּוִד מֶלֶךְ יִשְׂרָאֵל חַי וְקַיָּם.

Turn to three people and say to each:

שָׁלוֹם עֲלֵיכֶם.

They respond:

עֲלֵיכֶם שָׁלוֹם.

Say three times:

סִימָן טוֹב וּמַזָּל טוֹב יְהֵא לָנוּ וּלְכָל יִשְׂרָאֵל, אָמֵן.

קוֹל דּוֹדִי הִנֵּה־זֶה בָּא, מְדַלֵּג עַל־הֶהָרִים, מְקַפֵּץ עַל־הַגְּבָעוֹת: שיר
דּוֹמֶה דוֹדִי לִצְבִי אוֹ לְעֹפֶר הָאַיָּלִים, הִנֵּה־זֶה עוֹמֵד אַחַר כָּתְלֵנוּ, השירים ב
מַשְׁגִּיחַ מִן־הַחַלֹּנוֹת, מֵצִיץ מִן־הַחֲרַכִּים:

שִׁיר לַמַּעֲלוֹת A song of ascents. I lift my eyes up to the hills; from where *Ps. 121* will my help come? My help comes from the LORD, Maker of heaven and earth. He will not let your foot stumble; He who guards you does not slumber. See: the Guardian of Israel neither slumbers nor sleeps. The LORD is your Guardian; the LORD is your Shade at your right hand. The sun will not strike you by day, nor the moon by night. The LORD will guard you from all harm; He will guard your life. The LORD will guard your going and coming, now and for evermore.

הַלְלוּיָהּ Halleluya! Praise God in His holy place; praise Him in the heav- *Ps. 150* ens of His power. Praise Him for His mighty deeds; praise Him for His surpassing greatness. Praise Him with blasts of the ram's horn; praise Him with the harp and lyre. Praise Him with timbrel and dance; praise Him with strings and flute. Praise Him with clashing cymbals; praise Him with resounding cymbals. Let all that breathes praise the LORD. Halleluya!

תָּנָא In the academy of Rabbi Yishmael it was taught: Were the people of *Sanhedrin* Israel privileged to greet the presence of their heavenly Father only once *42a* a month, it would have been sufficient for them. Abaye said: Therefore it [the blessing of the moon] should be said standing. Who is this coming *Song. 8* up from the desert, leaning on her beloved?

וִיהִי May it be Your will, LORD my God and God of my ancestors, to make good the deficiency of the moon, so that it is no longer in its diminished state. May the light of the moon be like the light of the sun and like the light of the seven days of creation as it was before it was diminished, as it says, "The two great luminaries." And may there be fulfilled for us the *Gen. 1* verse: "They shall seek the LORD their God, and David their king." Amen. *Hos. 3*

לַמְנַצֵּחַ For the conductor of music. With stringed instruments, a psalm. *Ps. 67* A song. May God be gracious to us and bless us. May He make His face shine on us, Selah. Then will Your way be known on earth, Your salvation among all the nations. Let the peoples praise You, God; let all peoples praise You. Let nations rejoice and sing for joy, for You judge the peoples with equity, and guide the nations of the earth, Selah. Let the peoples praise You, God; let all peoples praise You. The earth has yielded its harvest. May God, our God, bless us. God will bless us, and all the ends of the earth will fear Him.

תהלים קכא
שִׁיר לַמַּעֲלוֹת, אֶשָּׂא עֵינַי אֶל־הֶהָרִים, מֵאַיִן יָבֹא עֶזְרִי: עֶזְרִי מֵעִם
יהוה, עֹשֵׂה שָׁמַיִם וָאָרֶץ: אַל־יִתֵּן לַמּוֹט רַגְלֶךָ, אַל־יָנוּם שֹׁמְרֶךָ:
הִנֵּה לֹא־יָנוּם וְלֹא יִישָׁן, שׁוֹמֵר יִשְׂרָאֵל: יהוה שֹׁמְרֶךָ, יהוה צִלְּךָ
עַל־יַד יְמִינֶךָ: יוֹמָם הַשֶּׁמֶשׁ לֹא־יַכֶּכָּה, וְיָרֵחַ בַּלָּיְלָה: יהוה יִשְׁמָרְךָ
מִכָּל־רָע, יִשְׁמֹר אֶת־נַפְשֶׁךָ: יהוה יִשְׁמָר־צֵאתְךָ וּבוֹאֶךָ, מֵעַתָּה
וְעַד־עוֹלָם:

תהלים קנ
הַלְלוּיָהּ, הַלְלוּ־אֵל בְּקָדְשׁוֹ, הַלְלוּהוּ בִּרְקִיעַ עֻזּוֹ: הַלְלוּהוּ בִגְבוּרֹתָיו,
הַלְלוּהוּ כְּרֹב גֻּדְלוֹ: הַלְלוּהוּ בְּתֵקַע שׁוֹפָר, הַלְלוּהוּ בְּנֵבֶל וְכִנּוֹר:
הַלְלוּהוּ בְּתֹף וּמָחוֹל, הַלְלוּהוּ בְּמִנִּים וְעֻגָב: הַלְלוּהוּ בְצִלְצְלֵי־שָׁמַע,
הַלְלוּהוּ בְּצִלְצְלֵי תְרוּעָה: כֹּל הַנְּשָׁמָה תְּהַלֵּל יָהּ, הַלְלוּיָהּ:

סנהדרין מב
תָּנָא דְּבֵי רַבִּי יִשְׁמָעֵאל: אִלְמָלֵי לֹא זָכוּ יִשְׂרָאֵל אֶלָּא לְהַקְבִּיל פְּנֵי
אֲבִיהֶם שֶׁבַּשָּׁמַיִם פַּעַם אַחַת בַּחֹדֶשׁ, דַּיָּם. אָמַר אַבַּיֵּי: הִלְכָּךְ צָרִיךְ
שיר
השירים ח
לְמֵימְרָא מְעֻמָּד. מִי זֹאת עֹלָה מִן־הַמִּדְבָּר, מִתְרַפֶּקֶת עַל־דּוֹדָהּ:

וִיהִי רָצוֹן מִלְּפָנֶיךָ יהוה אֱלֹהַי וֵאלֹהֵי אֲבוֹתַי, לְמַלֹּאת פְּגִימַת
הַלְּבָנָה וְלֹא יִהְיֶה בָּהּ שׁוּם מִעוּט. וִיהִי אוֹר הַלְּבָנָה כְּאוֹר הַחַמָּה
וּכְאוֹר שִׁבְעַת יְמֵי בְרֵאשִׁית, כְּמוֹ שֶׁהָיְתָה קֹדֶם מִעוּטָהּ, שֶׁנֶּאֱמַר:
בראשית א
הושע ג
אֶת־שְׁנֵי הַמְּאֹרֹת הַגְּדֹלִים: וְיִתְקַיֶּם בָּנוּ מִקְרָא שֶׁכָּתוּב: וּבִקְשׁוּ
אֶת־יהוה אֱלֹהֵיהֶם וְאֵת דָּוִד מַלְכָּם: אָמֵן.

תהלים סז
לַמְנַצֵּחַ בִּנְגִינֹת, מִזְמוֹר שִׁיר: אֱלֹהִים יְחָנֵּנוּ וִיבָרְכֵנוּ, יָאֵר פָּנָיו אִתָּנוּ
סֶלָה: לָדַעַת בָּאָרֶץ דַּרְכֶּךָ, בְּכָל־גּוֹיִם יְשׁוּעָתֶךָ: יוֹדוּךָ עַמִּים אֱלֹהִים,
יוֹדוּךָ עַמִּים כֻּלָּם: יִשְׂמְחוּ וִירַנְּנוּ לְאֻמִּים, כִּי־תִשְׁפֹּט עַמִּים מִישֹׁר,
וּלְאֻמִּים בָּאָרֶץ תַּנְחֵם סֶלָה: יוֹדוּךָ עַמִּים אֱלֹהִים, יוֹדוּךָ עַמִּים כֻּלָּם:
אֶרֶץ נָתְנָה יְבוּלָהּ, יְבָרְכֵנוּ אֱלֹהִים אֱלֹהֵינוּ: יְבָרְכֵנוּ אֱלֹהִים, וְיִירְאוּ
אוֹתוֹ כָּל־אַפְסֵי־אָרֶץ:

Stand while saying Aleinu. Bow at ˙.

עָלֵינוּ It is our duty to praise the Master of all, and ascribe greatness to the Author of creation, who has not made us like the nations of the lands nor placed us like the families of the earth; who has not made our portion like theirs, nor our destiny like all their multitudes. (For they worship vanity and emptiness, and pray to a god who cannot save.) ˙But we bow in worship and thank the Supreme King of kings, the Holy One, blessed be He, who extends the heavens and establishes the earth, whose throne of glory is in the heavens above, and whose power's Presence is in the highest of heights. He is our God; there is no other. Truly He is our King, there is none else, as it is written in His Torah: "You shall know and take to heart this day that the Lᴏʀᴅ is God, *Deut. 4* in heaven above and on earth below. There is no other."

Therefore, we place our hope in You, Lᴏʀᴅ our God, that we may soon see the glory of Your power, when You will remove abominations from the earth, and idols will be utterly destroyed, when the world will be perfected under the sovereignty of the Almighty, when all humanity will call on Your name, to turn all the earth's wicked toward You. All the world's inhabitants will realize and know that to You every knee must bow and every tongue swear loyalty. Before You, Lᴏʀᴅ our God, they will kneel and bow down and give honor to Your glorious name. They will all accept the yoke of Your kingdom, and You will reign over them soon and for ever. For the kingdom is Yours, and to all eternity You will reign in glory, as it is written in Your Torah: "The Lᴏʀᴅ will *Ex. 15* reign for ever and ever." ▸ And it is said: "Then the Lᴏʀᴅ shall be King over all *Zech. 14* the earth; on that day the Lᴏʀᴅ shall be One and His name One."

Some add:

Have no fear of sudden terror or of the ruin when it overtakes the wicked. Devise *Prov. 3* your strategy, but it will be thwarted; propose your plan, but it will not stand, for God *Is. 8* is with us. When you grow old, I will still be the same. When your hair turns gray, I *Is. 46* will still carry you. I made you, I will bear you, I will carry you, and I will rescue you.

MOURNER'S KADDISH

The following prayer, said by mourners, requires the presence of a minyan.
A transliteration can be found on page 699.

Mourner: יִתְגַּדַּל Magnified and sanctified may His great name be,
in the world He created by His will.
May He establish His kingdom
in your lifetime and in your days,
and in the lifetime of all the house of Israel,
swiftly and soon – and say: Amen.

Stand while saying עָלֵינוּ. *Bow at* ▾.

עָלֵינוּ לְשַׁבֵּחַ לַאֲדוֹן הַכֹּל, לָתֵת גְּדֻלָּה לְיוֹצֵר בְּרֵאשִׁית, שֶׁלֹּא עָשָׂנוּ כְּגוֹיֵי הָאֲרָצוֹת, וְלֹא שָׂמָנוּ כְּמִשְׁפְּחוֹת הָאֲדָמָה, שֶׁלֹּא שָׂם חֶלְקֵנוּ כָּהֶם וְגוֹרָלֵנוּ כְּכָל הֲמוֹנָם. (שֶׁהֵם מִשְׁתַּחֲוִים לְהֶבֶל וָרִיק וּמִתְפַּלְּלִים אֶל אֵל לֹא יוֹשִׁיעַ.)
▾וַאֲנַחְנוּ כּוֹרְעִים וּמִשְׁתַּחֲוִים וּמוֹדִים, לִפְנֵי מֶלֶךְ מַלְכֵי הַמְּלָכִים, הַקָּדוֹשׁ בָּרוּךְ הוּא, שֶׁהוּא נוֹטֶה שָׁמַיִם וְיוֹסֵד אָרֶץ, וּמוֹשַׁב יְקָרוֹ בַּשָּׁמַיִם מִמַּעַל, וּשְׁכִינַת עֻזּוֹ בְּגָבְהֵי מְרוֹמִים. הוּא אֱלֹהֵינוּ, אֵין עוֹד. אֱמֶת מַלְכֵּנוּ, אֶפֶס זוּלָתוֹ, כַּכָּתוּב בְּתוֹרָתוֹ, וְיָדַעְתָּ הַיּוֹם וַהֲשֵׁבֹתָ אֶל לְבָבֶךָ, כִּי יהוה הוּא הָאֱלֹהִים בַּשָּׁמַיִם מִמַּעַל וְעַל הָאָרֶץ מִתָּחַת, אֵין עוֹד:

דברים ד

עַל כֵּן נְקַוֶּה לְּךָ יהוה אֱלֹהֵינוּ, לִרְאוֹת מְהֵרָה בְּתִפְאֶרֶת עֻזֶּךָ, לְהַעֲבִיר גִּלּוּלִים מִן הָאָרֶץ, וְהָאֱלִילִים כָּרוֹת יִכָּרֵתוּן, לְתַקֵּן עוֹלָם בְּמַלְכוּת שַׁדַּי. וְכָל בְּנֵי בָשָׂר יִקְרְאוּ בִשְׁמֶךָ, לְהַפְנוֹת אֵלֶיךָ כָּל רִשְׁעֵי אָרֶץ. יַכִּירוּ וְיֵדְעוּ כָּל יוֹשְׁבֵי תֵבֵל, כִּי לְךָ תִּכְרַע כָּל בֶּרֶךְ, תִּשָּׁבַע כָּל לָשׁוֹן. לְפָנֶיךָ יהוה אֱלֹהֵינוּ יִכְרְעוּ וְיִפֹּלוּ, וְלִכְבוֹד שִׁמְךָ יְקָר יִתֵּנוּ, וִיקַבְּלוּ כֻלָּם אֶת עֹל מַלְכוּתֶךָ וְתִמְלֹךְ עֲלֵיהֶם מְהֵרָה לְעוֹלָם וָעֶד. כִּי הַמַּלְכוּת שֶׁלְּךָ הִיא וּלְעוֹלְמֵי עַד תִּמְלֹךְ בְּכָבוֹד, כַּכָּתוּב בְּתוֹרָתֶךָ, יהוה יִמְלֹךְ לְעֹלָם וָעֶד: ▸ וְנֶאֱמַר, וְהָיָה יהוה לְמֶלֶךְ עַל כָּל הָאָרֶץ, בַּיּוֹם הַהוּא יִהְיֶה יהוה אֶחָד וּשְׁמוֹ אֶחָד:

שמות טו
זכריה יד

Some add:

אַל תִּירָא מִפַּחַד פִּתְאֹם וּמִשֹּׁאַת רְשָׁעִים כִּי תָבֹא: עֻצוּ עֵצָה וְתֻפָר, דַּבְּרוּ דָבָר וְלֹא יָקוּם, כִּי עִמָּנוּ אֵל: וְעַד זִקְנָה אֲנִי הוּא, וְעַד שֵׂיבָה אֲנִי אֶסְבֹּל, אֲנִי עָשִׂיתִי וַאֲנִי אֶשָּׂא וַאֲנִי אֶסְבֹּל וַאֲמַלֵּט:

משלי ג
ישעיה ח
ישעיה מו

קדיש יתום

The following prayer, said by mourners, requires the presence of a מִנְיָן.
A transliteration can be found on page 699.

אבל יִתְגַּדַּל וְיִתְקַדַּשׁ שְׁמֵהּ רַבָּא (קהל: אָמֵן)

בְּעָלְמָא דִּי בְרָא כִרְעוּתֵהּ

וְיַמְלִיךְ מַלְכוּתֵהּ

בְּחַיֵּיכוֹן וּבְיוֹמֵיכוֹן וּבְחַיֵּי דְכָל בֵּית יִשְׂרָאֵל

בַּעֲגָלָא וּבִזְמַן קָרִיב, וְאִמְרוּ אָמֵן. (קהל: אָמֵן)

All: May His great name be blessed for ever and all time.

Mourner: Blessed and praised,
glorified and exalted,
raised and honored,
uplifted and lauded
be the name of the Holy One,
blessed be He,
beyond any blessing,
song, praise and consolation
uttered in the world –
and say: Amen.

May there be great peace from heaven,
and life for us and all Israel –
and say: Amen.

Bow, take three steps back, as if taking leave of the Divine Presence, then bow, first left, then right, then center, while saying:

May He who makes peace in His high places,
make peace for us and all Israel –
and say: Amen.

All sing:

טוֹבִים Good are the radiant stars our God created;
He formed them with knowledge,
understanding and deliberation.
He gave them strength and might
to rule throughout the world.

Full of splendor, radiating light,
beautiful is their splendor throughout the world.
Glad as they go forth, joyous as they return,
they fulfill with awe their Creator's will.

Glory and honor they give to His name,
jubilation and song at the mention of His majesty.
He called the sun into being and it shone with light.
He looked and fashioned the form of the moon.

קהל
ואבל: יְהֵא שְׁמֵהּ רַבָּא מְבָרַךְ לְעָלַם וּלְעָלְמֵי עָלְמַיָּא.

אבל: יִתְבָּרַךְ וְיִשְׁתַּבַּח וְיִתְפָּאַר
וְיִתְרוֹמַם וְיִתְנַשֵּׂא וְיִתְהַדָּר וְיִתְעַלֶּה וְיִתְהַלָּל
שְׁמֵהּ דְּקֻדְשָׁא בְּרִיךְ הוּא (קהל: בְּרִיךְ הוּא)
לְעֵלָּא מִן כָּל בִּרְכָתָא
/בעשרת ימי תשובה: לְעֵלָּא לְעֵלָּא מִכָּל בִּרְכָתָא/
וְשִׁירָתָא, תֻּשְׁבְּחָתָא וְנֶחֱמָתָא
דַּאֲמִירָן בְּעָלְמָא
וְאִמְרוּ אָמֵן. (קהל: אָמֵן)

יְהֵא שְׁלָמָא רַבָּא מִן שְׁמַיָּא
וְחַיִּים, עָלֵינוּ וְעַל כָּל יִשְׂרָאֵל
וְאִמְרוּ אָמֵן. (קהל: אָמֵן)

*Bow, take three steps back, as if taking leave of the Divine Presence,
then bow, first left, then right, then center, while saying:*

עֹשֶׂה שָׁלוֹם /בעשרת ימי תשובה: הַשָּׁלוֹם/ בִּמְרוֹמָיו
הוּא יַעֲשֶׂה שָׁלוֹם עָלֵינוּ וְעַל כָּל יִשְׂרָאֵל
וְאִמְרוּ אָמֵן. (קהל: אָמֵן)

All sing:

טוֹבִים מְאוֹרוֹת שֶׁבָּרָא אֱלֹהֵינוּ, יְצָרָם בְּדַעַת בְּבִינָה וּבְהַשְׂכֵּל
כֹּחַ וּגְבוּרָה נָתַן בָּהֶם, לִהְיוֹת מוֹשְׁלִים בְּקֶרֶב תֵּבֵל.

מְלֵאִים זִיו וּמְפִיקִים נֹגַהּ, נָאֶה זִיוָם בְּכָל הָעוֹלָם
שְׂמֵחִים בְּצֵאתָם וְשָׂשִׂים בְּבוֹאָם, עוֹשִׂים בְּאֵימָה רְצוֹן קוֹנָם.

פְּאֵר וְכָבוֹד נוֹתְנִים לִשְׁמוֹ, צָהֳלָה וְרִנָּה לְזֵכֶר מַלְכוּתוֹ
קָרָא לַשֶּׁמֶשׁ וַיִּזְרַח אוֹר, רָאָה וְהִתְקִין צוּרַת הַלְּבָנָה.

HAVDALA AT HOME

*On Motza'ei Yom Tov that is not a Motza'ei Shabbat, the first paragraph
and the blessings for the spices and flame are omitted.
Taking a cup of wine in the right hand, say:*

הִנֵּה Behold, God is my salvation. I will trust and not be afraid.   *Is. 12*
The Lord, the Lord, is my strength and my song.
He has become my salvation.
With joy you will draw water from the springs of salvation.
Salvation is the Lord's; on Your people is Your blessing, Selah.   *Ps. 3*
The Lord of hosts is with us, the God of Jacob is our stronghold, Selah. *Ps. 46*
Lord of hosts: happy is the one who trusts in You.   *Ps. 84*
Lord, save! May the King answer us on the day we call.   *Ps. 20*
For the Jews there was light and gladness, joy and honor – so may it be for us. *Esther 8*
I will lift the cup of salvation and call on the name of the Lord.   *Ps. 116*

When making Havdala for others, add:
Please pay attention, my masters.
Blessed are You, Lord our God, King of the Universe,
who creates the fruit of the vine.

Hold the spice box and say:
Blessed are You, Lord our God, King of the Universe,
who creates the various spices.

*Smell the spices and put the spice box down.
Lift the hands toward the flame of the Havdala candle and say:*
Blessed are You, Lord our God, King of the Universe,
who creates the lights of fire.

Holding the cup of wine again in the right hand, say:
בָּרוּךְ Blessed are You, Lord our God, King of the Universe,
who distinguishes between sacred and secular,
between light and darkness,
between Israel and the nations,
between the seventh day and the six days of work.
Blessed are You, Lord, who distinguishes between sacred and secular.

HAVDALA

Havdala is to the end of Shabbat what Kiddush is to the beginning: the marking of a transition from secular to holy time and vice versa. It is our way of
fulfilling the commandment to "Remember the Sabbath day," understood by

סדר הבדלה בבית

On מוצאי יום טוב that is not a מוצאי שבת, the first paragraph
and the blessings for the spices and flame are omitted.

Taking a cup of wine in the right hand, say:

ישעיה יב

הִנֵּה אֵל יְשׁוּעָתִי אֶבְטַח, וְלֹא אֶפְחָד
כִּי־עָזִּי וְזִמְרָת יָהּ יהוה, וַיְהִי־לִי לִישׁוּעָה:
וּשְׁאַבְתֶּם־מַיִם בְּשָׂשׂוֹן, מִמַּעַיְנֵי הַיְשׁוּעָה:

תהלים ג

לַיהוה הַיְשׁוּעָה, עַל־עַמְּךָ בִרְכָתֶךָ סֶּלָה:

תהלים מו

יהוה צְבָאוֹת עִמָּנוּ, מִשְׂגָּב לָנוּ אֱלֹהֵי יַעֲקֹב סֶלָה:

תהלים פד

יהוה צְבָאוֹת, אַשְׁרֵי אָדָם בֹּטֵחַ בָּךְ:

תהלים כ

יהוה הוֹשִׁיעָה, הַמֶּלֶךְ יַעֲנֵנוּ בְיוֹם־קָרְאֵנוּ:

אסתר ח

לַיְּהוּדִים הָיְתָה אוֹרָה וְשִׂמְחָה וְשָׂשֹׂן וִיקָר: כֵּן תִּהְיֶה לָּנוּ:

תהלים קטז

כּוֹס־יְשׁוּעוֹת אֶשָּׂא, וּבְשֵׁם יהוה אֶקְרָא:

When making הבדלה for others, add:

סַבְרִי מָרָנָן

בָּרוּךְ אַתָּה יהוה אֱלֹהֵינוּ מֶלֶךְ הָעוֹלָם, בּוֹרֵא פְּרִי הַגָּפֶן.

Hold the spice box and say:

בָּרוּךְ אַתָּה יהוה אֱלֹהֵינוּ מֶלֶךְ הָעוֹלָם, בּוֹרֵא מִינֵי בְשָׂמִים.

Smell the spices and put the spice box down.
Lift the hands toward the flame of the הבדלה candle and say:

בָּרוּךְ אַתָּה יהוה אֱלֹהֵינוּ מֶלֶךְ הָעוֹלָם, בּוֹרֵא מְאוֹרֵי הָאֵשׁ.

Holding the cup of wine again in the right hand, say:

בָּרוּךְ אַתָּה יהוה אֱלֹהֵינוּ מֶלֶךְ הָעוֹלָם
הַמַּבְדִּיל בֵּין קֹדֶשׁ לְחֹל, בֵּין אוֹר לְחֹשֶׁךְ
בֵּין יִשְׂרָאֵל לָעַמִּים
בֵּין יוֹם הַשְּׁבִיעִי לְשֵׁשֶׁת יְמֵי הַמַּעֲשֶׂה.
בָּרוּךְ אַתָּה יהוה, הַמַּבְדִּיל בֵּין קֹדֶשׁ לְחֹל.

הַמַּבְדִּיל He who distinguishes between sacred and secular,
may He forgive our sins.
May He multiply our offspring and wealth like the sand,
and like the stars at night.

The day has passed like a palm tree's shadow;
I call on God to fulfill what the watchman said: *Is. 21*
"Morning comes, though now it is night."

Your righteousness is as high as Mount Tabor. May You pass high over my sins.
[Let them be] like yesterday when it has passed, like a watch in the night.   *Ps. 90*

The time of offerings has passed. Would that I might rest.
I am weary with my sighing, every night I drench [with tears].   *Ps. 6*

Hear my voice; let it not be cast aside. Open for me the lofty gate.
My head is filled with the dew of dawn, my hair with raindrops of the night.   *Song. 5*

Heed my prayer, revered and awesome God.
When I cry, grant me deliverance at twilight,   *Prov. 7*
as the day fades, or in the darkness of the night.

I call to You, LORD: Save me. Make known to me the path of life.
Rescue me from misery before day turns to night.

Cleanse the defilement of my deeds, lest those who torment me say,
"Where is the God who made me, who gives cause for songs in the night?"   *Job 35*

We are in Your hands like clay: please forgive our sins, light and grave.
Day to day they pour forth speech,
and night to night [they communicate knowledge].

One of the key verbs in Genesis 1 is *b-d-l*, "to separate, distinguish, divide" –
the root of the word *Havdala*. It appears five times in the chapter. By inviting
human beings to engage in Havdala at the end of Shabbat, God invites us to
create worlds. Creation involves the ability to make distinctions, to rescue
order from chaos, to respect the integrity of creation. Havdala is thus not only
a human blessing over the end of the day of rest, but as it were a divine blessing over the days of work. The Creator invites us to be creative – but always
and only in a way that respects differences and distinctions, the laws of nature
and the moral law. The message of Havdala is: if we respect the integrity of
boundaries, we can turn chaos into order, darkness into light.

הַמַּבְדִּיל *He who distinguishes:* As we welcomed the arrival of Shabbat in song,
so we bid our farewell to it in song. This beautiful hymn, originally part of the
Ne'ila service on Yom Kippur, was composed by Isaac ibn Giat (1030–1089).

הַמַּבְדִּיל בֵּין קֹדֶשׁ לְחֹל, חַטֹּאתֵינוּ הוּא יִמְחֹל
זַרְעֵנוּ וְכַסְפֵּנוּ יַרְבֶּה כַחוֹל וְכַכּוֹכָבִים בַּלַּיְלָה.

יוֹם פָּנָה כְּצֵל תֹּמֶר, אֶקְרָא לָאֵל עָלַי גּוֹמֵר
אָמַר שֹׁמֵר, אָתָא בֹקֶר וְגַם־לָיְלָה:

ישעיה כא

צִדְקָתְךָ כְּהַר תָּבוֹר, עַל חֲטָאַי עָבוֹר תַּעֲבֹר
כְּיוֹם אֶתְמוֹל כִּי יַעֲבֹר, וְאַשְׁמוּרָה בַלָּיְלָה:

תהלים צ

חָלְפָה עוֹנַת מִנְחָתִי, מִי יִתֵּן מְנוּחָתִי
יָגַעְתִּי בְאַנְחָתִי, אַשְׂחֶה בְכָל־לָיְלָה:

תהלים ו

קוֹלִי בַּל יִנָּטֵל, פְּתַח לִי שַׁעַר הַמְנֻטָּל
שֶׁרֹּאשִׁי נִמְלָא טָל, קְוֻצּוֹתַי רְסִיסֵי לָיְלָה:

שיר השירים ה

הֵעָתֵר נוֹרָא וְאָיֹם, אֲשַׁוֵּעַ תְּנָה פִדְיוֹם
בְּנֶשֶׁף־בְּעֶרֶב יוֹם, בְּאִישׁוֹן לָיְלָה:

משלי ו

קְרָאתִיךָ יָהּ, הוֹשִׁיעֵנִי, אֹרַח חַיִּים תּוֹדִיעֵנִי
מִדַּלָּה תְבַצְּעֵנִי, מִיּוֹם עַד לָיְלָה.

טַהֵר טִנּוּף מַעֲשַׂי, פֶּן יֹאמְרוּ מַכְעִיסַי
אַיֵּה אֱלוֹהַּ עֹשָׂי, נֹתֵן זְמִרוֹת בַּלָּיְלָה:

איוב לה

נַחְנוּ בְיָדְךָ כַּחֹמֶר, סְלַח נָא עַל קַל וָחֹמֶר
יוֹם לְיוֹם יַבִּיעַ אֹמֶר, וְלַיְלָה לְּלָיְלָה:

תהלים יט

the sages to mean: "Remember it at the beginning and at the end" (*Pesaḥim* 106a) – in both cases over a cup of wine.

Its deeper meaning recalls the moment at which Adam and Eve, exiled from Eden because of their sin, prepared to enter, for the first time, the world outside, with its darkness and dangers. As a gift, God showed them how to make light. Hence the light of Havdala.

This profound parable is the reverse of the Greek myth of Prometheus – who stole fire from the gods and was sentenced to everlasting torment. Judaism taught that God wants and blesses human creativity. Day 8, for humans, was the counterpart to Day 1 for God. Just as God began creation by making light, so He taught humans how to make light – inviting them to become "His partners in the work of creation."

SHEMA BEFORE SLEEP AT NIGHT

הֲרֵינִי I hereby forgive anyone who has angered or provoked me or sinned against me, physically or financially or by failing to give me due respect, or in any other matter relating to me, involuntarily or willingly, inadvertently or deliberately, whether in word or deed: let no one incur punishment because of me.

בָּרוּךְ Blessed are You, LORD our God, King of the Universe, who makes the bonds of sleep fall on my eyes, and slumber on my eyelids. May it be Your will, LORD my God and God of my fathers, that You make me lie down in peace and arise in peace. Let not my imagination, bad dreams or troubling thoughts disturb me. May my bed be flawless before You. Enlighten my eyes lest I sleep the sleep of death, for it is You who illuminates the pupil of the eye. Blessed are You, LORD, who gives light to the whole world in His glory.

When saying all three paragraphs of Shema, say:
God, faithful King!

The following verse should be said aloud, while covering the eyes with the right hand:

Listen, Israel: the LORD is our God,
the LORD is One.

Deut. 6

Quietly: Blessed be the name of His glorious kingdom for ever and all time.

וְאָהַבְתָּ Love the LORD your God with all your heart, with all your soul, and with all your might. These words which I command you today shall be on your heart. Teach them repeatedly to your children, speaking of them when you sit at home and when you travel on the way, when you lie down and when you rise. Bind them as a sign on your hand, and they shall be an emblem between your eyes. Write them on the doorposts of your house and gates.

Deut. 6

---

from the evening service; (6) הַמַּלְאָךְ הַגֹּאֵל אֹתִי "May the angel who rescued me from all harm," a series of biblical verses about safety and security; (7) A verse about angels, based on "The LORD's angel encamps around those who fear Him, and He rescues them" (Psalm 34:8) and "He will command His angels about you, to guard you in all your ways" (Psalm 91:11); (8) Psalm 128, about work, recalling the phrase from Ecclesiastes (5:11), "Sweet is the sleep of one who labors"; (9) רִגְזוּ וְאַל־תֶּחֱטָאוּ "Tremble, and do not sin," from Psalm 4:5, mentioned in the Talmud (*Berakhot* 4b) as an appropriate verse before

קריאת שמע על המיטה

הֲרֵינִי מוֹחֵל לְכָל מִי שֶׁהִכְעִיס וְהִקְנִיט אוֹתִי אוֹ שֶׁחָטָא כְּנֶגְדִּי, בֵּין בְּגוּפִי בֵּין בְּמָמוֹנִי בֵּין בִּכְבוֹדִי בֵּין בְּכָל אֲשֶׁר לִי, בֵּין בְּאֹנֶס בֵּין בְּרָצוֹן, בֵּין בְּשׁוֹגֵג בֵּין בְּמֵזִיד, בֵּין בְּדִבּוּר בֵּין בְּמַעֲשֶׂה, וְלֹא יֵעָנֵשׁ שׁוּם אָדָם בְּסִבָּתִי.

בָּרוּךְ אַתָּה יהוה אֱלֹהֵינוּ מֶלֶךְ הָעוֹלָם, הַמַּפִּיל חֶבְלֵי שֵׁנָה עַל עֵינַי וּתְנוּמָה עַל עַפְעַפָּי. וִיהִי רָצוֹן מִלְּפָנֶיךָ, יהוה אֱלֹהַי וֵאלֹהֵי אֲבוֹתַי, שֶׁתַּשְׁכִּיבֵנִי לְשָׁלוֹם וְתַעֲמִידֵנִי לְשָׁלוֹם, וְאַל יְבַהֲלוּנִי רַעְיוֹנַי וַחֲלוֹמוֹת רָעִים וְהִרְהוּרִים רָעִים, וּתְהֵא מִטָּתִי שְׁלֵמָה לְפָנֶיךָ, וְהָאֵר עֵינַי פֶּן אִישַׁן הַמָּוֶת, כִּי אַתָּה הַמֵּאִיר לְאִישׁוֹן בַּת עָיִן. בָּרוּךְ אַתָּה יהוה, הַמֵּאִיר לָעוֹלָם כֻּלּוֹ בִּכְבוֹדוֹ.

When saying all three paragraphs of שמע, say:

אֵל מֶלֶךְ נֶאֱמָן

The following verse should be said aloud, while covering the eyes with the right hand:

דברים ו

שְׁמַע יִשְׂרָאֵל, יהוה אֱלֹהֵינוּ, יהוה ׀ אֶחָד:

Quietly בָּרוּךְ שֵׁם כְּבוֹד מַלְכוּתוֹ לְעוֹלָם וָעֶד.

דברים ו

וְאָהַבְתָּ אֵת יהוה אֱלֹהֶיךָ, בְּכָל־לְבָבְךָ וּבְכָל־נַפְשְׁךָ וּבְכָל־מְאֹדֶךָ: וְהָיוּ הַדְּבָרִים הָאֵלֶּה, אֲשֶׁר אָנֹכִי מְצַוְּךָ הַיּוֹם, עַל־לְבָבֶךָ: וְשִׁנַּנְתָּם לְבָנֶיךָ וְדִבַּרְתָּ בָּם, בְּשִׁבְתְּךָ בְּבֵיתֶךָ וּבְלֶכְתְּךָ בַדֶּרֶךְ, וּבְשָׁכְבְּךָ וּבְקוּמֶךָ: וּקְשַׁרְתָּם לְאוֹת עַל־יָדֶךָ וְהָיוּ לְטֹטָפֹת בֵּין עֵינֶיךָ: וּכְתַבְתָּם עַל־מְזוּזוֹת בֵּיתֶךָ וּבִשְׁעָרֶיךָ:

SHEMA BEFORE SLEEP AT NIGHT

Just as our first words in the morning should be words of prayer, so should our last at night. The night prayers consist of: (1) a prayer for peaceful sleep and a safe awakening, mentioned in the Talmud (*Berakhot* 60b); (2) the first paragraph of the Shema, ensuring these words are with us וּבְשָׁכְבְּךָ "when we lie down"; (3) Psalm 91, a prayer for protection from danger; (4) Psalm 3, chosen because of its reference to night: "I lie down to sleep and I wake again, for the LORD supports me"; (5) הַשְׁכִּיבֵנוּ "Help us lie down" – three paragraphs

וִיהִי May the pleasantness of the LORD our God be upon us. Establish for us *Ps. 90* the work of our hands, O establish the work of our hands.

יֹשֵׁב He who lives in the shelter of the Most High dwells in the shadow of the *Ps. 91* Almighty. I say of God, my Refuge and Stronghold, my LORD in whom I trust, that He will save you from the fowler's snare and the deadly pestilence. With His pinions He will cover you, and beneath His wings you will find shelter; His faithfulness is an encircling shield. You need not fear terror by night, nor the arrow that flies by day; not the pestilence that stalks in darkness, nor the plague that ravages at noon. A thousand may fall at your side, ten thousand at your right hand, but it will not come near you. You will only look with your eyes and see the punishment of the wicked. Because you said, "The LORD is my Refuge," taking the Most High as your shelter, no harm will befall you, no plague come near your tent, for He will command His angels about you, to guard you in all your ways. They will lift you in their hands, lest your foot stumble on a stone. You will tread on lions and vipers; you will trample on young lions and snakes. [God says:] "Because he loves Me, I will rescue him; I will protect him, because he acknowledges My name. When he calls on Me, I will answer him; I will be with him in distress, I will deliver him and bring him honor. With long life I will satisfy him and show him My salvation.

With long life I will satisfy him and show him My salvation.

יהוה LORD, how numerous are my enemies, how many rise against me. Many *Ps. 3* say of me: "There is no help for him in God," Selah. But You, LORD, are a shield around me. You are my glory; You raise my head high. I cry aloud to the LORD, and He answers me from His holy mountain, Selah. I lie down to sleep and I wake again, for the LORD supports me. I will not fear the myriad forces ranged against me on all sides. Arise, LORD, save me, O my God; strike all my enemies across the cheek; break the teeth of the wicked. From the LORD comes deliverance; may Your blessing rest upon Your people, Selah.

הַשְׁכִּיבֵנוּ Help us lie down, O LORD our God, in peace, and rise up, O our King, to life. Spread over us Your canopy of peace. Direct us with Your good counsel, and save us for the sake of Your name. Shield us and remove from us every enemy, plague, sword, famine and sorrow. Remove the adversary from before and behind us. Shelter us in the shadow of Your wings, for You, God, are our Guardian and Deliverer; You, God, are a gracious and compassionate King. Guard our going out and our coming in, for life and peace, from now and for ever.

וִיהִי נֹעַם אֲדֹנָי אֱלֹהֵינוּ עָלֵינוּ וּמַעֲשֵׂה יָדֵינוּ כּוֹנְנָה עָלֵינוּ וּמַעֲשֵׂה יָדֵינוּ תהלים צ
כּוֹנְנֵהוּ:

יֹשֵׁב בְּסֵתֶר עֶלְיוֹן, בְּצֵל שַׁדַּי יִתְלוֹנָן: אֹמַר לַיהוה מַחְסִי וּמְצוּדָתִי, אֱלֹהַי תהלים צא
אֶבְטַח־בּוֹ: כִּי הוּא יַצִּילְךָ מִפַּח יָקוּשׁ, מִדֶּבֶר הַוּוֹת: בְּאֶבְרָתוֹ יָסֶךְ לָךְ,
וְתַחַת־כְּנָפָיו תֶּחְסֶה, צִנָּה וְסֹחֵרָה אֲמִתּוֹ: לֹא־תִירָא מִפַּחַד לָיְלָה, מֵחֵץ
יָעוּף יוֹמָם: מִדֶּבֶר בָּאֹפֶל יַהֲלֹךְ, מִקֶּטֶב יָשׁוּד צָהֳרָיִם: יִפֹּל מִצִּדְּךָ אֶלֶף,
וּרְבָבָה מִימִינֶךָ, אֵלֶיךָ לֹא יִגָּשׁ: רַק בְּעֵינֶיךָ תַבִּיט, וְשִׁלֻּמַת רְשָׁעִים תִּרְאֶה:
כִּי־אַתָּה יהוה מַחְסִי, עֶלְיוֹן שַׂמְתָּ מְעוֹנֶךָ: לֹא־תְאֻנֶּה אֵלֶיךָ רָעָה, וְנֶגַע
לֹא־יִקְרַב בְּאָהֳלֶךָ: כִּי מַלְאָכָיו יְצַוֶּה־לָּךְ, לִשְׁמָרְךָ בְּכָל־דְּרָכֶיךָ: עַל־כַּפַּיִם
יִשָּׂאוּנְךָ, פֶּן־תִּגֹּף בָּאֶבֶן רַגְלֶךָ: עַל־שַׁחַל וָפֶתֶן תִּדְרֹךְ, תִּרְמֹס כְּפִיר וְתַנִּין:
כִּי בִי חָשַׁק וַאֲפַלְּטֵהוּ, אֲשַׂגְּבֵהוּ כִּי־יָדַע שְׁמִי: יִקְרָאֵנִי וְאֶעֱנֵהוּ, עִמּוֹ־אָנֹכִי
בְצָרָה, אֲחַלְּצֵהוּ וַאֲכַבְּדֵהוּ: אֹרֶךְ יָמִים אַשְׂבִּיעֵהוּ, וְאַרְאֵהוּ בִּישׁוּעָתִי:
אֹרֶךְ יָמִים אַשְׂבִּיעֵהוּ, וְאַרְאֵהוּ בִּישׁוּעָתִי:

יהוה מָה־רַבּוּ צָרָי, רַבִּים קָמִים עָלָי: רַבִּים אֹמְרִים לְנַפְשִׁי, אֵין יְשׁוּעָתָה תהלים ג
לּוֹ בֵאלֹהִים, סֶלָה: וְאַתָּה יהוה מָגֵן בַּעֲדִי, כְּבוֹדִי וּמֵרִים רֹאשִׁי: קוֹלִי
אֶל־יהוה אֶקְרָא, וַיַּעֲנֵנִי מֵהַר קָדְשׁוֹ, סֶלָה: אֲנִי שָׁכַבְתִּי וָאִישָׁנָה, הֱקִיצוֹתִי
כִּי יהוה יִסְמְכֵנִי: לֹא־אִירָא מֵרִבְבוֹת עָם, אֲשֶׁר סָבִיב שָׁתוּ עָלָי: קוּמָה
יהוה, הוֹשִׁיעֵנִי אֱלֹהַי, כִּי־הִכִּיתָ אֶת־כָּל־אֹיְבַי לֶחִי, שִׁנֵּי רְשָׁעִים שִׁבַּרְתָּ:
לַיהוה הַיְשׁוּעָה, עַל־עַמְּךָ בִרְכָתֶךָ סֶּלָה:

הַשְׁכִּיבֵנוּ, יהוה אֱלֹהֵינוּ, לְשָׁלוֹם. וְהַעֲמִידֵנוּ, מַלְכֵּנוּ, לְחַיִּים. וּפְרֹשׂ עָלֵינוּ
סֻכַּת שְׁלוֹמֶךָ, וְתַקְּנֵנוּ בְּעֵצָה טוֹבָה מִלְּפָנֶיךָ, וְהוֹשִׁיעֵנוּ לְמַעַן שְׁמֶךָ. וְהָגֵן
בַּעֲדֵנוּ, וְהָסֵר מֵעָלֵינוּ אוֹיֵב, דֶּבֶר וְחֶרֶב וְרָעָב וְיָגוֹן. וְהָסֵר שָׂטָן מִלְּפָנֵינוּ
וּמֵאַחֲרֵינוּ, וּבְצֵל כְּנָפֶיךָ תַּסְתִּירֵנוּ, כִּי אֵל שׁוֹמְרֵנוּ וּמַצִּילֵנוּ אָתָּה, כִּי אֵל מֶלֶךְ
חַנּוּן וְרַחוּם אָתָּה. וּשְׁמֹר צֵאתֵנוּ וּבוֹאֵנוּ לְחַיִּים וּלְשָׁלוֹם מֵעַתָּה וְעַד עוֹלָם.

---

sleep; and (10) Adon Olam / "Lᴏʀᴅ of the Universe," said here because of
its closing lines with their reference to entrusting our souls and bodies to
God's safekeeping at night.

בָּרוּךְ Blessed is the Lord by day, blessed is the Lord by night. Blessed is the Lord when we lie down; blessed is the Lord when we rise. For in Your hand are the souls of the living and the dead, [as it is written:] "In His hand *Job 12* is every living soul, and the breath of all mankind." Into Your hand I entrust *Ps. 31* my spirit: You redeemed me, Lord, God of truth. Our God in heaven, bring unity to Your name, establish Your kingdom constantly and reign over us for ever and all time.

יִרְאוּ May our eyes see, our hearts rejoice, and our souls be glad in Your true salvation, when Zion is told, "Your God reigns." The Lord is King, the Lord was King, and the Lord will be King for ever and all time. For sovereignty is Yours, and to all eternity You will reign in glory, for we have no king but You.

הַמַּלְאָךְ May the angel who rescued me from all harm, bless these boys. May *Gen. 48* they be called by my name and the names of my fathers Abraham and Isaac, and may they increase greatly on the earth.

וַיֹּאמֶר He said, "If you listen carefully to the voice of the Lord your God and *Ex. 15* do what is right in His eyes, if you pay attention to His commandments and keep all His statutes, I will not bring on you any of the diseases I brought on the Egyptians, for I am the Lord who heals you." The Lord said to the *Zech. 3* accuser, "The Lord shall rebuke you, accuser. The Lord who has chosen Jerusalem shall rebuke you! Is not this man a burning stick snatched from the fire?" Look! It is Solomon's bed, escorted by sixty warriors, the noblest *Song. 3* of Israel, all of them wearing the sword, experienced in battle, each with his sword at his side, prepared for the terror of the nights.

Say three times:

יְבָרֶכְךָ May the Lord bless you and protect you. *Num. 6*
May the Lord make His face shine on you and be gracious to you.
May the Lord turn His face toward you and grant you peace.

Say three times:

הִנֵּה See – the Guardian of Israel neither slumbers nor sleeps. *Ps. 121*

Say three times:

לִישׁוּעָתְךָ For Your salvation I hope, Lord. *Gen. 49*
I hope, Lord, for Your salvation.
Lord, for Your salvation I hope.

בָּרוּךְ יהוה בַּיּוֹם, בָּרוּךְ יהוה בַּלַּיְלָה, בָּרוּךְ יהוה בְּשָׁכְבֵּנוּ, בָּרוּךְ יהוה
בְּקוּמֵנוּ. כִּי בְיָדְךָ נַפְשׁוֹת הַחַיִּים וְהַמֵּתִים. אֲשֶׁר בְּיָדוֹ נֶפֶשׁ כָּל־חָי, וְרוּחַ
כָּל־בְּשַׂר־אִישׁ. בְּיָדְךָ אַפְקִיד רוּחִי, פָּדִיתָה אוֹתִי יהוה אֵל אֱמֶת: אֱלֹהֵינוּ
שֶׁבַּשָּׁמַיִם, יַחֵד שִׁמְךָ וְקַיֵּם מַלְכוּתְךָ תָּמִיד, וּמְלֹךְ עָלֵינוּ לְעוֹלָם וָעֶד.

איוב יב
תהלים לא

יִרְאוּ עֵינֵינוּ וְיִשְׂמַח לִבֵּנוּ, וְתָגֵל נַפְשֵׁנוּ בִּישׁוּעָתְךָ בֶּאֱמֶת, בֶּאֱמֹר לְצִיּוֹן
מָלַךְ אֱלֹהָיִךְ. יהוה מֶלֶךְ, יהוה מָלָךְ, יהוה יִמְלֹךְ לְעוֹלָם וָעֶד. כִּי הַמַּלְכוּת
שֶׁלְּךָ הִיא, וּלְעוֹלְמֵי עַד תִּמְלֹךְ בְּכָבוֹד, כִּי אֵין לָנוּ מֶלֶךְ אֶלָּא אָתָּה.

בראשית מח

הַמַּלְאָךְ הַגֹּאֵל אֹתִי מִכָּל־רָע יְבָרֵךְ אֶת־הַנְּעָרִים, וְיִקָּרֵא בָהֶם שְׁמִי וְשֵׁם
אֲבֹתַי אַבְרָהָם וְיִצְחָק, וְיִדְגּוּ לָרֹב בְּקֶרֶב הָאָרֶץ:

שמות טו

וַיֹּאמֶר אִם־שָׁמוֹעַ תִּשְׁמַע לְקוֹל יהוה אֱלֹהֶיךָ, וְהַיָּשָׁר בְּעֵינָיו תַּעֲשֶׂה,
וְהַאֲזַנְתָּ לְמִצְוֹתָיו וְשָׁמַרְתָּ כָּל־חֻקָּיו, כָּל־הַמַּחֲלָה אֲשֶׁר־שַׂמְתִּי בְמִצְרַיִם
לֹא־אָשִׂים עָלֶיךָ, כִּי אֲנִי יהוה רֹפְאֶךָ: וַיֹּאמֶר יהוה אֶל־הַשָּׂטָן, יִגְעַר יהוה

זכריה ג

בְּךָ הַשָּׂטָן, וְיִגְעַר יהוה בְּךָ הַבֹּחֵר בִּירוּשָׁלָם, הֲלוֹא זֶה אוּד מֻצָּל מֵאֵשׁ:
הִנֵּה מִטָּתוֹ שֶׁלִּשְׁלֹמֹה, שִׁשִּׁים גִּבֹּרִים סָבִיב לָהּ, מִגִּבֹּרֵי יִשְׂרָאֵל: כֻּלָּם

שיר
השירים ג

אֲחֻזֵי חֶרֶב, מְלֻמְּדֵי מִלְחָמָה, אִישׁ חַרְבּוֹ עַל־יְרֵכוֹ מִפַּחַד בַּלֵּילוֹת:

Say three times:

במדברו

יְבָרֶכְךָ יהוה וְיִשְׁמְרֶךָ:
יָאֵר יהוה פָּנָיו אֵלֶיךָ וִיחֻנֶּךָּ:
יִשָּׂא יהוה פָּנָיו אֵלֶיךָ וְיָשֵׂם לְךָ שָׁלוֹם:

Say three times:

תהלים קכא

הִנֵּה לֹא־יָנוּם וְלֹא יִישָׁן שׁוֹמֵר יִשְׂרָאֵל:

Say three times:

בראשית מט

לִישׁוּעָתְךָ קִוִּיתִי יהוה:
קִוִּיתִי יהוה לִישׁוּעָתְךָ:
יהוה לִישׁוּעָתְךָ קִוִּיתִי:

Say three times:

בְּשֵׁם In the name of the LORD, God of Israel:
may Michael be at my right hand,
Gabriel, at my left;
in front of me, Uriel,
behind me, Raphael;
and above my head the Presence of God.

שִׁיר הַמַּעֲלוֹת A song of ascents.   *Ps. 128*
Happy are all who fear the LORD, who walk in His ways.
When you eat the fruit of your labor, happy and fortunate are you.
Your wife shall be like a fruitful vine within your house;
your sons like olive saplings around your table.
So shall the man who fears the LORD be blessed.
May the LORD bless you from Zion;
may you see the good of Jerusalem all the days of your life;
and may you live to see your children's children. Peace be on Israel!

Say three times:

רִגְזוּ Tremble, and do not sin.   *Ps. 4*
Search your heart as you lie on your bed, and be silent. Selah.

אֲדוֹן עוֹלָם LORD of the Universe,
who reigned before the birth of any thing;
when by His will all things were made,
then was His name proclaimed King.
And when all things shall cease to be,
He alone will reign in awe.
He was, He is, and He shall be glorious for evermore.
He is One, there is none else, alone, unique, beyond compare;
Without beginning, without end, His might, His rule are everywhere.
He is my God; my Redeemer lives.
He is the Rock on whom I rely –
my banner and my safe retreat, my cup, my portion when I cry.
Into His hand my soul I place, when I awake and when I sleep.
The LORD is with me, I shall not fear;
body and soul from harm will He keep.

Say three times:

בְּשֵׁם יהוה אֱלֹהֵי יִשְׂרָאֵל

מִימִינִי מִיכָאֵל, וּמִשְּׂמֹאלִי גַּבְרִיאֵל

וּמִלְּפָנַי אוּרִיאֵל, וּמֵאֲחוֹרַי רְפָאֵל

וְעַל רֹאשִׁי שְׁכִינַת אֵל.

תהלים קכח

שִׁיר הַמַּעֲלוֹת, אַשְׁרֵי כָּל־יְרֵא יהוה, הַהֹלֵךְ בִּדְרָכָיו:
יְגִיעַ כַּפֶּיךָ כִּי תֹאכֵל, אַשְׁרֶיךָ וְטוֹב לָךְ:
אֶשְׁתְּךָ כְּגֶפֶן פֹּרִיָּה בְּיַרְכְּתֵי בֵיתֶךָ
בָּנֶיךָ כִּשְׁתִלֵי זֵיתִים, סָבִיב לְשֻׁלְחָנֶךָ:
הִנֵּה כִי־כֵן יְבֹרַךְ גָּבֶר יְרֵא יהוה:
יְבָרֶכְךָ יהוה מִצִּיּוֹן, וּרְאֵה בְּטוּב יְרוּשָׁלָ͏ִם, כֹּל יְמֵי חַיֶּיךָ:
וּרְאֵה־בָנִים לְבָנֶיךָ, שָׁלוֹם עַל־יִשְׂרָאֵל:

Say three times:

תהלים ד

רִגְזוּ וְאַל־תֶּחֱטָאוּ
אִמְרוּ בִלְבַבְכֶם עַל־מִשְׁכַּבְכֶם, וְדֹמּוּ סֶלָה:

אֲדוֹן עוֹלָם אֲשֶׁר מָלַךְ בְּטֶרֶם כָּל־יְצִיר נִבְרָא.
לְעֵת נַעֲשָׂה בְחֶפְצוֹ כֹּל אֲזַי מֶלֶךְ שְׁמוֹ נִקְרָא.
וְאַחֲרֵי כִּכְלוֹת הַכֹּל לְבַדּוֹ יִמְלֹךְ נוֹרָא.
וְהוּא הָיָה וְהוּא הֹוֶה וְהוּא יִהְיֶה בְּתִפְאָרָה.
וְהוּא אֶחָד וְאֵין שֵׁנִי לְהַמְשִׁיל לוֹ לְהַחְבִּירָה.
בְּלִי רֵאשִׁית בְּלִי תַכְלִית וְלוֹ הָעֹז וְהַמִּשְׂרָה.
וְהוּא אֵלִי וְחַי גֹּאֲלִי וְצוּר חֶבְלִי בְּעֵת צָרָה.
וְהוּא נִסִּי וּמָנוֹס לִי מְנָת כּוֹסִי בְּיוֹם אֶקְרָא.
בְּיָדוֹ אַפְקִיד רוּחִי בְּעֵת אִישַׁן וְאָעִירָה.
וְעִם רוּחִי גְּוִיָּתִי יהוה לִי וְלֹא אִירָא.

מועדים
FESTIVALS

Hallel

*On Ḥanukka, Yom HaAtzma'ut and Yom Yerushalayim, Full Hallel is said.
On Rosh Ḥodesh Half Hallel is said. See laws 132–133.*

בָּרוּךְ Blessed are You, LORD our God, King of the Universe,
who has made us holy through His commandments
and has commanded us to recite the Hallel.

הַלְלוּיָהּ Halleluya! Servants of the LORD, give praise; praise the name   Ps. 113
of the LORD. Blessed be the name of the LORD now and for evermore.
From the rising of the sun to its setting, may the LORD's name be
praised. High is the LORD above all nations; His glory is above the
heavens. Who is like the LORD our God, who sits enthroned so high,
yet turns so low to see the heavens and the earth? ‣ He raises the poor
from the dust and the needy from the refuse heap, giving them a place
alongside princes, the princes of His people. He makes the woman in
a childless house a happy mother of children. Halleluya!

---

at every epoch and at every trouble – may it not come to them! – and when
they are redeemed, they recite it in thanks for their delivery" (*Pesaḥim* 117a).
That is why we say it on Yom HaAtzma'ut and Yom Yerushalayim, the two
most transformative events of modern Jewish history, in the faith that it is not
human beings alone who shape the destiny of our people, but God working
in and through His children.

Because of its association with history, Hallel is not said on Rosh HaShana
or Yom Kippur, days dedicated less to national remembrance than to judgment, repentance and forgiveness.

מְקִימִי מֵעָפָר דָּל *He raises the poor from the dust:* A verse reminiscent of Hannah's prayer after the birth of her child (1 Sam. 2:8). The religions of the ancient world were deeply conservative, designed to vindicate and perpetuate
hierarchies of power. Judaism, believing that human dignity is the prerogative
of everyone, was an ongoing protest against such inequalities. God's greatness is evident in the fact that He can lift the poor and the needy to a place
of honor alongside princes.

סֵדֶר הַלֵּל

On ראש חודש, יום ירושלים and יום העצמאות, חנוכה הלל שלם is said. On
הלל בדילוג is said. See laws 132–133.

בָּרוּךְ אַתָּה יהוה אֱלֹהֵינוּ מֶלֶךְ הָעוֹלָם
אֲשֶׁר קִדְּשָֽׁנוּ בְּמִצְוֺתָיו וְצִוָּֽנוּ לִקְרֹא אֶת הַהַלֵּל.

הַלְלוּיָהּ, הַלְלוּ עַבְדֵי יהוה, הַלְלוּ אֶת־שֵׁם יהוה: יְהִי שֵׁם יהוה
מְבֹרָךְ, מֵעַתָּה וְעַד־עוֹלָם: מִמִּזְרַח־שֶׁמֶשׁ עַד־מְבוֹאוֹ, מְהֻלָּל שֵׁם
יהוה: רָם עַל־כָּל־גּוֹיִם יהוה, עַל הַשָּׁמַֽיִם כְּבוֹדוֹ: מִי כַּיהוה אֱלֹהֵֽינוּ,
הַמַּגְבִּיהִי לָשֶֽׁבֶת: הַמַּשְׁפִּילִי לִרְאוֹת, בַּשָּׁמַֽיִם וּבָאָֽרֶץ: ◄ מְקִימִי
מֵעָפָר דָּל, מֵאַשְׁפֹּת יָרִים אֶבְיוֹן: לְהוֹשִׁיבִי עִם־נְדִיבִים, עִם נְדִיבֵי
עַמּוֹ: מוֹשִׁיבִי עֲקֶֽרֶת הַבַּֽיִת, אֵם־הַבָּנִים שְׂמֵחָה, הַלְלוּיָהּ:

תהלים קיג

HALLEL

Psalms 113–118 – known as the Egyptian Hallel because of the reference in
the second paragraph to the exodus from Egypt – are among the earliest
prayers written to be recited in the Temple on days of national celebration.
They were sung as accompaniment to the Pesaḥ sacrifice, and early rabbinic
sources suggest that they were said on the pilgrimage festivals: Pesaḥ, Shavuot and Sukkot.

By the Talmudic era, a shortened form (known as "Half Hallel") was in
use for Rosh Ḥodesh and the last six days of Pesaḥ. The Full Hallel was not
said on Rosh Ḥodesh, because it is not a full festival, and on the last days of
Pesaḥ because (a) the main event of the exodus took place on the first day,
and (b) the miracle of the seventh day, the division of the Reed Sea, involved
suffering for the Egyptians. According to the Talmud (*Megilla* 10b; *Sanhedrin* 39b), when the angels wished to sing the Song at the Sea, God refused,
saying: "Shall you sing a song while My creatures are drowning in the sea?"

Hallel is a choral symphony of faith in the presence of God in history.
The sages said that the prophets "enacted that the Israelites should recite it

בְּצֵאת When Israel came out of Egypt, the house of Jacob from a   *Ps. 114*
people of foreign tongue, Judah became His sanctuary, Israel His
dominion. The sea saw and fled; the Jordan turned back. The mountains skipped like rams, the hills like lambs. ‣ Why was it, sea, that you
fled? Jordan, why did you turn back? Why, mountains, did you skip
like rams, and you, hills, like lambs? It was at the presence of the Lord,
Creator of the earth, at the presence of the God of Jacob, who turned
the rock into a pool of water, flint into a flowing spring.

Omit on Rosh Ḥodesh (except on Ḥanukka):

לֹא לָנוּ Not to us, Lord, not to us, but to Your name give glory, for Your   *Ps. 115*
love, for Your faithfulness. Why should the nations say, "Where now is
their God?" Our God is in heaven; whatever He wills He does. Their
idols are silver and gold, made by human hands. They have mouths
but cannot speak; eyes but cannot see. They have ears but cannot
hear; noses but cannot smell. They have hands but cannot feel; feet
but cannot walk. No sound comes from their throat. Those who make
them become like them; so will all who trust in them. ‣ Israel, trust in
the Lord – He is their Help and their Shield. House of Aaron, trust in
the Lord – He is their Help and their Shield. You who fear the Lord,
trust in the Lord – He is their Help and their Shield.

יהוה זְכָרָנוּ The Lord remembers us and will bless us. He will bless
the house of Israel. He will bless the house of Aaron. He will bless
those who fear the Lord, small and great alike. May the Lord give
you increase: you and your children. May you be blessed by the Lord,
Maker of heaven and earth. ‣ The heavens are the Lord's, but the earth
He has given over to mankind. It is not the dead who praise the Lord,
nor those who go down to the silent grave. But we will bless the Lord,
now and for ever. Halleluya!

_____

yet imperfect, ideals. Idolatry is the worship of the part instead of the whole,
one aspect of the universe in place of the Creator of all who transcends all.

יִרְאֵי יהוה *You who fear the Lord:* This may refer to converts to Judaism
(Rashi), or God-fearers among the nations (Ibn Ezra).

וְהָאָרֶץ נָתַן לִבְנֵי־אָדָם *But the earth He has given over to mankind:* "Given over"
rather than "given": placed in the guardianship of mankind. We do not own

תהלים קיד

בְּצֵאת יִשְׂרָאֵל מִמִּצְרָיִם, בֵּית יַעֲקֹב מֵעַם לֹעֵז: הָיְתָה יְהוּדָה
לְקָדְשׁוֹ, יִשְׂרָאֵל מַמְשְׁלוֹתָיו: הַיָּם רָאָה וַיָּנֹס, הַיַּרְדֵּן יִסֹּב לְאָחוֹר:
הֶהָרִים רָקְדוּ כְאֵילִים, גְּבָעוֹת כִּבְנֵי־צֹאן: ‹ מַה־לְּךָ הַיָּם כִּי תָנוּס,
הַיַּרְדֵּן תִּסֹּב לְאָחוֹר: הֶהָרִים תִּרְקְדוּ כְאֵילִים, גְּבָעוֹת כִּבְנֵי־צֹאן:
מִלִּפְנֵי אָדוֹן חוּלִי אָרֶץ, מִלִּפְנֵי אֱלוֹהַּ יַעֲקֹב: הַהֹפְכִי הַצּוּר אֲגַם־
מָיִם, חַלָּמִישׁ לְמַעְיְנוֹ־מָיִם:

Omit on ראש חודש (*except on* חנוכה):

תהלים קטו

לֹא לָנוּ יהוה לֹא לָנוּ, כִּי־לְשִׁמְךָ תֵּן כָּבוֹד, עַל־חַסְדְּךָ עַל־אֲמִתֶּךָ: לָמָּה
יֹאמְרוּ הַגּוֹיִם אַיֵּה־נָא אֱלֹהֵיהֶם: וֵאלֹהֵינוּ בַשָּׁמָיִם, כֹּל אֲשֶׁר־חָפֵץ
עָשָׂה: עֲצַבֵּיהֶם כֶּסֶף וְזָהָב, מַעֲשֵׂה יְדֵי אָדָם: פֶּה־לָהֶם וְלֹא יְדַבֵּרוּ,
עֵינַיִם לָהֶם וְלֹא יִרְאוּ: אָזְנַיִם לָהֶם וְלֹא יִשְׁמָעוּ, אַף לָהֶם וְלֹא יְרִיחוּן:
יְדֵיהֶם וְלֹא יְמִישׁוּן, רַגְלֵיהֶם וְלֹא יְהַלֵּכוּ, לֹא־יֶהְגּוּ בִּגְרוֹנָם: כְּמוֹהֶם יִהְיוּ
עֹשֵׂיהֶם, כֹּל אֲשֶׁר־בֹּטֵחַ בָּהֶם: ‹ יִשְׂרָאֵל בְּטַח בַּיהוה, עֶזְרָם וּמָגִנָּם
הוּא: בֵּית אַהֲרֹן בִּטְחוּ בַיהוה, עֶזְרָם וּמָגִנָּם הוּא: יִרְאֵי יהוה בִּטְחוּ
בַיהוה, עֶזְרָם וּמָגִנָּם הוּא:

יהוה זְכָרָנוּ יְבָרֵךְ, יְבָרֵךְ אֶת־בֵּית יִשְׂרָאֵל, יְבָרֵךְ אֶת־בֵּית אַהֲרֹן:
יְבָרֵךְ יִרְאֵי יהוה, הַקְּטַנִּים עִם־הַגְּדֹלִים: יֹסֵף יהוה עֲלֵיכֶם, עֲלֵיכֶם
וְעַל־בְּנֵיכֶם: בְּרוּכִים אַתֶּם לַיהוה, עֹשֵׂה שָׁמַיִם וָאָרֶץ: ‹ הַשָּׁמַיִם
שָׁמַיִם לַיהוה, וְהָאָרֶץ נָתַן לִבְנֵי־אָדָם: לֹא הַמֵּתִים יְהַלְלוּ־יָהּ, וְלֹא
כָּל־יֹרְדֵי דוּמָה: וַאֲנַחְנוּ נְבָרֵךְ יָהּ, מֵעַתָּה וְעַד־עוֹלָם, הַלְלוּיָהּ:

בְּצֵאת יִשְׂרָאֵל מִמִּצְרָיִם *When Israel came out of Egypt:* A lyrical account of how
nature itself trembled and rejoiced at the exodus, when the supreme Power
intervened to rescue the powerless.

כְּמוֹהֶם יִהְיוּ עֹשֵׂיהֶם *Those who make them become like them:* Worshiping imper-
sonal objects or forces eventually dehumanizes a culture and those who are
part of it. Whether what is worshiped is an icon, a ruler, a race or a political
ideology, the final outcome is the sacrifice of human lives on the altar of high,

Omit on Rosh Ḥodesh (except on Ḥanukka):

אָהַבְתִּי I love the LORD, for He hears my voice, my pleas. He turns His *Ps. 116*
ear to me whenever I call. The bonds of death encompassed me, the
anguish of the grave came upon me, I was overcome by trouble and
sorrow. Then I called on the name of the LORD: "LORD, I pray, save my
life." Gracious is the LORD, and righteous; our God is full of compassion. The LORD protects the simple hearted. When I was brought low,
He saved me. My soul, be at peace once more, for the LORD has been
good to you. For You have rescued me from death, my eyes from weeping, my feet from stumbling. ‣ I shall walk in the presence of the LORD
in the land of the living. I had faith, even when I said, "I am greatly
afflicted," even when I said rashly, "All men are liars."

מָה־אָשִׁיב How can I repay the LORD for all His goodness to me? I will
lift the cup of salvation and call on the name of the LORD. I will fulfill
my vows to the LORD in the presence of all His people. Grievous in
the LORD's sight is the death of His devoted ones. Truly, LORD, I am
Your servant; I am Your servant, the son of Your maidservant. You set
me free from my chains. ‣ To You I shall bring a thanksgiving-offering
and call on the LORD by name. I will fulfill my vows to the LORD in
the presence of all His people, in the courts of the House of the LORD,
in your midst, Jerusalem. Halleluya!

מָה־אָשִׁיב *How can I repay?* A rhetorical question: we can never repay God's
kindnesses to us. All that we have is His. The very fact that we exist is due to
His creative love. All we can do is express our thanks.

כּוֹס־יְשׁוּעוֹת אֶשָּׂא *I will lift the cup of salvation:* A reference to the wine-libation
accompanying a thanksgiving-offering (Rashi). Alternatively, I will hold a
feast of thanksgiving at which I will raise a glass of wine in thanks to God.

יָקָר בְּעֵינֵי יהוה, הַמָּוְתָה לַחֲסִידָיו *Grievous in the LORD's sight is the death of His
devoted ones:* this is Rashi's understanding of the text; others translate it as
"Precious in the LORD's sight." God does not wish His devoted ones to die.
As the previous two paragraphs have made clear, God is the God of life; only
idolatrous cultures worship death.

בֶּן־אֲמָתֶךָ *The son of Your maidservant:* Serving You comes naturally because
my mother did likewise (Radak). A father teaches us "the discipline of

Omit on ראש חודש *(except on* חנוכה*):*   תהלים קטז

אָהַבְתִּי, כִּי־יִשְׁמַע יהוה, אֶת־קוֹלִי תַּחֲנוּנָי: כִּי־הִטָּה אָזְנוֹ לִי, וּבְיָמַי
אֶקְרָא: אֲפָפוּנִי חֶבְלֵי־מֶוֶת, וּמְצָרֵי שְׁאוֹל מְצָאוּנִי, צָרָה וְיָגוֹן אֶמְצָא:
וּבְשֵׁם־יהוה אֶקְרָא, אָנָּה יהוה מַלְּטָה נַפְשִׁי: חַנּוּן יהוה וְצַדִּיק, וֵאלֹהֵינוּ
מְרַחֵם: שֹׁמֵר פְּתָאיִם יהוה, דַּלּוֹתִי וְלִי יְהוֹשִׁיעַ: שׁוּבִי נַפְשִׁי לִמְנוּחָיְכִי,
כִּי־יהוה גָּמַל עָלָיְכִי: כִּי חִלַּצְתָּ נַפְשִׁי מִמָּוֶת, אֶת־עֵינִי מִן־דִּמְעָה,
אֶת־רַגְלִי מִדֶּחִי: אֶתְהַלֵּךְ לִפְנֵי יהוה, בְּאַרְצוֹת הַחַיִּים: הֶאֱמַנְתִּי כִּי
אֲדַבֵּר, אֲנִי עָנִיתִי מְאֹד: אֲנִי אָמַרְתִּי בְחָפְזִי, כָּל־הָאָדָם כֹּזֵב:

מָה־אָשִׁיב לַיהוה, כָּל־תַּגְמוּלוֹהִי עָלָי: כּוֹס־יְשׁוּעוֹת אֶשָּׂא, וּבְשֵׁם
יהוה אֶקְרָא: נְדָרַי לַיהוה אֲשַׁלֵּם, נֶגְדָה־נָּא לְכָל־עַמּוֹ: יָקָר בְּעֵינֵי
יהוה, הַמָּוְתָה לַחֲסִידָיו: אָנָּה יהוה כִּי־אֲנִי עַבְדֶּךָ, אֲנִי־עַבְדְּךָ
בֶּן־אֲמָתֶךָ, פִּתַּחְתָּ לְמוֹסֵרָי: ‹ לְךָ־אֶזְבַּח זֶבַח תּוֹדָה, וּבְשֵׁם יהוה
אֶקְרָא: נְדָרַי לַיהוה אֲשַׁלֵּם, נֶגְדָה־נָּא לְכָל־עַמּוֹ: בְּחַצְרוֹת בֵּית
יהוה, בְּתוֹכֵכִי יְרוּשָׁלָיִם, הַלְלוּיָהּ:

---

the earth; we hold it in trust from God and there are conditions to that trust,
namely that we respect the earth's integrity and the dignity of the human
person; in short, that we honor God's laws.

אָהַבְתִּי *I love the LORD:* This and the next paragraph form a single psalm. The
psalmist turns from the collective to the individual. God has saved him from
crisis and he gives public voice to his thanks. This prayer was included in Hallel because it spoke to the many among the pilgrims to Jerusalem who had
vowed to bring thanksgiving-offerings, as is clear from the next paragraph.
The juxtaposition of the individual and the collective is a significant feature
of biblical texts generally. The Hebrew prophets and poets never saw the
nation as an abstraction and the people an amorphous mass. The individual
never loses his or her significance even in the presence of vast gatherings.
אֲנִי אָמַרְתִּי בְחָפְזִי, כָּל־הָאָדָם כֹּזֵב *Even when I said rashly, "All men are liars":* the
commentators relate this to King David who, when forced to flee from Saul,
felt betrayed by everyone. Alternatively: "Even when I was fleeing for my life,
I knew that those [who preached despair] were false" (Radak).

הַלְלוּ Praise the Lord, all nations; acclaim Him, all you peoples;   Ps. 117
for His loving-kindness to us is strong,
and the Lord's faithfulness is everlasting.
Halleluya!

The following verses are chanted by the Leader.
At the end of each verse, the congregation responds, "Thank the Lord
for He is good; His loving-kindness is for ever." See law 133.

הוֹדוּ Thank the Lord for He is good;   His loving-kindness is for ever.   Ps. 118
Let Israel say   His loving-kindness is for ever.
Let the house of Aaron say   His loving-kindness is for ever.
Let those who fear the Lord say   His loving-kindness is for ever.

מִן־הַמֵּצַר In my distress I called on the Lord. The Lord answered me
and set me free. The Lord is with me; I will not be afraid. What can
man do to me? The Lord is with me. He is my Helper. I will see the
downfall of my enemies. It is better to take refuge in the Lord than
to trust in man. It is better to take refuge in the Lord than to trust
in princes. The nations all surrounded me, but in the Lord's name I
drove them off. They surrounded me on every side, but in the Lord's
name I drove them off. They surrounded me like bees, they attacked
me as fire attacks brushwood, but in the Lord's name I drove them
off. They thrust so hard against me, I nearly fell, but the Lord came
to my help. The Lord is my strength and my song; He has become
my salvation. Sounds of song and salvation resound in the tents of

---

has been for so long the guardian of prophecy and transmitted it to the rest
of the world – such a nation cannot be destroyed. The Jew is everlasting as
eternity itself" (Tolstoy).

הוֹדוּ לַיהוה כִּי־טוֹב *Thank the Lord for He is good:* This verse was first recited by
King David when he brought the Ark to Jerusalem (1 Chr. 16:34).

מִן־הַמֵּצַר *In my distress… set me free:* The terms mean, respectively, "straits,
confined space" and "broad space, expanse." The psalmist writes that he felt
hemmed in by enemies; his eventual victory brings a sense of spaciousness
and freedom.

תהלים קיז

הַלְלוּ אֶת־יהוה כָּל־גּוֹיִם, שַׁבְּחוּהוּ כָּל־הָאֻמִּים:
כִּי גָבַר עָלֵינוּ חַסְדּוֹ, וֶאֱמֶת־יהוה לְעוֹלָם
הַלְלוּיָהּ:

The following verses are chanted by the שְׁלִיחַ צִבּוּר.
At the end of each verse, the קהל responds: הוֹדוּ לַיהוה כִּי־טוֹב, כִּי לְעוֹלָם חַסְדּוֹ. See law 133.

תהלים קיח

כִּי לְעוֹלָם חַסְדּוֹ:	הוֹדוּ לַיהוה כִּי־טוֹב
כִּי לְעוֹלָם חַסְדּוֹ:	יֹאמַר־נָא יִשְׂרָאֵל
כִּי לְעוֹלָם חַסְדּוֹ:	יֹאמְרוּ־נָא בֵית־אַהֲרֹן
כִּי לְעוֹלָם חַסְדּוֹ:	יֹאמְרוּ־נָא יִרְאֵי יהוה

מִן־הַמֵּצַר קָרָאתִי יָּהּ, עָנָנִי בַמֶּרְחָב יָהּ: יהוה לִי לֹא אִירָא, מַה־
יַּעֲשֶׂה לִי אָדָם: יהוה לִי בְּעֹזְרָי, וַאֲנִי אֶרְאֶה בְשֹׂנְאָי: טוֹב לַחֲסוֹת
בַּיהוה, מִבְּטֹחַ בָּאָדָם: טוֹב לַחֲסוֹת בַּיהוה, מִבְּטֹחַ בִּנְדִיבִים:
כָּל־גּוֹיִם סְבָבְוּנִי, בְּשֵׁם יהוה כִּי אֲמִילַם: סַבְּוּנִי גַם־סְבָבְוּנִי, בְּשֵׁם
יהוה כִּי אֲמִילַם: סַבְּוּנִי כִדְבֹרִים, דֹּעֲכוּ כְּאֵשׁ קוֹצִים, בְּשֵׁם יהוה
כִּי אֲמִילַם: דָּחֹה דְחִיתַנִי לִנְפֹּל, וַיהוה עֲזָרָנִי: עָזִּי וְזִמְרָת יָהּ,

thought as well as the discipline of action"; a mother teaches us the "living experience" of the commandments, their "flavor, scent and warmth." From her we learn "to feel the presence of the Almighty." "The fathers knew much about the Shabbat; the mothers lived the Shabbat, experienced her presence, and perceived her beauty and splendor" (Rabbi Joseph Soloveitchik).

הַלְלוּ אֶת־יהוה כָּל־גּוֹיִם *Praise the Lord, all nations:* The shortest of all the psalms, a mere two verses. The psalmist speaks of the universal significance of Israel's history. It is not Israel alone, but all the nations, who will see in the story of this people, something beyond mere history. "The Jew is the emblem of eternity. He who neither slaughter nor torture of thousands of years could destroy, he who neither fire nor sword nor inquisition was able to wipe off the face of the earth, he who was the first to produce the oracles of God, who

the righteous: "The Lᴏʀᴅ's right hand has done mighty deeds. The
Lᴏʀᴅ's right hand is lifted high. The Lᴏʀᴅ's right hand has done
mighty deeds." I will not die but live, and tell what the Lᴏʀᴅ has done.
The Lᴏʀᴅ has chastened me severely, but He has not given me over
to death. ‣ Open for me the gates of righteousness that I may enter
them and thank the Lᴏʀᴅ. This is the gateway to the Lᴏʀᴅ; through
it, the righteous shall enter.

אוֹדְךָ‎ I will thank You, for You answered me, and became my salvation.
I will thank You, for You answered me, and became my salvation.

The stone the builders rejected has become the main cornerstone.
The stone the builders rejected has become the main cornerstone.

This is the Lᴏʀᴅ's doing; it is wondrous in our eyes.
This is the Lᴏʀᴅ's doing; it is wondrous in our eyes.

This is the day the Lᴏʀᴅ has made; let us rejoice and be glad in it.
This is the day the Lᴏʀᴅ has made; let us rejoice and be glad in it.

Leader followed by congregation:

אָנָּא‎ Lᴏʀᴅ, please, save us.
Lᴏʀᴅ, please, save us.
Lᴏʀᴅ, please, grant us success.
Lᴏʀᴅ, please, grant us success.

_____

אוֹדְךָ‎ *I will thank You:* This and the next eight verses, the last of Psalm 118, are
repeated. Litany – a prayer in which the Leader says a verse or phrase and the
congregation responds – was an aspect of worship in the Temple, and is developed most fully in the *hakafot*, processions around the synagogue, on Sukkot.

אֶבֶן מָאֲסוּ הַבּוֹנִים‎ *The stone the builders rejected:* This is a reference to the people
of Israel. Two of the first references to Israel in non-Jewish sources – the
Merneptah stele (Egypt, thirteenth century ʙᴄᴇ) and the Mesha stele (Moab,
ninth century ʙᴄᴇ) – both declare that Israel has been destroyed. Israel is the
people that outlives its obituaries.

וַיְהִי־לִי לִישׁוּעָה: קוֹל רִנָּה וִישׁוּעָה בְּאָהֳלֵי צַדִּיקִים, יְמִין יהוה
עֹשָׂה חָיִל: יְמִין יהוה רוֹמֵמָה, יְמִין יהוה עֹשָׂה חָיִל: לֹא־אָמוּת
כִּי־אֶחְיֶה, וַאֲסַפֵּר מַעֲשֵׂי יָהּ: יַסֹּר יִסְּרַנִּי יָּהּ, וְלַמָּוֶת לֹא נְתָנָנִי:
‹ פִּתְחוּ־לִי שַׁעֲרֵי־צֶדֶק, אָבֹא־בָם אוֹדֶה יָהּ: זֶה־הַשַּׁעַר לַיהוה,
צַדִּיקִים יָבֹאוּ בוֹ:

אוֹדְךָ כִּי עֲנִיתָנִי, וַתְּהִי־לִי לִישׁוּעָה:
אוֹדְךָ כִּי עֲנִיתָנִי, וַתְּהִי־לִי לִישׁוּעָה:

אֶבֶן מָאֲסוּ הַבּוֹנִים, הָיְתָה לְרֹאשׁ פִּנָּה:
אֶבֶן מָאֲסוּ הַבּוֹנִים, הָיְתָה לְרֹאשׁ פִּנָּה:

מֵאֵת יהוה הָיְתָה זֹּאת, הִיא נִפְלָאת בְּעֵינֵינוּ:
מֵאֵת יהוה הָיְתָה זֹּאת, הִיא נִפְלָאת בְּעֵינֵינוּ:

זֶה־הַיּוֹם עָשָׂה יהוה, נָגִילָה וְנִשְׂמְחָה בוֹ:
זֶה־הַיּוֹם עָשָׂה יהוה, נָגִילָה וְנִשְׂמְחָה בוֹ:

קָהֵל *followed by* שְׁלִיחַ צִבּוּר:

אָנָּא יהוה הוֹשִׁיעָה נָּא:
אָנָּא יהוה הוֹשִׁיעָה נָּא:
אָנָּא יהוה הַצְלִיחָה נָּא:
אָנָּא יהוה הַצְלִיחָה נָּא:

עָזִּי וְזִמְרָת יָהּ *The Lord is my strength and my song:* a quotation from *Shirat HaYam* (Ex. 15:2); it also appears in Isaiah 12:2.

פִּתְחוּ־לִי שַׁעֲרֵי־צֶדֶק *Open for me the gates of righteousness:* A reference to the gates of the Temple.

בָּרוּךְ Blessed is one who comes in the name of the LORD;
we bless you from the House of the LORD.
Blessed is one who comes in the name of the LORD;
we bless you from the House of the LORD.

The LORD is God; He has given us light. Bind the festival offering
with thick cords [and bring it] to the horns of the altar.
The LORD is God; He has given us light. Bind the festival offering
with thick cords [and bring it] to the horns of the altar.

You are my God and I will thank You; You are my God, I will exalt You.
You are my God and I will thank You; You are my God, I will exalt You.

Thank the LORD for He is good; His loving-kindness is for ever.
Thank the LORD for He is good; His loving-kindness is for ever.

יְהַלְלוּךָ All Your works will praise You, LORD our God, and Your
devoted ones – the righteous who do Your will, together with all Your
people the house of Israel – will joyously thank, bless, praise, glorify,
exalt, revere, sanctify, and proclaim the sovereignty of Your name,
our King. ‣ For it is good to thank You and fitting to sing psalms to
Your name, for from eternity to eternity You are God. Blessed are You,
LORD, King who is extolled with praises.

*On Rosh Ḥodesh say Full Kaddish on page 182 and continue the
service with the Reading of the Torah on page 158.*

*On weekday Ḥanukka (except Rosh Ḥodesh Tevet), Yom HaAtzma'ut and
Yom Yerushalayim, the service continues with Half Kaddish on page 156.*

אֵלִי אַתָּה *You are my God:* The words of one who is bringing the offering.
וְאוֹדֶךָ *And I will thank You:* alternatively, "I will acknowledge You." These are
words of dedication, meaning: This offering I bring is an expression of thanks
and acknowledgment to God for all His kindnesses to me.

יְהַלְלוּךָ *All Your works will praise You:* A concluding benediction, as at the end
of the Verses of Praise.

בָּרוּךְ הַבָּא בְּשֵׁם יהוה, בֵּרַכְנוּכֶם מִבֵּית יהוה:
בָּרוּךְ הַבָּא בְּשֵׁם יהוה, בֵּרַכְנוּכֶם מִבֵּית יהוה:

אֵל יהוה וַיָּאֶר לָנוּ, אִסְרוּ־חַג בַּעֲבֹתִים עַד־קַרְנוֹת הַמִּזְבֵּחַ:
אֵל יהוה וַיָּאֶר לָנוּ, אִסְרוּ־חַג בַּעֲבֹתִים עַד־קַרְנוֹת הַמִּזְבֵּחַ:

אֵלִי אַתָּה וְאוֹדֶךָּ, אֱלֹהַי אֲרוֹמְמֶךָּ:
אֵלִי אַתָּה וְאוֹדֶךָּ, אֱלֹהַי אֲרוֹמְמֶךָּ:

הוֹדוּ לַיהוה כִּי־טוֹב, כִּי לְעוֹלָם חַסְדּוֹ:
הוֹדוּ לַיהוה כִּי־טוֹב, כִּי לְעוֹלָם חַסְדּוֹ:

יְהַלְלוּךָ יהוה אֱלֹהֵינוּ כָּל מַעֲשֶׂיךָ, וַחֲסִידֶיךָ צַדִּיקִים עוֹשֵׂי רְצוֹנֶךָ,
וְכָל עַמְּךָ בֵּית יִשְׂרָאֵל בְּרִנָּה יוֹדוּ וִיבָרְכוּ וִישַׁבְּחוּ וִיפָאֲרוּ וִירוֹמְמוּ
וְיַעֲרִיצוּ וְיַקְדִּישׁוּ וְיַמְלִיכוּ אֶת שִׁמְךָ מַלְכֵּנוּ, • כִּי לְךָ טוֹב לְהוֹדוֹת
וּלְשִׁמְךָ נָאֶה לְזַמֵּר, כִּי מֵעוֹלָם וְעַד עוֹלָם אַתָּה אֵל. בָּרוּךְ אַתָּה
יהוה, מֶלֶךְ מְהֻלָּל בַּתִּשְׁבָּחוֹת.

On רֹאשׁ חֹדֶשׁ *say* קדיש שלם *on page 183 and continue
the service with* קריאת התורה *on page 159.*

On weekday חנוכה (*except* רֹאשׁ חֹדֶשׁ טבת), יוֹם הָעַצְמָאוּת *and* יוֹם יְרוּשָׁלַיִם,
the service continues with חצי קדיש *on page 157.*

בָּרוּךְ הַבָּא *Blessed is one who comes:* A blessing made by the priests to those
who came to worship in the Temple (Rashi, Radak). One of the tasks of the
priests was to bless the people who came in pilgrimage to the Temple to
make their offerings.

אִסְרוּ־חַג בַּעֲבֹתִים *Bind the festival offering with thick cords:* Alternatively, "Order
the festival procession with boughs, up to the horns of the altar," a reference
to the procession around the altar, with a lulav, on Sukkot (*Sukka* 45a).

Musaf for Rosh Ḥodesh

THE AMIDA

*The following prayer, until "in former years" on page 384, is said silently, standing
with feet together. If there is a minyan, the Amida is repeated aloud by the Leader.
Take three steps forward and at the points indicated by ˙, bend the knees at the first word,
bow at the second, and stand straight before saying God's name.*

When I proclaim the LORD's name, give glory to our God.   *Deut. 32*

O LORD, open my lips, so that my mouth may declare Your praise.   *Ps. 51*

PATRIARCHS

˙בָּרוּךְ Blessed are You, LORD our God and God of our fathers,

God of Abraham, God of Isaac and God of Jacob;

the great, mighty and awesome God, God Most High,

who bestows acts of loving-kindness and creates all,

who remembers the loving-kindness of the fathers and will bring

a Redeemer to their children's children

for the sake of His name, in love.

King, Helper, Savior, Shield:

˙Blessed are You, LORD, Shield of Abraham.

DIVINE MIGHT

אַתָּה גִבּוֹר You are eternally mighty, LORD.

You give life to the dead and have great power to save.

> *The phrase "He makes the wind blow and the rain fall" is added from
> Simḥat Torah until Pesaḥ. In Israel the phrase "He causes the dew
> to fall" is added from Pesaḥ until Shemini Atzeret. See laws 49–51.*

In fall & winter: He makes the wind blow and the rain fall.

*In Israel, in spring
& summer:*   He causes the dew to fall.

---

and seek to begin again. In Temple times a special offering was brought, of
which the Musaf prayer is a memory. The central blessing of the Amida begins
with a brief statement of the nature of the day, followed by a prayer for the
restoration of the Temple and its sacrifices, a biblical passage describing the
Rosh Ḥodesh offering, and a prayer that the new month be blessed for good.

מוסף לראש חודש

עמידה

The following prayer, until קְדֻשָּׁה on page 385, is said silently, standing
with feet together. If there is a מִנְיָן, the עֲמִידָה is repeated aloud by the שְׁלִיחַ צִבּוּר.
Take three steps forward and at the points indicated by ׳, bend the knees at the first word,
bow at the second, and stand straight before saying God's name.

דברים לב   כִּי שֵׁם יהוה אֶקְרָא, הָבוּ גֹדֶל לֵאלֹהֵינוּ:
תהלים נא   אֲדֹנָי, שְׂפָתַי תִּפְתָּח, וּפִי יַגִּיד תְּהִלָּתֶךָ:

אבות

בָּרוּךְ אַתָּה יהוה, אֱלֹהֵינוּ וֵאלֹהֵי אֲבוֹתֵינוּ
אֱלֹהֵי אַבְרָהָם, אֱלֹהֵי יִצְחָק, וֵאלֹהֵי יַעֲקֹב
הָאֵל הַגָּדוֹל הַגִּבּוֹר וְהַנּוֹרָא, אֵל עֶלְיוֹן
גּוֹמֵל חֲסָדִים טוֹבִים, וְקֹנֵה הַכֹּל
וְזוֹכֵר חַסְדֵי אָבוֹת
וּמֵבִיא גוֹאֵל לִבְנֵי בְנֵיהֶם לְמַעַן שְׁמוֹ בְּאַהֲבָה.
מֶלֶךְ עוֹזֵר וּמוֹשִׁיעַ וּמָגֵן.
בָּרוּךְ אַתָּה יהוה, מָגֵן אַבְרָהָם.

גבורות

אַתָּה גִּבּוֹר לְעוֹלָם, אֲדֹנָי
מְחַיֵּה מֵתִים אַתָּה, רַב לְהוֹשִׁיעַ

The phrase מַשִּׁיב הָרוּחַ is added from שמחת תורה until פסח.
In ארץ ישראל the phrase מוֹרִיד הַטָּל is added from פסח until שמיני עצרת. See laws 49–51.

בחוץ לארץ מַשִּׁיב הָרוּחַ וּמוֹרִיד הַגֶּשֶׁם / בארץ ישראל בקיץ מוֹרִיד הַטָּל

ADDITIONAL SERVICE FOR THE NEW MOON

The New Moon, like the New Year, is understood in Judaism as a time of
renewal and rededication, in which we pray for forgiveness and atonement

He sustains the living with loving-kindness,
and with great compassion revives the dead.
He supports the fallen, heals the sick, sets captives free,
and keeps His faith with those who sleep in the dust.
Who is like You, Master of might,
and to whom can You be compared,
O King who brings death and gives life,
and makes salvation grow?
Faithful are You to revive the dead.
Blessed are You, LORD, who revives the dead.

When saying the Amida silently, continue with "You are holy" on the next page.

KEDUSHA

*During the Leader's Repetition, the following is said standing
with feet together, rising on the toes at the words indicated by ˙.*

Cong. then	נְקַדֵּשׁ We will sanctify Your name on earth,
Leader:	as they sanctify it in the highest heavens,
	as is written by Your prophet,
	"And they [the angels] call to one another saying:

Is. 6

Cong. then	˙Holy, ˙holy, ˙holy is the LORD of hosts
Leader:	the whole world is filled with His glory."
	Those facing them say "Blessed – "

Cong. then	˙"Blessed is the LORD's glory from His place."
Leader:	And in Your holy Writings it is written thus:

Ezek. 3

Cong. then	˙"The LORD shall reign for ever. He is your God, Zion,
Leader:	from generation to generation, Halleluya!"

Ps. 146

Leader:	From generation to generation we will declare Your greatness,
	and we will proclaim Your holiness for evermore.
	Your praise, our God, shall not leave our mouth forever,
	for You, God, are a great and holy King.
	Blessed are You, LORD, the holy God.

The Leader continues with "You have given New Moons" on the next page.

---

construction of the Tabernacle. From the first month of the second year after
the exodus, the day the Tabernacle was dedicated, it became a women's festival
(Rashi, *Megilla* 22b; *Shulḥan Arukh* OḤ 417:1).

מְכַלְכֵּל חַיִּים בְּחֶסֶד

מְחַיֵּה מֵתִים בְּרַחֲמִים רַבִּים

סוֹמֵךְ נוֹפְלִים, וְרוֹפֵא חוֹלִים, וּמַתִּיר אֲסוּרִים

וּמְקַיֵּם אֱמוּנָתוֹ לִישֵׁנֵי עָפָר.

מִי כָמְוֹךָ, בַּעַל גְּבוּרוֹת, וּמִי דְּוֹמֶה לָּךְ

מֶלֶךְ, מֵמִית וּמְחַיֶּה וּמַצְמִיחַ יְשׁוּעָה.

וְנֶאֱמָן אַתָּה לְהַחֲיוֹת מֵתִים.

בָּרוּךְ אַתָּה יהוה, מְחַיֵּה הַמֵּתִים.

When saying the עמידה silently, continue with אַתָּה קָדוֹשׁ on the next page.

קדושה

During the חזרת הש״ץ, the following is said standing
with feet together, rising on the toes at the words indicated by ˙.

ישעיה ו

קהל
then
ש״ץ: נְקַדֵּשׁ אֶת שִׁמְךָ בָּעוֹלָם, כְּשֵׁם שֶׁמַּקְדִּישִׁים אוֹתוֹ בִּשְׁמֵי מָרוֹם
כַּכָּתוּב עַל יַד נְבִיאֶךָ: וְקָרָא זֶה אֶל־זֶה וְאָמַר

קהל
then
ש״ץ: קָדוֹשׁ, קָדוֹשׁ, קָדוֹשׁ, יהוה צְבָאוֹת, מְלֹא כָל־הָאָרֶץ כְּבוֹדוֹ:
לְעֻמָּתָם בָּרוּךְ יֹאמֵרוּ

יחזקאל ג

קהל
then
ש״ץ: בָּרוּךְ כְּבוֹד־יהוה מִמְּקוֹמוֹ:
וּבְדִבְרֵי קָדְשְׁךָ כָּתוּב לֵאמֹר

תהלים קמו

קהל
then
ש״ץ: יִמְלֹךְ יהוה לְעוֹלָם, אֱלֹהַיִךְ צִיּוֹן לְדֹר וָדֹר, הַלְלוּיָהּ:

ש״ץ: לְדוֹר וָדוֹר נַגִּיד גָּדְלֶךָ, וּלְנֵצַח נְצָחִים קְדֻשָּׁתְךָ נַקְדִּישׁ
וְשִׁבְחֲךָ אֱלֹהֵינוּ מִפִּינוּ לֹא יָמוּשׁ לְעוֹלָם וָעֶד
כִּי אֵל מֶלֶךְ גָּדוֹל וְקָדוֹשׁ אָתָּה.
בָּרוּךְ אַתָּה יהוה, הָאֵל הַקָּדוֹשׁ.

The שליח ציבור continues with רָאשֵׁי חֳדָשִׁים on the next page.

A midrashic tradition associates Rosh Ḥodesh with Jewish women, as a tribute to their faithfulness and to their generosity in providing gifts for the

HOLINESS

אַתָּה קָדוֹשׁ You are holy and Your name is holy,
and holy ones praise You daily, Selah!
Blessed are You, LORD, the holy God.

HOLINESS OF THE DAY

רָאשֵׁי חֳדָשִׁים You have given New Moons to Your people
as a time of atonement for all their offspring.
They would bring You offerings of goodwill,
and goats as sin-offerings for atonement.
May it serve as a remembrance for them all,
and a deliverance of their lives
from the hand of the enemy.
May You establish a new altar in Zion,
and may we offer on it
the New Moon burnt-offering,
and prepare goats in favor.
May we all rejoice in the Temple service,
and may the songs of David Your servant,
be heard in Your city,
chanted before Your altar.
Bestow on them everlasting love,
and remember the covenant of the fathers for their children.

וַהֲבִיאֵנוּ Bring us back, with song,
to Zion Your city,
and to Jerusalem Your Sanctuary with everlasting joy.
There we will prepare for You our obligatory offerings:
the regular daily offerings in their order,
and the additional offerings according to their law.

---

the moon shines with reflected light. So too with Israel: the light with which
we shine comes not from ourselves but from God, of whose glory we are but
a reflection (Seforno, Num. 28:11).

קדושת השם
אַתָּה קָדוֹשׁ וְשִׁמְךָ קָדוֹשׁ
וּקְדוֹשִׁים בְּכָל יוֹם יְהַלְלוּךָ סֶּלָה.
בָּרוּךְ אַתָּה יהוה, הָאֵל הַקָּדוֹשׁ.

קדושת היום
רָאשֵׁי חֳדָשִׁים לְעַמְּךָ נָתַתָּ
זְמַן כַּפָּרָה לְכָל תּוֹלְדוֹתָם
בִּהְיוֹתָם מַקְרִיבִים לְפָנֶיךָ זִבְחֵי רָצוֹן
וּשְׂעִירֵי חַטָּאת לְכַפֵּר בַּעֲדָם.
זִכָּרוֹן לְכֻלָּם יִהְיוּ, וּתְשׁוּעַת נַפְשָׁם מִיַּד שׂוֹנֵא.
מִזְבֵּחַ חָדָשׁ בְּצִיּוֹן תָּכִין
וְעוֹלַת רֹאשׁ חֹדֶשׁ נַעֲלֶה עָלָיו
וּשְׂעִירֵי עִזִּים נַעֲשֶׂה בְרָצוֹן
וּבַעֲבוֹדַת בֵּית הַמִּקְדָּשׁ נִשְׂמַח כֻּלָּנוּ
וּבְשִׁירֵי דָוִד עַבְדְּךָ הַנִּשְׁמָעִים בְּעִירֶךָ
הָאֲמוּרִים לִפְנֵי מִזְבְּחֶךָ.
אַהֲבַת עוֹלָם תָּבִיא לָהֶם, וּבְרִית אָבוֹת לַבָּנִים תִּזְכֹּר.

וַהֲבִיאֵנוּ לְצִיּוֹן עִירְךָ בְּרִנָּה
וְלִירוּשָׁלַיִם בֵּית מִקְדָּשְׁךָ בְּשִׂמְחַת עוֹלָם
וְשָׁם נַעֲשֶׂה לְפָנֶיךָ אֶת קָרְבְּנוֹת חוֹבוֹתֵינוּ
תְּמִידִים כְּסִדְרָם וּמוּסָפִים כְּהִלְכָתָם.

───────────────────────────────

רָאשֵׁי חֳדָשִׁים *You have given New Moons to Your people:* The Jewish people is
compared to the moon because, whereas the sun shines with its own light,

וְאֵת מוּסַף The additional offering of this New Moon day
we will prepare and offer to You
with love according to Your will's commandment,
as You have written for us in Your Torah
by Your own word, through Your servant Moses,
as it is said:

Num. 28

> "On your new moons,
> present as a burnt-offering to the LORD,
> two young bulls, one ram,
> and seven yearling lambs without blemish."

וּמִנְחָתָם And their meal-offerings and wine-libations as ordained:
three-tenths of an ephah for each bull,
two-tenths of an ephah for the ram,
one-tenth of an ephah for each lamb,
wine for the libations, a male goat for atonement,
and two regular daily offerings according to their law.

אֱלֹהֵינוּ O God and God of our ancestors,
renew for us the coming month for good and blessing,
 joy and gladness, deliverance and consolation,
sustenance and support,
life and peace,
pardon of sin and forgiveness of iniquity
(*From Marḥeshvan to Adar II in*
 a Jewish leap year (see page 692) and atonement of transgression).
For You have chosen Your people Israel from all nations,
and have instituted for them rules for the New Moon.
Blessed are You, LORD, who sanctifies Israel and the New Moons.

Ex. 12:2), hence the six double expressions of blessing. In a leap year there
are seven months before Nisan, hence a seventh expression is added from
Marḥeshvan to Adar II.

וְאֶת מוּסַף יוֹם רֹאשׁ הַחֹדֶשׁ הַזֶּה
נַעֲשֶׂה וְנַקְרִיב לְפָנֶיךָ בְּאַהֲבָה כְּמִצְוַת רְצוֹנֶךָ
כְּמוֹ שֶׁכָּתַבְתָּ עָלֵינוּ בְּתוֹרָתֶךָ
עַל יְדֵי מֹשֶׁה עַבְדֶּךָ מִפִּי כְבוֹדֶךָ
כָּאָמוּר

במדבר כחוּבְרָאשֵׁי חָדְשֵׁיכֶם תַּקְרִיבוּ עֹלָה לַיהוה
פָּרִים בְּנֵי־בָקָר שְׁנַיִם וְאַיִל אֶחָד
כְּבָשִׂים בְּנֵי־שָׁנָה שִׁבְעָה, תְּמִימִם:

וּמִנְחָתָם וְנִסְכֵּיהֶם כִּמְדֻבָּר
שְׁלֹשָׁה עֶשְׂרֹנִים לַפָּר, וּשְׁנֵי עֶשְׂרֹנִים לָאַיִל, וְעִשָּׂרוֹן לַכֶּבֶשׂ
וְיַיִן כְּנִסְכּוֹ, וְשָׂעִיר לְכַפֵּר, וּשְׁנֵי תְמִידִים כְּהִלְכָתָם.

אֱלֹהֵינוּ וֵאלֹהֵי אֲבוֹתֵינוּ
חַדֵּשׁ עָלֵינוּ אֶת הַחֹדֶשׁ הַזֶּה לְטוֹבָה וְלִבְרָכָה
לְשָׂשׂוֹן וּלְשִׂמְחָה, לִישׁוּעָה וּלְנֶחָמָה
לְפַרְנָסָה וּלְכַלְכָּלָה, לְחַיִּים וּלְשָׁלוֹם
לִמְחִילַת חֵטְא וְלִסְלִיחַת עָוֹן

(From אדר שני to מרחשון in a\
     Jewish leap year (see page 692)) וּלְכַפָּרַת פָּשַׁע

כִּי בְעַמְּךָ יִשְׂרָאֵל בָּחַרְתָּ מִכָּל הָאֻמּוֹת
וְחֻקֵּי רָאשֵׁי חֳדָשִׁים לָהֶם קָבָעְתָּ.
בָּרוּךְ אַתָּה יהוה, מְקַדֵּשׁ יִשְׂרָאֵל וְרָאשֵׁי חֳדָשִׁים.

וּלְכַפָּרַת פָּשַׁע *And atonement for transgression:* There are six months from Tishrei (Rosh HaShana, the beginning of the year) to Nisan (the first of months:

TEMPLE SERVICE

רְצֵה Find favor, Lord our God,
in Your people Israel and their prayer.
Restore the service to Your most holy House,
and accept in love and favor
the fire-offerings of Israel and their prayer.
May the service of Your people Israel always find favor with You
And may our eyes
witness Your return to Zion in compassion.
Blessed are You, Lord, who restores His Presence to Zion.

THANKSGIVING

Bow at the first nine words.

מוֹדִים We give thanks to You,
for You are the Lord our God
and God of our ancestors
for ever and all time.
You are the Rock of our lives,
Shield of our salvation
from generation to generation.
We will thank You and
declare Your praise for our lives,
which are entrusted into Your hand;
for our souls,
which are placed in Your charge;
for Your miracles
which are with us every day;
and for Your wonders and favors
at all times, evening, morning and midday.
You are good –
for Your compassion never fails.
You are compassionate –
for Your loving-kindnesses never cease.
We have always placed our hope in You.

*During the Leader's Repetition,
the congregation says quietly:*

מוֹדִים We give thanks to You,
for You are the
Lord our God
and God of our ancestors,
God of all flesh,
who formed us
and formed the universe.
Blessings and thanks
are due to Your great
and holy name for giving us
life and sustaining us.
May You continue
to give us life and sustain us;
and may You gather our
exiles to Your holy courts,
to keep Your decrees,
do Your will and serve You
with a perfect heart,
for it is for us
to give You thanks.
Blessed be God to whom
thanksgiving is due.

עבודה

רְצֵה יהוה אֱלֹהֵינוּ בְּעַמְּךָ יִשְׂרָאֵל, וּבִתְפִלָּתָם

וְהָשֵׁב אֶת הָעֲבוֹדָה לִדְבִיר בֵּיתֶךָ

וְאִשֵּׁי יִשְׂרָאֵל וּתְפִלָּתָם בְּאַהֲבָה תְקַבֵּל בְּרָצוֹן

וּתְהִי לְרָצוֹן תָּמִיד עֲבוֹדַת יִשְׂרָאֵל עַמֶּךָ.

וְתֶחֱזֶינָה עֵינֵינוּ בְּשׁוּבְךָ לְצִיּוֹן בְּרַחֲמִים.

בָּרוּךְ אַתָּה יהוה, הַמַּחֲזִיר שְׁכִינָתוֹ לְצִיּוֹן.

הודאה

Bow at the first five words.

During the הש״ץ חזרת הש״ץ,
the קהל *says quietly:*

מוֹדִים אֲנַחְנוּ לָךְ

שָׁאַתָּה הוּא יהוה אֱלֹהֵינוּ

וֵאלֹהֵי אֲבוֹתֵינוּ לְעוֹלָם וָעֶד.

צוּר חַיֵּינוּ, מָגֵן יִשְׁעֵנוּ

אַתָּה הוּא לְדוֹר וָדוֹר.

נוֹדֶה לְּךָ וּנְסַפֵּר תְּהִלָּתֶךָ

עַל חַיֵּינוּ הַמְּסוּרִים בְּיָדֶךָ

וְעַל נִשְׁמוֹתֵינוּ הַפְּקוּדוֹת לָךְ

וְעַל נִסֶּיךָ שֶׁבְּכָל יוֹם עִמָּנוּ

וְעַל נִפְלְאוֹתֶיךָ וְטוֹבוֹתֶיךָ

שֶׁבְּכָל עֵת, עֶרֶב וָבֹקֶר וְצָהֳרָיִם.

הַטּוֹב, כִּי לֹא כָלוּ רַחֲמֶיךָ

וְהַמְרַחֵם, כִּי לֹא תַמּוּ חֲסָדֶיךָ

מֵעוֹלָם קִוִּינוּ לָךְ.

מוֹדִים אֲנַחְנוּ לָךְ

שָׁאַתָּה הוּא יהוה אֱלֹהֵינוּ

וֵאלֹהֵי אֲבוֹתֵינוּ

אֱלֹהֵי כָל בָּשָׂר

יוֹצְרֵנוּ, יוֹצֵר בְּרֵאשִׁית.

בְּרָכוֹת וְהוֹדָאוֹת

לְשִׁמְךָ הַגָּדוֹל וְהַקָּדוֹשׁ

עַל שֶׁהֶחֱיִיתָנוּ וְקִיַּמְתָּנוּ.

כֵּן תְּחַיֵּנוּ וּתְקַיְּמֵנוּ

וְתֶאֱסֹף גָּלֻיּוֹתֵינוּ

לְחַצְרוֹת קָדְשֶׁךָ

לִשְׁמֹר חֻקֶּיךָ וְלַעֲשׂוֹת רְצוֹנֶךָ

וּלְעָבְדְּךָ בְּלֵבָב שָׁלֵם

עַל שֶׁאֲנַחְנוּ מוֹדִים לָךְ.

בָּרוּךְ אֵל הַהוֹדָאוֹת.

On Ḥanukka:

עַל הַנִּסִּים [We thank You also] for the miracles, the redemption, the mighty deeds, the salvations, and the victories in battle which You performed for our ancestors in those days, at this time.

בִּימֵי מַתִּתְיָהוּ In the days of Mattityahu, son of Yoḥanan, the High Priest, the Hasmonean, and his sons, the wicked Greek kingdom rose up against Your people Israel to make them forget Your Torah and to force them to transgress the statutes of Your will. It was then that You in Your great compassion stood by them in the time of their distress. You championed their cause, judged their claim, and avenged their wrong. You delivered the strong into the hands of the weak, the many into the hands of the few, the impure into the hands of the pure, the wicked into the hands of the righteous, and the arrogant into the hands of those who were engaged in the study of Your Torah. You made for Yourself great and holy renown in Your world, and for Your people Israel You performed a great salvation and redemption as of this very day. Your children then entered the holiest part of Your House, cleansed Your Temple, purified Your Sanctuary, kindled lights in Your holy courts, and designated these eight days of Ḥanukka for giving thanks and praise to Your great name.

Continue with "For all these things."

וְעַל כֻּלָּם For all these things may Your name be blessed and exalted, our King, continually, for ever and all time.
Let all that lives thank You, Selah! and praise Your name in truth, God, our Savior and Help, Selah!
▸Blessed are You, Lord, whose name is "the Good" and to whom thanks are due.

When saying the Amida silently, continue with "Grant peace" on the next page.

The following is said by the Leader during the Repetition of the Amida.
In Israel, if Kohanim bless the congregation, turn to page 386. See laws 62–69.

Our God and God of our fathers, bless us with the threefold blessing in the Torah, written by the hand of Moses Your servant and pronounced by Aaron and his sons the priests, Your holy people, as it is said:

May the Lord bless you and protect you. *Num. 6*
    Cong: May it be Your will.
May the Lord make His face shine on you and be gracious to you.
    Cong: May it be Your will.
May the Lord turn His face toward you, and grant you peace.
    Cong: May it be Your will.

The Leader continues with "Grant peace" on the next page.

בחנוכה:

עַל הַנִּסִּים וְעַל הַפֻּרְקָן וְעַל הַגְּבוּרוֹת וְעַל הַתְּשׁוּעוֹת וְעַל הַמִּלְחָמוֹת
שֶׁעָשִׂיתָ לַאֲבוֹתֵינוּ בַּיָּמִים הָהֵם בַּזְּמַן הַזֶּה.

בִּימֵי מַתִּתְיָהוּ בֶּן יוֹחָנָן כֹּהֵן גָּדוֹל חַשְׁמוֹנַאי וּבָנָיו, כְּשֶׁעָמְדָה מַלְכוּת יָוָן
הָרְשָׁעָה עַל עַמְּךָ יִשְׂרָאֵל לְהַשְׁכִּיחָם תּוֹרָתֶךָ וּלְהַעֲבִירָם מֵחֻקֵּי רְצוֹנֶךָ,
וְאַתָּה בְּרַחֲמֶיךָ הָרַבִּים עָמַדְתָּ לָהֶם בְּעֵת צָרָתָם, רַבְתָּ אֶת רִיבָם, דַּנְתָּ
אֶת דִּינָם, נָקַמְתָּ אֶת נִקְמָתָם, מָסַרְתָּ גִבּוֹרִים בְּיַד חַלָּשִׁים, וְרַבִּים בְּיַד
מְעַטִּים, וּטְמֵאִים בְּיַד טְהוֹרִים, וּרְשָׁעִים בְּיַד צַדִּיקִים, וְזֵדִים בְּיַד עוֹסְקֵי
תוֹרָתֶךָ, וּלְךָ עָשִׂיתָ שֵׁם גָּדוֹל וְקָדוֹשׁ בְּעוֹלָמֶךָ, וּלְעַמְּךָ יִשְׂרָאֵל עָשִׂיתָ
תְּשׁוּעָה גְדוֹלָה וּפֻרְקָן כְּהַיּוֹם הַזֶּה. וְאַחַר כֵּן בָּאוּ בָנֶיךָ לִדְבִיר בֵּיתֶךָ,
וּפִנּוּ אֶת הֵיכָלֶךָ, וְטִהֲרוּ אֶת מִקְדָּשֶׁךָ, וְהִדְלִיקוּ נֵרוֹת בְּחַצְרוֹת קָדְשֶׁךָ,
וְקָבְעוּ שְׁמוֹנַת יְמֵי חֲנֻכָּה אֵלּוּ, לְהוֹדוֹת וּלְהַלֵּל לְשִׁמְךָ הַגָּדוֹל.

Continue with וְעַל כֻּלָּם.

וְעַל כֻּלָּם יִתְבָּרַךְ וְיִתְרוֹמַם שִׁמְךָ מַלְכֵּנוּ תָּמִיד לְעוֹלָם וָעֶד.
וְכֹל הַחַיִּים יוֹדוּךָ סֶּלָה, וִיהַלְלוּ אֶת שִׁמְךָ בֶּאֱמֶת
הָאֵל יְשׁוּעָתֵנוּ וְעֶזְרָתֵנוּ סֶלָה.
יבָּרוּךְ אַתָּה יהוה, הַטּוֹב שִׁמְךָ וּלְךָ נָאֶה לְהוֹדוֹת.

When saying the עמידה *silently, continue with* שִׂים שָׁלוֹם *on the next page.*

The following is said by the שליח ציבור *during the* חזרת הש״ץ.
In ארץ ישראל, *if* כהנים *say* ברכת כהנים, *turn to page 387. See laws 62–69.*

אֱלֹהֵינוּ וֵאלֹהֵי אֲבוֹתֵינוּ, בָּרְכֵנוּ בַבְּרָכָה הַמְשֻׁלֶּשֶׁת בַּתּוֹרָה, הַכְּתוּבָה עַל יְדֵי מֹשֶׁה
עַבְדֶּךָ, הָאֲמוּרָה מִפִּי אַהֲרֹן וּבָנָיו כֹּהֲנִים עַם קְדוֹשֶׁךָ, כָּאָמוּר:

במדברו

יְבָרֶכְךָ יהוה וְיִשְׁמְרֶךָ:   קהל: כֵּן יְהִי רָצוֹן

יָאֵר יהוה פָּנָיו אֵלֶיךָ וִיחֻנֶּךָּ:   קהל: כֵּן יְהִי רָצוֹן

יִשָּׂא יהוה פָּנָיו אֵלֶיךָ וְיָשֵׂם לְךָ שָׁלוֹם: קהל: כֵּן יְהִי רָצוֹן

The שליח ציבור *continues with* שִׂים שָׁלוֹם *on the next page.*

PEACE

שִׂים שָׁלוֹם Grant peace, goodness and blessing,
grace, loving-kindness and compassion
to us and all Israel Your people.
Bless us, our Father, all as one, with the light of Your face,
for by the light of Your face You have given us, LORD our God,
the Torah of life and love of kindness,
righteousness, blessing, compassion, life and peace.
May it be good in Your eyes to bless Your people Israel
at every time, in every hour, with Your peace.
Blessed are You, LORD, who blesses His people Israel with peace.

The following verse concludes the Leader's Repetition of the Amida.
Some also say it here as part of the silent Amida. See law 60.

May the words of my mouth and the meditation of my heart   *Ps. 19*
find favor before You, LORD, my Rock and Redeemer.

אֱלֹהַי My God, guard my tongue from evil   *Berakhot*
and my lips from deceitful speech.   *17a*
To those who curse me, let my soul be silent;
may my soul be to all like the dust.
Open my heart to Your Torah and let my soul pursue Your commandments.
As for all who plan evil against me,
swiftly thwart their counsel and frustrate their plans.

> Act for the sake of Your name; act for the sake of Your right hand;
> act for the sake of Your holiness; act for the sake of Your Torah.

That Your beloved ones may be delivered,   *Ps. 60*
save with Your right hand and answer me.
May the words of my mouth and the meditation of my heart   *Ps. 19*
find favor before You, LORD, my Rock and Redeemer.

Bow, take three steps back, then bow, first left, then right, then center, while saying:

May He who makes peace in His high places,
make peace for us and all Israel – and say: Amen.

יְהִי רָצוֹן May it be Your will, LORD our God and God of our ancestors, that the Temple
be rebuilt speedily in our days, and grant us a share in Your Torah. And there we will
serve You with reverence, as in the days of old and as in former years. Then the offering   *Mal. 3*
of Judah and Jerusalem will be pleasing to the LORD as in the days of old and as in
former years.

> *After the Leader's Repetition, the service continues with Full Kaddish (page 182),*
> *followed by Aleinu (page 184), the Daily Psalm (page 188) and Barekhi Nafshi (page 194).*

ברכת שלום

שִׂים שָׁלוֹם טוֹבָה וּבְרָכָה

חֵן וָחֶסֶד וְרַחֲמִים עָלֵינוּ וְעַל כָּל יִשְׂרָאֵל עַמֶּךָ.

בָּרְכֵנוּ אָבִינוּ כֻּלָּנוּ כְּאֶחָד בְּאוֹר פָּנֶיךָ

כִּי בְאוֹר פָּנֶיךָ נָתַתָּ לָּנוּ יהוה אֱלֹהֵינוּ

תּוֹרַת חַיִּים וְאַהֲבַת חֶסֶד וּצְדָקָה וּבְרָכָה וְרַחֲמִים וְחַיִּים וְשָׁלוֹם.

וְטוֹב בְּעֵינֶיךָ לְבָרֵךְ אֶת עַמְּךָ יִשְׂרָאֵל

בְּכָל עֵת וּבְכָל שָׁעָה בִּשְׁלוֹמֶךָ.

בָּרוּךְ אַתָּה יהוה, הַמְבָרֵךְ אֶת עַמּוֹ יִשְׂרָאֵל בַּשָּׁלוֹם.

The following verse concludes the חזרת הש״ץ.
Some also say it here as part of the silent עמידה. *See law 60.*

תהלים יט יִהְיוּ לְרָצוֹן אִמְרֵי־פִי וְהֶגְיוֹן לִבִּי לְפָנֶיךָ, יהוה צוּרִי וְגֹאֲלִי:

ברכות יז. אֱלֹהַי, נְצֹר לְשׁוֹנִי מֵרָע וּשְׂפָתַי מִדַּבֵּר מִרְמָה

וְלִמְקַלְלַי נַפְשִׁי תִדֹּם, וְנַפְשִׁי כֶּעָפָר לַכֹּל תִּהְיֶה.

פְּתַח לִבִּי בְּתוֹרָתֶךָ, וּבְמִצְוֹתֶיךָ תִּרְדֹּף נַפְשִׁי.

וְכָל הַחוֹשְׁבִים עָלַי רָעָה מְהֵרָה הָפֵר עֲצָתָם וְקַלְקֵל מַחֲשַׁבְתָּם.

עֲשֵׂה לְמַעַן שְׁמֶךָ, עֲשֵׂה לְמַעַן יְמִינֶךָ

עֲשֵׂה לְמַעַן קְדֻשָּׁתֶךָ, עֲשֵׂה לְמַעַן תּוֹרָתֶךָ.

תהלים ס לְמַעַן יֵחָלְצוּן יְדִידֶיךָ, הוֹשִׁיעָה יְמִינְךָ וַעֲנֵנִי:

תהלים יט יִהְיוּ לְרָצוֹן אִמְרֵי־פִי וְהֶגְיוֹן לִבִּי לְפָנֶיךָ, יהוה צוּרִי וְגֹאֲלִי:

Bow, take three steps back, then bow, first left, then right, then center, while saying:

עֹשֶׂה שָׁלוֹם בִּמְרוֹמָיו

הוּא יַעֲשֶׂה שָׁלוֹם עָלֵינוּ וְעַל כָּל יִשְׂרָאֵל, וְאִמְרוּ אָמֵן.

יְהִי רָצוֹן מִלְּפָנֶיךָ יהוה אֱלֹהֵינוּ וֵאלֹהֵי אֲבוֹתֵינוּ, שֶׁיִּבָּנֶה בֵּית הַמִּקְדָּשׁ בִּמְהֵרָה
בְיָמֵינוּ, וְתֵן חֶלְקֵנוּ בְּתוֹרָתֶךָ, וְשָׁם נַעֲבָדְךָ בְּיִרְאָה כִּימֵי עוֹלָם וּכְשָׁנִים קַדְמֹנִיּוֹת.
מלאכי ג וְעָרְבָה לַיהוה מִנְחַת יְהוּדָה וִירוּשָׁלָ͏ִם כִּימֵי עוֹלָם וּכְשָׁנִים קַדְמֹנִיּוֹת:

After the חזרת הש״ץ, *the service continues with* קדיש שלם (*page 183*),
followed by בָּרְכִי נַפְשִׁי (*page 189*) *and* שִׁיר שֶׁל יוֹם (*page 185*), עָלֵינוּ (*page 195*).

BIRKAT KOHANIM IN ISRAEL

*In Israel, the following is said by the Leader during the Repetition of the Amida
when Kohanim bless the congregation. If there is more than one Kohen,
a member of the congregation calls: (See laws 62–69.)*

Kohanim!

The Kohanim respond:

Blessed are You, Lord our God, King of the Universe, who has made us holy with
the holiness of Aaron, and has commanded us to bless His people Israel with love.

The Leader calls word by word, followed by the Kohanim:

יְבָרֶכְךָ May the LORD bless you and protect you. (*Cong:* Amen.)   *Num. 6*

May the LORD make His face shine on you
and be gracious to you. (*Cong:* Amen.)

May the LORD turn His face toward you,
and grant you peace. (*Cong:* Amen.)

The Leader continues with "Grant peace" below.

The congregation says:	*The Kohanim say:*
אַדִּיר Majestic One on high who dwells in power: You are peace and Your name is peace. May it be Your will to bestow on us and on Your people the house of Israel, life and blessing as a safeguard for peace.	רִבּוֹנוֹ Master of the Universe: we have done what You have decreed for us. So too may You deal with us as You have promised us. Look down from Your holy dwelling place, from heaven, and bless Your people Israel and the land You have given us as You promised on oath to our ancestors, a land flowing with milk and honey.

Deut. 26

The Leader continues:

שִׂים שָׁלוֹם Grant peace, goodness and blessing, grace, loving-kindness and
compassion to us and all Israel Your people. Bless us, our Father, all as one, with
the light of Your face, for by the light of Your face You have given us, LORD our
God, the Torah of life and love of kindness, righteousness, blessing, compassion,
life and peace. May it be good in Your eyes to bless Your people Israel at every
time, in every hour, with Your peace.

Between Rosh In the book of life, blessing, peace and prosperity,
HaShana & may we and all Your people the house of Israel
Yom Kippur: be remembered and written before You for a good life, and for peace.

Blessed are You, LORD, who blesses His people Israel with peace.

The following verse concludes the Leader's Repetition of the Amida. See law 60.

May the words of my mouth and the meditation of my heart   *Ps. 19*
find favor before You, LORD, my Rock and Redeemer.

ברכת כהנים בארץ ישראל

In ארץ ישראל, the following is said by the שליח ציבור during the חזרת הש״ץ when כהנים say ברכת כהנים. If there is more than one כהן, a member of the קהל calls: (See laws 62–69)

כֹּהֲנִים

The כהנים respond:

בָּרוּךְ אַתָּה יהוה אֱלֹהֵינוּ מֶלֶךְ הָעוֹלָם, אֲשֶׁר קִדְּשָׁנוּ בִּקְדֻשָּׁתוֹ שֶׁל אַהֲרֹן וְצִוָּנוּ לְבָרֵךְ אֶת עַמּוֹ יִשְׂרָאֵל בְּאַהֲבָה.

The שליח ציבור calls word by word, followed by the כהנים:

במדברו

יְבָרֶכְךָ יהוה וְיִשְׁמְרֶךָ: קהל: אָמֵן

יָאֵר יהוה פָּנָיו אֵלֶיךָ וִיחֻנֶּךָּ: קהל: אָמֵן

יִשָּׂא יהוה פָּנָיו אֵלֶיךָ וְיָשֵׂם לְךָ שָׁלוֹם: קהל: אָמֵן

The שליח ציבור continues with שים שלום below.

The קהל says:

אַדִּיר בַּמָּרוֹם שׁוֹכֵן בִּגְבוּרָה, אַתָּה שָׁלוֹם וְשִׁמְךָ שָׁלוֹם. יְהִי רָצוֹן שֶׁתָּשִׂים עָלֵינוּ וְעַל כָּל עַמְּךָ בֵּית יִשְׂרָאֵל חַיִּים וּבְרָכָה לְמִשְׁמֶרֶת שָׁלוֹם.

The כהנים say:

דברים ט

רִבּוֹנוֹ שֶׁל עוֹלָם, עָשִׂינוּ מַה שֶּׁגָּזַרְתָּ עָלֵינוּ, אַף אַתָּה עֲשֵׂה עִמָּנוּ כְּמוֹ שֶׁהִבְטַחְתָּנוּ. הַשְׁקִיפָה מִמְּעוֹן קָדְשְׁךָ מִן הַשָּׁמַיִם, וּבָרֵךְ אֶת־עַמְּךָ אֶת־יִשְׂרָאֵל, וְאֵת הָאֲדָמָה אֲשֶׁר נָתַתָּה לָנוּ, כַּאֲשֶׁר נִשְׁבַּעְתָּ לַאֲבֹתֵינוּ, אֶרֶץ זָבַת חָלָב וּדְבָשׁ:

The שליח ציבור continues:

שִׂים שָׁלוֹם טוֹבָה וּבְרָכָה, חֵן וָחֶסֶד וְרַחֲמִים עָלֵינוּ וְעַל כָּל יִשְׂרָאֵל עַמֶּךָ. בָּרְכֵנוּ אָבִינוּ כֻּלָּנוּ כְּאֶחָד בְּאוֹר פָּנֶיךָ, כִּי בְאוֹר פָּנֶיךָ נָתַתָּ לָּנוּ יהוה אֱלֹהֵינוּ, תּוֹרַת חַיִּים וְאַהֲבַת חֶסֶד, וּצְדָקָה וּבְרָכָה וְרַחֲמִים וְחַיִּים וְשָׁלוֹם. וְטוֹב בְּעֵינֶיךָ לְבָרֵךְ אֶת עַמְּךָ יִשְׂרָאֵל, בְּכָל עֵת וּבְכָל שָׁעָה בִּשְׁלוֹמֶךָ.

בעשרת ימי תשובה: בְּסֵפֶר חַיִּים, בְּרָכָה וְשָׁלוֹם, וּפַרְנָסָה טוֹבָה, נִזָּכֵר וְנִכָּתֵב לְפָנֶיךָ, אֲנַחְנוּ וְכָל עַמְּךָ בֵּית יִשְׂרָאֵל, לְחַיִּים טוֹבִים וּלְשָׁלוֹם.

בָּרוּךְ אַתָּה יהוה, הַמְבָרֵךְ אֶת עַמּוֹ יִשְׂרָאֵל בַּשָּׁלוֹם.

The following verse concludes the חזרת הש״ץ. See law 60.

תהלים יט

יִהְיוּ לְרָצוֹן אִמְרֵי־פִי וְהֶגְיוֹן לִבִּי לְפָנֶיךָ, יהוה צוּרִי וְגֹאֲלִי:

ANNULMENT OF VOWS

On the morning before Rosh HaShana, one should annul
vows before three men, who sit as judges, saying:

שִׁמְעוּ נָא Listen, please, my masters (expert judges): every vow or oath or prohibition or restriction or ban that I have vowed or sworn, whether awake or in a dream, or that I swore with one of the holy names that may not be erased, or by the holy four-letter name of God, blessed be He, or any na- ziriteship that I accepted on myself, even a naziriteship like that of Samson, or any prohibition, even against enjoyment, whether I forbade it to myself or others, by any expression of prohibition, whether using the language of prohibition or restriction or ban, or any positive commitment, even to perform a [non-obligatory] commandment, that I undertook by way of a vow or voluntary undertaking or oath or naziriteship or any other such expression, whether it was done by handshake or vow or voluntary under- taking or commandment-mandated custom I have customarily practiced, or any utterance that I have verbalized, or any non-obligatory command- ment or good practice or conduct I have vowed and resolved in my heart to do, and have done three times without specifying that it does not have the force of a vow, whether it relates to myself or others, both those known to me and those I have already forgotten – regarding all of them, I hereby express my retroactive regret, and ask and seek their annulment from you, my eminences. For I fear that I may stumble and be trapped, Heaven forbid, in the sin of vows, oaths, naziriteships, bans, prohibitions, restrictions and agreements. I do not regret, Heaven forbid, the performance of the good deeds I have done. I regret, rather, having accepted them on myself in the language of vow, oath, naziriteship, prohibition, ban, restriction, agreement or acceptance of the heart.

Therefore I request annulment for them all.

Judaism is a religion that stresses the sanctity of language, especially when used to accept or impose obligations on oneself. Deep significance attaches to vows and other verbal undertakings: "If a man makes a vow to God, or makes an oath to obligate himself, he must not break his word. He must do everything he said" (Num. 30:3). In general, it is preferable not to invest voluntary commitments with the sacred status of a vow. "If you refrain from making a vow, you will not be guilty" (Deut. 23:23). "It is better not to vow than to make a vow and not fulfill it" (Eccl. 5:4).

הַתָּרַת נְדָרִים

On the morning before ראש השנה*, one should annul vows*
before three men, who sit as judges, saying:

שִׁמְעוּ נָא רַבּוֹתַי (דַּיָּנִים מֻמְחִים), כָּל נֶדֶר אוֹ שְׁבוּעָה אוֹ אִסָּר אוֹ קוֹנָם
אוֹ חֵרֶם שֶׁנָּדַרְתִּי אוֹ נִשְׁבַּעְתִּי בְּהָקִיץ אוֹ בַחֲלוֹם, אוֹ נִשְׁבַּעְתִּי בְּשֵׁמוֹת
הַקְּדוֹשִׁים שֶׁאֵינָם נִמְחָקִים וּבְשֵׁם הֲוָיָ״ה בָּרוּךְ הוּא, וְכָל מִינֵי נְזִירוּת
שֶׁקִּבַּלְתִּי עָלַי וַאֲפִלּוּ נְזִירוּת שִׁמְשׁוֹן, וְכָל שׁוּם אִסּוּר וַאֲפִלּוּ אִסּוּר הֲנָאָה
שֶׁאָסַרְתִּי עָלַי אוֹ עַל אֲחֵרִים בְּכָל לָשׁוֹן שֶׁל אִסּוּר בֵּין בִּלְשׁוֹן אִסּוּר אוֹ
חֵרֶם אוֹ קוֹנָם, וְכָל שׁוּם קַבָּלָה אֲפִלּוּ שֶׁל מִצְוָה שֶׁקִּבַּלְתִּי עָלַי בֵּין בִּלְשׁוֹן
נֶדֶר בֵּין בִּלְשׁוֹן נְדָבָה בֵּין בִּלְשׁוֹן שְׁבוּעָה בֵּין בִּלְשׁוֹן נְזִירוּת בֵּין בְּכָל
לָשׁוֹן, וְגַם הַנַּעֲשֶׂה בִּתְקִיעַת כָּף. בֵּין כָּל נֶדֶר וּבֵין כָּל נְדָבָה וּבֵין שׁוּם מִנְהָג
שֶׁל מִצְוָה שֶׁנָּהַגְתִּי אֶת עַצְמִי, וְכָל מוֹצָא שְׂפָתַי שֶׁיָּצָא מִפִּי אוֹ שֶׁנָּדַרְתִּי
וְגָמַרְתִּי בְּלִבִּי לַעֲשׂוֹת שׁוּם מִצְוָה מֵהַמִּצְוֹת אוֹ אֵיזוֹ הַנְהָגָה טוֹבָה אוֹ
אֵיזֶה דָבָר טוֹב שֶׁנָּהַגְתִּי שָׁלֹשׁ פְּעָמִים, וְלֹא הִתְנֵיתִי שֶׁיְּהֵא בְּלִי נֶדֶר. הֵן
דָּבָר שֶׁעָשִׂיתִי, הֵן עַל עַצְמִי הֵן עַל אֲחֵרִים, הֵן אוֹתָן הַיְדוּעִים לִי הֵן אוֹתָן
שֶׁכְּבָר שְׁכַחְתִּי. בְּכֻלְּהוֹן אִתְחֲרַטְנָא בְּהוֹן מֵעִקָּרָא, וְשׁוֹאֵל וּמְבַקֵּשׁ אֲנִי
מִמַּעֲלַתְכֶם הַתָּרָה עֲלֵיהֶם, כִּי יָרֵאתִי פֶּן אֶכָּשֵׁל וְנִלְכַּדְתִּי, חַס וְשָׁלוֹם,
בַּעֲוֹן נְדָרִים וּשְׁבוּעוֹת וּנְזִירוֹת וַחֲרָמוֹת וְאִסּוּרִין וְקוֹנָמוֹת וְהַסְכָּמוֹת. וְאֵין
אֲנִי תוֹהֵא, חַס וְשָׁלוֹם, עַל קִיּוּם הַמַּעֲשִׂים הַטּוֹבִים הָהֵם שֶׁעָשִׂיתִי, רַק
אֲנִי מִתְחָרֵט עַל קַבָּלַת הָעִנְיָנִים בִּלְשׁוֹן נֶדֶר אוֹ שְׁבוּעָה אוֹ נְזִירוּת אוֹ
אִסּוּר אוֹ חֵרֶם אוֹ קוֹנָם אוֹ הַסְכָּמָה אוֹ קַבָּלָה בְּלֵב, וּמִתְחָרֵט אֲנִי עַל זֶה
שֶׁלֹּא אָמַרְתִּי הִנְנִי עוֹשֶׂה דָבָר זֶה בְּלִי נֶדֶר וּשְׁבוּעָה וּנְזִירוּת וְחֵרֶם וְאִסּוּר
וְקוֹנָם וְקַבָּלָה בְּלֵב.
לָכֵן אֲנִי שׁוֹאֵל הַתָּרָה בְּכֻלְּהוֹן.

ANNULMENT OF VOWS

To avoid entering the High Holy Days under the pressure of unfulfilled undertakings to God, our custom is to annul or "release" vows on the morning before Rosh HaShana. A similar, though more solemn, ceremony takes place immediately prior to Yom Kippur in the form of *Kol Nidrei*.

I regret all these things I have mentioned, whether they related to monetary matters, or to the body or to the soul.

In relation to them all, I regret the language of vow, oath, naziriteship, prohibition, ban, penalty, and acceptance of the heart.

To be sure, according to the law, one who regrets and seeks annulment must specify the vow [from which he seeks release]. But please know, my masters, that it is impossible to specify them, for they are many. I do not seek release from vows that cannot be annulled. Therefore, may it be in your eyes as if I had specified them.

The judges say the following three times:

May all be permitted to you. May all be forgiven you. May all be allowed to you. There is now no vow, oath, naziriteship, ban, prohibition, penalty, ostracism, excommunication, or curse. There is now pardon, forgiveness and atonement. And just as the earthly court has granted permission, so may the heavenly court grant permission.

The one seeking annulment of vows says:

Behold I make a formal declaration before you that I cancel from now onward all vows and all oaths, naziriteships, prohibitions, penalties, bans, agreements and acceptances of the heart that I may accept upon myself, whether awake or in a dream, except a vow to fast that I undertake at the time of the afternoon prayer. If I forget the conditions of this declaration and make a vow from this day onward, as of now I retroactively regret them and declare them to be null and void, without effect or validity, and they shall have no force whatsoever. Regarding them all, I regret them from now and for ever.

---

a sacrifice. *Nezirut*, the acceptance, usually for a period of thirty days, of the status of a nazirite (Num. 6:1–21), involves abstaining from wine or grapes, cutting one's hair, or contact with a corpse.

The basis of release is regret: had one known what one knows now, one would not have undertaken the vow. The release is performed by three adult men sitting as a court, and its effect is retroactive: it is as if the vow had never been made. The entire process emphasizes the solemnity of verbal commitments. We must be true to our word and never lightly promise to do what we may not be able to fulfill.

אֲנִי מִתְחָרֵט עַל כָּל הַנֻּזְכָּר, בֵּין אִם הָיוּ הַמַּעֲשִׂים מְדֻבָּרִים הַנּוֹגְעִים בְּמָמוֹן,
בֵּין מֵהַדְּבָרִים הַנּוֹגְעִים בַּגּוּף, בֵּין מֵהַדְּבָרִים הַנּוֹגְעִים אֶל הַנְּשָׁמָה.

בְּכֻלְּהוֹן אֲנִי מִתְחָרֵט עַל לְשׁוֹן נֶדֶר וּשְׁבוּעָה וּנְזִירוּת וְאִסּוּר וְחֵרֶם וְקוֹנָם
וְקַבָּלָה בְלֵב.

וְהִנֵּה מִצַּד הַדִּין הַמִּתְחָרֵט וְהַמְבַקֵּשׁ הַתָּרָה צָרִיךְ לִפְרֹט לְפְרֵט הַנֶּדֶר, אַךְ דְּעוּ נָא
רַבּוֹתַי, כִּי אִי אֶפְשָׁר לְפָרְטָם, כִּי רַבִּים הֵם. וְאֵין אֲנִי מְבַקֵּשׁ הַתָּרָה עַל אוֹתָם
הַנְּדָרִים שֶׁאֵין לְהַתִּיר אוֹתָם, עַל כֵּן יִהְיוּ נָא בְּעֵינֵיכֶם כְּאִלּוּ הָיִיתִי פוֹרְטָם.

The judges say the following three times:

הַכֹּל יִהְיוּ מֻתָּרִים לָךְ, הַכֹּל מְחוּלִים לָךְ, הַכֹּל שְׁרוּיִים לָךְ. אֵין כָּאן לֹא
נֶדֶר וְלֹא שְׁבוּעָה וְלֹא נְזִירוּת וְלֹא חֵרֶם וְלֹא אִסּוּר וְלֹא קוֹנָם וְלֹא נִדּוּי
וְלֹא שַׁמְתָּא וְלֹא אָרוּר. אֲבָל יֵשׁ כָּאן מְחִילָה וּסְלִיחָה וְכַפָּרָה. וּכְשֵׁם
שֶׁמַּתִּירִים בְּבֵית דִּין שֶׁל מַטָּה, כָּךְ יִהְיוּ מֻתָּרִים מִבֵּית דִּין שֶׁל מַעְלָה.

The one seeking annulment of vows says:

הֲרֵי אֲנִי מוֹסֵר מוֹדָעָה לִפְנֵיכֶם, וַאֲנִי מְבַטֵּל מִכָּאן וּלְהַבָּא כָּל הַנְּדָרִים
וְכָל שְׁבוּעוֹת וּנְזִירוּת וְאִסּוּרִין וְקוֹנָמוֹת וַחֲרָמוֹת וְהַסְכָּמוֹת וְקַבָּלָה בְלֵב
שֶׁאֲקַבֵּל עָלַי בְּעַצְמִי, הֵן בְּהָקִיץ הֵן בַּחֲלוֹם, חוּץ מִנִּדְרֵי תַעֲנִית בִּשְׁעַת
מִנְחָה. וּבָאֵ אֲשֶׁכַּח לְתַנַּאי הֲזֹאת וְאֶדֹּר מֵהַיּוֹם עוֹד, מֵעַתָּה
אֲנִי מִתְחָרֵט עֲלֵיהֶם וּמַתְנֶה עֲלֵיהֶם שֶׁיִּהְיוּ כֻלָּן בְּטֵלִין וּמְבֻטָּלִין, לֹא
שְׁרִירִין וְלֹא קַיָּמִין, וְלֹא יְהוֹן חָלִין חָלוּן כְּלָל וּכְלָל. בְּכֻלָּן אִתְחַרַטְנָא בְהוֹן
מֵעַתָּה וְעַד עוֹלָם.

The undertakings involved here relate to vows made to God in respect
of behavior not categorically demanded or forbidden by Jewish law. The
declaration covers a range of such commitments. A *neder* is a vow forbidding something to oneself; an *isar* is a more general category of self-imposed
prohibition. A *shevu'a* is an oath relating to action rather than an object: a
promise to do or not to do a certain act. A *ḥerem* renders an object forbidden by designating it as sacred property; a *konam* designates it as if it were

KAPAROT

Taking a rooster (men), or a hen (women) in the right hand
(alternatively one may use money), say the following paragraph three times:

בְּנֵי אָדָם Children of men,
those who sat in darkness and the shadow of death,   *Ps. 107*
cruelly bound in iron chains –
He brought them out from darkness
and the shadow of death and broke open their chains.
Some were fools with sinful ways,
and suffered affliction because of their iniquities.
They found all food repulsive, and came close to the gates of death.
Then they cried to the Lᴏʀᴅ in their trouble,
and He saved them from their distress.
He sent His word and healed them; He rescued them from their destruction.
Let them thank the Lᴏʀᴅ for his loving-kindness
and His wondrous deeds for humankind.
If there is one angel out of a thousand in his defense,   *Job 33*
to declare his righteousness on his behalf, He will be gracious to him
and say, "Spare him from going down to the pit; I have found atonement."

A man revolves the rooster around his head and says:

זֶה חֲלִיפָתִי Let this be my exchange, let this be my substitute,
let this rooster go to death
while I go and enter a good, long life and peace.

A woman revolves the hen around her head and says:

זֹאת חֲלִיפָתִי Let this be my exchange, let this be my substitute,
let this hen go to death
while I go and enter a good, long life and peace.

If money is used, then revolve the money around the head and say:

אֵלּוּ חֲלִיפָתִי Let this be my exchange, let this be my substitute,
let this money go to charity
while I go and enter a good, long life and peace.

Temple). The symbolic transfer of sins recalls the rite of the goat on which the
High Priest confessed the sins of Israel on Yom Kippur (Leviticus, chapter 16).
Maimonides explains that though sins cannot be transferred, the rite had a
powerful psychological effect, signaling the act of distancing ourselves from
past wrongs. Many have the custom of donating money to charity instead.

סֵדֶר כַּפָּרוֹת

Taking a rooster (men), or a hen (women) in the right hand
(alternatively one may use money), say the following paragraph three times:

בְּנֵי אָדָם

תהלים קז

יֹשְׁבֵי חֹשֶׁךְ וְצַלְמָוֶת, אֲסִירֵי עֳנִי וּבַרְזֶל:

יוֹצִיאֵם מֵחֹשֶׁךְ וְצַלְמָוֶת, וּמוֹסְרוֹתֵיהֶם יְנַתֵּק:

אֱוִלִים מִדֶּרֶךְ פִּשְׁעָם, וּמֵעֲוֺנֹתֵיהֶם יִתְעַנּוּ:

כָּל־אֹכֶל תְּתַעֵב נַפְשָׁם, וַיַּגִּיעוּ עַד־שַׁעֲרֵי מָוֶת:

וַיִּזְעֲקוּ אֶל־יהוה בַּצַּר לָהֶם, מִמְּצֻקוֹתֵיהֶם יוֹשִׁיעֵם:

יִשְׁלַח דְּבָרוֹ וְיִרְפָּאֵם, וִימַלֵּט מִשְּׁחִיתוֹתָם:

יוֹדוּ לַיהוה חַסְדּוֹ, וְנִפְלְאוֹתָיו לִבְנֵי אָדָם:

איוב לג

אִם־יֵשׁ עָלָיו מַלְאָךְ מֵלִיץ אֶחָד מִנִּי־אָלֶף, לְהַגִּיד לְאָדָם יָשְׁרוֹ:

וַיְחֻנֶּנּוּ וַיֹּאמֶר פְּדָעֵהוּ מֵרֶדֶת שָׁחַת, מָצָאתִי כֹפֶר:

A man revolves the rooster around his head and says:

זֶה חֲלִיפָתִי, זֶה תְּמוּרָתִי, זֶה כַּפָּרָתִי.

זֶה הַתַּרְנְגוֹל יֵלֵךְ לְמִיתָה

וַאֲנִי אֵלֵךְ וְאֶכָּנֵס לְחַיִּים טוֹבִים אֲרֻכִּים וּלְשָׁלוֹם.

A woman revolves the hen around her head and says:

זֹאת חֲלִיפָתִי, זֹאת תְּמוּרָתִי, זֹאת כַּפָּרָתִי.

זֹאת הַתַּרְנְגֹלֶת תֵּלֵךְ לְמִיתָה

וַאֲנִי אֵלֵךְ וְאֶכָּנֵס לְחַיִּים טוֹבִים אֲרֻכִּים וּלְשָׁלוֹם.

If money is used, then revolve the money around the head and say:

אֵלּוּ חֲלִיפָתִי, אֵלּוּ תְּמוּרָתִי, אֵלּוּ כַּפָּרָתִי.

אֵלּוּ הַמָּעוֹת יֵלְכוּ לִצְדָקָה

וַאֲנִי אֵלֵךְ וְאֶכָּנֵס לְחַיִּים טוֹבִים אֲרֻכִּים וּלְשָׁלוֹם.

Kapparot: Literally "atonements," this ritual is first mentioned as a custom in
the ninth century. Opposed by some authorities, it was endorsed by others,
especially Jewish mystics. Traditionally a chicken was used, so that the rite
could not be confused with a sacrificial act (chickens were not offered in the

VIDUY FOR MINḤA OF EREV YOM KIPPUR

The following is said on Erev Yom Kippur (and by a bride and groom on the eve of their wedding), in the Amida before "My God, guard":

אֱלֹהֵינוּ Our God and God of our fathers,
let our prayer come before You,
and do not hide Yourself from our plea,
for we are not so arrogant or obstinate as to say before You,
Lord, our God and God of our fathers,
we are righteous and have not sinned,
for in truth, we and our fathers have sinned.

Strike the left side of the chest with the right fist while saying each of the sins:

אָשַׁמְנוּ We have sinned, we have acted treacherously,
we have robbed, we have spoken slander.
We have acted perversely, we have acted wickedly,
we have acted presumptuously, we have been violent, we have framed lies.

We have given bad advice, we have deceived, we have scorned,
we have rebelled, we have provoked, we have turned away,
we have committed iniquity, we have transgressed,
we have persecuted, we have been obstinate.

We have acted wickedly, we have corrupted,
we have acted abominably, we have strayed, we have led others astray.

סַרְנוּ We have turned away from Your commandments and good laws,
to no avail, for You are just in all that has befallen us,
for You have acted faithfully while we have done wickedly.

מַה נֹּאמַר What can we say before You, You who dwell on high?
What can we declare before You, You who abide in heaven?
Do You not know all, the hidden and revealed alike?

אַתָּה יוֹדֵעַ You know every secret since the world began,
and what is hidden deep inside every living thing.
You search each person's inner chambers examining conscience and mind.
Nothing is shrouded from You, and nothing is hidden, before Your eyes.
And so, may it be Your will, Lord our God and God of our ancestors,
that You forgive us all our sins,
pardon all our iniquities
and grant us atonement for all of our transgressions.

וידוי למנחה בערב יום הכיפורים

The following is said on ערב יום הכיפורים *(and by a* חתן *and* כלה *on
the eve of their wedding), in the Amida before* אֱלֹהַי, נְצֹר:

אֱלֹהֵינוּ וֵאלֹהֵי אֲבוֹתֵינוּ
תָּבוֹא לְפָנֶיךָ תְּפִלָּתֵנוּ, וְאַל תִּתְעַלַּם מִתְּחִנָּתֵנוּ.
שֶׁאֵין אֲנַחְנוּ עַזֵּי פָנִים וּקְשֵׁי עֹרֶף לוֹמַר לְפָנֶיךָ
יהוה אֱלֹהֵינוּ וֵאלֹהֵי אֲבוֹתֵינוּ
צַדִּיקִים אֲנַחְנוּ וְלֹא חָטָאנוּ. אֲבָל אֲנַחְנוּ וַאֲבוֹתֵינוּ חָטָאנוּ.

Strike the left side of the chest with the right fist while saying each of the sins:

אָשַׁמְנוּ, בָּגַדְנוּ, גָּזַלְנוּ, דִּבַּרְנוּ דְפִי
הֶעֱוִינוּ, וְהִרְשַׁעְנוּ, זַדְנוּ, חָמַסְנוּ, טָפַלְנוּ שֶׁקֶר
יָעַצְנוּ רָע, כִּזַּבְנוּ, לַצְנוּ, מָרַדְנוּ, נִאַצְנוּ, סָרַרְנוּ
עָוִינוּ, פָּשַׁעְנוּ, צָרַרְנוּ, קִשִּׁינוּ עֹרֶף
רָשַׁעְנוּ, שִׁחַתְנוּ, תִּעַבְנוּ, תָּעִינוּ, תִּעְתָּעְנוּ.

סַרְנוּ מִמִּצְוֹתֶיךָ וּמִמִּשְׁפָּטֶיךָ הַטּוֹבִים, וְלֹא שָׁוָה לָנוּ.
וְאַתָּה צַדִּיק עַל כָּל הַבָּא עָלֵינוּ
כִּי אֱמֶת עָשִׂיתָ, וַאֲנַחְנוּ הִרְשָׁעְנוּ.

מַה נֹּאמַר לְפָנֶיךָ יוֹשֵׁב מָרוֹם, וּמַה נְּסַפֵּר לְפָנֶיךָ שׁוֹכֵן שְׁחָקִים
הֲלֹא כָּל הַנִּסְתָּרוֹת וְהַנִּגְלוֹת אַתָּה יוֹדֵעַ.

אַתָּה יוֹדֵעַ רָזֵי עוֹלָם וְתַעֲלוּמוֹת סִתְרֵי כָּל חָי.
אַתָּה חוֹפֵשׂ כָּל חַדְרֵי בָטֶן וּבוֹחֵן כְּלָיוֹת וָלֵב.
אֵין דָּבָר נֶעְלָם מִמֶּךָּ וְאֵין נִסְתָּר מִנֶּגֶד עֵינֶיךָ.
וּבְכֵן, יְהִי רָצוֹן מִלְּפָנֶיךָ, יהוה אֱלֹהֵינוּ וֵאלֹהֵי אֲבוֹתֵינוּ
שֶׁתִּסְלַח לָנוּ עַל כָּל חַטֹּאתֵינוּ
וְתִמְחַל לָנוּ עַל כָּל עֲוֹנוֹתֵינוּ
וּתְכַפֶּר לָנוּ עַל כָּל פְּשָׁעֵינוּ.

Strike the left side of the chest with the right fist while saying each of the sins.

עַל חֵטְא For the sin we have sinned before You under duress or freewill,
and for the sin we have sinned before You in hardness of heart.

For the sin we have sinned before You unwittingly,
and for the sin we have sinned before You by an utterance of our lips.

For the sin we have sinned before You by unchastity,
and for the sin we have sinned before You openly or secretly.

For the sin we have sinned before You knowingly and deceitfully,
and for the sin we have sinned before You in speech.

For the sin we have sinned before You by wronging a neighbor,
and for the sin we have sinned before You by thoughts of the heart.

For the sin we have sinned before You in a gathering for immorality,
and for the sin we have sinned before You by insincere confession.

For the sin we have sinned before You by contempt for parents and teachers,
and for the sin we have sinned before You willfully or in error.

For the sin we have sinned before You by force,
and for the sin we have sinned before You by desecrating Your name.

For the sin we have sinned before You by impure lips,
and for the sin we have sinned before You by foolish speech.

For the sin we have sinned before You by the evil inclination,
and for the sin we have sinned before You knowingly or unwittingly.

> For all these, God of forgiveness,
> forgive us, pardon us, grant us atonement.

עַל חֵטְא *For the sin:* It is a custom to confess sins as part of the Afternoon Service before Yom Kippur so as to enter the holy of holies of Jewish time in the appropriate mood of penitence. Confession is an essential element of *teshuva*, "repentance," and according to Maimonides, its biblical source. God forgives our wrongs, but only if we acknowledge them as wrongs. The

Strike the left side of the chest with the right fist while saying each of the sins.

עַל חֵטְא שֶׁחָטָאנוּ לְפָנֶיךָ בְּאֹנֶס וּבְרָצוֹן

וְעַל חֵטְא שֶׁחָטָאנוּ לְפָנֶיךָ בְּאִמּוּץ הַלֵּב

עַל חֵטְא שֶׁחָטָאנוּ לְפָנֶיךָ בִּבְלִי דָעַת

וְעַל חֵטְא שֶׁחָטָאנוּ לְפָנֶיךָ בְּבִטּוּי שְׂפָתָיִם

עַל חֵטְא שֶׁחָטָאנוּ לְפָנֶיךָ בְּגִלּוּי עֲרָיוֹת

וְעַל חֵטְא שֶׁחָטָאנוּ לְפָנֶיךָ בְּגָלוּי וּבַסֵּתֶר

עַל חֵטְא שֶׁחָטָאנוּ לְפָנֶיךָ בְּדַעַת וּבְמִרְמָה

וְעַל חֵטְא שֶׁחָטָאנוּ לְפָנֶיךָ בְּדִבּוּר פֶּה

עַל חֵטְא שֶׁחָטָאנוּ לְפָנֶיךָ בְּהוֹנָאַת רֵעַ

וְעַל חֵטְא שֶׁחָטָאנוּ לְפָנֶיךָ בְּהִרְהוּר הַלֵּב

עַל חֵטְא שֶׁחָטָאנוּ לְפָנֶיךָ בּוְעִידַת זְנוּת

וְעַל חֵטְא שֶׁחָטָאנוּ לְפָנֶיךָ בְּוִדּוּי פֶּה

עַל חֵטְא שֶׁחָטָאנוּ לְפָנֶיךָ בְּזִלְזוּל הוֹרִים וּמוֹרִים

וְעַל חֵטְא שֶׁחָטָאנוּ לְפָנֶיךָ בְּזָדוֹן וּבִשְׁגָגָה

עַל חֵטְא שֶׁחָטָאנוּ לְפָנֶיךָ בְּחֹזֶק יָד

וְעַל חֵטְא שֶׁחָטָאנוּ לְפָנֶיךָ בְּחִלּוּל הַשֵּׁם

עַל חֵטְא שֶׁחָטָאנוּ לְפָנֶיךָ בְּטֻמְאַת שְׂפָתָיִם

וְעַל חֵטְא שֶׁחָטָאנוּ לְפָנֶיךָ בְּטִפְשׁוּת פֶּה

עַל חֵטְא שֶׁחָטָאנוּ לְפָנֶיךָ בְּיֵצֶר הָרָע

וְעַל חֵטְא שֶׁחָטָאנוּ לְפָנֶיךָ בְּיוֹדְעִים וּבְלֹא יוֹדְעִים

וְעַל כֻּלָּם אֱלוֹהַּ סְלִיחוֹת סְלַח לָנוּ, מְחַל לָנוּ, כַּפֶּר לָנוּ.

For the sin we have sinned before You by deceit and lies,
and for the sin we have sinned before You by bribery.

For the sin we have sinned before You by scorn,
and for the sin we have sinned before You by evil speech.

For the sin we have sinned before You in business,
and for the sin we have sinned before You with food and drink.

For the sin we have sinned before You by interest and extortion,
and for the sin we have sinned before You by being haughty.

For the sin we have sinned before You by the idle chatter of our lips,
and for the sin we have sinned before You by prying eyes.

For the sin we have sinned before You by arrogance,
and for the sin we have sinned before You by insolence.

> For all these, God of forgiveness,
> forgive us, pardon us, grant us atonement.

For the sin we have sinned before You by casting off the yoke,
and for the sin we have sinned before You by perverting judgment.

For the sin we have sinned before You by entrapping a neighbor,
and for the sin we have sinned before You by envy.

For the sin we have sinned before You by lack of seriousness,
and for the sin we have sinned before You by obstinacy.

For the sin we have sinned before You by running to do evil,
and for the sin we have sinned before You by gossip.

---

two forms of confession, *Ashamnu*, "We have been guilty" and *Al ḥet*, "For the sin," are both arranged as alphabetical acrostics, as if to say, we confess with every letter of the alphabet and for every possible transgression. Divine forgiveness makes it possible for us to admit our failings and engage in moral and spiritual growth, defeating the rationalizations and self-justifications that may otherwise imprison people in their past and their shortcomings.

עַל חֵטְא שֶׁחָטָאנוּ לְפָנֶיךָ בְּכַחַשׁ וּבְכָזָב
וְעַל חֵטְא שֶׁחָטָאנוּ לְפָנֶיךָ בְּכַפַּת שֹׁחַד

עַל חֵטְא שֶׁחָטָאנוּ לְפָנֶיךָ בְּלָצוֹן
וְעַל חֵטְא שֶׁחָטָאנוּ לְפָנֶיךָ בְּלָשׁוֹן הָרָע

עַל חֵטְא שֶׁחָטָאנוּ לְפָנֶיךָ בְּמַשָּׂא וּבְמַתָּן
וְעַל חֵטְא שֶׁחָטָאנוּ לְפָנֶיךָ בְּמַאֲכָל וּבְמִשְׁתֶּה

עַל חֵטְא שֶׁחָטָאנוּ לְפָנֶיךָ בְּנֶשֶׁךְ וּבְמַרְבִּית
וְעַל חֵטְא שֶׁחָטָאנוּ לְפָנֶיךָ בִּנְטִיַּת גָּרוֹן

עַל חֵטְא שֶׁחָטָאנוּ לְפָנֶיךָ בְּשִׂיחַ שִׂפְתוֹתֵינוּ
וְעַל חֵטְא שֶׁחָטָאנוּ לְפָנֶיךָ בְּשִׁקּוּר עָיִן

עַל חֵטְא שֶׁחָטָאנוּ לְפָנֶיךָ בְּעֵינַיִם רָמוֹת
וְעַל חֵטְא שֶׁחָטָאנוּ לְפָנֶיךָ בְּעַזּוּת מֵצַח

וְעַל כֻּלָּם אֱלוֹהַּ סְלִיחוֹת סְלַח לָנוּ, מְחַל לָנוּ, כַּפֶּר לָנוּ.

עַל חֵטְא שֶׁחָטָאנוּ לְפָנֶיךָ בִּפְרִיקַת עֹל
וְעַל חֵטְא שֶׁחָטָאנוּ לְפָנֶיךָ בִּפְלִילוּת

עַל חֵטְא שֶׁחָטָאנוּ לְפָנֶיךָ בִּצְדִיַּת רֵעַ
וְעַל חֵטְא שֶׁחָטָאנוּ לְפָנֶיךָ בְּצָרוּת עָיִן

עַל חֵטְא שֶׁחָטָאנוּ לְפָנֶיךָ בְּקַלּוּת רֹאשׁ
וְעַל חֵטְא שֶׁחָטָאנוּ לְפָנֶיךָ בְּקַשְׁיוּת עֹרֶף

עַל חֵטְא שֶׁחָטָאנוּ לְפָנֶיךָ בְּרִיצַת רַגְלַיִם לְהָרַע
וְעַל חֵטְא שֶׁחָטָאנוּ לְפָנֶיךָ בִּרְכִילוּת

For the sin we have sinned before You by vain oath,
and for the sin we have sinned before You by baseless hatred.

For the sin we have sinned before You by breach of trust,
and for the sin we have sinned before You by confusion of heart.

For all these, God of forgiveness,
forgive us, pardon us, grant us atonement.

וְעַל חֲטָאִים And for the sins for which we are liable to bring a burnt-offering,
and for the sins for which we are liable to bring a sin-offering,
and for the sins for which we are liable to bring an offering
according to our means,
and for the sins for which we are liable to bring a guilt-offering
for certain or possible sin,
and for the sins for which we are liable to lashes for rebellion,
and for the sins for which we are liable to forty lashes,
and for the sins for which we are liable to death by the hands of Heaven,
and for the sins for which we are liable to be cut off and childless,
and for the sins for which we are liable to the four death penalties
inflicted by the court: stoning, burning, beheading and strangling.

For positive and negative commandments,
whether they can be remedied by an act or not,
for sins known to us and for those that are unknown –
for those that are known,
we have already declared them before You
and confessed them to You;
and for those that are unknown,
before You they are revealed and known,
as it is said,
"The secret things belong to the LORD our God,   *Deut. 29*
but the things that are revealed are for us and our children for ever,
that we may fulfill all the words of this Torah."
For You are He who forgives Israel
and pardons the tribes of Yeshurun in every generation,
and besides You we have no king who pardons and forgives, only You.

עַל חֵטְא שֶׁחָטָאנוּ לְפָנֶיךָ בִּשְׁבוּעַת שָׁוְא
וְעַל חֵטְא שֶׁחָטָאנוּ לְפָנֶיךָ בְּשִׂנְאַת חִנָּם

עַל חֵטְא שֶׁחָטָאנוּ לְפָנֶיךָ בִּתְשׂוּמֶת יָד
וְעַל חֵטְא שֶׁחָטָאנוּ לְפָנֶיךָ בְּתִמְהוֹן לֵבָב

וְעַל כֻּלָּם אֱלוֹהַּ סְלִיחוֹת סְלַח לָנוּ, מְחַל לָנוּ, כַּפֶּר לָנוּ.

וְעַל חֲטָאִים שֶׁאָנוּ חַיָּבִים עֲלֵיהֶם עוֹלָה
וְעַל חֲטָאִים שֶׁאָנוּ חַיָּבִים עֲלֵיהֶם חַטָּאת
וְעַל חֲטָאִים שֶׁאָנוּ חַיָּבִים עֲלֵיהֶם קָרְבָּן עוֹלֶה וְיוֹרֵד
וְעַל חֲטָאִים שֶׁאָנוּ חַיָּבִים עֲלֵיהֶם אָשָׁם וַדַּאי וְתָלוּי
וְעַל חֲטָאִים שֶׁאָנוּ חַיָּבִים עֲלֵיהֶם מַכַּת מַרְדּוּת
וְעַל חֲטָאִים שֶׁאָנוּ חַיָּבִים עֲלֵיהֶם מַלְקוּת אַרְבָּעִים
וְעַל חֲטָאִים שֶׁאָנוּ חַיָּבִים עֲלֵיהֶם מִיתָה בִּידֵי שָׁמַיִם
וְעַל חֲטָאִים שֶׁאָנוּ חַיָּבִים עֲלֵיהֶם כָּרֵת וַעֲרִירִי
וְעַל חֲטָאִים שֶׁאָנוּ חַיָּבִים עֲלֵיהֶם אַרְבַּע מִיתוֹת בֵּית דִּין
סְקִילָה, שְׂרֵפָה, הֶרֶג, וְחֶנֶק.

עַל מִצְוַת עֲשֵׂה וְעַל מִצְוַת לֹא תַעֲשֶׂה.
בֵּין שֶׁיֵּשׁ בָּה קוּם עֲשֵׂה וּבֵין שֶׁאֵין בָּה קוּם עֲשֵׂה.
אֶת הַגְּלוּיִים לָנוּ וְאֶת שֶׁאֵינָם גְּלוּיִים לָנוּ
אֶת הַגְּלוּיִים לָנוּ, כְּבָר אֲמַרְנוּם לְפָנֶיךָ, וְהוֹדִינוּ לְךָ עֲלֵיהֶם
וְאֶת שֶׁאֵינָם גְּלוּיִים לָנוּ, לְפָנֶיךָ הֵם גְּלוּיִים וִידוּעִים
כַּדָּבָר שֶׁנֶּאֱמַר
דברים כט
הַנִּסְתָּרֹת לַיהוה אֱלֹהֵינוּ
וְהַנִּגְלֹת לָנוּ וּלְבָנֵינוּ עַד־עוֹלָם
לַעֲשׂוֹת אֶת־כָּל־דִּבְרֵי הַתּוֹרָה הַזֹּאת:
כִּי אַתָּה סָלְחָן לְיִשְׂרָאֵל וּמָחֳלָן לְשִׁבְטֵי יְשֻׁרוּן בְּכָל דּוֹר וָדוֹר
וּמִבַּלְעָדֶיךָ אֵין לָנוּ מֶלֶךְ מוֹחֵל וְסוֹלֵחַ אֶלָּא אָתָּה.

אֱלֹהַי My God,
before I was formed I was unworthy,
and now that I have been formed it is as if I had not been formed.
I am dust while alive,
how much more so when I am dead.
See, I am before You like a vessel filled with shame and disgrace.
May it be Your will, LORD my God and God of my fathers,
that I may sin no more,
and as for the sins I have committed before You,
erase them in Your great compassion,
but not by suffering or severe illness.

אֱלֹהַי My God,   *Berakhot*
guard my tongue from evil   *17a*
and my lips from deceitful speech.
To those who curse me, let my soul be silent;
may my soul be to all like the dust.
Open my heart to Your Torah
and let my soul pursue Your commandments.
As for all who plan evil against me,
swiftly thwart their counsel and frustrate their plans.
        Act for the sake of Your name; act for the sake of Your right hand;
            act for the sake of Your holiness; act for the sake of Your Torah.
That Your beloved ones may be delivered,   *Ps. 60*
save with Your right hand and answer me.
May the words of my mouth and the meditation of my heart   *Ps. 19*
find favor before You, LORD, my Rock and Redeemer.

Bow, take three steps back, then bow, first left, then right, then center, while saying:
May He who makes peace in His high places,
make peace for us and all Israel – and say: Amen.

יְהִי רָצוֹן May it be Your will, LORD our God and God of our ancestors,
that the Temple be rebuilt speedily in our days,
and grant us a share in Your Torah.
And there we will serve You with reverence,
as in the days of old and as in former years.
Then the offering of Judah and Jerusalem   *Mal. 3*
will be pleasing to the LORD as in the days of old and as in former years.

אֱלֹהַי

עַד שֶׁלֹּא נוֹצַרְתִּי אֵינִי כְדַאי
וְעַכְשָׁיו שֶׁנּוֹצַרְתִּי, כְּאִלּוּ לֹא נוֹצַרְתִּי
עָפָר אֲנִי בְּחַיָּי, קַל וָחֹמֶר בְּמִיתָתִי.
הֲרֵי אֲנִי לְפָנֶיךָ כִּכְלִי מָלֵא בוּשָׁה וּכְלִמָּה.
יְהִי רָצוֹן מִלְּפָנֶיךָ, יהוה אֱלֹהַי וֵאלֹהֵי אֲבוֹתַי
שֶׁלֹּא אֶחֱטָא עוֹד.
וּמַה שֶּׁחָטָאתִי לְפָנֶיךָ, מְחֹק בְּרַחֲמֶיךָ הָרַבִּים
אֲבָל לֹא עַל יְדֵי יִסּוּרִים וָחֳלָיִם רָעִים.

אֱלֹהַי

ברכות יז.

נְצֹר לְשׁוֹנִי מֵרָע וּשְׂפָתַי מִדַּבֵּר מִרְמָה
וְלִמְקַלְלַי נַפְשִׁי תִדֹּם, וְנַפְשִׁי כֶּעָפָר לַכֹּל תִּהְיֶה.
פְּתַח לִבִּי בְּתוֹרָתֶךָ, וּבְמִצְוֹתֶיךָ תִּרְדֹּף נַפְשִׁי.
וְכָל הַחוֹשְׁבִים עָלַי רָעָה
מְהֵרָה הָפֵר עֲצָתָם וְקַלְקֵל מַחֲשַׁבְתָּם.
עֲשֵׂה לְמַעַן שְׁמֶךָ, עֲשֵׂה לְמַעַן יְמִינֶךָ
עֲשֵׂה לְמַעַן קְדֻשָּׁתֶךָ, עֲשֵׂה לְמַעַן תּוֹרָתֶךָ.

תהלים ס
לְמַעַן יֵחָלְצוּן יְדִידֶיךָ, הוֹשִׁיעָה יְמִינְךָ וַעֲנֵנִי:
תהלים יט
יִהְיוּ לְרָצוֹן אִמְרֵי פִי וְהֶגְיוֹן לִבִּי לְפָנֶיךָ, יהוה צוּרִי וְגֹאֲלִי:

Bow, take three steps back, then bow, first left, then right, then center, while saying:

עֹשֶׂה שָׁלוֹם / בעשרת ימי תשובה: הַשָּׁלוֹם/ בִּמְרוֹמָיו
הוּא יַעֲשֶׂה שָׁלוֹם עָלֵינוּ וְעַל כָּל יִשְׂרָאֵל וְאִמְרוּ אָמֵן.

יְהִי רָצוֹן מִלְּפָנֶיךָ יהוה אֱלֹהֵינוּ וֵאלֹהֵי אֲבוֹתֵינוּ
שֶׁיִּבָּנֶה בֵּית הַמִּקְדָּשׁ בִּמְהֵרָה בְיָמֵינוּ, וְתֵן חֶלְקֵנוּ בְּתוֹרָתֶךָ
וְשָׁם נַעֲבָדְךָ בְּיִרְאָה כִּימֵי עוֹלָם וּכְשָׁנִים קַדְמֹנִיּוֹת.
מלאכי ג
וְעָרְבָה לַיהוה מִנְחַת יְהוּדָה וִירוּשָׁלָ͏ִם כִּימֵי עוֹלָם וּכְשָׁנִים קַדְמֹנִיּוֹת:

SERVICE FOR HANUKKA

On each of the eight nights of Hanukka, the lights of the menora are lit: one on the first night, two on the second, and so on. On the first night, the rightmost branch of the menora is used; on each subsequent night, an additional light is added to the left. Each night, the new light is lit first, then the others, moving rightwards. If possible, the menora should be displayed near a window so that it is visible from the street.

The lights are lit using a separate flame known as the shamash. The lighting should be carried out as soon as possible after nightfall. On Friday night, it must be done before the beginning of Shabbat. See laws 135–136. Before lighting the Hanukka lights, say:

בָּרוּךְ Blessed are You, Lᴏʀᴅ our God, King of the Universe, who has made us holy through His commandments, and has commanded us to light the Hanukka lights.

בָּרוּךְ Blessed are You, Lᴏʀᴅ our God, King of the Universe, who performed miracles for our ancestors in those days, at this time.

On the first night, add:

בָּרוּךְ Blessed are You, Lᴏʀᴅ our God, King of the Universe, who has given us life, sustained us, and brought us to this time.

---

is the anniversary of that ceremony of rededication, celebrating not only the military victory and the restoration of Jewish self-government, but also the spiritual victory of Jewish faith over enforced assimilation. Shortly afterward, it was decided to hold an annual eight-day celebration in memory of those events, including the recitation of Hallel.

One incident came to hold immense symbolic significance: the fact that among the debris of the Temple, a single cruse of oil was found, its seal intact, with which the menora – the Temple candelabrum – could be lit. The oil that would normally have lasted for one day burned for eight, the full period of the rededication ceremony. Even after the Temple was destroyed more than two centuries later by the Romans, the Hanukka lights bore witness to the fact that after the worst desecration, something pure remains, lighting a way to the future. The Hanukka lights became one of the great symbols of Jewish hope.

סדר הדלקת נרות חנוכה

On each of the eight nights of חנוכה, the lights of the חנוכיה are lit: one on the
first night, two on the second, and so on. On the first night, the rightmost branch
of the חנוכיה is used; on each subsequent night, an additional light is added to the
left. Each night, the new light is lit first, then the others, moving rightwards. If possible,
the חנוכיה should be displayed near a window so that it is visible from the street.
The lights are lit using a separate flame known as the שמש. The lighting should be
carried out as soon as possible after nightfall. On Friday night, it must be done before
the beginning of שבת. See laws 135–136. Before lighting the חנוכה lights, say:

בָּרוּךְ אַתָּה יהוה אֱלֹהֵינוּ מֶלֶךְ הָעוֹלָם
אֲשֶׁר קִדְּשָׁנוּ בְּמִצְוֹתָיו וְצִוָּנוּ לְהַדְלִיק נֵר שֶׁל חֲנֻכָּה.

בָּרוּךְ אַתָּה יהוה אֱלֹהֵינוּ מֶלֶךְ הָעוֹלָם
שֶׁעָשָׂה נִסִּים לַאֲבוֹתֵינוּ בַּיָּמִים הָהֵם בַּזְּמַן הַזֶּה.

On the first night, add:

בָּרוּךְ אַתָּה יהוה אֱלֹהֵינוּ מֶלֶךְ הָעוֹלָם
שֶׁהֶחֱיָנוּ וְקִיְּמָנוּ וְהִגִּיעָנוּ לַזְּמַן הַזֶּה.

ḤANUKKA

After the conquests of Alexander the Great, Israel came under the rule of
Greece, in the third century BCE under the Ptolemies, based in Egypt; then
in the second century BCE under the Seleucids, based in Syria. Beginning in
175 BCE, one of the Seleucid rulers, Antiochus Epiphanes, decided to embark
on a campaign of enforced Hellenization of the Jews in Israel. A gymnasium
was built at the foot of the Temple Mount. Temple funds were diverted to
Greek athletic and cultural events. Eventually, in 167 BCE, the public practice
of Judaism was forbidden and a statue of Zeus erected in the Temple. Many
Jews went to their death as martyrs rather than abandon their faith.

A group of pious Jews, led by an elderly priest, Mattityahu, and his sons –
including most famously Judah, known as the Maccabee – rose in revolt. Over
the next three years they fought a successful campaign, driving the Greek
forces out of Jerusalem and rededicating the desecrated Temple. Ḥanukka

After lighting the first light, say:

הַנֵּרוֹת הַלָּלוּ **We light these lights**
because of the miracles and wonders,
deliverances and victories
You performed for our ancestors in those days, at this time,
through Your holy priests.

Sofrim
ch. 3

Throughout the eight days of Ḥanukka
these lights are holy
and we are not permitted
to make any other use of them,
except to look at them,

that we may give thanks and praise to Your great name
for Your miracles, Your wonders and Your deliverances.

After all the lights are lit:

מָעוֹז צוּר **Refuge, Rock of my salvation:**
to You it is a delight to give praise.
Restore my House of prayer,
so that there I may offer You thanksgiving.
When You silence the loud-mouthed foe,
Then will I complete, with song and psalm, the altar's dedication.

Shabbat lights, those of Ḥanukka are not lit for the sake of the light they give,
but rather are lit in order to "publicize the miracle." A separate light or candle,
the *shamash*, is used to light the others, and is placed slightly higher, so that
if we benefit from the light, it is from the *shamash*, and not those that form
part of the mitzva itself.

מָעוֹז צוּר יְשׁוּעָתִי *Refuge, Rock of my salvation:* Composed in Germany in the
thirteenth century. The first letters of the verses spell out the name Mordekhai;
other than this we cannot identify the author. The first verse recalls the
rededication of the Temple and looks forward to its future restoration.

מסכת
סופרים
פרק ג

After lighting the first light, say:

הַנֵּרוֹת הַלָּלוּ אָנוּ מַדְלִיקִים
עַל הַנִּסִּים וְעַל הַנִּפְלָאוֹת וְעַל הַתְּשׁוּעוֹת וְעַל הַמִּלְחָמוֹת
שֶׁעָשִׂיתָ לַאֲבוֹתֵינוּ בַּיָּמִים הָהֵם בַּזְּמַן הַזֶּה
עַל יְדֵי כֹּהֲנֶיךָ הַקְּדוֹשִׁים.

וְכָל שְׁמוֹנַת יְמֵי חֲנֻכָּה
הַנֵּרוֹת הַלָּלוּ קֹדֶשׁ הֵם
וְאֵין לָנוּ רְשׁוּת לְהִשְׁתַּמֵּשׁ בָּהֶם
אֶלָּא לִרְאוֹתָם בִּלְבָד

כְּדֵי לְהוֹדוֹת וּלְהַלֵּל לְשִׁמְךָ הַגָּדוֹל
עַל נִסֶּיךָ וְעַל נִפְלְאוֹתֶיךָ וְעַל יְשׁוּעָתֶךָ.

After all the lights are lit:

לְךָ נָאֶה לְשַׁבֵּחַ	מָעוֹז צוּר יְשׁוּעָתִי
וְשָׁם תּוֹדָה נְזַבֵּחַ	תִּכּוֹן בֵּית תְּפִלָּתִי
מִצָּר הַמְנַבֵּחַ	לְעֵת תָּכִין מַטְבֵּחַ
חֲנֻכַּת הַמִּזְבֵּחַ.	אָז אֶגְמֹר בְּשִׁיר מִזְמוֹר

――――――――――――――――――――――――――――――――――――

They are lit at home, at nightfall or soon thereafter, preferably in a position where they can be seen by passersby. Our custom is to light one candle (or olive-oil lamp) on the first night, two on the second, and so on. The first candle is placed at the right of the menora; on each night, the first light to be lit is the leftmost.

הַנֵּרוֹת הַלָּלוּ *We light these lights:* A hymn about the holiness of the lights and why we light them. The text is known from the rabbinic tractate, *Sofrim*, though it has undergone some changes in the intervening centuries. וְאֵין לָנוּ רְשׁוּת לְהִשְׁתַּמֵּשׁ בָּהֶם *We are not permitted to make any other use of them:* Unlike

רָעוֹת Troubles sated my soul; my strength was spent with sorrow.
They embittered my life with hardship,
when I was enslaved under Egyptian rule.
But God with His great power
brought out His treasured people,
While Pharaoh's host and followers sank like a stone into the deep.

דְּבִיר He brought me to His holy abode,
but even there I found no rest.
The oppressor came and exiled me,
because I had served strange gods.
I had drunk poisoned wine. I almost perished.
Then Babylon fell, Zerubbabel came: within seventy years I was saved.

כְּרֹת The Agagite, son of Hammedatha,
sought to cut down the tall fir tree,
But it became a trap to him,
and his arrogance was brought to an end.
You raised the head of the Benjaminite,
and the enemy's name You blotted out.
His many sons and his household You hanged on the gallows.

יְוָנִים Then the Greeks gathered against me,
in the days of the Hasmoneans.
They broke down the walls of my towers,
and defiled all the oils.
But from the last remaining flask
a miracle was wrought for Your beloved.
Therefore the sages ordained these eight days for song and praise.

חֲשֹׂף Bare Your holy arm, and hasten the time of salvation.
Take retribution against the evil nation
on behalf of Your servants,
For the hour [of deliverance] has been too long delayed;
there seems no end to the evil days.
Thrust the enemy into the darkness of death,
and establish for us the seven Shepherds.

בְּיָגוֹן כֹּחִי כִּלָּה   רָעוֹת שָׂבְעָה נַפְשִׁי
בְּשִׁעְבּוּד מַלְכוּת עֶגְלָה   חַיַּי מֵרְרוּ בְּקֹשִׁי
הוֹצִיא אֶת הַסְּגֻלָּה   וּבְיָדוֹ הַגְּדוֹלָה
יָרְדוּ כְּאֶבֶן מְצוּלָה.   חֵיל פַּרְעֹה וְכָל זַרְעוֹ

וְגַם שָׁם לֹא שָׁקַטְתִּי   דְּבִיר קָדְשׁוֹ הֱבִיאַנִי
כִּי זָרִים עָבַדְתִּי   וּבָא נוֹגֵשׂ וְהִגְלַנִי
כִּמְעַט שֶׁעָבַרְתִּי   וְיֵין רַעַל מָסַכְתִּי
לְקֵץ שִׁבְעִים נוֹשַׁעְתִּי.   קֵץ בָּבֶל זְרֻבָּבֶל

אֲגָגִי בֶּן הַמְּדָתָא   כְּרוֹת קוֹמַת בְּרוֹשׁ בִּקֵּשׁ
וְגַאֲוָתוֹ נִשְׁבָּתָה   וְנִהְיְתָה לוֹ לְפַח וּלְמוֹקֵשׁ
וְאוֹיֵב שְׁמוֹ מָחִיתָ   רֹאשׁ יְמִינִי נִשֵּׂאתָ
עַל הָעֵץ תָּלִיתָ.   רֹב בָּנָיו וְקִנְיָנָיו

אֲזַי בִּימֵי חַשְׁמַנִּים   יְוָנִים נִקְבְּצוּ עָלַי
וְטִמְּאוּ כָּל הַשְּׁמָנִים   וּפָרְצוּ חוֹמוֹת מִגְדָּלַי
נַעֲשָׂה נֵס לַשּׁוֹשַׁנִּים   וּמִנּוֹתַר קַנְקַנִּים
קָבְעוּ שִׁיר וּרְנָנִים.   בְּנֵי בִינָה יְמֵי שְׁמוֹנָה

וְקָרֵב קֵץ הַיְשׁוּעָה   חֲשֹׂף זְרוֹעַ קָדְשֶׁךָ
מֵאֻמָּה הָרְשָׁעָה   נְקֹם נִקְמַת עֲבָדֶיךָ
וְאֵין קֵץ לִימֵי הָרָעָה   כִּי אָרְכָה לָנוּ הַשָּׁעָה
הָקֵם לָנוּ רוֹעִים שִׁבְעָה.   דְּחֵה אַדְמוֹן בְּצֵל צַלְמוֹן

The next four describe, sequentially, four crises and deliverances of Jewish history – slavery in Egypt, the Babylonian exile, Purim, and Ḥanukka itself. The last verse, missing from some manuscripts, may have been a later addition; alternatively it may have been part of the original text, but was censored by the non-Jewish authorities.

SERVICE FOR PURIM

*Before the reading of the Megilla, the congregation stands
and the Reader says the following three blessings:*

בָּרוּךְ Blessed are You, Lord our God, King of the Universe,
who has made us holy through His commandments,
and has commanded us about reading the Megilla.

בָּרוּךְ Blessed are You, Lord our God, King of the Universe,
who performed miracles for our ancestors
in those days at this time.

בָּרוּךְ Blessed are You, Lord our God, King of the Universe,
who has given us life, sustained us, and brought us to this time.

*The Megilla is read. When the reading is completed, the scroll is rolled up
and, if a minyan is present, the Reader continues:*

בָּרוּךְ Blessed are You, Lord our God, King of the Universe,
who pleads our cause, judges our claim, avenges our wrong,
brings retribution to our enemies, and punishes our foes.
Blessed are You, Lord,
who on behalf of His people Israel,
exacts punishment from all their foes,
the God who brings salvation.

The following is said after the night reading of the Megilla:

אֲשֶׁר הֵנִיא [God] frustrated the plan of the nations,
Thwarted the intentions of the crafty.
An evil man rose up against us,
An arrogant branch of Amalek's tree,
Haughty, rich, he dug his own pit.
His hubris became his own snare.
He was trapped in the trap he set for others.
Seeking to destroy, he was destroyed.
Haman shared his ancestors' hate,
And stirred against children the hostility of brothers.
He did not remember Saul's act of mercy,
his pity for Agag, through which a new enemy was born.
The wicked planned to cut off the righteous,
but the impure were defeated by the pure.

סדר קריאת המגילה בפורים

Before the reading of the מגילה, *the* קהל *stands*
and the קורא *says the following three blessings:*

בָּרוּךְ אַתָּה יהוה אֱלֹהֵינוּ מֶלֶךְ הָעוֹלָם
אֲשֶׁר קִדְּשָׁנוּ בְּמִצְוֹתָיו וְצִוָּנוּ עַל מִקְרָא מְגִלָּה.

בָּרוּךְ אַתָּה יהוה אֱלֹהֵינוּ מֶלֶךְ הָעוֹלָם
שֶׁעָשָׂה נִסִּים לַאֲבוֹתֵינוּ בַּיָּמִים הָהֵם בַּזְּמַן הַזֶּה.

בָּרוּךְ אַתָּה יהוה אֱלֹהֵינוּ מֶלֶךְ הָעוֹלָם
שֶׁהֶחֱיָנוּ וְקִיְּמָנוּ וְהִגִּיעָנוּ לַזְּמַן הַזֶּה.

The מגילה *is read. When the reading is completed, the scroll is rolled up*
and, if a מנין *is present, the* קורא *continues:*

בָּרוּךְ אַתָּה יהוה אֱלֹהֵינוּ מֶלֶךְ הָעוֹלָם
הָרָב אֶת רִיבֵנוּ, וְהַדָּן אֶת דִּינֵנוּ, וְהַנּוֹקֵם אֶת נִקְמָתֵנוּ
וְהַמְשַׁלֵּם גְּמוּל לְכָל אוֹיְבֵי נַפְשֵׁנוּ, וְהַנִּפְרָע לָנוּ מִצָּרֵינוּ.
בָּרוּךְ אַתָּה יהוה
הַנִּפְרָע לְעַמּוֹ יִשְׂרָאֵל מִכָּל צָרֵיהֶם, הָאֵל הַמּוֹשִׁיעַ.

The following is said after the night reading of the מגילה:

אֲשֶׁר הֵנִיא עֲצַת גּוֹיִם, וַיָּפֶר מַחְשְׁבוֹת עֲרוּמִים.
בְּקוּם עָלֵינוּ אָדָם רָשָׁע, נֵצֶר זָדוֹן מִזֶּרַע עֲמָלֵק.
גָּאָה בְעָשְׁרוֹ וְכָרָה לוֹ בּוֹר, וּגְדֻלָּתוֹ יָקְשָׁה לּוֹ לָכֶד.
דִּמָּה בְנַפְשׁוֹ לִלְכֹּד וְנִלְכָּד, בִּקֵּשׁ לְהַשְׁמִיד וְנִשְׁמַד מְהֵרָה.
הָמָן הוֹדִיעַ אֵיבַת אֲבוֹתָיו, וְעוֹרֵר שִׂנְאַת אַחִים לַבָּנִים.
וְלֹא זָכַר רַחֲמֵי שָׁאוּל, כִּי בְחֶמְלָתוֹ עַל אֲגָג נוֹלַד אוֹיֵב.
זָמַם רָשָׁע לְהַכְרִית צַדִּיק, וְנִלְכַּד טָמֵא בִּידֵי טָהוֹר.

PURIM

Purim is the annual remembrance and celebration of the events described
in the book of Esther. During the reign of Aḥashverosh of Persia, one of his

[Mordekhai's] goodness overcame the father's [Saul's] error,
　　but the evil [Haman] piled sin upon sin.
He hid in his heart his cunning schemes, intent on his evildoing.
He stretched out his hand against God's holy ones;
　　he spent his wealth to destroy every memory of them.
When Mordekhai saw the wrath go forth,
　　and Haman's decrees issued in Shushan,
he put on sackcloth, wrapped himself in mourning,
　　decreed a fast and sat on ashes.
"Who will arise to atone for error,
　　and find forgiveness for our ancestors' sins?"
A flower blossomed from the palm tree;
　　Hadassa arose to wake those who slept.
Her servants hastened Haman to come,
　　to serve him wine with the venom of serpents.
He had risen by his wealth, but fell by his evil.
　　He made the very gallows by which he was hanged.
All the inhabitants of the world were amazed
　　When Haman's ploy (*pur*) became our joy (*Purim*).
The righteous was saved from evil hands,
　　the perpetrator suffered the fate of his intended victim.
They undertook to celebrate Purim, and to rejoice on it year after year.
You heeded the prayer of Mordekhai and Esther;
　　and Haman and his sons were hanged on the gallows.

The following is said after both night and morning readings of the Megilla:

שׁוֹשַׁנַּת יַעֲקֹב The lily of Jacob rejoiced and was glad,
When, together, they saw Mordekhai robed in royal blue.
You have been their eternal salvation, their hope in every generation;
To make known that all who hope in You will not be put to shame,
All who trust in You will never be humiliated.
Cursed be Haman who sought to destroy me.
Blessed be Mordekhai the Yehudi.
Cursed be Zeresh, wife of him who terrified me.
Blessed be Esther [whose actions saved] me.
Cursed be all the wicked; blessed be all Israel.
And may Ḥarbona, too, be remembered for good.

*After the night reading, Ma'ariv continues with "You are Holy" to "great and glorious" on
pages 318–320 (on Motza'ei Shabbat, begin with "May the pleasantness" on page 316).
The Leader then continues with Full Kaddish on page 322 (omitting the line "May the
prayers and pleas"). (On Motza'ei Shabbat, continue with "May God give you" on page
324.) The service continues with Aleinu on page 332, and Mourner's Kaddish on page 334.
In the morning, continue with Ashrei on page 174 and "A redeemer will come" on page 178.*

חֶֽסֶד גָּבַר עַל שִׁגְגַת אָב, וְרֶשַׁע הוֹסִיף חֵטְא עַל חֲטָאָיו.

טָמַן בְּלִבּוֹ מַחְשְׁבוֹת עֲרוּמָיו, וַיִּתְמַכֵּר לַעֲשׂוֹת רָעָה.

יָדוֹ שָׁלַח בִּקְדוֹשֵׁי אֵל, כַּסְפּוֹ נָתַן לְהַכְרִית זִכְרָם.

כִּרְאוֹת מָרְדְּכַי כִּי יָצָא קֶֽצֶף, וְדָתֵי הָמָן נִתְּנוּ בְשׁוּשָׁן.

לָבַשׁ שַׂק וְקָשַׁר מִסְפֵּד וְגָזַר צוֹם וַיֵּֽשֶׁב עַל הָאֵֽפֶר.

מִי זֶה יַעֲמֹד לְכַפֵּר שִׁגְגָה, וְלִמְחֹל חַטַּאת עֲוֹן אֲבוֹתֵֽינוּ.

נֵץ פָּרַח מִלּוּלָב, הֵן הֲדַסָּה עָמְדָה לְעוֹרֵר יְשֵׁנִים.

סָרִיסֶֽיהָ הִבְהִֽילוּ לְהָמָן, לְהַשְׁקוֹתוֹ יֵין חֲמַת תַּנִּינִים.

עָמַד בְּעָשְׁרוֹ וְנָפַל בְּרִשְׁעוֹ, עָשָׂה לוֹ עֵץ וְנִתְלָה עָלָיו.

פִּיהֶם פָּתְחוּ כָּל יוֹשְׁבֵי תֵבֵל, כִּי פוּר הָמָן נֶהְפַּךְ לְפוּרֵֽנוּ.

צַדִּיק נֶחֱלַץ מִיַּד רָשָׁע, אוֹיֵב נִתַּן תַּֽחַת נַפְשׁוֹ.

קִיְּמוּ עֲלֵיהֶם לַעֲשׂוֹת פוּרִים וְלִשְׂמֹֽחַ בְּכָל שָׁנָה וְשָׁנָה.

רָאִֽיתָ אֶת תְּפִלַּת מָרְדְּכַי וְאֶסְתֵּר, הָמָן וּבָנָיו עַל הָעֵץ תָּלִֽיתָ:

The following is said after both night and morning readings of the מגילה:

שׁוֹשַֽׁנַּת יַעֲקֹב צָהֲלָה וְשָׂמֵֽחָה בִּרְאוֹתָם יַֽחַד תְּכֵֽלֶת מָרְדְּכָי.

תְּשׁוּעָתָם הָיִֽיתָ לָנֶֽצַח, וְתִקְוָתָם בְּכָל דּוֹר וָדוֹר.

לְהוֹדִֽיעַ שֶׁכָּל קֹוֶֽיךָ לֹא יֵבֹֽשׁוּ, וְלֹא יִכָּלְמוּ לָנֶֽצַח כָּל הַחוֹסִים בָּךְ.

אָרוּר הָמָן אֲשֶׁר בִּקֵּשׁ לְאַבְּדִי, בָּרוּךְ מָרְדְּכַי הַיְּהוּדִי.

אֲרוּרָה זֶֽרֶשׁ אֵֽשֶׁת מַפְחִידִי, בְּרוּכָה אֶסְתֵּר בַּעֲדִי.

אֲרוּרִים כָּל הָרְשָׁעִים, בְּרוּכִים כָּל יִשְׂרָאֵל, וְגַם חַרְבֽוֹנָה זָכוּר לַטּוֹב:

After the night reading, מעריב *continues with* וְאַתָּה קָדוֹשׁ *to* וְיַאְדִּיר *on pages 319–321* (*on* מוצאי שבת*, begin with* וִיהִי נֹֽעַם *on page 317*). *The* שליח ציבור *then continues with* וְיִתֵּן־לְךָ *on page 323* (*omitting the line* תִּתְקַבֵּל). (*On* מוצאי שבת*, continue with* קַדִּישׁ שָׁלֵם *on page 325.*) *The service continues with* עָלֵֽינוּ *on page 333, and* קַדִּישׁ יָתוֹם *on page 335.*

In the morning, continue with אַשְׁרֵי *on page 175 and* וּבָא לְצִיּוֹן *on page 179.*

senior officials, Haman, conspired to "destroy, kill and annihilate all the Jews, young and old, women and children, on a single day" (Esther 3:13) – the day chosen by the lottery (*pur*) that gives the festival its name. The Jews were saved by a combination of the defiance of Mordekhai and the plea of his cousin Esther, who had been taken into the royal harem and was a favorite of the king. Haman's plan was thwarted, and he and his sons were hanged on the gallows they had prepared for Mordekhai.

Memorial Day

*At the end of Shaḥarit, after Full Kaddish, the Ark is opened
and the following is said by some congregations:*

לַמְנַצֵּחַ For the conductor of music. Upon the death of Labben. A psalm of David. *Ps. 9*

I will thank You, Lᴏʀᴅ, with all my heart; I will tell of all Your wonders.

I will rejoice and exult in You; I will sing praise to Your name, Most High.

My enemies retreat; they stumble and perish before You.

For You have upheld my case and my cause; You have sat enthroned as righteous Judge.

You have rebuked nations and destroyed the wicked, blotting out their name for ever and all time.

The enemy are finished, ruined forever; You have overthrown their cities; even the memory of them is lost.

But the Lᴏʀᴅ abides forever; He has established His throne for judgment.

He will judge the world with righteousness, and try the cause of peoples with justice.

The Lᴏʀᴅ is a refuge for the oppressed, a stronghold in times of trouble.

Those who know Your name trust in You, for You, Lᴏʀᴅ, do not forsake those who seek You.

Sing praise to the Lᴏʀᴅ who dwells in Zion; tell the peoples of His deeds.

For He who avenges blood remembers; He does not forget the cry of the afflicted.

Have mercy on me, Lᴏʀᴅ, see how my enemies afflict me. Lift me up from the gates of death,

That in the gates of the Daughter of Zion I may tell all Your praises and rejoice in Your deliverance.

The nations have fallen into the pit they dug; their feet are caught in the net they hid.

The Lᴏʀᴅ is known by His justice; the wicked is ensnared by the work of his own hands. Reflect on this, Selah.

The wicked return to the grave, all the nations that forget God.

The needy will not be forgotten forever, nor the hope of the afflicted ever be lost.

Arise, Lᴏʀᴅ, let not man have power; let the nations be judged in Your presence.

Strike them with fear, Lᴏʀᴅ; let the nations know they are only men. Selah.

The Ark is closed.

סדר תפילת שחרית ליום הזיכרון

At the end of שחרית, after קדיש שלם, the ארון קודש is opened
and the following is said by some congregations:

תהלים ט

לַמְנַצֵּחַ עַל־מוּת לַבֵּן מִזְמוֹר לְדָוִד:

אוֹדֶה יהוה בְּכָל־לִבִּי, אֲסַפְּרָה כָּל־נִפְלְאוֹתֶיךָ:

אֶשְׂמְחָה וְאֶעֶלְצָה בָךְ, אֲזַמְּרָה שִׁמְךָ עֶלְיוֹן:

בְּשׁוּב־אוֹיְבַי אָחוֹר, יִכָּשְׁלוּ וְיֹאבְדוּ מִפָּנֶיךָ:

כִּי־עָשִׂיתָ מִשְׁפָּטִי וְדִינִי, יָשַׁבְתָּ לְכִסֵּא שׁוֹפֵט צֶדֶק:

גָּעַרְתָּ גוֹיִם אִבַּדְתָּ רָשָׁע, שְׁמָם מָחִיתָ לְעוֹלָם וָעֶד:

הָאוֹיֵב תַּמּוּ חֳרָבוֹת לָנֶצַח, וְעָרִים נָתַשְׁתָּ, אָבַד זִכְרָם הֵמָּה:

וַיהוה לְעוֹלָם יֵשֵׁב, כּוֹנֵן לַמִּשְׁפָּט כִּסְאוֹ:

וְהוּא יִשְׁפֹּט־תֵּבֵל בְּצֶדֶק, יָדִין לְאֻמִּים בְּמֵישָׁרִים:

וִיהִי יהוה מִשְׂגָּב לַדָּךְ, מִשְׂגָּב לְעִתּוֹת בַּצָּרָה:

וְיִבְטְחוּ בְךָ יוֹדְעֵי שְׁמֶךָ, כִּי לֹא־עָזַבְתָּ דֹרְשֶׁיךָ, יהוה:

זַמְּרוּ לַיהוה יֹשֵׁב צִיּוֹן, הַגִּידוּ בָעַמִּים עֲלִילוֹתָיו:

כִּי־דֹרֵשׁ דָּמִים אוֹתָם זָכָר, לֹא־שָׁכַח צַעֲקַת עֲנָוִים:

חָנְנֵנִי יהוה רְאֵה עָנְיִי מִשֹּׂנְאָי, מְרוֹמְמִי מִשַּׁעֲרֵי־מָוֶת:

לְמַעַן אֲסַפְּרָה כָּל־תְּהִלָּתֶיךָ, בְּשַׁעֲרֵי בַת־צִיּוֹן אָגִילָה בִּישׁוּעָתֶךָ:

טָבְעוּ גוֹיִם בְּשַׁחַת עָשׂוּ, בְּרֶשֶׁת־זוּ טָמָנוּ נִלְכְּדָה רַגְלָם:

נוֹדַע יהוה מִשְׁפָּט עָשָׂה, בְּפֹעַל כַּפָּיו נוֹקֵשׁ רָשָׁע, הִגָּיוֹן סֶלָה:

יָשׁוּבוּ רְשָׁעִים לִשְׁאוֹלָה, כָּל־גּוֹיִם שְׁכֵחֵי אֱלֹהִים:

כִּי לֹא לָנֶצַח יִשָּׁכַח אֶבְיוֹן, תִּקְוַת עֲנִיִּים תֹּאבַד לָעַד:

קוּמָה יהוה אַל־יָעֹז אֱנוֹשׁ, יִשָּׁפְטוּ גוֹיִם עַל־פָּנֶיךָ:

שִׁיתָה יהוה מוֹרָה לָהֶם, יֵדְעוּ גוֹיִם, אֱנוֹשׁ הֵמָּה סֶּלָה:

The ארון קודש is closed.

Memorial Prayer for Fallen Israeli Soldiers

אָבִינוּ שֶׁבַּשָּׁמַיִם Heavenly Father, God, Source of the spirits of all flesh,
remember, we pray You, the pure souls of our sons and daughters
who heroically gave their lives
in defense of the people and the Land.
Swifter than eagles, stronger than lions,
they fought for the liberation of their people and homeland,
sacrificing their lives for Israel's rebirth in its holy land.
They breathed a spirit of strength and courage
into the whole house of Israel,
in the Land and the Diaspora,
inspiring it to go forward toward its redemption and liberation.
Remember them, our God, for good,
together with the myriad holy ones and heroes of Israel from ancient times.
May their souls be bound in the bonds of everlasting life,
may the Garden of Eden be their resting place,
may they rest in peace
and receive their reward at the End of Days.
Amen.

לְדָוִד Of David. Blessed is the Lᴏʀᴅ, my Rock, who trains my hands for war, *Ps. 144*
my fingers for battle. He is my Benefactor, my Fortress, my Stronghold and my
Refuge, my Shield in whom I trust, He who subdues nations under me. Lᴏʀᴅ,
what is man that You care for him, what are mortals that You think of them? Man
is no more than a breath, his days like a fleeting shadow. Lᴏʀᴅ, part Your heavens
and come down; touch the mountains so that they pour forth smoke. Flash forth
lightning and scatter them; shoot Your arrows and panic them. Reach out Your
hand from on high; deliver me and rescue me from the mighty waters, from the
hands of strangers, whose every word is worthless, whose right hands are raised
in falsehood. To You, God, I will sing a new song; to You I will play music on a
ten-stringed harp. He who gives salvation to kings, who saved His servant David
from the cruel sword: may He deliver me and rescue me from the hands of strangers, whose every word is worthless, whose right hands are raised in falsehood.
Then our sons will be like saplings, well nurtured in their youth. Our daughters
will be like pillars carved for a palace. Our barns will be filled with every kind of
provision. Our sheep will increase by thousands, even tens of thousands in our
fields. Our oxen will draw heavy loads. There will be no breach in the walls, no
going into captivity, no cries of distress in our streets. Happy are the people for
whom this is so; happy are the people whose God is the Lᴏʀᴅ.

Memorial Prayer for Fallen Israeli Soldiers

אָבִינוּ שֶׁבַּשָּׁמַיִם, אֵל אֱלֹהֵי הָרוּחוֹת לְכָל בָּשָׂר

זְכֹר נָא אֶת הַנְּשָׁמוֹת הַזַּכּוֹת וְהַטְּהוֹרוֹת שֶׁל בָּנֵינוּ וּבְנוֹתֵינוּ

אֲשֶׁר הֶעֱרוּ אֶת נַפְשָׁם לָמוּת מוֹת גִּבּוֹרִים

בְּהֵחָלְצָם לְעֶזְרַת הָעָם וְהָאָרֶץ.

מִנְּשָׁרִים קַלּוּ מֵאֲרָיוֹת גָּבֵרוּ

בְּמִלְחַמְתָּם לְמַעַן שִׁחְרוּר עַמָּם וּמוֹלַדְתָּם.

בַּעֲלוֹתָם עַל מִזְבַּח תְּקוּמַת יִשְׂרָאֵל בְּאֶרֶץ קָדְשׁוֹ

הֵפִיחוּ רוּחַ עֹז גְּבוּרָה בְּכָל בֵּית יִשְׂרָאֵל בָּאָרֶץ וּבַתְּפוּצוֹת

וַיִּתְעוֹרֵר לְקִרְאַת גְּאֻלָּתוֹ וּפְדוּת נַפְשׁוֹ.

יִזָּכְרֵם אֱלֹהֵינוּ לְטוֹבָה

עִם רִבְבוֹת אַלְפֵי קְדוֹשֵׁי יִשְׂרָאֵל וְגִבּוֹרָיו מִימֵי עוֹלָם

בִּצְרוֹר הַחַיִּים יִצְרֹר אֶת נִשְׁמָתָם

בְּגַן עֵדֶן תְּהֵא מְנוּחָתָם

וְיָנוּחוּ בְּשָׁלוֹם עַל מִשְׁכָּבָם

וְיַעַמְדוּ לְגוֹרָלָם לְקֵץ הַיָּמִין.

אָמֵן.

לְדָוִד בָּרוּךְ יהוה צוּרִי הַמְלַמֵּד יָדַי לַקְרָב, אֶצְבְּעוֹתַי לַמִּלְחָמָה: חַסְדִּי וּמְצוּדָתִי תהלים קמד

מִשְׂגַּבִּי וּמְפַלְטִי לִי מָגִנִּי וּבוֹ חָסִיתִי הָרוֹדֵד עַמִּי תַחְתָּי: יהוה מָה־אָדָם וַתֵּדָעֵהוּ,

בֶּן־אֱנוֹשׁ וַתְּחַשְּׁבֵהוּ: אָדָם לַהֶבֶל דָּמָה יָמָיו כְּצֵל עוֹבֵר: יהוה הַט־שָׁמֶיךָ וְתֵרֵד

גַּע בֶּהָרִים וְיֶעֱשָׁנוּ: בְּרוֹק בָּרָק וּתְפִיצֵם, שְׁלַח חִצֶּיךָ וּתְהֻמֵּם: שְׁלַח יָדֶיךָ מִמָּרוֹם

פְּצֵנִי וְהַצִּילֵנִי מִמַּיִם רַבִּים מִיַּד בְּנֵי נֵכָר: אֲשֶׁר פִּיהֶם דִּבֶּר־שָׁוְא, וִימִינָם יְמִין

שָׁקֶר: אֱלֹהִים שִׁיר חָדָשׁ אָשִׁירָה לָּךְ, בְּנֵבֶל עָשׂוֹר אֲזַמְּרָה־לָּךְ: הַנּוֹתֵן תְּשׁוּעָה

לַמְּלָכִים הַפּוֹצֶה אֶת־דָּוִד עַבְדּוֹ מֵחֶרֶב רָעָה: פְּצֵנִי וְהַצִּילֵנִי מִיַּד בְּנֵי־נֵכָר אֲשֶׁר־

פִּיהֶם דִּבֶּר־שָׁוְא, וִימִינָם יְמִין שָׁקֶר: אֲשֶׁר בָּנֵינוּ כִּנְטִעִים מְגֻדָּלִים בִּנְעוּרֵיהֶם

בְּנוֹתֵינוּ כְזָוִיֹּת מְחֻטָּבוֹת תַּבְנִית הֵיכָל: מְזָוֵינוּ מְלֵאִים מְפִיקִים מִזַּן אֶל־זַן צֹאונֵנוּ

מַאֲלִיפוֹת מְרֻבָּבוֹת בְּחוּצוֹתֵינוּ: אַלּוּפֵינוּ מְסֻבָּלִים אֵין פֶּרֶץ וְאֵין יוֹצֵאת וְאֵין

צְוָחָה בִּרְחֹבֹתֵינוּ: אַשְׁרֵי הָעָם שֶׁכָּכָה לּוֹ אַשְׁרֵי הָעָם שֶׁיהוה אֱלֹהָיו:

Ma'ariv for Yom HaAtzma'ut

In Israel and many communities outside Israel the following is said before Ma'ariv:

הוֹדוּ Thank the LORD for He is good; His loving-kindness is for ever. *Ps. 107* Let those the LORD redeemed say this – those He redeemed from the enemy's hand, those He gathered from the lands, from east and west, from north and south. Some lost their way in desert wastelands, finding no way to a city where they could live. They were hungry and thirsty, and their spirit grew faint. Then they cried out to the LORD in their trouble, and He rescued them from their distress. He led them by a straight path to a city where they could live. Let them thank the LORD for His loving-kindness and His wondrous deeds for humankind, for He satisfies the thirsty and fills the hungry with good. Some sat in darkness and the shadow of death, cruelly bound in iron chains, for they had rebelled against God's words and despised the counsel of the Most High. He humbled their hearts with hard labor; they stumbled, and there was none to help. Then they cried to the LORD in their trouble, and He saved them from their distress. He brought them out from darkness and the shadow of death and broke open their chains. Let them thank the LORD for His loving-kindness and His wondrous deeds for humankind, for He shattered gates of bronze and broke their iron bars. Some were fools with sinful ways, and suffered affliction because of their iniquities. They found all food repulsive, and came close to the gates of death. Then they cried to the LORD in their trouble, and He saved them from their distress. He sent His word and healed them; He rescued them from their destruction. Let them thank the LORD for His loving-kindness and His wondrous

---

and his descendants were summoned to create a new kind of society, based on the sanctity of human life and the equal dignity of all, where they would be subject to the sovereignty of God alone, constantly conscious of the Divine Presence while striving to be true to the covenant that charged them with being "a kingdom of priests and a holy nation."

Nahmanides (commentary to Lev. 18:25) says that the primary fulfillment of all the commandments, not just those that relate to the land, occurs only

מעריב ליום העצמאות

In ארץ ישראל and many communities in חוץ לארץ the following is said before מעריב:

תהלים קז

הֹדוּ לַיהוה כִּי־טוֹב, כִּי לְעוֹלָם חַסְדּוֹ: יֹאמְרוּ גְּאוּלֵי יהוה, אֲשֶׁר גְּאָלָם מִיַּד־צָר: וּמֵאֲרָצוֹת קִבְּצָם, מִמִּזְרָח וּמִמַּעֲרָב, מִצָּפוֹן וּמִיָּם: תָּעוּ בַמִּדְבָּר, בִּישִׁימוֹן דֶּרֶךְ, עִיר מוֹשָׁב לֹא מָצָאוּ: רְעֵבִים גַּם־צְמֵאִים, נַפְשָׁם בָּהֶם תִּתְעַטָּף: וַיִּצְעֲקוּ אֶל־יהוה בַּצַּר לָהֶם, מִמְּצוּקוֹתֵיהֶם יַצִּילֵם: וַיַּדְרִיכֵם בְּדֶרֶךְ יְשָׁרָה, לָלֶכֶת אֶל־עִיר מוֹשָׁב: יוֹדוּ לַיהוה חַסְדּוֹ, וְנִפְלְאוֹתָיו לִבְנֵי אָדָם: כִּי־הִשְׂבִּיעַ נֶפֶשׁ שֹׁקֵקָה, וְנֶפֶשׁ רְעֵבָה מִלֵּא־טוֹב: יֹשְׁבֵי חֹשֶׁךְ וְצַלְמָוֶת, אֲסִירֵי עֳנִי וּבַרְזֶל: כִּי־הִמְרוּ אִמְרֵי־אֵל, וַעֲצַת עֶלְיוֹן נָאָצוּ: וַיַּכְנַע בֶּעָמָל לִבָּם, כָּשְׁלוּ וְאֵין עֹזֵר: וַיִּזְעֲקוּ אֶל־יהוה בַּצַּר לָהֶם, מִמְּצֻקוֹתֵיהֶם יוֹשִׁיעֵם: יוֹצִיאֵם מֵחֹשֶׁךְ וְצַלְמָוֶת, וּמוֹסְרוֹתֵיהֶם יְנַתֵּק: יוֹדוּ לַיהוה חַסְדּוֹ, וְנִפְלְאוֹתָיו לִבְנֵי אָדָם: כִּי־שִׁבַּר דַּלְתוֹת נְחֹשֶׁת, וּבְרִיחֵי בַרְזֶל גִּדֵּעַ: אֱוִלִים מִדֶּרֶךְ פִּשְׁעָם, וּמֵעֲוֹנֹתֵיהֶם יִתְעַנּוּ: כָּל־אֹכֶל תְּתַעֵב נַפְשָׁם, וַיַּגִּיעוּ עַד־שַׁעֲרֵי מָוֶת: וַיִּזְעֲקוּ אֶל־יהוה בַּצַּר לָהֶם, מִמְּצֻקוֹתֵיהֶם יוֹשִׁיעֵם: יִשְׁלַח דְּבָרוֹ וְיִרְפָּאֵם,

YOM HAATZMA'UT

Yom HaAtzma'ut, Israel's Independence Day, 5th Iyar 5708, marks the moment when the Jewish people recovered their independence and sovereignty after a lapse of some two thousand years. The longest exile ever endured by a people was at an end. For the first time in two millennia Jews had a home in the sense given by the poet Robert Frost, a place that, "when you have to go there, they have to take you in." Jews had once again returned to the arena of history as a self-determining nation in the land to which Abraham journeyed in his day, and Moses and the Israelites in theirs.

The significance of Israel to Judaism is more than geographical, historical and political. It is spiritual. Israel was and is the Holy Land to which Abraham

deeds for humankind. Let them sacrifice thanksgiving-offerings and tell His deeds with songs of joy. Those who go to sea in ships, plying their trade in the mighty waters, have seen the works of the LORD, His wondrous deeds in the deep. He spoke and stirred up a tempest that lifted high the waves. They rose to the heavens and plunged down to the depths; their souls melted in misery. They reeled and staggered like drunkards; all their skill was to no avail. Then they cried to the LORD in their trouble, and He brought them out of their distress. He stilled the storm to a whisper, and the waves of the sea grew calm. They rejoiced when all was quiet, then He guided them to their destination. Let them thank the LORD for His loving-kindness and His wondrous deeds for humankind. Let them exalt Him in the assembly of the people and praise Him in the council of the elders. He turns rivers into a desert, springs of water into parched land, fruitful land into a salt marsh, because of the wickedness of its inhabitants. He turns the desert into pools of water, parched land into flowing springs; He brings the hungry to live there, they build themselves a town in which to live. They sow fields and plant vineyards that yield a fruitful harvest; He blesses them, and they increase greatly, their herds do not decrease, though they had been few and brought low by oppression, adversity and sorrow. He pours contempt on nobles and makes them wander in a pathless waste. ‣ He lifts the destitute from poverty and enlarges their families like flocks. The upright see and rejoice, but the mouth of all wrongdoers is stopped. Whoever is wise, let him lay these things to heart, and reflect on the loving-kindness of the LORD.

יהוה מָלָךְ The LORD reigns, let the earth be glad. Let the many islands   Ps. 97
rejoice. Clouds and thick darkness surround Him; righteousness and justice are the foundation of His throne. Fire goes ahead of Him, consuming His enemies on every side. His lightning lights up the

---

the form of a just, gracious and compassionate social order. It is a code for "societal beatitude" (Rabbi Aharon Lichtenstein), and is predicated on a free, self-governing nation in its own land.

Though Jews, in the long centuries of their dispersion, were scattered over the face of the earth, only in Israel have they formed a majority and

וִימַלֵּט מִשְּׁחִיתוֹתָם: יוֹדוּ לַיהוה חַסְדּוֹ, וְנִפְלְאוֹתָיו לִבְנֵי אָדָם:
וְיִזְבְּחוּ זִבְחֵי תוֹדָה וִיסַפְּרוּ מַעֲשָׂיו בְּרִנָּה: יוֹרְדֵי הַיָּם בָּאֳנִיּוֹת,
עֹשֵׂי מְלָאכָה בְּמַיִם רַבִּים: הֵמָּה רָאוּ מַעֲשֵׂי יהוה, וְנִפְלְאוֹתָיו
בִּמְצוּלָה: וַיֹּאמֶר, וַיַּעֲמֵד רוּחַ סְעָרָה, וַתְּרוֹמֵם גַּלָּיו: יַעֲלוּ שָׁמַיִם,
יֵרְדוּ תְהוֹמוֹת, נַפְשָׁם בְּרָעָה תִתְמוֹגָג: יָחוֹגּוּ וְיָנוּעוּ כַּשִּׁכּוֹר, וְכָל־
חָכְמָתָם תִּתְבַּלָּע: וַיִּצְעֲקוּ אֶל־יהוה בַּצַּר לָהֶם, וּמִמְּצוּקֹתֵיהֶם
יוֹצִיאֵם: יָקֵם סְעָרָה לִדְמָמָה, וַיֶּחֱשׁוּ גַּלֵּיהֶם: וַיִּשְׂמְחוּ כִי־יִשְׁתֹּקוּ,
וַיַּנְחֵם אֶל־מְחוֹז חֶפְצָם: יוֹדוּ לַיהוה חַסְדּוֹ, וְנִפְלְאוֹתָיו לִבְנֵי אָדָם:
וִירוֹמְמוּהוּ בִּקְהַל־עָם, וּבְמוֹשַׁב זְקֵנִים יְהַלְלוּהוּ: יָשֵׂם נְהָרוֹת
לְמִדְבָּר, וּמֹצָאֵי מַיִם לְצִמָּאוֹן: אֶרֶץ פְּרִי לִמְלֵחָה, מֵרָעַת יֹשְׁבֵי
בָהּ: יָשֵׂם מִדְבָּר לַאֲגַם־מַיִם, וְאֶרֶץ צִיָּה לְמֹצָאֵי מָיִם: וַיּוֹשֶׁב שָׁם
רְעֵבִים, וַיְכוֹנְנוּ עִיר מוֹשָׁב: וַיִּזְרְעוּ שָׂדוֹת, וַיִּטְּעוּ כְרָמִים, וַיַּעֲשׂוּ
פְּרִי תְבוּאָה: וַיְבָרְכֵם וַיִּרְבּוּ מְאֹד, וּבְהֶמְתָּם לֹא יַמְעִיט: וַיִּמְעֲטוּ
וַיָּשֹׁחוּ, מֵעֹצֶר רָעָה וְיָגוֹן: שֹׁפֵךְ בּוּז עַל־נְדִיבִים, וַיַּתְעֵם בְּתֹהוּ
לֹא־דָרֶךְ: ‹ וַיְשַׂגֵּב אֶבְיוֹן מֵעוֹנִי, וַיָּשֶׂם כַּצֹּאן מִשְׁפָּחוֹת: יִרְאוּ
יְשָׁרִים וְיִשְׂמָחוּ, וְכָל־עַוְלָה קָפְצָה פִּיהָ: מִי־חָכָם וְיִשְׁמָר־אֵלֶּה,
וְיִתְבּוֹנְנוּ חַסְדֵי יהוה:

תהלים צז

יהוה מָלָךְ תָּגֵל הָאָרֶץ, יִשְׂמְחוּ אִיִּים רַבִּים: עָנָן וַעֲרָפֶל סְבִיבָיו,
צֶדֶק וּמִשְׁפָּט מְכוֹן כִּסְאוֹ: אֵשׁ לְפָנָיו תֵּלֵךְ, וּתְלַהֵט סָבִיב צָרָיו:

---

world; the earth sees and trembles. Mountains melt like wax before the LORD, before the LORD of all the earth. The heavens proclaim His righteousness, and all the peoples see His glory. All who worship images and boast in idols are put to shame. Bow down to Him, all you heavenly powers. Zion hears and rejoices, and the towns of Judah are glad because of Your judgments, LORD. For You, LORD, are supreme over all the earth; You are exalted far above all heavenly powers. Let those who love the LORD hate evil, for He protects the lives of His devoted ones, delivering them from the hand of the wicked. ‣ Light is sown for the righteous, and joy for the upright in heart. Rejoice in the LORD, you who are righteous, and give thanks to His holy name.

מִזְמוֹר A Psalm. Sing a new song to the LORD, for He has done won- _Ps. 98_ drous things; He has saved by His right hand and His holy arm. The LORD has made His salvation known; He has displayed His righteousness in the sight of the nations. He remembered His loving-kindness and faithfulness to the house of Israel; all the ends of the earth have seen the victory of our LORD. Shout for joy to the LORD, all the earth; burst into song, sing with joy, play music. Play music to the LORD on the harp – on the harp with the sound of singing. With trumpets and the sound of the shofar, shout for joy before the LORD, the King. ‣ Let the sea and all that is in it thunder, the world and all who live in it. Let the rivers clap their hands, the mountains sing together for joy – before the LORD, for He is coming to judge the earth. He will judge the world with justice, and the peoples with equity.

---

millennia recovered it again. Ravaged by the Holocaust a mere three years earlier, the declaration of Israel's independence was a remarkable act of faith, an everlasting symbol of the victory of life over death, hope over despair.

Some thirty-three centuries ago, Moses prophesied: "Even if you have been dispersed to the most distant land under the heavens, from there the LORD your God will gather you and bring you back" (Deut. 30:4), and so it happened. If, as we believe, there are events that bear the signature of Heaven, this surely was one. Therefore we give thanks to God for bringing the land back to the people, and the people back to the land – the land where our people was born in ancient times, and reborn in ours.

הֵאִירוּ בְרָקָיו תֵּבֵל, רָאֲתָה וַתָּחֵל הָאָרֶץ: הָרִים כַּדּוֹנַג נָמַסּוּ
מִלִּפְנֵי יהוה, מִלִּפְנֵי אֲדוֹן כָּל־הָאָרֶץ: הִגִּידוּ הַשָּׁמַיִם צִדְקוֹ,
וְרָאוּ כָל־הָעַמִּים כְּבוֹדוֹ: יֵבֹשׁוּ כָּל־עֹבְדֵי פֶסֶל הַמִּתְהַלְלִים
בָּאֱלִילִים, הִשְׁתַּחֲווּ־לוֹ כָּל־אֱלֹהִים: שָׁמְעָה וַתִּשְׂמַח צִיּוֹן,
וַתָּגֵלְנָה בְּנוֹת יְהוּדָה, לְמַעַן מִשְׁפָּטֶיךָ יהוה: כִּי־אַתָּה יהוה
עֶלְיוֹן עַל־כָּל־הָאָרֶץ, מְאֹד נַעֲלֵיתָ עַל־כָּל־אֱלֹהִים: אֹהֲבֵי יהוה
שִׂנְאוּ רָע, שֹׁמֵר נַפְשׁוֹת חֲסִידָיו, מִיַּד רְשָׁעִים יַצִּילֵם: ‹ אוֹר
זָרֻעַ לַצַּדִּיק, וּלְיִשְׁרֵי־לֵב שִׂמְחָה: שִׂמְחוּ צַדִּיקִים בַּיהוה, וְהוֹדוּ
לְזֵכֶר קָדְשׁוֹ:

תהלים צח

מִזְמוֹר, שִׁירוּ לַיהוה שִׁיר חָדָשׁ כִּי־נִפְלָאוֹת עָשָׂה, הוֹשִׁיעָה־לּוֹ
יְמִינוֹ וּזְרוֹעַ קָדְשׁוֹ: הוֹדִיעַ יהוה יְשׁוּעָתוֹ, לְעֵינֵי הַגּוֹיִם גִּלָּה
צִדְקָתוֹ: זָכַר חַסְדּוֹ וֶאֱמוּנָתוֹ לְבֵית יִשְׂרָאֵל, רָאוּ כָל־אַפְסֵי־אָרֶץ
אֵת יְשׁוּעַת אֱלֹהֵינוּ: הָרִיעוּ לַיהוה כָּל־הָאָרֶץ, פִּצְחוּ וְרַנְּנוּ וְזַמֵּרוּ:
זַמְּרוּ לַיהוה בְּכִנּוֹר, בְּכִנּוֹר וְקוֹל זִמְרָה: בַּחֲצֹצְרוֹת וְקוֹל שׁוֹפָר,
הָרִיעוּ לִפְנֵי הַמֶּלֶךְ יהוה: ‹ יִרְעַם הַיָּם וּמְלֹאוֹ, תֵּבֵל וְיֹשְׁבֵי בָהּ:
נְהָרוֹת יִמְחֲאוּ־כָף, יַחַד הָרִים יְרַנֵּנוּ: לִפְנֵי־יהוה כִּי בָא לִשְׁפֹּט
הָאָרֶץ, יִשְׁפֹּט־תֵּבֵל בְּצֶדֶק, וְעַמִּים בְּמֵישָׁרִים:

---

been able to rule and defend themselves. Only in Israel can a Jew speak a
Jewish language, see a Jewish landscape, walk where our ancestors walked
and continue the story they began. Only in Israel have Jews been able to live
as a nation shaping its own destiny, constructing a society according to its
own principles and laws.

Jews were the first to see God in history, to see the unfolding of events as
a meaningful narrative, the ongoing story of the covenant between God and
His people. The celebration of Yom HaAtzma'ut as a religious festival is part
of this faith. Never before had a people survived so long an exile, its identity
intact. Never before had a nation that had not known sovereignty for two

It is customary to sing:

הִתְעוֹרְרִי Wake up, wake up,
For your light has come: rise, shine!
Awake, awake, break out in song,
For the LORD's glory is revealed on you.

This is the day the LORD has made;   *Ps. 118*
let us rejoice and be glad in it.

לֹא תֵבֹשִׁי Do not be ashamed, do not be confounded.
Why be downcast? Why do you mourn?
In you the needy of My people find shelter,
And the city shall be rebuilt on its hill.

This is the day the LORD has made;
let us rejoice and be glad in it.

יָמִין Right and left you shall spread out,
And God you will revere.
Through the descendant of Peretz,
We shall rejoice and we shall be glad.

This is the day the LORD has made;
let us rejoice and be glad in it.

Ma'ariv for Weekdays (page 262) is said at this point, in the Yom Tov melody. After Full Kaddish,
the Ark is opened and the following is said responsively by the Leader and congregation.

Listen, Israel: the LORD is our God, the LORD is One.   *Deut. 6*

The following is said three times responsively:

The LORD, He is God.

The Leader says the following which is repeated by the congregation.

מִי שֶׁעָשָׂה May He who performed miracles for our ancestors and for us,
redeeming us from slavery to freedom,
grant us a complete redemption soon,
and gather in our dispersed people
from the four quarters of the earth,
so that all Israel may be united in friendship,
and let us say: Amen.

The Ark is closed.

It is customary to sing:

הִתְעוֹרְרִי הִתְעוֹרְרִי

כִּי בָא אוֹרֵךְ קוּמִי אוֹרִי

עוּרִי עוּרִי, שִׁיר דַּבֵּרִי

כְּבוֹד יהוה עָלַיִךְ נִגְלָה.

זֶה־הַיּוֹם עָשָׂה יהוה, נָגִילָה וְנִשְׂמְחָה בוֹ:

תהלים קיח

לֹא תֵבְשִׁי וְלֹא תִכָּלְמִי

מַה תִּשְׁתּוֹחֲחִי וּמַה תֶּהֱמִי

בָּךְ יֶחֱסוּ עֲנִיֵּי עַמִּי

וְנִבְנְתָה עִיר עַל תִּלָּהּ.

זֶה־הַיּוֹם עָשָׂה יהוה, נָגִילָה וְנִשְׂמְחָה בוֹ:

יָמִין וּשְׂמֹאל תִּפְרֹצִי

וְאֶת יהוה תַּעֲרִיצִי

עַל יַד אִישׁ בֶּן פַּרְצִי

וְנִשְׂמְחָה וְנָגִילָה.

זֶה־הַיּוֹם עָשָׂה יהוה, נָגִילָה וְנִשְׂמְחָה בוֹ:

מעריב לחול (*page 263*) *is said at this point, in the* יום טוב *melody. After* קדיש שלם,
the ארון קודש *is opened and the following is said responsively by the* שליח ציבור *and the* קהל.

דברים ו

שְׁמַע יִשְׂרָאֵל, יהוה אֱלֹהֵינוּ, יהוה אֶחָד:

The following is said three times responsively:

יהוה הוּא הָאֱלֹהִים.

The שליח ציבור *says the following which is repeated by the* קהל.

מִי שֶׁעָשָׂה נִסִּים לַאֲבוֹתֵינוּ וְלָנוּ

וּגְאָלָנוּ מֵעַבְדוּת לְחֵרוּת

הוּא יִגְאָלֵנוּ גְּאֻלָּה שְׁלֵמָה בְּקָרוֹב

וִיקַבֵּץ נִדָּחֵינוּ מֵאַרְבַּע כַּנְפוֹת הָאָרֶץ

חֲבֵרִים כָּל יִשְׂרָאֵל, וְנֹאמַר אָמֵן.

The ארון קודש *is closed.*

The Leader continues:

וְכִי־תָבֹאוּ When you go into battle in your land against an enemy who *Num. 10*
is attacking you, sound a staccato blast on the trumpets. Then you
will be remembered by the LORD your God and you will be delivered
from your enemies. On your days of rejoicing – your festivals and new
moon celebrations – you shall sound a note on the trumpets over your
burnt- and peace-offerings, and they will be a remembrance for you
before your God. I am the LORD your God.

The shofar is sounded with a Tekia Gedola and the following is said aloud:
Next year in Jerusalem rebuilt.

All:
May it be Your will, LORD our God and God of our fathers,
That as we have merited to witness the beginning of redemption,
So may we merit to hear the sound of the shofar
of our righteous anointed one, swiftly in our days.

All sing:

שִׁיר הַמַּעֲלוֹת A song of ascents. When the LORD brought back the exiles of *Ps. 126*
Zion we were like people who dream. Then were our mouths filled with laugh-
ter, and our tongues with songs of joy. Then was it said among the nations,
"The LORD has done great things for them." The LORD did do great things for
us and we rejoiced. Bring back our exiles, LORD, like streams in a dry land. May
those who sowed in tears, reap in joy. May one who goes out weeping, carrying
a bag of seed, come back with songs of joy, carrying his sheaves.

The Omer is counted (page 304), followed by Aleinu (page 298).

All sing:

אֲנִי מַאֲמִין I believe with perfect faith
in the coming of the Messiah,
and though he may delay,
I wait daily for his coming.

It is customary to greet each other with the following phrase:
Happy festival; to a complete redemption!

The שליח ציבור continues:

בְּמִדְבַּר וְכִי־תָבֹאוּ מִלְחָמָה בְּאַרְצְכֶם עַל־הַצַּר הַצֹּרֵר אֶתְכֶם, וַהֲרֵעֹתֶם בַּחֲצֹצְרֹת, וְנִזְכַּרְתֶּם לִפְנֵי יהוה אֱלֹהֵיכֶם, וְנוֹשַׁעְתֶּם מֵאֹיְבֵיכֶם: וּבְיוֹם שִׂמְחַתְכֶם וּבְמוֹעֲדֵיכֶם וּבְרָאשֵׁי חָדְשֵׁכֶם, וּתְקַעְתֶּם בַּחֲצֹצְרֹת עַל עֹלֹתֵיכֶם וְעַל זִבְחֵי שַׁלְמֵיכֶם, וְהָיוּ לָכֶם לְזִכָּרוֹן לִפְנֵי אֱלֹהֵיכֶם, אֲנִי יהוה אֱלֹהֵיכֶם:

The שופר is sounded with a תקיעה גדולה and the following is said aloud:

לְשָׁנָה הַבָּאָה בִּירוּשָׁלַיִם הַבְּנוּיָה.

All:

יְהִי רָצוֹן מִלְּפָנֶיךָ יהוה אֱלֹהֵינוּ וֵאלֹהֵי אֲבוֹתֵינוּ שֶׁכְּשֵׁם שֶׁזָּכִינוּ לְאַתְחַלְתָּא דִגְאֻלָּה כֵּן נִזְכֶּה לִשְׁמֹעַ קוֹל שׁוֹפָרוֹ שֶׁל מָשִׁיחַ צִדְקֵנוּ בִּמְהֵרָה בְיָמֵינוּ.

All sing:

תְּהִלִּים קכו שִׁיר הַמַּעֲלוֹת, בְּשׁוּב יהוה אֶת־שִׁיבַת צִיּוֹן, הָיִינוּ כְּחֹלְמִים: אָז יִמָּלֵא שְׂחוֹק פִּינוּ וּלְשׁוֹנֵנוּ רִנָּה, אָז יֹאמְרוּ בַגּוֹיִם הִגְדִּיל יהוה לַעֲשׂוֹת עִם־אֵלֶּה: הִגְדִּיל יהוה לַעֲשׂוֹת עִמָּנוּ, הָיִינוּ שְׂמֵחִים: שׁוּבָה יהוה אֶת־שְׁבִיתֵנוּ, כַּאֲפִיקִים בַּנֶּגֶב: הַזֹּרְעִים בְּדִמְעָה בְּרִנָּה יִקְצֹרוּ: הָלוֹךְ יֵלֵךְ וּבָכֹה נֹשֵׂא מֶשֶׁךְ־הַזָּרַע, בֹּא־יָבֹא בְרִנָּה נֹשֵׂא אֲלֻמֹּתָיו:

The עומר is counted (page 305), followed by עָלֵינוּ (page 299).

All sing:

אֲנִי מַאֲמִין בֶּאֱמוּנָה שְׁלֵמָה בְּבִיאַת הַמָּשִׁיחַ וְאַף עַל פִּי שֶׁיִּתְמַהְמֵהַּ עִם כָּל זֶה אֲחַכֶּה לּוֹ בְּכָל יוֹם שֶׁיָּבוֹא.

It is customary to greet each other with the following phrase:

מוֹעֲדִים לְשִׂמְחָה לִגְאֻלָּה שְׁלֵמָה

Shaḥarit for Yom HaAtzma'ut

Begin as on weekdays, from pages 4–58.
In Israel and many congregations outside Israel, Pesukei DeZimra of Yom Tov, below, are said.

A PSALM BEFORE VERSES OF PRAISE

מִזְמוֹר שִׁיר A psalm of David. A song for the dedication of the House. *Ps. 30* I will exalt You, Lᴏʀᴅ, for You have lifted me up, and not let my enemies rejoice over me. Lᴏʀᴅ, my God, I cried to You for help and You healed me. Lᴏʀᴅ, You lifted my soul from the grave; You spared me from going down to the pit. Sing to the Lᴏʀᴅ, you His devoted ones, and give thanks to His holy name. For His anger is for a moment, but His favor for a lifetime. At night there may be weeping, but in the morning there is joy. When I felt secure, I said, "I shall never be shaken." Lᴏʀᴅ, when You favored me, You made me stand firm as a mountain, but when You hid Your face, I was terrified. To You, Lᴏʀᴅ, I called; I pleaded with my Lᴏʀᴅ: "What gain would there be if I died and went down to the grave? Can dust thank You? Can it declare Your truth? Hear, Lᴏʀᴅ, and be gracious to me; Lᴏʀᴅ, be my help." You have turned my sorrow into dancing. ‣ You have removed my sackcloth and clothed me with joy, so that my soul may sing to You and not be silent. Lᴏʀᴅ my God, for ever will I thank You.

---

hitherto secure, was suddenly in danger. It was then that he prayed to God, "What gain would there be if I died and went down to the grave?...Can dust thank You?" So we, waking to the life of a new day, express our sense of joy, "so that my soul may sing to You and not be silent."

שחרית ליום העצמאות

Begin as on weekdays, from pages 5–59.
In ארץ ישראל *and many congregations in* חוץ לארץ, פסוקי דזמרה *of* יום טוב, *below, are said.*

מזמור לפני פסוקי דזמרה

תהלים ל

מִזְמוֹר שִׁיר־חֲנֻכַּת הַבַּיִת לְדָוִד: אֲרוֹמִמְךָ יהוה כִּי דִלִּיתָנִי,
וְלֹא־שִׂמַּחְתָּ אֹיְבַי לִי: יהוה אֱלֹהָי, שִׁוַּעְתִּי אֵלֶיךָ וַתִּרְפָּאֵנִי:
יהוה, הֶעֱלִיתָ מִן־שְׁאוֹל נַפְשִׁי, חִיִּיתַנִי מִיָּרְדִי־בוֹר: זַמְּרוּ לַיהוה
חֲסִידָיו, וְהוֹדוּ לְזֵכֶר קָדְשׁוֹ: כִּי רֶגַע בְּאַפּוֹ, חַיִּים בִּרְצוֹנוֹ, בָּעֶרֶב
יָלִין בֶּכִי וְלַבֹּקֶר רִנָּה: וַאֲנִי אָמַרְתִּי בְשַׁלְוִי, בַּל־אֶמּוֹט לְעוֹלָם:
יהוה, בִּרְצוֹנְךָ הֶעֱמַדְתָּה לְהַרְרִי עֹז, הִסְתַּרְתָּ פָנֶיךָ הָיִיתִי נִבְהָל:
אֵלֶיךָ יהוה אֶקְרָא, וְאֶל־אֲדֹנָי אֶתְחַנָּן: מַה־בֶּצַע בְּדָמִי, בְּרִדְתִּי
אֶל שָׁחַת, הֲיוֹדְךָ עָפָר, הֲיַגִּיד אֲמִתֶּךָ: שְׁמַע־יהוה וְחָנֵּנִי, יהוה
הֱיֵה־עֹזֵר לִי: הָפַכְתָּ מִסְפְּדִי לְמָחוֹל לִי, פִּתַּחְתָּ שַׂקִּי, וַתְּאַזְּרֵנִי
שִׂמְחָה: לְמַעַן יְזַמֶּרְךָ כָבוֹד וְלֹא יִדֹּם, יהוה אֱלֹהַי, לְעוֹלָם אוֹדֶךָּ:

מִזְמוֹר שִׁיר־חֲנֻכַּת הַבַּיִת *A song for the dedication of the House*: According to
Rashi, David wrote this psalm to be sung at the inauguration of the Temple,
though he knew it would only take place in the lifetime of his son, Solomon.
The psalm first entered the siddur as a prayer to be said on Ḥanukka, and was
later adopted as part of the daily prayers.

Its content is beautifully suited to be a bridge between the Morning Blessings and the *Pesukei DeZimra*. The connecting theme is the restoration of
life as a reason for giving praise. The Psalmist recounts a crisis when his life,

MOURNER'S KADDISH

The following prayer, said by mourners, requires the presence of a minyan.
A transliteration can be found on page 699.

Mourner: יִתְגַּדַּל Magnified and sanctified
may His great name be,
in the world He created by His will.
May He establish His kingdom
in your lifetime and in your days,
and in the lifetime of all the house of Israel,
swiftly and soon – and say: Amen.

All: May His great name be blessed for ever and all time.

Mourner: Blessed and praised, glorified and exalted,
raised and honored, uplifted and lauded
be the name of the Holy One,
blessed be He,
beyond any blessing,
song, praise and consolation
uttered in the world – and say: Amen.

May there be great peace from heaven,
and life for us and all Israel – and say: Amen.

Bow, take three steps back, as if taking leave of the Divine Presence,
then bow, first left, then right, then center, while saying:
May He who makes peace in His high places,
make peace for us and all Israel –
and say: Amen.

The most profound gift we can bring to the memory of one we have lost is
to be a source of blessing to the deceased by the good deeds we do in his or her
name. When we say Kaddish, we are the cause of the congregation saying, in
response, "May His great name be blessed for ever and all time." This, according to the Talmud, brings great pleasure to God. By causing the congregation
to praise God, we show that the recollection of the person we have lost moves
us to good deeds – and thus that their memory continues to be a blessing.

קדיש יתום

The following prayer, said by mourners, requires the presence of a מנין.
A transliteration can be found on page 699.

אבל: יִתְגַּדַּל וְיִתְקַדַּשׁ שְׁמֵהּ רַבָּא (קהל: אָמֵן)
בְּעָלְמָא דִּי בְרָא כִרְעוּתֵהּ
וְיַמְלִיךְ מַלְכוּתֵהּ
בְּחַיֵּיכוֹן וּבְיוֹמֵיכוֹן וּבְחַיֵּי דְכָל בֵּית יִשְׂרָאֵל
בַּעֲגָלָא וּבִזְמַן קָרִיב, וְאִמְרוּ אָמֵן. (קהל: אָמֵן)

קהל
ואבל: יְהֵא שְׁמֵהּ רַבָּא מְבָרַךְ לְעָלַם וּלְעָלְמֵי עָלְמַיָּא.

אבל: יִתְבָּרַךְ וְיִשְׁתַּבַּח וְיִתְפָּאַר
וְיִתְרוֹמַם וְיִתְנַשֵּׂא וְיִתְהַדָּר וְיִתְעַלֶּה וְיִתְהַלָּל
שְׁמֵהּ דְּקֻדְשָׁא בְּרִיךְ הוּא (קהל: בְּרִיךְ הוּא)
לְעֵלָּא מִן כָּל בִּרְכָתָא
וְשִׁירָתָא, תֻּשְׁבְּחָתָא וְנֶחֱמָתָא
דַּאֲמִירָן בְּעָלְמָא, וְאִמְרוּ אָמֵן. (קהל: אָמֵן)

יְהֵא שְׁלָמָא רַבָּא מִן שְׁמַיָּא
וְחַיִּים, עָלֵינוּ וְעַל כָּל יִשְׂרָאֵל, וְאִמְרוּ אָמֵן. (קהל: אָמֵן)

Bow, take three steps back, as if taking leave of the Divine Presence,
then bow, first left, then right, then center, while saying:

עֹשֶׂה שָׁלוֹם בִּמְרוֹמָיו
הוּא יַעֲשֶׂה שָׁלוֹם עָלֵינוּ וְעַל כָּל יִשְׂרָאֵל
וְאִמְרוּ אָמֵן. (קהל: אָמֵן)

MOURNER'S KADDISH

The paradox has long been noted that the mourner's Kaddish contains no
mention of death, bereavement or grief. In Judaism, we emerge from the pain
of loss by re-immersing ourselves in life – and thus in God, the source of all life.

PESUKEI DEZIMRA

The following introductory blessing to the Pesukei DeZimra (Verses of Praise) is said standing, while holding the two front tzitziot of the tallit. They are kissed and released at the end of the blessing at "songs of praise" (on the next page). From the beginning of this prayer to the end of the Amida, conversation is forbidden. See table on pages 695–697 for which congregational responses are permitted.

Some say:

I hereby prepare my mouth to thank, praise and laud my Creator, for the sake of the unification of the Holy One, blessed be He, and His Divine Presence, through that which is hidden and concealed, in the name of all Israel.

BLESSED IS HE
WHO SPOKE

and the world came into being, blessed is He.

> Blessed is He who creates the universe.
> Blessed is He who speaks and acts.
> Blessed is He who decrees and fulfills.
> Blessed is He who shows compassion to the earth.
> Blessed is He who shows compassion to all creatures.
> Blessed is He who gives a good reward
> to those who fear Him.
> Blessed is He who lives for ever and exists to eternity.
> Blessed is He who redeems and saves.
> Blessed is His name.

---

tal preparation beforehand, as well as a gradual leave-taking afterward. It is impossible to move directly from worldly concerns to the intense concentration required for genuine prayer, and vice versa. The verse cited in support of this practice is "Happy are they that dwell in Your House" (Psalm 84:5), and this verse occupies a prominent place at the heart of the Verses of Praise. In addition to the six psalms said on weekdays, nine extra psalms are added on Shabbat and Yom Tov.

בָּרוּךְ שֶׁאָמַר **Blessed is He:** An introductory blessing to the *Pesukei DeZimra*, in two parts. The first is a ten-part litany of praise to God as creator, each phrase introduced with the word "Blessed" (the second phrase, "Blessed is He," is

פסוקי דזמרה

The following introductory blessing to the פסוקי דזמרה is said standing, while holding the two
front ציציות of the טלית. They are kissed and released at the end of the blessing at בתשבחות
(on the next page). From the beginning of this prayer to the end of the עמידה, conversation
is forbidden. See table on pages 695–697 for which congregational responses are permitted.

Some say:

הֲרֵינִי מְזַמֵּן אֶת פִּי לְהוֹדוֹת וּלְהַלֵּל וּלְשַׁבֵּחַ אֶת בּוֹרְאִי, לְשֵׁם יִחוּד קֻדְשָׁא בְּרִיךְ
הוּא וּשְׁכִינְתֵּהּ עַל יְדֵי הַהוּא טָמִיר וְנֶעְלָם בְּשֵׁם כָּל יִשְׂרָאֵל.

בָּרוּךְ
שֶׁאָמַר
וְהָיָה הָעוֹלָם, בָּרוּךְ הוּא.

בָּרוּךְ עוֹשֶׂה בְרֵאשִׁית
בָּרוּךְ אוֹמֵר וְעוֹשֶׂה
בָּרוּךְ גּוֹזֵר וּמְקַיֵּם
בָּרוּךְ מְרַחֵם עַל הָאָרֶץ
בָּרוּךְ מְרַחֵם עַל הַבְּרִיּוֹת
בָּרוּךְ מְשַׁלֵּם שָׂכָר טוֹב לִירֵאָיו
בָּרוּךְ חַי לָעַד וְקַיָּם לָנֶצַח
בָּרוּךְ פּוֹדֶה וּמַצִּיל
בָּרוּךְ שְׁמוֹ

PESUKEI DEZIMRA / VERSES OF PRAISE
This section of the prayers is based on the Talmudic teaching (*Berakhot* 32a)
that "The pious men of old used to wait for an hour [before praying], they
prayed for an hour, and then waited again for an hour." Prayer requires men-

Blessed are You, Lord our God,
King of the Universe,
God, compassionate Father,
extolled by the mouth of His people,
praised and glorified by the tongue of His devoted ones
and those who serve Him.
With the songs of Your servant David
we will praise You, O Lord our God.
With praises and psalms
we will magnify and praise You, glorify You,
Speak Your name and proclaim Your kingship,
our King, our God, ▸ the only One, Giver of life to the worlds
the King whose great name is praised
and glorified to all eternity.
Blessed are You, Lord,
the King extolled with songs of praise.

הודו Thank the Lord, call on His name, make His acts known *1 Chr. 16*
among the peoples. Sing to Him, make music to Him, tell of all
His wonders. Glory in His holy name; let the hearts of those who
seek the Lord rejoice. Search out the Lord and His strength; seek
His presence at all times. Remember the wonders He has done,
His miracles, and the judgments He pronounced. Descendants of
Yisrael His servant, sons of Jacob His chosen ones: He is the Lord
our God. His judgments are throughout the earth. Remember

הודו *Thank the Lord*: The Bible gives us a vivid account (1 Chr. 15–16) of
the moment when this passage was first recited: when King David brought
the Ark of the Covenant to Jerusalem, newly established as the capital of
the Jewish state. The Ark, which had been captured by the Philistines, was
brought back by David to a temporary resting place. Later it was carried into
Jerusalem to scenes of great jubilation. As on other momentous occasions in
the life of biblical Israel, the leader (here David) reminds the people of the

בָּרוּךְ אַתָּה יהוה אֱלֹהֵינוּ מֶלֶךְ הָעוֹלָם
הָאֵל הָאָב הָרַחֲמָן הַמְהֻלָּל בְּפִי עַמּוֹ
מְשֻׁבָּח וּמְפֹאָר בִּלְשׁוֹן חֲסִידָיו וַעֲבָדָיו
וּבְשִׁירֵי דָוִד עַבְדֶּךָ
נְהַלֶּלְךָ יהוה אֱלֹהֵינוּ.
בִּשְׁבָחוֹת וּבִזְמִירוֹת
נְגַדֶּלְךָ וּנְשַׁבֵּחֲךָ וּנְפָאֶרְךָ
וְנַזְכִּיר שִׁמְךָ וְנַמְלִיכְךָ
מַלְכֵּנוּ אֱלֹהֵינוּ, ◂ יָחִיד חֵי הָעוֹלָמִים
מֶלֶךְ, מְשֻׁבָּח וּמְפֹאָר עֲדֵי עַד שְׁמוֹ הַגָּדוֹל
בָּרוּךְ אַתָּה יהוה, מֶלֶךְ מְהֻלָּל בַּתִּשְׁבָּחוֹת.

דברי הימים א׳ ט״ז

הוֹדוּ לַיהוה קִרְאוּ בִשְׁמוֹ, הוֹדִיעוּ בָעַמִּים עֲלִילֹתָיו: שִׁירוּ לוֹ,
זַמְּרוּ־לוֹ, שִׂיחוּ בְּכָל־נִפְלְאוֹתָיו: הִתְהַלְלוּ בְּשֵׁם קָדְשׁוֹ, יִשְׂמַח לֵב
מְבַקְשֵׁי יהוה: דִּרְשׁוּ יהוה וְעֻזּוֹ, בַּקְּשׁוּ פָנָיו תָּמִיד: זִכְרוּ נִפְלְאֹתָיו
אֲשֶׁר עָשָׂה, מֹפְתָיו וּמִשְׁפְּטֵי־פִיהוּ: זֶרַע יִשְׂרָאֵל עַבְדּוֹ, בְּנֵי יַעֲקֹב
בְּחִירָיו: הוּא יהוה אֱלֹהֵינוּ בְּכָל־הָאָרֶץ מִשְׁפָּטָיו: זִכְרוּ לְעוֹלָם

___

not a separate verse but originally a congregational response). The number ten corresponds to the ten times the word *VaYomer*, "And He said," appears in the story of creation in Genesis 1. Hence the rabbinic saying that "With ten utterances the world was created" (Avot 5:1).

Blessed are You: The second half of the blessing is a prelude to the biblical verses that follow, mainly from the Psalms ("With the Psalms of your servant David we will exalt you") but also from the books of Chronicles and Nehemiah ("extolled by the mouth of His people"). To emphasize the significance of this declaration, we recite it standing and, at the end, kiss the two front fringes of the tallit.

His covenant for ever, the word He commanded for a thousand generations. He made it with Abraham, vowed it to Isaac, and confirmed it to Jacob as a statute and to Israel as an everlasting covenant, saying, "To you I will give the land of Canaan as your allotted heritage." You were then small in number, few, strangers there, wandering from nation to nation, from one kingdom to another, but He let no man oppress them, and for their sake He rebuked kings: "Do not touch My anointed ones, and do My prophets no harm." Sing to the LORD, all the earth; proclaim His salvation daily. Declare His glory among the nations, His marvels among all the peoples. For great is the LORD and greatly to be praised; He is awesome beyond all heavenly powers. ▸ For all the gods of the peoples are mere idols; it was the LORD who made the heavens.

Before Him are majesty and splendor; there is strength and beauty in His holy place. Render to the LORD, families of the peoples, render to the LORD honor and might. Render to the LORD the glory due to His name; bring an offering and come before Him; bow down to the LORD in the splendor of holiness. Tremble before Him, all the earth; the world stands firm, it will not be shaken. Let the heavens rejoice and the earth be glad; let them declare among the nations, "The LORD is King." Let the sea roar, and all that is in it; let the fields be jubilant, and all they contain. Then the trees of the forest will sing for joy before the LORD, for He is coming to judge the earth. Thank the LORD for He is good; His loving-kindness is for ever. Say: "Save us, God of our salvation; gather us and rescue us from the nations, to acknowledge Your holy name and glory in Your praise. Blessed is the LORD, God of Israel, from this world to eternity." And let all the people say "Amen" and "Praise the LORD."

---

as an accompaniment to the sacrifices, from that day until the inauguration of the Temple in the time of Solomon.

בְּרִיתוֹ, דָּבָר צִוָּה לְאֶלֶף דּוֹר: אֲשֶׁר כָּרַת אֶת־אַבְרָהָם, וּשְׁבוּעָתוֹ
לְיִצְחָק: וַיַּעֲמִידֶהָ לְיַעֲקֹב לְחֹק, לְיִשְׂרָאֵל בְּרִית עוֹלָם: לֵאמֹר,
לְךָ אֶתֵּן אֶרֶץ־כְּנָעַן, חֶבֶל נַחֲלַתְכֶם: בִּהְיוֹתְכֶם מְתֵי מִסְפָּר,
כִּמְעַט וְגָרִים בָּהּ: וַיִּתְהַלְּכוּ מִגּוֹי אֶל־גּוֹי, וּמִמַּמְלָכָה אֶל־עַם
אַחֵר: לֹא־הִנְּיחַ לְאִישׁ לְעָשְׁקָם, וַיּוֹכַח עֲלֵיהֶם מְלָכִים: אַל־
תִּגְּעוּ בִמְשִׁיחָי, וּבִנְבִיאַי אַל־תָּרֵעוּ: שִׁירוּ לַיהוה כָּל־הָאָרֶץ,
בַּשְּׂרוּ מִיּוֹם־אֶל־יוֹם יְשׁוּעָתוֹ: סַפְּרוּ בַגּוֹיִם אֶת־כְּבוֹדוֹ, בְּכָל־
הָעַמִּים נִפְלְאֹתָיו: כִּי גָדוֹל יהוה וּמְהֻלָּל מְאֹד, וְנוֹרָא הוּא
עַל־כָּל־אֱלֹהִים: ‹ כִּי כָּל־אֱלֹהֵי הָעַמִּים אֱלִילִים, וַיהוה שָׁמַיִם
עָשָׂה:

הוֹד וְהָדָר לְפָנָיו, עֹז וְחֶדְוָה בִּמְקֹמוֹ: הָבוּ לַיהוה מִשְׁפְּחוֹת
עַמִּים, הָבוּ לַיהוה כָּבוֹד וָעֹז: הָבוּ לַיהוה כְּבוֹד שְׁמוֹ, שְׂאוּ מִנְחָה
וּבֹאוּ לְפָנָיו, הִשְׁתַּחֲווּ לַיהוה בְּהַדְרַת־קֹדֶשׁ: חִילוּ מִלְּפָנָיו כָּל־
הָאָרֶץ, אַף־תִּכּוֹן תֵּבֵל בַּל־תִּמּוֹט: יִשְׂמְחוּ הַשָּׁמַיִם וְתָגֵל הָאָרֶץ,
וְיֹאמְרוּ בַגּוֹיִם יהוה מָלָךְ: יִרְעַם הַיָּם וּמְלוֹאוֹ, יַעֲלֹץ הַשָּׂדֶה
וְכָל־אֲשֶׁר־בּוֹ: אָז יְרַנְּנוּ עֲצֵי הַיָּעַר, מִלִּפְנֵי יהוה, כִּי־בָא לִשְׁפּוֹט
אֶת־הָאָרֶץ: הוֹדוּ לַיהוה כִּי טוֹב, כִּי לְעוֹלָם חַסְדּוֹ: וְאִמְרוּ,
הוֹשִׁיעֵנוּ אֱלֹהֵי יִשְׁעֵנוּ, וְקַבְּצֵנוּ וְהַצִּילֵנוּ מִן־הַגּוֹיִם, לְהֹדוֹת
לְשֵׁם קָדְשֶׁךָ, לְהִשְׁתַּבֵּחַ בִּתְהִלָּתֶךָ: בָּרוּךְ יהוה אֱלֹהֵי יִשְׂרָאֵל
מִן־הָעוֹלָם וְעַד־הָעֹלָם, וַיֹּאמְרוּ כָל־הָעָם אָמֵן, וְהַלֵּל לַיהוה:

history of the nation, and its dependence on divine providence. The passage
ends with the response of the people: "And all the people said 'Amen' and
'Praise the LORD.'" According to *Seder Olam* (chapter 14), this passage was
recited daily (in two halves: one in the morning, the other in the afternoon)

▶ Exalt the LORD our God and bow before His footstool: He is holy. *Ps. 99*
Exalt the LORD our God and bow at His holy mountain; for holy
is the LORD our God.

He is compassionate. He forgives iniquity and does not destroy. *Ps. 78*
Repeatedly He suppresses His anger, not rousing His full wrath.
You, LORD: do not withhold Your compassion from me. May Your *Ps. 40*
loving-kindness and truth always guard me. Remember, LORD, *Ps. 25*
Your acts of compassion and love, for they have existed for ever.
Ascribe power to God, whose majesty is over Israel and whose *Ps. 68*
might is in the skies. You are awesome, God, in Your holy places.
It is the God of Israel who gives might and strength to the people,
may God be blessed. God of retribution, LORD, God of retribution, *Ps. 94*
appear. Arise, Judge of the earth, to repay the arrogant their just
deserts. Salvation belongs to the LORD; may Your blessing rest upon *Ps. 3*
Your people, Selah! ▶ The LORD of hosts is with us, the God of Jacob *Ps. 46*
is our stronghold, Selah! LORD of hosts, happy is the one who trusts *Ps. 84*
in You. LORD, save! May the King answer us on the day we call. *Ps. 20*

Save Your people and bless Your heritage; tend them and carry *Ps. 28*
them for ever. Our soul longs for the LORD; He is our Help and *Ps. 33*
Shield. For in Him our hearts rejoice, for in His holy name we have
trusted. May Your loving-kindness, LORD, be upon us, as we have
put our hope in You. Show us, LORD, Your loving-kindness and *Ps. 85*

---

we have more time to pray, and also because on Shabbat we reflect on God's
creation, a theme of many of the psalms. The Ashkenazi custom is to say nine.
Together with the six weekday psalms, they make fifteen, the number associated with the fifteen Songs of Ascents (Psalms 120–134), and the fifteen steps
in the Temple on which the Levites stood and sang their songs.

There is a striking feature to this sequence of additional psalms. According to one interpretation (Meiri) the phrase "a song of ascents" means one
begun softly and continued with ever-increasing volume. The extra psalms
begin in Psalm 19 with the universe singing a silent song ("their voice is not
heard") and end in Psalm 93 with a magnificent crescendo ("Mightier than
the noise of many waters").

תהלים צט
‹ רוֹמְמוּ יהוה אֱלֹהֵינוּ וְהִשְׁתַּחֲווּ לַהֲדֹם רַגְלָיו, קָדוֹשׁ הוּא: רוֹמְמוּ יהוה אֱלֹהֵינוּ וְהִשְׁתַּחֲווּ לְהַר קָדְשׁוֹ, כִּי־קָדוֹשׁ יהוה אֱלֹהֵינוּ:

תהלים עח
וְהוּא רַחוּם, יְכַפֵּר עָוֹן וְלֹא־יַשְׁחִית, וְהִרְבָּה לְהָשִׁיב אַפּוֹ, וְלֹא־יָעִיר כָּל־חֲמָתוֹ:

תהלים מ
אַתָּה יהוה לֹא־תִכְלָא רַחֲמֶיךָ מִמֶּנִּי, חַסְדְּךָ

תהלים כה
וַאֲמִתְּךָ תָּמִיד יִצְּרוּנִי: זְכֹר־רַחֲמֶיךָ יהוה וַחֲסָדֶיךָ, כִּי מֵעוֹלָם

תהלים סח
הֵמָּה: תְּנוּ עֹז לֵאלֹהִים, עַל־יִשְׂרָאֵל גַּאֲוָתוֹ, וְעֻזּוֹ בַּשְּׁחָקִים: נוֹרָא אֱלֹהִים מִמִּקְדָּשֶׁיךָ, אֵל יִשְׂרָאֵל הוּא נֹתֵן עֹז וְתַעֲצֻמוֹת לָעָם, בָּרוּךְ אֱלֹהִים:

תהלים צד
אֵל־נְקָמוֹת יהוה, אֵל נְקָמוֹת הוֹפִיעַ: הִנָּשֵׂא שֹׁפֵט הָאָרֶץ, הָשֵׁב גְּמוּל עַל־גֵּאִים:

תהלים ג
לַיהוה הַיְשׁוּעָה, עַל־עַמְּךָ בִרְכָתֶךָ סֶּלָה:

תהלים מו
‹ יהוה צְבָאוֹת עִמָּנוּ, מִשְׂגָּב לָנוּ אֱלֹהֵי יַעֲקֹב סֶלָה:

תהלים פד
תהלים כ
יהוה צְבָאוֹת, אַשְׁרֵי אָדָם בֹּטֵחַ בָּךְ: יהוה הוֹשִׁיעָה, הַמֶּלֶךְ יַעֲנֵנוּ בְיוֹם־קָרְאֵנוּ:

תהלים כח
הוֹשִׁיעָה אֶת־עַמֶּךָ, וּבָרֵךְ אֶת־נַחֲלָתֶךָ, וּרְעֵם וְנַשְּׂאֵם עַד־הָעוֹלָם:

תהלים לג
נַפְשֵׁנוּ חִכְּתָה לַיהוה, עֶזְרֵנוּ וּמָגִנֵּנוּ הוּא: כִּי־בוֹ יִשְׂמַח לִבֵּנוּ, כִּי בְשֵׁם קָדְשׁוֹ בָטָחְנוּ: יְהִי־חַסְדְּךָ יהוה עָלֵינוּ, כַּאֲשֶׁר

רוֹמְמוּ *Exalt the LORD our God*: A selection of verses from the book of Psalms, expressing hope and trust in God. The voice in these verses modulates from singular to plural, individual to nation. This frequent shift from public to private and back again is a distinctive feature of Jewish sensibility. We speak to God as individuals, from the depths of our being, yet we are also members of an extended family, a people, a nation, whose fate and destiny we share and on whose behalf we pray.

EXTRA PSALMS FOR SHABBAT AND YOM TOV

In the earliest siddurim, we already find the well-established custom of saying extra psalms on Shabbat and Yom Tov. This is because, work being forbidden,

grant us Your salvation. Arise, help us and redeem us for the sake *Ps. 44*
of Your love. I am the LORD your God who brought you up from *Ps. 81*
the land of Egypt: open your mouth wide and I will fill it. Happy *Ps. 144*
is the people for whom this is so; happy is the people whose God
the LORD. ‣ As for me, I trust in Your loving-kindness; my heart *Ps. 13*
rejoices in Your salvation. I will sing to the LORD for He has been
good to me.

> *The custom is to say the following psalm standing.*
>
> מִזְמוֹר A psalm of thanksgiving. Shout joyously to the LORD, all *Ps. 100*
> the earth. Serve the LORD with joy. Come before Him with jubi-
> lation. Know that the LORD is God. He made us and we are His.
> We are His people and the flock He tends. Enter His gates with
> thanksgiving, His courts with praise. Thank Him and bless His
> name. ‣ For the LORD is good, His loving-kindness is everlasting,
> and His faithfulness is for every generation.

לַמְנַצֵּחַ For the conductor of music. A psalm of David. The heavens *Ps. 19*
declare the glory of God; the skies proclaim the work of His hands.
Day to day they pour forth speech; night to night they communicate
knowledge. There is no speech, there are no words, their voice is
not heard. Yet their music carries throughout the earth, their words
to the end of the world. In them He has set a tent for the sun. It
emerges like a groom from his marriage chamber, rejoicing like a
champion about to run a race. It rises at one end of the heaven and
makes its circuit to the other: nothing is hidden from its heat. The
LORD's Torah is perfect, refreshing the soul. The LORD's testimony
is faithful, making the simple wise. The LORD's precepts are just,
gladdening the heart. The LORD's commandment is radiant, giving

---

and His revelation of the world-that-ought-to-be. קָוָּם *Yet their music:* literally
"their line," perhaps the reverberating string of a musical instrument. Alternatively, it may mean the line marking a boundary – a reference to the order
and "fearful symmetry" of the universe.

תהלים פה
תהלים מד יַחֲלְנוּ לָךְ: הַרְאֵנוּ יהוה חַסְדֶּךָ, וְיֶשְׁעֲךָ תִּתֶּן־לָנוּ: קוּמָה עֶזְרָתָה

תהלים פא לָנוּ, וּפְדֵנוּ לְמַעַן חַסְדֶּךָ: אָנֹכִי יהוה אֱלֹהֶיךָ הַמַּעַלְךָ מֵאֶרֶץ

תהלים קמד מִצְרָיִם, הַרְחֶב־פִּיךָ וַאֲמַלְאֵהוּ: אַשְׁרֵי הָעָם שֶׁכָּכָה לּוֹ, אַשְׁרֵי

תהלים יג הָעָם שֶׁיהוה אֱלֹהָיו: ‹ וַאֲנִי בְּחַסְדְּךָ בָטַחְתִּי, יָגֵל לִבִּי בִּישׁוּעָתֶךָ,
אָשִׁירָה לַיהוה, כִּי גָמַל עָלָי:

The custom is to say the following psalm standing.

תהלים ק מִזְמוֹר לְתוֹדָה, הָרִיעוּ לַיהוה כָּל־הָאָרֶץ: עִבְדוּ אֶת־יהוה
בְּשִׂמְחָה, בְּאוּ לְפָנָיו בִּרְנָנָה: דְּעוּ כִּי־יהוה הוּא אֱלֹהִים, הוּא
עָשָׂנוּ וְלוֹ אֲנַחְנוּ, עַמּוֹ וְצֹאן מַרְעִיתוֹ: בְּאוּ שְׁעָרָיו בְּתוֹדָה,
חֲצֵרֹתָיו בִּתְהִלָּה, הוֹדוּ לוֹ, בָּרְכוּ שְׁמוֹ: ‹ כִּי־טוֹב יהוה, לְעוֹלָם
חַסְדּוֹ, וְעַד־דֹּר וָדֹר אֱמוּנָתוֹ:

תהלים יט לַמְנַצֵּחַ מִזְמוֹר לְדָוִד: הַשָּׁמַיִם מְסַפְּרִים כְּבוֹד־אֵל, וּמַעֲשֵׂה
יָדָיו מַגִּיד הָרָקִיעַ: יוֹם לְיוֹם יַבִּיעַ אֹמֶר, וְלַיְלָה לְּלַיְלָה יְחַוֶּה־
דָּעַת: אֵין־אֹמֶר וְאֵין דְּבָרִים, בְּלִי נִשְׁמָע קוֹלָם: בְּכָל־הָאָרֶץ
יָצָא קַוָּם, וּבִקְצֵה תֵבֵל מִלֵּיהֶם, לַשֶּׁמֶשׁ שָׂם־אֹהֶל בָּהֶם: וְהוּא
כְּחָתָן יֹצֵא מֵחֻפָּתוֹ, יָשִׂישׂ כְּגִבּוֹר לָרוּץ אֹרַח: מִקְצֵה הַשָּׁמַיִם
מוֹצָאוֹ, וּתְקוּפָתוֹ עַל־קְצוֹתָם, וְאֵין נִסְתָּר מֵחַמָּתוֹ: תּוֹרַת יהוה
תְּמִימָה, מְשִׁיבַת נָפֶשׁ, עֵדוּת יהוה נֶאֱמָנָה, מַחְכִּימַת פֶּתִי:

לַמְנַצֵּחַ *Psalm 19. The heavens declare the glory of God:* A hymn of glory to the
universe as God's work and the Torah as God's word. In the first half of the
poem, the Psalmist speaks metaphorically of creation singing a song of praise
to its Creator, a silent song yet one that can be heard by those whose ears are
attuned to wonder. But God's word not only gives life to the natural universe:
it instructs the human universe, the world we make by our actions and reac-
tions. The Psalmist pours out his praise of God's creation of the world-that-is,

light to the eyes. The fear of the LORD is pure, enduring for ever.
The LORD's judgments are true, altogether righteous. More precious
than gold, than much fine gold. They are sweeter than honey, than
honey from the comb. Your servant, too, is careful of them, for in
observing them there is great reward. Yet who can discern his errors?
Cleanse me of hidden faults. Keep Your servant also from willful
sins; let them not have dominion over me. Then shall I be blameless,
and innocent of grave sin. ‣ May the words of my mouth and the
meditation of my heart find favor before You, LORD, my Rock and
my Redeemer.

לְדָוִד Of David. When he pretended to be insane before Abimelech,   *Ps. 34*
who drove him away, and he left.
I will bless the LORD at all times;
         His praise will be always on my lips.
My soul will glory in the LORD;
         let the lowly hear this and rejoice.
Magnify the LORD with me;
         let us exalt His name together.
I sought the LORD, and He answered me;
         He saved me from all my fears.
Those who look to Him are radiant;
         Their faces are never downcast.
This poor man called, and the LORD heard;
         He saved him from all his troubles.
The LORD's angel encamps around those who fear Him,
         and He rescues them.
Taste and see that the LORD is good;
         happy is the man who takes refuge in Him.
Fear the LORD, you His holy ones,
         for those who fear Him lack nothing.

Meals. It is also said on taking the Torah scroll out of the Ark. טַעֲמוּ וּרְאוּ *Taste
and see*: religious experience precedes religious understanding. God's good-

פִּקּוּדֵי יהוה יְשָׁרִים, מְשַׂמְּחֵי־לֵב, מִצְוַת יהוה בָּרָה, מְאִירַת
עֵינָיִם: יִרְאַת יהוה טְהוֹרָה, עוֹמֶדֶת לָעַד, מִשְׁפְּטֵי־יהוה אֱמֶת,
צָדְקוּ יַחְדָּו: הַנֶּחֱמָדִים מִזָּהָב וּמִפַּז רָב, וּמְתוּקִים מִדְּבַשׁ וְנֹפֶת
צוּפִים: גַּם־עַבְדְּךָ נִזְהָר בָּהֶם, בְּשָׁמְרָם עֵקֶב רָב: שְׁגִיאוֹת מִי־
יָבִין, מִנִּסְתָּרוֹת נַקֵּנִי: גַּם מִזֵּדִים חֲשֹׂךְ עַבְדֶּךָ, אַל־יִמְשְׁלוּ־בִי
אָז אֵיתָם, וְנִקֵּיתִי מִפֶּשַׁע רָב: ‹ יִהְיוּ לְרָצוֹן אִמְרֵי־פִי וְהֶגְיוֹן לִבִּי
לְפָנֶיךָ, יהוה, צוּרִי וְגֹאֲלִי:

תהלים לד

לְדָוִד, בְּשַׁנּוֹתוֹ אֶת־טַעְמוֹ לִפְנֵי אֲבִימֶלֶךְ, וַיְגָרְשֵׁהוּ וַיֵּלַךְ:
אֲבָרְכָה אֶת־יהוה בְּכָל־עֵת, תָּמִיד תְּהִלָּתוֹ בְּפִי:
בַּיהוה תִּתְהַלֵּל נַפְשִׁי, יִשְׁמְעוּ עֲנָוִים וְיִשְׂמָחוּ:
גַּדְּלוּ לַיהוה אִתִּי, וּנְרוֹמְמָה שְׁמוֹ יַחְדָּו:
דָּרַשְׁתִּי אֶת־יהוה וְעָנָנִי, וּמִכָּל־מְגוּרוֹתַי הִצִּילָנִי:
הִבִּיטוּ אֵלָיו וְנָהָרוּ, וּפְנֵיהֶם אַל־יֶחְפָּרוּ:
זֶה עָנִי קָרָא, וַיהוה שָׁמֵעַ, וּמִכָּל־צָרוֹתָיו הוֹשִׁיעוֹ:
חֹנֶה מַלְאַךְ־יהוה סָבִיב לִירֵאָיו, וַיְחַלְּצֵם:
טַעֲמוּ וּרְאוּ כִּי־טוֹב יהוה, אַשְׁרֵי הַגֶּבֶר יֶחֱסֶה־בּוֹ:
יְראוּ אֶת־יהוה קְדֹשָׁיו, כִּי־אֵין מַחְסוֹר לִירֵאָיו:

לְדָוִד *Psalm 34*: During the period that David was fleeing from King Saul, he
took refuge in the Philistine city of Gath. There, however, he was recognized
and his life was again in danger. Feigning insanity in order to appear harmless,
he was dismissed by the king and was able to escape (1 Sam. 21:11–16). The
psalm of thanksgiving that follows is constructed as an alphabetical acrostic. An extra verse has been added at the end to avoid closing on a negative
note. גַּדְּלוּ לַיהוה אִתִּי *Magnify the LORD with me*: this verse is taken by the sages
as the source of the institution of summoning to prayer, as in the Grace after

Young lions may grow weak and hungry,
>   but those who seek the LORD lack no good thing.
Come, my children, listen to me;
>   I will teach you the fear of the LORD.
Who desires life,
>   loving each day to see good?
Then guard your tongue from evil
>   and your lips from speaking deceit.
Turn from evil and do good;
>   seek peace and pursue it.
The eyes of the LORD are on the righteous
>   and His ears attentive to their cry;
The LORD's face is set against those who do evil,
>   to erase their memory from the earth.
The righteous cry out, and the LORD hears them;
>   delivering them from all their troubles.
The LORD is close to the brokenhearted,
>   and saves those who are crushed in spirit.
Many troubles may befall the righteous,
>   but the LORD delivers him from them all;
He protects all his bones,
>   so that none of them will be broken.
Evil will slay the wicked;
>   the enemies of the righteous will be condemned.
▸ The LORD redeems his servants;
>   none who take refuge in Him shall be condemned.

תְּפִלָּה לְמֹשֶׁה A prayer of Moses, the man of God. LORD, You have *Ps. 90* been our shelter in every generation. Before the mountains were born, before You brought forth the earth and the world, from ever-lasting to everlasting You are God. You turn men back to dust, saying, "Return, you children of men." For a thousand years in Your sight are like yesterday when it has passed, like a watch in the night. You sweep men away; they sleep. In the morning they are

כְּפִירִים רָשׁוּ וְרָעֵבוּ, וְדֹרְשֵׁי יהוה לֹא־יַחְסְרוּ כָל־טוֹב:

לְכוּ־בָנִים שִׁמְעוּ־לִי, יִרְאַת יהוה אֲלַמֶּדְכֶם:

מִי־הָאִישׁ הֶחָפֵץ חַיִּים, אֹהֵב יָמִים לִרְאוֹת טוֹב:

נְצֹר לְשׁוֹנְךָ מֵרָע, וּשְׂפָתֶיךָ מִדַּבֵּר מִרְמָה:

סוּר מֵרָע וַעֲשֵׂה־טוֹב, בַּקֵּשׁ שָׁלוֹם וְרָדְפֵהוּ:

עֵינֵי יהוה אֶל־צַדִּיקִים, וְאָזְנָיו אֶל־שַׁוְעָתָם:

פְּנֵי יהוה בְּעֹשֵׂי רָע, לְהַכְרִית מֵאֶרֶץ זִכְרָם:

צָעֲקוּ וַיהוה שָׁמֵעַ, וּמִכָּל־צָרוֹתָם הִצִּילָם:

קָרוֹב יהוה לְנִשְׁבְּרֵי־לֵב, וְאֶת־דַּכְּאֵי־רוּחַ יוֹשִׁיעַ:

רַבּוֹת רָעוֹת צַדִּיק, וּמִכֻּלָּם יַצִּילֶנּוּ יהוה:

שֹׁמֵר כָּל־עַצְמוֹתָיו, אַחַת מֵהֵנָּה לֹא נִשְׁבָּרָה:

תְּמוֹתֵת רָשָׁע רָעָה, וְשֹׂנְאֵי צַדִּיק יֶאְשָׁמוּ:

◂ פּוֹדֶה יהוה נֶפֶשׁ עֲבָדָיו, וְלֹא יֶאְשְׁמוּ כָּל־הַחֹסִים בּוֹ:

תהלים צ

תְּפִלָּה לְמֹשֶׁה אִישׁ־הָאֱלֹהִים, אֲדֹנָי, מָעוֹן אַתָּה הָיִיתָ לָּנוּ בְּדֹר
וָדֹר: בְּטֶרֶם הָרִים יֻלָּדוּ, וַתְּחוֹלֵל אֶרֶץ וְתֵבֵל, וּמֵעוֹלָם עַד־עוֹלָם
אַתָּה אֵל: תָּשֵׁב אֱנוֹשׁ עַד־דַּכָּא, וַתֹּאמֶר שׁוּבוּ בְנֵי־אָדָם: כִּי
אֶלֶף שָׁנִים בְּעֵינֶיךָ, כְּיוֹם אֶתְמוֹל כִּי יַעֲבֹר, וְאַשְׁמוּרָה בַלָּיְלָה:
זְרַמְתָּם, שֵׁנָה יִהְיוּ, בַּבֹּקֶר כֶּחָצִיר יַחֲלֹף: בַּבֹּקֶר יָצִיץ וְחָלָף,

---

ness has to be felt before it can be thought. נְצֹר לְשׁוֹנְךָ מֵרָע *Then guard your
tongue from evil*: the sages said about *lashon hara*, evil speech, that it harms
the one who says it, the one it is said about, and the one who gives credence
to it. בַּקֵּשׁ שָׁלוֹם וְרָדְפֵהוּ *Seek peace and pursue it*: "Seek peace where you are,
and pursue it elsewhere" (Yerushalmi, Pe'ah 1:1).

תְּפִלָּה לְמֹשֶׁה *Psalm 90*: A moving meditation on the eternity of God and the
shortness of our lives. זְרַמְתָּם *You sweep men away*: a succession of poetic

like grass newly grown: in the morning it flourishes and is new, but by evening it withers and dries up. For we are consumed by Your anger, terrified by Your fury. You have set our iniquities before You, our secret sins in the light of Your presence. All our days pass away in Your wrath, we spend our years like a sigh. The span of our life is seventy years, or if we are strong, eighty years; but the best of them is trouble and sorrow, for they quickly pass, and we fly away. Who can know the force of Your anger? Your wrath matches the fear due to You. Teach us rightly to number our days, that we may gain a heart of wisdom. Relent, O LORD! How much longer? Be sorry for Your servants. Satisfy us in the morning with Your loving-kindness, that we may sing and rejoice all our days. Grant us joy for as many days as You have afflicted us, for as many years as we saw trouble. Let Your deeds be seen by Your servants, and Your glory by their children. ▸ May the pleasantness of the LORD our God be upon us. Establish for us the work of our hands, O establish the work of our hands.

יֹשֵׁב בְּסֵתֶר He who lives in the shelter of the Most High dwells in   *Ps. 91*
the shadow of the Almighty. I say of the LORD, my Refuge and Stronghold, my God in whom I trust, that He will save you from the fowler's snare and the deadly pestilence. With His pinions He will cover you, and beneath His wings you will find shelter; His faithful-ness is an encircling shield. You need not fear terror by night, nor the arrow that flies by day; not the pestilence that stalks in darkness, nor the plague that ravages at noon. A thousand may fall at your side, ten thousand at your right hand, but it will not come near you. You will only look with your eyes and see the punishment of

---

the Divine Presence rest in the work of your hands" (Bemidbar Raba 12:9; quoted by Rashi on Exodus 39:43).

יֹשֵׁב בְּסֵתֶר *Psalm 91*: A prayer for protection from danger and harm. The psalm uses many images for God's protection. To those who trust in Him, He is shelter, shadow, refuge, stronghold. He protects us beneath His wings, and

לָעֶרֶב יְמוֹלֵל וְיָבֵשׁ: כִּי־כָלִינוּ בְאַפֶּךָ, וּבַחֲמָתְךָ נִבְהָלְנוּ: שַׁתָּ
עֲוֹנֹתֵינוּ לְנֶגְדֶּךָ, עֲלֻמֵנוּ לִמְאוֹר פָּנֶיךָ: כִּי כָל־יָמֵינוּ פָּנוּ בְעֶבְרָתֶךָ,
כִּלִּינוּ שָׁנֵינוּ כְמוֹ־הֶגֶה: יְמֵי־שְׁנוֹתֵינוּ בָהֶם שִׁבְעִים שָׁנָה, וְאִם
בִּגְבוּרֹת שְׁמוֹנִים שָׁנָה, וְרָהְבָּם עָמָל וָאָוֶן, כִּי־גָז חִישׁ וַנָּעֻפָה:
מִי־יוֹדֵעַ עֹז אַפֶּךָ, וּכְיִרְאָתְךָ עֶבְרָתֶךָ: לִמְנוֹת יָמֵינוּ כֵּן הוֹדַע,
וְנָבִא לְבַב חָכְמָה: שׁוּבָה יהוה עַד־מָתָי, וְהִנָּחֵם עַל־עֲבָדֶיךָ:
שַׂבְּעֵנוּ בַבֹּקֶר חַסְדֶּךָ, וּנְרַנְּנָה וְנִשְׂמְחָה בְּכָל־יָמֵינוּ: שַׂמְּחֵנוּ
כִּימוֹת עִנִּיתָנוּ, שְׁנוֹת רָאִינוּ רָעָה: יֵרָאֶה אֶל־עֲבָדֶיךָ פָעֳלֶךָ,
וַהֲדָרְךָ עַל־בְּנֵיהֶם: ‹ וִיהִי נֹעַם אֲדֹנָי אֱלֹהֵינוּ עָלֵינוּ, וּמַעֲשֵׂה
יָדֵינוּ כּוֹנְנָה עָלֵינוּ, וּמַעֲשֵׂה יָדֵינוּ כּוֹנְנֵהוּ:

תהלים צא

יֹשֵׁב בְּסֵתֶר עֶלְיוֹן, בְּצֵל שַׁדַּי יִתְלוֹנָן: אֹמַר לַיהוה מַחְסִי וּמְצוּדָתִי,
אֱלֹהַי אֶבְטַח־בּוֹ: כִּי הוּא יַצִּילְךָ מִפַּח יָקוּשׁ, מִדֶּבֶר הַוּוֹת:
בְּאֶבְרָתוֹ יָסֶךְ לָךְ, וְתַחַת־כְּנָפָיו תֶּחְסֶה, צִנָּה וְסֹחֵרָה אֲמִתּוֹ:
לֹא־תִירָא מִפַּחַד לָיְלָה, מֵחֵץ יָעוּף יוֹמָם: מִדֶּבֶר בָּאֹפֶל יַהֲלֹךְ,
מִקֶּטֶב יָשׁוּד צָהֳרָיִם: יִפֹּל מִצִּדְּךָ אֶלֶף, וּרְבָבָה מִימִינֶךָ, אֵלֶיךָ
לֹא יִגָּשׁ: רַק בְּעֵינֶיךָ תַבִּיט, וְשִׁלֻּמַת רְשָׁעִים תִּרְאֶה: כִּי־אַתָּה

images conveying the brevity of human life: it flows as fast as a swollen river; as quickly as a sleep or a dream; it is like grass in a parched land that withers by the end of the day; it is like a sigh, a mere breath, like a bird that briefly lands then flies away. The speed with which these metaphors succeed one another mirrors the rapidity with which the days and years pass. לִמְנוֹת יָמֵינוּ כֵּן הוֹדַע *Teach us rightly to number our days*: the moral at the heart of the psalm: Teach us to remember how short life is, that we may spend our time on the things that endure. וִיהִי נֹעַם אֲדֹנָי אֱלֹהֵינוּ עָלֵינוּ *May the pleasantness of the Lord our God be upon us*: according to the sages, this is the blessing Moses gave the Israelites when they finished constructing the Tabernacle, adding, "May

the wicked. Because you said "The LORD is my Refuge," taking the
Most High as your shelter, no harm will befall you, no plague will
come near your tent, for He will command His angels about you, to
guard you in all your ways. They will lift you in their hands, lest your
foot stumble on a stone. You will tread on lions and vipers, you will
trample on young lions and snakes. [God says] "Because he loves
Me, I will rescue him; I will protect him, because he acknowledges
My name. When he calls on Me, I will answer him, I will be with
him in distress, I will deliver him and bring him honor. ‣ With long
life I will satisfy him, and show him My salvation. With long life I
will satisfy him, and show him My salvation."

הַלְלוּיָהּ Halleluya! Praise the name of the LORD. Praise Him, you   *Ps. 135*
servants of the LORD who stand in the LORD's House, in the courtyards of the House of our God. Praise the LORD, for the LORD is
good; sing praises to His name, for it is lovely. For the LORD has
chosen Jacob as His own, Israel as his treasure. For I know that
the LORD is great, that our LORD is above all heavenly powers.
Whatever pleases the LORD, He does, in heaven and on earth, in
the seas and all the depths. He raises clouds from the ends of the
earth; He sends lightning with the rain; He brings out the wind
from His storehouses. He struck down the firstborn of Egypt, of
both man and animals. He sent signs and wonders into your midst,
Egypt – against Pharaoh and all his servants. He struck down many
nations and slew mighty kings: Siḥon, King of the Amorites, Og,

---

series of invocations said by a leader of prayer, together with congregational
responses. Psalm 136, with its refrain "His loving-kindness is for ever," is the
only psalm in which the congregational responses are set out in full, line by
line. In Psalm 135 the responses are likely to have been, for the first section,
"Halleluya" (Praise God), and for the last, "Bless the LORD" (*Pesaḥim* 118a).
Psalm 135 is structured in three parts: the first and last speak about the truth
of God and the falsity of idols, and the second about God's power over nature
and history. The first part is five verses long; the second, seven; the third, nine.
שֶׁהִכָּה בְּכוֹרֵי מִצְרָיִם *He struck down the firstborn of Egypt*: these lines are paral-

יהוה מַחְסִי, עֶלְיוֹן שַׂמְתָּ מְעוֹנֶךָ: לֹא־תְאֻנֶּה אֵלֶיךָ רָעָה, וְנֶגַע
לֹא־יִקְרַב בְּאָהֳלֶךָ: כִּי מַלְאָכָיו יְצַוֶּה־לָּךְ, לִשְׁמָרְךָ בְּכָל־דְּרָכֶיךָ:
עַל־כַּפַּיִם יִשָּׂאוּנְךָ, פֶּן־תִּגֹּף בָּאֶבֶן רַגְלֶךָ: עַל־שַׁחַל וָפֶתֶן תִּדְרֹךְ,
תִּרְמֹס כְּפִיר וְתַנִּין: כִּי בִי חָשַׁק וַאֲפַלְּטֵהוּ, אֲשַׂגְּבֵהוּ כִּי־יָדַע
שְׁמִי: יִקְרָאֵנִי וְאֶעֱנֵהוּ, עִמּוֹ אָנֹכִי בְצָרָה, אֲחַלְּצֵהוּ וַאֲכַבְּדֵהוּ:
‹ אֹרֶךְ יָמִים אַשְׂבִּיעֵהוּ, וְאַרְאֵהוּ בִּישׁוּעָתִי:
אֹרֶךְ יָמִים אַשְׂבִּיעֵהוּ, וְאַרְאֵהוּ בִּישׁוּעָתִי:

תהלים קלה

הַלְלוּיָהּ, הַלְלוּ אֶת־שֵׁם יהוה, הַלְלוּ עַבְדֵי יהוה: שֶׁעֹמְדִים
בְּבֵית יהוה, בְּחַצְרוֹת בֵּית אֱלֹהֵינוּ: הַלְלוּיָהּ כִּי־טוֹב יהוה, זַמְּרוּ
לִשְׁמוֹ כִּי נָעִים: כִּי־יַעֲקֹב בָּחַר לוֹ יָהּ, יִשְׂרָאֵל לִסְגֻלָּתוֹ: כִּי אֲנִי
יָדַעְתִּי כִּי־גָדוֹל יהוה, וַאֲדֹנֵינוּ מִכָּל־אֱלֹהִים: כֹּל אֲשֶׁר־חָפֵץ
יהוה עָשָׂה, בַּשָּׁמַיִם וּבָאָרֶץ, בַּיַּמִּים וְכָל־תְּהֹמוֹת: מַעֲלֶה נְשִׂאִים
מִקְצֵה הָאָרֶץ, בְּרָקִים לַמָּטָר עָשָׂה, מוֹצֵא־רוּחַ מֵאוֹצְרוֹתָיו:
שֶׁהִכָּה בְּכוֹרֵי מִצְרָיִם, מֵאָדָם עַד־בְּהֵמָה: שָׁלַח אוֹתֹת וּמֹפְתִים
בְּתוֹכֵכִי מִצְרָיִם, בְּפַרְעֹה וּבְכָל־עֲבָדָיו: שֶׁהִכָּה גּוֹיִם רַבִּים, וְהָרַג

encircles us like a shield. When we are in distress, He is with us. When we
are in danger, we are not alone. Trust defeats terror, and faith conquers fear.
The first speaker in the psalm is human; the second, God Himself (*Sanhedrin*
103a).

הַלְלוּיָהּ *Psalms 135–136*: Two psalms forming a single composite unit, similar in tone, vocabulary and literary structure to the group of Psalms 113–118
known as Hallel. Some sages (*Pesaḥim* 118a) called these two psalms "The
Great Hallel" to distinguish them from Psalms 113–118 which they called
"The Egyptian Hallel" since it contains a reference to the exodus from Egypt
(others confined the description to Psalm 136 alone). It is likely that both
were written for public worship in the Temple, and both are litanies: a

King of Bashan, and all the kingdoms of Canaan, giving their land as a heritage, a heritage for His people Israel. Your name, LORD, endures for ever; Your renown, LORD, for all generations. For the LORD will bring justice to His people, and have compassion on His servants. The idols of the nations are silver and gold, the work of human hands. They have mouths, but cannot speak; eyes, but cannot see; ears, but cannot hear; there is no breath in their mouths. Those who make them will become like them: so will all who trust in them. ‣ House of Israel, bless the LORD. House of Aaron, bless the LORD. House of Levi, bless the LORD. You who fear the LORD, bless the LORD. Blessed is the LORD from Zion, He who dwells in Jerusalem. Halleluya!

The custom is to stand for the following psalm.

הוֹדוּ Thank the LORD for He is good;	His loving-kindness is for ever.	*Ps. 136*
Thank the God of gods,	His loving-kindness is for ever.	
Thank the LORD of lords,	His loving-kindness is for ever.	
To the One who alone works great wonders,	His loving-kindness is for ever.	
Who made the heavens with wisdom,	His loving-kindness is for ever.	
Who spread the earth upon the waters,	His loving-kindness is for ever.	
Who made the great lights,	His loving-kindness is for ever.	
The sun to rule by day,	His loving-kindness is for ever.	
The moon and the stars to rule by night;	His loving-kindness is for ever.	
Who struck Egypt through their firstborn,	His loving-kindness is for ever.	

---

half of each verse, to which the congregation responded with the second half. As in several other psalms, the poem opens with cosmology and ends with history; it begins with God as Creator, and continues with God as Redeemer. The sages related the twenty-six verses of the psalm to the twenty-six generations between Adam and the Giving of the Torah – from creation to revelation. Because of its summary of the events of the exodus, it forms part of the Haggada on Pesaḥ.

מְלָכִים עֲצוּמִים: לְסִיחוֹן מֶלֶךְ הָאֱמֹרִי, וּלְעוֹג מֶלֶךְ הַבָּשָׁן, וּלְכֹל
מַמְלְכוֹת כְּנָעַן: וְנָתַן אַרְצָם נַחֲלָה, נַחֲלָה לְיִשְׂרָאֵל עַמּוֹ: יהוה
שִׁמְךָ לְעוֹלָם, יהוה זִכְרְךָ לְדֹר־וָדֹר: כִּי־יָדִין יהוה עַמּוֹ, וְעַל־
עֲבָדָיו יִתְנֶחָם: עֲצַבֵּי הַגּוֹיִם כֶּסֶף וְזָהָב, מַעֲשֵׂה יְדֵי אָדָם: פֶּה־
לָהֶם וְלֹא יְדַבֵּרוּ, עֵינַיִם לָהֶם וְלֹא יִרְאוּ: אָזְנַיִם לָהֶם וְלֹא יַאֲזִינוּ,
אַף אֵין־יֶשׁ־רוּחַ בְּפִיהֶם: כְּמוֹהֶם יִהְיוּ עֹשֵׂיהֶם, כֹּל אֲשֶׁר־בֹּטֵחַ
בָּהֶם: ◂ בֵּית יִשְׂרָאֵל בָּרְכוּ אֶת־יהוה, בֵּית אַהֲרֹן בָּרְכוּ אֶת־
יהוה: בֵּית הַלֵּוִי בָּרְכוּ אֶת־יהוה, יִרְאֵי יהוה בָּרְכוּ אֶת־יהוה:
בָּרוּךְ יהוה מִצִּיּוֹן, שֹׁכֵן יְרוּשָׁלָֽםִ, הַלְלוּיָהּ:

The custom is to stand for the following psalm.

כִּי לְעוֹלָם חַסְדּוֹ:	הוֹדוּ לַיהוה כִּי־טוֹב
כִּי לְעוֹלָם חַסְדּוֹ:	הוֹדוּ לֵאלֹהֵי הָאֱלֹהִים
כִּי לְעוֹלָם חַסְדּוֹ:	הוֹדוּ לַאֲדֹנֵי הָאֲדֹנִים
כִּי לְעוֹלָם חַסְדּוֹ:	לְעֹשֵׂה נִפְלָאוֹת גְּדֹלוֹת לְבַדּוֹ
כִּי לְעוֹלָם חַסְדּוֹ:	לְעֹשֵׂה הַשָּׁמַיִם בִּתְבוּנָה
כִּי לְעוֹלָם חַסְדּוֹ:	לְרֹקַע הָאָרֶץ עַל־הַמָּיִם
כִּי לְעוֹלָם חַסְדּוֹ:	לְעֹשֵׂה אוֹרִים גְּדֹלִים
כִּי לְעוֹלָם חַסְדּוֹ:	אֶת־הַשֶּׁמֶשׁ לְמֶמְשֶׁלֶת בַּיּוֹם
כִּי לְעוֹלָם חַסְדּוֹ:	אֶת־הַיָּרֵחַ וְכוֹכָבִים לְמֶמְשְׁלוֹת בַּלָּיְלָה
כִּי לְעוֹלָם חַסְדּוֹ:	לְמַכֵּה מִצְרַיִם בִּבְכוֹרֵיהֶם

תהלים קלו

leled in the next psalm. עֲצַבֵּי הַגּוֹיִם כֶּסֶף וְזָהָב. *The idols of the nations are silver and gold… You who fear the* LORD, *bless the* LORD: almost exactly paralleled in Hallel (Psalm 115:4–11).

הוֹדוּ *Psalm 136:* Originally in the Temple, the leader of prayer said the first

And brought out Israel from their midst,	His loving-kindness is for ever.
With a strong hand	
and outstretched arm,	His loving-kindness is for ever.
Who split the Reed Sea into parts,	His loving-kindness is for ever.
And made Israel pass through it,	His loving-kindness is for ever.
Casting Pharaoh and his army	
into the Reed Sea;	His loving-kindness is for ever.
Who led His people	
through the wilderness;	His loving-kindness is for ever.
Who struck down great kings,	His loving-kindness is for ever.
And slew mighty kings,	His loving-kindness is for ever.
Sihon, King of the Amorites,	His loving-kindness is for ever.
And Og, King of Bashan,	His loving-kindness is for ever.
And gave their land as a heritage,	His loving-kindness is for ever.
A heritage for His servant Israel;	His loving-kindness is for ever.
Who remembered us in our lowly state,	His loving-kindness is for ever.
And rescued us from our tormentors,	His loving-kindness is for ever.
▸ Who gives food to all flesh,	His loving-kindness is for ever.
Give thanks to the God of heaven.	His loving-kindness is for ever.

רַנְּנוּ Sing joyfully to the LORD, you righteous, for praise from the *Ps. 33* upright is seemly. Give thanks to the LORD with the harp; make music to Him on the ten-stringed lute. Sing Him a new song, play skillfully with shouts of joy. For the LORD's word is right, and all His deeds are done in faith. He loves righteousness and justice; the earth is full of the LORD's loving-kindness. By the LORD's word the heavens were made, and all their starry host by the breath of His mouth. He gathers the sea waters as a heap, and places the deep in storehouses. Let all the earth fear the LORD, and all the world's inhabitants stand in awe of Him. For He spoke, and it was; He commanded, and it stood firm. The LORD foils the plans of nations; He thwarts the intentions of peoples. The LORD's plans stand for ever, His heart's intents for all generations. Happy is the nation whose God is the

וַיּוֹצֵא יִשְׂרָאֵל מִתּוֹכָם	כִּי לְעוֹלָם חַסְדּוֹ:
בְּיָד חֲזָקָה וּבִזְרוֹעַ נְטוּיָה	כִּי לְעוֹלָם חַסְדּוֹ:
לְגֹזֵר יַם־סוּף לִגְזָרִים	כִּי לְעוֹלָם חַסְדּוֹ:
וְהֶעֱבִיר יִשְׂרָאֵל בְּתוֹכוֹ	כִּי לְעוֹלָם חַסְדּוֹ:
וְנִעֵר פַּרְעֹה וְחֵילוֹ בְיַם־סוּף	כִּי לְעוֹלָם חַסְדּוֹ:
לְמוֹלִיךְ עַמּוֹ בַּמִּדְבָּר	כִּי לְעוֹלָם חַסְדּוֹ:
לְמַכֵּה מְלָכִים גְּדֹלִים	כִּי לְעוֹלָם חַסְדּוֹ:
וַיַּהֲרֹג מְלָכִים אַדִּירִים	כִּי לְעוֹלָם חַסְדּוֹ:
לְסִיחוֹן מֶלֶךְ הָאֱמֹרִי	כִּי לְעוֹלָם חַסְדּוֹ:
וּלְעוֹג מֶלֶךְ הַבָּשָׁן	כִּי לְעוֹלָם חַסְדּוֹ:
וְנָתַן אַרְצָם לְנַחֲלָה	כִּי לְעוֹלָם חַסְדּוֹ:
נַחֲלָה לְיִשְׂרָאֵל עַבְדּוֹ	כִּי לְעוֹלָם חַסְדּוֹ:
שֶׁבְּשִׁפְלֵנוּ זָכַר לָנוּ	כִּי לְעוֹלָם חַסְדּוֹ:
וַיִּפְרְקֵנוּ מִצָּרֵינוּ	כִּי לְעוֹלָם חַסְדּוֹ:
‹ נֹתֵן לֶחֶם לְכָל־בָּשָׂר	כִּי לְעוֹלָם חַסְדּוֹ:
הוֹדוּ לְאֵל הַשָּׁמָיִם	כִּי לְעוֹלָם חַסְדּוֹ:

רַנְּנוּ צַדִּיקִים בַּיהוה, לַיְשָׁרִים נָאוָה תְהִלָּה: הוֹדוּ לַיהוה בְּכִנּוֹר, תהלים לג

בְּנֵבֶל עָשׂוֹר זַמְּרוּ־לוֹ: שִׁירוּ־לוֹ שִׁיר חָדָשׁ, הֵיטִיבוּ נַגֵּן בִּתְרוּעָה:
כִּי־יָשָׁר דְּבַר־יהוה, וְכָל־מַעֲשֵׂהוּ בֶּאֱמוּנָה: אֹהֵב צְדָקָה וּמִשְׁפָּט,
חֶסֶד יהוה מָלְאָה הָאָרֶץ: בִּדְבַר יהוה שָׁמַיִם נַעֲשׂוּ, וּבְרוּחַ פִּיו
כָּל־צְבָאָם: כֹּנֵס כַּנֵּד מֵי הַיָּם, נֹתֵן בְּאוֹצָרוֹת תְּהוֹמוֹת: יִירְאוּ
מֵיהוה כָּל־הָאָרֶץ, מִמֶּנּוּ יָגוּרוּ כָּל־יֹשְׁבֵי תֵבֵל: כִּי הוּא אָמַר
וַיֶּהִי, הוּא־צִוָּה וַיַּעֲמֹד: יהוה הֵפִיר עֲצַת־גּוֹיִם, הֵנִיא מַחְשְׁבוֹת

LORD, the people He has chosen as His own. From heaven the LORD looks down and sees all mankind; from His dwelling place He oversees all who live on earth. He forms the hearts of all, and discerns all their deeds. No king is saved by the size of his army; no warrior is delivered by great strength. A horse is a vain hope for deliverance; despite its great strength, it cannot save. The eye of the LORD is on those who fear Him, on those who place their hope in His unfailing love, to rescue their soul from death, and keep them alive in famine. Our soul waits for the LORD; He is our Help and Shield. ‣ In Him our hearts rejoice, for we trust in His holy name. Let Your unfailing love be upon us, LORD, as we have put our hope in You.

מִזְמוֹר שִׁיר A psalm. A song for the Sabbath day. It is good to thank *Ps. 92* the LORD and sing psalms to Your name, Most High – to tell of Your loving-kindness in the morning and Your faithfulness at night, to the music of the ten-stringed lyre and the melody of the harp. For You have made me rejoice by Your work, O LORD; I sing for joy at the deeds of Your hands. How great are Your deeds, LORD, and how very deep Your thoughts. A boor cannot know, nor can a fool understand, that though the wicked spring up like grass and all evildoers flourish, it is only that they may be destroyed for ever. But You, LORD, are eternally exalted. For behold Your enemies, LORD, behold Your enemies will perish; all evildoers will be scattered. You have raised my pride like that of a wild ox; I am anointed with fresh oil. My eyes shall look in triumph on my adversaries, my ears shall hear the downfall of the wicked who rise against me. ‣ The righteous will flourish like a palm tree and grow tall like a cedar in Lebanon. Planted in the LORD's House, blossoming in our God's courtyards, they will still bear fruit in old age, and stay vigorous and fresh, proclaiming that the LORD is upright: He is my Rock, in whom there is no wrong.

יהוה מָלָךְ The LORD reigns. He is robed in majesty. The LORD is *Ps. 93* robed, girded with strength. The world is firmly established; it

עַמִּים: עֲצַת יהוה לְעוֹלָם תַּעֲמֹד, מַחְשְׁבוֹת לִבּוֹ לְדֹר וָדֹר: אַשְׁרֵי הַגּוֹי אֲשֶׁר־יהוה אֱלֹהָיו, הָעָם בָּחַר לְנַחֲלָה לוֹ: מִשָּׁמַיִם הִבִּיט יהוה, רָאָה אֶת־כָּל־בְּנֵי הָאָדָם: מִמְּכוֹן־שִׁבְתּוֹ הִשְׁגִּיחַ, אֶל כָּל־יֹשְׁבֵי הָאָרֶץ: הַיֹּצֵר יַחַד לִבָּם, הַמֵּבִין אֶל־כָּל־מַעֲשֵׂיהֶם: אֵין־הַמֶּלֶךְ נוֹשָׁע בְּרָב־חָיִל, גִּבּוֹר לֹא־יִנָּצֵל בְּרָב־כֹּחַ: שֶׁקֶר הַסּוּס לִתְשׁוּעָה, וּבְרֹב חֵילוֹ לֹא יְמַלֵּט: הִנֵּה עֵין יהוה אֶל־יְרֵאָיו, לַמְיַחֲלִים לְחַסְדּוֹ: לְהַצִּיל מִמָּוֶת נַפְשָׁם, וּלְחַיּוֹתָם בָּרָעָב: נַפְשֵׁנוּ חִכְּתָה לַיהוה, עֶזְרֵנוּ וּמָגִנֵּנוּ הוּא: ‹ כִּי־בוֹ יִשְׂמַח לִבֵּנוּ, כִּי בְשֵׁם קָדְשׁוֹ בָטָחְנוּ: יְהִי־חַסְדְּךָ יהוה עָלֵינוּ, כַּאֲשֶׁר יִחַלְנוּ לָךְ:

תהלים צב
מִזְמוֹר שִׁיר לְיוֹם הַשַּׁבָּת: טוֹב לְהֹדוֹת לַיהוה, וּלְזַמֵּר לְשִׁמְךָ עֶלְיוֹן: לְהַגִּיד בַּבֹּקֶר חַסְדֶּךָ, וֶאֱמוּנָתְךָ בַּלֵּילוֹת: עֲלֵי־עָשׂוֹר וַעֲלֵי־נָבֶל, עֲלֵי הִגָּיוֹן בְּכִנּוֹר: כִּי שִׂמַּחְתַּנִי יהוה בְּפָעֳלֶךָ, בְּמַעֲשֵׂי יָדֶיךָ אֲרַנֵּן: מַה־גָּדְלוּ מַעֲשֶׂיךָ יהוה, מְאֹד עָמְקוּ מַחְשְׁבֹתֶיךָ: אִישׁ־בַּעַר לֹא יֵדָע, וּכְסִיל לֹא־יָבִין אֶת־זֹאת: בִּפְרֹחַ רְשָׁעִים כְּמוֹ עֵשֶׂב, וַיָּצִיצוּ כָּל־פֹּעֲלֵי אָוֶן, לְהִשָּׁמְדָם עֲדֵי־עַד: וְאַתָּה מָרוֹם לְעֹלָם יהוה: כִּי הִנֵּה אֹיְבֶיךָ יהוה, כִּי־הִנֵּה אֹיְבֶיךָ יֹאבֵדוּ, יִתְפָּרְדוּ כָּל־פֹּעֲלֵי אָוֶן: וַתָּרֶם כִּרְאֵים קַרְנִי, בַּלֹּתִי בְּשֶׁמֶן רַעֲנָן: וַתַּבֵּט עֵינִי בְּשׁוּרָי, בַּקָּמִים עָלַי מְרֵעִים תִּשְׁמַעְנָה אָזְנָי: ‹ צַדִּיק כַּתָּמָר יִפְרָח, כְּאֶרֶז בַּלְּבָנוֹן יִשְׂגֶּה: שְׁתוּלִים בְּבֵית יהוה, בְּחַצְרוֹת אֱלֹהֵינוּ יַפְרִיחוּ: עוֹד יְנוּבוּן בְּשֵׂיבָה, דְּשֵׁנִים וְרַעֲנַנִּים יִהְיוּ: לְהַגִּיד כִּי־יָשָׁר יהוה, צוּרִי, וְלֹא־עַוְלָתָה בּוֹ:

תהלים צג
יהוה מָלָךְ, גֵּאוּת לָבֵשׁ, לָבֵשׁ יהוה עֹז הִתְאַזָּר, אַף־תִּכּוֹן תֵּבֵל בַּל־תִּמּוֹט: נָכוֹן כִּסְאֲךָ מֵאָז, מֵעוֹלָם אָתָּה: נָשְׂאוּ נְהָרוֹת יהוה,

cannot be moved. Your throne stands firm as of old; You are eternal. Rivers lift up, LORD, rivers lift up their voice, rivers lift up their Crashing waves. ‣ Mightier than the noise of many waters, than the mighty waves of the sea is the LORD on high. Your testimonies are very sure; holiness adorns Your House, LORD, for evermore.

Continue with "May the LORD's glory" on page 70. Shirat HaYam (page 80)
is said verse by verse. After the Leader's Repetition, Full Hallel (page 360) is
said followed by Half Kaddish (page 156). On Thursdays the Torah is read
(page 158). On all days, the following Haftara is read. See law 146.

עוֹד הַיּוֹם **This day** he will halt at Nob; he will wave his hand, mountain   Is. 10:32–
of the daughter of Zion, hill of Jerusalem. See, the sovereign LORD of   12:6
hosts will lop off the boughs with an axe. The tall trees will be felled,
the lofty ones laid low. He will cut down the forest thickets with an
axe. Lebanon will fall before the Mighty One. A shoot will grow from
the stump of Jesse; from his roots a branch will bear fruit. The spirit
of the LORD will rest on him – a spirit of wisdom and understanding,
a spirit of counsel and power, a spirit of knowledge and the fear of the
LORD, and he will delight in the fear of the LORD. He will not judge
by what his eyes see, or decide by what his ears hear; with justice he
will judge the poor, and with equity defend humble in the land. He
will strike the earth with the rod of his mouth; with the breath of his
lips he will slay the wicked. Justice will be his belt and faithfulness the
sash around his waist. The wolf will live with the lamb, the leopard will
lie down with the kid, the calf and the lion and the yearling together;
and a little child will lead them. The cow will graze with the bear, their
young will lie down together, and the lion will eat straw like the ox.
An infant will play near the cobra's hole, and a young child put his
hand into the viper's nest. They will neither harm nor destroy on all
My holy mountain, for the earth will be full of the knowledge of the
LORD as the waters cover the sea. On that day the stock of Jesse will
stand as a banner for the peoples; nations will rally to him, and his
place of rest will be glorious. On that day the LORD will reach out His
hand a second time to reclaim the remnant that is left of His people
from Assyria, Lower Egypt, Pathros, Cush, Elam, Shinar, Hamath
and the islands of the sea. He will raise a banner for the nations and
gather the exiles of Israel; He will assemble the scattered people of

נָשְׂאוּ נְהָרוֹת קוֹלָם, יִשְׂאוּ נְהָרוֹת דָּכְיָם: ‹ מִקֹּלוֹת מַיִם רַבִּים,
אַדִּירִים מִשְׁבְּרֵי־יָם, אַדִּיר בַּמָּרוֹם יהוה: עֵדֹתֶיךָ נֶאֶמְנוּ מְאֹד
לְבֵיתְךָ נַאֲוָה־קֹּדֶשׁ, יהוה לְאֹרֶךְ יָמִים:

Continue with כָּבוֹד הָבוּ (page 81). שִׁירוּ הַיָּם (page 71) on is said verse by verse. After חֲזֹרָה
הַלֵּל שָׁלֵם, תשי״ן (page 361) is said followed by חֲצִי קַדִּישׁ (page 157). On Thursdays the
תּוֹרָה is read (page 159). On all days, the following הַפְטָרָה is read. See law 146.

יְשַׁעְיָה
יְלֹ״ב־יֹ״בוֹ עוֹד הַיּוֹם בְּנֹב לַעֲמֹד יְנֹפֵף יָדוֹ הַר בַּת־צִיּוֹן גִּבְעַת
יְרוּשָׁלָ͏ִם: הִנֵּה הָאָדוֹן יהוה צְבָאוֹת מְסָעֵף פֻּארָה
בְּמַעֲרָצָה וְרָמֵי הַקּוֹמָה גְּדֻעִים וְהַגְּבֹהִים יִשְׁפָּלוּ: וְנִקַּף סִבְכֵי
הַיַּעַר בַּבַּרְזֶל וְהַלְּבָנוֹן בְּאַדִּיר יִפּוֹל: וְיָצָא חֹטֶר מִגֶּזַע
יִשַׁי וְנֵצֶר מִשָּׁרָשָׁיו יִפְרֶה: וְנָחָה עָלָיו רוּחַ יהוה רוּחַ חָכְמָה וּבִינָה
רוּחַ עֵצָה וּגְבוּרָה רוּחַ דַּעַת וְיִרְאַת יהוה: וַהֲרִיחוֹ בְּיִרְאַת יהוה
וְלֹא־לְמַרְאֵה עֵינָיו יִשְׁפּוֹט וְלֹא־לְמִשְׁמַע אָזְנָיו יוֹכִיחַ: וְשָׁפַט
בְּצֶדֶק דַּלִּים וְהוֹכִיחַ בְּמִישׁוֹר לְעַנְוֵי־אָרֶץ וְהִכָּה־אֶרֶץ בְּשֵׁבֶט
פִּיו וּבְרוּחַ שְׂפָתָיו יָמִית רָשָׁע: וְהָיָה צֶדֶק אֵזוֹר מָתְנָיו וְהָאֱמוּנָה
אֵזוֹר חֲלָצָיו: וְגָר זְאֵב עִם־כֶּבֶשׂ וְנָמֵר עִם־גְּדִי יִרְבָּץ וְעֵגֶל וּכְפִיר
וּמְרִיא יַחְדָּו וְנַעַר קָטֹן נֹהֵג בָּם: וּפָרָה וָדֹב תִּרְעֶינָה יַחְדָּו יִרְבְּצוּ
יַלְדֵיהֶן וְאַרְיֵה כַּבָּקָר יֹאכַל־תֶּבֶן: וְשִׁעֲשַׁע יוֹנֵק עַל־חֻר פֶּתֶן
וְעַל מְאוּרַת צִפְעוֹנִי גָּמוּל יָדוֹ הָדָה: לֹא־יָרֵעוּ וְלֹא־יַשְׁחִיתוּ
בְּכָל־הַר קָדְשִׁי כִּי־מָלְאָה הָאָרֶץ דֵּעָה אֶת־יהוה כַּמַּיִם לַיָּם
מְכַסִּים: וְהָיָה בַּיּוֹם הַהוּא שֹׁרֶשׁ יִשַׁי אֲשֶׁר עֹמֵד לְנֵס
עַמִּים אֵלָיו גּוֹיִם יִדְרֹשׁוּ וְהָיְתָה מְנֻחָתוֹ כָּבוֹד: וְהָיָה ׀
בַּיּוֹם הַהוּא יוֹסִיף אֲדֹנָי ׀ שֵׁנִית יָדוֹ לִקְנוֹת אֶת־שְׁאָר עַמּוֹ אֲשֶׁר
יִשָּׁאֵר מֵאַשּׁוּר וּמִמִּצְרַיִם וּמִפַּתְרוֹס וּמִכּוּשׁ וּמֵעֵילָם וּמִשִּׁנְעָר
וּמֵחֲמָת וּמֵאִיֵּי הַיָּם: וְנָשָׂא נֵס לַגּוֹיִם וְאָסַף נִדְחֵי יִשְׂרָאֵל וּנְפֻצוֹת

Judah from the four quarters of the earth. Ephraim's jealousy will vanish, and Judah's harassment will end. Ephraim will not be jealous of Judah, nor will Judah be hostile toward Ephraim. They will swoop down on the slopes of Philistia to the west; together they will plunder the people to the east. Edom and Moab shall be subject to them, and the Ammonites shall obey them. The LORD will dry up the gulf of the Egyptian sea; with a scorching wind He will sweep His hand over the Euphrates River. He will break it up into seven streams so that people can cross over in sandals. There will be a highway for the remnant of His people that is left from Assyria, as there was for Israel when they came up from Egypt. In that day you will say: "I will praise You, O LORD. Although You were angry with me, Your anger has turned away and You have comforted me. Surely God is my salvation; I will trust and not be afraid. The LORD, the LORD, is my strength and my song; He has become my salvation." With joy you will draw water from the wells of salvation. In that day you will say: "Give thanks to the LORD, call on His name; make known among the nations what He has done, and proclaim that His name is exalted. Sing to the LORD, for He has done glorious things; let this be known to all the world. Shout aloud and sing for joy, people of Zion, for great is the Holy One of Israel among you."

The Prayer for the Welfare of the Canadian Goverment is on the next page.

PRAYER FOR THE WELFARE OF THE AMERICAN GOVERNMENT

The Leader says the following:

הַנּוֹתֵן תְּשׁוּעָה May He who gives salvation to kings and dominion to princes, whose kingdom is an everlasting kingdom, who delivers His servant David from the evil sword, who makes a way in the sea and a path through the mighty waters, bless and protect, guard and help, exalt, magnify and uplift the President, Vice President and all officials of this land. May the Supreme King of kings in His mercy put into their hearts and the hearts of all their counselors and officials, to deal kindly with us and all Israel. In their days and in ours, may Judah be saved and Israel dwell in safety, and may the Redeemer come to Zion. May this be His will, and let us say: Amen.

יְהוּדָה יְקַבֵּץ מֵאַרְבַּע כַּנְפוֹת הָאָרֶץ: וְסָרָה קִנְאַת אֶפְרַיִם וְצֹרְרֵי יְהוּדָה יִכָּרֵתוּ אֶפְרַיִם לֹא־יְקַנֵּא אֶת־יְהוּדָה וִיהוּדָה לֹא־יָצֹר אֶת־אֶפְרָיִם: וְעָפוּ בְכָתֵף פְּלִשְׁתִּים יָמָּה יַחְדָּו יָבֹזּוּ אֶת־בְּנֵי־ קֶדֶם אֱדוֹם וּמוֹאָב מִשְׁלוֹחַ יָדָם וּבְנֵי עַמּוֹן מִשְׁמַעְתָּם: וְהֶחֱרִים יְהוָה אֵת לְשׁוֹן יָם־מִצְרַיִם וְהֵנִיף יָדוֹ עַל־הַנָּהָר בַּעְיָם רוּחוֹ וְהִכָּהוּ לְשִׁבְעָה נְחָלִים וְהִדְרִיךְ בַּנְּעָלִים: וְהָיְתָה מְסִלָּה לִשְׁאָר עַמּוֹ אֲשֶׁר יִשָּׁאֵר מֵאַשּׁוּר כַּאֲשֶׁר הָיְתָה לְיִשְׂרָאֵל בְּיוֹם עֲלֹתוֹ מֵאֶרֶץ מִצְרָיִם: וְאָמַרְתָּ בַּיּוֹם הַהוּא אוֹדְךָ יְהוָה כִּי אָנַפְתָּ בִּי יָשֹׁב אַפְּךָ וּתְנַחֲמֵנִי: הִנֵּה אֵל יְשׁוּעָתִי אֶבְטַח וְלֹא אֶפְחָד כִּי־ עָזִּי וְזִמְרָת יָהּ יְהוָה וַיְהִי־לִי לִישׁוּעָה: וּשְׁאַבְתֶּם־מַיִם בְּשָׂשׂוֹן מִמַּעַיְנֵי הַיְשׁוּעָה: וַאֲמַרְתֶּם בַּיּוֹם הַהוּא הוֹדוּ לַיהוָה קִרְאוּ בִשְׁמוֹ הוֹדִיעוּ בָעַמִּים עֲלִילֹתָיו הַזְכִּירוּ כִּי נִשְׂגָּב שְׁמוֹ: זַמְּרוּ יְהוָה כִּי גֵאוּת עָשָׂה מוּדַעַת זֹאת בְּכָל־הָאָרֶץ: צַהֲלִי וָרֹנִּי יוֹשֶׁבֶת צִיּוֹן כִּי־גָדוֹל בְּקִרְבֵּךְ קְדוֹשׁ יִשְׂרָאֵל:

The Prayer for the Welfare of the Canadian Goverment is on the next page.

תפילה לשלום המלכות

The שליח ציבור says the following:

הַנּוֹתֵן תְּשׁוּעָה לַמְּלָכִים וּמֶמְשָׁלָה לַנְּסִיכִים, מַלְכוּתוֹ מַלְכוּת כָּל עוֹלָמִים, הַפּוֹצֶה אֶת דָּוִד עַבְדּוֹ מֵחֶרֶב רָעָה, הַנּוֹתֵן בַּיָּם דֶּרֶךְ וּבְמַיִם עַזִּים נְתִיבָה, הוּא יְבָרֵךְ וְיִשְׁמֹר וְיִנְצֹר וְיַעֲזֹר וִירוֹמֵם וִיגַדֵּל וִינַשֵּׂא לְמַעְלָה אֶת הַנָּשִׂיא וְאֶת מִשְׁנֵהוּ וְאֶת כָּל שָׂרֵי הָאָרֶץ הַזֹּאת. מֶלֶךְ מַלְכֵי הַמְּלָכִים, בְּרַחֲמָיו יִתֵּן בְּלִבָּם וּבְלֵב כָּל יוֹעֲצֵיהֶם וְשָׂרֵיהֶם לַעֲשׂוֹת טוֹבָה עִמָּנוּ וְעִם כָּל יִשְׂרָאֵל. בִּימֵיהֶם וּבְיָמֵינוּ תִּוָּשַׁע יְהוּדָה, וְיִשְׂרָאֵל יִשְׁכֹּן לָבֶטַח, וּבָא לְצִיּוֹן גּוֹאֵל. וְכֵן יְהִי רָצוֹן, וְנֹאמַר אָמֵן.

PRAYER FOR THE SAFETY OF THE AMERICAN MILITARY

The Leader says the following:

אַדִּיר בַּמָּרוֹם God on high who dwells in might, the King to whom peace belongs, look down from Your holy habitation and bless the soldiers of the American military forces who risk their lives for the sake of peace on earth. Be their shelter and stronghold, and let them not falter. Give them the strength and courage to thwart the plans of the enemy and end the rule of evil. May their enemies be scattered and their foes flee before them, and may they rejoice in Your salvation. Bring them back safely to their homes, as is written: "The LORD *Ps. 121* will guard you from all harm, He will guard your life. The LORD will guard your going and coming, now and for evermore." And may there be fulfilled for us the verse: "Nation shall not lift up sword against *Is. 2* nation, nor shall they learn war any more." Let all the inhabitants on earth know that sovereignty is Yours and Your name inspires awe over all You have created – and let us say: Amen.

PRAYER FOR THE WELFARE OF THE CANADIAN GOVERNMENT

The Leader says the following:

הַנּוֹתֵן תְּשׁוּעָה May He who gives salvation to kings and dominion to princes, whose kingdom is an everlasting kingdom, who delivers His servant David from the evil sword, who makes a way in the sea and a path through the mighty waters, bless and protect, guard and help, exalt, magnify and uplift the Prime Minister and all the elected and appointed officials of Canada. May the Supreme King of kings in His mercy put into their hearts and the hearts of all their counselors and officials, to deal kindly with us and all Israel. In their days and in ours, may Judah be saved and Israel dwell in safety, and may the Redeemer come to Zion. May this be His will, and let us say: Amen.

PRAYER FOR THE SAFETY OF THE CANADIAN MILITARY FORCES

The Leader says the following:

אַדִּיר בַּמָּרוֹם God on high who dwells in might, the King to whom peace belongs, look down from Your holy habitation and bless the soldiers of the Canadian Forces who risk their lives for the sake of

תפילה לשלום חיילי צבא ארצות הברית

The שליח ציבור *says the following:*

אַדִּיר בַּמָּרוֹם שׁוֹכֵן בִּגְבוּרָה, מֶלֶךְ שֶׁהַשָּׁלוֹם שֶׁלּוֹ, הַשְׁקִיפָה מִמְּעוֹן
קָדְשֶׁךָ, וּבָרֵךְ אֶת חַיָּלֵי צְבָא אַרְצוֹת הַבְּרִית, הַמְחָרְפִים נַפְשָׁם
בְּלֶכְתָּם לָשִׂים שָׁלוֹם בָּאָרֶץ. הֱיֵה נָא לָהֶם מַחֲסֶה וּמָעוֹז, וְאַל תִּתֵּן
לַמּוֹט רַגְלָם, חַזֵּק יְדֵיהֶם וְאַמֵּץ רוּחָם לְהָפֵר עֲצַת אוֹיֵב וּלְהַעֲבִיר
מֶמְשֶׁלֶת זָדוֹן, יָפוּצוּ אוֹיְבֵיהֶם וְיָנוּסוּ מְשַׂנְאֵיהֶם מִפְּנֵיהֶם, וְיִשְׂמְחוּ
בִּישׁוּעָתֶךָ. הֲשִׁיבֵם בְּשָׁלוֹם אֶל בֵּיתָם, כַּכָּתוּב בְּדִבְרֵי קָדְשֶׁךָ: יהוה
תהלים קכא יִשְׁמָרְךָ מִכָּל־רָע, יִשְׁמֹר אֶת־נַפְשֶׁךָ: יהוה יִשְׁמָר־צֵאתְךָ וּבוֹאֶךָ,
מֵעַתָּה וְעַד־עוֹלָם: וְקַיֵּם בָּנוּ מִקְרָא שֶׁכָּתוּב: לֹא־יִשָּׂא גוֹי אֶל־גּוֹי ישעיה ב
חֶרֶב, וְלֹא־יִלְמְדוּ עוֹד מִלְחָמָה: וְיֵדְעוּ כָּל יוֹשְׁבֵי תֵבֵל כִּי לְךָ מְלוּכָה
יָאָתָה, וְשִׁמְךָ נוֹרָא עַל כָּל מַה שֶּׁבָּרָאתָ. וְנֹאמַר אָמֵן.

תפילה לשלום המלכות

The שליח ציבור *says the following:*

הַנּוֹתֵן תְּשׁוּעָה לַמְּלָכִים וּמֶמְשָׁלָה לַנְּסִיכִים, מַלְכוּתוֹ מַלְכוּת כָּל
עוֹלָמִים, הַפּוֹצֶה אֶת דָּוִד עַבְדּוֹ מֵחֶרֶב רָעָה, הַנּוֹתֵן בַּיָּם דֶּרֶךְ וּבְמַיִם
עַזִּים נְתִיבָה, הוּא יְבָרֵךְ וְיִשְׁמֹר וְיִנְצֹר וְיַעֲזֹר וִירוֹמֵם וִיגַדֵּל וִינַשֵּׂא
לְמַעְלָה אֶת רֹאשׁ הַמֶּמְשָׁלָה וְאֶת כָּל שָׂרֵי הָאָרֶץ הַזֹּאת. מֶלֶךְ
מַלְכֵי הַמְּלָכִים, בְּרַחֲמָיו יִתֵּן בְּלִבָּם וּבְלֵב כָּל יוֹעֲצֵיהֶם וְשָׂרֵיהֶם
לַעֲשׂוֹת טוֹבָה עִמָּנוּ וְעִם כָּל יִשְׂרָאֵל. בִּימֵיהֶם וּבְיָמֵינוּ תִּוָּשַׁע
יְהוּדָה, וְיִשְׂרָאֵל יִשְׁכֹּן לָבֶטַח, וּבָא לְצִיּוֹן גּוֹאֵל. וְכֵן יְהִי רָצוֹן,
וְנֹאמַר אָמֵן.

תפילה לשלום חיילי צבא קנדה

The שליח ציבור *says the following:*

אַדִּיר בַּמָּרוֹם שׁוֹכֵן בִּגְבוּרָה, מֶלֶךְ שֶׁהַשָּׁלוֹם שֶׁלּוֹ, הַשְׁקִיפָה מִמְּעוֹן
קָדְשֶׁךָ, וּבָרֵךְ אֶת חַיָּלֵי צְבָא קָנָדָה, הַמְחָרְפִים נַפְשָׁם בְּלֶכְתָּם לָשִׂים

peace on earth. Be their shelter and stronghold, and let them not falter.
Give them the strength and courage to thwart the plans of the enemy
and end the rule of evil. May their enemies be scattered and their foes
flee before them, and may they rejoice in Your salvation. Bring them
back safely to their homes, as is written: "The LORD will guard you   Ps. 121
from all harm, He will guard your life. The LORD will guard your going
and coming, now and for evermore." And may there be fulfilled for
us the verse: "Nation shall not lift up sword against nation, nor shall   Is. 2
they learn war any more." Let all the inhabitants on earth know that
sovereignty is Yours and Your name inspires awe over all You have
created – and let us say: Amen.

PRAYER FOR THE STATE OF ISRAEL

The Leader says the following prayer:

אָבִינוּ שֶׁבַּשָּׁמַיִם Heavenly Father, Israel's Rock and Redeemer, bless the
State of Israel, the first flowering of our redemption. Shield it under
the wings of Your loving-kindness and spread over it the Tabernacle
of Your peace. Send Your light and truth to its leaders, ministers and
counselors, and direct them with good counsel before You.

Strengthen the hands of the defenders of our Holy Land; grant them
deliverance, our God, and crown them with the crown of victory.
Grant peace in the land and everlasting joy to its inhabitants.

As for our brothers, the whole house of Israel, remember them in all
the lands of our (*In Israel say:* their) dispersion, and swiftly lead us
(*In Israel say:* them) upright to Zion Your city, and Jerusalem Your
dwelling place, as is written in the Torah of Moses Your servant:
"Even if you are scattered to the furthermost lands under the heav-   Deut. 30
ens, from there the LORD your God will gather you and take you
back. The LORD your God will bring you to the land your ancestors
possessed and you will possess it; and He will make you more prosperous and numerous than your ancestors. Then the LORD your God

שָׁלוֹם בָּאָרֶץ. הֱיֵה נָא לָהֶם מַחֲסֶה וּמָעוֹז, וְאַל תִּתֵּן לַמּוֹט רַגְלָם, חַזֵּק
יְדֵיהֶם וְאַמֵּץ רוּחָם לְהָפֵר עֲצַת אוֹיֵב וּלְהַעֲבִיר מֶמְשֶׁלֶת זָדוֹן, יָפוּצוּ
אוֹיְבֵיהֶם וְיָנוּסוּ מְשַׂנְאֵיהֶם מִפְּנֵיהֶם, וְיִשְׂמְחוּ בִּישׁוּעָתֶךָ. הֲשִׁיבֵם
בְּשָׁלוֹם אֶל בֵּיתָם, כַּכָּתוּב בְּדִבְרֵי קָדְשֶׁךָ: יהוה יִשְׁמָרְךָ מִכָּל־רָע,   תהלים קכא
יִשְׁמֹר אֶת־נַפְשֶׁךָ: יהוה יִשְׁמָר־צֵאתְךָ וּבוֹאֶךָ, מֵעַתָּה וְעַד־עוֹלָם:
וְקַיֵּם בָּנוּ מִקְרָא שֶׁכָּתוּב: לֹא־יִשָּׂא גוֹי אֶל־גּוֹי חֶרֶב, וְלֹא־יִלְמְדוּ   ישעיה ב
עוֹד מִלְחָמָה: וְיֵדְעוּ כָּל יוֹשְׁבֵי תֵבֵל כִּי לְךָ מְלוּכָה יָאָתָה, וְשִׁמְךָ
נוֹרָא עַל כָּל מַה שֶּׁבָּרָאתָ. וְנֹאמַר אָמֵן.

תפילה לשלום מדינת ישראל

The שליח ציבור says the following prayer:

אָבִינוּ שֶׁבַּשָּׁמַיִם, צוּר יִשְׂרָאֵל וְגוֹאֲלוֹ, בָּרֵךְ אֶת מְדִינַת יִשְׂרָאֵל,
רֵאשִׁית צְמִיחַת גְּאֻלָּתֵנוּ. הָגֵן עָלֶיהָ בְּאֶבְרַת חַסְדֶּךָ וּפְרֹשׂ עָלֶיהָ
סֻכַּת שְׁלוֹמֶךָ, וּשְׁלַח אוֹרְךָ וַאֲמִתְּךָ לְרָאשֶׁיהָ, שָׂרֶיהָ וְיוֹעֲצֶיהָ,
וְתַקְּנֵם בְּעֵצָה טוֹבָה מִלְּפָנֶיךָ.

חַזֵּק אֶת יְדֵי מְגִנֵּי אֶרֶץ קָדְשֵׁנוּ, וְהַנְחִילֵם אֱלֹהֵינוּ יְשׁוּעָה וַעֲטֶרֶת
נִצָּחוֹן תְּעַטְּרֵם, וְנָתַתָּ שָׁלוֹם בָּאָרֶץ וְשִׂמְחַת עוֹלָם לְיוֹשְׁבֶיהָ.

וְאֶת אַחֵינוּ כָּל בֵּית יִשְׂרָאֵל, פְּקָד נָא בְּכָל אַרְצוֹת פְּזוּרֵינוּ,
וְתוֹלִיכֵנוּ / בארץ ישראל בְּאֶרֶץ ישראל פְּזוּרֵיהֶם, וְתוֹלִיכֵם/ מְהֵרָה קוֹמְמִיּוּת לְצִיּוֹן
עִירֶךָ וְלִירוּשָׁלַיִם מִשְׁכַּן שְׁמֶךָ, כַּכָּתוּב בְּתוֹרַת מֹשֶׁה עַבְדֶּךָ: אִם־   דברים ל
יִהְיֶה נִדַּחֲךָ בִּקְצֵה הַשָּׁמָיִם, מִשָּׁם יְקַבֶּצְךָ יהוה אֱלֹהֶיךָ וּמִשָּׁם
יִקָּחֶךָ: וֶהֱבִיאֲךָ יהוה אֱלֹהֶיךָ אֶל־הָאָרֶץ אֲשֶׁר־יָרְשׁוּ אֲבֹתֶיךָ
וִירִשְׁתָּהּ, וְהֵיטִבְךָ וְהִרְבְּךָ מֵאֲבֹתֶיךָ: וּמָל יהוה אֱלֹהֶיךָ אֶת־לְבָבְךָ

will open up your heart and the heart of your descendants, to love the Lord your God with all your heart and with all your soul, that you may live."

Unite our hearts to love and revere Your name and observe all the words of Your Torah, and swiftly send us Your righteous anointed one of the house of David, to redeem those who long for Your salvation.

Appear in Your glorious majesty over all the dwellers on earth, and let all who breathe declare: The Lord God of Israel is King and His kingship has dominion over all. Amen, Selah.

The Prayer for the State of Israel is followed by the Memorial for Fallen Israeli Soldiers (page 416) is said. The service then continues with Ashrei until the end of Shaḥarit (page 174). At the end of the service, sing:

אֲנִי מַאֲמִין I believe with perfect faith
in the coming of the Messiah,
and though he may delay,
I wait daily for his coming.

YOM YERUSHALAYIM

*At Minḥa before Yom Yerushalayim, Taḥanun is omitted.
In the evening, Ma'ariv for weekdays is said in the Yom Tov melody.
The Omer is counted. Many have the custom to add prayers
of thanksgiving at the end of Ma'ariv.*

*In Shaḥarit, many communities outside Israel and in Israel say
the Pesukei DeZimra of Yom Tov (page 428). After the Leader's Repetition,
Full Hallel (page 360) is said and the regular service continues.*

וְאֶת־לְבַב זַרְעֶךָ, לְאַהֲבָה אֶת־יהוה אֱלֹהֶיךָ בְּכָל־לְבָבְךָ וּבְכָל־
נַפְשְׁךָ, לְמַעַן חַיֶּיךָ:

וְיַחֵד לְבָבֵנוּ לְאַהֲבָה וּלְיִרְאָה אֶת שְׁמֶךָ, וְלִשְׁמֹר אֶת כָּל דִּבְרֵי
תוֹרָתֶךָ, וּשְׁלַח לָנוּ מְהֵרָה בֶן דָּוִד מְשִׁיחַ צִדְקֶךָ, לִפְדּוֹת מְחַכֵּי
קֵץ יְשׁוּעָתֶךָ.

וְהוֹפַע בַּהֲדַר גְּאוֹן עֻזֶּךָ עַל כָּל יוֹשְׁבֵי תֵבֵל אַרְצֶךָ וְיֹאמַר כֹּל אֲשֶׁר
נְשָׁמָה בְאַפּוֹ, יהוה אֱלֹהֵי יִשְׂרָאֵל מֶלֶךְ וּמַלְכוּתוֹ בַּכֹּל מָשָׁלָה,
אָמֵן סֶלָה.

The Prayer for the State of Israel is followed by the אזכרה *for Fallen Israeli
Soldiers (page 417) is said. The service then continues with* אַשְׁרֵי *and* וּבָא
לְצִיּוֹן *until the end of* שחרית *(page 175). At the end of the service, sing:*

אֲנִי מַאֲמִין בֶּאֱמוּנָה שְׁלֵמָה, בְּבִיאַת הַמָּשִׁיחַ
וְאַף עַל פִּי שֶׁיִּתְמַהְמֵהַּ
עִם כָּל זֶה אֲחַכֶּה לוֹ בְּכָל יוֹם שֶׁיָּבוֹא.

יום חירות ירושלים

At מנחה *before* יום ירושלים, תחנון *is omitted. In the evening,* מעריב לחול
is said in the יום טוב *melody. The* עומר *is counted. Many have the
custom to add prayers of thanksgiving at the end of* מעריב.

In שחרית *many communities in* ארץ ישראל *and in* חוץ לארץ *say
the* הלל שלם, חזרת הש״ץ *of* יום טוב *(page 429). After* פסוקי דזמרה
(page 361) is said and the regular service continues.

Seliḥot

Seliḥot are said on Fast Days. On Tisha B'Av, Kinot are said instead.
On the Fast of Gedalya, the Seliḥot for the Ten Days of Repentance are said.

SELIḤOT FOR THE TENTH OF TEVET

סְלַח לָנוּ Forgive us, our Father, for in our great foolishness we have blundered. Pardon us, our King, for our iniquities are many.

אֵל אֶרֶךְ You are a God slow to anger, You are called the Master of Compassion, and You have taught the way of repentance. May You remember today and every day the greatness of Your compassion and kindness, for the sake of the descendants of Your beloved ones. Turn toward us in compassion, for You are the Master of Compassion. We come before You in plea and prayer, as You in ancient times showed the humble one [Moses]. Turn from Your fierce anger, as is written in Your Torah. In the shadow of Your wings may we shelter and abide, as on the day when the LORD descended in the cloud. ‣ Overlook sin and wipe away guilt, as on the day when "He stood beside him there." Give ear to our pleading and listen to our speech, as on the day when "he called upon the name of the LORD," and in that place is said –

Congregation then Leader:

And the LORD passed by before him and proclaimed: Ex. 34

All say aloud:

יהוה The LORD, the LORD, compassionate and gracious God, slow to anger, abounding in loving-kindness and truth, extending loving-kindness to a thousand generations, forgiving iniquity, rebellion and sin, and absolving [the guilty who repent]. Forgive us our iniquity and our sin, and take us as Your inheritance.

Continue:

סְלַח לָנוּ Forgive us, our Father, for we have sinned. Pardon us, our King, for we have transgressed. For You, LORD, are good and forgiving, abounding in   Ps. 86 loving-kindness to all who call on You.

For with the LORD there is loving-kindness, and great is His power to redeem.   Ps. 130
LORD, save Israel from all its troubles. It is He who will redeem Israel from   Ps. 25
all its sins. The LORD redeems His servants; those who take refuge in Him   Ps. 130
shall not be condemned.   Ps. 34

סליחות

סליחות are said on Fast Days. On תשעה באב, קינות are said instead.
On צום גדליה, the סליחות for the עשרת ימי תשובה are said.

סליחות לעשרה בטבת

סְלַח לָנוּ, אָבִינוּ, כִּי בְּרֹב אִוַּלְתֵּנוּ שָׁגִינוּ.
מְחַל לָנוּ, מַלְכֵּנוּ, כִּי רַבּוּ עֲוֹנֵינוּ.

אֵל אֶרֶךְ אַפַּיִם אַתָּה, וּבַעַל הָרַחֲמִים נִקְרֵאתָ, וְדֶרֶךְ תְּשׁוּבָה הוֹרֵיתָ. גְּדֻלַּת
רַחֲמֶיךָ וַחֲסָדֶיךָ, תִּזְכֹּר הַיּוֹם וּבְכָל יוֹם לְזֶרַע יְדִידֶיךָ. תֵּפֶן אֵלֵינוּ בְּרַחֲמִים,
כִּי אַתָּה הוּא בַּעַל הָרַחֲמִים. בְּתַחֲנוּן וּבִתְפִלָּה פָּנֶיךָ נְקַדֵּם, כְּהוֹדַעְתָּ
לֶעָנָו מִקֶּדֶם. מֵחֲרוֹן אַפְּךָ שׁוּב, כְּמוֹ בְּתוֹרָתְךָ כָּתוּב. וּבְצֵל כְּנָפֶיךָ נֶחֱסֶה
וְנִתְלוֹנָן, כְּיוֹם וַיֵּרֶד יהוה בֶּעָנָן. ◄ תַּעֲבֹר עַל פֶּשַׁע וְתִמְחֶה אָשָׁם, כְּיוֹם
וַיִּתְיַצֵּב עִמּוֹ שָׁם. תַּאֲזִין שַׁוְעָתֵנוּ וְתַקְשִׁיב מֶנּוּ מַאֲמָר, כְּיוֹם וַיִּקְרָא בְשֵׁם
יהוה, וְשָׁם נֶאֱמַר:

שליח ציבור then קהל:

וַיַּעֲבֹר יהוה עַל־פָּנָיו וַיִּקְרָא

All say aloud:

יהוה, יהוה, אֵל רַחוּם וְחַנּוּן, אֶרֶךְ אַפַּיִם, וְרַב־חֶסֶד וֶאֱמֶת: נֹצֵר
חֶסֶד לָאֲלָפִים, נֹשֵׂא עָוֹן וָפֶשַׁע וְחַטָּאָה, וְנַקֵּה: וְסָלַחְתָּ לַעֲוֹנֵנוּ
וּלְחַטָּאתֵנוּ, וּנְחַלְתָּנוּ:

Continue:

תהלים פו

סְלַח לָנוּ אָבִינוּ כִּי חָטָאנוּ, מְחַל לָנוּ מַלְכֵּנוּ כִּי פָשָׁעְנוּ. כִּי־אַתָּה אֲדֹנָי טוֹב
וְסַלָּח, וְרַב־חֶסֶד לְכָל־קֹרְאֶיךָ:

תהלים קל
תהלים כה
תהלים קל
תהלים לד

כִּי־עִם־יהוה הַחֶסֶד, וְהַרְבֵּה עִמּוֹ פְדוּת: פָּדֵה אֱלֹהִים אֶת־יִשְׂרָאֵל מִכֹּל
צָרוֹתָיו: וְהוּא יִפְדֶּה אֶת־יִשְׂרָאֵל מִכֹּל עֲוֹנוֹתָיו: פֹּדֶה יהוה נֶפֶשׁ עֲבָדָיו,
וְלֹא יֶאְשְׁמוּ כָּל־הַחֹסִים בּוֹ:

כְּרַחֵם As a father has compassion for his children,
so, Lord, have compassion for us.
Salvation is the Lord's; on Your people is Your blessing, Selah! *Ps. 3*
The Lord of hosts is with us, the God of Jacob is our stronghold, Selah! *Ps. 46*
Lord of hosts, happy is the one who trusts in You. *Ps. 84*
Lord, save! May the King answer us on the day we call. *Ps. 20*

‣ Forgive, please, this people's iniquity, in the abundance of Your kindness, *Num. 14*
and as You have forgiven this people from the time of Egypt until now,
and there it is written:

Congregation then Leader:

And the Lord said, I have forgiven as you asked.

Continue:

הַטֵּה Give ear, my God and hear; open Your eyes and see our desolation, and the *Dan. 9*
city that bears Your name, for it is not on the strength of our righteousness that we
throw down our pleadings before You, but on the strength of Your great compassion. Lord, hear me; Lord, forgive; Lord, listen and act and do not delay – for
Your sake, my God; for Your city and Your people bear Your name.

Our God and God of our fathers:

אֶזְכְּרָה I shall recall the anguish that came to me; He inflicted three blows upon *Job 16*
me in this month. He cut me off, He veered me aside, He beat me – but now He
has finally drained me out. On the eighth of the month He darkened my right
and my left; I marked out all three days for fasting. The king of Greece forced
me to write the Torah in his tongue. The ploughmen have ploughed across my
back; they made the furrows long. I raged, on the ninth, in shame and disgrace,
my mantle of glory and my wreath were taken from me. The man who gave us
the words of Heaven was torn from us on that day – that was Ezra the Scribe. On
the tenth, Ezekiel the Seer, son of Buzi was commanded, "Write this happen-
ing in the scroll, for the remembrance of a people melted away and disgraced;
write this very day." The tenth was listed last among the fasts to show the order *Ezek. 24*
of the months. My own mouth gapes open with weeping and wailing, and this
chronicle of troubles burns within my heart – as the fugitive came to me and
said, "The city is crushed." For these things I have scattered dust upon my face.
I have spoken now of all four – would that I could shoot an arrow through my
heart. For these great torments, I have dug my own grave. "The Lord is righteous; *Lam. 1*
I have rebelled against His word." I have called out Your name as I grieve my
troubles. Witness my oppression and hear my voice in its entreaty. Hear my pleading, please, hasten my salvation. Do not block Your ears to my sighing, to my cry. *Lam. 3*
‣ In the month of Tevet I was stricken sorely. The world changed its course, from
where I stand. I was stubborn, I sinned – yet may He reveal His goodness to me;
the One who told the ocean, "Only thus far, come."

כְּרַחֵם אָב עַל בָּנִים, כֵּן תְּרַחֵם יהוה עָלֵינוּ.
תהלים ג לַיהוה הַיְשׁוּעָה, עַל־עַמְּךָ בִרְכָתֶךָ סֶּלָה:
תהלים מו יהוה צְבָאוֹת עִמָּנוּ, מִשְׂגָּב לָנוּ אֱלֹהֵי יַעֲקֹב סֶלָה:
תהלים פד יהוה צְבָאוֹת, אַשְׁרֵי אָדָם בֹּטֵחַ בָּךְ:
תהלים כ יהוה הוֹשִׁיעָה, הַמֶּלֶךְ יַעֲנֵנוּ בְיוֹם־קָרְאֵנוּ:

במדבר יד ‹ סְלַח־נָא לַעֲוֹן הָעָם הַזֶּה כְּגֹדֶל חַסְדֶּךָ
וְכַאֲשֶׁר נָשָׂאתָה לָעָם הַזֶּה מִמִּצְרַיִם וְעַד־הֵנָּה:
וְשָׁם נֶאֱמַר

קהל then שליח ציבור:

וַיֹּאמֶר יהוה, סָלַחְתִּי כִּדְבָרֶךָ:

Continue:

דניאל ט הַטֵּה אֱלֹהַי אָזְנְךָ וּשֲׁמָע, פְּקַח עֵינֶיךָ וּרְאֵה שֹׁמְמֹתֵינוּ וְהָעִיר אֲשֶׁר־נִקְרָא שִׁמְךָ
עָלֶיהָ, כִּי לֹא עַל־צִדְקֹתֵינוּ אֲנַחְנוּ מַפִּילִים תַּחֲנוּנֵינוּ לְפָנֶיךָ, כִּי עַל־רַחֲמֶיךָ
הָרַבִּים: אֲדֹנָי שְׁמָעָה, אֲדֹנָי סְלָחָה, אֲדֹנָי הַקְשִׁיבָה וַעֲשֵׂה אַל־תְּאַחַר, לְמַעַנְךָ
אֱלֹהַי, כִּי־שִׁמְךָ נִקְרָא עַל־עִירְךָ וְעַל־עַמֶּךָ:

אֱלֹהֵינוּ וֵאלֹהֵי אֲבוֹתֵינוּ

אֶזְכְּרָה מָצוֹק אֲשֶׁר קְרָאַנִי. בְּשָׁלֹשׁ מַכּוֹת בַּחֹדֶשׁ הַזֶּה הִכַּנִי. גְּדָעַנִי הֲנִיאַנִי
איוב טז הִכְאַנִי. אַךְ־עַתָּה הֶלְאָנִי: דְּעַכְנִי בִשְׁמוֹנָה בּוֹ שְׂמָאלִית וִימָנִית. הֲלֹא שְׁלָשְׁתָּן
קְבָעְתִּי תַעֲנִית. וּמֶלֶךְ יָוָן אֲנָסַנִי לִכְתֹּב דָּת, יְוָנִית. עַל גַּבַּי חָרְשׁוּ חוֹרְשִׁים,
הֶאֱרִיכוּ מַעֲנִית. זְעַמְתִּי בְּתִשְׁעָה בּוֹ בְּכִלְמָה וָחֵפֶר. חָשַׁךְ מֵעָלַי מְעִיל הוֹד
וָצֶפֶר. טָרֹף טֹרַף בּוֹ הַנּוֹתֵן אִמְרֵי שֶׁפֶר. הוּא עֶזְרָא הַסּוֹפֵר. יוֹם עֲשִׂירִי, צֻוָּה
בֶן בּוּזִי הַחֹזֶה. כְּתָב לְךָ בְּסֵפֶר הַמַּחֲזֶה. לִזְכְּרוֹן לְעָם נָמֵס וְנִבְזֶה. אֶת־עֶצֶם
יחזקאל כד הַיּוֹם הַזֶּה: מִנְּנִי סֵדֶר חֳדָשִׁים בַּעֲשָׂרָה בּוֹ הֻכְּתָה הָעִיר. נָהִי וָיְלֵל בְּמוֹ פִי אַפְעִיר.
סֵדֶר פֻּרְעָנוּת בְּתוֹךְ לְבָבִי יַבְעִיר. בְּבֹא אֵלַי הַפָּלִיט לֵאמֹר הֻכְּתָה הָעִיר. עַל
אֵלֶּה, עַל פְּנֵי אָבְךָ זֵרֵיתִי. פַּצְתִּי עַל אַרְבַּעְתָּן, לוּ חֵץ בִּלְבָבִי יָרֵיתִי. צָרוֹת עַל
איכה א אֵלֶּה, קֶבֶר לִי כְּרֵיתִי. צַדִּיק הוּא יהוה, כִּי פִיהוּ מָרֵיתִי: קָרָאתִי שִׁמְךָ, מִתְנַחֵם
עַל רָעָתִי. רְאֵה עָנְיִי וּשֲׁמַע קוֹל פְּגִיעָתִי. שְׁמַע תַּחֲנוּנִי, חִישׁ נָא יְשׁוּעָתִי.
איכה ג אַל־תִּתְעַלַּם אָזְנְךָ לְרַוְחָתִי לְשַׁוְעָתִי: ‹ יֶרַח טֵבֵת, מְאֹד לָקֵיתִי בוֹ. וְשֻׁתַּנּוּ
עָלַי סִדְרֵי נְתִיבוֹ. סָרַרְתִּי, פָּשַׁעְתִּי, יִגָּלֶה לִי טוּבוֹ. הָאוֹמֵר לַיָּם עַד פֹּה תָבוֹא.

אֵל מֶלֶךְ God, King who sits upon a throne of compassion, who acts with loving-kindness, who pardons the iniquities of His people, passing them before Him in order; who forgives sinners and pardons transgressors; who performs righteousness with all flesh and spirit, do not repay their bad actions in kind. ‣ God, You taught us to speak thirteen attributes: recall for us today the covenant of the thirteen attributes, as You in ancient times showed the humble one [Moses], as is written: The LORD descended in the cloud and stood with him there, and proclaimed in the name of the LORD: *Ex. 34*

Congregation then Leader:

And the LORD passed by before him and proclaimed: *Ex. 34*

All say aloud:

יהוה The LORD, the LORD, compassionate and gracious God, slow to anger, abounding in loving-kindness and truth, extending loving-kindness to a thousand generations, forgiving iniquity, rebellion and sin, and absolving [the guilty who repent]. Forgive us our iniquity and our sin, and take us as Your inheritance.

Continue:

סְלַח לָנוּ Forgive us, our Father, for we have sinned. Pardon us, our King, for we have transgressed. For You, LORD, are good and forgiving, abounding in loving-kindness to all who call on You. *Ps. 86*

God, nations came into Your inheritance, they made Your holy Sanctuary impure, they reduced Jerusalem to ruins. God, wanton people came up against us and a gang of oppressors sought out our lives, and did not place You before them. *Ps. 79*

כְּרַחֵם As a father has compassion for his children,
so, LORD, have compassion for us.

Salvation is the LORD's; on Your people is Your blessing, Selah! *Ps. 3*

The LORD of hosts is with us, the God of Jacob is our stronghold, Selah! *Ps. 46*

LORD of hosts, happy is the one who trusts in You. *Ps. 84*

LORD, save! May the King answer us on the day we call. *Ps. 20*

Our God and God of our fathers:

אֶבֶן הָרֹאשָׁה The Temple, Top Stone, is laid to ruin and ploughed over, and the Torah's heirs, Israel, a derision among nations. Within me an aching heart, sickened and pained – we are left as if fatherless, become like orphans. Israel, delicate and refined, fenced by lilies of the Law, has now become mournful, given over to assailants. The faithful city has become like a widow, the countless

אֵל מֶלֶךְ יוֹשֵׁב עַל כִּסֵּא רַחֲמִים, מִתְנַהֵג בַּחֲסִידוּת. מוֹחֵל עֲוֹנוֹת עַמּוֹ, מַעֲבִיר רִאשׁוֹן רִאשׁוֹן. מַרְבֶּה מְחִילָה לַחַטָּאִים, וּסְלִיחָה לַפּוֹשְׁעִים. עֹשֶׂה צְדָקוֹת עִם כָּל בָּשָׂר וָרוּחַ, לֹא כְרָעָתָם תִּגְמֹל. ⟩ אֵל, הוֹרֵיתָ לָּנוּ לוֹמַר שְׁלֹשׁ עֶשְׂרֵה, וּזְכָר לָנוּ הַיּוֹם בְּרִית שְׁלֹשׁ עֶשְׂרֵה, כְּמוֹ שֶׁהוֹדַעְתָּ לֶעָנָו מִקֶּדֶם, כְּמוֹ שֶׁכָּתוּב: וַיֵּרֶד יהוה בֶּעָנָן, וַיִּתְיַצֵּב עִמּוֹ שָׁם, וַיִּקְרָא בְשֵׁם, יהוה:

שמות לד

שליח ציבור then קהל:

וַיַּעֲבֹר יהוה עַל־פָּנָיו וַיִּקְרָא

שמות לד

All say aloud:

יהוה, יהוה, אֵל רַחוּם וְחַנּוּן, אֶרֶךְ אַפַּיִם, וְרַב־חֶסֶד וֶאֱמֶת: נֹצֵר חֶסֶד לָאֲלָפִים, נֹשֵׂא עָוֹן וָפֶשַׁע וְחַטָּאָה, וְנַקֵּה: וְסָלַחְתָּ לַעֲוֹנֵנוּ וּלְחַטָּאתֵנוּ, וּנְחַלְתָּנוּ:

Continue:

תהלים פו

סְלַח לָנוּ אָבִינוּ כִּי חָטָאנוּ, מְחַל לָנוּ מַלְכֵּנוּ כִּי פָשָׁעְנוּ. כִּי־אַתָּה אֲדֹנָי טוֹב וְסַלָּח, וְרַב־חֶסֶד לְכָל־קֹרְאֶיךָ:

תהלים עט

אֱלֹהִים בָּאוּ גוֹיִם בְּנַחֲלָתֶךָ, טִמְּאוּ אֶת־הֵיכַל קָדְשֶׁךָ, שָׂמוּ אֶת־יְרוּשָׁלַ͏ִם לְעִיִּים: אֱלֹהִים, זֵדִים קָמוּ עָלֵינוּ, וַעֲדַת עָרִיצִים בִּקְשׁוּ נַפְשֵׁנוּ, וְלֹא שָׂמוּךָ לְנֶגְדָּם.

כְּרַחֵם אָב עַל בָּנִים, כֵּן תְּרַחֵם יהוה עָלֵינוּ.

תהלים ג

לַיהוה הַיְשׁוּעָה, עַל־עַמְּךָ בִרְכָתֶךָ סֶּלָה:

תהלים מו

יהוה צְבָאוֹת עִמָּנוּ, מִשְׂגָּב לָנוּ אֱלֹהֵי יַעֲקֹב סֶלָה:

תהלים פד

יהוה צְבָאוֹת, אַשְׁרֵי אָדָם בֹּטֵחַ בָּךְ:

תהלים כ

יהוה הוֹשִׁיעָה, הַמֶּלֶךְ יַעֲנֵנוּ בְיוֹם־קָרְאֵנוּ:

אֱלֹהֵינוּ וֵאלֹהֵי אֲבוֹתֵינוּ

אֶבֶן הָרֹאשָׁה, לְעִיִּים וְלַחֲרִישָׁה, וְנוֹחֲלֵי מוֹרָשָׁה, מָנוֹד רֹאשׁ בַּלְאֻמִּים. בְּקָרְבִּי לֵב נִכְאָב, נְדַוֶּה וְנִדְאָב, נִשְׁאַרְנוּ כְּאֵין אָב, וְהָיִינוּ כִּיתוֹמִים. רַכָּה וְעֻנֻגָה, בַּשׁוֹשַׁנִּים סוּגָה, וְעַתָּה הִיא נוּגָה, מְסוּרָה בְּיַד קָמִים. דִּינְתָּה

descendants of Jacob have been sold for no price. Refined and delicate, worthy of royalty, they have been ploughed across in long furrows over many years and days. The house of Jacob is given over to plunder, to jeering and slander, and the joyous city to plantations of vines. Doused in poison by lawless ones, is the people once desired like offerings, like fragrant incense. They have despised and neglected the Torah of Moses Avi-Zanoaḥ, they can find no rest by night or by day. Awesome, highest God, may the desire arise in You to bring a year of recompense for Israel's strife. Renew our days as of old, Dwelling Place who is our God of old. And wash our red guilt white as wool; our stains as snow.
‣ Strengthen us in awe of You, and in the keeping of Your Law. And come to us, in Your salvation, God who is full of compassion.

אֵל מֶלֶךְ God, King who sits upon a throne of compassion, who acts with loving-kindness, who pardons the iniquities of His people, passing them before Him in order; who forgives sinners and pardons transgressors; who performs righteousness with all flesh and spirit, do not repay their bad actions in kind. ‣ God, You taught us to speak thirteen attributes: recall for us today the covenant of the thirteen attributes, as You in ancient times showed the humble one [Moses], as is written: The Lord descended in the cloud and stood with him there, and   *Ex. 34* proclaimed in the name of the Lord:

Congregation then Leader:
And the Lord passed by before him and proclaimed: *Ex. 34*

All say aloud:
יהוה The Lord, the Lord, compassionate and gracious God, slow to anger, abounding in loving-kindness and truth, extending loving-kindness to a thousand generations, forgiving iniquity, rebellion and sin, and absolving [the guilty who repent]. Forgive us our iniquity and our sin, and take us as Your inheritance.

Continue:
סְלַח לָנוּ Forgive us, our Father, for we have sinned. Pardon us, our King, for we have transgressed. For You, Lord, are good and forgiving, abounding in   *Ps. 86* loving-kindness to all who call on You.

The following is said responsively:
אֲבוֹתַי When my forebears trusted in the name of God, my Rock, they grew and were successful and also gave forth fruit.
And from the time when they were drawn away to walk with Him in enmity, they diminished and diminished until the tenth month.   *Gen. 8*

כְּאַלְמָנָה, קִרְיָה נֶאֱמָנָה, וְזֶרַע מִי מָנָה, נִמְכְּרוּ בְּלֹא דָמִים. מְעֻנָּגָה וְרַכָּה, צָלְחָה לַמְּלוּכָה, וּמַעֲנִיתָה אֲרֻכָּה, זֶה כַּמָּה שָׁנִים וְיָמִים. בֵּית יַעֲקֹב לְבִזָּה, לְלַעַג וּלְעִזָּה, וְהָעִיר הָעַלִּיזָה, לְמַטְּעֵי כְרָמִים. רְוּיָה תַרְעֵלָה, בְּיַד בְּנֵי עוֹלָה, הָרְצוּצָה כְעוֹלָה, וְכִקְטֹרֶת הַסַּמִּים. מָאֲסָה לְנֹחַ, תּוֹרַת אָבִי זָנוֹחַ, וְלֹא מָצְאָה מָנוֹחַ, לֵילוֹת וְגַם יָמִים. נוֹרָא אֵל עֶלְיוֹן, מִמְּךָ יְהִי צִבְיוֹן, לְהָשִׁיב לְרִיב צִיּוֹן, שְׁנַת שִׁלּוּמִים. חַדֵּשׁ יָמֵינוּ כְּקֶדֶם, מְעוֹנָה אֱלֹהֵי קֶדֶם, וְלַבֵּן כְּצֶמֶר אָדָם, וְכַשֶּׁלֶג כְּתָמִים. ◂ חַזְּקֵנוּ בְּיִרְאָתֶךָ, וּבְקִיּוּם תּוֹרָתֶךָ, וּפָקְדֵנוּ בִּישׁוּעָתֶךָ, אֵל מְלֵא רַחֲמִים.

אֵל מֶלֶךְ יוֹשֵׁב עַל כִּסֵּא רַחֲמִים, מִתְנַהֵג בַּחֲסִידוּת. מוֹחֵל עֲוֹנוֹת עַמּוֹ, מַעֲבִיר רִאשׁוֹן רִאשׁוֹן. מַרְבֶּה מְחִילָה לַחַטָּאִים, וּסְלִיחָה לַפּוֹשְׁעִים. עֹשֶׂה צְדָקוֹת עִם כָּל בָּשָׂר וָרוּחַ, לֹא כְרָעָתָם תִּגְמֹל. ◂ אֵל, הוֹרֵיתָ לָּנוּ לוֹמַר שְׁלֹשׁ עֶשְׂרֵה, וּזְכֹר לָנוּ הַיּוֹם בְּרִית שְׁלֹשׁ עֶשְׂרֵה, כְּמוֹ שֶׁהוֹדַעְתָּ לֶעָנָו מִקֶּדֶם, כְּמוֹ שֶׁכָּתוּב: וַיֵּרֶד יהוה בֶּעָנָן, וַיִּתְיַצֵּב עִמּוֹ שָׁם, וַיִּקְרָא בְשֵׁם, יהוה: שמות לד

שליח ציבור then קהל

וַיַּעֲבֹר יהוה עַל פָּנָיו וַיִּקְרָא:
שמות לד

All say aloud:

יהוה, יהוה, אֵל רַחוּם וְחַנּוּן, אֶרֶךְ אַפַּיִם, וְרַב־חֶסֶד וֶאֱמֶת: נֹצֵר חֶסֶד לָאֲלָפִים, נֹשֵׂא עָוֹן וָפֶשַׁע וְחַטָּאָה, וְנַקֵּה: וְסָלַחְתָּ לַעֲוֹנֵנוּ וּלְחַטָּאתֵנוּ, וּנְחַלְתָּנוּ:

Continue:

סְלַח לָנוּ אָבִינוּ כִּי חָטָאנוּ, מְחַל לָנוּ מַלְכֵּנוּ כִּי פָשָׁעְנוּ. כִּי־אַתָּה אֲדֹנָי טוֹב וְסַלָּח, וְרַב־חֶסֶד לְכָל־קֹרְאֶיךָ:   תהלים פו

The following is said responsively:

אֲבוֹתַי כִּי בָטְחוּ בְּשֵׁם אֱלֹהֵי צוּרִי
גָּדְלוּ וְהִצְלִיחוּ וְגַם עָשׂוּ פֶרִי
וּמֵעֵת הֻדְּחוּ וְהָלְכוּ עִמּוֹ קֶרִי
הָיוּ הָלוֹךְ וְחָסוֹר עַד הַחֹדֶשׁ הָעֲשִׂירִי.
בראשית ח

On the tenth, the king of Babylon laid siege on the city,
and beleaguered it. The chief of the army arrived,
and I was yielded to be trampled,
was tormented in fetters,
and from month to month my harp turned to grief.

Once like the first figs of a new tree,
they were the very first to be destroyed.
They spoke the names of others,
and sin closed their destiny.
They did not recognize God's face and were swept off by the flood –
agony like that of a first childbirth, soars up as high as Heaven.

God brought us a day of evil and siege,
ordered enemies about me to harvest my last fruits.
The day my heart was quelled, no strength to resist,
and He said to the prophet,
"Preach this to the rebellious house."

He took the cloak of authority from the judges at the gate.
His rage burned like fire
and He raised the crown away,
and He cast down the splendor of the Temple, Forest of Lebanon,
and rushing wind and storm make my flesh bristle and shiver.

Once you were called most beautiful;
now you are darkened,
for you have stumbled over iniquity
and your heart has turned back.
You have been attacked from behind,
have been weakened, once, then twice,
and even the slightest dressing or balm not offered you.

The Righteous One, perfect Rock,
who forgives iniquity almost too great to bear,
flew from the cherubs to the threshold,
and from there to a corner of the roof,
because of the iniquity marked out; the scream of it rose up,
their evil as abundant as a fruit-tree's crop.

בָּעֲשִׂירִי לַחֹדֶשׁ סָמַךְ מֶלֶךְ בָּבֶל
וְצָר עַל עִיר הַקֹּדֶשׁ, וְנִקְרַב רַב הַחוֹבֵל
נָתַתִּי הָדֵשׁ וְעִנִּיתִי בַכֶּבֶל
וְהָיָה מִדֵּי חֹדֶשׁ לָאֵבֶל כִּנּוֹרִי.

רֵאשִׁית בִּכּוּרָה לְרֵאשִׁית הַחֵרֶם
שֵׁם אֲחֵרִים הִזְכִּירָה, וְהֶעָוֹן גּוֹרֵם
פְּנֵי אֵל לֹא הִכִּירָה, וְשָׁטְפָה בְזֶרֶם
צָרָה כְּמַבְכִּירָה כְּעֵת בַּמָּרוֹם תַּמְרִיא.

הָאֱלֹהִים הֵבִיא יוֹם רָעָה וּמָצוֹר
צִוָּה צָרֵי סְבִיבִי עוֹלְלֵי לִבְצֹר
יוֹם הֵרַךְ לְבָבִי וְאֵין כֹּחַ לַעֲצֹר
וַדַּבֵּר אֶל נָבִיא, מְשֹׁל אֶל בֵּית הַמֶּרִי.

מִיּוֹשְׁבֵי שַׁעַר הֶעֱבִיר אַדֶּרֶת
חֲמָתוֹ כָּאֵשׁ בָּעַר, וְהָרִים עָטֶרֶת
וּמִלְּבָנוֹן יַעַר הִשְׁלִיךְ תִּפְאֶרֶת
וְרוּחַ סוֹעָה וָסַעַר תְּסַמֵּר שַׂעֲרַת בְּשָׂרִי.

יָפְיָפִית נִמְשַׁלְתְּ, וְעַתָּה קַדְוֹרַנִּית
בְּעָוֹן כִּי כָשַׁלְתְּ, וְלִבֵּךְ אֲחוֹרַנִּית
זְנַבוּךְ וְנֶחְשַׁלְתְּ רִאשׁוֹנָה וּשְׁנִית
וְהָחֵל לֹא חָדַלְתְּ מְעַט צָרִי.

צַדִּיק הַצּוּר תָּם, נָשָׂא עָוֹן נִלְאָה
מִכְּרוּב לְמַפְּתָן, לְפִנַּת גַּג דָּאָה
מֵעָוֹן הֻנְבַּתֶּם, וְצַעֲקַתְכֶם בָּאָה
רַבָּה רָעַתְכֶם כְּעֵץ עֹשֶׂה פֶּרִי.

The One who weighs the actions of people,
 strengthened all my attackers,
 for my days had been filled with malignant deeds,
 and in the shamefulness of my youth
 I forgot the good granted me,
 and the One who gives me my bread and water,
 my flax and my wool.

My attackers opened wide their mouths and swallowed up my legacy.
They overcame me utterly, drank my blood and gulped it down.
Strangers became my enemies, they injured my brothers –
strangers who called out, "Destroy, destroy!"
Descendants of Seir the Horite.

 They said, "Come, let us finish them off,
 and put an end to their memory."
 Jealous, vengeful God, grant retribution;
 let them load the burden of their own ruin.
 Pay them back for their actions
 and have their hopes disgrace them,
 like the baker who dreamt his dream
 of three baskets of white bread.

My wound was not softened, my bruise enough to kill me,
and my eyes have grown dim with watching for my bright-faced Love.
Is His anger even now not forever forgotten?
Why has He done this; why this burning rage?

 This God of mine is compassionate; He shall not forever reject.
 The days of my grief have grown long and still my heart sighs.
 Return, God, to my tent; do not abandon Your place.
 Close the days of my grief. Bring my recompense.

LORD who is the portion allotted me,
come to me quickly, help me,
and loosen my sackcloth,
wrap me around in joy,
and dazzle my darkness with Your light – light up
the twilight I once longed for, for it is You who are my lamp.

חַזֵּק כָּל קָמַי, תּוֹכֵן הָעֲלִילוֹת
כִּי מָלְאוּ יָמַי בְּרֹעַ מִפְעָלוֹת
וּמִבֹּשֶׁת עֲלוּמַי שָׁכַחְתִּי גְמוּלוֹת
נוֹתֵן לַחְמִי וּמֵימַי, פִּשְׁתִּי וְצַמְרִי.

קָמַי פִּיהֶם פָּעֲרוּ וְנַחֲלָתִי בִּלְּעוּ
מְאֹד עָלַי גָּבְרוּ וְדָמִי שָׁתוּ וְלָעוּ
נָכְרִים עָלַי צָרוּ וְאֶת אַחַי הֵרֵעוּ
הָאוֹמְרִים עָרוּ עָרוּ, בְּנֵי שֵׂעִיר הַחֹרִי.

אָמְרוּ לְכוּ נְכַלֵּם, וְנַשְׁבִּיתָה זִכְרָם
אֵל קַנּוֹא וְנוֹקֵם, גָּמְלֵם, יִשְׂאוּ אֶת שִׁבְרָם
כְּמַעֲשֵׂיהֶם שַׁלֵּם וְיֵבוֹשׁוּ מִשִּׁבְרָם
כְּאִישׁ חֲלוֹם חוֹלֵם שְׁלֹשָׁה סַלֵּי חֹרִי.

פְּצָעַי לֹא רֻכְּכָה וְחַבּוּרוֹתַי רֶצַח
וְעֵינַי הֻכְהֲתָה, צוֹפָה לְדוֹדִי צַח
הַעוֹד לֹא שָׁכְכָה חֲמָתוֹ לָנֶצַח
עַל מֶה עָשָׂה כָּכָה וּמֶה חֳרִי.

רַחוּם זֶה אֵלִי, אַל לָעַד תִּזְנַח
אָרְכוּ יְמֵי אֶבְלִי וְעוֹד לִבִּי נֶאֱנָח
שׁוּבָה אֶל לְאָהֳלִי, מִקּוֹמְךָ אֶל תַּנַּח
שַׁלֵּם יְמֵי אֶבְלִי כִּי תָבוֹא עַל שְׂכָרִי.

יהוה מְנָת חֶלְקִי, חוּשָׁה לִי לְעֶזְרָה
וּפִתַּחְתָּ שַׂקִּי, שִׂמְחָה לִי לְאֶזְרָה
וְתַגִּיהַּ אֶת חָשְׁכִּי בְּאוֹרְךָ לְהָאִירָה
אֶת נֵשֶׁף חִשְׁקִי, כִּי אַתָּה נֵרִי.

Redeem my soul from anguish and sighing,
grant Your people remission, my King and my Holy One.
And turn into relief the fast of Av;
into gladness and joy, the fast of Tammuz and the fast of Tevet.

Continue with "God, King who sits" on page 500.

SELIHOT FOR THE FAST OF ESTHER

סְלַח לָנוּ Forgive us, our Father, for in our great foolishness we have blundered. Pardon us, our King, for our iniquities are many.

אֵל אֶרֶךְ You are a God slow to anger, You are called the Master of Compassion, and You have taught the way of repentance. May You remember today and every day the greatness of Your compassion and kindness, for the sake of the descendants of Your beloved ones. Turn toward us in compassion, for You are the Master of Compassion. We come before You in plea and prayer, as You in ancient times showed the humble one [Moses]. Turn from Your fierce anger, as is written in Your Torah. In the shadow of Your wings may we shelter and abide, as on the day when the LORD descended in the cloud. ▸ Disregard transgression and erase guilt as on the day You stood with him [Moses] there. Hear our cry and heed our word, as on the day You proclaimed in the name of the LORD, and there it is written:

Congregation then Leader:

And the LORD passed by before him and proclaimed: *Ex. 34*

All say aloud:

יהוה The LORD, the LORD, compassionate and gracious God, slow to anger, abounding in loving-kindness and truth, extending loving-kindness to a thousand generations, forgiving iniquity, rebellion and sin, and absolving [the guilty who repent]. Forgive us our iniquity and our sin, and take us as Your inheritance.

Continue:

סְלַח לָנוּ Forgive us, our Father, for we have sinned. Pardon us, our King, for we have transgressed. For You, LORD, are good and forgiving, abounding in   *Ps. 86* loving-kindness to all who call on You.

מִיָּגוֹן וַאֲנָחָה, פְּדֵה אֵל אֶת נַפְשִׁי
עֲשֵׂה לְעַמְּךָ הַנָּחָה, מַלְכִּי וּקְדוֹשִׁי
תַּהֲפוֹךְ לִרְוָחָה אֶת צוֹם הַחֲמִישִׁי
לְשָׂשׂוֹן וּלְשִׂמְחָה, צוֹם הָרְבִיעִי וְצוֹם הָעֲשִׂירִי.

Continue with אֵל מֶלֶךְ יוֹשֵׁב on page 501.

סליחות לתענית אסתר

סְלַח לָנוּ, אָבִינוּ, כִּי בְרֹב אִוַּלְתֵּנוּ שָׁגִינוּ.
מְחַל לָנוּ, מַלְכֵּנוּ, כִּי רַבּוּ עֲוֹנֵינוּ.

אֵל אֶרֶךְ אַפַּיִם אַתָּה, וּבַעַל הָרַחֲמִים נִקְרֵאתָ, וְדֶרֶךְ תְּשׁוּבָה הוֹרֵיתָ. גְּדֻלַּת
רַחֲמֶיךָ וַחֲסָדֶיךָ, תִּזְכֹּר הַיּוֹם וּבְכָל יוֹם לְזֶרַע יְדִידֶיךָ. תֵּפֶן אֵלֵינוּ בְּרַחֲמִים,
כִּי אַתָּה הוּא בַּעַל הָרַחֲמִים. בְּתַחֲנוּן וּבִתְפִלָּה פָּנֶיךָ נְקַדֵּם, כְּהוֹדַעְתָּ
לֶעָנָו מִקֶּדֶם. מֵחֲרוֹן אַפְּךָ שׁוּב, כְּמוֹ בְּתוֹרָתְךָ כָּתוּב. וּבְצֵל כְּנָפֶיךָ נֶחֱסֶה
וְנִתְלוֹנָן, כְּיוֹם וַיֵּרֶד יהוה בֶּעָנָן. ‣ תַּעֲבֹר עַל פֶּשַׁע וְתִמְחֶה אָשָׁם, כְּיוֹם
וַיִּתְיַצֵּב עִמּוֹ שָׁם. תַּאֲזִין שַׁוְעָתֵנוּ וְתַקְשִׁיב מֶנּוּ מַאֲמָר, כְּיוֹם וַיִּקְרָא בְשֵׁם
יהוה, וְשָׁם נֶאֱמַר

שְׁלִיחַ צִבּוּר then קָהָל:

שמות לד

וַיַּעֲבֹר יהוה עַל־פָּנָיו וַיִּקְרָא

All say aloud:

יהוה, יהוה, אֵל רַחוּם וְחַנּוּן, אֶרֶךְ אַפַּיִם, וְרַב־חֶסֶד וֶאֱמֶת: נֹצֵר
חֶסֶד לָאֲלָפִים, נֹשֵׂא עָוֹן וָפֶשַׁע וְחַטָּאָה, וְנַקֵּה: וְסָלַחְתָּ לַעֲוֹנֵנוּ
וּלְחַטָּאתֵנוּ, וּנְחַלְתָּנוּ:

Continue:

תהלים פו

סְלַח לָנוּ אָבִינוּ כִּי חָטָאנוּ, מְחַל לָנוּ מַלְכֵּנוּ כִּי פָשָׁעְנוּ. כִּי־אַתָּה אֲדֹנָי טוֹב
וְסַלָּח, וְרַב־חֶסֶד לְכָל־קֹרְאֶיךָ:

We have waited patiently for the Lord, and He has turned toward us and heard *Is. 26*
our cry. And on the path of Your laws, Lord, we have waited for You, for it is
Your name and Your memory that are our souls' desire.

כְּרַחֵם As a father has compassion for his children,
so, Lord, have compassion for us.
Salvation is the Lord's; on Your people is Your blessing, Selah! *Ps. 3*
The Lord of hosts is with us, the God of Jacob is our stronghold, Selah! *Ps. 46*
Lord of hosts, happy is the one who trusts in You. *Ps. 84*
Lord, save! May the King answer us on the day we call. *Ps. 20*

‣ Forgive, please, this people's iniquity, in the abundance of Your kindness, *Num. 14*
   and as You have forgiven this people from the time of Egypt until now,
   and there it is written:

Congregation then Leader:
And the Lord said, I have forgiven as you asked.

Continue:

הַטֵּה Give ear, my God and hear; open Your eyes and see our desolation, and the *Dan. 9*
city that bears Your name, for it is not on the strength of our righteousness that we
throw down our pleadings before You, but on the strength of Your great compassion. Lord, hear me; Lord, forgive, Lord, listen and act and do not delay – for
Your sake, my God; for Your city and Your people bear Your name.

Our God and God of our fathers:

אָדָם When a man rose up against us, convulsions of trembling seized us. When he
attached himself to a government of flattery, we almost stumbled and fell. They cheer-
fully closed an agreement to sell us, as a person with an unwanted mound gives it away
quite freely to one with an unwanted pit. There was no defense. They said, "Come, let *Ps. 83*
us annihilate them from among nations: the name of Israel shall be recalled no more."
My eyes turned heavenward and I called on You to curse my enemies: "Cut off name
and remnant; expunge their name, let it rot. And be Enemy to my enemies; bring
them down in the very deceptions with which they deceived the people of Jacob."
And they said, "The Lord will not see; the God of Jacob will not comprehend." Yet *Ps. 94*
God tormented the scattered ones and made them mournful – but did not mean to
destroy them utterly. They were guilty on the face of things, and so He terrorized
them. By the taking off of a ring, He made them tremble. But God fulfilled the good
of His word, raising them up in the view of nations. "In their enemies' land He did *Lev. 26*
not reject them, and did not detest them to the point of destruction." He revealed the
premonition of events for a nation begrimed and scratched over. He wrote "I shall
surely hide (*astir*) Myself" to hint at Esther, and fragrant "pure myrrh," translated
"mar-dokh," to hint at Mordekhai; all to put an end to Haman on the morrow, "From
(*hamin*) the tree" foreshadowing his gallows. "In place of the thorn bush, shall rise *Is. 55*

קַוֵּה קִוִּינוּ יהוה, וַיֵּט אֵלֵינוּ וַיִּשְׁמַע שַׁוְעָתֵנוּ. אַף אֹרַח מִשְׁפָּטֶיךָ יהוה   ישעיה כו
קִוִּינוּךָ, לְשִׁמְךָ וּלְזִכְרְךָ תַּאֲוַת־נָפֶשׁ:

כְּרַחֵם אָב עַל בָּנִים, כֵּן תְּרַחֵם יהוה עָלֵינוּ.
לַיהוה הַיְשׁוּעָה, עַל־עַמְּךָ בִרְכָתֶךָ סֶּלָה: תהלים ג
יהוה צְבָאוֹת עִמָּנוּ, מִשְׂגָּב לָנוּ אֱלֹהֵי יַעֲקֹב סֶלָה: תהלים מו
יהוה צְבָאוֹת, אַשְׁרֵי אָדָם בֹּטֵחַ בָּךְ:   תהלים פד
יהוה הוֹשִׁיעָה, הַמֶּלֶךְ יַעֲנֵנוּ בְיוֹם־קָרְאֵנוּ:   תהלים כ

‹ סְלַח־נָא לַעֲוֹן הָעָם הַזֶּה כְּגֹדֶל חַסְדֶּךָ   במדבר יד
וְכַאֲשֶׁר נָשָׂאתָה לָעָם הַזֶּה מִמִּצְרַיִם וְעַד־הֵנָּה
וְשָׁם נֶאֱמַר

שליח ציבור then קהל:
וַיֹּאמֶר יהוה, סָלַחְתִּי כִּדְבָרֶךָ:

Continue:

הַטֵּה אֱלֹהַי אָזְנְךָ וּשֲׁמָע, פְּקַח עֵינֶיךָ וּרְאֵה שֹׁמְמֹתֵינוּ וְהָעִיר אֲשֶׁר־נִקְרָא   דניאל ט
שִׁמְךָ עָלֶיהָ, כִּי לֹא עַל־צִדְקֹתֵינוּ אֲנַחְנוּ מַפִּילִים תַּחֲנוּנֵינוּ לְפָנֶיךָ, כִּי עַל־
רַחֲמֶיךָ הָרַבִּים: אֲדֹנָי שְׁמָעָה, אֲדֹנָי סְלָחָה, אֲדֹנָי הַקְשִׁיבָה וַעֲשֵׂה אַל־
תְּאַחַר, לְמַעַנְךָ אֱלֹהַי, כִּי־שִׁמְךָ נִקְרָא עַל־עִירְךָ וְעַל־עַמֶּךָ:

אֱלֹהֵינוּ וֵאלֹהֵי אֲבוֹתֵינוּ

אָדָם בָּקוּם עָלֵינוּ, חֵיל אֲחָזַתְנוּ לָרַעַד. בְּהִסְתַּפְּחוֹ לְמַלְכוּת חָנֵף, כִּמְעַט
כָּשַׁלְנוּ לְמֵעַד. גָּמְרוּ לְמָכְרֵנוּ כְּהֵל חֲרִיץ וְחָרוּץ בְּלִי מִסְעָד. אָמְרוּ לְכוּ וְנַכְחִידֵם   תהלים פג
מִגּוֹי, וְלֹא־יִזָּכֵר שֵׁם־יִשְׂרָאֵל עוֹד: דִּלּוּ עֵינֵי לַמָּרוֹם, קְרָאתֶיךָ אוֹיְבֵי לָקֹב.
הֶכְרֵת שֵׁם וּשְׁאָר, וּמְחֵה שֵׁם לְרִקֹב. וְצֹר צוֹרְרֵי בְּנִכְלֵיהֶם אֲשֶׁר נִכְלוּ
לַעֲקֹב. וַיֹּאמְרוּ, לֹא יִרְאֶה־יָּהּ, וְלֹא־יָבִין אֱלֹהֵי יַעֲקֹב: זְרוּיִים עָנֹה עָנָּה וַיִּגָּה,   תהלים צד
וְלֹא מָלֵב לְכֻלּוּתָם. חָוּוּ לְפָנֶיךָ, וְרָדֵם בַּהֲסָרַת טַבַּעַת לְהַחֲלוֹתָם. טוֹב
דִּבְּרוּ הָקִם לְעֵינֵי הַגּוֹיִם לְהַעֲלוֹתָם. בְּאֶרֶץ אוֹיְבֵיהֶם לֹא־מְאַסְתִּים וְלֹא־   ויקרא כו

up a cypress, and in place of the nettle, shall rise up myrtle." The king who listened
to lies, dictated accusation and sorrow. He wrapped himself in priestly clothes, Aha-
suerus, having mistaken his reckoning of the End. He ordered "other vessels" to be
used, from the Quarry from which the world was hewn; and the devil too, came and   *Job 2*
placed himself among them. When the people in Shushan ate of their destroyer's
meat, the king opened his mouth wide to accuse them, to give them over into the
hands of the one who was ready to pay their price. The Rock, meanwhile, agreed
to write a letter to destroy their hope; "I said that I would yield them up, would put   *Deut. 32*
an end to their memory among mankind." The angels, messengers of peace, wept
bitterly, crying out, "Compassionate One, look to the covenant and do not break it,
pushing it away!" The Torah, too, heard of it and put on clothes of widowhood and
sorrow; and she laid her hands upon her head and walked along, crying as she went.   *II Sam. 13*
[Elijah] The Tishbite wrapped a covering of sackcloth around his waist. He hurried
and told the three fathers who sleep in the Cave of Makhpelah, and then hastened to
the Shepherd, [Moses] – "What do you mean by sleeping? Rouse yourself! Get up   *Jonah 1*
and call out to your God – perhaps He may change His mind!" He told [Mordekhai]
Bilshan of the pronouncement that had been sealed in clay – but not in blood. They
learnt from the example of Nineveh how to overturn anger after a decree; the son
of Kish knocked at the door of the school, and covered himself in sackcloth and sat   *Jonah 3*
down on the earth. For three days he gathered the children before him – thirsty, hidden from God – so that, in the voice of Jacob, they might weaken the hand of the
bold-faced king. His hands raised steadily to God, Mordekhai prayed, "Save us now
from insult; that he should not come and slaughter us, mothers and children together."   *Gen. 32*
Those and those, from all sides, the children of my mighty ones and teachers, all cried
out, and their plea rose up to the LORD. And God, when those plaintive calls reached
Him, asked, "And what is this bleating of sheep that meets My ears?" The shepherd   *I Sam. 15*
Moses answered Him, "These are the little ones of the holy offspring. LORD, save
ones condemned to die, from the evil enemy." The compassion of the Gracious One
was stirred, and He was moved to weep for what had happened. And so it was that   *II Kings 5*
when the King of Israel read the letter, He tore it to pieces. The Jew suspended sons
below and father above. Each man covered three *amot*; the fourth *amah* above was
space exposed. Mordekhai saw a double revenge, was delighted, and spoke praises:
"I was returned to my post and he was hanged!" Esther wrote with emphasis, that   *Gen. 41*
a Hallel of thanks should be read on that day; and what the beloved ones accepted
down below was established above. A banner shall be raised by those who bear witness, to make the wonder known now, as it was then. And at this time – may relief   *Esther 4*
and salvation rise up for the Jews.

אֵל מֶלֶךְ God, King who sits upon a throne of compassion, who acts with loving-kindness, who pardons the iniquities of His people, passing them before Him in order;
who forgives sinners and pardons transgressors; who performs righteousness with

גְּעַלְתִּים לְכַלֹּתָם: יָדַע רֶמֶז הַקּוֹרוֹת לְעָם מְעָפָּר וּמֶהָדָּס. כְּתָב הַסֵּתֶר
אַסְתִּיר וּמָר דְּרוֹר מְפֹרָדֵס. לְשַׁבֵּת הָמָן מִמַּחְרַת, הָמָן הָעֵץ קָנֶדֶס. תַּחַת
הַנַּעֲצוּץ יַעֲלֶה בְרוֹשׁ וְתַחַת הַסִּרְפָּד יַעֲלֶה הֲדַס: מַקְשִׁיב דְּבַר שֶׁקֶר כָּתָב
שְׁנָתָה וְעֵצֶב. נִתְעַטֵּף בְּבִגְדֵי שָׂרָד כְּטַעַם בְּמִנְיָן קֶצֶב. סָדַר לְהִשְׁתַּמֵּשׁ
בְּשׁוֹנִים כְּלֵי הַמַּחֲצָב. וַיָּבוֹא גַם הַשָּׂטָן בְּתֹכָם לְהִתְיַצֵּב: עַם הַנִּמְצָאִים
בְּשׁוּשָׁן, בְּאָכְלָם מִזְבַּח עוֹכְרָם. פָּעַר פִּיו לְהַשְׁטִינָם, וּלְהַסְגִּירָם בְּיַד
נוֹתֵן מִכְרָם. צַוּוּ הַסְּכִים לִכְתֹּב אִגֶּרֶת לְאַבֵּד שְׁבָרָם. אָמַרְתִּי אַפְאֵיהֶם,
אַשְׁבִּיתָה מֵאֱנוֹשׁ זִכְרָם: קְדוֹשִׁים מַלְאֲכֵי שָׁלוֹם מַר יִבְכָּיוּן בִּצְעָקָה.
רַחוּם הַבֵּט לַבְּרִית וְאַל תָּפֵר לְהָרִחִיקָה. שָׁמְעָה מוֹרָשָׁה, וַתִּלְבַּשׁ בִּגְדֵי
אַלְמְנוּת וּמוּעָקָה. וַתַּשֶּׂם יָדָהּ עַל רֹאשָׁהּ, וַתֵּלֶךְ הָלוֹךְ וְזָעָקָה: תֵּשְׁבִי שָׁם
אֵזוֹר שַׂק בְּמָתְנָיו תַּחְבָּשֶׁת. מַהֵר וְהוֹדַע יִשַׁי מִכַּפֵּל, אָבוֹת שְׁלֶשֶׁת. נָחַץ
לְרוֹעֶה, מַה לָּךְ נִרְדָּם לְהִתְעַשֵּׁת. קוּם קְרָא אֶל־אֱלֹהֶיךָ, אוּלַי יִתְעַשֵּׁת:
חוֹתָם טִיט אֲשֶׁר נַעֲשָׂה, לִבְלְשָׁן סֵפֶר. מִנְיָנָם לָמְדוּ לְאַחַר גְּזֵרָה כְּעַס
לְהָפֵר. בֶּן קִישׁ הִקִּישׁ דַּלְתוֹת בֵּית הַסֵּפֶר. וַיְכַס שַׂק, וַיֵּשֶׁב עַל־הָאֵפֶר:
רָבַץ תִּינוֹקוֹת לְפָנָיו יָמִים שְׁלֹשָׁה, צְמֵאִים וּמִכְפָּנִים. בְּקוֹל יַעֲקֹב לַחֲלֹשׁ
יְדֵי עַז פָּנִים. יָדָיו אֱמוּנָה לָאֵל, הַצִּילֵנִי נָא מֵעֶלְבּוֹנִים. פֶּן־יָבוֹא וְהִכַּנִי
אֵם עַל־בָּנִים: מִזֶּה אֵלֶּה וּמִזֶּה אֵלֶּה, בְּנֵי אֵיתָנִי וְרַבַּנִי. כֻּלָם צָעֲקוּ, וַתַּעַל
שַׁוְעָתָם אֶל יהוה. זֶה, לְקוֹל רְנוּן כְּבוֹא. זֶה, וּמֶה קוֹל הַצֹּאן הַזֶּה
בְּאָזְנָי: רוֹעֶה הֱשִׁיבוּ, הֵם קְטַנֵּי קֹדֶשׁ זֶרַע. זֶה, הַצֵּל לְקוּחִים לַמָּוֶת מֵאוֹיֵב
הָרָע. חַנּוּן נִכְמְרוּ רַחֲמָיו וַיְבַקֵּשׁ לְבַכּוֹת הַמַּאֲרָע. וַיְהִי כִּקְרֹא מֶלֶךְ־יִשְׂרָאֵל
אֶת־הַסֵּפֶר, וַיִּקְרַע: יְהוּדִי הוֹקִיעַ, יַלְדֵי תַלְמוּד לְמַטָּה וַאֲבִיהֶם לְמַעְלָה. אִישׁ
אִישׁ בְּשָׁלֹשׁ אַמּוֹת, וְהָרְבִיעִית אֲוִיר מֻגְלָה. מִשְׁנָה נָקָם חָזָה, וְשָׂמַח וְשָׁח
תְּהִלָּה. אָתֵי הֱשִׁיב עַל־בָּנָיו וְאוֹתוֹ תָלָה: ♦ וַתִּכְתֹּב אֶסְתֵּר תֹּקֶף, לִקְרֹא
כַּהֲלֵל מְהֻדֹּד. מִלְמַעְלָה קִיְּמוּ מַה שֶּׁקִּבְּלוּ לְמַטָּה דוֹדִים. נָס יְנוֹסֵס
לְפַרְסֵם כָּאן פִּלְאוֹ מְסֻחֲדִים. בָּעֵת הַזֹּאת רֶוַח וְהַצָּלָה יַעֲמוֹד לַיְּהוּדִים:

יְשַׁעְיָה נה

אִיּוֹב ב

דְּבָרִים לב

שְׁמוּאֵל ב' י"ג

יוֹנָה א'

יוֹנָה ג

בְּרֵאשִׁית לב

שְׁמוּאֵל א' ט"ו

מְלָכִים ב ה

בְּרֵאשִׁית מא

אֶסְתֵּר ד

אֵל מֶלֶךְ יוֹשֵׁב עַל כִּסֵּא רַחֲמִים, מִתְנַהֵג בַּחֲסִידוּת. מוֹחֵל עֲוֹנוֹת עַמּוֹ,
מַעֲבִיר רִאשׁוֹן רִאשׁוֹן. מַרְבֶּה מְחִילָה לַחַטָּאִים, וּסְלִיחָה לַפּוֹשְׁעִים. עֹשֶׂה

all flesh and spirit, do not repay their bad actions in kind. God, You taught us to speak thirteen attributes: recall for us today the covenant of the thirteen attributes, as You in ancient times showed the humble one [Moses], as is written: The LORD descended in the cloud and stood with him there, and proclaimed in the name of the LORD:

Congregation then Leader:

And the LORD passed by before him and proclaimed: *Ex. 34*

All say aloud:

יהוה The LORD, the LORD, compassionate and gracious God, slow to anger, abounding in loving-kindness and truth, extending loving-kindness to a thousand generations, forgiving iniquity, rebellion and sin, and absolving [the guilty who repent]. Forgive us our iniquity and our sin, and take us as Your inheritance.

Continue:

סְלַח לָנוּ Forgive us, our Father, for we have sinned. Pardon us, our King, for we have transgressed. For You, LORD, are good and forgiving, abounding in loving-   *Ps. 86* kindness to all who call on You.

כִּי־עִמְּךָ For in You there is a wellspring of life; in Your light shall we see light. As we   *Ps. 36* call You, God of our righteousness, answer us. In a narrow place You have opened out our horizon; be gracious to us and hear our prayer. And now let the strength   *Num. 14* of the LORD be great, as You have said.

כְּרַחֵם As a father has compassion for his children,
so, LORD, have compassion for us.
Salvation is the LORD's; on Your people is Your blessing, Selah!   *Ps. 3*
The LORD of hosts is with us, the God of Jacob is our stronghold, Selah!   *Ps. 46*
LORD of hosts, happy is the one who trusts in You.   *Ps. 84*
LORD, save! May the King answer us on the day we call.   *Ps. 20*

Our God and God of our fathers:

אַתָּה הָאֵל It is You who are the God of wonders. You have made known among nations Your terrifying strength. You redeemed Your people by might from torments, suppressed their foes with ignominious death, when the enemy rose to awaken strife, and seemed about to cut down the exquisite flowers, Israel. He plotted to measure out into the masters' treasuries, a hundred times the silver talents of the sockets in the Tabernacle. You warned Your lambs to announce the shekel offering early; You knew what would be. You warned us to be punctual, and to find a way to douse the fire of ones who sought to burn us. And so, those once

צִדְקוֹת עִם כָּל בָּשָׂר וָרְוּחַ, לֹא כְרָעָתָם תִּגְמֹל · אֵל, הוֹרֵיתָ לָּנוּ לוֹמַר שְׁלֹשׁ
עֶשְׂרֵה, וּזְכָר לָנוּ הַיּוֹם בְּרִית שְׁלֹשׁ עֶשְׂרֵה, כְּמוֹ שֶׁהוֹדַעְתָּ לֶעָנָו מִקֶּדֶם,
כְּמוֹ שֶׁכָּתוּב: וַיֵּרֶד יְהוָה בֶּעָנָן, וַיִּתְיַצֵּב עִמּוֹ שָׁם, וַיִּקְרָא בְשֵׁם, יהוה:

שליח ציבור then קהל:

| שמות לד

וַיַּעֲבֹר יְהוָה עַל־פָּנָיו וַיִּקְרָא

All say aloud:

יְהוָה, יהוה, אֵל רַחוּם וְחַנּוּן, אֶרֶךְ אַפַּיִם, וְרַב־חֶסֶד וֶאֱמֶת: נֹצֵר
חֶסֶד לָאֲלָפִים, נֹשֵׂא עָוֹן וָפֶשַׁע וְחַטָּאָה, וְנַקֵּה: וְסָלַחְתָּ לַעֲוֹנֵנוּ
וּלְחַטָּאתֵנוּ, וּנְחַלְתָּנוּ:

Continue:

תהלים פו | סְלַח לָנוּ אָבִינוּ כִּי חָטָאנוּ, מְחַל לָנוּ מַלְכֵּנוּ כִּי פָשָׁעְנוּ. כִּי־אַתָּה אֲדֹנָי טוֹב
וְסַלָּח, וְרַב־חֶסֶד לְכָל־קֹרְאֶיךָ:

תהלים לו | כִּי־עִמְּךָ מְקוֹר חַיִּים, בְּאוֹרְךָ נִרְאֶה־אוֹר: בְּקָרְאֵנוּ עֲנֵנוּ אֱלֹהֵי צִדְקֵנוּ,
במדבר יד | בַּצַּר הִרְחַבְתָּ לָּנוּ, חָנֵּנוּ וּשְׁמַע תְּפִלָּתֵנוּ. וְעַתָּה יִגְדַּל־נָא כֹּחַ אֲדֹנָי, כַּאֲשֶׁר
דִּבַּרְתָּ לֵאמֹר:

כְּרַחֵם אָב עַל בָּנִים, כֵּן תְּרַחֵם יהוה עָלֵינוּ.
תהלים ג | לַיהוָה הַיְשׁוּעָה, עַל־עַמְּךָ בִרְכָתֶךָ סֶּלָה:
תהלים מו | יְהוָה צְבָאוֹת עִמָּנוּ, מִשְׂגָּב לָנוּ אֱלֹהֵי יַעֲקֹב סֶלָה:
תהלים פד | יְהוָה צְבָאוֹת, אַשְׁרֵי אָדָם בֹּטֵחַ בָּךְ:
תהלים כ | יְהוָה הוֹשִׁיעָה, הַמֶּלֶךְ יַעֲנֵנוּ בְיוֹם־קָרְאֵנוּ:

אֱלֹהֵינוּ וֵאלֹהֵי אֲבוֹתֵינוּ

אַתָּה הָאֵל עוֹשֵׂה פְלָאוֹת, בָּעַמִּים הוֹדַעְתָּ עֻזֶּךָ עֹז נוֹרָאוֹת, גָּאַלְתָּ בִּזְרוֹעַ עַמְּךָ
מִתְלָאוֹת, דָּכִּיתָ צָרֵיהֶם בְּמוֹתֵי תַחֲלוּאוֹת. הָאוֹיֵב בְּקוּמוֹ לְעוֹרֵר מְדָנִים,
וְדָמָה לְהַכְרִית פִּרְחֵי עֲדָנִים, וְזָמַם לִשְׁקֹל לְגִנְזֵי אֲדוֹנִים, חֲלִיפֵי מְאַת כִּכְּרֵי

condemned to death – are marked out for resurrection. When (for appearances,) they worshiped a narrow image, they were yielded up to be clipped off: all those offshoots and grapes. Traps surrounded them on all sides; they turned their eyes to You, they were concealed in Your hiddenness. The lots were overturned, they ruled over their enemies, and the gallows was prepared to receive Haman the Agagite. God struck and swallowed the façade of covering that covered, and He entombed His people's enemies in darkness. Peace and truth were written on all sides; power of salvation, steady rock and fortress. The plunderer was plundered, he was caught in his own trap. The one who spoke against me was swept away; destroyed; eyed disdainfully. The people made celebrations, and these were fixed for all generations. Amalek had entered the Scriptures three times – how could there be a fourth? Yet on High it was agreed and here below it was sealed, and the reason for all that had been fixed, was inscribed in the scroll. Your hand is lifted high to forgive sinners. You set Mordekhai the Jew and Hadassah Esther in their place as saviors, and now their righteousness remains forever to delight us, and the study of their honor to recall to You those who were saved. Be zealous for Your name, Awesome and Sanctified One. Witness Your vineyard, destroyed, trampled; gather our scattered ones and their song to You will be renewed. Sustain them and revive them with the building of the Temple. ‣ And as You did awe-inspiring things in those days, so perform with us the wonder of salvation for all time. Find in Your presence our ransom, our appeasement – God, King who sits upon a throne of compassion.

God, King who sits upon a throne of compassion, who acts with loving-kindness, who pardons the iniquities of His people, passing them before Him in order; who forgives sinners and pardons transgressors; who performs righteousness with all flesh and spirit, do not repay their bad actions in kind. ‣ God, You taught us to speak thirteen attributes: recall for us today the covenant of the thirteen attributes, as You in ancient times showed the humble one [Moses], as is written: The LORD descended in the cloud and stood with him there, and proclaimed in the name of the LORD:

Congregation then Leader:

And the LORD passed by before him and proclaimed: *Ex. 34*

All say aloud:

יהוה The LORD, the LORD, compassionate and gracious God, slow to anger, abounding in loving-kindness and truth, extending loving-kindness to a thousand generations, forgiving iniquity, rebellion and sin, and absolving [the guilty who repent]. Forgive us our iniquity and our sin, and take us as Your inheritance.

אֲדָרִים. טְלָאֶיךָ הַזָּהַרְתָּ שְׁקָלֵיהֶם לְהַקְדִּים, יָדַעְתָּ הָעֲתִידוֹת וְדָרַשְׁתָּ
נִשְׁקָדִים, כָּבוּי לְהַמְצִיא לְלַהַב יוֹקְדִים, לְקוּחִים לַמָּוֶת לְתַחֵי נִפְקָדִים.
מַסֵּכָה צָרָה בְּעָבְדָם לְפָנִים, נִמְסְרוּ לְהָתֵז קַנְקָנוֹת וּגְפָנִים, סְבָבוּם מוֹקְשִׁים
בְּכָל דְּפָנִים, עֵינֵיהֶם לְךָ תוֹלִים וּבִסְתָרְךָ נִצְפָּנִים. פּוּר נֶהְפַּךְ בְּאוֹיְבִים
לִשְׁלֹט, צָלִיחָה הוֹכַן אֲגָגִי לִקְלֹט, קָלַע וּבָלַע פְּנֵי הַלּוֹט הַלּוֹט, רִיבִי עַם
בְּאַשְׁמַנִּים לַעֲלֹט. שָׁלוֹם וֶאֱמֶת נִכְתַּב מִכָּל צַד, תְּקֹף יֶשַׁע סֶלַע וּמִצָּד,
שׁוֹדֵד הַשָּׁדַד וּבִרְשִׁתּוֹ נוֹצַד, מְלָשְׁנֵי נִסְחַף נִצְמַת וְנִרְצַד. עָשׂוּ שִׂמְחוֹת
וְלַדּוֹרוֹת קְבָעוּם, וּמִקְרָאוֹת שָׁלְשׁוּם וְלֹא רְבָעוּם, נִסְכְּמוּ מִמַּעַל וּלְמַטָּה
טְבָעוּם, בַּסֵּפֶר נֶחֱקַק עַל מָה קְבָעוּם. רָמָה יָדְךָ לִסְלֹחַ לַפּוֹשְׁעִים, יְהוּדִי
וְהֲדַסָּה הֵקַמְתָּ מוֹשִׁיעִים, צִדְקָתָם עוֹמֶדֶת לָעַד לְשַׁעֲשׁוּעִים, חֵקֶר כְּבוֹדָם
לְהַזְכִּיר לַנּוֹשָׁעִים. קַנֵּא לִשְׁמְךָ נוֹרָא וְנִקְדָּשׁ, חֲזֵה כַרְמְךָ נֶהֱרַס וְנִדַּשׁ, זְרוּעֵינוּ
קַבֵּץ וְשִׂיב לְךָ יֵחָדֵשׁ, קַיֵּם וְהַחֲיֵם בְּבִנְיַן בֵּית הַמִּקְדָּשׁ. ‹ וְכַעֲשׂוֹתְךָ
נוֹרָאוֹת בְּאוֹתָן הַיָּמִים, אַתָּה הַפְלֵא תְּשׁוּעַת עוֹלָמִים, מְצוֹא לְפָנֶיךָ כֹּפֶר
וְתַנְחוּמִים, אֵל מֶלֶךְ יוֹשֵׁב עַל כִּסֵּא רַחֲמִים.

אֵל מֶלֶךְ יוֹשֵׁב עַל כִּסֵּא רַחֲמִים, מִתְנַהֵג בַּחֲסִידוּת. מוֹחֵל עֲוֹנוֹת עַמּוֹ,
מַעֲבִיר רִאשׁוֹן רִאשׁוֹן. מַרְבֶּה מְחִילָה לַחַטָּאִים, וּסְלִיחָה לַפּוֹשְׁעִים. עֹשֶׂה
צְדָקוֹת עִם כָּל בָּשָׂר וָרוּחַ, לֹא כְרָעָתָם תִּגְמֹל. ‹ אֵל, הוֹרֵיתָ לָּנוּ לוֹמַר שְׁלֹשׁ
עֶשְׂרֵה, וּזְכָר לָנוּ הַיּוֹם בְּרִית שְׁלֹשׁ עֶשְׂרֵה, כְּמוֹ שֶׁהוֹדַעְתָּ לֶעָנָו מִקֶּדֶם,
כְּמוֹ שֶׁכָּתוּב: וַיֵּרֶד יהוה בֶּעָנָן, וַיִּתְיַצֵּב עִמּוֹ שָׁם, וַיִּקְרָא בְשֵׁם, יהוה:

שליח ציבור then קהל:

שמות לד

וַיַּעֲבֹר יהוה עַל־פָּנָיו וַיִּקְרָא

All say aloud:

יהוה, יהוה, אֵל רַחוּם וְחַנּוּן, אֶרֶךְ אַפַּיִם, וְרַב־חֶסֶד וֶאֱמֶת: נֹצֵר
חֶסֶד לָאֲלָפִים, נֹשֵׂא עָוֹן וָפֶשַׁע וְחַטָּאָה, וְנַקֵּה: וְסָלַחְתָּ לַעֲוֹנֵנוּ
וּלְחַטָּאתֵנוּ, וּנְחַלְתָּנוּ:

Continue:

סְלַח לָנוּ Forgive us, our Father, for we have sinned. Pardon us, our King, for we
have transgressed. For You, Lord, are good and forgiving, abounding in loving- Ps. 86
kindness to all who call on You.

The following is said responsively:

Small of number we stand pleading before You: do not block Your ears to the
cry of people crushed. Listen to their entreaty from the Heaven where You
dwell, as You saved Your children in the days of Myrrh and Myrtle [Mordekhai
and Esther].

> On Israel's praises You sit enthroned, hearing their cry, listening to their
> prayer. Bringing healing even before the blow, counting it out to help the
> ones You have acquired; to settle their homes again.

A foe and enemy fixed his eyes like knives on Israel; he opened wide his
mouth to swallow up the humble man. He deliberated within him to destroy
Mordekhai's great community; in the letter, he etched his intent to destroy the
treasured people.

> You who take revenge upon foes and persist in Your claim against
> enemies; You measured them out with the very measure they used
> against Your loved ones. The fighter and his descendants were hanged,
> suspended; they were strung up together, like fish on a thread.

On the day on which the enemies hoped to lay carnage among the people You
harbor, the rule was overturned and bodies fell; they bore the brunt and fury of
Your rage – they were trodden underfoot and washed away.

> And so may Your name be raised up, exalted. Your glory covers all the
> highest heavens. As You lift the downtrodden, those yielded up as
> plunder, Your praise fills up the valleys to their very ends.

Consider our thoughts, now, and witness our suffering. Rise up, in Your rage,
against the bitter enemy. Master, we have called You from a narrow place.
Please, take us out into the open, and release us from anguish.

> Bring us much, abundant pardon. Hear our prayer, and what is crude in
> us – pass over. Bring down those who press us and fill them with horror.
> And as for us – do not forever withhold Your compassion.

Continue with "God, King who sits" on page 500.

Continue:

סְלַח לָנוּ אָבִינוּ כִּי חָטָאנוּ, מְחַל לָנוּ מַלְכֵּנוּ כִּי פָשֶׁעְנוּ.
כִּי־אַתָּה אֲדֹנָי טוֹב וְסַלָּח, וְרַב־חֶסֶד לְכָל־קֹרְאֶיךָ:

תהלים פו

The following is said responsively:

בַּמֶּה מִסְפַּר חֲלֵינוּ פָּנֶיךָ. לִשׁוּעַת נְבָאִים אֵל תַּעֲלֵם אָזְנֶךָ.
הַקְשֵׁב תְּחִנָּתָם מִשְׁמֵי מְעוֹנֶךָ. כְּבִימֵי מֹר וַהֲדַס הוֹשַׁעְתָּ בָּנֶיךָ.

תְּהִלּוֹת יִשְׂרָאֵל אַתָּה יוֹשֵׁב. שַׁוְעָתָם מַאֲזִין וְרַצָּתָם קוֹשֵׁב.
רְפָאוֹת לְמַחַץ מַקְדִּים וּמְחַשֵּׁב. קַנּוֹיֶךָ לְהֵיטִיב וּפְנֵיהֶם לְיַשֵּׁב.

צָר וְאוֹיֵב הִלְטִישׁ עֵינָיו. פִּיהוּ פָּעַר לְשָׁאוֹף עֲנָו.
עֲשָׂת בִּשְׁלוֹ לְהַשְׁמִיד קְהַל הֲמוֹנָיו. סְגֻל לְאַבֵּד חָרַת בְּנִשְׁתְּוָנָיו.

נוֹקֵם לְצָרִים וְנוֹטֵר לְאוֹיְבִים. מָדַדְתָּ מִדָּתָם כְּזֵדוּ לַאֲהוּבִים.
לוֹחֵם וְעֵינָיו הִתְלוּ מַצְלִיבִים. כְּבַחֲרוֹת דָּגִים חֹרְזוּ תְחוּבִים.

יוֹם אֲשֶׁר שַׂבְּרוּ צוֹרְרִים. טָבְחָה לָשִׁית בְּעַם נְצוּרִים.
חֻלְּפָה הַדַּת וְנָפְלוּ פְגָרִים. וְלָעֲפוּ זַעֲמוּ מוּבָסִים מְגֹרָרִים.

וּבְכֵן יִתְעַלֶּה שִׁמְךָ וְיִתְנַשֵּׂא. הוֹדְךָ שְׁמֵי שָׁמַיִם כִּסָּה.
דָּכִּים בְּרוּמְמֶךָ נְתוּנִים לִמְשִׁסָּה. גֵּיא וְאַפְסַיָּה תְּהִלָּתְךָ מְכֻסָּה.

בִּינָה הַגִּיעֵנוּ עַתָּה, וּרְאֵה בַצָּר. בְּאַפְּךָ קוּמָה עַל צוֹרֵר הַצָּר.
אָדוֹן, קְרָאָנוּךָ מִן הַמֵּצַר. אָנָּא הוֹצִיאֵנוּ לַמֶּרְחָב וְחַלְּצֵנוּ מִצָּר.

מְאֹד תַּרְבֶּה לָנוּ מְחִילָה. שְׁמַע תְּפִלָּה, וְהַעֲבֵר תִּפְלָה.
לוֹחֲצֵינוּ הַמְעֵד וּמַלְּאֵם חַלְחָלָה. מִמְּנוּ רַחֲמֶיךָ לָעַד לֹא תִכְלָא.

Continue with אֵל מֶלֶךְ יוֹשֵׁב *on page 501.*

SELIHOT FOR THE SEVENTEENTH OF TAMMUZ

סְלַח לָנוּ Forgive us, our Father, for in our great foolishness we have blundered. Pardon us, our King, for our iniquities are many.

אֵל אֶרֶךְ You are a God slow to anger, You are called the Master of Compassion, and You have taught the way of repentance. May You remember today and every day the greatness of Your compassion and kindness, for the sake of the descendants of Your beloved ones. Turn toward us in compassion, for You are the Master of Compassion. We come before You in plea and prayer, as You in ancient times showed the humble one [Moses]. Turn from Your fierce anger, as is written in Your Torah. In the shadow of Your wings may we shelter and abide, as on the day when the LORD descended in the cloud.
‣ Disregard transgression and erase guilt as on the day You stood with him [Moses] there. Hear our cry and heed our word, as on the day You proclaimed in the name of the LORD, and there it is written:

Congregation then Leader:
And the LORD passed by before him and proclaimed: *Ex. 34*

All say aloud:

יהוה The LORD, the LORD, compassionate and gracious God, slow to anger, abounding in loving-kindness and truth, extending loving-kindness to a thousand generations, forgiving iniquity, rebellion and sin, and absolving [the guilty who repent]. Forgive us our iniquity and our sin, and take us as Your inheritance.

Continue:

סְלַח לָנוּ Forgive us, our Father, for we have sinned. Pardon us, our King, for we have transgressed. For You, LORD, are good and forgiving, abounding in loving-kindness to all who call on You. *Ps. 86*

And do not let Him rest, until He establishes, until He makes Jerusalem *Is. 62* praise of all the earth. For in You there is a wellspring of life; in Your light shall *Ps. 36* we see light. Our God, we are ashamed of our actions, distraught at our sins.

כְּרַחֵם As a father has compassion for his children,
so, LORD, have compassion for us.
Salvation is the LORD's; on Your people is Your blessing, Selah! *Ps. 3*
The LORD of hosts is with us, the God of Jacob is our stronghold, Selah! *Ps. 46*

סליחות לשבעה עשר בתמוז

סְלַח לָנוּ, אָבִינוּ, כִּי בְרֹב אִוַּלְתֵּנוּ שָׁגִינוּ.
מְחַל לָנוּ, מַלְכֵּנוּ, כִּי רַבּוּ עֲוֹנֵינוּ.

אֵל אֶרֶךְ אַפַּיִם אַתָּה, וּבַעַל הָרַחֲמִים נִקְרֵאתָ, וְדֶרֶךְ תְּשׁוּבָה הוֹרֵיתָ. גְּדֻלַּת
רַחֲמֶיךָ וַחֲסָדֶיךָ, תִּזְכֹּר הַיּוֹם וּבְכָל יוֹם לְזֶרַע יְדִידֶיךָ. תֵּפֶן אֵלֵינוּ בְּרַחֲמִים,
כִּי אַתָּה הוּא בַּעַל הָרַחֲמִים. בְּתַחֲנוּן וּבִתְפִלָּה פָּנֶיךָ נְקַדֵּם, כְּהוֹדַעְתָּ
לֶעָנָו מִקֶּדֶם. מֵחֲרוֹן אַפְּךָ שׁוּב, כְּמוֹ בְתוֹרָתְךָ כָּתוּב. וּבְצֵל כְּנָפֶיךָ נֶחֱסֶה
וְנִתְלוֹנָן, כְּיוֹם וַיֵּרֶד יהוה בֶּעָנָן. ‹ תַּעֲבֹר עַל פֶּשַׁע וְתִמְחֶה אָשָׁם, כְּיוֹם
וַיִּתְיַצֵּב עִמּוֹ שָׁם. תַּאֲזִין שַׁוְעָתֵנוּ וְתַקְשִׁיב מֶנּוּ מַאֲמָר, כְּיוֹם וַיִּקְרָא בְשֵׁם
יהוה, וְשָׁם נֶאֱמַר:

שליח ציבור then קהל:

שמות לד
וַיַּעֲבֹר יהוה עַל פָּנָיו וַיִּקְרָא

All say aloud:

יהוה, יהוה, אֵל רַחוּם וְחַנּוּן, אֶרֶךְ אַפַּיִם, וְרַב־חֶסֶד וֶאֱמֶת: נֹצֵר
חֶסֶד לָאֲלָפִים, נֹשֵׂא עָוֹן וָפֶשַׁע וְחַטָּאָה, וְנַקֵּה: וְסָלַחְתָּ לַעֲוֹנֵנוּ
וּלְחַטָּאתֵנוּ, וּנְחַלְתָּנוּ:

Continue:

תהלים פו
סְלַח לָנוּ אָבִינוּ כִּי חָטָאנוּ, מְחַל לָנוּ מַלְכֵּנוּ כִּי פָשָׁעְנוּ. כִּי־אַתָּה אֲדֹנָי טוֹב
וְסַלָּח, וְרַב־חֶסֶד לְכָל־קֹרְאֶיךָ:

ישעיה סב
תהלים לו
וְאַל־תִּתְּנוּ דֳמִי לוֹ, עַד־יְכוֹנֵן וְעַד־יָשִׂים אֶת־יְרוּשָׁלִַם תְּהִלָּה בָּאָרֶץ: כִּי־
עִמְּךָ מְקוֹר חַיִּים, בְּאוֹרְךָ נִרְאֶה־אוֹר: אֱלֹהֵינוּ, בְּשְׁנוּ בְּמַעֲשֵׂינוּ וְנִכְלַמְנוּ
בַּעֲוֹנֵינוּ.

כְּרַחֵם אָב עַל בָּנִים, כֵּן תְּרַחֵם יהוה עָלֵינוּ.
תהלים ג
לַיהוה הַיְשׁוּעָה, עַל־עַמְּךָ בִרְכָתֶךָ סֶּלָה:
תהלים מו
יהוה צְבָאוֹת עִמָּנוּ, מִשְׂגָּב לָנוּ אֱלֹהֵי יַעֲקֹב סֶלָה:

Lord of hosts, happy is the one who trusts in You.   *Ps. 84*
Lord, save! May the King answer us on the day we call.   *Ps. 20*

▸ Forgive, please, this people's iniquity,   *Num. 14*
   in the abundance of Your kindness,
     and as You have forgiven this people from the time of Egypt until now,
     and there it is written:

Congregation then Leader:
And the Lord said, I have forgiven as you asked.

Continue:

הַטֵּה Give ear, my God and hear; open Your eyes and see our desolation, and the   *Dan. 9*
city that bears Your name, for it is not on the strength of our righteousness that we
throw down our pleadings before You, but on the strength of Your great compassion. Lord, hear me; Lord, forgive; Lord, listen and act and do not delay – for
Your sake, my God; for Your city and Your people bear Your name.

Our God and God of our fathers:

אָתָנוּ We come before You, Former of the winds. In our many iniquities our sighs
have grown heavy; the decrees against us powerful and our screams so many – for
on the Seventeenth of Tammuz, the Tablets were smashed. We have been exiled
from the House of Your choosing; our judgment was sealed, the decree laid
down. And the light has darkened over us – for on the Seventeenth of Tammuz,
the Torah scroll was burnt. Our enemies destroyed the Sanctuary, the Divine
Presence fled from Its corner, and we were yielded up to the hands of the wanton,
to be consumed – for on the Seventeenth of Tammuz, an idol was set up in the
Temple. We were scattered from city to city, and old and young of us were seized.
The place of our delight was destroyed, and fire raged through her – for on the
Seventeenth of Tammuz the city was broken through. The lethal foe took hold
of our Temple, and the cherubs, bride and bridegroom were deprived of all their
ornament. Because we angered You we were given up to destruction – for on the
Seventeenth of Tammuz, the daily offering ceased. All glory and praise there ended.
The enemy drew his sword and brandished its point against us; small children
and babies were prepared for the slaughter – for on the Seventeenth of Tammuz,
the offerings and sacrifices ceased. We rebelled against the One who inhabits the
Heavens, and so we were dispersed to all the corners of the world. All our dancing
was turned to lament – for on the Seventeenth of Tammuz, the Temple service
ended. We acted obstinately with You in the discord of tongues, and so our own
tongue has learnt lamentation; we have been abandoned in countless numbers – for
on the Seventeenth of Tammuz, sin decided our destiny. We have been dispersed
and found no relief, and so our sighs have multiplied within us; Rock, see how

תהלים פד

יהוה צְבָאוֹת, אַשְׁרֵי אָדָם בֹּטֵחַ בָּךְ:

תהלים כ

יהוה הוֹשִׁיעָה, הַמֶּלֶךְ יַעֲנֵנוּ בְיוֹם־קָרְאֵנוּ:

במדבר יד

‹ סְלַח־נָא לַעֲוֹן הָעָם הַזֶּה כְּגֹדֶל חַסְדֶּךָ
וְכַאֲשֶׁר נָשָׂאתָה לָעָם הַזֶּה מִמִּצְרַיִם וְעַד־הֵנָּה:
וְשָׁם נֶאֱמַר:

שליח ציבור then קהל:

וַיֹּאמֶר יהוה, סָלַחְתִּי כִּדְבָרֶךָ:

Continue:

דניאל ט

הַטֵּה אֱלֹהַי אָזְנְךָ וּשֲׁמָע, פְּקַח עֵינֶיךָ וּרְאֵה שֹׁמְמֹתֵינוּ וְהָעִיר אֲשֶׁר־נִקְרָא
שִׁמְךָ עָלֶיהָ, כִּי לֹא עַל־צִדְקֹתֵינוּ אֲנַחְנוּ מַפִּילִים תַּחֲנוּנֵינוּ לְפָנֶיךָ, כִּי
עַל־רַחֲמֶיךָ הָרַבִּים: אֲדֹנָי שְׁמָעָה, אֲדֹנָי סְלָחָה, אֲדֹנָי הַקְשִׁיבָה וַעֲשֵׂה
אַל־תְּאַחַר, לְמַעַנְךָ אֱלֹהַי, כִּי־שִׁמְךָ נִקְרָא עַל־עִירְךָ וְעַל־עַמֶּךָ:

אֱלֹהֵינוּ וֵאלֹהֵי אֲבוֹתֵינוּ

אָתָנוּ לְךָ יוֹצֵר רוּחוֹת, בְּרוֹב עֲוֹנֵינוּ כָּבְדוּ אֲנָחוֹת, גָּזְרוּ עָצְמוּ וְרַבּוּ צָרִיחוֹת,
כִּי בְּשִׁבְעָה עָשָׂר בְּתַמּוּז נִשְׁתַּבְּרוּ הַלֻּחוֹת. גָּלְינוּ מִבֵּית הַבְּחִירָה, דִּינֵנוּ
נֶחְתַּם וְנִגְזְרָה גְזֵרָה, וְחָשַׁךְ בַּעֲדֵנוּ אוֹרָה, כִּי בְּשִׁבְעָה עָשָׂר בְּתַמּוּז נִשְׂרְפָה
הַתּוֹרָה. הָרְסוּ אוֹיְבֵינוּ הַהֵיכָל, וּבָרְחָה שְׁכִינָה מִזָּוִית הַהֵיכָל, וְנִמְסַרְנוּ בִּידֵי
זֵדִים לְהִתְאַכָּל, כִּי בְּשִׁבְעָה עָשָׂר בְּתַמּוּז הֶעֱמַד הָעוֹבֵד צֶלֶם בַּהֵיכָל. זֵרוּנוּ מֵעִיר
אֶל עִיר, וְנִלְכַּד מִמֶּנּוּ רַב וְצָעִיר, חָרְבָה מְשׁוֹשֵׂנוּ וְאֵשׁ בָּהּ הַבְעִיר, כִּי
בְּשִׁבְעָה עָשָׂר בְּתַמּוּז הֻבְקְעָה הָעִיר. טִפַּח מִקְדָּשֵׁנוּ צַר הַמַּשְׁמִיד, וְנִטַּל
מֶנְחָתָן וְכַלָּה אֶצְעָדָה וְצָמִיד, יַעַן כְּעַסְנוּךָ נִתְּנוּ לְהַשְׁמִיד, כִּי בְּשִׁבְעָה עָשָׂר
בְּתַמּוּז בֻּטַּל הַתָּמִיד. כָּלָה מֶנּוּ כָּל הוֹד וְשֶׁבַח, חֻרְבּוּ שָׁלָף אוֹיֵב עָלֵינוּ
לָאֵבַח, לִהְיוֹת עוֹלָלִים וְיוֹנְקִים מוּכָנִים לַטָּבַח, כִּי בְּשִׁבְעָה עָשָׂר בְּתַמּוּז
בֻּטַּל עוֹלָה וָזֶבַח. מָרַדְנוּ לְשׁוֹכֵן מְעוֹנוֹת, לָכֵן נֶחְפַּזְרְנוּ בְּכָל פִּנּוֹת, נֶהְפַּךְ
מְחוֹלֵנוּ לְקִינוֹת, כִּי בְּשִׁבְעָה עָשָׂר בְּתַמּוּז בֻּטְלוּ קָרְבָּנוֹת. סָרַרְנוּ לְפָנֶיךָ
מֶרִיב לְשׁוֹנוֹת, לָכֵן לֻמַּדָּה לְשׁוֹנֵנוּ לוֹמַר קִינוֹת, עָזַבְנוּ בְּלִי לְהִמָּנוֹת, כִּי
בְּשִׁבְעָה עָשָׂר בְּתַמּוּז גָּרְמוּ לָנוּ עֲוֹנוֹת. פָּזַרְנוּ בְּלִי מְצוֹא רְוָחָה, לָכֵן רַבְּתָה

our souls have been bowed low – and turn our Seventeenth of Tammuz into gladness and joy. We have been obstinate and many calamities have met us; and so we have been yielded up to the plunder, have been pushed into the mud. See, LORD, and release us from disaster – and turn our Seventeenth of Tammuz into joy and gladness. ‣ Turn to us, You who reside on High, and gather in our scattered ones from the very ends of the earth. Say to Zion, "Come, get up," – and turn our Seventeenth of Tammuz to a day of salvation and comfort.

אֵל מֶלֶךְ God, King who sits upon a throne of compassion, who acts with loving-kindness, who pardons the iniquities of His people, passing them before Him in order; who forgives sinners and pardons transgressors; who performs righteousness with all flesh and spirit, do not repay their bad actions in kind. ‣ God, You taught us to speak thirteen attributes: recall for us today the covenant of the thirteen attributes, as You in ancient times showed the humble one [Moses], as is written: The LORD descended in the cloud and stood with him there, and proclaimed in the name of the LORD.

Congregation then Leader:

And the LORD passed by before him and proclaimed: Ex. 34

All say aloud:

יהוה The LORD, the LORD, compassionate and gracious God, slow to anger, abounding in loving-kindness and truth, extending loving-kindness to a thousand generations, forgiving iniquity, rebellion and sin, and absolving [the guilty who repent]. Forgive us our iniquity and our sin, and take us as Your inheritance.

Continue:

סְלַח לָנוּ Forgive us, our Father, for we have sinned. Pardon us, our King, for we have transgressed. For You, LORD, are good and forgiving, abounding in loving-kindness to all who call on You. Ps. 86

God, do not rest, do not be silent and do not be still, for Your enemies clamor Ps. 83
and those who hate You hold their heads high. God of retribution, Ps. 94
LORD; God of retribution, appear

כְּרַחֵם As a father has compassion for his children,
so, LORD, have compassion for us.

Salvation is the LORD's; on Your people is Your blessing, Selah! Ps. 3
The LORD of hosts is with us, the God of Jacob is our stronghold, Selah! Ps. 46
LORD of hosts: happy is the one who trusts in You. Ps. 84
LORD, save! May the King answer us on the day we call. Ps. 20

בָּנוּ אֲנָחָה, צוּר רְאֵה נַפְשֵׁנוּ כִּי שָׁחָה, וְשִׁבְעָה עָשָׂר בְּתַמּוּז הָפַךְ לָנוּ לְלָשׁוֹן
וּלְשִׂמְחָה. קְשֵׁינוּ עֹרֶף וְרַבְתָּה בָּנוּ אָסוֹן, לָכֵן נִתְּנוּ לַמַּשִׁסָּה וְרִפְשׁוֹן, רְאֵה
יהוה וְחַלְצֵנוּ מֵאָסוֹן, וְשִׁבְעָה עָשָׂר בְּתַמּוּז הָפַךְ לָנוּ לְשִׂמְחָה וּלְשָׂשׂוֹן.
‹ שַׁעֲנוּ שׁוֹכֵן רוּמָה, וְקַבֵּץ נְפוּצוֹתֵינוּ מִקְצוֹת אַדְמָה, תֹּאמַר לְצִיּוֹן קוּמָה,
וְשִׁבְעָה עָשָׂר בְּתַמּוּז הָפַךְ לָנוּ לְיוֹם יְשׁוּעָה וְנֶחָמָה.

אֵל מֶלֶךְ יוֹשֵׁב עַל כִּסֵּא רַחֲמִים, מִתְנַהֵג בַּחֲסִידוּת. מוֹחֵל עֲוֹנוֹת עַמּוֹ,
מַעֲבִיר רִאשׁוֹן רִאשׁוֹן. מַרְבֶּה מְחִילָה לַחַטָּאִים, וּסְלִיחָה לַפּוֹשְׁעִים. עֹשֶׂה
צְדָקוֹת עִם כָּל בָּשָׂר וָרוּחַ, לֹא כְרָעָתָם תִּגְמֹל. ‹ אֵל, הוֹרֵיתָ לָּנוּ לוֹמַר שְׁלֹשׁ
עֶשְׂרֵה, וּזְכָר לָנוּ הַיּוֹם בְּרִית שְׁלֹשׁ עֶשְׂרֵה, כְּמוֹ שֶׁהוֹדַעְתָּ לֶעָנָו מִקֶּדֶם,
כְּמוֹ שֶׁכָּתוּב: וַיֵּרֶד יהוה בֶּעָנָן וַיִּתְיַצֵּב עִמּוֹ שָׁם, וַיִּקְרָא בְשֵׁם, יהוה:

שליח ציבור then קהל

שמות לד

וַיַּעֲבֹר יהוה עַל־פָּנָיו וַיִּקְרָא

All say aloud:

יהוה, יהוה, אֵל רַחוּם וְחַנּוּן, אֶרֶךְ אַפַּיִם, וְרַב־חֶסֶד וֶאֱמֶת: נֹצֵר
חֶסֶד לָאֲלָפִים, נֹשֵׂא עָוֹן וָפֶשַׁע וְחַטָּאָה, וְנַקֵּה: וְסָלַחְתָּ לַעֲוֹנֵנוּ
וּלְחַטָּאתֵנוּ, וּנְחַלְתָּנוּ:

Continue:

תהלים פו

סְלַח לָנוּ אָבִינוּ כִּי חָטָאנוּ, מְחַל לָנוּ מַלְכֵּנוּ כִּי פָשָׁעְנוּ. כִּי־אַתָּה אֲדֹנָי טוֹב
וְסַלָּח, וְרַב־חֶסֶד לְכָל־קֹרְאֶיךָ:

תהלים פג

אֱלֹהִים אַל־דֳּמִי־לָךְ, אַל־תֶּחֱרַשׁ וְאַל־תִּשְׁקֹט אֵל: כִּי־הִנֵּה אוֹיְבֶיךָ יֶהֱמָיוּן,
וּמְשַׂנְאֶיךָ נָשְׂאוּ רֹאשׁ: אֵל־נְקָמוֹת יהוה, אֵל נְקָמוֹת הוֹפִיעַ:

תהלים צד

כְּרַחֵם אָב עַל בָּנִים, כֵּן תְּרַחֵם יהוה עָלֵינוּ.

תהלים ג

לַיהוה הַיְשׁוּעָה, עַל־עַמְּךָ בִרְכָתֶךָ סֶּלָה:

תהלים מו

יהוה צְבָאוֹת עִמָּנוּ, מִשְׂגָּב לָנוּ אֱלֹהֵי יַעֲקֹב סֶלָה:

תהלים פד

יהוה צְבָאוֹת, אַשְׁרֵי אָדָם בֹּטֵחַ בָּךְ:

תהלים כ

יהוה הוֹשִׁיעָה, הַמֶּלֶךְ יַעֲנֵנוּ בְיוֹם־קָרְאֵנוּ:

Our God and God of our fathers:

אָמַר It is bitterly that I weep, over the Hand raised against our ruins. I blasphemed Him in His House, in my unfaithfulness and thieving. The Holy Presence broke out and fled, flew ten stretches and rose up to the seventh Heaven. God cut me off, tormented me, burnt me, in the fourth month. He closed the time set for Him to break those young boys, who were like boughs just sprouting. He shot us with His arrows twice, melted and weakened us, as heedless women wept for Tammuz in the Temple. He condemned me and became Enemy to me, then, in the month of Tammuz. Five traps were laid for me, deep in the Scripture of sufferings sent. Those people overcame me for my impurity on the seventeenth of the month. For I was ensnared like a wretched bride, unfaithful beneath a wedding canopy of peace and success. I did not wait for Moses, my shepherd, until the sixth hour, and the Tablets were smashed. From His hand was I ornamented with jewelry of fine gold, brooch and bracelet. They flowed away on the day of His rage, when I corrupted my way, and denounced my faith. I broke off the order of His service and the constant supplies of the altar – from the Chamber of the Lambs, the daily offering is ended. Israel is crumbled to pieces, scattered, storm battered, oppressed. Likened to a ship without a captain, tossed about like a boat. You have taken her by the head for her sins, exposed her twice over to mourning and moaning. Her enemies waged war on her on this day, and the city was broken through again. She fled out like a chased gazelle to hide, when none sought her. They sharpened their tongues, they made her like a lamb, and left her wool and milk for all takers. She cries out for the cherished thing with which she was crowned: the beloved of her eyes eluded her as Apostomus burnt the Torah. A fool cursed those oppressed and broken to vex them; he taunted abject people: "They shall be consumed;" "God shall hide His face from seeing." When idols were placed in the Temple, God avenged one's hand at the hand of the other, a disgusting item consumed. This, at the time when He gathered anguish over us; for an image was set up in the Sanctuary of God. Miserable and plagued are these children, who were once the very first. Their troubles have come close on one another's heels these many years; stricken as if by the stings of bees and scorpions. They think their hope is gone, that as they sit in this darkness they have no more chance. • Zealous God, in Your restraint towards those who incite You they have flourished fat and succulent. Raise up those who still await You; let them stand firm always, like something planted, or carved out with love. It is on fast days that truth and peace are hewn out. May they become forever times of joy and celebration – festive days.

אֵל מֶלֶךְ God, King who sits upon a throne of compassion, who acts with loving-kindness, who pardons the iniquities of His people, passing them before Him in order; who forgives sinners and pardons transgressors; who performs righteousness with all flesh and spirit, do not repay their bad actions in kind. • God, You taught us to speak thirteen attributes: recall for us today the covenant of the thirteen attributes, as You in ancient times showed the humble one [Moses], as is written: The LORD descended in the cloud and stood with him there, and proclaimed in the name of the LORD:

Congregation then Leader:

And the LORD passed by before him and proclaimed: Ex. 34

אֱלֹהֵינוּ וֵאלֹהֵי אֲבוֹתֵינוּ

אָמַר בְּבֶכִי מִפְּנֵי יַד שְׁלוּחָה בָּעִי. בְּנָאֲצֵי בְּתוֹךְ בֵּיתוֹ בִּבְגָדֵי וְקָבְעִי. גָּח וּבָרַח וְנָסַע עֶשֶׂר וְעָלָה לַשְּׁבִיעִי. דָּמְנִי הֱצִיקֵנִי הִשִּׁיקֵנִי בַּחֹדֶשׁ הָרְבִיעִי. הֵבִיא מוֹעֵד בְּמִלֵּאתוֹ לְשַׁבֵּר בָּחוּרֵי גָּמוּז. וְרַבָּה בוֹ פְּגָעִים בְּמִסְמוֹס וּמִזְמוּז. וְבוּלוֹ כָּשֵׁר שֶׁעֻנּוֹת מַכְבּוֹת אֶת הַתַּמּוּז. חִזְּבֵנִי וְאֵיבֵנִי אָזַי בְּיָרֵחַ תַּמּוּז. טָמְנוּ פַחִים חֲמִשָּׁה בְּמִקְרָא תְלָאוֹת מְשֻׁלָּחוֹת. יָכְלוּ לִי בְּשִׁבְעָה עָשָׂר בּוֹ בְּאֵלֶּה לֹחוֹת. כִּי נוּקַשְׁתִּי כְּכַלָּה עֲלוּבָה בְּחֻפַּת שֻׁלָּהּ וְהַצְלָחוֹת. לְרוֹעִי לֹא הַמְתַּנְתִּי שֵׁשׁ, וְנִשְׁתַּבְּרוּ הַלֻּחוֹת. מִיָּדוֹ עָדְיִתִי חֲלִי כֶתֶם, אֶצְעָדָה וְצָמִיד. עַד בֹּיוֹם אַפּוֹ, כְּשַׁחֲתִי דַּרְכִּי לְהַשְׁמִיד. סֵדֶר עֲבוֹדָתוֹ וָקִיק מִזְבֵּחַ קִצְתִּי לְהַעֲמִיד. עַל כֵּן מִלִּשְׁכַּת הַטְּלָאִים בָּטֵל הַתָּמִיד. פּוֹר הִתְפּוֹרְרָה וְנִתְפּוֹזָה סְעָרָה עֻנְיָהּ. צִי נִמְשְׁלָה מִבְּלִי חוֹבֵל, וְנִטְרְפָה כָּאֳנִיָּה. קַהֲתָה בְּחִטָּאתָהּ בָּרִאשָׁה, וּבִכְפֹל תַּאֲנָה וַאֲנִיָּה. רִיבָהּ צָרֶיהָ כְּהַיּוֹם, וְהַבְּקָעָה הָעִיר בַּשְּׁמִנִיָּה. שָׁלְחוּ כִּצְבִי מֻדָּח מֵאֵין דּוֹרֵשׁ לְהַסְתִּירָה. שָׁנָּוּ לְשׁוֹנָם וּנְתָנוּהָ כְּשֶׁה, צְמָרָהּ וַחֲלָבָהּ לְהַתִּירָה. תִּצְעַק עַל כְּלִי חֶמְדָּה שֶׁבּוֹ נִכְתָּרָה. תַּחֲמוֹד עֵינֶיהָ נָצַל כְּשָׁרַף אַפּוֹטְטוֹמוֹס הַתּוֹרָה. חֶרֶף עֲשׁוּקִים וּרְצוּצִים בַּעֲבוּר הָרְעִימָם סָכָל. יְדִידִים בּוֹהֲיָהּ לְאֵכֹל וּבְהִסְתֵּר פָּנִים מִלְּהִסְתַּכֵּל. יַד הַשָּׁלִים מִכַּף שִׁקּוּצִים נֶאֱכָל. עֵת צָרָה כְּהַתְכַּנֵּס וְהָעֳמַד צֶלֶם בַּהֵיכָל. דְּוֵוִים סְגוּפִים בָּנִים הֶהְיוּ מִקֶּדֶם רִאשׁוֹנִים. סְמוּכוֹת צָרוֹתֵיהֶם זוֹ לָזוֹ כַּמֶּה שָׁנִים. לוּקִים כַּאֲשֶׁר תַּעֲשֶׂינָה הַדְּבוֹרִים, וְהָעֳקָרְבִים שׁוֹנִים. הוֹגִים אָבַד שִׂבְרָם וּבָטֵל שִׂכּוּיֵם בָּאִישׁוֹנִים. ◄ אֵל קַנָּא, בְּהִתְאַפֵּק בְּמַקְנִיאֶיךָ דְּשֵׁנִים רְטוֹבִים. מְחַכִּים תָּקִים עוֹמְדִים לְעוֹלָמִים, כִּנְטוּעִים מְחֻטָּבִים בָּאֲהָבִים. הָאֱמֶת וְהַשָּׁלוֹם בְּצוֹמוֹת חֲטוּבִים. נֶצַח הֱיוֹתָם לְשִׂמְחָה וּלְשָׂשׂוֹן וּלְמוֹעֲדִים טוֹבִים.

אֵל מֶלֶךְ יוֹשֵׁב עַל כִּסֵּא רַחֲמִים, מִתְנַהֵג בַּחֲסִידוּת. מוֹחֵל עֲוֹנוֹת עַמּוֹ, מַעֲבִיר רִאשׁוֹן רִאשׁוֹן. מַרְבֶּה מְחִילָה לַחַטָּאִים, וּסְלִיחָה לַפּוֹשְׁעִים. עֹשֶׂה צְדָקוֹת עִם כָּל בָּשָׂר וָרוּחַ, לֹא כְרָעָתָם תִּגְמֹל. ◄ אֵל, הוֹרֵיתָ לָנוּ לוֹמַר שְׁלֹשׁ עֶשְׂרֵה, וּזְכָר לָנוּ הַיּוֹם בְּרִית שְׁלֹשׁ עֶשְׂרֵה, כְּמוֹ שֶׁהוֹדַעְתָּ לֶעָנָו מִקֶּדֶם, כְּמוֹ שֶׁכָּתוּב: וַיֵּרֶד יהוה בֶּעָנָן, וַיִּתְיַצֵּב עִמּוֹ שָׁם, וַיִּקְרָא בְשֵׁם, יהוה:

שְׁלִיחַ צִבּוּר then קָהָל:
וַיַּעֲבֹר יהוה עַל־פָּנָיו וַיִּקְרָא

שמות לד

All say aloud:

יהוה The Lᴏʀᴅ, the Lᴏʀᴅ, compassionate and gracious God, slow to anger, abounding in loving-kindness and truth, extending loving-kindness to a thousand generations, forgiving iniquity, rebellion and sin, and absolving [the guilty who repent]. Forgive us our iniquity and our sin, and take us as Your inheritance.

Continue:

סְלַח לָנוּ Forgive us, our Father, for we have sinned. Pardon us, our King, for we have transgressed. For You, Lᴏʀᴅ, are good and forgiving, abounding in loving-kindness to all who call on You. *Ps. 86*

The following is said responsively:

Turn to this prisoner who has been yielded up,
to the hand of Babylon and then of Seir;
to You he has been calling all these years, and he pleads like a small child,
       on the day the enemy prevailed and the city was broken through.

And so I bow myself and strike my hands together,
on this day of five disasters that scattered me about,
for at the time of the golden calf, the Tablets left me.
And the daily offering was annulled, and they brought me away in a cage.
And an idol was placed in the Sanctuary that was my crowning glory,
and I was deprived of His counsel.
The meal-offering was ended, and Your Law – the foe sent it up in flames,
       on the day the enemy prevailed and the city was broken through.

I tremble terribly, I stand horrified, on the day the Lᴏʀᴅ pushed me aside,
And Sennacherib, the Viper of the north, swept me away like a deluge.
My light grew dark, and Sheshakh [Babylon] too, tossed me about like a ball.
And the hunter stretched out his hand, and the goat of Greece,
the hairy one of Rome,
       on the day the enemy prevailed and the city was broken through.

The glory of my heart, my Stronghold, will Your rage fume forever?
Will You not see this weary nation, blackened as if by the furnace?
Close, with the descendant of Peretz, the breach in my fence,
and, from among the thorns, pick out the lily.
Build the Temple, and return the borders of the Carmel and of Bashan.
And open Your eyes, exact vengeance from Etzer and Dishan.
Judge a people struck dumb, so that the damages be paid,
by the one who destroys, the one who burns –
       on the day the enemy prevailed and the city was broken through.

All say aloud:

יהוה, יהוה, אֵל רַחוּם וְחַנּוּן, אֶרֶךְ אַפַּיִם, וְרַב־חֶסֶד וֶאֱמֶת: נֹצֵר
חֶסֶד לָאֲלָפִים, נֹשֵׂא עָוֹן וָפֶשַׁע וְחַטָּאָה, וְנַקֵּה: וְסָלַחְתָּ לַעֲוֹנֵנוּ
וּלְחַטָּאתֵנוּ, וּנְחַלְתָּנוּ:

Continue:

סְלַח לָנוּ אָבִינוּ כִּי חָטָאנוּ, מְחַל לָנוּ מַלְכֵּנוּ כִּי פָשָׁעְנוּ. כִּי־אַתָּה אֲדֹנָי טוֹב   תהלים פו
וְסַלָּח, וְרַב־חֶסֶד לְכָל־קֹרְאֶיךָ:

The following is said responsively:

שֶׂה נֶאֱסָר, אֲשֶׁר נִמְסָר, בְּיַד בָּבֶל וְגַם שֵׂעִיר.
לְךָ יֶהֱמֶה, זֶה כַּמֶּה, וְיִתְחַנֵּן כְּבֶן צָעִיר.
יוֹם גָּבַר הָאוֹיֵב וַתִּבָּקַע הָעִיר.

לְאֹת אֹכַף, וְאֶסְפֹּק כַּף, בְּיוֹם חֲמֵשׁ פְּזוּרֵנִי.
וְעַל רֶגֶל הָעֵגֶל, הַלּוּחוֹת יְצָאוּנִי.
וְגַם הֻשְׁמַד הַתָּמִיד, וּבְסוּגַר הֱבִיאֵנִי.
וְהוּשַׁם אֵלַי בְּהֵיכָל כְּלִיל, וּמֵעֲצָתוֹ כִּלְאַנִי.
וְהַמִּנְחָה הוּנְחָה, וְדָתְךָ, צָר בָּאֵשׁ הִבְעִיר.
יוֹם גָּבַר הָאוֹיֵב וַתִּבָּקַע הָעִיר.

מְאֹד אֶתְחַל, וְאֶתְחַלְחַל, בְּיוֹם שַׁדַּי דְּחָפַנִי.
וְהַשְּׁפִיפוֹן מִצָּפוֹן, כְּשִׁבֹּלֶת שְׁטָפַנִי.
מְאוֹר חָשַׁךְ, וְגַם שֵׁשַׁךְ, כְּמוֹ כַדּוּר צְנָפַנִי.
וְהַצָּיַד שָׁלַח יָד, וְהִצְפִּיר וְהִשְׂעִיר.
יוֹם גָּבַר הָאוֹיֵב וַתִּבָּקַע הָעִיר.

הוֹד לִבִּי וּמִשְׂגַּבִּי, הֲלָעַד אַפְּךָ יֶעְשַׁן.
הֲלֹא תֵרָאֶה עִם גִּלְאֵה, אֲשֶׁר הַשְׁחַר כְּמוֹ כִבְשָׁן.
גְּדֹר פִּרְצֵי בְּבֶן פַּרְצִי, וּמֵחֵדֶק לְקֹט שׁוֹשָׁן.
בְּנֵה בֵית זְבוּל, וְהָשֵׁב גְּבוּל הַכַּרְמֶל וְהַבָּשָׁן.
וְעַיִן פְּקָח, וְנָקָם קַח מֵאֲצֶר וּמִדִּישָׁן.
שְׁפֹט אִלֵּם, וְאָז יְשֻׁלַּם הַמַּבְעֶה וְהַמַּבְעִיר.
יוֹם גָּבַר הָאוֹיֵב וַתִּבָּקַע הָעִיר.

On all days continue:

אֵל מֶלֶךְ God, King who sits upon a throne of compassion, who acts with loving-kindness, who pardons the iniquities of His people, passing them before Him in order; who forgives sinners and pardons transgressors; who performs righteousness with all flesh and spirit, do not repay their bad actions in kind. God, You taught us to speak thirteen attributes: recall for us today the covenant of the thirteen attributes, as You in ancient times showed the humble one [Moses], as is written: The Lord descended in the cloud and stood with him there, and proclaimed in the name of the Lord:

Congregation then Leader:

And the Lord passed by before him and proclaimed: *Ex. 34*

All say aloud:

יהוה The Lord, the Lord, compassionate and gracious God, slow to anger, abounding in loving-kindness and truth, extending loving-kindness to a thousand generations, forgiving iniquity, rebellion and sin, and absolving [the guilty who repent]. Forgive us our iniquity and our sin, and take us as Your inheritance.

Continue:

סְלַח לָנוּ Forgive us, our Father, for we have sinned. Pardon us, our King, for we have transgressed. For You, Lord, are good and forgiving, abounding in   *Ps. 86* loving-kindness to all who call on You.

זְכֹר Remember, Lord, Your compassion and loving-kindness,   *Ps. 25*
    for they are everlasting. Remember us, Lord, in favoring Your people;
    redeem us with Your salvation.

זְכֹר Remember Your congregation, the one that You acquired long ago,   *Ps. 74*
    the tribe of Your inheritance that You redeemed,
    this Mount Zion that You have dwelt in.

זְכֹר Remember, Lord, the fondness of Jerusalem; do not forever forget the
    love of Zion. You shall rise up and have compassion for Zion,   *Ps. 102*
    for now it is right to be gracious, for the time has come.

זְכֹר Remember, Lord, what the Edomites did on the day Jerusalem fell.   *Ps. 137*
    They said, "Tear it down, tear it down to its very foundations!"

זְכֹר Remember Abraham, Isaac and Jacob, to whom You swore by Your   *Ex. 32*
    own self, when You said to them, "I shall make Your descendants
    as numerous as the stars in the sky, and I shall give all this Land that
    I spoke of to your descendants, and they shall inherit it forever."

זְכֹר Remember Your servants, Abraham, Isaac and Jacob; do not attend to   *Deut. 9*
    the stubbornness of this people, to their wickedness or sinfulness.

On all days continue:

אֵל מֶלֶךְ יוֹשֵׁב עַל כִּסֵּא רַחֲמִים, מִתְנַהֵג בַּחֲסִידוּת. מוֹחֵל עֲוֹנוֹת עַמּוֹ, מַעֲבִיר רִאשׁוֹן רִאשׁוֹן. מַרְבֶּה מְחִילָה לַחַטָּאִים, וּסְלִיחָה לַפּוֹשְׁעִים. עֹשֶׂה צְדָקוֹת עִם כָּל בָּשָׂר וָרוּחַ, לֹא כְרָעָתָם תִּגְמֹל. ‧ אֵל, הוֹרֵיתָ לָּנוּ לוֹמַר שְׁלֹשׁ עֶשְׂרֵה, וּזְכֹר לָנוּ הַיּוֹם בְּרִית שְׁלֹשׁ עֶשְׂרֵה, כְּמוֹ שֶׁהוֹדַעְתָּ לֶעָנָו מִקֶּדֶם, כְּמוֹ שֶׁכָּתוּב: וַיֵּרֶד יהוה בֶּעָנָן, וַיִּתְיַצֵּב עִמּוֹ שָׁם, וַיִּקְרָא בְשֵׁם, יהוה:

שליח ציבור then קהל

וַיַּעֲבֹר יהוה עַל־פָּנָיו וַיִּקְרָא   שמות לד

All say aloud:

יהוה, יהוה, אֵל רַחוּם וְחַנּוּן, אֶרֶךְ אַפַּיִם, וְרַב־חֶסֶד וֶאֱמֶת: נֹצֵר חֶסֶד לָאֲלָפִים, נֹשֵׂא עָוֹן וָפֶשַׁע וְחַטָּאָה, וְנַקֵּה, וְסָלַחְתָּ לַעֲוֹנֵנוּ וּלְחַטָּאתֵנוּ, וּנְחַלְתָּנוּ:

Continue:

סְלַח לָנוּ אָבִינוּ כִּי חָטָאנוּ, מְחַל לָנוּ מַלְכֵּנוּ כִּי פָשָׁעְנוּ. כִּי־אַתָּה אֲדֹנָי טוֹב   תהלים פו
וְסַלָּח, וְרַב־חֶסֶד לְכָל־קֹרְאֶיךָ:

זְכֹר רַחֲמֶיךָ יהוה וַחֲסָדֶיךָ, כִּי מֵעוֹלָם הֵמָּה: תהלים כה
זָכְרֵנוּ יהוה בִּרְצוֹן עַמֶּךָ, פָּקְדֵנוּ בִּישׁוּעָתֶךָ:

זְכֹר עֲדָתְךָ קָנִיתָ קֶּדֶם, גָּאַלְתָּ שֵׁבֶט נַחֲלָתֶךָ,   תהלים עד
הַר־צִיּוֹן זֶה שָׁכַנְתָּ בּוֹ:

זְכֹר יהוה חִבַּת יְרוּשָׁלַָם, אַהֲבַת צִיּוֹן אַל תִּשְׁכַּח לָנֶצַח:
אַתָּה תָקוּם תְּרַחֵם צִיּוֹן, כִּי־עֵת לְחֶנְנָהּ, כִּי־בָא מוֹעֵד: תהלים קב

זְכֹר יהוה לִבְנֵי אֱדוֹם אֵת יוֹם יְרוּשָׁלָ͏ִם,   תהלים קלז
הָאוֹמְרִים עָרוּ עָרוּ, עַד הַיְסוֹד בָּהּ:

זְכֹר לְאַבְרָהָם לְיִצְחָק וּלְיִשְׂרָאֵל עֲבָדֶיךָ, אֲשֶׁר נִשְׁבַּעְתָּ לָהֶם בָּךְ   שמות לב
וַתְּדַבֵּר אֲלֵהֶם, אַרְבֶּה אֶת־זַרְעֲכֶם כְּכוֹכְבֵי הַשָּׁמָיִם
וְכָל־הָאָרֶץ הַזֹּאת אֲשֶׁר אָמַרְתִּי אֶתֵּן לְזַרְעֲכֶם, וְנָחֲלוּ לְעֹלָם:

זְכֹר לַעֲבָדֶיךָ לְאַבְרָהָם לְיִצְחָק וּלְיַעֲקֹב,   דברים ט
אַל־תֵּפֶן אֶל־קְשִׁי הָעָם הַזֶּה וְאֶל־רִשְׁעוֹ וְאֶל־חַטָּאתוֹ:

אֵל־נָא Please, do not hold against us the sin   *Num. 12*
that we committed so foolishly, that we have sinned.
We have sinned, our Rock; forgive us, our Creator.

Some say responsively (all continue with "Remember the covenant" on the next page):

אֵל נָא God, please, heal please, the diseases of this fruitful vine,
ashamed, disgraced and miserable are her fruits.
Redeem her from destruction and from the seeping wound;
answer us as You answered our father Abraham on Mount Moriah –

> We have sinned, our Rock;
> forgive us, our Creator.

Let the flags of the people redeemed by Your revealed arm,
be spared from plague; let them not be cut down,
and answer our call, and desire the creations of Your hands.
Answer us as You answered our fathers at the Reed Sea –

> We have sinned, our Rock;
> forgive us, our Creator.

Reveal now the merit of Abraham and Sarah,
the rock from which we were hewn.
Spare us from rage and lead us on a straight path.
Clear our impurity, and open our eyes to the light of Your Torah.
Answer us as You answered Joshua at Gilgal –

> We have sinned, our Rock;
> forgive us, our Creator.

LORD, witness the ashes of bound Isaac; make our cure spring up.
Put an end to plunder and brokenness, tempest and storm.
Teach us and make us wise with Your perfect word.
Answer us as You answered Samuel at Mitzpah –

> We have sinned, our Rock;
> forgive us, our Creator.

Jacob who emerged perfect from the womb – do not let his roots dry up.
Cleanse us of all stain and blemish, and do not have us wither.
Help us and we shall be saved,
and receive of Your ways of kindness.
Answer us as You answered Elijah on Mount Carmel –

> We have sinned, our Rock;
> forgive us, our Creator.

אֵל־נָא תָשֵׁת עָלֵינוּ חַטָּאת אֲשֶׁר נוֹאַלְנוּ וַאֲשֶׁר חָטָאנוּ:
חָטָאנוּ צוּרֵנוּ, סְלַח לֵנוּ יוֹצְרֵנוּ.

Some say responsively (all continue with זְכֹר לֵנוּ בְּרִית *on the next page):*

אֵל נָא, רְפָא נָא תַּחֲלוּאֵי גֶּפֶן פּוֹרִיָּה
בּוֹשָׁה וְחָפְרָה, וְאֻמְלַל פִּרְיָהּ
גְּאָלֶנָּה מִשַּׁחַת וּמִמַּכָּה טְרִיָּה.
עֲנֵנוּ כְּשֶׁעָנִיתָ לְאַבְרָהָם אָבִינוּ בְּהַר הַמּוֹרִיָּה.
חָטָאנוּ צוּרֵנוּ, סְלַח לֵנוּ יוֹצְרֵנוּ.

דִּגְלֵי עָם, פְּדוּיֵי בְזוֹרְעַ חָשׂוּף
הַצֵּל מִנֶּגֶף וְאַל יִהְיוּ לְשִׁסּוּף
וְתַעֲנֶה קְרִיאָתֵנוּ וּלְמַעֲשֵׂה יָדֶיךָ תִּכְסֹף
עֲנֵנוּ כְּשֶׁעָנִיתָ לַאֲבוֹתֵינוּ עַל יַם סוּף.
חָטָאנוּ צוּרֵנוּ, סְלַח לֵנוּ יוֹצְרֵנוּ.

זְכוּת צוּר חָצֵב הַיּוֹם לֵנוּ תַגֵּל
חָשְׁכֵנוּ מֵאֹנֶף וְנִחֲנוּ בְּיֹשֶׁר מַעְגָּל
טַהֵר טֻמְאָתֵנוּ וְלִמְאוֹר תּוֹרָתְךָ עֵינֵינוּ גַּל
עֲנֵנוּ כְּשֶׁעָנִיתָ לִיהוֹשֻׁעַ בַּגִּלְגָּל.
חָטָאנוּ צוּרֵנוּ, סְלַח לֵנוּ יוֹצְרֵנוּ.

יָהּ, רְאֵה דֶּשֶׁן עָקוּד, וְהַצְמַח לֵנוּ תְרוּפָה
כַּלֵּה שֹׁד וָשֶׁבֶר, סַעַר וְסוּפָה
לַמְּדֵנוּ וְחַכְּמֵנוּ אִמְרָתְךָ הַצְּרוּפָה
עֲנֵנוּ כְּשֶׁעָנִיתָ לִשְׁמוּאֵל בַּמִּצְפָּה.
חָטָאנוּ צוּרֵנוּ, סְלַח לֵנוּ יוֹצְרֵנוּ.

מִתַּמֵּם מְרַחֵם, שָׁרָשָׁיו אֵל תַּקְמֵל
נַקֵּנוּ מִכֶּתֶם וְשֶׁמֶץ, וְלֹא נֶאֱמַל
סַעֲדֵנוּ וְנִוָּשֵׁעָה, וְאָרְחוֹת חֲסָדֶיךָ נִגְמַל
עֲנֵנוּ כְּשֶׁעָנִיתָ לְאֵלִיָּהוּ בְּהַר הַכַּרְמֶל.
חָטָאנוּ צוּרֵנוּ, סְלַח לֵנוּ יוֹצְרֵנוּ.

Strengthen us by the righteousness of Moses, drawn from water,
and atone our crimes, wanton or foolish.
Free us from the terror of death that thrusts us back,
rule for our salvation; do not let us melt away in our sins.
Answer us as You answered Jonah in the belly of the fish –

> We have sinned, our Rock;
> forgive us, our Creator.

Remember Your devoted Aaron's sanctity,
for the sake of Israel of the pleasing steps.
Awaken Your compassion, for we are doubly stricken.
Return us resolutely to our awe of You, do not expose us.
Answer us as You answered David, and Solomon his son in Jerusalem –

> We have sinned, our Rock;
> forgive us, our Creator.

On the Fast of Esther add:
Answer those who call You; listen out from Your residence.
Hear the cry of those who call out to You, You who listen to the destitute.
Have compassion for Your children, as a father has for his.
Answer us as You answered Mordekhai and Esther:
and on a fifty-cubit gallows they hanged father and sons –

> We have sinned, our Rock.
> Forgive us, our Creator.

All continue:

וְכֹר Remember the covenant of our fathers, as You have said,   *Lev. 26*
  "I shall remember My covenant with Jacob, and My covenant
  with Isaac, and I shall remember My covenant with Abraham,
  and I shall remember the Land."

וְכֹר Remember the covenant of the early ones, as You have said,   *Lev. 26*
  "I shall remember for them the covenant of the early ones,
  those I took out of the Land of Egypt before the eyes of the nations,
  in order to be their God: I am the LORD."

עֲשֵׂה Deal kindly with us as You have promised, "Even so, when they are in the   *Lev. 26*
land of their enemies I shall not reject them and shall not detest them to the
point of destruction, to the point of breaking My covenant with them, for I
am the LORD their God." Restore our fortunes, and have compassion for us as
is written, "And God shall restore your fortunes and have compassion for you,   *Deut. 30*
and shall return and gather you in from all the nations among whom the LORD

עוֹדְדֵנוּ בְּצֶדֶק מָשׁוּי מִמַּיִם, וְכַפֵּר זָדוֹן וּמְשׁוּגָה
פְּדֵנוּ מִמְּהוּמַת מָוֶת, וְאָחוֹר בַּל נְסוֹגָה
צַוֵּה יְשׁוּעָתֵנוּ, וּבְעַוֹנוֹתֵינוּ אַל נִתְמוֹגָגָה
עֲנֵנוּ כְּשֶׁעָנִיתָ לְיוֹנָה בִּמְעֵי הַדָּגָה.
חָטָאנוּ צוּרֵנוּ, סְלַח לָנוּ יוֹצְרֵנוּ.

קִדַּשְׁתָּ אִישׁ חֲסִידֶךָ זְכֹר לִיפַת פְּעָמַיִם
רַחֲמֶיךָ תְּעוֹרֵר כִּי לָקִינוּ בְּכִפְלַיִם
שׁוּבֵנוּ תֹּקֶף לְיִרְאָתֶךָ וְלֹא נֶחְשַׁב שׁוֹלָיִם
עֲנֵנוּ כְּשֶׁעָנִיתָ לְדָוִד וְלִשְׁלֹמֹה בְּנוֹ בִּירוּשָׁלָיִם.
חָטָאנוּ צוּרֵנוּ, סְלַח לָנוּ יוֹצְרֵנוּ.

On תַּעֲנִית אֶסְתֵּר add:

תַּעֲנֶה לְקוֹרְאֶיךָ, וְהַסְכֵּת מִמְּעוֹנִים
תִּשְׁמַע שַׁוְעַת צוֹעֲקֶיךָ, שׁוֹמֵעַ אֶל אֶבְיוֹנִים
תְּרַחֵם עַל בָּנֶיךָ כְּרַחֵם אָב עַל בָּנִים
עֲנֵנוּ כְּמוֹ שֶׁעָנִיתָ לְמָרְדְּכַי וְאֶסְתֵּר
וְתָלוּ עַל עֵץ־חֲמִשִּׁים הָאָב עִם בָּנִים.
חָטָאנוּ צוּרֵנוּ, סְלַח לָנוּ יוֹצְרֵנוּ.

All continue:

זְכֹר לָנוּ בְּרִית אָבוֹת כַּאֲשֶׁר אָמַרְתָּ: וְזָכַרְתִּי אֶת־בְּרִיתִי יַעֲקוֹב   ויקרא כו
וְאַף אֶת־בְּרִיתִי יִצְחָק וְאַף אֶת־בְּרִיתִי אַבְרָהָם אֶזְכֹּר
וְהָאָרֶץ אֶזְכֹּר:

זְכֹר לָנוּ בְּרִית רִאשׁוֹנִים כַּאֲשֶׁר אָמַרְתָּ: וְזָכַרְתִּי לָהֶם בְּרִית רִאשֹׁנִים   ויקרא כו
אֲשֶׁר הוֹצֵאתִי־אֹתָם מֵאֶרֶץ מִצְרַיִם לְעֵינֵי הַגּוֹיִם
לִהְיוֹת לָהֶם לֵאלֹהִים, אֲנִי יהוה:

עֲשֵׂה עִמָּנוּ כְּמָה שֶׁהִבְטַחְתָּנוּ: וְאַף גַּם־זֹאת בִּהְיוֹתָם בְּאֶרֶץ אֹיְבֵיהֶם   ויקרא כו
לֹא־מְאַסְתִּים וְלֹא־גְעַלְתִּים לְכַלֹּתָם, לְהָפֵר בְּרִיתִי אִתָּם, כִּי אֲנִי יהוה
אֱלֹהֵיהֶם: הָשֵׁב שְׁבוּתֵנוּ וְרַחֲמֵנוּ כְּמָה שֶׁכָּתוּב: וְשָׁב יהוה אֱלֹהֶיךָ אֶת־   דברים ל

has scattered you." Gather those of us who have been distanced, as is written, "If your distanced ones are at the very ends of the heavens, from there shall *Deut. 30* the LORD your God gather you; from there shall He bring You." Wipe out our crimes as if they were a cloud, as if they were a haze, as is written, "I have wiped *Is. 44* out your crimes like a cloud, and as a haze your sins; come back to Me for I have redeemed you." Wipe out our crimes for Your sake, as You have said, "I, I am the *Is. 43* one who shall wipe out your crimes for My sake, and I shall not recall your sins." Whiten our sins as snow and as wool, as is written, "Come now, let us reason *Is. 1* together, says the LORD; If your sins are like scarlet, they shall be whitened like snow; should they be as red as crimson, they shall become like wool." Throw over us pure waters and purify us, as is written, "I shall throw pure waters over *Ezek. 36* you and you shall be pure. I shall purify you of all your impurities and of all your idolatry." Have compassion for us and do not destroy us, as is written, "For the *Deut. 4* LORD your God is a compassionate God; He will not cease to hold you and He will not destroy you, and will not forget the covenant of your fathers that He pledged to them." Circumcise our hearts to love Your name, as is written, "And the LORD will circumcise your heart and the heart of your descendants to *Deut. 30* love the LORD your God with all your heart and with all your soul, so that you shall live." Let us find You when we seek You, as is written, "And if from there *Deut. 4* you seek the LORD your God, you shall find Him, when you seek Him out with all your heart and with all your soul." Bring us to Your holy mountain, and let us rejoice in Your house of prayer, as is written, "I shall bring them to My holy *Is. 56* mountain, and I shall make them rejoice in My house of prayer; their offerings and their sacrifices will be accepted, desired on My altar, for My House will be called a house of prayer for all peoples."

The Ark is opened. The following until ◂ *is said responsively, verse by verse:*

שְׁמַע קוֹלֵנוּ Listen to our voice, LORD our God. Spare us and have compassion on us, and in compassion and favor accept our prayer. Turn us back, O LORD, *Lam. 5* to You, and we will return. Renew our days as of old. Do not cast us away from You, and do not take Your holy spirit from us. Do not cast us away in our old age; when our strength is gone do not desert us.◂ Do not desert us, LORD; our God, do not be distant from us. Give us a sign of good things, and those who hate us shall see it and be ashamed, for You, LORD, will help us and console us. Hear our speech, LORD, consider our thoughts. May the words of our mouths and the thoughts within our hearts be pleasing to You, LORD, our Rock and our Redeemer. For it is You, LORD, that we have longed for; You shall answer us, LORD our God.

The Ark is closed.

שְׁבוּתְךָ וְרִחֲמֶךָ, וְשָׁב וְקִבֶּצְךָ מִכָּל־הָעַמִּים אֲשֶׁר הֱפִיצְךָ יהוה אֱלֹהֶיךָ

דברים ל — שָׁמָּה: קַבֵּץ נִדָּחֵינוּ כְּמָה שֶׁכָּתוּב: אִם־יִהְיֶה נִדַּחֲךָ בִּקְצֵה הַשָּׁמָיִם, מִשָּׁם

יְקַבֶּצְךָ יהוה אֱלֹהֶיךָ וּמִשָּׁם יִקָּחֶךָ: מְחֵה פְשָׁעֵינוּ כְּעָב וְכֶעָנָן כְּמָה שֶׁכָּתוּב:

ישעיה מד — מָחִיתִי כָעָב פְּשָׁעֶיךָ וְכֶעָנָן חַטֹּאותֶיךָ, שׁוּבָה אֵלַי כִּי גְאַלְתִּיךָ: מְחֵה פְשָׁעֵינוּ

ישעיה מג — לְמַעַנְךָ כַּאֲשֶׁר אָמַרְתָּ: אָנֹכִי אָנֹכִי הוּא מֹחֶה פְשָׁעֶיךָ לְמַעֲנִי, וְחַטֹּאתֶיךָ

ישעיה א — לֹא אֶזְכֹּר: הַלְבֵּן חֲטָאֵינוּ כַּשֶּׁלֶג וְכַצֶּמֶר כְּמָה שֶׁכָּתוּב: לְכוּ־נָא וְנִוָּכְחָה

יֹאמַר יהוה, אִם־יִהְיוּ חֲטָאֵיכֶם כַּשָּׁנִים כַּשֶּׁלֶג יַלְבִּינוּ, אִם־יַאְדִּימוּ כַתּוֹלָע

יחזקאל לו — כַּצֶּמֶר יִהְיוּ: זְרֹק עָלֵינוּ מַיִם טְהוֹרִים וְטַהֲרֵנוּ כְּמָה שֶׁכָּתוּב: וְזָרַקְתִּי עֲלֵיכֶם

מַיִם טְהוֹרִים וּטְהַרְתֶּם, מִכֹּל טֻמְאוֹתֵיכֶם וּמִכָּל־גִּלּוּלֵיכֶם אֲטַהֵר אֶתְכֶם:

רַחֵם עָלֵינוּ וְאַל תַּשְׁחִיתֵנוּ כְּמָה שֶׁכָּתוּב: כִּי אֵל רַחוּם יהוה אֱלֹהֶיךָ, לֹא

דברים ד — יַרְפְּךָ וְלֹא יַשְׁחִיתֶךָ, וְלֹא יִשְׁכַּח אֶת־בְּרִית אֲבֹתֶיךָ אֲשֶׁר נִשְׁבַּע לָהֶם: מוֹל

אֶת לְבָבֵנוּ לְאַהֲבָה אֶת שְׁמֶךָ כְּמָה שֶׁכָּתוּב: וּמָל יהוה אֱלֹהֶיךָ אֶת־לְבָבְךָ

דברים ל — וְאֶת־לְבַב זַרְעֶךָ, לְאַהֲבָה אֶת־יהוה אֱלֹהֶיךָ בְּכָל־לְבָבְךָ וּבְכָל־נַפְשְׁךָ, לְמַעַן

חַיֶּיךָ: הִמָּצֵא לָנוּ בְּבַקָּשָׁתֵנוּ כְּמָה שֶׁכָּתוּב: וּבִקַּשְׁתֶּם מִשָּׁם אֶת־יהוה

דברים ד — אֱלֹהֶיךָ וּמָצָאתָ, כִּי תִדְרְשֶׁנּוּ בְּכָל־לְבָבְךָ וּבְכָל־נַפְשֶׁךָ: תְּבִיאֵנוּ אֶל הַר

קָדְשְׁךָ וְשַׂמְּחֵנוּ בְּבֵית תְּפִלָּתֶךָ כְּמָה שֶׁכָּתוּב: וַהֲבִיאוֹתִים אֶל־הַר קָדְשִׁי

ישעיה נו — וְשִׂמַּחְתִּים בְּבֵית תְּפִלָּתִי, עוֹלֹתֵיהֶם וְזִבְחֵיהֶם לְרָצוֹן עַל־מִזְבְּחִי, כִּי בֵיתִי

בֵית־תְּפִלָּה יִקָּרֵא לְכָל־הָעַמִּים:

The אֲרוֹן קוֹדֶשׁ *is opened. The following until* ▸ *is said responsively, verse by verse:*

שְׁמַע קוֹלֵנוּ, יהוה אֱלֹהֵינוּ, חוּס וְרַחֵם עָלֵינוּ וְקַבֵּל בְּרַחֲמִים וּבְרָצוֹן אֶת

איכה ה — תְּפִלָּתֵנוּ: הֲשִׁיבֵנוּ יהוה אֵלֶיךָ וְנָשׁוּבָה, חַדֵּשׁ יָמֵינוּ כְּקֶדֶם: אַל תַּשְׁלִיכֵנוּ

מִלְּפָנֶיךָ, וְרוּחַ קָדְשְׁךָ אַל תִּקַּח מִמֶּנּוּ: אַל תַּשְׁלִיכֵנוּ לְעֵת זִקְנָה, כִּכְלוֹת

כֹּחֵנוּ אַל תַּעַזְבֵנוּ: ▸ אַל תַּעַזְבֵנוּ יהוה, אֱלֹהֵינוּ אַל תִּרְחַק מִמֶּנּוּ: עֲשֵׂה

עִמָּנוּ אוֹת לְטוֹבָה, וְיִרְאוּ שׂוֹנְאֵינוּ וְיֵבֹשׁוּ, כִּי אַתָּה יהוה עֲזַרְתָּנוּ וְנִחַמְתָּנוּ:

אֲמָרֵינוּ הַאֲזִינָה יהוה, בִּינָה הֲגִיגֵנוּ: יִהְיוּ לְרָצוֹן אִמְרֵי פִינוּ וְהֶגְיוֹן לִבֵּנוּ

לְפָנֶיךָ, יהוה צוּרֵנוּ וְגֹאֲלֵנוּ: כִּי לְךָ יהוה הוֹחָלְנוּ, אַתָּה תַעֲנֶה אֲדֹנָי אֱלֹהֵינוּ:

The אֲרוֹן קוֹדֶשׁ *is closed.*

CONFESSION

אֱלֹהֵינוּ Our God and God of our fathers,
let our prayer come before You, and do not hide Yourself from our plea,
for we are not so arrogant or obstinate as to say before You,
Lord, our God and God of our fathers,
we are righteous and have not sinned,
for in truth, we and our fathers have sinned.

Strike the left side of the chest with the right fist while saying each of the sins.

אָשַׁמְנוּ We have been guilty, we have acted treacherously, we have
robbed, we have spoken slander. We have acted perversely, we have
acted wickedly, we have acted presumptuously, we have been violent,
we have framed lies. We have given bad advice, we have deceived, we
have scorned, we have rebelled, we have provoked, we have turned away,
we have committed iniquity, we have transgressed, we have persecuted,
we have been obstinate. We have acted wickedly, we have corrupted,
we have acted abominably, we have strayed, we have led others astray.

סַרְנוּ We have turned away from Your commandments, and good laws, to no
avail, for You are just in all that has befallen us, for You have acted faithfully   *Neh. 9*
while we have done wickedly.

הִרְשַׁעְנוּ We have been wicked and we have done wrong, and so we have not
been saved. Place it in our hearts to abandon the way of wickedness, and
hasten our salvation, as is written by Your prophet, "Let each wicked person   *Is. 55*
abandon his ways, each man of iniquity his thoughts, and let him come back
to the Lord and He will have compassion for him; back to our God for He
will forgive abundantly."

מְשִׁיחַ Your righteous anointed one said to You, "Who can discern his own   *Ps. 19*
mistakes? Cleanse me of my hidden faults." Cleanse us, Lord our God, of all
our sins, and purify us of all our impurities and throw clear waters over us to
purify us, as was written by Your prophet, "I shall throw clear waters over you   *Ezek. 36*
and you shall be pure. I shall purify you of all your impurities and of all your
idolatry." Your people, Your inheritance, famished of Your good, thirsting for
Your loving-kindness, craving Your salvation – they shall recognize and know
that compassion and forgiveness belong to the Lord our God.

On days when Tahanun is not said (such as on the morning of a Brit Mila, or when a bridegroom
is present), continue with Avinu Malkenu on page 138 followed by Half Kaddish (page 156).

וידוי

אֱלֹהֵינוּ וֵאלֹהֵי אֲבוֹתֵינוּ

תָּבֹא לְפָנֶיךָ תְּפִלָּתֵנוּ, וְאַל תִּתְעַלַּם מִתְּחִנָּתֵנוּ.

שֶׁאֵין אֲנוּ עַזֵּי פָנִים וּקְשֵׁי עֹרֶף לוֹמַר לְפָנֶיךָ

יהוה אֱלֹהֵינוּ וֵאלֹהֵי אֲבוֹתֵינוּ, צַדִּיקִים אֲנַחְנוּ וְלֹא חָטָאנוּ.

אֲבָל אֲנַחְנוּ וַאֲבוֹתֵינוּ חָטָאנוּ.

Strike the left side of the chest with the right fist while saying each of the sins.

אָשַׁמְנוּ, בָּגַדְנוּ, גָּזַלְנוּ, דִּבַּרְנוּ דֹפִי. הֶעֱוִינוּ, וְהִרְשַׁעְנוּ, זַדְנוּ, חָמַסְנוּ,

טָפַלְנוּ שֶׁקֶר. יָעַצְנוּ רָע, כִּזַּבְנוּ, לַצְנוּ, מָרַדְנוּ, נִאַצְנוּ, סָרַרְנוּ,

עָוִינוּ, פָּשַׁעְנוּ, צָרַרְנוּ, קִשִּׁינוּ עֹרֶף. רָשַׁעְנוּ, שִׁחַתְנוּ, תִּעַבְנוּ,

תָּעִינוּ, תִּעְתָּעְנוּ.

סַרְנוּ מִמִּצְוֹתֶיךָ וּמִמִּשְׁפָּטֶיךָ הַטּוֹבִים, וְלֹא שָׁוָה לָנוּ. וְאַתָּה צַדִּיק עַל   נחמיה ט

כָּל־הַבָּא עָלֵינוּ, כִּי־אֱמֶת עָשִׂיתָ וַאֲנַחְנוּ הִרְשָׁעְנוּ.

הִרְשַׁעְנוּ וּפָשַׁעְנוּ לָכֵן לֹא נוֹשָׁעְנוּ. וְתֵן בְּלִבֵּנוּ לַעֲזֹב דֶּרֶךְ רֶשַׁע, וְחִישׁ

לָנוּ יֶשַׁע, כַּכָּתוּב עַל יַד נְבִיאֶךָ: יַעֲזֹב רָשָׁע דַּרְכּוֹ וְאִישׁ אָוֶן מַחְשְׁבֹתָיו,   ישעיה נה

וְיָשֹׁב אֶל־יהוה וִירַחֲמֵהוּ וְאֶל־אֱלֹהֵינוּ כִּי־יַרְבֶּה לִסְלוֹחַ:

מְשִׁיחַ צִדְקֶךָ אָמַר לְפָנֶיךָ: שְׁגִיאוֹת מִי־יָבִין, מִנִּסְתָּרוֹת נַקֵּנִי: נַקֵּנוּ יהוה   תהלים יט

אֱלֹהֵינוּ מִכָּל פְּשָׁעֵינוּ וְטַהֲרֵנוּ מִכָּל טֻמְאוֹתֵינוּ וּזְרֹק עָלֵינוּ מַיִם טְהוֹרִים

וְטַהֲרֵנוּ, כַּכָּתוּב עַל יַד נְבִיאֶךָ: וְזָרַקְתִּי עֲלֵיכֶם מַיִם טְהוֹרִים וּטְהַרְתֶּם,   יחזקאל לו

מִכֹּל טֻמְאוֹתֵיכֶם וּמִכָּל־גִּלּוּלֵיכֶם אֲטַהֵר אֶתְכֶם: עַמְּךָ וְנַחֲלָתְךָ רְעֵבֵי

טוּבְךָ, צְמֵאֵי חַסְדְּךָ, תְּאֵבֵי יִשְׁעֶךָ. יַכִּירוּ וְיֵדְעוּ, כִּי לַיהוה אֱלֹהֵינוּ

הָרַחֲמִים וְהַסְּלִיחוֹת.

On days when תחנון *is not said (such as on the morning of a* ברית מילה, *or when a* חתן
is present), continue with אבינו מלכנו *on page 139 followed by* חצי קדיש (*page 157*).

אֵל רַחוּם Compassionate God is Your name; Gracious God is Your name. We are called by Your name; LORD, act for the sake of Your name. Act for the sake of Your truth. Act for the sake of Your covenant. Act for the sake of Your greatness and glory. Act for the sake of Your Law. Act for the sake of Your majesty. Act for the sake of Your promise. Act for the sake of Your remembrance. Act for the sake of Your loving-kindness. Act for the sake of Your goodness. Act for the sake of Your oneness. Act for the sake of Your honor. Act for the sake of Your wisdom. Act for the sake of Your kingship. Act for the sake of Your eternity. Act for the sake of Your mystery. Act for the sake of Your might. Act for the sake of Your splendor. Act for the sake of Your righteousness. Act for the sake of Your holiness. Act for the sake of Your great compassion. Act for the sake of Your Presence. Act for the sake of Your praise. Act for the sake of those who loved You, who now dwell in the dust. Act for the sake of Abraham, Isaac and Jacob. Act for the sake of Moses and Aaron. Act for the sake of David and Solomon. Act for the sake of Jerusalem, Your holy city. Act for the sake of Zion, the dwelling place of Your glory. Act for the sake of the desolate site of Your Temple. Act for the sake of the ruins of Your altar. Act for the sake of those killed in sanctification of Your name. Act for the sake of those slaughtered over Your unity. Act for the sake of those who have gone through fire and water in sanctification of Your name. Act for the sake of suckling infants who have not sinned. Act for the sake of little ones just weaned who have done no wrong. Act for the sake of schoolchildren. Act for Your own sake if not for ours. Act for Your own sake, and save us.

עֲנֵנוּ Answer us, LORD, answer us. Answer us, our God, answer us. Answer us, our Father, answer us. Answer us, our Creator, answer us. Answer us, our Redeemer, answer us. Answer us, You who seek us, answer us. Answer us, God who is faithful, answer us. Answer us, You who are ancient and kind, answer us. Answer us, You who are pure and upright, answer us. Answer us, You who are alive and remain, answer us. Answer us, You who are good and do good, answer us. Answer us, You who know our impulses, answer us. Answer us, You who conquer rage, answer us. Answer us, You who clothe Yourself in righteousness, answer us. Answer us, Supreme King of kings, answer us. Answer us, You who are awesome and elevated, answer us. Answer us, You who forgive and pardon, answer us. Answer us, You who answer in times of trouble, answer us. Answer us, You who redeem and save, answer us. Answer us, You who are righteous and straightforward, answer us. Answer us, You who are close to those who call, answer us. Answer us, You who are compassionate and gracious, answer us. Answer us, You who listen to the destitute, answer us. Answer us, You who support the innocent, answer us. Answer us, God of our fathers, answer us. Answer us, God of Abraham, answer us. Answer us, Terror of Isaac, answer us. Answer us, Champion of Jacob, answer us. Answer us, Help of the tribes, answer us. Answer us, Stronghold of the mothers, answer us. Answer us, You who are slow to anger, answer us. Answer us, You who are lightly appeased, answer us. Answer us, You who answer at times of favor, answer us. Answer us, Father of orphans, answer us. Answer us, Justice of widows, answer us.

אֵל רַחוּם שְׁמֶךָ. אֵל חַנּוּן שְׁמֶךָ. בָּנוּ נִקְרָא שְׁמֶךָ. יהוה עֲשֵׂה לְמַעַן שְׁמֶךָ.
עֲשֵׂה לְמַעַן אֲמִתֶּךָ. עֲשֵׂה לְמַעַן בְּרִיתֶךָ. עֲשֵׂה לְמַעַן גׇּדְלְךָ וְתִפְאַרְתֶּךָ. עֲשֵׂה
לְמַעַן דָּתֶךָ. עֲשֵׂה לְמַעַן הוֹדֶךָ. עֲשֵׂה לְמַעַן וְעַדֶךָ. עֲשֵׂה לְמַעַן זִכְרֶךָ. עֲשֵׂה
לְמַעַן חַסְדֶּךָ. עֲשֵׂה לְמַעַן טוּבֶךָ. עֲשֵׂה לְמַעַן יִחוּדֶךָ. עֲשֵׂה לְמַעַן כְּבוֹדֶךָ.
עֲשֵׂה לְמַעַן לִמּוּדֶךָ. עֲשֵׂה לְמַעַן מַלְכוּתֶךָ. עֲשֵׂה לְמַעַן נִצְחֶךָ. עֲשֵׂה לְמַעַן
סוֹדֶךָ. עֲשֵׂה לְמַעַן עֻזֶּךָ. עֲשֵׂה לְמַעַן פְּאֵרֶךָ. עֲשֵׂה לְמַעַן צִדְקָתֶךָ. עֲשֵׂה
לְמַעַן קְדֻשָּׁתֶךָ. עֲשֵׂה לְמַעַן רַחֲמֶיךָ הָרַבִּים. עֲשֵׂה לְמַעַן שְׁכִינָתֶךָ. עֲשֵׂה
לְמַעַן תְּהִלָּתֶךָ. עֲשֵׂה לְמַעַן אוֹהֲבֶיךָ שׁוֹכְנֵי עָפָר. עֲשֵׂה לְמַעַן אַבְרָהָם
יִצְחָק וְיַעֲקֹב. עֲשֵׂה לְמַעַן מֹשֶׁה וְאַהֲרֹן. עֲשֵׂה לְמַעַן דָּוִד וּשְׁלֹמֹה. עֲשֵׂה
לְמַעַן יְרוּשָׁלַיִם עִיר קׇדְשֶׁךָ. עֲשֵׂה לְמַעַן צִיּוֹן מִשְׁכַּן כְּבוֹדֶךָ. עֲשֵׂה לְמַעַן
שִׁמְמוֹת הֵיכָלֶךָ. עֲשֵׂה לְמַעַן הֲרִיסוֹת מִזְבְּחֶךָ. עֲשֵׂה לְמַעַן הֲרוּגִים עַל שֵׁם
קׇדְשֶׁךָ. עֲשֵׂה לְמַעַן טְבוּחִים עַל יִחוּדֶךָ. עֲשֵׂה לְמַעַן בָּאֵי בָאֵשׁ וּבַמַּיִם
עַל קִדּוּשׁ שְׁמֶךָ. עֲשֵׂה לְמַעַן יוֹנְקֵי שָׁדַיִם שֶׁלֹּא חָטְאוּ. עֲשֵׂה לְמַעַן גְּמוּלֵי
חָלָב שֶׁלֹּא פָשָׁעוּ. עֲשֵׂה לְמַעַן תִּינוֹקוֹת שֶׁל בֵּית רַבָּן. עֲשֵׂה לְמַעַנְךָ אִם
לֹא לְמַעֲנֵנוּ. עֲשֵׂה לְמַעַנְךָ וְהוֹשִׁיעֵנוּ.

עֲנֵנוּ יהוה עֲנֵנוּ. עֲנֵנוּ אֱלֹהֵינוּ עֲנֵנוּ. עֲנֵנוּ אָבִינוּ עֲנֵנוּ. עֲנֵנוּ בּוֹרְאֵנוּ עֲנֵנוּ.
עֲנֵנוּ גוֹאֲלֵנוּ עֲנֵנוּ. עֲנֵנוּ דּוֹרְשֵׁנוּ עֲנֵנוּ. עֲנֵנוּ הָאֵל הַנֶּאֱמָן עֲנֵנוּ. עֲנֵנוּ וָתִיק
וְחָסִיד עֲנֵנוּ. עֲנֵנוּ זַךְ וְיָשָׁר עֲנֵנוּ. עֲנֵנוּ חַי וְקַיָּם עֲנֵנוּ. עֲנֵנוּ טוֹב וּמֵטִיב עֲנֵנוּ.
עֲנֵנוּ יוֹדֵעַ יֵצֶר עֲנֵנוּ. עֲנֵנוּ כּוֹבֵשׁ כְּעָסִים עֲנֵנוּ. עֲנֵנוּ לוֹבֵשׁ צְדָקוֹת עֲנֵנוּ.
עֲנֵנוּ מֶלֶךְ מַלְכֵי הַמְּלָכִים עֲנֵנוּ. עֲנֵנוּ נוֹרָא וְנִשְׂגָּב עֲנֵנוּ. עֲנֵנוּ סוֹלֵחַ וּמוֹחֵל
עֲנֵנוּ. עֲנֵנוּ עוֹנֶה בְּעֵת צָרָה עֲנֵנוּ. עֲנֵנוּ פּוֹדֶה וּמַצִּיל עֲנֵנוּ. עֲנֵנוּ צַדִּיק וְיָשָׁר
עֲנֵנוּ. עֲנֵנוּ קָרוֹב לְקוֹרְאָיו עֲנֵנוּ. עֲנֵנוּ רַחוּם וְחַנּוּן עֲנֵנוּ. עֲנֵנוּ שׁוֹמֵעַ אֶל
אֶבְיוֹנִים עֲנֵנוּ. עֲנֵנוּ תּוֹמֵךְ תְּמִימִים עֲנֵנוּ. עֲנֵנוּ אֱלֹהֵי אֲבוֹתֵינוּ עֲנֵנוּ. עֲנֵנוּ
אֱלֹהֵי אַבְרָהָם עֲנֵנוּ. עֲנֵנוּ פַּחַד יִצְחָק עֲנֵנוּ. עֲנֵנוּ אֲבִיר יַעֲקֹב עֲנֵנוּ. עֲנֵנוּ
עֶזְרַת הַשְּׁבָטִים עֲנֵנוּ. עֲנֵנוּ מִשְׂגָּב אִמָּהוֹת עֲנֵנוּ. עֲנֵנוּ קָשֶׁה לִכְעֹס עֲנֵנוּ.
עֲנֵנוּ רַךְ לִרְצוֹת עֲנֵנוּ. עֲנֵנוּ עוֹנֶה בְּעֵת רָצוֹן עֲנֵנוּ. עֲנֵנוּ אֲבִי יְתוֹמִים עֲנֵנוּ.
עֲנֵנוּ דַּיַּן אַלְמָנוֹת עֲנֵנוּ.

מִי שֶׁעָנָה The One who answered Abraham our father on Mount Moriah –
                        answer us.

The One who answered Isaac his son, when he was bound upon
                        the altar – answer us.

The One who answered Jacob in Beth-El – answer us.

The One who answered Joseph in prison – answer us.

The One who answered our fathers at the Reed Sea – answer us.

The One who answered Moses at Horeb – answer us.

The One who answered Aaron over his firepan – answer us.

The One who answered Pinehas when he stood up from among
                        the congregation – answer us.

The One who answered Joshua at Gilgal – answer us.

The One who answered Samuel at Mitzpah – answer us.

The One who answered David and Solomon his son in Jerusalem –
                        answer us.

The One who answered Elijah on Mount Carmel – answer us.

The One who answered Elisha at Jericho – answer us.

The One who answered Jonah in the belly of the fish – answer us.

The One who answered Hezekiah the king of Judah in his illness –
                        answer us.

The One who answered Hananiah, Mishael and Azariah in the
                        furnace of fire – answer us.

The One who answered Daniel in the lions' den – answer us.

The One who answered Mordekhai and Esther in Shushan the
                        capital city – answer us.

The One who answered Ezra in his exile – answer us.

The One who answered so many righteous, devoted, innocent and
                        upright people – answer us.

רַחֲמָנָא Loving God, who answers the oppressed: answer us.

Loving God, who answers the broken hearted: answer us.

Loving God, who answers those of humbled spirit: answer us.

Loving God, answer us.

Loving God, spare; Loving God, release; Loving God, save us.

Loving God, have compassion for us now, swiftly,
                        at a time soon coming.

Continue with "Avinu Malkenu" on page 138.

מִי שֶׁעָנָה לְאַבְרָהָם אָבִינוּ בְּהַר הַמּוֹרִיָּה, הוּא יַעֲנֵנוּ.

מִי שֶׁעָנָה לְיִצְחָק בְּנוֹ כְּשֶׁנֶּעֱקַד עַל גַּבֵּי הַמִּזְבֵּחַ, הוּא יַעֲנֵנוּ.

מִי שֶׁעָנָה לְיַעֲקֹב בְּבֵית אֵל, הוּא יַעֲנֵנוּ.

מִי שֶׁעָנָה לְיוֹסֵף בְּבֵית הָאֲסוּרִים, הוּא יַעֲנֵנוּ.

מִי שֶׁעָנָה לַאֲבוֹתֵינוּ עַל יַם סוּף, הוּא יַעֲנֵנוּ.

מִי שֶׁעָנָה לְמֹשֶׁה בְּחוֹרֵב, הוּא יַעֲנֵנוּ.

מִי שֶׁעָנָה לְאַהֲרֹן בַּמַּחְתָּה, הוּא יַעֲנֵנוּ.

מִי שֶׁעָנָה לְפִינְחָס בְּקוּמוֹ מִתּוֹךְ הָעֵדָה, הוּא יַעֲנֵנוּ.

מִי שֶׁעָנָה לִיהוֹשֻׁעַ בַּגִּלְגָּל, הוּא יַעֲנֵנוּ.

מִי שֶׁעָנָה לִשְׁמוּאֵל בַּמִּצְפָּה, הוּא יַעֲנֵנוּ.

מִי שֶׁעָנָה לְדָוִד וּשְׁלֹמֹה בְנוֹ בִּירוּשָׁלַיִם, הוּא יַעֲנֵנוּ.

מִי שֶׁעָנָה לְאֵלִיָּהוּ בְּהַר הַכַּרְמֶל, הוּא יַעֲנֵנוּ.

מִי שֶׁעָנָה לֶאֱלִישָׁע בִּירִיחוֹ, הוּא יַעֲנֵנוּ.

מִי שֶׁעָנָה לְיוֹנָה בִּמְעֵי הַדָּגָה, הוּא יַעֲנֵנוּ.

מִי שֶׁעָנָה לְחִזְקִיָּהוּ מֶלֶךְ יְהוּדָה בְּחָלְיוֹ, הוּא יַעֲנֵנוּ.

מִי שֶׁעָנָה לַחֲנַנְיָה מִישָׁאֵל וַעֲזַרְיָה בְּתוֹךְ כִּבְשַׁן הָאֵשׁ, הוּא יַעֲנֵנוּ.

מִי שֶׁעָנָה לְדָנִיֵּאל בְּגוֹב הָאֲרָיוֹת, הוּא יַעֲנֵנוּ.

מִי שֶׁעָנָה לְמָרְדְּכַי וְאֶסְתֵּר בְּשׁוּשַׁן הַבִּירָה, הוּא יַעֲנֵנוּ.

מִי שֶׁעָנָה לְעֶזְרָא בַּגּוֹלָה, הוּא יַעֲנֵנוּ.

מִי שֶׁעָנָה לְכָל הַצַּדִּיקִים וְהַחֲסִידִים וְהַתְּמִימִים וְהַיְשָׁרִים, הוּא יַעֲנֵנוּ.

רַחֲמָנָא דְּעָנֵי לַעֲנִיֵּי עֲנֵינָן.

רַחֲמָנָא דְּעָנֵי לִתְבִירֵי לִבָּא עֲנֵינָן.

רַחֲמָנָא דְּעָנֵי לְמַכִּיכֵי רוּחָא עֲנֵינָן.

רַחֲמָנָא עֲנֵינָן.

רַחֲמָנָא חוּס, רַחֲמָנָא פְּרֹק, רַחֲמָנָא שֵׁיזִב.

רַחֲמָנָא רַחֵם עֲלָן, הַשְׁתָּא בַּעֲגָלָא וּבִזְמַן קָרִיב.

Continue with אבינו מלכנו *on page 139.*

ברכות
GIVING THANKS

THE MEAL AND ITS BLESSINGS

On washing hands before eating bread (see laws 148–152):

Blessed are You, LORD our God, King of the Universe,
who has made us holy through His commandments,
and has commanded us about washing hands.

Before eating bread:

Blessed are You, LORD our God, King of the Universe,
who brings forth bread from the earth.

BIRKAT HAMAZON / GRACE AFTER MEALS

On days when Taḥanun is said:

עַל־נַהֲרוֹת By the rivers of Babylon we sat and wept as we remembered Zion. There on   Ps. 137
the willow trees we hung up our harps, for there our captors asked us for songs, our
tormentors, for amusement, said: "Sing us one of the songs of Zion!" How can we sing
the LORD's song on foreign soil? If I forget you, Jerusalem, may my right hand forget
its skill. May my tongue cling to the roof of my mouth if I do not remember you, if I do
not set Jerusalem above my highest joy. Remember, LORD, what the Edomites did on
the day Jerusalem fell. They said, "Tear it down, tear it down to its very foundations!"
Daughter of Babylon, doomed to destruction, happy is he who repays you for what
you have done to us, who seizes your infants and dashes them against the rocks.

On days when Taḥanun is omitted (see full list on page 144):

שִׁיר הַמַּעֲלוֹת A song of ascents. When the LORD brought back the exiles of   Ps. 126
Zion we were like people who dream. Then were our mouths filled with laugh-
ter, and our tongues with songs of joy. Then was it said among the nations,
"The LORD has done great things for them." The LORD did do great things for
us and we rejoiced. Bring back our exiles, LORD, like streams in a dry land.
May those who sowed in tears, reap in joy. May one who goes out weeping,
carrying a bag of seed, come back with songs of joy, carrying his sheaves.

The original form of Grace consisted of three blessings, which move sequentially from the universal to the particular. In the first, we thank God for
sustaining the world and all that lives. The second is national: we thank God
for the land of Israel as well as for the other blessings of Jewish life: the covenant and its sign, circumcision, and the Torah. The third turns to Jerusalem.
The fourth paragraph is a later addition: according to the Talmud (*Berakhot*
48b), it was added after the Bar Kokhba rebellion, c. 135 CE. Over the course
of time, it has expanded considerably.

סדר סעודה וברכותיה

On washing hands before eating bread (see laws 148–152):

בָּרוּךְ אַתָּה יהוה אֱלֹהֵינוּ מֶלֶךְ הָעוֹלָם
אֲשֶׁר קִדְּשָׁנוּ בְּמִצְוֹתָיו וְצִוָּנוּ עַל נְטִילַת יָדָיִם.

Before eating bread:

בָּרוּךְ אַתָּה יהוה אֱלֹהֵינוּ מֶלֶךְ הָעוֹלָם, הַמּוֹצִיא לֶחֶם מִן הָאָרֶץ.

בִּרְכַּת הַמָּזוֹן

On days when תחנון *is said:*

תהלים קלז

עַל־נַהֲרוֹת בָּבֶל, שָׁם יָשַׁבְנוּ גַּם־בָּכִינוּ, בְּזָכְרֵנוּ אֶת־צִיּוֹן: עַל־עֲרָבִים בְּתוֹכָהּ תָּלִינוּ כִּנֹּרוֹתֵינוּ: כִּי שָׁם שְׁאֵלוּנוּ שׁוֹבֵינוּ דִּבְרֵי־שִׁיר וְתוֹלָלֵינוּ שִׂמְחָה, שִׁירוּ לָנוּ מִשִּׁיר צִיּוֹן: אֵיךְ נָשִׁיר אֶת־שִׁיר־יהוה עַל אַדְמַת נֵכָר: אִם־אֶשְׁכָּחֵךְ יְרוּשָׁלִָם, תִּשְׁכַּח יְמִינִי: תִּדְבַּק לְשׁוֹנִי לְחִכִּי אִם־לֹא אֶזְכְּרֵכִי, אִם־לֹא אַעֲלֶה אֶת־יְרוּשָׁלִַם עַל רֹאשׁ שִׂמְחָתִי: זְכֹר יהוה לִבְנֵי אֱדוֹם אֵת יוֹם יְרוּשָׁלִָם, הָאֹמְרִים עָרוּ עָרוּ עַד הַיְסוֹד בָּהּ: בַּת־בָּבֶל הַשְּׁדוּדָה, אַשְׁרֵי שֶׁיְּשַׁלֶּם־לָךְ אֶת־גְּמוּלֵךְ שֶׁגָּמַלְתְּ לָנוּ: אַשְׁרֵי שֶׁיֹּאחֵז וְנִפֵּץ אֶת־עֹלָלַיִךְ אֶל־הַסָּלַע:

On days when תחנון *is omitted (see full list on page 145):*

תהלים קכו

שִׁיר הַמַּעֲלוֹת, בְּשׁוּב יהוה אֶת־שִׁיבַת צִיּוֹן, הָיִינוּ כְּחֹלְמִים: אָז יִמָּלֵא שְׂחוֹק פִּינוּ וּלְשׁוֹנֵנוּ רִנָּה, אָז יֹאמְרוּ בַגּוֹיִם הִגְדִּיל יהוה לַעֲשׂוֹת עִם־אֵלֶּה: הִגְדִּיל יהוה לַעֲשׂוֹת עִמָּנוּ, הָיִינוּ שְׂמֵחִים: שׁוּבָה יהוה אֶת־שְׁבִיתֵנוּ, כַּאֲפִיקִים בַּנֶּגֶב: הַזֹּרְעִים בְּדִמְעָה בְּרִנָּה יִקְצֹרוּ: הָלוֹךְ יֵלֵךְ וּבָכֹה נֹשֵׂא מֶשֶׁךְ־הַזָּרַע, בֹּא־יָבֹא בְרִנָּה נֹשֵׂא אֲלֻמֹּתָיו:

BIRKAT HAMAZON / GRACE AFTER MEALS
Grace after Meals is specifically mandated by the Torah itself: "You shall eat and be satisfied and bless the LORD your God" (Deut. 8:10). Thanksgiving, Moses taught the Israelites, is central to Jewish life, "lest your heart grow haughty and you forget the LORD your God … and you say to yourselves, 'My own power and the might of my own hand have won this wealth for me'" (ibid, vv. 14–17). Bereft of a sense of gratitude and of a power higher than humans, nations, like individuals, eventually decay.

Some say:

תְּהִלַּת My mouth shall speak the praise of God, and all creatures shall bless   Ps. 145
His holy name for ever and all time. We will bless God now and for ever.   Ps. 115
Halleluya! Thank the LORD for He is good; His loving-kindness is for ever.   Ps. 136
Who can tell of the LORD's mighty acts and make all His praise be heard?   Ps. 106

ZIMMUN / INVITATION

For the zimmun said at a wedding or during the week of Sheva Berakhot, see page 584. At a Brit, see page 562. In the house of a mourner when there are three or more men, see page 610.

When three or more men say Birkat HaMazon together, the following zimmun is said. When three or more women say Birkat HaMazon, substitute "Friends" for "Gentlemen." The leader should ask permission from those with precedence to lead the Birkat HaMazon.

Leader   Gentlemen, let us say grace.

Others   May the name of the LORD be blessed from now and for ever.   Ps. 113

Leader   May the name of the LORD be blessed from now and for ever.
With your permission, (my father and teacher / my mother and
                    teacher / the Kohanim present / our teacher the Rabbi /
                    the master of this house / the mistress of this house)
my masters and teachers,
let us bless (*in a minyan:* our God,) the One
from whose food we have eaten.

Others   Blessed be (*in a minyan:* our God,) the One
from whose food we have eaten, and by whose goodness we live.

People present who have not taken part in the meal say:
*Blessed be (*in a minyan:* our God,) the One
whose name is continually blessed for ever and all time.

Leader   Blessed be (*in a minyan:* our God,) the One
from whose food we have eaten, and by whose goodness we live.
Blessed be He, and blessed be His name.

---

to join in the act of praise is similar to the recitation of *Barekhu*, "Bless the
LORD," with which morning and evening services begin. It emphasizes the
essentially communal nature of prayer in Judaism. In addition to the regular
zimmun here, there are special forms of *zimmun* for (1) a wedding meal, (2)
a meal after a circumcision, and (3) a meal in a house of mourning.

Some say:

תְּהִלַּת יהוה יְדַבֶּר פִּי, וִיבָרֵךְ כָּל־בָּשָׂר שֵׁם קָדְשׁוֹ לְעוֹלָם וָעֶד: וַאֲנַחְנוּ תהלים קמה תהלים קטו
נְבָרֵךְ יָהּ מֵעַתָּה וְעַד־עוֹלָם, הַלְלוּיָהּ: הוֹדוּ לַיהוה כִּי־טוֹב, כִּי לְעוֹלָם תהלים קלו
חַסְדּוֹ: מִי יְמַלֵּל גְּבוּרוֹת יהוה, יַשְׁמִיעַ כָּל־תְּהִלָּתוֹ: תהלים קו

סדר הזימון

For the זימון *said at a wedding or during the week of* שבע ברכות*,* *see page 585.*
At a ברית*,* *see page 563.* *In a* בית אבל *when there are three or more men,* *see page 611.*

When three or more men say ברכת המזון *together, the following* זימון *is said.*
When three or more women say ברכת המזון*, substitute* חֲבֵרוֹתַי *for* רַבּוֹתַי*.*
The leader should ask permission from those with precedence to lead the ברכת המזון*.*

Leader רַבּוֹתַי, נְבָרֵךְ.

Others יְהִי שֵׁם יהוה מְבֹרָךְ מֵעַתָּה וְעַד־עוֹלָם: תהלים קיג

Leader יְהִי שֵׁם יהוה מְבֹרָךְ מֵעַתָּה וְעַד־עוֹלָם:
בִּרְשׁוּת (אָבִי מוֹרִי / אִמִּי מוֹרָתִי / כֹּהֲנִים / מוֹרֵנוּ הָרַב /
בַּעַל הַבַּיִת הַזֶּה / בַּעֲלַת הַבַּיִת הַזֶּה)
מָרָנָן וְרַבָּנָן וְרַבּוֹתַי
נְבָרֵךְ (במנין: אֱלֹהֵינוּ) שֶׁאָכַלְנוּ מִשֶּׁלּוֹ.

Others בָּרוּךְ (במנין: אֱלֹהֵינוּ) שֶׁאָכַלְנוּ מִשֶּׁלּוֹ וּבְטוּבוֹ חָיִינוּ.

**People present who have not taken part in the meal say:*

*בָּרוּךְ (במנין: אֱלֹהֵינוּ) וּמְבֹרָךְ שְׁמוֹ תָּמִיד לְעוֹלָם וָעֶד.

Leader בָּרוּךְ (במנין: אֱלֹהֵינוּ) שֶׁאָכַלְנוּ מִשֶּׁלּוֹ וּבְטוּבוֹ חָיִינוּ.
בָּרוּךְ הוּא וּבָרוּךְ שְׁמוֹ.

ZIMMUN

A meal at which there are three adult males requires a formal invitation, *zimmun*, to say Grace. The Talmud derives this from the verse, "Magnify the LORD with me; let us exalt His name together" (Psalm 34:4). A slightly longer version is used when at least ten are present. The act of inviting those present

BLESSING OF NOURISHMENT

בָּרוּךְ Blessed are You, LORD our God, King of the Universe,
who in His goodness feeds the whole world
with grace, kindness and compassion.
He gives food to all living things,
for His kindness is for ever.
Because of His continual great goodness,
we have never lacked food,
nor may we ever lack it, for the sake of His great name.
For He is God who feeds and sustains all,
does good to all,
and prepares food for all creatures He has created.
Blessed are You, LORD, who feeds all.

BLESSING OF LAND

נוֹדֶה We thank You, LORD our God,
for having granted as a heritage to our ancestors
a desirable, good and spacious land;
for bringing us out, LORD our God, from the land of Egypt,
freeing us from the house of slavery;
for Your covenant which You sealed in our flesh;
for Your Torah which You taught us;
for Your laws which You made known to us;
for the life, grace and kindness You have bestowed on us;
and for the food by which You continually feed and sustain us,
every day, every season, every hour.

נוֹדֶה *We thank:* After thanking God for the land, the paragraph goes on to
add thanks for God's other kindnesses to Israel: the exodus from Egypt, the
covenant and its sign, circumcision, the giving of the Torah and the commandments. On Ḥanukka and Purim, *Al HaNissim* ("[We thank You also]
for the miracles") is said here, as it is in the Amida in the parallel paragraph
of "Thanks" (*Modim*).

ברכת הזן

בָּרוּךְ אַתָּה יהוה אֱלֹהֵינוּ מֶלֶךְ הָעוֹלָם
הַזָּן אֶת הָעוֹלָם כֻּלּוֹ בְּטוּבוֹ
בְּחֵן בְּחֶסֶד וּבְרַחֲמִים
הוּא נוֹתֵן לֶחֶם לְכָל בָּשָׂר
כִּי לְעוֹלָם חַסְדּוֹ.
וּבְטוּבוֹ הַגָּדוֹל, תָּמִיד לֹא חָסַר לָנוּ
וְאַל יֶחְסַר לָנוּ מָזוֹן לְעוֹלָם וָעֶד
בַּעֲבוּר שְׁמוֹ הַגָּדוֹל.
כִּי הוּא אֵל זָן וּמְפַרְנֵס לַכֹּל
וּמֵטִיב לַכֹּל
וּמֵכִין מָזוֹן לְכָל בְּרִיּוֹתָיו אֲשֶׁר בָּרָא.
בָּרוּךְ אַתָּה יהוה, הַזָּן אֶת הַכֹּל.

ברכת הארץ

נוֹדֶה לְךָ, יהוה אֱלֹהֵינוּ
עַל שֶׁהִנְחַלְתָּ לַאֲבוֹתֵינוּ אֶרֶץ חֶמְדָּה טוֹבָה וּרְחָבָה
וְעַל שֶׁהוֹצֵאתָנוּ יהוה אֱלֹהֵינוּ מֵאֶרֶץ מִצְרַיִם
וּפְדִיתָנוּ מִבֵּית עֲבָדִים
וְעַל בְּרִיתְךָ שֶׁחָתַמְתָּ בִּבְשָׂרֵנוּ
וְעַל תּוֹרָתְךָ שֶׁלִּמַּדְתָּנוּ
וְעַל חֻקֶּיךָ שֶׁהוֹדַעְתָּנוּ
וְעַל חַיִּים חֵן וָחֶסֶד שֶׁחוֹנַנְתָּנוּ
וְעַל אֲכִילַת מָזוֹן שָׁאַתָּה זָן וּמְפַרְנֵס אוֹתָנוּ תָּמִיד
בְּכָל יוֹם וּבְכָל עֵת וּבְכָל שָׁעָה.

On Ḥanukka:

עַל הַנִּסִּים [We thank You also] for the miracles, the redemption, the mighty deeds, the salvations, and the victories in battle which You performed for our ancestors in those days, at this time.

בִּימֵי מַתִּתְיָהוּ In the days of Mattityahu, son of Yoḥanan, the High Priest, the Hasmonean, and his sons, the wicked Greek kingdom rose up against Your people Israel to make them forget Your Torah and to force them to transgress the statutes of Your will. It was then that You in Your great compassion stood by them in the time of their distress. You championed their cause, judged their claim, and avenged their wrong. You delivered the strong into the hands of the weak, the many into the hands of the few, the impure into the hands of the pure, the wicked into the hands of the righteous, and the arrogant into the hands of those who were engaged in the study of Your Torah. You made for Yourself great and holy renown in Your world, and for Your people Israel You performed a great salvation and redemption as of this very day. Your children then entered the holiest part of Your House, cleansed Your Temple, purified Your Sanctuary, kindled lights in Your holy courts, and designated these eight days of Ḥanukka for giving thanks and praise to Your great name.

Continue with "For all this."

On Purim:

עַל הַנִּסִּים [We thank You also] for the miracles, the redemption, the mighty deeds, the salvations, and the victories in battle which You performed for our ancestors in those days, at this time.

בִּימֵי מָרְדְּכַי In the days of Mordekhai and Esther, in Shushan the capital, the wicked Haman rose up against them and sought to destroy, slay and exterminate all the Jews, young and old, children and women, on one day, the thirteenth day of the twelfth month, which is the month of Adar, and to plunder their possessions. Then You in Your great compassion thwarted his counsel, frustrated his plans, and caused his scheme to recoil on his own head, so that they hanged him and his sons on the gallows.   *Esther 3*

Continue with "For all this."

וְעַל הַכֹּל For all this, Lᴏʀᴅ our God, we thank and bless You.
May Your name be blessed continually
by the mouth of all that lives, for ever and all time –
for so it is written: "You will eat and be satisfied, then you shall   *Deut. 8*
bless the Lᴏʀᴅ your God for the good land He has given you."
Blessed are You, Lᴏʀᴅ, for the land and for the food.

בַּחֲנֻכָּה:

עַל הַנִּסִּים וְעַל הַפֻּרְקָן וְעַל הַגְּבוּרוֹת וְעַל הַתְּשׁוּעוֹת וְעַל הַמִּלְחָמוֹת שֶׁעָשִׂיתָ לַאֲבוֹתֵינוּ בַּיָּמִים הָהֵם בַּזְּמַן הַזֶּה.

בִּימֵי מַתִּתְיָהוּ בֶּן יוֹחָנָן כֹּהֵן גָּדוֹל חַשְׁמוֹנַאי וּבָנָיו, כְּשֶׁעָמְדָה מַלְכוּת יָוָן הָרְשָׁעָה עַל עַמְּךָ יִשְׂרָאֵל לְהַשְׁכִּיחָם תּוֹרָתֶךָ וּלְהַעֲבִירָם מֵחֻקֵּי רְצוֹנֶךָ, וְאַתָּה בְּרַחֲמֶיךָ הָרַבִּים עָמַדְתָּ לָהֶם בְּעֵת צָרָתָם, רַבְתָּ אֶת רִיבָם, דַּנְתָּ אֶת דִּינָם, נָקַמְתָּ אֶת נִקְמָתָם, מָסַרְתָּ גִבּוֹרִים בְּיַד חַלָּשִׁים, וְרַבִּים בְּיַד מְעַטִּים, וּטְמֵאִים בְּיַד טְהוֹרִים, וּרְשָׁעִים בְּיַד צַדִּיקִים, וְזֵדִים בְּיַד עוֹסְקֵי תוֹרָתֶךָ, וּלְךָ עָשִׂיתָ שֵׁם גָּדוֹל וְקָדוֹשׁ בְּעוֹלָמֶךָ, וּלְעַמְּךָ יִשְׂרָאֵל עָשִׂיתָ תְּשׁוּעָה גְדוֹלָה וּפֻרְקָן כְּהַיּוֹם הַזֶּה. וְאַחַר כֵּן בָּאוּ בָנֶיךָ לִדְבִיר בֵּיתֶךָ, וּפִנּוּ אֶת הֵיכָלֶךָ, וְטִהֲרוּ אֶת מִקְדָּשֶׁךָ, וְהִדְלִיקוּ נֵרוֹת בְּחַצְרוֹת קָדְשֶׁךָ, וְקָבְעוּ שְׁמוֹנַת יְמֵי חֲנֻכָּה אֵלּוּ, לְהוֹדוֹת וּלְהַלֵּל לְשִׁמְךָ הַגָּדוֹל.

Continue with וְעַל הַכֹּל.

בְּפוּרִים:

עַל הַנִּסִּים וְעַל הַפֻּרְקָן וְעַל הַגְּבוּרוֹת וְעַל הַתְּשׁוּעוֹת וְעַל הַמִּלְחָמוֹת שֶׁעָשִׂיתָ לַאֲבוֹתֵינוּ בַּיָּמִים הָהֵם בַּזְּמַן הַזֶּה.

אֶסְתֵּר ג

בִּימֵי מָרְדְּכַי וְאֶסְתֵּר בְּשׁוּשַׁן הַבִּירָה, כְּשֶׁעָמַד עֲלֵיהֶם הָמָן הָרָשָׁע, בִּקֵּשׁ לְהַשְׁמִיד לַהֲרֹג וּלְאַבֵּד אֶת־כָּל־הַיְּהוּדִים מִנַּעַר וְעַד־זָקֵן טַף וְנָשִׁים בְּיוֹם אֶחָד, בִּשְׁלוֹשָׁה עָשָׂר לְחֹדֶשׁ שְׁנֵים־עָשָׂר, הוּא־חֹדֶשׁ אֲדָר, וּשְׁלָלָם לָבוֹז: וְאַתָּה בְּרַחֲמֶיךָ הָרַבִּים הֵפַרְתָּ אֶת עֲצָתוֹ, וְקִלְקַלְתָּ אֶת מַחֲשַׁבְתּוֹ, וַהֲשֵׁבוֹתָ לּוֹ גְּמוּלוֹ בְּרֹאשׁוֹ, וְתָלוּ אוֹתוֹ וְאֶת בָּנָיו עַל הָעֵץ.

Continue with וְעַל הַכֹּל.

וְעַל הַכֹּל, יהוה אֱלֹהֵינוּ

אֲנַחְנוּ מוֹדִים לָךְ וּמְבָרְכִים אוֹתָךְ

יִתְבָּרַךְ שִׁמְךָ בְּפִי כָּל חַי תָּמִיד לְעוֹלָם וָעֶד

דְּבָרִים ח

כַּכָּתוּב: וְאָכַלְתָּ וְשָׂבָעְתָּ, וּבֵרַכְתָּ אֶת־יהוה אֱלֹהֶיךָ

עַל־הָאָרֶץ הַטֹּבָה אֲשֶׁר נָתַן־לָךְ:

בָּרוּךְ אַתָּה יהוה, עַל הָאָרֶץ וְעַל הַמָּזוֹן.

BLESSING FOR JERUSALEM

רַחֵם נָא Have compassion, please, Lᴏʀᴅ our God,
on Israel Your people,
on Jerusalem Your city,
on Zion the dwelling place of Your glory,
on the royal house of David Your anointed,
and on the great and holy House that bears Your name.
Our God, our Father,
tend us, feed us,
sustain us and support us,
relieve us and send us relief,
Lᴏʀᴅ our God,
swiftly from all our troubles.
Please, Lᴏʀᴅ our God, do not make us dependent
on the gifts or loans of other people,
but only on Your full, open, holy and generous hand
so that we may suffer neither shame nor humiliation
for ever and all time.

> *On Rosh Ḥodesh, say:*
>
> אֱלֹהֵינוּ Our God and God of our ancestors,
> may there rise, come, reach, appear, be favored, heard, regarded
> and remembered before You, our recollection and remembrance,
> as well as the remembrance of our ancestors,
> and of the Messiah son of David Your servant,
> and of Jerusalem Your holy city,
> and of all Your people the house of Israel –
> for deliverance and well-being, grace,
> loving-kindness and compassion, life and peace,
> on this day of Rosh Ḥodesh.
> On it remember us, Lᴏʀᴅ our God, for good;
> recollect us for blessing, and deliver us for life.
> In accord with Your promise of salvation and compassion,
> spare us and be gracious to us;
> have compassion on us and deliver us,
> for our eyes are turned to You because You are God,
> gracious and compassionate.

ברכת ירושלים

רַחֶם נָא, יהוה אֱלֹהֵינוּ

עַל יִשְׂרָאֵל עַמֶּךָ

וְעַל יְרוּשָׁלַיִם עִירֶךָ

וְעַל צִיּוֹן מִשְׁכַּן כְּבוֹדֶךָ

וְעַל מַלְכוּת בֵּית דָּוִד מְשִׁיחֶךָ

וְעַל הַבַּיִת הַגָּדוֹל וְהַקָּדוֹשׁ שֶׁנִּקְרָא שִׁמְךָ עָלָיו.

אֱלֹהֵינוּ, אָבִינוּ, רְעֵנוּ, זוּנֵנוּ, פַּרְנְסֵנוּ וְכַלְכְּלֵנוּ

וְהַרְוִיחֵנוּ, וְהַרְוַח לָנוּ יהוה אֱלֹהֵינוּ מְהֵרָה מִכָּל צָרוֹתֵינוּ.

וְנָא אַל תַּצְרִיכֵנוּ, יהוה אֱלֹהֵינוּ

לֹא לִידֵי מַתְּנַת בָּשָׂר וָדָם

וְלֹא לִידֵי הַלְוָאָתָם

כִּי אִם לְיָדְךָ הַמְּלֵאָה, הַפְּתוּחָה, הַקְּדוֹשָׁה וְהָרְחָבָה

שֶׁלֹּא נֵבוֹשׁ וְלֹא נִכָּלֵם לְעוֹלָם וָעֶד.

On ראש חודש, say:

אֱלֹהֵינוּ וֵאלֹהֵי אֲבוֹתֵינוּ

יַעֲלֶה וְיָבֹא וְיַגִּיעַ, וְיֵרָאֶה וְיֵרָצֶה וְיִשָּׁמַע

וְיִפָּקֵד וְיִזָּכֵר זִכְרוֹנֵנוּ וּפִקְדוֹנֵנוּ, וְזִכְרוֹן אֲבוֹתֵינוּ

וְזִכְרוֹן מָשִׁיחַ בֶּן דָּוִד עַבְדֶּךָ

וְזִכְרוֹן יְרוּשָׁלַיִם עִיר קָדְשֶׁךָ

וְזִכְרוֹן כָּל עַמְּךָ בֵּית יִשְׂרָאֵל

לְפָנֶיךָ, לִפְלֵיטָה לְטוֹבָה, לְחֵן וּלְחֶסֶד וּלְרַחֲמִים

לְחַיִּים וּלְשָׁלוֹם בְּיוֹם רֹאשׁ הַחֹדֶשׁ הַזֶּה.

זָכְרֵנוּ יהוה אֱלֹהֵינוּ בּוֹ לְטוֹבָה

וּפָקְדֵנוּ בּוֹ לִבְרָכָה, וְהוֹשִׁיעֵנוּ בּוֹ לְחַיִּים.

וּבִדְבַר יְשׁוּעָה וְרַחֲמִים, חוּס וְחָנֵּנוּ וְרַחֵם עָלֵינוּ, וְהוֹשִׁיעֵנוּ

כִּי אֵלֶיךָ עֵינֵינוּ, כִּי אֵל חַנּוּן וְרַחוּם אָתָּה.

In the house of a mourner, "Comfort" on page 610 is substituted for the next two paragraphs.

וּבְנֵה And may Jerusalem the holy city
be rebuilt soon, in our time.
Blessed are You, LORD, who in His compassion
will rebuild Jerusalem. Amen.

BLESSING OF GOD'S GOODNESS

בָּרוּךְ Blessed are You, LORD our God, King of the Universe –
God our Father, our King, our Sovereign,
our Creator, our Redeemer, our Maker,
our Holy One, the Holy One of Jacob.
He is our Shepherd, Israel's Shepherd,
the good King who does good to all.
Every day He has done, is doing, and will do good to us.
He has acted, is acting, and will always act
kindly toward us for ever,
granting us grace, kindness and compassion, relief and rescue,
prosperity, blessing, redemption and comfort,
sustenance and support, compassion,
life, peace and all good things,
and of all good things may He never let us lack.

---

the Romans gave permission to the Jews to bury their dead. The failure
of the Bar Kokhba rebellion was one of the low points of Jewish history.
According to the Roman historian Dio, 580,000 Jews died in the fighting
and many others by starvation. Nine hundred and eighty-five towns, villages and settlements were destroyed. Jerusalem was leveled to the ground
and rebuilt as a Roman city, Aelia Capitolina. The fact that the sages were
able to salvage a fragment of consolation from the fact that the dead were
not denied the dignity of burial is testimony to an extraordinary ability to
survive catastrophe and preserve the lineaments of hope. The passage is
built around threefold references to God's kingship, goodness and bestowal
of kindness.

In the house of a mourner, נַחֵם *on page 611 is substituted for the next two paragraphs.*

וּבְנֵה יְרוּשָׁלַיִם עִיר הַקֹּדֶשׁ בִּמְהֵרָה בְיָמֵינוּ.
בָּרוּךְ אַתָּה יהוה, בּוֹנֵה בְרַחֲמָיו יְרוּשָׁלָיִם, אָמֵן.

ברכת הטוב והמטיב

בָּרוּךְ אַתָּה יהוה אֱלֹהֵינוּ מֶלֶךְ הָעוֹלָם
הָאֵל אָבִינוּ, מַלְכֵּנוּ, אַדִּירֵנוּ
בּוֹרְאֵנוּ, גּוֹאֲלֵנוּ, יוֹצְרֵנוּ, קְדוֹשֵׁנוּ, קְדוֹשׁ יַעֲקֹב
רוֹעֵנוּ, רוֹעֵה יִשְׂרָאֵל, הַמֶּלֶךְ הַטּוֹב וְהַמֵּטִיב לַכֹּל
שֶׁבְּכָל יוֹם וָיוֹם
הוּא הֵיטִיב, הוּא מֵטִיב, הוּא יֵיטִיב לָנוּ
הוּא גְמָלָנוּ, הוּא גוֹמְלֵנוּ, הוּא יִגְמְלֵנוּ לָעַד
לְחֵן וּלְחֶסֶד וּלְרַחֲמִים, וּלְרֶוַח, הַצָּלָה וְהַצְלָחָה
בְּרָכָה וִישׁוּעָה, נֶחָמָה, פַּרְנָסָה וְכַלְכָּלָה
וְרַחֲמִים וְחַיִּים וְשָׁלוֹם וְכָל טוֹב, וּמִכָּל טוּב לְעוֹלָם אַל יְחַסְּרֵנוּ.

וּבְנֵה יְרוּשָׁלַיִם *And may Jerusalem.* The third blessing speaks of Jerusalem, home of God's glory, as well as the Davidic monarchy and the Temple, for the restoration of which we pray. As is often the case in the siddur, Jerusalem is associated with the divine attribute of compassion, reflecting the words of Zechariah: "Therefore, this is what the LORD says: I will return to Jerusalem with compassion, and there My House will be rebuilt" (1:16). According to tradition, the Divine Presence never left Jerusalem, even when the city lay in ruins. בּוֹנֵה בְרַחֲמָיו יְרוּשָׁלַיִם, אָמֵן *Who in His compassion will rebuild Jerusalem. Amen:* the unusual appearance of the word *Amen* in this passage (normally we do not say it after our own blessings) signals that this was originally the end of Grace.

בָּרוּךְ *Blessed:* A later addition, dated by the Talmud (*Berakhot* 48b) to the period following the Bar Kokhba rebellion when, after a long delay,

ADDITIONAL REQUESTS

הָרַחֲמָן May the Compassionate One reign over us
  for ever and all time.
May the Compassionate One be blessed
  in heaven and on earth.
May the Compassionate One be praised
  from generation to generation,
  be glorified by us to all eternity,
  and honored among us for ever and all time.
May the Compassionate One
  grant us an honorable livelihood.
May the Compassionate One break the yoke from our neck
  and lead us upright to our land.
May the Compassionate One send us many blessings to this house
  and this table at which we have eaten.
May the Compassionate One send us Elijah the prophet –
  may he be remembered for good –
  to bring us good tidings of salvation and consolation.
May the Compassionate One bless the state of Israel,
  first flowering of our redemption.
May the Compassionate One bless
  the members of Israel's Defense Forces,
  who stand guard over our land.

A guest says:

יְהִי רָצוֹן May it be Your will that the master of this house shall not
suffer shame in this world, nor humiliation in the World to Come.
May all he owns prosper greatly, and may his and our possessions
be successful and close to hand. Let not the Accuser hold sway
over his deeds or ours, and may no thought of sin, iniquity or
transgression enter him or us from now and for evermore.

---

sages, is how Abraham and Sarah brought monotheism to the world. They
would provide hospitality to strangers. When the meal was over, and the
guests would begin to thank them, Abraham would reply, "Thank the One
from whom all we have enjoyed has come."

בקשות נוספות

הָרַחֲמָן הוּא יִמְלֹךְ עָלֵינוּ לְעוֹלָם וָעֶד.

הָרַחֲמָן הוּא יִתְבָּרַךְ בַּשָּׁמַיִם וּבָאָרֶץ.

הָרַחֲמָן הוּא יִשְׁתַּבַּח לְדוֹר דּוֹרִים, וְיִתְפָּאַר בָּנוּ לָעַד וּלְנֵצַח נְצָחִים וְיִתְהַדַּר בָּנוּ לָעַד וּלְעוֹלְמֵי עוֹלָמִים.

הָרַחֲמָן הוּא יְפַרְנְסֵנוּ בְּכָבוֹד.

הָרַחֲמָן הוּא יִשְׁבֹּר עֻלֵּנוּ מֵעַל צַוָּארֵנוּ וְהוּא יוֹלִיכֵנוּ קוֹמְמִיּוּת לְאַרְצֵנוּ.

הָרַחֲמָן הוּא יִשְׁלַח לָנוּ בְּרָכָה מְרֻבָּה בַּבַּיִת הַזֶּה וְעַל שֻׁלְחָן זֶה שֶׁאָכַלְנוּ עָלָיו.

הָרַחֲמָן הוּא יִשְׁלַח לָנוּ אֶת אֵלִיָּהוּ הַנָּבִיא זָכוּר לַטּוֹב וִיבַשֶּׂר לָנוּ בְּשׂוֹרוֹת טוֹבוֹת יְשׁוּעוֹת וְנֶחָמוֹת.

הָרַחֲמָן הוּא יְבָרֵךְ אֶת מְדִינַת יִשְׂרָאֵל, רֵאשִׁית צְמִיחַת גְּאֻלָּתֵנוּ.

הָרַחֲמָן הוּא יְבָרֵךְ אֶת חַיָּלֵי צְבָא הַהֲגָנָה לְיִשְׂרָאֵל הָעוֹמְדִים עַל מִשְׁמַר אַרְצֵנוּ.

A guest says:

יְהִי רָצוֹן שֶׁלֹּא יֵבוֹשׁ בַּעַל הַבַּיִת בָּעוֹלָם הַזֶּה, וְלֹא יִכָּלֵם לָעוֹלָם הַבָּא, וְיִצְלַח מְאֹד בְּכָל נְכָסָיו, וְיִהְיוּ נְכָסָיו וּנְכָסֵינוּ מֻצְלָחִים וּקְרוֹבִים לָעִיר, וְאַל יִשְׁלֹט שָׂטָן לֹא בְּמַעֲשֵׂה יָדָיו וְלֹא בְּמַעֲשֵׂה יָדֵינוּ. וְאַל יִזְדַּקֵּר לֹא לְפָנָיו וְלֹא לְפָנֵינוּ שׁוּם דְּבַר הִרְהוּר חֵטְא, עֲבֵרָה וְעָוֹן, מֵעַתָּה וְעַד עוֹלָם.

───────────────────────────────

הָרַחֲמָן *May the Compassionate One:* A series of additional prayers, dating from the Geonic period. The oldest is the one in which a guest invokes blessings on the hosts and their family. This is immediately preceded by a prayer that Elijah may come and announce the coming of the Messiah. The juxtaposition is striking: we bring redemption by acts of hospitality. This, according to the

הָרַחֲמָן May the Compassionate One bless –

> *When eating at one's own table, say (include the words in parentheses that apply):*
> me, (my wife/husband, / my father, my teacher / my mother,
> my teacher/ my children,) and all that is mine,

> *A guest at someone else's table says (include the words in parentheses that apply):*
> the master of this house, him (and his wife,
> the mistress of this house / and his children,) and all that is his,

> *Children at their parents' table say (include the words in parentheses that apply):*
> my father, my teacher, (master of this house,) and my mother,
> my teacher, (mistress of this house,) them, their household,
> their children, and all that is theirs.

> *For all other guests, add:*
> and all the diners here,

אוֹתָנוּ – together with us and all that is ours.
Just as our forefathers
Abraham, Isaac and Jacob were blessed in all, from all, with all,
so may He bless all of us together with a complete blessing,
and let us say: Amen.

בַּמָּרוֹם On high, may grace be invoked for them and for us,
as a safeguard of peace.
May we receive a blessing from the LORD
and a just reward from the God of our salvation,
and may we find grace and good favor in the eyes of God and man.

At a circumcision feast add here "May the Compassionate One bless the father" on page 564.

> *On Rosh Ḥodesh:* May the Compassionate One renew this month for us,
> for good and blessing.

הָרַחֲמָן May the Compassionate One make us worthy
of the Messianic Age and life in the World to Come.
He gives great / *On Rosh Ḥodesh:* He is a tower of / salvation to His king, *II Sam. 22*
showing kindness to His anointed,
to David and his descendants for ever.

הָרַחֲמָן הוּא יְבָרֵךְ

When eating at one's own table, say (include the words in parentheses that apply):

אוֹתִי (וְאֶת אִשְׁתִּי / וְאֶת בַּעְלִי / וְאֶת אָבִי מוֹרִי /
וְאֶת אִמִּי מוֹרָתִי / וְאֶת זַרְעִי) וְאֶת כָּל אֲשֶׁר לִי.

A guest at someone else's table says (include the words in parentheses that apply):

אֶת בַּעַל הַבַּיִת הַזֶּה, אוֹתוֹ (וְאֶת אִשְׁתּוֹ בַּעֲלַת הַבַּיִת הַזֶּה /
וְאֶת זַרְעוֹ) וְאֶת כָּל אֲשֶׁר לוֹ.

Children at their parents' table say (include the words in parentheses that apply):

אֶת אָבִי מוֹרִי (בַּעַל הַבַּיִת הַזֶּה), וְאֶת אִמִּי מוֹרָתִי (בַּעֲלַת הַבַּיִת
הַזֶּה), אוֹתָם וְאֶת בֵּיתָם וְאֶת זַרְעָם וְאֶת כָּל אֲשֶׁר לָהֶם

For all other guests, add:

וְאֶת כָּל הַמְּסֻבִּין כָּאן

אוֹתָנוּ וְאֶת כָּל אֲשֶׁר לָנוּ
כְּמוֹ שֶׁנִּתְבָּרְכוּ אֲבוֹתֵינוּ, אַבְרָהָם יִצְחָק וְיַעֲקֹב, בַּכֹּל, מִכֹּל, כֹּל,
כֵּן יְבָרֵךְ אוֹתָנוּ כֻּלָּנוּ יַחַד בִּבְרָכָה שְׁלֵמָה, וְנֹאמַר אָמֵן.

בַּמָּרוֹם יְלַמְּדוּ עֲלֵיהֶם וְעָלֵינוּ זְכוּת שֶׁתְּהֵא לְמִשְׁמֶרֶת שָׁלוֹם
וְנִשָּׂא בְרָכָה מֵאֵת יהוה וּצְדָקָה מֵאֱלֹהֵי יִשְׁעֵנוּ
וְנִמְצָא חֵן וְשֵׂכֶל טוֹב בְּעֵינֵי אֱלֹהִים וְאָדָם.

At a meal after a ברית *add here* הָרַחֲמָן הוּא יְבָרֵךְ אֲבִי הַיֶּלֶד *on page 565.*

בראש חודש: הָרַחֲמָן הוּא יְחַדֵּשׁ עָלֵינוּ
אֶת הַחֹדֶשׁ הַזֶּה לְטוֹבָה וְלִבְרָכָה.

הָרַחֲמָן הוּא יְזַכֵּנוּ לִימוֹת הַמָּשִׁיחַ וּלְחַיֵּי הָעוֹלָם הַבָּא
מַגְדִּל/ On ראש חודש מִגְדּוֹל/ יְשׁוּעוֹת מַלְכּוֹ
וְעֹשֶׂה־חֶסֶד לִמְשִׁיחוֹ, לְדָוִד וּלְזַרְעוֹ עַד־עוֹלָם:

שמואל ב׳ כב

He who makes peace in His high places,
may He make peace for us and all Israel,
and let us say: Amen.

יְרַאוּ Fear the LORD, you His holy ones;   Ps. 34
those who fear Him lack nothing.
Young lions may grow weak and hungry,
but those who seek the LORD
lack no good thing.
Thank the LORD for He is good;   Ps. 118
His loving-kindness is for ever.
You open Your hand,   Ps. 145
and satisfy every living thing with favor.
Blessed is the person   Jer. 17
who trusts in the LORD,
whose trust is in the LORD alone.
Once I was young, and now I am old,   Ps. 37
yet I have never watched
a righteous man forsaken
or his children begging for bread.
The LORD will give His people strength.   Ps. 29
The LORD will bless His people with peace.

*If Birkat HaMazon was made on a cup of wine, then the blessing over wine is made and
the majority of the cup is drunk, after which Al HaMihya, on the next page, is said.*

At a wedding or Sheva Berakhot, turn to page 582.

---

evil that shall come unto my people? Or how can I watch the destruction
of my kindred?" (8:6). The verb there means "stand as a passive witness to."
Taken in this sense, Psalm 37:25 should be understood as, "When the righteous was forsaken or his children forced to search for bread, I never merely
stood and watched." Understood thus, it is a warning against being a mere
bystander while other people suffer. It thus brings the Grace to a symmetri-
cal close: It began by speaking of God's goodness in feeding the hungry and
ends with an injunction for us to do likewise. This too is part of "walking in
God's ways."

עֹשֶׂה שָׁלוֹם בִּמְרוֹמָיו
הוּא יַעֲשֶׂה שָׁלוֹם עָלֵינוּ וְעַל כָּל יִשְׂרָאֵל
וְאִמְרוּ אָמֵן.

תהלים לד
יְראוּ אֶת־יהוה קְדֹשָׁיו
כִּי־אֵין מַחְסוֹר לִירֵאָיו:
כְּפִירִים רָשׁוּ וְרָעֵבוּ
וְדֹרְשֵׁי יהוה לֹא־יַחְסְרוּ כָל־טוֹב:

תהלים קיח
הוֹדוּ לַיהוה כִּי־טוֹב
כִּי לְעוֹלָם חַסְדּוֹ:

תהלים קמה
פּוֹתֵחַ אֶת־יָדֶךָ
וּמַשְׂבִּיעַ לְכָל־חַי רָצוֹן:

ירמיה יז
בָּרוּךְ הַגֶּבֶר אֲשֶׁר יִבְטַח בַּיהוה
וְהָיָה יהוה מִבְטַחוֹ:

תהלים לז
נַעַר הָיִיתִי גַּם־זָקַנְתִּי
וְלֹא־רָאִיתִי צַדִּיק נֶעֱזָב וְזַרְעוֹ מְבַקֶּשׁ־לָחֶם:

תהלים כט
יהוה עֹז לְעַמּוֹ יִתֵּן
יהוה יְבָרֵךְ אֶת־עַמּוֹ בַשָּׁלוֹם:

If ברכת המזון *was made on a cup of wine, then* בּוֹרֵא פְּרִי הַגֶּפֶן *is said and the majority of the cup is drunk, after which* ברכה מעין שלוש*,* on the next page, is said.

At a wedding or* שבע ברכות*, turn to page 583.

נַעַר הָיִיתִי *Once I was young:* The standard translation of this verse (Psalm 37:25) is "I was young and now am old and I have not seen the righteous forsaken or his children searching for bread." I have translated it here according to a fine insight, author unknown, suggesting that the verb *ra'iti* should be understood in the sense in which it appears in the book of Esther, when Esther, pleading on behalf of Jewry, says: "For how can I watch the

Before eating food, other than bread or matza,
made from the five species of grain (wheat, barley, rye, oats and spelt), or rice:

Blessed are You, the LORD our God, King of the Universe,
who creates the various kinds of nourishment.

Before drinking wine or grape juice:

Blessed are You, LORD our God, King of the Universe,
who creates the fruit of the vine.

Before eating fruit that grows on trees:

Blessed are You, LORD our God, King of the Universe,
who creates the fruit of the tree.

Before eating vegetables, or fruit that does not grow on trees:

Blessed are You, LORD our God, King of the Universe,
who creates the fruit of the ground.

Before eating other food or drinking other liquids:

Blessed are You, LORD our God, King of the Universe,
by whose word all things came to be.

Before eating fruit for the first time in a season, the following is said.
This blessing is also said when buying or wearing a new garment of significant value
(e.g. a dress or suit); entering a new home for the first time; or hearing personal good news.

Blessed are You, LORD our God, King of the Universe,
who has given us life, sustained us, and brought us to this time.

BLESSING AFTER FOOD – AL HAMIḤYA

Grace after eating from the "seven species" of produce with which Israel is blessed: food made from
the five grains (but not bread); wine or grape juice; grapes, figs, pomegranates, olives or dates.

בָּרוּךְ Blessed are You, LORD our God, King of the Universe,

After grain products *(but not bread or matza):*	*After wine or grape juice:*	*After grapes, figs, olives, pomegranates or dates:*
for the nourishment and sustenance,	for the vine and the fruit of the vine,	for the tree and the fruit of the tree,

After grain products (but not bread or matza), and wine or grape juice:
for the nourishment and sustenance
and for the vine and the fruit of the vine,

---

(1) food made from wheat, barley, rye, oats or spelt; (2) grape wine or juice;
or (3) grapes, figs, pomegranates, olives or dates.

Before eating food, other than bread or מצה,
made from the five species of grain (wheat, barley, rye, oats and spelt), or rice:

בָּרוּךְ אַתָּה יהוה אֱלֹהֵינוּ מֶלֶךְ הָעוֹלָם, בּוֹרֵא מִינֵי מְזוֹנוֹת.

Before drinking wine or grape juice:

בָּרוּךְ אַתָּה יהוה אֱלֹהֵינוּ מֶלֶךְ הָעוֹלָם, בּוֹרֵא פְּרִי הַגָּפֶן.

Before eating fruit that grows on trees:

בָּרוּךְ אַתָּה יהוה אֱלֹהֵינוּ מֶלֶךְ הָעוֹלָם, בּוֹרֵא פְּרִי הָעֵץ.

Before eating vegetables, or fruit that does not grow on trees:

בָּרוּךְ אַתָּה יהוה אֱלֹהֵינוּ מֶלֶךְ הָעוֹלָם, בּוֹרֵא פְּרִי הָאֲדָמָה.

Before eating other food or drinking other liquids:

בָּרוּךְ אַתָּה יהוה אֱלֹהֵינוּ מֶלֶךְ הָעוֹלָם, שֶׁהַכֹּל נִהְיָה בִּדְבָרוֹ.

Before eating fruit for the first time in a season, the following שֶׁהֶחֱיָנוּ *is said.*
This blessing is also said when buying or wearing a new garment of significant value
(e.g. a dress or suit); entering a new home for the first time; or hearing personal good news.

בָּרוּךְ אַתָּה יהוה אֱלֹהֵינוּ מֶלֶךְ הָעוֹלָם
שֶׁהֶחֱיָנוּ וְקִיְּמָנוּ וְהִגִּיעָנוּ לַזְּמַן הַזֶּה.

ברכה מעין שלוש

*Grace after eating from the "seven species" of produce with which Israel is blessed: food made from
the five grains (but not bread); wine or grape juice; grapes, figs, pomegranates, olives, or dates.*

בָּרוּךְ אַתָּה יהוה אֱלֹהֵינוּ מֶלֶךְ הָעוֹלָם, עַל

After grapes, figs, olives, pomegranates or dates:	*After wine or grape juice:*	*After grain products (but not bread or* מצה*):*
הָעֵץ וְעַל פְּרִי הָעֵץ	הַגֶּפֶן וְעַל פְּרִי הַגֶּפֶן	הַמִּחְיָה וְעַל הַכַּלְכָּלָה

After grain products (but not bread or מצה*), and wine or grape juice:*

הַמִּחְיָה וְעַל הַכַּלְכָּלָה וְעַל הַגֶּפֶן וְעַל פְּרִי הַגֶּפֶן

_____

עַל הַמִּחְיָה *A blessing after other food or drink:* Known as the "three-in-one" blessing, this prayer summarizes the first three paragraphs of the Grace after Meals. It is said after consuming any of the "seven kinds" of produce for which Israel is praised in the Torah (Deut. 8:8) other than bread or matza, namely:

and for the produce of the field; for the desirable, good and spacious land that You willingly gave as heritage to our ancestors, that they might eat of its fruit and be satisfied with its goodness. Have compassion, please, LORD our God, on Israel Your people, on Jerusalem, Your city, on Zion the home of Your glory, on Your altar and Your Temple. May You rebuild Jerusalem, the holy city swiftly in our time, and may You bring us back there, rejoicing in its rebuilding, eating from its fruit, satisfied by its goodness, and blessing You for it in holiness and purity.

> *On Rosh Ḥodesh:* Remember us for good
> on this day of the New Moon.

For You, God, are good and do good to all and we thank You for the land

After grain products (but not bread or matza):	*After wine or grape juice:*	*After grapes, figs, olives, pomegranates or dates:*
and for the nourishment.	and for the fruit of the vine.	and for the fruit.
Blessed are You, LORD, for the land and for the nourishment.	Blessed are You, LORD, for the land and for the fruit of the vine.	Blessed are You, LORD, for the land and for the fruit.

> *After grain products (but not bread or matza), and wine or grape juice:*
> and for the nourishment and for the fruit of the vine.
> Blessed are You, LORD,
> for the land and for the nourishment
> and the fruit of the vine.

BLESSING AFTER FOOD – BOREH NEFASHOT

> *After food or drink that does not require Birkat HaMazon or*
> *Al HaMihya – such as meat, fish, dairy products, vegetables, beverages,*
> *or fruit other than grapes, figs, pomegranates, olives or dates – say:*

בָּרוּךְ Blessed are You, LORD our God, King of the Universe,
who creates the many forms of life and their needs.
For all You have created
to sustain the life of all that lives,
blessed be He, Giver of life to the worlds.

וְעַל תְּנוּבַת הַשָּׂדֶה וְעַל אֶרֶץ חֶמְדָּה טוֹבָה וּרְחָבָה, שֶׁרָצִיתָ וְהִנְחַלְתָּ
לַאֲבוֹתֵינוּ לֶאֱכֹל מִפִּרְיָהּ וְלִשְׂבֹּעַ מִטּוּבָהּ. רַחֶם נָא יהוה אֱלֹהֵינוּ עַל
יִשְׂרָאֵל עַמֶּךָ וְעַל יְרוּשָׁלַיִם עִירֶךָ וְעַל צִיּוֹן מִשְׁכַּן כְּבוֹדֶךָ וְעַל מִזְבְּחֶךָ
וְעַל הֵיכָלֶךָ. וּבְנֵה יְרוּשָׁלַיִם עִיר הַקֹּדֶשׁ בִּמְהֵרָה בְיָמֵינוּ, וְהַעֲלֵנוּ לְתוֹכָהּ
וְשַׂמְּחֵנוּ בְּבִנְיָנָהּ וְנֹאכַל מִפִּרְיָהּ וְנִשְׂבַּע מִטּוּבָהּ, וּנְבָרֶכְךָ עָלֶיהָ בִּקְדֻשָּׁה
וּבְטָהֳרָה.

בראש חודש: וְזָכְרֵנוּ לְטוֹבָה בְּיוֹם רֹאשׁ הַחֹדֶשׁ הַזֶּה

כִּי אַתָּה יהוה טוֹב וּמֵטִיב לַכֹּל, וְנוֹדֶה לְּךָ עַל הָאָרֶץ

After grapes, figs, olives, pomegranates or dates:	*After wine or grape juice:*	*After grain products (but not bread or מצה):*
וְעַל הַפֵּרוֹת.**	וְעַל פְּרִי הַגָּפֶן.*	וְעַל הַמִּחְיָה.
בָּרוּךְ אַתָּה יהוה עַל הָאָרֶץ וְעַל הַפֵּרוֹת.**	בָּרוּךְ אַתָּה יהוה עַל הָאָרֶץ וְעַל פְּרִי הַגָּפֶן.*	בָּרוּךְ אַתָּה יהוה עַל הָאָרֶץ וְעַל הַמִּחְיָה.

After grain products (but not bread or מצה), and wine or grape juice:

וְעַל הַמִּחְיָה וְעַל פְּרִי הַגָּפֶן.*

בָּרוּךְ אַתָּה יהוה, עַל הָאָרֶץ וְעַל הַמִּחְיָה וְעַל פְּרִי הַגָּפֶן.*

*If the wine is from ארץ ישראל, then substitute גִּפְנָהּ for הַגָּפֶן.
**If the fruit is from ארץ ישראל, then substitute פֵּרוֹתֶיהָ for הַפֵּרוֹת.

בורא נפשות

After food or drink that does not require ברכת המזון or
מעין שלוש – such as meat, fish, dairy products, vegetables, beverages,
or fruit other than grapes, figs, pomegranates, olives or dates – say:

בָּרוּךְ אַתָּה יהוה אֱלֹהֵינוּ מֶלֶךְ הָעוֹלָם
בּוֹרֵא נְפָשׁוֹת רַבּוֹת וְחֶסְרוֹנָן
עַל כָּל מַה שֶּׁבָּרָאתָ לְהַחֲיוֹת בָּהֶם נֶפֶשׁ כָּל חָי.
בָּרוּךְ חֵי הָעוֹלָמִים.

BLESSINGS

BLESSINGS ON MITZVOT

In Israel on separating teruma and first tithe (if there is doubt as to whether the teruma and first tithe have been taken, the following blessing is not said, but the subsequent declaration is):

Blessed are You, Lord our God, King of the Universe,
who has made us holy through His commandments,
and has commanded us to separate *terumot* and tithes.

Whatever [of the allocated portion] is more than one in a hundred of everything here, is hereby declared to be *teruma gedola* [the priestly portion] and is the northern portion. The one in a hundred that remains here, together with nine equal portions on the upper side of this produce are declared to be the first [levitical] tithe. The one in a hundred I have made first tithe is hereby declared to be *terumat maaser* [the tithe-of-the-tithe set aside for the priests]. Nine other equal portions on the lower side of the produce are declared to be second tithe, but if this produce must have the tithe of the poor separated from it, let them be the tithe of the poor.

In Israel on separating and redeeming the second tithe (if there is doubt as to whether the second tithe has been taken, the following blessing is not said, but the subsequent declaration is):

Blessed are You, Lord our God, King of the Universe,
who has made us holy through His commandments,
and has commanded us about the redemption of the second tithe.

This second tithe, together with its additional fifth,
is hereby redeemed by one *peruta* of the coins I have set aside
for the redemption of the second tithe.

On taking ḥalla:

Blessed are You, Lord our God, King of the Universe,
who has made us holy through His commandments,
and has commanded us to set aside ḥalla from the dough.

On redeeming fourth-year fruit:

Blessed are You, Lord our God, King of the Universe,
who has made us holy through His commandments,
and has commanded us about the redemption of fruit of the fourth year.

---

commanded us about…" The most common explanation – though there are exceptions – is that the former is used when fulfilling a commandment which I personally am obligated to do, while the latter relates to fulfilling a commandment on behalf of others (as when a *mohel* circumcises a child on behalf of its parents).

ברכות

ברכות המצוות

In ארץ ישראל *on separating* תרומה *and* מעשר ראשון (*if there is doubt as to whether the* תרומה *and* מעשר ראשון *have been taken, the following blessing is not said, but the subsequent declaration is*):

בָּרוּךְ אַתָּה יהוה אֱלֹהֵינוּ מֶלֶךְ הָעוֹלָם, אֲשֶׁר קִדְּשָׁנוּ בְּמִצְוֹתָיו
וְצִוָּנוּ לְהַפְרִישׁ תְּרוּמוֹת וּמַעַשְׂרוֹת.

מַה שֶּׁהוּא יוֹתֵר מֵאֶחָד מִמֵּאָה מִן הַכֹּל שֶׁיֵּשׁ כָּאן, הֲרֵי הוּא תְּרוּמָה גְדוֹלָה בִּצְפוֹנוֹ,
וְהָאֶחָד מִמֵּאָה שֶׁנִּשְׁאַר כָּאן עִם תִּשְׁעָה חֲלָקִים כְּמוֹהוּ בְּצַד הָעֶלְיוֹן שֶׁל הַפֵּרוֹת
הַלָּלוּ, הֲרֵי הֵם מַעֲשֵׂר רִאשׁוֹן. אוֹתוֹ הָאֶחָד מִמֵּאָה שֶׁעֲשִׂיתִיו מַעֲשֵׂר רִאשׁוֹן הֲרֵי
הוּא תְּרוּמַת מַעֲשֵׂר. עוֹד תִּשְׁעָה חֲלָקִים כְּאֵלֶּה בְּצַד הַתַּחְתּוֹן שֶׁל הַפֵּרוֹת הֲרֵי הֵם
מַעֲשֵׂר שֵׁנִי, וְאִם הֵם חַיָּבִים בְּמַעֲשַׂר עָנִי, הֲרֵי הֵם מַעֲשַׂר עָנִי.

In ארץ ישראל *on separating and redeeming the* מעשר שני (*if there is doubt as to whether the* מעשר שני *has been taken, the following blessing is not said, but the subsequent declaration is*):

בָּרוּךְ אַתָּה יהוה אֱלֹהֵינוּ מֶלֶךְ הָעוֹלָם, אֲשֶׁר קִדְּשָׁנוּ בְּמִצְוֹתָיו
וְצִוָּנוּ עַל פִּדְיוֹן מַעֲשֵׂר שֵׁנִי.

מַעֲשֵׂר שֵׁנִי זֶה, הוּא וְחֻמְשׁוֹ, הֲרֵי הוּא מְחֻלָּל עַל פְּרוּטָה אַחַת מִן הַמַּטְבֵּעַ שֶׁיִּחַדְתִּי
לְפִדְיוֹן מַעֲשֵׂר שֵׁנִי.

On taking חלה:

בָּרוּךְ אַתָּה יהוה אֱלֹהֵינוּ מֶלֶךְ הָעוֹלָם, אֲשֶׁר קִדְּשָׁנוּ בְּמִצְוֹתָיו
וְצִוָּנוּ לְהַפְרִישׁ חַלָּה מִן הָעִסָּה.

On redeeming נטע רבעי:

בָּרוּךְ אַתָּה יהוה אֱלֹהֵינוּ מֶלֶךְ הָעוֹלָם, אֲשֶׁר קִדְּשָׁנוּ בְּמִצְוֹתָיו
וְצִוָּנוּ עַל פִּדְיוֹן נֶטַע רְבָעִי.

BLESSINGS ON MITZVOT

Most mitzvot, except those "between man and man," require a blessing prior
to their performance. The blessing is, in effect, the declaration of an intention
to fulfill the commandment, an expression of *kavana*, sacred intent. There
are two basic formulae, "Who has commanded us to…" and "Who has

On fixing a mezuza to the doorpost:
Blessed are You, LORD our God, King of the Universe,
who has made us holy through His commandments,
and has commanded us to affix the mezuza.

On making a protective railing around one's roof, or a fence around a pit:
Blessed are You, LORD our God, King of the Universe,
who has made us holy through His commandments,
and has commanded us to to affix a guard-rail.

A woman on ritual immersion:
Blessed are You, LORD our God, King of the Universe,
who has made us holy through His commandments,
and has commanded us about ritual immersion.

On immersing utensils made by or bought from a gentile:
Blessed are You, LORD our God, King of the Universe,
who has made us holy through His commandments,
and has commanded us about immersing a vessel (vessels).

BLESSINGS ON PLEASURES, SIGHTS AND SOUNDS

On wearing new clothes:
Blessed are You, LORD our God, King of the Universe, who clothes the naked.

On smelling fragrant shrubs or trees:
Blessed are You, LORD our God, King of the Universe,
who creates fragrant trees.

On smelling fragrant herbs, grasses or flowers:
Blessed are You, LORD our God, King of the Universe,
who creates fragrant plants.

On smelling fragrant fruit:
Blessed are You, LORD our God, King of the Universe,
who gives pleasant fragrance to fruits.

On smelling persimmon oil:
Blessed are You, LORD our God, King of the Universe,
who creates pleasing perfume.

On all other scents:
Blessed are You, LORD our God, King of the Universe,
who creates the various spices.

On seeing the wonders of nature, such as lightning, and on the 28-year solar cycle:
Blessed are You, LORD our God, King of the Universe, Author of creation.

On fixing a מזוזה to the doorpost:

בָּרוּךְ אַתָּה יהוה אֱלֹהֵינוּ מֶלֶךְ הָעוֹלָם, אֲשֶׁר קִדְּשָׁנוּ בְּמִצְוֹתָיו
וְצִוָּנוּ לִקְבֹּעַ מְזוּזָה.

On making a protective railing around one's roof, or a fence around a pit:

בָּרוּךְ אַתָּה יהוה אֱלֹהֵינוּ מֶלֶךְ הָעוֹלָם, אֲשֶׁר קִדְּשָׁנוּ בְּמִצְוֹתָיו
וְצִוָּנוּ לַעֲשׂוֹת מַעֲקֶה.

A woman on ritual immersion:

בָּרוּךְ אַתָּה יהוה אֱלֹהֵינוּ מֶלֶךְ הָעוֹלָם, אֲשֶׁר קִדְּשָׁנוּ בְּמִצְוֹתָיו
וְצִוָּנוּ עַל הַטְּבִילָה.

On immersing utensils made by or bought from a gentile:

בָּרוּךְ אַתָּה יהוה אֱלֹהֵינוּ מֶלֶךְ הָעוֹלָם, אֲשֶׁר קִדְּשָׁנוּ בְּמִצְוֹתָיו
וְצִוָּנוּ עַל טְבִילַת כְּלִי (כֵּלִים).

ברכות הנהנין, הראייה והשמיעה

On wearing new clothes:

בָּרוּךְ אַתָּה יהוה אֱלֹהֵינוּ מֶלֶךְ הָעוֹלָם, מַלְבִּישׁ עֲרֻמִּים.

On smelling fragrant shrubs or trees:

בָּרוּךְ אַתָּה יהוה אֱלֹהֵינוּ מֶלֶךְ הָעוֹלָם, בּוֹרֵא עֲצֵי בְשָׂמִים.

On smelling fragrant herbs, grasses or flowers:

בָּרוּךְ אַתָּה יהוה אֱלֹהֵינוּ מֶלֶךְ הָעוֹלָם, בּוֹרֵא עִשְׂבֵי בְשָׂמִים.

On smelling fragrant fruit:

בָּרוּךְ אַתָּה יהוה אֱלֹהֵינוּ מֶלֶךְ הָעוֹלָם, הַנּוֹתֵן רֵיחַ טוֹב בַּפֵּרוֹת.

On smelling persimmon oil:

בָּרוּךְ אַתָּה יהוה אֱלֹהֵינוּ מֶלֶךְ הָעוֹלָם, בּוֹרֵא שֶׁמֶן עָרֵב.

On all other scents:

בָּרוּךְ אַתָּה יהוה אֱלֹהֵינוּ מֶלֶךְ הָעוֹלָם, בּוֹרֵא מִינֵי בְשָׂמִים.

On seeing the wonders of nature, such as lightning, and ברכת החמה:

בָּרוּךְ אַתָּה יהוה אֱלֹהֵינוּ מֶלֶךְ הָעוֹלָם, עוֹשֶׂה מַעֲשֵׂה בְרֵאשִׁית.

On hearing thunder or experiencing a hurricane:
Blessed are You, LORD our God, King of the Universe,
whose power and might fill the world.

On seeing a rainbow:
Blessed are You, LORD our God, King of the Universe,
who remembers the covenant, is faithful to the covenant, and fulfills His word.

On seeing the ocean or the Mediterranean Sea for the first time in thirty days:
Blessed are You, LORD our God, King of the Universe,
who has made the great sea.

On seeing trees blossoming for the first time in the year:
Blessed are You, LORD our God, King of the Universe,
who has withheld nothing from His world,
but has created in it beautiful creatures and trees for human beings to enjoy.

On seeing beautiful scenes of nature:
Blessed are You, LORD our God, King of the Universe,
who has [created] such things in His world.

On seeing unusual people or animals:
Blessed are You, LORD our God, King of the Universe,
who makes [all] creatures different.

On hearing good news from which others as well as oneself will benefit:
Blessed are You, LORD our God, King of the Universe,
who is good and does good.

On hearing bad news, and said by a mourner before the ritual tearing of the garment:
Blessed are You, LORD our God, King of the Universe, the true Judge.

On seeing an outstanding Torah scholar:
Blessed are You, LORD our God, King of the Universe,
who has shared of His wisdom with those who revere Him.

On seeing an outstanding secular scholar:
Blessed are You, LORD our God, King of the Universe,
who has given of His wisdom with human beings.

On seeing a Monarch or Head of State:
Blessed are You, LORD our God, King of the Universe,
who has given of His glory to human beings.

---

sensibility. The Judaic mind moves instinctively from nature to its Creator, a
movement that is evident throughout the book of Psalms and many of the
prophetic and wisdom texts.

On hearing thunder or experiencing a hurricane:

בָּרוּךְ אַתָּה יהוה אֱלֹהֵינוּ מֶלֶךְ הָעוֹלָם, שֶׁכֹּחוֹ וּגְבוּרָתוֹ מָלֵא עוֹלָם.

On seeing a rainbow:

בָּרוּךְ אַתָּה יהוה אֱלֹהֵינוּ מֶלֶךְ הָעוֹלָם
זוֹכֵר הַבְּרִית וְנֶאֱמָן בִּבְרִיתוֹ וְקַיָּם בְּמַאֲמָרוֹ.

On seeing the ocean or the Mediterranean Sea for the first time in thirty days:

בָּרוּךְ אַתָּה יהוה אֱלֹהֵינוּ מֶלֶךְ הָעוֹלָם, שֶׁעָשָׂה אֶת הַיָּם הַגָּדוֹל.

On seeing trees blossoming for the first time in the year:

בָּרוּךְ אַתָּה יהוה אֱלֹהֵינוּ מֶלֶךְ הָעוֹלָם
שֶׁלֹּא חִסַּר בְּעוֹלָמוֹ כְּלוּם
וּבָרָא בוֹ בְּרִיּוֹת טוֹבוֹת וְאִילָנוֹת טוֹבִים לְהַנּוֹת בָּהֶם בְּנֵי אָדָם.

On seeing beautiful scenes of nature:

בָּרוּךְ אַתָּה יהוה אֱלֹהֵינוּ מֶלֶךְ הָעוֹלָם, שֶׁכָּכָה לוֹ בְּעוֹלָמוֹ.

On seeing unusual people or animals:

בָּרוּךְ אַתָּה יהוה אֱלֹהֵינוּ מֶלֶךְ הָעוֹלָם, מְשַׁנֶּה הַבְּרִיּוֹת.

On hearing good news from which others as well as oneself will benefit:

בָּרוּךְ אַתָּה יהוה אֱלֹהֵינוּ מֶלֶךְ הָעוֹלָם, הַטּוֹב וְהַמֵּיטִיב.

On hearing bad news, and said by a mourner before the ritual tearing of the garment:

בָּרוּךְ אַתָּה יהוה אֱלֹהֵינוּ מֶלֶךְ הָעוֹלָם, דַּיַּן הָאֱמֶת.

On seeing an outstanding Torah scholar:

בָּרוּךְ אַתָּה יהוה אֱלֹהֵינוּ מֶלֶךְ הָעוֹלָם, שֶׁחָלַק מֵחָכְמָתוֹ לִירֵאָיו.

On seeing an outstanding secular scholar:

בָּרוּךְ אַתָּה יהוה אֱלֹהֵינוּ מֶלֶךְ הָעוֹלָם, שֶׁנָּתַן מֵחָכְמָתוֹ לְבָשָׂר וָדָם.

On seeing a Monarch or Head of State:

בָּרוּךְ אַתָּה יהוה אֱלֹהֵינוּ מֶלֶךְ הָעוֹלָם, שֶׁנָּתַן מִכְּבוֹדוֹ לְבָשָׂר וָדָם.

BLESSINGS ON VARIOUS OCCASIONS

These blessings, many of which are to be said on encountering dramatic or sublime phenomena of nature, synthesize aesthetic sense with spiritual

On seeing 600,000 Jews together in Israel:
Blessed are You, LORD our God, King of the Universe,
who knows all secrets.

On seeing Jewish settlements in Israel:
Blessed are You, LORD our God, King of the Universe,
who establishes the border of the widow.

On seeing the place where miracles occurred to the Jewish people:
Blessed are You, LORD our God, King of the Universe,
who performed miracles for our ancestors in this place.

*On seeing the place where miracles occurred to oneself
or one's family (insert the relevant words):*
Blessed are You, LORD our God, King of the Universe,
who performed a miracle
for me (my father / my mother / my ancestors)
in this place.

ADDITIONAL BLESSINGS

After relieving oneself and washing one's hands, say:
Blessed are You, LORD our God, King of the Universe, who formed man in
wisdom and created in him many orifices and cavities. It is revealed and known
before the throne of Your glory that were one of them to be ruptured or blocked,
it would be impossible to survive and stand before You. Blessed are You, LORD,
Healer of all flesh who does wondrous deeds.

On visiting a cemetery, or seeing a Jewish grave, for the first time in thirty days:
Blessed are You, LORD our God, King of the Universe, who formed you in
judgment, who nourished and sustained you in judgment, who brought death
on you in judgment, who knows the number of you all in judgment, and who
in the future will restore you to life in judgment. Blessed are You, LORD, who
revives the dead.

You are eternally mighty, LORD. You give life to the dead and have great power
to save. He sustains the living with loving-kindness, and with great compassion
revives the dead. He supports the fallen, heals the sick, sets captives free, and
keeps His faith with those who sleep in the dust. Who is like You, Master of
might, and to whom can You be compared, O King who brings death and gives
life, and makes salvation grow? Faithful are You to revive the dead.

On seeing 600,000 Jews together in ארץ ישראל:

בָּרוּךְ אַתָּה יהוה אֱלֹהֵינוּ מֶלֶךְ הָעוֹלָם
חֲכַם הָרָזִים.

On seeing Jewish settlements in ארץ ישראל:

בָּרוּךְ אַתָּה יהוה אֱלֹהֵינוּ מֶלֶךְ הָעוֹלָם
מַצִּיב גְּבוּל אַלְמָנָה.

On seeing the place where miracles occurred to the Jewish people:

בָּרוּךְ אַתָּה יהוה אֱלֹהֵינוּ מֶלֶךְ הָעוֹלָם
שֶׁעָשָׂה נִסִּים לַאֲבוֹתֵינוּ בַּמָּקוֹם הַזֶּה.

On seeing the place where miracles occurred to oneself or one's family (insert the relevant words):

בָּרוּךְ אַתָּה יהוה אֱלֹהֵינוּ מֶלֶךְ הָעוֹלָם
שֶׁעָשָׂה לִי (לְאָבִי/לְאִמִּי/לַאֲבוֹתַי) נֵס בַּמָּקוֹם הַזֶּה.

ברכות נוספות

After relieving oneself and washing one's hands, say:

בָּרוּךְ אַתָּה יהוה אֱלֹהֵינוּ מֶלֶךְ הָעוֹלָם, אֲשֶׁר יָצַר אֶת הָאָדָם בְּחָכְמָה, וּבָרָא
בוֹ נְקָבִים נְקָבִים, חֲלוּלִים חֲלוּלִים. גָּלוּי וְיָדוּעַ לִפְנֵי כִסֵּא כְבוֹדֶךָ, שֶׁאִם יִפָּתֵחַ
אֶחָד מֵהֶם אוֹ יִסָּתֵם אֶחָד מֵהֶם, אִי אֶפְשַׁר לְהִתְקַיֵּם וְלַעֲמוֹד לְפָנֶיךָ. בָּרוּךְ
אַתָּה יהוה, רוֹפֵא כָל בָּשָׂר וּמַפְלִיא לַעֲשׂוֹת.

On visiting a cemetery, or seeing a Jewish grave, for the first time in thirty days:

בָּרוּךְ אַתָּה יהוה אֱלֹהֵינוּ מֶלֶךְ הָעוֹלָם, אֲשֶׁר יָצַר אֶתְכֶם בַּדִּין, וְזָן וְכִלְכֵּל
אֶתְכֶם בַּדִּין, וְהֵמִית אֶתְכֶם בַּדִּין, וְיוֹדֵעַ מִסְפַּר כֻּלְּכֶם בַּדִּין, וְהוּא עָתִיד
לְהַחֲיוֹתְכֶם וּלְקַיֵּם אֶתְכֶם בַּדִּין. בָּרוּךְ אַתָּה יהוה, מְחַיֵּה הַמֵּתִים.

אַתָּה גִּבּוֹר לְעוֹלָם אֲדֹנָי, מְחַיֵּה מֵתִים אַתָּה, רַב לְהוֹשִׁיעַ, מְכַלְכֵּל חַיִּים
בְּחֶסֶד, מְחַיֵּה מֵתִים בְּרַחֲמִים רַבִּים, סוֹמֵךְ נוֹפְלִים, וְרוֹפֵא חוֹלִים, וּמַתִּיר
אֲסוּרִים, וּמְקַיֵּם אֱמוּנָתוֹ לִישֵׁנֵי עָפָר. מִי כָמוֹךָ בַּעַל גְּבוּרוֹת וּמִי דּוֹמֶה לָּךְ,
מֶלֶךְ מֵמִית וּמְחַיֶּה וּמַצְמִיחַ יְשׁוּעָה, וְנֶאֱמָן אַתָּה לְהַחֲיוֹת מֵתִים.

PRAYER IN TIMES OF URGENCY

*In special cases of urgency only (see law 55), the following short form
of the Amida may be said. First say the first three blessings of the Amida
from "O Lord" on page 108 until "the holy God" page 114, then say:*

הֲבִינֵנוּ Grant us understanding, Lord our God, to know Your ways.

Sensitize our hearts so that we may revere You,

and forgive us so that we may be redeemed.

Keep us far from suffering

and satisfy us with the pastures of Your land.

Gather our scattered people from the four quarters of the earth.

May those who go astray be judged according to Your will:

raise Your hand against the wicked.

May the righteous rejoice in the rebuilding of Your city,

the restoration of Your Temple,

the flowering of Your servant David's glory,

and the radiant light of the son of Jesse, Your anointed.

May You answer us even before we call.

Blessed are You, Lord,

who hears prayer.

Continue with the final three blessings from "Find favor" on page 126 until the end.

*In extreme cases where there is no time to say the abbreviated Amida above,
one may say the following. However, if prayer is then possible
at a later time, one should say the complete Amida.*

צְרְכֵי The needs of Your people Israel are many,

and their patience is thin.

May it be Your will, Lord our God and God of our ancestors,

to give each one of them enough to sustain him,

and to every single body, all that it lacks –

and perform what is right in Your eyes.

Blessed are You, Lord,

who listens to prayer.

תפילה לשעת הדחק

In special cases of urgency only (see law 55), the following short form
of the עמידה of the ברכות may be said. First say the first three ברכות
of the עמידה on page 109 until הַקָּדוֹשׁ on page 115, then say:
אֲדֹנָי, שְׂפָתַי תִּפְתָּח from

הֲבִינֵנוּ יהוה אֱלֹהֵינוּ לָדַעַת דְּרָכֶיךָ

וּמוֹל אֶת לְבָבֵנוּ לְיִרְאָתֶךָ

וְתִסְלַח לָנוּ לִהְיוֹת גְּאוּלִים

וְרַחֲקֵנוּ מִמַּכְאוֹב

וְדַשְּׁנֵנוּ בִּנְאוֹת אַרְצֶךָ

וּנְפוּצוֹתֵינוּ מֵאַרְבַּע תְּקַבֵּץ

וְהַתּוֹעִים עַל דַּעְתְּךָ יִשָּׁפֵטוּ

וְעַל הָרְשָׁעִים תָּנִיף יָדֶךָ

וְיִשְׂמְחוּ צַדִּיקִים בְּבִנְיַן עִירֶךָ וּבְתִקּוּן הֵיכָלֶךָ

וּבִצְמִיחַת קֶרֶן לְדָוִד עַבְדֶּךָ

וּבַעֲרִיכַת נֵר לְבֶן יִשַׁי מְשִׁיחֶךָ, טֶרֶם נִקְרָא אַתָּה תַעֲנֶה.

בָּרוּךְ אַתָּה יהוה, שׁוֹמֵעַ תְּפִלָּה.

Continue with the final three ברכות, from רְצֵה on page 127 until the end.

In extreme cases where there is no time to say the abbreviated עמידה above,
one may say the following. However, if prayer is then possible
at a later time, one should say the complete עמידה.

צָרְכֵי עַמְּךָ יִשְׂרָאֵל מְרֻבִּים וְדַעְתָּם קְצָרָה.

יְהִי רָצוֹן מִלְּפָנֶיךָ יהוה אֱלֹהֵינוּ וֵאלֹהֵי אֲבוֹתֵינוּ

שֶׁתִּתֵּן לְכָל אֶחָד וְאֶחָד כְּדֵי פַרְנָסָתוֹ

וּלְכָל גְּוִיָּה וּגְוִיָּה דֵּי מַחְסוֹרָהּ

וְהַטּוֹב בְּעֵינֶיךָ עֲשֵׂה.

בָּרוּךְ אַתָּה יהוה, שׁוֹמֵעַ תְּפִלָּה.

SERVICE AT THE CONSECRATION OF A HOUSE

מִזְמוֹר A psalm of David. A song for the dedication of the House. I will *Ps. 30*
exalt You, LORD, for You have lifted me up, and not let my enemies
rejoice over me. LORD, my God, I cried to You for help and You
healed me. LORD, You lifted my soul from the grave; You spared me
from going down to the pit. Sing to the LORD, you His devoted ones,
and give thanks to His holy name. For His anger is for a moment,
but His favor for a lifetime. At night there may be weeping, but in
the morning there is joy. When I felt secure, I said, "I shall never be
shaken." LORD, when You favored me, You made me stand firm as a
mountain, but when You hid Your face, I was terrified. To You, LORD,
I called; I pleaded with my LORD: "What gain would there be if I died
and went down to the grave? Can dust thank You? Can it declare Your
truth? Hear, LORD, and be gracious to me; LORD, be my help." You
have turned my sorrow into dancing. You have removed my sackcloth
and clothed me with joy, so that my soul may sing to You and not be
silent. LORD my God, for ever will I thank You.

מִזְמוֹר A Psalm of David. LORD, who may dwell in Your tent? Who *Ps. 15*
may live on Your holy mountain? One who walks in integrity, does
what is right, and speaks the truth from his heart; who has no malice
on his tongue, does no wrong to his fellow, nor casts a slur on his
neighbor; who scorns those who are vile, but honors those who
fear the LORD; who keeps his oath even when it hurts; who does
not demand interest on his loans and never takes a bribe against the
innocent. One who does these things will never be shaken.

Solomon Hirschell; another was compiled by Chief Rabbi Dr. Hermann
Adler, which is the basis of the present text.

Where appropriate, the ceremony should begin with the fixing of mezuzot
with the appropriate blessing, together with *Sheheḥeyanu* (page 541 and 535).

Psalm 30 is then recited because of its superscription, "A song for the dedication of the House." Psalm 15 speaks of the qualities required for "dwelling
in the tent" of God – "tent" being understood by the sages (as in "How beautiful
are your tents, Jacob") as a metaphor for the Jewish home.

סדר חנוכת הבית

מִזְמוֹר שִׁיר־חֲנֻכַּת הַבַּיִת לְדָוִד: אֲרוֹמִמְךָ יהוה כִּי דִלִּיתָנִי, וְלֹא־ תהלים ל
שִׂמַּחְתָּ אֹיְבַי לִי: יהוה אֱלֹהָי, שִׁוַּעְתִּי אֵלֶיךָ וַתִּרְפָּאֵנִי: יהוה,
הֶעֱלִיתָ מִן־שְׁאוֹל נַפְשִׁי, חִיִּיתַנִי מִיָּרְדִי־בוֹר: זַמְּרוּ לַיהוה חֲסִידָיו,
וְהוֹדוּ לְזֵכֶר קָדְשׁוֹ: כִּי רֶגַע בְּאַפּוֹ, חַיִּים בִּרְצוֹנוֹ, בָּעֶרֶב יָלִין בֶּכִי
וְלַבֹּקֶר רִנָּה: וַאֲנִי אָמַרְתִּי בְשַׁלְוִי, בַּל־אֶמּוֹט לְעוֹלָם: יהוה, בִּרְצוֹנְךָ
הֶעֱמַדְתָּה לְהַרְרִי עֹז, הִסְתַּרְתָּ פָנֶיךָ הָיִיתִי נִבְהָל: אֵלֶיךָ יהוה
אֶקְרָא, וְאֶל־אֲדֹנָי אֶתְחַנָּן: מַה־בֶּצַע בְּדָמִי, בְּרִדְתִּי אֶל שָׁחַת,
הֲיוֹדְךָ עָפָר, הֲיַגִּיד אֲמִתֶּךָ: שְׁמַע־יהוה וְחָנֵּנִי, יהוה הֱיֵה־עֹזֵר לִי:
הָפַכְתָּ מִסְפְּדִי לְמָחוֹל לִי, פִּתַּחְתָּ שַׂקִּי, וַתְּאַזְּרֵנִי שִׂמְחָה: לְמַעַן
יְזַמֶּרְךָ כָבוֹד וְלֹא יִדֹּם, יהוה אֱלֹהַי, לְעוֹלָם אוֹדֶךָּ:

מִזְמוֹר לְדָוִד, יהוה מִי־יָגוּר בְּאָהֳלֶךָ, מִי־יִשְׁכֹּן בְּהַר קָדְשֶׁךָ: הוֹלֵךְ תהלים טו
תָּמִים וּפֹעֵל צֶדֶק, וְדֹבֵר אֱמֶת בִּלְבָבוֹ: לֹא־רָגַל עַל־לְשֹׁנוֹ, לֹא־
עָשָׂה לְרֵעֵהוּ רָעָה, וְחֶרְפָּה לֹא־נָשָׂא עַל־קְרֹבוֹ: נִבְזֶה בְּעֵינָיו
נִמְאָס, וְאֶת־יִרְאֵי יהוה יְכַבֵּד, נִשְׁבַּע לְהָרַע וְלֹא יָמִר: כַּסְפּוֹ לֹא־
נָתַן בְּנֶשֶׁךְ, וְשֹׁחַד עַל־נָקִי לֹא־לָקָח, עֹשֵׂה אֵלֶּה, לֹא יִמּוֹט לְעוֹלָם:

SERVICE AT THE CONSECRATION OF A HOUSE

The Torah mentions the dedication of a house: "The officials shall say to the
troops: Has anyone built a new house and not dedicated it? Let him go home,
or he may die in battle and someone else may dedicate it" (Deut. 20:5). There
are also descriptions of the consecration of the altar (Numbers, chapter 7)
and of the Temple (1 Kings, chapter 8).

No formal ceremony for the consecration of a house is mentioned in the
early rabbinic literature, other than saying Sheheḥeyanu ("Who has given us
life, sustained us, and brought us to this day") and the blessing on fixing the
mezuza. The current ceremony is a longstanding part of Anglo-Jewish custom. A service for the consecration of a house was compiled by Chief Rabbi

רִבּוֹן הָעוֹלָם Master of the Universe, look down from Your holy dwelling place, and in compassion and favor accept the prayer and plea of Your children, who are gathered here to consecrate this house, and to offer You their thanksgiving for all the kindness and truth You have shown them. Please do let not Your kindness depart, nor Your covenant of Your peace be removed from them. Shield this their home so that no evil befalls it. May illness and sadness never come near it, nor the sound of sorrow be heard within its walls. May the members of this household live together in this home in fellowship and friendship. May they love and revere You, hold fast to You, meditating in Your Torah, and living faithfully by its commandments.

Where appropriate, add the words in parentheses:

הָרֵק Bestow Your blessings on the owner of this house. LORD bless his resources and find favor in the work of his hands. Keep him far from sin and transgression. May Your tender love be upon him, and establish the work of our hands. May Your kindness be with his wife, she who watches over the affairs of her household, knowing that it is the God-fearing woman who deserves praise. (Bestow on their sons and daughters a spirit of wisdom and understanding. Lead them in the path of Your commandments, so that all who see them recognise that they are children blessed by the LORD, knowing Your Torah and revering You.) Protect them from all evil; protect their lives. May this [Your promise] be fulfilled in them: "You will be blessed when you come in, and blessed when you go out." And as we have been able to consecrate the house, so together may we witness the consecration of the great and holy Temple in Jerusalem Your city, city of our sacred assemblies, swiftly in our days. Amen.

Deut. 33

Prov. 31

Is. 61

Deut. 28

---

greater than receiving the Divine Presence. And it is where we create *shelom bayit,* "peace in the home," from which, we believe, flows peace to the world (See Maimonides, Laws of Ḥanukka 4:14).

רִבּוֹן הָעוֹלָם, הַשְׁקִיפָה מִמְּעוֹן קָדְשֶׁךָ, וְקַבֵּל בְּרַחֲמִים וּבְרָצוֹן
אֶת תְּפִלַּת בָּנֶיךָ וְתַחֲנוּנָם, אֲשֶׁר הִתְאַסְּפוּ פֹּה לַחֲנֹךְ אֶת הַבַּיִת
הַזֶּה וּלְהַקְרִיב לְפָנֶיךָ אֶת תּוֹדָתָם עַל כָּל הַחֶסֶד וְהָאֱמֶת אֲשֶׁר
עָשִׂיתָ אִתָּם. אָנָּא חַסְדְּךָ מֵאִתָּם אַל יָמוּשׁ, וּבְרִית שְׁלוֹמְךָ
אַל תָּמוֹט. הָגֵן בְּעַד בֵּית מְגוּרֵיהֶם, לֹא תְאֻנֶּה אֵלָיו רָעָה, וְנֶגַע
וְצַעַר לֹא יִקְרְבוּ אֵלָיו, וְלֹא יִשָּׁמַע קוֹל צְוָחָה בְּתוֹכוֹ. זַכֵּה אֶת
בְּנֵי הַבַּיִת לָשֶׁבֶת בְּמִשְׁכְּנָם בְּאַחֲוָה וְרֵעוּת, לְאַהֲבָה וּלְיִרְאָה
אוֹתְךָ וּלְדָבְקָה בָּךְ, לַהֲגוֹת בְּתוֹרָתְךָ וּלְקַיֵּם מִצְוֹתֶיךָ.

Where appropriate, add the words in parentheses:

הָרֵק בִּרְכוֹתֶיךָ עַל בַּעַל הַבַּיִת. בָּרֵךְ יהוה חֵילוֹ, וּפֹעַל יָדָיו   דברים לג
תִּרְצֶה: הַרְחִיקֵהוּ מִידֵי עֲבֵרָה וְעָוֹן, וִיהִי נֹעַם עָלָיו, וּמַעֲשֵׂה
יָדָיו כּוֹנְנֵהוּ. יְהִי נָא חַסְדְּךָ אֶת אִשְׁתּוֹ, צוֹפִיָּה הֲלִיכוֹת בֵּיתָהּ:   משלי לא
וְתֵדַע כִּי, אִשָּׁה יִרְאַת־יהוה הִיא תִתְהַלָּל: (הוֹפַע עַל בְּנֵיהֶם
וּבְנוֹתֵיהֶם רוּחַ חָכְמָה וּבִינָה, הַדְרִיכֵם בִּנְתִיב מִצְוֹתֶיךָ, וְכָל־   ישעיה סא
רוֹאֵיהֶם יַכִּירוּם כִּי הֵם זֶרַע בֵּרַךְ יהוה, בְּרוּכִים בַּתּוֹרָה וּבְיִרְאַת
שָׁמַיִם.) שָׁמְרֵם מִכָּל רָע, שְׁמֹר אֶת נַפְשָׁם, וִיקַיֵּם בָּהֶם: בָּרוּךְ   דברים כח
אַתָּה בְּבֹאֶךָ, וּבָרוּךְ אַתָּה בְּצֵאתֶךָ: וְכַאֲשֶׁר זָכִינוּ לַחֲנֹךְ אֶת
הַבַּיִת הַזֶּה עַתָּה, כֵּן נִזְכֶּה גַם יַחַד לִרְאוֹת חֲנֻכַּת הַבַּיִת הַגָּדוֹל
וְהַקָּדוֹשׁ בִּירוּשָׁלַיִם עִירְךָ, קִרְיַת מוֹעֲדֵינוּ, בִּמְהֵרָה בְיָמֵינוּ, אָמֵן.

רבּוֹן הָעוֹלָם **Master of the Universe:** A prayer of thanksgiving, followed by
prayers for the welfare of those who will live in the house. The sanctity of the
home is fundamental to Judaism. It is where we celebrate the love between
husband and wife – which is symbolic of the love between God and Israel.
It is where, with God's blessing, parents pass on their faith and teachings to
their children. It is where we practice hospitality, said by the sages to be even

THE TRAVELER'S PRAYER

If one intends to return home on the same day, add the words in parentheses:

יְהִי רָצוֹן May it be Your will,
Lord our God and God of our fathers,
to lead us to peace, direct our steps to peace,
guide us to peace, and bring us to our desired destination in life,
joy and peace
(and bring us back to our home in peace).
Rescue us from any enemy or ambush on the way,
and from all afflictions that trouble the world.
Send blessing to the work of our hands,
and let us find grace, kindness and compassion
from You and from all who see us.
Hear our pleas,
for You are a God who hears prayer and pleas.
Blessed are You, Lord, who listens to prayer.

May the Lord guard your going out and your return,   Ps. 121
from now and for all time.

Repeat three times:

וַיַּעֲקֹב And Jacob went on his way   Gen. 32
and angels of God met him.
When he saw them, Jacob said, "This is God's camp"
and he named the place Maḥanaim [two camps].

Repeat three times:

יְבָרֶכְךָ May the Lord bless you and protect you.   Num. 6
May the Lord make His face shine on you and be gracious to you.
May the Lord turn His face toward you and grant you peace.

שִׁיר לַמַּעֲלוֹת A song of ascents. I lift my eyes up to the hills; from where will   Ps. 121
my help come? My help comes from the Lord, Maker of heaven and earth.
He will not let your foot stumble; He who guards you does not slumber.
See: the Guardian of Israel neither slumbers nor sleeps. The Lord is your
Guardian; the Lord is your Shade at your right hand. The sun will not strike
you by day, nor the moon by night. The Lord will guard you from all harm;
He will guard your life. The Lord will guard your going and coming, now
and for evermore.

תפילת הדרך

If one intends to return home on the same day, add the words in parentheses:

יְהִי רָצוֹן מִלְּפָנֶיךָ, יהוה אֱלֹהֵינוּ וֵאלֹהֵי אֲבוֹתֵינוּ
שֶׁתּוֹלִיכֵנוּ לְשָׁלוֹם, וְתַצְעִידֵנוּ לְשָׁלוֹם, וְתַדְרִיכֵנוּ לְשָׁלוֹם
וְתַגִּיעֵנוּ לִמְחוֹז חֶפְצֵנוּ לְחַיִּים וּלְשִׂמְחָה וּלְשָׁלוֹם
(וְתַחֲזִירֵנוּ לְבֵיתֵנוּ לְשָׁלוֹם)
וְתַצִּילֵנוּ מִכַּף כָּל אוֹיֵב וְאוֹרֵב בַּדֶּרֶךְ
וּמִכָּל מִינֵי פֻּרְעָנִיּוֹת הַמִּתְרַגְּשׁוֹת לָבוֹא לָעוֹלָם
וְתִשְׁלַח בְּרָכָה בְּמַעֲשֵׂה יָדֵינוּ
וְתִתְּנֵנוּ לְחֵן וּלְחֶסֶד וּלְרַחֲמִים בְּעֵינֶיךָ וּבְעֵינֵי כָל רוֹאֵינוּ
וְתִשְׁמַע קוֹל תַּחֲנוּנֵינוּ
כִּי אֵל שׁוֹמֵעַ תְּפִלָּה וְתַחֲנוּן אַתָּה.
בָּרוּךְ אַתָּה יהוה, שׁוֹמֵעַ תְּפִלָּה.

תהלים קכא

יהוה יִשְׁמָר־צֵאתְךָ וּבוֹאֶךָ, מֵעַתָּה וְעַד־עוֹלָם:

Repeat three times:

בראשית לב

וְיַעֲקֹב הָלַךְ לְדַרְכּוֹ, וַיִּפְגְּעוּ־בוֹ מַלְאֲכֵי אֱלֹהִים:
וַיֹּאמֶר יַעֲקֹב כַּאֲשֶׁר רָאָם, מַחֲנֵה אֱלֹהִים זֶה
וַיִּקְרָא שֵׁם־הַמָּקוֹם הַהוּא מַחֲנָיִם:

Repeat three times:

במדברו

יְבָרֶכְךָ יהוה וְיִשְׁמְרֶךָ:
יָאֵר יהוה פָּנָיו אֵלֶיךָ וִיחֻנֶּךָּ:
יִשָּׂא יהוה פָּנָיו אֵלֶיךָ וְיָשֵׂם לְךָ שָׁלוֹם:

תהלים קכא

שִׁיר לַמַּעֲלוֹת, אֶשָּׂא עֵינַי אֶל־הֶהָרִים, מֵאַיִן יָבֹא עֶזְרִי: עֶזְרִי מֵעִם יהוה,
עֹשֵׂה שָׁמַיִם וָאָרֶץ: אַל־יִתֵּן לַמּוֹט רַגְלֶךָ, אַל־יָנוּם שֹׁמְרֶךָ: הִנֵּה לֹא־יָנוּם
וְלֹא יִישָׁן, שׁוֹמֵר יִשְׂרָאֵל: יהוה שֹׁמְרֶךָ, יהוה צִלְּךָ עַל־יַד יְמִינֶךָ: יוֹמָם
הַשֶּׁמֶשׁ לֹא־יַכֶּכָּה, וְיָרֵחַ בַּלָּיְלָה: יהוה יִשְׁמָרְךָ מִכָּל־רָע, יִשְׁמֹר אֶת־נַפְשֶׁךָ:
יהוה יִשְׁמָר־צֵאתְךָ וּבוֹאֶךָ, מֵעַתָּה וְעַד־עוֹלָם:

מעגל החיים

THE CYCLE OF LIFE

BRIT MILA

When the baby is brought in, all stand and say:
Blessed is he who comes.

The mohel (in some congregations, all) say (in Israel omit):

וַיְדַבֵּר The LORD spoke to Moses, saying: Pinehas the son of Elazar, the *Num. 25* son of Aaron the priest, turned back My rage from the children of Israel, when he was zealous for Me among them, and I did not annihilate the children of Israel in My own zeal. And so tell him, that I now give him My covenant for peace.

The following verses, through "LORD, please, grant us success," are only said in Israel.

Mohel: Happy are those You choose and bring near to dwell in Your courts. *Ps. 65*

All: May we be sated with the goodness of Your House,
Your holy Temple.

The father takes the baby in his hands and says quietly:

אִם אֶשְׁכָּחֵךְ If I forget you, O Jerusalem, may my right hand forget *Ps. 137* its skill. May my tongue cling to the roof of my mouth, if I do not remember you, if I do not set Jerusalem above my highest joy.

The father says aloud, followed by the congregation:

Listen, Israel: the LORD is our God, the LORD is One. *Deut. 6*

The Mohel, followed by the congregation, recites each of the following three phrases:

The LORD is King, the LORD was King,
the LORD shall be King for ever and all time.
LORD, please, save us. *Ps. 118*
LORD, please, grant us success.

The baby is placed on Eliyahu's seat, and the Mohel says:

This is the throne of Elijah the prophet, may he be remembered for good.

The Mohel continues:

לִישׁוּעָתְךָ For Your salvation I wait, O LORD. I await Your deliverance, *Gen. 49* LORD, and I observe Your commandments. Elijah, angel of the covenant, *Ps. 119* behold: yours is before you. Stand at my right hand and be close to me.

סדר ברית מילה

When the baby is brought in, all stand and say:

בָּרוּךְ הַבָּא.

The מוהל (in some congregations, all) say (in ארץ ישראל omit):

וַיְדַבֵּר יהוה אֶל־מֹשֶׁה לֵּאמֹר: פִּינְחָס בֶּן־אֶלְעָזָר בֶּן־אַהֲרֹן הַכֹּהֵן
הֵשִׁיב אֶת־חֲמָתִי מֵעַל בְּנֵי־יִשְׂרָאֵל, בְּקַנְאוֹ אֶת־קִנְאָתִי בְּתוֹכָם,
וְלֹא־כִלִּיתִי אֶת־בְּנֵי־יִשְׂרָאֵל בְּקִנְאָתִי: לָכֵן אֱמֹר, הִנְנִי נֹתֵן לוֹ אֶת־
בְּרִיתִי שָׁלוֹם:

(במדבר כה)

The following verses, through אָנָּא יהוה הַצְלִיחָה נָא are only said in Israel.

המוהל: אַשְׁרֵי תִּבְחַר וּתְקָרֵב, יִשְׁכֹּן חֲצֵרֶיךָ
הקהל: נִשְׂבְּעָה בְּטוּב בֵּיתֶךָ, קְדֹשׁ הֵיכָלֶךָ:

(תהלים סה)

The father takes the baby in his hands and says quietly:

אִם־אֶשְׁכָּחֵךְ יְרוּשָׁלָ͏ִם, תִּשְׁכַּח יְמִינִי: תִּדְבַּק לְשׁוֹנִי לְחִכִּי
אִם־לֹא אֶזְכְּרֵכִי, אִם־לֹא אַעֲלֶה אֶת־יְרוּשָׁלַ͏ִם עַל רֹאשׁ שִׂמְחָתִי:

(תהלים קלז)

The father says aloud, followed by the קהל:

שְׁמַע יִשְׂרָאֵל, יהוה אֱלֹהֵינוּ, יהוה אֶחָד:

(דברים ו)

The מוהל, followed by the קהל, repeats each of the following three phrases:

יהוה מֶלֶךְ, יהוה מָלָךְ, יהוה יִמְלֹךְ לְעֹלָם וָעֶד.
אָנָּא יהוה הוֹשִׁיעָה נָּא
אָנָּא יהוה הַצְלִיחָה נָּא:

(תהלים קיח)

The baby is placed on the כסא של אליהו, and the מוהל says:

זֶה הַכִּסֵּא שֶׁל אֵלִיָּהוּ הַנָּבִיא זָכוּר לַטּוֹב.

The מוהל continues:

לִישׁוּעָתְךָ קִוִּיתִי יהוה: שִׂבַּרְתִּי לִישׁוּעָתְךָ יהוה, וּמִצְוֹתֶיךָ עָשִׂיתִי:
אֵלִיָּהוּ מַלְאַךְ הַבְּרִית, הִנֵּה שֶׁלְּךָ לְפָנֶיךָ, עֲמֹד עַל יְמִינִי וְסָמְכֵנִי.

(בראשית מט / תהלים קיט)

I await Your deliverance, LORD. I rejoice in Your word like one who finds   *Ps. 119*
much spoil. Those who love Your Torah have great peace, and there is
no stumbling block before them. Happy are those You choose and bring   *Ps. 65*
near to dwell in Your courts.

All respond:

May we be sated with the goodness of Your House, Your holy Temple.

The baby is placed on the knees of the Sandak, and the Mohel says:

בָּרוּךְ Blessed are You, LORD our God, King of the Universe,
who has made us holy through His commandments,
and has commanded us concerning circumcision.

Immediately after the circumcision, the father says:

בָּרוּךְ Blessed are You, LORD our God, King of the Universe,
who has made us holy through His commandments,
and has commanded us to bring him [our son]
into the covenant of Abraham, our father.

In Israel the father adds (some outside Israel add it as well):

בָּרוּךְ Blessed are You, LORD our God, King of the Universe,
who has given us life, sustained us, and brought us to this time.

All respond:

אָמֵן Amen. Just as he has entered into the covenant,
so may he enter into Torah, marriage and good deeds.

---

the covenant of Abraham, our father – a separate blessing, referring not to the
circumcision itself, but what it is a sign of – namely entry into the life of the
covenant, under the sheltering wings of the Divine Presence (*Arukh HaShulḥan,
Yoreh De'ah* 365:2); (3) *Who made the beloved one* [*Isaac*] *holy from the womb* – a
blessing of acknowledgment. Isaac was the first child to have a circumcision at
the age of eight days. He was consecrated before birth, Abraham having been
told that it would be Isaac who would continue the covenant (Gen. 17:19–21).

כְּשֵׁם שֶׁנִּכְנַס לַבְּרִית *Just as he has entered into the covenant:* Mentioned already in
early rabbinic sources as the response of those present. The three phrases
refer to the duties of a parent to a child: (1) to teach him Torah; (2) to ensure
that he marries; and (3) to train him to do good deeds, as the Torah says in
the case of Abraham: "For I have singled him out so that he may instruct his
children and his posterity to keep the way of the LORD by doing what is just
and right" (Gen. 18:19).

שַׂשְׂתִּי לִישׁוּעָתְךָ יהוה: שָׂשׂ אָנֹכִי עַל־אִמְרָתֶךָ, כְּמוֹצֵא שָׁלָל רָב: תהלים קיט

שָׁלוֹם רָב לְאֹהֲבֵי תוֹרָתֶךָ, וְאֵין־לָמוֹ מִכְשׁוֹל: אַשְׁרֵי תִּבְחַר וּתְקָרֵב, תהלים סה

יִשְׁכֹּן חֲצֵרֶיךָ:

All respond:

נִשְׂבְּעָה בְּטוּב בֵּיתֶךָ, קְדֹשׁ הֵיכָלֶךָ:

The baby is placed on the knees of the סנדק*, and the* מוהל *says:*

בָּרוּךְ אַתָּה יהוה אֱלֹהֵינוּ מֶלֶךְ הָעוֹלָם

אֲשֶׁר קִדְּשָׁנוּ בְּמִצְוֹתָיו וְצִוָּנוּ עַל הַמִּילָה.

Immediately after the circumcision, the father says:

בָּרוּךְ אַתָּה יהוה אֱלֹהֵינוּ מֶלֶךְ הָעוֹלָם, אֲשֶׁר קִדְּשָׁנוּ בְּמִצְוֹתָיו

וְצִוָּנוּ לְהַכְנִיסוֹ בִּבְרִיתוֹ שֶׁל אַבְרָהָם אָבִינוּ.

In ארץ ישראל *the father adds (some in* חוץ לארץ *add it as well):*

בָּרוּךְ אַתָּה יהוה אֱלֹהֵינוּ מֶלֶךְ הָעוֹלָם

שֶׁהֶחֱיָנוּ וְקִיְּמָנוּ וְהִגִּיעָנוּ לַזְּמַן הַזֶּה.

All respond:

אָמֵן. כְּשֵׁם שֶׁנִּכְנַס לַבְּרִית, כֵּן יִכָּנֵס לְתוֹרָה וּלְחֻפָּה וּלְמַעֲשִׂים טוֹבִים.

SERVICE AT A CIRCUMCISION

Since the days of Abraham (Gen. 17:4–14), circumcision has been the sign, for Jewish males, of the covenant between God and His people. Despite the fact that the law was restated by Moses (Lev. 12:3), it remains known as the "Covenant of Abraham." The ceremony – always performed on the eighth day, even on Shabbat, unless there are medical reasons for delay – marks the entry of the child into the covenant of Jewish fate and destiny. The duty of circumcision devolves, in principle, on the father of the child; in practice it is performed only by a qualified *mohel*.

בָּרוּךְ *Blessed are You:* There are three blessings to be said at a circumcision: (1) *And has commanded us concerning circumcision* – a blessing over the commandment itself, the "about" formula signaling that the *mohel* is performing the commandment on behalf of the father; (2) *To bring him [our son] into*

*After the circumcision has been completed, the Mohel
(or another honoree) takes a cup of wine and says:*

בָּרוּךְ Blessed are You, LORD our God, King of the Universe, who creates the fruit of the vine.

בָּרוּךְ Blessed are You, LORD our God, King of the Universe, who made the beloved one [Isaac] holy from the womb, marked the decree of circumcision in his flesh, and gave his descendants the seal and sign of the holy covenant. As a reward for this, the Living God, our Portion, our Rock, did order deliverance from destruction for the beloved of our flesh, for the sake of His covenant that He set in our flesh. Blessed are You, LORD, who establishes the covenant.

אֱלֹהֵינוּ Our God and God of our fathers, preserve this child to his father and mother, and let his name be called in Israel (*baby's name* son of *father's name*). May the father rejoice in the issue of his body, and the mother be glad with the fruit of her womb, as is written, "May your *Prov. 23* father and mother rejoice, and she who bore you be glad." And it is said, "Then I passed by you and saw you downtrodden in your blood, and I *Ezek. 16* said to you: In your blood, live; and I said to you: In your blood, live."

וְנֶאֱמַר And it is said, "He remembered His covenant for ever; the *Ps. 105* word He ordained for a thousand generations; the covenant He made with Abraham and gave on oath to Isaac, confirming it as a statute for Jacob, an everlasting covenant for Israel." And it is said, "And Abraham circumcised his son Isaac at the age of eight days, as *Gen. 21* God had commanded him." Thank the LORD for He is good; His *Ps. 118* loving-kindness is for ever.

All respond:

Thank the LORD for He is good; His loving-kindness is for ever.

The Mohel (or honoree) continues:

May this child (*baby's name* son of *father's name*) become great. Just as he has entered into the covenant, so may he enter into Torah, marriage and good deeds.

*The Sandak also drinks some of the wine; some drops are given to the baby.
The cup is then sent to the mother, who also drinks from it.*

All say Aleinu on page 184, and Mourner's Kaddish on page 186.

After the circumcision has been completed, the מוהל
(or another honoree) takes a cup of wine and says:

בָּרוּךְ אַתָּה יהוה אֱלֹהֵינוּ מֶלֶךְ הָעוֹלָם, בּוֹרֵא פְּרִי הַגָּפֶן.

בָּרוּךְ אַתָּה יהוה אֱלֹהֵינוּ מֶלֶךְ הָעוֹלָם, אֲשֶׁר קִדֵּשׁ יְדִיד מִבֶּטֶן,
וְחֹק בִּשְׁאֵרוֹ שָׂם, וְצֶאֱצָאָיו חָתַם בְּאוֹת בְּרִית קֹדֶשׁ. עַל כֵּן
בִּשְׂכַר זֹאת, אֵל חַי חֶלְקֵנוּ צוּרֵנוּ צִוָּה לְהַצִּיל יְדִידוּת שְׁאֵרֵנוּ
מִשַּׁחַת, לְמַעַן בְּרִיתוֹ אֲשֶׁר שָׂם בִּבְשָׂרֵנוּ. בָּרוּךְ אַתָּה יהוה,
כּוֹרֵת הַבְּרִית.

אֱלֹהֵינוּ וֵאלֹהֵי אֲבוֹתֵינוּ, קַיֵּם אֶת הַיֶּלֶד הַזֶּה לְאָבִיו וּלְאִמּוֹ,
וְיִקָּרֵא שְׁמוֹ בְּיִשְׂרָאֵל (פלוני בֶּן פלוני). יִשְׂמַח הָאָב בְּיוֹצֵא חֲלָצָיו וְתָגֵל
אִמּוֹ בִּפְרִי בִטְנָהּ, כַּכָּתוּב: יִשְׂמַח־אָבִיךָ וְאִמֶּךָ, וְתָגֵל יוֹלַדְתֶּךָ: | משלי כג

וְנֶאֱמַר: וָאֶעֱבֹר עָלַיִךְ וָאֶרְאֵךְ מִתְבּוֹסֶסֶת בְּדָמָיִךְ, וָאֹמַר לָךְ | יחזקאל טז
בְּדָמַיִךְ חֲיִי, וָאֹמַר לָךְ בְּדָמַיִךְ חֲיִי:

וְנֶאֱמַר: זָכַר לְעוֹלָם בְּרִיתוֹ, דָּבָר צִוָּה לְאֶלֶף דּוֹר: אֲשֶׁר כָּרַת אֶת־ | תהלים קה
אַבְרָהָם, וּשְׁבוּעָתוֹ לְיִשְׂחָק: וַיַּעֲמִידֶהָ לְיַעֲקֹב לְחֹק, לְיִשְׂרָאֵל
בְּרִית עוֹלָם: וְנֶאֱמַר: וַיָּמָל אַבְרָהָם אֶת־יִצְחָק בְּנוֹ בֶּן־שְׁמֹנַת | בראשית כא
יָמִים, כַּאֲשֶׁר צִוָּה אֹתוֹ אֱלֹהִים: הוֹדוּ לַיהוה כִּי־טוֹב, כִּי לְעוֹלָם | תהלים קיח
חַסְדּוֹ:

All respond:

הוֹדוּ לַיהוה כִּי־טוֹב, כִּי לְעוֹלָם חַסְדּוֹ:

The מוהל (or honoree) continues:

(פלוני בֶּן פלוני) זֶה הַקָּטֹן גָּדוֹל יִהְיֶה, כְּשֵׁם שֶׁנִּכְנַס לַבְּרִית, כֵּן יִכָּנֵס
לְתוֹרָה וּלְחֻפָּה וּלְמַעֲשִׂים טוֹבִים.

The סנדק also drinks some of the wine; some drops are given to the baby.
The cup is then sent to the mother, who also drinks from it.

All say עָלֵינוּ, *on page 185, and* קדיש יתום *on page 187.*

BIRKAT HAMAZON AT A BRIT MILA

Leader Gentlemen, let us say grace.

Others May the name of the Lord be blessed from now and for ever.   *Ps. 113*

Leader May the name of the Lord be blessed from now and for ever.

Leader then We give thanks to Your name among the faithful.
others Blessed are you to the Lord.

Leader With permission of the Almighty, awesome and revered,
a refuge in times of trouble,
Almighty, girded with strength –
majestic on high, the Lord.

Others We give thanks to Your name among the faithful.
Blessed are you to the Lord.

Leader With permission of the holy Torah,
pure and clear,
given to us as a heritage
by Moses the servant of the Lord.

Others We give thanks to Your name among the faithful.
Blessed are you to the Lord.

Leader With permission of the priests, the Levites,
I call upon the God of the Hebrews,
declaring His glory to the furthest isles,
and offering blessings to the Lord.

Others We give thanks to Your name among the faithful.
Blessed are you to the Lord.

---

from God, the Torah, Kohanim and Levites, and the assembled company,
dating from the Middle Ages. Originally said at other festive occasions, it has
come, over the course of time, to be associated specifically with the celebration of a circumcision.

ברכת המזון לברית מילה

Leader	רַבּוֹתַי נְבָרֵךְ.
Others	יְהִי שֵׁם יהוה מְבֹרָךְ מֵעַתָּה וְעַד־עוֹלָם:
Leader	יְהִי שֵׁם יהוה מְבֹרָךְ מֵעַתָּה וְעַד־עוֹלָם:
Leader then others	נוֹדֶה לְשִׁמְךָ בְּתוֹךְ אֱמוּנַי, בְּרוּכִים אַתֶּם לַיהוה.

תהלים קיג

בִּרְשׁוּת אֵל אָיֹם וְנוֹרָא — Leader
מִשְׂגָּב לְעִתּוֹת בַּצָּרָה
אֵל נֶאְזָר בִּגְבוּרָה
אַדִּיר בַּמָּרוֹם יהוה.

נוֹדֶה לְשִׁמְךָ בְּתוֹךְ אֱמוּנַי, בְּרוּכִים אַתֶּם לַיהוה. — Others

בִּרְשׁוּת הַתּוֹרָה הַקְּדוֹשָׁה — Leader
טְהוֹרָה הִיא וְגַם פְּרוּשָׁה
צִוָּה לָנוּ מוֹרָשָׁה
מֹשֶׁה עֶבֶד יהוה.

נוֹדֶה לְשִׁמְךָ בְּתוֹךְ אֱמוּנַי, בְּרוּכִים אַתֶּם לַיהוה. — Others

בִּרְשׁוּת הַכֹּהֲנִים וְהַלְוִיִּם — Leader
אֶקְרָא לֵאלֹהֵי הָעִבְרִיִּים
אֲהוֹדֶנּוּ בְּכָל אִיִּים
אֲבָרְכָה אֶת יהוה.

נוֹדֶה לְשִׁמְךָ בְּתוֹךְ אֱמוּנַי, בְּרוּכִים אַתֶּם לַיהוה. — Others

---

BIRKAT HAMAZON AT A BRIT MILA

נוֹדֶה לְשִׁמְךָ בְּתוֹךְ אֱמוּנַי *We give thanks to Your name among the faithful:* A highly stylized form of the invitation to say Grace, asking permission respectively

Leader With the permission of the rabbis, teachers and friends,
I open my lips with song,
saying from my innermost being:
"Blessed is he that comes in the name of the LORD."

Others We give thanks to Your name among the faithful.
Blessed are you to the LORD.

Leader With your permission, my masters and teachers,
let us bless (*in a minyan:* our God,) the One
from whose food we have eaten.

Others Blessed be (*in a minyan:* our God,) the One
from whose food we have eaten,
and by whose goodness we live.

Leader Blessed be (*in a minyan:* our God,) the One
from whose food we have eaten,
and by whose goodness we live.
Blessed be He, and blessed be His name.

*Continue with Birkat HaMazon on page 520 until
"in the eyes of God and man" on page 530. Then continue:*

Someone other than the father says:

הָרַחֲמָן May the Compassionate One
bless the father and mother of this child.
May they be worthy to raise him,
educate him, and train him in wisdom.
From this eighth day onward may his blood be accepted,
and may the LORD his God be with him always.

Someone other than the Sandak says:

הָרַחֲמָן May the Compassionate One bless him [the Sandak]
who assisted in the covenant of circumcision
and rejoiced to do this pious deed.
May God doubly reward him for his deed,
exalting him ever higher.

Leader   בִּרְשׁוּת מָרָנָן וְרַבָּנָן וְרַבּוֹתַי

אֶפְתְּחָה בְּשִׁיר פִּי וּשְׂפָתַי

וְתֹאמַרְנָה עַצְמוֹתַי

בָּרוּךְ הַבָּא בְּשֵׁם יהוה.

Others   נוֹדֶה לְשִׁמְךָ בְּתוֹךְ אֱמוּנַי, בְּרוּכִים אַתֶּם לַיהוה.

Leader   בִּרְשׁוּת מָרָנָן וְרַבָּנָן וְרַבּוֹתַי

נְבָרֵךְ (במנין: אֱלֹהֵינוּ) שֶׁאָכַלְנוּ מִשֶּׁלוֹ.

Others   בָּרוּךְ (במנין: אֱלֹהֵינוּ) שֶׁאָכַלְנוּ מִשֶּׁלוֹ וּבְטוּבוֹ חָיִינוּ.

Leader   בָּרוּךְ (במנין: אֱלֹהֵינוּ) שֶׁאָכַלְנוּ מִשֶּׁלוֹ וּבְטוּבוֹ חָיִינוּ.

בָּרוּךְ הוּא וּבָרוּךְ שְׁמוֹ.

Continue with ברכת המזון *on page 521 until* וְאָדָם בְּעֵינֵי אֱלֹהִים *on page 531. Then continue:*

Someone other than the father says:

הָרַחֲמָן הוּא יְבָרֵךְ אֲבִי הַיֶּלֶד וְאִמּוֹ

וְיִזְכּוּ לְגַדְּלוֹ וּלְחַנְּכוֹ וּלְחַכְּמוֹ

מִיּוֹם הַשְּׁמִינִי וָהָלְאָה יֵרָצֶה דָמוֹ

וִיהִי יהוה אֱלֹהָיו עִמּוֹ.

Someone other than the סנדק *says:*

הָרַחֲמָן הוּא יְבָרֵךְ בַּעַל בְּרִית הַמִּילָה

אֲשֶׁר שָׂשׂ לַעֲשׂוֹת צֶדֶק בְּגִילָה

וִישַׁלֵּם פָּעֳלוֹ וּמַשְׂכֻּרְתּוֹ כְּפוּלָה

וְיִתְּנֵהוּ לְמַעְלָה לְמָעְלָה.

הָרַחֲמָן *May the Compassionate One:* A series of special blessings for the parents of the child, the *Sandak,* the child, and the *mohel.* The fifth and sixth are prayers for the coming of the Messiah, and for Elijah, who is believed to be

הָרַחֲמָן May the Compassionate One
bless the tender child, circumcised on his eighth day.
May his heart and hands be firm with God,
and may he be worthy to witness the Divine Presence
three times a year.

Someone other than the Mohel says:

הָרַחֲמָן May the Compassionate One
bless him who performed the circumcision,
and fulfilled every part of the precept.
The service of the faint-hearted would not be acceptable
if he failed to perform
the three essentials of the precept.

הָרַחֲמָן May the Compassionate One
send us His anointed, blameless in life,
through the merit of this child
groomed by the blood of circumcision,
to proclaim good news and consolations
to the unique people scattered
and dispersed among the nations.

הָרַחֲמָן May the Compassionate One
send us the righteous priest,
who was taken into hiding,
until a throne, bright as the sun, radiant as a diamond,
is prepared for him;
the prophet who covered his face with his mantle
and wrapped himself in it [when God declared]:
My covenant is with him for life and peace.

*Continue with "May the Compassionate One make us
worthy of the Messianic Age" on page 530.*

*On Rosh Ḥodesh continue with "May the Compassionate
One renew this month" on page 530.*

הָרַחֲמָן הוּא יְבָרֵךְ רַךְ הַנִּמּוֹל לִשְׁמוֹנָה
וְיִהְיוּ יָדָיו וְלִבּוֹ לָאֵל אֱמוּנָה
וְיִזְכֶּה לִרְאוֹת פְּנֵי הַשְּׁכִינָה
שָׁלֹשׁ פְּעָמִים בַּשָּׁנָה.

Someone other than the מוהל *says:*

הָרַחֲמָן הוּא יְבָרֵךְ הַמָּל בְּשַׂר הָעָרְלָה
וּפָרַע וּמָצַץ דְּמֵי הַמִּילָה
אִישׁ הַיָּרֵא וְרַךְ הַלֵּבָב עֲבוֹדָתוֹ פְּסוּלָה
אִם שָׁלֹשׁ אֵלֶּה לֹא יַעֲשֶׂה לָהּ.

הָרַחֲמָן הוּא יִשְׁלַח לָנוּ מְשִׁיחוֹ הוֹלֵךְ תָּמִים
בִּזְכוּת חֲתַן לַמּוּלוֹת דָּמִים
לְבַשֵּׂר בְּשׂוֹרוֹת טוֹבוֹת וְנִחוּמִים
לְעַם אֶחָד מְפֻזָּר וּמְפֹרָד בֵּין הָעַמִּים.

הָרַחֲמָן הוּא יִשְׁלַח לָנוּ כֹּהֵן צֶדֶק אֲשֶׁר לֻקַּח לְעֵילוֹם
עַד הוּכַן כִּסְאוֹ כַּשֶּׁמֶשׁ וְיַהֲלוֹם
וַיָּלֶט פָּנָיו בְּאַדַּרְתּוֹ וַיִּגְלוֹם
בְּרִיתִי הָיְתָה אִתּוֹ הַחַיִּים וְהַשָּׁלוֹם.

Continue with הָרַחֲמָן הוּא יְזַכֵּנוּ לִימוֹת הַמָּשִׁיחַ *on page 531.*
On ראש חודש *continue with* הָרַחֲמָן הוּא יְחַדֵּשׁ *on page 531.*

---

present at the circumcision. The author has left his name, Abraham, in an acrostic formed by the initial letters of the third-to-last word in the first line of the first five blessings.

REDEMPTION OF THE FIRSTBORN

A firstborn male child, must be redeemed on the 31st day of his birth – unless the father is a Kohen or Levi, or the mother is a daughter of a Kohen or a Levi. If the 31st day falls on Shabbat or Yom Tov, the ceremony is postponed to the following weekday.

The father, presenting his child to the Kohen, declares:

זֶה This is my firstborn son, the first issue of his mother's womb. The Holy One, blessed be He, has commanded us to redeem him, as is said,

> "Those who are to be redeemed, you must redeem from   *Num. 18*
> the age of one month, at the fixed price of five shekels of
> silver by the sacred standard, which is twenty gerahs to
> the shekel."

And it is also stated,

> "Consecrate to Me every firstborn; the first of every womb   *Ex. 13*
> among the people of Israel, whether of man or beast,
> belongs to Me."

The Kohen checks with the mother that this is her firstborn, and then asks if she has miscarried before this child. If her answer is no, he asks the father:

מַאי Which do you prefer:
to give me your firstborn son,
the first birth of his mother,
or to redeem him for five selas
as you are bound to do according to the Torah?

---

prescribes a ceremony of redemption, in which the father of the child makes a monetary offering to a Kohen, symbolically exchanging it for his son. The substance of the ceremony has not changed since biblical times, though its wording is first mentioned in the Talmud.

מַאי בָּעִית טְפֵי *Which do you prefer:* A notional question. In fact, the father has no choice but to redeem the child. The question is asked to ensure that the father understands the nature of the ceremony. The present text is in Aramaic, but it can be said in any language.

סדר פדיון הבן

A firstborn male child, must be redeemed on the 31st day of his birth – unless the father
is a כהן or לוי, or the mother is a daughter of a כהן or a לוי. If the 31st day falls
on שבת or יום טוב, the ceremony is postponed to the following weekday.

The father, presenting his child to the כהן, declares:

זֶה בְּנִי בְכוֹרִי הוּא פֶּטֶר רֶחֶם לְאִמּוֹ
וְהַקָּדוֹשׁ בָּרוּךְ הוּא צִוָּה לִפְדּוֹתוֹ
שֶׁנֶּאֱמַר

וּפְדוּיָו מִבֶּן־חֹדֶשׁ תִּפְדֶּה, בְּעֶרְכְּךָ כֶּסֶף חֲמֵשֶׁת שְׁקָלִים   במדבר יח
בְּשֶׁקֶל הַקֹּדֶשׁ, עֶשְׂרִים גֵּרָה הוּא:

וְנֶאֱמַר   שמות יג

קַדֶּשׁ־לִי כָל־בְּכוֹר פֶּטֶר כָּל־רֶחֶם בִּבְנֵי יִשְׂרָאֵל בָּאָדָם
וּבַבְּהֵמָה, לִי הוּא:

The כהן checks with the mother that this is her firstborn, and then asks if she
has miscarried before this child. If her answer is no, he asks the father:

מַאי בָּעֵית טְפֵי
לִתֵּן לִי בִּנְךָ בְּכוֹרְךָ שֶׁהוּא פֶּטֶר רֶחֶם לְאִמּוֹ
אוֹ בָּעֵית לִפְדּוֹתוֹ בְּעַד חֲמֵשׁ סְלָעִים
כִּדְמְחַיְּבַתְּ מִדְּאוֹרַיְתָא.

REDEMPTION OF THE FIRSTBORN
According to the Torah, firstborn males originally carried a special sanctity.
Their lives spared during the last of the ten plagues, the firstborns were to
become God's special ministers, who would dedicate themselves to His
service. (The supreme biblical example is Samuel, dedicated to God by his
mother Hannah, 1 Sam. 1:11.) After the sin of the golden calf, that responsibility was transferred to the Levites, the only tribe that did not take part in the
sin (Num. 3:11–13). In memory of the earlier sanctity, however, the Torah

The father replies:

חָפֵץ I wish to redeem my son.
I present you with the cost of his redemption
which I am bound to give according to the Torah.

Holding the redemption money, the father says:

בָּרוּךְ Blessed are You, Lᴏʀᴅ our God, King of the Universe,
who has made us holy through His commandments,
and has commanded us concerning the redemption of a son.

בָּרוּךְ Blessed are You, Lᴏʀᴅ our God, King of the Universe,
who has given us life, sustained us, and brought us to this time.

The redemption money is given to the Kohen, who then returns the child to his father.
The Kohen takes a cup of wine and says:

בָּרוּךְ Blessed are You, Lᴏʀᴅ our God, King of the Universe,
who creates the fruit of the vine.

Placing his right hand on the head of the child, the Kohen blesses him as follows:

יְשִׂמְךָ May God make you like   Gen. 48
Ephraim and Manasseh.
May the Lᴏʀᴅ bless you and protect you.   Num. 6
May the Lᴏʀᴅ make His face shine on you
and be gracious to you.
May the Lᴏʀᴅ turn His face toward you
and grant you peace.
The Lᴏʀᴅ is your Guardian;   Ps. 121
the Lᴏʀᴅ is your protection at your right hand.
The Lᴏʀᴅ will guard you against all harm.
He will guard your life.
For length of days, years of life, and peace   Prov. 3
He will increase for you.

The father replies:

חָפֵץ אֲנִי לִפְדּוֹת אֶת בְּנִי

וְהֵילָךְ דְּמֵי פִדְיוֹנוֹ כְּדִמְחַיַבְנָא מִדְּאוֹרַיְתָא.

Holding the redemption money, the father says:

בָּרוּךְ אַתָּה יהוה אֱלֹהֵינוּ מֶלֶךְ הָעוֹלָם

אֲשֶׁר קִדְּשָׁנוּ בְּמִצְוֹתָיו וְצִוָּנוּ עַל פִּדְיוֹן הַבֵּן.

בָּרוּךְ אַתָּה יהוה אֱלֹהֵינוּ מֶלֶךְ הָעוֹלָם

שֶׁהֶחֱיָנוּ וְקִיְּמָנוּ וְהִגִּיעָנוּ לַזְּמַן הַזֶּה.

The redemption money is given to the כהן, who then returns the child to his father.
The כהן takes a cup of wine and says:

בָּרוּךְ אַתָּה יהוה אֱלֹהֵינוּ מֶלֶךְ הָעוֹלָם, בּוֹרֵא פְּרִי הַגָּפֶן.

Placing his right hand on the head of the child, the כהן blesses him as follows:

בראשית מח · יְשִׂמְךָ אֱלֹהִים כְּאֶפְרַיִם וְכִמְנַשֶּׁה:

במדבר ו · יְבָרֶכְךָ יהוה וְיִשְׁמְרֶךָ:

יָאֵר יהוה פָּנָיו אֵלֶיךָ וִיחֻנֶּךָּ:

יִשָּׂא יהוה פָּנָיו אֵלֶיךָ וְיָשֵׂם לְךָ שָׁלוֹם:

תהלים קכא · יהוה שֹׁמְרֶךָ, יהוה צִלְּךָ עַל יַד יְמִינֶךָ:

יהוה יִשְׁמָרְךָ מִכָּל רָע, יִשְׁמֹר אֶת נַפְשֶׁךָ:

משלי ג · כִּי אֹרֶךְ יָמִים וּשְׁנוֹת חַיִּים וְשָׁלוֹם יוֹסִיפוּ לָךְ:

THANKSGIVING PRAYER AFTER CHILDBIRTH

On entering the synagogue, say:

וַאֲנִי As for me, by Your great love,   Ps. 5
I will come into Your House.
I will bow down toward Your holy Temple in awe of You.

אָהַבְתִּי I love the LORD, for He hears my voice, my pleas.   Ps. 116
He turns His ear to me whenever I call.
The bonds of death encompassed me,
the anguish of the grave came upon me,
I was overcome by trouble and sorrow.
Then I called on the name of the LORD: "LORD, I pray, save my life."
Gracious is the LORD, and righteous; our God is full of compassion.
The LORD protects the simple hearted.
When I was brought low, He saved me.
My soul, be at peace once more,
for the LORD has been good to you.
For You have rescued me from death,
my eyes from weeping, my feet from stumbling.
I shall walk in the presence of the LORD in the land of the living.
I had faith, even when I said, "I am greatly afflicted,"
even when I said rashly, "All men are liars."

מָה־אָשִׁיב How can I repay the LORD for all His goodness to me?   Ps. 116
To You I shall bring a thanksgiving-offering
and call on the LORD by name.
I will fulfill my vows to the LORD in the presence of all His people,
in the courts of the House of the LORD,
in your midst, Jerusalem. Halleluya!

The above prayer is composed of the following elements: (1) a prayer on entry
to the synagogue; (2) verses of thanksgiving from Hallel; (3) the blessing
"Who bestows good things" (*HaGomel*) together with the congregational
response; and (4) prayers for recovery from the pains of birth, and for success in raising the child.

סדר תפילה ליולדת

On entering the בית כנסת, say:

תהלים ה

וַאֲנִי בְּרֹב חַסְדְּךָ אָבוֹא בֵיתֶךָ
אֶשְׁתַּחֲוֶה אֶל־הֵיכַל־קָדְשְׁךָ בְּיִרְאָתֶךָ:

תהלים קטז

אָהַבְתִּי, כִּי־יִשְׁמַע יהוה, אֶת־קוֹלִי תַּחֲנוּנָי:

כִּי־הִטָּה אָזְנוֹ לִי, וּבְיָמַי אֶקְרָא:

אֲפָפוּנִי חֶבְלֵי־מָוֶת, וּמְצָרֵי שְׁאוֹל מְצָאוּנִי, צָרָה וְיָגוֹן אֶמְצָא:

וּבְשֵׁם־יהוה אֶקְרָא, אָנָּה יהוה מַלְּטָה נַפְשִׁי:

חַנּוּן יהוה וְצַדִּיק, וֵאלֹהֵינוּ מְרַחֵם:

שֹׁמֵר פְּתָאיִם יהוה, דַּלּוֹתִי וְלִי יְהוֹשִׁיעַ:

שׁוּבִי נַפְשִׁי לִמְנוּחָיְכִי, כִּי־יהוה גָּמַל עָלָיְכִי:

כִּי חִלַּצְתָּ נַפְשִׁי מִמָּוֶת, אֶת־עֵינִי מִן־דִּמְעָה, אֶת־רַגְלִי מִדֶּחִי:

אֶתְהַלֵּךְ לִפְנֵי יהוה, בְּאַרְצוֹת הַחַיִּים:

הֶאֱמַנְתִּי כִּי אֲדַבֵּר, אֲנִי עָנִיתִי מְאֹד:

אֲנִי אָמַרְתִּי בְחָפְזִי, כָּל־הָאָדָם כֹּזֵב:

תהלים קטז

מָה־אָשִׁיב לַיהוה, כָּל־תַּגְמוּלוֹהִי עָלָי:

לְךָ־אֶזְבַּח זֶבַח תּוֹדָה, וּבְשֵׁם יהוה אֶקְרָא:

נְדָרַי לַיהוה אֲשַׁלֵּם, נֶגְדָה־נָּא לְכָל־עַמּוֹ:

בְּחַצְרוֹת בֵּית יהוה, בְּתוֹכֵכִי יְרוּשָׁלָ͏ִם, הַלְלוּיָהּ:

THANKSGIVING PRAYER AFTER CHILDBIRTH

In Temple times, mothers would offer a sacrifice after the birth of a child (Lev. 12:6–8). No record exists of a formal prayer offered on such occasions: there may have been no fixed text. Hannah's prayer after the birth of Samuel (1 Sam. 2:1–10) is, however, a powerful example of such a song of thanksgiving.

The mother says:

בָּרוּךְ Blessed are You, LORD our God, King of the Universe,
who bestows good things on the unworthy,
who has bestowed on me much good.

All respond:

אָמֵן Amen. May He who bestowed much good on you,
continue to bestow on you much good. Selah.

אָנָּא O great, mighty and revered God. By Your great love I now come into
Your House, to offer You a thanksgiving-offering for all the good You have
bestowed on me. Travail beset me, pains seized me. In my distress I cried to
You, and from Your habitation You heard my voice and helped me. You healed
all my sickness, and crowned me with kindness and compassion. Until now
Your mercy has helped me. I pray to You, God, never forsake me. Bestow Your
blessing upon Your handmaid. Strengthen and support me together with my
husband, that we may raise

For a boy:

הַיֶּלֶד the boy that has been born to us, to revere You and serve You
in truth, and to walk in the path of righteousness. Protect our tender
child in all his ways. Favor him with knowledge, understanding and
discernment, and let his portion be in Your Torah, so that he may
sanctify Your great name, and become a comfort to us as we grow
old. As for me, may my prayer come to You, LORD, at a time of favor. *Ps. 69*
O God, in Your great love, answer me with Your faithful salvation.

For a girl:

הַיַּלְדָּה the girl that has been born to us, to revere You and serve You
in truth, and to walk in the path of righteousness. Protect our tender
child in all her ways. Favor her with knowledge, understanding and
discernment, and let her portion be in Your Torah, so that she may
sanctify Your great name, and become a comfort to us as we grow
old. As for me, may my prayer come to You, LORD, at a time of favor. *Ps. 69*
O God, in Your great love, answer me with Your faithful salvation.

If the baby is brought to the synagogue, the Rabbi says the following blessings over him/her:

יְבָרֶכְךָ May the LORD bless you and protect you. *Num. 6*
May the LORD make His face shine on you and be gracious to you.
May the LORD turn His face toward you and grant you peace.

The mother says:

בָּרוּךְ אַתָּה יהוה אֱלֹהֵינוּ מֶלֶךְ הָעוֹלָם
הַגּוֹמֵל לְחַיָּבִים טוֹבוֹת, שֶׁגְּמָלַנִי כָּל טוֹב.

All respond:

אָמֵן. מִי שֶׁגְּמָלֵךְ כָּל טוֹב, הוּא יִגְמָלֵךְ כָּל טוֹב, סֶלָה.

אָנָּא הָאֵל הַגָּדוֹל הַגִּבּוֹר וְהַנּוֹרָא, בְּרֹב חַסְדְּךָ אָבוֹא בֵיתֶךָ, לִזְבֹּחַ לְךָ זֶבַח
תּוֹדָה עַל כָּל הַטּוֹבוֹת אֲשֶׁר גְּמַלְתָּ עָלָי. אֲפָפְוּנִי חֲבָלִים וְצִירִים אֲחָזְוּנִי,
בַּצַּר לִי קָרָאתִי אֵלֶיךָ, וְשָׁמַעְתָּ מֵהֵיכָלֶךָ קוֹלִי וְהָיִיתָ בְּעוֹזְרִי, רִפֵּאתָ
לְכָל תַּחֲלוּאַי, עֲטַרְתָּנִי חֶסֶד וְרַחֲמִים, עַד הֵנָּה עֲזָרְוּנִי רַחֲמֶיךָ, אָנָּא אַל
תִּטְּשֵׁנִי לָנֶצַח. הוֹאֵל אֱלוֹהַּ, וּבָרֵךְ אֶת אֲמָתֶךָ, חַזְּקִנִי וְאַמְּצֵנִי, אוֹתִי וְאֶת
בַּעְלִי, וְנַגְדֵּל אֶת

For a boy:

הַיֶּלֶד אֲשֶׁר יֻלַּד לָנוּ, לְיִרְאָתֶךָ וּלְעָבְדְּךָ בֶּאֱמֶת, וְלָלֶכֶת אֹרַח
מֵישָׁרִים. שְׁמֹר אֶת הַיֶּלֶד הָרַךְ בְּכָל דְּרָכָיו, חָנֵּהוּ דֵּעָה בִּינָה
וְהַשְׂכֵּל, וְתֵן חֶלְקוֹ בְּתוֹרָתֶךָ, וִיקַדֵּשׁ אֶת שִׁמְךָ הַגָּדוֹל, וְהָיָה לָנוּ
לְמֵשִׁיב נֶפֶשׁ בִּימֵי שֵׂיבָתֵנוּ. וַאֲנִי תְפִלָּתִי־לְךָ יהוה עֵת רָצוֹן,
אֱלֹהִים בְּרָב־חַסְדֶּךָ, עֲנֵנִי בֶּאֱמֶת יִשְׁעֶךָ:   תהלים סט

For a girl:

הַיַּלְדָּה אֲשֶׁר יֻלְּדָה לָנוּ, לְיִרְאָתֶךָ וּלְעָבְדְּךָ בֶּאֱמֶת, וְלָלֶכֶת אֹרַח
מֵישָׁרִים. שְׁמֹר אֶת הַיַּלְדָּה הָרַכָּה בְּכָל דְּרָכֶיהָ, חָנֶּהָ דֵּעָה בִּינָה
וְהַשְׂכֵּל, וְתֵן חֶלְקָהּ בְּתוֹרָתֶךָ, וּתְקַדֵּשׁ אֶת שִׁמְךָ הַגָּדוֹל, וְהָיְתָה
לָנוּ לִמְשִׁיבַת נֶפֶשׁ בִּימֵי שֵׂיבָתֵנוּ. וַאֲנִי תְפִלָּתִי־לְךָ יהוה עֵת רָצוֹן,
אֱלֹהִים בְּרָב־חַסְדֶּךָ, עֲנֵנִי בֶּאֱמֶת יִשְׁעֶךָ:   תהלים סט

If the baby is brought to the בית כנסת, *the Rabbi says the following blessings over him/her:*

יְבָרֶכְךָ יהוה וְיִשְׁמְרֶךָ: יָאֵר יהוה פָּנָיו אֵלֶיךָ וִיחֻנֶּךָּ:   במדברו
יִשָּׂא יהוה פָּנָיו אֵלֶיךָ, וְיָשֵׂם לְךָ שָׁלוֹם:

ZEVED HABAT

The mother or father says:

יוֹנָתִי My dove in the clefts of the rock,
in the hiding places of the mountain side,
show me your face, let me hear your voice;
for your voice is sweet, and your face is lovely.

Song 2

If this is their first daughter, they add:

אַחַת There is one alone, my dove, my perfect one,
her mother's only child,
the favorite of the one who bore her.
Maidens see her and called her blessed;
queens and concubines praise her.

Song 6

The Rabbi says:

מִי שֶׁבֵּרַךְ He who blessed our ancestors,
Abraham, Isaac and Jacob, Moses and Aaron, David and Solomon,
Sarah, Rebecca, Rachel and Leah –
may He bless (*mother's name* daughter of *her mother's name*),
who has given birth.

If the baby has already been named in the synagogue:

and her newborn daughter, (*baby's name* daughter of *father's name*),
born in favor.

If the baby has not been named in the synagogue:

and her newborn daughter, born in favor, whose name in Israel
shall be called (*baby's name* daughter of *father's name*).

Bless, we pray to You, her parents
that they may have the merit to raise her to the Torah,
to the marriage canopy and to good deeds; and let us say: Amen.

---

her life. If food is served at the ceremony, the meal has religious significance
(*seudat mitzva*), and should be accompanied by words of Torah.

יוֹנָתִי *My dove in the clefts of the rock:* Song of Songs 2:14. אַחַת הִיא *There is one alone:* Song of Songs 6:9.

סדר זבד הבת

The mother or father says:

שיר
השירים ב

יוֹנָתִי בְּחַגְוֵי הַסֶּלַע, בְּסֵתֶר הַמַּדְרֵגָה
הַרְאִינִי אֶת־מַרְאַיִךְ, הַשְׁמִיעִנִי אֶת־קוֹלֵךְ
כִּי־קוֹלֵךְ עָרֵב וּמַרְאֵיךְ נָאוֶה:

If this is their first daughter, they add:

שיר
השירים ו

אַחַת הִיא יוֹנָתִי תַמָּתִי
אַחַת הִיא לְאִמָּה, בָּרָה הִיא לְיוֹלַדְתָּהּ
רָאוּהָ בָנוֹת וַיְאַשְּׁרוּהָ, מְלָכוֹת וּפִילַגְשִׁים וַיְהַלְלוּהָ:

The Rabbi says:

מִי שֶׁבֵּרַךְ אֲבוֹתֵינוּ אַבְרָהָם יִצְחָק וְיַעֲקֹב
מֹשֶׁה וְאַהֲרֹן דָּוִד וּשְׁלֹמֹה, שָׂרָה רִבְקָה רָחֵל וְלֵאָה
הוּא יְבָרֵךְ אֶת הָאִשָּׁה הַיּוֹלֶדֶת (פלונית בת פלונית)

If the baby has already been named in the בית כנסת:

וְאֶת בִּתָּהּ (פלונית בת פלוני) שֶׁנּוֹלְדָה לָהּ בְּמַזָּל טוֹב.

If the baby has not been named in the בית כנסת:

וְאֶת בִּתָּהּ שֶׁנּוֹלְדָה לָהּ בְּמַזָּל טוֹב
וְיִקָּרֵא שְׁמָהּ בְּיִשְׂרָאֵל (פלונית בת פלוני).

אָנָּא בָּרֵךְ אֶת אָבִיהָ וְאֶת אִמָּהּ
וְיִזְכּוּ לְגַדְּלָהּ לְתוֹרָה וּלְחֻפָּה וּלְמַעֲשִׂים טוֹבִים, וְנֹאמַר אָמֵן.

ZEVED HABAT

There has long been a custom among Sephardim – increasingly adopted by Ashkenazim – to mark the birth of a daughter with a special ceremony known as *Zeved HaBat* ("the gift of a daughter"), during which the baby is named and blessed. We give expression to our thanks to God for the miracle of a new life, and pray that His blessings should accompany her through the course of

The parents bless the child:

יְשִׂמֵךְ May God make you like Sarah, Rebecca, Rachel and Leah.

May the Lord bless you and protect you.

May the Lord make His face shine on you and be gracious to you.

May the Lord turn His face toward you and grant you peace.

Num. 6

וִיהִי רָצוֹן May it be the will of our Father in heaven,

that He set in your heart the love and awe of Him all your days,

so that you do not come to sin.

May your desire be for the Torah and the commandments.

May your eyes look straight before you;

may your mouth speak wisdom

and your heart meditate in awe;

may your hands be occupied with the commandments

and may your feet run to do the will of your Father in heaven.

If grandparents are present, they say the following blessing:

הָאֱלֹהִים May God before whom my fathers

Abraham and Isaac walked –

God who has been my Shepherd all my life to this day,

the angel who has rescued me from all harm –

may He bless the children.

May they be called by my name

and the names of my fathers Abraham and Isaac,

and may they increase greatly on earth.

Gen. 48

All say:

Our sister, may you grow to become thousands of myriads.

Gen. 24

הָאֱלֹהִים אֲשֶׁר הִתְהַלְּכוּ אֲבֹתַי לְפָנָיו *May God before whom my fathers:* the blessing given by Jacob to the children of Joseph (Gen. 48:15–16), the only instance in the Torah of a grandparent blessing grandchildren. אֲחֹתֵנוּ *Our sister:* the blessing given to Rebecca by her family (Gen. 24:60).

The parents bless the child:

יְשִׂמֵךְ אֱלֹהִים כְּשָׂרָה רִבְקָה רָחֵל וְלֵאָה.

במדבר ו

יְבָרֶכְךָ יהוה וְיִשְׁמְרֶךָ:

יָאֵר יהוה פָּנָיו אֵלֶיךָ וִיחֻנֶּךָּ:

יִשָּׂא יהוה פָּנָיו אֵלֶיךָ, וְיָשֵׂם לְךָ שָׁלוֹם:

וִיהִי רָצוֹן מִלִּפְנֵי אָבִינוּ שֶׁבַּשָּׁמַיִם, שֶׁיִּתֵּן בְּלִבֵּךְ אַהֲבָתוֹ וְיִרְאָתוֹ
וְתִהְיֶה יִרְאַת יהוה עַל פָּנֵיִךְ כָּל יָמַיִךְ שֶׁלֹּא תֶחֱטָאִי
וִיהִי חֶשְׁקֵךְ בַּתּוֹרָה וּבַמִּצְוֹת.
עֵינַיִךְ לְנֹכַח יַבִּיטוּ, פִּיךְ יְדַבֵּר חָכְמוֹת וְלִבֵּךְ יֶהְגֶּה אֵימוֹת
יָדַיִךְ יַעַסְקוּ בְּמִצְוֹת
וְרַגְלַיִךְ יָרוּצוּ לַעֲשׂוֹת רְצוֹן אָבִיךְ שֶׁבַּשָּׁמַיִם.

If grandparents are present, they say the following blessing:

בראשית מח

הָאֱלֹהִים אֲשֶׁר הִתְהַלְּכוּ אֲבֹתַי לְפָנָיו, אַבְרָהָם וְיִצְחָק
הָאֱלֹהִים הָרֹעֶה אֹתִי, מֵעוֹדִי עַד־הַיּוֹם הַזֶּה:
הַמַּלְאָךְ הַגֹּאֵל אֹתִי מִכָּל־רָע, יְבָרֵךְ אֶת־הַנְּעָרִים
וְיִקָּרֵא בָהֶם שְׁמִי, וְשֵׁם אֲבֹתַי אַבְרָהָם וְיִצְחָק
וְיִדְגּוּ לָרֹב בְּקֶרֶב הָאָרֶץ:

All say:

בראשית כד

אֲחֹתֵנוּ, אַתְּ הֲיִי לְאַלְפֵי רְבָבָה:

יְשִׂמֵךְ *May God make you like:* the traditional blessing given by parents to
daughters. יְבָרֶכְךָ יהוה *May the Lord bless you:* the Priestly Blessing (Num.
6:24–26).

וִיהִי רָצוֹן *May it be the will:* Taken from a traditional blessing given by parents
to children on the eve of Yom Kippur.

MARRIAGE SERVICE

BLESSINGS OF BETROTHAL

The Rabbi performing the ceremony takes a cup of wine and says:

בָּרוּךְ Blessed are You, LORD our God, King of the Universe, who creates the fruit of the vine.

בָּרוּךְ Blessed are You, LORD our God, King of the Universe, who has made us holy through His commandments, and has commanded us concerning forbidden unions, forbidding us those who are betrothed, permitting us those who are wedded to us through the rite of the canopy and sacred covenant of marriage. Blessed are You, LORD, who sanctifies His people Israel by the rite of the canopy and sacred covenant of marriage.

The bride and bridegroom both drink from the wine. The bridegroom takes the ring and, holding it ready to be placed on the forefinger of the bride's right hand, says:

הֲרֵי Behold you are consecrated to me by this ring
in accordance with the law of Moses and of Israel.

He then places the ring on the forefinger of the bride's right hand. The Ketuba is read and the bridegroom hands it to the bride. A second cup of wine is taken, and over it, the Sheva Berakhot on the next page are said; the same person should preferably say the first two.

---

blessings said over a cup of wine, and nowadays they are separated by the reading of the marriage contract (*Ketuba*). The betrothal blessing spells out the fact that both ceremonies must be observed for the marriage to be complete.

הֲרֵי אַתְּ מְקֻדֶּשֶׁת לִי *Behold you are consecrated to me:* The declaration accompanying the giving of the ring by the groom to the bride. The use of the word "consecration" in the context of marriage signals the sacred nature of the bond between the partners. כְּדָת מֹשֶׁה וְיִשְׂרָאֵל *The law of Moses and of Israel:* the bridegroom undertakes to honor his obligations according to both biblical (Moses) and rabbinic (Israel) law.

THE MARRIAGE CONTRACT

Read in its original Aramaic, it spells out the duty of a Jewish husband to his wife, to "work for, honor, support and maintain" her, and to meet all financial obligations arising out of the marriage. The *Ketuba* dates back more than two thousand years, and was intended to secure the bride's legal rights within the marriage. It is made binding by the bridegroom raising an object, usually a handkerchief, in the presence of two witnesses. These witnesses sign the document, which is also usually signed by the bridegroom.

סדר קידושין ונישואין

ברכות האירוסין

The קידושין מסדר *takes a cup of wine and says:*

בָּרוּךְ אַתָּה יהוה אֱלֹהֵינוּ מֶלֶךְ הָעוֹלָם, בּוֹרֵא פְּרִי הַגָּפֶן.

בָּרוּךְ אַתָּה יהוה אֱלֹהֵינוּ מֶלֶךְ הָעוֹלָם, אֲשֶׁר קִדְּשָׁנוּ בְּמִצְוֹתָיו וְצִוָּנוּ עַל הָעֲרָיוֹת, וְאָסַר לָנוּ אֶת הָאֲרוּסוֹת, וְהִתִּיר לָנוּ אֶת הַנְּשׂוּאוֹת לָנוּ עַל יְדֵי חֻפָּה וְקִדּוּשִׁין. בָּרוּךְ אַתָּה יהוה, מְקַדֵּשׁ עַמּוֹ יִשְׂרָאֵל עַל יְדֵי חֻפָּה וְקִדּוּשִׁין.

The חתן *and* כלה *both drink from the wine. The* חתן *takes the ring and,*
holding it ready to be placed on the forefinger of the כלה's *right hand, says:*

הֲרֵי אַתְּ מְקֻדֶּשֶׁת לִי בְּטַבַּעַת זוֹ כְּדַת מֹשֶׁה וְיִשְׂרָאֵל.

He then places the ring on the forefinger of the כלה's *right hand. The* כתובה *is read and*
the חתן *hands it to the* כלה. *A second cup of wine is taken, and over it, the* שבע ברכות
on the next page are said; the same person should preferably say the first two.

MARRIAGE SERVICE

"The LORD God said: It is not good for man to be alone, I will make a partner suited to him…That is why a man leaves his father and mother and attaches himself to his wife, and they become one flesh" (Gen. 2:18, 2:24). Marriage is one of the supreme institutions of Judaism, the first mentioned in the Bible, and the one spoken of by the prophets in their deepest moments as the most compelling metaphor for God's relationship with His people. In marriage, the bridegroom and bride pledge themselves to one another in a bond of loyalty and love, each respecting the integrity of the other while joining their destinies to achieve together what neither could achieve alone. The very word ḥayyim, "life," in Hebrew is plural, as if to suggest that life, at its fullest, is to be shared. Marriage is the moralization of passion, love translated into a covenant of mutual responsibility through which, by sharing our vulnerabilities, we redeem our solitude and discover strength.

בָּרוּךְ *Blessed are You:* Marriage originally took the form of two distinct moments. The first, *Erusin* or *Kiddushin*, "betrothal," joined the couple in a mutual pledge. Bride and groom then returned to their respective families. A year or so later, the bride would be brought under the bridal canopy to the groom and they would begin their life together. This was called *Nissu'in*, and was accompanied by its own blessings. During the upheavals of Jewish life in the early Middle Ages, the two ceremonies were brought together. Each involves

THE SEVEN BLESSINGS OF MARRIAGE

When saying the Seven Blessings after Birkat HaMazon, begin with the second blessing. The first blessing, that over the wine, is recited at the end.

בָּרוּךְ Blessed are You, LORD our God, King of the Universe,
who creates the fruit of the vine.

בָּרוּךְ Blessed are You, LORD our God, King of the Universe,
who has created all for His glory.

בָּרוּךְ Blessed are You, LORD our God, King of the Universe,
Creator of mankind.

בָּרוּךְ Blessed are You, LORD our God, King of the Universe,
who made humanity in His image, the image of His likeness,
and out of His very self formed a building for eternity.
Blessed are You, LORD, Creator of mankind.

שׂוֹשׂ Bring great happiness and joy to one who was barren [Zion],
as her children return to her in joy.
Blessed are You, LORD, who gladdens Zion through her children.

שַׂמֵּחַ Bring great joy to these loving friends,
as You gave joy to Your creations in the Garden of Eden.
Blessed are You, LORD, who gives joy to the bridegroom and bride.

בָּרוּךְ Blessed are You, LORD our God, King of the Universe,
who created joy and gladness, bridegroom and bride,
happiness and jubilation, cheer and delight,
love, fellowship, peace and friendship.
Soon, LORD our God, may there be heard in the cities of Judah,
and in the streets of Jerusalem, the sounds of joy and gladness,
the sounds of the bridegroom and bride,
the joyous sounds of bridegrooms from their wedding canopy and of
young people at their feasts of song.
Blessed are You, LORD,
who makes the bridegroom rejoice with the bride.

---

become "a building for eternity" through their descendants. The fifth movingly speaks about the Jewish people (Zion) as a whole, renewed through this marriage of her children. The sixth prays that the bride and groom should find joy together and bring joy to God. The seventh and longest brings all of these themes together, invoking the words of the prophet Jeremiah (33:10–11) that in the future there will be heard "the sounds of joy and gladness, the sounds of bridegroom and bride."

שבע ברכות הנשואין

When saying the שבע ברכות *after* ברכת המזון*, begin with the second blessing. The first blessing, that over the wine, is recited at the end.*

בָּרוּךְ אַתָּה יהוה אֱלֹהֵינוּ מֶלֶךְ הָעוֹלָם, בּוֹרֵא פְּרִי הַגָּפֶן.

בָּרוּךְ אַתָּה יהוה אֱלֹהֵינוּ מֶלֶךְ הָעוֹלָם, שֶׁהַכֹּל בָּרָא לִכְבוֹדוֹ.

בָּרוּךְ אַתָּה יהוה אֱלֹהֵינוּ מֶלֶךְ הָעוֹלָם, יוֹצֵר הָאָדָם.

בָּרוּךְ אַתָּה יהוה אֱלֹהֵינוּ מֶלֶךְ הָעוֹלָם

אֲשֶׁר יָצַר אֶת הָאָדָם בְּצַלְמוֹ, בְּצֶלֶם דְּמוּת תַּבְנִיתוֹ
וְהִתְקִין לוֹ מִמֶּנּוּ בִּנְיַן עֲדֵי עַד.

בָּרוּךְ אַתָּה יהוה, יוֹצֵר הָאָדָם.

שׂוֹשׂ תָּשִׂישׂ וְתָגֵל הָעֲקָרָה בְּקִבּוּץ בָּנֶיהָ לְתוֹכָהּ בְּשִׂמְחָה.
בָּרוּךְ אַתָּה יהוה, מְשַׂמֵּחַ צִיּוֹן בְּבָנֶיהָ.

שַׂמֵּחַ תְּשַׂמַּח רֵעִים הָאֲהוּבִים כְּשַׂמֵּחֲךָ יְצִירְךָ בְּגַן עֵדֶן מִקֶּדֶם.
בָּרוּךְ אַתָּה יהוה, מְשַׂמֵּחַ חָתָן וְכַלָּה.

בָּרוּךְ אַתָּה יהוה אֱלֹהֵינוּ מֶלֶךְ הָעוֹלָם

אֲשֶׁר בָּרָא שָׂשׂוֹן וְשִׂמְחָה, חָתָן וְכַלָּה
גִּילָה, רִנָּה, דִּיצָה וְחֶדְוָה, אַהֲבָה וְאַחֲוָה וְשָׁלוֹם וְרֵעוּת.
מְהֵרָה יהוה אֱלֹהֵינוּ
יִשָּׁמַע בְּעָרֵי יְהוּדָה וּבְחוּצוֹת יְרוּשָׁלַיִם
קוֹל שָׂשׂוֹן וְקוֹל שִׂמְחָה, קוֹל חָתָן וְקוֹל כַּלָּה
קוֹל מִצְהֲלוֹת חֲתָנִים מֵחֻפָּתָם וּנְעָרִים מִמִּשְׁתֵּה נְגִינָתָם.
בָּרוּךְ אַתָּה יהוה, מְשַׂמֵּחַ הֶחָתָן עִם הַכַּלָּה.

SHEVA BERAKHOT / THE SEVEN BLESSINGS

These blessings, accompanying the second stage of the marriage, date back to early rabbinic times. After the blessing over wine, the remaining six benedictions move sequentially from the universal to the particular. The second praises God as Creator of all. The third speaks of His creation of man. The fourth alludes to the second chapter of Genesis in which God, seeing that the man was alone, formed "out of His very self" a partner so that they could

The bride and bridegroom both drink from the wine.

The bridegroom breaks a glass in memory of the destruction of the Temple. Some say the following beforehand:

אִם־אֶשְׁכָּחֵךְ If I forget you, O Jerusalem, may my right hand forget its skill. *Ps. 137*
May my tongue cling to the roof of my mouth if I do not remember you,
if I do not set Jerusalem above my highest joy.

ZIMMUN AFTER A WEDDING
OR SHEVA BERAKHOT FEAST

The leader takes a cup of wine in his hand and says:

Leader Gentlemen, let us say grace.

Others May the name of the LORD be blessed from now and for ever. *Ps. 113*

Leader May the name of the LORD be blessed from now and for ever.

Banish grief and anger. Let even the mute celebrate in song.
Guide us in the paths of righteousness.
Hear the blessing of the children of Aaron.

Add the appropriate words in parentheses (see page 518):

With your permission, (my father and teacher / my mother and
teacher / the Kohanim present / our teacher the Rabbi / the master
of this house / the mistress of this house) my masters and teachers,
let us bless our God, in whose dwelling place is joy,
from whose food we have eaten.

Others Blessed be our God in whose dwelling place is joy,
from whose food we have eaten, and by whose goodness we live.

Leader Blessed be our God in whose dwelling place is joy,
from whose food we have eaten, and by whose goodness we live.
Blessed be He, and blessed be His name.

*Continue with Birkat HaMazon on page 520, at the end of which say the
Sheva Berakhot (on previous page) over a cup of wine, beginning with the second blessing,
"who has created all," and ending with the first blessing, that over the wine.*

GRACE AFTER THE WEDDING FEAST
The special invocation, with its phrase "in whose dwelling place is joy," is
mentioned in the Talmud (*Ketubot* 8a). דְּוַי הָסֵר וְגַם חָרוֹן *Banish grief and anger:*
a poem written by the tenth-century linguist and poet, Dunash ben Labrat.
The initial letters of the four phrases spell out his name.

The חתן and כלה both drink from the wine.

The חתן breaks a glass in memory of the destruction of the
בית המקדש. Some say the following beforehand:

תהלים קלז

אִם־אֶשְׁכָּחֵךְ יְרוּשָׁלָ͏ִם, תִּשְׁכַּח יְמִינִי: תִּדְבַּק לְשׁוֹנִי לְחִכִּי אִם־לֹא אֶזְכְּרֵכִי,
אִם־לֹא אַעֲלֶה אֶת־יְרוּשָׁלַ͏ִם עַל רֹאשׁ שִׂמְחָתִי:

זימון לסעודת שבע ברכות

The leader takes a cup of wine in his hand and says:

Leader   רַבּוֹתַי, נְבָרֵךְ.

תהלים קיג   Others   יְהִי שֵׁם יהוה מְבֹרָךְ מֵעַתָּה וְעַד־עוֹלָם:

Leader   יְהִי שֵׁם יהוה מְבֹרָךְ מֵעַתָּה וְעַד־עוֹלָם:

וְאָז אִלֵּם בְּשִׁיר יָרֹן.   דְּוַי הָסֵר וְגַם חָרוֹן

שָׁעָה בִּרְכַּת בְּנֵי אַהֲרֹן.   נַחֲנוּ בְמַעְגְּלֵי צֶדֶק

Add the appropriate words in parentheses (see page 519):

בִּרְשׁוּת (אָבִי מוֹרִי / אִמִּי מוֹרָתִי / כֹּהֲנִים / מוֹרֵנוּ הָרַב /
בַּעַל הַבַּיִת הַזֶּה / בַּעֲלַת הַבַּיִת הַזֶּה) מָרָנָן וְרַבָּנָן וְרַבּוֹתַי
נְבָרֵךְ אֱלֹהֵינוּ שֶׁהַשִּׂמְחָה בִּמְעוֹנוֹ וְשֶׁאָכַלְנוּ מִשֶּׁלּוֹ.

Others   בָּרוּךְ אֱלֹהֵינוּ שֶׁהַשִּׂמְחָה בִּמְעוֹנוֹ, שֶׁאָכַלְנוּ מִשֶּׁלּוֹ וּבְטוּבוֹ חָיִינוּ.

Leader   בָּרוּךְ אֱלֹהֵינוּ שֶׁהַשִּׂמְחָה בִּמְעוֹנוֹ, שֶׁאָכַלְנוּ מִשֶּׁלּוֹ וּבְטוּבוֹ חָיִינוּ.
בָּרוּךְ הוּא וּבָרוּךְ שְׁמוֹ.

Continue with ברכת המזון on page 521, at the end of which say the
שבע ברכות (on previous page) over a cup of wine, beginning with the second blessing,
בּוֹרֵא פְּרִי הַגֶּפֶן, and ending with the first blessing, שֶׁהַכֹּל בָּרָא לִכְבוֹדוֹ.

BREAKING THE GLASS

An ancient custom, reminding us that while the Temple remains unbuilt, our
joy cannot be complete. It has become a custom to preface this by reciting
the verse from Psalm 137, "If I forget you, O Jerusalem," said by the exiles in
Babylon after the destruction of the First Temple.

PRAYER FOR RECOVERY FROM ILLNESS

מִזְמוֹר לְדָוִד A psalm of David. The LORD is my Shepherd, I shall not want. He makes me lie down in green pastures. He leads me beside the still waters. He refreshes my soul. He guides me in the paths of righteousness for His name's sake. Though I walk through the valley of the shadow of death, I will fear no evil, for You are with me; Your rod and Your staff, they comfort me. You set a table before me in the presence of my enemies; You anoint my head with oil; my cup is filled to overflowing. May goodness and kindness follow me all the days of my life, and may I live in the House of the LORD for evermore. *Ps. 23*

לְדָוִד By David. Bless the LORD, my soul; with all my being I bless His holy name. Bless the LORD, my soul, and forget none of His benefits. He forgives all your sins. He heals all your ills. He redeems your life from the pit. He crowns you with love and compassion. He satisfies your soul with good things, so that your youth is renewed like the eagle's. The LORD is righteous in all He does; He brings justice to all the oppressed. He made known His ways to Moses, His deeds to the people of Israel. The LORD is compassionate and gracious, slow to anger, abounding in love. He will not always accuse or nurse His anger for ever. He has not treated us as our sins deserve, or repaid us according to our misdeeds. For as high as the heavens are above the earth, so great is His love for those who fear Him. As far as the east is from the west, so far has He removed our transgressions from us. As a father has compassion on his children, so the LORD has compassion on those who fear Him. For He knows how we are formed; He remembers that we are dust. As for man, his days are like grass; like a flower of the field he flourishes. For a wind passes over it and it is gone, and its place knows it no more. But the kindness of the LORD is for all eternity to those who fear Him; His righteousness is with their children's children – with those who keep His covenant, and remember to obey His precepts. The LORD has established His throne in heaven, and His kingdom rules over all. Bless the LORD, you His angels, mighty in power, who do His bidding, who obey His word. Bless the LORD, all you His host, the ministers who do His will. Bless the LORD, all His works, everywhere in His dominion. Bless the LORD, my soul. *Ps. 103*

לַמְנַצֵּחַ For the conductor of music. A psalm of David. O LORD, You have examined me and You know me. You know when I sit and when I rise; You understand my thoughts from afar. You encompass my going out and lying down. You are familiar with all my ways. Before a word is on my tongue, You, LORD, know it all. You keep close guard behind and before me. You have laid Your hand upon me. Knowledge so wonderful is beyond me; so high, it is *Ps. 139*

תפילה לחולה

תהלים כג

מִזְמוֹר לְדָוִד, יְהֹוָה רֹעִי לֹא אֶחְסָר: בִּנְאוֹת דֶּשֶׁא יַרְבִּיצֵנִי, עַל־מֵי מְנֻחוֹת
יְנַהֲלֵנִי: נַפְשִׁי יְשׁוֹבֵב, יַנְחֵנִי בְמַעְגְּלֵי־צֶדֶק לְמַעַן שְׁמוֹ: גַּם כִּי־אֵלֵךְ בְּגֵיא
צַלְמָוֶת לֹא־אִירָא רָע, כִּי־אַתָּה עִמָּדִי, שִׁבְטְךָ וּמִשְׁעַנְתֶּךָ הֵמָּה יְנַחֲמֻנִי:
תַּעֲרֹךְ לְפָנַי שֻׁלְחָן נֶגֶד צֹרְרָי, דִּשַּׁנְתָּ בַשֶּׁמֶן רֹאשִׁי, כּוֹסִי רְוָיָה: אַךְ טוֹב
וָחֶסֶד יִרְדְּפוּנִי כָּל־יְמֵי חַיָּי, וְשַׁבְתִּי בְּבֵית־יְהֹוָה לְאֹרֶךְ יָמִים:

תהלים קג

לְדָוִד, בָּרְכִי נַפְשִׁי אֶת־יְהֹוָה, וְכָל־קְרָבַי אֶת־שֵׁם קָדְשׁוֹ: בָּרְכִי נַפְשִׁי אֶת־
יְהֹוָה, וְאַל־תִּשְׁכְּחִי כָּל־גְּמוּלָיו: הַסֹּלֵחַ לְכָל־עֲוֹנֵכִי, הָרֹפֵא לְכָל־תַּחֲלֻאָיְכִי:
הַגּוֹאֵל מִשַּׁחַת חַיָּיְכִי, הַמְעַטְּרֵכִי חֶסֶד וְרַחֲמִים: הַמַּשְׂבִּיעַ בַּטּוֹב עֶדְיֵךְ,
תִּתְחַדֵּשׁ כַּנֶּשֶׁר נְעוּרָיְכִי: עֹשֵׂה צְדָקוֹת יְהֹוָה, וּמִשְׁפָּטִים לְכָל־עֲשׁוּקִים:
יוֹדִיעַ דְּרָכָיו לְמֹשֶׁה, לִבְנֵי יִשְׂרָאֵל עֲלִילוֹתָיו: רַחוּם וְחַנּוּן יְהֹוָה, אֶרֶךְ
אַפַּיִם וְרַב־חָסֶד: לֹא־לָנֶצַח יָרִיב, וְלֹא לְעוֹלָם יִטּוֹר: לֹא כַחֲטָאֵינוּ עָשָׂה
לָנוּ, וְלֹא כַעֲוֹנֹתֵינוּ גָּמַל עָלֵינוּ: כִּי כִגְבֹהַּ שָׁמַיִם עַל־הָאָרֶץ, גָּבַר חַסְדּוֹ
עַל־יְרֵאָיו: כִּרְחֹק מִזְרָח מִמַּעֲרָב, הִרְחִיק מִמֶּנּוּ אֶת־פְּשָׁעֵינוּ: כְּרַחֵם אָב
עַל־בָּנִים, רִחַם יְהֹוָה עַל־יְרֵאָיו: כִּי־הוּא יָדַע יִצְרֵנוּ, זָכוּר כִּי־עָפָר אֲנָחְנוּ:
אֱנוֹשׁ כֶּחָצִיר יָמָיו, כְּצִיץ הַשָּׂדֶה כֵּן יָצִיץ: כִּי רוּחַ עָבְרָה־בּוֹ וְאֵינֶנּוּ, וְלֹא־
יַכִּירֶנּוּ עוֹד מְקוֹמוֹ: וְחֶסֶד יְהֹוָה מֵעוֹלָם וְעַד־עוֹלָם עַל־יְרֵאָיו, וְצִדְקָתוֹ
לִבְנֵי בָנִים: לְשֹׁמְרֵי בְרִיתוֹ, וּלְזֹכְרֵי פִקֻּדָיו לַעֲשׂוֹתָם: יְהֹוָה בַּשָּׁמַיִם הֵכִין
כִּסְאוֹ, וּמַלְכוּתוֹ בַּכֹּל מָשָׁלָה: בָּרְכוּ יְהֹוָה מַלְאָכָיו, גִּבֹּרֵי כֹחַ עֹשֵׂי דְבָרוֹ,
לִשְׁמֹעַ בְּקוֹל דְּבָרוֹ: בָּרְכוּ יְהֹוָה כָּל־צְבָאָיו, מְשָׁרְתָיו עֹשֵׂי רְצוֹנוֹ: בָּרְכוּ
יְהֹוָה כָּל־מַעֲשָׂיו, בְּכָל־מְקֹמוֹת מֶמְשַׁלְתּוֹ, בָּרְכִי נַפְשִׁי אֶת־יְהֹוָה:

תהלים קלט

לַמְנַצֵּחַ לְדָוִד מִזְמוֹר, יְהֹוָה חֲקַרְתַּנִי וַתֵּדָע: אַתָּה יָדַעְתָּ שִׁבְתִּי וְקוּמִי,
בַּנְתָּה לְרֵעִי מֵרָחוֹק: אָרְחִי וְרִבְעִי זֵרִיתָ, וְכָל־דְּרָכַי הִסְכַּנְתָּה: כִּי אֵין
מִלָּה בִּלְשׁוֹנִי, הֵן יְהֹוָה יָדַעְתָּ כֻלָּהּ: אָחוֹר וָקֶדֶם צַרְתָּנִי, וַתָּשֶׁת עָלַי
כַּפֶּכָה: פְּלִיאָה דַעַת מִמֶּנִּי, נִשְׂגְּבָה לֹא־אוּכַל לָהּ: אָנָה אֵלֵךְ מֵרוּחֶךָ, וְאָנָה
מִפָּנֶיךָ אֶבְרָח: אִם־אֶסַּק שָׁמַיִם שָׁם אָתָּה, וְאַצִּיעָה שְּׁאוֹל הִנֶּךָ: אֶשָּׂא
כַנְפֵי־שָׁחַר, אֶשְׁכְּנָה בְּאַחֲרִית יָם: גַּם־שָׁם יָדְךָ תַנְחֵנִי, וְתֹאחֲזֵנִי יְמִינֶךָ:

above my reach. Where can I escape from Your spirit? Where can I flee from Your presence? If I climb to heaven, You are there; if I make my bed in the underworld, You are there. If I rise on the wings of the dawn, if I settle on the far side of the sea, even there Your hand will guide me, Your right hand will hold me fast. Were I to say, "Surely the darkness will hide me, and light become night around me," to You the darkness would not be dark; night is light as day; to You dark and light are one. For You created my innermost being; You knitted me together in my mother's womb. I praise You because I am awesomely, wondrously made; wonderful are Your works; I know that full well. My frame was not hidden from You when I was formed in the secret place, woven in the depths of the earth. Your eyes saw my unformed body. All the days ordained for me were written in Your book before one of them came to be. How precious to me are Your thoughts, God, how vast in number they are. Were I to count them, they would outnumber the grains of the sand. I awake and I am still with You. God, if only You would slay the wicked – away from me, you bloodthirsty men. They speak of You with evil intent; Your adversaries misuse Your name. Do I not hate those who hate You, Lord, and loathe those who rise up against You? I have nothing but hatred for them; I count them my enemies. Search me, God, and know my heart; test me and know my innermost thoughts. See if there is grief in the way I follow, and lead me in the everlasting way.

תְּפִלָּה לְעָנִי A prayer of one who is afflicted, when he is faint, and pours out his   *Ps. 102*
anguish before the Lord. Lord, hear my prayer and let my cry come before You. Do not hide Your face from me in my day of distress. Turn Your ear toward me; answer me swiftly on the day I call.

אָנָּא Please, Lord, Healer of all flesh, have pity on me, and support me on my sick bed, in Your great love, for I am weak. Send relief and healing to me and to the others of Your children who are sick. Heal my pain and renew my youth as the eagle's. Grant wisdom to the physician that he may cure my illness, so that my healing may spring up swiftly. Hear my prayer, prolong my life, and let me complete my years in happiness, so that I may be able to serve You and keep Your precepts with a perfect heart. Grant me the understanding to know that this bitter trial has come upon me for my welfare. Let me not reject Your discipline or spurn Your rebuke.

---

sages consist of three psalms long associated with deliverance from harm, together with two prayers, one for healing, the other for forgiveness, since, our tradition tells us, illness is a time for self-examination and rededication.

וָאֹמַר אַךְ־חְשֶׁךְ יְשׁוּפֵנִי, וְלַיְלָה אוֹר בַּעֲדֵנִי: גַּם־חְשֶׁךְ לֹא־יַחְשִׁיךְ מִמֶּךָ,
וְלַיְלָה כַּיּוֹם יָאִיר, כַּחֲשֵׁיכָה כָּאוֹרָה: כִּי־אַתָּה קָנִיתָ כִלְיֹתָי, תְּסֻכֵּנִי בְּבֶטֶן
אִמִּי: אוֹדְךָ עַל כִּי נוֹרָאוֹת נִפְלֵיתִי, נִפְלָאִים מַעֲשֶׂיךָ, וְנַפְשִׁי יֹדַעַת מְאֹד:
לֹא־נִכְחַד עָצְמִי מִמֶּךָ, אֲשֶׁר־עֻשֵּׂיתִי בַסֵּתֶר, רֻקַּמְתִּי בְּתַחְתִּיּוֹת אָרֶץ:
גָּלְמִי רָאוּ עֵינֶיךָ, וְעַל־סִפְרְךָ כֻּלָּם יִכָּתֵבוּ, יָמִים יֻצָּרוּ, וְלוֹ אֶחָד בָּהֶם: וְלִי
מַה־יָּקְרוּ רֵעֶיךָ אֵל, מֶה עָצְמוּ רָאשֵׁיהֶם: אֶסְפְּרֵם מֵחוֹל יִרְבּוּן, הֱקִיצֹתִי
וְעוֹדִי עִמָּךְ: אִם־תִּקְטֹל אֱלוֹהַּ רָשָׁע, וְאַנְשֵׁי דָמִים סוּרוּ מֶנִּי: אֲשֶׁר יֹמְרוּךָ
לִמְזִמָּה, נָשׂוּא לַשָּׁוְא עָרֶיךָ: הֲלוֹא־מְשַׂנְאֶיךָ יהוה אֶשְׂנָא, וּבִתְקוֹמְמֶיךָ
אֶתְקוֹטָט: תַּכְלִית שִׂנְאָה שְׂנֵאתִים, לְאוֹיְבִים הָיוּ לִי: חָקְרֵנִי אֵל וְדַע לְבָבִי,
בְּחָנֵנִי וְדַע שַׂרְעַפָּי: וּרְאֵה אִם־דֶּרֶךְ־עֹצֶב בִּי, וּנְחֵנִי בְּדֶרֶךְ עוֹלָם:

תהלים קב

תְּפִלָּה לְעָנִי כִי־יַעֲטֹף, וְלִפְנֵי יהוה יִשְׁפֹּךְ שִׂיחוֹ: יהוה שִׁמְעָה תְפִלָּתִי,
וְשַׁוְעָתִי אֵלֶיךָ תָבוֹא: אַל־תַּסְתֵּר פָּנֶיךָ מִמֶּנִּי בְּיוֹם צַר לִי, הַטֵּה־אֵלַי אָזְנֶךָ,
בְּיוֹם אֶקְרָא מַהֵר עֲנֵנִי:

אָנָּא יהוה רוֹפֵא כָל בָּשָׂר, רַחֵם עָלַי, וְסַעֲדֵנִי בְּחַסְדְּךָ הַגָּדוֹל עַל עֶרֶשׂ
דְּוָי, כִּי אֻמְלַל אָנִי. שְׁלַח לִי תְּרוּפָה וּתְעָלָה, בְּתוֹךְ שְׁאָר חוֹלֵי יִשְׂרָאֵל.
רְפָא אֶת מַכְאוֹבִי, וְחַדֵּשׁ כַּנֶּשֶׁר נְעוּרָי. תֵּן בִּינָה לָרוֹפֵא, וְיַגֵּהַּ מִמֶּנִּי מְזוֹרִי,
וַאֲרוּכָתִי מְהֵרָה תִצְמָח. שְׁמַע תְּפִלָּתִי, וְהוֹסֵף יָמִים עַל יָמַי, וַאֲכַלֶּה שְׁנוֹתַי
בַּנְּעִימִים, לְמַעַן אוּכַל לַעֲבֹד אוֹתְךָ, וְלִשְׁמֹר פִּקּוּדֶיךָ בְּלֵב שָׁלֵם. הֲבִינֵנִי
וְאֵדְעָה, כִּי לְשְׁלוֹמִי מַר לִי מָר. וְאַל אֱמָאֵס אֶת מוּסָרֶךָ, וּבְתוֹכַחְתְּךָ אַל
אָקוּץ.

PRAYER FOR RECOVERY FROM ILLNESS

Since the birth of faith, people have turned to God "who heals the broken-hearted and binds up their wounds" for strength and recovery in times of sickness. Many of the psalms are supreme examples of such prayers. There is a deep connection, still not fully understood by medical science, between "healing of the spirit and healing of the body." Prayer, said the sages, is not a substitute for medicine, but neither is medicine a substitute for prayer: both have their part to play in the healing process. Prayer gives strength, as does the knowledge that God is close to all who call on Him in truth. The above pas-

אֱלֹוהַ סְלִיחוֹת God of forgiveness, gracious and compassionate, slow to anger, abounding in love, I acknowledge before You with a broken and contrite heart that I have sinned and done evil in Your sight. I hereby repent of my evil and turn to You in complete repentance. Help me, God of my salvation, that I may not turn to folly again, but instead walk before You in truth and integrity. Gladden Your servant's heart, for to You, LORD, I lift up my soul. Ps. 86 Heal me, LORD, and I will be healed, save me and I will be saved, for You are Jer. 17 my glory. Amen and Amen!

THANKSGIVING PRAYER
AFTER RECOVERY FROM ILLNESS

Say Psalms 23 and 103 on page 586. Then continue with:

אָנָּא O great, mighty and awesome God: By Your great love I come before You to offer thanks for all the good You have bestowed on me. In my distress I called to You and You answered me; from my sick bed I cried to You, and You heard my voice and my pleas. You chastened me severely, LORD, but You did not hand me over to death. In Your love and compassion You lifted my soul from the grave. For Your anger is for a moment, Your favor for a lifetime. At night there may be weeping, but in the morning there is joy. The living, Is. 38 only the living, praise You as I do this day. My soul which You have redeemed shall tell of Your wonders to the children of men. Blessed are You, the faithful Healer of all flesh.

אֵל רַחוּם O God, compassionate and gracious, who grants favors to the undeserving: I am not worthy of all the kindness You have shown to me until now. Purify, please, my heart that I may be worthy to walk before You in the way of the upright. Extend Your help to Your servant. Grant me the strength and resolution to overcome my weakness, and bless me with physical health. Keep sorrow and grief far from me; protect me from all harm, and guide me with Your counsel. May the sun of righteousness shine for me, bringing healing in its wings. May the words of my mouth and the meditation of my heart find Ps. 19 favor before You, O LORD, my Rock and my Redeemer. Amen.

---

life-threatening, the *HaGomel* blessing (page 163) should be said on the first occasion one is able to attend the synagogue, either weekday, Shabbat or Festival.

אֱלוֹהַּ סְלִיחוֹת, חַנּוּן וְרַחוּם אֶרֶךְ אַפַּיִם וְרַב חֶסֶד, מוֹדֶה אֲנִי לְפָנֶיךָ בְּלֵב
נִשְׁבָּר וְנִדְכֶּה כִּי חָטָאתִי, וְהָרַע בְּעֵינֶיךָ עָשִׂיתִי. הִנֵּה נִחַמְתִּי עַל רָעָתִי,
וְאָשׁוּב בִּתְשׁוּבָה שְׁלֵמָה לְפָנֶיךָ. עָזְרֵנִי אֱלֹהֵי יִשְׁעִי, וְלֹא אָשׁוּב לְכִסְלָה,
וְאֶתְהַלֵּךְ לְפָנֶיךָ בֶּאֱמֶת וּבְתָמִים. שַׂמֵּחַ נֶפֶשׁ עַבְדֶּךָ, כִּי־אֵלֶיךָ אֲדֹנָי,   תהלים פו
נַפְשִׁי אֶשָּׂא: רְפָאֵנִי יהוה וְאֵרָפֵא, הוֹשִׁיעֵנִי וְאִוָּשֵׁעָה, כִּי תְהִלָּתִי אָתָּה: ירמיה יז
אָמֵן וְאָמֵן.

תפילה לעומד מחליו

Say תהלים כג and קג on page 587. Then continue with:

אָנָּא הָאֵל הַגָּדוֹל הַגִּבּוֹר וְהַנּוֹרָא, בְּרֹב חֲסָדֶךָ אָבוֹא לְפָנֶיךָ לְהוֹדוֹת
לְךָ עַל כָּל הַטּוֹבוֹת אֲשֶׁר גְּמַלְתָּ עָלַי. מִן הַמֵּצַר קְרָאתִיךָ וַתַּעֲנֵנִי, מֵעֶרֶשׂ
דְּוַי שִׁוַּעְתִּי אֵלֶיךָ, וַתִּשְׁמַע אֶת קוֹלִי תַּחֲנוּנִי. יִסֹּר יִסְּרַתַּנִי יָהּ, וְלַמָּוֶת לֹא
נְתַתָּנִי. בְּאַהֲבָתְךָ וּבְחֶמְלָתְךָ הֶעֱלִיתָ מִן שְׁאוֹל נַפְשִׁי. כִּי רֶגַע בְּאַפֶּךָ,
חַיִּים בִּרְצוֹנוֹ, בָּעֶרֶב יָלִין בֶּכִי וְלַבֹּקֶר רִנָּה. חַי חַי הוּא יוֹדֶךָ, כָּמוֹנִי הַיּוֹם: ישעיה לח
וְנַפְשִׁי אֲשֶׁר פָּדִיתָ, תְּסַפֵּר נִפְלְאוֹתֶיךָ לִבְנֵי אָדָם. בָּרוּךְ אַתָּה, רוֹפֵא נֶאֱמָן
לְכָל בָּשָׂר.

אֵל רַחוּם וְחַנּוּן, הַגּוֹמֵל לְחַיָּבִים טוֹבוֹת, קָטֹנְתִּי מִכֹּל הַחֲסָדִים אֲשֶׁר
עָשִׂיתָ עִם עַבְדְּךָ עַד הֵנָּה. אָנָּא טַהֵר לִבָּבִי, וְזַכֵּנִי לָלֶכֶת בְּדֶרֶךְ יְשָׁרִים לְפָנֶיךָ,
וּמְשֹׁךְ עָזְרְךָ לְעַבְדֶּךָ. חַזְּקֵנִי וְאַמְּצֵנִי מֵרִפְיוֹן, וּבְחִלּוּץ עֲצָמוֹת תְּבָרְכֵנִי.
הַרְחֵק מֵעָלַי כָּל צָרָה וְתוּגָה, שָׁמְרֵנִי מִכָּל רָע, וּבַעֲצָתְךָ תַּנְחֵנִי. וְזָרְחָה לִי
שֶׁמֶשׁ צְדָקָה, וּמַרְפֵּא בִּכְנָפֶיהָ. יִהְיוּ לְרָצוֹן אִמְרֵי־פִי וְהֶגְיוֹן לִבִּי לְפָנֶיךָ,   תהלים יט
יהוה צוּרִי וְגֹאֲלִי: אָמֵן.

_____

THANKSGIVING PRAYER AFTER RECOVERY FROM ILLNESS

No less important than prayer *for* recovery is thanksgiving *after* recovery.
There are many psalms which share this theme; two are suggested here, together with a thanksgiving prayer. If the illness is felt to have been potentially

CONFESSION BEFORE DEATH

The following confession is said by one near death.
He or she should be told: "Do not fear. Many confessed their sins, and then recovered.
Everyone who does confess has reward in the World to Come" (Shabbat 32a).

מוֹדֶה אֲנִי I acknowledge before You, LORD my God and God of my ancestors, that my cure and my death are in Your hands. May it be Your will to send me a perfect healing. Yet if my death is fully determined by You, I accept it in love at Your hand. May my death be an atonement for all the sins, iniquities and transgressions I have committed before You. Grant me of the great happiness that is stored up for the righteous. Make known to me the path of life, in Your *Ps. 16* presence is fullness of joy; at Your right hand bliss for evermore.

אֲבִי יְתוֹמִים Father of orphans and Justice of widows, protect my cherished family, whose souls are bound with mine. Into Your hand I entrust my spirit. *Ps. 31* May You redeem me, LORD, God of truth. Amen and Amen.

When the end is approaching, the following should be said.

Repeat three times:

The LORD is King, the LORD was King,
and the LORD will be King for ever and ever.

Repeat three times:

Blessed be the name of His glorious
kingdom for ever and all time.

Repeat seven times:

The LORD, He is God.

Once:

Listen, Israel: the LORD is our God, the LORD is One. *Deut. 6*

(*Shabbat* 32a). These prayers are supreme testimonies of faith, as the human soul reaches upward to the world of souls.

וידוי שכיב מרע

The following confession is said by one near death.
He or she should be told: "Do not fear. Many confessed their sins, and then recovered.
Everyone who does confess has reward in the World to Come" (Shabbat 32a).

מוֹדֶה אֲנִי לְפָנֶיךָ, יְהוה אֱלֹהַי וֵאלֹהֵי אֲבוֹתַי, שֶׁרְפוּאָתִי וּמִיתָתִי בְּיָדֶךָ. יְהִי רָצוֹן מִלְּפָנֶיךָ, שֶׁתִּרְפָּאֵנִי רְפוּאָה שְׁלֵמָה, וְאִם אָמוּת, תְּהִי מִיתָתִי כַּפָּרָה עַל כָּל חֲטָאִים וַעֲוֹנוֹת וּפְשָׁעִים שֶׁחָטָאתִי וְשֶׁעָוִיתִי וְשֶׁפָּשַׁעְתִּי לְפָנֶיךָ. וְזַכֵּנִי לְעוֹלָם הַבָּא הַצָּפוּן לַצַּדִּיקִים. תּוֹדִיעֵנִי אֹרַח חַיִּים, שֹׂבַע שְׂמָחוֹת אֶת־פָּנֶיךָ, נְעִימוֹת בִּימִינְךָ נֶצַח:

תהלים טז

אֲבִי יְתוֹמִים וְדַיַּן אַלְמָנוֹת, הָגֵן בְּעַד קְרוֹבַי הַיְקָרִים, אֲשֶׁר נַפְשִׁי קְשׁוּרָה בְּנַפְשָׁם. בְּיָדְךָ אַפְקִיד רוּחִי, פָּדִיתָה אוֹתִי יְהוה אֵל אֱמֶת: אָמֵן וְאָמֵן.

תהלים לא

When the end is approaching, the following should be said.

Repeat three times:

יְהוה מֶלֶךְ, יְהוה מָלָךְ, יְהוה יִמְלֹךְ לְעוֹלָם וָעֶד.

Repeat three times:

בָּרוּךְ שֵׁם כְּבוֹד מַלְכוּתוֹ לְעוֹלָם וָעֶד.

Repeat seven times:

יְהוה הוּא הָאֱלֹהִים.

Once:

שְׁמַע יִשְׂרָאֵל, יְהוה אֱלֹהֵינוּ, יְהוה אֶחָד:

דברים ו

CONFESSION BEFORE DEATH
"One who confesses and renounces his sins finds mercy" (Prov. 28:13). "When a person is sick and close to death, he or she is told: make a confession"

FUNERAL SERVICE

עֲקַבְיָא Akavya ben Mahalalel said: Reflect on three things and you will avoid transgression: Know where you came from, where you are going, and before whom you will have to give an account and reckoning. "Where you came from" – from a putrid drop. "Where you are going" – to a place of dust, worms and maggots. "And before whom you will have to give an account and reckoning" – before the Supreme King of kings, the Holy One, blessed be He.

Mishna
Avot 3:1

While on the way to the grave, say:

יֹשֵׁב בְּסֵתֶר He who lives in the shelter of the Most High dwells in the shadow of the Almighty. I say of the LORD, my Refuge and Stronghold, my God in whom I trust, that He will save you from the fowler's snare and the deadly pestilence. With His pinions He will cover you, and beneath His wings you will find shelter; His faithfulness is an encircling shield. You need not fear terror by night, nor the arrow that flies by day; not the pestilence that stalks in darkness, nor the plague that ravages at noon. A thousand may fall at your side, ten thousand at your right hand, but it will not come near you. You will only look with your eyes and see the punishment of the wicked. Because you said "The LORD is my Refuge," taking the Most High as your shelter, no harm will befall you, no plague will come near your tent, for He will command His angels about you, to guard you in all your ways. They will lift you in their hands, lest your foot stumble on a stone. You will tread on lions and vipers, you will trample on young lions and snakes. [God says] "Because he loves Me, I will rescue him; I will protect him, because he acknowledges My name. When he calls on Me, I will answer him, I will be with him in distress, I will deliver him and bring him honor. With long life I will satisfy him, and show him My salvation. With long life I will satisfy him, and show him My salvation."

Ps. 91

---

there is suffering and death, we reaffirm our faith, tried and tested though it may be, that there is an ultimate order and justice in the universe. הַצּוּר *The Rock:* a symbol, taken from the Song of Moses (Deut. 32) signifying the eternity of God in the face of the transience of life.

לוויית המת

משנה
אבות ג: א
עֲקַבְיָא בֶּן מַהֲלַלְאֵל אוֹמֵר: הִסְתַּכֵּל בִּשְׁלֹשָׁה דְבָרִים, וְאֵין אַתָּה
בָא לִידֵי עֲבֵרָה. דַּע מֵאַיִן בָּאתָ, וּלְאָן אַתָּה הוֹלֵךְ, וְלִפְנֵי מִי אַתָּה
עָתִיד לִתֵּן דִּין וְחֶשְׁבּוֹן. מֵאַיִן בָּאתָ, מִטִּפָּה סְרוּחָה. וּלְאָן אַתָּה
הוֹלֵךְ, לִמְקוֹם עָפָר, רִמָּה וְתוֹלֵעָה. וְלִפְנֵי מִי אַתָּה עָתִיד לִתֵּן דִּין
וְחֶשְׁבּוֹן, לִפְנֵי מֶלֶךְ מַלְכֵי הַמְּלָכִים, הַקָּדוֹשׁ בָּרוּךְ הוּא.

While on the way to the grave, say:

תהלים צא
יֹשֵׁב בְּסֵתֶר עֶלְיוֹן, בְּצֵל שַׁדַּי יִתְלוֹנָן: אֹמַר לַיהוה מַחְסִי וּמְצוּדָתִי,
אֱלֹהַי אֶבְטַח־בּוֹ: כִּי הוּא יַצִּילְךָ מִפַּח יָקוּשׁ, מִדֶּבֶר הַוּוֹת: בְּאֶבְרָתוֹ
יָסֶךְ לָךְ, וְתַחַת־כְּנָפָיו תֶּחְסֶה, צִנָּה וְסֹחֵרָה אֲמִתּוֹ: לֹא־תִירָא מִפַּחַד
לָיְלָה, מֵחֵץ יָעוּף יוֹמָם: מִדֶּבֶר בָּאֹפֶל יַהֲלֹךְ, מִקֶּטֶב יָשׁוּד צָהֳרָיִם:
יִפֹּל מִצִּדְּךָ אֶלֶף, וּרְבָבָה מִימִינֶךָ, אֵלֶיךָ לֹא יִגָּשׁ: רַק בְּעֵינֶיךָ תַבִּיט,
וְשִׁלֻּמַת רְשָׁעִים תִּרְאֶה: כִּי־אַתָּה יהוה מַחְסִי, עֶלְיוֹן שַׂמְתָּ מְעוֹנֶךָ:
לֹא־תְאֻנֶּה אֵלֶיךָ רָעָה, וְנֶגַע לֹא־יִקְרַב בְּאָהֳלֶךָ: כִּי מַלְאָכָיו יְצַוֶּה־
לָּךְ, לִשְׁמָרְךָ בְּכָל־דְּרָכֶיךָ: עַל־כַּפַּיִם יִשָּׂאוּנְךָ, פֶּן־תִּגֹּף בָּאֶבֶן רַגְלֶךָ:
עַל־שַׁחַל וָפֶתֶן תִּדְרֹךְ, תִּרְמֹס כְּפִיר וְתַנִּין: כִּי בִי חָשַׁק וַאֲפַלְּטֵהוּ,
אֲשַׂגְּבֵהוּ כִּי־יָדַע שְׁמִי: יִקְרָאֵנִי וְאֶעֱנֵהוּ, עִמּוֹ אָנֹכִי בְצָרָה, אֲחַלְּצֵהוּ
וַאֲכַבְּדֵהוּ: אֹרֶךְ יָמִים אַשְׂבִּיעֵהוּ, וְאַרְאֵהוּ בִּישׁוּעָתִי:
אֹרֶךְ יָמִים אַשְׂבִּיעֵהוּ, וְאַרְאֵהוּ בִּישׁוּעָתִי:

Bereavement is doubly devastating. One who was part of our life is no longer
there and our world threatens to fall apart. And we come face to face with
mortality itself, the knowledge that all that lives, dies. At such times, prayer
helps us make the transition from *aninut*, the inarticulate shock of grief, to
avelut, the work of mourning and recovering faith in life (R. Joseph Soloveitchik). *Tzidduk HaDin*, "The Acceptance of Judgment" (on next page), is the
ultimate act of humility in the face of loss. Though we cannot understand why

After the funeral, the following is said, except on days on which Taḥanun
is omitted, or after nightfall. Some say the following before the funeral.

THE ACCEPTANCE OF JUDGMENT

הַצוּר The Rock, His work is perfect, for all His ways are just;   *Deut. 32*
A faithful God who does no wrong, righteous and fair is He.

The Rock, perfect in every deed:
Who can say to Him, "What have You done?"
He rules below and above. He brings death and gives life,   *1 Sam. 2*
bringing down to the grave and raising up again.

The Rock, perfect in every act:
Who can say to Him, "Why do You so act?"
You who speak and act: show us kindness we do not deserve,
and in the merit of the one who was bound like a lamb, hear us and act.

Righteous in all His ways, the Rock who is perfect,
slow to anger and full of compassion,
please have pity and spare parents and children,
for Yours, LORD, are forgiveness and compassion.

You are righteous, LORD, in bringing death and giving life.
In Your hand is the safekeeping of all spirits.
Far be it from You to erase our remembrance.
May Your eyes be open to us in compassion,
for Yours, LORD, are compassion and forgiveness.

If one lives for a year or a thousand years,
what does it profit him? He shall be as if he had never been.
Blessed is the true Judge who brings death and gives life.

Blessed is He for His judgment is true, and in His sight He surveys all.
He repays man in accord with his account and just desert,
and all must render acknowledgment to His name.

We know, LORD, that Your judgment is just.
You are just when You speak and fair when You judge.
It is not for us to criticize Your manner of judgment.
You are righteous, LORD, and Your judgments are fair.   *Ps. 119*

After the funeral, the following is said, except on days on which תחנון
is omitted, or after nightfall. Some say the following before the funeral.

צדוק הדין

דברים לב

הַצּוּר תָּמִים פָּעֳלוֹ, כִּי כָל־דְּרָכָיו מִשְׁפָּט
אֵל אֱמוּנָה וְאֵין עָוֶל, צַדִּיק וְיָשָׁר הוּא:

הַצּוּר תָּמִים בְּכָל פֹּעַל, מִי יֹאמַר לוֹ מַה תִּפְעָל

שמואל א׳ ב

הַשַּׁלִּיט בְּמַטָּה וּבְמַעַל. מֵמִית וּמְחַיֶּה, מוֹרִיד שְׁאוֹל וַיָּעַל:

הַצּוּר תָּמִים בְּכָל מַעֲשֶׂה, מִי יֹאמַר לוֹ מַה תַּעֲשֶׂה
הָאוֹמֵר וְעוֹשֶׂה, חֶסֶד חִנָּם לָנוּ תַעֲשֶׂה
וּבִזְכוּת הַנֶּעֱקַד כְּשֶׂה, הַקְשִׁיבָה וַעֲשֵׂה.

צַדִּיק בְּכָל דְּרָכָיו הַצּוּר תָּמִים, אֶרֶךְ אַפַּיִם וּמָלֵא רַחֲמִים
חֲמָל נָא וְחוּס נָא עַל אָבוֹת וּבָנִים
כִּי לְךָ אָדוֹן הַסְּלִיחוֹת וְהָרַחֲמִים.

צַדִּיק אַתָּה יהוה לְהָמִית וּלְהַחֲיוֹת
אֲשֶׁר בְּיָדְךָ פִּקְדוֹן כָּל רוּחוֹת, חָלִילָה לְךָ זִכְרוֹנֵנוּ לִמְחוֹת
וְיִהְיוּ נָא עֵינֶיךָ בְּרַחֲמִים עָלֵינוּ פְקוּחוֹת
כִּי לְךָ אָדוֹן הָרַחֲמִים וְהַסְּלִיחוֹת.

אָדָם אִם בֶּן שָׁנָה יִהְיֶה, אוֹ אֶלֶף שָׁנִים יִחְיֶה
מַה יִּתְרוֹן לוֹ, כְּלֹא הָיָה יִהְיֶה
בָּרוּךְ דַּיַּן הָאֱמֶת, מֵמִית וּמְחַיֶּה.

בָּרוּךְ הוּא כִּי אֱמֶת דִּינוֹ, וּמְשׁוֹטֵט הַכֹּל בְּעֵינוֹ
וּמְשַׁלֵּם לְאָדָם חֶשְׁבּוֹנוֹ וְדִינוֹ, וְהַכֹּל לִשְׁמוֹ הוֹדָיָה יִתֵּנוּ.

יָדַעְנוּ יהוה כִּי צֶדֶק מִשְׁפָּטֶךָ, תִּצְדַּק בְּדָבְרֶךָ וְתִזְכֶּה בְשָׁפְטֶךָ
תהלים קיט

וְאֵין לְהַרְהֵר אַחַר מִדַּת שָׁפְטֶךָ. צַדִּיק אַתָּה יהוה, וְיָשָׁר מִשְׁפָּטֶיךָ:

True Judge, Judge of righteousness and truth:
Blessed is the true Judge for all His judgments are righteous and true.

In Your hand is the soul of every living thing. Your right hand and
power are full of righteousness.
Have compassion on the remnant of the flock of those who serve You,
and say to the angel [of death], "Stay your hand."

Great in counsel and mighty in deed,   *Jer. 32*
Your eyes are open to all the ways of men,
giving each according to his ways and the fruit of his deeds:

to proclaim that the LORD is upright;   *Ps. 92*
He is my Rock, in whom there is no wrong.

The LORD has given and the LORD has taken away: *Job 1*
blessed be the name of the LORD.

He is compassionate; He forgives iniquity and does not destroy.   *Ps. 78*
Repeatedly He suppresses His anger, not rousing His full wrath.

The following Kaddish, said by the mourners, requires the presence of a minyan.

Mourner: Magnified and sanctified may His great name be,
          in the world that will in future be renewed,
          reviving the dead and raising them up to eternal life.
          He will rebuild the city of Jerusalem
          and in it reestablish His Temple.
          He will remove alien worship from the earth
          and restore to its place the worship of Heaven.
          Then the Holy One, blessed be He,
          will reign in His sovereignty and splendor.
          May it be in your lifetime and in your days,
          and in the lifetime of all the House of Israel,
          swiftly and soon – and say: Amen.

All: May His great name be blessed for ever and all time.

---

tion of the dead. Death is not final: it is a prelude to eternal life and eventual
rebirth.

דַּיַּן אֱמֶת, שׁוֹפֵט צֶדֶק וֶאֱמֶת

בָּרוּךְ דַּיַּן הָאֱמֶת, שֶׁכָּל מִשְׁפָּטָיו צֶדֶק וֶאֱמֶת.

נֶפֶשׁ כָּל חַי בְּיָדֶךָ, צֶדֶק מָלְאָה יְמִינְךָ וְיָדֶךָ

רַחֵם עַל פְּלֵטַת צֹאן עֲבָדֶיךָ, וְתֹאמַר לַמַּלְאָךְ הֶרֶף יָדֶךָ.

ירמיה לב
גְּדֹל הָעֵצָה וְרַב הָעֲלִילִיָּה

אֲשֶׁר־עֵינֶיךָ פְקֻחוֹת עַל־כָּל־דַּרְכֵי בְּנֵי אָדָם

לָתֵת לְאִישׁ כִּדְרָכָיו, וְכִפְרִי מַעֲלָלָיו:

תהלים צב
לְהַגִּיד כִּי־יָשָׁר יהוה, צוּרִי וְלֹא־עַוְלָתָה בּוֹ:

איוב א
יהוה נָתַן וַיהוה לָקָח, יְהִי שֵׁם יהוה מְבֹרָךְ:

תהלים עח
וְהוּא רַחוּם, יְכַפֵּר עָוֹן וְלֹא־יַשְׁחִית

וְהִרְבָּה לְהָשִׁיב אַפּוֹ, וְלֹא־יָעִיר כָּל־חֲמָתוֹ:

The following קדיש, said by the mourners, requires the presence of a מנין.

אבל יִתְגַּדַּל וְיִתְקַדַּשׁ שְׁמֵהּ רַבָּא (קהל: אָמֵן)

בְּעָלְמָא דְּהוּא עָתִיד לְאִתְחַדָּתָא

וּלְאַחֲיָאָה מֵתַיָּא, וּלְאַסָּקָא יָתְהוֹן לְחַיֵּי עָלְמָא

וּלְמִבְנֵא קַרְתָּא דִירוּשְׁלֵם, וּלְשַׁכְלְלָא הֵיכְלֵהּ בְּגַוַּהּ

וּלְמֶעְקַר פֻּלְחָנָא נֻכְרָאָה מֵאַרְעָא

וְלַאֲתָבָא פֻּלְחָנָא דִשְׁמַיָּא לְאַתְרֵהּ

וְיַמְלִיךְ קֻדְשָׁא בְּרִיךְ הוּא בְּמַלְכוּתֵהּ וִיקָרֵהּ

בְּחַיֵּיכוֹן וּבְיוֹמֵיכוֹן וּבְחַיֵּי דְּכָל בֵּית יִשְׂרָאֵל

בַּעֲגָלָא וּבִזְמַן קָרִיב, וְאִמְרוּ אָמֵן. (קהל: אָמֵן)

קהל
ואבל: יְהֵא שְׁמֵהּ רַבָּא מְבָרַךְ לְעָלַם וּלְעָלְמֵי עָלְמַיָּא.

─────────────────────────────────

The long Kaddish, said only by a mourner after the funeral and by one who completes a tractate of the Oral Law, is unique in its reference to the resurrec-

Mourner: Blessed and praised, glorified and exalted,
raised and honored, uplifted and lauded
be the name of the Holy One, blessed be He,
beyond any blessing,
song, praise and consolation
uttered in the world – and say: Amen.

May there be great peace from heaven,
and life for us and all Israel – and say: Amen.

Bow, take three steps back, as if taking leave of the Divine Presence,
then bow, first left, then right, then center, while saying:

May He who makes peace in His high places,
make peace for us and all Israel – and say: Amen.

After the funeral, those present form two rows, the mourners pass
between them, and the following is said to them:

May the Almighty comfort you among the
other mourners of Zion and Jerusalem.

Some conclude with:

May you have no further grief.

Some have the custom to pick blades of grass and throw them over their shoulders, saying:

May they of the city grow like the grass of the earth.   *Ps. 72*

Or:

Remember that we are dust.   *Ps. 103*

After leaving the cemetery, it is customary to wash one's hands and say:

He will destroy death for ever, and the Lord God will wipe away   *Is. 25*
the tears from all faces and remove the reproach of His people from
the whole earth, for the Lord has spoken.

הַמָּקוֹם יְנַחֵם *May the Almighty comfort you:* By comforting the mourners, we
help reintegrate them into the community of the living, and into the larger
hope that just as Jerusalem will be rebuilt, so will our fractured lives.

אבל: יִתְבָּרַךְ וְיִשְׁתַּבַּח וְיִתְפָּאַר

וְיִתְרוֹמַם וְיִתְנַשֵּׂא וְיִתְהַדָּר וְיִתְעַלֶּה וְיִתְהַלָּל

שְׁמֵהּ דְּקֻדְשָׁא בְּרִיךְ הוּא (קהל: בְּרִיךְ הוּא)

לְעֵלָּא מִן כָּל בִּרְכָתָא

/בעשרת ימי תשובה: לְעֵלָּא לְעֵלָּא מִכָּל בִּרְכָתָא/

וְשִׁירָתָא, תֻּשְׁבְּחָתָא וְנֶחֱמָתָא

דַּאֲמִירָן בְּעָלְמָא, וְאִמְרוּ אָמֵן. (קהל: אָמֵן)

יְהֵא שְׁלָמָא רַבָּא מִן שְׁמַיָּא

וְחַיִּים, עָלֵינוּ וְעַל כָּל יִשְׂרָאֵל, וְאִמְרוּ אָמֵן. (קהל: אָמֵן)

*Bow, take three steps back, as if taking leave of the Divine Presence,
then bow, first left, then right, then center, while saying:*

עֹשֶׂה שָׁלוֹם/בעשרת ימי תשובה: הַשָּׁלוֹם/ בִּמְרוֹמָיו

הוּא יַעֲשֶׂה שָׁלוֹם, עָלֵינוּ וְעַל כָּל יִשְׂרָאֵל

וְאִמְרוּ אָמֵן. (קהל: אָמֵן)

*After the funeral, those present form two rows, the mourners pass
between them, and the following is said to them:*

הַמָּקוֹם יְנַחֵם אוֹתְךָ/אוֹתָךְ/אֶתְכֶם

בְּתוֹךְ שְׁאָר אֲבֵלֵי צִיּוֹן וִירוּשָׁלָיִם.

Some conclude with:

וְלֹא תוֹסִיפוּ לְדַאֲבָה עוֹד.

Some have the custom to pick blades of grass and throw them over their shoulders, saying:

תהלים עב

וְיָצִיצוּ מֵעִיר כְּעֵשֶׂב הָאָרֶץ:

Or:

תהלים קג

זְכוֹר כִּי־עָפָר אֲנָחְנוּ:

After leaving the cemetery, it is customary to wash one's hands and say:

ישעיה כה

בִּלַּע הַמָּוֶת לָנֶצַח, וּמָחָה אֲדֹנָי יֱהֹוִה דִּמְעָה מֵעַל כָּל־פָּנִים, וְחֶרְפַּת

עַמּוֹ יָסִיר מֵעַל כָּל־הָאָרֶץ, כִּי יהוה דִּבֵּר:

PRAYER IN A HOUSE OF MOURNING

After the regular service, the following psalm is read in a house of mourning during the shiva week. On those days on which Taḥanun is not said, Psalm 16 (below) is substituted.

לַמְנַצֵּחַ For the conductor of music. Of the sons of Koraḥ. A sacred song. Hear *Ps. 49* this, all you peoples. Listen, all inhabitants of the world, low and high, rich and poor alike. My mouth will speak words of wisdom; the utterance of my heart will give understanding. I listen with care to a parable; I expound my mystery to the music of the harp. Why should I fear when evil days come, when the wickedness of my foes surrounds me, trusting in their wealth, boasting of their great riches? No man can redeem his brother or pay God the price of his release, for the ransom of a life is costly; no payment is ever enough that would let him live for ever, never seeing the grave. For all can see that wise men die, that the foolish and senseless all perish and leave their wealth to others. They think their houses will remain for ever, their dwellings for all generations; they give their names to their estates. But man, despite his splendor, does not endure; he is like the beasts that perish. Such is the fate of the foolish and their followers who approve their words, Selah. Like sheep they are destined for the grave: death will be their shepherd. The upright will rule over them in the morning. Their forms will decay in the grave, far from their mansions. But God will redeem my life from the grave; He will surely take me to Himself, Selah. Do not be overawed when a man grows rich, when the glory of his house increases, for he will take nothing with him when he dies; his wealth will not descend with him. Though while he lived he counted himself blessed – men always praise you when you prosper – he will join the generation of his ancestors who will never again see the light. A man who, despite his splendor, lacks understanding, is like the beasts that perish.

On those days on which Taḥanun is not said, substitute:

מִכְתָּם לְדָוִד A musical composition of David. Protect me, God, for in You I *Ps. 16* have found refuge. I have said to the Lord: You are my Lord: from You alone comes the good I enjoy. All my delight is in the holy ones, the mighty in the land. Those who run after other gods multiply their sorrows. I shall never offer them libations of blood, nor will their names pass my lips. The Lord

---

מִכְתָּם לְדָוִד *Psalm 16.* On days when *Taḥanun* is not said, we recite this psalm, quite different in mood from Psalm 49. The psalm reflects that, despite our loss, we are here, alive, and with much for which to thank God. This is a poem of reaffirmation.

תפילה בבית האבל

After the regular service, the following psalm is read in a house of mourning during the שבעה week. On those days on which תחנון is not said, טו תהלים (below) is substituted.

תהלים מט

לַמְנַצֵּחַ לִבְנֵי־קֹרַח מִזְמוֹר: שִׁמְעוּ־זֹאת כָּל־הָעַמִּים, הַאֲזִינוּ כָּל־יֹשְׁבֵי חָלֶד: גַּם־בְּנֵי אָדָם, גַּם־בְּנֵי־אִישׁ, יַחַד עָשִׁיר וְאֶבְיוֹן: פִּי יְדַבֵּר חָכְמוֹת, וְהָגוּת לִבִּי תְבוּנוֹת: אַטֶּה לְמָשָׁל אָזְנִי, אֶפְתַּח בְּכִנּוֹר חִידָתִי: לָמָּה אִירָא בִּימֵי רָע, עֲוֹן עֲקֵבַי יְסוּבֵּנִי: הַבֹּטְחִים עַל־חֵילָם, וּבְרֹב עָשְׁרָם יִתְהַלָּלוּ: אָח לֹא־פָדֹה יִפְדֶּה אִישׁ, לֹא־יִתֵּן לֵאלֹהִים כָּפְרוֹ: וְיֵקַר פִּדְיוֹן נַפְשָׁם, וְחָדַל לְעוֹלָם: וִיחִי־עוֹד לָנֶצַח, לֹא יִרְאֶה הַשָּׁחַת: כִּי יִרְאֶה חֲכָמִים יָמוּתוּ, יַחַד כְּסִיל וָבַעַר יֹאבֵדוּ, וְעָזְבוּ לַאֲחֵרִים חֵילָם: קִרְבָּם בָּתֵּימוֹ לְעוֹלָם, מִשְׁכְּנֹתָם לְדוֹר וָדֹר, קָרְאוּ בִשְׁמוֹתָם עֲלֵי אֲדָמוֹת: וְאָדָם בִּיקָר בַּל־יָלִין, נִמְשַׁל כַּבְּהֵמוֹת נִדְמוּ: זֶה דַרְכָּם, כֵּסֶל לָמוֹ, וְאַחֲרֵיהֶם בְּפִיהֶם יִרְצוּ סֶלָה: כַּצֹּאן לִשְׁאוֹל שַׁתּוּ, מָוֶת יִרְעֵם, וַיִּרְדּוּ בָם יְשָׁרִים לַבֹּקֶר, וְצוּרָם לְבַלּוֹת שְׁאוֹל מִזְּבֻל לוֹ: אַךְ־אֱלֹהִים יִפְדֶּה נַפְשִׁי מִיַּד שְׁאוֹל, כִּי יִקָּחֵנִי סֶלָה: אַל־תִּירָא כִּי־יַעֲשִׁר אִישׁ, כִּי־יִרְבֶּה כְּבוֹד בֵּיתוֹ: כִּי לֹא בְמוֹתוֹ יִקַּח הַכֹּל, לֹא־יֵרֵד אַחֲרָיו כְּבוֹדוֹ: כִּי־נַפְשׁוֹ בְּחַיָּיו יְבָרֵךְ, וְיוֹדֻךָ כִּי־תֵיטִיב לָךְ: תָּבוֹא עַד־דּוֹר אֲבוֹתָיו, עַד־נֵצַח לֹא יִרְאוּ־אוֹר: אָדָם בִּיקָר וְלֹא יָבִין, נִמְשַׁל כַּבְּהֵמוֹת נִדְמוּ:

On those days on which תחנון is not said, substitute:

תהלים טז

מִכְתָּם לְדָוִד, שָׁמְרֵנִי אֵל כִּי־חָסִיתִי בָךְ: אָמַרְתְּ לַיהוה, אֲדֹנָי אָתָּה, טוֹבָתִי בַּל־עָלֶיךָ: לִקְדוֹשִׁים אֲשֶׁר־בָּאָרֶץ הֵמָּה, וְאַדִּירֵי כָּל־חֶפְצִי־בָם: יִרְבּוּ עַצְּבוֹתָם אַחֵר מָהָרוּ, בַּל־אַסִּיךְ נִסְכֵּיהֶם מִדָּם, וּבַל־אֶשָּׂא אֶת־שְׁמוֹתָם

PRAYER IN A HOUSE OF MOURNING

לַמְנַצֵּחַ *Psalm 49.* Repentance is part of the process of mourning (Maimonides). Confronted with an awareness of our mortality, we begin to rethink our priorities, knowing that what occupy our energies and thoughts much of the time, are often matters of relatively minor significance when weighed against the fullness of eternity and the brevity of our lives on earth. Psalm 49 is a most powerful expression of this idea. What lives on after us is not our wealth but the ideals for which we live and the good we do.

is my allotted portion and my cup: You direct my fate. The lines have fallen for me in pleasant places; I am well content with my inheritance. I will bless the LORD who has guided me; at night my innermost being admonishes me. I have set the LORD before me at all times. He is at my right hand: I shall not be shaken. Therefore my heart is glad, my spirit rejoices, and my body rests secure. For You will not abandon me to the grave, nor let Your faithful one see the pit. You will teach me the path of life. In Your presence is fullness of joy; at Your right hand, bliss for evermore.

MEMORIAL PRAYER

אָנָּא O LORD and King, full of compassion, God of the spirits of all flesh, in whose hand are the souls of the living and the dead, receive, we pray You, in Your great love the soul of

> *For a man, say:*
>
> (*name* son of *father's name*) who has been gathered to his people. Have mercy on him, pardon all his transgressions, for there is no one *Eccl. 7* so righteous on earth as to have done only good and never sinned. Remember the righteousness that he did, and let his reward be with him, his recompense before him. O shelter his soul in the shadow of Your wings. Make known to him the path of life. In Your presence is fullness of joy, at Your right hand bliss for evermore. Bestow upon him the great goodness that is stored up for the righteous.

> *For a woman, say:*
>
> (*name* daughter of *father's name*) who has been gathered to her people. Have mercy on her, pardon all her transgressions, for there is no one *Eccl. 7* so righteous on earth as to have done only good and never sinned. Remember the righteousness that she did, and let her reward be with her, her recompense before her. O shelter her soul in the shadow of Your wings. Make known to her the path of life. In Your presence is fullness of joy, at Your right hand bliss for evermore. Bestow upon her the great goodness that is stored up for the righteous.

> *For a boy, say:*
>
> (*name* son of *father's name*) who has been gathered to his people. Remember the righteousness that he did, and let his reward be with him, his recompense before him. O shelter his soul in the shadow of Your wings. Make known to him the path of life. In Your presence is fullness of joy, at Your right hand bliss for evermore. Bestow upon him the great goodness that is stored up for the righteous.

עַל־שְׂפָתָי: יהוה, מְנָת־חֶלְקִי וְכוֹסִי, אַתָּה תּוֹמִיךְ גּוֹרָלִי: חֲבָלִים נָפְלוּ־לִי בַּנְּעִמִים, אַף־נַחֲלַת שָׁפְרָה עָלָי: אֲבָרֵךְ אֶת־יהוה אֲשֶׁר יְעָצָנִי, אַף־לֵילוֹת יִסְּרוּנִי כִלְיוֹתָי: שִׁוִּיתִי יהוה לְנֶגְדִּי תָמִיד, כִּי מִימִינִי בַּל־אֶמּוֹט: לָכֵן שָׂמַח לִבִּי וַיָּגֶל כְּבוֹדִי, אַף־בְּשָׂרִי יִשְׁכֹּן לָבֶטַח: כִּי לֹא־תַעֲזֹב נַפְשִׁי לִשְׁאוֹל, לֹא־ תִתֵּן חֲסִידְךָ לִרְאוֹת שָׁחַת: תּוֹדִיעֵנִי אֹרַח חַיִּים, שֹׂבַע שְׂמָחוֹת אֶת־פָּנֶיךָ, נְעִמוֹת בִּימִינְךָ נֶצַח:

אזכרה

אָנָּא יהוה מֶלֶךְ מָלֵא רַחֲמִים, אֱלֹהֵי הָרוּחוֹת לְכָל בָּשָׂר, אֲשֶׁר בְּיָדְךָ נַפְשׁוֹת הַחַיִּים וְהַמֵּתִים, אָנָּא קַבֵּל בְּחַסְדְּךָ הַגָּדוֹל אֶת נִשְׁמַת

For a man, say:

(פלוני בֶּן פלוני) אֲשֶׁר נֶאֱסַף אֶל עַמָּיו. חוּס וַחֲמֹל עָלָיו, סְלַח וּמְחַל לְכָל פְּשָׁעָיו. כִּי אָדָם אֵין צַדִּיק בָּאָרֶץ, אֲשֶׁר יַעֲשֶׂה־טּוֹב וְלֹא יֶחֱטָא: זְכֹר לוֹ צִדְקָתוֹ אֲשֶׁר עָשָׂה, וִיהִי שְׂכָרוֹ אִתּוֹ, וּפְעֻלָּתוֹ לְפָנָיו. אָנָּא הַסְתֵּר אֶת נִשְׁמָתוֹ בְּצֵל כְּנָפֶיךָ, הוֹדִיעֵהוּ אֹרַח חַיִּים, שֹׂבַע שְׂמָחוֹת אֶת פָּנֶיךָ, נְעִמוֹת בִּימִינְךָ נֶצַח, וְתַשְׁפִּיעַ לוֹ מֵרֹב טוּב הַצָּפוּן לַצַּדִּיקִים.   קהלת׃

For a woman, say:

(פלונית בַּת פלוני) אֲשֶׁר נֶאֶסְפָה אֶל עַמֶּיהָ. חוּס וַחֲמֹל עָלֶיהָ, סְלַח וּמְחַל לְכָל פְּשָׁעֶיהָ. כִּי אָדָם אֵין צַדִּיק בָּאָרֶץ, אֲשֶׁר יַעֲשֶׂה־טּוֹב וְלֹא יֶחֱטָא: זְכֹר לָהּ צִדְקָתָהּ אֲשֶׁר עָשָׂתָה, וִיהִי שְׂכָרָהּ אִתָּהּ, וּפְעֻלָּתָהּ לְפָנֶיהָ. אָנָּא הַסְתֵּר אֶת נִשְׁמָתָהּ בְּצֵל כְּנָפֶיךָ, הוֹדִיעָהּ אֹרַח חַיִּים, שֹׂבַע שְׂמָחוֹת אֶת פָּנֶיךָ, נְעִמוֹת בִּימִינְךָ נֶצַח, וְתַשְׁפִּיעַ לָהּ מֵרֹב טוּב הַצָּפוּן לַצַּדִּיקִים.   קהלת׃

For a boy, say:

(פלוני בֶּן פלוני) אֲשֶׁר נֶאֱסַף אֶל עַמָּיו. זְכֹר לוֹ צִדְקָתוֹ אֲשֶׁר עָשָׂה, וִיהִי שְׂכָרוֹ אִתּוֹ, וּפְעֻלָּתוֹ לְפָנָיו. אָנָּא הַסְתֵּר אֶת נִשְׁמָתוֹ בְּצֵל כְּנָפֶיךָ, הוֹדִיעֵהוּ אֹרַח חַיִּים, שֹׂבַע שְׂמָחוֹת אֶת פָּנֶיךָ, נְעִמוֹת בִּימִינְךָ נֶצַח, וְתַשְׁפִּיעַ לוֹ מֵרֹב טוּב הַצָּפוּן לַצַּדִּיקִים.

For a girl, say:

(*name* daughter of *father's name*) who has been gathered to her people. Remember the righteousness that she did, and let her reward be with her, her recompense before her. O shelter her soul in the shadow of Your wings. Make known to her the path of life. In Your presence is fullness of joy, at Your right hand bliss for evermore. Bestow upon her the great goodness that is stored up for the righteous.

As it is written, "How great is Your goodness which You have stored up for   *Ps. 31* those who revere You, which You bestow on those that trust in You before the children of men."

אָנָּא May the Lord who heals the brokenhearted and binds up their wounds, grant consolation to the mourners.

For a young boy, add:
May the death of this boy
mark the end of all anguish and sorrow for his parents.

For a young girl, add:
May the death of this girl
mark the end of all anguish and sorrow for her parents.

If the mourners have children, add the words in parentheses:
חַזְקֵם Strengthen and support them in the day of their sadness and grief; and remember them (and their children) for a long and good life. Put into their hearts love and reverence for You, so that they may serve You with a perfect heart; and let their end be peace. Amen.

כְּאִישׁ As a mother comforts her son,   *Is. 66*
so will I comfort you;
and in Jerusalem you shall find comfort.
Your sun shall no more set,   *Is. 60*
your moon shall no more withdraw itself,
for the Lord shall be your everlasting light,
and your days of mourning shall be ended.
He will destroy death for ever;   *Is. 25*
and the Lord God will wipe away the tears from all faces,
and remove the reproach of His people from the whole earth;
for the Lord has spoken it.

For a girl, say:

(פלונית בַּת פלוני) אֲשֶׁר נֶאֶסְפָה אֶל עַמֶּיהָ. זְכוֹר לָהּ צִדְקָתָהּ אֲשֶׁר
עָשְׂתָה, וִיהִי שְׂכָרָהּ אִתָּהּ, וּפְעֻלָּתָהּ לְפָנֶיהָ. אָנָּא הַסְתֵּר אֶת נִשְׁמָתָהּ
בְּצֵל כְּנָפֶיךָ, הוֹדִיעֶהָ אֹרַח חַיִּים, שֹׂבַע שְׂמָחוֹת אֶת פָּנֶיךָ, נְעִימוֹת
בִּימִינְךָ נֶצַח, וְתַשְׁפִּיעַ לָהּ מֵרַב טוּב הַצָּפוּן לַצַּדִּיקִים.

כְּמוֹ שֶׁכָּתוּב: מָה רַב טוּבְךָ אֲשֶׁר־צָפַנְתָּ לִּירֵאֶיךָ, פָּעַלְתָּ לַחֹסִים בָּךְ נֶגֶד תהלים לא
בְּנֵי אָדָם:

אָנָּא יהוה, הָרוֹפֵא לִשְׁבוּרֵי לֵב וּמְחַבֵּשׁ לְעַצְּבוֹתָם, שַׁלֵּם נִחוּמִים לָאֲבֵלִים.

For a young boy, add:

וּתְהִי פְּטִירַת הַיֶּלֶד הַזֶּה קֵץ לְכָל צָרָה וְצוּקָה לְאָבִיו וּלְאִמּוֹ.

For a young girl, add:

וּתְהִי פְּטִירַת הַיַּלְדָּה הַזֹּאת קֵץ לְכָל צָרָה וְצוּקָה לְאָבִיהָ וּלְאִמָּהּ.

If the mourners have children, add the words in parentheses:

חַזְּקֵם וְאַמְּצֵם בְּיוֹם אָבְלָם וִיגוֹנָם, וְזָכְרֵם (וּזְכֹר אֶת בְּנֵי בֵיתָם) לְחַיִּים
טוֹבִים וַאֲרֻכִּים. תֵּן בְּלִבָּם יִרְאָתְךָ וְאַהֲבָתְךָ לְעָבְדְּךָ בְּלֵבָב שָׁלֵם, וּתְהִי
אַחֲרִיתָם שָׁלוֹם, אָמֵן.

ישעיה סו כְּאִישׁ אֲשֶׁר אִמּוֹ תְּנַחֲמֶנּוּ
כֵּן אָנֹכִי אֲנַחֶמְכֶם
וּבִירוּשָׁלַם תְּנֻחָמוּ:
ישעיה ס לֹא־יָבוֹא עוֹד שִׁמְשֵׁךְ, וִירֵחֵךְ לֹא יֵאָסֵף
כִּי יהוה יִהְיֶה־לָּךְ לְאוֹר עוֹלָם
וְשָׁלְמוּ יְמֵי אֶבְלֵךְ:
ישעיה כה בִּלַּע הַמָּוֶת לָנֶצַח
וּמָחָה אֲדֹנָי יֱהֹוִה דִּמְעָה מֵעַל כָּל־פָּנִים
וְחֶרְפַּת עַמּוֹ יָסִיר מֵעַל כָּל־הָאָרֶץ
כִּי יהוה דִּבֵּר:

MOURNER'S KADDISH

The following prayer, said by mourners, requires the presence of a minyan.
A transliteration can be found on page 699.

Mourner: יִתְגַּדַּל Magnified and sanctified
may His great name be,
in the world He created by His will.
May He establish His kingdom
in your lifetime and in your days,
and in the lifetime of all the house of Israel,
swiftly and soon –
and say: Amen.

All: May His great name be blessed
for ever and all time.

Mourner: Blessed and praised,
glorified and exalted,
raised and honored,
uplifted and lauded
be the name of the Holy One,
blessed be He,
beyond any blessing,
song, praise and consolation
uttered in the world –
and say: Amen.

May there be great peace from heaven,
and life for us and all Israel –
and say: Amen.

Bow, take three steps back, as if taking leave of the Divine Presence,
then bow, first left, then right, then center, while saying:
May He who makes peace in His high places,
make peace for us and all Israel –
and say: Amen.

קדיש יתום

The following prayer, said by mourners, requires the presence of a מִנְיָן.
A transliteration can be found on page 699.

אבל: יִתְגַּדַּל וְיִתְקַדַּשׁ שְׁמֵהּ רַבָּא (קהל: אָמֵן)
בְּעָלְמָא דִּי בְרָא כִרְעוּתֵהּ
וְיַמְלִיךְ מַלְכוּתֵהּ
בְּחַיֵּיכוֹן וּבְיוֹמֵיכוֹן וּבְחַיֵּי דְכָל בֵּית יִשְׂרָאֵל
בַּעֲגָלָא וּבִזְמַן קָרִיב
וְאִמְרוּ אָמֵן. (קהל: אָמֵן)

קהל ואבל: יְהֵא שְׁמֵהּ רַבָּא מְבָרַךְ לְעָלַם וּלְעָלְמֵי עָלְמַיָּא.

אבל: יִתְבָּרַךְ וְיִשְׁתַּבַּח וְיִתְפָּאַר
וְיִתְרוֹמַם וְיִתְנַשֵּׂא וְיִתְהַדָּר וְיִתְעַלֶּה וְיִתְהַלָּל
שְׁמֵהּ דְּקֻדְשָׁא בְּרִיךְ הוּא (קהל: בְּרִיךְ הוּא)
לְעֵלָּא מִן כָּל בִּרְכָתָא / בעשרת ימי תשובה: לְעֵלָּא לְעֵלָּא מִכָּל בִּרְכָתָא/
וְשִׁירָתָא, תֻּשְׁבְּחָתָא וְנֶחֱמָתָא
דַּאֲמִירָן בְּעָלְמָא
וְאִמְרוּ אָמֵן. (קהל: אָמֵן)

יְהֵא שְׁלָמָא רַבָּא מִן שְׁמַיָּא
וְחַיִּים, עָלֵינוּ וְעַל כָּל יִשְׂרָאֵל
וְאִמְרוּ אָמֵן. (קהל: אָמֵן)

*Bow, take three steps back, as if taking leave of the Divine Presence,
then bow, first left, then right, then center, while saying:*

עֹשֶׂה שָׁלוֹם / בעשרת ימי תשובה: הַשָּׁלוֹם / בִּמְרוֹמָיו
הוּא יַעֲשֶׂה שָׁלוֹם עָלֵינוּ וְעַל כָּל יִשְׂרָאֵל
וְאִמְרוּ אָמֵן. (קהל: אָמֵן)

BIRKAT HAMAZON IN A HOUSE OF MOURNING

Leader Gentlemen, let us say grace.
Others May the name of the Lord be blessed from now and for ever.   *Ps. 113*
Leader May the name of the Lord be blessed from now and for ever.
          With your permission,
          let us bless the One who comforts mourners
          from whose food we have eaten.
Others Blessed be the One who comforts mourners,
          from whose food we have eaten, and by whose goodness we live.

> *People present who have not taken part in the meal say:*
> *Blessed be the One who comforts mourners,
>   whose name is continually blessed for ever and all time.*

Leader Blessed be the One who comforts mourners,
          from whose food we have eaten, and by whose goodness we live.
          Blessed be He, and blessed be His name.

*Continue with Birkat HaMazon on page 520 until
"And may Jerusalem" on page 526. Then say:*

נַחֵם Comfort, O Lord our God, the mourners of Jerusalem and those
who mourn here. Grant them consolation in their mourning and gladness
in their grief, as it is said, "As a mother comforts her son, so will I comfort   *Is. 66*
you, and in Jerusalem you shall find comfort." Blessed are You, Lord,
who brings comfort to Zion through the rebuilding of Jerusalem. Amen.

בָּרוּךְ Blessed are You, Lord our God, King of the Universe – God our
Father, our King, our Sovereign, our Creator, our Redeemer, our Maker,
our Holy One, the Holy One of Jacob. He is our Shepherd, Israel's
Sheperd, our living King who is good and does good, the true God, the
true Judge, who judges righteously and takes back souls in judgment. He
rules the world according to His will, for all His ways are just, and we
are His people and His servants. For everything, we are duty bound to
acknowledge and bless Him. May He who repairs the breaches in Israel,
repair this breach in us and grant us life and peace. May He always bestow
on us grace, kindness, compassion and all good things. Of all that is good,
may He never let us lack.

Continue with "May the Compassionate One reign" on page 528.

ברכת המזון בבית האבל

Leader	רַבּוֹתַי, נְבָרֵךְ.

תהלים קיג

Others	יְהִי שֵׁם יהוה מְבֹרָךְ מֵעַתָּה וְעַד־עוֹלָם:
Leader	יְהִי שֵׁם יהוה מְבֹרָךְ מֵעַתָּה וְעַד־עוֹלָם:

בִּרְשׁוּת רַבּוֹתַי, נְבָרֵךְ מְנַחֵם אֲבֵלִים שֶׁאָכַלְנוּ מִשֶּׁלּוֹ.

Others	בָּרוּךְ מְנַחֵם אֲבֵלִים, שֶׁאָכַלְנוּ מִשֶּׁלּוֹ וּבְטוּבוֹ חָיִינוּ.

People present who have not taken part in the meal say:

*בָּרוּךְ מְנַחֵם אֲבֵלִים, וּמְבֹרָךְ שְׁמוֹ תָּמִיד לְעוֹלָם וָעֶד.

Leader	בָּרוּךְ מְנַחֵם אֲבֵלִים, שֶׁאָכַלְנוּ מִשֶּׁלּוֹ וּבְטוּבוֹ חָיִינוּ.

בָּרוּךְ הוּא וּבָרוּךְ שְׁמוֹ.

Continue with בְּרַכַּת הַמָּזוֹן *on page 521 until* וּבְנֵה יְרוּשָׁלַיִם *on page 527. Then say:*

ישעיה סו

נַחֵם יהוה אֱלֹהֵינוּ אֶת אֲבֵלֵי יְרוּשָׁלַיִם, וְאֶת הָאֲבֵלִים הַמִּתְאַבְּלִים בָּאֵבֶל הַזֶּה. נַחֲמֵם מֵאֶבְלָם וְשַׂמְּחֵם מִיגוֹנָם, כָּאָמוּר: כְּאִישׁ אֲשֶׁר אִמּוֹ תְּנַחֲמֶנּוּ, כֵּן אָנֹכִי אֲנַחֶמְכֶם וּבִירוּשָׁלַיִם תְּנֻחָמוּ: בָּרוּךְ אַתָּה יהוה, מְנַחֵם צִיּוֹן בְּבִנְיַן יְרוּשָׁלַיִם. אָמֵן.

בָּרוּךְ אַתָּה יהוה אֱלֹהֵינוּ מֶלֶךְ הָעוֹלָם, הָאֵל אָבִינוּ מַלְכֵּנוּ אַדִּירֵנוּ בּוֹרְאֵנוּ גּוֹאֲלֵנוּ יוֹצְרֵנוּ קְדוֹשֵׁנוּ קְדוֹשׁ יַעֲקֹב, רוֹעֵנוּ רוֹעֵה יִשְׂרָאֵל, הַמֶּלֶךְ הַטּוֹב וְהַמֵּטִיב. אֵל אֱמֶת, דַּיָּן אֱמֶת, שׁוֹפֵט צֶדֶק, לוֹקֵחַ נְפָשׁוֹת בְּמִשְׁפָּט, וְשַׁלִּיט בְּעוֹלָמוֹ לַעֲשׂוֹת בּוֹ כִּרְצוֹנוֹ, כִּי כָל דְּרָכָיו מִשְׁפָּט, וַאֲנַחְנוּ עַמּוֹ וַעֲבָדָיו, וְעַל הַכֹּל אֲנַחְנוּ חַיָּבִים לְהוֹדוֹת לוֹ וּלְבָרְכוֹ. גּוֹדֵר פִּרְצוֹת יִשְׂרָאֵל, הוּא יִגְדֹּר אֶת הַפִּרְצָה הַזֹּאת מֵעָלֵינוּ לְחַיִּים וּלְשָׁלוֹם. הוּא יִגְמְלֵנוּ לָעַד חֵן וָחֶסֶד וְרַחֲמִים וְכָל טוֹב, וּמִכָּל טוֹב לְעוֹלָם אַל יְחַסְּרֵנוּ.

Continue with הָרַחֲמָן הוּא יִמְלֹךְ *on page 529.*

קריאת התורה
TORAH READINGS

קריאת התורה
לימי שני וחמישי

THE READING OF THE TORAH
FOR MONDAYS AND THURSDAYS

בראשית   BERESHIT

בראשית א: א-כג

בְּרֵאשִׁ֖ית בָּרָ֣א אֱלֹהִ֑ים אֵ֥ת הַשָּׁמַ֖יִם וְאֵ֥ת הָאָֽרֶץ: וְהָאָ֗רֶץ הָיְתָ֥ה תֹ֙הוּ֙ וָבֹ֔הוּ וְחֹ֖שֶׁךְ עַל־פְּנֵ֣י תְה֑וֹם וְר֣וּחַ אֱלֹהִ֔ים מְרַחֶ֖פֶת עַל־פְּנֵ֥י הַמָּֽיִם: וַיֹּ֥אמֶר אֱלֹהִ֖ים יְהִ֣י א֑וֹר וַֽיְהִי־אֽוֹר: וַיַּ֧רְא אֱלֹהִ֛ים אֶת־הָא֖וֹר כִּי־ט֑וֹב וַיַּבְדֵּ֣ל אֱלֹהִ֔ים בֵּ֥ין הָא֖וֹר וּבֵ֥ין הַחֹֽשֶׁךְ: וַיִּקְרָ֨א אֱלֹהִ֤ים ׀ לָאוֹר֙ י֔וֹם וְלַחֹ֖שֶׁךְ קָ֣רָא לָ֑יְלָה וַֽיְהִי־עֶ֥רֶב וַֽיְהִי־בֹ֖קֶר י֥וֹם אֶחָֽד:

לוי   וַיֹּ֣אמֶר אֱלֹהִ֔ים יְהִ֥י רָקִ֖יעַ בְּת֣וֹךְ הַמָּ֑יִם וִיהִ֣י מַבְדִּ֔יל בֵּ֥ין מַ֖יִם לָמָֽיִם: וַיַּ֣עַשׂ אֱלֹהִים֮ אֶת־הָֽרָקִיעַ֒ וַיַּבְדֵּ֗ל בֵּ֤ין הַמַּ֙יִם֙ אֲשֶׁר֙ מִתַּ֣חַת לָרָקִ֔יעַ וּבֵ֣ין הַמַּ֔יִם אֲשֶׁ֖ר מֵעַ֣ל לָרָקִ֑יעַ וַֽיְהִי־כֵֽן: וַיִּקְרָ֧א אֱלֹהִ֛ים לָרָקִ֖יעַ שָׁמָ֑יִם וַֽיְהִי־עֶ֥רֶב וַֽיְהִי־בֹ֖קֶר י֥וֹם שֵׁנִֽי:

ישראל   וַיֹּ֣אמֶר אֱלֹהִ֗ים יִקָּו֨וּ הַמַּ֜יִם מִתַּ֤חַת הַשָּׁמַ֙יִם֙ אֶל־מָק֣וֹם אֶחָ֔ד וְתֵרָאֶ֖ה הַיַּבָּשָׁ֑ה וַֽיְהִי־כֵֽן: וַיִּקְרָ֨א אֱלֹהִ֤ים ׀ לַיַּבָּשָׁה֙ אֶ֔רֶץ וּלְמִקְוֵ֥ה הַמַּ֖יִם קָרָ֣א יַמִּ֑ים וַיַּ֥רְא אֱלֹהִ֖ים כִּי־טֽוֹב: וַיֹּ֣אמֶר אֱלֹהִ֗ים תַּֽדְשֵׁ֤א הָאָ֙רֶץ֙ דֶּ֔שֶׁא עֵ֚שֶׂב מַזְרִ֣יעַ זֶ֔רַע עֵ֣ץ פְּרִ֞י עֹ֤שֶׂה פְּרִי֙ לְמִינ֔וֹ אֲשֶׁ֥ר זַרְעוֹ־ב֖וֹ עַל־הָאָ֑רֶץ וַֽיְהִי־כֵֽן: וַתּוֹצֵ֨א הָאָ֜רֶץ דֶּ֠שֶׁא עֵ֣שֶׂב מַזְרִ֤יעַ זֶ֙רַע֙ לְמִינֵ֔הוּ וְעֵ֧ץ עֹֽשֶׂה־פְּרִ֛י אֲשֶׁ֥ר זַרְעוֹ־ב֖וֹ לְמִינֵ֑הוּ וַיַּ֥רְא אֱלֹהִ֖ים כִּי־טֽוֹב: וַֽיְהִי־עֶ֥רֶב וַֽיְהִי־בֹ֖קֶר י֥וֹם שְׁלִישִֽׁי:

Some extend the ישראל *portion on the Thursday reading:*

וַיֹּ֣אמֶר אֱלֹהִ֗ים יְהִ֤י מְאֹרֹת֙ בִּרְקִ֣יעַ הַשָּׁמַ֔יִם לְהַבְדִּ֕יל בֵּ֥ין הַיּ֖וֹם וּבֵ֣ין הַלָּ֑יְלָה וְהָי֤וּ לְאֹתֹת֙ וּלְמ֣וֹעֲדִ֔ים וּלְיָמִ֖ים וְשָׁנִֽים: וְהָי֤וּ לִמְאוֹרֹת֙ בִּרְקִ֣יעַ הַשָּׁמַ֔יִם לְהָאִ֖יר עַל־הָאָ֑רֶץ וַֽיְהִי־כֵֽן: וַיַּ֣עַשׂ אֱלֹהִ֔ים אֶת־שְׁנֵ֥י הַמְּאֹרֹ֖ת הַגְּדֹלִ֑ים אֶת־הַמָּא֤וֹר הַגָּדֹל֙ לְמֶמְשֶׁ֣לֶת הַיּ֔וֹם וְאֶת־הַמָּא֤וֹר הַקָּטֹן֙ לְמֶמְשֶׁ֣לֶת הַלַּ֔יְלָה וְאֵ֖ת הַכּֽוֹכָבִֽים: וַיִּתֵּ֥ן אֹתָ֛ם אֱלֹהִ֖ים בִּרְקִ֣יעַ הַשָּׁמָ֑יִם לְהָאִ֖יר עַל־הָאָֽרֶץ: וְלִמְשֹׁל֙ בַּיּ֣וֹם וּבַלַּ֔יְלָה

וּלֲהַבְדִּיל בֵּין הָאוֹר וּבֵין הַחֹשֶׁךְ וַיַּרְא אֱלֹהִים כִּי־טֽוֹב: וַֽיְהִי־עֶרֶב וַֽיְהִי־בֹקֶר
יוֹם רְבִיעִֽי:
וַיֹּאמֶר אֱלֹהִים יִשְׁרְצוּ הַמַּיִם שֶׁרֶץ נֶפֶשׁ חַיָּה וְעוֹף יְעוֹפֵף עַל־הָאָרֶץ עַל־פְּנֵי
רְקִיעַ הַשָּׁמָֽיִם: וַיִּבְרָא אֱלֹהִים אֶת־הַתַּנִּינִם הַגְּדֹלִים וְאֵת כָּל־נֶפֶשׁ הַֽחַיָּה ׀
הָֽרֹמֶשֶׂת אֲשֶׁר שָֽׁרְצוּ הַמַּיִם לְמִֽינֵהֶם וְאֵת כָּל־עוֹף כָּנָף לְמִינֵהוּ וַיַּרְא אֱלֹהִים
כִּי־טֽוֹב: וַיְבָרֶךְ אֹתָם אֱלֹהִים לֵאמֹר פְּרוּ וּרְבוּ וּמִלְאוּ אֶת־הַמַּיִם בַּיַּמִּים וְהָעוֹף
יִרֶב בָּאָֽרֶץ: וַֽיְהִי־עֶרֶב וַֽיְהִי־בֹקֶר יוֹם חֲמִישִֽׁי:

NOAH

נח

בראשית ו:
ט-כב
אֵלֶּה תּֽוֹלְדֹת נֹחַ נֹחַ אִישׁ צַדִּיק תָּמִים הָיָה בְּדֹֽרֹתָיו אֶת־הָֽאֱלֹהִים הִֽתְהַלֶּךְ־
נֹֽחַ: וַיּוֹלֶד נֹחַ שְׁלֹשָׁה בָנִים אֶת־שֵׁם אֶת־חָם וְאֶת־יָֽפֶת: וַתִּשָּׁחֵת הָאָרֶץ
לִפְנֵי הָֽאֱלֹהִים וַתִּמָּלֵא הָאָרֶץ חָמָֽס: וַיַּרְא אֱלֹהִים אֶת־הָאָרֶץ וְהִנֵּה נִשְׁחָתָה
כִּֽי־הִשְׁחִית כָּל־בָּשָׂר אֶת־דַּרְכּוֹ עַל־הָאָֽרֶץ: וַיֹּאמֶר אֱלֹהִים
לְנֹחַ קֵץ כָּל־בָּשָׂר בָּא לְפָנַי כִּֽי־מָֽלְאָה הָאָרֶץ חָמָס מִפְּנֵיהֶם וְהִנְנִי מַשְׁחִיתָם
אֶת־הָאָֽרֶץ: עֲשֵׂה לְךָ תֵּבַת עֲצֵי־גֹפֶר קִנִּים תַּֽעֲשֶׂה אֶת־הַתֵּבָה וְכָֽפַרְתָּ אֹתָהּ
מִבַּיִת וּמִחוּץ בַּכֹּֽפֶר: וְזֶה אֲשֶׁר תַּֽעֲשֶׂה אֹתָהּ שְׁלֹשׁ מֵאוֹת אַמָּה אֹרֶךְ הַתֵּבָה
חֲמִשִּׁים אַמָּה רָחְבָּהּ וּשְׁלֹשִׁים אַמָּה קֽוֹמָתָֽהּ: צֹהַר ׀ תַּֽעֲשֶׂה לַתֵּבָה וְאֶל־אַמָּה
תְּכַלֶּנָּה מִלְמַעְלָה וּפֶתַח הַתֵּבָה בְּצִדָּהּ תָּשִׂים תַּחְתִּיִּם שְׁנִיִּם וּשְׁלִשִׁים תַּֽעֲשֶֽׂהָ:
לוי
*וַֽאֲנִי הִנְנִי מֵבִיא אֶת־הַמַּבּוּל מַיִם עַל־הָאָרֶץ לְשַׁחֵת כָּל־בָּשָׂר אֲשֶׁר־בּוֹ
רוּחַ חַיִּים מִתַּחַת הַשָּׁמָיִם כֹּל אֲשֶׁר־בָּאָרֶץ יִגְוָֽע: וַהֲקִֽמֹתִי אֶת־בְּרִיתִי אִתָּךְ
וּבָאתָ אֶל־הַתֵּבָה אַתָּה וּבָנֶיךָ וְאִשְׁתְּךָ וּנְשֵֽׁי־בָנֶיךָ אִתָּֽךְ: וּמִכָּל־הָחַי מִכָּל־
ישראל
בָּשָׂר שְׁנַיִם מִכֹּל תָּבִיא אֶל־הַתֵּבָה לְהַֽחֲיֹת אִתָּךְ זָכָר וּנְקֵבָה יִֽהְיֽוּ: *מֵֽהָעוֹף
לְמִינֵהוּ וּמִן־הַבְּהֵמָה לְמִינָהּ מִכֹּל רֶמֶשׂ הָֽאֲדָמָה לְמִינֵהוּ שְׁנַיִם מִכֹּל יָבֹאוּ
אֵלֶיךָ לְהַֽחֲיֽוֹת: וְאַתָּה קַח־לְךָ מִכָּל־מַֽאֲכָל אֲשֶׁר יֵֽאָכֵל וְאָֽסַפְתָּ אֵלֶיךָ וְהָיָה
לְךָ וְלָהֶם לְאָכְלָֽה: וַיַּעַשׂ נֹחַ כְּכֹל אֲשֶׁר צִוָּה אֹתוֹ אֱלֹהִים כֵּן עָשָֽׂה:

LEKH LEKHA

לך לך

בראשית יב:
א-ג
וַיֹּאמֶר יְהֹוָה אֶל־אַבְרָם לֶךְ־לְךָ מֵֽאַרְצְךָ וּמִמּֽוֹלַדְתְּךָ וּמִבֵּית אָבִיךָ אֶל־הָאָרֶץ
אֲשֶׁר אַרְאֶֽךָּ: וְאֶֽעֶשְׂךָ לְגוֹי גָּדוֹל וַאֲבָרֶכְךָ וַאֲגַדְּלָה שְׁמֶךָ וֶהְיֵה בְּרָכָֽה: וַאֲבָֽרְכָה

לוי מְבָרַכֶיךָ וּמְקַלֶּלְךָ אָאֹר וְנִבְרְכוּ בְךָ כֹּל מִשְׁפְּחֹת הָאֲדָמָה: ⁴וַיֵּלֶךְ אַבְרָם כַּאֲשֶׁר
דִּבֶּר אֵלָיו יְהֹוָה וַיֵּלֶךְ אִתּוֹ לוֹט וְאַבְרָם בֶּן־חָמֵשׁ שָׁנִים וְשִׁבְעִים שָׁנָה בְּצֵאתוֹ
מֵחָרָן: ⁵וַיִּקַּח אַבְרָם אֶת־שָׂרַי אִשְׁתּוֹ וְאֶת־לוֹט בֶּן־אָחִיו וְאֶת־כָּל־רְכוּשָׁם
אֲשֶׁר רָכָשׁוּ וְאֶת־הַנֶּפֶשׁ אֲשֶׁר־עָשׂוּ בְחָרָן וַיֵּצְאוּ לָלֶכֶת אַרְצָה כְּנַעַן וַיָּבֹאוּ
אַרְצָה כְּנָעַן: ⁶וַיַּעֲבֹר אַבְרָם בָּאָרֶץ עַד מְקוֹם שְׁכֶם עַד אֵלוֹן מוֹרֶה וְהַכְּנַעֲנִי
אָז בָּאָרֶץ: ⁷וַיֵּרָא יְהֹוָה אֶל־אַבְרָם וַיֹּאמֶר לְזַרְעֲךָ אֶתֵּן אֶת־הָאָרֶץ הַזֹּאת וַיִּבֶן
שָׁם מִזְבֵּחַ לַיהֹוָה הַנִּרְאֶה אֵלָיו: ⁸וַיַּעְתֵּק מִשָּׁם הָהָרָה מִקֶּדֶם לְבֵית־אֵל וַיֵּט
אָהֳלֹה בֵּית־אֵל מִיָּם וְהָעַי מִקֶּדֶם וַיִּבֶן־שָׁם מִזְבֵּחַ לַיהֹוָה וַיִּקְרָא בְּשֵׁם יְהֹוָה:
⁹וַיִּסַּע אַבְרָם הָלוֹךְ וְנָסוֹעַ הַנֶּגְבָּה:

ישראל ¹⁰וַיְהִי רָעָב בָּאָרֶץ וַיֵּרֶד אַבְרָם מִצְרַיְמָה לָגוּר שָׁם כִּי־כָבֵד הָרָעָב בָּאָרֶץ:
¹¹וַיְהִי כַּאֲשֶׁר הִקְרִיב לָבוֹא מִצְרָיְמָה וַיֹּאמֶר אֶל־שָׂרַי אִשְׁתּוֹ הִנֵּה־נָא יָדַעְתִּי
כִּי אִשָּׁה יְפַת־מַרְאֶה אָתְּ: ¹²וְהָיָה כִּי־יִרְאוּ אֹתָךְ הַמִּצְרִים וְאָמְרוּ אִשְׁתּוֹ זֹאת
וְהָרְגוּ אֹתִי וְאֹתָךְ יְחַיּוּ: ¹³אִמְרִי־נָא אֲחֹתִי אָתְּ לְמַעַן יִיטַב־לִי בַעֲבוּרֵךְ וְחָיְתָה
נַפְשִׁי בִּגְלָלֵךְ:

VAYERA וירא

¹וַיֵּרָא אֵלָיו יְהֹוָה בְּאֵלֹנֵי מַמְרֵא וְהוּא יֹשֵׁב פֶּתַח־הָאֹהֶל כְּחֹם הַיּוֹם: ²וַיִּשָּׂא
עֵינָיו וַיַּרְא וְהִנֵּה שְׁלֹשָׁה אֲנָשִׁים נִצָּבִים עָלָיו וַיַּרְא וַיָּרָץ לִקְרָאתָם מִפֶּתַח
הָאֹהֶל וַיִּשְׁתַּחוּ אָרְצָה: ³וַיֹּאמַר אֲדֹנָי אִם־נָא מָצָאתִי חֵן בְּעֵינֶיךָ אַל־נָא
תַעֲבֹר מֵעַל עַבְדֶּךָ: ⁴יֻקַּח־נָא מְעַט־מַיִם וְרַחֲצוּ רַגְלֵיכֶם וְהִשָּׁעֲנוּ תַּחַת הָעֵץ:
⁵וְאֶקְחָה פַת־לֶחֶם וְסַעֲדוּ לִבְּכֶם אַחַר תַּעֲבֹרוּ כִּי־עַל־כֵּן עֲבַרְתֶּם עַל־עַבְדְּכֶם
לוי וַיֹּאמְרוּ כֵּן תַּעֲשֶׂה כַּאֲשֶׁר דִּבַּרְתָּ: ⁶וַיְמַהֵר אַבְרָהָם הָאֹהֱלָה אֶל־שָׂרָה וַיֹּאמֶר
מַהֲרִי שְׁלֹשׁ סְאִים קֶמַח סֹלֶת לוּשִׁי וַעֲשִׂי עֻגוֹת: ⁷וְאֶל־הַבָּקָר רָץ אַבְרָהָם
וַיִּקַּח בֶּן־בָּקָר רַךְ וָטוֹב וַיִּתֵּן אֶל־הַנַּעַר וַיְמַהֵר לַעֲשׂוֹת אֹתוֹ: ⁸וַיִּקַּח חֶמְאָה
וְחָלָב וּבֶן־הַבָּקָר אֲשֶׁר עָשָׂה וַיִּתֵּן לִפְנֵיהֶם וְהוּא־עֹמֵד עֲלֵיהֶם תַּחַת הָעֵץ
ישראל וַיֹּאכֵלוּ: ⁹וַיֹּאמְרוּ אֵלָיו אַיֵּה שָׂרָה אִשְׁתֶּךָ וַיֹּאמֶר הִנֵּה בָאֹהֶל: ¹⁰וַיֹּאמֶר שׁוֹב
אָשׁוּב אֵלֶיךָ כָּעֵת חַיָּה וְהִנֵּה־בֵן לְשָׂרָה אִשְׁתֶּךָ וְשָׂרָה שֹׁמַעַת פֶּתַח הָאֹהֶל
וְהוּא אַחֲרָיו: ¹¹וְאַבְרָהָם וְשָׂרָה זְקֵנִים בָּאִים בַּיָּמִים חָדַל לִהְיוֹת לְשָׂרָה אֹרַח
כַּנָּשִׁים: ¹²וַתִּצְחַק שָׂרָה בְּקִרְבָּהּ לֵאמֹר אַחֲרֵי בְלֹתִי הָיְתָה־לִּי עֶדְנָה וַאדֹנִי

זָקֵן: וַיֹּאמֶר יְהוָה אֶל־אַבְרָהָם לָמָּה זֶּה צָחֲקָה שָׂרָה לֵאמֹר הַאַף אֻמְנָם אֵלֵד
וַאֲנִי זָקַנְתִּי: הֲיִפָּלֵא מֵיהוָה דָּבָר לַמּוֹעֵד אָשׁוּב אֵלֶיךָ כָּעֵת חַיָּה וּלְשָׂרָה בֵן:

HAYYEI SARA
חיי שרה

בראשית כג
א-טז

וַיִּהְיוּ חַיֵּי שָׂרָה מֵאָה שָׁנָה וְעֶשְׂרִים שָׁנָה וְשֶׁבַע שָׁנִים שְׁנֵי חַיֵּי שָׂרָה: וַתָּמָת
שָׂרָה בְּקִרְיַת אַרְבַּע הִוא חֶבְרוֹן בְּאֶרֶץ כְּנָעַן וַיָּבֹא אַבְרָהָם לִסְפֹּד לְשָׂרָה
וְלִבְכֹּתָהּ: וַיָּקָם אַבְרָהָם מֵעַל פְּנֵי מֵתוֹ וַיְדַבֵּר אֶל־בְּנֵי־חֵת לֵאמֹר: גֵּר־וְתוֹשָׁב
אָנֹכִי עִמָּכֶם תְּנוּ לִי אֲחֻזַּת־קֶבֶר עִמָּכֶם וְאֶקְבְּרָה מֵתִי מִלְּפָנָי: וַיַּעֲנוּ בְנֵי־חֵת
אֶת־אַבְרָהָם לֵאמֹר לוֹ: שְׁמָעֵנוּ ׀ אֲדֹנִי נְשִׂיא אֱלֹהִים אַתָּה בְּתוֹכֵנוּ בְּמִבְחַר
קְבָרֵינוּ קְבֹר אֶת־מֵתֶךָ אִישׁ מִמֶּנּוּ אֶת־קִבְרוֹ לֹא־יִכְלֶה מִמְּךָ מִקְּבֹר מֵתֶךָ:
וַיָּקָם אַבְרָהָם וַיִּשְׁתַּחוּ לְעַם־הָאָרֶץ לִבְנֵי־חֵת: וַיְדַבֵּר אִתָּם לֵאמֹר אִם־יֵשׁ
אֶת־נַפְשְׁכֶם לִקְבֹּר אֶת־מֵתִי מִלְּפָנַי שְׁמָעוּנִי וּפִגְעוּ־לִי בְּעֶפְרוֹן בֶּן־צֹחַר:
וְיִתֶּן־לִי אֶת־מְעָרַת הַמַּכְפֵּלָה אֲשֶׁר־לוֹ אֲשֶׁר בִּקְצֵה שָׂדֵהוּ בְּכֶסֶף מָלֵא יִתְּנֶנָּה
לִי בְּתוֹכְכֶם לַאֲחֻזַּת־קָבֶר: וְעֶפְרוֹן יֹשֵׁב בְּתוֹךְ בְּנֵי־חֵת וַיַּעַן עֶפְרוֹן הַחִתִּי
אֶת־אַבְרָהָם בְּאָזְנֵי בְנֵי־חֵת לְכֹל בָּאֵי שַׁעַר־עִירוֹ לֵאמֹר: לֹא־אֲדֹנִי שְׁמָעֵנִי
הַשָּׂדֶה נָתַתִּי לָךְ וְהַמְּעָרָה אֲשֶׁר־בּוֹ לְךָ נְתַתִּיהָ לְעֵינֵי בְנֵי־עַמִּי נְתַתִּיהָ לָּךְ
קְבֹר מֵתֶךָ: וַיִּשְׁתַּחוּ אַבְרָהָם לִפְנֵי עַם־הָאָרֶץ: וַיְדַבֵּר אֶל־עֶפְרוֹן בְּאָזְנֵי עַם־
הָאָרֶץ לֵאמֹר אַךְ אִם־אַתָּה לוּ שְׁמָעֵנִי נָתַתִּי כֶּסֶף הַשָּׂדֶה קַח מִמֶּנִּי וְאֶקְבְּרָה
אֶת־מֵתִי שָׁמָּה: וַיַּעַן עֶפְרוֹן אֶת־אַבְרָהָם לֵאמֹר לוֹ: אֲדֹנִי שְׁמָעֵנִי אֶרֶץ אַרְבַּע
מֵאֹת שֶׁקֶל־כֶּסֶף בֵּינִי וּבֵינְךָ מַה־הִוא וְאֶת־מֵתְךָ קְבֹר: וַיִּשְׁמַע אַבְרָהָם אֶל־
עֶפְרוֹן וַיִּשְׁקֹל אַבְרָהָם לְעֶפְרֹן אֶת־הַכֶּסֶף אֲשֶׁר דִּבֶּר בְּאָזְנֵי בְנֵי־חֵת אַרְבַּע
מֵאוֹת שֶׁקֶל כֶּסֶף עֹבֵר לַסֹּחֵר:

לוי

ישראל

TOLEDOT
תולדות

בראשית
כה:יט-כו:ה

וְאֵלֶּה תּוֹלְדֹת יִצְחָק בֶּן־אַבְרָהָם אַבְרָהָם הוֹלִיד אֶת־יִצְחָק: וַיְהִי יִצְחָק בֶּן־
אַרְבָּעִים שָׁנָה בְּקַחְתּוֹ אֶת־רִבְקָה בַּת־בְּתוּאֵל הָאֲרַמִּי מִפַּדַּן אֲרָם אֲחוֹת לָבָן
הָאֲרַמִּי לוֹ לְאִשָּׁה: וַיֶּעְתַּר יִצְחָק לַיהוָה לְנֹכַח אִשְׁתּוֹ כִּי עֲקָרָה הִוא וַיֵּעָתֶר
לוֹ יְהוָה וַתַּהַר רִבְקָה אִשְׁתּוֹ: וַיִּתְרֹצְצוּ הַבָּנִים בְּקִרְבָּהּ וַתֹּאמֶר אִם־כֵּן לָמָּה
זֶּה אָנֹכִי וַתֵּלֶךְ לִדְרֹשׁ אֶת־יְהוָה: וַיֹּאמֶר יְהוָה לָהּ שְׁנֵי גֹיִים בְּבִטְנֵךְ וּשְׁנֵי

לוי

גוים

לְאֻמִּים מִמֵּעַיִךְ יִפָּרֵדוּ וּלְאֹם מִלְאֹם יֶאֱמָץ וְרַב יַעֲבֹד צָעִיר: וַיִּמְלְאוּ יָמֶיהָ
לָלֶדֶת וְהִנֵּה תוֹמִם בְּבִטְנָהּ: וַיֵּצֵא הָרִאשׁוֹן אַדְמוֹנִי כֻּלּוֹ כְּאַדֶּרֶת שֵׂעָר וַיִּקְרְאוּ
שְׁמוֹ עֵשָׂו: וְאַחֲרֵי־כֵן יָצָא אָחִיו וְיָדוֹ אֹחֶזֶת בַּעֲקֵב עֵשָׂו וַיִּקְרָא שְׁמוֹ יַעֲקֹב
וְיִצְחָק בֶּן־שִׁשִּׁים שָׁנָה בְּלֶדֶת אֹתָם: ישראל וַיִּגְדְּלוּ הַנְּעָרִים וַיְהִי עֵשָׂו אִישׁ יֹדֵעַ צַיִד
אִישׁ שָׂדֶה וְיַעֲקֹב אִישׁ תָּם יֹשֵׁב אֹהָלִים: וַיֶּאֱהַב יִצְחָק אֶת־עֵשָׂו כִּי־צַיִד בְּפִיו
וְרִבְקָה אֹהֶבֶת אֶת־יַעֲקֹב: וַיָּזֶד יַעֲקֹב נָזִיד וַיָּבֹא עֵשָׂו מִן־הַשָּׂדֶה וְהוּא עָיֵף:
וַיֹּאמֶר עֵשָׂו אֶל־יַעֲקֹב הַלְעִיטֵנִי נָא מִן־הָאָדֹם הָאָדֹם הַזֶּה כִּי עָיֵף אָנֹכִי עַל־
כֵּן קָרָא־שְׁמוֹ אֱדוֹם: וַיֹּאמֶר יַעֲקֹב מִכְרָה כַיּוֹם אֶת־בְּכֹרָתְךָ לִי: וַיֹּאמֶר עֵשָׂו
הִנֵּה אָנֹכִי הוֹלֵךְ לָמוּת וְלָמָּה־זֶּה לִי בְּכֹרָה: וַיֹּאמֶר יַעֲקֹב הִשָּׁבְעָה לִּי כַּיּוֹם
וַיִּשָּׁבַע לוֹ וַיִּמְכֹּר אֶת־בְּכֹרָתוֹ לְיַעֲקֹב: וְיַעֲקֹב נָתַן לְעֵשָׂו לֶחֶם וּנְזִיד עֲדָשִׁים
וַיֹּאכַל וַיֵּשְׁתְּ וַיָּקָם וַיֵּלַךְ וַיִּבֶז עֵשָׂו אֶת־הַבְּכֹרָה:

וַיְהִי רָעָב בָּאָרֶץ מִלְּבַד הָרָעָב הָרִאשׁוֹן אֲשֶׁר הָיָה בִּימֵי אַבְרָהָם וַיֵּלֶךְ יִצְחָק
אֶל־אֲבִימֶלֶךְ מֶלֶךְ־פְּלִשְׁתִּים גְּרָרָה: וַיֵּרָא אֵלָיו יהוה וַיֹּאמֶר אַל־תֵּרֵד מִצְרָיְמָה
שְׁכֹן בָּאָרֶץ אֲשֶׁר אֹמַר אֵלֶיךָ: גּוּר בָּאָרֶץ הַזֹּאת וְאֶהְיֶה עִמְּךָ וַאֲבָרְכֶךָּ כִּי־לְךָ
וּלְזַרְעֲךָ אֶתֵּן אֶת־כָּל־הָאֲרָצֹת הָאֵל וַהֲקִמֹתִי אֶת־הַשְּׁבֻעָה אֲשֶׁר נִשְׁבַּעְתִּי
לְאַבְרָהָם אָבִיךָ: וְהִרְבֵּיתִי אֶת־זַרְעֲךָ כְּכוֹכְבֵי הַשָּׁמַיִם וְנָתַתִּי לְזַרְעֲךָ אֵת כָּל־
הָאֲרָצֹת הָאֵל וְהִתְבָּרֲכוּ בְזַרְעֲךָ כֹּל גּוֹיֵי הָאָרֶץ: עֵקֶב אֲשֶׁר־שָׁמַע אַבְרָהָם
בְּקֹלִי וַיִּשְׁמֹר מִשְׁמַרְתִּי מִצְוֹתַי חֻקּוֹתַי וְתוֹרֹתָי:

VAYETZEH

ויצא

בראשית
כ"ח:י-כב
וַיֵּצֵא יַעֲקֹב מִבְּאֵר שָׁבַע וַיֵּלֶךְ חָרָנָה: וַיִּפְגַּע בַּמָּקוֹם וַיָּלֶן שָׁם כִּי־בָא הַשֶּׁמֶשׁ
וַיִּקַּח מֵאַבְנֵי הַמָּקוֹם וַיָּשֶׂם מְרַאֲשֹׁתָיו וַיִּשְׁכַּב בַּמָּקוֹם הַהוּא: וַיַּחֲלֹם וְהִנֵּה
סֻלָּם מֻצָּב אַרְצָה וְרֹאשׁוֹ מַגִּיעַ הַשָּׁמָיְמָה וְהִנֵּה מַלְאֲכֵי אֱלֹהִים עֹלִים וְיֹרְדִים
לוי בּוֹ: וְהִנֵּה יהוה נִצָּב עָלָיו וַיֹּאמַר אֲנִי יהוה אֱלֹהֵי אַבְרָהָם אָבִיךָ וֵאלֹהֵי יִצְחָק
הָאָרֶץ אֲשֶׁר אַתָּה שֹׁכֵב עָלֶיהָ לְךָ אֶתְּנֶנָּה וּלְזַרְעֶךָ: וְהָיָה זַרְעֲךָ כַּעֲפַר הָאָרֶץ
וּפָרַצְתָּ יָמָּה וָקֵדְמָה וְצָפֹנָה וָנֶגְבָּה וְנִבְרֲכוּ בְךָ כָּל־מִשְׁפְּחֹת הָאֲדָמָה וּבְזַרְעֶךָ:
וְהִנֵּה אָנֹכִי עִמָּךְ וּשְׁמַרְתִּיךָ בְּכֹל אֲשֶׁר־תֵּלֵךְ וַהֲשִׁבֹתִיךָ אֶל־הָאֲדָמָה הַזֹּאת כִּי
לֹא אֶעֱזָבְךָ עַד אֲשֶׁר אִם־עָשִׂיתִי אֵת אֲשֶׁר־דִּבַּרְתִּי לָךְ: וַיִּיקַץ יַעֲקֹב מִשְּׁנָתוֹ

וַיֹּאמֶר אָכֵן יֵשׁ יְהֹוָה בַּמָּקוֹם הַזֶּה וְאָנֹכִי לֹא יָדָעְתִּי: וַיִּירָא וַיֹּאמַר מַה־נּוֹרָא

הַמָּקוֹם הַזֶּה אֵין זֶה כִּי אִם־בֵּית אֱלֹהִים וְזֶה שַׁעַר הַשָּׁמָיִם: *וַיַּשְׁכֵּם יַעֲקֹב   ישראל

בַּבֹּקֶר וַיִּקַּח אֶת־הָאֶבֶן אֲשֶׁר־שָׂם מְרַאֲשֹׁתָיו וַיָּשֶׂם אֹתָהּ מַצֵּבָה וַיִּצֹק שֶׁמֶן

עַל־רֹאשָׁהּ: וַיִּקְרָא אֶת־שֵׁם־הַמָּקוֹם הַהוּא בֵּית־אֵל וְאוּלָם לוּז שֵׁם־הָעִיר

לָרִאשֹׁנָה: וַיִּדַּר יַעֲקֹב נֶדֶר לֵאמֹר אִם־יִהְיֶה אֱלֹהִים עִמָּדִי וּשְׁמָרַנִי בַּדֶּרֶךְ הַזֶּה

אֲשֶׁר אָנֹכִי הוֹלֵךְ וְנָתַן־לִי לֶחֶם לֶאֱכֹל וּבֶגֶד לִלְבֹּשׁ: וְשַׁבְתִּי בְשָׁלוֹם אֶל־בֵּית

אָבִי וְהָיָה יְהֹוָה לִי לֵאלֹהִים: וְהָאֶבֶן הַזֹּאת אֲשֶׁר־שַׂמְתִּי מַצֵּבָה יִהְיֶה בֵּית

אֱלֹהִים וְכֹל אֲשֶׁר תִּתֶּן־לִי עַשֵּׂר אֲעַשְּׂרֶנּוּ לָךְ:

VAYISHLAḤ   וישלח

בראשית
לב:ג-יב

וַיִּשְׁלַח יַעֲקֹב מַלְאָכִים לְפָנָיו אֶל־עֵשָׂו אָחִיו אַרְצָה שֵׂעִיר שְׂדֵה אֱדוֹם: וַיְצַו

אֹתָם לֵאמֹר כֹּה תֹאמְרוּן לַאדֹנִי לְעֵשָׂו כֹּה אָמַר עַבְדְּךָ יַעֲקֹב עִם־לָבָן גַּרְתִּי

וָאֵחַר עַד־עָתָּה: וַיְהִי־לִי שׁוֹר וַחֲמוֹר צֹאן וְעֶבֶד וְשִׁפְחָה וָאֶשְׁלְחָה לְהַגִּיד

לַאדֹנִי לִמְצֹא־חֵן בְּעֵינֶיךָ: *וַיָּשֻׁבוּ הַמַּלְאָכִים אֶל־יַעֲקֹב לֵאמֹר בָּאנוּ אֶל־   לוי

אָחִיךָ אֶל־עֵשָׂו וְגַם הֹלֵךְ לִקְרָאתְךָ וְאַרְבַּע־מֵאוֹת אִישׁ עִמּוֹ: וַיִּירָא יַעֲקֹב

מְאֹד וַיֵּצֶר לוֹ וַיַּחַץ אֶת־הָעָם אֲשֶׁר־אִתּוֹ וְאֶת־הַצֹּאן וְאֶת־הַבָּקָר וְהַגְּמַלִּים

לִשְׁנֵי מַחֲנוֹת: וַיֹּאמֶר אִם־יָבוֹא עֵשָׂו אֶל־הַמַּחֲנֶה הָאַחַת וְהִכָּהוּ וְהָיָה הַמַּחֲנֶה

הַנִּשְׁאָר לִפְלֵיטָה: *וַיֹּאמֶר יַעֲקֹב אֱלֹהֵי אָבִי אַבְרָהָם וֵאלֹהֵי אָבִי יִצְחָק יְהֹוָה   ישראל

הָאֹמֵר אֵלַי שׁוּב לְאַרְצְךָ וּלְמוֹלַדְתְּךָ וְאֵיטִיבָה עִמָּךְ: קָטֹנְתִּי מִכֹּל הַחֲסָדִים

וּמִכָּל־הָאֱמֶת אֲשֶׁר עָשִׂיתָ אֶת־עַבְדֶּךָ כִּי בְמַקְלִי עָבַרְתִּי אֶת־הַיַּרְדֵּן הַזֶּה

וְעַתָּה הָיִיתִי לִשְׁנֵי מַחֲנוֹת: הַצִּילֵנִי נָא מִיַּד אָחִי מִיַּד עֵשָׂו כִּי־יָרֵא אָנֹכִי

אֹתוֹ פֶּן־יָבוֹא וְהִכַּנִי אֵם עַל־בָּנִים: וְאַתָּה אָמַרְתָּ הֵיטֵב אֵיטִיב עִמָּךְ וְשַׂמְתִּי

אֶת־זַרְעֲךָ כְּחוֹל הַיָּם אֲשֶׁר לֹא־יִסָּפֵר מֵרֹב:

VAYESHEV   וישב

בראשית
לז:א-יא

וַיֵּשֶׁב יַעֲקֹב בְּאֶרֶץ מְגוּרֵי אָבִיו בְּאֶרֶץ כְּנָעַן: אֵלֶּה ׀ תֹּלְדוֹת יַעֲקֹב יוֹסֵף

בֶּן־שְׁבַע־עֶשְׂרֵה שָׁנָה הָיָה רֹעֶה אֶת־אֶחָיו בַּצֹּאן וְהוּא נַעַר אֶת־בְּנֵי בִלְהָה

וְאֶת־בְּנֵי זִלְפָּה נְשֵׁי אָבִיו וַיָּבֵא יוֹסֵף אֶת־דִּבָּתָם רָעָה אֶל־אֲבִיהֶם: וְיִשְׂרָאֵל

לוי אָהַב אֶת־יוֹסֵף מִכָּל־בָּנָיו כִּי־בֶן־זְקֻנִים הוּא לוֹ וְעָשָׂה לוֹ כְּתֹנֶת פַּסִּים: ‏*וַיִּרְאוּ
אֶחָיו כִּי־אֹתוֹ אָהַב אֲבִיהֶם מִכָּל־אֶחָיו וַיִּשְׂנְאוּ אֹתוֹ וְלֹא יָכְלוּ דַּבְּרוֹ לְשָׁלֹם:
וַיַּחֲלֹם יוֹסֵף חֲלוֹם וַיַּגֵּד לְאֶחָיו וַיּוֹסִפוּ עוֹד שְׂנֹא אֹתוֹ: וַיֹּאמֶר אֲלֵיהֶם שִׁמְעוּ־
נָא הַחֲלוֹם הַזֶּה אֲשֶׁר חָלָמְתִּי: וְהִנֵּה אֲנַחְנוּ מְאַלְּמִים אֲלֻמִּים בְּתוֹךְ הַשָּׂדֶה
וְהִנֵּה קָמָה אֲלֻמָּתִי וְגַם־נִצָּבָה וְהִנֵּה תְסֻבֶּינָה אֲלֻמֹּתֵיכֶם וַתִּשְׁתַּחֲוֶיןָ לַאֲלֻמָּתִי:

ישראל ‏*וַיֹּאמְרוּ לוֹ אֶחָיו הֲמָלֹךְ תִּמְלֹךְ עָלֵינוּ אִם־מָשׁוֹל תִּמְשֹׁל בָּנוּ וַיּוֹסִפוּ עוֹד
שְׂנֹא אֹתוֹ עַל־חֲלֹמֹתָיו וְעַל־דְּבָרָיו: וַיַּחֲלֹם עוֹד חֲלוֹם אַחֵר וַיְסַפֵּר אֹתוֹ
לְאֶחָיו וַיֹּאמֶר הִנֵּה חָלַמְתִּי חֲלוֹם עוֹד וְהִנֵּה הַשֶּׁמֶשׁ וְהַיָּרֵחַ וְאַחַד עָשָׂר
כּוֹכָבִים מִשְׁתַּחֲוִים לִי: וַיְסַפֵּר אֶל־אָבִיו וְאֶל־אֶחָיו וַיִּגְעַר־בּוֹ אָבִיו וַיֹּאמֶר לוֹ
מָה הַחֲלוֹם הַזֶּה אֲשֶׁר חָלָמְתָּ הֲבוֹא נָבוֹא אֲנִי וְאִמְּךָ וְאַחֶיךָ לְהִשְׁתַּחֲוֹת לְךָ
אָרְצָה: וַיְקַנְאוּ־בוֹ אֶחָיו וְאָבִיו שָׁמַר אֶת־הַדָּבָר:

מקץ
MIKETZ

בראשית
מא: א-יד

וַיְהִי מִקֵּץ שְׁנָתַיִם יָמִים וּפַרְעֹה חֹלֵם וְהִנֵּה עֹמֵד עַל־הַיְאֹר: וְהִנֵּה מִן־הַיְאֹר
עֹלֹת שֶׁבַע פָּרוֹת יְפוֹת מַרְאֶה וּבְרִיאֹת בָּשָׂר וַתִּרְעֶינָה בָּאָחוּ: וְהִנֵּה שֶׁבַע
פָּרוֹת אֲחֵרוֹת עֹלוֹת אַחֲרֵיהֶן מִן־הַיְאֹר רָעוֹת מַרְאֶה וְדַקּוֹת בָּשָׂר וַתַּעֲמֹדְנָה
אֵצֶל הַפָּרוֹת עַל־שְׂפַת הַיְאֹר: וַתֹּאכַלְנָה הַפָּרוֹת רָעוֹת הַמַּרְאֶה וְדַקֹּת הַבָּשָׂר

לוי אֵת שֶׁבַע הַפָּרוֹת יְפֹת הַמַּרְאֶה וְהַבְּרִיאֹת וַיִּיקַץ פַּרְעֹה: ‏*וַיִּישָׁן וַיַּחֲלֹם שֵׁנִית
וְהִנֵּה ׀ שֶׁבַע שִׁבֳּלִים עֹלוֹת בְּקָנֶה אֶחָד בְּרִיאוֹת וְטֹבוֹת: וְהִנֵּה שֶׁבַע שִׁבֳּלִים
דַּקּוֹת וּשְׁדוּפֹת קָדִים צֹמְחוֹת אַחֲרֵיהֶן: וַתִּבְלַעְנָה הַשִּׁבֳּלִים הַדַּקּוֹת אֵת

ישראל שֶׁבַע הַשִּׁבֳּלִים הַבְּרִיאוֹת וְהַמְּלֵאוֹת וַיִּיקַץ פַּרְעֹה וְהִנֵּה חֲלוֹם: ‏*וַיְהִי בַבֹּקֶר
וַתִּפָּעֶם רוּחוֹ וַיִּשְׁלַח וַיִּקְרָא אֶת־כָּל־חַרְטֻמֵּי מִצְרַיִם וְאֶת־כָּל־חֲכָמֶיהָ וַיְסַפֵּר
פַּרְעֹה לָהֶם אֶת־חֲלֹמוֹ וְאֵין־פּוֹתֵר אוֹתָם לְפַרְעֹה: וַיְדַבֵּר שַׂר הַמַּשְׁקִים אֶת־
פַּרְעֹה לֵאמֹר אֶת־חֲטָאַי אֲנִי מַזְכִּיר הַיּוֹם: פַּרְעֹה קָצַף עַל־עֲבָדָיו וַיִּתֵּן אֹתִי
בְּמִשְׁמַר בֵּית שַׂר הַטַּבָּחִים אֹתִי וְאֵת שַׂר הָאֹפִים: וַנַּחַלְמָה חֲלוֹם בְּלַיְלָה
אֶחָד אֲנִי וָהוּא אִישׁ כְּפִתְרוֹן חֲלֹמוֹ חָלָמְנוּ: וְשָׁם אִתָּנוּ נַעַר עִבְרִי עֶבֶד לְשַׂר
הַטַּבָּחִים וַנְּסַפֶּר־לוֹ וַיִּפְתָּר־לָנוּ אֶת־חֲלֹמֹתֵינוּ אִישׁ כַּחֲלֹמוֹ פָּתָר: וַיְהִי כַּאֲשֶׁר
פָּתַר־לָנוּ כֵּן הָיָה אֹתִי הֵשִׁיב עַל־כַּנִּי וְאֹתוֹ תָלָה: וַיִּשְׁלַח פַּרְעֹה וַיִּקְרָא אֶת־
יוֹסֵף וַיְרִיצֻהוּ מִן־הַבּוֹר וַיְגַלַּח וַיְחַלֵּף שִׂמְלֹתָיו וַיָּבֹא אֶל־פַּרְעֹה:

VAYIGASH
ויגש

בראשית
מד:יח-ל

וַיִּגַּ֨שׁ אֵלָ֜יו יְהוּדָ֗ה וַיֹּ֘אמֶר֮ בִּ֣י אֲדֹנִי֒ יְדַבֶּר־נָ֨א עַבְדְּךָ֤ דָבָר֙ בְּאָזְנֵ֣י אֲדֹנִ֔י וְאַל־יִ֥חַר אַפְּךָ֖ בְּעַבְדֶּ֑ךָ כִּ֥י כָמ֖וֹךָ כְּפַרְעֹֽה: אֲדֹנִ֣י שָׁאַ֔ל אֶת־עֲבָדָ֖יו לֵאמֹ֑ר הֲיֵשׁ־לָכֶ֥ם אָ֖ב אוֹ־אָֽח: וַנֹּ֙אמֶר֙ אֶל־אֲדֹנִ֔י יֶשׁ־לָ֙נוּ֙ אָ֣ב זָקֵ֔ן וְיֶ֥לֶד זְקֻנִ֖ים קָטָ֑ן וְאָחִ֣יו מֵ֗ת וַיִּוָּתֵ֨ר ה֤וּא לְבַדּ֙וֹ לְאִמּ֔וֹ וְאָבִ֖יו אֲהֵבֽוֹ: *וַתֹּ֙אמֶר֙ אֶל־עֲבָדֶ֔יךָ הוֹרִדֻ֖הוּ אֵלָ֑י וְאָשִׂ֥ימָה עֵינִ֖י לוי

עָלָֽיו: וַנֹּ֙אמֶר֙ אֶל־אֲדֹנִ֔י לֹא־יוּכַ֥ל הַנַּ֖עַר לַעֲזֹ֣ב אֶת־אָבִ֑יו וְעָזַ֥ב אֶת־אָבִ֖יו וָמֵֽת: וַתֹּ֙אמֶר֙ אֶל־עֲבָדֶ֔יךָ אִם־לֹ֥א יֵרֵ֛ד אֲחִיכֶ֥ם הַקָּטֹ֖ן אִתְּכֶ֑ם לֹ֥א תֹסִפ֖וּן לִרְא֥וֹת פָּנָֽי:

וַיְהִי֙ כִּ֣י עָלִ֔ינוּ אֶֽל־עַבְדְּךָ֖ אָבִ֑י וַנַּ֨גֶּד־ל֔וֹ אֵ֖ת דִּבְרֵ֥י אֲדֹנִֽי: *וַיֹּ֖אמֶר אָבִ֑ינוּ שֻׁ֖בוּ ישראל

שִׁבְרוּ־לָ֖נוּ מְעַט־אֹֽכֶל: וַנֹּ֕אמֶר לֹ֥א נוּכַ֖ל לָרֶ֑דֶת אִם־יֵ֩שׁ אָחִ֨ינוּ הַקָּטֹ֤ן אִתָּ֙נוּ֙ וְיָרַ֔דְנוּ כִּי־לֹ֣א נוּכַ֗ל לִרְאוֹת֙ פְּנֵ֣י הָאִ֔ישׁ וְאָחִ֥ינוּ הַקָּטֹ֖ן אֵינֶ֥נּוּ אִתָּֽנוּ: וַיֹּ֛אמֶר עַבְדְּךָ֥ אָבִ֖י אֵלֵ֑ינוּ אַתֶּ֣ם יְדַעְתֶּ֔ם כִּ֥י שְׁנַ֖יִם יָֽלְדָה־לִּ֥י אִשְׁתִּֽי: וַיֵּצֵ֤א הָֽאֶחָד֙ מֵֽאִתִּ֔י וָאֹמַ֕ר אַ֖ךְ טָרֹ֣ף טֹרָ֑ף וְלֹ֥א רְאִיתִ֖יו עַד־הֵֽנָּה: וּלְקַחְתֶּ֧ם גַּם־אֶת־זֶ֛ה מֵעִ֥ם פָּנַ֖י וְקָרָ֣הוּ אָס֑וֹן וְהֽוֹרַדְתֶּ֧ם אֶת־שֵׂיבָתִ֛י בְּרָעָ֖ה שְׁאֹֽלָה: וְעַתָּ֗ה כְּבֹאִי֙ אֶל־עַבְדְּךָ֣ אָבִ֔י וְהַנַּ֖עַר אֵינֶ֣נּוּ אִתָּ֑נוּ וְנַפְשׁ֖וֹ קְשׁוּרָ֥ה בְנַפְשֽׁוֹ:

VAYHI
ויחי

בראשית
מז:כח-מח:ט

וַיְחִ֤י יַֽעֲקֹב֙ בְּאֶ֣רֶץ מִצְרַ֔יִם שְׁבַ֥ע עֶשְׂרֵ֖ה שָׁנָ֑ה וַיְהִ֤י יְמֵֽי־יַֽעֲקֹב֙ שְׁנֵ֣י חַיָּ֔יו שֶׁ֣בַע שָׁנִ֔ים וְאַרְבָּעִ֥ים וּמְאַ֖ת שָׁנָֽה: וַיִּקְרְב֣וּ יְמֵֽי־יִשְׂרָאֵל֘ לָמוּת֒ וַיִּקְרָ֣א ׀ לִבְנ֣וֹ לְיוֹסֵ֗ף וַיֹּ֤אמֶר לוֹ֙ אִם־נָ֨א מָצָ֤אתִי חֵן֙ בְּעֵינֶ֔יךָ שִֽׂים־נָ֥א יָדְךָ֖ תַּ֣חַת יְרֵכִ֑י וְעָשִׂ֤יתָ עִמָּדִי֙ חֶ֣סֶד וֶֽאֱמֶ֔ת אַל־נָ֥א תִקְבְּרֵ֖נִי בְּמִצְרָֽיִם: וְשָֽׁכַבְתִּי֙ עִם־אֲבֹתַ֔י וּנְשָׂאתַ֙נִי֙ מִמִּצְרַ֔יִם וּקְבַרְתַּ֖נִי בִּקְבֻֽרָתָ֑ם וַיֹּאמַ֕ר אָֽנֹכִ֖י אֶֽעֱשֶׂ֥ה כִדְבָרֶֽךָ: וַיֹּ֗אמֶר הִשָּֽׁבְעָה֙ לִ֔י וַיִּשָּׁבַ֖ע ל֑וֹ וַיִּשְׁתַּ֥חוּ יִשְׂרָאֵ֖ל עַל־רֹ֥אשׁ הַמִּטָּֽה:

וַיְהִ֗י אַֽחֲרֵי֙ הַדְּבָרִ֣ים הָאֵ֔לֶּה וַיֹּ֣אמֶר לְיוֹסֵ֔ף הִנֵּ֥ה אָבִ֖יךָ חֹלֶ֑ה וַיִּקַּ֞ח אֶת־שְׁנֵ֤י בָנָיו֙ לוי

עִמּ֔וֹ אֶת־מְנַשֶּׁ֖ה וְאֶת־אֶפְרָֽיִם: וַיַּגֵּ֣ד לְיַֽעֲקֹ֔ב וַיֹּ֕אמֶר הִנֵּ֛ה בִּנְךָ֥ יוֹסֵ֖ף בָּ֣א אֵלֶ֑יךָ וַיִּתְחַזֵּק֙ יִשְׂרָאֵ֔ל וַיֵּ֖שֶׁב עַל־הַמִּטָּֽה: וַיֹּ֤אמֶר יַֽעֲקֹב֙ אֶל־יוֹסֵ֔ף אֵ֥ל שַׁדַּ֛י נִרְאָֽה־אֵלַ֥י בְּל֖וּז בְּאֶ֣רֶץ כְּנָ֑עַן וַיְבָ֖רֶךְ אֹתִֽי: *וַיֹּ֣אמֶר אֵלַ֗י הִנְנִ֤י מַפְרְךָ֙ וְהִרְבִּיתִ֔ךָ וּנְתַתִּ֖יךָ ישראל

לִקְהַ֣ל עַמִּ֑ים וְנָ֨תַתִּ֜י אֶת־הָאָ֧רֶץ הַזֹּ֛את לְזַרְעֲךָ֥ אַֽחֲרֶ֖יךָ אֲחֻזַּ֥ת עוֹלָֽם: וְעַתָּ֡ה שְׁנֵֽי־בָנֶיךָ֩ הַנּֽוֹלָדִ֨ים לְךָ֜ בְּאֶ֣רֶץ מִצְרַ֗יִם עַד־בֹּאִ֥י אֵלֶ֛יךָ מִצְרַ֖יְמָה לִי־הֵ֑ם אֶפְרַ֙יִם֙ וּמְנַשֶּׁ֔ה כִּרְאוּבֵ֥ן וְשִׁמְע֖וֹן יִֽהְיוּ־לִֽי: וּמֽוֹלַדְתְּךָ֛ אֲשֶׁר־הוֹלַ֥דְתָּ אַֽחֲרֵיהֶ֖ם לְךָ֣ יִֽהְי֑וּ

עַל שֵׁם אֲחֵיהֶם יִקָּרְאוּ בְּנַחֲלָתָם: וַאֲנִי ׀ בְּבֹאִי מִפַּדָּן מֵתָה עָלַי רָחֵל בְּאֶרֶץ
כְּנַעַן בַּדֶּרֶךְ בְּעוֹד כִּבְרַת־אֶרֶץ לָבֹא אֶפְרָתָה וָאֶקְבְּרֶהָ שָּׁם בְּדֶרֶךְ אֶפְרָת
הִוא בֵּית לָחֶם: וַיַּרְא יִשְׂרָאֵל אֶת־בְּנֵי יוֹסֵף וַיֹּאמֶר מִי־אֵלֶּה: וַיֹּאמֶר יוֹסֵף
אֶל־אָבִיו בָּנַי הֵם אֲשֶׁר־נָתַן־לִי אֱלֹהִים בָּזֶה וַיֹּאמַר קָחֶם־נָא אֵלַי וַאֲבָרֲכֵם:

שמות

שמות
א:א-ג

וְאֵלֶּה שְׁמוֹת בְּנֵי יִשְׂרָאֵל הַבָּאִים מִצְרָיְמָה אֵת יַעֲקֹב אִישׁ וּבֵיתוֹ בָּאוּ:
רְאוּבֵן שִׁמְעוֹן לֵוִי וִיהוּדָה: יִשָּׂשכָר זְבוּלֻן וּבִנְיָמִן: דָּן וְנַפְתָּלִי גָּד וְאָשֵׁר:
וַיְהִי כָּל־נֶפֶשׁ יֹצְאֵי יֶרֶךְ־יַעֲקֹב שִׁבְעִים נָפֶשׁ וְיוֹסֵף הָיָה בְמִצְרָיִם: וַיָּמָת יוֹסֵף
וְכָל־אֶחָיו וְכֹל הַדּוֹר הַהוּא: וּבְנֵי יִשְׂרָאֵל פָּרוּ וַיִּשְׁרְצוּ וַיִּרְבּוּ וַיַּעַצְמוּ בִּמְאֹד
מְאֹד וַתִּמָּלֵא הָאָרֶץ אֹתָם:

לוי

וַיָּקָם מֶלֶךְ־חָדָשׁ עַל־מִצְרָיִם אֲשֶׁר לֹא־יָדַע אֶת־יוֹסֵף: וַיֹּאמֶר אֶל־עַמּוֹ הִנֵּה עַם
בְּנֵי יִשְׂרָאֵל רַב וְעָצוּם מִמֶּנּוּ: הָבָה נִתְחַכְּמָה לוֹ פֶּן־יִרְבֶּה וְהָיָה כִּי־תִקְרֶאנָה
מִלְחָמָה וְנוֹסַף גַּם־הוּא עַל־שֹׂנְאֵינוּ וְנִלְחַם־בָּנוּ וְעָלָה מִן־הָאָרֶץ: וַיָּשִׂימוּ
עָלָיו שָׂרֵי מִסִּים לְמַעַן עַנֹּתוֹ בְּסִבְלֹתָם וַיִּבֶן עָרֵי מִסְכְּנוֹת לְפַרְעֹה אֶת־פִּתֹם
וְאֶת־רַעַמְסֵס: וְכַאֲשֶׁר יְעַנּוּ אֹתוֹ כֵּן יִרְבֶּה וְכֵן יִפְרֹץ וַיָּקֻצוּ מִפְּנֵי בְּנֵי יִשְׂרָאֵל:

ישראל

*וַיַּעֲבִדוּ מִצְרַיִם אֶת־בְּנֵי יִשְׂרָאֵל בְּפָרֶךְ: וַיְמָרְרוּ אֶת־חַיֵּיהֶם בַּעֲבֹדָה קָשָׁה
בְּחֹמֶר וּבִלְבֵנִים וּבְכָל־עֲבֹדָה בַּשָּׂדֶה אֵת כָּל־עֲבֹדָתָם אֲשֶׁר־עָבְדוּ בָהֶם
בְּפָרֶךְ: וַיֹּאמֶר מֶלֶךְ מִצְרַיִם לַמְיַלְּדֹת הָעִבְרִיֹּת אֲשֶׁר שֵׁם הָאַחַת שִׁפְרָה וְשֵׁם
הַשֵּׁנִית פּוּעָה: וַיֹּאמֶר בְּיַלֶּדְכֶן אֶת־הָעִבְרִיּוֹת וּרְאִיתֶן עַל־הָאָבְנָיִם אִם־בֵּן
הוּא וַהֲמִתֶּן אֹתוֹ וְאִם־בַּת הִוא וָחָיָה: וַתִּירֶאןָ הַמְיַלְּדֹת אֶת־הָאֱלֹהִים וְלֹא
עָשׂוּ כַּאֲשֶׁר דִּבֶּר אֲלֵיהֶן מֶלֶךְ מִצְרָיִם וַתְּחַיֶּיןָ אֶת־הַיְלָדִים:

וארא

שמות
ו:ב-ג

וַיְדַבֵּר אֱלֹהִים אֶל־מֹשֶׁה וַיֹּאמֶר אֵלָיו אֲנִי יְהוָה: וָאֵרָא אֶל־אַבְרָהָם אֶל־יִצְחָק
וְאֶל־יַעֲקֹב בְּאֵל שַׁדָּי וּשְׁמִי יְהוָה לֹא נוֹדַעְתִּי לָהֶם: וְגַם הֲקִמֹתִי אֶת־בְּרִיתִי
אִתָּם לָתֵת לָהֶם אֶת־אֶרֶץ כְּנָעַן אֵת אֶרֶץ מְגֻרֵיהֶם אֲשֶׁר־גָּרוּ בָהּ: וְגַם ׀ אֲנִי
שָׁמַעְתִּי אֶת־נַאֲקַת בְּנֵי יִשְׂרָאֵל אֲשֶׁר מִצְרַיִם מַעֲבִדִים אֹתָם וָאֶזְכֹּר אֶת־

בְּרִיתִי: *לָכֵ֞ן אֱמֹ֣ר לִבְנֵֽי־יִשְׂרָאֵל֮ אֲנִ֣י יְהֹוָה֒ וְהוֹצֵאתִ֣י אֶתְכֶ֗ם מִתַּ֙חַת֙ סִבְלֹ֣ת לוי
מִצְרַ֔יִם וְהִצַּלְתִּ֥י אֶתְכֶ֖ם מֵעֲבֹֽדָתָ֑ם וְגָאַלְתִּ֤י אֶתְכֶם֙ בִּזְר֣וֹעַ נְטוּיָ֔ה וּבִשְׁפָטִ֖ים
גְּדֹלִֽים: וְלָקַחְתִּ֨י אֶתְכֶ֥ם לִי֙ לְעָ֔ם וְהָיִ֥יתִי לָכֶ֖ם לֵֽאלֹהִ֑ים וִֽידַעְתֶּ֗ם כִּ֣י אֲנִ֤י יְהֹוָה֙
אֱלֹ֣הֵיכֶ֔ם הַמּוֹצִ֣יא אֶתְכֶ֔ם מִתַּ֖חַת סִבְל֥וֹת מִצְרָֽיִם: וְהֵבֵאתִ֤י אֶתְכֶם֙ אֶל־הָאָ֔רֶץ
אֲשֶׁ֤ר נָשָׂ֙אתִי֙ אֶת־יָדִ֔י לָתֵ֣ת אֹתָ֔הּ לְאַבְרָהָ֥ם לְיִצְחָ֖ק וּֽלְיַעֲקֹ֑ב וְנָתַתִּ֨י אֹתָ֥הּ לָכֶ֛ם
מֽוֹרָשָׁ֖ה אֲנִ֥י יְהֹוָֽה: וַיְדַבֵּ֥ר מֹשֶׁ֛ה כֵּ֖ן אֶל־בְּנֵ֣י יִשְׂרָאֵ֑ל וְלֹ֤א שָֽׁמְעוּ֙ אֶל־מֹשֶׁ֔ה
מִקֹּ֣צֶר ר֔וּחַ וּמֵעֲבֹדָ֖ה קָשָֽׁה:

וַיְדַבֵּ֥ר יְהֹוָ֖ה אֶל־מֹשֶׁ֥ה לֵּאמֹֽר: בֹּ֣א דַבֵּ֔ר אֶל־פַּרְעֹ֖ה מֶ֣לֶךְ מִצְרָ֑יִם וִֽישַׁלַּ֥ח אֶת־ ישראל
בְּנֵֽי־יִשְׂרָאֵ֖ל מֵֽאַרְצֽוֹ: וַיְדַבֵּ֣ר מֹשֶׁ֔ה לִפְנֵ֥י יְהֹוָ֖ה לֵאמֹ֑ר הֵ֤ן בְּנֵֽי־יִשְׂרָאֵל֙ לֹֽא־שָׁמְע֣וּ
אֵלַ֔י וְאֵיךְ֙ יִשְׁמָעֵ֣נִי פַרְעֹ֔ה וַאֲנִ֖י עֲרַ֥ל שְׂפָתָֽיִם:

וַיְדַבֵּ֣ר יְהֹוָ֔ה אֶל־מֹשֶׁ֖ה וְאֶֽל־אַהֲרֹ֑ן וַיְצַוֵּם֙ אֶל־בְּנֵ֣י יִשְׂרָאֵ֔ל וְאֶל־פַּרְעֹ֖ה מֶ֣לֶךְ
מִצְרָ֑יִם לְהוֹצִ֥יא אֶת־בְּנֵֽי־יִשְׂרָאֵ֖ל מֵאֶ֥רֶץ מִצְרָֽיִם:

וַיֹּ֤אמֶר יְהֹוָה֙ אֶל־מֹשֶׁ֔ה בֹּ֖א אֶל־פַּרְעֹ֑ה כִּֽי־אֲנִ֞י הִכְבַּ֤דְתִּי אֶת־לִבּוֹ֙ וְאֶת־לֵ֣ב שמות
עֲבָדָ֔יו לְמַ֗עַן שִׁתִ֛י אֹתֹתַ֥י אֵ֖לֶּה בְּקִרְבּֽוֹ: וּלְמַ֡עַן תְּסַפֵּר֩ בְּאׇזְנֵ֨י בִנְךָ֜ וּבֶן־בִּנְךָ֗ אֵ֣ת יֵ׳ֹא-יֵ״א
אֲשֶׁ֤ר הִתְעַלַּ֙לְתִּי֙ בְּמִצְרַ֔יִם וְאֶת־אֹתֹתַ֖י אֲשֶׁר־שַׂ֣מְתִּי בָ֑ם וִֽידַעְתֶּ֖ם כִּֽי־אֲנִ֥י יְהֹוָֽה:
וַיָּבֹ֨א מֹשֶׁ֣ה וְאַהֲרֹן֮ אֶל־פַּרְעֹה֒ וַיֹּֽאמְר֣וּ אֵלָ֗יו כֹּֽה־אָמַ֤ר יְהֹוָה֙ אֱלֹהֵ֣י הָֽעִבְרִ֔ים
עַד־מָתַ֣י מֵאַ֔נְתָּ לֵעָנֹ֖ת מִפָּנָ֑י שַׁלַּ֥ח עַמִּ֖י וְיַֽעַבְדֻֽנִי: *כִּ֣י אִם־מָאֵ֣ן אַתָּה֮ לְשַׁלֵּ֣חַ לוי
אֶת־עַמִּי֒ הִנְנִ֣י מֵבִ֥יא מָחָ֛ר אַרְבֶּ֖ה בִּגְבֻלֶֽךָ: וְכִסָּה֙ אֶת־עֵ֣ין הָאָ֔רֶץ וְלֹ֥א יוּכַ֖ל
לִרְאֹ֣ת אֶת־הָאָ֑רֶץ וְאָכַ֣ל ׀ אֶת־יֶ֣תֶר הַפְּלֵטָ֗ה הַנִּשְׁאֶ֤רֶת לָכֶם֙ מִן־הַבָּרָ֔ד וְאָכַל֙
אֶת־כׇּל־הָעֵ֔ץ הַצֹּמֵ֥חַ לָכֶ֖ם מִן־הַשָּׂדֶֽה: וּמָלְא֨וּ בָתֶּ֜יךָ וּבָתֵּ֣י כׇל־עֲבָדֶ֗יךָ וּבָתֵּ֣י
כׇל־מִצְרַ֔יִם אֲשֶׁ֨ר לֹא־רָא֤וּ אֲבֹתֶ֙יךָ֙ וַֽאֲב֣וֹת אֲבֹתֶ֔יךָ מִיּ֗וֹם הֱיוֹתָם֙ עַל־הָ֣אֲדָמָ֔ה
עַ֖ד הַיּ֣וֹם הַזֶּ֑ה וַיִּ֥פֶן וַיֵּצֵ֖א מֵעִ֥ם פַּרְעֹֽה: וַיֹּֽאמְרוּ֩ עַבְדֵ֨י פַרְעֹ֜ה אֵלָ֗יו עַד־מָתַי֙ ישראל
יִהְיֶ֨ה זֶ֥ה לָ֙נוּ֙ לְמוֹקֵ֔שׁ שַׁלַּח֙ אֶת־הָ֣אֲנָשִׁ֔ים וְיַֽעַבְד֖וּ אֶת־יְהֹוָ֣ה אֱלֹֽהֵיהֶ֑ם הֲטֶ֣רֶם
תֵּדַ֔ע כִּ֥י אָבְדָ֖ה מִצְרָֽיִם: וַיּוּשַׁ֞ב אֶת־מֹשֶׁ֤ה וְאֶֽת־אַהֲרֹן֙ אֶל־פַּרְעֹ֔ה וַיֹּ֣אמֶר
אֲלֵהֶ֗ם לְכ֥וּ עִבְד֖וּ אֶת־יְהֹוָ֣ה אֱלֹֽהֵיכֶ֑ם מִ֥י וָמִ֖י הַהֹֽלְכִֽים: וַיֹּ֣אמֶר מֹשֶׁ֔ה בִּנְעָרֵ֥ינוּ
וּבִזְקֵנֵ֖ינוּ נֵלֵ֑ךְ בְּבָנֵ֨ינוּ וּבִבְנוֹתֵ֜נוּ בְּצֹאנֵ֤נוּ וּבִבְקָרֵ֙נוּ֙ נֵלֵ֔ךְ כִּ֥י חַג־יְהֹוָ֖ה לָֽנוּ: וַיֹּ֣אמֶר

אֱלֹהִים יְהִי כֵן יְהוָה עִמָּכֶם כַּאֲשֶׁר אֲשַׁלַּח אֶתְכֶם וְאֶת־טַפְּכֶם רְאוּ כִּי רָעָה
נֶגֶד פְּנֵיכֶם: לֹא כֵן לְכוּ־נָא הַגְּבָרִים וְעִבְדוּ אֶת־יְהוָֹה כִּי אֹתָהּ אַתֶּם מְבַקְשִׁים
וַיְגָרֶשׁ אֹתָם מֵאֵת פְּנֵי פַרְעֹה:

בשלח

BESHALLAH

שמות י״ג: י״ז-י״ח וַיְהִי בְּשַׁלַּח פַּרְעֹה אֶת־הָעָם וְלֹא־נָחָם אֱלֹהִים דֶּרֶךְ אֶרֶץ פְּלִשְׁתִּים כִּי קָרוֹב
הוּא כִּי ׀ אָמַר אֱלֹהִים פֶּן־יִנָּחֵם הָעָם בִּרְאֹתָם מִלְחָמָה וְשָׁבוּ מִצְרָיְמָה: וַיַּסֵּב
אֱלֹהִים ׀ אֶת־הָעָם דֶּרֶךְ הַמִּדְבָּר יַם־סוּף וַחֲמֻשִׁים עָלוּ בְנֵי־יִשְׂרָאֵל מֵאֶרֶץ
מִצְרָיִם: וַיִּקַּח מֹשֶׁה אֶת־עַצְמוֹת יוֹסֵף עִמּוֹ כִּי הַשְׁבֵּעַ הִשְׁבִּיעַ אֶת־בְּנֵי יִשְׂרָאֵל
לֵאמֹר פָּקֹד יִפְקֹד אֱלֹהִים אֶתְכֶם וְהַעֲלִיתֶם אֶת־עַצְמֹתַי מִזֶּה אִתְּכֶם: וַיִּסְעוּ
מִסֻּכֹּת וַיַּחֲנוּ בְאֵתָם בִּקְצֵה הַמִּדְבָּר: וַיהוָה הֹלֵךְ לִפְנֵיהֶם יוֹמָם בְּעַמּוּד עָנָן
לַנְחֹתָם הַדֶּרֶךְ וְלַיְלָה בְּעַמּוּד אֵשׁ לְהָאִיר לָהֶם לָלֶכֶת יוֹמָם וָלָיְלָה: לֹא־יָמִישׁ
עַמּוּד הֶעָנָן יוֹמָם וְעַמּוּד הָאֵשׁ לָיְלָה לִפְנֵי הָעָם:

לוי וַיְדַבֵּר יְהוָֹה אֶל־מֹשֶׁה לֵּאמֹר: דַּבֵּר אֶל־בְּנֵי יִשְׂרָאֵל וְיָשֻׁבוּ וְיַחֲנוּ לִפְנֵי פִּי
הַחִירֹת בֵּין מִגְדֹּל וּבֵין הַיָּם לִפְנֵי בַּעַל צְפֹן נִכְחוֹ תַחֲנוּ עַל־הַיָּם: וְאָמַר פַּרְעֹה
לִבְנֵי יִשְׂרָאֵל נְבֻכִים הֵם בָּאָרֶץ סָגַר עֲלֵיהֶם הַמִּדְבָּר: וְחִזַּקְתִּי אֶת־לֵב־פַּרְעֹה
וְרָדַף אַחֲרֵיהֶם וְאִכָּבְדָה בְּפַרְעֹה וּבְכָל־חֵילוֹ וְיָדְעוּ מִצְרַיִם כִּי־אֲנִי יְהוָֹה וַיַּעֲשׂוּ
כֵן:

ישראל וַיֻּגַּד לְמֶלֶךְ מִצְרַיִם כִּי בָרַח הָעָם וַיֵּהָפֵךְ לְבַב פַּרְעֹה וַעֲבָדָיו אֶל־הָעָם
וַיֹּאמְרוּ מַה־זֹּאת עָשִׂינוּ כִּי־שִׁלַּחְנוּ אֶת־יִשְׂרָאֵל מֵעָבְדֵנוּ: וַיֶּאְסֹר אֶת־רִכְבּוֹ
וְאֶת־עַמּוֹ לָקַח עִמּוֹ: וַיִּקַּח שֵׁשׁ־מֵאוֹת רֶכֶב בָּחוּר וְכֹל רֶכֶב מִצְרָיִם וְשָׁלִשִׁם
עַל־כֻּלּוֹ: וַיְחַזֵּק יְהוָֹה אֶת־לֵב פַּרְעֹה מֶלֶךְ מִצְרַיִם וַיִּרְדֹּף אַחֲרֵי בְּנֵי יִשְׂרָאֵל
וּבְנֵי יִשְׂרָאֵל יֹצְאִים בְּיָד רָמָה:

יתרו

YITRO

שמות י״ח: א׳-ב׳ וַיִּשְׁמַע יִתְרוֹ כֹהֵן מִדְיָן חֹתֵן מֹשֶׁה אֵת כָּל־אֲשֶׁר עָשָׂה אֱלֹהִים לְמֹשֶׁה
וּלְיִשְׂרָאֵל עַמּוֹ כִּי־הוֹצִיא יְהוָֹה אֶת־יִשְׂרָאֵל מִמִּצְרָיִם: וַיִּקַּח יִתְרוֹ חֹתֵן
מֹשֶׁה אֶת־צִפֹּרָה אֵשֶׁת מֹשֶׁה אַחַר שִׁלּוּחֶיהָ: וְאֵת שְׁנֵי בָנֶיהָ אֲשֶׁר שֵׁם הָאֶחָד
גֵּרְשֹׁם כִּי אָמַר גֵּר הָיִיתִי בְּאֶרֶץ נָכְרִיָּה: וְשֵׁם הָאֶחָד אֱלִיעֶזֶר כִּי־אֱלֹהֵי אָבִ

בְּעֶזְרִי וַיַּצִּלֵנִי מֵחֶרֶב פַּרְעֹה: *וַיָּבֹא יִתְרוֹ חֹתֵן מֹשֶׁה וּבָנָיו וְאִשְׁתּוֹ אֶל־מֹשֶׁה   לוי
אֶל־הַמִּדְבָּר אֲשֶׁר־הוּא חֹנֶה שָׁם הַר הָאֱלֹהִים: וַיֹּאמֶר אֶל־מֹשֶׁה אֲנִי חֹתֶנְךָ
יִתְרוֹ בָּא אֵלֶיךָ וְאִשְׁתְּךָ וּשְׁנֵי בָנֶיהָ עִמָּהּ: וַיֵּצֵא מֹשֶׁה לִקְרַאת חֹתְנוֹ וַיִּשְׁתַּחוּ
וַיִּשַּׁק־לוֹ וַיִּשְׁאֲלוּ אִישׁ־לְרֵעֵהוּ לְשָׁלוֹם וַיָּבֹאוּ הָאֹהֱלָה: וַיְסַפֵּר מֹשֶׁה לְחֹתְנוֹ
אֵת כָּל־אֲשֶׁר עָשָׂה יְהוָה לְפַרְעֹה וּלְמִצְרַיִם עַל אוֹדֹת יִשְׂרָאֵל אֵת כָּל־הַתְּלָאָה
אֲשֶׁר מְצָאָתַם בַּדֶּרֶךְ וַיַּצִּלֵם יְהוָה: *וַיִּחַדְּ יִתְרוֹ עַל כָּל־הַטּוֹבָה אֲשֶׁר־עָשָׂה   ישראל
יְהוָה לְיִשְׂרָאֵל אֲשֶׁר הִצִּילוֹ מִיַּד מִצְרָיִם: וַיֹּאמֶר יִתְרוֹ בָּרוּךְ יְהוָה אֲשֶׁר הִצִּיל
אֶתְכֶם מִיַּד מִצְרַיִם וּמִיַּד פַּרְעֹה אֲשֶׁר הִצִּיל אֶת־הָעָם מִתַּחַת יַד־מִצְרָיִם:
עַתָּה יָדַעְתִּי כִּי־גָדוֹל יְהוָה מִכָּל־הָאֱלֹהִים כִּי בַדָּבָר אֲשֶׁר זָדוּ עֲלֵיהֶם: וַיִּקַּח
יִתְרוֹ חֹתֵן מֹשֶׁה עֹלָה וּזְבָחִים לֵאלֹהִים וַיָּבֹא אַהֲרֹן וְכֹל ׀ זִקְנֵי יִשְׂרָאֵל לֶאֱכָל־
לֶחֶם עִם־חֹתֵן מֹשֶׁה לִפְנֵי הָאֱלֹהִים:

MISHPATIM   משפטים

וְאֵלֶּה הַמִּשְׁפָּטִים אֲשֶׁר תָּשִׂים לִפְנֵיהֶם: כִּי תִקְנֶה עֶבֶד עִבְרִי שֵׁשׁ שָׁנִים   שמות כא
יַעֲבֹד וּבַשְּׁבִעִת יֵצֵא לַחָפְשִׁי חִנָּם: אִם־בְּגַפּוֹ יָבֹא בְּגַפּוֹ יֵצֵא אִם־בַּעַל אִשָּׁה   א-יט
הוּא וְיָצְאָה אִשְׁתּוֹ עִמּוֹ: אִם־אֲדֹנָיו יִתֶּן־לוֹ אִשָּׁה וְיָלְדָה־לוֹ בָנִים אוֹ בָנוֹת
הָאִשָּׁה וִילָדֶיהָ תִּהְיֶה לַאדֹנֶיהָ וְהוּא יֵצֵא בְגַפּוֹ: וְאִם־אָמֹר יֹאמַר הָעֶבֶד
אָהַבְתִּי אֶת־אֲדֹנִי אֶת־אִשְׁתִּי וְאֶת־בָּנָי לֹא אֵצֵא חָפְשִׁי: וְהִגִּישׁוֹ אֲדֹנָיו
אֶל־הָאֱלֹהִים וְהִגִּישׁוֹ אֶל־הַדֶּלֶת אוֹ אֶל־הַמְּזוּזָה וְרָצַע אֲדֹנָיו אֶת־אָזְנוֹ
בַּמַּרְצֵעַ וַעֲבָדוֹ לְעֹלָם: *וְכִי־יִמְכֹּר אִישׁ אֶת־בִּתּוֹ לְאָמָה לֹא   לוי
תֵצֵא כְּצֵאת הָעֲבָדִים: אִם־רָעָה בְּעֵינֵי אֲדֹנֶיהָ אֲשֶׁר־לא יְעָדָהּ וְהֶפְדָּהּ לְעַם   לוי
נָכְרִי לֹא־יִמְשֹׁל לְמָכְרָהּ בְּבִגְדוֹ־בָהּ: וְאִם־לִבְנוֹ יִיעָדֶנָּה כְּמִשְׁפַּט הַבָּנוֹת
יַעֲשֶׂה־לָּהּ: אִם־אַחֶרֶת יִקַּח־לוֹ שְׁאֵרָהּ כְּסוּתָהּ וְעֹנָתָהּ לֹא יִגְרָע: וְאִם־שְׁלָשׁ־
אֵלֶּה לֹא יַעֲשֶׂה לָהּ וְיָצְאָה חִנָּם אֵין כָּסֶף: *מַכֵּה אִישׁ וָמֵת מוֹת   ישראל
יוּמָת: וַאֲשֶׁר לֹא צָדָה וְהָאֱלֹהִים אִנָּה לְיָדוֹ וְשַׂמְתִּי לְךָ מָקוֹם אֲשֶׁר יָנוּס
שָׁמָּה: וְכִי־יָזִד אִישׁ עַל־רֵעֵהוּ לְהָרְגוֹ בְעָרְמָה מֵעִם מִזְבְּחִי
תִּקָּחֶנּוּ לָמוּת: וּמַכֵּה אָבִיו וְאִמּוֹ מוֹת יוּמָת: וְגֹנֵב
אִישׁ וּמְכָרוֹ וְנִמְצָא בְיָדוֹ מוֹת יוּמָת: וּמְקַלֵּל אָבִיו וְאִמּוֹ מוֹת

וְכִי־יְרִיבֻן אֲנָשִׁים וְהִכָּה־אִישׁ אֶת־רֵעֵהוּ בְּאֶבֶן אוֹ בְאֶגְרֹף יומת:
וְלֹא יָמוּת וְנָפַל לְמִשְׁכָּב: אִם־יָקוּם וְהִתְהַלֵּךְ בַּחוּץ עַל־מִשְׁעַנְתּוֹ וְנִקָּה הַמַּכֶּה
רַק שִׁבְתּוֹ יִתֵּן וְרַפֹּא יְרַפֵּא:

תרומה
TERUMA

וַיְדַבֵּר יְהוָֹה אֶל־מֹשֶׁה לֵּאמֹר: דַּבֵּר אֶל־בְּנֵי יִשְׂרָאֵל וְיִקְחוּ־לִי תְּרוּמָה מֵאֵת
כָּל־אִישׁ אֲשֶׁר יִדְּבֶנּוּ לִבּוֹ תִּקְחוּ אֶת־תְּרוּמָתִי: וְזֹאת הַתְּרוּמָה אֲשֶׁר תִּקְחוּ
מֵאִתָּם זָהָב וָכֶסֶף וּנְחֹשֶׁת: וּתְכֵלֶת וְאַרְגָּמָן וְתוֹלַעַת שָׁנִי וְשֵׁשׁ וְעִזִּים: וְעֹרֹת
אֵילִם מְאָדָּמִים וְעֹרֹת תְּחָשִׁים וַעֲצֵי שִׁטִּים: שֶׁמֶן לַמָּאֹר בְּשָׂמִים לְשֶׁמֶן
הַמִּשְׁחָה וְלִקְטֹרֶת הַסַּמִּים: אַבְנֵי־שֹׁהַם וְאַבְנֵי מִלֻּאִים לָאֵפֹד וְלַחֹשֶׁן: וְעָשׂוּ
לִי מִקְדָּשׁ וְשָׁכַנְתִּי בְּתוֹכָם: כְּכֹל אֲשֶׁר אֲנִי מַרְאֶה אוֹתְךָ אֵת תַּבְנִית הַמִּשְׁכָּן
וְאֵת תַּבְנִית כָּל־כֵּלָיו וְכֵן תַּעֲשׂוּ:   *וְעָשׂוּ אֲרוֹן עֲצֵי שִׁטִּים אַמָּתַיִם
וָחֵצִי אָרְכּוֹ וְאַמָּה וָחֵצִי רָחְבּוֹ וְאַמָּה וָחֵצִי קֹמָתוֹ: וְצִפִּיתָ אֹתוֹ זָהָב טָהוֹר
מִבַּיִת וּמִחוּץ תְּצַפֶּנּוּ וְעָשִׂיתָ עָלָיו זֵר זָהָב סָבִיב: וְיָצַקְתָּ לּוֹ אַרְבַּע טַבְּעֹת
זָהָב וְנָתַתָּה עַל אַרְבַּע פַּעֲמֹתָיו וּשְׁתֵּי טַבָּעֹת עַל־צַלְעוֹ הָאֶחָת וּשְׁתֵּי טַבָּעֹת
עַל־צַלְעוֹ הַשֵּׁנִית: וְעָשִׂיתָ בַדֵּי עֲצֵי שִׁטִּים וְצִפִּיתָ אֹתָם זָהָב: וְהֵבֵאתָ אֶת־
הַבַּדִּים בַּטַּבָּעֹת עַל צַלְעֹת הָאָרֹן לָשֵׂאת אֶת־הָאָרֹן בָּהֶם: בְּטַבְּעֹת הָאָרֹן
יִהְיוּ הַבַּדִּים לֹא יָסֻרוּ מִמֶּנּוּ: וְנָתַתָּ אֶל־הָאָרֹן אֵת הָעֵדֻת אֲשֶׁר אֶתֵּן אֵלֶיךָ:

תצוה
TETZAVEH

וְאַתָּה תְּצַוֶּה | אֶת־בְּנֵי יִשְׂרָאֵל וְיִקְחוּ אֵלֶיךָ שֶׁמֶן זַיִת זָךְ כָּתִית לַמָּאוֹר
לְהַעֲלֹת נֵר תָּמִיד: בְּאֹהֶל מוֹעֵד מִחוּץ לַפָּרֹכֶת אֲשֶׁר עַל־הָעֵדֻת יַעֲרֹךְ
אֹתוֹ אַהֲרֹן וּבָנָיו מֵעֶרֶב עַד־בֹּקֶר לִפְנֵי יְהוָֹה חֻקַּת עוֹלָם לְדֹרֹתָם מֵאֵת בְּנֵי
יִשְׂרָאֵל: וְאַתָּה הַקְרֵב אֵלֶיךָ אֶת־אַהֲרֹן אָחִיךָ וְאֶת־בָּנָיו אִתּוֹ מִתּוֹךְ
בְּנֵי יִשְׂרָאֵל לְכַהֲנוֹ־לִי אַהֲרֹן נָדָב וַאֲבִיהוּא אֶלְעָזָר וְאִיתָמָר בְּנֵי אַהֲרֹן: וְעָשִׂיתָ
בִגְדֵי־קֹדֶשׁ לְאַהֲרֹן אָחִיךָ לְכָבוֹד וּלְתִפְאָרֶת: וְאַתָּה תְּדַבֵּר אֶל־כָּל־חַכְמֵי־לֵב
אֲשֶׁר מִלֵּאתִיו רוּחַ חָכְמָה וְעָשׂוּ אֶת־בִּגְדֵי אַהֲרֹן לְקַדְּשׁוֹ לְכַהֲנוֹ־לִי: וְאֵלֶּה
הַבְּגָדִים אֲשֶׁר יַעֲשׂוּ חֹשֶׁן וְאֵפוֹד וּמְעִיל וּכְתֹנֶת תַּשְׁבֵּץ מִצְנֶפֶת וְאַבְנֵט וְעָשׂוּ
בִגְדֵי־קֹדֶשׁ לְאַהֲרֹן אָחִיךָ וּלְבָנָיו לְכַהֲנוֹ־לִי: וְהֵם יִקְחוּ אֶת־הַזָּהָב וְאֶת־הַתְּכֵלֶת

וְאֶת־הָאַרְגָּמָן וְאֶת־תּוֹלַעַת הַשָּׁנִי וְאֶת־הַשֵּׁשׁ:

לוי ◦ וַיַּעֲשׂוּ אֶת־הָאֵפֹד זָהָב תְּכֵלֶת וְאַרְגָּמָן תּוֹלַעַת שָׁנִי וְשֵׁשׁ מָשְׁזָר מַעֲשֵׂה חֹשֵׁב:

שְׁתֵּי כְתֵפֹת חֹבְרֹת הָיָה־לּוֹ אֶל־שְׁנֵי קְצוֹתָו וְחֻבָּר: וְחֵשֶׁב אֲפֻדָּתוֹ אֲשֶׁר עָלָיו

כְּמַעֲשֵׂהוּ מִמֶּנּוּ הָיָה זָהָב תְּכֵלֶת וְאַרְגָּמָן וְתוֹלַעַת שָׁנִי וְשֵׁשׁ מָשְׁזָר: וַיַּעֲשׂוּ

ישראל ◦ אֶת־אַבְנֵי הַשֹּׁהַם מֻסַבֹּת מִשְׁבְּצֹת זָהָב מְפֻתָּחֹת פִּתּוּחֵי חוֹתָם עַל־שְׁמוֹת בְּנֵי יִשְׂרָאֵל: *שִׁשָּׁה מִשְּׁמֹתָם עַל

הָאֶבֶן הָאֶחָת וְאֶת־שְׁמוֹת הַשִּׁשָּׁה הַנּוֹתָרִים עַל־הָאֶבֶן הַשֵּׁנִית כְּתוֹלְדֹתָם:

מַעֲשֵׂה חָרַשׁ אֶבֶן פִּתּוּחֵי חֹתָם תְּפַתַּח אֶת־שְׁתֵּי הָאֲבָנִים עַל־שְׁמֹת בְּנֵי

יִשְׂרָאֵל מֻסַבֹּת מִשְׁבְּצֹת זָהָב תַּעֲשֶׂה אֹתָם: וְשַׂמְתָּ אֶת־שְׁתֵּי הָאֲבָנִים עַל

כִּתְפֹת הָאֵפֹד אַבְנֵי זִכָּרֹן לִבְנֵי יִשְׂרָאֵל וְנָשָׂא אַהֲרֹן אֶת־שְׁמוֹתָם לִפְנֵי יְהוָה

עַל־שְׁתֵּי כְתֵפָיו לְזִכָּרֹן:

KI TISSA   כי תשא

שמות ◦ וַיְדַבֵּר יְהוָה אֶל־מֹשֶׁה לֵּאמֹר: כִּי תִשָּׂא אֶת־רֹאשׁ בְּנֵי־יִשְׂרָאֵל לִפְקֻדֵיהֶם
ל:יא–כא

וְנָתְנוּ אִישׁ כֹּפֶר נַפְשׁוֹ לַיהוָה בִּפְקֹד אֹתָם וְלֹא־יִהְיֶה בָהֶם נֶגֶף בִּפְקֹד אֹתָם:

זֶה ׀ יִתְּנוּ כָּל־הָעֹבֵר עַל־הַפְּקֻדִים מַחֲצִית הַשֶּׁקֶל בְּשֶׁקֶל הַקֹּדֶשׁ עֶשְׂרִים

גֵּרָה הַשֶּׁקֶל מַחֲצִית הַשֶּׁקֶל תְּרוּמָה לַיהוָה: *כֹּל הָעֹבֵר עַל־הַפְּקֻדִים מִבֶּן לוי ◦

עֶשְׂרִים שָׁנָה וָמָעְלָה יִתֵּן תְּרוּמַת יְהוָה: הֶעָשִׁיר לֹא־יַרְבֶּה וְהַדַּל לֹא יַמְעִיט

מִמַּחֲצִית הַשָּׁקֶל לָתֵת אֶת־תְּרוּמַת יְהוָה לְכַפֵּר עַל־נַפְשֹׁתֵיכֶם: וְלָקַחְתָּ

אֶת־כֶּסֶף הַכִּפֻּרִים מֵאֵת בְּנֵי יִשְׂרָאֵל וְנָתַתָּ אֹתוֹ עַל־עֲבֹדַת אֹהֶל מוֹעֵד וְהָיָה

לִבְנֵי יִשְׂרָאֵל לְזִכָּרוֹן לִפְנֵי יְהוָה לְכַפֵּר עַל־נַפְשֹׁתֵיכֶם:

ישראל ◦ וַיְדַבֵּר יְהוָה אֶל־מֹשֶׁה לֵּאמֹר: וְעָשִׂיתָ כִּיּוֹר נְחֹשֶׁת וְכַנּוֹ נְחֹשֶׁת לְרָחְצָה וְנָתַתָּ

אֹתוֹ בֵּין־אֹהֶל מוֹעֵד וּבֵין הַמִּזְבֵּחַ וְנָתַתָּ שָׁמָּה מָיִם: וְרָחֲצוּ אַהֲרֹן וּבָנָיו מִמֶּנּוּ

אֶת־יְדֵיהֶם וְאֶת־רַגְלֵיהֶם: בְּבֹאָם אֶל־אֹהֶל מוֹעֵד יִרְחֲצוּ־מַיִם וְלֹא יָמֻתוּ אוֹ

בְגִשְׁתָּם אֶל־הַמִּזְבֵּחַ לְשָׁרֵת לְהַקְטִיר אִשֶּׁה לַיהוָה: וְרָחֲצוּ יְדֵיהֶם וְרַגְלֵיהֶם

וְלֹא יָמֻתוּ וְהָיְתָה לָהֶם חָק־עוֹלָם לוֹ וּלְזַרְעוֹ לְדֹרֹתָם:

VAYAK-HEL   ויקהל

שמות ◦ וַיַּקְהֵל מֹשֶׁה אֶת־כָּל־עֲדַת בְּנֵי יִשְׂרָאֵל וַיֹּאמֶר אֲלֵהֶם אֵלֶּה הַדְּבָרִים אֲשֶׁר
לה:א–ב

צִוָּה יְהוָה לַעֲשֹׂת אֹתָם: שֵׁשֶׁת יָמִים תֵּעָשֶׂה מְלָאכָה וּבַיּוֹם הַשְּׁבִיעִי יִהְיֶה

לָכֶ֣ם קֹ֗דֶשׁ שַׁבַּ֧ת שַׁבָּת֛וֹן לַיהוָֹ֖ה כָּל־הָעֹשֶׂ֥ה ב֛וֹ מְלָאכָ֖ה יוּמָֽת: לֹא־תְבַעֲר֣וּ אֵ֔שׁ בְּכֹ֖ל מֹשְׁבֹֽתֵיכֶ֑ם בְּי֖וֹם הַשַּׁבָּֽת:

לוי וַיֹּ֣אמֶר מֹשֶׁ֗ה אֶל־כָּל־עֲדַ֧ת בְּנֵֽי־יִשְׂרָאֵ֛ל לֵאמֹ֑ר זֶ֣ה הַדָּבָ֔ר אֲשֶׁר־צִוָּ֥ה יהוָ֖ה לֵאמֹֽר: קְח֨וּ מֵֽאִתְּכֶ֤ם תְּרוּמָה֙ לַֽיהֹוָ֔ה כֹּ֚ל נְדִ֣יב לִבּ֔וֹ יְבִיאֶ֕הָ אֵ֖ת תְּרוּמַ֣ת יהוָ֑ה זָהָ֥ב וָכֶ֖סֶף וּנְחֹֽשֶׁת: וּתְכֵ֧לֶת וְאַרְגָּמָ֛ן וְתוֹלַ֥עַת שָׁנִ֖י וְשֵׁ֥שׁ וְעִזִּֽים: וְעֹרֹ֨ת אֵילִ֧ם מְאָדָּמִ֛ים וְעֹרֹ֥ת תְּחָשִׁ֖ים וַעֲצֵ֥י שִׁטִּֽים: וְשֶׁ֖מֶן לַמָּא֑וֹר וּבְשָׂמִים֙ לְשֶׁ֣מֶן הַמִּשְׁחָ֔ה וְלִקְטֹ֖רֶת הַסַּמִּֽים: וְאַ֨בְנֵי־שֹׁ֔הַם וְאַבְנֵ֖י מִלֻּאִ֑ים לָאֵפ֖וֹד וְלַחֹֽשֶׁן: וְכָל־חֲכַם־לֵ֖ב

ישראל בָּכֶ֑ם יָבֹ֣אוּ וְיַעֲשׂ֔וּ אֵ֛ת כָּל־אֲשֶׁ֥ר צִוָּ֖ה יהוָֹֽה: *אֶת־הַ֨מִּשְׁכָּ֔ן אֶת־אָהֳל֖וֹ וְאֶת־מִכְסֵ֑הוּ אֶת־קְרָסָיו֙ וְאֶת־קְרָשָׁ֔יו אֶת־בְּרִיחָ֕ו אֶת־עַמֻּדָ֖יו וְאֶת־אֲדָנָֽיו: אֶת־הָֽאָרֹ֥ן וְאֶת־בַּדָּ֖יו אֶת־הַכַּפֹּ֑רֶת וְאֵ֖ת פָּרֹ֥כֶת הַמָּסָֽךְ: אֶת־הַשֻּׁלְחָ֥ן וְאֶת־בַּדָּ֖יו וְאֶת־כָּל־כֵּלָ֑יו וְאֵ֖ת לֶ֥חֶם הַפָּנִֽים: וְאֶת־מְנֹרַ֧ת הַמָּא֛וֹר וְאֶת־כֵּלֶ֖יהָ וְאֶת־נֵֽרֹתֶ֑יהָ וְאֵ֖ת שֶׁ֥מֶן הַמָּאֽוֹר: וְאֶת־מִזְבַּ֤ח הַקְּטֹ֨רֶת֙ וְאֶת־בַּדָּ֔יו וְאֵת֙ שֶׁ֣מֶן הַמִּשְׁחָ֔ה וְאֵ֖ת קְטֹ֣רֶת הַסַּמִּ֑ים וְאֶת־מָסַ֥ךְ הַפֶּ֖תַח לְפֶ֥תַח הַמִּשְׁכָּֽן: אֵ֣ת ׀ מִזְבַּ֣ח הָעֹלָ֗ה וְאֶת־מִכְבַּ֤ר הַנְּחֹ֨שֶׁת֙ אֲשֶׁר־ל֔וֹ אֶת־בַּדָּ֖יו וְאֶת־כָּל־כֵּלָ֑יו אֶת־הַכִּיֹּ֖ר וְאֶת־כַּנּֽוֹ: אֵ֣ת קַלְעֵ֣י הֶֽחָצֵ֗ר אֶת־עַמֻּדָ֖יו וְאֶת־אֲדָנֶ֑יהָ וְאֵ֕ת מָסַ֖ךְ שַׁ֥עַר הֶחָצֵֽר: אֶת־יִתְדֹ֧ת הַמִּשְׁכָּ֛ן וְאֶת־יִתְדֹ֥ת הֶחָצֵ֖ר וְאֶת־מֵֽיתְרֵיהֶֽם: אֶת־בִּגְדֵ֥י הַשְּׂרָ֖ד לְשָׁרֵ֣ת בַּקֹּ֑דֶשׁ אֶת־בִּגְדֵ֤י הַקֹּ֨דֶשׁ֙ לְאַֽהֲרֹ֣ן הַכֹּהֵ֔ן וְאֶת־בִּגְדֵ֥י בָנָ֖יו לְכַהֵֽן: וַיֵּ֥צְא֛וּ כָּל־עֲדַ֥ת בְּנֵֽי־יִשְׂרָאֵ֖ל מִלִּפְנֵ֥י מֹשֶֽׁה:

PEKUDEI

פקודי

שמות לח:כא–לט:א

אֵ֣לֶּה פְקוּדֵ֤י הַמִּשְׁכָּן֙ מִשְׁכַּ֣ן הָֽעֵדֻ֔ת אֲשֶׁ֥ר פֻּקַּ֖ד עַל־פִּ֣י מֹשֶׁ֑ה עֲבֹדַת֙ הַלְוִיִּ֔ם בְּיַד֙ אִֽיתָמָ֔ר בֶּן־אַהֲרֹ֖ן הַכֹּהֵֽן: וּבְצַלְאֵ֛ל בֶּן־אוּרִ֥י בֶן־ח֖וּר לְמַטֵּ֣ה יְהוּדָ֑ה עָשָׂ֕ה אֵ֛ת כָּל־אֲשֶׁר־צִוָּ֥ה יהוָ֖ה אֶת־מֹשֶֽׁה: וְאִתּ֗וֹ אָהֳלִיאָ֞ב בֶּן־אֲחִיסָמָ֛ךְ לְמַטֵּה־דָ֖ן חָרָ֣שׁ וְחֹשֵׁ֑ב וְרֹקֵ֗ם בַּתְּכֵ֨לֶת֙ וּבָֽאַרְגָּמָ֔ן וּבְתוֹלַ֥עַת הַשָּׁנִ֖י וּבַשֵּֽׁשׁ: *כָּל־הַזָּהָ֗ב הֶֽעָשׂוּי֙ לַמְּלָאכָ֔ה בְּכֹ֖ל מְלֶ֣אכֶת הַקֹּ֑דֶשׁ וַיְהִ֣י ׀ זְהַ֣ב הַתְּנוּפָ֗ה תֵּ֤שַׁע וְעֶשְׂרִים֙ כִּכָּ֔ר וּשְׁבַ֥ע מֵא֛וֹת וּשְׁלֹשִׁ֥ים שֶׁ֖קֶל בְּשֶׁ֥קֶל הַקֹּֽדֶשׁ: וְכֶ֛סֶף פְּקוּדֵ֥י הָעֵדָ֖ה מְאַ֣ת כִּכָּ֑ר וְאֶ֜לֶף וּשְׁבַ֤ע מֵאוֹת֙ וַחֲמִשָּׁ֣ה וְשִׁבְעִ֔ים שֶׁ֖קֶל בְּשֶׁ֥קֶל הַקֹּֽדֶשׁ: בֶּ֚קַע לַגֻּלְגֹּ֔לֶת מַחֲצִ֥ית הַשֶּׁ֖קֶל בְּשֶׁ֣קֶל הַקֹּ֑דֶשׁ לְכֹ֨ל הָעֹבֵ֜ר עַל־הַפְּקֻדִ֗ים מִבֶּ֨ן עֶשְׂרִ֤ים שָׁנָה֙

וַמַעֲלֶה לְשֵׁשׁ־מֵאוֹת אֶלֶף וּשְׁלֹשֶׁת אֲלָפִים וַחֲמֵשׁ מֵאוֹת וַחֲמִשִּׁים: וַיְהִי
מְאַת כִּכַּר הַכֶּסֶף לָצֶקֶת אֵת אַדְנֵי הַקֹּדֶשׁ וְאֵת אַדְנֵי הַפָּרֹכֶת מְאַת אֲדָנִים
לִמְאַת הַכִּכָּר כִּכָּר לָאָדֶן: *וְאֶת־הָאֶלֶף וּשְׁבַע הַמֵּאוֹת וַחֲמִשָּׁה וְשִׁבְעִים ישראל
עָשָׂה וָוִים לָעַמּוּדִים וְצִפָּה רָאשֵׁיהֶם וְחִשַּׁק אֹתָם: וּנְחֹשֶׁת הַתְּנוּפָה שִׁבְעִים
כִּכָּר וְאַלְפַּיִם וְאַרְבַּע־מֵאוֹת שָׁקֶל: וַיַּעַשׂ בָּהּ אֶת־אַדְנֵי פֶּתַח אֹהֶל מוֹעֵד
וְאֵת מִזְבַּח הַנְּחֹשֶׁת וְאֶת־מִכְבַּר הַנְּחֹשֶׁת אֲשֶׁר־לוֹ וְאֵת כָּל־כְּלֵי הַמִּזְבֵּחַ:
וְאֶת־אַדְנֵי הֶחָצֵר סָבִיב וְאֶת־אַדְנֵי שַׁעַר הֶחָצֵר וְאֵת כָּל־יִתְדֹת הַמִּשְׁכָּן
וְאֶת־כָּל־יִתְדֹת הֶחָצֵר סָבִיב: וּמִן־הַתְּכֵלֶת וְהָאַרְגָּמָן וְתוֹלַעַת הַשָּׁנִי עָשׂוּ
בִגְדֵי־שְׂרָד לְשָׁרֵת בַּקֹּדֶשׁ וַיַּעֲשׂוּ אֶת־בִּגְדֵי הַקֹּדֶשׁ אֲשֶׁר לְאַהֲרֹן כַּאֲשֶׁר צִוָּה
יְהוָה אֶת־מֹשֶׁה:

VAYIKRA
ויקרא

וַיִּקְרָא אֶל־מֹשֶׁה וַיְדַבֵּר יְהוָה אֵלָיו מֵאֹהֶל מוֹעֵד לֵאמֹר: דַּבֵּר אֶל־בְּנֵי יִשְׂרָאֵל ויקרא
וְאָמַרְתָּ אֲלֵהֶם אָדָם כִּי־יַקְרִיב מִכֶּם קָרְבָּן לַיהוָה מִן־הַבְּהֵמָה מִן־הַבָּקָר א׳,א-ג
וּמִן־הַצֹּאן תַּקְרִיבוּ אֶת־קָרְבַּנְכֶם: אִם־עֹלָה קָרְבָּנוֹ מִן־הַבָּקָר זָכָר תָּמִים
יַקְרִיבֶנּוּ אֶל־פֶּתַח אֹהֶל מוֹעֵד יַקְרִיב אֹתוֹ לִרְצֹנוֹ לִפְנֵי יְהוָה: וְסָמַךְ יָדוֹ עַל
רֹאשׁ הָעֹלָה וְנִרְצָה לוֹ לְכַפֵּר עָלָיו: וְשָׁחַט אֶת־בֶּן הַבָּקָר לִפְנֵי יְהוָה וְהִקְרִיבוּ לוי
בְּנֵי אַהֲרֹן הַכֹּהֲנִים אֶת־הַדָּם וְזָרְקוּ אֶת־הַדָּם עַל־הַמִּזְבֵּחַ סָבִיב אֲשֶׁר־פֶּתַח
אֹהֶל מוֹעֵד: וְהִפְשִׁיט אֶת־הָעֹלָה וְנִתַּח אֹתָהּ לִנְתָחֶיהָ: וְנָתְנוּ בְּנֵי אַהֲרֹן
הַכֹּהֵן אֵשׁ עַל־הַמִּזְבֵּחַ וְעָרְכוּ עֵצִים עַל־הָאֵשׁ: וְעָרְכוּ בְּנֵי אַהֲרֹן הַכֹּהֲנִים
אֵת הַנְּתָחִים אֶת־הָרֹאשׁ וְאֶת־הַפָּדֶר עַל־הָעֵצִים אֲשֶׁר עַל־הָאֵשׁ אֲשֶׁר עַל־
הַמִּזְבֵּחַ: וְקִרְבּוֹ וּכְרָעָיו יִרְחַץ בַּמָּיִם וְהִקְטִיר הַכֹּהֵן אֶת־הַכֹּל הַמִּזְבֵּחָה עֹלָה
אִשֵּׁה רֵיחַ־נִיחֹחַ לַיהוָה: *וְאִם־מִן־הַצֹּאן קָרְבָּנוֹ מִן־הַכְּשָׂבִים ישראל
אוֹ מִן־הָעִזִּים לְעֹלָה זָכָר תָּמִים יַקְרִיבֶנּוּ: וְשָׁחַט אֹתוֹ עַל יֶרֶךְ הַמִּזְבֵּחַ צָפֹנָה
לִפְנֵי יְהוָה וְזָרְקוּ בְּנֵי אַהֲרֹן הַכֹּהֲנִים אֶת־דָּמוֹ עַל־הַמִּזְבֵּחַ סָבִיב: וְנִתַּח אֹתוֹ
לִנְתָחָיו וְאֶת־רֹאשׁוֹ וְאֶת־פִּדְרוֹ וְעָרַךְ הַכֹּהֵן אֹתָם עַל־הָעֵצִים אֲשֶׁר עַל־הָאֵשׁ
אֲשֶׁר עַל־הַמִּזְבֵּחַ: וְהַקֶּרֶב וְהַכְּרָעַיִם יִרְחַץ בַּמָּיִם וְהִקְרִיב הַכֹּהֵן אֶת־הַכֹּל
וְהִקְטִיר הַמִּזְבֵּחָה עֹלָה הוּא אִשֵּׁה רֵיחַ נִיחֹחַ לַיהוָה:

TZAV
צו

ויקרא
ו:א-יא

וַיְדַבֵּר יְהוָה אֶל־מֹשֶׁה לֵּאמֹר: צַו אֶת־אַהֲרֹן וְאֶת־בָּנָיו לֵאמֹר זֹאת תּוֹרַת
הָעֹלָה הִוא הָעֹלָה עַל מוֹקְדָה עַל־הַמִּזְבֵּחַ כָּל־הַלַּיְלָה עַד־הַבֹּקֶר וְאֵשׁ הַמִּזְבֵּחַ
תּוּקַד בּוֹ: וְלָבַשׁ הַכֹּהֵן מִדּוֹ בַד וּמִכְנְסֵי־בַד יִלְבַּשׁ עַל־בְּשָׂרוֹ וְהֵרִים אֶת־הַדֶּשֶׁן

לוי

אֲשֶׁר תֹּאכַל הָאֵשׁ אֶת־הָעֹלָה עַל־הַמִּזְבֵּחַ וְשָׂמוֹ אֵצֶל הַמִּזְבֵּחַ: *וּפָשַׁט אֶת־
בְּגָדָיו וְלָבַשׁ בְּגָדִים אֲחֵרִים וְהוֹצִיא אֶת־הַדֶּשֶׁן אֶל־מִחוּץ לַמַּחֲנֶה אֶל־מָקוֹם
טָהוֹר: וְהָאֵשׁ עַל־הַמִּזְבֵּחַ תּוּקַד־בּוֹ לֹא תִכְבֶּה וּבִעֵר עָלֶיהָ הַכֹּהֵן עֵצִים בַּבֹּקֶר
בַּבֹּקֶר וְעָרַךְ עָלֶיהָ הָעֹלָה וְהִקְטִיר עָלֶיהָ חֶלְבֵי הַשְּׁלָמִים: אֵשׁ תָּמִיד תּוּקַד
עַל־הַמִּזְבֵּחַ לֹא תִכְבֶּה: *וְזֹאת תּוֹרַת הַמִּנְחָה הַקְרֵב אֹתָהּ

ישראל

בְּנֵי־אַהֲרֹן לִפְנֵי יְהוָה אֶל־פְּנֵי הַמִּזְבֵּחַ: וְהֵרִים מִמֶּנּוּ בְּקֻמְצוֹ מִסֹּלֶת הַמִּנְחָה
וּמִשַּׁמְנָהּ וְאֵת כָּל־הַלְּבֹנָה אֲשֶׁר עַל־הַמִּנְחָה וְהִקְטִיר הַמִּזְבֵּחַ רֵיחַ נִיחֹחַ
אַזְכָּרָתָהּ לַיהוָה: וְהַנּוֹתֶרֶת מִמֶּנָּה יֹאכְלוּ אַהֲרֹן וּבָנָיו מַצּוֹת תֵּאָכֵל בְּמָקוֹם
קָדֹשׁ בַּחֲצַר אֹהֶל־מוֹעֵד יֹאכְלוּהָ: לֹא תֵאָפֶה חָמֵץ חֶלְקָם נָתַתִּי אֹתָהּ מֵאִשָּׁי
קֹדֶשׁ קָדָשִׁים הִוא כַּחַטָּאת וְכָאָשָׁם: כָּל־זָכָר בִּבְנֵי אַהֲרֹן יֹאכְלֶנָּה חָק־עוֹלָם
לְדֹרֹתֵיכֶם מֵאִשֵּׁי יְהוָה כֹּל אֲשֶׁר־יִגַּע בָּהֶם יִקְדָּשׁ:

SHEMINI
שמיני

ויקרא
ט:א-טז

וַיְהִי בַּיּוֹם הַשְּׁמִינִי קָרָא מֹשֶׁה לְאַהֲרֹן וּלְבָנָיו וּלְזִקְנֵי יִשְׂרָאֵל: וַיֹּאמֶר אֶל־אַהֲרֹן
קַח־לְךָ עֵגֶל בֶּן־בָּקָר לְחַטָּאת וְאַיִל לְעֹלָה תְּמִימִם וְהַקְרֵב לִפְנֵי יְהוָה: וְאֶל־
בְּנֵי יִשְׂרָאֵל תְּדַבֵּר לֵאמֹר קְחוּ שְׂעִיר־עִזִּים לְחַטָּאת וְעֵגֶל וָכֶבֶשׂ בְּנֵי־שָׁנָה
תְּמִימִם לְעֹלָה: וְשׁוֹר וָאַיִל לִשְׁלָמִים לִזְבֹּחַ לִפְנֵי יְהוָה וּמִנְחָה בְּלוּלָה בַשָּׁמֶן
כִּי הַיּוֹם יְהוָה נִרְאָה אֲלֵיכֶם: וַיִּקְחוּ אֵת אֲשֶׁר צִוָּה מֹשֶׁה אֶל־פְּנֵי אֹהֶל מוֹעֵד
וַיִּקְרְבוּ כָּל־הָעֵדָה וַיַּעַמְדוּ לִפְנֵי יְהוָה: וַיֹּאמֶר מֹשֶׁה זֶה הַדָּבָר אֲשֶׁר־צִוָּה יְהוָה

לוי

תַּעֲשׂוּ וְיֵרָא אֲלֵיכֶם כְּבוֹד יְהוָה: *וַיֹּאמֶר מֹשֶׁה אֶל־אַהֲרֹן קְרַב אֶל־הַמִּזְבֵּחַ
וַעֲשֵׂה אֶת־חַטָּאתְךָ וְאֶת־עֹלָתֶךָ וְכַפֵּר בַּעַדְךָ וּבְעַד הָעָם וַעֲשֵׂה אֶת־קָרְבַּן
הָעָם וְכַפֵּר בַּעֲדָם כַּאֲשֶׁר צִוָּה יְהוָה: וַיִּקְרַב אַהֲרֹן אֶל־הַמִּזְבֵּחַ וַיִּשְׁחַט אֶת־
עֵגֶל הַחַטָּאת אֲשֶׁר־לוֹ: וַיַּקְרִבוּ בְּנֵי אַהֲרֹן אֶת־הַדָּם אֵלָיו וַיִּטְבֹּל אֶצְבָּעוֹ
בַּדָּם וַיִּתֵּן עַל־קַרְנוֹת הַמִּזְבֵּחַ וְאֶת־הַדָּם יָצַק אֶל־יְסוֹד הַמִּזְבֵּחַ: וְאֶת־הַחֵלֶב
וְאֶת־הַכְּלָיֹת וְאֶת־הַיֹּתֶרֶת מִן־הַכָּבֵד מִן־הַחַטָּאת הִקְטִיר הַמִּזְבֵּחָה כַּאֲשֶׁר

צִוָּה יְהוָה אֶת־מֹשֶׁה: *וְאֶת־הַבָּשָׂר וְאֶת־הָעוֹר שָׂרַף בָּאֵשׁ מִחוּץ לַמַּחֲנֶה: וַיִּשְׁחַט אֶת־הָעֹלָה וַיַּמְצִאוּ בְּנֵי אַהֲרֹן אֵלָיו אֶת־הַדָּם וַיִּזְרְקֵהוּ עַל־הַמִּזְבֵּחַ סָבִיב: וְאֶת־הָעֹלָה הִמְצִיאוּ אֵלָיו לִנְתָחֶיהָ וְאֶת־הָרֹאשׁ וַיַּקְטֵר עַל־הַמִּזְבֵּחַ: וַיִּרְחַץ אֶת־הַקֶּרֶב וְאֶת־הַכְּרָעָיִם וַיַּקְטֵר עַל־הָעֹלָה הַמִּזְבֵּחָה: וַיַּקְרֵב אֵת קָרְבַּן הָעָם וַיִּקַּח אֶת־שְׂעִיר הַחַטָּאת אֲשֶׁר לָעָם וַיִּשְׁחָטֵהוּ וַיְחַטְּאֵהוּ כָּרִאשׁוֹן: וַיַּקְרֵב אֶת־הָעֹלָה וַיַּעֲשֶׂהָ כַּמִּשְׁפָּט:

תזריע
TAZRIA

וַיְדַבֵּר יְהוָה אֶל־מֹשֶׁה לֵּאמֹר: דַּבֵּר אֶל־בְּנֵי יִשְׂרָאֵל לֵאמֹר אִשָּׁה כִּי תַזְרִיעַ וְיָלְדָה זָכָר וְטָמְאָה שִׁבְעַת יָמִים כִּימֵי נִדַּת דְּוֹתָהּ תִּטְמָא: וּבַיּוֹם הַשְּׁמִינִי יִמּוֹל בְּשַׂר עָרְלָתוֹ: וּשְׁלֹשִׁים יוֹם וּשְׁלֹשֶׁת יָמִים תֵּשֵׁב בִּדְמֵי טָהֳרָה בְּכָל־ קֹדֶשׁ לֹא־תִגָּע וְאֶל־הַמִּקְדָּשׁ לֹא תָבֹא עַד־מְלֹאת יְמֵי טָהֳרָהּ: *וְאִם־נְקֵבָה תֵלֵד וְטָמְאָה שְׁבֻעַיִם כְּנִדָּתָהּ וְשִׁשִּׁים יוֹם וְשֵׁשֶׁת יָמִים תֵּשֵׁב עַל־דְּמֵי טָהֳרָה: וּבִמְלֹאת ׀ יְמֵי טָהֳרָהּ לְבֵן אוֹ לְבַת תָּבִיא כֶּבֶשׂ בֶּן־שְׁנָתוֹ לְעֹלָה וּבֶן־יוֹנָה אוֹ־תֹר לְחַטָּאת אֶל־פֶּתַח אֹהֶל־מוֹעֵד אֶל־הַכֹּהֵן: וְהִקְרִיבוֹ לִפְנֵי יְהוָה וְכִפֶּר עָלֶיהָ וְטָהֲרָה מִמְּקֹר דָּמֶיהָ זֹאת תּוֹרַת הַיֹּלֶדֶת לַזָּכָר אוֹ לַנְּקֵבָה: וְאִם־לֹא תִמְצָא יָדָהּ דֵּי שֶׂה וְלָקְחָה שְׁתֵּי־תֹרִים אוֹ שְׁנֵי בְּנֵי יוֹנָה אֶחָד לְעֹלָה וְאֶחָד לְחַטָּאת וְכִפֶּר עָלֶיהָ הַכֹּהֵן וְטָהֵרָה:

וַיְדַבֵּר יְהוָה אֶל־מֹשֶׁה וְאֶל־אַהֲרֹן לֵאמֹר: אָדָם כִּי־יִהְיֶה בְעוֹר־בְּשָׂרוֹ שְׂאֵת אוֹ־סַפַּחַת אוֹ בַהֶרֶת וְהָיָה בְעוֹר־בְּשָׂרוֹ לְנֶגַע צָרָעַת וְהוּבָא אֶל־אַהֲרֹן הַכֹּהֵן אוֹ אֶל־אַחַד מִבָּנָיו הַכֹּהֲנִים: וְרָאָה הַכֹּהֵן אֶת־הַנֶּגַע בְּעוֹר־הַבָּשָׂר וְשֵׂעָר בַּנֶּגַע הָפַךְ ׀ לָבָן וּמַרְאֵה הַנֶּגַע עָמֹק מֵעוֹר בְּשָׂרוֹ נֶגַע צָרַעַת הוּא וְרָאָהוּ הַכֹּהֵן וְטִמֵּא אֹתוֹ: וְאִם־בַּהֶרֶת לְבָנָה הִוא בְּעוֹר בְּשָׂרוֹ וְעָמֹק אֵין־מַרְאֶהָ מִן־הָעוֹר וּשְׂעָרָה לֹא־הָפַךְ לָבָן וְהִסְגִּיר הַכֹּהֵן אֶת־הַנֶּגַע שִׁבְעַת יָמִים: וְרָאָהוּ הַכֹּהֵן בַּיּוֹם הַשְּׁבִיעִי וְהִנֵּה הַנֶּגַע עָמַד בְּעֵינָיו לֹא־פָשָׂה הַנֶּגַע בָּעוֹר וְהִסְגִּירוֹ הַכֹּהֵן שִׁבְעַת יָמִים שֵׁנִית:

מצורע
METZORA

וַיְדַבֵּר יְהוָה אֶל־מֹשֶׁה לֵּאמֹר: זֹאת תִּהְיֶה תּוֹרַת הַמְּצֹרָע בְּיוֹם טָהֳרָתוֹ

וְהוּבָא אֶל־הַכֹּהֵן: וְיָצָא הַכֹּהֵן אֶל־מִחוּץ לַמַּחֲנֶה וְרָאָה הַכֹּהֵן וְהִנֵּה נִרְפָּא
נֶגַע־הַצָּרַעַת מִן־הַצָּרוּעַ: וְצִוָּה הַכֹּהֵן וְלָקַח לַמִּטַּהֵר שְׁתֵּי־צִפֳּרִים חַיּוֹת
טְהֹרוֹת וְעֵץ אֶרֶז וּשְׁנִי תוֹלַעַת וְאֵזֹב: וְצִוָּה הַכֹּהֵן וְשָׁחַט אֶת־הַצִּפּוֹר הָאֶחָת
לוי   אֶל־כְּלִי־חֶרֶשׂ עַל־מַיִם חַיִּים: אֶת־הַצִּפֹּר הַחַיָּה יִקַּח אֹתָהּ וְאֶת־עֵץ הָאֶרֶז
וְאֶת־שְׁנִי הַתּוֹלַעַת וְאֶת־הָאֵזֹב וְטָבַל אוֹתָם וְאֵת ׀ הַצִּפֹּר הַחַיָּה בְּדַם הַצִּפֹּר
הַשְּׁחֻטָה עַל הַמַּיִם הַחַיִּים: וְהִזָּה עַל הַמִּטַּהֵר מִן־הַצָּרַעַת שֶׁבַע פְּעָמִים
וְטִהֲרוֹ וְשִׁלַּח אֶת־הַצִּפֹּר הַחַיָּה עַל־פְּנֵי הַשָּׂדֶה: וְכִבֶּס הַמִּטַּהֵר אֶת־בְּגָדָיו
וְגִלַּח אֶת־כָּל־שְׂעָרוֹ וְרָחַץ בַּמַּיִם וְטָהֵר וְאַחַר יָבוֹא אֶל־הַמַּחֲנֶה וְיָשַׁב מִחוּץ
לְאָהֳלוֹ שִׁבְעַת יָמִים: וְהָיָה בַיּוֹם הַשְּׁבִיעִי יְגַלַּח אֶת־כָּל־שְׂעָרוֹ אֶת־רֹאשׁוֹ
וְאֶת־זְקָנוֹ וְאֵת גַּבֹּת עֵינָיו וְאֶת־כָּל־שְׂעָרוֹ יְגַלֵּחַ וְכִבֶּס אֶת־בְּגָדָיו וְרָחַץ אֶת־
ישראל   בְּשָׂרוֹ בַּמַּיִם וְטָהֵר: *וּבַיּוֹם הַשְּׁמִינִי יִקַּח שְׁנֵי־כְבָשִׂים תְּמִימִם וְכַבְשָׂה אַחַת
בַּת־שְׁנָתָהּ תְּמִימָה וּשְׁלֹשָׁה עֶשְׂרֹנִים סֹלֶת מִנְחָה בְּלוּלָה בַשֶּׁמֶן וְלֹג אֶחָד
שָׁמֶן: וְהֶעֱמִיד הַכֹּהֵן הַמְטַהֵר אֵת הָאִישׁ הַמִּטַּהֵר וְאֹתָם לִפְנֵי יְהוָה פֶּתַח
אֹהֶל מוֹעֵד: וְלָקַח הַכֹּהֵן אֶת־הַכֶּבֶשׂ הָאֶחָד וְהִקְרִיב אֹתוֹ לְאָשָׁם וְאֶת־לֹג
הַשָּׁמֶן וְהֵנִיף אֹתָם תְּנוּפָה לִפְנֵי יְהוָה:

AHAREI MOT   אחרי מות

ויקרא   וַיְדַבֵּר יְהוָה אֶל־מֹשֶׁה אַחֲרֵי מוֹת שְׁנֵי בְּנֵי אַהֲרֹן בְּקָרְבָתָם לִפְנֵי־יְהוָה וַיָּמֻתוּ:
טז:א–יז   וַיֹּאמֶר יְהוָה אֶל־מֹשֶׁה דַּבֵּר אֶל־אַהֲרֹן אָחִיךָ וְאַל־יָבֹא בְכָל־עֵת אֶל־הַקֹּדֶשׁ
מִבֵּית לַפָּרֹכֶת אֶל־פְּנֵי הַכַּפֹּרֶת אֲשֶׁר עַל־הָאָרֹן וְלֹא יָמוּת כִּי בֶּעָנָן אֵרָאֶה
עַל־הַכַּפֹּרֶת: בְּזֹאת יָבֹא אַהֲרֹן אֶל־הַקֹּדֶשׁ בְּפַר בֶּן־בָּקָר לְחַטָּאת וְאַיִל
לְעֹלָה: כְּתֹנֶת־בַּד קֹדֶשׁ יִלְבָּשׁ וּמִכְנְסֵי־בַד יִהְיוּ עַל־בְּשָׂרוֹ וּבְאַבְנֵט בַּד
יַחְגֹּר וּבְמִצְנֶפֶת בַּד יִצְנֹף בִּגְדֵי־קֹדֶשׁ הֵם וְרָחַץ בַּמַּיִם אֶת־בְּשָׂרוֹ וּלְבֵשָׁם:
וּמֵאֵת עֲדַת בְּנֵי יִשְׂרָאֵל יִקַּח שְׁנֵי־שְׂעִירֵי עִזִּים לְחַטָּאת וְאַיִל אֶחָד לְעֹלָה:
לוי   וְהִקְרִיב אַהֲרֹן אֶת־פַּר הַחַטָּאת אֲשֶׁר־לוֹ וְכִפֶּר בַּעֲדוֹ וּבְעַד בֵּיתוֹ: *וְלָקַח
אֶת־שְׁנֵי הַשְּׂעִירִם וְהֶעֱמִיד אֹתָם לִפְנֵי יְהוָה פֶּתַח אֹהֶל מוֹעֵד: וְנָתַן אַהֲרֹן
עַל־שְׁנֵי הַשְּׂעִירִם גּוֹרָלוֹת גּוֹרָל אֶחָד לַיהוָה וְגוֹרָל אֶחָד לַעֲזָאזֵל: וְהִקְרִיב
אַהֲרֹן אֶת־הַשָּׂעִיר אֲשֶׁר עָלָה עָלָיו הַגּוֹרָל לַיהוָה וְעָשָׂהוּ חַטָּאת: וְהַשָּׂעִיר
אֲשֶׁר עָלָה עָלָיו הַגּוֹרָל לַעֲזָאזֵל יָעֳמַד־חַי לִפְנֵי יְהוָה לְכַפֵּר עָלָיו לְשַׁלַּח

אֹתוֹ לַעֲזָאזֵל הַמִּדְבָּרָה: וְהִקְרִיב אַהֲרֹן אֶת־פַּר הַחַטָּאת אֲשֶׁר־לוֹ וְכִפֶּר

בַּעֲדוֹ וּבְעַד בֵּיתוֹ וְשָׁחַט אֶת־פַּר הַחַטָּאת אֲשֶׁר־לוֹ: *וְלָקַח מְלֹא־הַמַּחְתָּה ישראל

גַּחֲלֵי־אֵשׁ מֵעַל הַמִּזְבֵּחַ מִלִּפְנֵי יהוה וּמְלֹא חָפְנָיו קְטֹרֶת סַמִּים דַּקָּה וְהֵבִיא

מִבֵּית לַפָּרֹכֶת: וְנָתַן אֶת־הַקְּטֹרֶת עַל־הָאֵשׁ לִפְנֵי יהוה וְכִסָּה ׀ עֲנַן הַקְּטֹרֶת

אֶת־הַכַּפֹּרֶת אֲשֶׁר עַל־הָעֵדוּת וְלֹא יָמוּת: וְלָקַח מִדַּם הַפָּר וְהִזָּה בְאֶצְבָּעוֹ

עַל־פְּנֵי הַכַּפֹּרֶת קֵדְמָה וְלִפְנֵי הַכַּפֹּרֶת יַזֶּה שֶׁבַע־פְּעָמִים מִן־הַדָּם בְּאֶצְבָּעוֹ:

וְשָׁחַט אֶת־שְׂעִיר הַחַטָּאת אֲשֶׁר לָעָם וְהֵבִיא אֶת־דָּמוֹ אֶל־מִבֵּית לַפָּרֹכֶת

וְעָשָׂה אֶת־דָּמוֹ כַּאֲשֶׁר עָשָׂה לְדַם הַפָּר וְהִזָּה אֹתוֹ עַל־הַכַּפֹּרֶת וְלִפְנֵי הַכַּפֹּרֶת:

וְכִפֶּר עַל־הַקֹּדֶשׁ מִטֻּמְאֹת בְּנֵי יִשְׂרָאֵל וּמִפִּשְׁעֵיהֶם לְכָל־חַטֹּאתָם וְכֵן יַעֲשֶׂה

לְאֹהֶל מוֹעֵד הַשֹּׁכֵן אִתָּם בְּתוֹךְ טֻמְאֹתָם: וְכָל־אָדָם לֹא־יִהְיֶה ׀ בְּאֹהֶל מוֹעֵד

בְּבֹאוֹ לְכַפֵּר בַּקֹּדֶשׁ עַד־צֵאתוֹ וְכִפֶּר בַּעֲדוֹ וּבְעַד בֵּיתוֹ וּבְעַד כָּל־קְהַל יִשְׂרָאֵל:

KEDOSHIM

קדושים

ויקרא
יט:א-יד

וַיְדַבֵּר יהוה אֶל־מֹשֶׁה לֵּאמֹר: דַּבֵּר אֶל־כָּל־עֲדַת בְּנֵי־יִשְׂרָאֵל וְאָמַרְתָּ אֲלֵהֶם

קְדֹשִׁים תִּהְיוּ כִּי קָדוֹשׁ אֲנִי יהוה אֱלֹהֵיכֶם: אִישׁ אִמּוֹ וְאָבִיו תִּירָאוּ וְאֶת־

שַׁבְּתֹתַי תִּשְׁמֹרוּ אֲנִי יהוה אֱלֹהֵיכֶם: אַל־תִּפְנוּ אֶל־הָאֱלִילִם וֵאלֹהֵי מַסֵּכָה

לֹא תַעֲשׂוּ לָכֶם אֲנִי יהוה אֱלֹהֵיכֶם: *וְכִי תִזְבְּחוּ זֶבַח שְׁלָמִים לַיהוה לִרְצֹנְכֶם לוי

תִּזְבָּחֻהוּ: בְּיוֹם זִבְחֲכֶם יֵאָכֵל וּמִמָּחֳרָת וְהַנּוֹתָר עַד־יוֹם הַשְּׁלִישִׁי בָּאֵשׁ יִשָּׂרֵף:

וְאִם הֵאָכֹל יֵאָכֵל בַּיּוֹם הַשְּׁלִישִׁי פִּגּוּל הוּא לֹא יֵרָצֶה: וְאֹכְלָיו עֲוֹנוֹ יִשָּׂא כִּי־

אֶת־קֹדֶשׁ יהוה חִלֵּל וְנִכְרְתָה הַנֶּפֶשׁ הַהִוא מֵעַמֶּיהָ: וּבְקֻצְרְכֶם אֶת־קְצִיר

אַרְצְכֶם לֹא תְכַלֶּה פְּאַת שָׂדְךָ לִקְצֹר וְלֶקֶט קְצִירְךָ לֹא תְלַקֵּט: וְכַרְמְךָ לֹא

תְעוֹלֵל וּפֶרֶט כַּרְמְךָ לֹא תְלַקֵּט לֶעָנִי וְלַגֵּר תַּעֲזֹב אֹתָם אֲנִי יהוה אֱלֹהֵיכֶם:

*לֹא תִּגְנֹבוּ וְלֹא־תְכַחֲשׁוּ וְלֹא־תְשַׁקְּרוּ אִישׁ בַּעֲמִיתוֹ: וְלֹא־תִשָּׁבְעוּ בִשְׁמִי ישראל

לַשָּׁקֶר וְחִלַּלְתָּ אֶת־שֵׁם אֱלֹהֶיךָ אֲנִי יהוה: לֹא־תַעֲשֹׁק אֶת־רֵעֲךָ וְלֹא תִגְזֹל

לֹא־תָלִין פְּעֻלַּת שָׂכִיר אִתְּךָ עַד־בֹּקֶר: לֹא־תְקַלֵּל חֵרֵשׁ וְלִפְנֵי עִוֵּר לֹא תִתֵּן

מִכְשֹׁל וְיָרֵאתָ מֵּאֱלֹהֶיךָ אֲנִי יהוה:

EMOR

אמור

ויקרא
כא:א-ט

וַיֹּאמֶר יהוה אֶל־מֹשֶׁה אֱמֹר אֶל־הַכֹּהֲנִים בְּנֵי אַהֲרֹן וְאָמַרְתָּ אֲלֵהֶם לְנֶפֶשׁ

לֹא־יִטַּמָּא בְּעַמָּיו: כִּי אִם־לִשְׁאֵרוֹ הַקָּרֹב אֵלָיו לְאִמּוֹ וּלְאָבִיו וְלִבְנוֹ וּלְבִתּוֹ
וּלְאָחִיו: וְלַאֲחֹתוֹ הַבְּתוּלָה הַקְּרוֹבָה אֵלָיו אֲשֶׁר לֹא־הָיְתָה לְאִישׁ לָהּ יִטַּמָּא:

יקרא לֹא יִטַּמָּא בַּעַל בְּעַמָּיו לְהֵחַלּוֹ: לֹא־יִקְרְחָה קָרְחָה בְּרֹאשָׁם וּפְאַת זְקָנָם
לֹא יְגַלֵּחוּ וּבִבְשָׂרָם לֹא יִשְׂרְטוּ שָׂרָטֶת: קְדֹשִׁים יִהְיוּ לֵאלֹהֵיהֶם וְלֹא יְחַלְּלוּ
שֵׁם אֱלֹהֵיהֶם כִּי אֶת־אִשֵּׁי יהוה לֶחֶם אֱלֹהֵיהֶם הֵם מַקְרִיבִם וְהָיוּ קֹדֶשׁ:

לוי אִשָּׁה זֹנָה וַחֲלָלָה לֹא יִקָּחוּ וְאִשָּׁה גְּרוּשָׁה מֵאִישָׁהּ לֹא יִקָּחוּ כִּי־קָדֹשׁ הוּא
לֵאלֹהָיו: וְקִדַּשְׁתּוֹ כִּי־אֶת־לֶחֶם אֱלֹהֶיךָ הוּא מַקְרִיב קָדֹשׁ יִהְיֶה־לָּךְ כִּי קָדוֹשׁ
אֲנִי יהוה מְקַדִּשְׁכֶם: וּבַת אִישׁ כֹּהֵן כִּי תֵחֵל לִזְנוֹת אֶת־אָבִיהָ הִיא מְחַלֶּלֶת
בָּאֵשׁ תִּשָּׂרֵף: וְהַכֹּהֵן הַגָּדוֹל מֵאֶחָיו אֲשֶׁר־יוּצַק עַל־רֹאשׁוֹ שֶׁמֶן
הַמִּשְׁחָה וּמִלֵּא אֶת־יָדוֹ לִלְבֹּשׁ אֶת־הַבְּגָדִים אֶת־רֹאשׁוֹ לֹא יִפְרָע וּבְגָדָיו לֹא
יִפְרֹם: וְעַל כָּל־נַפְשֹׁת מֵת לֹא יָבֹא לְאָבִיו וּלְאִמּוֹ לֹא יִטַּמָּא: וּמִן־הַמִּקְדָּשׁ
לֹא יֵצֵא וְלֹא יְחַלֵּל אֵת מִקְדַּשׁ אֱלֹהָיו כִּי נֵזֶר שֶׁמֶן מִשְׁחַת אֱלֹהָיו עָלָיו אֲנִי
יהוה: *וְהוּא אִשָּׁה בִבְתוּלֶיהָ יִקָּח: אַלְמָנָה וּגְרוּשָׁה וַחֲלָלָה זֹנָה אֶת־אֵלֶּה
ישראל לֹא יִקָּח כִּי אִם־בְּתוּלָה מֵעַמָּיו יִקַּח אִשָּׁה: וְלֹא־יְחַלֵּל זַרְעוֹ בְּעַמָּיו כִּי אֲנִי
יהוה מְקַדְּשׁוֹ:

בהר

BEHAR

ויקרא וַיְדַבֵּר יהוה אֶל־מֹשֶׁה בְּהַר סִינַי לֵאמֹר: דַּבֵּר אֶל־בְּנֵי יִשְׂרָאֵל וְאָמַרְתָּ
כה:א-ג אֲלֵהֶם כִּי תָבֹאוּ אֶל־הָאָרֶץ אֲשֶׁר אֲנִי נֹתֵן לָכֶם וְשָׁבְתָה הָאָרֶץ שַׁבָּת לַיהוה:
שֵׁשׁ שָׁנִים תִּזְרַע שָׂדֶךָ וְשֵׁשׁ שָׁנִים תִּזְמֹר כַּרְמֶךָ וְאָסַפְתָּ אֶת־תְּבוּאָתָהּ:

לוי *וּבַשָּׁנָה הַשְּׁבִיעִת שַׁבַּת שַׁבָּתוֹן יִהְיֶה לָאָרֶץ שַׁבָּת לַיהוה שָׂדְךָ לֹא תִזְרָע
וְכַרְמְךָ לֹא תִזְמֹר: אֵת סְפִיחַ קְצִירְךָ לֹא תִקְצוֹר וְאֶת־עִנְּבֵי נְזִירֶךָ לֹא תִבְצֹר
שְׁנַת שַׁבָּתוֹן יִהְיֶה לָאָרֶץ: וְהָיְתָה שַׁבַּת הָאָרֶץ לָכֶם לְאָכְלָה לְךָ וּלְעַבְדְּךָ
וְלַאֲמָתֶךָ וְלִשְׂכִירְךָ וּלְתוֹשָׁבְךָ הַגָּרִים עִמָּךְ: וְלִבְהֶמְתְּךָ וְלַחַיָּה אֲשֶׁר בְּאַרְצֶךָ
ישראל תִּהְיֶה כָל־תְּבוּאָתָהּ לֶאֱכֹל: *וְסָפַרְתָּ לְךָ שֶׁבַע שַׁבְּתֹת שָׁנִים
שֶׁבַע שָׁנִים שֶׁבַע פְּעָמִים וְהָיוּ לְךָ יְמֵי שֶׁבַע שַׁבְּתֹת הַשָּׁנִים תֵּשַׁע וְאַרְבָּעִים
שָׁנָה: וְהַעֲבַרְתָּ שׁוֹפַר תְּרוּעָה בַּחֹדֶשׁ הַשְּׁבִעִי בֶּעָשׂוֹר לַחֹדֶשׁ בְּיוֹם הַכִּפֻּרִים
תַּעֲבִירוּ שׁוֹפָר בְּכָל־אַרְצְכֶם: וְקִדַּשְׁתֶּם אֵת שְׁנַת הַחֲמִשִּׁים שָׁנָה וּקְרָאתֶם
דְּרוֹר בָּאָרֶץ לְכָל־יֹשְׁבֶיהָ יוֹבֵל הִוא תִּהְיֶה לָכֶם וְשַׁבְתֶּם אִישׁ אֶל־אֲחֻזָּתוֹ

‏וְאִישׁ אֶל־מִשְׁפַּחְתּוֹ תָּשֻׁבוּ: יוֹבֵל הִוא שְׁנַת הַחֲמִשִּׁים שָׁנָה תִּהְיֶה לָכֶם לֹא
‏תִזְרָעוּ וְלֹא תִקְצְרוּ אֶת־סְפִיחֶיהָ וְלֹא תִבְצְרוּ אֶת־נְזִרֶיהָ: כִּי יוֹבֵל הִוא קֹדֶשׁ
‏תִּהְיֶה לָכֶם מִן־הַשָּׂדֶה תֹּאכְלוּ אֶת־תְּבוּאָתָהּ: בִּשְׁנַת הַיּוֹבֵל הַזֹּאת תָּשֻׁבוּ
‏אִישׁ אֶל־אֲחֻזָּתוֹ:

BEHUKKOTAI   ‏בחקתי

‏אִם־בְּחֻקֹּתַי תֵּלֵכוּ וְאֶת־מִצְוֹתַי תִּשְׁמְרוּ וַעֲשִׂיתֶם אֹתָם: וְנָתַתִּי גִשְׁמֵיכֶם בְּעִתָּם
‏וְנָתְנָה הָאָרֶץ יְבוּלָהּ וְעֵץ הַשָּׂדֶה יִתֵּן פִּרְיוֹ: וְהִשִּׂיג לָכֶם דַּיִשׁ אֶת־בָּצִיר וּבָצִיר
‏יַשִּׂיג אֶת־זָרַע וַאֲכַלְתֶּם לַחְמְכֶם לָשֹׂבַע וִישַׁבְתֶּם לָבֶטַח בְּאַרְצְכֶם: *וְנָתַתִּי
‏שָׁלוֹם בָּאָרֶץ וּשְׁכַבְתֶּם וְאֵין מַחֲרִיד וְהִשְׁבַּתִּי חַיָּה רָעָה מִן־הָאָרֶץ וְחֶרֶב
‏לֹא־תַעֲבֹר בְּאַרְצְכֶם: וּרְדַפְתֶּם אֶת־אֹיְבֵיכֶם וְנָפְלוּ לִפְנֵיכֶם לֶחָרֶב: וְרָדְפוּ
‏מִכֶּם חֲמִשָּׁה מֵאָה וּמֵאָה מִכֶּם רְבָבָה יִרְדֹּפוּ וְנָפְלוּ אֹיְבֵיכֶם לִפְנֵיכֶם לֶחָרֶב:
‏וּפָנִיתִי אֲלֵיכֶם וְהִפְרֵיתִי אֶתְכֶם וְהִרְבֵּיתִי אֶתְכֶם וַהֲקִימֹתִי אֶת־בְּרִיתִי אִתְּכֶם:
‏*וַאֲכַלְתֶּם יָשָׁן נוֹשָׁן וְיָשָׁן מִפְּנֵי חָדָשׁ תּוֹצִיאוּ: וְנָתַתִּי מִשְׁכָּנִי בְּתוֹכְכֶם וְלֹא־
‏תִגְעַל נַפְשִׁי אֶתְכֶם: וְהִתְהַלַּכְתִּי בְּתוֹכְכֶם וְהָיִיתִי לָכֶם לֵאלֹהִים וְאַתֶּם תִּהְיוּ־לִי
‏לְעָם: אֲנִי יְהוָה אֱלֹהֵיכֶם אֲשֶׁר הוֹצֵאתִי אֶתְכֶם מֵאֶרֶץ מִצְרַיִם מִהְיֹת לָהֶם
‏עֲבָדִים וָאֶשְׁבֹּר מֹטֹת עֻלְּכֶם וָאוֹלֵךְ אֶתְכֶם קוֹמְמִיּוּת:

BEMIDBAR   ‏במדבר

‏וַיְדַבֵּר יְהוָה אֶל־מֹשֶׁה בְּמִדְבַּר סִינַי בְּאֹהֶל מוֹעֵד בְּאֶחָד לַחֹדֶשׁ הַשֵּׁנִי בַּשָּׁנָה
‏הַשֵּׁנִית לְצֵאתָם מֵאֶרֶץ מִצְרַיִם לֵאמֹר: שְׂאוּ אֶת־רֹאשׁ כָּל־עֲדַת בְּנֵי־יִשְׂרָאֵל
‏לְמִשְׁפְּחֹתָם לְבֵית אֲבֹתָם בְּמִסְפַּר שֵׁמוֹת כָּל־זָכָר לְגֻלְגְּלֹתָם: מִבֶּן עֶשְׂרִים
‏שָׁנָה וָמַעְלָה כָּל־יֹצֵא צָבָא בְּיִשְׂרָאֵל תִּפְקְדוּ אֹתָם לְצִבְאֹתָם אַתָּה וְאַהֲרֹן:
‏וְאִתְּכֶם יִהְיוּ אִישׁ אִישׁ לַמַּטֶּה אִישׁ רֹאשׁ לְבֵית־אֲבֹתָיו הוּא: *וְאֵלֶּה שְׁמוֹת
‏הָאֲנָשִׁים אֲשֶׁר יַעַמְדוּ אִתְּכֶם לִרְאוּבֵן אֱלִיצוּר בֶּן־שְׁדֵיאוּר: לְשִׁמְעוֹן שְׁלֻמִיאֵל
‏בֶּן־צוּרִישַׁדָּי: לִיהוּדָה נַחְשׁוֹן בֶּן־עַמִּינָדָב: לְיִשָּׂשכָר נְתַנְאֵל בֶּן־צוּעָר:
‏לִזְבוּלֻן אֱלִיאָב בֶּן־חֵלֹן: לִבְנֵי יוֹסֵף לְאֶפְרַיִם אֱלִישָׁמָע בֶּן־עַמִּיהוּד לִמְנַשֶּׁה
‏גַּמְלִיאֵל בֶּן־פְּדָהצוּר: לְבִנְיָמִן אֲבִידָן בֶּן־גִּדְעֹנִי: לְדָן אֲחִיעֶזֶר בֶּן־עַמִּישַׁדָּי:
‏לְאָשֵׁר פַּגְעִיאֵל בֶּן־עָכְרָן: לְגָד אֶלְיָסָף בֶּן־דְּעוּאֵל: לְנַפְתָּלִי אֲחִירַע בֶּן־

‏ויקרא
‏כו:יג–‏ג

‏לוי

‏ישראל

‏במדבר
‏א:א–‏יט

‏לוי

קְרוּאֵי עֵינָן: אֵלֶּה קְרִיאֵי הָעֵדָה נְשִׂיאֵי מַטּוֹת אֲבוֹתָם רָאשֵׁי אַלְפֵי יִשְׂרָאֵל הֵם:
ישראל *וַיִּקַּח מֹשֶׁה וְאַהֲרֹן אֵת הָאֲנָשִׁים הָאֵלֶּה אֲשֶׁר נִקְּבוּ בְּשֵׁמוֹת: וְאֵת כָּל־הָעֵדָה
הִקְהִילוּ בְּאֶחָד לַחֹדֶשׁ הַשֵּׁנִי וַיִּתְיַלְדוּ עַל־מִשְׁפְּחֹתָם לְבֵית אֲבֹתָם בְּמִסְפַּר
שֵׁמוֹת מִבֶּן עֶשְׂרִים שָׁנָה וָמַעְלָה לְגֻלְגְּלֹתָם: כַּאֲשֶׁר צִוָּה יְהוָה אֶת־מֹשֶׁה
וַיִּפְקְדֵם בְּמִדְבַּר סִינָי:

NASO נשא

במדבר ד:כא–לז וַיְדַבֵּר יְהוָה אֶל־מֹשֶׁה לֵּאמֹר: נָשֹׂא אֶת־רֹאשׁ בְּנֵי גֵרְשׁוֹן גַּם־הֵם לְבֵית אֲבֹתָם
לְמִשְׁפְּחֹתָם: מִבֶּן שְׁלֹשִׁים שָׁנָה וָמַעְלָה עַד בֶּן־חֲמִשִּׁים שָׁנָה תִּפְקֹד אוֹתָם
כָּל־הַבָּא לִצְבֹא צָבָא לַעֲבֹד עֲבֹדָה בְּאֹהֶל מוֹעֵד: זֹאת עֲבֹדַת מִשְׁפְּחֹת
לוי הַגֵּרְשֻׁנִּי לַעֲבֹד וּלְמַשָּׂא: *וְנָשְׂאוּ אֶת־יְרִיעֹת הַמִּשְׁכָּן וְאֶת־אֹהֶל מוֹעֵד מִכְסֵהוּ
וּמִכְסֵה הַתַּחַשׁ אֲשֶׁר־עָלָיו מִלְמָעְלָה וְאֶת־מָסַךְ פֶּתַח אֹהֶל מוֹעֵד: וְאֵת קַלְעֵי
הֶחָצֵר וְאֶת־מָסַךְ ׀ פֶּתַח ׀ שַׁעַר הֶחָצֵר אֲשֶׁר עַל־הַמִּשְׁכָּן וְעַל־הַמִּזְבֵּחַ סָבִיב
וְאֵת מֵיתְרֵיהֶם וְאֶת־כָּל־כְּלֵי עֲבֹדָתָם וְאֵת כָּל־אֲשֶׁר יֵעָשֶׂה לָהֶם וְעָבָדוּ:
עַל־פִּי אַהֲרֹן וּבָנָיו תִּהְיֶה כָּל־עֲבֹדַת בְּנֵי הַגֵּרְשֻׁנִּי לְכָל־מַשָּׂאָם וּלְכֹל עֲבֹדָתָם
וּפְקַדְתֶּם עֲלֵהֶם בְּמִשְׁמֶרֶת אֵת כָּל־מַשָּׂאָם: זֹאת עֲבֹדַת מִשְׁפְּחֹת בְּנֵי הַגֵּרְשֻׁנִּי
ישראל בְּאֹהֶל מוֹעֵד וּמִשְׁמַרְתָּם בְּיַד אִיתָמָר בֶּן־אַהֲרֹן הַכֹּהֵן: *בְּנֵי מְרָרִי
לְמִשְׁפְּחֹתָם לְבֵית־אֲבֹתָם תִּפְקֹד אֹתָם: מִבֶּן שְׁלֹשִׁים שָׁנָה וָמַעְלָה וְעַד בֶּן־
חֲמִשִּׁים שָׁנָה תִּפְקְדֵם כָּל־הַבָּא לַצָּבָא לַעֲבֹד אֶת־עֲבֹדַת אֹהֶל מוֹעֵד: וְזֹאת
מִשְׁמֶרֶת מַשָּׂאָם לְכָל־עֲבֹדָתָם בְּאֹהֶל מוֹעֵד קַרְשֵׁי הַמִּשְׁכָּן וּבְרִיחָיו וְעַמּוּדָיו
וַאֲדָנָיו: וְעַמּוּדֵי הֶחָצֵר סָבִיב וְאַדְנֵיהֶם וִיתֵדֹתָם וּמֵיתְרֵיהֶם לְכָל־כְּלֵיהֶם וּלְכֹל
עֲבֹדָתָם וּבְשֵׁמֹת תִּפְקְדוּ אֶת־כְּלֵי מִשְׁמֶרֶת מַשָּׂאָם: זֹאת עֲבֹדַת מִשְׁפְּחֹת בְּנֵי
מְרָרִי לְכָל־עֲבֹדָתָם בְּאֹהֶל מוֹעֵד בְּיַד אִיתָמָר בֶּן־אַהֲרֹן הַכֹּהֵן:

Some extend the ישראל portion:

וַיִּפְקֹד מֹשֶׁה וְאַהֲרֹן וּנְשִׂיאֵי הָעֵדָה אֶת־בְּנֵי הַקְּהָתִי לְמִשְׁפְּחֹתָם וּלְבֵית אֲבֹתָם:
מִבֶּן שְׁלֹשִׁים שָׁנָה וָמַעְלָה וְעַד בֶּן־חֲמִשִּׁים שָׁנָה כָּל־הַבָּא לַצָּבָא לַעֲבֹדָה
בְּאֹהֶל מוֹעֵד: וַיִּהְיוּ פְקֻדֵיהֶם לְמִשְׁפְּחֹתָם אַלְפַּיִם שְׁבַע מֵאוֹת וַחֲמִשִּׁים: אֵלֶּה
פְקוּדֵי מִשְׁפְּחֹת הַקְּהָתִי כָּל־הָעֹבֵד בְּאֹהֶל מוֹעֵד אֲשֶׁר פָּקַד מֹשֶׁה וְאַהֲרֹן
עַל־פִּי יְהוָה בְּיַד־מֹשֶׁה:

בהעלותך

BEHAALOTEKHA

במדבר
ח:א-יד

וַיְדַבֵּ֥ר יְהוָ֖ה אֶל־מֹשֶׁ֥ה לֵּאמֹֽר: דַּבֵּר֙ אֶֽל־אַהֲרֹ֔ן וְאָמַרְתָּ֖ אֵלָ֑יו בְּהַעֲלֹֽתְךָ֙ אֶת־הַנֵּרֹ֔ת אֶל־מוּל֙ פְּנֵ֣י הַמְּנוֹרָ֔ה יָאִ֖ירוּ שִׁבְעַ֥ת הַנֵּרֽוֹת: וַיַּ֤עַשׂ כֵּן֙ אַהֲרֹ֔ן אֶל־מוּל֙ פְּנֵ֣י הַמְּנוֹרָ֔ה הֶעֱלָ֖ה נֵרֹתֶ֑יהָ כַּֽאֲשֶׁ֛ר צִוָּ֥ה יְהוָ֖ה אֶת־מֹשֶֽׁה: וְזֶ֨ה מַֽעֲשֵׂ֤ה הַמְּנֹרָה֙ מִקְשָׁ֣ה זָהָ֔ב עַד־יְרֵכָ֥הּ עַד־פִּרְחָ֖הּ מִקְשָׁ֣ה הִ֑וא כַּמַּרְאֶ֗ה אֲשֶׁ֨ר הֶרְאָ֤ה יְהוָה֙ אֶת־מֹשֶׁ֔ה כֵּ֥ן עָשָׂ֖ה אֶת־הַמְּנֹרָֽה:

לוי

וַיְדַבֵּ֥ר יְהוָ֖ה אֶל־מֹשֶׁ֥ה לֵּאמֹֽר: קַ֚ח אֶת־הַֽלְוִיִּ֔ם מִתּ֖וֹךְ בְּנֵ֣י יִשְׂרָאֵ֑ל וְטִֽהַרְתָּ֖ אֹתָֽם: וְכֹ֨ה־תַֽעֲשֶׂ֤ה לָהֶם֙ לְטַֽהֲרָ֔ם הַזֵּ֥ה עֲלֵיהֶ֖ם מֵ֣י חַטָּ֑את וְהֶעֱבִ֤ירוּ תַ֨עַר֙ עַל־כָּל־בְּשָׂרָ֔ם וְכִבְּס֥וּ בִגְדֵיהֶ֖ם וְהִטֶּהָֽרוּ: וְלָֽקְחוּ֙ פַּ֣ר בֶּן־בָּקָ֔ר וּמִנְחָת֔וֹ סֹ֖לֶת בְּלוּלָ֣ה בַשָּׁ֑מֶן וּפַר־שֵׁנִ֥י בֶן־בָּקָ֖ר תִּקַּ֥ח לְחַטָּֽאת: וְהִקְרַבְתָּ֙ אֶת־הַ֣לְוִיִּ֔ם לִפְנֵ֖י אֹ֣הֶל מוֹעֵ֑ד וְהִ֨קְהַלְתָּ֔ אֶֽת־כָּל־עֲדַ֖ת בְּנֵ֥י יִשְׂרָאֵֽל: ★וְהִקְרַבְתָּ֥ אֶת־הַלְוִיִּ֖ם לִפְנֵ֣י יְהוָ֑ה וְסָֽמְכ֧וּ בְנֵֽי־יִשְׂרָאֵ֛ל אֶת־יְדֵיהֶ֖ם עַל־הַֽלְוִיִּֽם: וְהֵנִיף֩ אַֽהֲרֹ֨ן אֶת־הַֽלְוִיִּ֤ם תְּנוּפָה֙ לִפְנֵ֣י יְהוָ֔ה מֵאֵ֖ת בְּנֵ֣י יִשְׂרָאֵ֑ל וְהָי֕וּ לַֽעֲבֹ֖ד אֶת־עֲבֹדַ֥ת יְהוָֽה: וְהַ֨לְוִיִּ֜ם יִסְמְכ֤וּ אֶת־יְדֵיהֶם֙ עַ֚ל רֹ֣אשׁ הַפָּרִ֔ים וַֽ֠עֲשֵׂה אֶת־הָֽאֶחָ֨ד חַטָּ֜את וְאֶת־הָֽאֶחָ֤ד עֹלָה֙ לַֽיהוָ֔ה לְכַפֵּ֖ר עַל־הַֽלְוִיִּֽם: וְהַֽעֲמַדְתָּ֙ אֶת־הַ֣לְוִיִּ֔ם לִפְנֵ֥י אַֽהֲרֹ֖ן וְלִפְנֵ֣י בָנָ֑יו וְהֵֽנַפְתָּ֥ אֹתָ֛ם תְּנוּפָ֖ה לַֽיהוָֽה: וְהִבְדַּלְתָּ֙ אֶת־הַ֣לְוִיִּ֔ם מִתּ֖וֹךְ בְּנֵ֣י יִשְׂרָאֵ֑ל וְהָ֥יוּ לִ֖י הַֽלְוִיִּֽם:

שלח

SHELAḤ

במדבר
יג:א-כ

וַיְדַבֵּ֥ר יְהוָ֖ה אֶל־מֹשֶׁ֥ה לֵּאמֹֽר: שְׁלַח־לְךָ֣ אֲנָשִׁ֗ים וְיָתֻ֨רוּ֙ אֶת־אֶ֣רֶץ כְּנַ֔עַן אֲשֶׁר־אֲנִ֥י נֹתֵ֖ן לִבְנֵ֣י יִשְׂרָאֵ֑ל אִ֣ישׁ אֶחָד֩ אִ֨ישׁ אֶחָ֜ד לְמַטֵּ֤ה אֲבֹתָיו֙ תִּשְׁלָ֔חוּ כֹּ֖ל נָשִׂ֥יא בָהֶֽם: וַיִּשְׁלַ֨ח אֹתָ֥ם מֹשֶׁ֛ה מִמִּדְבַּ֥ר פָּארָ֖ן עַל־פִּ֣י יְהוָ֑ה כֻּלָּ֣ם אֲנָשִׁ֔ים רָאשֵׁ֥י בְנֵֽי־יִשְׂרָאֵ֖ל הֵֽמָּה:

לוי

★וְאֵ֖לֶּה שְׁמוֹתָ֑ם לְמַטֵּ֣ה רְאוּבֵ֔ן שַׁמּ֖וּעַ בֶּן־זַכּֽוּר: לְמַטֵּ֣ה שִׁמְע֔וֹן שָׁפָ֖ט בֶּן־חוֹרִֽי: לְמַטֵּ֣ה יְהוּדָ֔ה כָּלֵ֖ב בֶּן־יְפֻנֶּֽה: לְמַטֵּ֣ה יִשָּׂשֹׂכָ֔ר יִגְאָ֖ל בֶּן־יוֹסֵֽף: לְמַטֵּ֥ה אֶפְרָ֖יִם הוֹשֵׁ֥עַ בִּן־נֽוּן: לְמַטֵּ֣ה בִנְיָמִ֔ן פַּלְטִ֖י בֶּן־רָפֽוּא: לְמַטֵּ֣ה זְבוּלֻ֔ן גַּדִּיאֵ֖ל בֶּן־סוֹדִֽי: לְמַטֵּ֣ה יוֹסֵ֣ף לְמַטֵּ֣ה מְנַשֶּׁ֔ה גַּדִּ֖י בֶּן־סוּסִֽי: לְמַטֵּ֣ה דָ֔ן עַמִּיאֵ֖ל בֶּן־גְּמַלִּֽי: לְמַטֵּ֣ה אָשֵׁ֔ר סְתוּ֖ר בֶּן־מִֽיכָאֵֽל: לְמַטֵּ֣ה נַפְתָּלִ֔י נַחְבִּ֖י בֶּן־וָפְסִֽי: לְמַטֵּ֣ה גָ֔ד גְּאוּאֵ֖ל בֶּן־מָכִֽי: אֵ֗לֶּה שְׁמ֤וֹת הָֽאֲנָשִׁים֙ אֲשֶׁר־שָׁלַ֣ח מֹשֶׁ֔ה לָת֖וּר אֶת־הָאָ֑רֶץ וַיִּקְרָ֥א מֹשֶׁ֛ה לְהוֹשֵׁ֥עַ בִּן־נ֖וּן יְהוֹשֻֽׁעַ:

ישראל

★וַיִּשְׁלַ֤ח אֹתָם֙ מֹשֶׁ֔ה לָת֖וּר אֶת־אֶ֣רֶץ כְּנָ֑עַן וַיֹּ֣אמֶר אֲלֵהֶ֗ם עֲל֥וּ זֶה֙ בַּנֶּ֔גֶב וַֽעֲלִיתֶ֖ם אֶת־הָהָֽר: וּרְאִיתֶ֥ם

אֶת־הָאָ֜רֶץ מַה־הִ֗וא וְאֶת־הָעָם֙ הַיֹּשֵׁ֣ב עָלֶ֔יהָ הֶחָזָ֥ק הוּא֙ הֲרָפֶ֔ה הַמְעַ֥ט ה֖וּא
אִם־רָ֑ב וּמָ֣ה הָאָ֗רֶץ אֲשֶׁר־הוּא֙ יֹשֵׁ֣ב בָּ֔הּ הֲטוֹבָ֥ה הִ֖וא אִם־רָעָ֑ה וּמָ֣ה הֶֽעָרִ֗ים
אֲשֶׁר־הוּא֙ יוֹשֵׁ֣ב בָּהֵ֔נָּה הַבְּמַֽחֲנִ֖ים אִ֥ם בְּמִבְצָרִֽים: וּמָ֣ה הָ֠אָ֠רֶץ הַשְּׁמֵנָ֨ה הִ֜וא
אִם־רָזָ֗ה הֲיֵֽשׁ־בָּ֥הּ עֵץ֙ אִם־אַ֔יִן וְהִ֨תְחַזַּקְתֶּ֔ם וּלְקַחְתֶּ֖ם מִפְּרִ֣י הָאָ֑רֶץ וְהַ֨יָּמִ֔ים
יְמֵ֖י בִּכּוּרֵ֥י עֲנָבִֽים:

וַיִּקַּ֣ח קֹ֔רַח בֶּן־יִצְהָ֥ר בֶּן־קְהָ֖ת בֶּן־לֵוִ֑י וְדָתָ֨ן וַֽאֲבִירָ֜ם בְּנֵ֧י אֱלִיאָ֛ב וְא֥וֹן בֶּן־
פֶּ֖לֶת בְּנֵ֥י רְאוּבֵֽן: וַיָּקֻ֨מוּ֙ לִפְנֵ֣י מֹשֶׁ֔ה וַֽאֲנָשִׁ֥ים מִבְּנֵֽי־יִשְׂרָאֵ֖ל חֲמִשִּׁ֣ים וּמָאתָ֑יִם
נְשִׂיאֵ֥י עֵדָ֛ה קְרִאֵ֥י מוֹעֵ֖ד אַנְשֵׁי־שֵֽׁם: וַיִּקָּֽהֲל֞וּ עַל־מֹשֶׁ֣ה וְעַֽל־אַֽהֲרֹ֗ן וַיֹּֽאמְר֣וּ
אֲלֵהֶם֮ רַב־לָכֶם֒ כִּ֤י כׇל־הָֽעֵדָה֙ כֻּלָּ֣ם קְדֹשִׁ֔ים וּבְתוֹכָ֖ם יְהֹוָ֑ה וּמַדּ֥וּעַ תִּֽתְנַשְּׂא֖וּ
עַל־קְהַ֥ל יְהֹוָֽה: וַיִּשְׁמַ֣ע מֹשֶׁ֔ה וַיִּפֹּ֖ל עַל־פָּנָֽיו: וַיְדַבֵּ֨ר אֶל־קֹ֜רַח וְאֶֽל־כׇּל־עֲדָתוֹ֮
לֵאמֹר֒ בֹּ֠קֶר וְיֹדַ֨ע יְהֹוָ֧ה אֶת־אֲשֶׁר־ל֛וֹ וְאֶת־הַקָּד֖וֹשׁ וְהִקְרִ֣יב אֵלָ֑יו וְאֵ֛ת אֲשֶׁ֥ר
יִבְחַר־בּ֖וֹ יַקְרִ֥יב אֵלָֽיו: זֹ֖את עֲשׂ֑וּ קְחוּ־לָכֶ֣ם מַחְתּ֔וֹת קֹ֖רַח וְכׇל־עֲדָתֽוֹ: וּתְנ֣וּ
בָהֵ֣ן ׀ אֵ֗שׁ וְשִׂ֨ימוּ עֲלֵיהֶ֥ן ׀ קְטֹ֨רֶת֙ לִפְנֵ֤י יְהֹוָה֙ מָחָ֔ר וְהָיָ֗ה הָאִ֛ישׁ אֲשֶׁר־יִבְחַ֥ר
יְהֹוָ֖ה ה֣וּא הַקָּד֑וֹשׁ רַב־לָכֶ֖ם בְּנֵ֥י לֵוִֽי: וַיֹּ֥אמֶר מֹשֶׁ֖ה אֶל־קֹ֑רַח שִׁמְעוּ־נָ֖א בְּנֵ֥י
לֵוִֽי: הַמְעַ֣ט מִכֶּ֗ם כִּֽי־הִבְדִּיל֩ אֱלֹהֵ֨י יִשְׂרָאֵ֤ל אֶתְכֶם֙ מֵֽעֲדַ֣ת יִשְׂרָאֵ֔ל לְהַקְרִ֥יב
אֶתְכֶ֖ם אֵלָ֑יו לַֽעֲבֹ֗ד אֶת־עֲבֹדַת֙ מִשְׁכַּ֣ן יְהֹוָ֔ה וְלַֽעֲמֹ֛ד לִפְנֵ֥י הָֽעֵדָ֖ה לְשָֽׁרְתָֽם:
וַיַּקְרֵב֙ אֹֽתְךָ֔ וְאֶת־כׇּל־אַחֶ֥יךָ בְנֵֽי־לֵוִ֖י אִתָּ֑ךְ וּבִקַּשְׁתֶּ֖ם גַּם־כְּהֻנָּֽה: לָכֵ֗ן אַתָּה֙
וְכׇל־עֲדָ֣תְךָ֔ הַנֹּֽעָדִ֖ים עַל־יְהֹוָ֑ה וְאַֽהֲרֹ֣ן מַה־ה֔וּא כִּ֥י תַלִּ֖ינוּ עָלָֽיו: וַיִּשְׁלַ֣ח מֹשֶׁ֔ה
לִקְרֹ֛א לְדָתָ֥ן וְלַֽאֲבִירָ֖ם בְּנֵ֣י אֱלִיאָ֑ב וַיֹּֽאמְר֖וּ לֹ֥א נַֽעֲלֶֽה: הַמְעַ֗ט כִּ֤י הֶֽעֱלִיתָ֙נוּ֙
מֵאֶ֨רֶץ זָבַ֤ת חָלָב֙ וּדְבַ֔שׁ לַֽהֲמִיתֵ֖נוּ בַּמִּדְבָּ֑ר כִּֽי־תִשְׂתָּרֵ֥ר עָלֵ֖ינוּ גַּם־הִשְׂתָּרֵֽר:

וַיְדַבֵּ֣ר יְהֹוָ֔ה אֶל־מֹשֶׁ֥ה וְאֶֽל־אַֽהֲרֹ֖ן לֵאמֹֽר: זֹ֚את חֻקַּ֣ת הַתּוֹרָ֔ה אֲשֶׁר־צִוָּ֖ה יְהֹוָ֣ה
לֵאמֹ֑ר דַּבֵּ֣ר ׀ אֶל־בְּנֵ֣י יִשְׂרָאֵ֗ל וְיִקְח֣וּ אֵלֶ֩יךָ֩ פָרָ֨ה אֲדֻמָּ֜ה תְּמִימָ֗ה אֲשֶׁ֤ר אֵֽין־בָּהּ֙
מ֔וּם אֲשֶׁ֛ר לֹֽא־עָלָ֥ה עָלֶ֖יהָ עֹֽל: וּנְתַתֶּ֣ם אֹתָ֔הּ אֶל־אֶלְעָזָ֖ר הַכֹּהֵ֑ן וְהוֹצִ֤יא אֹתָהּ֙
אֶל־מִח֣וּץ לַֽמַּחֲנֶ֔ה וְשָׁחַ֥ט אֹתָ֖הּ לְפָנָֽיו: וְלָקַ֞ח אֶלְעָזָ֧ר הַכֹּהֵ֛ן מִדָּמָ֖הּ בְּאֶצְבָּע֑וֹ
וְהִזָּ֞ה אֶל־נֹ֨כַח פְּנֵ֤י אֹֽהֶל־מוֹעֵד֙ מִדָּמָ֔הּ שֶׁ֖בַע פְּעָמִֽים: וְשָׂרַ֥ף אֶת־הַפָּרָ֖ה לְעֵינָ֑יו

אֶת־עֹרָהּ וְאֶת־בְּשָׂרָהּ וְאֶת־דָּמָהּ עַל־פִּרְשָׁהּ יִשְׂרֹף: וְלָקַח הַכֹּהֵן עֵץ אֶרֶז
וְאֵזוֹב וּשְׁנִי תוֹלָעַת וְהִשְׁלִיךְ אֶל־תּוֹךְ שְׂרֵפַת הַפָּרָה: ⋆וְכִבֶּס בְּגָדָיו הַכֹּהֵן
וְרָחַץ בְּשָׂרוֹ בַּמַּיִם וְאַחַר יָבֹא אֶל־הַמַּחֲנֶה וְטָמֵא הַכֹּהֵן עַד־הָעָרֶב: וְהַשֹּׂרֵף
אֹתָהּ יְכַבֵּס בְּגָדָיו בַּמַּיִם וְרָחַץ בְּשָׂרוֹ בַּמָּיִם וְטָמֵא עַד־הָעָרֶב: וְאָסַף ׀ אִישׁ
טָהוֹר אֵת אֵפֶר הַפָּרָה וְהִנִּיחַ מִחוּץ לַמַּחֲנֶה בְּמָקוֹם טָהוֹר וְהָיְתָה לַעֲדַת
בְּנֵי־יִשְׂרָאֵל לְמִשְׁמֶרֶת לְמֵי נִדָּה חַטָּאת הִוא: ⋆וְכִבֶּס הָאֹסֵף אֶת־אֵפֶר הַפָּרָה
אֶת־בְּגָדָיו וְטָמֵא עַד־הָעָרֶב וְהָיְתָה לִבְנֵי יִשְׂרָאֵל וְלַגֵּר הַגָּר בְּתוֹכָם לְחֻקַּת
עוֹלָם: הַנֹּגֵעַ בְּמֵת לְכָל־נֶפֶשׁ אָדָם וְטָמֵא שִׁבְעַת יָמִים: הוּא יִתְחַטָּא־בוֹ
בַּיּוֹם הַשְּׁלִישִׁי וּבַיּוֹם הַשְּׁבִיעִי יִטְהָר וְאִם־לֹא יִתְחַטָּא בַּיּוֹם הַשְּׁלִישִׁי וּבַיּוֹם
הַשְּׁבִיעִי לֹא יִטְהָר: כָּל־הַנֹּגֵעַ בְּמֵת בְּנֶפֶשׁ הָאָדָם אֲשֶׁר־יָמוּת וְלֹא יִתְחַטָּא
אֶת־מִשְׁכַּן יְהֹוָה טִמֵּא וְנִכְרְתָה הַנֶּפֶשׁ הַהִוא מִיִּשְׂרָאֵל כִּי מֵי נִדָּה לֹא־זֹרַק
עָלָיו טָמֵא יִהְיֶה עוֹד טֻמְאָתוֹ בוֹ: זֹאת הַתּוֹרָה אָדָם כִּי־יָמוּת בְּאֹהֶל כָּל־
הַבָּא אֶל־הָאֹהֶל וְכָל־אֲשֶׁר בָּאֹהֶל יִטְמָא שִׁבְעַת יָמִים: וְכֹל כְּלִי פָתוּחַ אֲשֶׁר
אֵין־צָמִיד פָּתִיל עָלָיו טָמֵא הוּא: וְכֹל אֲשֶׁר־יִגַּע עַל־פְּנֵי הַשָּׂדֶה בַּחֲלַל־חֶרֶב
אוֹ בְמֵת אוֹ־בְעֶצֶם אָדָם אוֹ בְקָבֶר יִטְמָא שִׁבְעַת יָמִים: וְלָקְחוּ לַטָּמֵא מֵעֲפַר
שְׂרֵפַת הַחַטָּאת וְנָתַן עָלָיו מַיִם חַיִּים אֶל־כֶּלִי:

BALAK

וַיַּרְא בָּלָק בֶּן־צִפּוֹר אֵת כָּל־אֲשֶׁר־עָשָׂה יִשְׂרָאֵל לָאֱמֹרִי: וַיָּגָר מוֹאָב מִפְּנֵי
הָעָם מְאֹד כִּי רַב־הוּא וַיָּקָץ מוֹאָב מִפְּנֵי בְּנֵי יִשְׂרָאֵל: וַיֹּאמֶר מוֹאָב אֶל־זִקְנֵי
מִדְיָן עַתָּה יְלַחֲכוּ הַקָּהָל אֶת־כָּל־סְבִיבֹתֵינוּ כִּלְחֹךְ הַשּׁוֹר אֵת יֶרֶק הַשָּׂדֶה
וּבָלָק בֶּן־צִפּוֹר מֶלֶךְ לְמוֹאָב בָּעֵת הַהִוא: ⋆וַיִּשְׁלַח מַלְאָכִים אֶל־בִּלְעָם
בֶּן־בְּעֹר פְּתוֹרָה אֲשֶׁר עַל־הַנָּהָר אֶרֶץ בְּנֵי־עַמּוֹ לִקְרֹא־לוֹ לֵאמֹר הִנֵּה עַם
יָצָא מִמִּצְרַיִם הִנֵּה כִסָּה אֶת־עֵין הָאָרֶץ וְהוּא יֹשֵׁב מִמֻּלִי: וְעַתָּה לְכָה־נָּא
אָרָה־לִּי אֶת־הָעָם הַזֶּה כִּי־עָצוּם הוּא מִמֶּנִּי אוּלַי אוּכַל נַכֶּה־בּוֹ וַאֲגָרְשֶׁנּוּ
מִן־הָאָרֶץ כִּי יָדַעְתִּי אֵת אֲשֶׁר־תְּבָרֵךְ מְבֹרָךְ וַאֲשֶׁר תָּאֹר יוּאָר: וַיֵּלְכוּ זִקְנֵי
מוֹאָב וְזִקְנֵי מִדְיָן וּקְסָמִים בְּיָדָם וַיָּבֹאוּ אֶל־בִּלְעָם וַיְדַבְּרוּ אֵלָיו דִּבְרֵי בָלָק:
⋆וַיֹּאמֶר אֲלֵיהֶם לִינוּ פֹה הַלַּיְלָה וַהֲשִׁבֹתִי אֶתְכֶם דָּבָר כַּאֲשֶׁר יְדַבֵּר יְהֹוָה אֵלָי
וַיֵּשְׁבוּ שָׂרֵי־מוֹאָב עִם־בִּלְעָם: וַיָּבֹא אֱלֹהִים אֶל־בִּלְעָם וַיֹּאמֶר מִי הָאֲנָשִׁים

הָאֵ֖לֶּה עִמָּ֑ךְ: וַיֹּ֨אמֶר בִּלְעָ֜ם אֶל־הָ֣אֱלֹהִ֗ים בָּלָ֧ק בֶּן־צִפֹּ֛ר מֶ֥לֶךְ מוֹאָ֖ב שָׁלַ֥ח
אֵלָֽי: הִנֵּ֤ה הָעָם֙ הַיֹּצֵ֣א מִמִּצְרַ֔יִם וַיְכַ֖ס אֶת־עֵ֣ין הָאָ֑רֶץ עַתָּ֗ה לְכָ֤ה קָֽבָה־לִּי֙ אֹת֔וֹ
אוּלַ֥י אוּכַ֛ל לְהִלָּ֥חֶם בּ֖וֹ וְגֵרַשְׁתִּֽיו: וַיֹּ֨אמֶר אֱלֹהִ֜ים אֶל־בִּלְעָ֗ם לֹ֤א תֵלֵךְ֙ עִמָּהֶ֔ם
לֹ֥א תָאֹ֖ר אֶת־הָעָ֑ם כִּ֥י בָר֖וּךְ הֽוּא:

וַיְדַבֵּ֥ר יְהֹוָ֖ה אֶל־מֹשֶׁ֥ה לֵּאמֹֽר: פִּֽינְחָ֨ס בֶּן־אֶלְעָזָ֜ר בֶּן־אַהֲרֹ֣ן הַכֹּהֵ֗ן הֵשִׁ֤יב
אֶת־חֲמָתִי֙ מֵעַ֣ל בְּנֵֽי־יִשְׂרָאֵ֔ל בְּקַנְא֥וֹ אֶת־קִנְאָתִ֖י בְּתוֹכָ֑ם וְלֹֽא־כִלִּ֥יתִי אֶת־
בְּנֵֽי־יִשְׂרָאֵ֖ל בְּקִנְאָתִֽי: לָכֵ֖ן אֱמֹ֑ר הִנְנִ֨י נֹתֵ֥ן ל֛וֹ אֶת־בְּרִיתִ֖י שָׁלֽוֹם: *וְהָ֤יְתָה לּ֙וֹ
וּלְזַרְע֣וֹ אַחֲרָ֔יו בְּרִ֖ית כְּהֻנַּ֣ת עוֹלָ֑ם תַּ֗חַת אֲשֶׁ֤ר קִנֵּא֙ לֵֽאלֹהָ֔יו וַיְכַפֵּ֖ר עַל־בְּנֵ֥י
יִשְׂרָאֵֽל: וְשֵׁם֩ אִ֨ישׁ יִשְׂרָאֵ֜ל הַמֻּכֶּ֗ה אֲשֶׁ֤ר הֻכָּה֙ אֶת־הַמִּדְיָנִ֔ית זִמְרִ֖י בֶּן־סָל֑וּא
נְשִׂ֥יא בֵֽית־אָ֖ב לַשִּׁמְעֹנִֽי: וְשֵׁ֨ם הָֽאִשָּׁ֧ה הַמֻּכָּ֛ה הַמִּדְיָנִ֖ית כָּזְבִּ֣י בַת־צ֑וּר רֹ֣אשׁ
אֻמּ֥וֹת בֵּית־אָ֛ב בְּמִדְיָ֖ן הֽוּא:

וַיְדַבֵּ֥ר יְהֹוָ֖ה אֶל־מֹשֶׁ֥ה לֵּאמֹֽר: צָר֖וֹר אֶת־הַמִּדְיָנִ֑ים וְהִכִּיתֶ֖ם אוֹתָֽם: כִּֽי־
צֹרְרִ֥ים הֵ֛ם לָכֶ֖ם בְּנִכְלֵיהֶ֑ם אֲשֶׁר־נִכְּל֧וּ לָכֶ֛ם עַל־דְּבַר־פְּע֑וֹר וְעַל־דְּבַ֞ר כָּזְבִּ֣י
בַת־נְשִׂ֤יא מִדְיָן֙ אֲחֹתָ֔ם הַמֻּכָּ֥ה בְיֽוֹם־הַמַּגֵּפָ֖ה עַל־דְּבַר־פְּעֽוֹר: וַיְהִ֖י אַחֲרֵ֥י
הַמַּגֵּפָֽה

וַיֹּ֨אמֶר יְהֹוָ֜ה אֶל־מֹשֶׁ֗ה וְאֶ֧ל אֶלְעָזָ֛ר בֶּן־אַהֲרֹ֥ן הַכֹּהֵ֖ן לֵאמֹֽר: שְׂא֞וּ אֶת־רֹ֣אשׁ ׀
כׇּל־עֲדַ֣ת בְּנֵֽי־יִשְׂרָאֵ֗ל מִבֶּ֨ן עֶשְׂרִ֥ים שָׁנָ֛ה וָמַ֖עְלָה לְבֵ֣ית אֲבֹתָ֑ם כׇּל־יֹצֵ֥א צָבָ֖א
בְּיִשְׂרָאֵֽל: וַיְדַבֵּ֨ר מֹשֶׁ֜ה וְאֶלְעָזָ֤ר הַכֹּהֵן֙ אֹתָ֔ם בְּעַֽרְבֹ֣ת מוֹאָ֑ב עַל־יַרְדֵּ֥ן יְרֵח֖וֹ
לֵאמֹֽר: מִבֶּ֨ן עֶשְׂרִ֥ים שָׁנָ֛ה וָמַ֖עְלָה כַּאֲשֶׁ֨ר צִוָּ֤ה יְהֹוָה֙ אֶת־מֹשֶׁ֔ה וּבְנֵ֖י יִשְׂרָאֵ֔ל
הַיֹּצְאִ֖ים מֵאֶ֥רֶץ מִצְרָֽיִם:

וַיְדַבֵּ֤ר מֹשֶׁה֙ אֶל־רָאשֵׁ֣י הַמַּטּ֔וֹת לִבְנֵ֥י יִשְׂרָאֵ֖ל לֵאמֹ֑ר זֶ֣ה הַדָּבָ֔ר אֲשֶׁ֖ר צִוָּ֥ה
יְהֹוָֽה: אִישׁ֩ כִּֽי־יִדֹּ֨ר נֶ֜דֶר לַֽיהֹוָ֗ה אֽוֹ־הִשָּׁ֤בַע שְׁבֻעָה֙ לֶאְסֹ֤ר אִסָּר֙ עַל־נַפְשׁ֔וֹ
לֹ֥א יַחֵ֖ל דְּבָר֑וֹ כְּכׇל־הַיֹּצֵ֥א מִפִּ֖יו יַעֲשֶֽׂה: וְאִשָּׁ֕ה כִּֽי־תִדֹּ֥ר נֶ֙דֶר֙ לַֽיהֹוָ֔ה וְאָסְרָ֥ה
אִסָּ֖ר בְּבֵ֣ית אָבִ֑יהָ בִּנְעֻרֶֽיהָ: וְשָׁמַ֨ע אָבִ֜יהָ אֶת־נִדְרָ֗הּ וֶֽאֱסָרָהּ֙ אֲשֶׁ֣ר אָֽסְרָ֣ה
עַל־נַפְשָׁ֔הּ וְהֶחֱרִ֥ישׁ לָ֖הּ אָבִ֑יהָ וְקָ֙מוּ֙ כׇּל־נְדָרֶ֔יהָ וְכׇל־אִסָּ֛ר אֲשֶׁר־אָסְרָ֥ה

עַל־נַפְשָׁהּ יָקוּם: וְאִם־הֵנִיא אָבִיהָ אֹתָהּ בְּיוֹם שָׁמְעוֹ כָּל־נְדָרֶיהָ וֶאֱסָרֶיהָ
אֲשֶׁר־אָסְרָה עַל־נַפְשָׁהּ לֹא יָקוּם וַיהוָה יִסְלַח־לָהּ כִּי־הֵנִיא אָבִיהָ אֹתָהּ:
וְאִם־הָיוֹ תִהְיֶה לְאִישׁ וּנְדָרֶיהָ עָלֶיהָ אוֹ מִבְטָא שְׂפָתֶיהָ אֲשֶׁר אָסְרָה עַל־
נַפְשָׁהּ: וְשָׁמַע אִישָׁהּ בְּיוֹם שָׁמְעוֹ וְהֶחֱרִישׁ לָהּ וְקָמוּ נְדָרֶיהָ וֶאֱסָרֶהָ אֲשֶׁר־
אָסְרָה עַל־נַפְשָׁהּ יָקֻמוּ: וְאִם בְּיוֹם שְׁמֹעַ אִישָׁהּ יָנִיא אוֹתָהּ וְהֵפֵר אֶת־נִדְרָהּ
אֲשֶׁר עָלֶיהָ וְאֵת מִבְטָא שְׂפָתֶיהָ אֲשֶׁר אָסְרָה עַל־נַפְשָׁהּ וַיהוָה יִסְלַח־לָהּ:
*וְנֵדֶר אַלְמָנָה וּגְרוּשָׁה כֹּל אֲשֶׁר־אָסְרָה עַל־נַפְשָׁהּ יָקוּם עָלֶיהָ: וְאִם־בֵּית לוי
אִישָׁהּ נָדָרָה אוֹ־אָסְרָה אִסָּר עַל־נַפְשָׁהּ בִּשְׁבֻעָה: וְשָׁמַע אִישָׁהּ וְהֶחֱרִשׁ לָהּ
לֹא הֵנִיא אֹתָהּ וְקָמוּ כָּל־נְדָרֶיהָ וְכָל־אִסָּר אֲשֶׁר־אָסְרָה עַל־נַפְשָׁהּ יָקוּם:
וְאִם־הָפֵר יָפֵר אֹתָם ׀ אִישָׁהּ בְּיוֹם שָׁמְעוֹ כָּל־מוֹצָא שְׂפָתֶיהָ לִנְדָרֶיהָ וּלְאִסַּר
נַפְשָׁהּ לֹא יָקוּם אִישָׁהּ הֲפֵרָם וַיהוָה יִסְלַח־לָהּ: *כָּל־נֵדֶר וְכָל־שְׁבֻעַת אִסָּר ישראל
לְעַנֹּת נָפֶשׁ אִישָׁהּ יְקִימֶנּוּ וְאִישָׁהּ יְפֵרֶנּוּ: וְאִם־הַחֲרֵשׁ יַחֲרִישׁ לָהּ אִישָׁהּ
מִיּוֹם אֶל־יוֹם וְהֵקִים אֶת־כָּל־נְדָרֶיהָ אוֹ אֶת־כָּל־אֱסָרֶיהָ אֲשֶׁר עָלֶיהָ הֵקִים
אֹתָם כִּי־הֶחֱרִשׁ לָהּ בְּיוֹם שָׁמְעוֹ: וְאִם־הָפֵר יָפֵר אֹתָם אַחֲרֵי שָׁמְעוֹ וְנָשָׂא
אֶת־עֲוֹנָהּ: אֵלֶּה הַחֻקִּים אֲשֶׁר צִוָּה יְהוָה אֶת־מֹשֶׁה בֵּין אִישׁ לְאִשְׁתּוֹ בֵּין־
אָב לְבִתּוֹ בִּנְעֻרֶיהָ בֵּית אָבִיהָ:

MASEI   מסעי

במדבר
לג:א-נג
אֵלֶּה מַסְעֵי בְנֵי־יִשְׂרָאֵל אֲשֶׁר יָצְאוּ מֵאֶרֶץ מִצְרַיִם לְצִבְאֹתָם בְּיַד־מֹשֶׁה
וְאַהֲרֹן: וַיִּכְתֹּב מֹשֶׁה אֶת־מוֹצָאֵיהֶם לְמַסְעֵיהֶם עַל־פִּי יְהוָה וְאֵלֶּה מַסְעֵיהֶם
לְמוֹצָאֵיהֶם: וַיִּסְעוּ מֵרַעְמְסֵס בַּחֹדֶשׁ הָרִאשׁוֹן בַּחֲמִשָּׁה עָשָׂר יוֹם לַחֹדֶשׁ
הָרִאשׁוֹן מִמָּחֳרַת הַפֶּסַח יָצְאוּ בְנֵי־יִשְׂרָאֵל בְּיָד רָמָה לְעֵינֵי כָּל־מִצְרָיִם:
*וּמִצְרַיִם מְקַבְּרִים אֵת אֲשֶׁר הִכָּה יְהוָה בָּהֶם כָּל־בְּכוֹר וּבֵאלֹהֵיהֶם עָשָׂה לוי
יְהוָה שְׁפָטִים: וַיִּסְעוּ בְנֵי־יִשְׂרָאֵל מֵרַעְמְסֵס וַיַּחֲנוּ בְּסֻכֹּת: וַיִּסְעוּ מִסֻּכֹּת
וַיַּחֲנוּ בְאֵתָם אֲשֶׁר בִּקְצֵה הַמִּדְבָּר: *וַיִּסְעוּ מֵאֵתָם וַיָּשָׁב עַל־פִּי הַחִירֹת אֲשֶׁר ישראל
עַל־פְּנֵי בַּעַל צְפוֹן וַיַּחֲנוּ לִפְנֵי מִגְדֹּל: וַיִּסְעוּ מִפְּנֵי הַחִירֹת וַיַּעַבְרוּ בְתוֹךְ־הַיָּם
הַמִּדְבָּרָה וַיֵּלְכוּ דֶּרֶךְ שְׁלֹשֶׁת יָמִים בְּמִדְבַּר אֵתָם וַיַּחֲנוּ בְּמָרָה: וַיִּסְעוּ מִמָּרָה
וַיָּבֹאוּ אֵילִמָה וּבְאֵילִם שְׁתֵּים עֶשְׂרֵה עֵינֹת מַיִם וְשִׁבְעִים תְּמָרִים וַיַּחֲנוּ־שָׁם:
וַיִּסְעוּ מֵאֵילִם וַיַּחֲנוּ עַל־יַם־סוּף:

Some extend the לוי portion:

וַיִּסְעוּ מִיַּם־סוּף וַיַּחֲנוּ בְּמִדְבַּר־סִין: וַיִּסְעוּ מִמִּדְבַּר־סִין וַיַּחֲנוּ בְּדָפְקָה: וַיִּסְעוּ
מִדָּפְקָה וַיַּחֲנוּ בְּאָלוּשׁ: וַיִּסְעוּ מֵאָלוּשׁ וַיַּחֲנוּ בִּרְפִידִם וְלֹא־הָיָה שָׁם מַיִם לָעָם
לִשְׁתּוֹת: וַיִּסְעוּ מֵרְפִידִם וַיַּחֲנוּ בְּמִדְבַּר סִינָי: וַיִּסְעוּ מִמִּדְבַּר סִינָי וַיַּחֲנוּ בְּקִבְרֹת
הַתַּאֲוָה: וַיִּסְעוּ מִקִּבְרֹת הַתַּאֲוָה וַיַּחֲנוּ בַּחֲצֵרֹת: וַיִּסְעוּ מֵחֲצֵרֹת וַיַּחֲנוּ בְּרִתְמָה:
וַיִּסְעוּ מֵרִתְמָה וַיַּחֲנוּ בְּרִמֹּן פָּרֶץ: וַיִּסְעוּ מֵרִמֹּן פָּרֶץ וַיַּחֲנוּ בְּלִבְנָה: וַיִּסְעוּ
מִלִּבְנָה וַיַּחֲנוּ בְּרִסָּה: וַיִּסְעוּ מֵרִסָּה וַיַּחֲנוּ בִּקְהֵלָתָה: וַיִּסְעוּ מִקְּהֵלָתָה וַיַּחֲנוּ
בְּהַר־שָׁפֶר: וַיִּסְעוּ מֵהַר־שָׁפֶר וַיַּחֲנוּ בַּחֲרָדָה: וַיִּסְעוּ מֵחֲרָדָה וַיַּחֲנוּ בְּמַקְהֵלֹת:
וַיִּסְעוּ מִמַּקְהֵלֹת וַיַּחֲנוּ בְּתָחַת: וַיִּסְעוּ מִתָּחַת וַיַּחֲנוּ בְּתָרַח: וַיִּסְעוּ מִתָּרַח וַיַּחֲנוּ
בְּמִתְקָה: וַיִּסְעוּ מִמִּתְקָה וַיַּחֲנוּ בְּחַשְׁמֹנָה: וַיִּסְעוּ מֵחַשְׁמֹנָה וַיַּחֲנוּ בְּמֹסֵרוֹת:
וַיִּסְעוּ מִמֹּסֵרוֹת וַיַּחֲנוּ בִּבְנֵי יַעֲקָן: וַיִּסְעוּ מִבְּנֵי יַעֲקָן וַיַּחֲנוּ בְּחֹר הַגִּדְגָּד: וַיִּסְעוּ
מֵחֹר הַגִּדְגָּד וַיַּחֲנוּ בְּיָטְבָתָה: וַיִּסְעוּ מִיָּטְבָתָה וַיַּחֲנוּ בְּעַבְרֹנָה: וַיִּסְעוּ מֵעַבְרֹנָה
וַיַּחֲנוּ בְּעֶצְיֹן גָּבֶר: וַיִּסְעוּ מֵעֶצְיֹן גָּבֶר וַיַּחֲנוּ בְמִדְבַּר־צִן הִוא קָדֵשׁ: וַיִּסְעוּ
מִקָּדֵשׁ וַיַּחֲנוּ בְּהֹר הָהָר בִּקְצֵה אֶרֶץ אֱדוֹם: וַיַּעַל אַהֲרֹן הַכֹּהֵן אֶל־הֹר הָהָר
עַל־פִּי יְהוָה וַיָּמָת שָׁם בִּשְׁנַת הָאַרְבָּעִים לְצֵאת בְּנֵי־יִשְׂרָאֵל מֵאֶרֶץ מִצְרַיִם
בַּחֹדֶשׁ הַחֲמִישִׁי בְּאֶחָד לַחֹדֶשׁ: וְאַהֲרֹן בֶּן־שָׁלֹשׁ וְעֶשְׂרִים וּמְאַת שָׁנָה בְּמֹתוֹ
בְּהֹר הָהָר: וַיִּשְׁמַע הַכְּנַעֲנִי מֶלֶךְ עֲרָד וְהוּא־יֹשֵׁב בַּנֶּגֶב בְּאֶרֶץ
כְּנַעַן בְּבֹא בְּנֵי יִשְׂרָאֵל: וַיִּסְעוּ מֵהֹר הָהָר וַיַּחֲנוּ בְּצַלְמֹנָה: וַיִּסְעוּ מִצַּלְמֹנָה
וַיַּחֲנוּ בְּפוּנֹן: וַיִּסְעוּ מִפּוּנֹן וַיַּחֲנוּ בְּאֹבֹת: וַיִּסְעוּ מֵאֹבֹת וַיַּחֲנוּ בְּעִיֵּי הָעֲבָרִים
בִּגְבוּל מוֹאָב: וַיִּסְעוּ מֵעִיִּים וַיַּחֲנוּ בְּדִיבֹן גָּד: וַיִּסְעוּ מִדִּיבֹן גָּד וַיַּחֲנוּ בְּעַלְמֹן
דִּבְלָתָיְמָה: וַיִּסְעוּ מֵעַלְמֹן דִּבְלָתָיְמָה וַיַּחֲנוּ בְּהָרֵי הָעֲבָרִים לִפְנֵי נְבוֹ: וַיִּסְעוּ
מֵהָרֵי הָעֲבָרִים וַיַּחֲנוּ בְּעַרְבֹת מוֹאָב עַל יַרְדֵּן יְרֵחוֹ: וַיַּחֲנוּ עַל־הַיַּרְדֵּן מִבֵּית
הַיְשִׁמֹת עַד אָבֵל הַשִּׁטִּים בְּעַרְבֹת מוֹאָב: *וַיְדַבֵּר יְהוָה אֶל־* **ישראל**
מֹשֶׁה בְּעַרְבֹת מוֹאָב עַל־יַרְדֵּן יְרֵחוֹ לֵאמֹר: דַּבֵּר אֶל־בְּנֵי יִשְׂרָאֵל וְאָמַרְתָּ
אֲלֵהֶם כִּי אַתֶּם עֹבְרִים אֶת־הַיַּרְדֵּן אֶל־אֶרֶץ כְּנָעַן: וְהוֹרַשְׁתֶּם אֶת־כָּל־יֹשְׁבֵי
הָאָרֶץ מִפְּנֵיכֶם וְאִבַּדְתֶּם אֵת כָּל־מַשְׂכִּיֹּתָם וְאֵת כָּל־צַלְמֵי מַסֵּכֹתָם תְּאַבֵּדוּ
וְאֵת כָּל־בָּמוֹתָם תַּשְׁמִידוּ: וְהוֹרַשְׁתֶּם אֶת־הָאָרֶץ וִישַׁבְתֶּם־בָּהּ כִּי לָכֶם נָתַתִּי
אֶת־הָאָרֶץ לָרֶשֶׁת אֹתָהּ:

DEVARIM

דברים

אֵ֣לֶּה הַדְּבָרִ֗ים אֲשֶׁ֨ר דִּבֶּ֤ר מֹשֶׁה֙ אֶל־כׇּל־יִשְׂרָאֵ֔ל בְּעֵ֖בֶר הַיַּרְדֵּ֑ן בַּמִּדְבָּ֣ר בָּעֲרָבָ֡ה
מ֣וֹל סוּף֩ בֵּֽין־פָּארָ֨ן וּבֵֽין־תֹּ֜פֶל וְלָבָ֤ן וַחֲצֵרֹת֙ וְדִ֣י זָהָ֔ב: אַחַ֨ד עָשָׂ֥ר יוֹם֙ מֵֽחֹרֵ֔ב
דֶּ֖רֶךְ הַר־שֵׂעִ֑יר עַ֖ד קָדֵ֥שׁ בַּרְנֵֽעַ: וַיְהִי֙ בְּאַרְבָּעִ֣ים שָׁנָ֔ה בְּעַשְׁתֵּֽי־עָשָׂ֥ר חֹ֖דֶשׁ
בְּאֶחָ֣ד לַחֹ֑דֶשׁ דִּבֶּ֤ר מֹשֶׁה֙ אֶל־בְּנֵ֣י יִשְׂרָאֵ֔ל כְּ֠כֹ֠ל אֲשֶׁ֨ר צִוָּ֧ה יְהֹוָ֛ה אֹת֖וֹ אֲלֵהֶֽם:

לוי

אַֽחֲרֵ֣י הַכֹּת֗וֹ אֵ֚ת סִיחֹן֙ מֶ֣לֶךְ הָֽאֱמֹרִ֔י אֲשֶׁ֥ר יוֹשֵׁ֖ב בְּחֶשְׁבּ֑וֹן וְאֵ֗ת ע֚וֹג מֶ֣לֶךְ
הַבָּשָׁ֔ן אֲשֶׁר־יוֹשֵׁ֥ב בְּעַשְׁתָּרֹ֖ת בְּאֶדְרֶֽעִי: בְּעֵ֥בֶר הַיַּרְדֵּ֖ן בְּאֶ֣רֶץ מוֹאָ֑ב הוֹאִ֣יל
מֹשֶׁ֔ה בֵּאֵ֛ר אֶת־הַתּוֹרָ֥ה הַזֹּ֖את לֵאמֹֽר: יְהֹוָ֧ה אֱלֹהֵ֛ינוּ דִּבֶּ֥ר אֵלֵ֖ינוּ בְּחֹרֵ֣ב לֵאמֹ֑ר
רַב־לָכֶ֥ם שֶׁ֖בֶת בָּהָ֥ר הַזֶּֽה: פְּנ֣וּ ׀ וּסְע֣וּ לָכֶ֗ם וּבֹ֨אוּ הַ֥ר הָֽאֱמֹרִי֮ וְאֶל־כׇּל־שְׁכֵנָיו֒
בָּעֲרָבָ֥ה בָהָ֛ר וּבַשְּׁפֵלָ֥ה וּבַנֶּ֖גֶב וּבְח֣וֹף הַיָּ֑ם אֶ֤רֶץ הַֽכְּנַעֲנִי֙ וְהַלְּבָנ֔וֹן עַד־הַנָּהָ֥ר
הַגָּדֹ֖ל נְהַר־פְּרָֽת: רְאֵ֛ה נָתַ֥תִּי לִפְנֵיכֶ֖ם אֶת־הָאָ֑רֶץ בֹּ֚אוּ וּרְשׁ֣וּ אֶת־הָאָ֔רֶץ

ישראל

אֲשֶׁ֣ר נִשְׁבַּ֣ע יְ֠הֹוָ֠ה לַאֲבֹ֨תֵיכֶ֜ם לְאַבְרָהָ֨ם לְיִצְחָ֤ק וּֽלְיַעֲקֹב֙ לָתֵ֣ת לָהֶ֔ם וּלְזַרְעָ֖ם
אַחֲרֵיהֶֽם: וָֽאֹמַ֣ר אֲלֵכֶ֔ם בָּעֵ֥ת הַהִ֖וא לֵאמֹ֑ר לֹֽא־אוּכַ֥ל לְבַדִּ֖י שְׂאֵ֥ת אֶתְכֶֽם:
יְהֹוָ֥ה אֱלֹֽהֵיכֶ֖ם הִרְבָּ֣ה אֶתְכֶ֑ם וְהִנְּכֶ֣ם הַיּ֔וֹם כְּכוֹכְבֵ֥י הַשָּׁמַ֖יִם לָרֹֽב: יְהֹוָ֞ה אֱלֹהֵ֣י
אֲבֽוֹתֵכֶ֗ם יֹסֵ֧ף עֲלֵיכֶ֛ם כָּכֶ֖ם אֶ֣לֶף פְּעָמִ֑ים וִיבָרֵ֣ךְ אֶתְכֶ֔ם כַּאֲשֶׁ֖ר דִּבֶּ֥ר לָכֶֽם:

VA'ET-HANAN

ואתחנן

וָאֶתְחַנַּ֖ן אֶל־יְהֹוָ֑ה בָּעֵ֥ת הַהִ֖וא לֵאמֹֽר: אֲדֹנָ֣י יֱהֹוִ֗ה אַתָּ֤ה הַֽחִלּ֙וֹתָ֙ לְהַרְא֣וֹת
אֶֽת־עַבְדְּךָ֔ אֶ֨ת־גׇּדְלְךָ֔ וְאֶת־יָדְךָ֖ הַחֲזָקָ֑ה אֲשֶׁ֤ר מִי־אֵל֙ בַּשָּׁמַ֣יִם וּבָאָ֔רֶץ אֲשֶׁר־
יַעֲשֶׂ֥ה כְמַעֲשֶׂ֖יךָ וְכִגְבֽוּרֹתֶֽךָ: אֶעְבְּרָה־נָּ֗א וְאֶרְאֶה֙ אֶת־הָאָ֣רֶץ הַטּוֹבָ֔ה אֲשֶׁ֖ר
בְּעֵ֣בֶר הַיַּרְדֵּ֑ן הָהָ֥ר הַטּ֛וֹב הַזֶּ֖ה וְהַלְּבָנֹֽן: וַיִּתְעַבֵּ֨ר יְהֹוָ֥ה בִּי֙ לְמַ֣עַנְכֶ֔ם וְלֹ֥א

לוי

שָׁמַ֖ע אֵלָ֑י וַיֹּ֨אמֶר יְהֹוָ֤ה אֵלַי֙ רַב־לָ֔ךְ אַל־תּ֗וֹסֶף דַּבֵּ֥ר אֵלַ֛י ע֖וֹד בַּדָּבָ֥ר הַזֶּֽה:
עֲלֵ֣ה ׀ רֹ֣אשׁ הַפִּסְגָּ֗ה וְשָׂ֥א עֵינֶ֛יךָ יָ֧מָּה וְצָפֹ֛נָה וְתֵימָ֥נָה וּמִזְרָ֖חָה וּרְאֵ֣ה בְעֵינֶ֑יךָ
כִּי־לֹ֥א תַעֲבֹ֖ר אֶת־הַיַּרְדֵּ֥ן הַזֶּֽה: וְצַ֥ו אֶת־יְהוֹשֻׁ֖עַ וְחַזְּקֵ֣הוּ וְאַמְּצֵ֑הוּ כִּי־ה֣וּא
יַעֲבֹ֗ר לִפְנֵי֙ הָעָ֣ם הַזֶּ֔ה וְהוּא֙ יַנְחִ֣יל אוֹתָ֔ם אֶת־הָאָ֖רֶץ אֲשֶׁ֥ר תִּרְאֶֽה: וַנֵּ֣שֶׁב
בַּגָּ֔יְא מ֖וּל בֵּ֥ית פְּעֽוֹר:

וְעַתָּ֣ה יִשְׂרָאֵ֗ל שְׁמַ֤ע אֶל־הַֽחֻקִּים֙ וְאֶל־הַמִּשְׁפָּטִ֔ים אֲשֶׁ֧ר אָנֹכִ֛י מְלַמֵּ֥ד אֶתְכֶ֖ם
לַעֲשׂ֑וֹת לְמַ֣עַן תִּֽחְי֗וּ וּבָאתֶם֙ וִֽירִשְׁתֶּ֣ם אֶת־הָאָ֔רֶץ אֲשֶׁ֧ר יְהֹוָ֛ה אֱלֹהֵ֥י אֲבֹתֵיכֶ֖ם

נֹתֵן לָכֶם: לֹא תֹסִפוּ עַל־הַדָּבָר אֲשֶׁר אָנֹכִי מְצַוֶּה אֶתְכֶם וְלֹא תִגְרְעוּ מִמֶּנּוּ לִשְׁמֹר אֶת־מִצְוֹת יְהוָה אֱלֹהֵיכֶם אֲשֶׁר אָנֹכִי מְצַוֶּה אֶתְכֶם: עֵינֵיכֶם הָרֹאוֹת אֵת אֲשֶׁר־עָשָׂה יְהוָה בְּבַעַל פְּעוֹר כִּי כָל־הָאִישׁ אֲשֶׁר הָלַךְ אַחֲרֵי בַעַל־ פְּעוֹר הִשְׁמִידוֹ יְהוָה אֱלֹהֶיךָ מִקִּרְבֶּךָ: וְאַתֶּם הַדְּבֵקִים בַּיהוָה אֱלֹהֵיכֶם חַיִּים כֻּלְּכֶם הַיּוֹם: *רְאֵה | לִמַּדְתִּי אֶתְכֶם חֻקִּים וּמִשְׁפָּטִים כַּאֲשֶׁר צִוַּנִי יְהוָה אֱלֹהָי לַעֲשׂוֹת כֵּן בְּקֶרֶב הָאָרֶץ אֲשֶׁר אַתֶּם בָּאִים שָׁמָּה לְרִשְׁתָּהּ: וּשְׁמַרְתֶּם וַעֲשִׂיתֶם כִּי הִוא חָכְמַתְכֶם וּבִינַתְכֶם לְעֵינֵי הָעַמִּים אֲשֶׁר יִשְׁמְעוּן אֵת כָּל־ הַחֻקִּים הָאֵלֶּה וְאָמְרוּ רַק עַם־חָכָם וְנָבוֹן הַגּוֹי הַגָּדוֹל הַזֶּה: כִּי מִי־גוֹי גָּדוֹל אֲשֶׁר־לוֹ אֱלֹהִים קְרֹבִים אֵלָיו כַּיהוָה אֱלֹהֵינוּ בְּכָל־קָרְאֵנוּ אֵלָיו: וּמִי גּוֹי גָּדוֹל אֲשֶׁר־לוֹ חֻקִּים וּמִשְׁפָּטִים צַדִּיקִם כְּכֹל הַתּוֹרָה הַזֹּאת אֲשֶׁר אָנֹכִי נֹתֵן לִפְנֵיכֶם הַיּוֹם:

ישראל

עקב
EKEV

וְהָיָה | עֵקֶב תִּשְׁמְעוּן אֵת הַמִּשְׁפָּטִים הָאֵלֶּה וּשְׁמַרְתֶּם וַעֲשִׂיתֶם אֹתָם וְשָׁמַר יְהוָה אֱלֹהֶיךָ לְךָ אֶת־הַבְּרִית וְאֶת־הַחֶסֶד אֲשֶׁר נִשְׁבַּע לַאֲבֹתֶיךָ: וַאֲהֵבְךָ וּבֵרַכְךָ וְהִרְבֶּךָ וּבֵרַךְ פְּרִי־בִטְנְךָ וּפְרִי־אַדְמָתֶךָ דְּגָנְךָ וְתִירֹשְׁךָ וְיִצְהָרֶךָ שְׁגַר־ אֲלָפֶיךָ וְעַשְׁתְּרֹת צֹאנֶךָ עַל הָאֲדָמָה אֲשֶׁר־נִשְׁבַּע לַאֲבֹתֶיךָ לָתֶת לָךְ: בָּרוּךְ תִּהְיֶה מִכָּל־הָעַמִּים לֹא־יִהְיֶה בְךָ עָקָר וַעֲקָרָה וּבִבְהֶמְתֶּךָ: וְהֵסִיר יְהוָה מִמְּךָ כָּל־חֹלִי וְכָל־מַדְוֵי מִצְרַיִם הָרָעִים אֲשֶׁר יָדַעְתָּ לֹא יְשִׂימָם בָּךְ וּנְתָנָם בְּכָל־שֹׂנְאֶיךָ: וְאָכַלְתָּ אֶת־כָּל־הָעַמִּים אֲשֶׁר יְהוָה אֱלֹהֶיךָ נֹתֵן לָךְ לֹא־תָחוֹס עֵינְךָ עֲלֵיהֶם וְלֹא תַעֲבֹד אֶת־אֱלֹהֵיהֶם כִּי־מוֹקֵשׁ הוּא לָךְ: כִּי תֹאמַר בִּלְבָבְךָ רַבִּים הַגּוֹיִם הָאֵלֶּה מִמֶּנִּי אֵיכָה אוּכַל לְהוֹרִישָׁם: לֹא תִירָא מֵהֶם זָכֹר תִּזְכֹּר אֵת אֲשֶׁר־עָשָׂה יְהוָה אֱלֹהֶיךָ לְפַרְעֹה וּלְכָל־מִצְרָיִם: הַמַּסֹּת הַגְּדֹלֹת אֲשֶׁר־רָאוּ עֵינֶיךָ וְהָאֹתֹת וְהַמֹּפְתִים וְהַיָּד הַחֲזָקָה וְהַזְּרֹעַ הַנְּטוּיָה אֲשֶׁר הוֹצִאֲךָ יְהוָה אֱלֹהֶיךָ כֵּן־יַעֲשֶׂה יְהוָה אֱלֹהֶיךָ לְכָל־הָעַמִּים אֲשֶׁר־אַתָּה יָרֵא מִפְּנֵיהֶם: וְגַם אֶת־הַצִּרְעָה יְשַׁלַּח יְהוָה אֱלֹהֶיךָ בָּם עַד־אֲבֹד הַנִּשְׁאָרִים וְהַנִּסְתָּרִים מִפָּנֶיךָ: לֹא תַעֲרֹץ מִפְּנֵיהֶם כִּי־יְהוָה אֱלֹהֶיךָ בְּקִרְבֶּךָ אֵל גָּדוֹל וְנוֹרָא: *וְנָשַׁל יְהוָה אֱלֹהֶיךָ אֶת־הַגּוֹיִם הָאֵל מִפָּנֶיךָ מְעַט מְעָט לֹא תוּכַל כַּלֹּתָם מַהֵר פֶּן־תִּרְבֶּה עָלֶיךָ חַיַּת הַשָּׂדֶה: וּנְתָנָם יְהוָה אֱלֹהֶיךָ לְפָנֶיךָ וְהָמָם

דברים
ז:יב-חי

לוי

מְהוּמָה גְדֹלָה עַד הִשָּׁמְדָם: וְנָתַן מַלְכֵיהֶם בְּיָדֶךָ וְהַאֲבַדְתָּ אֶת־שְׁמָם מִתַּחַת הַשָּׁמָיִם לֹא־יִתְיַצֵּב אִישׁ בְּפָנֶיךָ עַד הִשְׁמִדְךָ אֹתָם: פְּסִילֵי אֱלֹהֵיהֶם תִּשְׂרְפוּן בָּאֵשׁ לֹא־תַחְמֹד כֶּסֶף וְזָהָב עֲלֵיהֶם וְלָקַחְתָּ לָךְ פֶּן תִּוָּקֵשׁ בּוֹ כִּי תוֹעֲבַת יְהוָה אֱלֹהֶיךָ הוּא: וְלֹא־תָבִיא תוֹעֵבָה אֶל־בֵּיתֶךָ וְהָיִיתָ חֵרֶם כָּמֹהוּ שַׁקֵּץ ׀ תְּשַׁקְּצֶנּוּ וְתַעֵב ׀ תְּתַעֲבֶנּוּ כִּי־חֵרֶם הוּא:

כָּל־הַמִּצְוָה אֲשֶׁר אָנֹכִי מְצַוְּךָ הַיּוֹם תִּשְׁמְרוּן לַעֲשׂוֹת לְמַעַן תִּחְיוּן וּרְבִיתֶם וּבָאתֶם וִירִשְׁתֶּם אֶת־הָאָרֶץ אֲשֶׁר־נִשְׁבַּע יְהוָה לַאֲבֹתֵיכֶם: וְזָכַרְתָּ אֶת־כָּל־ הַדֶּרֶךְ אֲשֶׁר הוֹלִיכֲךָ יְהוָה אֱלֹהֶיךָ זֶה אַרְבָּעִים שָׁנָה בַּמִּדְבָּר לְמַעַן עַנֹּתְךָ לְנַסֹּתְךָ לָדַעַת אֶת־אֲשֶׁר בִּלְבָבְךָ הֲתִשְׁמֹר מִצְוֹתָו אִם־לֹא: וַיְעַנְּךָ וַיַּרְעִבֶךָ וַיַּאֲכִלְךָ אֶת־הַמָּן אֲשֶׁר לֹא־יָדַעְתָּ וְלֹא יָדְעוּן אֲבֹתֶיךָ לְמַעַן הוֹדִיעֲךָ כִּי לֹא עַל־הַלֶּחֶם לְבַדּוֹ יִחְיֶה הָאָדָם כִּי עַל־כָּל־מוֹצָא פִי־יְהוָה יִחְיֶה הָאָדָם: _{ישראל} *שִׂמְלָתְךָ לֹא בָלְתָה מֵעָלֶיךָ וְרַגְלְךָ לֹא בָצֵקָה זֶה אַרְבָּעִים שָׁנָה: וְיָדַעְתָּ עִם־ לְבָבֶךָ כִּי כַּאֲשֶׁר יְיַסֵּר אִישׁ אֶת־בְּנוֹ יְהוָה אֱלֹהֶיךָ מְיַסְּרֶךָּ: וְשָׁמַרְתָּ אֶת־מִצְוֹת יְהוָה אֱלֹהֶיךָ לָלֶכֶת בִּדְרָכָיו וּלְיִרְאָה אֹתוֹ: כִּי יְהוָה אֱלֹהֶיךָ מְבִיאֲךָ אֶל־אֶרֶץ טוֹבָה אֶרֶץ נַחֲלֵי מָיִם עֲיָנֹת וּתְהֹמֹת יֹצְאִים בַּבִּקְעָה וּבָהָר: אֶרֶץ חִטָּה וּשְׂעֹרָה וְגֶפֶן וּתְאֵנָה וְרִמּוֹן אֶרֶץ־זֵית שֶׁמֶן וּדְבָשׁ: אֶרֶץ אֲשֶׁר לֹא בְמִסְכֵּנֻת תֹּאכַל־בָּהּ לֶחֶם לֹא־תֶחְסַר כֹּל בָּהּ אֶרֶץ אֲשֶׁר אֲבָנֶיהָ בַרְזֶל וּמֵהֲרָרֶיהָ תַּחְצֹב נְחֹשֶׁת: וְאָכַלְתָּ וְשָׂבָעְתָּ וּבֵרַכְתָּ אֶת־יְהוָה אֱלֹהֶיךָ עַל־הָאָרֶץ הַטֹּבָה אֲשֶׁר נָתַן־לָךְ:

ראה   RE'EH

_{דברים}
_{יא:כו-יב:י}
רְאֵה אָנֹכִי נֹתֵן לִפְנֵיכֶם הַיּוֹם בְּרָכָה וּקְלָלָה: אֶת־הַבְּרָכָה אֲשֶׁר תִּשְׁמְעוּ אֶל־ מִצְוֹת יְהוָה אֱלֹהֵיכֶם אֲשֶׁר אָנֹכִי מְצַוֶּה אֶתְכֶם הַיּוֹם: וְהַקְּלָלָה אִם־לֹא תִשְׁמְעוּ אֶל־מִצְוֹת יְהוָה אֱלֹהֵיכֶם וְסַרְתֶּם מִן־הַדֶּרֶךְ אֲשֶׁר אָנֹכִי מְצַוֶּה אֶתְכֶם הַיּוֹם לָלֶכֶת אַחֲרֵי אֱלֹהִים אֲחֵרִים אֲשֶׁר לֹא־יְדַעְתֶּם: וְהָיָה כִּי יְבִיאֲךָ יְהוָה אֱלֹהֶיךָ אֶל־הָאָרֶץ אֲשֶׁר־אַתָּה בָא־שָׁמָּה לְרִשְׁתָּהּ וְנָתַתָּה אֶת־הַבְּרָכָה עַל־הַר גְּרִזִים וְאֶת־הַקְּלָלָה עַל־הַר עֵיבָל: הֲלֹא־הֵמָּה בְּעֵבֶר הַיַּרְדֵּן אַחֲרֵי דֶּרֶךְ מְבוֹא הַשֶּׁמֶשׁ בְּאֶרֶץ הַכְּנַעֲנִי הַיֹּשֵׁב בָּעֲרָבָה מוּל הַגִּלְגָּל אֵצֶל אֵלוֹנֵי מֹרֶה: כִּי אַתֶּם עֹבְרִים אֶת־הַיַּרְדֵּן לָבֹא לָרֶשֶׁת אֶת־הָאָרֶץ אֲשֶׁר־יְהוָה אֱלֹהֵיכֶם

לוי נָתַן לָכֶם וִירִשְׁתֶּם אֹתָהּ וִישַׁבְתֶּם־בָּהּ: *וּשְׁמַרְתֶּם לַעֲשׂוֹת אֵת כָּל־הַחֻקִּים
וְאֶת־הַמִּשְׁפָּטִים אֲשֶׁר אָנֹכִי נֹתֵן לִפְנֵיכֶם הַיּוֹם: אֵלֶּה הַחֻקִּים וְהַמִּשְׁפָּטִים
אֲשֶׁר תִּשְׁמְרוּן לַעֲשׂוֹת בָּאָרֶץ אֲשֶׁר נָתַן יהוה אֱלֹהֵי אֲבֹתֶיךָ לְךָ לְרִשְׁתָּהּ
כָּל־הַיָּמִים אֲשֶׁר־אַתֶּם חַיִּים עַל־הָאֲדָמָה: אַבֵּד תְּאַבְּדוּן אֶת־כָּל־הַמְּקֹמוֹת
אֲשֶׁר עָבְדוּ־שָׁם הַגּוֹיִם אֲשֶׁר אַתֶּם יֹרְשִׁים אֹתָם אֶת־אֱלֹהֵיהֶם עַל־הֶהָרִים
הָרָמִים וְעַל־הַגְּבָעוֹת וְתַחַת כָּל־עֵץ רַעֲנָן: וְנִתַּצְתֶּם אֶת־מִזְבְּחֹתָם וְשִׁבַּרְתֶּם
אֶת־מַצֵּבֹתָם וַאֲשֵׁרֵיהֶם תִּשְׂרְפוּן בָּאֵשׁ וּפְסִילֵי אֱלֹהֵיהֶם תְּגַדֵּעוּן וְאִבַּדְתֶּם
אֶת־שְׁמָם מִן־הַמָּקוֹם הַהוּא: לֹא־תַעֲשׂוּן כֵּן לַיהוה אֱלֹהֵיכֶם: כִּי אִם־אֶל־
הַמָּקוֹם אֲשֶׁר־יִבְחַר יהוה אֱלֹהֵיכֶם מִכָּל־שִׁבְטֵיכֶם לָשׂוּם אֶת־שְׁמוֹ שָׁם
ישראל לְשִׁכְנוֹ תִדְרְשׁוּ וּבָאתָ שָּׁמָּה: *וַהֲבֵאתֶם שָׁמָּה עֹלֹתֵיכֶם וְזִבְחֵיכֶם וְאֵת
מַעְשְׂרֹתֵיכֶם וְאֵת תְּרוּמַת יֶדְכֶם וְנִדְרֵיכֶם וְנִדְבֹתֵיכֶם וּבְכֹרֹת בְּקַרְכֶם וְצֹאנְכֶם:
וַאֲכַלְתֶּם־שָׁם לִפְנֵי יהוה אֱלֹהֵיכֶם וּשְׂמַחְתֶּם בְּכֹל מִשְׁלַח יֶדְכֶם אַתֶּם וּבָתֵּיכֶם
אֲשֶׁר בֵּרַכְךָ יהוה אֱלֹהֶיךָ: לֹא תַעֲשׂוּן כְּכֹל אֲשֶׁר אֲנַחְנוּ עֹשִׂים פֹּה הַיּוֹם
אִישׁ כָּל־הַיָּשָׁר בְּעֵינָיו: כִּי לֹא־בָאתֶם עַד־עָתָּה אֶל־הַמְּנוּחָה וְאֶל־הַנַּחֲלָה
אֲשֶׁר־יהוה אֱלֹהֶיךָ נֹתֵן לָךְ: וַעֲבַרְתֶּם אֶת־הַיַּרְדֵּן וִישַׁבְתֶּם בָּאָרֶץ אֲשֶׁר־
יהוה אֱלֹהֵיכֶם מַנְחִיל אֶתְכֶם וְהֵנִיחַ לָכֶם מִכָּל־אֹיְבֵיכֶם מִסָּבִיב וִישַׁבְתֶּם־
בֶּטַח:

SHOFETIM
שופטים

דברים שֹׁפְטִים וְשֹׁטְרִים תִּתֶּן־לְךָ בְּכָל־שְׁעָרֶיךָ אֲשֶׁר יהוה אֱלֹהֶיךָ נֹתֵן לְךָ לִשְׁבָטֶיךָ
טז:יח-יז:יב וְשָׁפְטוּ אֶת־הָעָם מִשְׁפַּט־צֶדֶק: לֹא־תַטֶּה מִשְׁפָּט לֹא תַכִּיר פָּנִים וְלֹא־תִקַּח
שֹׁחַד כִּי הַשֹּׁחַד יְעַוֵּר עֵינֵי חֲכָמִים וִיסַלֵּף דִּבְרֵי צַדִּיקִם: צֶדֶק צֶדֶק תִּרְדֹּף לְמַעַן
לוי תִּחְיֶה וְיָרַשְׁתָּ אֶת־הָאָרֶץ אֲשֶׁר־יהוה אֱלֹהֶיךָ נֹתֵן לָךְ: *לֹא־
תִטַּע לְךָ אֲשֵׁרָה כָּל־עֵץ אֵצֶל מִזְבַּח יהוה אֱלֹהֶיךָ אֲשֶׁר תַּעֲשֶׂה־לָּךְ: וְלֹא־
תָקִים לְךָ מַצֵּבָה אֲשֶׁר שָׂנֵא יהוה אֱלֹהֶיךָ: לֹא־תִזְבַּח לַיהוה
אֱלֹהֶיךָ שׁוֹר וָשֶׂה אֲשֶׁר יִהְיֶה בוֹ מוּם כֹּל דָּבָר רָע כִּי תוֹעֲבַת יהוה אֱלֹהֶיךָ
הוּא: כִּי־יִמָּצֵא בְקִרְבְּךָ בְּאַחַד שְׁעָרֶיךָ אֲשֶׁר־יהוה אֱלֹהֶיךָ נֹתֵן
לָךְ אִישׁ אוֹ־אִשָּׁה אֲשֶׁר יַעֲשֶׂה אֶת־הָרַע בְּעֵינֵי יהוה־אֱלֹהֶיךָ לַעֲבֹר בְּרִיתוֹ:
וַיֵּלֶךְ וַיַּעֲבֹד אֱלֹהִים אֲחֵרִים וַיִּשְׁתַּחוּ לָהֶם וְלַשֶּׁמֶשׁ ׀ אוֹ לַיָּרֵחַ אוֹ לְכָל־צְבָא

הַשָּׁמַיִם אֲשֶׁר לֹא־צִוִּיתִי: וְהֻגַּד־לְךָ וְשָׁמָעְתָּ וְדָרַשְׁתָּ הֵיטֵב וְהִנֵּה אֱמֶת נָכוֹן הַדָּבָר נֶעֶשְׂתָה הַתּוֹעֵבָה הַזֹּאת בְּיִשְׂרָאֵל: וְהוֹצֵאתָ אֶת־הָאִישׁ הַהוּא אוֹ אֶת־הָאִשָּׁה הַהִוא אֲשֶׁר עָשׂוּ אֶת־הַדָּבָר הָרָע הַזֶּה אֶל־שְׁעָרֶיךָ אֶת־הָאִישׁ אוֹ אֶת־הָאִשָּׁה וּסְקַלְתָּם בָּאֲבָנִים וָמֵתוּ: עַל־פִּי ׀ שְׁנַיִם עֵדִים אוֹ שְׁלֹשָׁה עֵדִים יוּמַת הַמֵּת לֹא יוּמַת עַל־פִּי עֵד אֶחָד: יַד הָעֵדִים תִּהְיֶה־בּוֹ בָרִאשֹׁנָה לַהֲמִיתוֹ וְיַד כָּל־הָעָם בָּאַחֲרֹנָה וּבִעַרְתָּ הָרָע מִקִּרְבֶּךָ:

כִּי יִפָּלֵא מִמְּךָ דָבָר לַמִּשְׁפָּט בֵּין־דָּם ׀ לְדָם בֵּין־דִּין לְדִין וּבֵין נֶגַע לָנֶגַע דִּבְרֵי רִיבֹת בִּשְׁעָרֶיךָ וְקַמְתָּ וְעָלִיתָ אֶל־הַמָּקוֹם אֲשֶׁר יִבְחַר יְהוָה אֱלֹהֶיךָ בּוֹ: וּבָאתָ אֶל־הַכֹּהֲנִים הַלְוִיִּם וְאֶל־הַשֹּׁפֵט אֲשֶׁר יִהְיֶה בַּיָּמִים הָהֵם וְדָרַשְׁתָּ וְהִגִּידוּ לְךָ אֵת דְּבַר הַמִּשְׁפָּט: וְעָשִׂיתָ עַל־פִּי הַדָּבָר אֲשֶׁר יַגִּידוּ לְךָ מִן־הַמָּקוֹם הַהוּא אֲשֶׁר יִבְחַר יְהוָה וְשָׁמַרְתָּ לַעֲשׂוֹת כְּכֹל אֲשֶׁר יוֹרוּךָ: *עַל־פִּי הַתּוֹרָה אֲשֶׁר ישראל יוֹרוּךָ וְעַל־הַמִּשְׁפָּט אֲשֶׁר־יֹאמְרוּ לְךָ תַּעֲשֶׂה לֹא תָסוּר מִן־הַדָּבָר אֲשֶׁר־יַגִּידוּ לְךָ יָמִין וּשְׂמֹאל: וְהָאִישׁ אֲשֶׁר־יַעֲשֶׂה בְזָדוֹן לְבִלְתִּי שְׁמֹעַ אֶל־הַכֹּהֵן הָעֹמֵד לְשָׁרֶת שָׁם אֶת־יְהוָה אֱלֹהֶיךָ אוֹ אֶל־הַשֹּׁפֵט וּמֵת הָאִישׁ הַהוּא וּבִעַרְתָּ הָרָע מִיִּשְׂרָאֵל: וְכָל־הָעָם יִשְׁמְעוּ וְיִרָאוּ וְלֹא יְזִידוּן עוֹד:

KI TETZEH   כי תצא

כִּי־תֵצֵא לַמִּלְחָמָה עַל־אֹיְבֶיךָ וּנְתָנוֹ יְהוָה אֱלֹהֶיךָ בְּיָדֶךָ וְשָׁבִיתָ שִׁבְיוֹ: וְרָאִיתָ דברים בַּשִּׁבְיָה אֵשֶׁת יְפַת־תֹּאַר וְחָשַׁקְתָּ בָהּ וְלָקַחְתָּ לְךָ לְאִשָּׁה: וַהֲבֵאתָהּ אֶל־ כא:י–כא תּוֹךְ בֵּיתֶךָ וְגִלְּחָה אֶת־רֹאשָׁהּ וְעָשְׂתָה אֶת־צִפָּרְנֶיהָ: וְהֵסִירָה אֶת־שִׂמְלַת שִׁבְיָהּ מֵעָלֶיהָ וְיָשְׁבָה בְּבֵיתֶךָ וּבָכְתָה אֶת־אָבִיהָ וְאֶת־אִמָּהּ יֶרַח יָמִים וְאַחַר כֵּן תָּבוֹא אֵלֶיהָ וּבְעַלְתָּהּ וְהָיְתָה לְךָ לְאִשָּׁה: וְהָיָה אִם־לֹא חָפַצְתָּ בָּהּ וְשִׁלַּחְתָּהּ לְנַפְשָׁהּ וּמָכֹר לֹא־תִמְכְּרֶנָּה בַּכָּסֶף לֹא־תִתְעַמֵּר בָּהּ תַּחַת אֲשֶׁר עִנִּיתָהּ:   *כִּי־תִהְיֶיןָ לְאִישׁ שְׁתֵּי נָשִׁים הָאַחַת אֲהוּבָה וְהָאַחַת לוי שְׂנוּאָה וְיָלְדוּ־לוֹ בָנִים הָאֲהוּבָה וְהַשְּׂנוּאָה וְהָיָה הַבֵּן הַבְּכוֹר לַשְּׂנִיאָה: וְהָיָה בְּיוֹם הַנְחִילוֹ אֶת־בָּנָיו אֵת אֲשֶׁר־יִהְיֶה לוֹ לֹא יוּכַל לְבַכֵּר אֶת־בֶּן־הָאֲהוּבָה עַל־פְּנֵי בֶן־הַשְּׂנוּאָה הַבְּכֹר: כִּי אֶת־הַבְּכֹר בֶּן־הַשְּׂנוּאָה יַכִּיר לָתֶת לוֹ פִּי שְׁנַיִם בְּכֹל אֲשֶׁר־יִמָּצֵא לוֹ כִּי־הוּא רֵאשִׁית אֹנוֹ לוֹ מִשְׁפַּט הַבְּכֹרָה: *כִּי־ ישראל יִהְיֶה לְאִישׁ בֵּן סוֹרֵר וּמוֹרֶה אֵינֶנּוּ שֹׁמֵעַ בְּקוֹל אָבִיו וּבְקוֹל אִמּוֹ וְיִסְּרוּ אֹתוֹ

וְלֹא יִשְׁמַע אֲלֵיהֶם: וְתָפְשׂוּ בוֹ אָבִיו וְאִמּוֹ וְהוֹצִיאוּ אֹתוֹ אֶל־זִקְנֵי עִירוֹ וְאֶל־
שַׁעַר מְקֹמוֹ: וְאָמְרוּ אֶל־זִקְנֵי עִירוֹ בְּנֵנוּ זֶה סוֹרֵר וּמֹרֶה אֵינֶנּוּ שֹׁמֵעַ בְּקֹלֵנוּ
זוֹלֵל וְסֹבֵא: וּרְגָמֻהוּ כָּל־אַנְשֵׁי עִירוֹ בָאֲבָנִים וָמֵת וּבִעַרְתָּ הָרָע מִקִּרְבֶּךָ
וְכָל־יִשְׂרָאֵל יִשְׁמְעוּ וְיִרָאוּ:

KI TAVO   כי תבוא

וְהָיָה כִּי־תָבוֹא אֶל־הָאָרֶץ אֲשֶׁר יְהוָה אֱלֹהֶיךָ נֹתֵן לְךָ נַחֲלָה וִירִשְׁתָּהּ   דברים
וְיָשַׁבְתָּ בָּהּ: וְלָקַחְתָּ מֵרֵאשִׁית ׀ כָּל־פְּרִי הָאֲדָמָה אֲשֶׁר תָּבִיא מֵאַרְצְךָ אֲשֶׁר   כו:א־טו
יְהוָה אֱלֹהֶיךָ נֹתֵן לָךְ וְשַׂמְתָּ בַטֶּנֶא וְהָלַכְתָּ אֶל־הַמָּקוֹם אֲשֶׁר יִבְחַר יְהוָה
אֱלֹהֶיךָ לְשַׁכֵּן שְׁמוֹ שָׁם: וּבָאתָ אֶל־הַכֹּהֵן אֲשֶׁר יִהְיֶה בַּיָּמִים הָהֵם וְאָמַרְתָּ
אֵלָיו הִגַּדְתִּי הַיּוֹם לַיהוָה אֱלֹהֶיךָ כִּי־בָאתִי אֶל־הָאָרֶץ אֲשֶׁר נִשְׁבַּע יְהוָה
לַאֲבֹתֵינוּ לָתֶת לָנוּ: *וְלָקַח הַכֹּהֵן הַטֶּנֶא מִיָּדֶךָ וְהִנִּיחוֹ לִפְנֵי מִזְבַּח יְהוָה   לוי
אֱלֹהֶיךָ: וְעָנִיתָ וְאָמַרְתָּ לִפְנֵי ׀ יְהוָה אֱלֹהֶיךָ אֲרַמִּי אֹבֵד אָבִי וַיֵּרֶד מִצְרַיְמָה
וַיָּגָר שָׁם בִּמְתֵי מְעָט וַיְהִי־שָׁם לְגוֹי גָּדוֹל עָצוּם וָרָב: וַיָּרֵעוּ אֹתָנוּ הַמִּצְרִים
וַיְעַנּוּנוּ וַיִּתְּנוּ עָלֵינוּ עֲבֹדָה קָשָׁה: וַנִּצְעַק אֶל־יְהוָה אֱלֹהֵי אֲבֹתֵינוּ וַיִּשְׁמַע
יְהוָה אֶת־קֹלֵנוּ וַיַּרְא אֶת־עָנְיֵנוּ וְאֶת־עֲמָלֵנוּ וְאֶת־לַחֲצֵנוּ: וַיּוֹצִאֵנוּ יְהוָה
מִמִּצְרַיִם בְּיָד חֲזָקָה וּבִזְרֹעַ נְטוּיָה וּבְמֹרָא גָּדֹל וּבְאֹתוֹת וּבְמֹפְתִים: וַיְבִאֵנוּ
אֶל־הַמָּקוֹם הַזֶּה וַיִּתֶּן־לָנוּ אֶת־הָאָרֶץ הַזֹּאת אֶרֶץ זָבַת חָלָב וּדְבָשׁ: וְעַתָּה
הִנֵּה הֵבֵאתִי אֶת־רֵאשִׁית פְּרִי הָאֲדָמָה אֲשֶׁר־נָתַתָּה לִּי יְהוָה וְהִנַּחְתּוֹ לִפְנֵי
יְהוָה אֱלֹהֶיךָ וְהִשְׁתַּחֲוִיתָ לִפְנֵי יְהוָה אֱלֹהֶיךָ: וְשָׂמַחְתָּ בְכָל־הַטּוֹב אֲשֶׁר נָתַן־
לְךָ יְהוָה אֱלֹהֶיךָ וּלְבֵיתֶךָ אַתָּה וְהַלֵּוִי וְהַגֵּר אֲשֶׁר בְּקִרְבֶּךָ: *כִּי   ישראל
תְכַלֶּה לַעְשֵׂר אֶת־כָּל־מַעְשַׂר תְּבוּאָתְךָ בַּשָּׁנָה הַשְּׁלִישִׁת שְׁנַת הַמַּעֲשֵׂר
וְנָתַתָּה לַלֵּוִי לַגֵּר לַיָּתוֹם וְלָאַלְמָנָה וְאָכְלוּ בִשְׁעָרֶיךָ וְשָׂבֵעוּ: וְאָמַרְתָּ לִפְנֵי
יְהוָה אֱלֹהֶיךָ בִּעַרְתִּי הַקֹּדֶשׁ מִן־הַבַּיִת וְגַם נְתַתִּיו לַלֵּוִי וְלַגֵּר לַיָּתוֹם וְלָאַלְמָנָה
כְּכָל־מִצְוָתְךָ אֲשֶׁר צִוִּיתָנִי לֹא־עָבַרְתִּי מִמִּצְוֹתֶיךָ וְלֹא שָׁכָחְתִּי: לֹא־אָכַלְתִּי
בְאֹנִי מִמֶּנּוּ וְלֹא־בִעַרְתִּי מִמֶּנּוּ בְּטָמֵא וְלֹא־נָתַתִּי מִמֶּנּוּ לְמֵת שָׁמַעְתִּי בְּקוֹל
יְהוָה אֱלֹהָי עָשִׂיתִי כְּכֹל אֲשֶׁר צִוִּיתָנִי: הַשְׁקִיפָה מִמְּעוֹן קָדְשְׁךָ מִן־הַשָּׁמַיִם
וּבָרֵךְ אֶת־עַמְּךָ אֶת־יִשְׂרָאֵל וְאֵת הָאֲדָמָה אֲשֶׁר נָתַתָּה לָנוּ כַּאֲשֶׁר נִשְׁבַּעְתָּ
לַאֲבֹתֵינוּ אֶרֶץ זָבַת חָלָב וּדְבָשׁ:

NITZAVIM
נצבים

דברים
כט:ט–כח

אַתֶּם נִצָּבִים הַיּוֹם כֻּלְּכֶם לִפְנֵי יְהֹוָה אֱלֹהֵיכֶם רָאשֵׁיכֶם שִׁבְטֵיכֶם זִקְנֵיכֶם
וְשֹׁטְרֵיכֶם כֹּל אִישׁ יִשְׂרָאֵל: טַפְּכֶם נְשֵׁיכֶם וְגֵרְךָ אֲשֶׁר בְּקֶרֶב מַחֲנֶיךָ מֵחֹטֵב
עֵצֶיךָ עַד שֹׁאֵב מֵימֶיךָ: לְעָבְרְךָ בִּבְרִית יְהֹוָה אֱלֹהֶיךָ וּבְאָלָתוֹ אֲשֶׁר יְהֹוָה
אֱלֹהֶיךָ כֹּרֵת עִמְּךָ הַיּוֹם: *לְמַעַן הָקִים־אֹתְךָ הַיּוֹם ׀ לוֹ לְעָם וְהוּא יִהְיֶה־לְּךָ לוי
לֵאלֹהִים כַּאֲשֶׁר דִּבֶּר־לָךְ וְכַאֲשֶׁר נִשְׁבַּע לַאֲבֹתֶיךָ לְאַבְרָהָם לְיִצְחָק וּלְיַעֲקֹב:
וְלֹא אִתְּכֶם לְבַדְּכֶם אָנֹכִי כֹּרֵת אֶת־הַבְּרִית הַזֹּאת וְאֶת־הָאָלָה הַזֹּאת: כִּי
אֶת־אֲשֶׁר יֶשְׁנוֹ פֹּה עִמָּנוּ עֹמֵד הַיּוֹם לִפְנֵי יְהֹוָה אֱלֹהֵינוּ וְאֵת אֲשֶׁר אֵינֶנּוּ פֹּה
עִמָּנוּ הַיּוֹם: *כִּי־אַתֶּם יְדַעְתֶּם אֵת אֲשֶׁר־יָשַׁבְנוּ בְּאֶרֶץ מִצְרָיִם וְאֵת אֲשֶׁר־ ישראל
עָבַרְנוּ בְּקֶרֶב הַגּוֹיִם אֲשֶׁר עֲבַרְתֶּם: וַתִּרְאוּ אֶת־שִׁקּוּצֵיהֶם וְאֵת גִּלֻּלֵיהֶם
עֵץ וָאֶבֶן כֶּסֶף וְזָהָב אֲשֶׁר עִמָּהֶם: פֶּן־יֵשׁ בָּכֶם אִישׁ אוֹ־אִשָּׁה אוֹ מִשְׁפָּחָה
אוֹ־שֵׁבֶט אֲשֶׁר לְבָבוֹ פֹנֶה הַיּוֹם מֵעִם יְהֹוָה אֱלֹהֵינוּ לָלֶכֶת לַעֲבֹד אֶת־אֱלֹהֵי
הַגּוֹיִם הָהֵם פֶּן־יֵשׁ בָּכֶם שֹׁרֶשׁ פֹּרֶה רֹאשׁ וְלַעֲנָה: וְהָיָה בְּשָׁמְעוֹ אֶת־דִּבְרֵי
הָאָלָה הַזֹּאת וְהִתְבָּרֵךְ בִּלְבָבוֹ לֵאמֹר שָׁלוֹם יִהְיֶה־לִּי כִּי בִּשְׁרִרוּת לִבִּי אֵלֵךְ
לְמַעַן סְפוֹת הָרָוָה אֶת־הַצְּמֵאָה: לֹא־יֹאבֶה יְהֹוָה סְלֹחַ לוֹ כִּי אָז יֶעְשַׁן אַף־
יְהֹוָה וְקִנְאָתוֹ בָּאִישׁ הַהוּא וְרָבְצָה בּוֹ כָּל־הָאָלָה הַכְּתוּבָה בַּסֵּפֶר הַזֶּה וּמָחָה
יְהֹוָה אֶת־שְׁמוֹ מִתַּחַת הַשָּׁמָיִם: וְהִבְדִּילוֹ יְהֹוָה לְרָעָה מִכֹּל שִׁבְטֵי יִשְׂרָאֵל
כְּכֹל אָלוֹת הַבְּרִית הַכְּתוּבָה בְּסֵפֶר הַתּוֹרָה הַזֶּה: וְאָמַר הַדּוֹר הָאַחֲרוֹן בְּנֵיכֶם
אֲשֶׁר יָקוּמוּ מֵאַחֲרֵיכֶם וְהַנָּכְרִי אֲשֶׁר יָבֹא מֵאֶרֶץ רְחוֹקָה וְרָאוּ אֶת־מַכּוֹת
הָאָרֶץ הַהִוא וְאֶת־תַּחֲלֻאֶיהָ אֲשֶׁר־חִלָּה יְהֹוָה בָּהּ: גָּפְרִית וָמֶלַח שְׂרֵפָה כָל־
אַרְצָהּ לֹא תִזָּרַע וְלֹא תַצְמִחַ וְלֹא־יַעֲלֶה בָהּ כָּל־עֵשֶׂב כְּמַהְפֵּכַת סְדֹם וַעֲמֹרָה
אַדְמָה וּצְבֹיִים אֲשֶׁר הָפַךְ יְהֹוָה בְּאַפּוֹ וּבַחֲמָתוֹ: וְאָמְרוּ כָּל־הַגּוֹיִם עַל־מֶה וצבוים
עָשָׂה יְהֹוָה כָּכָה לָאָרֶץ הַזֹּאת מֶה חֳרִי הָאַף הַגָּדוֹל הַזֶּה: וְאָמְרוּ עַל אֲשֶׁר
עָזְבוּ אֶת־בְּרִית יְהֹוָה אֱלֹהֵי אֲבֹתָם אֲשֶׁר כָּרַת עִמָּם בְּהוֹצִיאוֹ אֹתָם מֵאֶרֶץ
מִצְרָיִם: וַיֵּלְכוּ וַיַּעַבְדוּ אֱלֹהִים אֲחֵרִים וַיִּשְׁתַּחֲווּ לָהֶם אֱלֹהִים אֲשֶׁר לֹא־יְדָעוּם
וְלֹא חָלַק לָהֶם: וַיִּחַר־אַף יְהֹוָה בָּאָרֶץ הַהִוא לְהָבִיא עָלֶיהָ אֶת־כָּל־הַקְּלָלָה
הַכְּתוּבָה בַּסֵּפֶר הַזֶּה: וַיִּתְּשֵׁם יְהֹוָה מֵעַל אַדְמָתָם בְּאַף וּבְחֵמָה וּבְקֶצֶף גָּדוֹל
וַיַּשְׁלִכֵם אֶל־אֶרֶץ אַחֶרֶת כַּיּוֹם הַזֶּה: הַנִּסְתָּרֹת לַיהֹוָה אֱלֹהֵינוּ וְהַנִּגְלֹת לָנוּ
וּלְבָנֵינוּ עַד־עוֹלָם לַעֲשׂוֹת אֶת־כָּל־דִּבְרֵי הַתּוֹרָה הַזֹּאת:

וילך

VAYELEKH

דברים
לא:א-ג

וַיֵּלֶךְ מֹשֶׁה וַיְדַבֵּר אֶת־הַדְּבָרִים הָאֵלֶּה אֶל־כָּל־יִשְׂרָאֵל: וַיֹּאמֶר אֲלֵהֶם בֶּן־
מֵאָה וְעֶשְׂרִים שָׁנָה אָנֹכִי הַיּוֹם לֹא־אוּכַל עוֹד לָצֵאת וְלָבוֹא וַיהוָה אָמַר אֵלַי
לֹא תַעֲבֹר אֶת־הַיַּרְדֵּן הַזֶּה: יְהוָה אֱלֹהֶיךָ הוּא ׀ עֹבֵר לְפָנֶיךָ הוּא־יַשְׁמִיד
אֶת־הַגּוֹיִם הָאֵלֶּה מִלְּפָנֶיךָ וִירִשְׁתָּם יְהוֹשֻׁעַ הוּא עֹבֵר לְפָנֶיךָ כַּאֲשֶׁר דִּבֶּר

לוי

יְהוָה: וְעָשָׂה יְהוָה לָהֶם כַּאֲשֶׁר עָשָׂה לְסִיחוֹן וּלְעוֹג מַלְכֵי הָאֱמֹרִי וּלְאַרְצָם
אֲשֶׁר הִשְׁמִיד אֹתָם: וּנְתָנָם יְהוָה לִפְנֵיכֶם וַעֲשִׂיתֶם לָהֶם כְּכָל־הַמִּצְוָה
אֲשֶׁר צִוִּיתִי אֶתְכֶם: חִזְקוּ וְאִמְצוּ אַל־תִּירְאוּ וְאַל־תַּעַרְצוּ מִפְּנֵיהֶם כִּי ׀

ישראל

יְהוָה אֱלֹהֶיךָ הוּא הַהֹלֵךְ עִמָּךְ לֹא יַרְפְּךָ וְלֹא יַעַזְבֶךָּ: *וַיִּקְרָא
מֹשֶׁה לִיהוֹשֻׁעַ וַיֹּאמֶר אֵלָיו לְעֵינֵי כָל־יִשְׂרָאֵל חֲזַק וֶאֱמָץ כִּי אַתָּה תָּבוֹא
אֶת־הָעָם הַזֶּה אֶל־הָאָרֶץ אֲשֶׁר נִשְׁבַּע יְהוָה לַאֲבֹתָם לָתֵת לָהֶם וְאַתָּה
תַּנְחִילֶנָּה אוֹתָם: וַיהוָה הוּא ׀ הַהֹלֵךְ לְפָנֶיךָ הוּא יִהְיֶה עִמָּךְ לֹא יַרְפְּךָ
וְלֹא יַעַזְבֶךָּ לֹא תִירָא וְלֹא תֵחָת: וַיִּכְתֹּב מֹשֶׁה אֶת־הַתּוֹרָה הַזֹּאת וַיִּתְּנָהּ
אֶל־הַכֹּהֲנִים בְּנֵי לֵוִי הַנֹּשְׂאִים אֶת־אֲרוֹן בְּרִית יְהוָה וְאֶל־כָּל־זִקְנֵי יִשְׂרָאֵל:
וַיְצַו מֹשֶׁה אוֹתָם לֵאמֹר מִקֵּץ ׀ שֶׁבַע שָׁנִים בְּמֹעֵד שְׁנַת הַשְּׁמִטָּה בְּחַג
הַסֻּכּוֹת: בְּבוֹא כָל־יִשְׂרָאֵל לֵרָאוֹת אֶת־פְּנֵי יְהוָה אֱלֹהֶיךָ בַּמָּקוֹם אֲשֶׁר
יִבְחָר תִּקְרָא אֶת־הַתּוֹרָה הַזֹּאת נֶגֶד כָּל־יִשְׂרָאֵל בְּאָזְנֵיהֶם: הַקְהֵל אֶת־
הָעָם הָאֲנָשִׁים וְהַנָּשִׁים וְהַטַּף וְגֵרְךָ אֲשֶׁר בִּשְׁעָרֶיךָ לְמַעַן יִשְׁמְעוּ וּלְמַעַן
יִלְמְדוּ וְיָרְאוּ אֶת־יְהוָה אֱלֹהֵיכֶם וְשָׁמְרוּ לַעֲשׂוֹת אֶת־כָּל־דִּבְרֵי הַתּוֹרָה
הַזֹּאת: וּבְנֵיהֶם אֲשֶׁר לֹא־יָדְעוּ יִשְׁמְעוּ וְלָמְדוּ לְיִרְאָה אֶת־יְהוָה אֱלֹהֵיכֶם
כָּל־הַיָּמִים אֲשֶׁר אַתֶּם חַיִּים עַל־הָאֲדָמָה אֲשֶׁר אַתֶּם עֹבְרִים אֶת־הַיַּרְדֵּן שָׁמָּה
לְרִשְׁתָּהּ:

HA'AZINU

האזינו

דברים
לב:א-ח

וְתִשְׁמַע הָאָרֶץ אִמְרֵי־פִי:	הַאֲזִינוּ הַשָּׁמַיִם וַאֲדַבֵּרָה
תִּזַּל כַּטַּל אִמְרָתִי	יַעֲרֹף כַּמָּטָר לִקְחִי
וְכִרְבִיבִים עֲלֵי־עֵשֶׂב:	כִּשְׂעִירִם עֲלֵי־דֶשֶׁא
הָבוּ גֹדֶל לֵאלֹהֵינוּ:	כִּי שֵׁם יְהוָה אֶקְרָא

לוי

כִּי כָל־דְּרָכָיו מִשְׁפָּט	*הַצּוּר תָּמִים פָּעֳלוֹ
צַדִּיק וְיָשָׁר הוּא:	אֵל אֱמוּנָה וְאֵין עָוֶל
דּוֹר עִקֵּשׁ וּפְתַלְתֹּל:	שִׁחֵת לוֹ לֹא בָּנָיו מוּמָם
עַם נָבָל וְלֹא חָכָם	ה לַיהוה תִּגְמְלוּ־זֹאת
הוּא עָשְׂךָ וַיְכֹנְנֶךָ:	הֲלוֹא־הוּא אָבִיךָ קָּנֶךָ

Some start the לוי portion here:

ישראל

בִּינוּ שְׁנוֹת דֹּר־וָדֹר	*זְכֹר יְמוֹת עוֹלָם
זְקֵנֶיךָ וְיֹאמְרוּ לָךְ:	שְׁאַל אָבִיךָ וְיַגֵּדְךָ
בְּהַפְרִידוֹ בְּנֵי אָדָם	בְּהַנְחֵל עֶלְיוֹן גּוֹיִם
לְמִסְפַּר בְּנֵי יִשְׂרָאֵל:	יַצֵּב גְּבֻלֹת עַמִּים
יַעֲקֹב חֶבֶל נַחֲלָתוֹ:	כִּי חֵלֶק יהוה עַמּוֹ
וּבְתֹהוּ יְלֵל יְשִׁמֹן	יִמְצָאֵהוּ בְּאֶרֶץ מִדְבָּר
יִצְּרֶנְהוּ כְּאִישׁוֹן עֵינוֹ:	יְסֹבְבֶנְהוּ יְבוֹנְנֵהוּ
עַל־גּוֹזָלָיו יְרַחֵף	כְּנֶשֶׁר יָעִיר קִנּוֹ
יִשָּׂאֵהוּ עַל־אֶבְרָתוֹ:	יִפְרֹשׂ כְּנָפָיו יִקָּחֵהוּ
וְאֵין עִמּוֹ אֵל נֵכָר:	יהוה בָּדָד יַנְחֶנּוּ

Most finish here; some start the ישראל portion here:

במתי

וַיֹּאכַל תְּנוּבֹת שָׂדָי	*יַרְכִּבֵהוּ עַל־במותי אָרֶץ
וְשֶׁמֶן מֵחַלְמִישׁ צוּר:	וַיֵּנִקֵהוּ דְבַשׁ מִסֶּלַע
עִם־חֵלֶב כָּרִים	חֶמְאַת בָּקָר וַחֲלֵב צֹאן
עִם־חֵלֶב כִּלְיוֹת חִטָּה	וְאֵילִים בְּנֵי־בָשָׁן וְעַתּוּדִים
וַיִּשְׁמַן יְשֻׁרוּן וַיִּבְעָט	וְדַם־עֵנָב תִּשְׁתֶּה־חָמֶר:
וַיִּטֹּשׁ אֱלוֹהַּ עָשָׂהוּ	שָׁמַנְתָּ עָבִיתָ כָּשִׂיתָ
יַקְנִאֻהוּ בְּזָרִים	וַיְנַבֵּל צוּר יְשֻׁעָתוֹ:
יִזְבְּחוּ לַשֵּׁדִים לֹא אֱלֹהַּ	בְּתוֹעֵבֹת יַכְעִיסֻהוּ:
חֲדָשִׁים מִקָּרֹב בָּאוּ	אֱלֹהִים לֹא יְדָעוּם
צוּר יְלָדְךָ תֶּשִׁי	לֹא שְׂעָרוּם אֲבֹתֵיכֶם:
	וַתִּשְׁכַּח אֵל מְחֹלְלֶךָ:

VEZOT HABERAKHA וזאת הברכה

דברים
ל״ג:א–ה

וְזֹאת הַבְּרָכָה אֲשֶׁר בֵּרַךְ מֹשֶׁה אִישׁ הָאֱלֹהִים אֶת־בְּנֵי יִשְׂרָאֵל לִפְנֵי מוֹתוֹ: וַיֹּאמַר יְהוָה מִסִּינַי בָּא וְזָרַח מִשֵּׂעִיר לָמוֹ הוֹפִיעַ מֵהַר פָּארָן וְאָתָה מֵרִבְבֹת אֵשׁ דָּת קֹדֶשׁ מִימִינוֹ אשדת לָמוֹ: אַף חֹבֵב עַמִּים כָּל־קְדֹשָׁיו בְּיָדֶךָ וְהֵם תֻּכּוּ לְרַגְלֶךָ יִשָּׂא מִדַּבְּרֹתֶיךָ: תּוֹרָה צִוָּה־לָנוּ מֹשֶׁה מוֹרָשָׁה קְהִלַּת יַעֲקֹב: וַיְהִי בִישֻׁרוּן מֶלֶךְ בְּהִתְאַסֵּף רָאשֵׁי עָם יַחַד שִׁבְטֵי יִשְׂרָאֵל: יְחִי רְאוּבֵן וְאַל־יָמֹת וִיהִי מְתָיו מִסְפָּר: וְזֹאת לִיהוּדָה וַיֹּאמַר שְׁמַע יְהוָה קוֹל יְהוּדָה וְאֶל־עַמּוֹ תְּבִיאֶנּוּ יָדָיו רָב לוֹ וְעֵזֶר מִצָּרָיו תִּהְיֶה:

לוי וּלְלֵוִי אָמַר תֻּמֶּיךָ וְאוּרֶיךָ לְאִישׁ חֲסִידֶךָ אֲשֶׁר נִסִּיתוֹ בְּמַסָּה תְּרִיבֵהוּ עַל־מֵי מְרִיבָה: הָאֹמֵר לְאָבִיו וּלְאִמּוֹ לֹא רְאִיתִיו וְאֶת־אֶחָיו לֹא הִכִּיר וְאֶת־בָּנָו לֹא יָדָע כִּי שָׁמְרוּ אִמְרָתֶךָ וּבְרִיתְךָ יִנְצֹרוּ: יוֹרוּ מִשְׁפָּטֶיךָ לְיַעֲקֹב וְתוֹרָתְךָ לְיִשְׂרָאֵל יָשִׂימוּ קְטוֹרָה בְּאַפֶּךָ וְכָלִיל עַל־מִזְבְּחֶךָ: בָּרֵךְ יְהוָה חֵילוֹ וּפֹעַל יָדָיו תִּרְצֶה מְחַץ מָתְנַיִם קָמָיו וּמְשַׂנְאָיו מִן־יְקוּמוּן: לְבִנְיָמִן אָמַר יְדִיד יְהוָה

ישראל יִשְׁכֹּן לָבֶטַח עָלָיו חֹפֵף עָלָיו כָּל־הַיּוֹם וּבֵין כְּתֵפָיו שָׁכֵן: *וּלְיוֹסֵף אָמַר מְבֹרֶכֶת יְהוָה אַרְצוֹ מִמֶּגֶד שָׁמַיִם מִטָּל וּמִתְּהוֹם רֹבֶצֶת תָּחַת: וּמִמֶּגֶד תְּבוּאֹת שָׁמֶשׁ וּמִמֶּגֶד גֶּרֶשׁ יְרָחִים: וּמֵרֹאשׁ הַרְרֵי־קֶדֶם וּמִמֶּגֶד גִּבְעוֹת עוֹלָם: וּמִמֶּגֶד אֶרֶץ וּמְלֹאָהּ וּרְצוֹן שֹׁכְנִי סְנֶה תָּבוֹאתָה לְרֹאשׁ יוֹסֵף וּלְקָדְקֹד נְזִיר אֶחָיו: בְּכוֹר שׁוֹרוֹ הָדָר לוֹ וְקַרְנֵי רְאֵם קַרְנָיו בָּהֶם עַמִּים יְנַגַּח יַחְדָּו אַפְסֵי־אָרֶץ וְהֵם רִבְבוֹת אֶפְרַיִם וְהֵם אַלְפֵי מְנַשֶּׁה:

קריאת התורה לראש חודש,
לתעניות ציבור, לחנוכה ולפורים

THE READING OF THE TORAH FOR ROSH ḤODESH,
FAST DAYS, ḤANUKKA AND PURIM

READING FOR ROSH ḤODESH   קריאה לראש חודש

For the כהן, *the first three verses are read up to* עֹלָה תָמִיד. *For the* לוי, *the third verse is repeated and starts with* וְאָמַרְתָּ לָהֶם. *For* שלישי, *continue from* עֹלַת תָּמִיד *up to* וְנִסְכָּה. *For* רביעי, *read from* וּבְרָאשֵׁי חָדְשֵׁיכֶם *until the end. In* אֶרֶץ יִשְׂרָאֵל, *some read as follows: For the* כהן *read until* שלישי, *for the* לוי *read from* אֶת־הַכֶּבֶשׂ *until* נִחֹחַ לַה׳, *for* שלישי, *the last verse is repeated and starts at* עֹלַת תָּמִיד *up to* וְנִסְכָּה, *and for* רביעי, *from* וּבְרָאשֵׁי חָדְשֵׁיכֶם *until the end. On* שבת ראש חודש, *the* כהן *reads until* רְבִיעִת הַהִין, *the* לוי *reads the portion for* שלישי *and the* שלישי *the portion of* רביעי; *the fourth* עולה *reads the appropriate day of* חנוכה *on page 658.*

במדבר
כח:א-טו

וַיְדַבֵּר יְהוָה אֶל־מֹשֶׁה לֵּאמֹר: צַו אֶת־בְּנֵי יִשְׂרָאֵל וְאָמַרְתָּ אֲלֵהֶם אֶת־

קָרְבָּנִי לַחְמִי לְאִשַּׁי רֵיחַ נִיחֹחִי תִּשְׁמְרוּ לְהַקְרִיב לִי בְּמוֹעֲדוֹ:   וְאָמַרְתָּ **לוי**

לָהֶם זֶה הָאִשֶּׁה אֲשֶׁר תַּקְרִיבוּ לַיהוָה כְּבָשִׂים בְּנֵי־שָׁנָה תְמִימִם שְׁנַיִם לַיּוֹם

עֹלָה תָמִיד:* אֶת־הַכֶּבֶשׂ אֶחָד תַּעֲשֶׂה בַבֹּקֶר וְאֵת הַכֶּבֶשׂ הַשֵּׁנִי תַּעֲשֶׂה   עד כאן לכהן

בֵּין הָעַרְבָּיִם: וַעֲשִׂירִית הָאֵיפָה סֹלֶת לְמִנְחָה בְּלוּלָה בְּשֶׁמֶן כָּתִית רְבִיעִת

הַהִין: *עֹלַת תָּמִיד הָעֲשֻׂיָה בְּהַר סִינַי לְרֵיחַ נִיחֹחַ אִשֶּׁה לַיהוָה: וְנִסְכּוֹ   **שלישי**

רְבִיעִת הַהִין לַכֶּבֶשׂ הָאֶחָד בַּקֹּדֶשׁ הַסֵּךְ נֶסֶךְ שֵׁכָר לַיהוָה: וְאֵת הַכֶּבֶשׂ

הַשֵּׁנִי תַּעֲשֶׂה בֵּין הָעַרְבָּיִם כְּמִנְחַת הַבֹּקֶר וּכְנִסְכּוֹ תַּעֲשֶׂה אִשֵּׁה רֵיחַ נִיחֹחַ

לַיהוָה:

וּבְיוֹם הַשַּׁבָּת שְׁנֵי־כְבָשִׂים בְּנֵי־שָׁנָה תְּמִימִם וּשְׁנֵי עֶשְׂרֹנִים סֹלֶת מִנְחָה בְּלוּלָה

בַשֶּׁמֶן וְנִסְכּוֹ: עֹלַת שַׁבַּת בְּשַׁבַּתּוֹ עַל־עֹלַת הַתָּמִיד וְנִסְכָּהּ:

וּבְרָאשֵׁי חָדְשֵׁיכֶם תַּקְרִיבוּ עֹלָה לַיהוָה פָּרִים בְּנֵי־בָקָר שְׁנַיִם וְאַיִל אֶחָד   **רביעי**

כְּבָשִׂים בְּנֵי־שָׁנָה שִׁבְעָה תְּמִימִם: וּשְׁלֹשָׁה עֶשְׂרֹנִים סֹלֶת מִנְחָה בְּלוּלָה

בַשֶּׁמֶן לַפָּר הָאֶחָד וּשְׁנֵי עֶשְׂרֹנִים סֹלֶת מִנְחָה בְּלוּלָה בַשֶּׁמֶן לָאַיִל הָאֶחָד:

וְעִשָּׂרֹן עִשָּׂרוֹן סֹלֶת מִנְחָה בְּלוּלָה בַשֶּׁמֶן לַכֶּבֶשׂ הָאֶחָד עֹלָה רֵיחַ נִיחֹחַ

אִשֶּׁה לַיהוָה: וְנִסְכֵּיהֶם חֲצִי הַהִין יִהְיֶה לַפָּר וּשְׁלִישִׁת הַהִין לָאַיִל וּרְבִיעִת

הַהִין לַכֶּבֶשׂ יָיִן זֹאת עֹלַת חֹדֶשׁ בְּחָדְשׁוֹ לְחָדְשֵׁי הַשָּׁנָה: וּשְׂעִיר עִזִּים אֶחָד

לְחַטָּאת לַיהוָה עַל־עֹלַת הַתָּמִיד יֵעָשֶׂה וְנִסְכּוֹ:

READING FOR FAST DAYS

קריאה לתענית ציבור

The following is read on a תענית ציבור *(except* תשעה באב*) in both* שחרית *and* מנחה.
At מנחה, *the person called up for* שלישי *also reads the* הפטרה.

It is customary for the קהל *to say aloud the passages marked
by arrows, followed by the* קורא *(see law 113).*

שמות לב:
יא-יד

וַיְחַל מֹשֶׁה אֶת־פְּנֵי יהוה אֱלֹהָיו וַיֹּאמֶר לָמָה יהוה יֶחֱרֶה אַפְּךָ בְּעַמֶּךָ
אֲשֶׁר הוֹצֵאתָ מֵאֶרֶץ מִצְרַיִם בְּכֹחַ גָּדוֹל וּבְיָד חֲזָקָה: לָמָּה יֹאמְרוּ מִצְרַיִם
לֵאמֹר בְּרָעָה הוֹצִיאָם לַהֲרֹג אֹתָם בֶּהָרִים וּלְכַלֹּתָם מֵעַל פְּנֵי הָאֲדָמָה ◄ שׁוּב
מֵחֲרוֹן אַפֶּךָ וְהִנָּחֵם עַל־הָרָעָה לְעַמֶּךָ: ◄ זְכֹר לְאַבְרָהָם לְיִצְחָק וּלְיִשְׂרָאֵל
עֲבָדֶיךָ אֲשֶׁר נִשְׁבַּעְתָּ לָהֶם בָּךְ וַתְּדַבֵּר אֲלֵהֶם אַרְבֶּה אֶת־זַרְעֲכֶם כְּכוֹכְבֵי
הַשָּׁמָיִם וְכָל־הָאָרֶץ הַזֹּאת אֲשֶׁר אָמַרְתִּי אֶתֵּן לְזַרְעֲכֶם וְנָחֲלוּ לְעֹלָם: וַיִּנָּחֶם
מנחה יהוה עַל־הָרָעָה אֲשֶׁר דִּבֶּר לַעֲשׂוֹת לְעַמּוֹ:

שמות לד:א-י
לוי

וַיֹּאמֶר יהוה אֶל־מֹשֶׁה פְּסָל־לְךָ שְׁנֵי־לֻחֹת אֲבָנִים כָּרִאשֹׁנִים וְכָתַבְתִּי עַל־
הַלֻּחֹת אֶת־הַדְּבָרִים אֲשֶׁר הָיוּ עַל־הַלֻּחֹת הָרִאשֹׁנִים אֲשֶׁר שִׁבַּרְתָּ: וֶהְיֵה
נָכוֹן לַבֹּקֶר וְעָלִיתָ בַבֹּקֶר אֶל־הַר סִינַי וְנִצַּבְתָּ לִי שָׁם עַל־רֹאשׁ הָהָר: וְאִישׁ
לֹא־יַעֲלֶה עִמָּךְ וְגַם־אִישׁ אַל־יֵרָא בְּכָל־הָהָר גַּם־הַצֹּאן וְהַבָּקָר אַל־יִרְעוּ
ישראל אֶל־מוּל הָהָר הַהוּא: ◄ וַיִּפְסֹל שְׁנֵי־לֻחֹת אֲבָנִים כָּרִאשֹׁנִים וַיַּשְׁכֵּם מֹשֶׁה בַבֹּקֶר
וַיַּעַל אֶל־הַר סִינַי כַּאֲשֶׁר צִוָּה יהוה אֹתוֹ וַיִּקַּח בְּיָדוֹ שְׁנֵי לֻחֹת אֲבָנִים: וַיֵּרֶד
יהוה בֶּעָנָן וַיִּתְיַצֵּב עִמּוֹ שָׁם וַיִּקְרָא בְשֵׁם יהוה: וַיַּעֲבֹר יהוה ׀ עַל־פָּנָיו וַיִּקְרָא
◄ יהוה ׀ יהוה אֵל רַחוּם וְחַנּוּן אֶרֶךְ אַפַּיִם וְרַב־חֶסֶד וֶאֱמֶת: נֹצֵר חֶסֶד לָאֲלָפִים
נֹשֵׂא עָוֹן וָפֶשַׁע וְחַטָּאָה וְנַקֵּה לֹא יְנַקֶּה פֹּקֵד ׀ עֲוֹן אָבוֹת עַל־בָּנִים וְעַל־בְּנֵי
בָנִים עַל־שִׁלֵּשִׁים וְעַל־רִבֵּעִים: וַיְמַהֵר מֹשֶׁה וַיִּקֹּד אַרְצָה וַיִּשְׁתָּחוּ: וַיֹּאמֶר
אִם־נָא מָצָאתִי חֵן בְּעֵינֶיךָ אֲדֹנָי יֵלֶךְ־נָא אֲדֹנָי בְּקִרְבֵּנוּ כִּי עַם־קְשֵׁה־עֹרֶף
הוּא ◄ וְסָלַחְתָּ לַעֲוֹנֵנוּ וּלְחַטָּאתֵנוּ וּנְחַלְתָּנוּ: ◄ וַיֹּאמֶר הִנֵּה אָנֹכִי כֹּרֵת בְּרִית
נֶגֶד כָּל־עַמְּךָ אֶעֱשֶׂה נִפְלָאֹת אֲשֶׁר לֹא־נִבְרְאוּ בְכָל־הָאָרֶץ וּבְכָל־הַגּוֹיִם
וְרָאָה כָל־הָעָם אֲשֶׁר־אַתָּה בְקִרְבּוֹ אֶת־מַעֲשֵׂה יהוה כִּי־נוֹרָא הוּא אֲשֶׁר
אֲנִי עֹשֶׂה עִמָּךְ:

ברכות ההפטרה

Before reading the הפטרה, *the person called up for* מפטיר *says:*

בָּרוּךְ אַתָּה יהוה אֱלֹהֵינוּ מֶלֶךְ הָעוֹלָם אֲשֶׁר בָּחַר בִּנְבִיאִים טוֹבִים, וְרָצָה

בְּדִבְרֵיהֶם הַנֶּאֱמָרִים בֶּאֱמֶת. בָּרוּךְ אַתָּה יהוה, הַבּוֹחֵר בַּתּוֹרָה וּבְמֹשֶׁה עַבְדּוֹ וּבְיִשְׂרָאֵל עַמּוֹ וּבִנְבִיאֵי הָאֱמֶת וָצֶדֶק.

After the הפטרה, the person called up for מפטיר says the following blessings:

בָּרוּךְ אַתָּה יהוה אֱלֹהֵינוּ מֶלֶךְ הָעוֹלָם, צוּר כָּל הָעוֹלָמִים, צַדִּיק בְּכָל הַדּוֹרוֹת, הָאֵל הַנֶּאֱמָן, הָאוֹמֵר וְעֹשֶׂה, הַמְדַבֵּר וּמְקַיֵּם, שֶׁכָּל דְּבָרָיו אֱמֶת וָצֶדֶק. נֶאֱמָן אַתָּה הוּא יהוה אֱלֹהֵינוּ וְנֶאֱמָנִים דְּבָרֶיךָ, וְדָבָר אֶחָד מִדְּבָרֶיךָ אָחוֹר לֹא יָשׁוּב רֵיקָם, כִּי אֵל מֶלֶךְ נֶאֱמָן (וְרַחֲמָן) אָתָּה. בָּרוּךְ אַתָּה יהוה, הָאֵל הַנֶּאֱמָן בְּכָל דְּבָרָיו.

רַחֵם עַל צִיּוֹן כִּי הִיא בֵּית חַיֵּינוּ, וְלַעֲלוּבַת נֶפֶשׁ תּוֹשִׁיעַ בִּמְהֵרָה בְיָמֵינוּ. בָּרוּךְ אַתָּה יהוה, מְשַׂמֵּחַ צִיּוֹן בְּבָנֶיהָ.

שַׂמְּחֵנוּ יהוה אֱלֹהֵינוּ בְּאֵלִיָּהוּ הַנָּבִיא עַבְדֶּךָ, וּבְמַלְכוּת בֵּית דָּוִד מְשִׁיחֶךָ, בִּמְהֵרָה יָבוֹא וְיָגֵל לִבֵּנוּ. עַל כִּסְאוֹ לֹא יֵשֵׁב זָר, וְלֹא יִנְחֲלוּ עוֹד אֲחֵרִים אֶת כְּבוֹדוֹ, כִּי בְשֵׁם קָדְשְׁךָ נִשְׁבַּעְתָּ לּוֹ שֶׁלֹּא יִכְבֶּה נֵרוֹ לְעוֹלָם וָעֶד. בָּרוּךְ אַתָּה יהוה, מָגֵן דָּוִד.

HAFTARA FOR FAST DAYS   הפטרה לתענית ציבור

ישעיה
נה:ו–נו:ח

דִּרְשׁוּ יהוה בְּהִמָּצְאוֹ קְרָאֻהוּ בִּהְיוֹתוֹ קָרוֹב: יַעֲזֹב רָשָׁע דַּרְכּוֹ וְאִישׁ אָוֶן מַחְשְׁבֹתָיו וְיָשֹׁב אֶל־יהוה וִירַחֲמֵהוּ וְאֶל־אֱלֹהֵינוּ כִּי־יַרְבֶּה לִסְלוֹחַ: כִּי לֹא מַחְשְׁבוֹתַי מַחְשְׁבוֹתֵיכֶם וְלֹא דַרְכֵיכֶם דְּרָכָי נְאֻם יהוה: כִּי־גָבְהוּ שָׁמַיִם מֵאָרֶץ כֵּן גָּבְהוּ דְרָכַי מִדַּרְכֵיכֶם וּמַחְשְׁבֹתַי מִמַּחְשְׁבֹתֵיכֶם: כִּי כַּאֲשֶׁר יֵרֵד הַגֶּשֶׁם וְהַשֶּׁלֶג מִן־הַשָּׁמַיִם וְשָׁמָּה לֹא יָשׁוּב כִּי אִם־הִרְוָה אֶת־הָאָרֶץ וְהוֹלִידָהּ וְהִצְמִיחָהּ וְנָתַן זֶרַע לַזֹּרֵעַ וְלֶחֶם לָאֹכֵל: כֵּן יִהְיֶה דְבָרִי אֲשֶׁר יֵצֵא מִפִּי לֹא־יָשׁוּב אֵלַי רֵיקָם כִּי אִם־עָשָׂה אֶת־אֲשֶׁר חָפַצְתִּי וְהִצְלִיחַ אֲשֶׁר שְׁלַחְתִּיו: כִּי־בְשִׂמְחָה תֵצֵאוּ וּבְשָׁלוֹם תּוּבָלוּן הֶהָרִים וְהַגְּבָעוֹת יִפְצְחוּ לִפְנֵיכֶם רִנָּה

וְתַחַת וְכָל־עֲצֵי הַשָּׂדֶה יִמְחֲאוּ־כָף: תַּחַת הַנַּעֲצוּץ יַעֲלֶה בְרוֹשׁ תַּחַת הַסִּרְפַּד יַעֲלֶה הֲדַס וְהָיָה לַיהוה לְשֵׁם לְאוֹת עוֹלָם לֹא יִכָּרֵת: כֹּה אָמַר יהוה שִׁמְרוּ מִשְׁפָּט וַעֲשׂוּ צְדָקָה כִּי־קְרוֹבָה יְשׁוּעָתִי לָבוֹא וְצִדְקָתִי לְהִגָּלוֹת: אַשְׁרֵי אֱנוֹשׁ יַעֲשֶׂה־זֹּאת וּבֶן־אָדָם יַחֲזִיק בָּהּ שֹׁמֵר שַׁבָּת מֵחַלְּלוֹ וְשֹׁמֵר יָדוֹ מֵעֲשׂוֹת כָּל־רָע: וְאַל־יֹאמַר בֶּן־הַנֵּכָר הַנִּלְוָה אֶל־יהוה לֵאמֹר הַבְדֵּל

כִּי יַבְדִּילַנִי יהוה מֵעַל עַמּוֹ וְאַל־יֹאמַר הַסָּרִיס הֵן אֲנִי עֵץ יָבֵשׁ:

כֹּה ׀ אָמַ֣ר יְהֹוָ֗ה לַסָּֽרִיסִים֙ אֲשֶׁ֤ר יִשְׁמְרוּ֙ אֶת־שַׁבְּתוֹתַ֔י וּבָחֲר֖וּ בַּאֲשֶׁ֣ר חָפָ֑צְתִּי
וּמַחֲזִיקִ֖ים בִּבְרִיתִֽי: וְנָתַתִּ֨י לָהֶ֜ם בְּבֵיתִ֤י וּבְחֽוֹמֹתַי֙ יָ֣ד וָשֵׁ֔ם ט֖וֹב מִבָּנִ֣ים
וּמִבָּנ֑וֹת שֵׁ֤ם עוֹלָם֙ אֶתֶּן־ל֔וֹ אֲשֶׁ֖ר לֹ֥א יִכָּרֵֽת: וּבְנֵ֣י הַנֵּכָ֗ר הַנִּלְוִ֤ים
עַל־יְהֹוָה֙ לְשָׁ֣רְת֔וֹ וּֽלְאַהֲבָה֙ אֶת־שֵׁ֣ם יְהֹוָ֔ה לִהְי֥וֹת ל֖וֹ לַעֲבָדִ֑ים כָּל־שֹׁמֵ֤ר
שַׁבָּת֙ מֵֽחַלְּל֔וֹ וּמַחֲזִיקִ֖ים בִּבְרִיתִֽי: וַהֲבִֽיאוֹתִ֞ים אֶל־הַ֣ר קָדְשִׁ֗י וְשִׂמַּחְתִּים֙
בְּבֵ֣ית תְּפִלָּתִ֔י עוֹלֹתֵיהֶ֧ם וְזִבְחֵיהֶ֛ם לְרָצ֖וֹן עַֽל־מִזְבְּחִ֑י כִּ֣י בֵיתִ֗י בֵּית־תְּפִלָּ֥ה
יִקָּרֵ֖א לְכָל־הָעַמִּֽים: נְאֻם֙ אֲדֹנָ֣י יְהֹוִ֔ה מְקַבֵּ֖ץ נִדְחֵ֣י יִשְׂרָאֵ֑ל ע֛וֹד אֲקַבֵּ֥ץ עָלָ֖יו
לְנִקְבָּצָֽיו:

READING FOR TISHA B'AV

The following is read during שחרית of תשעה באב. The person called up for שלישי also
reads the הפטרה. At מנחה, the קריאת התורה and הפטרה are those for regular Fast Days.

דברים
ד:כה-מ

כִּֽי־תוֹלִ֤יד בָּנִים֙ וּבְנֵ֣י בָנִ֔ים וְנֽוֹשַׁנְתֶּ֖ם בָּאָ֑רֶץ וְהִשְׁחַתֶּ֗ם וַעֲשִׂ֤יתֶֽם פֶּ֨סֶל֙ תְּמ֣וּנַת
כֹּ֔ל וַעֲשִׂיתֶ֥ם הָרַ֛ע בְּעֵינֵ֥י יְהֹוָֽה־אֱלֹהֶ֖יךָ לְהַכְעִיסֽוֹ: הַעִידֹ֩תִי֩ בָכֶ֨ם הַיּ֜וֹם אֶת־
הַשָּׁמַ֣יִם וְאֶת־הָאָ֗רֶץ כִּֽי־אָבֹ֣ד תֹּאבֵדוּן֮ מַהֵר֒ מֵעַ֣ל הָאָ֔רֶץ אֲשֶׁ֨ר אַתֶּ֜ם עֹבְרִ֧ים
אֶת־הַיַּרְדֵּ֛ן שָׁ֖מָּה לְרִשְׁתָּ֑הּ לֹֽא־תַאֲרִיכֻ֤ן יָמִים֙ עָלֶ֔יהָ כִּֽי־הִשָּׁמֵ֖ד תִּשָּׁמֵדֽוּן:
וְהֵפִ֧יץ יְהֹוָ֛ה אֶתְכֶ֖ם בָּֽעַמִּ֑ים וְנִשְׁאַרְתֶּם֙ מְתֵ֣י מִסְפָּ֔ר בַּגּוֹיִ֕ם אֲשֶׁ֨ר יְנַהֵ֧ג יְהֹוָ֛ה
אֶתְכֶ֖ם שָֽׁמָּה: וַעֲבַדְתֶּם־שָׁ֣ם אֱלֹהִ֔ים מַעֲשֵׂ֖ה יְדֵ֣י אָדָ֑ם עֵ֣ץ וָאֶ֔בֶן אֲשֶׁ֤ר לֹֽא־
יִרְאוּן֙ וְלֹ֣א יִשְׁמְע֔וּן וְלֹ֥א יֹֽאכְל֖וּן וְלֹ֥א יְרִיחֻֽן: וּבִקַּשְׁתֶּ֥ם מִשָּׁ֛ם אֶת־יְהֹוָ֥ה אֱלֹהֶ֖יךָ
וּמָצָ֑אתָ כִּ֣י תִדְרְשֶׁ֔נּוּ בְּכָל־לְבָבְךָ֖ וּבְכָל־נַפְשֶֽׁךָ: *בַּצַּ֣ר לְ֠ךָ֠ וּמְצָא֗וּךָ כֹּל֙ הַדְּבָרִ֣ים

לוי

הָאֵ֔לֶּה בְּאַחֲרִית֙ הַיָּמִ֔ים וְשַׁבְתָּ֙ עַד־יְהֹוָ֣ה אֱלֹהֶ֔יךָ וְשָׁמַעְתָּ֖ בְּקֹלֽוֹ: כִּ֣י אֵ֤ל
רַחוּם֙ יְהֹוָ֣ה אֱלֹהֶ֔יךָ לֹ֥א יַרְפְּךָ֖ וְלֹ֣א יַשְׁחִיתֶ֑ךָ וְלֹ֤א יִשְׁכַּח֙ אֶת־בְּרִ֣ית אֲבֹתֶ֔יךָ
אֲשֶׁ֥ר נִשְׁבַּ֖ע לָהֶֽם: כִּ֣י שְׁאַל־נָא֩ לְיָמִ֨ים רִֽאשֹׁנִ֜ים אֲשֶׁר־הָי֣וּ לְפָנֶ֗יךָ לְמִן־הַיּוֹם֙
אֲשֶׁר֩ בָּרָ֨א אֱלֹהִ֤ים ׀ אָדָם֙ עַל־הָאָ֔רֶץ וּלְמִקְצֵ֥ה הַשָּׁמַ֖יִם וְעַד־קְצֵ֣ה הַשָּׁמָ֑יִם
הֲנִֽהְיָ֗ה כַּדָּבָ֤ר הַגָּדוֹל֙ הַזֶּ֔ה א֖וֹ הֲנִשְׁמַ֥ע כָּמֹֽהוּ: הֲשָׁמַ֣ע עָם֩ ק֨וֹל אֱלֹהִ֜ים מְדַבֵּ֧ר
מִתּֽוֹךְ־הָאֵ֛שׁ כַּאֲשֶׁר־שָׁמַ֥עְתָּ אַתָּ֖ה וַיֶּֽחִי: א֣וֹ ׀ הֲנִסָּ֣ה אֱלֹהִ֗ים לָ֠ב֠וֹא לָקַ֨חַת ל֣וֹ
גוֹי֮ מִקֶּ֣רֶב גּוֹי֒ בְּמַסֹּת֩ בְּאֹתֹ֨ת וּבְמֽוֹפְתִ֜ים וּבְמִלְחָמָ֗ה וּבְיָ֤ד חֲזָקָה֙ וּבִזְר֣וֹעַ נְטוּיָ֔ה
וּבְמֽוֹרָאִ֖ים גְּדֹלִ֑ים כְּ֠כֹ֠ל אֲשֶׁר־עָשָׂ֨ה לָכֶ֜ם יְהֹוָ֧ה אֱלֹהֵיכֶ֛ם בְּמִצְרַ֖יִם לְעֵינֶֽיךָ:

ישראל

אַתָּה֙ הָרְאֵ֣תָ לָדַ֔עַת כִּ֥י יְהֹוָ֖ה ה֣וּא הָאֱלֹהִ֑ים אֵ֥ין ע֖וֹד מִלְּבַדּֽוֹ: *מִן־הַשָּׁמַ֛יִם

הִשְׁמִיעֲךָ אֶת־קֹלוֹ לְיַסְּרֶךָ וְעַל־הָאָרֶץ הֶרְאֲךָ אֶת־אִשּׁוֹ הַגְּדוֹלָה וּדְבָרָיו
שָׁמַעְתָּ מִתּוֹךְ הָאֵשׁ: וְתַחַת כִּי אָהַב אֶת־אֲבֹתֶיךָ וַיִּבְחַר בְּזַרְעוֹ אַחֲרָיו
וַיּוֹצִאֲךָ בְּפָנָיו בְּכֹחוֹ הַגָּדֹל מִמִּצְרָיִם: לְהוֹרִישׁ גּוֹיִם גְּדֹלִים וַעֲצֻמִים מִמְּךָ
מִפָּנֶיךָ לַהֲבִיאֲךָ לָתֶת־לְךָ אֶת־אַרְצָם נַחֲלָה כַּיּוֹם הַזֶּה: וְיָדַעְתָּ הַיּוֹם וַהֲשֵׁבֹתָ
אֶל־לְבָבֶךָ כִּי יְהוָה הוּא הָאֱלֹהִים בַּשָּׁמַיִם מִמַּעַל וְעַל־הָאָרֶץ מִתָּחַת אֵין
עוֹד: וְשָׁמַרְתָּ אֶת־חֻקָּיו וְאֶת־מִצְוֹתָיו אֲשֶׁר אָנֹכִי מְצַוְּךָ הַיּוֹם אֲשֶׁר יִיטַב לְךָ
וּלְבָנֶיךָ אַחֲרֶיךָ וּלְמַעַן תַּאֲרִיךְ יָמִים עַל־הָאֲדָמָה אֲשֶׁר יְהוָה אֱלֹהֶיךָ נֹתֵן לְךָ
כָּל־הַיָּמִים:

HAFTARA FOR TISHA B'AV
הפטרה לתשעה באב

ירמיהו
ח:יג–ט:כג

אָסֹף אֲסִיפֵם נְאֻם־יְהוָה אֵין עֲנָבִים בַּגֶּפֶן וְאֵין תְּאֵנִים בַּתְּאֵנָה וְהֶעָלֶה נָבֵל
וָאֶתֵּן לָהֶם יַעַבְרוּם: עַל־מָה אֲנַחְנוּ יֹשְׁבִים הֵאָסְפוּ וְנָבוֹא אֶל־עָרֵי הַמִּבְצָר
וְנִדְּמָה־שָּׁם כִּי יְהוָה אֱלֹהֵינוּ הֲדִמָּנוּ וַיַּשְׁקֵנוּ מֵי־רֹאשׁ כִּי חָטָאנוּ לַיהוָה:
קַוֵּה לְשָׁלוֹם וְאֵין טוֹב לְעֵת מַרְפֵּה וְהִנֵּה בְעָתָה: מִדָּן נִשְׁמַע נַחְרַת סוּסָיו
מִקּוֹל מִצְהֲלוֹת אַבִּירָיו רָעֲשָׁה כָּל־הָאָרֶץ וַיָּבוֹאוּ וַיֹּאכְלוּ אֶרֶץ וּמְלוֹאָהּ עִיר
וְיֹשְׁבֵי בָהּ: כִּי הִנְנִי מְשַׁלֵּחַ בָּכֶם נְחָשִׁים צִפְעֹנִים אֲשֶׁר אֵין־לָהֶם לָחַשׁ וְנִשְּׁכוּ
אֶתְכֶם נְאֻם־יְהוָה: מַבְלִיגִיתִי עֲלֵי יָגוֹן עָלַי לִבִּי דַוָּי: הִנֵּה־קוֹל
שַׁוְעַת בַּת־עַמִּי מֵאֶרֶץ מַרְחַקִּים הַיהוָה אֵין בְּצִיּוֹן אִם־מַלְכָּהּ אֵין בָּהּ מַדּוּעַ
הִכְעִסוּנִי בִּפְסִלֵיהֶם בְּהַבְלֵי נֵכָר: עָבַר קָצִיר כָּלָה קָיִץ וַאֲנַחְנוּ לוֹא נוֹשָׁעְנוּ:
עַל־שֶׁבֶר בַּת־עַמִּי הָשְׁבָּרְתִּי קָדַרְתִּי שַׁמָּה הֶחֱזִקָתְנִי: הַצֳרִי אֵין בְּגִלְעָד אִם־
רֹפֵא אֵין שָׁם כִּי מַדּוּעַ לֹא עָלְתָה אֲרֻכַת בַּת־עַמִּי: מִי־יִתֵּן רֹאשִׁי
מַיִם וְעֵינִי מְקוֹר דִּמְעָה וְאֶבְכֶּה יוֹמָם וָלַיְלָה אֵת חַלְלֵי בַת־עַמִּי: מִי־יִתְּנֵנִי
בַמִּדְבָּר מְלוֹן אֹרְחִים וְאֶעֶזְבָה אֶת־עַמִּי וְאֵלְכָה מֵאִתָּם כִּי כֻלָּם מְנָאֲפִים עֲצֶרֶת
בֹּגְדִים: וַיַּדְרְכוּ אֶת־לְשׁוֹנָם קַשְׁתָּם שֶׁקֶר וְלֹא לֶאֱמוּנָה גָּבְרוּ בָאָרֶץ כִּי מֵרָעָה
אֶל־רָעָה יָצָאוּ וְאֹתִי לֹא־יָדָעוּ נְאֻם־יְהוָה: אִישׁ מֵרֵעֵהוּ הִשָּׁמֵרוּ וְעַל־כָּל־
אָח אַל־תִּבְטָחוּ כִּי כָל־אָח עָקוֹב יַעְקֹב וְכָל־רֵעַ רָכִיל יַהֲלֹךְ: וְאִישׁ בְּרֵעֵהוּ
יְהָתֵלּוּ וֶאֱמֶת לֹא יְדַבֵּרוּ לִמְּדוּ לְשׁוֹנָם דַּבֶּר־שֶׁקֶר הַעֲוֵה נִלְאוּ:   לֵכֵן כֹּה
בְּתוֹךְ מִרְמָה בְּמִרְמָה מֵאֲנוּ דַעַת־אוֹתִי נְאֻם־יְהוָה:
אָמַר יְהוָה צְבָאוֹת הִנְנִי צוֹרְפָם וּבְחַנְתִּים כִּי־אֵיךְ אֶעֱשֶׂה מִפְּנֵי בַּת־עַמִּי:

שָׁחוּט חֵץ שׁוֹחֵט לְשׁוֹנָם מִרְמָה דִבֵּר בְּפִיו שָׁלוֹם אֶת־רֵעֵהוּ יְדַבֵּר וּבְקִרְבּוֹ יָשִׂים אָרְבּוֹ: הַעַל־אֵלֶּה לֹא־אֶפְקָד־בָּם נְאֻם־יהוה אִם בְּגוֹי אֲשֶׁר־כָּזֶה לֹא תִתְנַקֵּם נַפְשִׁי: עַל־הֶהָרִים אֶשָּׂא בְכִי וָנֶהִי וְעַל־נְאוֹת מִדְבָּר קִינָה כִּי נִצְּתוּ מִבְּלִי־אִישׁ עֹבֵר וְלֹא שָׁמְעוּ קוֹל מִקְנֶה מֵעוֹף הַשָּׁמַיִם וְעַד־בְּהֵמָה נָדְדוּ הָלָכוּ: וְנָתַתִּי אֶת־יְרוּשָׁלִַם לְגַלִּים מְעוֹן תַּנִּים וְאֶת־עָרֵי יְהוּדָה אֶתֵּן שְׁמָמָה מִבְּלִי יוֹשֵׁב: מִי־הָאִישׁ הֶחָכָם וְיָבֵן אֶת־זֹאת וַאֲשֶׁר דִּבֶּר פִּי־יהוה אֵלָיו וְיַגִּדָהּ עַל־מָה אָבְדָה הָאָרֶץ נִצְּתָה כַמִּדְבָּר מִבְּלִי עֹבֵר: וַיֹּאמֶר יהוה עַל־עָזְבָם אֶת־תּוֹרָתִי אֲשֶׁר נָתַתִּי לִפְנֵיהֶם וְלֹא־שָׁמְעוּ בְקוֹלִי וְלֹא־הָלְכוּ בָהּ: וַיֵּלְכוּ אַחֲרֵי שְׁרִרוּת לִבָּם וְאַחֲרֵי הַבְּעָלִים אֲשֶׁר לִמְּדוּם אֲבוֹתָם: לָכֵן כֹּה־אָמַר יהוה צְבָאוֹת אֱלֹהֵי יִשְׂרָאֵל הִנְנִי מַאֲכִילָם אֶת־הָעָם הַזֶּה לַעֲנָה וְהִשְׁקִיתִים מֵי־רֹאשׁ: וַהֲפִצוֹתִים בַּגּוֹיִם אֲשֶׁר לֹא יָדְעוּ הֵמָּה וַאֲבוֹתָם וְשִׁלַּחְתִּי אַחֲרֵיהֶם אֶת־הַחֶרֶב עַד כַּלּוֹתִי אוֹתָם: כֹּה אָמַר יהוה צְבָאוֹת הִתְבּוֹנְנוּ וְקִרְאוּ לַמְקוֹנְנוֹת וּתְבוֹאֶינָה וְאֶל־הַחֲכָמוֹת שִׁלְחוּ וְתָבוֹאנָה: וּתְמַהֵרְנָה וְתִשֶּׂנָה עָלֵינוּ נֶהִי וְתֵרַדְנָה עֵינֵינוּ דִּמְעָה וְעַפְעַפֵּינוּ יִזְּלוּ־מָיִם: כִּי קוֹל נְהִי נִשְׁמַע מִצִּיּוֹן אֵיךְ שֻׁדָּדְנוּ בֹּשְׁנוּ מְאֹד כִּי־עָזַבְנוּ אָרֶץ כִּי הִשְׁלִיכוּ מִשְׁכְּנוֹתֵינוּ: כִּי־ שְׁמַעְנָה נָשִׁים דְּבַר־יהוה וְתִקַּח אָזְנְכֶם דְּבַר־פִּיו וְלַמֵּדְנָה בְנוֹתֵיכֶם נֶהִי וְאִשָּׁה רְעוּתָהּ קִינָה: כִּי־עָלָה מָוֶת בְּחַלּוֹנֵינוּ בָּא בְּאַרְמְנוֹתֵינוּ לְהַכְרִית עוֹלָל מִחוּץ בַּחוּרִים מֵרְחֹבוֹת: דַּבֵּר כֹּה נְאֻם־יהוה וְנָפְלָה נִבְלַת הָאָדָם כְּדֹמֶן עַל־פְּנֵי הַשָּׂדֶה וּכְעָמִיר מֵאַחֲרֵי הַקֹּצֵר וְאֵין מְאַסֵּף: כֹּה אָמַר יהוה אַל־יִתְהַלֵּל חָכָם בְּחָכְמָתוֹ וְאַל־יִתְהַלֵּל הַגִּבּוֹר בִּגְבוּרָתוֹ אַל־יִתְהַלֵּל עָשִׁיר בְּעָשְׁרוֹ: כִּי אִם־בְּזֹאת יִתְהַלֵּל הַמִּתְהַלֵּל הַשְׂכֵּל וְיָדֹעַ אוֹתִי כִּי אֲנִי יהוה עֹשֶׂה חֶסֶד מִשְׁפָּט וּצְדָקָה בָּאָרֶץ כִּי־בְאֵלֶּה חָפַצְתִּי נְאֻם־יהוה:

FIRST DAY OF HANUKKA   קריאה ליום הראשון של חנוכה

במדבר
ז:א- יז

וַיְהִי בְּיוֹם כַּלּוֹת מֹשֶׁה לְהָקִים אֶת־הַמִּשְׁכָּן וַיִּמְשַׁח אֹתוֹ וַיְקַדֵּשׁ אֹתוֹ וְאֶת־ כָּל־כֵּלָיו וְאֶת־הַמִּזְבֵּחַ וְאֶת־כָּל־כֵּלָיו וַיִּמְשָׁחֵם וַיְקַדֵּשׁ אֹתָם: וַיַּקְרִיבוּ נְשִׂיאֵי יִשְׂרָאֵל רָאשֵׁי בֵּית אֲבֹתָם הֵם נְשִׂיאֵי הַמַּטֹּת הֵם הָעֹמְדִים עַל־הַפְּקֻדִים: וַיָּבִיאוּ אֶת־קָרְבָּנָם לִפְנֵי יהוה שֵׁשׁ־עֶגְלֹת צָב וּשְׁנֵי־עָשָׂר בָּקָר עֲגָלָה עַל־שְׁנֵי

הַנְּשִׂאִים וְשׁוֹר לָאֶחָד וַיַּקְרִיבוּ אוֹתָם לִפְנֵי הַמִּשְׁכָּן: וַיֹּאמֶר יהוה אֶל־מֹשֶׁה
לֵּאמֹר: קַח מֵאִתָּם וְהָיוּ לַעֲבֹד אֶת־עֲבֹדַת אֹהֶל מוֹעֵד וְנָתַתָּה אוֹתָם אֶל־
הַלְוִיִּם אִישׁ כְּפִי עֲבֹדָתוֹ: וַיִּקַּח מֹשֶׁה אֶת־הָעֲגָלֹת וְאֶת־הַבָּקָר וַיִּתֵּן אוֹתָם
אֶל־הַלְוִיִּם: אֵת ׀ שְׁתֵּי הָעֲגָלֹת וְאֵת אַרְבַּעַת הַבָּקָר נָתַן לִבְנֵי גֵרְשׁוֹן כְּפִי
עֲבֹדָתָם: וְאֵת ׀ אַרְבַּע הָעֲגָלֹת וְאֵת שְׁמֹנַת הַבָּקָר נָתַן לִבְנֵי מְרָרִי כְּפִי עֲבֹדָתָם
בְּיַד אִיתָמָר בֶּן־אַהֲרֹן הַכֹּהֵן: וְלִבְנֵי קְהָת לֹא נָתָן כִּי־עֲבֹדַת הַקֹּדֶשׁ עֲלֵהֶם
בַּכָּתֵף יִשָּׂאוּ: וַיַּקְרִיבוּ הַנְּשִׂאִים אֵת חֲנֻכַּת הַמִּזְבֵּחַ בְּיוֹם הִמָּשַׁח אֹתוֹ וַיַּקְרִיבוּ
הַנְּשִׂיאִם אֶת־קָרְבָּנָם לִפְנֵי הַמִּזְבֵּחַ: וַיֹּאמֶר יהוה אֶל־מֹשֶׁה נָשִׂיא אֶחָד לַיּוֹם
נָשִׂיא אֶחָד לַיּוֹם יַקְרִיבוּ אֶת־קָרְבָּנָם לַחֲנֻכַּת הַמִּזְבֵּחַ:

לוי

*וַיְהִי־
הַמַּקְרִיב בַּיּוֹם הָרִאשׁוֹן אֶת־קָרְבָּנוֹ נַחְשׁוֹן בֶּן־עַמִּינָדָב לְמַטֵּה יְהוּדָה: וְקָרְבָּנוֹ
קַעֲרַת־כֶּסֶף אַחַת שְׁלֹשִׁים וּמֵאָה מִשְׁקָלָהּ מִזְרָק אֶחָד כֶּסֶף שִׁבְעִים שֶׁקֶל
בְּשֶׁקֶל הַקֹּדֶשׁ שְׁנֵיהֶם ׀ מְלֵאִים סֹלֶת בְּלוּלָה בַשֶּׁמֶן לְמִנְחָה: כַּף אַחַת
עֲשָׂרָה זָהָב מְלֵאָה קְטֹרֶת: *פַּר אֶחָד בֶּן־בָּקָר אַיִל אֶחָד כֶּבֶשׂ־אֶחָד בֶּן־

ישראל

שְׁנָתוֹ לְעֹלָה: שְׂעִיר־עִזִּים אֶחָד לְחַטָּאת: וּלְזֶבַח הַשְּׁלָמִים בָּקָר שְׁנַיִם
אֵילִם חֲמִשָּׁה עַתּוּדִים חֲמִשָּׁה כְּבָשִׂים בְּנֵי־שָׁנָה חֲמִשָּׁה זֶה קָרְבַּן נַחְשׁוֹן
בֶּן־עַמִּינָדָב:

SECOND DAY OF ḤANUKKA   קריאה ליום השני של חנוכה

In ארץ ישראל, for שלישי repeat the first paragraph: בַּיּוֹם הַשֵּׁנִי until נְתַנְאֵל בֶּן־צוּעָר.

במדבר
ז:יח-כט

בַּיּוֹם הַשֵּׁנִי הִקְרִיב נְתַנְאֵל בֶּן־צוּעָר נְשִׂיא יִשָּׂשכָר: הִקְרִב אֶת־קָרְבָּנוֹ קַעֲרַת־
כֶּסֶף אַחַת שְׁלֹשִׁים וּמֵאָה מִשְׁקָלָהּ מִזְרָק אֶחָד כֶּסֶף שִׁבְעִים שֶׁקֶל בְּשֶׁקֶל
הַקֹּדֶשׁ שְׁנֵיהֶם ׀ מְלֵאִים סֹלֶת בְּלוּלָה בַשֶּׁמֶן לְמִנְחָה: כַּף אַחַת עֲשָׂרָה זָהָב

לוי

מְלֵאָה קְטֹרֶת: *פַּר אֶחָד בֶּן־בָּקָר אַיִל אֶחָד כֶּבֶשׂ־אֶחָד בֶּן־שְׁנָתוֹ לְעֹלָה:
שְׂעִיר־עִזִּים אֶחָד לְחַטָּאת: וּלְזֶבַח הַשְּׁלָמִים בָּקָר שְׁנַיִם אֵילִם חֲמִשָּׁה עַתֻּדִים
חֲמִשָּׁה כְּבָשִׂים בְּנֵי־שָׁנָה חֲמִשָּׁה זֶה קָרְבַּן נְתַנְאֵל בֶּן־צוּעָר:

ישראל

בַּיּוֹם הַשְּׁלִישִׁי נָשִׂיא לִבְנֵי זְבוּלֻן אֱלִיאָב בֶּן־חֵלֹן: קָרְבָּנוֹ קַעֲרַת־כֶּסֶף אַחַת
שְׁלֹשִׁים וּמֵאָה מִשְׁקָלָהּ מִזְרָק אֶחָד כֶּסֶף שִׁבְעִים שֶׁקֶל בְּשֶׁקֶל הַקֹּדֶשׁ שְׁנֵיהֶם ׀
מְלֵאִים סֹלֶת בְּלוּלָה בַשֶּׁמֶן לְמִנְחָה: כַּף אַחַת עֲשָׂרָה זָהָב מְלֵאָה קְטֹרֶת:
פַּר אֶחָד בֶּן־בָּקָר אַיִל אֶחָד כֶּבֶשׂ־אֶחָד בֶּן־שְׁנָתוֹ לְעֹלָה: שְׂעִיר־עִזִּים אֶחָד

לְחַטָּאת: וּלְזֶבַח הַשְּׁלָמִים בָּקָר שְׁנַיִם אֵילִם חֲמִשָּׁה עַתּוּדִים חֲמִשָּׁה כְּבָשִׂים בְּנֵי־שָׁנָה חֲמִשָּׁה זֶה קָרְבַּן אֱלִיאָב בֶּן־חֵלֹן:

THIRD DAY OF ḤANUKKA · קריאה ליום השלישי של חנוכה

In ארץ ישראל, *for* שלישי *repeat the first paragraph:* בַּיּוֹם הַשְּׁלִישִׁי *until* אֱלִיאָב בֶּן־חֵלֹן.

במדבר ז:כד-לה

בַּיּוֹם הַשְּׁלִישִׁי נָשִׂיא לִבְנֵי זְבוּלֻן אֱלִיאָב בֶּן־חֵלֹן: קָרְבָּנוֹ קַעֲרַת־כֶּסֶף אַחַת שְׁלֹשִׁים וּמֵאָה מִשְׁקָלָהּ מִזְרָק אֶחָד כֶּסֶף שִׁבְעִים שֶׁקֶל בְּשֶׁקֶל הַקֹּדֶשׁ שְׁנֵיהֶם ׀ מְלֵאִים סֹלֶת בְּלוּלָה בַשֶּׁמֶן לְמִנְחָה: כַּף אַחַת עֲשָׂרָה זָהָב מְלֵאָה קְטֹרֶת:

לוי

*פַּר אֶחָד בֶּן־בָּקָר אַיִל אֶחָד כֶּבֶשׂ־אֶחָד בֶּן־שְׁנָתוֹ לְעֹלָה: שְׂעִיר־עִזִּים אֶחָד לְחַטָּאת: וּלְזֶבַח הַשְּׁלָמִים בָּקָר שְׁנַיִם אֵילִם חֲמִשָּׁה עַתֻּדִים חֲמִשָּׁה כְּבָשִׂים בְּנֵי־שָׁנָה חֲמִשָּׁה זֶה קָרְבַּן אֱלִיאָב בֶּן־חֵלֹן:

ישראל

בַּיּוֹם הָרְבִיעִי נָשִׂיא לִבְנֵי רְאוּבֵן אֱלִיצוּר בֶּן־שְׁדֵיאוּר: קָרְבָּנוֹ קַעֲרַת־כֶּסֶף אַחַת שְׁלֹשִׁים וּמֵאָה מִשְׁקָלָהּ מִזְרָק אֶחָד כֶּסֶף שִׁבְעִים שֶׁקֶל בְּשֶׁקֶל הַקֹּדֶשׁ שְׁנֵיהֶם ׀ מְלֵאִים סֹלֶת בְּלוּלָה בַשֶּׁמֶן לְמִנְחָה: כַּף אַחַת עֲשָׂרָה זָהָב מְלֵאָה קְטֹרֶת: פַּר אֶחָד בֶּן־בָּקָר אַיִל אֶחָד כֶּבֶשׂ־אֶחָד בֶּן־שְׁנָתוֹ לְעֹלָה: שְׂעִיר־עִזִּים אֶחָד לְחַטָּאת: וּלְזֶבַח הַשְּׁלָמִים בָּקָר שְׁנַיִם אֵילִם חֲמִשָּׁה עַתֻּדִים חֲמִשָּׁה כְּבָשִׂים בְּנֵי־שָׁנָה חֲמִשָּׁה זֶה קָרְבַּן אֱלִיצוּר בֶּן־שְׁדֵיאוּר:

FOURTH DAY OF ḤANUKKA · קריאה ליום הרביעי של חנוכה

In ארץ ישראל, *for* שלישי *repeat the first paragraph:* בַּיּוֹם הָרְבִיעִי *until* אֱלִיצוּר בֶּן־שְׁדֵיאוּר.

במדבר ז:ל-מא

בַּיּוֹם הָרְבִיעִי נָשִׂיא לִבְנֵי רְאוּבֵן אֱלִיצוּר בֶּן־שְׁדֵיאוּר: קָרְבָּנוֹ קַעֲרַת־כֶּסֶף אַחַת שְׁלֹשִׁים וּמֵאָה מִשְׁקָלָהּ מִזְרָק אֶחָד כֶּסֶף שִׁבְעִים שֶׁקֶל בְּשֶׁקֶל הַקֹּדֶשׁ שְׁנֵיהֶם ׀ מְלֵאִים סֹלֶת בְּלוּלָה בַשֶּׁמֶן לְמִנְחָה: כַּף אַחַת עֲשָׂרָה זָהָב מְלֵאָה

לוי

קְטֹרֶת: *פַּר אֶחָד בֶּן־בָּקָר אַיִל אֶחָד כֶּבֶשׂ־אֶחָד בֶּן־שְׁנָתוֹ לְעֹלָה: שְׂעִיר־עִזִּים אֶחָד לְחַטָּאת: וּלְזֶבַח הַשְּׁלָמִים בָּקָר שְׁנַיִם אֵילִם חֲמִשָּׁה עַתֻּדִים חֲמִשָּׁה כְּבָשִׂים בְּנֵי־שָׁנָה חֲמִשָּׁה זֶה קָרְבַּן אֱלִיצוּר בֶּן־שְׁדֵיאוּר:

ישראל

בַּיּוֹם הַחֲמִישִׁי נָשִׂיא לִבְנֵי שִׁמְעוֹן שְׁלֻמִיאֵל בֶּן־צוּרִישַׁדָּי: קָרְבָּנוֹ קַעֲרַת־כֶּסֶף אַחַת שְׁלֹשִׁים וּמֵאָה מִשְׁקָלָהּ מִזְרָק אֶחָד כֶּסֶף שִׁבְעִים שֶׁקֶל בְּשֶׁקֶל הַקֹּדֶשׁ שְׁנֵיהֶם ׀ מְלֵאִים סֹלֶת בְּלוּלָה בַשֶּׁמֶן לְמִנְחָה: כַּף אַחַת עֲשָׂרָה זָהָב מְלֵאָה

קְטֹרֶת: פַּר אֶחָד בֶּן־בָּקָר אַיִל אֶחָד כֶּבֶשׂ אֶחָד בֶּן־שְׁנָתוֹ לְעֹלָה: שְׂעִיר־עִזִּים
אֶחָד לְחַטָּאת: וּלְזֶבַח הַשְּׁלָמִים בָּקָר שְׁנַיִם אֵילִם חֲמִשָּׁה עַתּוּדִים חֲמִשָּׁה
כְבָשִׂים בְּנֵי־שָׁנָה חֲמִשָּׁה זֶה קָרְבַּן שְׁלֻמִיאֵל בֶּן־צוּרִישַׁדָּי:

FIFTH DAY OF HANUKKA   קריאה ליום החמישי של חנוכה

שְׁלֻמִיאֵל בֶּן־צוּרִישַׁדָּי *In* אֶרֶץ ישראל, *for* שלישי *repeat the first paragraph:* בַּיּוֹם הַחֲמִישִׁי *until* שְׁלֻמִיאֵל בֶּן־צוּרִישַׁדָּי.

במדבר
ז:לו-מו
בַּיּוֹם הַחֲמִישִׁי נָשִׂיא לִבְנֵי שִׁמְעוֹן שְׁלֻמִיאֵל בֶּן־צוּרִישַׁדָּי: קָרְבָּנוֹ קַעֲרַת־
כֶּסֶף אַחַת שְׁלֹשִׁים וּמֵאָה מִשְׁקָלָהּ מִזְרָק אֶחָד כֶּסֶף שִׁבְעִים שֶׁקֶל בְּשֶׁקֶל
הַקֹּדֶשׁ שְׁנֵיהֶם ׀ מְלֵאִים סֹלֶת בְּלוּלָה בַשֶּׁמֶן לְמִנְחָה: כַּף אַחַת עֲשָׂרָה זָהָב
מְלֵאָה קְטֹרֶת: *פַּר אֶחָד בֶּן־בָּקָר אַיִל אֶחָד כֶּבֶשׂ אֶחָד בֶּן־שְׁנָתוֹ לְעֹלָה: לוי
שְׂעִיר־עִזִּים אֶחָד לְחַטָּאת: וּלְזֶבַח הַשְּׁלָמִים בָּקָר שְׁנַיִם אֵילִם חֲמִשָּׁה עַתּוּדִים
חֲמִשָּׁה כְבָשִׂים בְּנֵי־שָׁנָה חֲמִשָּׁה זֶה קָרְבַּן שְׁלֻמִיאֵל בֶּן־צוּרִישַׁדָּי:

ישראל
בַּיּוֹם הַשִּׁשִּׁי נָשִׂיא לִבְנֵי גָד אֶלְיָסָף בֶּן־דְּעוּאֵל: קָרְבָּנוֹ קַעֲרַת־כֶּסֶף אַחַת
שְׁלֹשִׁים וּמֵאָה מִשְׁקָלָהּ מִזְרָק אֶחָד כֶּסֶף שִׁבְעִים שֶׁקֶל בְּשֶׁקֶל הַקֹּדֶשׁ שְׁנֵיהֶם ׀
מְלֵאִים סֹלֶת בְּלוּלָה בַשֶּׁמֶן לְמִנְחָה: כַּף אַחַת עֲשָׂרָה זָהָב מְלֵאָה קְטֹרֶת:
פַּר אֶחָד בֶּן־בָּקָר אַיִל אֶחָד כֶּבֶשׂ אֶחָד בֶּן־שְׁנָתוֹ לְעֹלָה: שְׂעִיר־עִזִּים אֶחָד
לְחַטָּאת: וּלְזֶבַח הַשְּׁלָמִים בָּקָר שְׁנַיִם אֵילִם חֲמִשָּׁה עַתּוּדִים חֲמִשָּׁה כְבָשִׂים
בְּנֵי־שָׁנָה חֲמִשָּׁה זֶה קָרְבַּן אֶלְיָסָף בֶּן־דְּעוּאֵל:

קריאה ליום הששי של חנוכה וראש חודש
SIXTH DAY OF HANUKKA AND ROSH ḤODESH

The sixth day is ראש חודש טבת. *Two* ספרי תורה *are taken out of the* ארון קודש. *From the
first, read the* בַּיּוֹם הַשִּׁשִּׁי *for* ראש חודש קריאת התורה (*page 653*), *from the second, read*:

במדבר
ז:מב-מז
בַּיּוֹם הַשִּׁשִּׁי נָשִׂיא לִבְנֵי גָד אֶלְיָסָף בֶּן־דְּעוּאֵל: קָרְבָּנוֹ קַעֲרַת־כֶּסֶף אַחַת
שְׁלֹשִׁים וּמֵאָה מִשְׁקָלָהּ מִזְרָק אֶחָד כֶּסֶף שִׁבְעִים שֶׁקֶל בְּשֶׁקֶל הַקֹּדֶשׁ שְׁנֵיהֶם ׀
מְלֵאִים סֹלֶת בְּלוּלָה בַשֶּׁמֶן לְמִנְחָה: כַּף אַחַת עֲשָׂרָה זָהָב מְלֵאָה קְטֹרֶת:
פַּר אֶחָד בֶּן־בָּקָר אַיִל אֶחָד כֶּבֶשׂ אֶחָד בֶּן־שְׁנָתוֹ לְעֹלָה: שְׂעִיר־עִזִּים אֶחָד
לְחַטָּאת: וּלְזֶבַח הַשְּׁלָמִים בָּקָר שְׁנַיִם אֵילִם חֲמִשָּׁה עַתּוּדִים חֲמִשָּׁה כְבָשִׂים
בְּנֵי־שָׁנָה חֲמִשָּׁה זֶה קָרְבַּן אֶלְיָסָף בֶּן־דְּעוּאֵל:

קריאה ליום השביעי של חנוכה וראש חודש
SEVENTH DAY OF ḤANUKKA AND ROSH ḤODESH

If the seventh day is also ראש חודש, then two ספרי תורה are taken out of the ארון קודש. From the first, read the קריאת התורה for ראש חודש (page 653), from the second, read בַּיּוֹם הַשְּׁבִיעִי:

במדבר
כח-נג:

בַּיּוֹם הַשְּׁבִיעִי נָשִׂיא לִבְנֵי אֶפְרָיִם אֱלִישָׁמָע בֶּן־עַמִּיהוּד: קָרְבָּנוֹ קַעֲרַת־כֶּסֶף אַחַת שְׁלֹשִׁים וּמֵאָה מִשְׁקָלָהּ מִזְרָק אֶחָד כֶּסֶף שִׁבְעִים שֶׁקֶל בְּשֶׁקֶל הַקֹּדֶשׁ שְׁנֵיהֶם ׀ מְלֵאִים סֹלֶת בְּלוּלָה בַשֶּׁמֶן לְמִנְחָה: כַּף אַחַת עֲשָׂרָה זָהָב מְלֵאָה קְטֹרֶת: פַּר אֶחָד בֶּן־בָּקָר אַיִל אֶחָד כֶּבֶשׂ־אֶחָד בֶּן־שְׁנָתוֹ לְעֹלָה: שְׂעִיר־עִזִּים אֶחָד לְחַטָּאת: וּלְזֶבַח הַשְּׁלָמִים בָּקָר שְׁנַיִם אֵילִם חֲמִשָּׁה עַתֻּדִים חֲמִשָּׁה כְּבָשִׂים בְּנֵי־שָׁנָה חֲמִשָּׁה זֶה קָרְבַּן אֱלִישָׁמָע בֶּן־עַמִּיהוּד:

SEVENTH DAY OF ḤANUKKA
קריאה ליום השביעי של חנוכה

If the seventh day is not ראש חודש, then read as below. In ארץ ישראל
for שלישי repeat the first paragraph: בַּיּוֹם הַשְּׁבִיעִי *until* אֱלִישָׁמָע בֶּן־עַמִּיהוּד:

במדבר
כח-נט:

בַּיּוֹם הַשְּׁבִיעִי נָשִׂיא לִבְנֵי אֶפְרָיִם אֱלִישָׁמָע בֶּן־עַמִּיהוּד: קָרְבָּנוֹ קַעֲרַת־כֶּסֶף אַחַת שְׁלֹשִׁים וּמֵאָה מִשְׁקָלָהּ מִזְרָק אֶחָד כֶּסֶף שִׁבְעִים שֶׁקֶל בְּשֶׁקֶל הַקֹּדֶשׁ שְׁנֵיהֶם ׀ מְלֵאִים סֹלֶת בְּלוּלָה בַשֶּׁמֶן לְמִנְחָה: כַּף אַחַת עֲשָׂרָה זָהָב מְלֵאָה

לוי

קְטֹרֶת: *פַּר אֶחָד בֶּן־בָּקָר אַיִל אֶחָד כֶּבֶשׂ־אֶחָד בֶּן־שְׁנָתוֹ לְעֹלָה: שְׂעִיר־עִזִּים אֶחָד לְחַטָּאת: וּלְזֶבַח הַשְּׁלָמִים בָּקָר שְׁנַיִם אֵילִם חֲמִשָּׁה עַתֻּדִים חֲמִשָּׁה כְּבָשִׂים בְּנֵי־שָׁנָה חֲמִשָּׁה זֶה קָרְבַּן אֱלִישָׁמָע בֶּן־עַמִּיהוּד:

ישראל

בַּיּוֹם הַשְּׁמִינִי נָשִׂיא לִבְנֵי מְנַשֶּׁה גַּמְלִיאֵל בֶּן־פְּדָהצוּר: קָרְבָּנוֹ קַעֲרַת־כֶּסֶף אַחַת שְׁלֹשִׁים וּמֵאָה מִשְׁקָלָהּ מִזְרָק אֶחָד כֶּסֶף שִׁבְעִים שֶׁקֶל בְּשֶׁקֶל הַקֹּדֶשׁ שְׁנֵיהֶם ׀ מְלֵאִים סֹלֶת בְּלוּלָה בַשֶּׁמֶן לְמִנְחָה: כַּף אַחַת עֲשָׂרָה זָהָב מְלֵאָה קְטֹרֶת: פַּר אֶחָד בֶּן־בָּקָר אַיִל אֶחָד כֶּבֶשׂ־אֶחָד בֶּן־שְׁנָתוֹ לְעֹלָה: שְׂעִיר־עִזִּים אֶחָד לְחַטָּאת: וּלְזֶבַח הַשְּׁלָמִים בָּקָר שְׁנַיִם אֵילִם חֲמִשָּׁה עַתֻּדִים חֲמִשָּׁה כְּבָשִׂים בְּנֵי־שָׁנָה חֲמִשָּׁה זֶה קָרְבַּן גַּמְלִיאֵל בֶּן־פְּדָהצוּר:

EIGHTH DAY OF ḤANUKKA
קריאה ליום השמיני של חנוכה

במדבר
כד-חד:

בַּיּוֹם הַשְּׁמִינִי נָשִׂיא לִבְנֵי מְנַשֶּׁה גַּמְלִיאֵל בֶּן־פְּדָהצוּר: קָרְבָּנוֹ קַעֲרַת־כֶּסֶף אַחַת שְׁלֹשִׁים וּמֵאָה מִשְׁקָלָהּ מִזְרָק אֶחָד כֶּסֶף שִׁבְעִים שֶׁקֶל בְּשֶׁקֶל הַקֹּדֶשׁ

שְׁנֵיהֶם ׀ מְלֵאִים סֹלֶת בְּלוּלָה בַשֶּׁמֶן לְמִנְחָה: כַּף אַחַת עֲשָׂרָה זָהָב מְלֵאָה
קְטֹרֶת: *פַּר אֶחָד בֶּן־בָּקָר אַיִל אֶחָד כֶּבֶשׂ־אֶחָד בֶּן־שְׁנָתוֹ לְעֹלָה: שְׂעִיר־עִזִּים לֵוִי
אֶחָד לְחַטָּאת: וּלְזֶבַח הַשְּׁלָמִים בָּקָר שְׁנַיִם אֵילִם חֲמִשָּׁה עַתֻּדִים חֲמִשָּׁה
כְּבָשִׂים בְּנֵי־שָׁנָה חֲמִשָּׁה זֶה קָרְבַּן גַּמְלִיאֵל בֶּן־פְּדָהצוּר:

בַּיּוֹם הַתְּשִׁיעִי נָשִׂיא לִבְנֵי בִנְיָמִן אֲבִידָן בֶּן־גִּדְעֹנִי: קָרְבָּנוֹ קַעֲרַת־כֶּסֶף אַחַת יִשְׂרָאֵל
שְׁלֹשִׁים וּמֵאָה מִשְׁקָלָהּ מִזְרָק אֶחָד כֶּסֶף שִׁבְעִים שֶׁקֶל בְּשֶׁקֶל הַקֹּדֶשׁ שְׁנֵיהֶם ׀
מְלֵאִים סֹלֶת בְּלוּלָה בַשֶּׁמֶן לְמִנְחָה: כַּף אַחַת עֲשָׂרָה זָהָב מְלֵאָה קְטֹרֶת:
פַּר אֶחָד בֶּן־בָּקָר אַיִל אֶחָד כֶּבֶשׂ־אֶחָד בֶּן־שְׁנָתוֹ לְעֹלָה: שְׂעִיר־עִזִּים אֶחָד
לְחַטָּאת: וּלְזֶבַח הַשְּׁלָמִים בָּקָר שְׁנַיִם אֵילִם חֲמִשָּׁה עַתֻּדִים חֲמִשָּׁה כְּבָשִׂים
בְּנֵי־שָׁנָה חֲמִשָּׁה זֶה קָרְבַּן אֲבִידָן בֶּן־גִּדְעֹנִי:

בַּיּוֹם הָעֲשִׂירִי נָשִׂיא לִבְנֵי דָן אֲחִיעֶזֶר בֶּן־עַמִּישַׁדָּי: קָרְבָּנוֹ קַעֲרַת־כֶּסֶף אַחַת
שְׁלֹשִׁים וּמֵאָה מִשְׁקָלָהּ מִזְרָק אֶחָד כֶּסֶף שִׁבְעִים שֶׁקֶל בְּשֶׁקֶל הַקֹּדֶשׁ שְׁנֵיהֶם ׀
מְלֵאִים סֹלֶת בְּלוּלָה בַשֶּׁמֶן לְמִנְחָה: כַּף אַחַת עֲשָׂרָה זָהָב מְלֵאָה קְטֹרֶת:
פַּר אֶחָד בֶּן־בָּקָר אַיִל אֶחָד כֶּבֶשׂ־אֶחָד בֶּן־שְׁנָתוֹ לְעֹלָה: שְׂעִיר־עִזִּים אֶחָד
לְחַטָּאת: וּלְזֶבַח הַשְּׁלָמִים בָּקָר שְׁנַיִם אֵילִם חֲמִשָּׁה עַתֻּדִים חֲמִשָּׁה כְּבָשִׂים
בְּנֵי־שָׁנָה חֲמִשָּׁה זֶה קָרְבַּן אֲחִיעֶזֶר בֶּן־עַמִּישַׁדָּי:

בַּיּוֹם עַשְׁתֵּי עָשָׂר יוֹם נָשִׂיא לִבְנֵי אָשֵׁר פַּגְעִיאֵל בֶּן־עָכְרָן: קָרְבָּנוֹ קַעֲרַת־כֶּסֶף
אַחַת שְׁלֹשִׁים וּמֵאָה מִשְׁקָלָהּ מִזְרָק אֶחָד כֶּסֶף שִׁבְעִים שֶׁקֶל בְּשֶׁקֶל הַקֹּדֶשׁ
שְׁנֵיהֶם ׀ מְלֵאִים סֹלֶת בְּלוּלָה בַשֶּׁמֶן לְמִנְחָה: כַּף אַחַת עֲשָׂרָה זָהָב מְלֵאָה
קְטֹרֶת: פַּר אֶחָד בֶּן־בָּקָר אַיִל אֶחָד כֶּבֶשׂ־אֶחָד בֶּן־שְׁנָתוֹ לְעֹלָה: שְׂעִיר־עִזִּים
אֶחָד לְחַטָּאת: וּלְזֶבַח הַשְּׁלָמִים בָּקָר שְׁנַיִם אֵילִם חֲמִשָּׁה עַתֻּדִים חֲמִשָּׁה
כְּבָשִׂים בְּנֵי־שָׁנָה חֲמִשָּׁה זֶה קָרְבַּן פַּגְעִיאֵל בֶּן־עָכְרָן:

בַּיּוֹם שְׁנֵים עָשָׂר יוֹם נָשִׂיא לִבְנֵי נַפְתָּלִי אֲחִירַע בֶּן־עֵינָן: קָרְבָּנוֹ קַעֲרַת־כֶּסֶף
אַחַת שְׁלֹשִׁים וּמֵאָה מִשְׁקָלָהּ מִזְרָק אֶחָד כֶּסֶף שִׁבְעִים שֶׁקֶל בְּשֶׁקֶל הַקֹּדֶשׁ
שְׁנֵיהֶם ׀ מְלֵאִים סֹלֶת בְּלוּלָה בַשֶּׁמֶן לְמִנְחָה: כַּף אַחַת עֲשָׂרָה זָהָב מְלֵאָה
קְטֹרֶת: פַּר אֶחָד בֶּן־בָּקָר אַיִל אֶחָד כֶּבֶשׂ־אֶחָד בֶּן־שְׁנָתוֹ לְעֹלָה: שְׂעִיר־עִזִּים
אֶחָד לְחַטָּאת: וּלְזֶבַח הַשְּׁלָמִים בָּקָר שְׁנַיִם אֵילִם חֲמִשָּׁה עַתֻּדִים חֲמִשָּׁה
כְּבָשִׂים בְּנֵי־שָׁנָה חֲמִשָּׁה זֶה קָרְבַּן אֲחִירַע בֶּן־עֵינָן:

זֹאת ׀ חֲנֻכַּת הַמִּזְבֵּחַ בְּיוֹם הִמָּשַׁח אֹתוֹ מֵאֵת נְשִׂיאֵי יִשְׂרָאֵל קַעֲרֹת כֶּסֶף

שְׁתֵּים עֶשְׂרֵה מִזְרְקֵי־כֶסֶף שְׁנֵים עָשָׂר כַּפּוֹת זָהָב שְׁתֵּים עֶשְׂרֵה: שְׁלֹשִׁים
וּמֵאָה הַקְּעָרָה הָאַחַת כֶּסֶף וְשִׁבְעִים הַמִּזְרָק הָאֶחָד כָּל כֶּסֶף הַכֵּלִים אַלְפַּיִם
וְאַרְבַּע־מֵאוֹת בְּשֶׁקֶל הַקֹּדֶשׁ: כַּפּוֹת זָהָב שְׁתֵּים־עֶשְׂרֵה מְלֵאֹת קְטֹרֶת
עֲשָׂרָה עֲשָׂרָה הַכַּף בְּשֶׁקֶל הַקֹּדֶשׁ כָּל־זְהַב הַכַּפּוֹת עֶשְׂרִים וּמֵאָה: כָּל־
הַבָּקָר לָעֹלָה שְׁנֵים עָשָׂר פָּרִים אֵילִם שְׁנֵים־עָשָׂר כְּבָשִׂים בְּנֵי־שָׁנָה שְׁנֵים
עָשָׂר וּמִנְחָתָם וּשְׂעִירֵי עִזִּים שְׁנֵים עָשָׂר לְחַטָּאת: וְכֹל בְּקַר ׀ זֶבַח הַשְּׁלָמִים
עֶשְׂרִים וְאַרְבָּעָה פָּרִים אֵילִם שִׁשִּׁים עַתֻּדִים שִׁשִּׁים כְּבָשִׂים בְּנֵי־שָׁנָה שִׁשִּׁים
זֹאת חֲנֻכַּת הַמִּזְבֵּחַ אַחֲרֵי הִמָּשַׁח אֹתוֹ: וּבְבֹא מֹשֶׁה אֶל־אֹהֶל מוֹעֵד לְדַבֵּר
אִתּוֹ וַיִּשְׁמַע אֶת־הַקּוֹל מִדַּבֵּר אֵלָיו מֵעַל הַכַּפֹּרֶת אֲשֶׁר עַל־אֲרֹן הָעֵדֻת מִבֵּין
שְׁנֵי הַכְּרֻבִים וַיְדַבֵּר אֵלָיו:

וַיְדַבֵּר יהוה אֶל־מֹשֶׁה לֵּאמֹר: דַּבֵּר אֶל־אַהֲרֹן וְאָמַרְתָּ אֵלָיו בְּהַעֲלֹתְךָ אֶת־
הַנֵּרֹת אֶל־מוּל פְּנֵי הַמְּנוֹרָה יָאִירוּ שִׁבְעַת הַנֵּרוֹת: וַיַּעַשׂ כֵּן אַהֲרֹן אֶל־מוּל
פְּנֵי הַמְּנוֹרָה הֶעֱלָה נֵרֹתֶיהָ כַּאֲשֶׁר צִוָּה יהוה אֶת־מֹשֶׁה: וְזֶה מַעֲשֵׂה הַמְּנֹרָה
מִקְשָׁה זָהָב עַד־יְרֵכָהּ עַד־פִּרְחָהּ מִקְשָׁה הִוא כַּמַּרְאֶה אֲשֶׁר הֶרְאָה יהוה
אֶת־מֹשֶׁה כֵּן עָשָׂה אֶת־הַמְּנֹרָה:

PURIM   קריאה לפורים

וַיָּבֹא עֲמָלֵק וַיִּלָּחֶם עִם־יִשְׂרָאֵל בִּרְפִידִם: וַיֹּאמֶר מֹשֶׁה אֶל־יְהוֹשֻׁעַ בְּחַר־   שמות
לָנוּ אֲנָשִׁים וְצֵא הִלָּחֵם בַּעֲמָלֵק מָחָר אָנֹכִי נִצָּב עַל־רֹאשׁ הַגִּבְעָה וּמַטֵּה   יז:ח-טז
הָאֱלֹהִים בְּיָדִי: וַיַּעַשׂ יְהוֹשֻׁעַ כַּאֲשֶׁר אָמַר־לוֹ מֹשֶׁה לְהִלָּחֵם בַּעֲמָלֵק וּמֹשֶׁה
אַהֲרֹן וְחוּר עָלוּ רֹאשׁ הַגִּבְעָה: וְהָיָה כַּאֲשֶׁר יָרִים מֹשֶׁה יָדוֹ וְגָבַר יִשְׂרָאֵל   לוי
וְכַאֲשֶׁר יָנִיחַ יָדוֹ וְגָבַר עֲמָלֵק: וִידֵי מֹשֶׁה כְּבֵדִים וַיִּקְחוּ־אֶבֶן וַיָּשִׂימוּ תַחְתָּיו
וַיֵּשֶׁב עָלֶיהָ וְאַהֲרֹן וְחוּר תָּמְכוּ בְיָדָיו מִזֶּה אֶחָד וּמִזֶּה אֶחָד וַיְהִי יָדָיו אֱמוּנָה
עַד־בֹּא הַשָּׁמֶשׁ: וַיַּחֲלֹשׁ יְהוֹשֻׁעַ אֶת־עֲמָלֵק וְאֶת־עַמּוֹ לְפִי־חָרֶב:
וַיֹּאמֶר יהוה אֶל־מֹשֶׁה כְּתֹב זֹאת זִכָּרוֹן בַּסֵּפֶר וְשִׂים בְּאָזְנֵי יְהוֹשֻׁעַ כִּי־מָחֹה   ישראל
אֶמְחֶה אֶת־זֵכֶר עֲמָלֵק מִתַּחַת הַשָּׁמָיִם: וַיִּבֶן מֹשֶׁה מִזְבֵּחַ וַיִּקְרָא שְׁמוֹ יהוה ׀
נִסִּי: וַיֹּאמֶר כִּי־יָד עַל־כֵּס יָהּ מִלְחָמָה לַיהוה בַּעֲמָלֵק מִדֹּר דֹּר:

הלכות תפילה

GATES TO PRAYER

The text (*nusaḥ*) of the siddur that we use today is based on the siddur of the Geonim, primarily *Seder Rav Amram Gaon* from the ninth century. The *nusaḥ* we call "*Nusaḥ Ashkenaz*" refers to the prayer texts and customs of Ashkenazi Jewry, which included the Jews of Germany and northern France. When Ashkenazi Jews moved eastward, they brought their practices with them to Poland and Russia, as well as Lithuania, Bohemia, Moravia, Austro-Hungary, Romania and the Balkans. Similarly, Ashkenazi Jews moved westward to Switzerland, France, Belgium, Holland, Northern Italy, England and, lastly, to Israel and America.

There is no single, authoritative version of *Nusaḥ Ashkenaz*. Certain differences in *nusaḥ* developed between the Jews of western Germany and eastern Germany (known today as *Minhag Polin*). For the most part, *Minhag Polin* is what Ashkenazi Jews follow today. But not exclusively. In the eighteenth century, Ḥasidic Jews adopted a new *nusaḥ* based on the Ari (R. Isaac Luria, 1534–1572), which strongly resembles the *nusaḥ* of Sephardi Jewry. As a result, many Jews of Ashkenazi descent now follow what is called "*Nusaḥ Sepharad*." Another variation on *Nusaḥ Ashkenaz* was developed by the Vilna Gaon (R. Eliyahu b. Shelomo, 1720–1797) and is called "*Minhag HaGra*." Students of the Vilna Gaon who moved to Israel in the nineteenth century brought *Minhag HaGra* with them, and it is the dominant Ashkenazi practice in Israel today.

In this Siddur we have tried to present *Nusaḥ Ashkenaz* as it is typically practiced in Ashkenazi congregations in the United States and Israel, with the differences noted in the instructions. Some practices referred to as "Israeli" are also followed by select congregations in the United States. In the pages below, we also note certain practices of *Nusaḥ Sepharad* which have become more common in Ashkenazi circles.

Rabbi Eli D. Clark

DAILY PRAYER

ON WAKING

1 The custom is to say מוֹדֶה אֲנִי immediately on waking, even before washing hands [משנ״ב אורח, א:ח].

Laws of Washing Hands; בִּרְכַּת אֲשֶׁר יָצַר; אֱלֹהַי נְשָׁמָה

2 Upon waking, one is obligated to wash hands [שבת, קח]. Some hold that one should not walk four *amot* (around six feet) prior to washing hands [משנ״ב אורח, א:ב (בשם הזוהר)].

3 According to some authorities, there is a separate obligation to wash hands prior to prayer [ערוהי"ש אורח, ד: ה]. One who washes and says the blessing of עַל נְטִילַת יָדַיִם after waking, does not repeat the blessing when washing prior to prayer [רמ״א אורח, ו: ב].

4 Hands should preferably be washed using a cup, but a cup is not required [שו״ע ורמ״א, אורח, ד, ז]. The custom is to pour water from the cup onto the right hand, then the left, and repeat a total of three times [משנ״ב, שם: י]. Where water is unavailable, one may clean one's hands using any appropriate material; in that case, the blessing is changed to עַל נְקִיּוּת יָדַיִם [שו״ע אורח, ד: כב].

5 The blessing of עַל נְטִילַת יָדַיִם may be said before drying one's hands or afterward [משנ״ב, ד: ב].

6 A number of reasons have been offered for washing hands upon waking. The Gemara states that, during the night, hands are enveloped by an "evil vapor," רוּחַ רעה, which is removed by washing one's hands [שבת, קח]. In addition, there is a concern that, while sleeping, one's hands may have touched an unclean part of the body [ראי"ש ברכות, פ"ט: כג]. Finally, it is noted that a person who wakes is

like a newborn; therefore, one needs to sanctify oneself by washing [שו״ת רשב״א
ח׳א, קצא].

7 The blessing of אֲשֶׁר יָצַר should be said each time after relieving oneself. It is
recommended that one should go to the bathroom immediately after washing
hands, then say the blessings of עַל נְטִילַת יָדַיִם followed by אֲשֶׁר יָצַר. However, even if
one does not relieve oneself, one is permitted to say אֲשֶׁר יָצַר after washing hands
[רמ״א אורח, ד:א]. One should not postpone going to the bathroom [שו״ע אורח, ג:יז].

8 According to the Gemara, the blessing of אֱלֹהַי נְשָׁמָה should be said upon waking [ברכות, ס:]. The contemporary custom is to say אֱלֹהַי נְשָׁמָה immediately after
אֲשֶׁר יָצַר [משנ״ב, שם:יב]. However, some rule that one who stays up all night should
not say אֱלֹהַי נְשָׁמָה and the blessing הַמַּעֲבִיר שֵׁנָה מֵעֵינַי, and should instead hear them
from others [משנ״ב, מו:כד].

9 The custom is to say the *Birkhot HaTorah* after אֲשֶׁר יָצַר, because one should
not read or recite Torah verses before making the requisite blessings on Torah
study [שו״ע ורמ״א, אורח:מו, מז:ט].

Laws of Tzitzit

10 Putting on a four-cornered garment with tzitzit attached fulfills an affirmative
mitzva from the Torah. The obligation applies only during the daytime [מנחות, מג].
Since wearing tzitzit is a time-bound mitzva, women are exempt [שו״ע אורח, יז:ב].

11 The accepted practice is to wear a *tallit katan* all day long and to wear a *tallit
gadol* during Shaḥarit [שו״ע אורח, כד:א]. The dominant Ashkenazi custom is to
begin wearing a *tallit gadol* when one marries [משנ״ב, יז:י], but Jews of German
and Sephardi descent begin wearing the *tallit gadol* at an earlier age. Nevertheless, the custom is to wear a *tallit gadol* – even if unmarried – when acting as
Shaliaḥ Tzibbur, reading from or being called up to the Torah, opening the Ark
or performing *hagbaha* or *gelila*.

12 One should put on the *tallit katan* immediately upon dressing. One should first
examine the strings of the tzitzit to ensure that they are not torn [שו״ע אורח, ח:ט].
Then, while standing [שו״ע אורח, ח:א], one should say the blessing of עַל מִצְוַת צִיצִית
and immediately put on the garment [רמ״א אורח, ח:ו]. One does not say the blessing if (a) one is about to put on a *tallit gadol*, and (b) one will have in mind the
tallit katan when saying the blessing on the *tallit gadol*. On the other hand, if
there is a substantial interruption between the time one puts on the *tallit katan*
and one puts on the *tallit gadol*, one should say the separate blessing on the
tallit katan [שו״ע אורח, ח:יג].

13 The blessing on tzitzit may be said at daybreak, but not before [רמ״א או״ח, יח:ג].

14 Similarly with the *tallit gadol*, one should first examine the strings, then while standing, say the blessing לְהִתְעַטֵּף בְּצִיצִית and put on the *tallit gadol*. The word לְהִתְעַטֵּף means to wrap oneself; one should initially wrap the *tallit gadol* around to cover one's head and face for a few moments, after which it is sufficient that it cover the torso [מג״א, ח:ב].

15 If one removes the *tallit gadol* for any reason, one should repeat the blessing when putting the tallit back on [שו״ע או״ח, ח:יד]. The blessing is not repeated if the *tallit gadol* is put back on soon after taking it off, and either (a) one was wearing a *tallit katan* all along, or (b) one's original intention was to put the tallit back on shortly [משנ״ב, שם:לז].

16 If one's head is otherwise covered, there is no requirement to cover one's head with the *tallit gadol* [ט״ז או״ח, ח:ג]. Some authorities nevertheless require married men to cover their heads with the *tallit gadol* throughout Shaḥarit, because it promotes reverence in prayer [בה״ג או״ח, ח:ג (בשם הרדב״ז)]. Others have the custom to cover their heads during the Amida only, or from *Barekhu* through the end of the Amida. Unmarried persons should not wear the *tallit gadol* over their heads [קידושין, כט:].

Laws of Tefillin

17 Putting on tefillin fulfills an affirmative mitzva from the Torah. The obligation applies only on weekdays [שו״ע או״ח, לא]. Since wearing tefillin is a time-bound mitzva, women are exempt [שו״ע או״ח, לח:ג].

18 One puts on tefillin after the tallit, because the former are more sacred, and we follow the principle of "ascending in sanctity" (מַעֲלִין בְּקוֹדֶשׁ) [שו״ע או״ח, כה:א].

19 The *tefillin shel yad* is worn on the weaker arm, meaning that right-handed people wear it on the left arm, and left-handed people wear it on the right arm [שו״ע או״ח, כז:ו].

20 The *tefillin shel yad* is put on first, by placing the box on the biceps near the elbow joint, angled toward the heart, and saying the blessing לְהָנִיחַ תְּפִלִּין. One then tightens the strap around the muscle and wraps the strap around the forearm seven times. Without speaking or otherwise becoming distracted [שו״ע או״ח, כה:ט–י], one places the *tefillin shel rosh* on the head above the hairline, centered over the nose, and says the blessing עַל מִצְוַת תְּפִלִּין. One then adjusts the straps, so that the knot rests at the base of the skull and the two straps hang down the front of one's chest, and says בָּרוּךְ שֵׁם כְּבוֹד מַלְכוּתוֹ לְעוֹלָם וָעֶד [רמ״א או״ח, כה:ה].

Finally, one wraps the strap of the *tefillin shel yad* around the fingers, while saying וְאֵרַשְׂתִּיךְ (See page 17).

21 The box of the *tefillin shel yad* and the *tefillin shel rosh* must rest directly on the arm and head respectively, without any barrier between them [שו"ע אורח, כו: ד]. This rule does not apply to the straps of the tefillin [רמ"א שם].

22 One should regularly touch first the *tefillin shel yad*, then the *tefillin shel rosh*, so as to remain conscious that one is wearing them. In particular, one should touch the appropriate tefillin when saying the relevant verses of the Shema [שו"ע אורח, כח: א] (see law 40). It is also customary to touch them when saying the verse פּוֹתֵחַ אֶת יָדֶךָ during *Ashrei*.

23 At a minimum, tefillin should be worn while saying the Shema and the Amida [שו"ע אורח, כה: ד]. The custom is to keep them on until one has heard the *Kedusha* three times and Kaddish four times [רמ"א שם: ע], which means that one should not remove the tefillin until after the Mourner's Kaddish following *Aleinu* [משנ"ב, שם: נ]. In theory, one should wear tefillin all day. The custom, however, is to take the tefillin off after praying, because it is difficult to maintain a constant awareness of the tefillin and the requisite purity of mind and body throughout the day [שו"ע אורח, ל: ב].

24 The order in which one removes tefillin is the reverse of the order in which they were put on. Thus, one first unwinds the strap of the *tefillin shel yad* from one's fingers, then removes the *tefillin shel rosh* and wraps it in its case. One then unwinds the *tefillin shel yad* from the arm, removes the box from the muscle and wraps the tefillin in its case [שו"ע אורח, כח: ב]. This entire process should be performed standing up [משנ"ב, כח: ו].

SERVICES

Laws of Birkhot HaShaḥar and Pesukei DeZimra

25 According to the Gemara [ברכות, ס:], Birkhot HaShaḥar (Morning Blessings) were originally said separately, in conjunction with the performance of the associated activity. Thus, upon dressing one would say the blessing of מַלְבִּישׁ עֲרֻמִּים, and upon standing up one would say the blessing of זוֹקֵף כְּפוּפִים. However, the custom now is to say all of the blessings together in the synagogue [שו"ע אורח, מו: ב].

26 The insertion of the verse (or verses) of Shema after *Birkhot HaShaḥar* was not meant to satisfy the individual's obligation to say the Shema every morning [רמ״א שם: ט]. However, as discussed in further detail in law 33, the three paragraphs of Shema must be said within the first half of the morning (measured as ¼ of the time from daybreak to nightfall). Since some congregations hold Shaḥarit services late, especially on Shabbat, and as such the communal recitation of the Shema in Shaḥarit may take place too late to fulfill the halakhic obligation, under such circumstances it is recommended to say all three paragraphs of Shema after *Birkhot HaShaḥar* [משנ״ב, שם: לא].

27 One should say the biblical verses describing the קרבן תמיד (page 45), preferably with the congregation [רמ״א אריח, מח]. Some authorities require one to stand [משניב, שם: ב].

28 The fifth chapter of מסכת זבחים and the ברייתא דרבי ישמעאל were added after the biblical passages regarding sacrifices to institutionalize the daily study of Scripture, Mishna and Gemara [שו״ע אריח, נ: א].

29 Saying Kaddish, *Barekhu* or *Kedusha* requires the presence of a *minyan* (ten adult males) [שו״ע אריח, נה: א].

30 One should not utter idle speech from the beginning of the words בָּרוּךְ אַתָּה יהוה in *Barukh SheAmar* until one completes the Amida [שו״ע אריח, נא: ד]. Certain responses are permitted, as detailed in the chart on pages 695–697.

31 If one comes late to the synagogue, one may skip all, or portions, of *Pesukei DeZimra*, as follows:

a If there is sufficient time, say *Barukh SheAmar*, Psalms 145–150, and *Yishtabaḥ*.

b If there is less time, say *Barukh SheAmar*, Psalms 145, 148, 150, and *Yishtabaḥ*.

c If there is less time, say *Barukh SheAmar*, Psalm 145, and *Yishtabaḥ*.

d If there is less time, omit *Pesukei DeZimra* altogether. Complete the rest of the service with the congregation, then say *Pesukei DeZimra* privately, omitting *Burukh SheAmar* and *Yishtabaḥ* [רמ״א ושו״ע אריח, נב].

Morning Shema – קריאת שמע של שחרית

32 Saying the three paragraphs of the Shema each morning and each night fulfills an affirmative mitzva from the Torah. Since saying the Shema is a time-bound mitzva, women are exempt [שו״ע אריח, ע: ג]. Nevertheless, women are required to say the first verse to express their acceptance of עול מלכות שמים ("the yoke of the kingdom of Heaven") [ב״ח, שם]. Women are permitted to say the Shema and its preceding and following blessings [משניב, שם: ב].

33 There is a set time period every morning during which the Shema may be said. The optimal time is immediately before sunrise, when there is assumed to be sufficient light to recognize an acquaintance from a distance of four *amot* (around 6 feet). If necessary, the Shema may be said from daybreak [שו״ע או״ח, נח:ג]. After sunrise, the earlier the Shema is said, the better [שם:ב]. At the latest, the Shema must be said during the first quarter of the day (in halakhic terminology, three halakhic "hours," where each hour represents 1/12 of the day [שם:א]. After that time, one is permitted to say the Shema with the blessings during the fourth halakhic "hour," that is, until the end of the first third of the day. After that, the Shema may be said without the blessings, but this does not fulfill the mitzva [שם:ו].

34 If one says the Shema without its preceding and following blessings, one has still fulfilled the mitzva. However, one should say the blessings afterward, preferably repeating the Shema as well [שו״ע או״ח, ס:ב].

35 The Shema must be said with concentration and awe [שו״ע או״ח, סא:א]. Each word and syllable should be pronounced correctly and carefully, without slurring consonants [שו״ע או״ח, סא: טו-כא].

36 Some authorities ruled that one should say the Shema with *Ta'amei HaMikra*. Today, however, most people do not do so [שו״ע ורמ״א, שם: כד].

37 The custom is to cover the eyes with the right hand while saying the first verse, so as not look at anything that might disturb one's concentration [שו״ע או״ח, סא:ה].

38 It is customary to draw out one's pronunciation of the letters ח and ד in the word אֶחָד to emphasize God's sovereignty over creation [שו״ע או״ח, סא:ו].

39 The sentence בָּרוּךְ שֵׁם כְּבוֹד מַלְכוּתוֹ לְעוֹלָם וָעֶד is said quietly, because it does not appear in the biblical text of the Shema [שו״ע שם: יג; משנ״ב, שם: ל].

40 As discussed in law 22 above, the custom is to touch the *tefillin shel yad* when saying וּקְשַׁרְתָּם לְאוֹת עַל־יָדֶךָ and to touch the *tefillin shel rosh* when saying וְהָיוּ לְטֹטָפֹת בֵּין עֵינֶיךָ [שו״ע או״ח, כח:א].

41 If one enters the synagogue and hears the congregation about to begin saying the Shema, one is required to say the first verse of the Shema together with the congregation [שו״ע או״ח, סה:ב].

Laws of the Shaḥarit Amida

42 There is a set time period every morning during which the Amida may be said. In general, the Amida should be said at or after sunrise. At the latest, the Amida should be said during the first third of the day, (four halakhic "hours"). If the Amida was said between daybreak and sunrise, the mitzva has been fulfilled. If

necessary, it is permissible to say the Amida after the first third of the day, but before midday [שו"ע או"ח, פט:א].

43 One who must leave for work (or a journey) before sunrise is permitted to say the Amida from daybreak [שו"ע שם סע"ח]. If one did not say the Shaḥarit Amida prior to midday, one should say the Minḥa Amida twice [משנ"ב, שם:סיק"ז].

44 One should not eat or drink before saying the Amida, although drinking water is permitted. Moreover, anyone who needs to eat or drink in order to concentrate on his prayers is permitted to do so [שו"ע או"ח, פט:ג-ד].

45 The Amida is said facing the site of the Temple in Jerusalem. Thus, outside Israel, one faces the land of Israel; inside Israel, one faces Jerusalem; and inside Jerusalem, one faces the Temple Mount [שו"ע או"ח, צד:א]. If one is praying in a synagogue, one should pray facing the Ark [משנ"ב, שם:סיק"י].

46 The Amida is said standing with feet together in imitation of the angels who, according to tradition, present the appearance of having only one leg [ברכות, י, רש"י, ד"ה זורגליהם]. One should bow one's head and imagine one is standing in the Temple, like a servant before his master [שו"ע או"ח, צה:א-ב].

47 One who is traveling in a vehicle should, if possible, say the Amida standing; if this is not possible, one is permitted to sit [שו"ע או"ח, צד:ה].

48 When saying the Shaḥarit Amida, one may not allow any interruption or disruption between the conclusion of the blessing גָּאַל יִשְׂרָאֵל and the introductory words to the Amida [שו"ע או"ח, סו:ח; שם, קיא:א]. This includes not responding to Kaddish, Barekhu, Kedusha or Modim [רמ"א שם]. One may also answer "Amen" if one hears someone else concluding the blessing גָּאַל יִשְׂרָאֵל [רמ"א או"ח, סו:ז].

Laws of מַשִּׁיב הָרוּחַ

49 One begins saying מַשִּׁיב הָרוּחַ in Musaf of Shemini Atzeret and continues until Musaf of the first day of Pesaḥ [שו"ע או"ח, קיד:א].

50 If one forgets to say מַשִּׁיב הָרוּחַ in its proper place but realizes before beginning the words of the blessing מְחַיֵּה הַמֵּתִים, one should immediately say מַשִּׁיב הָרוּחַ and continue with the rest of the blessing. If one realizes the omission immediately after completing the blessing מְחַיֵּה הַמֵּתִים, one should say מַשִּׁיב הָרוּחַ and continue with the following blessing. If one realizes the omission after beginning the words אַתָּה קָדוֹשׁ, one must repeat the Amida from the beginning [שו"ע או"ח, קיד:ו].

51 If one forgets to say מַשִּׁיב הָרוּחַ but says מוֹרִיד הַטָּל (as is the custom in Israel, and that of Nusaḥ Sepharad, in the spring and summer months), one need not repeat the Amida [שו"ע או"ח, קיד:ה]. If there is doubt whether one said מַשִּׁיב הָרוּחַ,

the presumption is as follows: within the first thirty days from *Shemini Atzeret*, one should assume that one forgot to say מַשִּׁיב הָרוּחַ. After thirty days, one should assume that one said מַשִּׁיב הָרוּחַ [שו״ע או״ח, קיד: ח].

Laws of וְתֵן טַל וּמָטָר לִבְרָכָה

52 In most years, during Ma'ariv on the evening of the 4th of December, one begins to say וְתֵן טַל וּמָטָר לִבְרָכָה in the ninth blessing of the Amida. In the year preceding a civil leap year, one begins to say וְתֵן טַל וּמָטָר לִבְרָכָה one day later, on the night of the 5th of December [שו״ע או״ח, קיז: א].

53 If one forgets to say וְתֵן טַל וּמָטָר לִבְרָכָה in its proper place but realizes before saying God's name in the ninth blessing (מְבָרֵךְ הַשָּׁנִים), one should immediately say וְתֵן טַל וּמָטָר לִבְרָכָה and continue with the rest of the blessing. If one realizes the omission after completing the blessing, מְבָרֵךְ הַשָּׁנִים, one should say וְתֵן טַל וּמָטָר לִבְרָכָה prior to the words כִּי אַתָּה שׁוֹמֵעַ in the sixteenth blessing (שׁוֹמֵעַ תְּפִלָּה). If one realizes the omission after beginning the seventeenth blessing (רְצֵה), one must repeat the Amida from the beginning of the ninth blessing (מְבָרֵךְ הַשָּׁנִים). If one realizes the omission after completing the Amida, one must repeat the entire Amida [שו״ע או״ח, קיז: ה].

54 If there is doubt whether one properly said וְתֵן טַל וּמָטָר לִבְרָכָה, the presumption is as follows: within the first thirty days from December 4th (or 5th), one should assume that one forgot to say וְתֵן טַל וּמָטָר לִבְרָכָה. After thirty days, one should assume that one said וְתֵן טַל וּמָטָר לִבְרָכָה.

Laws of Havinenu

55 When circumstances require, one is permitted to substitute a special paragraph (*Havinenu*, page 547) for the thirteen middle blessings of the Amida. This is only permitted in exceptional cases, such as when one is incapable of concentrating during a full-length Amida or expects interruptions. One says this abbreviated form of the Amida while standing, and one does not need to repeat the full-length Amida afterward. *Havinenu* is not said during the winter months or on Motza'ei Shabbat [שו״ע או״ח, קי: א].

Laws of חזרת הש״ץ

56 During the Repetition of the Amida, the congregation is required to listen attentively to the blessings and respond "Amen" [שו״ע או״ח, קכד: ד].

57 In order to begin the Repetition of the Amida, at least nine men are required to be listening attentively [שם].

58 Some require the congregation to stand during the Repetition of the Amida [רמ״א, שם].

59 Under extenuating circumstances, the *Shaliaḥ Tzibbur* may begin saying the Amida aloud, while the congregation says the Amida quietly along with him. The *Kedusha* is said aloud in the customary fashion and, after the *Shaliaḥ Tzibbur* finishes the blessing הָאֵל הַקָּדוֹשׁ, he and the congregation continue saying the Amida quietly [רמ״א, שם:ב].

60 At the conclusion of the Repetition of the Amida, it is recommended that the *Shaliaḥ Tzibbur* say quietly the verse יִהְיוּ לְרָצוֹן אִמְרֵי פִי, except when Full Kaddish immediately follows the Repetition of the Amida [משנ״ב קכגכא]. Some also say this verse during the individual's silent Amida.

Laws of Kedusha

61 There are different customs regarding what the congregation says during the *Kedusha*: (1) The congregation says only the biblical verses (קָדוֹשׁ...; בָּרוּךְ...; יִמְלֹךְ...) [שו״ע אורח, קכה:א]; (2) The congregation says every word of the *Kedusha*, with the *Shaliaḥ Tzibbur* repeating each sentence [בה״ג, שם (בשם האר״י)]; (3) The congregation says נְקַדֵּשׁ and all the biblical verses [ערוה״ש, שם:ב].

Laws of Birkat Kohanim

62 The Kohen has an affirmative obligation from the Torah to bless the congregation, provided there are at least ten males aged 13 or over (including the Kohen himself) [שו״ע אורח, קכח:א-ב].

63 The Kohen is required to wash his hands (without a blessing) before saying *Birkat Kohanim*. It is customary for a Levi to pour the water [שם, ו]. If there is no water, or if the Kohen did not have enough time to wash, he may say *Birkat Kohanim*, provided that: (a) he washed his hands before Shaḥarit, and (b) since washing for Shaḥarit he has not touched anything unclean, even his own shoes [משנ״ב, שם:כ].

64 Each Kohen removes his shoes before ascending to say *Birkat Kohanim* [שם,ה]. When the *Shaliaḥ Tzibbur* begins רְצֵה, the Kohanim ascend to the Ark and stand with their backs to the congregation [שם, ח:ו-ז]. After the congregation answers "Amen" to the blessing הַטּוֹב שִׁמְךָ וּלְךָ נָאֶה לְהוֹדוֹת, if there is more than one Kohen, the *Shaliaḥ Tzibbur* calls out "Kohanim," and they turn around and say the blessing. If only one Kohen has ascended to the Ark, he starts the blessing without being prompted [שם:י-יא]. The *Shaliaḥ Tzibbur* does not answer "Amen" at the end of the blessing [משנ״ב, שם:עא].

65 The *Shaliaḥ Tzibbur* reads each word of *Birkat Kohanim* and the Kohanim repeat it in unison. At the end of each verse, the congregation answers "Amen" [שו״ע, שם: יג]. The *Shaliaḥ Tzibbur* does not answer "Amen" at the end of each verse [שו״ע, שם: יט].

66 If the *Shaliaḥ Tzibbur* is himself a Kohen, some rule that he should not say the blessing, unless no other Kohanim are in the synagogue [שו״ע, שם: יט]. However, the custom today is for the *Shaliaḥ Tzibbur* to participate in the blessing [משנ״ב, שם: עה].

67 During *Birkat Kohanim*, the congregation should stand silently with eyes lowered and concentrate on the words of the Kohanim. One should not look at the faces or hands of the Kohanim [שו״ע, שם: כג].

68 In most congregations in Israel, *Birkat Kohanim* is said every day in Shaḥarit and, where applicable, in Musaf. It is also said in Minḥa on a fast day [שו״ע אריח, קכח: א]. *Birkat Kohanim* is not said in Shaḥarit of Tisha B'Av or in a mourner's house [משנ״ב, קכא: ו], although in Jerusalem, the custom is to say *Birkat Kohanim* even in a mourner's house [גשר החיים, כ: ה]. On those occasions and when no Kohen is present, the *Shaliaḥ Tzibbur* says אֱלֹהֵינוּ וֵאלֹהֵי אֲבוֹתֵינוּ (page 133).

69 The custom outside Israel and in certain northern Israeli congregations, is for the *Shaliaḥ Tzibbur* to say אֱלֹהֵינוּ וֵאלֹהֵי אֲבוֹתֵינוּ instead of the Kohanim saying *Birkat Kohanim*, except in Musaf of Yom Tov [רמ״א אריח, קכח: מד].

Laws of Taḥanun

70 נפילת אפים ("Lowering the Head," pages 153/253) is said immediately after the Shaḥarit Amida on Sundays, Tuesdays, Wednesdays and Fridays, and after the Minḥa Amida on every weekday except for Friday. In Shaḥarit on Mondays and Thursdays, *Taḥanun* begins with וְהוּא רַחוּם (page 145), and יהוה אֱלֹהֵי יִשְׂרָאֵל (page 153) is added.

71 On fast days (except on Tisha B'Av, when neither *Avinu Malkenu* nor *Taḥanun* is said) and during the *Aseret Yemei Teshuva*, *Avinu Malkenu* (page 139) is said before *Taḥanun*.

72 One should not speak between the Amida and נפילת אפים [שו״ע אריח, קלא: א].

73 נפילת אפים should be said while sitting [שם: ב], with one's head lowered against one's weaker forearm. If one is wearing tefillin however, one lays one's head against the arm lacking tefillin [שו״ע ורמ״א, שם: א]. The head is lowered only where there is a Sefer Torah [רמ״א, שם: ב], except in Jerusalem, where the custom is to lower the head in any case [שו״ת אגרות משה יו״ד ח״ג, קכט (ב)].

74 For days on which *Taḥanun* is not said, see list on page 145 [שו״ע ורמ״א או״ח, קל״א: ד' [משנ״ב, שם: ט].

Laws of Torah Reading

75 To ensure that the Torah is read at least once every three days, Moses established the public reading of the Torah on Shabbat, Yom Tov, Ḥol HaMo'ed, Rosh Ḥodesh, and Monday and Thursday mornings. Ezra added the public reading in Shabbat Minḥa [רמב״ם הלכות תפילה פי״ב ה״א].

76 On weekdays and Shabbat Minḥa, three people are called up [שו״ע או״ח, קל״ה: א']. On Shabbat morning, seven are called up, though additional individuals (*hosafot*) may also be called [שו״ע או״ח, רפ״ב: א']. On Yom Kippur morning, six are called up, five on Yom Tov, and four on Ḥol HaMo'ed and Rosh Ḥodesh.

77 If a Kohen is present, he is called up first. If a Levi is also present, he is called up second; for subsequent *aliyot*, one calls up a Yisrael [שו״ע או״ח, קל״ה: ג']. If a Kohen is present but a Levi is not, the same Kohen is called up for the first two *aliyot* [שם: ח']. If a Levi is present and a Kohen is not, the Levi need not be called up, but if the Levi is called up, he should be first [שו״ע ורמ״א או״ח, קל״ה: ו'].

78 Other individuals who are given priority for an *aliya* include: a bridegroom on his wedding day; a Bar Mitzva; the father of a newborn baby; one commemorating a parent's *yahrzeit*; and a person obligated to say *Birkat HaGomel* [בהׅ״ל, קל״ו: ד׳יה ׳יכשבת׳].

79 It is considered bad luck to call up two brothers or a father and son one after the other [שו״ע או״ח, קמ״א: ו']. While the custom is to avoid the practice, if one is called up after one's brother or father, one should accept the *aliya*.

80 One who is called up to the Torah should take the shortest route to the *bima* [שו״ע, שם: ו']. He should open the scroll to locate where the *aliya* begins. Still holding the handle, he should say the blessing, taking care to look away from the Torah (or close the scroll or his eyes), so as not to appear to be reading the blessing from the scroll itself [שו״ע ורמ״א או״ח, קל״ט: ד'].

81 If, after the blessing is said, the *ba'al koreh* discovers that the blessing was said over the wrong passage of the Torah, the scroll is rolled to the correct location and the *oleh* repeats the blessing. The blessing does not need to be repeated if the correct passage was visible when the blessing was said [שו״ע או״ח, קמ״: ג' [משנ״ב, שם: ט].

82 The Torah is read standing [שו״ע או״ח, קמ״א: א']. The *oleh* is also required to stand. The rest of the congregation is not obligated to stand, but it is proper to do so [עיוה״ש, שם: ב'].

83 The *oleh* should read the words quietly along with the *ba'al koreh* [ב:שרע אורח,קמא].

84 If the *ba'al koreh* makes an error that affects the meaning of the words, he needs to reread the Torah portion from the location of the error [שרע ורמ"א אורח, קמב:א].

85 If an error is found in the Torah scroll, the reading is stopped, a new scroll is brought out, and the reading is continued from the location of the error [שרע אורח,קמג:ד]. It is not required to call up all of the *aliyot* a second time to read from the new scroll, but if the remainder of the reading can be divided into the appropriate number of *aliyot* for that day, it is preferable to do so [משנ"ב, שם:טו].

86 It is customary to say a prayer for a sick person (מִי שֶׁבֵּרַךְ, page 165) at the conclusion of the Torah reading, or between *aliyot*.

87 After completing the reading from a Torah scroll, the open scroll is raised and displayed to the entire congregation. The congregation says וְזֹאת הַתּוֹרָה (page 169) [שרע ורמ"א אורח,קלד:ב].

Laws of Birkat HaGomel

88 After being saved from mortal danger, one should say *Birkat HaGomel* [שרע אורח,ריט: א,ו-ז; משנ"ב, שם:לב] (see page 163). The blessing should be said no later than three days after the event [שרע, שם:ו]. *Birkat HaGomel* is said only in the presence of a *minyan*; the custom is to say the blessing after the Torah reading [שם:ג]. If one will not be in the presence of *minyan* within three days, one is permitted to say the blessing without a *minyan* [משנ"ב, שם:ח].

89 A husband may say *Birkat HaGomel* for his wife, or a father for his children [משנ"ב, שם:יז]. But, according to most authorities, it is preferable that a woman say *Birkat HaGomel* for herself in the presence of a *minyan*.

Laws of Mourner's Kaddish

90 The Mourner's Kaddish is generally said after specific chapters of Psalms at the beginning and end of a service. It is said by one who is either (a) in mourning for a relative, or (b) commemorating the *yahrzeit* of a relative. When no such person is present, the Mourner's Kaddish is generally omitted, except after *Aleinu* at the end of Shaḥarit [רמ"א אורח,קלב:ב], when it is said by one whose parents have died or whose parents do not object to their child saying the Mourner's Kaddish [שם].

91 Historically, the Mourner's Kaddish was said by one individual. A set of rules developed for allocating among different mourners the various opportunities

for saying it [ביאור הלכה, שם; קונטרס מאמר קדישין, י]. Today, most congregations allow group recitation of the Mourner's Kaddish. In such cases, they should say the words in unison [סידור יעב"ץ].

Laws of the Minḥa Amida

92 There is a set time period every afternoon during which the Minḥa Amida may be said. At the earliest, one may say the Amida one half of a halakhic "hour" from midday (a halakhic hour is ¹⁄₁₂ of the day measured from daybreak to nightfall). At the latest, the Amida must be said before nightfall. It is preferable to say the Amida at least 3½ halakhic "hours" after midday [שו"ע אורח, רל"ג: א].

93 One should wash hands before saying Minḥa, even if they are not dirty; but if no water is available, one need not wash [שו"ע אורח, רל"ג: ב]. No blessing is said on the hand-washing.

Laws of the Evening Shema and Ma'ariv

94 There is a set time period every night during which the Shema may be said. At the earliest, one may say the Shema from nightfall [שו"ע אורח, רל"ה: א]. It is preferable to say the Shema before midnight (measured from nightfall to daybreak), but one is permitted to say the Shema until daybreak [שם: ב].

95 Some congregations hold Ma'ariv services early, with the result that the communal recitation of the Shema in Ma'ariv may take place too early to fulfill the halakhic obligation. Under such circumstances, one should repeat all three paragraphs of Shema after nightfall [שו"ע, שם: א].

96 If one enters the synagogue and hears the congregation about to begin saying the Amida, one should say the Amida together with the congregation, then afterward say the Shema with its preceding and following blessings [שו"ע אורח, רל"ו: ג].

97 After the blessings of the Shema, the congregation says בָּרוּךְ יהוה לְעוֹלָם (page 273), except in Israel. One who begins Ma'ariv late should omit בָּרוּךְ יהוה לְעוֹלָם in order to say the Amida with the congregation, then say בָּרוּךְ יהוה לְעוֹלָם after Ma'ariv, without the final blessing [משנ"ב, שם: יא].

Laws of Sefirat HaOmer

98 One counts the Omer for a given day after nightfall. The custom is to count standing up [שו"ע אורח, תפ"ט: א].

99 One who forgets to count at night may count prior to nightfall of the following day, although no blessing is said when counting during daylight hours [שם:ו].

100 One who forgets to count for an entire 24-hour period continues counting the Omer from the following day, but without the blessing [שם:ח].

Laws of the Sefirat HaOmer Period

101 During the period of counting the Omer, certain mourning rituals are observed: one does not cut one's hair, shave, listen to music, or hold weddings and other parties [שו"ע ורמ"א אר"ח, תצג: א-ג]. Some permit shaving during this period. These practices commemorate a plague that killed twelve thousand pairs of students of Rabbi Akiva who, the Talmud says, did not honor one another properly. The Ashkenazi community intensified these mourning customs in the wake of the pogroms of the First Crusade, which took place in Iyar and Sivan in the year 1096 (4856).

102 Different communities observe these customs during different periods: (1) from the end of Pesaḥ to the 18th of Iyar (Lag BaOmer), (2) from the 1st of Iyar until the 3rd of Sivan, (3) during the entire period from the end of Pesaḥ until the 3rd of Sivan.

Laws of Motza'ei Shabbat

103 In some congregations, Psalms 144 and 67 (pages 315–317) are sung before Ma'ariv.

104 Ma'ariv: as for weekdays (page 263). In the fourth blessing of the Amida, אַתָּה חוֹנַנְתָּנוּ (page 281) is added [שו"ע אר"ח, רצד: א]. On Rosh Ḥodesh, יַעֲלֶה וְיָבוֹא (page 289) is added in the seventeenth blessing. If one forgets either of these additions, one does not repeat the Amida [שם]. After the silent Amida, unless Yom Tov falls in the following week, the Shaliaḥ Tzibbur says Half Kaddish and the congregation says וְאַתָּה קָדוֹשׁ and וִיהִי נֹעַם (pages 317–319) [רמ"א אר"ח, רצה: א]. The Shaliaḥ Tzibbur then says Full Kaddish. From the second day of Pesaḥ until Shavuot, the Omer is counted (page 305). Some have the custom to say וְיִתֶּן לְךָ (page 325) [שם]. In most congregations, the Shaliaḥ Tzibbur says Havdala [שו"ע]. The congregation says Aleinu, followed by Mourner's Kaddish. From the 1st of Elul to Shemini Azeret, Psalm 27 is said (page 303).

105 After nightfall, one may not perform labor until one says Havdala or hears it said. If one says אַתָּה חוֹנַנְתָּנוּ in Ma'ariv (page 281), one may perform labor after nightfall prior to Havdala [רמ"א אר"ח, רצט: י].

106 Each month, one says Kiddush Levana (page 337) on seeing the New Moon at night. Kiddush Levana may be said from the eve of the fourth day of the new month until the middle day of the month. By custom, it is said on the first Motza'ei Shabbat that falls within the time span, preferably outdoors with a *minyan*. [שו"ע ורמ"א או"ח, תכו].

107 Havdala is said at home if (a) one did not say אַתָּה חוֹנַנְתָּנוּ or hear Havdala in the synagogue; (b) one said אַתָּה חוֹנַנְתָּנוּ or heard Havdala, but intended not to fulfill one's obligation; or (c) someone at home did not yet hear Havdala [שו"ע או"ח, רצו; משנ"ב, שם:לב]. Women may say Havdala for themselves [משנ"ב, שם:לה-לו]. If one forgets to say Havdala on Motza'ei Shabbat, one may say it as late as Tuesday night.

108 After Shabbat, one should eat a meal, the *Melaveh Malka*, as a way of marking the end of Shabbat [שו"ע או"ח, ש:א].

Laws of Keri'at Shema al HaMita (the Shema Before Sleep at Night)

109 *Keri'at Shema al HaMita* should be said before retiring, when one is feeling sleepy [משנ"ב או"ח, רלט:ג], after which one should not eat, drink or speak [רמ"א שם:א].

FAST DAYS

Minor Fast days

110 On a minor fast day the fast begins at dawn [שו"ע או"ח, תקנ:ב]. One is permitted to wake before dawn to eat and drink, but only if one had the intention to do so before going to sleep [שו"ע או"ח, תקסד:א].

111 Eating and drinking are forbidden, but other activities (bathing, wearing leather shoes) are permitted [שו"ע או"ח, תקנ:ב]. Pregnant and nursing women are exempt from fasting [רמ"א, שם:א].

112 Shaharit: The recitation of *Selihot* precedes Shaharit for weekdays. The additions for *Aseret Yemei Teshuva* are said. During the Repetition of the Amida, the *Shaliah Tzibbur* says the paragraph עֲנֵנוּ between the seventh and eighth blessings (page 117) [שו"ע או"ח, תקסו:ד]. This is followed by *Avinu Malkenu* and *Tahanun*.

113 Torah Reading (page 654): The Torah is read only if at least six people (according to some: three people) are fasting. Only people who are fasting are called up. It is customary for the congregation to say the following passages aloud: the last seven words of Ex. 32:12: שׁוּב מֵחֲרוֹן אַפֶּךָ, וְהִנָּחֵם עַל־הָרָעָה לְעַמֶּךָ, the "Thirteen Attributes of Mercy": יהוה יהוה אֵל רַחוּם וְחַנּוּן אֶרֶךְ אַפַּיִם וְרַב־חֶסֶד וֶאֱמֶת: נֹצֵר חֶסֶד לָאֲלָפִים נֹשֵׂא

וְסָלַחְתָּ לַעֲוֹנֵנוּ וּלְחַטָּאתֵנוּ וּנְחַלְתָּנוּ, and the last four words of Ex. 34:9: "וְסָלַחְתָּ לַעֲוֹנֵנוּ וּלְחַטָּאתֵנוּ וּנְחַלְתָּנוּ" [משניב, שם (ג)].

114 Minḥa: After *Ashrei* and Half Kaddish, the Torah is read. The reading is the same as that of the morning. The third *oleh* reads the Haftara (page 655) [רמ״א, שם]. After the Torah is returned to the Ark, the *Shaliaḥ Tzibbur* says Half Kaddish, and Minḥa Amida for weekdays is said.

115 During the silent recitation of the Amida, those who are fasting say the paragraph עֲנֵנוּ as part of the sixteenth blessing, שׁוֹמֵעַ תְּפִלָּה (page 243); during the Repetition of the Amida, the *Shaliaḥ Tzibbur* says עֲנֵנוּ between the seventh and eighth blessings, as in the morning (page 237). After the blessing הַטּוֹב שִׁמְךָ וּלְךָ נָאֶה לְהוֹדוֹת, the *Shaliaḥ Tzibbur* says the paragraph relating to *Birkat Kohanim* (page 249). For the final blessings of the Amida, שִׂים שָׁלוֹם is said instead of שָׁלוֹם רָב. After the Amida, the congregation says *Avinu Malkenu*. This is followed by *Taḥanun*, Full Kaddish and *Aleinu*.

Tisha B'Av (9th of Av)

116 According to the Mishna (*Ta'anit* 4:6), the fast of the 9th of Av commemorates five calamities that befell the Jewish people on that date: (1) God decreed that the children of Israel would not be allowed to enter the land of Israel, (2) the First Temple was destroyed, (3) the Second Temple was destroyed, (4) Beitar was captured, and (5) Jerusalem was plowed over.

117 The fast begins at sunset. In addition to eating and drinking, one is prohibited from washing and anointing oneself and from wearing leather shoes. Marital relations are likewise forbidden. One abstains from Torah study, except for topics such as mourning laws, *Eikha*, Job, and the unhappy portions of Jeremiah [שו״ע אורח, תקנד:א-ב]. One does not greet other people or inquire after their welfare [שם: כ].

118 Ma'ariv: for weekdays. The Amida is followed by Full Kaddish, the reading of *Eikha* and the recitation of *Kinot*. The congregation says וְאַתָּה קָדוֹשׁ (page 319), followed by Full Kaddish (omitting the line beginning תִּתְקַבֵּל), *Aleinu* (page 333), and Mourner's Kaddish. When Tisha B'Av falls on Motza'ei Shabbat, וַיְהִי נֹעַם is omitted.

119 If the fast falls (or is observed) on Motza'ei Shabbat, וַיְהִי נֹעַם is omitted, and Havdala is not said. The blessing בּוֹרֵא מְאוֹרֵי הָאֵשׁ is said on a flame [שו״ע אורח, תקנו:א].

120 Shaḥarit: Neither tallit nor tefillin is worn in the morning [שו״ע אורח, תקנה: א]. During the Repetition of the Amida, the *Shaliaḥ Tzibbur* says עֲנֵנוּ between the seventh and eighth blessings (page 117). *Taḥanun* is omitted.

121 Torah Reading: page 656. Three men are called up. The third *oleh* reads the

Haftara: page 657 [רמ״א אורח תקנד, ד]. Afterwards, the first three blessings following the Haftara (page 655) are said. After the Torah is returned to the Ark, *Kinot* are said. This is followed by *Ashrei*, וּבָא לְצִיּוֹן (omitting the verse וַאֲנִי זֹאת בְּרִיתִי, see page 179), Full Kaddish (omitting the line beginning תִּתְקַבַּל), *Aleinu*, and Mourner's Kaddish.

122 During Minḥa both tallit and tefillin are worn.

123 Minḥa starts with the Daily Psalm (pages 189–195), *Ashrei* and Half Kaddish. The Torah is read: page 654. Three men are called up; the third reads the Haftara: page 655. After the Torah is returned to the Ark, the *Shaliaḥ Tzibbur* says Half Kaddish.

124 During the silent recitation of the Amida (page 231), the congregation says נַחֵם as part of the fourteenth blessing (בּוֹנֵה יְרוּשָׁלָיִם), עֲנֵנוּ as part of the sixteenth blessing (שׁוֹמֵעַ תְּפִלָּה) (unless one is not fasting), and שִׂים שָׁלוֹם in place of שָׁלוֹם רָב (page 249). During the Repetition of the Amida, the *Shaliaḥ Tzibbur* says עֲנֵנוּ between the seventh (גּוֹאֵל יִשְׂרָאֵל) and eighth (רוֹפֵא חוֹלֵי עַמּוֹ יִשְׂרָאֵל) blessings, נַחֵם as part of the fourteenth blessing, the paragraph relating to *Birkat Kohanim* [שו״ע ורמ״א אורח, תקנז:א], and שִׂים שָׁלוֹם. Minḥa ends with Full Kaddish and *Aleinu*.

125 After Ma'ariv, *Kiddush Levana* is said (page 337). When Tisha B'Av begins on Motza'ei Shabbat, Havdala is said on Sunday night, preferably over a cup of wine or grape juice; no blessing is made over spices or a flame.

126 Although the fast is broken after nightfall, it is customary to continue the other mourning customs until midday of the 10th of Av. However, if the 10th of Av falls on Friday, one is permitted to bathe and otherwise prepare for Shabbat prior to midday [רמ״א אורח, תקנח:א].

ROSH ḤODESH PRAYER

127 On Rosh Ḥodesh, יַעֲלֶה וְיָבוֹא is added to the seventeenth blessing of the Amida (רְצֵה) in Ma'ariv, Shaḥarit and Minḥa [שו״ע אורח, תכב:א], and to the third blessing of *Birkat HaMazon* (page 525) [שם, תכד:א].

128 If one forgets to say יַעֲלֶה וְיָבוֹא in its proper place in the Amida, but realizes before beginning the blessing הַמַּחֲזִיר שְׁכִינָתוֹ לְצִיּוֹן, one should immediately say יַעֲלֶה וְיָבוֹא and continue with the rest of the blessing. If one realizes the omission immediately after completing the blessing הַמַּחֲזִיר שְׁכִינָתוֹ לְצִיּוֹן, one should say יַעֲלֶה וְיָבוֹא and continue with the following blessing. If one realizes the omission after beginning the words מוֹדִים אֲנַחְנוּ לָךְ, one must repeat the Amida from the

beginning of the seventeenth blessing (from the word רְצֵה). If one realizes the omission after completing the Amida, one must repeat the Amida from the beginning [שוֹע אוֹרַח, תכב:א].

129 If one forgets to say יַעֲלֶה וְיָבֹא in Ma'ariv, one does not repeat the Amida [שם].

130 Shaḥarit: as for weekdays, although one adds special verses for Rosh Ḥodesh in the *Korbanot* (page 51) [שוֹע אוֹרַח, תבא:א]. יַעֲלֶה וְיָבֹא is added to the Amida (laws 127–128). After the Repetition of the Amida, *Taḥanun* is omitted, and the congregation says Half Hallel [שוֹע אוֹרַח, תכב:ב], followed by Full Kaddish.

131 Torah reading: page 653. Four men are called up [שוֹע אוֹרַח, תכב:ב]. Note that the second *aliya* begins by repeating the last verse of the first *aliya* [שוֹע אוֹרַח, תכב:ג]. Half Kaddish is said before the Torah is returned to the Ark. The service continues with *Ashrei*, וּבָא לְצִיּוֹן and Half Kaddish. The tefillin are then removed [שוֹע אוֹרַח, תכב:ד], and the congregation says Musaf for Rosh Ḥodesh. This is followed by *Aleinu*, Mourner's Kaddish, the Daily Psalm, Psalm 104 (בָּרְכִי נַפְשִׁי), and Mourner's Kaddish.

Laws of Hallel

132 Hallel is said standing [שוֹע אוֹרַח, תכב:ו]. On Rosh Ḥodesh and the last six days of Pesaḥ, the abridged form, Half Hallel, is said [שוֹע אוֹרַח, תכב:ב; תצ:ד], omitting the first halves of Psalm 115 (לֹא לָנוּ) and Psalm 116 (אָהַבְתִּי, כִּי יִשְׁמַע).

133 At the beginning of Psalm 118 (הוֹדוּ לַיהוה כִּי טוֹב, page 367), it is customary for the *Shaliaḥ Tzibbur* to say each of the four verses out loud, and the congregation responds with [הוֹדוּ לַיהוה כִּי טוֹב, כִּי לְעוֹלָם חַסְדּוֹ מֹשֶׁנב תכב, כ]. Some advise the congregation to quietly say each verse with the *Shaliaḥ Tzibbur*.

ḤANUKKA (25th of Kislev–2nd of Tevet)

134 On Ḥanukka, עַל הַנִּסִּים is added to the Amida in Ma'ariv, Shaḥarit and Minḥa, as well as the second blessing of *Birkat HaMazon*. If one forgets to say עַל הַנִּסִּים, one does not repeat the Amida or *Birkat HaMazon* [שוֹע אוֹרַח, תרפב:א].

135 It is customary to light Ḥanukka lights in the synagogue, either before or after Ma'ariv of each evening of Ḥanukka. The procedure is identical to that of lighting in the home, as described below, except that the lights should be placed along the southern wall of the synagogue.

136 After Ma'ariv, Ḥanukka lights are lit in the home. On the first night, three blessings are said: (1) שֶׁעָשָׂה נִסִּים, (2) לְהַדְלִיק נֵר שֶׁל חֲנֻכָּה, ("Who performed miracles")

and (3) שֶׁהֶחֱיָנוּ (page 405). On subsequent nights, only the first two blessings are said [שרע אורח, תרעו:א]. When adding lights each night, the new light is always added to the left. The newest candle is lit first, and one then lights the rest of the lights from left to right.

PURIM *(14th of Adar)*

137 On Purim, עַל הַנִּסִּים is added to the Amida in Ma'ariv, Shaḥarit and Minḥa, as well as the second blessing of *Birkat HaMazon*. If one forgets to say עַל הַנִּסִּים, one does not repeat the Amida or *Birkat HaMazon* [שרע אורח, תרצג:ב].

138 Ma'ariv: for weekdays. After recitation of the Amida, the *Shaliaḥ Tzibbur* says the Full Kaddish. The Reader of the Megilla says three blessings: (1) עַל מִקְרָא מְגִלָּה ("about reading the Megilla"), (2) שֶׁעָשָׂה נִסִּים ("Who performed miracles") and (3) שֶׁהֶחֱיָנוּ (page 411). The Megilla is read and the concluding blessing, הָרָב אֶת רִיבֵנוּ is said. The congregation says אֲשֶׁר הֵנִיא and concludes with a joyous singing of שׁוֹשַׁנַּת יַעֲקֹב. The *Shaliaḥ Tzibbur* leads the congregation in saying וִיהִי נֹעַם and וְאַתָּה קָדוֹשׁ (page 319). On Motza'ei Shabbat, this is preceded by וִיהִי נֹעַם (page 317) [שרע אורח, תרצג:א]. This is followed by Full Kaddish (omitting the sentence beginning תִּתְקַבֵּל), and *Aleinu* [משרב, שם:א]. On Motza'ei Shabbat, however, וְיִתֶּן לְךָ (page 325) and Havdala precede *Aleinu* [עורה"ש, שם:ג].

139 Women are obligated to hear the reading of the Megilla [שרע אורח, תרפט:א].

140 Shaḥarit: for weekdays. After the Repetition of the Amida, the *Shaliaḥ Tzibbur* says Half Kaddish and the Torah is taken from the Ark. The Torah reading (page 664) is followed by Half Kaddish and returning the Torah to the Ark [שרע אורח, תרצד:ד]. The Megilla reading is repeated, with the introductory blessings and the concluding blessing. אֲשֶׁר הֵנִיא is not said a second time, but שׁוֹשַׁנַּת יַעֲקֹב is. The congregation says *Ashrei* and וּבָא לְצִיּוֹן, followed by Full Kaddish, *Aleinu*, the Daily Psalm and Mourner's Kaddish.

141 On Purim day, one is commanded to fulfill the mitzvot of מַתָּנוֹת לָאֶבְיוֹנִים (gifts to the poor – *tzedaka* given to at least two poor people) [שרע אורח, תרצד:א]; מִשְׁלוֹחַ מָנוֹת (sending at least two portions of food to one person) [שם, תרצה:ד]; and סְעֻדַּת פּוּרִים (the Purim feast), at which one should drink "until he cannot distinguish between 'Cursed be Haman' and 'Blessed be Mordekhai'" [שם, תרצה:ב].

Shushan Purim (15th of Adar)

142 Both *Taḥanun* and לַמְנַצֵּחַ are omitted [שרע אורח, תרעו:א].

YOM HAATZMA'UT (5TH OF IYAR)

143 If the 5th of Iyar falls on Friday or Shabbat, Yom HaAtzma'ut is moved back to the preceding Thursday. If the 5th of Iyar falls on a Monday, Yom HaAtzma'ut is postponed to Tuesday.

144 On Yom HaAtzma'ut, the mourning customs of *Sefirat HaOmer* are suspended. It is permissible to cut one's hair, shave, attend parties, celebrate weddings and bar/bat mitzvas, and listen to music. The custom is to permit shaving and cutting one's hair before nightfall in honor of the holiday.

145 Ma'ariv: Customs differ (see pages 419–427). The service adopted by the Israeli Chief Rabbinate is as follows: selections from Psalms and other readings precede Ma'ariv for weekdays. It is customary for the *Shaliaḥ Tzibbur* to lead Ma'ariv using melodies associated with Yom Tov. After the Amida, the *Shaliaḥ Tzibbur* says Full Kaddish. Responsive readings and Psalm 126 to the tune of *"HaTikva"* follow. The service concludes with the counting of the Omer, *Aleinu*, Mourner's Kaddish and communal singing of אֲנִי מַאֲמִין.

146 Shaḥarit: *Pesukei DeZimra* as for Shabbat and Yom Tov, with the addition of מִזְמוֹר לְתוֹדָה (page 441). נִשְׁמַת is not said. After יהוה מֶלֶךְ (page 455), prayers continue with Shaḥarit for weekdays (page 71). The Repetition of the Amida by the *Shaliaḥ Tzibbur* is followed by Hallel and Half Kaddish. On a Thursday (see law 143,) the Torah is taken from the Ark and the appropriate section of the Torah is read. After the Torah reading, Half Kaddish is said. Haftara is said without blessings (page 457). The Prayer for the State of Israel (page 463) is said, followed by the Memorial Prayer for fallen soldiers (page 417). Shaḥarit continues as for weekdays (page 175). At the end of the service, the congregation sings אֲנִי מַאֲמִין (page 465).

147 *Taḥanun* is omitted during Shaḥarit and Minḥa on the 5th of Iyar, even if Yom HaAtzma'ut is celebrated on a different day.

LAWS OF HAND-WASHING,
HAMOTZI AND BIRKAT HAMAZON

148 Before eating bread, one is required to wash one's hands [שו״ע או״ח, קנח:א]. After washing but before drying the hands, one says the blessing עַל נְטִילַת יָדָיִם; however, if one forgot, one may say the blessing after one's hands are dry [רמ״א, שם:א]. One should dry one's hands carefully before touching the bread [שו״ע, שם:יב].

149 Hands should be washed using a cup or other container that holds at least a *revi'it* (about 4.4 ounces) of liquid [שו״ע או״ח, קנט:א]. Holding one's hands under flowing water is not valid [שו״ע, שם:ו].

150 One should wash each hand up to the wrist, although the minimum requirement is to wash the fingers up to the knuckle furthest from the nail [שו״ע או״ח, קסא:ד]. Hands should be free of dirt or other material that one normally removes. In addition, rings should be removed before washing [שם:א-ג].

151 If the hands are clean, it is sufficient to pour water once on each hand [שו״ע או״ח, קסב:ב], but twice on each hand is preferable [מ״ב שם, כא].

152 After washing, one should take care not to allow one's wet hands to touch the unwashed hands of another. If they do so, one must dry them and wash them again [שו״ע שם, ד].

153 If one makes the blessing הַמּוֹצִיא לֶחֶם מִן הָאָרֶץ on bread, no blessing need be said on foods that are part of the meal. If one eats foods that are not eaten with bread or are not part of the meal, such as fruit eaten as dessert, they require a separate blessing [שו״ע, קעז:א].

154 If wine is served during the meal, the blessing בּוֹרֵא פְּרִי הַגָּפֶן must be said, as the blessing on bread does not cover wine [שו״ע או״ח, קעד:א]. But if wine is drunk before the meal (or as part of Kiddush), the blessing need not be repeated when drinking wine during the meal [שם:ד].

155 One should not remove bread from the table until after *Birkat HaMazon* is said [שו״ע או״ח, קפ:א].

156 Prior to saying *Birkat HaMazon*, one should wash the grime off one's fingers with *mayim aḥaronim* [שו״ע או״ח, קפא:א]. Some have the custom not to wash with *mayim aḥaronim*, because the original reasons for the practice no longer apply [שם, י; משנ״ב שם, כב], but a fastidious person who washes after a meal should wash with *mayim aḥaronim* before *Birkat HaMazon* [שו״ע שם].

157 Women are obligated to say *Birkat HaMazon* [שו״ע או״ח, קפו:א].

158 *Birkat HaMazon* should be said where one ate. If one forgot to say *Birkat*

HaMazon and went elsewhere, one should return to the site of the meal to say *Birkat HaMazon*. If one cannot return to the site of the meal, one is permitted to say *Birkat HaMazon* as soon as one remembers to do so [שו"ע ורמ"א או"ח, קפד: ד; משנ"ב, שם:ו].

159 If one forgets to say *Birkat HaMazon* at the end of the meal, it must be said afterward, so long as one does not feel hungry [שו"ע או"ח, קפד: ד]. If one wants to eat again, one may wash hands and say הַמּוֹצִיא again; the subsequent *Birkat HaMazon* then covers the first meal as well [רמ"א או"ח, קעח: ב].

160 On Ḥanukka or Purim, one adds עַל הַנִּסִּים (page 523) to the second blessing. If one forgets עַל הַנִּסִּים, one is not required to repeat *Birkat HaMazon* [שו"ע או"ח, תרפב: א; שו"ע ורמ"א או"ח, תרצה: ג].

161 On Rosh Ḥodesh one adds יַעֲלֶה וְיָבוֹא (page 525) to the third blessing. If one forgets the required addition on Rosh Ḥodesh, one is not required to repeat *Birkat HaMazon* [שם:ו].

162 If one started eating while it was Rosh Ḥodesh, and continued the meal after sunset, one still says the additions to *Birkat HaMazon* [שם].

163 If three adult males eat a meal together, they are required to preface *Birkat HaMazon* with *zimmun* (page 519). If women are present, they are required to join in the *zimmun* as well. Three adult females may also form a *zimmun*, but are not obligated to do so. If ten or more males are present, the word אֱלֹהֵינוּ is added to the formula [שו"ע או"ח, קצב: א].

164 *Zimmun* is required if all three participants ate bread. If only two participants ate bread, but a third person either eats a *kezayit* (about 1.5 ounces) of any food, or drinks a *revi'it* (about 4.4 ounces) of any beverage (other than water), the three should say *zimmun* [שו"ע או"ח, קצז: ג; משנ"ב, שם: כב].

165 Even if the participants are not sitting together, as long as some of the participants can see each other, they can join together in a *zimmun* [שו"ע או"ח, קצה: א].

166 If one of the three participants said *Birkat HaMazon* by himself, he may still join the other two to make a *zimmun*, but if two of them (or all three) said *Birkat HaMazon* by themselves, then no *zimmun* may be said [שו"ע או"ח, קצג: א].

167 At a *Sheva Berakhot* meal, a special addition is made to the *zimmun* (page 585) [שו"ע אבה"ע, סב: יג; עורה"ש, שם: יח], and the *Sheva Berakhot* (page 583) are said after *Birkat HaMazon* [שו"ע, שם].

168 At the meal after a *Brit Mila*, a special *zimmun* (page 563) is said, and

a series of prayers (pages 565–567) is added before the end of *Birkat HaMazon*.

169 At a meal in a house of mourning, a special addition is made to the *zimmun*, and the third and fourth blessings are changed (page 611) [עֻרוה"ש יו"ד, שעט: א–ב].

PRAYER IN A HOUSE OF MOURNING

170 The following prayers are omitted when praying in a house of mourning during the days of *shiva*:

a *Korbanot* (קרבנות) – omitted only by the mourners themselves [משנ"ב אורח, א: יז]

b *Taḥanun* [שו"ע אורח, קלא: ד]

c Hallel, except when Rosh Ḥodesh falls on Shabbat [משנ"ב, שם: כ]. On Ḥanukka, those who are not mourning should say Hallel on returning home.

d *El Erekh Apayim* אֵל אֶרֶךְ אַפַּיִם [משנ"ב, שם: לה]

e Psalm 20 (לַמְנַצֵּחַ) [שם]

f *Pirkei Avot* or *Barekhi Nafshi* on Shabbat – omitted only by the mourners themselves [אשי ישראל, לו: צו]

g *Birkat Kohanim* in Israel (see law 68)

171 In a house of mourning, it is customary to say Psalm 49 after the Daily Psalm; on days on which no *Taḥanun* is said, Psalm 16 is said instead (page 603).

A HALAKHIC GUIDE TO PRAYER
FOR VISITORS TO ISRAEL

GENERAL RULES
PUBLIC VS. PRIVATE CONDUCT

172 For halakhic purposes, the definition of "visitor" is one who intends to
return to his place of origin within one year [משנ״ב, קי״ו: ה]. Unmarried students may be considered visitors as long as they are supported by their
parents [שו״ת אגרות משה אורח חיב, ח״ב, קא].

173 In general, a visitor to Israel should continue to follow his or her customs
in private. In public, however, one should avoid conduct that deviates from
local practice [שו״ע אורח, תס״ח: ד; משנ״ב, שם: יד]. Hence, a visitor to Israel should
generally pray in accordance with his non-Israeli customs. This rule is
limited, however, to one's private prayers.

174 If one is serving as *Shaliaḥ Tzibbur*, one is required to pray in accordance
with the local Israeli custom. This includes, for example, repeating the
Amida according to Israeli practice: saying מוֹרִיד הַטָּל in the summer, saying וְתֵן טַל וּמָטָר לִבְרָכָה from the 7th of Marḥeshvan onward, and saying *Ein
Keloheinu* at the end of weekday Shaḥarit (page 199).

175 In Israel (and in some congregations outside Israel), *Taḥanun* is not said
from *Isru Ḥag* of Simḥat Torah until Rosh Ḥodesh Marḥeshvan, and from
Isru Ḥag of Shavuot until the 12th of Sivan.

176 Even if one is not serving as *Shaliaḥ Tzibbur*, a visitor praying with Israelis
should say the following prayers, because of their public nature, following
local Israeli custom:

a Many Israeli congregations (some daily, others only on Mondays and Thursdays) adopt the Sephardi custom of saying *Viduy* and the יג מידות (the Thirteen Attributes of Mercy) prior to *Taḥanun* in *Shaḥarit* (page 137). One who prays in such a congregation must say at least the יג מידות [שות אגרות משה אורח חיג, פט].

b *Birkat Kohanim* is said daily in *Shaḥarit* and *Musaf*, in *Minḥa* on fast days, although not in certain communities in northern Israel.

c *Barekhu* is said at the end of weekday *Shaḥarit* (except on Mondays and Thursdays) and at the end of *Ma'ariv*.

d In the Rabbis' *Kaddish*, the word קדישׁא is added after the words דִי בְאַתְרָא.

Laws of וְתֵן טַל וּמָטָר לִבְרָכָה

177 If one is visiting Israel on the 7th of Marḥeshvan, when Israeli residents begin saying וְתֵן טַל וּמָטָר לִבְרָכָה, and one intends to remain in Israel until after the 4th (or 5th) of December, when nonresidents of Israel begin saying וְתֵן טַל וּמָטָר לִבְרָכָה, one should also begin to say וְתֵן טַל וּמָטָר לִבְרָכָה. If, however, one intends to leave Israel before then, there are two opinions: (a) while one remains in Israel one should say וְתֵן טַל וּמָטָר לִבְרָכָה, but upon leaving Israel one need not continue saying it [בהיטב אורח, קו:ד], and (b) while one remains in Israel one should add וְתֵן טַל וּמָטָר לִבְרָכָה to the blessing of שׁוֹמֵעַ תְּפִלָּה [אשי ישראל, כג: לא (בשם רשׁי׳ אויערבאך)].

178 If, between the 7th of Marḥeshvan and the 4th (or 5th) of December, one forgets to say וְתֵן טַל וּמָטָר לִבְרָכָה, one need not repeat the Amida [שות בצל החכמה חיא, סב].

Laws of Purim

179 In Jerusalem, Purim is celebrated on the 15th of Adar (Shushan Purim). Outside Jerusalem, Purim is celebrated on the 14th of Adar. For a resident of Jerusalem, the day of Purim is an ordinary day: one performs none of the obligations relating to Purim and one says the regular weekday prayers, although one omits *Taḥanun*.

180 One is considered a resident of Jerusalem for these purposes if one is present in Jerusalem at dawn on the morning of the 15th of Adar. Similarly, one is considered a non-resident of Jerusalem for these purposes if one is outside Jerusalem at dawn on the 14th of Adar. There is, however, an opinion that the determining factor is one's intention on the preceding evening [משניב, תרפח:יג].

181 As a practical matter, a person who stays overnight outside Jerusalem on Purim eve, but stays overnight in Jerusalem on Shushan Purim eve, is obligated to celebrate Purim twice – first on the 14th of Adar, along with non-residents of Jerusalem, and then on the 15th of Adar, along with residents of Jerusalem. Conversely, a person who stays overnight in Jerusalem on Purim eve but stays overnight outside Jerusalem on Shushan Purim eve would have no obligation to celebrate Purim at all.

182 Special rules apply to residents of Jerusalem when Shushan Purim falls on Shabbat, a situation known as *Purim Meshulash*. On Thursday night and Friday morning (14th Adar), the Megilla is read, as is the practice outside Jerusalem. On Friday one also performs the mitzva of מַתְּנוֹת לָאֶבְיוֹנִים (gifts to the poor). On Shabbat one adds עַל הַנִּסִּים to both the Amida and *Birkat HaMazon*. For Maftir one reads the Torah portion for Purim (page 664). The Haftara is as for Shabbat Zakhor: 1 Sam. 15:2–34. On Sunday one performs the mitzva of מִשְׁלוֹחַ מָנוֹת (sending food portions) and סְעוּדַת פּוּרִים (the Purim feast), but one does not add עַל הַנִּסִּים to the Amida or *Birkat HaMazon* [שו״ע או״ח, תרפ״ח:ו].

JEWISH LEAP YEARS

The words וּלְכַפָּרַת פֶּשַׁע *are added in the* מוּסַף of חוֹדֶשׁ רֹאשׁ עֲמִידָה
during the months of מַרְחֶשְׁוָן *to* שֵׁנִי אֲדָר *in Jewish leap years.*

JEWISH YEAR	CIVIL YEAR
5776	2015–2016
5779	2018–2019
5782	2021–2022
5784	2023–2024
5787	2026–2027
5790	2029–2030
5793	2032–2033
5795	2034–2035
5798	2037–2038

TEXTUAL VARIANTS

Note: The text of this Siddur reflects the accumulation of centuries of debate and deliberation on matters of meaning, syntax and grammar. Below is a table which compares, with respect to selected passages, the text of this Siddur with alternate readings that are also endorsed by practice or noted halakhic authorities.

Page	Koren Text	Alternate Text
25	...הנו אדון עולם, וְכָל נוֹצֶר Behold He is Master of the Universe; and every creature...	...הנו אדון עולם לְכָל נוֹצֶר Behold He is Master of the Universe; to every creature...
39	...הַמְקַדֵּשׁ אֶת שְׁמוֹ ברבים. ...who sanctifies His name among the multitudes.	...מְקַדֵּשׁ אֶת שְׁמְךָ ברבים. ... who sanctifies Your name among the multitudes.
Kaddish	...יִתְגַּדַּל וְיִתְקַדַּשׁ Magnified and sanctified...(Aramaic)	...יִתְגַּדֵּל וְיִתְקַדֵּשׁ Magnified and sanctified...(Hebrew)
Kaddish	...לְעֵלָּא לְעֵלָּא above and beyond...	לְעֵלָּא וּלְעֵלָּא above and beyond...
Kaddish	...עֹשֶׂה הַשָּׁלוֹם May He who makes the peace...	...עֹשֶׂה שָׁלוֹם May He who makes peace...
Rabbis' Kaddish	...יַעֲשֶׂה בְרַחֲמָיו שלום ...in His compassion make peace	...בְּרַחֲמָיו יַעֲשֶׂה שלום ...in His compassion make peace
65	...הַמְהֻלָּל בְּפִי עמו ...extolled by the mouth of His people	...הַמְהֻלָּל בְּפֶה עמו ...extolled by the mouth of His people
93	בשפה ברורה ובנעימה, קְדֻשָּׁה כולם כאחד ...in pure speech and melody, All as one proclaim His holiness...	בשפה ברורה, ובנעימה קְדוֹשָׁה כולם כאחד ...in pure speech and holy melody. All as one proclaim...
Amida	משיב הרוח ומוריד הַגֶּשֶׁם He makes the wind blow and the rain fall.	משיב הרוּחַ וּמוֹרִיד הַגֶּשֶׁם He makes the wind blow and the rain fall.
Amida	...וְשַׂבְּעֵנוּ מְטוּבָהּ ...and from its goodness satisfy us	...וְשַׂבְּעֵנוּ מְטוּבְךָ ...and from Your goodness satisfy us
Amida	...וְכֹל אוֹיְבֵי עַמְּךָ ...all Your people's enemies	...וְכֹל אוֹיְבֶיךָ ...all Your enemies...
Amida	...ושים חלקנו עמהם, וּלְעוֹלָם לֹא נֵבוֹשׁ Set our lot with them, so that we may never be ashamed...	...ושים חלקנו עמהם לְעוֹלָם, וְלֹא נֵבוֹשׁ Set our lot with them forever, so that we may not be ashamed...

Page	Koren Text	Alternate Text
Amida	**ואשי** השב את העבודה לדביר ביתך, **ישראל ותפלתם** באהבה תקבל ברצון. Restore the service to Your most holy House, and accept in love and favor the fire-offerings of Israel and their prayer.	והשב את העבודה לדביר ביתך **ואשי ישראל. ותפלתם באהבה** תקבל ברצון. Restore the service and the fire-offerings of Israel to Your most holy House, and in love and favor accept their prayer.
Amida	...על הנסים For the miracles...	...ועל הנסים And for the miracles...
Amida	ברכנו בברכה המשלשת **בתורה,** הכתובה... bless us with the threefold blessing in the Torah, written...	ברכנו בברכה המשלשת, **בתורה** הכתובה... bless us with the threefold blessing, written in the Torah...
139	וזכרנו **בזכרון** טוב לפניך. ...remember us with a memory of favorable deeds before You.	וזכרנו **בזכרון** טוב לפניך. ...remember us with a favorable memory before You.
265	אל חי **וקיים תמיד,** ימלך עלינו... May the living and forever enduring God rule over us...	אל חי וקים, **תמיד ימלך** עלינו... May the living and enduring God rule over us for ever...
275	המלך **בכבודו תמיד,** ימלך עלינו... the King who in His constant glory will reign over us...	המלך בכבודו, **תמיד ימלך** עלינו... the King who in His glory will constantly reign over us...
305–313	היום ___ ימים בעמר. Today is the ___ day of the Omer.	היום ___ ימים לעמר. Today is the ___ day of the Omer.
377	וזכרן לכלם **יהיו, ותשועת** נפשם... May it serve as a remembrance for them all, and a deliverance...	וזכרן לכלם **היו, תשועת** נפשם... It served as a remembrance for them all, and a deliverance...
413	... ברוכים כל **ישראל.** ...blessed be all Israel.	...ברוכים **הצדיקים.** ...blessed be all the righteous.
413	ארורים כל הרשעים, ברוכים כל ישראל. Cursed be all the wicked; blessed be all Israel.	אין Omitted
525	...כי אל רחום וחנון אתה. ...because You are God, gracious and compassionate.	... כי **מלך** רחום וחנון אתה. ...because You are God, gracious and compassionate King.
527	...בונה **ברחמיו** ירושלים אמן. ...who in His compassion will rebuild Jerusalem.	... בונה ירושלים אמן. ...who will rebuild Jerusalem.
561	אל חי...**צוה** להציל ידידות שארנו משחת. the Living God...did order deliverance from destruction for the beloved of our flesh.	אל חי...**צוה** להציל ידידות שארנו משחת. the Living God...order deliverance from destruction for the beloved of our flesh.

TABLE OF PERMITTED RESPONSES

	Pesukei DeZimra (from Barukh SheAmar to Yishtabah)	Within a paragraph of the Shema or the preceding blessings[1]	Between the paragraphs of the Shema or the preceding blessings	Between concluding the blessing גָּאַל יִשְׂרָאֵל and beginning the Amida[2]
אָמֵן יְהֵא שְׁמֵהּ רַבָּא; אָמֵן following דַּאֲמִירָן בְּעָלְמָא[3]	Permissible	Permissible	Permissible	Forbidden שוע אורח סו, ט, ח [משוב נא, ח]
אָמֵן following any blessing	Permissible	Forbidden	Permissible	Forbidden[4]
בָּרוּךְ הוּא וּבָרוּךְ שְׁמוֹ; בְּרִיךְ הוּא	Forbidden[5]	Forbidden	Forbidden	Forbidden
Tallit	Put on the tallit, but say the blessing between paragraphs [משוב נג, ה]	Put on the tallit, but say the blessing after the Amida שוע ורמיא [אורח סו, ב]	Put on the tallit, but say the blessing after the Amida	Forbidden [שוע אורח סו, ח]
Tefillin	Put on the tefillin, but say the blessings between sections [משוב נג, ו]	Before the Shema: forbidden; within the Shema, put on the tefillin and say the blessing [משוב סו, טו]	Permissible	Put on the tefillin, but say the blessings after the Amida שוע אורח סו, ח

---

1. The paragraphs are as follows: from the blessing יוֹצֵר אוֹר to יוֹצֵר הַמְּאוֹרוֹת; from אַהֲבָה רַבָּה or אַהֲבַת עוֹלָם to Shema; from Shema to בְּשַׁעֲרֶיךָ; from שְׁמַע to וְהָיָה אִם שָׁמֹעַ; from עַל-הָאָרֶץ to וַיֹּאמֶר to גָּאַל יִשְׂרָאֵל [שוע אורח סו, ה]. Responses permitted within a paragraph are also permissible within a verse, though it is preferable to respond only at the end of a thought.

2. Some rule that on Shabbat one may respond to Kaddish, Barekhu, Kedusha or Modim [רמיא אורח קיא, א]. See law 48.

3. Only these are required responses; the other responses of אָמֵן in Kaddish are only a custom [משוב סו, יז].

4. One may answer אָמֵן if one hears another concluding the blessing גָּאַל יִשְׂרָאֵל [רמיא אורח סו, ז].

5. These responses are only a custom, as they are not mentioned in the Gemara [משוב נא, ח].

	Pesukei DeZimra (from Barukh SheAmar to Yishtabah)	Within a paragraph of the Shema or the preceding blessings[1]	Between the paragraphs of the Shema or the preceding blessings	Between concluding the blessing גָּאַל יִשְׂרָאֵל and beginning the Amida[2]
Barekhu[6]	Permissible	Permissible	Permissible	Forbidden
Shema	Say the first verse with the congregation [משנ״ב סו, יא]	Forbidden, except to close one's eyes and sing the melody of the Shema	Forbidden, except to close one's eyes and sing the melody of the Shema[7] [שו״ע או״ח סה, ב]	Forbidden
Kedusha	Permissible[8] [משנ״ב נא, ח]	Say only the verses beginning בָּרוּךְ and קָדוֹשׁ	Say only the verses beginning בָּרוּךְ and קָדוֹשׁ	Forbidden [משנ״ב סו, יז]
הָאֵל after אָמֵן and שׁוֹמֵעַ הַקָּדוֹשׁ and תְּפִלָּה	Permissible	Permissible	Permissible	Forbidden [תר״א או״ח סו, ו]
Modim DeRabanan	Permissible	Say only the words מוֹדִים אֲנַחְנוּ לָךְ	Say only the words מוֹדִים אֲנַחְנוּ לָךְ	Forbidden [משנ״ב סו, כ]
Being called up to the Torah[9]	Permissible	Permissible – but not in the middle of the first verse of the Shema or בָּרוּךְ שֵׁם כְּבוֹד מַלְכוּתוֹ לְעוֹלָם וָעֶד	Permissible	Forbidden [משנ״ב סו, כו]

6. Whether before the blessings of the Shema or before the Reading of the Torah. The blessings said by the עוֹלֶה are like any other blessing [משנ״ב סו, יח].
7. If the congregation is saying *Aleinu*, one should stand and bow with them [ערוהי״ש או״ח סו,ז].
8. Say only the biblical verses [אשר ישראל פט״ע, לא; see law 61].
9. The Gabba'im should not call up to the Torah one who is in the middle of prayer; however, if only one Kohen is present, he may be called up. Likewise, if only one person knows how to read the Torah, he may interrupt his prayers in order to be the *ba'al koreh* [משנ״ב סו, כו].

	Pesukei DeZimra (from Barukh SheAmar to Yishtabaḥ)	Within a paragraph of the Shema or the preceding blessings[1]	Between the paragraphs of the Shema or the preceding blessings	Between concluding the blessing גָּאַל יִשְׂרָאֵל and beginning the Amida[2]
אֲשֶׁר יָצַר	Say the blessing between paragraphs [בהי"ל, נא די' ה צרי']	Wash one's hands, but say the blessing after the Amida	Wash one's hands, but say the blessing after the Amida	Wash one's hands, but say the blessing after the Amida [משנ"ב ס, כג]
Blessing on thunder or lightning	Permissible	Forbidden	Permissible, if the opportunity may not recur	Forbidden [משנ"ב סו, יט]

GENERAL RULES

MA'ARIV

The rules regarding responses are identical to those of Shaharit. After the blessing שׁוֹמֵר עַמּוֹ יִשְׂרָאֵל לָעַד until Half Kaddish, is considered to be between paragraphs, even in the middle of בָּרוּךְ יהוה לְעוֹלָם אָמֵן וְאָמֵן [ביאור הלכה סו די'ה ואלו].

HALLEL

The laws regarding responses during Hallel are identical to those of the Shema [שו"ע או"ח תפח,א]. If a Lulav is brought in the middle of Hallel, one should say the blessing between paragraphs of Hallel [משנ"ב תרמד,ז].

REMOVING A CRYING CHILD

One should remove a crying child from the synagogue even while saying the Amida, in order to avoid disturbing others who are praying [אשי ישראל פל"ב, יג (בשם החזון איש)].

KADDISH DURING PESUKEI DEZIMRA

A mourner is permitted to say Kaddish during *Pesukei DeZimra*, if he will be unable to say it afterwards [אשי ישראל פט"ו הערה קט].

RABBIS' KADDISH

Mourner: Yitgadal ve-yitkadash shemeh raba. (*Cong:* Amen)
Be-alema di vera khir'uteh, ve-yamlikh malkhuteh,
be-ḥayyeikhon, uv-yomeikhon,
uv-ḥayyei de-khol beit Yisrael,
ba-agala uvi-zman kariv,
ve-imru Amen. (*Cong:* Amen)

All: Yeheh shemeh raba mevarakh le'alam ul-alemei alemaya.

Mourner: Yitbarakh ve-yishtabaḥ ve-yitpa'ar ve-yitromam ve-yitnaseh
ve-yit-hadar ve-yit'aleh ve-yit-hallal
shemeh dekudsha, berikh hu. (*Cong:* Berikh hu)
Le-ela min kol birkhata
/*Between Rosh HaShana & Yom Kippur:* Le-ela le-ela mi-kol birkhata/
ve-shirata, tushbeḥata ve-neḥemata, da-amiran be-alema,
ve-imru, Amen. (*Cong:* Amen)

Al Yisrael, ve-al rabanan,
ve-al talmideihon, ve-al kol talmidei talmideihon,
ve-al kol man de-asekin be-oraita
di be-atra (*In Israel:* kadisha) ha-dein ve-di be-khol atar va-atar,
yeheh lehon ul-khon shelama raba,
ḥina ve-ḥisda, ve-raḥamei,
ve-ḥayyei arikhei, um-zonei re-viḥei,
u-furkana min kodam avuhon di vish-maya,
ve-imru Amen. (*Cong:* Amen)

Yeheh shelama raba min shemaya
ve-ḥayyim (tovim) aleinu ve-al kol Yisrael,
ve-imru Amen. (*Cong:* Amen)

*Bow, take three steps back, as if taking leave of the Divine Presence,
then bow, first left, then right, then center, while saying:*
Oseh shalom/*Between Rosh HaShana & Yom Kippur:* ha-shalom/
bim-romav,
hu ya'aseh ve-raḥamav shalom aleinu, ve-al kol Yisrael,
ve-imru Amen. (*Cong:* Amen)

MOURNER'S KADDISH

Mourner: Yitgadal ve-yitkadash shemeh raba. (*Cong:* Amen)
Be-alema di vera khir'uteh, ve-yamlikh malkhuteh,
be-ḥayyeikhon, uv-yomeikhon,
uv-ḥayyei de-khol beit Yisrael,
ba-agala uvi-zman kariv,
ve-imru Amen. (*Cong:* Amen)

All: Yeheh shemeh raba mevarakh le'alam ul-alemei alemaya.

Mourner: Yitbarakh ve-yishtabaḥ ve-yitpa'ar ve-yitromam ve-yitnaseh
ve-yit-hadar ve-yit'aleh ve-yit-hallal
shemeh dekudsha, berikh hu. (*Cong:* Berikh hu)
Le-ela min kol birkhata
/*Between Rosh HaShana & Yom Kippur:* Le-ela le-ela mi-kol birkhata/
ve-shirata, tushbeḥata ve-neḥemata, da-amiran be-alema,
ve-imru, Amen. (*Cong:* Amen)

Yeheh shelama raba min shemaya
ve-ḥayyim aleinu ve-al kol Yisrael,
ve-imru Amen. (*Cong:* Amen)

*Bow, take three steps back, as if taking leave of the Divine Presence,
then bow, first left, then right, then center, while saying:*
Oseh shalom/*Between Rosh HaShana & Yom Kippur:* ha-shalom/
bim-romav,
hu ya'aseh shalom aleinu, ve-al kol Yisrael,
ve-imru Amen. (*Cong:* Amen)

קורן ירושלים